CRITICAL SURVEY
OF
LONG FICTION

CRITICAL SURVEY

OF

LONG FICTION

Second Revised Edition

Volume 8

Essays

Index

Editor, Second Revised Edition   #631574
Carl Rollyson
Baruch College, City University of New York

Editor, First Edition, English and Foreign Language Series
Frank N. Magill

SALEM PRESS, INC.
Pasadena, California   Hackensack, New Jersey

Managing Editor: Christina J. Moose
Research Supervisor: Jeffry Jensen
Acquisitions Editor: Mark Rehn
Photograph Editor: Karrie Hyatt
Manuscript Editors: Lauren M. D'Andrea, Doug Long
Research Assistant: Jun Ohnuki
Production Editor: Cynthia Beres
Layout: William Zimmerman
Graphics: Yasmine Cordoba

Copyright © 2000, by Salem Press, Inc.

Some of the essays in this work, which have been updated, originally appeared in the following Salem Press publications: *Critical Survey of Long Fiction, English Language Series, Revised Edition* (1991), *Critical Survey of Long Fiction, Foreign Language Series* (1984).

Library of Congress Cataloging-in-Publication Data

Critical survey of long fiction / editor, Carl Rollyson ; editor, English and foreign language series, Frank N. Magill.—2nd rev. ed.

p. cm.

"The current reference work both updates and substantially adds to the previous editions of the Critical survey from which it is partially drawn: the Critical survey of long fiction. English language series, revised edition (1991) and the Critical survey of long fiction. Foreign language series (1984)"—Publisher's note.

Includes bibliographical references and index.

ISBN 0-89356-890-2 (v. 8 : alk. paper) — ISBN 0-89356-882-1 (set : alk. paper)

1. Fiction—History and criticism. 2. Fiction—Bio-bibliography—Dictionaries. I. Rollyson, Carl E. (Carl Edmund) II. Magill, Frank Northen, 1907-1997.

PN3451.C75 2000
809.3—dc21   00-020195

First Printing

PRINTED IN THE UNITED STATES OF AMERICA

CONTENTS

CRITICAL SURVEY

OF

LONG FICTION

LONG FICTION
IN
HISTORY

LONG FICTION IN THE ANCIENT GRECO-ROMAN WORLD

The novel has often been described as a modern genre with little in common with the prose fiction of other periods and cultures. The relationship between the modern novel and the prose fiction of the ancient Greeks and Romans is particularly problematic. In *The Novel Before the Novel* (1977), Arthur Heiserman admits that it is anachronistic to categorize ancient prose works as fiction novels. Ian Watt, an influential scholar, begins his study of the novel in *The Rise of the Novel: Studies in Defoe, Richardson, and Fielding* (1957) with eighteenth, or, at the earliest, seventeenth century prose fiction. In *The Ancient Novel* (1995), however, Niklas Holzberg argues that the works of ancient authors such as Xenophon of Ephesus and Apuleius easily fit the broad modern definition of the novel.

Differences in style, form, and content among modern novelists have made any critical definition of the genre difficult. The questions "What makes a good novel?" and "Is this work really a novel?" can be answered only by arbitrary critical rules, for a major feature of the genre appears to be its inability to be restricted or characterized. The novel becomes what it wants to be: descriptive, narrative, or dramatic; ironic, serious, or ambiguous in tone; historical or imaginary; purely entertaining, didactic, or both. As a result, critics such as Robert Scholes and Robert A. Kellogg in *The Nature of Narrative* (1966) have stressed the diverse and changing nature of the novel form. In *The Ancient Romances: A Literary-Historical Account of Their Origin* (1967), Ben Edwin Perry calls the genre "formless," and in *The Search for the Ancient Novel* (1994), James Tatum describes ancient fiction as oxymoronic because of its many contradictory features. A better description of such a varied genre would be polymorphic, or "many-formed." The protean tendencies of the novel are, perhaps, its defining characteristic.

The ambiguity of the genre applies not only to its form, but also to its name. The ancient Greeks, who supplied the terms "epic," "drama," and "lyric," never created a word for their prose fiction, which was obliquely referred to as "fictional" (*plasmatika*), "dramatic" (*dramatika*), or, according to Chariton of Aphrodisias, "erotic sufferings" (*erotika pathemata*). Because they were written not in the standard Latin of the time but in the vernacular of the Romance languages, the adventure stories of the medieval period, such as *Chanson de Roland* (c. 1100; *Song of Roland*, 1880), were called "romances," which, in the form *roman*, supplied the term for all forms of long prose fiction in French and German. In Spanish and English, however, the words "novel" and *novela* (from *novus*, or "new," in Latin) were created to distinguish from the more idealistic romance a form of prose fiction on contemporary or realistic subjects. As a result, the European languages present a variety of terms for long prose fiction, including "romance," *roman*, "novel," and "novella." The confusion is especially acute in English, which has retained both "romance" and "novel." In theory, "romance" is used for long fiction that is "ideal" and "remote from contemporary life," while "novel" applies to works that are "realistic" and "contemporary." Yet the distinction is often difficult to apply. Further, the term "romance" itself refers equally to both the chivalric epics of the medieval period and a popular genre of paperback fiction.

The uncertain terminology surrounding long prose fiction is particularly evident with the surviving ancient Greek examples of the genre. Most modern critics call these works "romances" because of their idealistic qualities, and they imply a generic gap between the Greek romances and the modern novel that reinforces the view of the novel as a modern creation; yet many of the features considered characteristic of the modern novel can, in fact, be found in ancient prose fiction. Psychological development of character, time sequencing, narrative form, and realism or verisimilitude (especially an insistence on the illusion of real experiences) are contained in the so-called Greek romances as well as in the modern novel. Ancient prose fiction, like its modern counterpart, tends to incorporate into its fabric many literary forms and modes, so that both, to a certain extent, can be called polymorphic. For these reasons, the term "novel" will be applied in this essay to both ancient and modern examples of long prose fiction.

History and criticism of the Greek novel

The Greek novel received little contemporary critical attention, probably because ancient critics did not consider it a serious literary form, and modern critics have often been more interested in the literary precursors and origins of the Greek novel than in the works themselves.

Erwin Rohde's monumental study of the genre, *Der griechische Roman und seine Vorläufer* (1876, 1960; the Greek novel and its antecedents), established the theory that the form was a phenomenon of the mid-second through sixth centuries C.E. and was especially the product of rhetorical schools. In particular, Rohde linked the Greek novel with the Second Sophistic, a second century C.E. cultural movement which sought a return to the literary models and language of fifth century B.C.E. Athens.

Papyrus finds of Greek novels, however, have proved Rohde wrong. This genre originated much earlier than Rohde imagined, at least as early as the first century B.C.E., and the extant novels represent only a few examples of a very popular and thriving literary form. A distinction must now be made between the novels of Heliodorus, Achilles Tatius, and Longus, which show many characteristics of the Second Sophistic, and those of Chariton and Xenophon, which predate this period and are therefore called "non-Sophistic" or "pre-Sophistic." Despite major alterations in Rohde's theories, however, his emphasis on the rhetorical features of the Greek novel is still valid. Rhetorical tropes, set speeches, and legal argumentation as taught in ancient schools of rhetoric are indeed an important aspect of the surviving novels, even if the schools themselves can no longer be called the originators of the novel form.

Realization that the Greek novel developed in the late Hellenistic world of the second and first centuries B.C.E. has led to many hypotheses on the sociological background of the genre. Perry has suggested that the diverse nature of the novel reflected the varied literary tastes of the cosmopolitan Hellenistic society that gave it birth, in the same way that the more

fixed Greek epic served the needs of an earlier, more uniform age. For Perry, any talk about the "development" of the Greek novel is useless; the genre did not gradually evolve, but was a sudden, deliberate creation of an individual unknown author. Tomas Hägg, in *Den Antika Romanen* (1980; *The Novel in Antiquity*, 1983), associates the earliest novels with a rise in literacy in the late Hellenistic Age and plausibly conjectures that these novels were usually recited in small groups rather than read silently and were probably circulated, if not created, by scribes. The evidence suggests that the Greek novel was a popular rather than serious literary form, originally meant to entertain rather than to edify. Only in its later, Sophistic manifestations does the novel display clear didactic and sophisticated tendencies.

Another theory on the origin of the Greek novel is that of Reinhold Merkelbach in *Roman und Mysterium in der Antike* (1962; novel and mystery in antiquity). Merkelbach associates the novels with various religious sects, especially with the Egyptian cult of Isis, and makes these novels into mystery texts. According to this view, the regular plot of the Greek novel, with its themes of separation, trial, and reunion, parallels the message of the ancient mystery religions, and the text becomes religiously symbolic. While the religious interest in the novels is a valid observation, it is unlikely that Greek novels arose from such a monolithic, theological purpose.

Graham Anderson used Sumerian texts to suggest the Near Eastern origin of the Greek romance. Similarly, Laurence M. Wills compared Greek novels to prose works in the Jewish tradition—such as the biblical books of Tobit, Esther, and Judith—and concluded that both the Greek and the Jewish narrative form, thriving simultaneously in the first century B.C.E., sprang from the same tradition of popular literature in the eastern Mediterranean.

The polymorphic nature of the Greek novel is also suggested by the many literary antecedents proposed for the genre. The influence of the Greek epic, especially of Homer's *Odyssey* (c. 800 B.C.E.), is evident in the Greek novel of all periods. Chariton has his characters retell the story at the end of his novel in the same way as Homer has Odysseus retell his odyssey to Penelope in *Odyssey* 23. Achilles Tatius's use of the first-person narrative may be traced back to a similar technique in *Odyssey* 9 to 12. Heliodorus's debt to Homer for beginning *in medias res* is unquestionable. He also imitates Homer in book 7 when the hero almost fails to recognize the heroine because she, like Odysseus, is dressed in rags.

The frequent description of their works as dramas by Chariton, Achilles Tatius, and Heliodorus points also to the influence of the Greek theater on the novel. Similarities between the two genres are numerous. The Aristotelian dramatic terms "peripeteia" (reversal) and "anagnorisis" (recognition) readily apply to the plots of Greek novels, with their frequent and sudden changes of situation and with their inevitable reunions of the main characters to their separated lovers and their families. In Heliodorus, the dramatic recognition by the Ethiopian king and queen that the heroine is their daughter has many parallels in Greek drama (for example, Euripides' *Ion*). Furthermore, the "romantic dramas" of Euripides, such as *Ion*, *Helen*, and *Iphigenia in Tauris* (all c. 412 B.C.E.), are, like the novels, filled with intrigues, love, foreign settings, and happy endings. The Greek novels also share themes with the Greek New Comedy as exemplified by Menander, from which the genre may have derived another feature—the stock character of the intelligent slave upon whom the ingenuous protagonist relies for help.

It is, perhaps, to ancient historiography that the Greek novel owes the most. The modern world's distinction between "fiction" and "history" was not generally made in the ancient world, where myths and legends were not distinguished from eyewitness accounts of actual events and where the historian was not expected to recount what was actually said, but what ought to have been said. Herodotus is a good example, for the "father of history" blends into his historical framework not only the events surrounding the war between the Persians and the Greeks in the early fifth century B.C.E., but also numerous undocumented legends and stories. Such a priority of storytelling over historical method undoubtedly influenced the Greek novel, which does not hesitate to blend historical and fictional elements. Chariton, for example,

centers his novel on the apparently fictional daughter of a historical personage, Hemocrates, known from books 6 and 7 of Thucydides's *Historiae* (c. 424-404 B.C.E.; *Eight Books of the Peloponnesian Wars*, 1629).

The Greek novel's debt to the historian Xenophon of Athens can be seen not only in Chariton's imitation of Xenophon's prose style but also in parallels between several novels and the *Cyropaedia* (c. 430-355 B.C.E.; also as *Kuruo paideía*, c. 360 B.C.E.; English translation, 1632) of Xenophon. This work, a didactic, fictional biography of a Persian prince, shares themes of travel and love with the Greek novels. The semibiographical *Cyropaedia* also suggests another path leading toward the development of the Greek novel, a path that leads through the ancient tradition of biography and the *Alexander Romance* (c. 300 C.E.).

Finally, Rohde's famous study notes the influence of Greek travel tales and erotic poetry on the novel. Fantastic tales of adventure, such as those by Euhemerus, Iambulus, and, especially, Antonius Diogenes's *Ta uper Thoulēn apista* (c. 100 C.E., twenty-four books; *Marvels Beyond Thule*, 1989), were popular in the Hellenistic period and undoubtedly satisfied the same yearning for the exotic which can be found in the Greek novels. The erotic poetry of the Hellenistic age, with its emphasis on local legends about the varying fortunes of young lovers, shares with the Greek novels a similar depiction of the violent eruption of young love. Examples of such tales survive in the *Erotica pathemata* (erotic tales) of Parthenius, written during the first century B.C.E. and accessible in J. M. Edmonds's English translation of Longus's *Daphnis and Chloë* (1916).

Such broad literary debts indicate that the Greek novel did not originate from any single genre; rather, Greek novelists were able to incorporate features from different literary contexts into the fabric of their texts. Modern novelists do much the same.

THE GREEK NOVEL: A SURVEY

In addition to five extant novels, fragments or summaries survive from several other novels. Even these few short pieces provide enough information to create a fuller picture of the genre and its development. Unless otherwise noted, all the material discussed is available in English translation in B. P. Reardon's *Collected Ancient Greek Novels* (1989). The earliest fragments come from the so-called *Ninus Romance* by an unknown author from about the first century B.C.E. The plot of this novel apparently centered on the adventures of the legendary Assyrian king Ninus and his love for Semiramis, identifiable with the real Assyrian queen, Sammu-rāmat, who built the famous Hanging Gardens of Babylon. The author's evident alteration of historical fact— Sammu-rāmat's real husband was King Shamshi-Adad (823-810 B.C.E.)—parallels the blend of legend and history that can also be found in Chariton's extant novel.

A similar trend can be seen in the fragments of a later novel, the *Parthenope Romance* (also known as *Metiochus and Perthenope*), dated to the second century C.E., by another unknown novelist. In this work, as in Chariton, the principal characters are offspring of prominent figures in Greek history: The heroine, Parthenope, is the daughter of Polycrates, the tyrant of Samos (fl. 540-522 B.C.E.), and the hero, Metiochus, is the son of Miltiades, the Athenian general at the Battle of Marathon (490 B.C.E.). In the extant fragments, the lovers Parthenope and Metiochus are participating in a symposium, or drinking party, at which the topic is the nature of love. One is reminded here of the infamous discussion at the end of book 2 of Achilles Tatius on the advantages of homosexual versus heterosexual love.

Fragments from two other works, the *Phoenicia* (also known as *Phoenician Story*) of Lollianus and the *Iolaus* fragment (by an unknown author), both of the second century C.E., are significant for their highly erotic contents. The graphic scene of deflowering in the *Phoenicia* and the vulgar language found in the *Iolaus* contrast sharply with the virtuous poise of the extant novels and suggest that the genre as a whole may have treated the love theme in a more varied fashion than the extant novels suggest.

The *Babyloniaca* (*Rhodanes et Simonis*) survives only in a Byzantine summary. The author, Iamblichus (fl. 161-180 C.E.), was not a Greek, but a Hellenized Oriental, a background that partly accounts for his novel's Eastern setting. Babylon, also the setting for the *Ninus Romance* and books 5 and 6 of Chariton, clearly satisfied the novel reader's taste for the exotic. Iamblichus's plot is similar to those of the extant novels: Two young lovers, Rhodanes and Simonis, suffer the hardships of jealousy and separation but are eventually reunited happily, and Rhodanes becomes King of Babylon.

While papyrus evidence suggests that *Peri Chairean kai Kalliroēn* (c. second century C.E.; *The Loves of Chareas and Callirrhoe*, 1764), in eight books, by Chariton of Aphrodisias, was extremely popular in the ancient world, this novel was the last of the five extant Greek novels to be published in the modern world. Its *editio princeps*, or first printed edition, was in 1750.

Rohde once called Chariton's work the product of the fifth or sixth century C.E., but it is now considered the earliest extant complete novel and can be dated around 125 C.E. or even as early as the first century B.C.E. Some independent archaeological evidence has even been found for the author, Chariton, in his native city of Aphrodisias in ancient Caria (southwest Turkey). In his novel, Chariton identifies himself as the legal secretary to the rhetorician Athenegoras, and Chariton's professional interests are evident especially in the public and legal speeches that highlight his novel. The action of the novel begins with a festival of Aphrodite, the Greek goddess of love, in Syracuse, Sicily, where, historically, the cult of that goddess was not important, and it is possible that Aphrodite's dominance throughout Chariton's novel may in fact be caused by the prominence of Aphrodite in Aphrodisias, her eponymous city and Chariton's home.

Chariton's story centers on two handsome Syracusan youths, the offspring of political rivals, who fall in love at first sight during Aphrodite's festival and are married only after their fathers are persuaded at a public assembly to put aside their feud. The parallels to the plot of William Shakespeare's *Romeo and Juliet* (1596) include not only the Capulet-Montague theme but also a false death and burial of the heroine, who is kicked by her jealous husband and knocked unconscious. Chariton shares this treatment of mistaken death and burial with several other Greek novelists, including Achilles Tatius and Heliodorus. Callirhoe awakes in her tomb only to be carried off by the pirate Theron and sold as a slave in Miletus (eastern Turkey). Chariton's vivid psychological study of Callirhoe's new master, Dionysius, is noteworthy. Recently bereft of a beloved wife, Dionysius is torn between his sudden passion for a new slave and his loyalties to his dead wife, between the absolute power of a master over his slave and the complete subjection of a lover to his beloved. Chariton's portrayal of Dionysius in such emotional turmoil displays a psychological perception usually associated only with modern novels.

While the heroines of all the other Greek novels remain resolutely faithful to their lovers, Callirhoe, upon learning that she is pregnant with Chaereas's child, agrees to marry the childless Dionysius and passes her child off as his. Callirhoe's decision to remarry, albeit based upon her difficult circumstances, has been called an act of betrayal of Chaereas. It is also a hint that the standard of absolute chastity that applies to the other extant novels is not a rule of the genre but an accident of preservation.

Chaereas eventually learns that his wife is still alive and follows her to Miletus, where he is attacked by pirates and sold into slavery to Mithridates, the Persian governor of Caria (Chariton's homeland), who, himself, has fallen in love with the heroine. This complicated, spiraling love triangle eventually leads to Babylon and the court of Artaxerxes II (404-359 B.C.E.), where a great trial determines the disposition of Callirhoe. The king himself becomes enamored of the girl, but, before he can force her to join his harem, he himself is enjoined to leave Babylon to deal with an Egyptian revolt. Chaereas becomes a general for the Egyptians, eventually defeats the king, and wins back his wife. The exciting military scenes are paralleled in the *Ninus Romance* as well as in Heliodorus. The novel ends with the triumphant return of the protagonists to Syracuse where all the events are recapitulated at another public assembly. Chariton is particularly fond of these scenes of public deliberation, which occur throughout his novel and create within the framework of the plot a collective voice with which Chariton's readers can readily identify.

Chariton's form is unusual in that it is a mixture of prose and verse. This type of composition, called Menippean after its inventor, the cynic philosopher Menippus of Gadara (fl. 250 B.C.E.), was particularly popular among Latin authors, including the novelist Petronius, but is not otherwise common in extant Greek novels. Chariton writes an educated Greek in the simple but dramatic style called Asianism very popular in his time. His novel, lacking the Attic tendencies of the Second Sophistic, is technically called pre- or non-Sophistic. Chariton also demonstrates a particular fondness for Homer, whose epic dialect is frequently quoted and whose epic techniques, including formulas or repeated phrases, are often imitated. (For a more detailed discussion of the author, see Gareth Schmeling's *Chariton*, 1974.)

Approximately contemporary with Chariton is the *Ephesiaca* (second or third century B.C.E.; *Ephesian History: Or, The Love Adventures of Abracoman and Anthia*, 1727; better known as *Ephesian Tale*), in five books, of Xenophon of Ephesus. Nothing is known of the author. His association with Ephesus may result solely from the fact that his story begins and ends in that important ancient city; his name may even be a mere pseudonym, perhaps meant to honor the great Athenian historian by that name. Some scholars suspect the surviving text to be an epitome or summary of a longer work, but this cannot be proven. Like the text of Chariton, Xenophon's novel was published in the modern world only belatedly; its *editio princeps* was in 1726.

Of the five extant Greek novels, Xenophon's is the least popular today and is often criticized as crudely written and developed. In contrast to Chariton's careful psychological studies, Xenophon's characters are often mere puppets in a complicated series of adventurous episodes.

Xenophon's plot has several features in common with Chariton's. The Ephesian hero and heroine, Habrocomes and Anthia, fall in love at a religious festival and are soon married. Sent away from Ephesus because of an oracle, the newlyweds are captured by pirates and enslaved in Tyre. A double love triangle developing between the couple and their masters leads to a separation that is not resolved until the end of the novel. Prior to their reunion on the island of Rhodes, the couple travels separately throughout the eastern half of the Mediterranean, and they are put through a series of trials, tests of fidelity, and escapes from near death.

Several Euripidean parallels can be noted in the novel. Like Hippolytus, Habrocomes is fanatically dedicated to chastity at the beginning of the novel and later gets entangled in a Hippolytus-Phaedra-Theseus triangle in which his mistress first attempts unsuccessfully to seduce him and then falsely accuses him of rape. A nearly certain Euripidean imitation, this time of the *Electra*, is the marriage of Anthia to a goatherd who honors her chastity.

Religious elements are particularly strong in Xenophon. The fate of the protagonists is sealed by an oracle, and the deities Artemis of Ephesus, Helius (the sun) of Rhodes, and Isis of Egypt play dominant roles.

A distinctive feature of this novel is the appearance of two stories-within-stories that are among the more memorable incidents of the book. The tale of the pirate Hippothoos's unfortunate homosexual love affair in book 3 contrasts with the happier but bizarre story of the necrophiliac Aigaleus and his wife, Thelxinoe, in book 5. Both tales, recounted in the first person to Habrocomes, highlight the overall love theme of the novel in much the same way that Lucius Apuleius (c. 125-c. 185 C.E.) employs tales in his *Metamorphoses* (c. 160 C.E.; English translation, 1566; also known as *The Golden Ass*). (Schmeling's *Xenophon of Ephesus*, 1980, is a good source for further study.)

Ta katà Leukippēn kaì Kleitophōnta (*Leucippe and Cleitophon*), in eight books, of the Alexandrian orator Achilles Tatius, was once considered a fifth century C.E. parody of Heliodorus's novel, but papyrus finds have made necessary a much earlier date, approximately 170 C.E., which makes imitation of Heliodorus virtually impossible. While Achilles Tatius is now dated close in time to the novels of Chariton and Xenophon, his book is stylistically a world apart and reflects, with its simple language and

use of literary figures, the learned influence of the Second Sophistic. The *editio princeps* of Achilles Tatius appeared in 1601, but the work was known in Latin translation fifty years earlier.

The plot of this novel takes place, in succession, in Tyre, Egypt, and Ephesus. The three settings correspond loosely to the three stages of the story: love, separation, and reunion. As in the other novels, the plot is complicated by several near or apparent deaths and love triangles threatening the union of the lovers. Like Chariton, Achilles Tatius includes a thrilling trial scene, but here the hero is falsely condemned to death for murdering the heroine. Achilles Tatius's effort to create surprise and suspense at every possible turn is also reflected in Leucippe's three near-deaths: the first as a ritual victim at a sacrifice, the second by poisoning, and the third by beheading.

Achilles Tatius is fond of long digressions, mostly in the form of *ecphrasis*, or careful description reflecting the author's learned style. In fact, the novel begins with an *ecphrasis* of a painting of the rape of Europa. This description is not a mere digression for its own sake; it not only broadly parallels the plot but also serves to introduce the hero to the author, who meets Cleitophon while looking at the painting. Like Chariton, the Alexandrian Achilles Tatius can let local pride intrude into his novel. The magnificent description of the city of Alexandria at the beginning of book 5 could only have been written by a patriot. Other digressions can be zoological (as a description of the hippopotamus in book 4) or erotic (as a debate on homosexual versus heterosexual love in book 2).

The most striking feature of Achilles Tatius's novel is narrative form: Cleitophon himself is presented as relating the story to the author. This first-person narrative underscores the contemporaneity of Achilles Tatius's story. Leucippe and Cleitophon's experiences occurred recently enough for the hero himself to relay them to the author, while all the other extant novels recall events of the distant past. Although Cleitophon is narrating after the fact and knows how incidents will turn out, he never intrudes into the story as an omniscient narrator. Rather, the reader is forced to experience events as Cleitophon did at the time, without benefit of hindsight. Thus, when the hero sees Leucippe sacrificed before his eyes, the reader sees only what Cleitophon sees and only learns the happy truth of her escape when he does.

This narrative perspective also creates, between author and hero, a distance permitting Cleitophon to relate events without the author intruding his own comments and views. The reader is thus introduced directly to Cleitophon's bumbling affairs; his aborted deflowering of Leucippe and their disastrous elopement in book 2 and his unheroic acquiescence to Melite's advances in book 5 make Cleitophon's escapades quite similar in tone to the adventures of Petronius's antihero Encolpius or to Henry Fielding's *The History of Tom Jones, a Foundling* (1749). It is, perhaps, this mock-heroic perspective that has made many scholars erroneously believe *Leucippe and Cleitophon* to be a parody of Heliodorus's novel.

The *Ethiopica* (*Ethiopian Story*, 1961; also as *An Aethiopean History*, 1569, reprinted 1895) in ten books of Heliodorus of Emesa, datable as early as 225 C.E. (but a late fourth century date is also possible), brings to a fruitful climax the ancient novel tradition. Heliodorus so masterfully reworked the diverse elements of the form that his novel remained very popular in late antiquity and in medieval Byzantium, was admired in the Renaissance, and became an early model for the prose authors of the seventeenth century. Heliodorus was the first Greek novelist to become available in the Renaissance; his *editio princeps* was in 1534. A 1547 French translation by Jacques Amyot and a 1569 English translation by Thomas Underdowne did much to put Heliodorus into the mainstream of Renaissance literary activity.

The Syrian Heliodorus presents a novel that is the most exotic of its extant Greek counterparts. The heroine, Charicleia, is actually the abandoned daughter of the king and queen of Ethiopia, and the denouement of the novel is the dramatic recognition of the girl by her parents. Anagnorisis is achieved in classical fashion by means of birth tokens left with the girl when she was abandoned as an infant (recalling the recognition scenes in many Greek dramas, including Euripides' *Ion*). "Ethiopia" to Heliodorus and his readers meant not the geographic bounds of the modern nation, but the ancient kingdom of Nubia, located in the modern Sudan. The novel, in fact, ends in the capital of ancient Nubia, Meroë, and, except for events in Greece recounted after the fact, all the action of the book takes place along the Nile. Heliodorus has managed to restrict the broad wanderings of the genre's typical protagonists, but, like so many of his predecessors, features a faraway place in his novel.

The battle scene, found in earlier novels such as those of Chariton and the *Ninus Romance*, is used to great effect by Heliodorus, whose description in book 9 of the siege of Syene is perhaps modeled on the siege of Nisibis in 350 C.E. recounted by Julian the Apostate and is filled with elaborate detail and suspense. This *ecphrasis*, as well as that of a procession at Delphi in book 3, reminds one also of the careful descriptions found in Achilles Tatius.

Heliodorus's novel is also exotic in terms of religious sentiment. The Eastern sun cult, popular in the author's native Emesa and apparently important in Meroë as well, is central to the story. Religious syncretism, common in antiquity, is evident in the association of the sun god with Apollo, whose shrine at Delphi plays a critical role in the history of the hero and heroine. Charicleia's protector, Calasiris, is both a priest of Helius (the sun) and a gymnosophist, an Egyptian wise man. Heliodorus, whose name in Greek means "sun-gift," ends his novel by describing himself as a descendant of the sun.

In no other ancient novels are the protagonists so resolutely chaste. Chastity takes on a deeply religious meaning in *Ethiopian Story*, where Charicleia's virtue is closely associated with her worship of Artemis and Isis.

Characterization in Heliodorus can be particularly complex. Several of the characters present multiple sides to their very human and very realistic personalities. The religious convictions of both Charicleia and Calasiris are intermingled with tendencies toward deception difficult for the modern reader to understand. Theagenes, resolutely chaste and stoic even under torture when his virtue is threatened, lacks a similar fortitude when faced with mere servitude or certain death. He is ingenuous and often unable to understand his beloved's deceptions of others, such as Charicleia's deceit of Thyamis at the end of book 1. Thyamis, the brigand son of the priest Calasiris, temporarily compromises his religious background with the life of a pirate. While some of the minor characters are mere stereotypes, others, such as the Athenian Cnemon, are carefully developed in a sympathetic manner.

Heliodorus's artistry is particularly evident in his narrative technique. The novel begins with a brilliant use of *in medias res*. An omniscient narrator describes the aftermath of a bitter battle. The only survivors, a wounded young man and the beautiful young woman nursing him, turn out to be the protagonists, Theagenes and Charicleia. Their full identities and the circumstances surrounding the battle come to light only much later in the narrative. Heliodorus's failure to narrate events in the chronological order standard in the other extant novels creates an intense suspense that is heightened at the end of book 1 when the brigand Thyamis apparently murders Charicleia. Only in the next book does the reader learn that Thyamis murdered the wrong woman, but not before the hero, Theagenes, also mistakes the corpse for that of Charicleia.

The unusual beginning naturally leads to the use of flashback to bring the reader up-to-date. The flashback is dramatically achieved through a conversation between Calasiris and Cnemon in which the priest recounts past events in the first person. In this instance, Heliodorus is probably imitating the *Odyssey* with its central flashback narrated by Odysseus himself. The affinity of Heliodorus's technique to that of the modern cinema has often been noted; it is surprising that no producer has yet put *Ethiopian Story* on the screen.

Calasiris's story itself is not chronologically straightforward. In books 3 to 5, he narrates first how Theagenes and Charicleia met at Delphi and fell in love; then he goes back further in time to relate Charicleia's birth and history; finally, he returns to the first narrative string to describe the escape of the protagonists from Delphi, their capture by pirates, and, at last, the circumstances surrounding the carnage with which book 1 began. Thus, only at the end of book 5 does the reader receive all the background information necessary to comprehend the events described in book 1.

Like Xenophon, Heliodorus uses the story-within-a-story technique, but his are much more tightly bound into the fabric of the novel. Most notably, the story of Cnemon, recounted in book 1, proves in several ways to be linked with the story of the protagonists.

Heliodorus's intricate narrative form is paralleled by a baroque language. The ancient passion for rhetoric results here in complicated sentence structures with multiple pairs of balanced subordinate clauses. Heliodorus's diction is often poetic and oblique, as even a casual examination of the battle scene in book 1 indicates: severed limbs quiver; wine goblets become missiles; wine is mixed with blood; the bloody wound of Theagenes makes his white cheek more brilliant; and Theagenes mistakes the living Charicleia for a benevolent ghost. (A good introduction to Heliodorus in English is that of Gerald N. Sandy, 1982.)

Daphnis and Chloë, in four books, stands out in many ways from the other four extant Greek novels yet has much in common with them. Little is known about the author, Longus of Lesbos, whose association with Lesbos may merely result from the setting of Longus's story, chosen, perhaps, because of the traditional links between the island of Lesbos and the love theme. Dating is mere conjecture: from the late second to the middle of the third century C.E. Of the Greek novels, *Daphnis and Chloë* is probably the best known today. It was translated into French by Amyot, in 1559, and the *editio princeps* of the Greek text appeared in 1598.

Longus's tale, like that of the other novels, is of young love with the standard themes of separation of the lovers, jealousy, love rivals (both heterosexual and homosexual), and eventual union of the lovers at the end. What is distinctive is the novel's simple, bucolic setting. The entire action takes place on the island of Lesbos—quite a contrast with the multiple changes of scene in Xenophon's *Ephesian Tale*. The protagonists, a goatherd and a shepherdess, function in the peaceful, natural surroundings of the Lesbian countryside. The conventional pirate raid is permitted to intrude into this pastoral setting, but only abortively. Pan, the rural deity who oversees the fates of both Daphnis and Chloë, miraculously saves the heroine from the pirates before the ship has left Lesbian waters. The author clearly owes much to the pastoral poetic tradition best known today through Theocritus's *Idylls* (1566; English translation, 1684) and Vergil's *Eclogues* (43-37 B.C.E.; also known as *Bucolics*; English translation 1575), in which "Daphnis" is both a conventional shepherd name and a mythic figure. The artificiality of this poetry, in which the simple setting is described in a highly sophisticated, indirect language, is reflected in the stylized, poetic language of Longus, whose novel, like those of Achilles Tatius and Heliodorus, is labeled "Sophistic." Yet, within this artificial context, Longus's vivid characterization of the stirrings of adolescent love is striking and psychologically perceptive.

The temporal structure of the novel is not so much controlled by a succession of events as it is by the changes of the seasons, followed through nearly two cycles. The story begins in spring with the first signs of pubescent passion. Winter brings snow and isolation to the lovers. The following spring finds an entirely innocent and sexually naïve pair of lovers trying to consummate their love by imitating their flocks. Summer provides more practical sexual experience to Daphnis, who is successfully seduced by the wife of a neighboring farmer. Here Longus follows all the other extant novelists except Heliodorus in suggesting or admitting an affair on the part of the male protagonist, but Chloë, like the heroines of Achilles Tatius and Heliodorus, remains unquestionably innocent until her marriage to Daphnis. The second autumn leads to the recognitions of the foundling protagonists by wealthy, aristocratic, urban parents. Their anagnorises, accomplished via the necessary tokens, are appropriately occasioned by a harvest festival. Daphnis and Chloë, rejecting the city life of their newly found parents, are eventually married among their beloved flocks and lead a bucolic existence for the rest of their lives. Here, again, Longus diverges from his colleagues, who tell their readers nothing about the protagonists' lives following their happy reunions. Daphnis and Chloë are said to have had children, a boy and a girl, and to have "grown old together." (For a more detailed discussion of Longus's novel, see W. E. McCulloh, *Longus*, 1970.)

The foregoing survey of the five extant Greek novels and the fragments of several others has demonstrated that the Greek novel tradition functioned in a context of conventionality. The themes are repetitious: young lovers, separated on long journeys and tested in terms of their virtue and fidelity by various temptations, are eventually reunited, usually under the guidance of a protective deity. Conventional, too, is the rhetorical style and the borrowings from other genres. Yet over this monotony is laid a pattern of variety that is a controlling feature of the genre. The protagonists, it turns out, are not always completely virtuous. The time is usually, but not always, the distant past. The tone is not consistently ideal; there are occasional elements of irony and comedy. Characterization differs significantly from novelist to novelist. The mode of presentation, while always narrative, varies from the simple omniscient narrative technique of Chariton, Xenophon, and Longus to the more sophisticated first-person narrative of Achilles Tatius and the extremely complicated combination of third- and first-person narratives in Heliodorus. Each author strives via a different technique to establish the authenticity of his story: by associating the main characters with historical personages (Chariton), by documentary inscription (Xenophon), or even by personal witness (Achilles Tatius). Each author seeks variety as a means of creating suspense and surprise and of establishing his credentials for novelty and originality within the genre. From this point of view, the Greek novel, like its modern counterpart, is indeed polymorphic, open to a diversity of form, theme, and expression.

THE ROMAN NOVEL

Until papyrus fragments radically altered the late dating of the Greek novels, the two extant Latin works of long prose fiction, the *Satyricon* (c. 60; *The Satyricon*, 1694) of Petronius Arbiter and the *Metamorphoses* of Lucius Apuleius, were thought to have been written before the rise of the Greek novel and thus were considered uniquely Roman creations, independent of the Greek romance tradition. With the realization that the Greek novel arose in the late Hellenistic period, at least as early as the first century B.C.E., it is now necessary to view both Petronius's novel of the first century C.E. and Apuleius's work of the late second century in the context of a thriving tradition of novel composition in the Mediterranean world. Both of these works, while unquestionably Roman and original creations, arose out of the peculiar symbiotic relationship of Greek and Latin literature. From the outset of literary Latin writing in the third century B.C.E., the influence of the older and more established Greek literature upon Latin authors is constant and strong. Latin writers strove to emulate their Greek counterparts and, at the same time, to create a uniquely Roman literature of high quality.

The literary background to the *Satyricon* and the *Metamorphoses* is a case in point. Petronius and Apuleius both produce original works, but only out of the Greco-Roman literary tradition. Several diverse genres have been proposed as building blocks for the Roman novels. The most prominent source is the Greek novel. While the comic, down-to-earth tone of the Roman novel, usually described as comic or even picaresque, is quite distinct from the generally romantic, idealistic mood of the Greek novel, the Roman novel shares many themes with its Greek counterpart. The Roman novel, however, takes these themes and turns them upside down. This is especially true of the *Satyricon*, which is, among other things, "a parody of the Greek ideal world" according to Hägg. The same is true, to a lesser degree, of the *Metamorphoses*. Both Latin works contain the themes of travel, divine protection/disfavor, and, especially, love—which are central to the Greek novel— but treat them in a different way. The virtuous heterosexual relationship normally depicted in the Greek novel becomes, in Petronius, a disastrously comic homosexual *ménage à trois*, and, in Apuleius, wanton sexuality leads to the transformation of the hero into an ass. Such differences in tone have generally caused the Greek works to be called ideal romances and the Roman ones comic novels, but their structural similarities and historical links cannot be ignored. Greek papyri such as those of Lollianus and the

Iolaus fragment have even suggested the existence of a Greek comic novel tradition contemporary with the Roman.

Besides the Greek novel, several other genres are important to the development of the novel in Latin. The epic tradition, represented in Rome by both Homer and Vergil, is an inevitable source of literary material for both Petronius and Apuleius, who each create heroes who are the inverse of the epic mold. The bumbling adventures of the naïve Petronian antihero Encolpius and the Apuleian Lucius are striking contrasts to the heroes of epic and have much in common with the blunders of Achilles Tatius's Cleitophon and with the picaresque heroes of seventeenth and eighteenth century novelists.

The influence of the Roman stage, especially of the popular low comedy of the mime, also can be seen on Petronius and Apuleius. The mime, a short, comic skit about everyday life with stock characters using colloquial language, gave the Roman novel its contemporary scenes and characters, its often "low" or realistic tone, and, in Petronius, its sometimes unliterary, colloquial Latin.

The erotic Milesian tales, a collection of racy short stories originating with the Greek Aristides of Miletus in 100 B.C.E. and early translated into Latin, was undoubtedly a model, if not a source, for the often indecorous tales inserted by both Petronius and Apuleius into their works. Several of these tales, including Petronius's "Widow of Ephesus" and Apuleius's "Tale of the Jealous Husband and the Tub" (*Metamorphoses*, 9, 38)—a tale later borrowed by Giovanni Boccaccio in *Decameron: O, Prencipe Galetto* (1349-1351; *The Decameron*, 1620)—have developed independent literary lives of their own. It is difficult to judge from the fragmentary remains of the *Satyricon* how many short stories Petronius blended into his novel and how closely these tales were related to the plot, but all the tales in Apuleius can be interpreted as part of the larger work. Apuleius, if not Petronius, took the short story tradition and incorporated it integrally into the novel form. Parallel use of such stories-within-stories can be seen in the Greek novelists Xenophon and Heliodorus and in modern authors such as Fielding.

Finally, Roman satire exerted a major influence upon the Latin novel, especially upon Petronius. Inasmuch as the Greeks lacked examples of the genre, the Romans claimed satire as their own creation, which, as developed by Lucilius, Varro, Horace, and Juvenal, was primarily a medley, conversational in tone with an emphasis upon variety of form, tone, and character. While the best-known Latin satirists, Horace and Juvenal, wrote exclusively in verse, the first century B.C.E. satirist Varro of Reate wrote in a combination of prose and verse called Menippean satire, and Petronius, following Varro's example, wrote the *Satyricon* in the prosimetric form. Of the Greek novelists, only Chariton used both prose and verse. Prosimetry aside, both Petronius and Apuleius owe to Roman satire the diversity and variety that is so evident in their novels. Roman satire also offered an often biting commentary on contemporary Roman society that Petronius readily followed. Such variety or polymorphy is a feature that the Latin novelists shared with their Greek and modern colleagues.

Any discussion of the antecedents to the Roman novel must also mention the 1967 work of Ben Edwin Perry, who argues for the Roman novel, as he does for the Greek, that there was no gradual development of the Latin novel; rather, he claims that both the *Satyricon* and the *Metamorphoses* were individual creations written to serve the unique literary purposes of their authors. Perry's theory remains a caveat for those who overemphasize the literary debts of Petronius and Apuleius instead of their originality.

The *Satyricon* of Petronius survives only in extensive fragments filling about 140 modern pages. The original work may have been at least five times that size. Nearly one-third of the extant *Satyricon* is devoted to the famous "Cena Trimalchionis" ("Trimalchio's Feast"). It is generally agreed by scholars that the author of the *Satyricon* was the Petronius Arbiter who is mentioned in Tacitus (*Annals* 16, 28-29) as Nero's minister of etiquette (*arbiter elegantiae*) and was forced to commit suicide in 66 C.E. The man of polished and elegant voluptuousness, whose very death was so charmingly staged, transferred his personal qualities into his work, which is a perfect product of the licentious elegance of the Neronian age.

Petronius's fragments, without the "Cena," were first published in 1482; the "Cena" did not emerge from obscurity until the mid-seventeenth century. Several good modern English translations are available, including that of William Arrowsmith (1959).

The title of the novel is somewhat disputed. Most manuscripts render it *Satyricon*, which seems to refer to the Greek satyr and thus to associate the work with the lascivious nature of that mythological beast. Other manuscripts give the mongrel form *Satiricon*, which could only be the Latin word *satira*, or "satire," transformed into Greek. P. G. Walsh has suggested convincingly that Petronius's title is meant to be ambiguous, that in the novel Petronius is consciously combining the traditions of Greek comic fiction (*Satyricon*) with Roman satire (*Satiricon*). This interpretation goes far in explaining the diverse elements of this novel, with its sympathetic but comic antihero Encolpius, his homosexual passion for Giton, the pathetically comic figure of Trimalchio (whose development owes much to the figure of the bore in Roman satire), and the ironic depictions of the rhetor Agamemnon and the poet Eumolpus. Each of these characters is unquestionably a blend of literary antecedents and contemporary caricatures which makes the novel both topical to its first century C.E. readers and sometimes arcane to twentieth century readers, who often miss the allusions. Contemporaneity is also a feature that distinguishes the Roman novel from its more ideal Greek cousin, which usually chooses the distant past as its temporal setting.

The extensive poetry of Eumolpus contained in the text is also a source of controversy. Eumolpus's verses, especially those on the sack of Troy and on the Roman Civil War, are interpreted by Perry to be serious literary creations that are, in fact, the excuse for the novel itself. Perry argues that Petronius, living at the dangerous court of Nero, could produce his serious literature only within the context of a farce and that the *Satyricon* provided the ideal outlet for Petronius's literary genius. Walsh, on the other hand, argues that the poems of Eumolpus are not insertions by Petronius but are meant to be Eumolpus's own verses, ironically in character with the poetic caricature created by Petronius. For Walsh, the *Satyricon* is intentionally a burlesque, not only of contemporary Roman life, but also of much Greco-Roman literature, including the Greek novel.

The *Metamorphoses*, or *The Golden Ass*, in eleven books, is dated to the second half of the second century C.E. The author, Lucius Apuleius, was a native of Madaura in North Africa, studied law at Carthage and Athens, and was fluent in both Latin and Greek. His career as a lawyer brought him fame and respect in his native Africa. His unsuccessful prosecution for witchcraft (c. 158 C.E.), on which his extant *Apologia* (158-159 C.E.; English translation, 1909) is based, as well as the themes of sorcery in the *Metamorphoses*, led to the medieval belief that he was a wizard. The *Metamorphoses* was one of the first classical texts published in the Renaissance; its *editio princeps* appeared in 1469. The famous English translation of 1566 by William Adlington, *The Golden Asse* (revised 1915), is still usable today.

Apuleius derived the kernel of his story, the adventures of a man transformed into an ass, directly from a Greek source: a prose story associated with the Greek satirist Lucian (c. 120-c. 185 C.E.). Lucian's *Metamorphoses* survives only in an abridged edition, called the *Onos* or *The Ass* (English translation, 1989). Lucian's tale, filled with sex and magic, undoubtedly springs from the Milesian type of story already discussed. Comparison of the extant *Onos* with Apuleius's novel shows that Apuleius closely followed the plot of his original, but added much in terms of characterization. Apuleius's hero, Lucius, is much more developed than in the Greek version, but this impression may be a result of the abridgement of the Greek text. More significantly, Apuleius weaves into the plot a series of short stories, including "Cupid and Psyche," that were not in his original source. Completely Apuleian, too, is the climax of religious conversion in book 11. In the Greek version, the retransformation of Lucius back into his true shape occurs when the ass eats some roses; in Apuleius, the metamorphosis only occurs through the intervention of the Egyptian deity Isis, and the novel ends with the hero dedicating his life to her.

The intent of Apuleius's work has caused much debate. At the beginning of the first book, Apuleius addresses his reader directly and describes his tale as "diverse stories in the Milesian fashion" that will "delight your gracious ears with a pleasant tale." The entertaining goal of the work is reinforced at the end of this introduction, where the reader is asked to "pay attention; you will be amused." Many scholars, including Perry, take Apuleius's words at face value and argue that the work is meant exclusively for entertainment.

Other scholars emphasize the intense religiosity of the last book and argue that, while entertaining, the work also has a didactic purpose. Walsh thus sees the *Metamorphoses* simultaneously as entertainment, as fable (especially in "Cupid and Psyche"), and as religious apologia. According to this interpretation, the diverse tales that Apuleius incorporates into his work are not merely amusing anecdotes; rather, each serves to develop the message of the work—the danger of excessive eroticism and curiosity versus religious faith as the sole source of personal salvation.

The *Metamorphoses* is a unique blend of the comic and the ideal, of entertainment and of edification. The hero, Lucius, is both an amusing bungler and, ironically, a moral exemplum. Female characters in the tales are both intensely sexual, as in the Milesian tales, and also admirably virtuous, as in the Greek novel tradition. Using variations of tone and theme, Apuleius has thus created a unique example of ancient long fiction. The *Metamorphoses*, in itself, exemplifies the polymorphic character of the novel form of which it is a significant ancient example. (The best introduction to both Petronius and Apuleius is Walsh, 1970.)

Other ancient long fiction

A survey of the novel in the ancient world would be incomplete without a brief discussion of other forms of long fiction, which Tomas Hägg has shown to have close ties with the novel form.

Marvels Beyond Thule, in twenty-four books, by Antonius Diogenes (fl. 100 C.E.), is an example of the travel literature popular in antiquity. While the work only survives in a medieval summary, many parallels to the ancient novels can be noted: travel, separation, apparent death, and reunion. Significantly, the love motif appears to have been secondary in Diogenes, who emphasizes, as the title suggests, incredible adventures beyond the end of the world. He apparently wove together a complicated narrative consisting of first-person narrative within first-person narrative.

The *Alexander Romance*, attributed falsely to the fourth century B.C.E. historian Callisthenes, is an excellent example of the way fiction and history could be blended in the ancient world. The author, called Pseudo-Callisthenes, and writing sometime around the fourth century C.E., seems to have started with a Hellenistic prose biography of Alexander the Great and to have added material gathered from an epistolary romance about the king (dated about 100 B.C.E. and now lost) as well as from several separate longer letters from Alexander to his mother or to his teacher Aristotle. These last letters include descriptions of the king's adventures in India and at the ends of the world, especially his encounter with the gymnosophists of India (recalling the gymnosophists in Heliodorus). The affinities of this peculiar historiography with the Greek novel tradition are based upon the travel motif as well as the fictionalization of historical events. The *Alexander Romance* survives in several Greek and Latin versions from late antiquity (fourth to sixth centuries) as well as in many medieval vernacular forms that indicate the popularity of the book in the medieval period. The romance has been translated into English by Ken Dowden in Reardon's *Collected Ancient Greek Novels*.

Also well-known in the Middle Ages were the so-called *Troy Romances* of Dictys of Crete and Dares of Phrygia, which were written about the second century C.E. (English translation, 1966). These works—both Dictys's *Ephemeris belli Troiani* (fourth century C.E.; diary of the Trojan War) and Dares's *De excidio Troiae historia* (fifth century C.E., probably written during second or third century C.E.; English translation, 1553)—claimed to be historical accounts of historical events. If the *Alexander Romance* could treat history like fiction, the *Troy Romances* could treat myth like history. So, too, could the ancient novelists.

The anonymous *Historia Apollonii regis Tyri* (c. third century C.E.; *The Old English Apollonius of Tyre*, 1958) is another piece of ancient long fiction

extremely popular in the Middle Ages and widely translated into the vernacular. The surviving Latin version, dating from the fifth or sixth centuries, is probably derived from an original Greek version of the third century to which Christian elements were joined. The plot and style are very similar to Xenophon's *Ephesian Tale* and display the typical novel's blend of love, travel, and adventure, to which folktale motifs such as the suitor contest have been added. The story of Apollonius thus provides an important link between the Greek novel form and the "darkness" of the Middle Ages. An accessible English translation, by Gerald N. Sandy, is in Reardon's *Collected Ancient Greek Novels*.

The popular Menippean satire must also be mentioned as another example of ancient long fiction. The prosimetric form was not only employed in the classical novels of Petronius and Chariton but also in important works of late antiquity: the fifth century allegory *De nuptiis Philologiae et Mercurii* (*On the Marriage of Mercury and Philology*, 1977) of Martianus Capella (fl. late fourth to early fifth century) and the sixth century philosophical work *De consolatione philosophiae* (510-524 C.E.; The Boke of Boecius, Called the Comforte of Philosophye, 1556) by Anicius Manlius Severinus Boethius (c. 480-c. 524). These works, fictional in the way Plato's philosophical presentation of the historical Socrates is fictional, demonstrate the variegated purposes and forms of ancient fiction.

A final form of long prose fiction shows an important link between the "pagan" novel and early Christian literature. The thematic and structural similarities between the Greek novels and such fictional works as *Paul and Thecla* from the *Apocryphal Acts of the Apostles* (both dating around the second century) and the *Recognitions* (written c. 200 and attributed to Clement of Rome; English translation, 1890) have been discussed by Hägg. Both works use the novelistic themes of travel, love, separation, and reunion in order to introduce Christian themes to the popular audience. The same motifs can be seen transmitted into the hagiographic literature of the medieval period. Such lives of the saints as the popular *Barlaam and Joasaph* have proved, upon examination, to be more fiction than fact. The classical disregard for historical fact, the blending of history and fiction—also notable in the ancient novel—continues in this Christian literature well past the medieval period.

The continuity and influence of the genre

While the Sophistic Greek novels of Heliodorus, Achilles Tatius, and Longus, as well as the two Roman novels, were certainly known and read in late antiquity, there is no evidence that any new novels of this type were written after Heliodorus. There are several possible reasons for this. Certainly, the political and social upheavals of late antiquity resulted in a gradual decline in literacy, and logically, in a decrease in potential readers of the novel. Also important is the rise of Christianity. While the Greek novels of Heliodorus and Achilles Tatius were admired for their moral edification and praise of virginity, demand for these "pagan" works was inevitably displaced by more Christian fiction, such as *Paul and Thecla.*

During the medieval period, there is little indication that any of the ancient novels were known in the West, but the Greek Sophistic novels continued to be read and enjoyed in the Greek Byzantine empire. Achilles Tatius and Heliodorus received the praise of Photius, the learned ninth century Byzantine Patriarch, and of Michael Psellus, the eleventh century philosopher and diplomat. The twelfth century revival during the Comnenian Dynasty saw the appearance of four Byzantine novels modeled on ancient tales: those of Hysmine and Hysminias, by Eustathius Mackrembolites; *Rhodantes et Dosiclis amores,* by Theodorus Prodromus; Aristandros and Callithea, by Constantius Manasses; and Drosilla and Charicles, by Nicetas Eugenianus. Despite the innovation that all but the first were written in verse rather than in prose, each retains a classical, "pagan" setting as well as many of the standard novelistic themes. Byzantine novels continued to be written nearly until the Fall of Constantinople in 1453, but in these later novels, the genre had already begun to transform under the influences of medieval and folktale traditions and even through Western contacts, especially the Crusades. The impact of these relatively obscure Byzantine novels upon Western literature through cultural links has been little studied, but is another potential bond between the ancient and modern genres.

The *Metamorphoses* of Apuleius was the first ancient novel to reemerge in the West. The novel had a wide circulation from about 1100 onward in Italy and reached France and Great Britain by the thirteenth century. One of the first Latin texts to be published, the *Metamorphoses* gained a large reading public and exerted great influence during the Renaissance. The admiration of Boccaccio, who uses three of Apuleius's tales in his *Decameron,* makes Apuleius an important source, especially for stories about cuckolded husbands, in the history of the modern novella or short story. Apuleius's "Cupid and Psyche" has had broad independent influence beginning with Boccaccio's retelling in his *Genealogia deorum gentilium* (1350-1375; *The Genealogies of the Gods,* 1472). Since then, "Cupid and Psyche" has been fashioned into epic, drama, ballet, opera, poetic letter, and painting throughout Europe. Apuleius is also influential both in the rise of a popular literature of the ass, especially in Renaissance Italy, and in the development of the picaresque novel, particularly in Spain. Mateo Alemán's *Guzmán de Alfarache* (1599-1604; *The Rogue: Or, The Life of Guzman de Alfarache,* 1622) is modeled, to a certain extent, upon the adventures of Apuleius's Lucius. Through such Spanish rogue literature, the Roman novel exerts its influence on the novels of other European languages, including Alain-René Lesage's *Histoire de Gil Blas de Santillane* (1715-1735; *The History of Gil Blas of Santillane,* 1716, 1735) and Henry Fielding's *The History of the Adventures of Joseph Andrews, and of His Friend Mr. Abraham Adams* (1742; commonly known as *Joseph Andrews*).

Petronius's influence in the Renaissance was more subtle than Apuleius's but not insignificant. The fragmentary and often scandalous nature of his novel meant that few had direct contact with the *Satyricon* during this period, but enough was known of Petronius and his novel to encourage imitation of Petronius's mood and structure and to explain the similarities between the *Satyricon* and modern comic novels such as Fielding's. Petronius's novel has even been adapted to the cinema in a famous screenplay by Italian director Federico Fellini (1969).

The three Sophistic Greek novels were all known in the West, either in the original or in translation, by the mid-sixteenth century. Several translations, especially those of Heliodorus by Amyot and by Underdowne, were widely read and particularly influential. Heliodorus, in fact, quickly became a critical model for the Renaissance, which ranked the *Ethiopian Story* together with Aristotle's *Poetics* (334-323 B.C.E.) and Horace's *Ars poetica* (c. 17 B.C.E.; *The Art of Poetry*, 1567). The appeal of Apuleius and Heliodorus in the Renaissance results, to a great extent, from the ability of both writers to combine entertainment with edification, the Horatian principles of *utile* (useful) and *dulci* (sweet), which were so precious to the Renaissance. Heliodorus received commendation for his instructional value, both as moral and literary standard, from such Renaissance critics as his French translator Amyot, the great classical scholar J. C. Scaliger, the Italian poet Torquato Tasso, and the Spanish theorist López Pinciano. Critical praise inevitably led to imitation. Some of the more famous and influential works with Heliodoran features include Sir Philip Sidney's pastoral *New Arcadia* (1590), Honoré d'Urfé's *L'Astrée* (1607-1628; *Astrea*, 1657-1658), and Miguel de Cervantes's *Los trabajos de Persiles y Sigismunda* (1617; *The Travels of Persiles and Sigismunda: A Northern History*, 1619). The seventeenth century saw Heliodorus's modern heyday, when he gained the admiration of even the French Classical dramatist Jean Racine, but, with the gradual rejection of edification as a primary literary goal in the late seventeenth century, Heliodorus's influence quickly waned and has never recovered.

Longus's *Daphnis and Chloë* has maintained its own sphere of modern influence, especially over the sometime popular pastoral. In 1831, the novel even received the glowing commendation of Johann Wolfgang von Goethe for its "perfection" and "great beauty." The work has been particularly favored by European book illustrators of the nineteenth and twentieth centuries.

The pre-Sophistic Greek novels of Xenophon and Chariton were not known again in Europe until the eighteenth century and thus have not affected modern literature in the way Heliodorus or Apuleius have. It has been suggested by Paul Turner, however, that the influence of the text of Xenophon rediscovered in 1727 can be seen in the novels of that period, including Fielding's *Joseph Andrews*, *The History of the Life of the Late Mr. Jonathan Wild the Great* (1743, 1754), and *Tom Jones*, and even in Charlotte Brontë's *Jane Eyre* (1847). The similarities of plot between the Greek novel and these modern novels is at least a modest caution to those who deny any link between the ancient and modern novel traditions.

Thomas J. Sienkewicz

BIBLIOGRAPHY

Anderson, Graham. *Ancient Fiction: The Novel in the Graeco-Roman World*. Totowa, N.J.: Barnes & Noble, 1984. This broad examination of the ancient novel begins with the quest for the origin of the Greek novel and uses some Sumerian texts to suggest the Near Eastern roots of the tradition. Also includes chapters on topics such as narrative, love, character, myth, history, sex, and structure in the Greek novels, as well as a chapter on Petronius's *Satyricon* and two chapters on Apuleius's *The Golden Ass*.

Hägg, Tomas. *The Novel in Antiquity*. Berkeley: University of California Press, 1983. Offers the general English reader an outstanding introduction to the ancient novel. Hägg includes chapters on the genre in antiquity, plot summaries and analyses of the extant Greek novels, the social context and readership of these novels, their literary antecedents, historical novels, hagiographic novels, Roman comic novels, and the influence of the Greek novel in the Renaissance. Particularly useful to the novice is an introductory note on terms, a map, and seventy-nine black-and-white illustrations depicting ancient artwork and artifacts as well as woodcuts and prints from early modern editions of the novels. In an appendix Hägg uses such modern book illustrations in order to outline the plot of Longus's *Daphnis and Chloe*.

Haight, Elizabeth H. *Essays on Ancient Fiction*. New

York: Longman, 1936. Reprint. Freeport, N.Y.: Books for Libraries, 1966. These five essays intended for the general reader deal with Eastern tales in Greco-Roman prose literature, narratives in Latin elegiac inscriptions, the influence of satire on the Roman novel, Seneca's *Controversiae* as an example of prose fiction in the late first century B.C.E., and the narrative art of Apuleius.

Holzberg, Niklas. *The Ancient Novel: An Introduction.* Translated by Christine Jackson-Holzberg. London: Routledge, 1995. A general overview of the genre with chapters on characteristics and definition of the genre, the historical development of ancient prose fiction, the idealistic Greek novel in the early Roman empire, the Greco-Roman comic-realistic novels, and idealistic Greek novels in the second century C.E.

Konstan, David. *Sexual Symmetry: Love in the Ancient Novel and Related Genres.* Princeton, N.J.: Princeton University Press, 1994. A Brown University professor examines the ways in which erotic relationships are represented in Greek and Roman novels, related ancient genres such as epic tragedy, and early modern novels such as Samuel Richardson's *Pamela.* Argues that the ancient novels celebrate the ideal personal love in marriage that became popular in the early Roman Empire.

Perry, Ben Edwin. *The Ancient Romances: A Literary-Historical Account of Their Origin.* Berkeley: University of California Press, 1967. This influential scholarly study of the origin of the Greco-Roman novel tradition is divided into two parts. In the first, Perry argues that the first Greek romance was the conscious creation of an individual author in the late Hellenistic period. In the second, he examines features of comic or burlesque romances like Petronius's *Satyricon,* Lucian's *Metamorphoses,* and Apuleius's *Metamorphoses.*

Schmeling, Gareth L., ed. *The Novel in the Ancient World.* New York: Brill, 1996. This scholarly collection of essays covers a wide range of topics related to the ancient novel, including genre, origin, readership, characterization, religion, the portrayal of women and foreigners, and the influence of these works in later periods. Also includes individual essays on each of the major ancient authors and twelve maps illustrating the routes followed by the characters in these novels.

Tatum, James, ed. *The Search for the Ancient Novel.* Baltimore: The Johns Hopkins University Press, 1994. This collection of twenty-four scholarly articles includes studies on the origin of the ancient novel, the use of parody and imitation in the genre, the romance or pastoral form, idealized love, representations of reality, religion, and later influence.

Walsh, P. G. *The Roman Novel.* Cambridge: Cambridge University Press, 1970. In this scholarly study of the Roman comic novel, Walsh examines the literary antecedents and sophistication of works like Petronius's *Satyricon* and Apuleius's *Metamorphoses.* Includes separate studies of the *Satyricon,* the *Dinner of Trimalcio,* the *Metamorphoses,* and the tale of "Cupid and Psyche," as well as a chapter on the influence of these works on later European literature. In appendices Walsh discusses the date of *Satyricon* and biographical details concerning Apuleius and provides the Greek text of an aretology of the Egyptian goddess Isis who plays in important role in Apuleius' novel.

Wills, Lawrence M. *The Jewish Novel in the Ancient World.* Ithaca, N.Y.: Cornell University Press, 1995. Examines several examples of prose fiction in the Jewish tradition, including the biblical books of Daniel, Susanna, Tobit, Esther, and Judith as well as the nonbiblical *Joseph and Aseneth* and other Jewish historical novels. Wills notes similarities between these works and other prose fiction in the eastern Mediterranean, especially that of the Greeks and the Sumerians, and argues that all of these novels spring from a literary tradition popular in the first century B.C.E.

ORIGINS AND DEVELOPMENT OF THE NOVEL BEFORE 1740

The English-speaking world has long considered 1740, the year in which Samuel Richardson's *Pamela: Or, Virtue Rewarded* was published, pivotal in the development of the novel, a broad term that, for several centuries, has been applied to many different forms of long fiction. Richardson's first novel remains a convenient landmark in the history of the form because, at least in England, it went further than any previous work in exploring an individual character's "sensibility," that wonderful mix of perception, culture, logic, sentiment, passion, and myriad other traits that define one's individuality. *Pamela* has been called the first intellectual novel, that subgenre in which most of the greatest novelists of the nineteenth and twentieth centuries worked.

Nevertheless, while 1740 is an important date in the development of one type of novel, to see all earlier novels as primitive ancestors of *Pamela* would distort the history of this multifarious form. The novel followed substantially different lines of development in Spain, France, and England, three countries notable for their contributions to the early growth of this form in Europe. Moreover, different types of novels exist side by side in every period, each type appealing to a different taste, much as different types of the novel flourish today. Finally, certain earlier works have exerted as profound and lasting an influence on the novel in Europe as that attributed to *Pamela*.

The massive, thousand-page *Genji monogatari* (c. 1004; *The Tale of Genji*, 1925-1933) appeared in Japan hundreds of years before the genre developed in the West. The author, Murasaki Shikibu, was a lady-in-waiting to the empress. This first great novel in the history of world literature would have little influence on the Western novel because of the isolation of Japan and Western Europe at the time. Also, the woman novelist would not emerge in the West for another seven hundred years; thereafter, women's contributions to the novel would emerge along with men's, especially during the eighteenth and nineteenth centuries.

THE SIXTEENTH CENTURY

It could be argued the Sir Thomas Malory's *Le Morte d'Arthur* (1485; the death of Arthur) marks the beginning of the English novel, followed closely by Sir Thomas More's *De Optimo Reipublicae Statu, deque Nova Insula Utopia* (1516; *Utopia*, 1551). Scholars of the genre, however, have usually excluded these works. *Le Morte d'Arthur*, somewhat inaccurately titled, is a translation of selected and condensed romances from the French. The plot is rambling and unfocused, unlike the novel as a form. *Utopia* is a much more unified work of prose, but More composed it in Latin, thus placing it technically, and literally, outside English literature.

Whereas the French novel underwent constant refinement during the century and a half preceding 1740, with French writers producing masterpieces at intervals throughout the period, the English novel flowered briefly before 1600, then lay dormant for more than one century until it was revitalized by Daniel Defoe. The seventeenth century in England produced but one work of genius in the form, John Bunyan's *The Pilgrim's Progress from This World to That Which Is to Come* (1678, 1684; more commonly known as *The Pilgrim's Progress*), a novel ignored by contemporary literary society because of its style and theme.

Though overshadowed by the unsurpassed drama of the Elizabethans, the 1580's and 1590's saw an outpouring of original fictional narratives, including one voluminous work and a host of shorter works in the pastoral and satiric modes. Like the French one decade later, English writers were heavily influenced by translations of the late Greek romances, as well as by the satires of the humanists, the pastorals of Jacopo Sannazaro and Jorge de Montemayor, and the tragic love *novelle* of Matteo Bandello. Other influential sources were the manuals of courtly behavior and noble ethics written by the Italians Baldassare Castiglione (*Il libro del cortegiano*, 1528; *The Book of the Courtier*, 1561) and Stefano Guazzo (*La civil conversatione* (1574; *Civil Conversation*, 1581-1586). These inspired similar guides in England and provided a format of learned discourse imitated by writers of fiction.

The most distinctive feature of the English novels of that time is their commitment to moral improvement by the individual and by the state as a whole. Since, with the exception of Sir Philip Sidney, the principal novelists of that time were sons of the middle class, much of their writing was suffused with middle-class values: hard work, thrift, cautious ambition. As the period advanced, fictional works became more overtly addressed to the middle class, with more middle-class characters taking principal roles. In the 1580's, this bourgeois appeal typically took the form of the romance intended to instruct the upwardly mobile reader in courtly ways; later, satire held sway, a satire moved by the spirit of reform rather than the resigned contempt of the Spanish picaresques.

The most influential fiction early in this period was John Lyly's *Euphues, the Anatomy of Wit* (1578), actually less a novel than a moral handbook for wealthy, budding scholars. In it, bright, young Euphues exchanges academic arguments with wise old Eubolus on the issue of worldly experience versus the codified wisdom of the ages. Euphues fails to heed Eubolus's sage advice and decides to taste the world, only to become the emotional captive of Lucilla, a courtesan who strips him of his money and dignity. A chastened Euphues vows to spend the rest of his life contemplating philosophy and warning the young. *Euphues, the Anatomy of Wit* was a continuing hit with a wide audience, and Lyly's peculiar style established a fashion that persisted for a decade. Called "euphuism," this style features the culling of exotic lore from the pseudohistories of the ancients, primarily the Roman scholar Pliny. In euphuistic argumentation, these strange bits are used as evidence for or against certain courses of action. That euphuism succeeded where other linguistic experiments such as "marivaudage" failed shows the hunger of Lyly's audience for a mode of discourse that would make them appear learned.

Lyly's most enthusiastic follower was Robert Greene, a highly original novelist in his own right who composed an amazing variety of euphuistic

romances between 1580 and 1587. In such Greene works as *Mamillia* (1583, 1593), *The Mirror of Modesty* (1584), *Morando: The Tritameron of Love* (1584, 1587), and *Euphues His Censure to Philautus* (1587), one can see most clearly the amalgamation of sources—Italian *novelle*, the Bible, Castiglione, Greek epic—in Elizabethan fiction. Unlike Lyly, however, Greene brings to these romances a spirit of comic realism that invests his characters with greater fullness and sympathy than Lyly's characters. Greene's later romances (such as *Menaphon*, 1589, and *Greene's Never Too Late*, 1590) reject euphuism in favor of a somewhat colloquial conversational style better suited to his more realistic characters.

When Greene turned away from Lyly in 1588, he was responding to the new fashion for pastoral love stories established by Sidney's huge romance, *Arcadia*, which had been circulating in manuscript since 1580 but was not published until 1590 (revised in 1593 and 1598). *Arcadia*, an aristocratic work similar to Honoré d'Urfé's *L'Astrée* (1607-1628, 1925; *Astrea*, 1657-1658), shows the blending of the Greek romances, with their pastoral and heroic elements, and the intensely emotional love pastorals of Sannazaro and the Elizabethan sonneteers, including Sidney himself. There is a good deal of the chivalric spirit present here, too, as knightly combats, with armor and emblems vividly described, are the primary means of settling disputes. Amid the shipwrecks, kidnapings, heroic rescues, and seemingly endless love laments of the sexually frustrated heroes, Musidorus and Pyrocles, two genuinely sympathetic characters emerge: Amphialus and his wife Parthenia. Theirs is a tragic tale of the Homeric conflict between a soldier's sense of duty and his regard for his wife, whose desire for his safety leads her to endanger herself and ultimately lose her life. The power of this story within *Arcadia* derives from Sidney's almost Shakespearean refusal to take sides—his willingness to let the story unfold and allow the reader to judge. Had the novel's main plot—his heroes' often silly attempts to win the favor of a pair of princesses—been exchanged for a serious investigation of ethical issues, Sidney might have produced a work of the stature of Miguel de Cervantes's *El ingenioso hidalgo don Quixote de la Mancha* (1605, 1615; *The History of the Valorous and Wittie Knight-Errant, Don Quixote of the Mancha*, 1612-1620; better known as *Don Quixote de la Mancha*). Cervantes' novel—one of the greatest in literary history—has had an influence upon popular fiction, drama, and film in the West that can scarcely be overstated.

Thomas Shelton translated part 1 of *Don Quixote de la Mancha* into English shortly after its original publication. Poet and playwright William Shakespeare may well have read Shelton's translation. In fact, some scholars have speculated that one of Shakespeare's lost plays was a dramatization of *Don Quixote de la Mancha*. Henry Fielding imitated the manner of Cervantes in *The History of the Adventures of Joseph Andrews, and of His Friend Mr. Abraham Adams* (1742; commonly known as *Joseph Andrews*). Fielding also composed a ballad-opera entitled *Don Quixote in England* (pr., pb. 1734). Tobias Smollett, Daniel Defoe, and many later English writers paid the tribute of imitation to the knight of La Mancha.

Among the traits that limited Sidney as a novelist was his contempt for the common people, as shown in *Arcadia* in several episodes that caricature plebeians as stupid, greedy, and bestial. Since the future of publishing in England meant appealing to the powerful London middle class, it was inevitable that novels would emerge with middle-class heroes and heroines. Greene's later romances are of this category, as are the works of Thomas Deloney, a silk weaver, whose *The Pleasant History of John Winchcomb in His Younger Days Called Jack of Newbery* (1597; better known as *Jack of Newbery*) and *Thomas of Reading: Or, The Six Worthy Yeomen of the West* (c. 1600) feature romanticized artisan heroes within vividly authentic backgrounds of English town and rural life.

Deloney's contribution to English literary history was much disputed by scholars of the twentieth century. Although some considered him "an astonishing genius" and others disregarded him entirely, most current critics and historians take a middle view of Deloney's significance as a prose writer. While not a genius, Deloney was one of the first English authors to write for and about the rising middle class. His

perceptiveness of the prevailing literary climate, whether educated or merely fortuitous, was accurate, for his popularity among the middle class was unsurpassed. His works, within only a few years of their publication, were literally read out of existence. Contemporary fiction's debt to Deloney is substantial, for his portrayal of middle-class values, concerns, and language are the roots of the modern novel.

That Deloney became a spokesman for the middle class was only a portion of his accomplishment. Another reason for the popularity of his works was that they were written in prose. Prior to Deloney's time, written works were composed in verse or dramatic form, making the exploration of rising social issues a laborious chore. Less artificial, prose fiction better addressed such subject matter, and Deloney proved himself a more talented master of the form than most prose fiction writers of his time.

What makes Deloney's fiction outstanding are his skillful use of dialogue and his excellent characterizations. Presenting three-dimensional middle-class characters drawn from his hard-working colleagues, Deloney engages them in dialogue fit for the stage. Instead of the lofty language familiar only to kings and nobles, however, he captures the idiomatic speech and straightforwardness of the common people of his day.

Deloney's plot development is less remarkable, although it should not be lightly dismissed. *Jack of Newbery*, considered his most unified prose work, is a tale about a young man who works for a wealthy clothier and eventually becomes the master of the business when the owner dies, leaving the conscientious young Jack (known as John) to marry the widow. The majority of the work centers on John's adventures after his wife has died and he has become a wealthy man. *Thomas of Reading* is a less unified work, yet it reaches a level of plot sophistication higher than that of *Jack of Newbery*. In it, King Henry I is made aware of the value of the clothing industry in England, and by deliberately supporting the clothiers, he enables them to raise their social positions. Such a change in social status was finally an attainable goal for the working class, and thus a tale of this type appealed to a wide audience.

While many of Deloney's characters typically grasp the beneficent hand of capitalism, Deloney ensures that they do not succumb to the snobbishness common to those who already enjoy aristocratic freedoms. After diligently earning their wealth, these protagonists liberally distribute it, thus allowing the entire community to prosper from their good fortune. Despite such indirect moralizing, Deloney was accepted as the militant spokesman for the middle class, and the political disjunction between his views and those of Sidney gives evidence of the social rift that would lead to civil war in the next century.

Class and religious tensions—the fires fanned by economic decline—were already sparking sharp satires, some obviously political, others less partisan in their scourge of social abuse. In the latter group are Greene's tales of "connycatching" (1591-1592), which purport to expose the methods of actual thieves and con artists so that decent citizens may beware. These contributed to the development of fiction in England because Greene's reproving tone is a thin veil for his real interest in exploring the romantic, sympathetic side of the criminal stereotype. Such characters as Ned Browne, Nan the whore, Laurence the cutpurse, and Cuthbert Connycatcher blend the *picaros* with the courageous imps of the medieval jestbooks. The candor and colloquial discourse of these stories created a fashion for rogue books that persisted through the seventeenth century and influenced Defoe.

Brilliantly capitalizing on the connycatching fad was Greene's boon companion Thomas Nashe, one of literature's sharpest tongues and quickest wits. After achieving notoriety through vicious anti-Puritan pamphlets and personal attacks on literary foes, Nashe penned the age's premier satiric novel, *The Unfortunate Traveller: Or, The Life of Jack Wilton* (1594). Lacking the fellow feeling of a Lazaro, a Gil Blas, or even one of Greene's connycatchers, Nashe's Jack Wilton astounds the reader with the range of his amoral exploits and the depth of his depravity. He satirizes through deeds, not only words: He outcheats the greatest cheats, plots the deaths of murderers, tortures the heartlessly cruel. Though he makes a perfunctory repentance at the end of the novel, Jack is a thorough villain who satirizes not from a sense of moral outrage but because his clever foes are so gullible or have the audacity to be as villainous as he. His attacks on Italy, for example, are inspired by the Italians' allegedly unquenchable thirst for vengeance, a trait that Jack has much reason to fear.

Just as outrageous as Jack's character is Nashe's cast of minor figures: King Henry VIII, Thomas More, Erasmus, and most other notables of the early sixteenth century. Jack spends a good deal of the novel as the servant of Henry Howard, the earl of Surrey, and together they romp through dangerous escapades. History as rewritten by Thomas Nashe is a pageant composed for Jack Wilton, poor in birth but inexhaustibly rich in wit. The plot and the person are incredible, but Nashe so deftly appeals to the cynical reader that it is easy to see this book as a realistic fiction rather than what might more accurately be described as a fantasy of revenge. The dark tragedies of Cyril Tourneur, John Webster, George Chapman, and Thomas Middleton in the Jacobean years partake of this same spirit and were surely influenced by *The Unfortunate Traveller.*

THE SEVENTEENTH CENTURY

Because satiric fiction of the next decades returned to the pattern and subject matter of the connycatching works, prose writers who followed Nashe perhaps found his brilliance inimitable. The best of these writers, Thomas Dekker, presented collections of jests and stories carefully describing the shifts of London thieves and beggars in his *The Bellman of London* (1608) and *Lanthorn and Candlelight* (1608, 1609; revised as *O per se O*), both heavy-handed condemnations of the outlaws from the perspective of the outraged citizen demanding protection. Dekker affects neither Greene's sympathy nor Nashe's worldly wise cynicism. Because his works create no real characters, they cannot really be said to be novels.

Just as the French religious wars of the sixteenth century precluded the growth of the novel in that country, so the strides in English fiction taken during the Elizabethan years were halted during the seventeenth century as the economy worsened and religious tensions increased. Though novel readers continued to demand reprints of Elizabethan fictions, no significant works in this genre were produced in England until well after the Restoration of the monarchy in 1660. The appetite for novels during the first two-thirds of the century was satisfied by translations of contemporary French works, with *L'Astrée* and the heroic novels of Madame de Scudéry enjoying great popularity. Ironically, when the century did produce a great English novelist, John Bunyan, he was ignored by the readers of French novels because of his allegorical method and his Puritan views.

Bunyan's masterpiece, *The Pilgrim's Progress*, was partly written during his second imprisonment for unauthorized preaching. This occurred some six years after his first imprisonment (1660-1672), during which he had written his spiritual autobiography, *Grace Abounding to the Chief of Sinners* (1666), an intensely moving study reminiscent of Saint Augustine's *Confessiones* (397-400; *Confessions*, 1620). It would be misleading to say that *The Pilgrim's Progress* was influenced by any literary source except the Bible, since the uneducated Bunyan is not known to have been familiar with any other of the earlier seminal works. This partly explains why Bunyan's style avoids affectations that make most fiction of this period undigestible for modern readers. Also, Bunyan wrote for an audience as simple as himself, one that did not demand the veneer of learning applied by aristocratic writers.

If the Bible did influence Bunyan's masterpiece, one can find in Revelation the source for his use of the dream-vision framework, as well as such features as the castlelike heaven, the goal of Christian's journey. The allegorical hindrances that the pilgrim encounters on his trek, such as the Castle of Despair and the Hill of Difficulty, seem original with Bunyan, though certainly the mode of the allegorical journey is familiar from Edmund Spenser's *The Faerie Queene* (1590, 1596), a work probably known to Bunyan. Undeniably original are Bunyan's characters, such as Timorous, Mistrust, and Talkative, who not only embody the vices for which they are named but also talk as authentically as actual people in whom one recognizes these dominant traits. The ar-

guments of these characters are so plausible that the reader sympathizes with the character Christian's frequent doubts about how to proceed and whom to believe. Moreover, Bunyan's characterizations are so concise, his observations so exact, that a character's presence for one or two pages is sufficient to keep him or her sharply defined in the reader's memory. For example, though Christian is accompanied by Faithful through only a small portion of part 1 of *The Pilgrim's Progress*, one builds up enough sympathy for this character to feel shocked when he is murdered by the citizens of Vanity Fair.

Bunyan as a novelist works so economically, so unselfconsciously, that the reader quickly loses the sense of artifice, even though the work is in an unorthodox form. In other words, *The Pilgrim's Progress* is one of those rare works of fiction that readers usually do not regard as fiction because they apprehend it as truth. Passing directly into the cultural mainstream of the people without having been authorized, as it were, by literary society, Bunyan's allegory can be said to have influenced most English writers since the mid-eighteenth century, although its traces are often hard to mark because it has been so well assimilated.

Beginning just after the appearance of *The Pilgrim's Progress*, though in no way inspired by Bunyan's work, the novelistic career of Aphra Behn appealed to the aristocratic and city audience to which Bunyan gave no thought. Predictably, her novels and stories follow the French heroic pattern, with its idealized, beautiful characters and exotic settings. In her best work, *Three Histories* (1688), a collection that includes the notable *Oroonoko: Or, The History of the Royal Slave*, Behn adds a wrinkle that makes her heroic works irresistible: The stories purport to be true, and she includes sufficient London names and places to make the assertion believable. At a time when London society craved gossip about the fashionable and saw the *roman à clef* as a way to satisfy that craving, readers preferred to accept the illusion of allegedly real people performing impossibly heroic acts rather than explicit fiction attempting the accurate portrayal of reality. In *Oroonoko*, for example, a pair of African lovers (with ideal European aristocratic manners) are swept across continents and oceans from one harrowing scrape to another until both are murdered. Despite the implausibility of the events, readers accepted Behn's claim that the incidents actually occurred.

THE EARLY EIGHTEENTH CENTURY

Behn's popularity occasioned many imitators. In competition with them were the writers of sensational accounts of authentic voyages to exotic places. Both forms appealed to the taste, present in every age, for examples of individual survival or death in the midst of calamitous events. It was to suit this taste that the most famous adventure novel of modern times, Daniel Defoe's *The Life and Strange Surprizing Adventures of Robinson Crusoe, of York, Mariner, Written by Himself* (1719; more commonly known as *Robinson Crusoe*), was written. Drawing on numerous accounts of travelers' shipwrecks, isolation, and survival, Defoe created a study of the individual in collision with environment that surpassed in realism any previous English fiction, except perhaps *The Pilgrim's Progress*. Defoe's *Robinson Crusoe* and *The Fortunes and Misfortunes of the Famous Moll Flanders, Written from Her Own Memorandums* (1722; more commonly known as *Moll Flanders*) created a fashion for realistic characterization that made possible the character studies of Richardson, Fielding, and their successors.

Firmly established as a journalist, political propagandist, and editor of popular periodicals, Defoe brought to the writing of *Robinson Crusoe* an unerring sense of public taste and a sure knack for the detail or turn of phrase that would convince the reader of the authenticity of a story. Though the central fact of the book, an Englishman's survival on an uninhabited island for twenty-eight years, is as improbable as many of Behn's turns of plot, Defoe makes the entire story plausible by his scrupulous attention to even the tiniest fact of Crusoe's existence. Where Behn or one of her imitators would have focused on the emotional trauma of shipwreck and isolation, Defoe, eminently practical in all his endeavors, focuses on the mundane *how* of existence: how to ensure a supply of meat when all the powder and bullets are gone, how

to make a shovel without iron, how to bake bread without an oven. Nevertheless, Defoe does not slight Crusoe the moral and emotional creature; perhaps the greatest masterstroke of the novel is that Defoe first makes the reader confront and gradually accept the narrator's aloneness then presents the fearsome truth that Crusoe is not alone. Though Defoe's sincerity as an ethical writer has often been questioned, there is nothing feigned about Crusoe's confused response to his savage visitors. Behn's *Oroonoko* has been called the first novel to make equality of the races an issue, but Crusoe's profound dilemma over his proper reaction to the Indians' cannibalism is a more authentic grappling with the issue than is Behn's portrait of the dark-skinned slaves as noble innocents.

Following the immediate success of *Robinson Crusoe*, Defoe wrote two sequels in the same year, one a series of further adventures and the other Crusoe's reflections on his miraculous life. Meanwhile, Defoe's prolific imagination was at work on a new project, the "private history" of a London woman who, originally a poor orphan, grows up to lead an exciting, inevitably scandalous life before finally achieving security and station. *Moll Flanders* differs in plot and setting from *Robinson Crusoe*, but the psychological authenticity of this purportedly true memoir is brought about by standard Defoe methods. Where Crusoe lovingly recounts his ingenious solutions to minute logistical problems, Moll recalls verbatim the coolly calculated speeches, the nuances of dress and gesture, that had been either her making or undoing in romantic affairs. These are Moll's tools of survival just as surely as Crusoe's odds and ends are his, and Defoe, through his everlastingly coy narrator, convinces the reader that her predicament within society is perhaps more precarious than Crusoe's without. Moreover, one accepts the extremity of her situation because she, like Crusoe, wastes few words bewailing it, instead moving immediately from the recognition of disaster to the search for means to survive. One does not pity Moll; rather, one sees oneself in her plight and soon comes unconsciously to share her values.

The reader accepts Moll's authenticity as an autobiographer because she is neither more nor less conscious of her motives than one would expect her to be. She is intuitively ethical, knowing that her need for money does not justify her thievery, especially from people no better off than she is; nevertheless, she is not so aware of herself as to realize that her panic-stricken repentance in Newgate is not real. Neither she nor Defoe are hiding tongue in cheek when she vows to live honestly, then immediatcly lies. When, at the end, Moll, rich and secure, says that she and her husband (the fourth of five, but the only one surviving) will spend the rest of their days in penitence, the reader can stand back and chuckle. With the realization that it would be useless to demand that the protagonist be more introspective, the reader understands that Defoe has established Moll's character to be the child of a society where money is everything and only the rich can afford to be morally precise. The greatness of the novel is that Defoe never mentions this point; the closest Moll comes to this is to say that a woman without a dowry is lost and that a woman without looks or a dowry is truly lost.

The irony of the novel is that Defoe, in his preface, would have the reader believe that *Moll Flanders* is a story of despicable deeds fervently repented rather than one of inevitable deeds and a sprinkling of penitent words. With his eye on the prejudices of his audience, he could not bring himself to say that Moll could not repent because society could not forgive and because it was really society that nccdcd repentance. He, like his flesh-and-blood heroine, dared give the lie to his public time and again, in one "true" history after another, but he, like she, dared not take off the mask.

Not much later, on the Continent, Voltaire produced *Histoire de Charles XII* (1731; *The History of Charles XII*, 1732). His interest in the extraordinary character of Sweden's great soldier-king moved Voltaire to write the king's biography, but he did so emphasizing details of the monarch's personal, not public, life. Thus, the history reads like a novel, and Voltaire would eventually use the techniques developed in writing this book in his creation of two philosophical novels at midcentury. By the third decade of the eighteenth century, then, Defoe had successfully

exploited fiction disguised as history, and Voltaire had written history that read like good fiction.

Christopher J. Thaiss, updated by Patrick Adcock

BIBLIOGRAPHY

Gilman, Stephen. *The Novel According to Cervantes.* Berkeley: University of California Press, 1989. *Don Quixote* not only influenced great picaresque novels that would later be written in English (including Henry Fielding's *The History of Tom Jones, a Foundling*, 1749, and Mark Twain's *Adventures of Huckleberry Finn*, 1884) but also firmly established several stock characters for generations of popular novels, plays, and films: the comic sidekick, the idealized and unresponsive maiden loved by the hero, and the elusive villain orchestrating the hero's woes from the shadows.

Hill, Christopher. *A Tinker and a Poor Man: John Bunyan and His Church.* New York: Knopf, 1989. Examines the political, social, and theological background of *The Pilgrim's Progress*, thc one indisputably great English novel of the seventeenth century. Two long chapters are devoted to a detailed analysis of thc novcl.

Sambrook, James. *The Eighteenth Century: The Intellectual and Cultural Context of English Literature, 1700-1789.* 2d ed. White Plains, N.Y.: Longman, 1994. A good introduction to the intellectual currents of eighteenth century England. Traces thc impact of social, political, and aesthetic thought upon the literature of the period, including the novel.

Sill, Geoffrey M. *Defoe and the Idea of Fiction, 1713-1719.* Newark: University of Delaware Press, 1983. Concentrates on the period during which Defoe managed to establish himself as a writer more or less free of political connections. Also provides sound information regarding the novelist's activities during the six years preceding thc appearance of his first "honest cheat," the supposedly true history of *Robinson Crusoe*.

Smith, Grahame. *The Novel and Society: Defoe to George Eliot.* Totowa, N.J.: Barnes & Noble, 1984. The first seventy-one pages of this book are devoted to a broad discussion of the relationship of literature—in its several forms in different countries during different periods—to society, followed by an examination of Daniel Defoe, Tobias Smollett, and the rise of the novel in England. From page seventy-two (chapter 3) onward, the author discusses Samuel Richardson and novelists who wrote between 1740 and the late nineteenth century.

Tatum, James, ed. *The Search for the Ancient Novel*. Baltimore: Johns Hopkins University Press, 1994. Twenty-four essays tracing the influence of ancient Greek, Roman, Byzantine, and Arab romances, pastorals, and tales upon such novelists as François Rabelais, Miguel de Cervantes, Samuel Richardson, and Frances Burney.

Williamson, Marilyn L. *Raising Their Voices, 1650-1750*. Detroit: Wayne State University Press, 1990. Discusses the contributions of women to the Enlightenment in England. Aphra Behn, though breaking no new intellectual ground, firmly established the place of women in the field of novel writing. *Oroonoko: Or, The History of the Royal Slave* was popular and proved that any woman who could give the public sensational adventures occurring in exotic or glamorous settings would find a reading audience. Although, in the next century, the gothic romance was introduced into England by a man, Horace Walpole, it soon became the domain of women novelists and has remained so ever since.

ORIGINS AND DEVELOPMENT OF THE NOVEL, 1740-1890

No primary genre of literature has been so often defined and redefined as the novel, and still, no consensus has been reached. Several scholars have suggested that the only valid definition of the novel is the history of the genre itself. The origins of the modern novel, however—the novel as it appears in bookstores today, encompassing both serious fiction and best-sellers—are more easily traced. The modern novel in the eighteenth century and its rise in the nineteenth coincided with the rise of the middle class. In consequence, as Ian Watt observes in *The Rise of the Novel* (1957), one of the paramount features of the novel has been its focus on a detailed re-creation of the bourgeois interior: the clothes, the furnishings, the belongings of the middle class. The novel is also distinguished, Watt points out, by its emphasis on individual characterization, an emphasis that can be related to the social and political movements of the eighteenth and nineteenth centuries. These movements recognize the dignity of the individual and the equality of all people. Despite all its transmutations and variations, the novel today performs the same function it has served since the eighteenth century: It offers reports (to borrow a title from Anthony Trollope) on *The Way We Live Now*.

Since American literature was, in its early stages, merely an outgrowth of English literature, this survey will treat the development of the English novel before turning to the history of the form in America. It is well to note at the outset, however, that there are several notable differences between the English and the American novel. While generalizations about "the novel" in a given nation must always be hedged, it is true that, as Richard Chase observes in *The American Novel and Its Tradition* (1957), "The American novel tends to rest in contradictions and among extreme ranges of experience," while "the English novel has followed the middle way." Frederick R. Karl, in *A Reader's Guide to the Nineteenth Century British Novel* (1972), argues that "unlike the American novel, the English novel principally takes place in time, not space." He then maintains that the "temporal" emphasis of the English novel, as opposed to the

"spatial" aspect of the American novel, is related to the greater "blandness" of English fiction, since people who live in a restricted space must pay closer attention to time and also must modify their behavior more rigorously than those who occupy large areas, feel no sense of crowding, and need give much less heed to the passage of time and the markings of its flow.

More important than such dissimilarities, though, are the general likenesses, one of the most significant being the tendency traced in Erich Kahler's study, *The Inward Turn of Narrative* (1972). Kahler's thesis is that throughout the eighteenth and nineteenth centuries, the consciousness of Westerners turned more toward an inner vision of reality, and that the novel reflects this slow but momentous shift in human attention. As Watt indicates, the "realism of the novel allows a more immediate imitation of individual experience" than do other literary forms, and "this surely explains why the majority of readers in the last two hundred years have found in the novel the literary form which most closely satisfies their wishes for a close correspondence between life and art."

The narrative element of the novel can be traced back to preliterate eras when storytellers recounted long narratives, such as the Sumerian *Gilgamesh Epic*, which dates to about 2000 B.C.E. In some ways, Gilgamesh is not so different from the protagonist of a contemporary novel. During the course of the epic, he changes: He grows, then declines. Initially, he is a bad, oppressive king. Then, under the beneficent influence of his dear friend, Enkidu, he grows into a good king whose reign is marked by great deeds. At Enkidu's death, Gilgamesh is overcome by grief and despair. He undertakes an arduous journey in search of the secret of everlasting life. When he finds, then loses the secret, he returns to Uruk, sickens, and dies.

Such narratives, however, were in the form of verse, which facilitated memorization; narrative prose fiction was a much later development. Precursors of the modern novel can be found in every literate culture, ranging from Greek romances such as Chariton's *Peri Chairean kai Kalliroēn* (c. second century C.E.; *The*

Loves of Chareas and Callirrhoe, 1764) to *Genji monogatari* (c. 1004; *The Tale of Genji*, 1925-1933), written by Murasaki Shikibu in eleventh century Japan. Like a novelist of the nineteenth or twentieth century, Murasaki portrays her society in exquisite detail. It is not, however, a bourgeois society; it is the society of the Imperial Court. The novel as it is now known, however, began in the eighteenth century, following related but distinct lines of development in England, Spain, and on the Continent.

EIGHTEENTH CENTURY BACKGROUND

Many factors contributed to the birth of the English novel in the eighteenth century. An important social phenomenon was the growing trend of country people gravitating to the cities, especially London. Although no reliable figures are available, it is certain that the population of London multiplied several times from 1660 to 1740. With the growth of the city came the attendant blessings and curses: a more rapid and wider spread of ideas, an easier dissemination of reading material, the development of a more commercial society (although England's economy remained primarily agrarian until the Industrial Revolution), as well as the miseries of urban crime (which had been flourishing since the Elizabethan era, but never so widely), unhealthy living conditions, insufficient housing, disease, and what has been called the greatest social curse of the period, the high incidence of drunkenness. As late as 1780, infant and child mortality was still at a shockingly high level; it was rare for a family to have more than half of its children reach adulthood.

Such a lively and perilous time was, in a sense, made for Daniel Defoe (1660-1731), regarded by many critics as the first significant English novelist. As a small businessman (often a failed one), occasional spy, prolific writer under various names in a number of genres, a Dissenter (one who refused to accept the Established Church of England, though still a Protestant), and generally energetic citizen (who was accused of being a Trimmer, a person who switched from Whig to Tory, or vice versa), Defoe seems to represent nearly all the conditions that prepared the way for the appearance and popular acceptance of the English novel. These conditions include an emphasis on the individual, both as a social entity and a being with a soul, and an interest in his daily affairs (Defoe displays this emphasis clearly in *The Fortunes and Misfortunes of the Famous Moll Flanders, Written from Her Own Memorandums*, 1722), the treatment of narrative in measured time rather than in eternal time (thus the novel deals with events in a more specific temporal frame than that of the heroic romance—Henry Fielding's *The History of Tom Jones, a Foundling*, 1749, is perhaps the quintessential example of such a careful temporal treatment). Other conditions in Defoe's works that prepared readers for the novel are people seen acting in a real setting, which includes earning a living, eating, drinking, and making love; an interest in improving one's social and economic status, usually by legal means, but not exclusively so (Moll Flanders tries to live honestly, but circumstances force her into thievery); a growing independence, of children from parents, citizens from their government, parishioners from the Church, and everyone from traditional ideas and beliefs, especially those received from the past and from authoritative sources; an emphasis on interior scenes and urban experiences (though the countryside was to figure prominently in the English novel for two centuries, much of the most important action takes place indoors, with the most detailed description being saved for interiors—the classic later example of this accent is the work of Charles Dickens, 1812-1870); and finally, an unprecedented attention to the interests and aspirations of women.

As a man of his age, Defoe represents as well as anyone that most significant fact about the English novel: It is the ultimate expression of the middle class. No literary form was written and read by the ever-growing middle class as much as the novel. By the time Samuel Richardson (1689-1761) published *Pamela: Or, Virtue Rewarded* (1740-1741), the reading public was rapidly expanding, though it was still very small by modern standards. Again, no reliable numbers are available, but scholarly estimates indicate a figure of about seventy or eighty thousand, which was only 1 or 2 percent of the total population. The figure increased as the century waned, but even by 1800, only a small fraction of the population, perhaps some 100,000 people, were capable of reading a novel.

The same process was under way in the East, though probably at a somewhat lesser rate. Between 1740 and 1750, Cao Xueqin, or Ts'ao Hsüeh-Ch'in (1715-1763), born into a once-prominent family then in decline, wrote the first eighty chapters of *Hong-lou Meng* (1792; *Dream of the Red Chamber*, 1929; also as *The Story of the Stone*, 1973-1986; also as *A Dream of Red Mansions*, 1978). A second writer, Gao E (c. 1740-c. 1815), added another forty chapters and published the final version in 1791. This classic novel embodies the cultural identity of China at the middle of the eighteenth century.

1740 TO 1764

In 1740, potential novel-readers were chiefly interested in family life, the details of everyday living, and the problems of morality on an individual basis. Wide generalizations concerning what constituted ethical conduct, as were found in Alexander Pope's poetry, may have been widely quoted, but they were not taken much to heart; also, the novel could do what no verse essay by even so skilled a versifier as Pope could do: It could show morality being lived. Richardson's *Pamela* satisfied these interests, and the book was extremely popular. The fact that Richardson tells most of the story by way of letters is an indication of the particularity of detail and expression and the interest in the individual that engaged the attention of readers near the middle of the century.

As to the economy and the stability of the government, the nation was in reasonably good condition. At this point, England was enjoying a rewarding trade relationship with its colonies in the New World and was in the initial stages of the process of taking over India. The wars in which it engaged took place on foreign soil. George II (1683-1760) was not a skilled ruler, but the country was controlled chiefly by ministers, who were intent on keeping or increasing their power, always with an eye, however, to avoiding open conflict with the people. The most notable civil disorder of the era (not counting the abortive attempts to restore the Stuarts to the throne, which had

little effect on the lives of ordinary citizens) were the Gordon Riots, an anti-Catholic outburst, which did not take place until 1780 and were confined to small sections of London, lasting but a few days.

Although called the Age of Reason and although the official philosophy was one of rationalism, the actual lives of most people were not at all lived according to such theories; this fact is more clearly reflected in the novel than in any other form of literature. The best-known heroes of the early novel are either criminals, such as Moll, or rebels against a hostile society, such as Clarissa and Sophia Western from *Tom Jones* (the former running away from home and being drugged and seduced, the latter also escaping from her father and nearly being raped). Tom Jones is turned out of his benefactor's house on very slender evidence of wrongdoing; he is then beaten, robbed, and almost hanged, and it takes almost eight hundred pages to establish his innocence. (Typical of the increasingly middle-class morality of the time, one of the chief themes of *Tom Jones* is that virtue is what a person owes to others, while prudence is what one owes oneself.) These works deal primarily with the lives of one or two central characters, further evidence of the eighteenth century emphasis on the individual.

Individuality, as a concern and thematic focus, is most strikingly advanced in the entertaining but often nearly surrealistic *The Life and Opinions of Tristram Shandy, Gent.* (1759-1767), by Laurence Sterne (1713-1768). Some critics believe that Sterne's book did more than any other to open the way for the later psychological novel. This concern was also indicated by the spread of Methodism, whose first meetings were held in 1729. In its early stages, before it hardened into an established denomination, it was an emotional movement that went back to the individualistic roots of Protestantism. The focus on the life of the individual is also reflected in the earlier, and continuing, enthusiasm for biography. Defoe augmented this tradition by basing *The Life and Strange Surprizing Adventures of Robinson Crusoe, of York, Mariner, Written by Himself* (1719) largely on the experience of the Scottish sailor Alexander Selkirk, who was marooned on an island for some four and a half years. Typically, Defoe transforms Crusoe into a resourceful, God-fearing middle-class person who hardly changes at all during more than twenty-five years on the fictional island—unlike Selkirk, who emerged from his experience in a half-bestial state.

Along with an increasing emphasis on the particulars of people's lives, the early novel depended heavily on a flexible, readable prose style that was far from the inflated expression of the romances of earlier times. Much of the brevity and liveliness of this "new" style was the product of journalists and "hack" writers, who were compelled to produce considerable quantities of material for an unliterary audience in short periods. Defoe is again a classic example. He did not start writing long fiction until he was sixty, by which time he had produced hundreds of expository works of a very readable nature, most of them published in periodicals. On a more lofty plane, but still of a vigorous composition, were the widely admired informal essays of Joseph Addison (1672-1719) and Richard Steele (1672-1729), published chiefly in the popular periodicals *The Tatler* (1709-1711) and *The Spectator* (1711-1712). The styles of Richardson and Fielding (1707-1754) are also somewhat more elevated, as befits the stories of more socially eminent characters (Fielding was the more "literary," having had a superior education and an admirable career in the law, along with previous experience as a successful dramatist); but Tobias Smollett (1721-1771) wrote in a very plain style, displaying the "common touch" to a high degree and attaining a much enjoyed earthy humor.

One reason that prose fiction sold so well during this era was the Licensing Act of 1737, directed at the theater, which amounted to a form of censorship enforced by a sensitive government under the leadership of Prime Minister Sir Robert Walpole, who had been the butt of several satirical passages in popular plays. In effect, this law forced Fielding to turn from drama to the novel; it also encouraged bland theater, thus winning a greater readership for contentious periodicals, such as the famous *Spectator Papers*, by Addison and Steele, which led a growing list of well-written and topical journals. The emphasis on individualism during this period was further reflected in the new es-

teem for portraiture, leading to illustrious careers for such great portrait painters as Sir Joshua Reynolds (1723-1792), a popular member of Samuel Johnson's celebrated Club, and Thomas Gainsborough (1727-1788). Johnson's group, which met more or less regularly in the 1760's and 1770's, was a culmination of another eighteenth century tendency that exhibits the desire of people to come to know others on a quasi-individual basis: the popularity of the coffeehouses, establishments where upper-middle-class men gathered to discuss events of the day, the latest articles in the current periodicals, and one another. One of Johnson's salient criticisms of men he did not like was that they were "unclubbable."

Since the novel was written chiefly for the middle class and selected most of its characters from the ranks of this group, it reflects the lamentable fact that nearly all the truly charitable work that was done during this mid-century period (and there was an unfortunate paucity of it, by modern standards) was accomplished by the middle class. It was this stratum of society that instituted the parish groups that gave to the poor and looked after unwed mothers and orphaned offspring (though, as *Moll Flanders* clearly demonstrates, the care was woefully inadequate for many). The two institutions that would be expected to take the lead in such endeavors simply failed to do so in any meaningful fashion until the next century; they were the government and the church, both of which were more determined to promulgate their primacy and power than to form any effective organized assistance for the unfortunate members of society. Foreign wars and economic shifts created a large body of such people; indeed, former military people who become idlers appear as minor characters in decades of British fiction.

Perhaps the chief cultural irony of this period is that the novel both protested against the conditions of society and yet depended on them for its existence. The cosmic concerns expressed by earlier writers (John Milton, 1608-1674, is perhaps the most obvious example) did not attract the interest of readers as they had. People were more interested in how to get along, live both successfully and morally, and come to terms with the rapidly changing times. For such guidance, it was not the philosophers or great poets to whom most readers turned, but the novelists, for these middle-class authors spoke to the real needs and concerns of their readers. Addressing this issue, Johnson's moral strictures against licentious material in the newly popular novels were severe but were based on a genuine concern for the virtue of the readership, many of whom were "the young, the ignorant, and the idle." Apart from the ethical aspect of this influential declaration of concern, Johnson's remarks, in an essay published in *The Rambler* in 1750, also reveal the great effect that fiction was having on a number of its readers, who, Johnson notes, "regulate their own practice" on the models of the leading characters in novels.

One of the few major historical events that captured the imagination of the everyday reader was the voyage around the world from 1740 to 1744 of George Anson (1697-1762) and, later, the Pacific explorations from 1768 to 1779 of James Cook (1728-1779). Thus, the passages in Smollett's *The Adventures of Roderick Random* (1748) dealing with the hero's experience on a naval vessel were of considerable relevance to the novel reader. As the feats of explorers and colonizers became known, a greater sense of empire, as well as the recognition of ever-increasing opportunities for trade, began to be felt in the populace. England's navy, strong for centuries, was now the guardian of a lively British maritime commerce around the world, with the colonies providing invaluable raw materials and opening areas for further colonization and economic development for enterprising adventurers.

1764 TO 1800

The date 1764 is of special significance in the history of long fiction because it clearly marks the beginning of a distinct change in the direction of English culture, especially as reflected in the novel. The first genuine gothic novel (the novel of suspense, terror, exotic setting, and effects) was published in that year. *The Castle of Otranto* (1765), by Horace Walpole (1717-1797), enjoyed an enormous success and signaled a shift in public taste toward the exotic, the extraordinary, and violent passions—toward the Ro-

mantic movement, adumbrations of which can be found this early.

Another early sign of Romanticism is a different sort of novel, also the first of its kind: *The Vicar of Wakefield* (1766), by Oliver Goldsmith (1728-1774), regarded as the harbinger of the novel of sensibility, another signal of the Romantic "temperament." These two impulses, the gothic and the sentimental, were to gain an even greater hold on the interests and reading habits of the late eighteenth century English. Further evidence of this shift in enthusiasm can be found in a seemingly unrelated art, that of architecture. The early eighteenth century had seen the construction of practically designed and constructed buildings, with symmetrical proportions and even measurements (the double cube was a popular design)—a kind of "proper" organization also found in the well-trimmed and geometrically planned formal gardens (the topiary art reached its highest point in this era). The later age preferred wild countrysides spotted with ruined or half-ruined castles or rude country dwellings, charming in their quaint rusticity. These "wild" settings became increasingly common in novels and were a staple feature of the Romantic novel to come.

Another important stand of Romanticism was anticipated by the publication of Bishop Thomas Percy's *Reliques of Ancient English Poetry* (1765), which brought to its clearest exposure an interest in the medieval past, which had been growing since early in the century. The enormous popularity of the volume by Percy (1729-1811) testified also to the wider interest in ancient and exotic poetry that came to characterize Romanticism. Further, nature, which was to play so large a part in later novels—notably those of the Romantic Sir Walter Scott—is secondary to the concern for human welfare, especially in terms of emotional states.

Such pre-Romantic tendencies were not confined to England. One of the most popular novels of sensibility was *Die Leiden des jungen Werthers* (1774; *The Sorrows of Young Werther*, 1779) by Johann Wolfgang von Goethe (1749-1832), a pathetic tale of unrequited love and sad but eloquent protestations of passion and self-pity. It has been claimed that the suicide rate among young readers rose sharply soon after this novel was published. Goethe's novel reveals a typical connection between the novels of sensibility and gothicism in that much of the scenery in his tale is wild and "natural." The pre-Romantic tendencies revealed in these novels can also be discovered in the often socially critical, homespun Scottish poetry of Robert Burns (1759-1796) and the mystic verses of William Blake (1757-1827).

Probably the most extreme manifestation of sensibility is to be found in Henry Mackenzie's *The Man of Feeling* (1771); in this short novel, the hero falls to weeping more than fifty times. All this sentimentality (which was, in later novels, to be the basis of some extremely humorous satire, as in Jane Austen's *Northanger Abbey*, 1818) was in part an expression of the flowering social consciousness of the age. This sense of an imperative to develop sensitivities to the needs and concerns of others allied itself with the perennial didactic element in the novel and in the national consciousness. Just as the early novelists often claimed a morally elevating purpose in order to have their works accepted by the public and not roundly condemned from the pulpit, so the writers of this era genuinely believed that their novels were stimulating readers to loftier sentiments and more generous acts. In Parliament, the moving and eloquent speeches by the liberal Edmund Burke (1729-1797), many of which were devoted to opposing the government's narrow-minded policy of taxation in the American colonies, officially ratified the growing belief that people had a right to be helped by others and that the willingness to do so was a sacred duty for any who were able. A popular phrase in the novel of sensibility asserted that the true gentleman "was never an indifferent spectator of misery in others." This attitude assumed, of course, that human nature was essentially benevolent, a notion that did not take hold in popular fiction until this period.

The notion that human nature is, if uncorrupted by evil forces, naturally good was urged upon the English nation by the influential French philosopher Jean-Jacques Rousseau (1712-1778), whose asseveration that humans in their natural state are moral gave rise to a widespread discussion of the doctrine of the "noble savage." This theory relates to the whole atmosphere of primitivism that is found in the ballad revival (intensified by Percy's volume) and associated phenomena, such as the novel of ideas, a genre that usually endorsed liberal educational and social concepts. Typical of the genre was Thomas Day's *The History of Sandford and Merton* (1783-1789), a humorless tract in the form of a novel that tries to prove that a "natural" education is better than an excessively structured one and that morality is always rewarded. Many of the novels of ideas dealt with education in Rousseauistic terms, but the most striking novel of liberal tendencies was William Godwin's *Things as They Are: Or, The Adventures of Caleb Williams*, 1794 (also known as *The Adventures of Caleb Williams: Or, Things as They Are*; best known as *Caleb Williams*), which has the distinction of being one of the earliest novels of propaganda and also perhaps the first novel of crime and detection.

These novels of social concern illustrate an important phenomenon of the period: The novel was beginning to occupy a position that had formerly been held by the drama. While a few excellent satires can be found near the close of the century—such as Goldsmith's *She Stoops to Conquer: Or, The Mistakes of a Night* (1773) and Richard Brinsley Sheridan's *The Rivals* (1775) and *The School for Scandal* (1777)—generally, the burgeoning concern for human rights and social reform is to be found most fully developed in the novel, though a number of poems also revealed such concerns. In *English Literature from Dryden to Burns* (1948), Alan D. McKillop argues that the novel "entails a critical or analytical attitude toward characters represented under actual or conceivable social conditions" and that the "critical attitude is directed toward both individual character and the social situation." The book suggests the way in which the novel was coming ever closer to the real lives of its readers as the eighteenth century came to a close. Despite the excesses of the sentimental novel and the novel of terror, the central trend of prose fiction was toward an attempt to grasp and come to terms with the world as it had to be dealt with by individual people every day.

Perhaps the best example of this tendency is the

work of Frances "Fanny" Burney (1752-1840), whose moralistic but readable novels of domestic life contain a great deal of sensible advice—either by demonstration or declaration—for their readers, especially young women. The extensive readership attained by her novels illustrates another aspect of the times: More women were beginning to read and write novels. Burney had a great many followers in the field of domestic fiction. This trend helped to prepare the way for the woman who is, in the view of numerous critics, the best female novelist in the language, Jane Austen (1775-1817).

In 1759 the fierce French satirist Voltaire (1694-1778), Rousseau's arch-philosophical and literary enemy, had published his masterpiece of dark comedy, *Candide: Ou, L'Optimisme* (*Candide: Or, All for the Best*, 1759). This fast-moving combination of farce and biting satire sweeps its naïve hero along from one disaster to another, each of which evokes from the reader laughter rather than feelings of horror. One character is hanged, a second has a sword thrust into his belly up to the hilt, and a third is repeatedly raped and stabbed. All reappear later in the novel, not only still alive but also little the worse for wear. The plot races from Europe to South America, back to Europe, and finally to the Middle East. Voltaire's influence on the English novel extended well into the twentieth century. *Candide*—like comic novels about rootless and irreverent young people—*Decline and Fall* (1928) and *Vile Bodies* (1930) by Evelyn Waugh (1903-1966), *Afternoon Men* (1931) by Anthony Powell (born 1905), and *Highland Fling* (1931) by Nancy Mitford (1904-1973)—flourished for a time and constituted almost a "school" of the period.

It could be argued that, for common people, the Industrial Revolution—which might be said to date from 1769, the year of James Watt's first patent for a steam engine—was more important than any political unrest. For intellectuals, however, among them many novelists, the disappointment over the Reign of Terror, which was seen as a betrayal of the worthy liberal sentiments that had inspired the revolution, was deep and of great duration. The youthful William Wordsworth (1770-1850) was among the most grimly unsettled of the poets to be shocked by the

bloody course that the insurrection took; the young Sir Walter Scott (1771-1832), though not as morbidly struck as the poet, was deeply disappointed. The reason for the perhaps greater significance of the industrial advance among the lower and middle classes was that individual lives were more directly affected. This fact is of signal importance in the development of the English novel, because this genre, as no other, concentrates on the inner lives of people. Whether the author achieves a detailed delineation of the thoughts and emotions of a character (as does Richardson) or a clear demonstration of the character's motives by action (as in Fielding), the novel depended on single people, both in their relationships with others and in their interpretation of the meaning of their own lives, for most of its interest and value. This dependency was to increase in the ages following the eighteenth century. That the trend was to be informed by what could be considered a semirevolutionary bent (the single person pitted against society or a tradition) was only the predictable result of the tenor of the times.

1800 TO 1832

The first decades of the nineteenth century were the peak of Romanticism in English literature, its chief exemplars being the five great Romantic poets John Keats (1795-1821), Percy Bysshe Shelley (1792-1822), William Wordsworth (1770-1850), George Gordon, Lord Byron (1788-1824), and Samuel Taylor Coleridge (1772-1834). All of these artists wrote verse that emphasized the imaginative intuition of the individual as the way to achieve truth.

Sir Walter Scott was a powerful force in the popularization of both Romantic poetry and the Romantic novel. His *Minstrelsy of the Scottish Border* (1802-1803) capitalized on the widening interest in old ballads and folktales, especially of the rural type. Scott turned to the novel as an act of self-defense when Byron became so popular that the verse of other poets could no longer command an adequate market. At the time, Scott had no idea of what a favor was being accorded him. The publication of *Waverley: Or, 'Tis Sixty Years Since* (1814), the first of the so-called Waverley novels—all of which are set in the past and many of which provide insightful, if not fully accurate, visions of historical events and people—marked the commencement of a groundswell of enthusiasm among readers for depictions of wild Scottish scenery and vigorous actions performed by impossibly virtuous and somewhat leaden heroes in the defense of improbably sweet and chaste heroines. Scott's talent for characterization was never highly praised, except in his portraits of lower-class characters such as thieves, pirates, and gypsies, but his powers of description were unequaled in his day. In his better works, such as *The Heart of Midlothian* (1818) and *The Bride of Lammermoor* (1819), he attained gothic effects that rival those in any of the novels in the genre, even the works of Ann Radcliffe (1764-1823) and Charles Robert Maturin (1780-1824).

While verse was the prevailing form during the Romantic period, the novel was still popular; the growth of the population, especially in cities, and the proliferation of lending libraries permitted a wider dissemination of fiction and thus greater economic rewards for writing and publishing novels. There was, however, still a stigma attached to both the writing and the reading of fiction. Scott published his first several novels anonymously, and Jane Austen took considerable pains to conceal from all but members of her family that she was actually writing novels. A period that can boast the wide sweep and narrative drive of Scott's historical fiction and the elegant but barbed domestic vignettes of Austen is rich indeed.

An additional aspect of the novel in this era was the fairly new emphasis on regional fiction. Maria Edgeworth (1767-1849) dealt with the problems, charms, and complexities of life in Ireland with sensitivity and perception. Relations between Ireland and England had been strained since the time of Elizabeth I. Edgeworth offered some penetrating arguments in favor of the Irish side of the question, most notably on the injustice of the English practice of absentee landlordism. Although satire was not the predominant tone of the fiction of the period, the novels of Thomas Love Peacock (1785-1866) provide an entertaining vision of the romance as seen through more modern eyes, with lively touches of humor. The very titles of some of

his most popular works indicate the nature of his approach: *Headlong Hall* (1816), *Nightmare Abbey* (1818), and *Crotchet Castle* (1831).

1832 TO 1870: THE EARLY VICTORIAN AGE

Although Victoria did not gain the throne until 1837, several events suggest the year 1832 as a suitable date to designate the opening of the era that bears her name. It is well to note, however, that the designation indicates how mixed and complex the cultural and historical period was. It followed epochs that were identified according to their obvious characteristics: the Age of Reason, the Enlightenment, the Age of Pope, the Age of Johnson, the Romantic age. A seventy-year period named after the reigning monarch is something of an evasion, but the era was so complicated and contradictory that the choice is understandable. As Walter Houghton notes in *The Victorian Frame of Mind* (1957), "Studies in this area have emphasized only a few characteristics, notably moral earnestness and optimism, to the obscuring of others, equally important, like enthusiasm and anxiety." He goes on to explain how difficult it is to capture the spirit of the period because it is composed of so many divergent and, at times, contradictory elements.

Indeed, anxiety was underlying a great deal of the surface optimism for which Victorian England is famous. Thus, the celebrated attack by Matthew Arnold (1822-1888) on the ignorant remark about the era's wonderful condition by an English industrialist makes a great deal of sense. Another indication of the anxiety and conflict that pervaded the period can be found in the Oxford, or Tractarian, movement, which started in 1833 and persevered until 1841. It was an attempt to elevate the position of the Church (in that time, this meant always the Church of England, the Anglican Church) in the lives of the people. There were complicated theological and even political reasons for the zeal of the reformers, but one can perceive in this intense conviction that there was a need for such a radical change, an aura of uncertainty and even anxiety about the cultural substance of the life of the time.

The novelist who, for many readers, epitomizes

the Victorian Age, Charles Dickens (1812-1870), published his first major work between 1836 and 1837. *Pickwick Papers* (originally published as *The Posthumous Papers of the Pickwick Club*) demonstrates an additional aspect of the Victorian "personality": a delightful sense of humor, chiefly based on charming eccentricity of character. It is typical of the age, however, that the tone of Dickens's novels almost steadily darkened throughout his lifetime. Indeed, one can trace an increasing tendency toward grimness as the century passed in novelists from Dickens through Thomas Hardy (1840-1928).

In part, the increasing pessimism of the Victorian age reflected a growing awareness of urban blight, of the complex consequences of the Industrial Revolution. There were few novels specifically about industry, but Dickens's impassioned plea for more humanity and less materialism, as found in *Hard Times* (1854; originally published as *Hard Times for These Times*), was echoed in the works of lesser writers who were popular in their day. Dickens protested against a variety of social abuses, from inhuman schools for poor children, as in *Oliver Twist* (1837-1839), to the corruption and inefficiency of the courts of chancery, as in *Bleak House* (1852-1853); particularly intense was his resistance to the cruel working conditions created by the factory system, presented most sharply in *The Old Curiosity Shop* (1840-1841), a work whose excessive emotional stress causes it to cross the border into bathos, a common failing of the era's novels. Despite these social concerns, the central thrust of the novel in the Victorian period remained toward a revelation of the ways by which more or less common people attempted to meet the challenges of life, generally on an individual basis. The principal tone tended to be comic in the early years of the period, growing more somber as the decades passed, and ending with the cold pessimism of Thomas Hardy.

The spiritual crises that afflicted many of the artists and thinkers of the Victorian era—particularly the conflicts with Charles Darwin's evolutionary hypothesis, but also with other challenges to orthodox Christianity, such as Higher Criticism of biblical texts—lent the later novels of this period a philo-

sophical depth and seriousness unprecedented in English fiction. The most impressive novelist who wrote in this vein was George Eliot (1819-1880), in whose works one of Thomas Carlyle's most iterated principles is demonstrated repeatedly: the assertion that life can take on its true meaning only when the individual is willing to renounce earthly glory and material possessions. The theme of renunciation that resounds through *Adam Bede* (1859), *The Mill on the Floss* (1860), *Silas Marner* (1861), and *Middlemarch* (1871-1872) is an echo of the same stress placed by Carlyle (1795-1881) on this human recognition of limited claims and the virtue of humility. These two "philosophers" of the period, Carlyle being the earlier, reveal two diverging tendencies in the Victorian attitude toward prominent people. While Carlyle (in his famous essay *On Heroes, Hero-Worship, and the Heroic in History*, 1841) praises the "hero" in history as the kind of person who makes historical events happen, Eliot presents her leading characters as simple people who demonstrate the Victorian trend away from the usual vision of the lofty, noble, aristocratic hero of the past, as in Scott's historical novels. As Mario Praz establishes in *The Hero in Eclipse in Victorian Fiction* (1956), the romantic hero gave way to the middle-class man or woman who exhibited worthy moral traits, some bravery, and a lack of egotism. Such central characters allowed Eliot and a host of lesser writers to explore the intellectual and emotional depths of people who appear common (they certainly occupy common places in society) but display profound levels of sensitivity and spiritual resources. Eliot's often noted remark that she found God inconceivable but duty indispensable illustrates a typical attitude of many of the respected authors of the middle and later Victorian period.

1870 TO 1890: THE LATE VICTORIAN AGE

This era, referred to as the late Victorian age, usually includes the last decade of the century; it is also known as the Realistic period. The generation opened with the death of Dickens in 1870 and the publication of Darwin's *The Descent of Man* in 1871, a work that further elucidated the theory of evolution, which by this time was more generally accepted. In the same year, one of Hardy's early novels, *Desperate Remedies*, appeared. This gloomy title not only indicates the grim philosophy that Hardy revealed in nearly all of his novels but also suggests the plight of many of the inhabitants of Great Britain, who had encountered several political and cultural "realities": the repressive policies of Lord Palmerston, prime minister in 1855-1858 and 1859-1865; the positivistic interpretation of history in the works of Hippolyte Taine (1828-1893), whose *History of English Literature* was translated in 1873; and the naturalism of Émile Zola (1840-1902). The potato famine that had struck Ireland in 1846 was a harbinger of the hard times to strike the rest of the British Isles. As the previously expanding economy began to slow down and settle into less expansive patterns, the competition from other industrial nations, especially the United States and Germany, began to take a severe toll. The near monopoly in international trade that England had enjoyed for decades was irrevocably broken. For the laboring classes, the results were catastrophic. There were extended periods of unemployment, and the rate of emigration, before but a trickle, rapidly rose. It is estimated that some twenty thousand English citizens emigrated to America in 1886 and that an even greater number left in the following two-year period.

An inevitable result of the ruptures in the previously booming economy was the increased interest in socialistic projects and leaders. In 1880 three Labor Party candidates won seats in Parliament; soon afterward, several socialistic organizations were founded, the most remarkable being the Fabian Society, started in 1884, which was later to count H. G. Wells (1866-1946) and George Bernard Shaw (1856-1950) among its members. The disorder in society that this sort of expedient implies was indeed present. Faith in a number of institutions, such as the Church, the Monarchy, Parliament, the economic system, religion, and even science, began to wane.

By an odd, but not unique, quirk of psychology, the novels of Anthony Trollope (1815-1882) found their popularity largely on the basis of their calm tone, the certitude of a pleasant outcome (now and then, Trollope stops the story to inform the reader that there is no cause for anxiety, since he has arranged it so that all will be well), and the relatively trivial concerns of the characters, many of whom are country parsons with very little of serious import in their actions and conversation. This phenomenon was repeated during the anxious days of World War II, when Trollope was again popular. This impulse to escape was to be expressed in a much different manner in the 1890's by the Decadents, who championed "art for art's sake" on the theory that art is far above life and therefore should not soil its hands trying to deal with it. The most famous of the Decadents was Oscar Wilde (1856-1900), whose semigothic supernatural novel *The Picture of Dorian Gray* (1891) was a sort of fictional announcement of the bizarre extremes of this movement.

Thus, while the empire was expanding abroad, life at home for the lower classes—the upper middle class was not harmed much by the unemployment and the emigration—was not prosperous. The resistance among writers to the principles of expansion of the empire and the heartless exploitation of both foreign and domestic laborers was vocal. In the novel, one finds such impassioned propagandistic works as Hardy's *The Mayor of Casterbridge* (1886) and George Gissing's *Workers in the Dawn* (1880).

From a more purely literary standpoint, however, the age was a rich one, as the novel achieved a wider scope and a greater depth than it had yet known. Though George Eliot is best known for her novels of domestic life, such as *Middlemarch*, she also took up social causes with an intensity and thoughtfulness not found before in the English novel—the prime example is *Daniel Deronda* (1876), which deals with "the Jewish question." Although England had had a skilled Jewish prime minister, Benjamin Disraeli (1804-1881), in office for several long periods in the nineteenth century, anti-Semitism was still widespread and often institutionally sanctioned. Eliot, along with Hardy and George Meredith (1828-1909) in particular, also helped create what was to become known as the psychological novel. Certainly, foreign writers of the realistic school—most notably the French realists Honoré de Balzac (1799-1850), Stendhal (Marie-Henri Beyle, 1783-1842), and Gustave Flaubert (1821-

1880)—had assisted in opening the paths to psychological realism, but the English novelists of the late nineteenth century carried this tendency to a lofty height. British literary historians occasionally enjoy claiming that the American-born Henry James (1843-1916), who could be classified as the most insightful of all psychological realists, was more of an English novelist than an American one, since he lived the last thirty-five years of his life in England and wrote a great deal more about English society than he did about that of his native land. The claim is hotly contested, however, by students of the novel in the United States, and there is much in James's work that proclaims its author as essentially American, wherever he chose to reside.

The period ended with the death of Robert Browning (1812-1889). This most Victorian of writers, whose optimistic poems are so well known as to mislead casual readers, is a fitting representative of the era that, to a large degree, ended when his life did. The way was already prepared for the more modern writings of later poets such as Rudyard Kipling (1865-1936), a severe critic of the empire-building practices of the government, and William Butler Yeats (1865-1939). The novelists to follow included Robert Louis Stevenson (1850-1894), Joseph Conrad (1857-1924), Arnold Bennett (1867-1931), and D. H. Lawrence (1885-1930). The works of these authors, and of the other imposing figures who were to carry this magnificent genre down to the present, would not, however, have been possible without the efforts of the countless writers of long fiction who opened the avenues of what F. R. Leavis has aptly called *The Great Tradition* (1964).

BACKGROUND OF THE AMERICAN NOVEL

By general consent, the first American novel was *The Power of Sympathy* (1789), very probably by William Hill Brown (the matter of authorship is somewhat obscured by the assignment of the book to Sarah Wentworth Morton for a number of years); it was not published until 1789. There had been numerous literary achievements of varying aesthetic merit since the founding of the two earliest settlements in what were to be the colonies: one at Jamestown, Vir-

ginia, in 1607, and the other at Plymouth, Massachusetts, in 1620. No memorable fiction was produced, however, until late in the next century. Most of the earliest works were practical, semihistorical pieces, such as Captain John Smith's *A True Relation of Such Occurrences and Accidents of Noate as Hath Hapned in Virginia Since the First Planting of That Collony* (1608) and *A Description of New England: Or, Observations and Discoveries of Captain John Smith* (1616). A substantial body of religious literature began to appear, including the famous *Bay Psalm Book* (1640), which had the distinction of being the first book to be printed in America, Roger Williams's *Bloudy Tenent of Persecution, for Cause of Conscience, Discussed* (1644), the poetry of Edward Taylor (c. 1645-1729), and the fiery sermons and tracts of Increase Mather (one of whose titles, *Case of Conscience Concerning Evil Spirits*, 1693, provides an indication of the force of the Puritan tendency in these writings) and Cotton Mather (1663-1728). These and similar works, well into the eighteenth century, provided information, attitudes, some impressive poetic imagery, and much moralizing; what they almost entirely lacked was any recognizable belletristic quality. This was especially true of the prose. Fiction did not begin to find a general readership until the second half of the eighteenth century, and most of the fiction published at that time in the colonies was either British (because no international copyright law existed, much importing and pirating of novels from the mother country occurred) or closely based on British models, chiefly novels by Daniel Defoe, Samuel Richardson, and Henry Fielding.

The delay in the appearance of native fiction of high quality is usually attributed to a variety of causes, both cultural (a heavy dependence by the colonies on Britain for literary forms and techniques endured until long after the American Revolution, 1776-1781) and natural (the enormous land mass of the "new" continent and the regionality it stimulated). Many scholars believe that the primary reason for the delayed and tentative beginning of American long fiction, apart from the influence of British examples, was simply the absence of an indigenous culture rich in tradition; in Henry James's formulation

(*Hawthorne*, 1879), it requires "an accumulation of history and custom . . . to form a suggestion for the novelist."

On the other side of the situation, it has been noted that this paucity of social and historical substance compelled American novelists to discover or create other bases for their themes, founded on more abstract material. The result, claim the scholars who are favorably impressed by this phenomenon, was a fiction rich in symbolism and allegory, a literature abundant in metaphysical significance and elevated by a textual density. Of special interest in this connection is the massive achievement of *Moby Dick: Or, The Whale* (1851), in which Herman Melville (1819-1891) created a symbol of evil (or, some readers believe, of something far more complex) that may represent the highest attainment in the English language of a thematic expression. Nathaniel Hawthorne's "romances," as he wished his fictions to be designated, are almost by definition apart from the British genre of the realistic novel of social life. It is inviting to speculate about what Mark Twain (1835-1910) would think, given his preliminary instructions to readers to eschew a search for any motive, moral, or plot (with a dire warning of severe punishment for offenders), of the current scholarly attention given to *Adventures of Huckleberry Finn* (1884), which discovers in the novel archetypal characters (such as Jim, who is interpreted as a surrogate, spiritual father to Huck) and events (such as the journey down the Mississippi River, which has been elucidated as a recapitulation of the quest motif found in primitive myth). In *Form and Fable in American Fiction* (1961), Daniel Hoffman makes a persuasive case for the enormous reliance of American novelists on folklore and the extensive utilization of allegorical and symbolic modes of signification.

Since America comprises such a vast expanse of territory, and since this area includes regions settled by people with diverse backgrounds and ambitions, it has been customary to divide the country into several sections, noting the most imposing characteristics of each. The differences among these regions are striking evidence of the geographical reasons for what is often perceived as the rich variety of American litera-

ture. For a considerable time, the cultural life of America was synonymous with the cultural life of New England, and Boston was judged the cultural capital of the country as well as its publishing center—the first printing press in America was established in Cambridge in 1639—until well into the nineteenth century, when it relinquished that distinction to New York. More isolated by topographical features than any other major division of the nation, New England was marked by an often-overstated Puritan fervor and a moralistic emphasis. The middle states—usually regarded as including New York, New Jersey, Pennsylvania, and perhaps Maryland and Delaware—were distinguished by the great diversity of their settlers and the resulting manifold qualities of thought and concerns. By contrast, the South developed a more homogeneous culture, a sort of feudal society based on the establishment of slavery. From a literary standpoint, the chief cultural benefit of the plantation system was that it allowed the growth of a leisured class of "aristocrats" who had the time and the education to read widely and write articulately.

The last general division in the national consciousness, which was soon to be broken into constituent regions, was the West, an area that was unknown, untraveled, and thus possessed, for the first settlers and many later immigrants, an awesome charm. As the frontier moved west, more and more was learned that removed the mystery from the land, but until late in the nineteenth century, the image of the West held by many Americans and foreign visitors was still marked by a sense of romance, unreality, freedom, and unlimited opportunity. A measure of the linguistic importance of this regional aspect of America may be seen in the fact that, at the First Continental Congress in 1774, many of the delegates were frustrated because they found themselves nearly unable to comprehend the speech of other members.

In establishing the periods of American literature, great variance is found, and there are quarrels regarding most delineations of the periods. The wisest deduction would appear to be that American literature is so complex, despite the evident relative simplicity of the nation's history and culture, that clear separations are just not possible or, perhaps, legitimate. Furthermore, the person who most historians agree was the first American professional author, Charles Brockden Brown (1771-1810), did not publish until near the end of the eighteenth century, and then he was only moderately successful. This account denotes the difficulty of the situation in American letters for a serious novelist. As in England, the novel in America was chiefly the product of middle-class authors and the reading material of middle-class citizens. These middle-class writers, however, were not as close to social and political subjects as their British counterparts. The current explanation for this distance is that there existed a severe tension between several pairs of opposing impulses and enthusiasms. Among these, the more obvious are those between the intense desire for freedom and the fact of slavery, the opposing attractions of Romanticism and rationalism, and the antagonism between the desire for economic power and what Leslie Fiedler calls "the need for cultural autonomy." One result of these tensions and the difficulty of obtaining a unified vision of American society was that the most important authors tended to resort to forms of escape, distancing them from the people. James Fenimore Cooper (1789-1851) escaped to the frontier, Hawthorne fled to the past with his insightful studies of the Puritan ethos, Melville found liberation in distant settings and on the sea, Mark Twain escaped to the near past and the West, and Henry James went to Europe in order to find suitable subject matter for his art.

1789 TO 1820

Several conditions prevailed prior to that period in England that hindered the development of the novel there. These conditions also existed, but with greater impact, in the Colonies until the time of the American Revolution and afterward, lessening as the decades passed; they are important in understanding why the American novel did not develop as fast as its European model. Apart from the problem of colonial, later state, loyalties (Alexander Cowie, in *The Rise of the American Novel*, 1948, points out that most citizens, even after a national identity had been established, would declare their "country" as the state

from which they came), there was a scattered population, making the dissemination of books difficult and expensive; an uneven and low level of public education, an area in which America lagged sadly behind Europe; and finally, a lack of publishers. Although, in the last decade of the eighteenth century, more than fifty new magazines were published, few had any chance of persisting, and almost all were content either to print fiction from abroad or focus on practical, expository material. This emphasis on the pragmatic had a further dampening effect on the production of worthy native fiction.

The early American novels that were set in America and dealt with distinctively American concerns were almost entirely of a moralistic nature, since the moral strictures that had militated against lively, imaginative novels in England were felt in America as well; in some regions, mainly New England, they were felt with even more force than in Britain. As a consequence, the fiction that was turned out well into the nineteenth century tended to be both didactic and imitative of English forms, such as the novel of domestic life, the sentimental novel (these categories often overlapped), the gothic romance, and the historical novel.

William Hill Brown's *The Power of Sympathy* (1789) fits into the category of the novel of domestic life with more than a suggestion of the qualities of the sentimental novel, and it has a heavily moralistic dedication; yet it is replete with sensational elements such as near incest, seduction, abduction, and violence. The influence both of the story of Moll Flanders—the low-born protagonist of Defoe's tale of suffering, thievery, and intrigue—and of Richardson's account of the grim adventures of the upper-middle class Clarissa Harlowe is seen here. Of an equally lively nature but better written—Brown's style is ponderous and much in the vein of the lesser English authors of the eighteenth century—is Susanna Rowson's popular *Charlotte: A Tale of Truth* (1791; published in the United States as *Charlotte Temple*, 1797), which also displays the effects of the pressure of a Puritan morality and probably a sympathetic reading by the author of the works of Fanny Burney. Other novels of this type, written chiefly by women, established this subgenre in American literature for decades to come.

The gothic romance, while it was presented in some impressive early examples, mostly those of Charles Brockden Brown, did not flourish as had the domestic and sentimental novels. The most apparent reason for this weakness was the lack of didactic themes. The gothic setting and plot did not encourage moralizing on the author's part. There was also often a touch of the picaresque in these productions, which tended to discourage moral lessons. Like the British models, such as William Beckford's *Vathek: An Arabian Tale* (1786; original French edition, 1787) and Matthew Gregory Lewis's *The Monk: A Romance* (1796; also published as *Ambrosio: Or, The Monk*), the American gothic novel developed a body of gothic machinery designed to terrify. As in England, the form stimulated a number of parodies of its most extreme features: unlikely plots, bizarre settings, and unwholesome characters whose actions often descend into the lunatic.

As a reaction against these types developed in the form of the early historical novel, marked by the introduction of American Indians as important characters, the level of the quality of fiction in the New World began to rise, but at a slow pace. It is noteworthy that it was not until nearly fifty years after the American Revolution that American novelists dealt significantly and seriously with the event. The delay was once again largely the result of a powerful British cultural influence on the new nation. When that influence was overcome, and as the country commenced to become more unified (improved roads and modes of travel had a great deal to do with this advance), the ground was laid for the important achievements of writers.

1820 TO 1865

The unrest at the heart of the American novel, especially in the nineteenth century, is particularly evident in the work of James Fenimore Cooper (1784-1851). It is not so evident in a lesser book, such as *Satanstoe: Or, The Littlepage Manuscripts, a Tale of the Colony* (1845), as in the more famous novels: *The Last of the Mohicans: A Narrative of 1757* (1826), *The Prairie: A Tale* (1827), *The Pathfinder: Or, The Inland Sea* (1840), and *The Deerslayer: Or, The*

First Warpath (1841)—the central titles in his famous Leatherstocking Tales, which recount the adventures of one of the most influential characters in early American fiction, the redoubtable Natty Bumppo. Cooper's presentation of this interesting personage's experiences on the frontier could be said to have brought about the development of the Western genre, or at least to have brought it to the highest point to which it aspired (the culmination of the trend may perhaps be found in Owen Wister's *The Virginian*, 1902, which, while a more sophisticated work, still emphasizes the virtues of Western heroes in contrast with the evils and corruption of the East). As Richard Chase, in *The American Novel and Its Tradition* (1957), declares, Cooper is at his best when he can "accept without anxiety or thought the vivid contradictions of Natty Bumppo and his way of life." Chase and many other literary historians point out that the unrest was the result of unresolved disunities in a nation that had been formed largely from disparate elements: progressive thinkers and conservative traditions, European influence and American innovation, and what would later be termed the "highbrow" versus the "lowbrow."

Such oppositions might well be expected in a new country whose physical borders were still expanding, with new states being added every several years, and whose population was still being enlarged by immigration at a rapid pace: More than fifty million people traveled to America from Europe and Asia during the nineteenth century. The lack of serenity in American political and economic life was mirrored by its artistic sphere. A sort of inferiority complex in the arts persisted in the United States long after the insulting remark by the British writer Sidney Smith in 1820: "In the four quarters of the globe, who reads an American book? Or goes to an American play? Or looks at an American picture or statue?" Many Americans were forced to agree that the artistic accomplishments of the new nation were slight. As late as the 1840's, Margaret Fuller (1810-1850), the scholarly author and friend of most of the transcendentalists (whose most illustrious member was Ralph Waldo Emerson, 1803-1882), asserted that, in order for America to produce a literature of its own, "an original idea must animate this nation." Few of these fresh concepts were to be found in a culture that was influenced by Europe and whose chief concerns were advancing its political growth and consolidating its economy.

Into this wasteland of artistic sterility, as many viewed it, came the imposing figure of Nathaniel Hawthorne, who turned to his Puritan forebears for material to be used in some of the finest short stories and at least two of the most impressive novels (*The Scarlet Letter*, 1850, and *The House of the Seven Gables*, 1851) to be created in the nineteenth century. One of Hawthorne's ancestors had been a judge at the Salem witch trials and had participated in the condemnation to ghastly torture of innocent women. The sensitive descendant of this old, honored, and guilty family could not rid himself of the sense of wrongdoing and, fortunately for his art, developed a haunting penetration into the nature of good and evil. Also of benefit to his writing was a more distinctive and loftier prose style than had been attained previously. Many scholars would concur with Irving Howe's judgment in *The Literature of America: Nineteenth Century* (1970), that Hawthorne is "the first great American novelist."

Howe and others see the Puritan influence elsewhere as well, in the works of writers as diverse as Herman Melville and Mark Twain. These authors were not only producing American novels of high quality, but they were also helping to legitimize the acceptance of American fiction in the United States. Their success was partially a result of nonartistic phenomena, such as the fact that the population of the nation, in 1840, was roughly four times what it had been at the time of the American Revolution and that the territory controlled by the country was enlarged by about the same proportion. Prosperity was causing people to take pride in their accomplishments and also providing more leisure in which to read fiction. While the stress on personal advancement sometimes took the form of immoral self-aggrandizement, there was a countervailing impulse toward endorsement of the leveling effects of democracy. This conflict, like so many others appearing in the United States toward the middle of the nineteenth

century, can be discovered as an underlying theme in the better novels of Melville: *Redburn: His First Voyage* (1849), *White-Jacket: Or, The World in a Man-of-War* (1850), *Moby Dick* (1851), and *Billy Budd, Foretopman* (a novella not published until 1924 but now considered one of his finest works).

The mid-century also saw the growth of "local-color" fiction, which ranged in the following decades from the Western sketches of Bret Harte (1836-1902) to the poetic realism of Sarah Orne Jewett (1849-1909). To some extent, the local colorists were preserving or re-creating a simpler, preindustrial America in the nostalgic mood of Twain's *The Adventures of Tom Sawyer* (1876). Though Twain produced only one generally accepted masterpiece, *Adventures of Huckleberry Finn*, the influence of nearly all of his stories, especially the early ones, was enormous. It is perhaps not too much to say that this emotionally troubled author (particularly in his later years) assisted America in realizing how much it had lost by the westward spread of civilization.

Harriet Beecher Stowe (1811-1896), a then little-known writer from the civilized East, fond of reading the romances of Sir Walter Scott, has been credited with awakening the conscience of the North to the horrors of slavery. *Uncle Tom's Cabin: Or, Life Among the Lowly* (1852) is hardly a great book, and its dependence on romantic elements is at times humorous, or would be were the subject of the novel not so unhappy. Abraham Lincoln was no doubt exaggerating when he remarked, upon meeting Stowe, that he was pleased to greet the little lady who had started the big war, but there is no question that this novel contributed greatly to the abolitionist movement. In so doing, it proved that a work of fiction could have a profound social and political effect on the nation.

The post-Civil War period, satirically named "The Gilded Age" by Twain and his collaborator Charles Dudley Warner (1829-1900) in their 1873 novel of that title, was also perceived, especially by later historians, as the age of realism. There had been novels with realistic elements before the war, but the forthright recognition by novelists of the harsh realities of the Reconstruction period tends to justify that designation. James emphasized psychological realism. While he did live mostly in Europe and often wrote about Europeans, he never lost his interest in the American personality; his novels are filled with fascinating American characters, often seen in conflict with, or corrupted by, the older society of Europe, such as the charming Isabel Archer of *The Portrait of a Lady* (1880-1881) and the very American Christopher Newman of *The American* (1876-1877). Even when James was writing chiefly about European characters who visit America, as in *The Europeans* (1878), one might say that the attentive reader gleans more information about the nature of American morals and attitudes, as with the Wentworth family in that story, than about those of the foreign characters. James's psychological realism influenced his good friend and constant admirer William Dean Howells (1837-1920), most notably in *The Rise of Silas Lapham* (1885). Howells was much more concerned with external reality and much cruder in his treatment of emotional nuances than was James.

Indeed, under the influence of naturalism, Howells went so far as to claim that art should be eliminated altogether and fiction turned into a sort of factual, semiscientific report of life as it is. He never attained this goal, but some of the naturalistic writers came close to doing so: Howells's influence on Frank Norris (1870-1902), Stephen Crane (1871-1900), and Theodore Dreiser (1871-1945) was considerable. In a larger way, James and Twain affected the course of American long fiction for a longer time. As depth psychology came into vogue, the examinations of characters' motives and states of mind so highly evolved in James's novels—the later ones, such as *The Wings of the Dove* (1902) and *The Ambassadors* (1903) are especially impressive for this achievement—became very influential. Although his popularity with readers has never equaled Twain's, James had a powerful effect on later writers.

The spread of literacy, which accelerated sharply after the Civil War, helped create a market for fiction, and a great number of minor authors emerged. Some of them had superior credentials, such as the historical novelist Francis Marion Crawford (1854-1909), who, during his travels and studies, attained a reason-

able fluency in more than fifteen languages. Most of these authors are, unfortunately, little read today. Stylistically, the most prominent influence on the period was Twain, to whom, much later, both William Faulkner and Ernest Hemingway admitted a debt. In another way, Twain encouraged the advance of the naturalist movement, which has been defined as realism with predilection for the nasty, by his increasing pessimism. This gloomy outlook, largely the result of business reverses (Twain was a poor businessman, and the expanding economy encouraged unwise investments), can readily be seen in the naturalistic writers.

The dejection in Twain's later work, most sharply revealed in the posthumously published *Mark Twain's Mysterious Stranger Manuscripts* (1969), was not without valid cause. The Gilded Age had followed what some experts consider the first experience of truly modern warfare, characterized by the participation of large numbers of civilians, the massing and action of large bodies of troops, and the phenomenon of individual battles often being decided on the basis of extensive massacres; also, it has been judged the first war in which victory was primarily the result of an industrial superiority. The epoch was modern in other ways as well, which, though not so bloody, were distressing: The growth of the economy created new industries and sudden fortunes, and it also brought into being a new class of urban poor and the beginnings of extensive slum areas. These grim conditions inevitably led to clashes between corporations and nonorganized workers, thus impelling the rapid expansion of the labor movement.

By 1890 the United States was well on its way to becoming a modern country, with all the blessings and curses that such a development implies. As usual, the novelists tended to fix their attention on the curses; yet this penchant could be regarded as something of a duty for novelists, especially in the modern era. When the liberal educator and writer Thomas Wentworth Higginson (1823-1911) was asked how one could best learn about "American society in its formative process," he recommended reading the novels of Howells. It might not be too much to say that Americans who desire to understand the most significant trends in the early development of their nation and their people would be well advised to peruse the novels produced by their own varied and energetic culture.

Fred B. McEwen, updated by Patrick Adcock

BIBLIOGRAPHY

Blackall, Eric A. *The Novels of the German Romantics*. Ithaca, N.Y.: Cornell University Press, 1983. Blackall argues that between 1795 and 1830, most notably in Germany, a complete revolution in the conception of the form of the novel took place. Here were the beginnings of the novel that moved away from linear, chronological narrative featuring finality toward a fragmented, ambiguous presentation. According to Blackall, the German Romantics declared the novel a poetic form, whereas in the eighteenth century it had been considered a prose form. The writings of Friedrich Schlegel, E. T. A. Hoffmann, Joseph von Eichendorff, and others are discussed.

Clayton, Jay. *Romantic Vision and the Novel*. Cambridge, England: Cambridge University Press, 1987. Clayton pursues the theme of transcendence in the English novel—the capacity to go beyond or rise above the bounds of ordinary experience. He cites *Mansfield Park* (1814), by Jane Austen; *Wuthering Heights* (1847), by Emily Brontë; *Little Dorritt* (1855-1857), by Charles Dickens; *Adam Bede*, by George Eliot; and *Women in Love* (1920), by D. H. Lawrence (the only novel from the twentieth century that Clayton discusses).

Ellis, Markman. *The Politics of Sensibility: Race, Gender, and Commerce in the Sentimental Novel*. New York: Cambridge University Press, 1996. Part of the Cambridge Studies in Romanticism series, this is a thoughtful examination of the sentimental novel. Politics, race, slavery, and the treatment of women in fiction are considered.

Harris, Sharon M., ed. *Redefining the Political Novel: American Women Writers, 1797-1901*. Knoxville: University of Tennessee Press, 1995. The political novel is one of the enduring forms in American fiction. This book features nine essays discussing the contribution of women writers to the genre.

Two essays deal with famous authors: Louisa May Alcott and Mary E. Wilkins Freeman. The other seven essays examine the work of less well known, but deserving, female novelists.

Holbrook, David. *The Novel and Authenticity*. London: Vision Press, 1987. Holbrook's thesis is that the contemporary novel is too often a vehicle for inauthenticity, no longer characterized by moral concern and a quest for truth but too often launching a "deliberate assault on values, meaning, and truth." In developing this interesting and controversial theory, he devotes his introduction and the first two chapters to novels of moral concern and authenticity: *Mansfield Park*, by Jane Austen, and *What Maisie Knew* (1897) and *The Awkward Age* (1897-1899), by Henry James. The balance of the book is devoted to later novels featuring nihilism and inauthenticity.

Horsman, Alan. *The Victorian Novel*. Oxford History of English Literature 13. Oxford, England: Oxford University Press, 1990. The time frame addressed is the period from the death of Walter Scott in September of 1832 to the death of George Eliot in December of 1880. Of the book's ten chapters, six are devoted to the major novelists Eliot, William Makepeace Thackeray, the Brontës (Charlotte, Emily, and Anne), Charles Dickens, Anthony Trollope, and George Meredith. Also contains a chronological table and a select bibliography.

Pearce, Richard. *The Novel in Motion: An Approach to Modern Fiction*. Columbus: Ohio State University Press, 1983. The author asserts that movement, an obsession of modern consciousness, dominates the modern novel. He begins his argument with the eighteenth century novelists Daniel Defoe, Samuel Richardson, and Henry Fielding, to whom he devotes his first chapter, along with Charles Dickens. The remaining chapters deal with the twentieth century novel and film.

Perosa, Sergio. *American Theories of the Novel: 1793-1903*. New York: New York University Press, 1983. The author begins with a discussion of the colonial background of the American novel. He follows these observations with chapters titled "The Debate over Realism in the 1870's and

1880's," "Henry James and the Art of Fiction," "Genteel Realism and Regionalism," "Naturalism, Veritism, and Impressionism," and "The New Romance."

Richter, David H. *The Progress of Romance: Literary Historiography and the Gothic Novel*. Columbus: Ohio State University Press, 1996. This volume examines the gothic genre in detail.

ORIGINS AND DEVELOPMENT OF THE NOVEL, 1890-1980

The environment in England during the 1880's and 1890's was an especially fertile one for the development of new trends in literature. As the century came to a close, all the giants of the novel, except George Meredith, had either died or stopped writing. Even Thomas Hardy, who can be justly classified as either "Victorian" or "modern," quit writing prose in 1895 and turned to poetry. The great Victorian poets, too, were disappearing: Matthew Arnold died in 1888, Robert Browning in 1889, and Alfred, Lord Tennyson in 1890. The Victorian stage, for decades the province of producers and directors who spared no expense to provide "spectacle" to audiences whose penchant for grand performances demanded ever greater mechanical wonders on the boards, was becoming the province of men such as George Bernard Shaw. His plays, while amusing at times, generally abandoned the grandiose for the middle class and did so with a striking (and sometimes disturbing) sense of realism. Upstarts such as Oscar Wilde and Walter Pater were turning their backs on "traditional" subjects in art and presenting material that could only be described by the general populace as "decadent." The younger generation of writers had turned away from their English ancestors, seeking inspiration from French novelists whose naturalistic treatment of subjects glorified the commonplace and vulgar while minimizing the good in traditional morality; Honoré de Balzac and Émile Zola became the luminaries whom budding authors copied with dedication and fidelity. Among this generation of writers and readers, the Victorian notion of "high seriousness" was giving way to a concern for subjects only whispered about during the heyday of that glorious queen who gave her name to the period. That aging lady still occupied the throne, but everyone knew that she was to die soon, and with her would pass an "age" in English life.

THE AMERICAN NOVEL: 1880-1900

On the other side of the Atlantic, the novel was also undergoing a transformation. By the close of the nineteenth century, most American novelists had declared their independence from their English forebears. Whether one agrees with Ernest Hemingway that "all American literature springs from one book," Mark Twain's *Adventures of Huckleberry Finn* (1884), it is nevertheless true that by the 1880's, American writers had turned to their own country for literary inspiration. The heritage of the American past, the attitudes and concerns of the founding fathers and the Puritan heritage they had bequeathed to their heirs, the legends of the original American Indian inhabitants of the land, and the particular curiosities associated with the various regions of the country had supplanted earlier tendencies to anglicize American situations and frontier characters. Whereas the Indians in James Fenimore Cooper's Leatherstocking Tales speak (and often act) like eighteenth century gentlemen, those of late century novelists exhibit no such artificiality. American writers had become interested in American society, a society that had, in a period of barely more than one century, grown from adolescent imitation of the English culture that had given it birth to an adult life that was in many ways different from that of its parent.

While Britishers such as Matthew Arnold could dismiss America as "uninteresting" and an expatriate such as Henry James lament the absence of castles, kings, and monuments that in Europe heralded a link to the past of a thousand or more years, most American writers of the last decades of the nineteenth century took a look around them, found what they saw of interest to themselves and to their countrymen, and wrote about it with fidelity not to British literary tradition but to their own growing awareness of the unique qualities of their own country. The absence of a society that dated back a thousand years may have made it difficult for Americans to write "social novels" in the manner of Jane Austen, George Meredith, or George Eliot, for, as Alfred Kazin has observed, the social novel most often flourishes in a society "deeply settled," one that "knows itself thoroughly" and "takes itself for granted."

What American writers lacked may have been a handicap in the 1830's, but by the 1880's they had abandoned their attempts to imitate their British counterparts; instead, they turned to the problems and the people around them for inspiration and found ample material for their work. The American experience had been, for almost three hundred years, one of change and development, characterized by the ever-present challenge to conquer the frontier. America was not, and had in fact never been, one society, but was rather a collage of many; its various regions—South, Northeast, Midwest, Pacific Coast—developed separate cultures in which political homogeneity was often the only common link to other areas in the vast expanse of yet unsubdued country. American novelists, turning from romance to realism, found their subjects in the various regions about which they chose to write. As a consequence, novelists as diverse as William Dean Howells and Mark Twain were both "realists" in depicting the American scene, though they differ significantly in subject matter and technique. Both treat American life, but life in the Northeast was quite different from that in the far West or along the Mississippi River. Hence, the modern American novel, born of a drive to portray a country and its people realistically, became for almost half a century a novel of regions and subcultures.

By the end of the nineteenth century, the novel had gained acceptance in America as a serious literary form, but even then there was strong sentiment among readers that novels were purely entertainment, unless some explicit moral was woven into the narrative. Beginning in the 1880's, however, a young American, a New Yorker by birth, a Bostonian by upbringing, and an expatriate by choice, began to change that perception, both in his homeland and in England.

HENRY JAMES

Henry James may well be considered the first modern critic of the novel, and since the modern novel is the product of self-conscious artists who are concerned with their craft as well as their message, it is well to begin a discussion of the development of the modern novel with James. Considering his own works to be art as well as social commentary, James spent four decades explaining, in essays and prefaces

he affixed to the collected edition of his works, how good prose fiction may be identified and judged. James's essay "The Art of Fiction" (1884), written as an answer to Walter Besant's essay of the same title, comes closer than any other document published during the final decades of the nineteenth century to being a manifesto for the modern novelist. Besant's essay had summarized the Victorian position on the role and limits of the novel: It was to provide wholesome entertainment, treat certain subjects only, avoid others at all costs, attempt verisimilitude but not at the expense of moral education, provide swift and unrelenting justice for moral offenders (especially where sexual transgressions were involved), and support the aims of society at large. In "The Art of Fiction," James struck out against almost all of these notions. The only requirement a novelist has, he says, is that he be "interesting." "We must grant the artist his subject matter," he insists, and judge the value of the work by the artist's success in executing his own design. No subject should be taboo, James argues, no artificial strictures should be placed on the novelist's creativity as long as that talent is put in the service of depicting life as it really is. Where Besant had tried to develop appropriate classifications for novels (similar to those used to describe various forms of poetry), James swept away such prescriptive categories, claiming that novelists must be free to explore incidents and characters and develop their stories in such a way as to be pleasing to the reader.

James fancied himself the consummate realist, interested in portraying life as it is lived by sensitive individuals full of thought and reflection. Much like Jane Austen, he limited his artistic gaze to a narrow segment of society, foregoing the panoramic techniques of the romancer and the historical novelist and avoiding the sweeping pronouncements of the social novelist to explore the nuances of social life among the upper classes. James has been called the first international novelist, and he was undoubtedly the first major figure to explore the clash of American and European cultures; in *The American* (1876-1877), *The Portrait of a Lady* (1880-1881), *The Ambassadors* (1903), *The Golden Bowl* (1904), and numerous other works, he presents American men and women, usually naïve and filled with the optimism characteristic of their countrymen, confronting the wiser but more jaded men and women of England and the Continent.

A late masterpiece, *The Golden Bowl*, may serve as an example of James's method. In that novel, a young American girl, Maggie Verver, falls in love with an Italian nobleman, Prince Amerigo. Amerigo is charmed by her naïveté but apparently prefers the company of her more worldly wise and well-traveled American friend Charlotte Stant, with whom Amerigo has apparently had an affair some time before. Because Maggie is rich, he agrees to marry her, and only after the two are already married does Maggie discover the true nature of the relationship between her friend and her husband. At the end of this sordid tale of social intrigue and betrayal, Maggie emerges victorious—after a fashion. Charlotte marries Maggie's father and returns with him to America, leaving to the heroine a prince who is apparently reformed enough to recognize where his loyalty should lie. In winning, however, Maggie loses, too; her father, whom she adores, returns to America, never to see her again, and she is at best a sadder and wiser woman for the "victory."

As an allegory of the conflict of cultures, James's novel is largely pessimistic about the modern condition. Such an attitude is clearly characteristic of the realists in general, who, looking scientifically at the contemporary scene, found little to cheer about in the present condition of society. These men and women were willing to openly express their displeasure, despite the threat of censure from a reading public accustomed to having their literary lessons presented either in romantic garb or in stark allegorical narrative. James and his contemporaries who examined the American or British scene under their figurative microscopes would not allow their readers to maintain a comfortable distance from their subject.

James's novels and his critical pronouncements signaled a change in the attitude toward the novel shared by several of his contemporaries who were just beginning to regard themselves as artists as well as (or rather than) social reformers or educators, or mere entertainers. From James, it is only a short step to Joseph Conrad, who declared in his preface to *The Nigger of the "Narcissus"* (1897) that "any work which aspires to the condition of art must carry its justification in every line." Conrad's own works testify to his constant concern for selecting the right word or phrase to characterize the situation he chooses to create. Always the careful observer of men in conditions that tested their fortitude and challenged their values, Conrad wrote of the sea as a constant metaphor for the human condition in general. In his works, events take on a significance beyond the literal, but Conrad is no simple allegorist whose story serves as an excuse for presenting a philosophical proposition. For the most part, his men and women are interesting as people, not as mere representations of abstract principles. In *Heart of Darkness* (serial 1899, book 1902), for example, the "horror" that Kurtz sees as he lies on his deathbed in the heart of Africa strikes the reader as especially poignant because no one in the story is really larger than life; the simple possibility that men could be so corrupted makes the tale a chilling commentary on the tenuousness of civilization as a means of staving off the bestial side of human nature.

Writers such as James and Conrad concerned themselves with the structure of their works, with choosing incident and detail to give the works a sense of balance and completeness that satisfies the reader's aesthetic sensibilities. Quietly, these novelists were redefining their readership: No longer would they write for the general audience (though they may have claimed to do so), but rather for those discerning few who could detect what James would call in another essay "the figure in the carpet." No longer would plot, action, and moral pronouncement be the glue to bind the parts of the novel to the whole or to solidify the bond between the reader and writer. The artist was becoming aware that he could communicate with his reader—albeit a certain kind of reader—by other means: patterns of images that would themselves suggest larger themes than the story conveyed (symbolism, leitmotif), conscious attempts to balance or juxtapose incidents and characters whose stories are often unrelated on the literal level, and clear links with the great literature or folk culture of the past. The fragmentation of the audience for fiction, which had begun at least a decade before James began writing, became complete by the decade after he died.

While James was abroad writing pronouncements on the status of American and British fiction, his friend and contemporary William Dean Howells remained at home and did the same. Using his position as editor of several popular magazines, Howells influenced the taste of countless readers by promoting the kind of fiction he believed best suited the public's needs. Like James, he was a realist: His own novels display a careful concern for realistic presentation of information, often a meticulous attention to detail and an extraordinary accumulation of facts, and a concern for the contemporary social and political milieu in his own country. Howells, less daring than James, remained faithful to nineteenth century moral ideals and practices; hence, his realistic vision is limited by his moral sensibilities. In *The Rise of Silas Lapham* (1885), for example, Howells combines his penchant for providing realistic detail with his strong sense of moral purpose to create a portrait of American society and American business that shows how the drive for material betterment can often lead to spiritual poverty and, eventually, to ruin both in this world and possibly in the next. As a portrait of American commerce it is most unflattering, but it is typical both of Howells's own outlook and that of many other realistic novelists who were looking around them and finding little to like in the contemporary scene.

THOMAS HARDY AND THEODORE DREISER

Two novelists, one English, one American, may serve to characterize the naturalistic movement in the English-language novel during this period of transition from Victorian to modern sensibilities. Like other naturalists, both Thomas Hardy and Theodore Dreiser were followers of the school of realism: Their works are filled with minute descriptions of ordinary places and events, with scenes and characters from the middle and lower classes, and neither makes any attempt to glorify his heroes and heroines by raising them to epic proportion.

Thomas Hardy's novels, usually set in the Wessex district of England, depict the life of common folks who struggle to eke out an existence against an unforgiving nature. Influenced by the theories of Charles Darwin and Herbert Spencer, Hardy displays in his novels a world where natural selection and determinism are the primary moving forces and where chance is ever present to ruin the best design of even the best men. *The Mayor of Casterbridge* (1886) offers a good example of Hardy's philosophy of determinism and the role that chance plays in human lives. In this novel, Michael Henchard, a man of strong will but somewhat irrational temperament (in the opening scene, a drunken Henchard sells his wife and daughter), rises by his own industry to become a wealthy farmer and prominent citizen in his local community. As chance would have it, however, he soon falls victim to a series of setbacks: He finds his wife again and, believing he should win her back to make restitution for his earlier behavior, abandons a woman who loves him; he loses all his money to another farmer, largely because the weather favors the other's crops, loses his wife again to this rival, who also supplants him as mayor of the town, and is reduced at the end of the novel to a penniless beggar who wanders off to die alone on the barren countryside.

This note of extreme pessimism characterizes Hardy's other works and is, in fact, typical of many naturalistic novelists. The work of Frank Norris in the United States, especially in a novel such as *McTeague* (1899), bears a striking resemblance to Hardy's fiction. Like most naturalists, Hardy ignored the Victorian conventions prescribing subject matter for fiction and turned to issues that would eventually cause him to be rejected by the British public of his day. In *Tess of the D'Urbervilles* (1891), his heroine, forced to yield to a young nobleman who abandons her after he has used her, suffers the fate one would expect for prostitutes in Victorian England; Hardy's Tess, however, evokes not horror but pity in the reader, a feeling that apparently made many Victorian readers uncomfortable. In *Jude the Obscure* (1895), Hardy abandoned any pretense of dealing out Victorian justice or shying away from taboo subjects. In this novel, he frankly and sympathetically treats the extramarital, adulterous relationship of Jude Fawley and Sue Bridehead. They struggle to maintain a life built on genuine love in a society whose conventions work against their ever being happy. As in other Hardy novels, chance intervenes to bring misery to both hero and heroine, destroying them for no apparent reason. *Jude the Obscure* was Hardy's last novel, for he was sternly criticized for his open treatment of adultery, a subject he felt he had only touched on and not fully explored in this work. Disappointed that the public was unwilling to face contemporary issues head-on, Hardy abandoned the novel and turned to poetry.

The kind of restraints that caused Hardy to abandon the novel worked against American novelists as well; Theodore Dreiser's experience is a good example. Dreiser was initially stymied in his attempts to publish *Sister Carrie*, which was finally published in 1900, because that work dealt openly with the problems of an impoverished girl who becomes a man's mistress as a means of preserving her life. The book was derided in numerous literary and religious circles, for it suggested that submission to evil, even in an extremity, did not necessarily lead to a life of ignominy. Unlike Hardy's Tess, Carrie succeeds by using her wits and feminine charm. Without the least hint that he believes his heroine has been wrong in her actions, Dreiser traces Carrie's rise to prominence in society, while simultaneously portraying the decline and eventual suicide of her original benefactor, Hurstwood. There is in this novel, and in most of Dreiser's others, a strong implication that the common person in the United States can succeed only by abandoning the platitudes preached both in the pulpit and the public forum and that those who succeed do so at the expense of others.

Regardless of the methods one uses, however, there is no guarantee of success. In the greatest of his novels, *An American Tragedy* (1925), Dreiser portrays the sad results of the American Dream gone awry. His protagonist, Clyde Griffiths, a shallow young man, self-centered and greedy for the "good things in life," enters the world of business and society to find that success depends much more upon birth and chance than upon honest striving for advancement. Clyde is made to look like a fool in the high society where he seeks membership. Through foolish behavior, he causes a girl who really loves him to become pregnant. When he discovers that she is a hindrance to his chances to climb the social ladder, he plots to kill her, only to discover that he is too much the coward to commit the deed. Cruel chance does for him what he cannot do for himself, however, as the girl accidentally falls from a boat and drowns (the kind of death Clyde had planned for her). Ironically, Clyde is accused of committing the crime he had plotted but failed to carry out and is eventually convicted.

It is impossible not to see an intellectual kinship between Dreiser and Hardy, both of whose characters succeed or fail according to circumstances over which they have no control. The works of these novelists provide some of the finest statements of naturalism, the stepchild of scientific determinism and literary realism.

THE EDWARDIAN NOVEL

The death of Queen Victoria in 1901 and the ascension of Edward VII marked the beginning of a new political age in England, but the fiction of the next two decades continued to show strong ties to that which had preceded it. On more than one occasion, the literature of the period has been disparagingly dismissed as mere journalism. That journalistic style, however, was often a facade that covered serious treatments of problems plaguing England as it entered the new century. Novelists in early twentieth century England, much more than their fellow artists in the United States, felt the impact of the intellectual advances that had been made during the preceding century. Living in what John Batchelor, in *The Edwardian Novelists* (1982), has called "a contracting moral universe, in which the received moral imperatives had lost their urgency," they attempted to find substitutes for religious imperatives in secular ones. Duty in society replaced obedience to God as the principle of right living for many Edwardians, and novelists reflected that attitude in their works.

Heroes were needed, of course, but heroism seemed impossible in the modern environment. Further, the English countryside that had provided a wholesome counterpart to the squalor of the city for earlier novelists was fast disappearing as suburbs spread out around the metropolitan areas. The growth of the suburbs was paralleled by the retreat of the empire, as Great Britain's worldwide system of colonial enterprise was clearly in danger of falling apart. The "glory that was England" under Victoria was fading, and the impending conflict with Germany, foreseen as early as 1900, caused concern among the populace and influenced the works of Edwardian novelists. The period was characterized by a general anxiety about the state of the individual and society. The major figures of the period—John Galsworthy, Arnold Bennett, H. G. Wells, Ford Madox Ford, E. M. Forster—adopted the form of the novel that their Victorian predecessors had bequeathed them, but they were living in a society quite changed both intellectually and politically. It is small wonder that one of the most popular images in Edwardian novels is the abyss.

On the popular front, two voices emerged as the spokesmen for the novel in England: Arnold Bennett and John Galsworthy. Bennett's popularity was important to him, and some critics have complained that he prostituted a fine talent in order to satisfy his desire to be regarded as a social lion. A disciple of realism, in his best works, such as *The Old Wives' Tale* (1908), he demonstrates a keen eye for detail and an ability to make the lives of commonplace people interesting and significant. He and Galsworthy did much to popularize the chronicle novel, multiple volumes dealing with the same character or group of characters. Others among his works, such as *The Grand Babylon Hotel* (1902; published in the United States as *T. Racksole and Daughter*), are predecessors of the modern documentary novels that explore life in particular institutions or forms of business. Galsworthy achieved success as both a playwright and a novelist, giving Edwardian England a portrait of its Victorian heritage and its contemporary problems in his famous series, *The Forsyte Saga* (1922).

Both Galsworthy and Bennett paid close attention to external detail, but their unwillingness or inability to explore the motivations and inner feelings of char-

acters with the same sensitivity made them targets for writers who believed that the job of the artist was not to substitute for the photographer but to explore the reality of experience that could not be seen on the surface. Virginia Woolf's famous essay "Mr. Bennett and Mrs. Brown" (1924) provided the rationale for certain post-World War I novelists to reject traditional realism.

Ford and Forster bridged the gap between the Edwardian period and the 1920's. Ford had achieved recognition during the early years of the war with the publication of *The Good Soldier* (1915), but in his Tietjens sequence of four novels (1924-1928), he examined the changes that had occurred in society and their effect on the hero, whom he has carefully drawn to represent the traditionally good English gentleman. Forster published four novels before 1910, all of them typical English social novels that are, at times, melodramatic. His most significant work, *A Passage to India*, did not appear until 1924, and while the style and method of narration recall his own earlier works and those of the novelists of the turn of the century, the book's theme reflects both the effects that the war had on sensibilities in England and a timeless concern for the paradox of human experience that Forster shared with other members of the literary circle to which he belonged, the Bloomsbury Group (which included Woolf). More than in any of his other novels, Forster depicts in *A Passage to India* a certain tragic quality about human life. One of his characters, Mrs. Moore, reflects at one point in the novel that "Pathos, piety, courage—they exist, but are identical, and so is filth. Everything exists, nothing has value." For anything in life to have value, man must make that thing worthwhile; no values are preordained. That philosophy, the product of modern science strengthened by the experiences of World War I, links Forster to as unlikely a colleague as Ernest Hemingway, whose characters often express the same idea and act to establish meaning for their own lives in the face of certain defeat.

THE AMERICAN NOVEL: 1900-1920

During this same period in the United States, the novelists who rose to prominence were often much like their British counterparts. In *The Modern Novel in Britain and the United States* (1964), Walter Allen called the first two decades of the twentieth century a period of comparative sterility in American fiction. If one excludes Henry James and Theodore Dreiser, that description may be just, for no giant of American literature emerged until after World War I. The American populace was being swept away by sensationalism, as the new journalists captured the country's interest with their exposés of business, politics, and life in the cities and the country. Novelists such as Upton Sinclair achieved popular acclaim for fiction that called attention to the rot at the core of American institutions; Sinclair's *The Jungle* (1906), which graphically displayed the horrors of the meatpacking industry, was read for its sociological impact as much as its literary merit. It became fashionable for the novelist to look deeply into the American scene and expose the corruption or absence of value in institutions that had long been considered honorable.

Among American novelists who focused their gaze in this fashion, none was more popular than Sinclair Lewis, whose works consistently drew attention to the inadequacies of the American dream. Like Dreiser and Sherwood Anderson, Lewis was a Midwesterner by birth. A student of the American realists, he concentrated on mid-America, depicting the pettiness and emptiness of life in what was generally regarded as the bastion of modern American morality in *Main Street: The Story of Carol Kennicott* (1920), *Babbitt* (1922), and other earlier works. Lewis pointed out to Americans and readers abroad (where he achieved a certain degree of popularity) that the heartland of America was filled with George Babbitts, whose lives consisted of belonging to clubs that gave members status by telling them what to think, men whose advancement in society was always at the expense of someone less fortunate. Lewis was awarded the Nobel Prize in Literature in 1930, the first American so honored.

There were others writing in the United States during this period whose works were less sensational but of considerable literary merit. Edith Wharton, a writer of the Jamesian school of social realism,

turned to East Coast society for her subject and created novels that rival James's for their penetrating insights into social situations and the impact on character that society can have. The American penchant for local color and regionalism continued unabated, and among novelists who provided this kind of literature were Willa Cather and Ellen Glasgow. In her stories of the Nebraska plains where she was reared, the Virginia area where she was born, and other regions, Cather constantly reminded her readers of the plight of the individual in modern society. Her insight into contemporary America rivals, and often surpasses, that of Sinclair Lewis. Glasgow's region was the old South, where she was born and reared. Her stories showed the fixation of the South on its past, and her vision was pessimistic. A fine novelist in her own right, she is also important as a forerunner of the southern writers who were to form a literary subculture in the United States during the later decades of the twentieth century.

World War I provided a distinct dividing line between the nineteenth century sensibility and the new age in both England and the United States. Although Americans had had, in their Civil War, a preview of the kind of destruction modern warfare could produce, few people in either country were psychologically prepared for the carnage of World War I. In both countries, the postwar period was characterized by rapid social change and a heightened sense of the tenuousness of modern life in the face of total war. Though it is hard to offer a generalization that can encompass all English and American novelists, it is safe to say that in both countries the 1920's were characterized by a certain gaiety of spirit that masked a genuine disillusionment with institutions and in Britain with the class system. This feverish gaiety gave way to the Great Depression, reflected in British and American novels by a growing sense of concern for the future of a society based on capitalism, a growing trend toward social violence, and an increasing tendency to look for solutions to social problems outside the existing political frameworks that had been functioning in these countries for so long.

There were, as one might expect, a large number of novels written about the war itself, many of them by men who had taken part in the fighting. Several of these novels have taken their place among the modern classics: John Dos Passos's *Three Soldiers* (1921) and Hemingway's *A Farewell to Arms* (1929) fall into this category. The impact of the war on the literature of the next decades extended far beyond the novelists whose works deal directly with battlefield events. Institutions that had stood for a century or more had been shaken by the four-year conflict. The worth of the individual, already called into question by the discoveries and theories of nineteenth century science, had been almost shattered by the wholesale destruction that the machinery of modern warfare had wreaked. Such events left many sensitive young men and women in shock, and those who turned to the novel as a means of expressing their dismay reflected the general disillusionment of the populaces of both countries.

MODERNISM

The breakdown of public agreement about what is significant in human life, the new view of the nature of consciousness introduced by the study of psychology, and a desire to discover new ways to reach their audience caused writers of the post-World War I period to experiment with the form of the novel. In fact, the period immediately following the end of hostilities on the Continent can best be described as the age of experimentation. The tendency to try new ways of representing reality is most noticeable in novelists who abandoned traditional narrative conventions, adopting instead the method suggested by William James in his discussions on psychology. Determining that reality cannot best be portrayed by a simple recitation of physical detail, these writers attempted to put down on paper the thought processes of characters, to re-create the stream of consciousness. The term "stream of consciousness" was first used by William James as a metaphor to describe the way thoughts pass through the mind just below the surface level, prior to their being formulated into intelligible patterns that are normally expressed as sentences. The technique of limiting the perspective of the novel to a single character was nothing new: Daniel Defoe's *The Life and Strange Surprizing Adventures of Robinson Crusoe, of York, Mariner, Written*

by Himself (1719) makes use of the first-person narrator, as do myriad other eighteenth and nineteenth century works. That one could further limit the perspective, and hence more closely approximate the way in which reality was really apprehended, was first argued explicitly by Henry James, who, in the preface to *The Ambassadors*, discussed his method of limiting his descriptions to whatever might impinge on the "center of consciousness" of his hero. James's hero, however, is presented as having already formulated his thoughts, so that what one reads in a James novel are the intellectual reflections of a character who has observed something outside himself, rather than the record of those impressions as they first impinge upon his consciousness. The great experimenters in the modern novel—Dorothy Richardson, Virginia Woolf, and James Joyce in Britain, and William Faulkner in the United States—attempted to record the stream of consciousness itself.

In her essay "Mr. Bennett and Mrs. Brown," Woolf observed that "human character changed" decisively "on or about December 1910." Despite the whimsical precision of her statement, the sentiment was real; during the decade from 1910 to 1920, a number of literary figures, captivated by the new way of apprehending reality, began experimenting with the form of the novel. Woolf herself provided a key to understanding both the purpose and method of the new movement. In an essay appropriately entitled "Modern Fiction" (1925), she dismissed the efforts of Galsworthy, Bennett, and Wells as materialistic, condemning them for "spend[ing] immense skill and immense industry making the trivial and the transitory appear the true and the enduring" without capturing life as it really exists. Those novelists were hidebound by the tradition of the novel, which had always found in external events and relationships the proper material for fiction; if one should look within, Woolf says, "life, it seems, is very far from being 'like this.'" Instead, Woolf says, life is the action of the mind in contact with the outside world:

The mind receives . . . impressions—trivial, fantastic, evanescent, or engraved with the sharpness of steel. From all sides they come, an incessant shower of innumerable atoms. . . . Life is not a series of gig lamps symmetrically arranged; but a luminous halo, a semi-transparent envelope surrounding us from the beginning of consciousness to the end.

The job of the writer is to abandon conventions and seek to display this inner life: "Is it not the task of the novelist," Woolf continues, "to convey this varying, this unknown and uncircumscribed spirit, whatever aberration or complexity it may display, with as little mixture of the alien and external as possible? We are not pleading merely for courage and sincerity; we are suggesting that the proper stuff of fiction is a little other than custom would have us believe it."

In her own novels, Woolf repeatedly tried to capture life as a series of impressions upon the mind of sensitive characters such as Mrs. Ramsay in *To the Lighthouse* (1927) or Bernard in *The Waves* (1931). Abandoning conventional concerns for plot, Woolf tried to reproduce, through asyntactical language, parenthetical digressions, juxtaposed sentences whose meanings appear to have no causal relationship, and other similar techniques, the immediacy of the human mind encountering the world around it.

When Woolf wrote "Modern Fiction," she was not introducing a theory so much as commenting upon the works of novelists who had recently entered the literary scene. Early experimenters included Dorothy Richardson, who attempted to capture *in toto* the workings of a single, ordinary mind. Miriam, the heroine of Richardson's twelve-volume *Pilgrimage* (1938, 1967), is revealed to the reader solely through the associative patterns of thoughts that race through her consciousness as she goes about her ordinary tasks. Though Richardson's notions of psychology may be pre-Freudian and though she may avoid with a curious Victorian reticence certain subjects and actions that no doubt would have been on her heroine's mind at some time, she is nevertheless an important figure in the development of stream-of-consciousness fiction. Another early experimenter whose novels reflect her awareness of Freudian psychology was May Sinclair. Better than Richardson, Sinclair seems to have understood the real frustrations of women in late Victorian England, and she captures the psychological turmoil

of her characters in narratives that are a curious blend of the Jamesian center of consciousness and Richardson's more free-form technique.

Unquestionably the greatest experimenter in this age of the experimental novel was James Joyce. His *A Portrait of the Artist as a Young Man* (serial 1914-1915, book 1916), a semiautobiographical work about the upbringing of a young Irish Catholic Dubliner, is told with a degree of objectivity hitherto unknown in novels. Not once does the author intrude to tell the reader how he should respond to the hero's actions; even descriptive adjectives are carefully omitted so that the reader is forced to interpret feeling and motive directly from action and speech. The same penchant for authorial self-effacement characterizes Joyce's later masterpieces, *Ulysses* (1922) and *Finnegans Wake* (1939). In these, Joyce abandons the conventions of plot and narrative to present events in a method best described as collage: Incidents are set in parallel, compared and contrasted so that meaning must be inferred, gleaned by the reader in the act of judging the text itself, not from authorial intrusions telling him what to believe or what to make of this strange mixture of dialogue, stream-of-consciousness narrative, soliloquies, dramatic vignettes, and other curious interjections of prose that often mystify all but the most careful, attentive reader.

In *Ulysses*, Joyce resorts to a device typical of many modern authors who aim not at the general reader but at one who brings to the work a strong background in classical and modern literature. By suggesting correspondences between his work and Homer's *Odyssey* (c. 800 B.C.E.), Joyce forces the reader to look for parallels between the world of modern Dublin and the mythic world of Homer's poem. The drive to raise the significance of modern events to the level of myth has become commonplace among many novelists who consider themselves serious artists, and the works of writers as diverse as Albert Camus and William Faulkner share this tendency to some degree.

In *Finnegans Wake* the tendency toward myth is still present, but punning and other forms of wordplay dominate that work and have baffled most readers, leading to the production of numerous handbooks explaining what Joyce "means" in his novel. Some critics have thrown up their hands at *Finnegans Wake*, dismissing it in exasperation as not a novel at all. Its "narrative" is circular (the book begins in mid-sentence and ends with the first half of that sentence), and even the stream-of-consciousness method seems secondary to Joyce's continual play with the multiple meaning of words. In fact, *Finnegans Wake* is often cited as the primary example of what is wrong with the experimental novel by critics and novelists who adhere to the more traditional methods of narrative and who feel that the novel should not abandon its historical function as a bearer of news about the way people live.

Experimentation with form was not confined to writers in England or on the Continent. A number of American novelists quickly adopted wholly or in part the techniques of stream of consciousness or other methods of nontraditional narration. Dos Passos used a kind of collage of narrative forms to achieve the panoramic effect he sought as a means of capturing the expanse and variety of his native land in his *U.S.A.* trilogy (1937). Faulkner carried on experiments with the form of the novel that included juxtaposing stream of consciousness with traditional narrative techniques (*The Sound and the Fury*, 1929), collecting disparate stories with related themes to form a single work (*Go Down, Moses*, 1942), or presenting two seemingly unrelated stories in parallel (*The Wild Palms*, 1939). Adding an elaborate style to these other rhetorical devices, Faulkner moved the novel in the direction of modern poetry, where the reader is often called upon to work to discover meaning amid a collection of images. Use of stream of consciousness and other nontraditional techniques has now become commonplace in modern fiction.

D. H. Lawrence

The reaction to experimentation with form has been strident, perhaps more vehement in England than in America. Since 1923, when D. H. Lawrence dismissed the efforts of Joyce, Richardson, and Woolf as "childish" and "absorbedly self-conscious" in his essay "Surgery for the Novel—or a Bomb," many critics and novelists have lashed out against the trend

to abandon the intellectual bond between the writer and the general reader. Novelists who believe in the efficacy of fiction as social documentary have been loudest in their protests, and their work has remained close in both form and content to the traditional novel as written by their eighteenth and nineteenth century forebears. In *The Realists* (1978) C. P. Snow, always a staunch believer in the value of the story in the novel, described the trend to "regard novels, and compose novels, as verbal puzzles to be worked out by persons cleverer than the original writer" as a sign of a "period of decline not only in the art itself, but also in the society from which it derives." It is no wonder that Snow's own novels, especially those in the *Strangers and Brothers* series (1940; reissued as *George Passant*, 1972) are traditionally realistic chronicles of English society that focus on intellectual dilemmas and social quandaries faced by men and women who are immediately recognizable to the reader. The swing back toward more traditional forms of narrative after World War II was hailed by British critic Paul West, who saw the return to convention as a kind of recovery after sickness: "The English novel has recovered from the flux, and only Lawrence Durrell makes much use of it."

Though he distrusted the experimental fiction of his time, D. H. Lawrence now is ranked as a great innovator himself. Along with Woolf and Joyce, he stands as a preeminent figure of the period between the wars. Like Joyce, he had already published a work of some distinction before the war, distinctly exhibiting modern sensibilities in his first autobiographical novel *Sons and Lovers* (1913). Though similar in some respects to the traditional *Bildungsroman*, *Sons and Lovers* clearly shows the influence of Freudian theories of psychology; in it, Lawrence depicts the classical Oedipal conflict. In the 1920's, an age that glorified anti-intellectualism, Lawrence was right at home. He rebelled against the modern industrial society because it had, in his view, cheapened the quality of human experience. Intellectualism was at best a form of escape from the fullness of life's experiences, and at worst it ruined all that was worthwhile in life; not surprisingly, almost all of Lawrence's villains are intellectuals. Only those who felt deeply and acted vigorously (even violently) were worthy of praise.

The theories of Sigmund Freud and other psychologists had made the world aware of the submerged part of the human mind that often drove people to actions they could not explain, and Lawrence found in these theories fertile ground for his works. In a style often reminiscent of Romantic poetry, Lawrence tried to convey the power that these subliminal urges had to drive men and women to act. Unlike Joyce or Woolf, he did not abandon conventional narrative techniques or traditional forms of organization for his works; in fact, *The Rainbow* (1915), one of his best novels, is in many respects a fine chronicle novel in the fashion of Galsworthy or Bennett. Lawrence was always interested, however, in trying to convey what Eliseo Vivas called the "felt quality of experience," "the ebb and flow of the affective life, particularly the felt quality of erotic passion and of religious emotion." As much as any novelist of the period, Lawrence created in his works powerful symbols that could evoke multiple levels of meaning for discerning readers. A man of strong passions himself, he was ultimately disappointed with the public response to his works, complaining on one occasion that his "psychological" stuff simply did not sell well. What did sell well was *Lady Chatterley's Lover* (1928) but for the wrong reasons—the book developed a reputation as a pornographic masterpiece.

The brilliance of Joyce, Woolf, and Lawrence has often overshadowed the accomplishments of other British novelists whose careers were contemporary with theirs. Aldous Huxley, the preeminent exponent of the novel of ideas, published his first novels in the years immediately following the armistice. Though remembered by succeeding generations principally for *Brave New World* (1932), his dystopian analysis of a future society controlled by scientists, Huxley explored the problems of post-World War I Britain in a number of provocative novels, including *Antic Hay* (1923) and *Crome Yellow* (1921). Through careful selection of character types and careful construction of plots that juxtapose characters in situations where they must talk with one another at length, Huxley managed to satirize the more extreme forms of English character and society while retaining a focus on what he saw as an irreconcilable problem: Human actions, however noble, inevitably lead to frustration and evil, and humankind's highest intellectual and artistic aspirations exist in beings that have inescapable biological urges and needs.

Joining Huxley among the ranks of the social comedians were Evelyn Waugh and Anthony Powell. Both were skilled crafters of the novel, and Waugh especially donned the satirist's mantle to shock people into recognizing the moral vacuity of modern life. Graham Greene first surfaced as a novelist concerned with the social condition of his country; he quickly turned to popular forms of the day—the thriller, for example—taking them over for his own use and making them the vehicles for serious discussion of moral and theological questions. While none of these novelists practiced experimentation in forms that matched the works of Joyce or Woolf, they often displayed the marks of influence in their close treatment of the inner psychology of character. A host of minor novelists round out the complement of figures whose works provide an insight into the post-World War I period: David Garnett, T. F. Powys, J. C. Powys, William Gehardi, and others all wrote novels that reflect the impact of contemporary events and ideas. L. H. Myers, whose best work was done in the 1930's, was a product of this period. Richard Hughes's *A High Wind in Jamaica* (1929) provided one of the most original treatments of childhood in any British novel. A bleaker vision of maturation appears in William Golding's *Lord of the Flies* (1954), in which the author examines the responses of a group of isolated young boys who react to their first encounter with the darkness dormant in the human heart.

The rebellion in the novel that became evident in the new experiments with form extended far beyond technical boundaries. As Irving Howe has observed, "modern novelists," those who began writing after the earlier works of Henry James had been published, "had been committed to a peculiarly anxious and persistent search for values." The novelists of the 1920's and 1930's tested values by juxtaposing their characters against a set of fixed social norms—the business community, the political hierarchy, the wealthy class.

The values of these social groups were clearly identifiable and often open to question. Certainly, in the period between the two world wars, there was ample reason to challenge the worn-out institutions that had led Europe and the United States into a frenzy of destruction and had wreaked havoc over a continent. Many of the young novelists of the period, especially those in the United States, did exactly that.

F. SCOTT FITZGERALD AND ERNEST HEMINGWAY

The prominent American novelists of the 1920's were F. Scott Fitzgerald and Ernest Hemingway. Fitzgerald's novels generally reflect the moral degeneracy of the jazz age; his characters, often *nouveau riche*, often pretenders to social status, are usually defeated because they aspire to false values. Fitzgerald's *The Great Gatsby* (1925) remains the best illustration of the sad decay of the American Dream. The hero, Jay Gatsby, is a self-made man from the West who has come east to reap all the benefits that money can buy. He appears to possess unlimited riches, and he attempts to buy his way into Long Island society through lavish parties and extravagant affairs at his home. The secret to his success, however, is "dirty money": He made his fortune as a bootlegger, changed his name to avoid his Jewish heritage, and never achieved the one thing he really wanted, the love of his sweetheart from more innocent days, Daisy, who is now the wife of the boorish Tom Buchanan. Gatsby's world comes tumbling down around him when, through a series of misadventures, he is murdered by the husband of Tom Buchanan's mistress. Yet for all his pretensions and foibles, Gatsby himself is drawn quite sympathetically by Fitzgerald. It is hard to dislike him, and his brand of heroism has a certain charm about it that suggests that the old virtues of the American character, so often derided as both unobtainable and psychologically damaging, are a tragic alternative to the sterility of life in American high society of the Jazz Age. For Fitzgerald, there appeared to be no way of winning.

The importance of Hemingway to American literature cannot be overestimated. During the 1920's, Hemingway developed three things that were to ensure his success: a writing style characterized by a simplicity unmatched by any writer of equal stature before or after him; a "code" or philosophy by which men must live and die if they wish to be great; and a lifestyle, based in part on the code, that was to gain him notoriety for several decades and make him as controversial for his personal life as for his fiction. Like many writers of his generation, he had gone to the war, and its experiences had made an indelible impression on him. Unlike many of them, however, Hemingway found a certain dignity in violent action; it was one way for humans to express themselves in defiance against a universe that seemed not to care for the individual. His novels, beginning with *The Sun Also Rises* in 1926, develop in fiction the "code" that Hemingway himself lived by publicly: gusto for life, distrust for institutions, commitment to duty. His *A Farewell to Arms* may be the best novel about World War I and ranks with Stephen Crane's *The Red Badge of Courage: An Episode of the American Civil War* (1895) as one of the finest American war novels ever written. When he turned his attention to the Spanish Civil War in the mid-1930's, Hemingway again produced in *For Whom the Bell Tolls* (1940) a literary work that captures at once the futility of war and the opportunities for true heroism that war offers the brave.

Hemingway wrote for four decades, always clinging to his original artistic premise that good art must be simple and suggestive. A late work, *The Old Man and the Sea* (1952), shows Hemingway's method of simplicity at its best: The hero, an old fisherman who has failed to catch anything for eighty-four days, goes out alone into the Gulf Stream off Florida, where he hooks a magnificent fish and finally lands him after a three-day battle, only to have the carcass eaten by sharks on the trip back to his dock. The reader suffers with the hero, feels his triumph at the catch, and experiences his despair when the fish is taken away by the agents of nature. One is left with a curious feeling, however, that the hero has triumphed despite the apparent failure; this feeling is precisely the one that Hemingway sought to convey in all of his works.

It soon became fashionable for young novelists to imitate the Hemingway style, spare prose devoid of complex sentences and elaborate rhetoric. Hundreds of popular adventure stories, filled with toughs and soldiers of fortune, rogues from every walk of life, filled bookstands across the country; some writers and readers even went so far as to try to adopt the Hemingway code as a model for living. Since the virtues he promoted—courage in the face of overwhelming odds, bravery, self-sufficiency—were the ones that had traditionally been associated with the American hero, Hemingway soon developed a large following both among the general public and in academic circles. Always subject to criticism for his aggressively masculine persona, Hemingway has been judged with increasing severity as the values that he incarnated have become increasingly unfashionable. His legacy to American literature, however—and indeed, to world literature—cannot be ignored.

THE GREAT DEPRESSION

With the Depression, many young novelists turned their attention to social and political issues with renewed interest. Any hope that may have begun to grow during the 1920's was shattered during this decade of mass unemployment and the growing spread of fascism. In the United States novelists concerned with the plight of victims of the Depression used realistic methods to graphically depict the effects of economic privation. James T. Farrell's *Studs Lonigan: A Trilogy* (1935) is one of the best of a number of American works during the period that present, according to Walter Allen, "a corrupt and vicious social order that [the novelist believed] must be destroyed." Farrell was one of a number of writers on both sides of the Atlantic who adopted communism as an alternative to the capitalistic society that was apparently responsible for the condition of life in the Western world in the 1930's.

During the same period, another significant American novelist first began to publish. John Steinbeck's *In Dubious Battle* (1936) deals directly with the problems of workers and the possibilities and restrictions communism offered. From Steinbeck, the United States received its greatest literary treatment of the effects of the Depression. *The Grapes of Wrath* (1939) is the story of the Joad family, poor farmers who leave the Dust Bowl of Oklahoma for a better life in California only to find that conditions there are no better, sometimes worse. Because the plight of the Joads and the other families in the novel appeared so typical and because their stories were presented so poignantly (often melodramatically), *The Grapes of Wrath* became a parable of the American migrant. Much like early works of Charles Dickens or Harriet Beecher Stowe's *Uncle Tom's Cabin: Or, Life Among the Lowly* (1852), the novel provided a rallying point for reformers, a propaganda piece in the hands of those attempting to aid the victims of a decade of hard living and almost inhuman suffering.

While a group of daring young men and women in England were experimenting with the form of the novel and their counterparts in the United States were fulfilling their role as members of the Lost Generation, a large number of writers, less concerned with artistry than with entertainment, continued to provide the public with what is now referred to as "popular literature." Much of the best-seller material of the 1920's and 1930's lasted no more than a season. One form of popular fiction, however, rose to a new level of prominence and achieved notice for its artistry from contemporary critics and in succeeding decades. Detective fiction, fathered by Edgar Allan Poe almost one century earlier and brought to fame by Sir Arthur Conan Doyle at the beginning of the twentieth century, reached a new level of artistic merit during the period between the wars. In England Dorothy Sayers and Agatha Christie entered the literary scene, creating detective heroes who would rival the legendary Sherlock Holmes in the public eye. In the United States Dashiell Hammett led the way for a number of gifted storytellers whose brand of detective thriller differed noticeably from the British version of the genre. The genteel, intellectual pursuit of the criminal, characteristic of Sayers's Lord Peter Wimsey and Christie's Hercule Poirot, was replaced by the tough-guy tactics of hard-boiled characters such as Hammett's Sam Spade. In England, Graham Greene explored in his thrillers, especially *Brighton Rock* (1938), the violent world that had recently received much attention in the newspapers. During the next fifty years, bookstores and public libraries were filled with the novels of these early mystery writers and their many successors; the works of the best of them— writers such as Hammett, Raymond Chandler, and Ross Macdonald—gradually achieved the recognition generally reserved for mainstream fiction. The novels of English writer P. D. James, who began publishing mysteries in the 1970's, have been considered equal in literary merit to those of her contemporaries writing more mainstream fiction.

THE SOUTHERN NOVEL

During this period of exceptional literary activity, the publication of a group of novels by a single Mississippi author highlighted the emergence of southern fiction. William Faulkner had been writing for a decade and had already published three novels and several short stories when *The Sound and the Fury* appeared in 1929. It was followed in rapid succession by *As I Lay Dying* (1930), *Sanctuary* (1931), *Light in August* (1932), and *Absalom, Absalom!* (1936), all of which depicted the fate of the South through the lives of generations of men and women in Faulkner's mythical Yoknapatawpha County. Earlier novels and stories had provided some details about these characters, and later ones, notably *Go Down, Moses* (1942), *Requiem for a Nun* (1951), and the trilogy consisting of *The Hamlet* (1940), *The Town* (1957), and *The Mansion* (1959), round out the portrait of a community that is representative of its region in a way that is unlike any other work by an American author.

Faulkner also dealt with philosophical issues that may have been apparent only to one steeped in traditions such as those found in the South; what he had learned and what he attempted to portray both in his stories and through the texture of his prose was the inextricable link between past and present. The evils upon which southern society had been built, especially the evil of slavery, remain to entrap those who try to put the past behind them. Comprehensive in his view of society, Faulkner presents a cast of characters from all walks of life who share the plight of the southerner and who are ultimately destroyed by it: the Compsons, the Sutpens, and African Americans such as Charles Bon (*Absalom, Absalom!*) and Joe Christmas (*Light in August*). He also presents charac-

ters who endure, such as Dilsey the black housekeeper, the poor farm girl Lena (*Light in August*), and the chameleonlike Snopes family, who attain the reader's grudging admiration for their stubbornness and adaptability, despite their overriding amorality.

Faulkner stands at the forefront of a group of southern writers, many of whom emerged during the period between the wars and were influenced in one way or another by the Fugitives, a coterie of artists and academics founded early in the twentieth century at Vanderbilt University in Nashville, Tennessee. Allen Tate and Robert Penn Warren, both members of this group, wrote works that attempted to define and explain the special conditions that set the South apart from the rest of the United States. Warren's *All the King's Men* (1946), a fiction based on the political career of Louisiana demagogue Huey Long, achieved popular success and has been critically acclaimed for its sensitive portrait of the characters whose lives fall under the spell of the political tyrant. Carson McCullers, like Faulkner, focuses on the rural and smalltown South, presenting a kaleidoscope of characters, many of them physically impaired, to suggest the moral condition of the region. Flannery O'Connor fuses the grotesque and the transcendent in a distinctively southern vision that has exercised a great influence on contemporary fiction writers, not only in the South but also in the other regions.

THE WAR NOVEL

The end of the 1930's found the world once again aroused to arms in a conflict that, like its predecessor, would change the shape of both serious and popular fiction. The novelists' reaction to World War II, however, was quite different from what it had been to World War I. Before England's and, later, the United States' first encounters with the realities of modern warfare, people had shared a tenuous kind of idealism; the novels of the post-World War I period reflected the disillusionment, horror, and cynicism of those who had seen for the first time what such a war was really like. Works about World War I were often crude, but the sentiments they expressed were shocking to their audience. The novels of World War II, by contrast, were more sophisticated, but serious novelists found themselves reacting to a different kind of problem from that which had faced their predecessors after World War I.

During the first two decades after World War II, a great many war novels were published, far more than had been generated in the 1920's and 1930's. Many of these works, however, were merely popular potboilers, not serious attempts to investigate the causes or conditions of the conflict. Among novels that did make an attempt to come to grips with the impact of World War II on those who participated in it, Norman Mailer's *The Naked and the Dead* (1948) offered the best portrait of life in battle as it affects men of different geographical and ideological backgrounds. In Mailer's work, one can see the irony that characterizes many of the new war novels. Through a careful juxtaposition of scenes, Mailer depicts the common soldier plodding through the seemingly meaningless tasks that war brings and the grand strategy of those in charge. The goal of the army in this novel is the capture of an island in the Pacific. That goal is achieved not through brilliant planning or heroic action, but rather through accident and blundering. To make matters worse, the success of the army accomplishes nothing to help the war effort. Mailer's novel is a study in the effects of power in men's lives and the changes that war may bring into their lives, but it does not appear to be saying something new about the nature of modern warfare.

Mailer's inability to offer something new is characteristic of many writers of this period. The novelists writing about World War II lacked the advantage of "shock value" as a means of gaining their readers' attention and sympathy. Although the machinery of mass destruction was more devastating than in World War I, World War II produced almost no real surprises except for the destructive power of the atomic bomb, which has been one of the most pervasive, if subtle, influences on literature since the 1940's.

THE POSTWAR NOVEL

The explosion of the atomic bomb provides a new dividing line for fiction, but one must be careful not to insist too strongly that all literature changed immediately and irrevocably after August, 1945. As had

happened after World War I, both in England and the United States, many novelists who had established their reputations before the conflict continued to publish during the first postwar decade, and much of their work followed themes worked out either completely or partially in earlier novels. Greene continued to explore religious and moral questions under the guise of thrillers. Waugh continued to write satire. Anthony Powell, who had published five novels in the 1930's, began his masterpiece, *A Dance to the Music of Time*, a series of twelve novels published between 1951 and 1975. Hemingway's novels of the late 1940's and 1950's show little advance in theme over those of the 1930's. Faulkner continued his saga of the Yoknapatawpha County, crystallizing a world within the borders of this Mississippi region.

The new voices in literature were different, though; the young novelist now faced the horror that at any time, humans could conceivably destroy themselves; the ultimate achievement of Western civilization was, sadly, the perfection of destruction. The novels that deal directly with the possibility and the effects of a nuclear holocaust have been surprisingly few. The subject has not lacked treatment in nonfiction, but in fiction, it has been largely the purview of popular novelists whose sensationalistic treatment has titillated the reading public and aroused momentary curiosity or fear without providing serious study of either the problem or its potential solution. With but few exceptions, the modern writer, choosing to avoid direct confrontation with the issue, has opted instead to examine the experience of people who live daily in the shadow of the threat that total destruction poses.

The Cold War and the threat of nuclear holocaust did give rise to a host of thrillers—spy stories, tales of adventures and intrigue, conventional mysteries—that adapted the traditional formulas that had made these kinds of novels popular since the beginning of the century. The international spy novel achieved a new level of prominence, and Ian Fleming's slim volumes about a British intelligence agent gave his own country and the United States a new hero, James Bond. A combination of bravado, exceptional knowledge and intelligence, charm, and sex appeal made Bond and the dozens of other characters who populate the world of the spy novel immediate successes with the mass reading public that sought escapism rather than serious investigation of modern problems. Not all spy novels, however, are to be dismissed as escapist fare written in the slapdash manner of the Bond saga. The novels of John le Carré, for example, distinguished works by any standards, capture the ambience of the Cold War years, the "climate of betrayal," with great authority and insight.

Perhaps the primary issue for the artist of this period became the assertion of the self in a society that promoted anonymity. The group of new writers who emerged after World War II in Britain have often been classed with their fellow dramatists as the Angry Young Men. Writing about a society in which mobility among classes was becoming much easier, novelists such as John Wain, Kingsley Amis, John Braine, and Doris Lessing struck out against institutions that remained to signal the vestiges of class distinction. Some, like Amis, turned to comedy as the medium for social commentary. Others, Lessing among them, composed sociological dramas in which the line between fiction and reportage is often blurred.

Curiously, many of these writers turned away from the experimental methods of the giants of literature in the preceding generation, finding that older forms of narrative better suited their purposes. The British novels of the 1950's and after often appeared to be throwbacks to their predecessors of a century or more: Picaresque, farce, even the massive sweep of society that characterized the Victorian novel appeared once again in the hands of men and women whose avowed purpose was to hold the mirror up to contemporary society.

What makes these novelists quite different from their predecessors is the relativism—moral as well as social—that characterizes their fiction. Even the novelists of the 1920's and 1930's wrote with a sense that absolutes may exist, or indeed did exist. That certainty is almost completely absent in the works of the new generation. The heroes of post-World War II novels are most likely to be existential people given to establishing their own norms and defining their existence by setting themselves up against the flux of experience that they encounter. Beneath the comedy

of Amis's *Lucky Jim* (1954) or the political rantings of Lessing's early novels is a strain of metaphysical existentialism that links these works to those of Camus and Jean-Paul Sartre as closely as their form or ostensible subject may link them to their British ancestors.

The reason for this is simple. As James Gindin has observed, "Almost all the contemporary novels are searches for identity, efforts on the part of the hero to understand and to define who or what he is." The search to find or define the self, to establish an identity that sets one apart from mass society, is often the goal of modern heroes. Unlike their predecessors, however, modern heroes are often self-questioning, a kind of antihero given to failure and sometimes the victim of acute neurosis or even paranoia.

The protagonist as antihero is a staple of works of John Updike, perhaps the most prolific and controversial American novelist of the postwar period. A chameleon writer who excels in short and long fiction, poetry, and essays, Updike has produced a major work annually since 1957. Principally concerned with domestic issues and questions of morality and convention, Updike has combined exceptional insight into American society and the human condition with a unique command of style to produce novels that highlight the individual's difficulty in establishing a sense of self-hood and self-worth in a post-industrial society.

In virtually every one of his novels, Updike concerns himself with questions of religion and sex, two issues that for him define the human condition in its spiritual and physical dimensions. Updike's most extensive analysis of the problems common people face in modern society are four novels detailing the life of Harry Angstrom, a character affectionately known to family and friends as Rabbit. *Rabbit, Run* (1960), the first in the series, depicts Angstrom's life in a small Pennsylvania town where the boom caused by industrialism is fading. Noted only for his basketball prowess in high school, Rabbit is unable to cope with the pressures of adulthood. Married to a woman almost as immature as himself, he constantly runs away from his responsibilities to his wife, newborn baby, and job. Rabbit longs for the nostalgia of his youth, when he was important and when others handled his problems for him. In subsequent novels in the series, *Rabbit Redux* (1971), *Rabbit Is Rich* (1981), and *Rabbit at Rest* (1990), Rabbit begins to understand his weaknesses and comes to accept the sad comedy of his existence. Updike also uses this series of novels to critique changes in American society from the end of World War I through the decade of the 1980's. Throughout the series, Updike presents his unsophisticated, materialistic, and often self-centered protagonist with great sympathy, making him a reflection of many in modern society who also long for a less complex time when answers to ethical, epistemological, and theological questions were more readily forthcoming.

One of the more common methods adopted by postwar novelists to portray the conflict between the individual and society is the use of an outsider as hero or protagonist. A great number of American novels have such characters as heroes: Truman Capote's homosexuals, Saul Bellow's and Bernard Malamud's Jews, and the black heroes of James Baldwin and Ralph Ellison.

Two novelists who emerged in the 1950's, Saul Bellow and Bernard Malamud, may serve to represent the course that writers in the mainstream of modern fiction took for the next three decades. As observers and recorders of modern American society, both Bellow and Malamud captured the essential frustration that the individual feels when facing the leviathan that modern society has become. In the case of Bellow, much of his fiction is influenced by his Jewish background, but that often provides merely a point of departure for works that explore the modern condition in much broader terms. His *The Adventures of Augie March* (1953), for example, a picaresque novel set in the era of the Great Depression, displays the universal struggle of the individual to free himself from the shackles of society. In *Henderson the Rain King* (1959), Bellow's hero abandons modern society in favor of a more primitive mode of living in Africa, in order to be reborn, as it were, into a new life of self-awareness and to develop a deeper appreciation for himself and others.

Bernard Malamud—like Bellow, of Jewish background—introduced his heritage into his novels with great advantage in works such as *The Assistant* (1957). In the novel, the universal problem of the human desire to achieve moral excellence is treated with great irony, as the hero, an assistant in a small store run by a Jewish family, first tries to take advantage of the family members (robbing from the store, seducing the daughter) but later undergoes a change of heart and carries on the business when the father dies. The hero's acceptance of others' burdens gives the story a particularly poignant quality that, though it borders on the melodramatic, never becomes so.

In the case of both writers, the hero is often on the fringe of society (Bellow's Augie March) or a subgroup of society (the Gentile assistant in Malamud's novel) or consciously abandons modern, urban society to find personal meaning for his life outside it (Henderson). In almost every case, the individual is tested to establish meaning for his life outside of or against society, not within it—suggesting that to meld with the society is to become faceless, a kind of nonperson who counts for nothing. Because life has meaning only in the here and now (the existentialist view certainly dominates these works), the nonperson who fades into the anonymity of the mass society is lost forever. A rage to assert the self against the forces that foster anonymity burns within the heart of many modern heroes.

As a result, it is not surprising to find social causes that promote individual identity and individual worth being celebrated in novels that treat the question of identity. During the 1950's and 1960's in the United States, several works of significance about the plight of African Americans made a mark on the literary scene. As African Americans became more aware of their heritage, they learned that black people had been writing literature for as long as they had been living in America and that works depicting the black experience had been circulating for some time. Only a few, such as Richard Wright's *Native Son* (1940) and Ralph Ellison's *Invisible Man* (1952), had received widespread critical attention. Fine works such as Arna Bontemps's *Black Thunder* (1936), a historical novel about Gabriel Prosser's aborted slave rebellion in the early nineteenth century, had gone largely unnoticed. The interest in black studies generated during the late 1960's and the 1970's, among Americans both black and white, led to the "discovery" of numerous writers whose works have expanded the boundaries of American fiction.

The larger problems of the human search for identity could be most poignantly displayed by writers who had themselves been the victims of discrimination that caused them to *be* nonpersons, and these authors produced powerful testimonies to the struggle that oppressed people face in preserving their identity and dignity in a world hostile toward them. Critic Tony Tanner called Ellison's *Invisible Man* "quite simply the most profound novel about American identity since the war." Among black writers who began to receive acclaim in the 1950's, James Baldwin emerged as a major literary figure whose writing presented the black experience candidly and forcefully in novels that are artistically excellent. Baldwin's ability to portray the anger and the pathos of his characters without preaching or moralizing makes works such as *Go Tell It on the Mountain* (1953) and *The Fire Next Time* (1963) stand out among the thousands of post-World War II books that dramatize contemporary American social problems.

While a number of major novelists were exploring contemporary issues in traditional forms, others, employing a method designated as "fabulation" by the critic Robert Scholes, abandoned attempts at verisimilitude and opted instead to create conscious artifices that moved "away from direct representation of the surface of reality" but approached "actual human life by way of ethically controlled fantasy." Many important novelists, among them William Gass, Robert Coover, Kurt Vonnegut, Donald Barthelme, and John Barth, produced works that clearly share the qualities of fabulation: concern with design and structure, use of the absurd or surreal, a tendency toward allegory, and formal and narrative characteristics of the Romance tradition as opposed to those normally associated with the novel. At the center of the aesthetic of the fabulators is a belief expressed succinctly by one of their exemplars, John Hawkes, that "the true enemies of the novel [are] plot, character, setting, and theme." For Hawkes, "structure—verbal and psycho-

logical coherence" is the primary concern. For such writers, realism is no more than one of many formal constructs available to the novelist.

Laurence W. Mazzeno

BIBLIOGRAPHY

Allen, Walter. *The Modern Novel in Britain and the United States*. New York: E. P. Dutton, 1964. Writing about novelists who published after World War I, Allen provides detailed discussions of major and minor figures on both sides of the Atlantic. Rather than looking for common themes and selecting works representative of specific trends, Allen examines writers individually and within their historical context.

Batchelor, John. *The Edwardian Novelists*. London: Duckworth, 1982. Concentrating on the major British novelists of the first decades of the twentieth century, Batchelor explains how these figures form a bridge between their Victorian forebears and the modern novelists who followed them.

Breen, Jennifer. *In Her Own Write: Twentieth-Century Women's Fiction*. New York: St. Martin's Press, 1990. Breen offers a method of reading novels that privileges the values and aspirations of women. Though she focuses on British novelists, her discussion provides a method for examining American women novelists as well.

Donald, Miles. *The American Novel in the Twentieth Century*. Totowa, N.J.: Barnes & Noble, 1978. Miles discusses major American novelists beginning with commentary on the post-World War I giants F. Scott Fitzgerald, Ernest Hemingway, and John Dos Passos, whom he calls traditional because they continue to explore themes that occupied American novelists of the late nineteenth century. He follows with provocative chapters on William Faulkner and John Updike, minority novelists, the Jewish American novel, and popular fiction.

Gindin, James. *Postwar British Fiction: New Accents and Attitudes*. Berkeley: University of California Press, 1962. Gindin explores the persistence of British novelists' concern with conduct and class, noting how World War II changed both the political and social climate in England. Gindin is expressly concerned with the heroes created by novelists such as Allan Sillitoe, Kingsley Amis, Doris Lessing, John Wain, Iris Murdoch, and William Golding.

Klein, Marcus, ed. *The American Novel Since World War II*. New York: Fawcett, 1969. This collection of essays by a number of distinguished critics provides analysis of the social and political background to novels written during the period 1940-1960. Includes a section on the underground novel, writings protesting mainstream American values.

McCormick, John. *Fiction as Knowledge: The Modern Post-romantic Novel*. New Brunswick, N.J.: Transaction Publishers, 1999. Examines the stream-of-consciousness novel, the rise of the antihero, and metaphysical and epistemological themes.

Sage, Lorna. *Women in the House of Fiction: Post-War Women Novelists*. New York: Routledge, 1992. Relying on feminist criticism, Sage reviews the work of nearly two dozen women whose works have shaped what she believes is a new, alternative tradition in fiction. Her survey includes Continental as well as British and American writers.

Scholes, Robert. *Fabulation and Metafiction*. Urbana: University of Illinois Press, 1979. Scholes examines a strong trend among post-World War II novelists to return to the techniques of romancers and creators of fables to provide insight into the modern condition. Central to his study are the works of writers such as Lawrence Durrell, John Barth, Kurt Vonnegut, and Bernard Malamud.

Spiller, Robert E. *The Cycle of American Literature: An Essay in Historical Criticism*. New York: Macmillan, 1955. Although dated in some respects, Spiller's review of American literature provides insight into the development of the modern American novel by analyzing it in the context of its nineteenth century forebears. His discussions of Theodore Dreiser, Ernest Hemingway, William Faulkner, and Thomas Wolfe help explain the social context in which these authors wrote and the political and literary milieu that helped shape their fiction.

Stamirowska, K. *Representations of Reality in the Post-war English Novel, 1957-1975*. Kraków: Universitas, 1992. Examines realism in postwar fiction in Great Britain.

POSTCOLONIAL LONG FICTION

A discussion of postcolonial literature must first acknowledge the scope and complexity of the term "postcolonial." Temporally, the term designates any national literature written after the nation gained independence from a colonizing power. According to this definition, all literature written in the United States after 1776 could qualify as postcolonial. Because the United States has occupied the position of an economic and political world power since the nineteenth century, however, it is today regarded more as a historically colonizing force than as a former colony of Great Britain. Within this field of literary studies, "postcolonial" refers to those nations that gained independence between the last quarter of the nineteenth century and the 1960's.

Geographically, "postcolonial" is a global term: It designates nations of the Caribbean, Central and South America, Africa, the South Pacific islands, and Malaysia. It applies equally to India, Ireland, Australia, New Zealand, Canada, and the Philippines. The colonizing powers to which these countries were subjected and with which they continue to contend after gaining independence are Great Britain, France, Spain, Portugal, Belgium, Germany, and the United States.

Postcolonial studies are not limited by geography or time, however. They treat a broad span of concerns: the functioning of different empires during the colonial period and varying administrative systems left as legacies to the former colonies; the specific conditions under which independence was gained in each case; cultural, economic, and linguistic imperialism that persists after independence; and the local concerns of education, government, citizenship, and identity.

Postcolonial literature tends to address opposition against imperial forces as it seeks to define autonomous national identity. In that quest, postcolonial literature explores issues of cultural alienation, and it struggles to expresses the specificity and particularities of indigenous cultures in a language that is not generally the original language of the indigenous people but rather the language of the former colonizer. The Kenyan writer Ngugi wa Thiong'o decided in 1981, after his imprisonment and exile for co-authoring and producing two Gikuyu-language plays that criticized the postcolonial Kenyan government, to switch from English to Gikuyu as the language for his writing. Similarly, the Irishman Samuel Beckett chose to live in France and write in French because this location and language did not carry the baggage of Ireland's struggles for independence from Britain. For many postcolonial writers, then, to write in the language of the colonizing power is an act of acceptance and acquiescence to that power, even if that power is no longer physically present.

The issue of language is complex, however. Although writing in the language of the colonizers implies some complicity with their power and cultural dominance, there are questions of circulation and counterdiscourse to consider. Can the circulation and readership of Ngugi's writings be as wide in Gikuyu as in English? Can the postcolonial voice of resistance against dominance and hegemony of the empire be heard in a Caribbean patois? To express postcolonial struggles and establish national identity in the language of the colonizing powers—English, French, or Spanish—is to form a counterdiscourse that can be heard at the center of the empire.

To express oneself in a language that is not one's own, a language that does not belong to one's land but has been violently imposed upon it, is a source of tension that gives rise not only to feelings of alienation and uncertainty regarding the legitimacy of the mother tongue but also to confusion regarding identity. To what degree is a citizen from India truly Indian, having been educated in English, writing in English, and even communicating with fellow Indians in the language of the British Empire? Although India possesses national identity, history, literature, and cultural practices, how can these remain purely Indian after two hundred years of British rule? Just as postcolonial Indian literature finds expression in English, not in one of the hundreds of Indian languages, so does it strive to define and establish an identity that can no longer be pure. This postindependence, postcolonial identity must admit that it is a hybrid, a mix of colonial and national identities transmitted through education, government, religion, and social practices.

The dynamics of foregrounding and theorizing a plurality of identities, mixing of cultures, interdependence between colonizer and colonized, as well as localized political concerns, create a reciprocity between postcolonial fiction and postcolonial theory. The interdependent development of postcolonial fiction and theory constitutes postcolonialism.

The association with poststructuralism and postmodernism is not accidental: These schools of literary and cultural criticism serve to validate the margins of artistic production by deconstructing centers of truth. These forms of criticism posit that truth, meaning, and identity are never axiomatic; they are in a constant state of production, wholly dependent on the context in which they appear. Postcolonial theorists stress that colonial identity is created by the ruling, colonizing powers. For example, Edward W. Said's seminal work *Orientalism* (1978) argues that the "Orient" is a set of images and assumptions constructed by the Western literary canon and projected onto colonized nations. Along with Said, Gayatri Chakravorty Spivak and Homi K. Bhabha argue that these fabricated, projected images of the Oriental "other" provide a framework and support for the enlightened European subject. India's Subaltern Studies group, led by Ranajit Guha and Spivak, rereads the history of British occupation for the purposes of asserting versions of cultural identity free from imperial constructions. Just as the Oriental other was given form through writing, so the postcolonial subject seeks expression through literature. With each postcolonial novel that is written, a new version of postcolonial subjectivity is told, and a new theory of cultural difference as well as political and intellectual autonomy is formulated. In postcolonialism, fiction and theory work together to define, shape, and stretch each other's boundaries.

Principal themes that postcolonial fiction develops are exile and alienation; rebellion, struggle, and opposition against colonial powers; and mixing or confusion of identities, multiculturalism, and establishing cultural autonomy free from imperial forces.

EXILE AND ALIENATION

Exile and alienation are represented both physically and figuratively in postcolonial fiction. Exile occurs when the protagonist or other character, usually a member of an indigenous people subjected to the colonial power, travels to the land of the colonizers for the purpose of education or finding work. Becoming a marginal member of society in the colonizing nation, the subject takes on certain characteristics and values of the oppressing culture. Thereafter, returning to the land of birth is nearly impossible because of psychological changes experienced while the postcolonial subject was away. Physical exile also occurs for political reasons: The subject either acts out against the government and is sent away or chooses to leave the homeland because colonial and postcolonial rules have wreaked such change on the native environment that it becomes unlivable.

Figuratively, the theme of exile is expressed as alienation and represents a search for the self. Colonial conditions in the native land render native culture, language, and education inferior to the culture and governing systems of the colonizers. Such cultural repression and validation of the imperial other provoke in the postcolonial protagonist an identity crisis and prompt him or her to search for a legitimate and positive image of the self. In order to embark on this quest for the self, the protagonist must first be split, shattered, or called into question, leading to his or her alienation from society. Alienation is similar to exile in that the subject is no longer "at home" either physically or psychologically in the native land. Physical alienation occurs when an otherwise respectable inhabitant of the native land is considered criminal or subversive by colonial law, leading to the subject's imprisonment or the revocation of societal privileges. More often, alienation is represented as psychological in postcolonial fiction: It is the state of not belonging, of not having a true home. Postcolonial subjects are alienated by Eurocentric, imperial systems that will never fully accept them, either culturally or racially; at the same time, they are alienated by native cultures that have either acquiesced to the colonial system or rejected them because they speak the language of the colonizers or have received the education of the empire.

One of the most in-depth explorations of cultural exile and quest for the self is presented in James Joyce's *Ulysses* (1922). Although its main characters, Stephen Dedalus, Leopold Bloom, and Molly Bloom, never leave Dublin, the novel draws a modern parallel to Homer's *Odyssey*, the epic story of a man's alienation from his home, exile to strange lands, and search for a way back home (metaphorically, a search for the self). On the surface, Joyce's novel does not appear to be concerned with Ireland's struggle for freedom from centuries of British rule. The action of the novel takes place in one day; the plot consists in Bloom and Stephen going about their day and in Bloom making his way home. Yet the novel operates on many levels—literally, metaphorically, and mythically—one of which emerges from its many references to the British occupation of Ireland and the Irish struggle for political autonomy. Following Bloom in his journey through Dublin, the novel depicts his departure from home and his return to home at the end as an exploration of Irish subjectivity. What the reader discovers, as the many layers of meaning unravel, is that Bloom is neither a pure Irishman nor a pure product of British colonial rule. The novel makes references to Bloom's Jewish descent; his wife Molly grew up on the British island of Gibraltar, the geographical gateway for British imperial expansion; and Bloom's English is a multicultural mix of Irishisms and Italian and Greek words. This modern odyssey with colonial concerns shows that a search for the self leads to the revelation of an identity that is not culturally pure. The novel also shows that as soon as one leaves home, all notions of a pure, unified self are lost.

A prototypical novel of exile and alienation is George Lamming's *In the Castle of My Skin* (1953). This autobiographical *Bildungsroman* presents the author's childhood in Barbados from his point of view at the age of twenty-three while living in London. He is led into retrospection by the alienation he experiences in the capital of the colonizers. The

childhood that he revisits and that forms the narrative chronologically parallels the last stages of colonialism in the Caribbean and unfolds against the backdrop of rising nationalism. The author's childhood development meaningfully parallels the loss of cultural innocence as destructive floods, a general strike across the island, and riots mark his ninth year, and the land of the village is sold to business just before he takes his first job in neighboring Trinidad. As the protagonist leaves Barbados, his village falls apart, thus producing an analogy between loss of childhood innocence and the disruption of cultural identity, between exile and alienation and the destruction of native lands by colonization. Only from the point of view of physical and spiritual alienation can the narrator look back and understand the destruction of his homeland. Only from this state of exile can he narrate his story; the only home to which he can return is the one that is rendered fictional, the one that constitutes his story. As the title suggests, in the state of exile that colonialism has forced upon him, the narrator is left with only his body, which has become his home.

The theme of alienation and exclusion of people not only from a dominant culture but also from their own land, language, and cultural practices has extended the boundaries of postcolonial literature to include feminist concerns regarding the oppression of women by men. Anita Desai's novel *Fire on the Mountain* (1977) addresses the cultural and social alienation of women in India with an unusual twist on the theme of exile. The novel's protagonist, Nanda Kaul, has retired to a mountaintop in the Punjab after fulfilling the duties of wife and mother. This exile into retirement in her old age foreshadows the transformative exile that awaits Nanda. The novel first depicts her as the image of Indian womanly perfection: stately, gentle, upstanding, and refined in her manners. Nanda paints her life as a young woman in the colors of happiness: her childhood, what her parents offered her as a child in a society that typically holds girls in contempt, and her marriage. By the end of the narrative, she reveals the unhappy reality of her past: Her father was usually absent when she was a child, and he never brought home nice gifts; her husband never loved or respected her, and he kept a mistress throughout his marriage to Nanda; and she never enjoyed a closeness with her children, who were in fact responsible for placing her atop a mountain in order to be rid of her. So that Nanda's story not appear to be tragic or out of the ordinary for women in India, the novel presents a minor character, Ila Das, whose life story is indeed tragic and unlucky. Ila is a childhood friend of Nanda who has not grown up; she is vulgar, ill-mannered, and rather stupid. Ila has also been unlucky: Her father died when she was young, her mother was an invalid, and her brothers squandered the family fortune. Nanda and her husband rescued Ila many times from poverty by procuring jobs for her that she failed to keep. She is well intentioned but has no social graces to compensate for her lack of survival skills. One day, just after having tea with Nanda, Ila is raped and killed in the streets. This event marks a turning point for Nanda, who admits to the social alienation she has experienced her whole life. She then performs the exit ritual and becomes one with the fire god, Agni, the bearer of the flame of eternal life, by walking into ardent coals. Her act of exile from the physical realm represents her alienation, at the same time raising her life to a higher, symbolic, transformative level.

STRUGGLE AND OPPOSITION

Aside from the themes of alienation, exile, confusion of identity, and search for the self, postcolonial fiction is also characterized by tensions between colonizer and colonized, or between the old colonial society and the emerging postcolonial one. These multiple themes that seek to define the postcolonial condition are often present in and overlap within the same novel, but it is just as often the case that one theme stands out above the others.

When the theme of social and political tension upstages the others, it can take the form of direct confrontation between colonizer and colonized. For example, in E. M. Forster's novel *A Passage to India* (1924), colonial tensions make their way to the courtroom when the respectable Indian citizen Dr. Aziz is accused of attacking a visiting Englishwoman, Adela Quested, during a friendly outing to some regionally

famous caves. Everyone in town takes a side as the polemics surrounding the trial against Aziz reach an explosive level. The Indians believe strongly in Aziz's innocence, while the occupying British remain convinced that Aziz is a local savage incapable of restraining himself around a white woman. The trial marks the climax of the novel, and the turning point occurs when Adela Quested takes the witness stand only to waver in her testimony and withdraw her charges against Aziz. Here, colonial tensions are played out on a symbolically legal level; the confrontation between colonized and colonizer is expressed as a life-or-death issue of guilt or innocence to be decided by emotional fervor and resentment of the colonial situation only thinly veiled by justice. In the end, justice prevails in that Quested recants her accusation, but the readiness of the British to bring Aziz to trial and the Indians' protest against such an act of oppressive power reveal the prejudices, and exemplify the hatred and mistrust, that colonialism promotes on each of the opposing sides. The novel encapsulates colonial hatred and mistrust in a legal issue, the trial, yet it is a legal issue—one country's government forcibly taking over another country's rights to govern itself—that provokes this hatred and mistrust.

In the novel *Things Fall Apart* (1958), by the Nigerian author Chinua Achebe, struggle, confrontation, and rebellion define the novel from start to finish. The protagonist, Okonkwo, is leader of an Igbo village and has built a reputation from his youth as a great wrestler. He develops fierce, warriorlike ways in opposition to his father, who died a man of weak, "woman-like" character. Okonkwo is a strict ruler, adhering closely to the traditions of his religion and culture. He does not defy tradition when community elders command the execution of his adopted son; he obediently accepts the traditional punishment of seven years of exile when he inadvertently kills a clansman. Okonkwo is a warrior whose principal cause is to preserve his culture even at the expense of rebelling against his father and, at times, cruelly beating his wives. Ironically, in obeying the dictates of tradition, by serving the sentence of exile, Okonkwo allows his culture to be destroyed. During the seven years of his absence, British missionaries move in and proselytize members of the village. In exile, Okonkwo learns from a friend that when a neighboring village killed a missionary, more white men came and annihilated its entire population. Okonkwo returns to his community to find that a district commissioner, a representative of the British government, has established a council. The climax of the novel stems from a conflict of religious interests: When the villagers burn down the missionaries' church because of sacrilege committed against their religion by a convert, the commissioner performs an act of retribution by imprisoning a group of Igbo men, including Okonkwo, until a fine is collectively paid. In the final confrontation between colonized and colonizer, Okonkwo kills a British messenger knowing immediately after the fact that this reckless act of violence has ruined the possibility of successfully combatting the British with warriorlike integrity. The district commissioner comes to Okonkwo's home to arrest and punish him for the murder, but he finds the warrior hanging from a tree, having committed suicide. The novel ends with the commissioner's musings about how to integrate Okonkwo's story as either a chapter or a paragraph in his book *The Pacification of the Primitive Tribes of the Lower Niger*.

Achebe's novel depicts struggle and conflict within the Igbo community before and during colonization. It is precisely this contrast, as well as the focus on customs and interpersonal relations in the village, that sends a message: Conflict and struggle among the Igbo people of this community prior to colonization did indeed exist but could be reckoned with and resolved; with colonization came the destruction of Igbo religion and conflicts that did not lead to resolution but to violence and death. The last words of the novel, the title of the district commissioner's book, reflect the British appropriation of African history: The chronicle of an Igbo village and the life of its leader becomes, by the end of the novel, a mere chapter or less in the history of British colonization.

MULTICULTURALISM AND IDENTITY

Colonial rule—the control and assimilation of other nations, their cultures and histories—was not executed without conflict, struggle, and opposition; furthermore, it has left its subjects, colonized people, in a state of alienation and either physical or psychological exile from places that were once unquestionably their homes. While colonialism has created two distinct categories of people, colonized and colonizer, each on the opposite side of the power divide, historically it has also caused a blending of races, languages, cultures, and systems of beliefs and values. This mixing of cultures is another principal theme in postcolonial fiction, and it is often developed in the broader context of establishing identity. With what identity are the people of a colonized nation left after centuries of foreign occupation and rule during which their neighbors were exported for labor or they themselves left home in search of legitimizing education and experience in Europe? On what cultural identity can an Indian family, for example, depend when the parents speak Hindi yet their children speak only English? What historical legitimacy can a community enjoy when its history has been rewritten by colonizers and when its laws have been overruled by the laws of a foreign land?

The need for an identity that is not imposed by occupying forces comes from a lack that is created by the violent intrusion and disruption of "home" by foreign powers. In V. S. Naipaul's *A House for Mr. Biswas* (1961), the house that a Hindu resident of Trinidad, Mr. Biswas, insists on buying but cannot afford becomes a symbol of independence and identity. His is an unlucky life fraught with poverty, lack of love, and failure. Analogous to oppressive, colonizing powers is the Tulsi clan to whom Biswas's wife remains faithful and who hold him in contempt. Having had enough of homelessness and rambling, Biswas buys the house, which is no better than a shack, and it stands for his pride, a fortress of autonomy towering above the prejudice and cultural oppression from which he suffers. His house also symbolizes the poverty and weakness that minorities experience in establishing cultural autonomy. The house of Mr. Biswas, who represents minorities in general, is a metaphor for his identity: It is at once poor and ramshackle, yet it belongs solely to him.

Salman Rushdie's *The Satanic Verses* (1988) deals with the issue of establishing cultural identity in postcolonial Britain and India in more complex terms. Regarding the formation of the postcolonial subject, this novel underscores ambivalence and posits that identity is composed through hybridity. Neither the British subject nor the Indian subject is constituted in a culturally pure fashion; the identities of both consist in effects and qualities of the other. Postcolonial identity is split between the cultural identity produced in the land of the colonizers and that of the colonized land, between British history and Indian history, between formation under British rule, with its concomitant values and customs, and the values and customs of the indigenous culture. From the moment the two cultures meet and clash as part of the colonizing project, neither culture can remain pure or unaffected.

The Satanic Verses expresses this process in terms of good and evil. Rushdie blurs the distinction between the colonizers as evil and the colonized as good by transforming the characteristics of the two protagonists, Gibreel Farishta and Saladin Chamcha. Gibreel was a poor orphan who became a movie star in Bombay. He achieved stardom by acting the parts of Hindu gods in theological films, and all the women of Bombay desire him. Aside from the divine roles he plays and the archangel his name denotes, he develops the physical attributes of an angel. After the start of the novel, he quickly acquires a halo and the power to entrance whomever he meets. In terms of postcolonial subjectivity, Gibreel initially represents the purity of Indian culture and identity, but by the end of the novel Gibreel has become disturbed and delusional, transforming into Azraeel, the angel of death. Gibreel parades around London blowing Azraeel's trumpet, provoking fires, and pronouncing destruction. Thematically, Gibreel is in London to colonize the land of the colonizer. As archangel, he fancies himself the harbinger of change for humanity, and he declares to the city of London that he intends to "tropicalize" it. In transforming from benevolent angel into the angel of death and destruction, Gibreel represents the absolutist system of values imposed on India by the British. Gibreel, the postcolonial subject, is both good and evil; he is both the culturally pure colonial native and a violent, invading force. His

insanity and subsequent death suggest that such absolute, inflexible identities lead to totalitarianism and destruction. In order to thrive, the postcolonial subject must be constituted by a working blend of cultural attributes.

By contrast, Saladin Chamcha is a "brown Englishman," an Indian made in Britain. Bombay-born, he was sent to English schools as a boy, and there he remained. He has made a career taking on the voices for inanimate objects in British television commercials as well as for the animated cartoon character Maxim Alien. Saladin proves to have the most malleable of British accents, which can pass for a catsup bottle, proud Englishman, or alien at will. He has expelled the Indian from himself—lifestyle, face, and voice—and represents the postcolonial Indian subject who has completely subscribed to British ways. It is not surprising that shortly after the start of the novel Saladin begins to grow horns. As the Indian who has betrayed his culture and national identity, Saladin is a product of postcolonial evil. He metamorphoses into a full-blown, eight-foot, goat-like devil. Just as Gibreel undergoes a qualitative transformation from good to bad angel, so Saladin rehumanizes himself upon admitting his hatred for "Mister Perfecto," Gibreel, who betrayed Saladin at the time of the latter's unjustified arrest. In the end it is Saladin who makes of himself a successful postcolonial subject: Having received a British education and understanding the position of fellow immigrants in London, he returns to his native Bombay, to his dying father's side, and there he decides to stay.

The start of the novel presents the situation that brings Saladin and Gibreel together. They take the same plane to London from India, and the plane is hijacked by a group of Sikh militant separatists. They spend more than one hundred days hovering over the British isle until the plane explodes; Saladin and Gibreel are the sole survivors. As they descend toward English soil, the two protagonists are transmuted into devil and angel, first passing through a state of being one. The process of uniting Saladin and Gibreel in order to separate them as devil and angel represents the cultural and symbolic splitting of the postcolonial subject. The novel then proceeds to render ambiguous their respective identities as Gibreel becomes a demonic angel and Saladin develops his sense of humanity through his experience as a devil. Above all, the novel posits that postcolonial identity is not stable, absolute, or fixed; it is always in a process of renegotiating itself depending on context and particular experiences. The postcolonial subject is neither a culturally pure colonized native nor a completely converted object of colonizing discipline and control. Postcolonial identity is necessarily a dynamic blend of the qualities, mentalities, and cultural formations of both colonized and colonizer.

Postcolonial fiction is not limited to the themes of exile and alienation, struggle and opposition, and cultural hybridity. Many postcolonial novelists have developed other themes, such as American and European enslavement of Africans; the historical oppression of black people in the United States; the forced assimilation in North America of minority cultures such as Native Americans, Latinos, and Asian immigrants; North Africans and their descendants in France; and Turkish immigrants in Germany. Regardless of the topic or setting, however, the postcolonial novel concerns itself with the cultural and political situation created by the colonial project, the necessarily violent and oppressive encounter between colonizer and colonized.

Nirmala Singh

BIBLIOGRAPHY

Ashcroft, Bill, Gareth Griffiths, and Helen Tiffin. *The Empire Writes Back: Theory and Practice in Post-Colonial Literatures*. London: Routledge, 1989. One of the most important categorical studies of postcolonial fiction in English. The authors define the genre in its relation to English literary studies, divide postcolonial fiction in English among critical models, define and examine textual strategies in producing this fiction, offer critical analyses of exemplary works, and discuss various postcolonial literary theories according to geographic divisions.

Bhabha, Homi K. *The Location of Culture*. London: Routledge, 1994. Twelve essays, including the widely read "DissemiNation: Time, Narrative and the Margins of the Modern Nation," that examine the formation of the colonial subject, whether colonizer or colonized. One of the principal aims of Bhabha's work is to reveal the possibilities for developing a minority discourse and expressing cultural difference.

Mohanram, Radhika, and Gita Rajan, eds. *English Postcoloniality: Literatures from Around the World*. Westport, Conn.: Greenwood Press, 1996. A collection of essays that discuss postcolonial literature in English according to regional cultures. The final section addresses indigenous literatures.

Parker, Michael, and Roger Starkey, eds. *Postcolonial Literatures*. New York: St. Martin's Press, 1995. A collection of essays by various critics offering textual analyses of postcolonial works by Chinua Achebe, Ngugi wa Thiong'o, Anita Desai, and Derek Walcott.

Said, Edward W. *Orientalism*. New York: Pantheon, 1978. A classic and boldly critical study of European cultural imperialism. Said argues that the intellectual and artistic formation of the "Oriental other" by the West was the necessary precursor for physical colonization. Said exposes and denounces European discursive constructions of the Orient in literature and history that persist and continue to colonize the literary imagination.

Spivak, Gayatri Chakravorty. *In Other Worlds: Essays in Cultural Politics*. London: Methuen, 1987. A collection of Spivak's essays divided into three sections. The first explores feminist strategies for rereading canonical literature. The second section critically examines French feminism and the production of ideology in Western universities. The third develops methods for reading Third World literature by analyzing the work of Indian author Mahasweta Devi and the Subaltern Studies group.

CONTEMPORARY LONG FICTION

It is generally agreed that the postmodern period of world literature begins immediately following the end of World War II and extends at least through the fall of the Berlin Wall and the dissolution of the Soviet Union. Perhaps this period of the novel's development is identified most of all with experimentation. Worldwide, postmodern novels have flown in the face of much that preceded them, yet the novel remains an evolving, thriving genre. Testimony to its vitality is to be found in how this somewhat Eurocentric, male-dominated genre of literature now counts among its preeminent practitioners women from countries not traditionally identified with the novel at its best, and evidence of this vitality is to be found as well in new schools of novelizing such as Magical Realism.

To appreciate such a turn of events in the novel's development, one must know something about the history of the novel and its traditions. The novel is the only genre today that cannot also be found among the classic literatures of Rome and Greece. It emerged as a budding literary form while philosophical thought and everyday life were undergoing changes of staggering breadth during the Age of Enlightenment in the seventeenth century. The Age of Enlightenment championed human reason at a time when God and the Church had begun to recede from the forefront of European consciousness as the defining elements of human existence, as evidenced by philosopher René Descartes's famous statement, "I think, therefore I am." A new formulation of value and worth was in the offing as well, one imposed by humanity rather than by the heavens. Rising in tandem with the gold standard, international trade, and modern economics, the novel found its initial audience and practitioners amid a flowering, newly educated, secular middle class that had begun to appear on the horizons of mercantile Europe at about the same time.

Like the flourishing mercantile environment from which it sprang, the novel has traditionally championed individual initiative, choosing for its protagonists not high-ranking nobility, as was true of the literatures of ancient Rome and Greece, but rather unremarkable, often common men and women with recognizable emotional and physical desires. These characters resembled the reader. With their capacity to reason, such protagonists were given the opportunity to understand the world around them and, through such understanding, the chance to satisfy their physical needs and emotional desires by choosing one alternative over another. What brings readers to a novel may well be the chance it gives them to participate in the wishes, dreams, desires, and emotions of its characters, but what propels a novel forward is the characters' decision-making process and their capacity to make well-informed choices. By bringing to bear what they have learned in the past on the current situations in which they find themselves, the protagonists of traditional novels have the opportunity to control their destinies in ways that would have boggled the minds of the ancients, held in the grip of the fates as they were. The linear concept of time—that is, that a past bears directly on a present that allows one to determine a future—came hand in hand with a new sense of space that emerged with the Enlightenment thought of Descartes, Baruch Spinoza, Thomas Hobbes, and John Locke. As world trade flourished and as the globe became navigable through spatial coordinates such as longitude and latitude, this new and relatively sophisticated sense of space was reflected in the novel as a literary form.

The conventional novels that grew out of the Enlightenment reflected the age's confidence in the ability to navigate a world based in scientific laws. Conventionally, the first 10 to 20 percent of a novel introduces the reader to the major characters, especially protagonist, and locates those characters in a particular time and a particular spatial realm. Then follows an event, choice, or dilemma—something that sets the plot into motion. Plot development begins as a character responds to this initial event, choosing A over B in an attempt to resolve a dilemma. That choice is usually successful only in part, resulting in a new event, choice, or dilemma to which the protagonist must respond. How well the characters fare in manipulating their circumstances to achieve their goals is eventually determined by some central and final occurrence, the climax of the plot. The reader's identification with the characters compels the reader's interest. Moreover, novels suppose not only an ever-changing world but ever-changing characters as well. The reader expects the characters—at least the protagonist and the central characters—to change and evolve emotionally and intellectually as they live through the experiences the novel puts before them.

THE NEW NOVEL

The single most important change in the novel after World War II was the degree to which it challenged and reacted against what the novel had been traditionally. Within a decade of the war's end, signs were afoot that the modernist period of literature—a literary movement that had begun after World War I—had probably run its course. The watchword of the modernists had been "alienation." As the Industrial Revolution of the mid-nineteenth century had flowered at the beginning of the twentieth century, momentous changes had taken place that called for new ways of understanding the world and the people in it. A machine age was beginning. For the first time in the history of Western civilization, large numbers of people were abandoning the rural environment and agrarian life in favor of cities and a life of mercantilism premised upon the mass manufacture of material goods. If the literature of the period is to be trusted, this shift wrenched humankind from the most trusted human verities and demand new ways of conceiving what it meant to be human.

Within a decade of the end of World War II, modernism's "alienation" seemed to be transmogrifying into something other. New watchwords such as "isolation" and "anxiety" were in the offing, and new, postmodern considerations came to the fore. With the development of the atomic bomb, humankind had in its hands enough power to destroy civilization. Fundamental concepts from the Age of Enlightenment—attempts to understand one's world through temporal and spatial coordinates, as well as through cause and effect relationships; assumptions of the primacy of reason in the human experience; and assumptions of the primacy of the individual—were challenged, questioned, and defied by the new generation of novelists that appeared after 1945.

This change has been reflected in a wide variety of names, most of them suggesting reaction against the status quo or rebellion against constraint. American critics called it "antiliterature" or the "antinovel," while in France experimental forms of fiction were variously labeled *écriture blanche*, *chosisme*, *école du regard*, or *école de minuit*; in both Europe and the United States, the form eventually came to be called the *nouveau roman*, or, loosely translated, the new novel.

Spearheaded by French authors—among them Samuel Beckett, Alain Robbe-Grillet, Nathalie Sarraute, Michel Butor, Claude Simon, Robert Pinget, Marguerite Duras, and Jean Cayrol—the *nouveau roman* was to have far-reaching, liberating effects on the novel in the decades ahead. The *nouveau roman* looked not to the world at large for its subject matter but rather to the consciousness of its protagonists, for it grew out of an assumption that, in an unstable world, only human consciousness can be known for certain. Conventions of plotting, characterization, and narrative based on linear time and stable space were put to the side as writers explored the workings of minds struggling to structure, often through language, a world that, in the wake of two world wars, defied comprehension.

With *Murphy* (1938), *Watt* (1953), and his mid-1950's trilogy of novels—*Molloy* (1951; English translation, 1955), *Malone meurt* (1951; *Malone Dies*, 1956), and *L'Innommable* (1953; *The Unnamable*, 1958)—Samuel Beckett set out what would be his primary novelistic interests over the next twenty-five years. Beckett's focus is human solitude, and, understandably, the protagonists of his novels are often monologists. They are generally incapacitated, crippled, and immobile, doing their best to understand where they are and how they got there. Readers generally meet them just as their bodies are dying or, more precisely, at the point when they become aware of the dying process, yet their minds race on, refusing to quit even though their flesh is prepared to surrender. Unable to distinguish between illusion and

reality or between memories of actual events and fig-
ments of their imaginations, they speak in a void,
gradually becoming more aware of their own narrative voices and the futility of their need to tell their
stories when no one is there to listen. That does not
stop them from speaking. It should. Certainly they
would like it to. Their consciousness will not allow
it, however. Despite all odds, human consciousness
needs to make sense of experience; hence, their
monologues continue to their final, dying breath. As
Beckett writes in the concluding lines of *The Unnamable*, "You must go on, I can't go on, I'll go on,
you must say words as long as there are any, until
they find me, until they say me."

Alain Robbe-Grillet, perhaps the most articulate
spokesman for the New Novel (as attested by his
1963 *Pour un nouveau roman*; *For a New Novel*,
1965), dealt with similar issues. Robbe-Grillet's first
novel, *Les Gommes* (1953; *The Erasers*, 1964), was
published while he was freshly associated with the
influential French publishing house Éditions de
Minuit, but it was *Le Voyeur* (1955; *The Voyeur*,
1958), which won the Prix des Critiques, that
brought Robbe-Grillet to world prominence. Robbe-
Grillet announced shortly after its publication, "What
is important for me in the novel is structure." His
plots appear, in their first few pages, to be conventional, but as one reads, one enters a plot of labyrinthine complexities—One of Robbe-Grillet's later
novels, in fact, is titled *Dans le labyrinthe* (1959; *In
the Labyrinth*, 1960). There is no dramatic conclusion, no logical climax to his plots; rather, one enters
a narrative in which attempts to comprehend events
through chronology and space, and through cause
and effect relationships, lead only to dead ends.

Nathalie Sarraute's first postwar work of importance was *Martereau*, published in 1953 (English
translation, 1959). However, it was the short story
collection *Tropismes* (1939, 1957; *Tropisms*, 1963)
with which she is most often identified. The "tropisms" of the title are fleeting responses to the world,
the experiences people sense in themselves that are
not translatable into language. Her concern is how
Western thought teaches people to privilege language, reason, and what cannot be known through

the five senses, and how it subjugates tropisms to the
level of "whim" or "emotion." People's real lives are
being lived on levels of consciousness that they have
been trained to ignore. Sarraute's novels contain story
lines and characters of sorts; however, like Robbe-
Grillet, her foremost concern is demonstrating that
readers are too willing to trust the artifice of fiction.

PREEMINENT WOMEN NOVELISTS

The novel flowered internationally following
World War II. Despite all that has been written about
the decline of print literature and the rise of elec-
tronic media after 1945, the depth and breadth of talented novelists has arguably never been greater than
in this single period. Witness Sarraute and Robbe-
Grillet in France, the Soviet Union's Alexander Sol-
zhenitzyn, India's Salman Rushdie, Germany's Günter Grass and Heinrich Böll, and Mexico's Carlos
Fuentes; the trend continued as a younger generation of enormously talented novelists, England's Graham Swift and Julian Barnes to name but two, began
to take their rightful place in world letters. Many
women may be counted among the preeminent novelists of the postwar period, particularly South Africa's
Doris Lessing and Nadine Gordimer, Canada's Margaret Atwood, and Chile's Isabel Allende. That these
women hail from countries not normally identified
with the forefront of the Western world's letters at-
tests to the growing internationalization of the novel.

Lessing's two most widely read novels are *The
Golden Notebook* (1962) and *The Four-Gated City*
(1969). First published before the feminist movement
had received high recognition, *The Golden Notebook*
became a feminist landmark, an ambitious, unyield-
ing account of the political, personal, and professional lives of writer Anna Wulf. Attempting to reconcile her inner self with the self that she shows to
the world at large, Wulf turns to her notebooks. The
struggle to define herself as a woman and as a person
is played out in four different notebooks: one for her
political self, another for her personal self, a third for
herself as an author confounded by writer's block,
and a fourth, the "golden notebook" of the title, in
which she brings the other three together.

This idea of creating a whole that is more than the

sum of its parts is central to Lessing's writing, as is maintaining one's mental stability in an unstable world. Both themes are dealt with in Lessing's *The Four-Gated City*, the fifth and last installment of her *Children of Violence* pentology, five works published individually as *Martha Quest* (1952), *A Proper Marriage* (1954), *A Ripple from the Storm* (1958), *Landlocked* (1965, 1991), and *The Four-Gated City*. Lessing's protagonist, Martha Quest, is her most compelling and certainly most complex heroine. The pentology follows Martha from her youth as a rebellious teenager through her middle age, during which she copes with teenagers of her own. A woman not unlike what is known about Lessing from her autobiography *Walking in the Shade* (1997), Martha takes up residence in London and becomes politicized as she finds herself involved in the communist scares of the period and deeply involved in the lives of people she encounters. Many of Martha's actions are daring, risky, and sometimes foolish, for experience is Martha's goal—to experience life in a manner different from how, as a woman, she has been taught to live. Commitment, however, is the lesson to be taken to heart. The act of commitment stands apart from politics, from the cause itself; Lessing suggests that in a world of contradiction and confusion, commitment is the only way to affirm life in a particularly human fashion.

Gordimer, who won the Nobel Prize in Literature in 1991, published the novel *Burger's Daughter* in 1979. Its protagonist, Rosa Burger, has survived her two politically active parents, both of whom suffered for their antiapartheid convictions. With her parents dead, Rosa struggles to find her place in her culture and reconcile her parents' legacy with the current political climate of her homeland, discovering as she does that every private act carries with it a public dimension. Many of these same concerns are dealt with in Gordimer's *The House Gun* (1998). Its protagonists are the Lindgards, Harald and Claudia, a middle-aged, upper-class couple living in postapartheid South Africa who are forced to confront their country's legacy of violence and racism when their son Duncan is arrested, imprisoned, and tried for the murder of his lover. Facing a postapartheid legal sys-

tem, the Lindgards hire a black attorney to be their son's representative, thinking that will be all they need, only to discover themselves becoming enmeshed in a legal and personal process in which they are powerless to act effectively or even understand what is going on. Imprisonment is the central theme of the book. The story explores the generational differences that separate parents from child, but it also explores the walls that the Lindgards have erected around themselves in order to avoid dealing with the darkest realities of South African culture.

Atwood's *Surfacing* (1972) is set in northern Quebec on a remote island. The nameless female protagonist, the protagonist's lover Joe, and their friends Anna and David set out to find the protagonist's father, who has been reported missing. Their search returns the protagonist to the area where she was raised; in the course of searching for her father, she finds, most of all, herself. She finds in her own psyche memories and levels of understanding that have little to do with the definition of herself she has established through her artwork and her social relationships. Atwood also deals with the ways in which women define themselves in such later novels as *Cat's Eye* (1989), *Alias Grace* (1996), and *The Handmaid's Tale* (1985).

The Handmaid's Tale, a thought-provoking, scathing, satire rather than a journey of self-discovery, is set at the millennium in the mythical Republic of Gilead. In this parody of the biblical story of Rachel, a social movement akin to America's Moral Majority has blurred the separation of church and state and institutionalized a mind-numbing version of domestic tranquility. Young women, including the protagonist Offred, are required to breed in order to repopulate a world devastated by birth control gone awry, ecological mismanagement, and nuclear fallout. Offred and the other handmaidens of Gilead remain uneducated and in positions of servitude, their primary—in fact their sole—social identity being their fertile ovaries.

Allende, a seasoned journalist, debuted as a novelist with *La casa de los espíritus* (1982; *The House of the Spirits*, 1985), a chronicle of three generations of the Trueba family in an unnamed South American country from the beginning of the twentieth century through the 1980's. The novel's central character is Clara del Valle-Trueba, a hypersensitive youngster who is just discovering her own telepathic powers. The death of her sister Rosa silences Clara for nearly a decade. When Rosa's fiancé, Esteban Trueba, returns to his homeland, Clara recognizes him as the figure who has been coming to her in her dreams and speaks for the first time since her sister's death. Esteban and Clara marry and take up residence in the house of the novel's title. In addition to bearing and raising a family, Clara fills the house with artists, spiritualists, and an assortment of other visionaries until the mansion becomes a world unto itself. However, Esteban's attachment to his estate points his attention outward to the world beyond his property. There, an amalgam of uneasy political forces is gradually drawing the country toward a volatile period of socialist reforms that threaten Esteban's hold on his land. Esteban fails to recognize what, for Clara, is the most fundamental tenet of life—namely, that what people seek to possess will, in the end, take possession of them, rather than the other way around. Consequently, over the years, Esteban's opposition to a socialist state draws him and his loved ones into political upheavals that jeopardize their lives, their property, and their love for one another.

MAGICAL REALISM

Allende attempted to reconcile the political novel with the epic in *The House of the Spirits*, just as she attempted to reconcile the effect of people on history and the effect of history on people, the private world of a family and the public world in which people's lives are finally lived, and the hold nature has on people's minds and the hold the supernatural maintains on their souls. Allende's subsequent novels, such as *El plan infinito* (1991; *The Infinite Plan*, 1993), have been somewhat less ambitious but no less skillfully written. Her prose is filled with vivid, often surprising imagery. To read her work is akin to waking from a dream only to find that one has not been dreaming, for her spiritual world is as faithfully and realistically rendered as are her accounts of revolutions.

Allende's work has been associated with Magical Realism, a genre of writing that appeared after World War II. Magical Realists make little or no distinction between the real and the surreal; characters seem to inhabit a world where the magical is no less substantial than the commonplace event. The term "Magical Realism" has been used to describe the work of a wide variety of fiction writers, such as Graham Swift, Sandra Cisneros, Peter Carey, Alusaine Dunbar, B. Kojo Laing, Milan Kundera, V. S. Naipaul, Tomaso Landolfi, Jorge Luis Borges, Italo Calvino, and Marina Maxwell. Ordinarily, however, Magical Realism as a description is reserved for the work of those writers who draw from particular South American and Spanish traditions of the absurd or the grotesque, predominantly Laura Esquivel, Horacio Quiroga, Carlos Fuentes, Alejo Carpentier, Roberto Gonzalez Eschevarria, Julio Cortázar, and José Saramago, who won the 1999 Nobel Prize in Literature.

Of the Magical Realists, Colombia's Gabriel García Márquez, who won the Nobel Prize in Literature in 1982, is perhaps the most well known to the general reading public. His novel *Cien años de soledad* (1967; *One Hundred Years of Solitude*, 1970), set in the village of Macondo in the South American lowlands of Colombia, relates the history of the Buendía family from about 1830 to 1930. The novel is less a family chronicle than a physical and metaphysical exploration of human life. García Márquez is capable of stunning physical description. In that sense, he demonstrates all the capacities of the finest of realist writers, but his aim is to demonstrate that a "realistic" depiction of the world is misleading. His sentences can run on for pages, making readers lose the point in the process. The family tree at the book's beginning proves of less help than expected: Several different characters share the same name at the same time, and the referents for pronouns such as "he" or "they" are often difficult, if not impossible, to locate. The past flows into the present without warning, and plot and subplot become so intertwined that it is nearly impossible to distinguish one from the other. One senses, however, that ordering principles exist beneath the apparent confusion.

García Márquez's depiction of life in the community of Macondo reveals that its political history is one of violence, mayhem, and chaos. Yet an order belies this chaos, if one is perceptive enough to detect it. In one of the novel's most famous sequences, for instance, a character is pushed up against a wall, then shot within view of his loved one, Rebecca, who exacts revenge by shooting someone else. In a long section rendered in minute and breathtaking detail, her victim's blood trickles through the town, finally passing by this victim's loved one, Ursula, just as she is separating thirty-six eggs in the course of baking bread. Ursula follows the trail in reverse, discovering, at last, her dead loved one and Rebecca.

The patterns that inform the world of García Márquez's *One Hundred Years of Solitude* have little to do with what can be learned from history books or courses in empirical science, much less what one expects to learn from a book-length family chronicle. This same worldview is to be found as well in his later novels, such as *El amor en los tiempos del cólera* (1985; *Love in the Time of Cholera*, 1988). The novel is set in a mythical country on the Caribbean coast of South America and accounts for about fifty years in the lives of its three main characters. As young men, Florentino Arizo and Juvenal Urbino fall in love with Femina Diaz. Although she marries Urbino, Arizo remains in love with her, and she becomes his primary reason for living. Upon the death of Urbino many years later, Arizo declares his feelings for Diaz at last, woos her as if she were still a young girl, and loves her in his bed despite the fact that her beauty has long passed.

One of the major themes of the novel is time. As measured by a calendar or a watch, many years pass in the course of the plot. For Arizo, however, no time has passed at all. Time is only meaningful if one can know how it is experienced, and, similarly, one can only understand the life Arizo has lived once they are given a privileged view of his heart. Arizo might appear to the world to be a lecher, for instance, or at the very least a libertine. He reports that he has brought to his bed more than six hundred women, and one of these was his ward, a fourteen-year-old girl. Femina, however, is the woman to whom he has been trying to make love. Paradoxically, by becoming Urbino's wife rather than Arizo's, she has become the center of Arizo's life in ways she could not have had she married him.

THE POSTMODERN AMERICAN NOVEL

Not surprisingly, much that changed in the novel worldwide after World War II also changed in the American novel—sometimes more so. Perhaps the most important development in American novels after the war, however, was the manner in which America itself and the place of its citizens within it were portrayed. What kind of country was the United States to become, now that Europe was disabled and the United States was so unthinkably strong? Was it possible that modernism's sense of alienation was now going to be institutionalized, employed, made part of the social infrastructure? Modernism had chronicled the assimilation of immigrants into the American grain. Much of that assimilation was complete by the end of World War II. Postmodern literature seemed to question the price at which this assimilation had come about. To participate in America as a "melting pot" had meant that those who travelled to the United States from distant lands gave up old ways of life in favor of new ones. New authors began to consider whether the melting pot was a myth and whether it was possible to completely give up one's roots and become, first and foremost, an American.

World War II cost some 350,000 Americans their lives in battle, and more than double that number were wounded; yet in a war that counted more than 50 million dead in all, America was spared much of the suffering endured by the nations of Europe. The United States emerged more prosperous and powerful than any other nation on earth. Change was in the air. This was true as well in literature. Thomas Wolfe had died in 1938; F. Scott Fitzgerald and Nathaniel West in 1940; Sherwood Anderson in 1941. Other modernist novelists who had been at the forefront of American letters since World War I, such as William Faulkner and Ernest Hemingway, had already done their best work, and though they would be lauded in the years ahead, they were stepping to the side as younger novelists sought a voice in literature, many of them military veterans, most of them university educated, and all of them coming into their own as adults. The first signal of this change was the publication of a spate of popular, middlebrow novels that appeared within a few years of the war's end that chronicled wartime experience: John Hersey's *A Bell for Adano* (1944), Gore Vidal's *Williwaw* (1946), John Horne Burns's *The Gallery* (1948), Irwin Shaw's *The Young Lions* (1948), James Gould Cozzens's *Guard of Honor* (1948), Herman Wouk's *The Caine Mutiny* (1951), and James Jones's *From Here to Eternity* (1951). It soon became clear that the new novelists were doing more than adding their voices to those of their elders, however. This generation brought to their work thematic concerns that were different in kind and degree from the novelists who had preceded them.

No three or four novels can demonstrate the depth and breadth of such matters, but perhaps Norman Mailer's *The Naked and the Dead* (1948), Ralph Ellison's *Invisible Man* (1952), and Saul Bellow's *The Adventures of Augie March* (1953) can serve as a place from which to begin. Though its form was seriously indebted to the work of modernist novelist John Dos Passos, Mailer's *The Naked and the Dead* was a war novel that touched upon what would become postmodern fare in the years ahead; it is arguably the first postmodern war novel in the American canon. Freudian thought had recently become a standard component of many liberal arts curricula in American universities, and the Harvard-educated Mailer made use of what he had learned. Mailer's platoon of soldiers tasked with taking an island in the Pacific during the final months of the war are drawn as characters with both conscious and unconscious levels to their psyches, characters only partially aware of their own motives and the motives of others. They are complicated and confused characters, unable to make their own experience of the United States coincide with the country's myths. They are drawn in ways that suggest that anxiety is a central feature of the human experience. Literature had always included fearful, anxious characters, but these were conditions that could be mitigated or overcome. Not so in Mailer's work. Postmodern people were anxiety-ridden figures, unable to understand or appreciate the complexities of their situations, ever aware that they had less control of their fate than they told.

More important, Mailer had his finger on what

would become a new and disturbing concept of the United States itself, one that would become familiar in American novels in the coming years. As the United States became the most powerful nation on earth, American authors began focusing on Americans who had less power than ever before in history. Postmodern Americans were forced to find their place in a culture that touted individualism and self-sufficiency yet denied both in practice as it attempted to enter an era of high technology, mass culture, and anonymous suburban life.

One of Mailer's characters, the brilliant General Cummings, continually debates the shape of the postwar world with his subordinate, Lieutenant Robert Hearn. Hearn argues that much of American military life is dangerously close to fascism. Cummings counters that fascism is singularly suited to meet the challenges of a country as rich and diverse as the United States will be in the years ahead. If anything, Cummings instructs him, the military environment is a preview of what the United States will be like after the war is over. It will continue to appear to be a free and democratic nation, paying lip service to the importance of the individual and other outmoded patriotic verities, but the truth of the matter will be otherwise. In order to harness the kinetic energy of the country so it can take its place as a world power in an age of high technology, American society will have to be rigidly structured from top to bottom. There will be little or no place for the free-thinking individual. People will be forced to accept their places in a "fear ladder," afraid and envious of their superiors and threatened by their subordinates' ambitions and eager to keep them in their place. According to Cummings, "the only morality of the future is a power morality, and a man who cannot find his adjustment to it is doomed. There's one thing about power. It can only flow from the top down."

The nameless protagonist of Ralph Ellison's *Invisible Man* is a black college student at an all-black southern institution funded by white benefactors and run by a distinguished black educator, Doctor Bledsoe. Early in the novel, the protagonist protests when Bledsoe moves to have him expelled unfairly. The protagonist threatens to make his case public. Bledsoe's speech is reminiscent of that of Mailer's General Cummings. Here, Cummings's "power morality" becomes Bledsoe's "power set-up":

Tell anyone you like," [Bledsoe] said. "I don't care . . . Power doesn't have to show off. Power is confident, self-assuring, self-starting, self-stopping, self-warming and self-justifying. . . . This is a power set-up, son, and I'm at the controls. You think about that. When you buck me, you're bucking against power, rich white folks' power, the nation's power—which means government power . . . You're nobody son, you don't exist—can't you see that?

These last few words direct a reader to the central conceit of the novel. Ellison's protagonist is as "invisible" to powerful black people as he is to powerful white people. He has no significant individual identity. As a person, he exists only insofar as he accepts a role in the agenda of the people in power.

A related concept is to be found in Saul Bellow's *The Adventures of Augie March*. Bellow first appeared on the literary scene with *Dangling Man* in 1944. For much of that novel, Bellow's protagonist, Joseph, "dangles" between two alternatives, both of which he finds unsatisfactory. As Joseph awaits induction into the U.S. Army, he tries to decide whether he should accept his induction notice and become part of an institution that he finds morally repugnant, or be true to his own conscience, suffer the immediate consequences, and accept that he will spend the rest of his life defined by this choice, always on the fringes of mainstream American community. Joseph's is a sticky decision to make, but it pales in comparison to the world faced by Augie March in *The Adventures of Augie March*. Augie's world is one of dizzying complexities. As the Jewish Augie March tries to take his place in mainstream American culture, he finds that good and evil, right and wrong, are simpleminded tenets. So is individual identity. In his way, Augie is as "invisible" as Ellison's protagonist. The only thing Augie can know for sure is that everyone seeks power. All people come to a given situation with their own agenda in hand, eager to make others a part of it, eager to offer them an identity that serves their immediate ends:

You invent a man who can stand before the terrible appearances. This way he can't get justice and he can't give justice, but he can life. And this is what humanity always does. It's made up of these inventors or artists, millions and millions of them, each in his own way trying to recruit other people to play a supporting role and sustain him in this make-believe. The great chiefs and leaders recruit the greatest number, and that's what their power is. There's one image that gets out in front to lead the rest and can impose its claim to being genuine with more force than the others. Then a huge invention, which is the invention of the world itself, and of nature, becomes . . . the actuality. That's the struggle of humanity, to recruit others to your version of what's real.

This identifiably postmodern consideration of the United States and American life in literature, in which individuals are defined by their incapacities as much as their strengths, by their confusions as much as their insights, became a predominant theme of novels written through the time of the war in Vietnam. No longer was the United States a country premised upon the rights and prerogatives of the individual. One had to take one's proper place in the culture, like it or not; predictably, the protagonists of American novels did not like it.

The postmodern era has been called the era of the "antihero." This would suggest that the protagonists of many novels are bounders, wasters, simpletons, and fools when, in fact, they demonstrate many of the same strengths as conventional heroes. What changes is that they are so rarely successful in achieving what they set out to do. This is another way of saying that what changes is not the American hero but America itself. The protagonists of novels published ten to fifteen years after World War II tested four central courses of action—assimilation, accommodation, flight, and rebellion—and found each to be as ineffective as the next.

Perhaps the two authors most associated with the perils and peculiar difficulties of assimilation into American culture after the war are John Updike and James Purdy. The issue surfaced with John Updike's *Rabbit, Run* (1960) and became a concern with which he would deal throughout his career, particularly the subsequent installments of the Rabbit Ang-strom series, *Rabbit Redux* (1971) and *Rabbit Is Rich* (1981). James Purdy staked a collateral claim to these concerns in his first published work, a collection of short stories titled *Color of Darkness* (1957), then explored it in more depth in such early novels as *Malcolm* (1959) and *Cabot Wright Begins* (1964). This theme has been explored by a wide variety of postmodern American fiction writers: Protagonists attempt to embrace the values of the culture, take their place, and make do with what they were given. This course of action is rarely, if ever, successful. The values of American culture are no longer clear, and they seem to center on money, mercantile success, upward social mobility, power, and secular values; even if one were to succeed, the victory would be a hollow one.

Another approach was to accommodate the culture, but only in part. This was the tactic explored by Ellison in *Invisible Man* and Bellow in *The Adventures of Augie March*. For a time it seemed to be the domain of Jewish American novelists, particularly Bellow, Philip Roth, Bernard Malamud, suggesting that accommodation was the domain of novelists focusing their attention on the search for the American Dream among minority groups. Accommodation, however, was explored by a wide range of authors, and the results were largely the same in each case: One plays a daily role, taking what one can from the marketplace but always keeping some of one's self in reserve, only to discover in the end that such a preservation of "self" is virtually impossible. Insofar as "we" accommodate culture, "we" become "them," whether or not "we" realize this is happening.

Flight was yet another response to the new American life. Protagonists in American novels had been fleeing civilized American life in favor of the frontier since the nineteenth century; in fact, such protagonists as James Fenimore Cooper's Natty Bumppo and Mark Twain's Huckleberry Finn were legendary for it. Flight, however, was no longer a possibility. The United States had become urbanized and suburbanized, and it no longer contained a frontier. Although this lack stopped many novelists dead in their tracks, others, such as William Burroughs and Richard Brau-

tigan, looked for less terrestrial alternatives and a re-definition of new and fertile landscapes. Burroughs's *The Naked Lunch* (1959; republished as *Naked Lunch*, 1962) explored drug addiction and retreat into the recesses of the human psyche, while Brautigan's *Trout Fishing in America* (1967) and *In Watermelon Sugar* (1968) offered the human imagination as the last frontier in which the America of mythology could be found.

Rebellion is as American as the United States itself, as is clear from the history of the American Revolution. Yet rebellion no longer seemed viable either. Novels no longer made it clear who the enemy was, and it was difficult to determine who to rebel against in order to prosper. Ken Kesey's *One Flew over the Cuckoo's Nest* (1962) articulated such dilemmas for the youthful countercultures of the turbulent 1960's, particularly the dilemma of the rebel. Kesey's protagonist, Randle Patrick McMurphy, checks himself into a mental institution in an attempt to get off a work detail during a sentence he is serving in prison. He does battle with Nurse Ratched, the supervisor of the mental ward to which he is committed. Prior to McMurphy's arrival, the narrator of the novel, Chief Bromden, has found a way to accommodate her and the ward she runs by passing himself off as deaf and dumb. McMurphy's presence brings Chief to his full senses, and McMurphy's willingness to confront and rebel against Nurse Ratched inspires Chief to daring, selfless acts of his own. Any pleasure of victory Chief might feel is tempered, however. After all, one nurse in one mental ward is not really the problem. In the novel, Mailer's "power morality" and Ellison's "power set-up" becomes what Chief calls the "Combine." Chief says about McMurphy,

> He says he don't think getting her out of the way would really make much difference; he says that there's something bigger making all this mess and goes on to try to say what he thinks it is. He finally gives up when he can't explain it. McMurphy doesn't know it, but he's onto what I realized a long time back, that it's not just the Big Nurse by herself, but it's the whole Combine, the nation-wide Combine that's the really big force, and the nurse is just a high-ranking official for them.

BLACK HUMOR

The problem Chief ponders is a familiar one in postmodern novels. If the Combine, rather than Nurse Ratched, is the enemy, how is one to rebel against it? The Combine is tantamount to postmodern American life itself. Therefore, the enemy is everywhere yet, paradoxically, nowhere to be found. Can acts of rebellion be heroic in a world so absurd, one in which the enemy is everywhere and nowhere, or are they simply self-destructive? These and similar questions became the focus of what has come to be called the black humor novel. It is marked by a darkness of authorial vision and an absurd, sometimes surreal, depiction of contemporary life. Mostly, however, it is definable through its sense of gallows humor. This school of darkly comic novels is generally considered to be a Cold War phenomenon, but the black humor novel first entered the American canon of letters at the end of the modernist period with the works of Nathaniel West: *A Cool Million: Or, The Dismantling of Lemuel Pitkin* (1934), *The Dream Life of Balso Snell* (1931), *Miss Lonelyhearts* (1933), and *The Day of the Locust* (1939). Among the most noteworthy postmodern practitioners of this form are James Purdy, John Hawkes, Jerome Charyn, Max Apple, Barry Hannah, Bruce Jay Friedman, J. P. Donleavy, Thomas Pynchon, Terry Southern, Vladimir Nabokov, William Gaddis, T. Coraghessan Boyle, Don DeLillo, and John Barth. Were one to choose a single novelist to be the dean of this school, however, it would probably have to be Joseph Heller. The title of Heller's first novel, *Catch-22* (1961), has literally become part of American lexicography—one can find it now in dictionaries. The title refers to a phenomenon one encounters when dealing with powerful bureaucratic institutions. Situations appear to offer the individual a choice between mutually exclusive alternatives, but there is always a "catch-22." Either alternative brings the same result: The institutions wins, the individual loses.

The novel recounts the wartime experiences of Yossarian, a U.S. Army Air Corps bombardier stationed in Italy during the last two years of World War II. Yossarian begins to realize that the occupying German forces are no more his enemy than the regime of which he is a part: Neither cares for his well-being, and both would just as soon see him dead. The most important distinction in the world is not between the Allies and the Axis or the Americans and the Germans, nor is it between right and wrong, the just and the unjust; rather, the world is only really divisible between those with power and those without it, and those without it will always lose. Yossarian spends much of the novel trying to survive by accommodating the whims of his commanding officers and the shifting winds of fate, reasoning that when one's enemies are everywhere, there is nowhere to flee and no one to rebel against. In the novel's final pages, however, he chooses a higher course. For much of the novel he has done everything in his power to get out of combat and be sent home. When that opportunity finally presents itself, he opts instead to perform one unselfish act, risking life and limb in the process, to save one child and take her to Sweden. He is told that what he intends to do will accomplish little of substance, but that, Yossarian realizes, is not the point. As a human, he knows that he is not relieved of the responsibility to behave humanely simply because the world no longer cares for humanity, nor is he relieved of responsibility for the evil of the world simply because it is not in his power to stop it. Yossarian thinks, "Someone had to do something sometime. Every victim was a culprit, every culprit a victim, and somebody had to stand up sometime to try to break the lousy chain of inherited habit that was imperiling them all."

METAFICTION

The form of *Catch-22* might be said to reflect its theme. The novel begins in the middle of Yossarian's tour of duty, then moves back and forth through time and space without warning or guidance on the part of the author. Such a curious sequencing of events is dizzying, even to those willing to read the novel repeatedly, but then, that is the point. That is precisely the kind of lesson Yossarian would have readers take to heart from what he has learned. Temporal and spatial coordinates no longer tell people where they are; when the world has gone mad, one bombing run is the same as any other, and one enemy the same as all the enemies one may encounter.

Such an authorial strategy has been termed "metafiction"; many postmodern novels share this impulse to play form and content against each other. However, this is not what is meant by metafiction per se. The metafictional novel is one that draws the reader's attention not only to the story being told but also to the means through which a novel tells a story. The metafictional novel reminds readers that the conventions of the traditional novel are just that—conventions, or formal properties that emerged several hundred years ago. Conventions of plot, character, setting, and theme are acts of artifice, a way of giving artistic structure to a depiction of human life; the metafictional novel suggests that such a conventional form of novelizing may have outlived its time.

Many of the foremost black humorists have found their place in the metafictional school, particularly John Barth, Robert Coover, Gilbert Sorrentino, Ronald Sukenick, Donald Barthelme, Thomas Pynchon, and Vladmir Nabokov. Both schools intend for readers to realize that life is less stable than they would like to let on and that precision is only approximate. Reason is a more limited means of comprehending life than people are apt to admit.

As surely as filmmaker Alfred Hitchcock made it a practice to appear momentarily in his own films, reminding viewers that, after all, it is only a movie they are watching, so metafictional novelists make sure that readers know they are there. Late in Pynchon's *Gravity's Rainbow* (1973), after readers have grappled with hundreds of characters and dozens of interwoven plots, the author declares that the reader "will want cause and effect," assuming, and rightly, that readers are at a point in the book when they are sure to be confused. Likewise, the narrative voice of Nabokov's *Ada or Ardor: A Family Chronicle* (1969), aware that the novel cannot be understood on one reading alone, steps forward and addresses the reader as "re-reader."

Published in 1958, John Barth's novel *The End of the Road* was the first to articulate the unique relationship between reader and writer that the metafictional novel posited:

Everyone is necessarily the hero of his own life story. *Hamlet* could be told from Polonius's point of view

and called *The Tragedy of Polonius, Lord Chamberlain of Denmark*. He didn't suppose he was a minor character in anything, I dare say . . . So in this sense fiction isn't a lie at all, but a true representation of the distortion that everyone makes of life. Now, not only are we the heroes of our own life stories—we're the ones who conceive the story, and give other people the essences of minor characters. But since no man's life story as a rule is ever one story with a coherent plot, we're always reconceiving just the sort of hero we are, and consequently just the sort of minor roles that other people are suppose to play.

The metafictional novel is self-conscious, then, but with a larger purpose in mind than drawing attention to itself alone. This is also to remind readers that everyone is a storyteller. People cast themselves as the protagonist in their tales, "star" in their own stories, as it were, attributing a particular *cause* to a particular *effect*; people assume that experiences they have had in the past can inform what they are experiencing at any given moment. They attribute motives to those around them, casting some in minor roles and others in larger roles such as villain or antagonist. They create narrative structures they know to be false, or at least not indisputable, in an attempt to understand the world around them and their place within it.

THE NATIVE AMERICAN NOVEL

Among the developments in the American novel during this period was the degree to which it began to privilege gender and ethnicity as defining factors in the American experience. New categories began to appear in literary criticism and on the shelves of bookstores: the Native American novel, the Asian American novel, the Latina/Latino novel, the African American novel, and the feminist novel. Novels written by those of Native American heritage, such as Louise Erdrich's *Love Medicine* (1984; revised and expanded 1993), have brought new and important perspectives to bear on the established canon of American literature. While only a few of these have earned a full position in that canon, any number of Native American novels would have to be counted among the more significant to be written after World

War II, among them James Welch's *Winter in the Blood* (1974) and *Fools Crow* (1986), Greg Sarris's *Watermelon Nights* (1998) and *Grand Avenue* (1994), Paula Gunn Allen's *The Woman Who Owned the Shadows* (1983), Michael Dorris's *A Yellow Raft in Blue Water* (1987), D'Arcy McNickle's *The Surrounded* (1936) and *Wind from an Enemy Sky* (1978), Linda Hogan's *Power* (1998) and *Mean Spirit* (1990), Gerald Vizenor's *Darkness in Saint Louis Bearheart* (1978; revised as *Bearheart: The Heirship Chronicles*, 1990), Louis Owens's *The Sharpest Sight* (1992), Thomas King's *Green Grass, Running Water* (1993), Leslie Marmon Silko's *Ceremony* (1977), N. Scott Momaday's *House Made of Dawn* (1968), and Guy Madison's *The Res* (1998).

Erdrich's *Love Medicine* was the first of these to receive widespread acclaim, garnering, among other honors, the National Book Critics Circle Award; it was also perhaps the first novel by a Native American to receive deep and widespread critical attention. The characters introduced in *Love Medicine* reappeared in such subsequent works as *The Beet Queen* (1986), *Tracks* (1988), and *The Bingo Palace* (1994). The lives of the families chronicled in her work span several generations. Later generations are inevitably caught between the world of white, industrialized America and that of Native American culture. Consequently, her youngest characters have a clearer idea of who they are not than they do of who they are. For instance, Lipsha Morrissey, the protagonist of *The Bingo Palace*, returns to his Chippewa reservation on the North Dakota plains after moving away to work in Fargo's sugar beet factories. His return to a winter powwow is chronicled in these words:

> We saw [Lipsha] edge against the wall to watch the whirling bright dancers, and immediately we had to notice that there was no place the coy could fit. He was not a tribal council honcho, not a powwow organizer, not a medic in the cop's car in the parking lot, no one we could trust with our life . . . He was not even one of those gathered at the soda machines outside the doors, the ones who wouldn't go into the warm and grassy air because of being drunk or too much in love or just bashful. He was not the Chippewa with the rings pierced in her nose or the old aunt with water

dripping through her fingers or the announcer with a ragged face and a drift of plumes on his indoor hat. He was none of these, only Lipsha, come home.

In the hope of bringing in revenue from beyond the reservation, the bingo palace of the title is being built on a sacred lake, and in the course of the novel both Lipsha and the reader come to understand that what a white man might perceive to be chance occurrence or luck is actually the doing of Lipsha's dead ancestors, now part of the spirit realm. Such a turn of events can come as no surprise to Erdrich's regular readers. Much in her work attempts to bridge the workings of contemporary America with those of Native American religion and tradition.

Something of the same might be said about the formal properties of her novels. For structure, her novels draw upon both the oral traditions of her Chippewa roots and the printed narrative patterns of American novels. *Love Medicine*, for instance, spans some fifty years. The lives of several Chippewa families during this period are presented in overlapping fragments, most from the mouths of the central characters. This is appropriate to a culture less affected by print than by an oral tradition, a culture where news comes in bits and pieces as what a white world might dismiss as "gossip," for each speaker modifies the account as he or she brings prejudices and unique perspectives to bear. The end result is the formation of a community based on shared experiences, one that transcends familial and tribal differences, and this perception is central to what Erdrich is about. While neither traditional tribal structures and ways of life nor the structures of white modern America seem to serve her characters, Erdrich holds out the possibility of yet a third sense of community, one that might serve as salvation for all of those involved.

THE ASIAN AMERICAN NOVEL

Among Asian American novels of importance are Gus Lee's *China Boy* (1991) and *Honor and Duty* (1994), Lisa See's *The Flower Net* (1997), Mako Yoshikawa's *One Hundred and One Ways* (1999), Maxine Hong Kingston's *Tripmaster Monkey: His Fake Book* (1989), Gish Jen's *Typical American*

(1992) and *Mona in the Promised Land* (1996), and Amy Tan's *The Hundred Secret Senses* (1995), *The Kitchen God's Wife* (1991), and *The Joy Luck Club* (1989). All of these deal with the clash of Western and Eastern cultures and explore this clash by placing their central characters in family units that extend for several generations. Jen's *Typical American*, for instance, explores how time, traditions, social boundaries, and social customs are central to the Chinese understanding of human experience: "Everywhere there are limits," one of her characters says. For Jen, those limits are central to understanding the Chinese world as it runs headlong into the United States. It is no wonder then that when her Chinese characters emigrate to the United States, they are baffled by what they find. At one point, a character's car is stolen, and what impresses him most is the way the thief drives. Unlike the speaker, the thief is completely comfortable behind the wheel, heedless of danger and anyone who might be in his way: "He was a natural driver for whom the wheel seemed a natural extension of his hands. Anyone would have thought he'd invented the automobile."

Amy Tan deals with similar matters in *The Joy Luck Club*. Set in San Francisco's Chinatown, the novel focuses on two generations of Asian women—Chinese mothers and their Chinese American daughters—and the bonds that hold them together as well as the tensions that force them apart. Foremost among these tensions is how the two generations view the world. For the mothers, the world is a cosmos of carefully balanced structures (ancestral hierarchies, for instance) and natural forces (earth, wind, fire, and water) in which people must find their proper place. With that place properly found, one achieves *nengkan*, a strength or capacity to survive and prosper. Says one of the narrators,

> It was this belief in their *nengkan* that had brought my parents to America. It had enabled them to have seven children and buy a house in the Sunset district with very little money. It had given them the confidence to believe their luck would never run out, that God was on their side, that the house gods had only benevolent things to report and our ancestors were pleased, that lifetime warranties meant our lucky streak would never

break, that all the elements were in balance, the right amount of wind and water.

Born and reared in China, the mothers in the novel take their immediate identity as women from their place in a family unit. For instance, many of their memories of China deal with being "orphaned" in one form or another, their greatest fear. In fact, they cannot perceive an identity apart from that unit. To their educated, liberated, Americanized daughters, such outmoded beliefs are just one step away from believing in magic dragons. For them, a woman's identity comes from taking charge of her own fate, not from finding her place in some larger, preestablished order, and certainly not from finding her place as a homemaker in her own family or as a dutiful daughter in her mother's.

Readers see what these two generations can only appreciate in part. Neither way of understanding the world and one's place in it is proportionately better than the other. Certainly the daughters are not happier for being liberated and Americanized. Their relationships with men are troubled and troubling; the rewards of the careers they choose leave them sleepless and unsatisfied. Readers come away from the narratives wishing that the daughters could speak as easily to their mothers as they seem to be able to speak to the readers.

THE LATINO/LATINA NOVEL

Rudolfo Anaya's *Bless Me, Última* (1972) and Tomás Rivera's *. . . y no se tragó la tierra/ . . . and the earth did not part* (1971; also known as *This Migrant Earth*, 1985; *. . . and the earth did not devour him*, 1987) both represent the essence of the Latino/Latina novel. Published within months of one another, these pioneering efforts in the establishment of a postwar Mexican American literature reaffirmed traditional verities at a time when so much of postmodern literature seemed to be putting them aside.

Rivera's characters try to reconcile their Catholicism and their belief in a higher pagan power with the cruelties and hardships that make up so much of their daily experience. Backbreaking manual labor is their life. They struggle to make sense of their experience by looking first to laboring for their own survival, then to the heavens, and finally to a nether world of good and evil spirits where pagan gods control the sun, droughts, rain, and floods. What is valued most of all in Rivera's work is human life and the dignities one can muster against all the things that go wrong. In one passage, the young protagonist is in danger of losing his father to illness. He has recently learned that he is in danger of losing his younger brother as well, and despite his mother's warnings, he curses God out of grief:

> He cursed God. Upon doing it he felt the fear instilled in him by time and by his parents. For a split second he saw the earth open up to devour him. But, although he didn't look down, he then felt himself walking on very solid ground; it was harder than he had ever felt it. Anger swelled up in him again and he released it by cursing God. Then he noticed that his little brother no longer appeared quite so ill . . . He was no longer worried about his father nor about his brother. All he looked forward to was the new day, the coolness of the morning . . . He left for work and he was faced with a very cool morning. There were clouds and for the first time he felt himself capable of doing and undoing whatever he chose. He looked toward the ground and he kicked it and said to it, Not yet, you can't eat me yet. Someday. But I won't know.

Much of this same sense of the world is found in *Bless Me, Última*. Anaya's novel is set in the Santa Rosa area of central New Mexico, midway between Albuquerque and Tucumcari, not far from New Mexico's nuclear testing grounds during a period in which nuclear testing was underway. It is a grown man's memoir of a time during his childhood when his grandmother, Ultima, came to live with his family. Ultima is a *curandera*, a sorceress who is in touch with a supernatural world of witches, both good and bad, and has magic at her fingertips. The story is set at a time in the boy's life when innocence has made him open-minded, when the wonders of nuclear power are no more or less amazing than his grandmother's magic; the boy tests these wonders, and others, against the Catholicism in which he is being raised and his father's secular way of life as a rancher. The novel ends with the protagonist struggling to make

sense of what he has experienced, aware, as an adult, that the answer must be found in a synthesis between a belief in God and a belief in the supernatural, between sacred beliefs and secular beliefs, between high technology and what the earth has to teach.

The Latino/Latina novel is much more diverse than many readers appreciate. While Anaya and Rivera are the most well known of Latino novelists, their work is not necessarily representative of a body of literature that includes José Antonio Villarreal's *Pocho* (1959), John Rechy's *City of Night* (1963), Alfredo Vea's *La Maravilla* (1993), Arturo Islas's *The Rain God: A Desert Tale* (1984), Maria Amparo Escandon's *Esperanza's Box of Saints* (1999), Oscar Hijuelos's *Mambo Kings Play Songs of Love* (1989) and *Empress of the Splendid Season* (1999), and Sandra Cisneros's *The House on Mango Street* (1984). For example, Cisneros's roots are Mexican American. Her setting is the American Southwest. *The House on Mango Street* is a fragmented narrative, a journal of civic events distilled by the author into stunning lyric moments. By contrast, the Pulitzer Prize-winning Hijuelos writes rather conventionally structured novels. Of Cuban descent, Hijuelos focuses on the collision of an immigrant's dreams with the realities of life in large, East Coast cities. How does one maintain a distinctly Cuban identity in a country where the key to survival seems to be to repeatedly reinvent oneself? How does one convey Cuban identity to one's children? His *Empress of the Splendid Season* explores the lives of one Cuban American family over fifty years, taking readers from pre-Fidel Castro Cuba to the 1990's by passing the narrative from one character's point of view to another's.

THE AFRICAN AMERICAN NOVEL

A relatively clear pattern can be found in the development of novels written by African American men. This literary tradition began with slave narratives in the nineteenth century, such as those of Frederick Douglass. It developed through the Harlem Renaissance of the 1920's—where jazz music influenced the poetry of Countée Cullen, Claude McKay, and others—and reached new heights just before and just after World War II with the novellas and novels of Richard Wright (*Uncle Tom's Children*, 1938, 1940; *Native Son*, 1940) and James Baldwin (*Go Tell It on the Mountain*, 1953; *Giovanni's Room*, 1956). After World War II, Ellison and younger writers such as Ernest J. Gaines (*A Gathering of Old Men*, 1983), David Bradley (*The Chaneysville Incident*, 1981), Charles Johnson (*Dreamer*, 1998), and Randell Kenan (*A Visitation of Spirits*, 1989) chronicled, in relatively conventional forms, the difficulties of finding personhood in a predominantly white culture while still keeping intact what is strongest about one's own heritage. Meanwhile, Amiri Baraka (*The System of Dante's Hell*, 1965), Ishmael Reed (*Yellow Back Radio Broke Down*, 1969; *Mumbo Jumbo*, 1972), and others began to experiment with language, blur the distinctions between conventional narrative forms, and explore alternative systems of beliefs.

No such clear developmental pattern can be found in the work of African American women novelists, yet the body of literature they have produced is impressive, including Toni Cade Bambara's *The Salt Eaters* (1980), Alice Walker's *The Color Purple* (1982), Gloria Naylor's *The Women of Brewster Place: A Novel in Seven Stories* (1982), and Jamaica Kincaid's *Lucy* (1990). Of the African American women writers who emerged after World War II, the greatest longevity was demonstrated by Paule Marshall, whose *Brown Girl, Brownstones* (1959) chronicled a young Caribbean girl's experiences as an immigrant in an American city. Although initially ignored, it was later reissued; Marshall's later work— *Praisesong for the Widow* (1983), *The Chosen Place, the Timeless People* (1969), and *Daughters* (1991)— fulfilled much, if not all, of its promise.

Toni Morrison, who won the Nobel Prize in Literature in 1993, has produced an impressive body of work: *The Bluest Eye* (1970), *Sula* (1973), *Song of Solomon* (1977), *Tar Baby* (1981), *Beloved* (1987), *Jazz* (1992), and *Paradise* (1998). Morrison's central concerns are the relationships between black men and women; the necessity for black women to find, within a community of women, new ways of understanding themselves beyond the identity taken from the men in their lives; and the manner in which these women pass on to their children what is best in themselves and their pasts. The Bible, myth, legend, and the supernatural play significant roles in her writing. She has explained that one of her intentions is

> to blend the acceptance of the supernatural and a profound rootedness in the real world at the same time with neither taking precedence over the other. It is indicative of the cosmology, the way in which Black people looked at the world. We are a very practical people, very down-to-earth, even shrewd people. But within that practicality we also accepted what I suppose could be called superstition and magic, which is another way of knowing things.

Morrison is certainly to be counted among the best novelists in the United States. *Beloved*, perhaps her finest novel, is a slave narrative and nineteenth century family saga that blends the natural and the supernatural. The title character is a ghost, the lost daughter of the novel's protagonist, Sethe, who escapes from brutal slave masters. Sethe kills the child when her masters catch her rather than allow Beloved to live a life of enslavement. Sethe subsequently spends her days trying "to beat back the past," without much success. The house in which she lives is filled by the child's restless spirit. Sethe's experiences as a slave remain so fresh in her memory that she calls them "rememories," for they are as present and immediate as any experience she might be having at the moment. The task Morrison sets her protagonist is to somehow get that past behind her and get on with her life.

This process begins when Beloved's spirit materializes. She appears on Sethe's property in the flesh, demanding a place in Sethe's life and her world. Beloved's presence threatens the thin hold Sethe has on her living daughter, Denver, as well as Sethe's relationship with a man, Paul D. It is only after Sethe can come to terms with Beloved that she can reaffirm her relationship with the two of them and step outside her house toward the future.

THE FEMINIST NOVEL

Several African American women novelists, such as Audre Lorde, Patricia J. Williams, and Barbara

Smith, are often classified as feminist writers. During the 1970's, feminist literature was associated with a particular left-of-center political agenda that connoted a call for political activism. Marge Piercy, Rita Mae Brown, Allison Lurie, Susan Fromberg Shaffer, and Erica Jong were included in this category. Readers often expected certain themes to be addressed, certain plot situations to be explored, and characters to develop in particular ways. However, the body of work produced by women novelists after World War II has been so much richer than these expectations that to speak of a feminist novel probably means a novel in which the main characters are female and the novel itself has been written by a woman who explores issues thought to bear more immediately on the lives of women than men.

Since World War II, numerous women have written novels of importance and been recognized for their achievements. The highly esteemed National Book Critics Circle Award provides an example: Alice McDermott's *Charming Billy* won in 1999, Alice Munro's *The Love of a Good Woman* won in 1998, Penelope Fitzgerald's *Blue Flower* won in 1997, and Gina Berriault's *Women in Their Beds* won in 1996. Women novelists seem to be rising to positions of parity in areas once dominated by males. Of Jewish American writers, Cynthia Ozick's work threatens to eclipse the later work of Roth or Bellow as chronicles of the Jewish experience. While skillful artisans with a wide and faithful following, such as Robert Stone, Thomas Berger, and John Irving, produced novels such as *Damascus Gate* (1998), *The Return of Little Big Man* (1999), and *A Widow for One Year* (1998), respectively, Rosellen Brown moved to the fore as the middlebrow novelist of her generation. Similarly, with novels such as *The Age of Grief: A Novella and Stories* (1987), *Barn Blind* (1980), *Ordinary Love and Good Will: Two Novellas* (1989), and her Pulitzer Prize-winning *A Thousand Acres* (1991), a novel based upon William Shakespeare's *King Lear* (1605- 1606), Jane Smiley demonstrates much literary breadth.

Literature is not a contest, of course; certainly it is not a war of the genders. To frame matters in these terms is simply to acknowledge that American

women novelists began to come into their own after World War II and suggest that the novels they have produced may be changing the American novel itself. One of the changes is the importance assigned to family. From its outset, the American novel has been most at home with lone male figures setting out on their own or with another male companion to perform heroic acts in the open spaces of America. Examples include Natty Bumppo and Chingachgook in the forests of the upper East Coast, Huckleberry Finn and Slave Jim floating south on the Mississippi, Ishmael and Queequeg shipping out aboard the Pequod to hunt whale, and later, Hemingway's characters at war on foreign shores or hunting in Africa; in any case, American novels have favored self-sufficient men establishing their presence far afield from where family really matters. If anything, wives, children, and family have been equated with the civilizing forces of middle-class life, which has been depicted as the proper domain of women rather than men. This tradition can still be seen in such contemporary novels as *One Flew over the Cuckoo's Nest*. When McMurphy seeks to restore the inmates of the asylum to a proper state of manhood, he removes them from the purview of the nurse, taking them out to sea "where men are men, and boats are boats."

Many women novelists have responded to the same postwar disorientation explored by lonely, isolated, anxious protagonists. Theirs is certainly not an affirmation of the middle-class nuclear family; if their books are to be trusted, the nuclear American family is in desperate trouble, maybe in irreparable shape. What they have proffered instead is an alternative to being lost and alone. A new kind of "tribal" family may be on the horizon, one in part composed of blood relationships but in larger part depending upon a loose community of people with shared experiences coming together in support of one another.

Another change in American novels concerns space, specifically interior, domesticated space. Literally and metaphorically, much in the American grain has pointed protagonists toward the open frontier. This was where real life was to be lived. What readers have longed for in protagonists is the great deed, and only in such an untrammeled space could an American protagonist impose himself fully on the landscape. Women novelists have provided a counterpoint. The title of Smiley's *A Thousand Acres*, for instance, refers to one thousand acres of rich farmland with which the patriarch of the family, Larry Cook, identifies a lifetime's work. It exists for him in time and space; he can touch it with his hands. Readers gradually realize that the defining moments in the family saga take place indoors, however, not out in the fields; to ignore this fact is to miss more than one-half of the story.

Yet another change is the ritual through which people create a community. Gossip, birthing, household chores, and preparing, serving, and eating food—matters that have been ignored or mocked in the American traditional novel—are now being given credence as paramount moments of human experience. In Smiley's *A Thousand Acres*, for instance, eating together signals more than filling one's stomach, just as preparing and serving food become defining moments in a family's well-being. To eat without being a community is to be a family in desperate trouble.

Finally, there seem to be two evolving views of the world that are apt to come into conflict with each other. It is often said that men are vilified in many novels by women, but, in fact, vilification is less the issue than how the men in these novels make sense of their lives. The men are much more trusting in the powers of logic and reason than are the women. Whether using myth, legend, the spirit world, the supernatural, or simply intuition—a "sixth" sense—the women are more likely to be open than men to an alternative mode of understanding.

THE NOVEL AFTER THE COLD WAR

The post-Cold War novel, which includes what might be called "postcolonial" literature, comprises the work of novelists such as Paul Scott (*The Raj Quartet*, 1979) and Salman Rushdie (*The Satanic Verses*, 1988), who explore Third World cultures as they emerge from domination by declining world empires. However, the term has also been used in regard to Charles Frazier's *Cold Mountain* (1997), a Civil War epic that chronicles with methodical detail the re-

alities of nineteenth century battle, and David Guterson's popular *Snow Falling on Cedars* (1994), which blends a World War II-era history of the American Northwest with an oddly lyrical murder mystery.

The novel after the Cold War changed from its earlier modernist and postmodernist manifestations. Postmodernism has been identified with a period of history during which the fate of the world was defined by the tensions between two new superpowers, the Soviet Union and the United States. This brings up questions of whether the collapse of the Soviet Union has caused the world, and its literature, to change diametrically, and whether a new era, a "post-postmodern" era, has begun. What is certain is that novels are changing, and they are proving to be much richer than the categories that have been employed in an attempt to appreciate them.

By privileging gender and ethnicity, critics may well have created categories that obscure as well as inform understanding of literature. The concerns of women and minorities as they have entered the literary arena may well be something still more profound. The interest in myth, legend, and the supernatural that has been linked to the cultural roots of the Latino/Latina novel, the Asian American novel, and the Native American novel may well be something broader, an attempt on the part of literature to find an alternative means of understanding human experience that transcends ethnic lines. In addition, the novel no longer has full faith in what an Age of Enlightenment had to teach. Reason is more limited than one might suspect in negotiating a confused and confusing world. Logic can take one only so far.

When it was first published, Jay McInerney's *Bright Lights, Big City* (1984) was hailed as his generation's anthem to life on the fast track. In retrospect, it may be something more. It may well be in line with precisely this sentiment. With the failure of his brief marriage and the departure of his bride, the protagonist loses his job and surrenders to a devastating cocaine addiction that he has been battling. Only after he has lost everything of value near the novel's climax does he begin to understand his dilemma. It is not the loss of his bride that has brought him to this point, but rather the death of his mother and his estrangement from his own family. He has brought disastrous values to the fast track of upwardly mobile, big city life, leaving him unprepared to cope with daily living. In the book's final moments, he is in front of a bakery at dawn. Strung out on drugs, he is reminded by the smell of baking bread of his last visit home while his mother was alive. A delivery man throws him a bag of bread as one might toss such a bag to an indigent. The novel ends with these words: "You get down on your knees and tear open the bag. The smell of warm dough envelops you. The first bite sticks in your throat and you almost gag. You will have to go slowly. You will have to learn everything all over again."

Jay Boyer

BIBLIOGRAPHY

Aldridge, John W. *Talents and Technicians*. New York: New York University Press, 1992. Aldridge is a noted American scholar whose *After the Lost Generation* was a landmark study of American modernism; a subsequent volume, *The American Novel and How We Live Now*, addressed the novel's transition from modernism to postmodernism. Dealing with the novels of Jay McInerney, Ann Beattie, Frederick Barthelme, Brett Easton Ellis, and others of their generation, this third volume takes the next logical step and addresses developments in American novels at the end of the twentieth century.

Geyh, Paula, ed. *Postmodern American Fiction: A Norton Anthology*. New York: W. W. Norton, 1997. The first volume of the Norton Anthology series devoted solely to postmodernism, this book is the best sampler available. It offers a wide range of readings and helpful guides with which to appreciate them.

Harvey, David. *The Condition of Postmodernity*. Oxford, England: Blackwell Publishing, 1990. This excellent book—which deals with postmodernity in art, architecture, economics, and post-World War II culture at large—is useful for establishing a context for one's reading of contemporary literature.

Sakrajda, Mira. *Postmodern Discourses of Love*. New York: Peter Lang, 1999. Part of the Studies in Literary Criticism and Theory series, this volume explores love and its absence in the work of Thomas Pynchon, John Barth, Robert Coover, and other contemporary novelists.

Tabbi, Joseph. *Postmodern Sublime*. Ithaca, N.Y.: Cornell University Press, 1995. This ambitious study addresses postmodern literature from Norman Mailer to the cyberpunk genre. Tabbi posits an ambivalence toward technology that unites otherwise disparate literary texts.

WORLD
LONG FICTION

AFRICAN LONG FICTION

The term "African," when applied in this essay to the novel and other literary genres, does not include the Arab states of the north or the peoples of European descent who may have settled in Africa. It refers to the black, indigenous peoples in the southern two-thirds of the continent who, to some extent, share a common culture. The geographical area extends from Senegal in the west to Kenya and Somalia in the east and southward to the Cape of Good Hope. It encompasses more than thirty-five countries, which are themselves often arbitrary divisions that cut across numerous tribal groups with different languages and customs. It might seem strange amid all of this diversity to speak of an African novel, rather than a Kenyan or a Yoruba novel, for example. A few countries, in fact—notably Nigeria—are already establishing their own written literary traditions. What makes the situation even more complicated is that African novels, with a few exceptions, have not been written in African but in European languages, such as French, English, or Portuguese. Thus most scholars, both African and foreign, attempting to understand the totality of the fiction, while not having to deal with multiple African languages, nevertheless do face a language barrier. Still, in spite of these obstacles and differences, the African novel is a meaningful and manageable category.

Though the history of written African prose goes back at least as far as Olaudah Equiano's *The Interesting Narrative of the Life of Olaudah Equiano: Or, Gustavus Vassa, the African, Written by Himself* (1789), that is, to the era of the slave trade, and even further than that if one includes the Islamic presence in the Sahel and cultural centers such as Timbuktu during the medieval period, the African novel itself is a relatively recent phenomenon—hardly more than fifty years old if one excludes isolated attempts earlier in the century. René Maran's *Batouala*, first published in 1921 (English translation, 1922), which pretends to be an attack on colonialism but actually reflects European perceptions, is a questionable choice as the first African novel. Its author, son of Guyanese parents but born in Martinique, did not spend an extended period of time in Africa until he was twenty-three. Other examples of prose fiction before the 1950's include the famous African tales of Birago Diop, various oral chronicles in written form, and novels derivative of the French. D. O. Fagunwa's *Ogboju Ode Ninu Igbo Irunmale* (1939; translated by Wole Soyinka as *Forest of a Thousand Daemons*, 1984), written in his native Yoruba, and Amos Tutuola's *The Palm-Wine Drinkard* (1952), written in Tutuola's own special brand of English, both transform traditional myths and legends into a longer structure that only approaches novel form but captures a truly African spirit

Though Peter Abrahams of South Africa anticipated the movement by about ten years with *Mine Boy* (1946), the true flowering of the novel proper came in the 1950's with Camara Laye's *L'Enfant noir* (1953; *The Dark Child*, 1954; also known as *The African Child*), Cyprian Ekwensi's *People of the City* (1954), and Chinua Achebe's *Things Fall Apart* (1958). Since that time, the novel has been a consistently popular form, especially in francophone and anglophone regions. From a plethora of rising novelists, a number have emerged as accomplished artists and have attained an international reputation and classic status. Among these writers from francophone countries are Cheikh Hamidou Kane and Ousmane Sembène of Senegal, Ferdinand Oyono and Mongo Beti of Cameroon, Camara Laye of Guinea, and Yambo Ouologuem of Mali. Anglophone novelists include Ayi Kwei Armah and Ama Ata Aidoo of Ghana; Buchi Emecheta, Chinua Achebe, Wole Soyinka, and Ben Okri of Nigeria; Ngugi wa Thiong'o and Grace Ogot of Kenya; Nuruddin Farah of Somalia; and Peter Abrahams, Ezekiel Mphahlele, Bessie Head, and Alex La Guma of South Africa. This impressive array of novelists is part of a genuine literary revival in Africa, coinciding with political resistance to colonialism after 1945 and the declarations of independence in the late 1950's and early 1960's. There is a nearly unanimous feeling of responsibility among these writers toward their own peoples, but also toward the continent as a whole. At the same time, they form an elite literary community that is acutely aware of itself, within which literary influences are common; they have begun to create a written African literary tradition. This fact, together with the brevity of its history, makes it still possible to view the African novel holistically.

Furthermore, in the contemporary world, being African as well as Senegalese or Ghanaian is a political reality. The African novel has developed within an international context; the novelists have undergone extensive exposure to the West, and the subject of the novels was, until the 1980's and 1990's, almost exclusively the impact of colonialism. There is a feeling of commonality among black Africans because they have shared the same history over the past several centuries: the slave trade, economic exploitation, colonialism, liberation, and political and economic instability during the postindependence years. They have undergone a common psychological experience. Whatever the particular tribal myths and customs might have been, the immediate problems of survival in the face of foreign intimidation have prompted a self-consciousness and a common purpose. In a sense, the West has made Black Africa aware of itself. The novel has played a significant role in this coming to awareness.

Finally, there is a powerful ideological factor responsible for African unity. Behind the violent initiation into the industrial age, there was not only an expansionist policy of exploitation and conquest but also an assumption that the old Africa was primitive and superstitious, that its cultures were markedly inferior to those cultures that colonized it. In order to counter and modify that image, certain African thinkers as early as the eighteenth century, but especially in the nineteenth and twentieth centuries, who had lived in the West and had received a Western education, challenged the primitive image and insisted on the value of their own culture.

Léopold Senghor of Senegal coined the term "negritude" to identify the black peoples of the world, including those peoples no longer living on the African continent. For him, it indicated the collective consciousness of the race. He distinguished African individuals by their different mode of consciousness:

Theirs was essentially an emotional response to things, not an intellectual one. Their reason was intuitive, not analytical. Rather than the Cartesian "I think, therefore I am," Senghor posited the African "I feel, I dance the other." This definition of the African was long perceived as a francophone response to the French assimilation policy that tried to create a French mentality among the colonized. Abiola Irele, however, convincingly showed in *The African Experience in Literature and Ideology* (1981) that the concept of an African personality—developed among anglophone Africans in the nineteenth century—was essentially the same, emphasizing the communal, religious sense of the world as characteristic of all Africans, regardless of tribe or region. Both concepts, the one epistemological, the other ontological, are Pan-African and have as their purpose the establishing of a positive, dynamic image for the oppressed peoples of the subcontinent. One must admit now that both are mythical or ideological creations of individual humans. They have, however, had a tremendous impact and are to some degree responsible for the sense of unity in Africa today. As a concept within the literary world, negritude, or the African personality, has had such influence and aroused such controversy as to warrant special attention.

NEGRITUDE AND THE NOVEL

The concept of negritude, perhaps because of its emotive and mystical dimension, originally found literary expression in poetry rather than fiction. Senghor himself was a poet as well as a philosophical apologist and political leader. Nevertheless, it appears as a basic assumption in the novel as well, especially those by such francophone writers as Cheikh Hamidou Kane, Camara Laye, and Mongo Beti. Kane's classic work, *L'Aventure ambiguë* (1961; *Ambiguous Adventure*, 1963), presents the tragic psychological and spiritual confrontation of two mentalities. Nurtured as a child within the rituals and mystical atmosphere of an African animism modified by Islam, in which he experienced a spiritual oneness with the universe, the hero, Samba Diallo, becomes a student in a French educational system that is characterized by Cartesian dualism. His fate is to end his life with no identity at all, torn between the two worlds. The only way he has to rejoin the universe that was once his is to die, a service symbolically performed by a madman on his home soil. Though Kane was himself from the French colony of Senegal, as is his hero, the novel seems designed to represent the archetypal situation of a Western-educated African during the 1950's. It laments the loss of spiritual fulfillment and, at the end, reasserts its primacy. Laye, in his autobiographical novel, *The Dark Child*, gives an even more complete picture of traditional life, this time in a Malinké village of French Guinea: the ancient customs, the daily presence of the supernatural, the animism, the honored craft of the goldsmith, and the terrifying ritual of circumcision.

Laye's second novel, one of the most impressive creations by an African writer, *Le Regard du roi* (1954; *The Radiance of the King*, 1956), is perhaps the most striking example of the concept of negritude incorporated into fiction. Laye dramatizes Senghor's idea that the West needs the imaginative and spiritual qualities of the black race as much as the African has needed the technical and intellectual lessons of the colonizers. The hero is a white man, Clarence, a rarity in African fiction. At the beginning of the novel, he is the typical arrogant expatriate, with the usual sense of superiority to the blacks around him—even though, with his careless sense that as a white man he is invulnerable, he is practically destitute. Laye puts him through a series of adventures, in particular a long symbolic journey through Africa and the life of a stud in a harem. His journey is in search of the African King, who holds court in the south. Though he originally believes that his race qualifies him to speak to the king, by the end he has cast off his Western assumptions about time, money, work, and inalienable rights and has humbled himself before the mysteries of things, of the senses, and of spiritual transcendence. Laye has thus done more than assert the difference between the West and Africa; he has dramatized the primacy of the senses and the spirit, which the West has lost but which the African still possesses.

Certainly not all francophone writers place such faith in the endurance of an African consciousness.

Though Mongo Beti often draws striking contrasts between the two cultures, his satiric purpose either throws emphasis on the insidious danger of Western education and religion or exposes the naïveté and vulnerability of traditional village life. In Beti's *Le Pauvre Christ de Bomba* (1956; *The Poor Christ of Bomba*, 1971), it is primarily the central character, the Reverend Father Drumont, who represents the intolerance and insensitivity of the Catholic Church as it attempts to stamp out pagan practices. By the end of the novel, as his failure to convert the natives drives him back to France, he comes to a notional awareness of the inadequacy of himself and his religion, but, as Eustace Palmer (in *The Growth of the African Novel*, 1979) has demonstrated, he remains blind to his real responsibility for the changes in Bomba and continues to sadistically project his frustrations through his punishments of the young girls at the mission who have violated his rule of chastity. Lying behind the Catholic vision of reality is the indigenous sense of the sacred and the natural purity of sex, but they seem already removed from their original state. The narrator, Dennis, an acolyte in the Mission of Drumont, has long since lost the mentality of the native village. He exits the novel to work for a Greek merchant.

In another of Beti's novels, *Mission terminée* (1957; *Mission Accomplished*, 1958; better known as *Mission to Kala*), the sixteen-year-old narrator, Jean-Marie, returns to his native village after attending school in the French educational system. He has recently failed his examination, and his education has obviously been incomplete, but the village perceives him as a hero. It is not Jean-Marie, however, who truly knows the world, but the peers he left behind. Gradually, he is initiated into the traditional life of the village and experiences sexual fulfillment. In making a comment on the degrees of usefulness in the education provided by the two societies, Beti assumes a negritudist view of traditional African life. Still, the description is double-edged. Beti satirizes the Kalans for their romanticizing of foreign learning and attacks the father in particular, as Palmer notes, for his authoritarian insistence on his son getting a Western education. The father's tyranny, which may reflect a flaw in the traditional society, drives Jean-Marie away. He, like so many other African heroes, is left wandering between the two worlds. Beti seems pessimistic about the African clinging to a traditional consciousness.

One francophone writer in particular, Yambo Ouologuem, completely rejects the notion of negritude; the naturalistic panorama of African history in his chronicle-novel, *Le Devoir de violence* (1968; *Bound to Violence*, 1971), unmasks the naked truth. What characterizes Africa (and humankind in general), according to myth, legend, and history, is a penchant for violence, sexual perversion, and political subjugation. Skepticism toward negritude, though it does not elsewhere reach this extreme, is most prevalent among anglophone writers, who have tended to see it as idealistic, needlessly theoretical, and impractical. This idea seems to reflect an "English" insistence on fact and may be the result, to some extent, of English education and English colonial policy. Chinua Achebe, for example, has written two novels that are anthropological rather than theoretical in emphasis: *Things Fall Apart* and *Arrow of God* (1964).

One Nigerian novelist, Wole Soyinka, attacked the concept of negritude directly with his now famous and influential statement that the tiger does not declare his "tigretude." Yet, ironically, Soyinka is among the most consistent defenders of African tradition. He objects to what he regards as the backward-looking, nostalgic flavor of the negritudist theory, as well as its vague simplicity and especially its implied acceptance and even glorification of the exploiter's myth about the African personality. Soyinka contends, in *Myth, Literature, and the African World* (1976), for example, that the blacks on the subcontinent are not simply intuitive, sensuous beings, but are as practical, analytical, and sophisticated as their Western counterparts. When he returns to the past and the essential African spirit, it is to recall and reinterpret the myths of his own Yoruban culture, to bring them alive within the contemporary setting. In his novels (as well as his plays), his modern characters are often embodiments of mythical figures; the creator or poet is the servant of the traditional Promethean-Dionysian god, Ogun, and the situations are repetitions of archetypal patterns.

Soyinka's first novel, *The Interpreters* (1965), captures this sense of the past impinging on the present. His "interpreters" are Western-educated Nigerians futilely trying to balance the two worlds in their psyches, to change a society that has imitated and perpetuated the worst features of the new and the old. Although Soyinka uses particular details from his own Yoruban myth and theology, his aim, as his political pronouncements indicate, is Pan-African. Soyinka's second novel, *Season of Anomy* (1973), although somewhat more sensational and melodramatic, follows archetypal patterns, including a paradisal view of precolonial Africa, that assume generalizations about the African continent and, at the same time, provide a point of contact with a foreign consciousness.

Another anglophone novelist, Ayi Kwei Armah, based two of his novels on the myth of an African way of life, kept alive by religious leaders, warrior priests, and their followers, who pass the secret down from generation to generation in anticipation of an age when the entire society will be ready to accept it. One is tempted to assume that Armah regards himself and other African intellectuals as members of this secret community. While Armah has a mythical imagination and pan-African aspirations, he does not fit easily into the negritudist concept of Africa. Ousmane Sembène, much more clearly, though a French-speaking African from Senegal, exhibits certain practical, political instincts that place him in the Anglophone camp. In Sembène's novel *Le Dernier de l'Empire* (1981; *The Last of the Empire*, 1983), the major character rejects Senghor's romantic vision of Africa in favor of native social values that are not simple responses to a myth of Africa perpetuated by white people. Though originally Marxist-inspired, as is evident in the earlier novels, Sembène seems to be envisioning a truly African socialism drawn from traditional sources. Again, however, even when the negritudist position is called into question, the alternative is not usually an insistence on local or provincial values but on values that include the entire subcontinent.

THE LANGUAGE PROBLEM

From the point of view of negritude, of the African personality, or of an alternative, there emerges a concept of Africa as one entity that has to some extent contributed to the shaping of an African novel. That is, African writers seem to have a consciousness of themselves that extends beyond their tribal origins or "national" identity. Theirs is a rather special situation in the modern world. What makes it even more special is the language they choose for their works. In the brief history of the African novel, practitioners have in most cases been at least bilingual. They have their own tribal language, which offers no written tradition, and they have the language of the European country that colonized their regions—in whose educational system they received their introduction to Western culture and literature. Almost without exception, African novelists have expressed themselves in the official European language. Obviously, the choice of a foreign linguistic medium to some extent works against the expression of an indigenous African personality, for it would seem extremely difficult to communicate the mentality of a tribe (or a race) without using the language in which the instinctive responses to life are learned. To put them into another language would be tantamount to translating the rhythms of native speech into a foreign idiom. This concept has raised the basic aesthetic problem that writing a novel in French, English, or Portuguese would seem to deny the importance of its Africanness.

Without dismissing the significance of this fact, one must also admit that the choice of a European language has, on the other hand, encouraged the crossing of tribal and national boundaries. Not that the use of a foreign tongue was entirely a matter of choice; certain conditions dictated it. It was through the study of the novel in the foreign idiom that Africans learned their craft. Their audience was not, in the initial stages of development, within Africa but in Europe, and indeed the early novels were largely addressed to a foreign clientele. They were satiric attacks on Western culture and defenses of a traditional African culture. In addition, financial realities dictated foreign publication. Now that there is a growing Western-educated elite in Africa, the idea of audi-

ence has been changing. Still, in order to speak to the entire continent, and not only to one tribe within one or two countries whose members happen to speak the language of the novelist, the international language has remained the primary medium of communication.

Sembène found film to be the effective means of using the local language, not the novel. Ngugi wa Thiong'o attempted, however, not only in his play *The Trial of Dedan Kimathi* (1976) but also in his novels *Caitaani Mutharaba-Ini* (1980; *Devil on the Cross*, 1982) and *Matigari ma Njiruungi* (1986; *Matigari*, 1989), to speak directly to the Gikuyu people in Kenya through initial publications in the indigenous language. *Devil on the Cross* was popular enough to go through three editions in Gikuyu; he then translated the novel into English, trying to preserve the native idiom. Written as it usually is, however, in the language of the colonizer, the African novel has had to contend with a corollary issue: whether it is, in fact, an appendage of the "mother country"—that is, an extension of French or English literature. One of the literary issues facing the African novel, then, is its uniqueness. Has the novelist been able to manipulate the language so that it has become an African medium, or is language itself so essentially a part of culture that Africans must use their own to express their Africanness? Dealt with in this way, the issue is not political but aesthetic, and it has plagued chauvinist sentiment since the inception of the novel in the 1950's.

Chinua Achebe was perhaps the most successful in dealing with the problem, both in his criticism (*Morning Yet on Creation Day*, 1975) and in his novels. The two set in a traditional village during the colonial era (*Things Fall Apart* and *Arrow of God*) overcome the barrier by imitating the pattern of Igbo thought in the structure of the English sentence, relying on images and figures of speech from the local setting, and sprinkling traditional proverbs throughout the narrative and dialogue. The two novels set in more modern times (*No Longer at Ease*, 1960, and *A Man of the People*, 1966) continue this practice to some extent, but they rely also on the pidgin English of contemporary Nigeria. Achebe's predecessor in

Nigeria, Amos Tutuola, who achieved a kind of notoriety through his use of ungrammatical, nonidiomatic English in *The Palm-Wine Drinkard*, raises his own aesthetic and generic problems. Some novelists, such as Achebe, Soyinka, Ngugi, and Ahmadou Kourouma, seem to have found a satisfactory linguistic compromise. Others have not seen the issue as crucial or have found different ways to reflect an African quality in the total structure and technique. While novelists in Africa have had to experiment with the form, a slowly developing tradition led away from formal realism toward Magical Realism in the 1980's and 1990's, influenced no doubt by Latin American authors.

THE MAJOR THEME: A QUEST FOR IDENTITY

Indeed, whatever else may be said to distinguish the African novel from its Western counterparts—whether a unique consciousness significantly modifies the conventional form—there can be no doubt about its content. The African novel has had as its subject the African experience, and formal realism has been one of the essential modes in presenting it. Colonialism is at the center of this experience. Western industrial society has forced Africa to repeat its 250-year transition within a matter of decades. The Western novel has developed over that same period; in Africa, as it evolved during the second half of the twentieth century, it became an instrument in Africa's response to the West's cultural and economic imperialism.

Formal realism has allowed African writers to describe their situation in a convincing manner and attack both foreign presumptions and local acquiescence. The novel, born of an economic era that stressed the reality of things, money, upward social mobility, materialism, and individualism, proved to be appropriate for the kind of existence the West was forcing Africa to live. The African novel is both description and critique, but it has an ultimate goal. Its subject, viewed holistically, is a search for identity. Africa presents a special instance of this significant theme in modern literature, which Robert Langbaum, in his study *The Mysteries of Identity* (1977), explores in such "romantic" figures as William Words-

worth, William Butler Yeats, and D. H. Lawrence. For Langbaum, identity and humanity are interchangeable. The denial of humanity by industrial and technological progress, however, is compounded in Africa by the attempt of the West over the past several centuries to assert its superiority in all aspects of culture. The West has put Africans in the position of denying the value of their past. In order to recover that past, defend it, put it into perspective, and deal with the modern threat and its consequences, novelists have examined the various stages of Africa's contact with the West. There are four periods in African history that have come under scrutiny: the precolonial era, when the African village was supposedly intact; the colonial era, during which the central motif was a conflict of cultures; the resistance movement and the establishment of independent states; and finally the ensuing period of self-rule, dominated by economic distress, political corruption, and what Ngugi calls "neocolonialism." In this final phase, experimental novelists began suggesting new directions in thought and aesthetics. A few novels during the last half of the twentieth century attempt to give a panoramic view of the whole, but most concentrated on one or two of these phases.

THE PRECOLONIAL ERA

Usually the attempt to re-create African society before the arrival of Europeans is a defense of African culture and hence of its humanity. Such depictions often seem highly idealistic and even improbable—thus the advantage of the novel form that uses formal realism to establish the illusion of reality. Laye, in *The Dark Child*, nostalgically describes experiences that were no doubt his own in a village untouched by the outside world. Everything takes place in an atmosphere of mystery, spiritual presences, magical interactions between humans and animals, and rituals that have real and sacred meanings. The absolute faith of the young narrator as he tells the actual events of his early life in unpretentious, simple language lends credibility to the implied argument that such occurrences actually happened. This is not legend, but "fact." The sacred nature of things is named as part of the identity of the old life.

The experience of Samba Diallo in Kane's *Ambiguous Adventure* is similar, though here Islam has become an integral part of African animism and encourages an even more mystical and metaphysical identification with cosmic forces and death. When Ngugi alludes to precolonial days, as in *The River Between* (1965), he also suggests an idyllic existence; rather than re-create it, however, he usually relies upon the myths and legends about the origins of Kenya. Armah, on the other hand, in both *Two Thousand Seasons* (1973) and *The Healers* (1978), makes a daring attempt to create a timeless society that maintains the values of community and self-sacrifice. Consisting as it does of exiles who become guerrillas fighting for the restoration of old Africa, it hardly becomes credible on a realistic level. In Armah's case, the moral purpose of the search makes the demand of formal realism almost irrelevant.

On the opposite end of the spectrum is Ouologuem's *Bound to Violence*, which argues that precolonial Africa was not essentially different from its subsequent history of sadism, violence, and treachery. It is difficult to see this novel as other than an attempt to debunk the nostalgic view of the past. An interpretation of traditional African culture that lies between the two extremes is that of Achebe, who strives to create an impression of complete objectivity. Rather than glorify the past, he takes pains to describe its daily life, the heroism and failings of ordinary inhabitants of the village. The legends become tales that mothers tell their children. The rituals have a perceivable function within the seasonal cycle. The proverbs are practical ways of dealing with other people, with natural forces, and with the gods. Though there are protagonists in both *Things Fall Apart* and *Arrow of God* who reflect the traditional life, and though one of them is, in fact, the chief priest of the tribe, Achebe does not insist upon a mystical reality among the Igbo to which European civilization is insensitive. Both protagonists are practical, pragmatic members of society whose downfall, nevertheless, results from the human failings of pride, stubbornness, and self-interest.

The emphasis in Achebe is not so much on the cultural values as it is on the humanity of the African,

which differs in no essential respect from that of the invading European, though the rhetorical argument of the novels emphasizes the African's humanity at the expense of the particular breed of Englishman representing the British Empire in Nigeria. Achebe's definition of Africa in precolonial times is a rational, ordered, self-sufficient society, with a legal system capable of coping with violations to the social order, a belief in a supreme being, and a concept of the gods as creations of humans, designed to serve human needs. It also recognizes that certain customs in traditional life were needlessly cruel and superstitious. The balancing of the virtues and failings makes the total picture believable and lends credibility to the underlying argument that the Western view of African primitivism is prejudicial and self-serving.

THE COLONIAL ERA: A CONFLICT OF CULTURES

Though numerous African novels attempt to identify traditional life, either through an extensive treatment, as in Achebe's works, or through brief glimpses of the recent or distant past, few confine themselves exclusively to that era, recognizing perhaps the impossibility of return and the necessity of redefining the African identity within an international context. In fact, until the mid-1960's, at which time most African states had achieved their independence, the dominant subject of the novel was the initial contact between Africa and the West and the disruption of tribal life. Underlying the conflict of cultures in these novels is racism on the part of the West, which the African was not prepared to cope with, making it difficult to reestablish a clear sense of self. European culture pervaded every part of African life. European mentality and the various institutions that reflected it—the church, education, the law, and the economic system—gradually insinuated themselves into the social fabric.

Achebe's *Things Fall Apart* is a classic example of the process, modified by the author's own premise that resilience and adaptation are essential for human survival. Okonkwo is an aggressive, ambitious individual who has difficulty accommodating himself even within his own traditional world, which is in most cases flexible enough to tolerate his defiance and admire his material success. His concern over his masculine image and his unpredictable resistance to authority—natural, supernatural, or human—prove to be his downfall, however, when it is not his own tribal custom that rises to chastise him but the foreign English authority. Okonkwo's life covers the crucial period of transition between the old and the new. Though he has passed his youth and achieved his social status within a traditional framework, he has to maintain his success and his image in a changing society.

During his enforced exile of seven years for accidentally killing a member of the clan, English institutions infiltrate his native village. He returns to see his own status diminished and his fellow villagers adopting English ways. When Achebe comments on this process, he presents the typical sequence experienced in practically every African country. The missionary moves in with a new religion and a new god. The clan innocently tolerates his presence and even ridicules him, because he attracts only the social outcasts and builds his church on accursed land. In spite of expectations, the church thrives and continues to make converts, one of whom is Okonkwo's own son, rebellious against his father's authoritarian treatment. Achebe calls the church the knife that cuts the ties binding the society together: Without spiritual cohesiveness, the tribe falls apart. Into this disintegrated society enters the government and its legal system. Now Okonkwo is in danger of violating not only his own social codes but also those of white people. It is when the English administration tries to establish control over the village that Okonkwo asserts his manhood—his sense of self defined by his life within traditional society. Okonkwo symbolically lashes out by attacking a representative of the new order and, rather than be humiliated by becoming a victim of English justice, hangs himself.

Meanwhile, the third significant institution has already begun its encroachment on the minds of the villagers: Okonkwo's Christian son has been receiving an English education. He has learned how to speak and write English—the crucial first step in the new system. When the novel ends, he is already studying in a teachers' college so that he can enter the ranks of a Westernized bureaucracy. Okonkwo is symbolic of the dying order. The issue in the novel is the inevitability of change, the necessity of adaptation, and the intense desire, nevertheless, to somehow retain a sense of one's integrity, which is certainly not to be found in the unattractive picture of English character that closes the novel, the district commissioner reducing the tragedies of the village and Okonkwo to one paragraph in his projected study, *The Pacification of the Primitive Tribes of the Lower Niger*.

In much more strident and emotional fashion, Ngugi traces the same process of English exploitation. His language becomes more and more that of a revolutionary, intensified by his disenchantment with Christianity, his Marxist ideology, and the particular nature of colonialism in Kenya, which attracted not only European and American industrialists but also settlers who bought and occupied fertile Kenyan lands and subjugated the inhabitants to the role of tenants. Ngugi's strategy is often to decry this exploitation of the land. To the Gikuyu tribe, land is sacred, its possession sanctioned by the gods. Ngugi draws a parallel between the biblical story of Eden and the Gikuyu myth that defines Kenya as the garden granted to descendants of the original parents. This appeal to myth and the sacred arouses passions that Achebe chooses not to inject into his works. Still, like Achebe, Ngugi points to the Christian Church as the initial culprit in the disasters that befall his country: Missionaries are the prophets of capitalism, and hence their message is tainted. They lull the inhabitants into an acceptance of the foreigner. The education they provide seems to be the wisdom of the future, to contain the "light" of salvation. *Weep Not, Child* (1964) has as its main motif the exposure of this panacea: Acceptance of Western education and religion means submission to Western imperialism.

It is primarily in *The River Between*, however, that Ngugi presents the head-to-head conflict between traditional culture and the new Christian faith. He symbolically uses a river to separate the adherents to traditional custom and the new Christian converts. The protagonist, Waiyaki, educated within the British system but sympathetic to the spiritual life of the past, tries to unite the two. His role is complicated by his being in love with the daughter of the pastor who puritanically leads the Christian element of the population. Like Achebe, Ngugi does not see the situation as a simple black-white melodrama. Waiyaki's defeat is at the hands of devious elements within traditional society, and the Christian intruder is not a white missionary but an African who has become obsessed by the Christian message. Thus, Ngugi's attack is directed as much against the dupes of Western imperialism—who become traitors to Kenya—as against the foreign force itself. Waiyaki himself carries within him the taint of his mission-school education: He is a messianic hero, his language is sprinkled with biblical images, and his fate is that of a "Christian" martyr who, however, achieves nothing.

It is difficult to determine whether, in this early novel, Ngugi admires the young romantic individualist or looks at him ironically for his narcissism and his want of political savvy. He nevertheless offers evidence that the alien society has infiltrated the consciousness of the people and has set the old and the new forces on a collision course that a simple romantic idealism cannot prevent. The great enemies of traditional culture, for Ngugi, are Christianity and capitalism. It is the former that occupies Ngugi in this early novel and attracts more and more of his venom as his pessimism and his social and political involvement deepen.

Perhaps the most devastating critique of Christianity's impact on African culture is Beti's *The Poor Christ of Bomba*. It presents a striking contrast between the natural, uninhibited sexual attitudes and social forms of the native people of Cameroon and the Church's absolute notions of sexual purity, abstinence, and monogamy. The Reverend Father Drumont's mission to convert the natives leads not to the virgin ideal but to either total rejection of his dogma or a deceitful subversion of it that spreads syphilis throughout the region. This has both a real and a symbolic significance. The Church has not really succeeded in establishing itself, but it may, nevertheless, have contaminated the rhythms of life it has tried to replace. The novel is also a philosophical analysis of the Catholic menace. In this *roman à thèse*, Father Drumont engages in periodic discussions with the local administrator, Vidal, who views Christianity in the skeptical European manner but who regards it as an essential weapon in the struggle against Marxism in Africa. Specifically, Vidal confirms Ngugi's and Achebe's contention that the role of the missionary is to soften the natives' resistance to political and economic exploitation. At the same time, he is convinced that the introduction of French civilization is for their own benefit.

Father Drumont had never shared these assumptions but had come to Cameroon as an idealist to save the natives for Christ, naïvely believing that his religion so clearly represented the truth that the lost, unfortunate natives would hunger after it. Whatever Father Drumont's failings may be at the end of his experience, he does eventually admit his ignorance and youthful innocence. In his last conversation with Vidal, he rejects his role as a prophet for capitalism. Besides, he has seen clearly that the natives' acceptance of Christianity is superficial, a purely formal one arising first out of curiosity, then out of fear and self-defense. He has never reached their souls. In addition, he recognizes that they have, almost from the start, seen through the subtle process of exploitation. Though he still makes statements that indicate an insensitivity toward their culture, he has begun to admit their intelligence and their humanity, thus emphasizing, as do other aspects of the novel, the dominant motif of colonial fiction—the insistence on an independent African identity.

These, then, are three among many African novels that treat the challenge to African identity during the initial conflict with the West. Where white characters appear, they are either stereotypes—thus reversing expectations and pointing up the depth of the African character by contrast—or, in the exceptional case of *The Poor Christ of Bomba*, complex individuals exposing the immorality and deficiency of the European in Africa. Here, it is the African who perceives and interprets human nature. These novels are set within the village, where white people are anomalies, albinos, ghosts riding their iron horses—comic precursors of doom. In these novels, one also finds the transition already beginning between the old and new orders. A few Africans have adopted Western ways, become Christian, joined the administration, learned to read and write. They have assumed an importance in society because they have the foreign government behind them. The black missionary is a potent force. It would appear that the only way to survive is to change allegiances.

Sembène, because of his atypical education and experiences among the poor, presents a special variation of the transition. His novel *O pays, mon beau peuple!* (1957; oh my country, my beautiful people) is also, for the most part, set in a rural community, the Casamance region of Senegal, but establishes its ties with the urban seat of government and with the "mother country," France. More important, it has as its protagonist Oumar Faye, a son of the region who has fought in the European wars, has had extensive experience in France, and has discovered and defended his identity among white people. He returns home to a people who have not yet learned that they can face up to the white political and economic leaders who are controlling their lives. His mission is to unite the farmers into a cooperative strong enough to resist pressures from the white businesspeople—a community effort that draws upon African and Marxist ideals—but also open enough to introduce technological knowledge from the West.

Again, white people tend to be stereotyped, but Sembène at least makes an attempt at compromise here, too, through a mixed marriage. Oumar brings back with him a Frenchwoman who sincerely joins in with the traditional life, eventually wins over Oumar's family, and ends the novel pregnant with a symbolic union of the two races and cultures. Sembène has obviously moved beyond a definition of the conflict toward a political and ideological solution. To some extent, he re-creates the traditional life in the family and in the fishing and farming communities, but his attitude, shaped as it is by contact with the West, tends to be critical of those customs that militate against reason, individualism, and practical adaptation to the contemporary world. Yet, through all of this, one continues to sense a loyalty to Africa, a love of the land, and a preservation of tradition.

Another group of novels transports the African to the city. These novels deal with a later stage of the colonial period and are mainly concerned with the phenomenon of alienation and disorientation. No longer surrounded by traditional custom, the protagonists must adapt to the white peoples' world. Perhaps the writer who deals with this situation most extensively is Cyprian Ekwensi. This prolific storyteller has attempted to describe practically every phase of African life, including the old precolonial era, but such accounts as found in his *Burning Grass* (1962), about the Fulani herdsmen of northern Nigeria, seem more like tales than novels.

One can almost say the same about his stories of city life: *Lokotown and Other Stories* (1966), *Jagua Nana* (1961), and *People of the City* (1954). This last-named novel introduces a common motif, the youth who has left the village and is trying to make his way in the city. Ekwensi's rather improbable (and Western) choice to make his hero, Amusa Sango, a crime reporter and a part-time trumpeter in a dance band nevertheless gives him the opportunity to introduce practically every facet of the city's teeming life. However, improbabilities, so uncharacteristic of what one expects in a novel, plague the development of Amusa's adventures.

Ekwensi defines Amusa as the most eligible bachelor in the entire metropolis of Lagos, anxious to achieve success but addicted to pleasure and especially to women. His irresistible charm (never made convincing) almost appears to be authorial wish-fulfillment, as not only the loose women of the city but also the respectable seek him out and involve him in seemingly inextricable situations. Aina, a Moll Flanders type, enters the novel as his mistress, soon goes to jail as a thief, and eventually uses her pregnancy (by another man) to appeal to his conscience, while her vindictive mother, thinking he is responsible for her imprisonment, unsuccessfully tries to implicate him in an illegal racket. Beatrice, a social climber who attaches herself to numerous successful men, but especially white men, also becomes Amusa's mistress. Then there is Elina, Amusa's childhood fiancé, whom he tries his best to abandon because she is plain and holds none of the excitement of city life. The fourth attraction is a well-educated, respectable girl, also named Beatrice for some curious symbolic reason, who apparently combines the best of two worlds but whom Amusa cannot marry until Aina has a miscarriage. Aina's mother suffers a miraculous change of heart, Beatrice the First is mauled to death by women whom she had slighted in her ambitious seductions, Amusa's own mother dies (leaving him to choose his own wife), and Beatrice the Second's fiancé commits suicide after failing his medical examinations. The novel ends as Amusa and Beatrice incredibly set off into the sunset in a lorry bound for Ghana (the Gold Coast).

Amusa's adventures have involved him in all the "romance" of the city: theft, murder, prostitution, political and economic corruption, and swindling and racketeering, as well as an election and a labor march mourning the death of a spiritual leader who is described as an African Gandhi. The message is clear that money has replaced the old values, in particular loyalty to relatives and to the people of one's own country. Amusa has to experience it all before he can accept the responsibility of doing something and becoming something—that is what his self-imposed exile is all about. It is difficult to take this romantic, melodramatic, chaotic novel seriously. Yet Ekwensi has written better works, and this is his first. For a long time it was pointed to as the first anglophone novel to be widely read outside Africa. It is thus historically important. It is also an unfortunate example of some of the worst elements in Western fiction and illustrates what appears to a Western reader to be a complete loss of an African perception. It is difficult to distinguish Amusa's goal of success from a Western one, or from Ekwensi's. His father's challenge to seek opportunities in the new world, to do something, to become something makes success a definition of one's humanity. Thus, *People of the City* is, above all, in both its story and its point of view, a record of the moral confusion that Western civilization has incited in such urban centers as Lagos in West Africa.

In *Jagua Nana*, Ekwensi is again in Lagos, and the protagonist is a female version of Amusa Sango, a forty-five-year-old prostitute with dreams of marrying into the elite. She plans to achieve her goal by sending her young lover, Freddie Namme, to England to get a degree in law. When he abandons her for a younger woman and then dies in a political vendetta, she returns to her native village and dreams of setting herself up as an independent merchant. Ekwensi fleshes out this skeletal plot with almost as many varied adventures as make up *People of the City* and with the same titillating sexual language. The male protagonist, Freddie, is even closer than Amusa to the fictional type that dominates the late colonial period, the young, Western-educated African—usually a "been-to"—whose main goal is to imitate white people, enter the elite of the city, drive a car, have money, and attract women. That is, he not only has rejected but also is ashamed of his past and wants to be completely independent of the old ties of loyalty. Unlike Amusa, Freddie must pay for his selfishness and betrayal with his own death, but this poetic justice is essentially melodramatic and, besides, is more than balanced by the heroine's survival and return to moral sanity.

Achebe, in *No Longer at Ease*, as one might expect, manages the experience of the "been-to" in a more controlled and convincing manner. Rather than allow the melodramatic elements to get out of hand, Achebe uses various devices, such as flashbacks, juxtaposition, point of view, irony, and humor, to force a judgment of the protagonist, Obi Okonkwo (grandson of the hero in *Things Fall Apart*). The novel begins with his trial and indictment, for example, and the plot moves inexorably toward a financial and moral indebtedness that tempts him into the widespread practice of accepting bribes. Though he begins his life in Lagos with a sense of mission, to remain above the prevailing moral corruption, he eventually succumbs but is not clever enough to succeed. Through Obi and his experience, Achebe indicts the entire Nigerian society for its unfair demands on the young, for the corruption of the older members in both the city and the native village, for the false values that have replaced the traditional ones, and for the vanity and naïve expectations of the young. Nor do the racist British bosses escape blame. *No Longer at Ease* may not have the firm sense of place and authority found in *Things Fall Apart* and *Arrow of God*, but it convincingly reveals the loss of identity and integrity in the transition from village to city.

Both Achebe and Ekwensi are Nigerians, with Lagos providing their common example of the new culture in Africa, but their perception is not essentially different from that of observers in other regions with somewhat different colonial histories. Lenrie Peters, from Gambia and Sierra Leone, describes a similar situation in his novel *The Second Round* (1965). In this case, however, the protagonist, Dr. Kawa, retains his integrity. He returns from England with his medical degree and with high ideals of serving his country but finds Freetown a divided city, European civilization having modified the traditional society. Uncomfortable in the superficial, materialistic environment and unable to satisfy the expectations of his mother and friends, Kawa decides to transfer to a country hospital in hopes of washing off the stain of moral contamination. In spite of his moral integrity and his attack on superficial Western values, Kawa remains a contemporary man. This novel is at a far remove from the negritudist perception of an African personality that one finds in the novels of Laye.

The same can be said of the novels of city life that come out of South Africa, an area that poses a special problem to readers of African literature. Until the 1990's, it represented an entrenched colonialism, a white minority that controlled the political, social, and economic situation under the system of apartheid. On the other hand, it has long been so highly industrialized that relations between the races resemble the American experience; the blacks who are writing are often far removed from their tribal roots. A return to an African identity does not appear to be the major motif.

This can, at least, be said for one of the country's most prolific novelists, Peter Abrahams, born in a Johannesburg slum, son of a black father and a colored mother. Early in his life, he made the breaking down of the color barrier a major conviction and goal, and rejected negritude, which seemed to glorify blackness and emphasize racial distinctions. For him, spiritual freedom and individualism, Western values with an early touch of Marxism, ignored distinctions of race. Eventually, as his later novels reveal, he argued that political freedom must precede individual freedom. His novel of city life, *Mine Boy*, written in his mid-twenties, already indicates these directions of his thought. Its purpose is to expose the evils of apartheid, which denies the humanity of blacks and either maims or kills them. Xuma, a strong young man from the country, comes to the city with illusions of money and success. He receives evidence of the city's destructiveness in the form of disheartened men and women, hears advice from Leah, a magnificent mother-protectress, but remains in his ignorance until he goes to work in the mines.

Once on the white peoples' ground, he begins to feel his inferiority. It requires the support and wisdom of his Irish boss, Paddy O'Shea—a Marxist and hence a rare example of tolerance among white people—before he recovers his sense of integrity. He then becomes aware of the political situation that will not allow him his humanity, and this, in turn, prompts him to lead a strike against his white bosses at the mine. Though still subject to apartheid law at the end of the novel, he declares himself a spokesman for his people—the role that Abrahams himself has assumed. Through all of this, it is evident that Abrahams makes no appeal to tribal values. It is the Westerner, Paddy O'Shea, who guides him, and, though Marxism may be at the root of the economic struggle, it is Western individualism that wins him over. Abrahams himself insists that racism, prejudice, and provincialism are prevalent in every culture and that international understanding and pluralism are the answer.

Abrahams's critique of society, in particular the city, is tame and romanticized in comparison with that of another South African, Alex La Guma, who relies extensively on realistic and naturalistic detail. His attack is almost exclusively against the evils of apartheid, which necessitates underground resistance (*In the Fog of the Seasons' End*, 1972) and results in large portions of the nonwhite population spending their lives in prison for politically or economically motivated crimes (*The Stone Country*, 1967). In the former novel, La Guma inserts a typical interrogation of a nonwhite by a white authority who details the endless regulations that control the nonwhite's movements within the country. Both of these novels deal with urban blacks, but La Guma's earlier work, the short novel *A Walk in the Night* (1962), gives the clearest picture of what it is like for a nonwhite to live in a South African city. It recounts the events of one evening in the life of a Coloured, Michael Adonis—a bitterly ironic choice of names—who has recently been fired from his factory job for speaking disrespectfully to his white superior.

Frustrated and angry, Michael wanders the streets, frequents old restaurants and bars, is interrogated by a policeman, comes into contact with the lower elements of society, and ends up at the house of his neighbor, Mr. Doughty, an old Irishman and formerly successful actor whom life has beaten into alcoholism. In a drunken fit of passion and resentment over Doughty's philosophizing, but especially over his whiteness, Michael hits him with a wine bottle and kills him. He has a series of psychological reactions to this, his first murder—rationalization, indifference, a sense of superiority, entrapment, and fear. Ironically, it is not Michael whom an informer names as the guilty party, but Willieboy, one of his acquaintances in the streets. In a brutal sequence of scenes, the police constable, Raalt, chases Willieboy like an animal, shoots him, and allows him to die in the back of his van while he stops to buy cigarettes on the way to the station. Michael has no idea that Willieboy has died in his place, that he is a "sacrificial victim." The old Irishman who futilely quotes William Shakespeare to Michael, describing life as the ghost of Hamlet's father walking the night, cannot become his spiritual father. The only culture in these streets is in the gangsters and cowboys at the cinema. Joe, the young vagabond who wanders through the novel, warns Michael to preserve his integrity, but this advice, too, fails.

Michael decides to join a band of thieves. Hope seems impossible. La Guma ends the novel with a cockroach gorging itself on a mixture of liquor and vomit in old Mr. Doughty's room; John Abrahams, the informer, living in shame and helplessness; Joe escaping the city for the sea; and the anonymous Frank Lorenzo, with his five children and his pregnant wife, Grace, looking to the dawn. The irony of Michael Adonis's name continues to the bitter end. The experience of the black South African is almost a thing apart. It seems closer to Ralph Ellison's *Invisible Man* (1952) than to colonial literature in the rest of Black Africa. Nevertheless, the need for community, which Michael is able to find only in a robber gang and which Joe seeks in Michael, is as real in its absence as in Armah's *The Beautyful Ones Are Not Yet Born* (1968). Identity within the community is an essential motif within these African novels.

FROM RESISTANCE TO INDEPENDENCE

The theme of resistance to apartheid, strongly suggested in such novels as *Mine Boy*, *A Walk in the Night*, and *The Stone Country* and treated directly by *In the Fog of the Seasons' End*, finds its parallels in the countries to the north. Throughout the colonial period, before the final achieving of independence in the early 1960's, there were pockets of resistance to foreign intervention. Armah presents this phenomenon mythically in *The Healers* and *Two Thousand Seasons*, the former concentrating on the defeat of the Ashanti during the British conquest of Ghana in the late nineteenth century, the latter tracing the resistance to exploitation over the past one thousand years. Armah raises the issue of the slave trade, a rarity in African fiction, and accuses his own people of complicity and betrayal in this and in the turning over of power to British authority. In both novels, however, he contends that a group of spiritual leaders has continued to preserve the old African traditions and has periodically engaged in guerrilla warfare in order to survive.

Mongo Beti of Cameroon attempts a more realistic account of the struggle in *Remember Reuben* (1973; English translation, 1980). It deals with the exploits of a trade union leader, who first opposes the French through political means but eventually must become a guerrilla leader. The novel has a romantic strain as well: Mor-Zamba, the true protagonist, attains heroic status in the eyes of his fellows. It is his realization that constitutes the message of the novel, that the struggle has nothing to do with individual personalities or personal gain, that the goal is not simply political power or economic control but African identity and spiritual independence of foreign cultural domination.

Meja Mwangi of Kenya, in his *Carcase for Hounds* (1974), relies even more than Beti on pure realistic detail. He examines the role of one particular group of Mau Mau fighters, the carryover of tribal ferocity into the struggle for liberation, and, in particular, the quest of the legendary General Haraka for the heads of tribal chiefs who side with the British. More gruesome, however, is the loyalty code that demands success or death. The novel ends with Kimamo, who functions as the main focus of narration, nursing his wounded and feverish general, watching him execute a fellow terrorist who has failed in a mission, and then watching his own execution for the same reason. The final paragraphs reintroduce the almost inevitable but ambiguous romantic note of the soul's survival in a paradisal afterlife in which Kimamo and General Haraka reunite. The hyena's sardonic chuckle, which had floated as a motif in earlier scenes, dimly qualifies the spiritual affirmation.

Some mythologizing of the resistance movement is almost inevitable. The resistance fighters must become heroes of legend, especially within the African context, in which such transformation is basic to the oral literature. Ngugi, in his resistance novel, however, has his legendary figure recede into the background and concentrates on the psychological realities of betrayal, deception, and cowardice. *A Grain of Wheat* (1967) is many things at once: a mythical but humanized treatment of the guerrilla fighter Kihika; a clever merger of Christian myth within the thematic structure of divine mission and Judas-like betrayal; and a satiric portrait of the anemic white administration in the last days of the colony. Its purpose, however, is to raise essential questions about motives and aspirations of the combatants and to suggest, finally, the ambiguity surrounding heroism, cowardice, and the personal struggle that is even more intense than the public one. Mugo, the betrayer of the legendary hero Kihika, endures the most intense moral struggle among the participants; ironically, his public avowal on the day of independence, which leads to his execution by people of less moral stature, is too late to

have any effect on the political situation. Gikonyo returns from a detention camp to find his wife pregnant by Karanja, a subordinate for the white administration. Despite the ambiguity surrounding her submission to Karanja, Ngugi seems to insist on her essential integrity and puts the burden on Gikonyo to accept her in an act of faith. Again, this struggle is as real in the novel as any directly connected with the resistance movement. Contained in *A Grain of Wheat* are the seeds of success and of failure in the postindependence society.

Like Ngugi, Sembène carries the resistance movement up to the moment of independence. His novel *Les Bouts de bois de Dieu* (1960; *God's Bits of Wood*, 1962) is a fictional account of an actual event in the Western Sudan, the railway strike of 1947-1948. He treats its success as a temporary triumph against oppressive French authority and treats its leaders as romanticized heroes. It is an epic portrayal relying upon realistic detail, romantic gesture, communal loyalty, and a touch of Marxist ideology. Sembène's next novel, *L'Harmattan, livre I: Référendum* (1964), treats events in an anonymous African country in the late 1950's. He shifts focus from the band of Marxist revolutionaries endorsing a vote for independence on the referendum to the personal and public life of Dr. Tangara, who sympathizes with their goal but not their ideology and methods and who must make a decision for or against them. Though the referendum results in independence in only one of the French colonies, the revolutionary forces have not lost heart, and the hesitant politicism of such rare humanistic figures as Dr. Tangara withdraws from the scene. Sembène in these novels is much less pessimistic about the future of Senegal than Ngugi is about the capacity of Kenyans to maintain a high level of resistance to the temptations of Western civilization. Like Sembène, Ngugi eventually turns to Marxism as an ideology that better suits the African sense of community, but more than Sembène, he desperately needs to recover and reinstate traditional African values—hence, perhaps, his deeper pessimism about the future.

This pessimism is also evident in two other novelists, Armah and Abrahams. Armah's *Why Are We So*

Blest? (1971) is a unique version of the revolutionary theme. The action takes place entirely outside black Africa. This universalizes the revolutionary struggle and, in fact, turns it into a conflict of races. The colonial situation in the sub-Sahara is essentially no different from that in America and North Africa, and Armah holds out no hope of success. Of the three protagonists, the white American girl, Aimée, has motives that are suspect; the young African student at Harvard, Modu, dies while naïvely trying to join the revolution; and the mature Solo, also an African, is too skeptical about revolution and the callous organization that runs it to commit himself. His contribution will apparently remain that of a philosophical literary exile.

Abrahams, in *A Wreath for Udomo* (1956), likewise carries the struggle outside Africa, to a core of political leaders residing in London. Their job is to conduct a propaganda campaign that forces the British government to turn power over to the indigenous population. Michael Udomo, in rather unconvincing fashion, soon becomes the center of the group, wresting power and influence from the country's idol, who has lost touch with the real political situation. Although he returns to "Pan-Africa" to prepare the way for Lanwood, by the time the latter arrives, Udomo is firmly established in the seat of power and has changed markedly from the rash, irresponsible youth he was in London to an astute politician, sure of himself and his goals. He no doubt represents the voice of Abrahams in the novel, but as a result, it brings both him and the author into conflict with the voice of tribalism. Udomo uses his power to modernize and industrialize his country; he works to defeat the tribe, which stands for everything evil, superstitious, and savage. This goal drives him to a temporary compromise with Pluralia (South Africa) and a betrayal of his best friend, who heads a resistance group within that country.

Whether such actions go beyond Abrahams's own convictions is difficult to say, but Udomo seems to retain his romantic image to the very end. Abrahams's pessimism does not, it would seem, arise from the necessity of compromise but from his awareness that the enemy, tribalism, is a powerful force. Udomo dies a sacrificial death at its hands in a savage and terrifying ritual ceremony. The intellectual of the novel, Paul Mahbi, in a letter to Lois, Udomo's white mistress whom he had abandoned for the African cause, composes an eloquent defense of his greatness in spite of his violation of private moralities. Whatever Abrahams's intentions, the conflict in the novel suggests the necessity of compromise between the new civilization and the old and makes one wonder if the tribe does not, after all, have values that Abrahams and Udomo do not allow to surface. In any case, *A Wreath for Udomo* is a remarkable novel, written as it was in 1956, some years before the majority of the African countries had achieved independence. It is prophetic in its anticipation of the internal struggles that were to ensue.

POSTINDEPENDENCE AND NEOCOLONIALISM

Fictional representations of the new African states, published between 1960 and the 1990's, have borne out Abrahams's fears. Return of political power to African hands has not been complete—for economic control has remained, for the most part, with international conglomerates and with "black Europeans" who reflect foreign interests. The new political leaders themselves have been corrupt or incapable of controlling the competing factions and often corrupt forces within the country. Another problem is the basic ideological conflict that Abrahams identifies. In practically every novel dealing with contemporary Africa, the temptations of Western materialism—the dream of social advancement, the status symbols, the luxuries of modern civilization and technology, and the power that makes their attainment possible—and the capitalistic ideology that lies behind them receive the brunt of the attack, but now it is not usually the foreigner who is the villain. The novelist points to the African who betrays his heritage. The rare individuals who maintain their integrity either have no visible or respected sanctions for their morality or more or less vaguely inherit it from the traditional past. In the most pessimistic of the novels, the individual becomes a helpless and alienated victim of corruption and various economic and sociopolitical forces. Among the many who have set their novels in the postcolonial period are the almost canonical figures in African literature: Armah, Aidoo, Achebe, Emecheta, Soyinka, Sembène, and Ngugi.

The most erudite novelist and critic of the contemporary scene is Wole Soyinka, the recipient of the Nobel Prize in Literature in 1986. His first novel, *The Interpreters*, is a masterpiece of virtuosity, ironic commentary, philosophical probing, and mythic intimations. Though it touches every level of society, it concentrates on the social elite: those people who belong to the hypocritical majority and the few intellectuals, educated abroad but spiritually bound to Africa, who try to act, to find a place for themselves, and to interpret their situation. They include Egbo, the son of a tribal chief whose dilemma is to reconcile his obligations to the past and the present and whose conflicting sexual attractions to the sensuous Simi and a young university student provide a specific locus for his choice. Egbo's return with the other interpreters to visit his tribal home vividly depicts the power of tradition over the minds of the descendants. His private encounter with Ogun—the Dionysian god of creation and destruction—puts him into spiritual contact with the natural world and is only one of many ways that the mythic impinges on the daily lives of the interpreters.

Kola, the painter, makes contact through his art—Ogun himself being the patron of artists—as he struggles to finish his masterpiece, a merging of contemporary personalities into the forms of the Yoruba gods. Egbo is Ogun, the god of contradictions, repeating the god's symbolic journey from the traditional world of spirits to the contemporary world of the living. Kola's sculpture, *The Wrestler*, is a heroic elevation of a comic incident involving another of the interpreters, Sekoni. This idealist and spiritual inspiration within the group is already dead but has become a legendary hero. After his attempt as an engineer to construct an electric power station in a rural community is rejected by provincial and corrupt politicians, he goes insane, for the power station represents for him not simply a technological achievement but a harnessing of natural power through human creativity and was to give meaning to his new life in Africa. This failure haunts the other interpreters. They

see his death in terms of a ritual sacrifice.

Sagoe seems in some respects to be a practical member of the group. As a reporter for a Lagos newspaper—a position he obtains in a strange and comic way—he investigates curious happenings in the city. He is also bound to one of the female protagonists in a relatively conventional fashion. Yet his strange and symbolic philosophy of "Voidancy"—spiritual elevation being achieved through complete relieving of the bowels—gives him an opposite dimension. The philosophy is not only comic playfulness, but it is also part of the motif of excrement and filth, of fertility and sterility, in contemporary Nigerian society. Finally, there is Bandele, apparently the cohesive force of the group. Generally a detached observer, quiet and pragmatic in his actions, he is a professor of English at the university and may be Soyinka's authorial voice, the *raisonneur*.

While these characters exist on many different levels, from the profoundly sacred to the farcical, the characters representing a hypocritical society reside in a world of satiric comedy, and Soyinka is brilliant as a Molière in exposing them to ridicule. Faseyi, Sir Derinola, Chief Winsala, Professor Oguazor, and Dr. Lumoye are "petrified" brains, concerned only with façades and trivia. Through them, Soyinka attacks the materialism and utilitarianism that inhibit the interpreters from realizing their creative energies within the social fabric. A third group of characters introduces the strange world of evangelical religions so prevalent in modern Nigeria and a common theme in Soyinka's other work. The interpreters visit the church of the prophet Lazarus, who claims to have risen from the dead. Soyinka seems to use the religious service—which is fraught with theatrics—as well as the other pseudo-Christian rites and avowals, to emphasize the quest for spiritual values in the void of contemporary life. The activities of the interpreters themselves are part of the same quest.

Rather than provide answers, however, the novel seems to end in paradox and mystery. There is a strange equation of disciples and thieves, of sinners and martyrs. The mystery of death and resurrection is present throughout the novel but reappears at the end with the symbolic, nightmarish drowning of Joe

Golder, a black American, in a vat of black dye. Golder, who has no identity, who is black and yet an American rather than an African, obsessively defends the principle of negritude. Yet Soyinka also identifies him as a homosexual and, in the eyes of Sagoe, as a pervert. While Soyinka defends the integrity of the African tradition, he does not make it a matter of color and rejects here as elsewhere the negritudist definition of the African. His vision of the African is complex. It is not even clear that he has intellectually sorted it out or wishes to do so in any dogmatic or analytical way. He states as much in his second novel, *Season of Anomy.*

The Interpreters ends as a night of severance: The disciples are separated, and the Savior has not come. The interpreters are "apostates," but to what, they are not sure: to the new world that demands their acquiescence, to the real or imagined past that still has a spiritual hold on them, or to the inner self as the final sanction for responsible and heroic action? Bandele usually remains quiet in the face of the irreligious society that sacrifices its young to the preservation of itself, but he is the one who gives the parting ironic shot: May they all live to bury their own daughters.

While Soyinka's first novel focuses on the lives of intellectuals during the early sixties, and his second, *Season of Anomy*, on the Nigerian Civil War (1967-1970), others writers such as Armah, Achebe, Ngugi, and Sembène turned their attention to the political leadership and its effect on the citizenry. Armah's *The Beautyful Ones Are Not Yet Born* looks at national corruption, as condoned and even encouraged by politicians, through the eyes of an unnamed protagonist, "the man," a controller in a railway office. He is the only moral force in the society, surrounded by images of filth and excrement, by fellow workers who take bribes, by a family whose material desires pressure him to do likewise, by a cynical "Teacher" friend who has retreated from society, and by a former schoolmate, Koomson—the main human symbol of social degradation, who has used corrupt means to rise to political prominence and who is using the man and his family in yet another of his illegal activities. Armah transforms the protagonist into a hero—a model of moral behavior—in the second

half of the novel when, after a military coup, with absolutely no ulterior motive, he risks his own life to save Koomson's. Armah's indictment of the new African leadership is achieved largely through scatological imagery and character foils: the indulgent materialism of Koomson and the reflective sensitivity and compassion of the man.

Achebe presents similar portraits of political leaders in *No Longer at Ease* and *A Man of the People*, but most impressively in his fifth novel, *Anthills of the Savannah* (1987). Using shifting points of view, overlapping time sequences, and periodic flashbacks, he focuses attention on incidents surrounding a military coup in present time in an imaginary African country (actually a thinly disguised Nigeria in the early 1980's). Kangan's president, familiarly known as Sam, has gone the way of other political figures in postcolonial Africa, abandoning his revolutionary ideals and abusing his newly gained power. The main characters are Sam's former schoolmates, who react in various ways to his betrayal: Chris, minister of information, who tries to guide Sam back to public responsibility; his friend Ikem, editor of the city newspaper, who attacks Sam in his columns; and Beatrice, a secretary and priestess in love with Chris and confidant of Ikem. When Sam refuses to acknowledge the needs of the people, specifically ignoring a delegation of elders from the drought-plagued north, a military junta assassinates him and assumes authority. At the end, with both Chris and Ikem dead, Beatrice hosts a symbolic communal meeting of friends that suggests the ideal future direction of the country. The novel reflects, through its various techniques, a contemporary experimentation with fictional form; through Beatrice the growing feminist voice in Africa; and through the use of myth, folktale, and legend the continuing attempt of novelists to explore the relevance of tradition in modern Africa.

Ngugi continued to develop as a novelist as well, and to respond in fresh ways to the post-colonial situation in Kenya. In *Devil on the Cross* and *Matigari* he asserted his indigenous culture by writing in his native Gikuyu before producing English versions and by adapting oral techniques to the novel form. Both works attack corruption of the neocolonialists. The former specifically targets Western capitalism and patriarchy, using griot narration, folktale monsters, ritual repetition, and a female folk hero to rouse the public against blatant abuses of power. The latter targets government and economic abuse through parabolic characters and stories that mix social satire and fantasy in a form of Magical Realism. A folk hero-father returns to his native country after fighting wars of revolution only to find that imperialist forces are still in power behind the scenes. In his search for truth and justice, he rescues a prostitute and a child-thief to form a new African family but is chased out of the country, wounded and perhaps killed, with only his "son" to carry on the cultural war. Likewise, Sembène, first in *Xala* (1973; English translation, 1976), then in *The Last of the Empire*, attacks neocolonialism from an African socialist perspective. *Xala* focuses on the chamber of commerce in Dakar, in particular on one representative member, El Hadji, who follows the typical literary pattern of neocolonial capitalists. He forgets his revolutionary ideals before independence and becomes a corrupt opportunist, taking advantage of the economic system to acquire wives, material possessions, and social standing. Sembène traces his gradual fall at the hands of the people he has disenfranchised and impoverished, led by a beggar-griot who, through the curse of impotence, reminds him of his crime, its human consequences, and the necessary cure: an identification with the community of Senegal. In *The Last of the Empire*, in a political plot similar to Achebe's *Anthills of the Savannah*, the "chamber" is that of the government, the ministers who serve under Léon, the president of Senegal. The main character is the minister of justice, the conscientious elder Cheikh Tidiane, who at the beginning of the narrative resigns his post just as Léon mysteriously disappears. The novel is itself a mystery, which gradually reveals the reason for the disappearance, exposes the egotistic struggles for power of Léon's subordinates, provides the stimulus for Tidiane's realization of his social role as writer-griot, and sets the stage for Sembène's own political agenda in support of feminism, social responsibility, and sanity in dealing with issues of religion, polygamy, property, and education. All of

these writers—Achebe, Armah, Ngugi, and Sembène—assume the role of traditional griot, assessing the needs of contemporary African society in the light of indigenous traditions and colonial influences.

Other voices on the literary scene include a second generation of male writers and a growing number of female writers to complement such established names as Aidoo, Emecheta, and Head. While they continue some of the same social and political themes, following the African aesthetic of writing for the people's sake, they also often exhibit a highly experimental style, sometimes resembling the Magical Realism of Latin American novelists. Among the most distinguished of the male artists are Ben Okri of Nigeria and Nuruddin Farah of Somalia. Farah published seven novels between 1970 and 1998, including *From a Crooked Rib* (1970), a sympathetic, even feminist, portrait of a Somali woman, and two sets of trilogies with political themes. The first of these six books, *Sweet and Sour Milk* (1979), led to his exile of almost twenty years from his native country. His works, fictional manifestations of Edward Said's "Orientalism" argument, are exquisitely written assertions of Somalian identity in the face of Western "othering" of so-called Third World peoples. Okri, who has expressed the wish to be known as a writer, not simply as an African writer, is a superb stylist who mixes realism with mythical and magical qualities that draw on African folk literature and themes. *The Famished Road* (1991) and *Songs of Enchantment* (1993), for example, present as the protagonist an *ogbangi* child, the literary prototype for which is Ezinma in Achebe's *Things Fall Apart*. His characters move through fabulous worlds reminiscent of Tutuola's narratives and African folktales. Okri won several literary prizes in recognition of his technical skills, and his moral commitment to the African people is a visible part of his fictional achievement. Several other writers emerged toward the end of the twentieth century, including Henri Lopès and Labou Tansi of the Congo, and Tierno Monénembo of Guinea.

One of the most encouraging signs in the literature of the last three decades of the twentieth century was the emergence of numerous women authors, including novelists. Few women of the first generation continued to write. Ama Ata Aidoo of Ghana was mainly known for her poems, short stories, and plays until 1977, when her 1966 African feminist novel, *Our Sister Killjoy: Or, Reflections from a Black-eyed Squint*, was finally published; in 1991 she published a second novel, *Changes: A Love Story*. Another West African writer, Emecheta of Nigeria, wrote some fifteen novels between 1976 (*The Bride Price*), and 1994 (*Kehinde*). Her most famous and important novel, *The Joys of Motherhood* (1979), offers a wrenching account of a wife and mother in the modern city of Lagos, bound by the tradition of polygamy and spousal inheritance that forces a second wife into her already established monogamous marriage. Grace Ogot of Kenya was the first and is perhaps the best known East African novelist. Her early novel, *The Promised Land* (1966), and her collection of literary folktales, *Land without Thunder* (1968), established the themes and folkloric style for her later works that deal with the impact of tradition on modern life and the plight of women. Her novel *The Graduate* (1980), about women in postcolonial Kenya, like her first, was written in English, but her later work, including *Miaha* (1983; *The Strange Bride*, 1989) and *Simbi Nyaima* (1983), perhaps influenced by her countryman Ngugi, was written in her native language, Luo. Among francophone women writers, Mariama Bâ followed up her widely read *Une si longue lettre* (1980; *So Long a Letter*, 1981), which raises serious questions about polygamy, with *Un Chant écarlate* (1981; Scarlet Song, 1986), which deals with mixed marriages within the particular cultural expectations of postcolonial Senegal.

Among women novelists of the second generation, two of the most productive are the anglophone writer from Zimbabwe, Yvonne Vera, and the francophone writer from Senegal, Aminata Sow Fall. Vera's novels include *Nehanda* (1993), *Without a Name* (1994), and *Under the Tongue* (1996). Her books are psychological studies of women in exile caught between a disturbing past and an uncertain future. Fall's novels—*Le Revenant* (1976; the ghost), *La Grève des battù, Ou, Les dechets humains* (1979; *The Beggars' Strike: Or, The Dregs of Society*, 1981), *L'Appel des arènes* (1982; the call of the arena), and *Ex-père de*

la nation (1987; ex-father of the nation)— focus on unstable socioeconomic and political situations that make victims of everyone in the society. *Ex-père de la nation* traces the life of an imprisoned former president of an African country to show that neither the "fathers" nor the "mothers" in Africa are fulfilling their nurturing roles. They promise no future for Africa until individuals assume communal responsibility. Other novelists that have received critical attention are Calixthe Beyala and Werewere Liking of Cameroon, Angèle Rawiri of Gabon, and Véronique Tadjo of Ivory Coast. They offer a variety of perspectives on the personal, familial, and social situation of women in Africa.

CONCLUSION: A CRITICAL EVALUATION

Throughout its brief history, the African novel can be characterized as theme and variation on the issue of identity. An internalized sense of inferiority and the threat of cultural extinction contributed to its rise, usually as a mode of defense and a means of preservation. What the novels often lament is the loss of community, and of customs, rituals, values, and sanctions that give meaning to an individual life. When the incursion of an alien culture began to destroy cultural cohesiveness, alienation was an inevitable result. While some novelists, such as La Guma and Mwangi, stress the anonymity that comes with the loss of tradition, others make an effort to integrate the past with the contemporary world. In any case, the novel is not only a literary phenomenon in Africa but also a social document that traces the history of Africa during the past one thousand years. Furthermore, as Kenneth Harrow has argued in *Thresholds of Change in African Literature: The Emergence of a Tradition* (1994), the written tradition is now at least fifty years old and has begun to build on itself. In these documents containing the gradual and then the sudden introduction of Africa to the West, that is, in these various commentaries on the threat to traditional African identity, one motif stands out, that of initiation.

In order to personalize the conflict, the novelist almost inevitably has created a narrator or a central character who undergoes an initiation experience.

This technique is a common theme in Western novels as well, but it seems particularly appropriate to Africa in its period of sudden transition to a society that still practiced age-old initiation rites as an integral part of its communal life. Eileen Julien, in fact, in *African Novels and the Question of Orality* (1992), sees initiation as one of three genres from the oral tradition still practiced by African male novelists. In *God's Bits of Wood*, Sembène explicitly states that participation in the protest march to Dakar is a realistic and practical substitute for the ritual of initiation. The usual pattern in the initiation process is a character's introduction to Western culture, ordinarily through education; a resulting split in personality and loyalties; alienation from the old community and a failure to integrate into the new one; at the extreme, a total exile from the country or a mental breakdown; and finally, in rare cases, a recovery and the beginning of efforts to reestablish ties or create a new community. Novels that end in alienation are likely to be realistic in mode; those novels that project a cure are likely to emphasize the archetypal aspects of the motif and rely on the romantic and mythic mode. No African novel, however, is written exclusively in one mode or the other. The novel that is perhaps the best example of the entire process is, ironically, *The Radiance of the King*, which forces a white man to discover the cultural realities of black Africa.

This is only one instance of the variety one finds in the African novel. Certainly there are other archetypal motifs. Initiation itself can merge gradually into the quest, as is the case with Soyinka's *Season of Anomy*. The sacrificial scapegoat is a common motif that arises out of the historical situation, though often the victim's death does not seem to have any immediate benefits, except perhaps in its effect within the fictional rhetoric. It is partly through the use of archetypes that the novelist, consciously or unconsciously, appeals to an international audience while reflecting local realities. The myth of paradise is a common device to contrast the old life with the new. In numerous novels, symbolism breaks through the realistic description. In some novels, local color—sociological and anthropological documentation—is

a significant part of the structure. In others, the novelist explores the psychological impact on a highly sensitive individual reared in one culture but educated into another. Often the primary purpose is social or political satire. Some novels are structured as histories in imitation of traditional chronicles told by the griots. Others are highly experimental, attempting to incorporate Western devices into the African context or carry over folk and mythic qualities from the past into the contemporary novel form.

In the light of this variety, it may seem somewhat surprising that the African novel has come under fire from Western critics, especially the formalists. African intellectuals have often been sensitive to outside criticism. Achebe is a case in point. They question whether the foreigner really has enough knowledge of African history, the African oral tradition, the African mentality, the contemporary situation, or, more particularly, the biographies and intentions of individual authors. Formalist critics would tend to downplay such factors anyway, and they complain that African novelists are so concerned with social purpose that they neglect aesthetic matters. Achebe's response is that the purpose of literature is first of all humanistic and that this obligation pertains especially in Africa. Some African critics, in fact, will turn on their own when the popular function is neglected. Soyinka, in particular, has come under criticism for his excessive concern with style and technique, in spite of the fact that he is obviously in the forefront of political activism.

Perhaps the best way to evaluate the African novel is through such a sociological critic as Kenneth Burke, who defines all literature as essentially a strategy to deal with reality. His emphasis is on the reality imitated, as is the case in the African novel, but he also stresses the importance of a complex strategy—how well and how convincingly it responds to the situation. This allows some latitude for the pedagogical function that Achebe sees as essential, for the satiric attacks on Western exploitation and African assimilation, and for the general quest for a new African image. This is somewhat the approach Eustace Palmer takes in his 1979 study, *The Growth of the African Novel*. The novel began as a response to a new situation; it has provided not only complex presentations of it but also a variety of strategies to deal with it. Significantly, Burke uses the proverb to illustrate the way literature deals with reality. It is a way of coping. Achebe himself defines the proverb as "the palm oil with which words are eaten." He and other African novelists respect the aesthetic medium, and some, including Achebe, Soyinka, Ngugi, Laye, Kane, Okri, and Farah, achieve a high level of artistry that deserves recognition, especially considering the short history of the form in Africa. The fact that the novelist uses that artistry primarily in the service of a humanistic and social purpose should not be an object of criticism but a source of admiration.

Thomas Banks

BIBLIOGRAPHY

Booker, M. Keith. *The African Novel in English.* Portsmouth, N.H.: Heinemann, 1998. In this collection Booker includes an introduction addressed specifically to a Western audience, a brief history of the African novel, and essays on eight anglophone African novels, four by men and four by women. The selections are intended to represent the variety in the African novel as well as the social and historical contexts of three different regions in Africa.

D'Almeida, Irène Assiba. *Francophone African Women Writers: Destroying the Emptiness of Silence.* Gainesville: University Press of Florida, 1994. While women had a literary voice in traditional Africa as storytellers and griots, until the end of the twentieth century they were silent as writers. D'Almeida's purpose is to help end that silence by discussing autobiographies and novels of a few francophone women published during the 1970's and 1980's as they try to define themselves and their roles on their own terms.

Gikandi, Simon. *Reading the African Novel.* London: James Currey, 1987. In categorizing several African novels according to types—parabolic, biographical, subjective, and political—Gikandi explores the ways that form and content work together in addressing such issues as social norms, values, and power conflicts in reshaping African

reality and in speaking to an African audience in the instructive storytelling tradition. Regardless of type, African novels are in some sense political and try to establish continuity between the mythical or historical past and the present.

Harrow, Kenneth W. *Thresholds of Change in African Literature: The Emergence of a Tradition.* Portsmouth, N.H.: Heinemann, 1994. Applying formal and deconstructive theory, Harrow traces the development of modern African fiction from the 1950's to the 1990's, from novels that witness to those that revolt, and finally to complex discourses that are not realistic or easily accessible. In analyzing works by Camara Laye, Chinua Achebe, Ferdinand Oyono, Yambo Ouologuem, Bessie Head, V. Y. Mudimbe, Wole Soyinka, Ahamadou Kourouma, Henri Lopès, and Sony Labou Tansi, he tries to identify a changing literature based on oral tradition, Western influence, social circumstances, and intertextual self-reflection.

Julien, Eileen. *African Novels and the Question of Orality.* Bloomington: Indiana University Press, 1992. Rather than simply validate the indigenous authenticity of modern African novels by demonstrating their oral qualities, Julien classifies them according to their traditional generic origins—the epic, the initiation story, and the fable. Among the mainly francophone novelists examined, she notes that only male writers seem to follow the forms. In every case the novels both use and vary the genre to fit contemporary circumstances, and the fable in particular adapts to the late twentieth century form of Magical Realism. What is more important for Julien is not authenticity but accountability to the African audience of the writer.

Ker, David I. *The African Novel and the Modernist Tradition.* New York: Peter Lang, 1997. In this comparative study of anglophone African novels, Ker attempts to show that the authors—Wole Soyinka, Kofi Awoonor, Ngugi Wa Thiong'o, Ayi Kwei Armah, and Gabriel Okara—consciously adapted British and American models by such experimental novelists as Henry James, James Joyce, and William Faulkner to an African cultural and historical context. He thus places African fiction within an international modernist setting but asserts that modernism's response to cultural chaos is particularly appropriate to postcolonial Africa.

Loflin, Christine. *African Horizons: The Landscapes of African Fiction*. Westport, Conn.: Greenwood Press, 1998. In responding to the common view that African novels do not include detailed landscapes, Loflin demonstrates that landscapes of various types are present: natural, communal, domestic, social, political, economic, and religious. These are landscapes—horizons—defined from within by the African novelists themselves, not dictated by Western perspectives.

Mortimer, Mildred. *Journeys Through the French African Novel*. Portsmouth, N.H.: Heinemann, 1990. Beginning with Joseph Conrad's journey up the Congo in *Heart of Darkness*, Mortimer traces the various fictional journeys of male and female novelists, discovering that, for the most part, male journeys are outer and female inner. Both lead to enlightenment or liberation, if not to happiness or public victory. Because of these fictional journeys, demonstrating that the African has a language, a voice, and a destiny, the contemporary's voyage into Africa is no longer colored by Conrad's primitive image.

Nfah-Abbenyi, Juliana Makuchi. *Gender in African Women's Writing: Identity, Sexuality, and Difference*. Bloomington: Indiana University Press, 1997. Nfah-Abbenyi's purpose is to use the novels of nine anglophone and francophone women writers to help redefine African feminist and postcolonial theory and to place the power of self-definition in the hands of the women themselves regarding such issues as education, home, politics, and sexuality. The message of these writers is that African women are not victims but have power and must assume responsibility over their own destiny.

Owomoyela, Oyekan, ed. *A History of Twentieth-Century African Literatures*. Lincoln: University of Nebraska Press, 1993. Among its thirteen essays on language and literature in Africa, three are specifically on fiction from West, East, and South Africa, and one is on francophone fiction. Others deal with larger issues relevant to an understanding of African fiction, such as culture and identity, the use of European rather than African languages, the development of women's writing, and the status of publishing in various regions of the continent.

Palmer, Eustace. *The Growth of the African Novel*. London: Heinemann, 1979. Palmer states as his purpose a critical coherency that is lacking in previous studies of the African novel. He argues that the novels from Tutuola's *The Palm-Wine Drinkard* in 1952 to Ngugi's *Petals of Blood* in 1977 should be evaluated within an African context both on social and human relevance and on aesthetic quality. His actual evaluation of the quality pays attention to such matters as structural coherence, character portrayal, and technique.

THE AUSTRALIAN NOVEL

Today Australian novels enjoy a wide reception around the world. Yet this recognition came slowly and took place for the most part after World War II. History helped the Australian novel to be accepted overseas.

Following the war, Australia shed its British cocoon and entered the larger world. In particular, it strengthened its relationship with the United States, a situation that not only influenced the country's social structure and literary art but also opened the door to an immense audience. Some observers suggest that the distribution of Australian films in the early 1980's and their popularity abroad helped to introduce Australian fiction to a larger readership. During this period, as well, government support of the arts increased, and novelists benefited through financial grants and subsidized publishing. The appearance of a major figure in Australian literature, Patrick White (1912-1990), also helped bring the Australian novel to world attention. Initially published and recognized in the United States and Great Britain, White received the Nobel Prize in Literature in 1973, the first Australian writer to do so.

The Australian novel emerged long before, however; while many of the nineteenth century novels hold more historical than literary interest, a few have become classics. During the first half of the twentieth century, several notable novelists published books that found an Australian readership and in some instances received attention overseas. Today, long after the appearance of White's last book in 1986, the literary scene remains a lively one.

CONVICTS AND SETTLERS: 1788-1900

Australia's European settlement got under way in 1788, when the First Fleet of convicts and their keepers arrived in Sydney Harbor. This brutal and uneducated society hardly encouraged literary production. Instead, those in charge kept diaries and wrote reports on the settlement's development, the exotic flora and fauna, the land's geographical oddities, and the Aboriginal inhabitants. In 1830 a novel did appear, *Quintus Servinton*, an undistinguished book by a convict, Henry Savery (1791-1842), an educated man who had been transported to Australia for forgery. Although the author died in Australia after further criminal activities, the book's hero, Quintus, makes a fortune in the new land and returns happily to England. This plot line characterized many of the novels that followed. Written by homesick settlers, not convicts, the books treated the colony's rugged life harshly and allowed their heroes to go home to England with money they had accumulated by exploiting the country's resources.

The Transportation System (the euphemism for sending English convicts to the colony) lasted into the 1830's. One other convict, James Tucker (c. 1808-1888), wrote a novel about his experiences. The manuscript, dated around 1845, was not discovered until the 1920's and first appeared in an authentic edition in 1952. Tucker's *Ralph Rashleigh*, unlike Savery's book, depicts the convicts as overcoming the injustice dealt them and showing pride in their new country, where they hoped to lead a better life. In spite of the significance of the convict settlement and its inherent drama, only one other novel from the nineteenth century treated the Transportation System fully, and it was written by a free British settler, Marcus Clarke (1846-1881). His novel, *For the Term of His Natural Life* (1882), records the misadventures of Rufus Dawes, transported to Australia on false charges to suffer every degradation the Transportation System had to offer. Clarke's fictional version of the convict experience is generally considered to be the most important Australian novel from the 1800's.

As the nineteenth century progressed, the makeup of the country altered. The Transportation System was disbanded, the old convicts vanished, and free settlers arrived with plans to stay and advance the colony, attracted by the discovery of gold and the fortunes to be made in sheep. They shunted aside the colony's ignominious beginnings as an embarrassing happenstance. It was not until the mid-twentieth century that novelists again addressed the convict experience, in books such as Eleanor Dark's *The Timeless Land* (1941), Hal Porter's *The Tilted Cross* (1961),

Thomas Keneally's *Bring Larks and Heroes* (1967) and *The Playmaker* (1987), Jessica Anderson's *The Commandant* (1975), and Patrick White's *A Fringe of Leaves* (1976).

A new theme had now emerged: life in the bush. This theme embraced the severity of a land tormented by fire, dust, drought, flies, and untold hardships. It also created the bushman: individualistic, brave, unpretentious, self-deprecating, and, above all, loyal to his fellows—a much-prized quality known as mateship. In this predominantly male world, the long-suffering female settler usually remained invisible. A Sydney newspaper, the *Bulletin*, established in 1880, encouraged a brand of literary nationalism that promoted literature by Australians and about Australians out in the bush. Ironically, most Australians lived in the growing cities, including many of those who wrote bush stories. Although little of the short fiction published by the *Bulletin* lasted long, the newspaper's literary theory had a profound impact on Australian literature well into the twentieth century.

Two noteworthy novels from this era, both of which could be called "bush romances," are *The Recollections of Geoffry Hamlyn* (1859), by Henry Kingsley (1830-1876), and *Robbery Under Arms* (1888), by Rolf Boldrewood (pseudonym for Thomas Alexander Browne, 1826-1915). Kingsley chronicles the fates of three families who confront unbounded misfortunes and personal calamities but at last prevail. Although it has often been dismissed as too British in its sensibility and too romantic in its approach, the novel successfuly captures a period in Australian history. More engaging and more faithful to Australia, *Robbery Under Arms* offers a lively narrative that follows the adventures and destruction of a gang of bushrangers: lawless men, sometimes former convicts, who pillaged and terrorized the countryside.

THE BUSH TRADITION: 1788-1900

On January 1, 1901, the six separate colonies on the vast continent united to become the Commonwealth of Australia. The move toward federation had started in the 1840's but did not gain momentum until the late 1800's. Through the nineteenth century literary advancement of the bush myth and the chauvinis-

tic attitudes it incorporated, writers had taken an active part in the political maneuvering that led to federation. In the nationalistic fervor that dominated at the turn of the century, it was generally assumed that Australian literature would focus on what was considered authentic Australia and genuine Australians—that is, the bush and its inhabitants. While this prescribed framework produced a body of forgettable fiction in the first half of the century, it also brought forth a number of memorable novels that adhered to the tradition but overcame its limitations.

One writer who mastered the bush tradition was Katharine Susannah Prichard (1883-1969). *The Black Opal* (1921), for example, deals with the rigors of opal mining, while *Working Bullocks* (1926) depicts the lumber industry. Both are set in Western Australia, and both are politically charged. A dedicated Communist, Prichard saw literature as a way to improve Australia's social structure. The most admired of her novels, *Coonardoo: The Well in the Shadow* (1929), examines the tragic encounter between the Aboriginal and the white settler and was one of the first books to treat the Aboriginal in a sympathetic and honest manner. Another writer who took up the conflict between Australia's white and Aboriginal inhabitants was Xavier Herbert (1901-1984). His first major work, *Capricornia* (1938), is set in the vast, unsettled Northern Territory and traces the day-to-day lives of its assorted and colorful inhabitants. A tireless proponent of the superiority of the bush over the city, Herbert may well have been the last member of the nationalistic movement and his monumental book *Poor Fellow My Country* (1976) the last of its novels. This sprawling, fourteen-hundred-page narrative expands on the setting and people in the earlier novel and indicts modern Australia for turning its back on the virtues that the bush myth embodies. Although she wrote several books recording bush life, Miles Franklin (1879-1954) remains best known for *My Brilliant Career* (1901), which was made into an internationally acclaimed film. This narrative undermines the romance of the bush by exposing how miserably women fared on the land. Barbara Baynton (1857-1929) also offers a striking alternative to the bush romance by showing that country life could be grim and oppressive, especially for women. These themes dominate her novel *Human Toll* (1907) and her collection of short stories *Bush Studies* (1902).

Some of the most lasting novels from this era, at least in popular terms, are the mystery tales of Arthur Upfield (1888-1964), who continued to publish into the 1960's. Relating the adventures of a half-white, half-Aboriginal detective, the books brim with bush lore and provide an honest account of Aboriginal life. Although not great literature, the novels are entertaining and continue to draw readers from around the world.

From a purely literary standpoint, though, the finest work to come from this period is *The Fortunes of Richard Mahony* (a trilogy first published as one volume in 1930), by Henry Handel Richardson (pseudonym for Ethel Florence Lindesay Robertson, 1870-1946). Interestingly, Richardson left Australia for Germany at age eighteen, then settled in England, where she spent the rest of her life, except for one brief visit to Australia. Although her other novels take Europe as a setting, *The Getting of Wisdom* (1910), a narrative based on Richardson's time in a Melbourne girls school that was made into a successful film, and the trilogy return to the Australia of her childhood. For the most part, Richardson based *The Fortunes of Richard Mahony* on her own family's intermingling of tragic and fortunate circumstances in Australia from the gold rush days of the 1850's to her father's death and their impoverishment in the 1880's. In painstaking detail, Richardson re-creates colonial society, both its strengths and its defects, and in particular scrutinizes the role of women. This absolutely Australian exposition of the dark and the bright sides of colonial life fulfills the bush tradition but at the same time subverts it.

DIVERGENCE OF THEME AND FORM: THE NOVEL
AFTER 1946

The bush myth in Australian fiction did not simply vanish in the postwar period. Its champions fought hard to maintain its literary conventions. That is one reason that Patrick White's work gained only limited recognition at home until he received the Nobel Prize in 1973. In a 1958 essay titled "The Pro-

digal Son," published in *Australian Letters*—a rebellious journal determined to promote cultural "modernism"—White called Australian critics "dingoes . . . howling unmercifully" and expressed his desire to prove the Australian novel as "not necessarily the dreary dun-coloured offspring of journalistic realism."

Although most of White's twelve novels are set in Australia, he handled the inherited materials in new ways by turning away from the realistic form of Australian fiction and moving into metaphysical realms. His first postwar novel, *The Tree of Man* (1955), unfolds the lives of an ordinary Australian farm couple, but at the same time it probes the possibilities of their inner being. On one level, the book consolidates the elements of the bush heritage—the tyrannies of nature, such as drought, bushfires, dust, and floods, along with the patience and understated valor of the pioneer. At the same time, the narrative undermines these conventions, reversing them to explore the visionary's longing. The same could be said of *Voss* (1957), which inverts the myth of heroism as it traces the Australian desert explorations of Voss, whose tortured journey evolves into a metaphysical one. White continued to give new meaning to sanctioned Australian materials in novel after novel, a practice that culminates in *A Fringe of Leaves* (1976), which retells an Australian legend of a woman captured by Aborigines. In this version an escaped convict rescues her. On the surface, the narrative resembles a classic bush romance, but in truth it deals with the deeper understanding its heroine gains through her trials. White's style, especially his tortured syntax, is inseparable from what is being said. In all respects, White opened up fresh possibilities for a fiction once characterized by stark realism.

While only a handful of Australian critics recognized the impact these novels would have on their literature, many emerging writers realized that they were no longer required to "write Australian," as Michael Wilding (born 1942) described the demands of the bush tradition. Wilding, Frank Moorhouse (born 1938), and Murray Bail (born 1941) write in an experimental fashion far exceeding White and base their work on the urban experience. Another writer, Thea Astley (born 1925), said in an interview that no

Australian novelist who picked up a pen after White began writing could escape his influence. Publishing her first novel in 1958, Astley remained faithful to the Australian stock-in-trade and to the landscape. Yet she employed these familiar rudiments to place her characters in a position to seek and possibly to find what she called the spiritual "center," a theme that dominates her work. Like White, she forsakes the cheerful bushmen and long-suffering pioneer women for what she called "misfits," those who confront an often bitter vision as they exorcise what Astley describes as the "sore fruit of their souls."

Even after Patrick White's death in 1990, some writers and critics complained that he continued to dominate Australian fiction like a colossus under whose shadow novelists must work. That is an exaggeration. Although his massive achievement will endure and remain a landmark in the Australian novel—and in the world novel in English—he freed novelists from the demand that they "write Australian." As a result, Australian fiction flourishes. Australian novelists are published abroad; their books are well reviewed and are honored with international awards. Two writers in particular, Peter Carey (born 1943) and David Malouf (born 1934), deserve special notice.

Carey writes mainly about Australia, and his work is distinguished by wit, flights of imagination, cosmopolitan traits, and a metaphysical dimension. Critics have compared him with Jorge Luis Borges and Gabriel García Márquez. In *Illywhacker* (1985), whose title comes from an Australian slang term for confidence artist, Carey undermines the national myth in a tour de force that demonstrates how lies dominate the nation's history. He received the Booker Prize for *Oscar and Lucinda* (1988), a novel about colonial Australia that moves from reality into the fanciful. In *The Unusual Life of Tristan Smith* (1994), Carey invents a postcolonial nation that resembles Australia, which is in conflict with another imaginary nation, a powerful country that brings to mind the United States. In *Jack Maggs* (1998), he revisits Charles Dickens's *Great Expectations* (1860-1861) to unfold the history of the Australian convict Magwitch, who figures peripherally in the original novel.

Equally original in his writing, Malouf sometimes sets his work in Europe but has placed his best novels foursquare in the Australian milieu. He examines the plight of the artist in a postcolonial society through the depiction of a painter in *Harland's Half Acre* (1984), and in *Remembering Babylon* (1993) and *The Conversations at Curlow Creek* (1996) he returns to the colonial era. Malouf does not handle that material in the prescribed manner of the bush tradition but uses the settlers, convicts, and bushrangers to make a contemporary statement. Publishing first as a poet, Malouf writes in a luminous poetic style. In 1993 he received the prestigious IMPAC Dublin Literary Award for *Remembering Babylon*.

No discussion of the Australian novel would be complete without attention to that enigmatic figure, Christina Stead (1902-1983). Born in Australia, she left for England in her mid-twenties and for the next forty years lived in Europe and the United States. At the end of her life she returned to Sydney, where she died. Except for *Seven Poor Men of Sydney* (1934), an impressionistic account of city life, and the first half of *For Love Alone* (1944), none of her fiction takes place in Australia. Her reputation depends in great part on *The Man Who Loved Children*, set in the Washington, D.C., area. First published in 1940 but largely ignored until it was reissued in 1965, the novel has since then become an international classic. Her highly original, penetrating, at once bold and subtle narrative style is unparalleled in the Australian novel. Long ignored in Australia, Stead has found a secure place in the national literary canon.

Although Australia's original inhabitants have figured in Australian fiction throughout its history—too often not very favorably or authentically—there were few or no known novels by Aboriginals to give a firsthand account of their lives in a colonized condition. The foremost Aboriginal writer is Mudrooroo (born 1939), who published as Colin Johnson until he took his tribal name in 1988. His first two novels, *Wild Cat Falling* (1965) and *Long Live Sandawara* (1979), are conventional in structure and depict alienated Aboriginal men living on the fringes of society. In one of his most noted works, *Doctor Wooreddy's Prescription for Enduring the Ending of the World* (1983), Mudrooroo relates the history of the Tasmanian Aboriginals who were slaughtered during the nineteenth century. He tells this sad story in an impressive and inventive way, as the title suggests. Since this novel appeared, he has continued to work in the postmodern mode while employing Aboriginal materials to make statements about the precarious condition of Aboriginality. Many other Aboriginal writers have emerged, excelling more fully in drama, poetry, and the short story than in the novel.

The bush tradition has faded. Realism has been replaced by a fiction employing a mixture of experimental techniques. Standardized prose has been transformed into a melange of styles. Patrick White is dead. The Australian novel, however, flourishes, an inheritor of the very traditions it has relegated to literary history.

Robert L. Ross

BIBLIOGRAPHY

Jones, Joseph, and Johanna Jones. *Australian Fiction.* Boston: Twayne, 1983. Surveys the development of Australian fiction and provides an extensive bibliography of novels and critical works, the latter partially annotated.

Scheckter, John. *The Australian Novel, 1830-1980: A Thematic Introduction.* New York: Peter Lang, 1998. Traces the development of the Australian novel from its beginning to 1980, with full discussions of many major works. Examines how specific themes have been repeated and refined over the years.

Walker, Shirley, ed. *Who Is She?* New York: St. Martin's Press, 1983. Considers the treatment of women by fifteen male and female novelists from the nineteenth century to the end of the twentieth century.

Willbanks, Ray. *Australian Voices: Writers and Their Work.* Austin: University of Texas Press, 1991. Provides in-depth interviews with sixteen contemporary Australian novelists who talk about their work and the state of the art in Australia.

Wolfe, Peter, ed. *Critical Essays on Patrick White.* Boston: G. K. Hall, 1990. In a long introduction, Wolfe surveys White's development. Critical essays examine various aspects of White's themes and style. A comprehensive introduction to White's work.

CENTRAL AND SOUTHEASTERN EUROPEAN LONG FICTION

The Central and Southeastern European literatures discussed in this section—Polish, Czech, Slovak, Hungarian, Serbian, Croatian, Slovenian, and Macedonian—have a long history. Yet their long fiction did not develop until the second half of the nineteenth century, long after the genre had established itself in Western literatures. To be sure, there have been earlier manifestations—in 1810 in Serbian literature, in 1836 in Hungarian, in the 1840's in Polish—but they were only beginnings, while the full bloom would come decades later. There is a valid reason for this delay. All of these countries lived under a similar historical handicap: They were all dominated, until some time in the nineteenth century, by a foreign power that prevented them from fulfilling their national potential. While the novel flourished in other, more fortunate nations, the Polish, Czech, Slovak, Hungarian, and South Slavic lands were either in the process of liberating themselves from a centuries-old yoke or were still under domination. For the same reason, the literary movements that prevailed in Western and Russian literatures in the eighteenth century and the first half of the nineteenth century came to Central and Southeastern European literatures decades later. Furthermore, all of these peoples found themselves, around the middle of the nineteenth century, in the midst of a powerful national revival, during which literature began to flourish suddenly and, understandably, in a somewhat emotional and romantic manner. It is normal that, at such times, genres other than the novel—poetry, drama, even the short story—occupy prominent positions. All of these factors contributed heavily to the slow rise of the novel in these literatures.

As these national reawakenings began to draw to a close, the novel began to grow. Because romanticism lingered and the euphoria of the national renaissance was still in the air, there were still romantic, patriotic, and historical novels. Thus, the national renaissance contributed after all to the growth of the novel in the second half of the nineteenth century, which would eventually—and organically—lead to a flood in the next decades. The flood swelled as realism reached these literatures, again belatedly, and social conditions and problems swayed writers to pay more attention to them. The readership, hitherto rather small, grew to the extent that it demanded more substantial works, such as the novel. It is no surprise, therefore, that the rise and full blossoming of the novel (quantitatively, if not qualitatively) coincided with the growth of social consciousness.

The enthusiasm centered on the national revival and the increased social awareness were, therefore, the two main forces that enabled the novel to come into its own in this area. There were, however, other common features. Because these societies were in the nineteenth century overwhelmingly rural, the novelists concentrated on the life of the peasants and identified with them. As these societies became more urbanized, the focus of the writers shifted accordingly; around the middle of the twentieth century, novels about city life—whether they focused on urbanites or on newcomers from the villages—greatly outnumbered those with rural themes. By the same token, as social problems sharpened, often to the point of confrontation, novelists' interest in these problems grew. Consequently, the number of socially engaged, even revolutionary, writers in this area is disproportionately large.

One additional common feature in all of these literatures is the interest in, and the influence of, larger and more advanced literatures, especially those of Western Europe, Russia, and the United States. There is no denial that these writers were, to a larger or lesser extent, shaped by the models abroad, despite their deep roots in the native soil. The earlier the period, the greater was that influence. Today, this process is still taking place, although on a much more sophisticated level and with an increasing mutuality.

Finally, similar historical circumstances have brought on similar literary developments, especially in the sequence of literary movements, almost always in the same order. The simple fact that these countries, except Yugoslavia to some degree, suffered the same political fate after World War II also accounts for similar literary experiences. All of these factors have led to striking similarities in the literatures, especially in the novel, of the entire region.

This is not to say that one should always speak about these literatures in the same breath. On the contrary, they arise from separate countries in which there are many differences in the ethnic, cultural, linguistic, and even historical sense. For example, the fact that Polish, Czech, Serbian, Croatian, Slovenian, and Macedonian literatures are Slavic does not make them interchangeable; one cannot be read intelligently by the readers of another (Serbian and Croatian are the only exceptions). Moreover, the fact that Slavic countries have often been closely connected through common or related historical experience does not eliminate the inevitable and often basic differences between them. Therefore, to speak of their literatures together or separately is simply a matter of personal preference or convenience.

Long fiction in the Central and Southeastern European countries reflects both the similarities and the differences of their respective literatures and is, perhaps more than any other genre, a true mirror of their successes and travails, their riches and limitations.

Vasa D. Mihailovich

THE POLISH NOVEL

While the history of the Polish novel in the strict sense goes back only a little further than two hundred years, the beginnings of Polish long fiction can be traced back as far as the Middle Ages and the Renaissance. The fifteenth and sixteenth centuries gave birth to numerous chronicles, hagiographies, legends, and apocrypha, in which the proportion of fictional and nonfictional elements varied. Even a genre as apparently factographic as the chronicle usually included fictional or fantastic passages, and apocrypha were purely fictional variations on biblical motifs. The subsequent development of long fiction in the late Renaissance and the long period of the baroque (which lasted approximately until the middle of the eighteenth century) moved along two distinctly different routes. In terms of the sociology of literature, the difference can be seen as a gradually widening rift between the cultural elite and the popular readership, as well as between "high" and "low" literary genres. The genre of

verse epic evolved from among the "high" genres to acquire the greatest significance in the seventeenth century. Of the "lower" genres, medieval legends and apocrypha developed into the special genre of "histories," popular tales loosely based on historical, mythological, or biblical plots. Meanwhile, nonfictional genres such as memoirs, itineraries, and diaries, which flourished particularly in the seventeenth century, also laid foundations for the emergence of the Polish novel, insofar as they provided it with specific models of construction and style.

The creation of the genre of the novel in Poland, however, would have been delayed still further if a sudden outburst of interest in Western literatures had not occurred around the middle of the eighteenth century. The period of the Enlightenment, which in Poland coincided with the reign of the last Polish king, Stanisław August Poniatowski (who reigned from 1764 to 1795), was marked by the rapidly increasing popularity of English, French, and German novels, which were read both in the original and in translations or loose adaptations; in particular, translations of Daniel Defoe, Jonathan Swift, Henry Fielding, Tobias Smollett, Samuel Richardson, Voltaire, Jean-Jacques Rousseau, Alain-René Lesage, and Johann Wolfgang von Goethe were available from about the 1760's.

Both foreign and native influences can be detected in the first Polish novel *sensu stricto*, *Mikołaja Doświadczyńskiego przypadki* (the adventures of Nicholas Doświadczyński), which was published in 1776 by the most prominent poet of the Polish Enlightenment, Ignacy Krasicki (1735-1801). In full accord with the didactic role assigned to literature in that epoch, with *Mikołaja Doświadczyńskiego przypadki*, Krasicki initiated the genre of the "educational novel," in which the central character goes through various stages in order to demonstrate how Prejudice and Error can be finally overcome by Reason. Krasicki's novel, a liberal mixture of satiric, realistic, utopian, and didactic elements, gave the initial stimulus to the more far-reaching experiments in the field of the newly created genre. Authors such as Dymitr Krajewski (1746-1817), Józef Kossakowski (1738-1794), and Stanisław Kostka Potocki (1752-1821) produced other educational novels and "novel-treatises";

Krasicki (in another novel), Franciszek Salezy Jezierski (1740-1791), and Anna Mostowska (c. 1762-1833) created the Polish version of the historical novel; the sentimental novel, sometimes including both elements of psychological insight and realistic portrayals of society, was represented by Ludwik Kropiński (1767-1844), Maria Wirtemberska (1768-1854), and Klementyna Tańska-Hoffmanowa (1798-1845); the novels closest to the realistic mode were written by Julian Ursyn Niemcewicz (1757-1841) and Fryderyk Skarbek (1792-1866), who was also influenced in other of his novels by the style of Lawrence Sterne.

In spite of the generally rationalistic character of the Enlightenment, the first Polish gothic novels (chiefly by Mostowska) also emerged; the most masterful example of this genre was that of Jan Potocki (1761-1815), *Manuscrit de Saragosse* (*The Saragossa Manuscript*, 1960), written in French between 1803 and 1815 and published in Polish as *Rękopis znaleziony w Saragossie* only in 1847. As far as its poetics was concerned, the Polish novel of the Enlightenment was characterized by its didactic purpose, personal narrator, and frequent use of "authenticating" devices (for example, epistolary or diaristic forms, or the convention of the "found manuscript").

In Poland, the subsequent epoch of Romanticism was the period of the greatest triumphs of the nonprosaic genres, such as poetry and poetic drama—though certain epic poems, such as the famous *Pan Tadeusz: Czyli, Ostatni Zajazd na litwie historia Szlachecka zr. 1811 i 1812 we dwunastu ksiegach wierszem* (1834; *Pan Tadeusz: Or, The Last Foray in Lithuania, a Tale of Gentlefolk in 1811 and 1812, in Twelve Books in Verse*, 1917), by Adam Mickiewicz (1798-1855), can be said to represent long fiction in verse. The novel, however, was far from insignificant in this period. On the contrary, the first half of the nineteenth century was marked by the rapid evolution of realistic techniques in the novel, developed principally under the powerful influence of Honoré de Balzac (Stendhal, Charles Dickens, and—in the field of the historical novel—Sir Walter Scott were also important influences). Another source of inspiration was the subjective and fantastic prose of Sterne, Nikolai Gogol, Jean Paul, and E. T. A. Hoffmann.

The towering figure in the Polish novel of the first half of the nineteenth century was Józef Ignacy Kraszewski (1812-1887), an amazingly prolific author of hundreds of novels ranging in subject matter from historical topics to contemporary life; his chief undertaking was an enormous sequence of novels that presented the history of Poland at various stages from its legendary beginnings until the end of the eighteenth century. Zygmunt Kaczkowski (1825-1896) was another important historical novelist of the period, while Józef Korzeniowski (1797-1863), Józef Dzierzkowski (1807-1865), and Walery Łoziński (1837-1861) were the most prominent novelists to deal with contemporary themes in a realistic manner. A special place is occupied by Ludwik Sztyrmer (1809-1886), who represented an extreme in his narrative subjectivism and fascination with psychopathology, and by Henryk Rzewuski (1791-1866), who drew from the seventeenth century tradition to create a specifically Polish genre of *gawęda* (a first-person tale told in "oral" style).

After the defeat of an uprising against Russia in 1863 and 1864, Polish literature entered the epoch of positivism, which was characterized, among other things, by an abrupt turn from poetry to prose. Realistic description of society's woes became the principal task of literature, and the novel seemed the most fit genre to perform it. Bolesław Prus (the pen name of Aleksander Głowacki, 1845-1912) was the most accomplished novelist of Polish positivism. A journalist turned fiction writer, he wrote a number of excellent novels, ranging in theme from that of *Faraon* (1897; *The Pharaoh and the Priest*, 1902), a novel on the mechanisms of political power as exemplified by ancient Egypt, to that of *Lalka* (1890; *The Doll*, 1972), a panorama of Polish society after the failure of the 1863 uprising. Eliza Orzeszkowa (1841-1910) was the most outspoken champion of positivist ideas among female writers; in several novels she dealt with specific social issues, such as the emancipation of women and the fate of the Jewish minority, while her chief work, *Nad Niemnem* (1888; on the bank of the Niemen), is another vast panorama of society's life. Henryk Sienkiewicz (1846-1916) was particularly well-known in the West, thanks to his novel on ancient Rome, *Quo vadis* (1896; *Quo Vadis: A Narrative of the Time of Nero*, 1896), which won him the Nobel Prize in Literature; in his own country, however, he enjoyed tremendous popularity for his novels on Poland's historical past, *Krzyżacy* (1900; *The Knights of the Cross*, 1900; also as *The Teutonic Knights*, 1943) and the trilogy consisting of *Ogniem i mieczem* (1884; *With Fire and Sword: An Historical Novel of Poland and Russia*, 1890), *Potop* (1886; *The Deluge: An Historical Novel of Poland, Sweden, and Russia*, 1891), and *Pan Wołodyjowski* (1887-1888; *Pan Michael: An Historical Novel of Poland, the Ukraine, and Turkey*, 1893).

The traditional kind of realism, which had reigned in the positivist novel, at the end of the nineteenth century developed, under the visible influence of Émile Zola, into the naturalistic trend in Polish fiction. This naturalism, however, was often heavily indebted to the poetics of Symbolism, which at the same time began to flourish in poetry. The most prominent fiction writer of the postpositivist generation, Stefan Zeromski (1864-1925), can be considered an inventor of a specific form of novel in which a realistic, sometimes naturalistic, vision is contrasted with a highly emotional, lyric style. Władysław Reymont (1867-1925), another Polish Nobel Prize winner, was close to naturalism in his unflinching portrayal of the industrial city of Lodz in *Ziemia obiecana* (1899; *The Promised Land*, 1927) and in his epic picture of peasant life in *Chłopi* (1904-1909; *The Peasants*, 1924-1925). Wacław Berent (1873-1940) also began his career as a naturalist, but he later devoted himself to seeking new technical solutions in both contemporary and historical fiction. His highly original novel *Ozimina* (1911; winter wheat), for instance, employs an innovative device of shifting points of view in order to present a cross section of Polish society's attitudes. Other experimental options in novelistic narration and construction were sought by Stanisław Brzozowski (1878-1911) and Karol Irzykowski (1873-1944), both of whom were better known for their literary criticism; it was only later that their novels began to be appreciated as they deserved to be.

In the interwar period of 1918 to 1939, Polish novelists continued their search for new technical devices and thematic areas, although there was no lack of fairly conservative solutions. Such an extreme of traditional storytelling was represented, for example, by Maria Dąbrowska (1889-1965) and her family saga *Noce i dnie* (1932-1934; nights and days). Two other female novelists, Zofia Nałkowska (1884-1954) and Maria Kuncewiczowa (born 1899), explored the theme of the subconscious with great subtlety. The works of Juliusz Kaden-Bandrowski (1885-1944) introduced a new kind of political novel, a combination of *roman à clef* with expressionistic deformation. The echoes of naturalism and expressionism could still be heard in the novels of Józef Wittlin (1896-1976) or Zbigniew Uniłowski (1909-1937). At the same time, the three perhaps most important fiction writers of the interwar period were, each in his own way, experimenters in both artistic philosophy and technique. Stanisław Ignacy Witkiewicz (1885-1939), in his loosely constructed novels such as *Nienasycenie* (1930; *Insatiability: A Novel in Two Parts*, 1977), offered a half catastrophic and half-grotesque prophecy of the approaching totalitarianism. Bruno Schulz (1892-1942) published two collections of short stories, which can be considered segments of a complex whole; the mythologized world of his private obsessions is reflected in a highly subjective narrative technique. Finally, Witold Gombrowicz (1904-1969), in his prewar novel *Ferdydurke* (1937; English translation, 1961)—complemented, after the war, by three other of his novels—concealed under a seemingly absurd plot a profound analysis of the mechanisms of interhuman relations.

In post-1944 Poland, long fiction retained its prominent place among other literary genres despite the censorship troubles that seemed to affect the novel more than any other genre. Although the reign of Socialist Realism (from 1949 to 1955) brought a visible decline in artistic quality of the novel, Polish fiction gained momentum after the 1956 "thaw" in cultural policies of the state, and it continues to vigorously seek new creative solutions. The most prominent postwar novelists are Jerzy Andrzejewski (1909-1983), who, after the realistic *Popiół i diament* (1948; *Ashes and Diamonds*, 1962), shifted toward parabolic fiction in *Ciemonosci kryją ziemię* (1957; *The Inquisitors*, 1960) and *Bramy raju* (1960; *The Gates of Paradise*, 1962) before returning to direct social criticism in *Miazga* (1972; the pulp); Kazimierz Brandys (born 1916), whose fiction often employs nonfictional genres, such as the diary, letter, and essay; Jacek Bocheński (born 1926), author of parabolic novels on ancient Rome; Tadeusz Konwicki (born 1926), who offered catastrophic and bitter visions of contemporary Poland in *Sennik współczesny* (1963; *A Dreambook for Our Time*, 1969), *Kompleks polski* (1977; *The Polish Complex*, 1981), and *Mała apokalipsa* (1979; *A Minor Apocalypse*, 1983); Julian Stryjkowski (born 1905), author of *Austeria* (1966; *The Inn*, 1971) and other novels that revive the history of Jews in Poland; Tadeusz Parnicki (born 1908), a unique innovator in the field of the historical novel; and Stanisław Lem (born 1921), an equally original writer of science fiction and philosophical parables. Among a younger generation, Adam Zagajewski (born 1945), Janusz Głowacki (born 1938), and Janusz Anderman (born 1949) scored artistic successes with their novels on contemporary Poland.

Stanisław Barańczak

THE CZECH NOVEL

Although Czech literature is the oldest of the Slavic literatures, its long fiction appeared relatively late, in the nineteenth century. This may be the result of the twofold handicap of the Czech culture mentioned by the great Czech critic Arne Novák (1889-1939): religion and nationalism.

Religion, particularly dissenting religion, or Protestantism, mixed with the national cause, first isolated Bohemia from the European cultural context, and when, during the Counter-Reformation, it was forcibly reattached to it, the national cause suffered. The latter meant that Czech publications were discouraged, and only at the end of the eighteenth century and then gloriously in the nineteenth did a national revival take place. This revival invested literature with tremendous responsibilities: Literature represented the nation. It set out with a grand aim to prevent the nation from perishing, and it accom-

plished that goal. It also laid the foundations for the future independent state. This nation-building role was fulfilled primarily by poetry; fiction had a relatively less prominent part in it. Nevertheless, considering the shortness of time, Czech fiction developed remarkably quickly and in astonishing variety, perhaps as a result of the central position occupied by the Czechs in the reigning cultural and particularly literary world at the time. Czechs were aware of the German culture as well as the triumphs of the Russian novels. They read the English as well as the French masters. Most important, the Czech novel embarked on a mission that continues to this day and that could be considered the most notable of all literary endeavors: the mission of self-discovery. It is in this vein that the first Czech masterpiece of note must be approached.

Humbly entitled *Babička* (1855; *The Grandmother*, 1891), this novel by Božena Němcová (1820-1862) is a portrait of her grandmother, whose gift was the power to transform the life of her grandchildren, who were doomed by modest circumstances. Hailed as the major fictional artistic legacy of the post-Romantic era, the novel succeeds in bringing to life an admirable character whose grace, charm, and wit has endeared Němcová to generations of readers.

A direct antithesis to Němcová is another female writer, Karolina Světlá (1830-1899). While Němcová still represents a woman who honors tradition, occasionally transcending it in the name of love, Světlá is a feminist often compared to George Sand and George Eliot. Contemporary problems, set against a background of country settings and picturesque local customs, are typical of her fiction. Representative of this type of novel is her *Vesnický román* (1867; a village romance), which proved to be a generic predecessor of a group of novels by writers predominantly concerned with the village novel but who belong to a later generation, such as Karel V. Rais (1859-1926), Vilém Mrštík (1863-1912), and Josef Holeček (1853-1929).

In fact, the novels of Světlá foreshadow, in a curiously incomplete and often frustrating manner, the main directions of Czech fiction in the nineteenth century: the social, the village, and the historical, to list the main ones.

An attempt has been made to place *The Grand-mother* into the category of the social novel, but the works of Gustav Pfleger Moravský (1833-1875), Matej Anastasia Šimáček (1860-1913), and Josef Karel Šlejhar (1864-1914) better exemplify this type.

By far the most influential type of novel written in the nineteenth century was the historical novel. Here, the Czech Protestant cause—its defeat and what followed it—proved irresistible to nationalist-minded Czech novelists: V. Beneš Třebízský (1849-1884), Zikmund Winter (1846-1912), and, most important, Alois Jirásek (1851-1930).

Jirásek covered the whole range of Czech history, and his importance is analogous to that of Henryk Sienkiewicz in Poland. It is no exaggeration to say that Jirásek consciously blended historical material into myths designed to augment the nation-building that was going on in his lifetime. That this effort was often accompanied by distortions, simplifications, and whitewashing, to say nothing of the fact that it ignored the obviously negative consequences of at least some historical Czech actions, is beyond doubt. Also beyond doubt is Jirásek's powerful historical vision, his ability to project himself to distant times and to grasp or re-create the motivation of historical characters in a spellbinding and often emotionally moving manner. This is true of his *Proti všem* (1893; against everyone) and his trilogy *Bratrstvo* (1899-1908; the brethren), as well as of his numerous historical novels, with the exception of those treating a more recent, revivalist past, such as his tetralogy *U nás* (1896-1903; in our land).

The period of realism announced in the work of K. Čapek-Chod (1860-1927) can be understood either as a transitional period leading up to the three most important interwar novelists, Jaroslav Hašek (1883-1923), Karel Čapek (1890-1938), and Vladislav Vančura (1891-1942), or as the beginning of an as yet unconcluded period of realism of many different varieties.

Hašek's *Osudy dobrého vojáka Švejka ve světove valky* (1921-1923; *The Good Soldier: Švejk*, 1930; also as *The Good Soldier Švejk and His Fortunes in the World War*, 1973) is a masterpiece of the satiric novel, while Čapek's trilogy, comprising *Hordubal*

(1933; English translation, 1934), *Povětroň* (1934; *Meteor*, 1935), and *Obyčejný život* (1934; *An Ordinary Life*, 1936), offers a fine example of the philosophical novel. Vančura's experimentation was stylistic and, of the three, is least accessible to a foreign reader; these three authors taken together represent a firm foundation for the flourishing of the novel after World War II.

Somewhat isolated seems Jaroslav Durych (1886-1962), a brilliant novelist who is an antipode to Jirásek in his own historical novels concerned with the same Hussite period, to which Durych takes a contrasting, Catholic approach.

The novel, as well as all literature, suffered after the communist takeover in 1948, when a large-scale Sovietization of cultural life was enforced, together with the absurd requirements of Socialist Realism: to write in a way that would not anger the authorities. The tragic 1950's ended in gradual liberalization and the appearance of three great novelists: Bohumil Hrabal (born 1914), Josef Škvorecký (born 1924), and Milan Kundera (born 1929). Hrabal is a narrative genius with an unerring eye for the surreal and the grotesque in everyday life. In his fiction, accidents, violence, sex, and drinking are mixed with sentimentalism and the moving pathos of unexpected lyric passages. Even though after initial prohibition Hrabal was allowed to publish, he was forced to make many compromises with state censors, as is evident in those works that are published abroad.

Škvorecký and Kundera, in that order, were forced to emigrate after the liberalization of the 1960's abruptly ended in the Soviet invasion of Czechoslovakia in 1968. This exile was a mixed blessing; Whatever the discomforts of the authors, the world gained two great novelists. Kundera's *Le Livre du rire et de l'oubli* (1979; *The Book of Laughter and Forgetting*, 1980; in Czech as *Kniha smíchu a zapomnění*, 1981) and, even more, his *L'Insoutenable Légèreté de l'être* (1984; *The Unbearable Lightness of Being*, 1984; in Czech as *Nesnesitelná lehkost bytí*, 1985), as well as his many essays published in leading literary magazines in the West, have made him the leading spokesman for the endangered entity of Central Europe, whose roots and sympathies lie in the West. Kundera's prose carries the influence of Hašek, Čapek, and Vančura into a synthesis always grounded in a philosophical theme approached with irony and sometimes even misanthropy.

Škvorecký's *Zbabělci* (1958; *The Cowards*, 1970) is a masterpiece of dramatic action seen through the eyes of an adolescent interested in girls and jazz. Much more ambitious, but less successful, is his *Příběh inženyra lidskych duší* (1977; *The Engineer of Human Souls: An Entertainment on the Old Themes of Life, Women, Fate, Dreams, the Working Class, Secret Agents, Love, and Death*, 1984), in which the narrator, like Škovrecký himself, an émigré Czech professor at a university in Toronto, deals with personal and political problems with the help of his experiences under the Nazi and then communist regime in Bohemia. Škvorecký's work, although informed by a powerful intellect, is less elaborate and less pretentious than the work of Hrabal and Kundera. A quiet sense of rationality and moderation radiates from Škvorecký's writing, which is infused with a gentle humor.

Hrabal, Kundera, and Škvorecký are worthy successors to Hašek, Čapek, and Vančura. Their achievement marks the solid establishment of a tradition of long fiction that is entirely Czech—not only self-sufficient but also in a position to enter and influence world literature. In the case of Kundera, such influence is already apparent.

Peter Petro

THE SLOVAK NOVEL

Slovak literature, and consequently Slovak fiction, is less well-known than the neighboring Czech fiction. This could be a negative consequence of having a binational state. The country was, until it split into the Czech Republic and Slovakia in 1993, known as Czechoslovakia, and if one thought about translating anything of "its" literature, one thought first of Czech literature. The world is less aware of the existence of the "other" literature. There are still some encyclopedias that carry articles about Czechoslovakian literature, even though no such entity exists.

In fact, there is, besides very good poetry, interesting and occasionally brilliant fiction to be found in Slovak literature. It is very much unlike the fiction of any of its neighbors, perhaps because it reflects radically different living conditions: Slovakia, like Switzerland, is a country of mountains, of shepherds and lumberjacks, but also of rapidly growing cities, the capital of which, Bratislava, always had a cosmopolitan atmosphere because of its German and Hungarian population. The center of gravity of Slovak fiction then, not surprisingly, lies in the exploitation of the geographical fact that it derives from a country of mountains. The Slovak village novel is characteristically concerned with unspoiled, natural people; the traditional lifestyle of the people of the mountains is juxtaposed to the artificial existence offered by the cities. This contrast is particularly well-developed and fortified by an indigenous Slovak tradition of so-called lyric prose. Indeed, while there are urban Slovak novels and experimental novels that betray common Central European—that is, Western—heritage, the main accomplishment of Slovak long fiction is the development and establishment of the rich genre of lyric prose.

Jozef Ignác Bajza (1755-1836) stands at the beginning of Slovak prose with his novel *René mládenca prihodi a skúsenosti* (1783; the adventures and experiences of the young man René), published even before the codification of the Slovak language (1843). The novel bears traces of the influence of Voltaire and Christoph Martin Wieland.

The first half of the nineteenth century was taken up with the gradual establishment of the revivalist movement, expressed in literature mainly through poetry. Prose reaffirmed itself in the second half of the century with *Reštaurácia* (1860; the elections), by Ján Kalinčiak (1822-1871), wherein the world of the Slovak gentry's life is pictured in Hungary before 1848, the revolutionary year. The problem of Slovak politics in the absence of a Slovak state (for Slovakia was then a part of Hungary) is indirectly posed through the gentle satire of manners and politics.

Far more valuable are the works of a leading man of letters, Svetozár Hurban Vajanský (1847-1916), who dealt sensitively with a wide range of problems—social, domestic, national, and philosophical—

in his *Letiace tiene* (1883; fleeting shadows) and *Suchá ratolest'* (1884; the withered branch).

Martin Kukučín (1860-1928), often considered the best Slovak novelist, spent much of his life abroad, forced by unbearable conditions to leave his motherland. Indeed, millions of his fellow Slovaks began leaving their country toward the end of the nineteenth century, settling in the United States, Canada, and elsewhere in such numbers that, one hundred years later, there were more Slovaks abroad than in Slovakia. Kukučín's work, in five volumes, *Mat' volá* (1926-1927; mother is calling), deals with the fate of Croatian emigrants in Latin America, but his short stories, plays, and other novels are firmly rooted in Slovak soil.

A follower of Kukučín and in many respects his superior in the scope, quality, and the ambitiousness of his novelistic enterprise is Jozef Cíger-Hronský (1896-1961), best known for his novel *Jozef Mak* (1933; English translation, 1984), which deals with the life of a silent villager in a sensitive, lyric manner imbued with a pathos based on a Christian worldview. Among Hronský's other novels, particularly brilliant are two in which one can trace connections with *Jozef Mak*, thus establishing a "trilogy": *Pisár Gráč* (1940; Gráč the clerk) and *Andreas Búr Majster* (1948; Andreas Búr, master). This trilogy of masterpieces is unequaled in Slovak literature. No one has matched Hronský's ability to capture the "spirit" or the "essence" of Slovak existence and to express what it meant to be a Slovak in some key and dramatic periods of the modern history of Slovakia.

Milo Urban (1904-1982) received considerable attention for his *Živý bič* (1927; the living whip), which, together with Hronský's *Jozef Mak*, belongs among the outstanding novels of the interwar period. This period was particularly rich and represents an explosion of talents and styles: the decadent experimentation of Gejza Vámoši (1901-1956), the proletarian novels of Peter Jilemnický (1901-1949), and the gradual establishment of lyric prose through the work of L. Ondrejov (1901-1962), M. Figuli (born 1909), F. Švantner (1912-1950), and Dobroslav Chrobák (1907-1951).

After 1948, the communist takeover slowed down the promising coming-of-age of the Slovak long fiction but could not stop its development in the hands of F. Hečko (1905-1960), Franko Král' (1903-1955), and their younger followers, such as Vladimír Mináč (born 1922) and Dominik Tatarka (born 1913), who later developed into a fiercely independent spirit best known for his *Prútené kreslá* (1962; straw chairs) and *Démon súhlasu* (1963; the demon of acquiescence).

Strangely enough, the most successful and original of a newer generation of Slovak novelists, Vincent Šikula (born 1936), tries to link up with the prewar novel; his model is Hronský. This is clear from his trilogy *Majstri, Muškát, Vilma* (1976-1979; masters, geranium, Vilma).

The various ups and downs of communist literary politics during the late twentieth century notwithstanding, Slovak literature continued to flourish, even though the price may have been a compromise—flight into history or even the inability to publish. This paradoxical situation can be explained by a strong showing of new talent and a great variety of approaches observable in the incoming novelistic production. Nor is it always the kind of literature that would be faithful to the beginnings, or to its mountainous geography, which inspired the novelists to look inward with pride and find the purity and model among the simple mountain folk. Today Slovak fiction bears all the attributes of modern urban literature. The worthy exceptions to this "follow the West" movement, such as Šikula, prove, nevertheless, that a much surer way for future Slovak literature would be the movement back to roots, a movement which, at any rate, has always been present in it.

Peter Petro

THE HUNGARIAN NOVEL

In contrast with Western Europe, where the history of the modern novel had its beginnings with the rise of the Third Estate, in Hungary this genre appeared around the end of the eighteenth century, at the time when a sizable and nationally conscious native bourgeoisie did not yet exist. The most bourgeois of literary forms was thus championed by the more enlightened representatives of the privileged classes.

Another peculiarity of late eighteenth century Hungarian literary life was that while nearly every intellectual realized the necessity to develop a sovereign national cultural atmosphere, imitations of Western European forms continued to prevail. In the case of the novel, the example of the English model, with its moderate, moralizing sentimentality, and of the French writers, with their cooler, rational detachment, were particularly strong influences. The German trends were also prominent on the scene, but, in part because of the uncomfortable presence of Habsburg domination, a number of Hungarian writers were reluctant to follow them.

In accordance with what many Hungarian intellectuals adopted as their motto, "The chief hope of a country's happiness lies through knowledge," the earliest novels were earmarked by enlightened curiosity and newly gained erudition. The various aspects of Neoclassicism were mixed with the baroque and rococo elements of the Habsburg culture, while faint signs of sentimental and Romantic attitudes foreshadowed the developments that were to take place during the nineteenth century.

There was an increasing popular interest in the novel, but it was available to Hungarian readers mostly in the form of poor translations (or, more often, adaptations) based upon foreign works of questionable value. The term *roman* even acquired a pejorative connotation among some intellectuals, who criticized the genre as much for its "immorality" as for its lack of aesthetic standards. Among the earliest examples of original Hungarian novels, the most successful were those that catered to the sentimental outlook of the women readers and the nationalistic pride of the men. Thus, in a country where lyric and narrative poetry were traditionally considered the chief forms of literary expression, the novel was well on its way to becoming the new, modern national epic.

After the beginning of the nineteenth century, a small but determined group of intellectuals initiated a thorough reform of the Hungarian language. They emphasized originality, individuality, and new aesthetic principles, and they revealed their concern for the development of a less feudalistic and tradition-bound society by coining phrases and words to fit timely concepts, thus opposing the linguistic (and social) isolationism of their opponents. They may have broken some of the rules of grammar and "offended the spirit of the language," as their critics claimed, but the majority of their linguistic innovations passed into literary and everyday use. Their campaign also brought literature to the center of Hungarian public life. Shrewd publishers offered more and more novels, in order to satisfy popular demand. The quality of these writings improved rather slowly, and imitations and adaptations continued to prevail for decades; nevertheless, by the 1840's a number of significant novels dealing with the social problems of the past and the present appeared. Exhibiting the positive influence of the French and English Romantics, Hungarian writers introduced well-drawn characters in fast-paced action, and their manner of depiction also became more convincing.

Besides offering plenty of adventure and excitement to the readers, Romanticism was also in perfect accord with the birth or revival of national consciousness sweeping Europe during the nineteenth century. One important aspect of this process was that men of letters made the study of folk life and folk literature one of their aims, in order to depict better the lives of, and eventually to give voice to the long-neglected aspirations of, the commoners. In Hungary, this trend held out the promise of a more democratic approach to national characterization as well as to literary activity in general. Romantic philosophy was domesticated by equating the concept of True Man with that of the True Hungarian. During what came to be called an "era of the people," populist aesthetic principles and practices came to prevail, and increasingly realistic elements were introduced into the essentially Romantic prose of the mid-nineteenth century. To a certain extent, this was true even in the case of Mór Jókai (1825-1904), the greatest and most prolific Romantic storyteller of Hungary, whose imaginative power, spontaneously allied with the prevailing sentiments of his countrymen, was supremely responsible for the creation of many national illusions.

Romanticism continued to dominate the Hungarian novel, even though there were writers, most notably József Eötvös (1813-1871), whose works approached in quality the best that European realism had to offer. The problems and contradictions of society, however, became the central theme of long fiction only after the 1867 Compromise between the Habsburg ruler and his formerly rebellious Hungarian subjects. Influenced by imported positivist, utilitarian, and even socialist ideas, a number of middle-class writers came to view themselves as members of an "unnecessary" generation and vented their feelings of disappointment in a flood of bitterly critical *Bildungsromane.*

After the policies of Dualist Hungary achieved a certain degree of "consolidation," the tendencies toward objective realism and social criticism again were neglected. Johann Strauss the Younger's operetta *Der Zigeunerbaron* (1885; *The Gypsy Baron,* 1954), based on an 1885 Jókai novel of the same title, could with some justification be considered the representative artistic creation of the period. The anecdotal approach of Jókai and his followers was so prevalent that, even as the *fin de siècle* brought more of the problems of society to the surface, Hungarian writers clung to the genre of the melancholy, resignation-filled short story in their presentation of the new realities. Kálmán Mikszáth (1847-1910) may be considered the most successful exception: In his novels, the influence of the best and worst traits (imaginative, dramatic narration and anecdotal provincialism) of Jókai were gradually replaced by a bitingly critical, though never combative, strain of social satire. As the first major Hungarian writer whose Romanticism was subordinated to realism, the influence of Mikszáth on subsequent generations of prose writers was decisive.

Many Hungarian writers were associated with the literary journalism of the growing cities, and this experience was instrumental in their adopting subjective and relative aesthetic values and, consequently, shocking their audiences with adventurous free-association techniques. They struggled hard in order to successfully present their society, which was troubled by sharp contradictions between the glitter of Budapest and the squalor of the villages, between the impressive economic growth and the self-destructive pro-

cess of mass emigration, and between the prevalence of national complacency and the intellectual ferment brought about by an illustrious generation of thinkers and artists. The periodical *Nyugat* (meaning "west"), published from 1908 to 1941, financed by "new money," and cultivated mostly by urban intellectuals, attracted a loose coalition of artistic and literary talent, difficult to classify into any single category but strongly influenced by the fashionable "isms" of contemporary Western Europe. Paying more attention to style than to content, and remaining a largely apolitical platform throughout its existence, *Nyugat* (and the publishing house associated with it) rejected many conventions and provided an independent forum for every new, exciting trend and idea. The *Nyugat* novelists were served by the principle that in literature anything was justified if the writer had the talent to achieve his intended effect.

The literature of Hungary during the interwar period is frequently labeled as nationalistic and conservative, but a conscientious examination reveals that many kinds of writings, including even those of the noncommunist Left, were allowed to reach the readers, and critical realism continued to be in ascendance. Having shed some of their nationalistic presumptions and addressing instead the issues of modern human existence, the best of Hungary's writers strove to make their public aware of the burning need to alter their society. Since realism was relatively late arriving in Hungary, its energies were still fresh, and the extreme social polarization lent it a special virulence. The works of Zsigmond Móricz (1879-1942) stand out with their carefully balanced duality: They bore the stamp of naturalism in presenting the joys and sorrows of poor people's lives, while they continually affirmed the idealistic, nearly prophetic commitment of the writer to improving the lot of the underprivileged. An entire generation of writers following Móricz's lead, and their ethnocentric orientation continues to make its effect felt even in today's Hungarian prose.

The neopopulists of the 1930's advocated a "third road" course for Hungary and proclaimed the potentials of peasantry for leading a national revival. Their "revolution of quality" was to prepare the country for the changes that were foreseeable after the end of the war. On the other hand, the writings of the important novelists among the "urbanists" were marked by a desire to reveal the unsettling dichotomy between surface appearance and reality and by an ability to capture the substance of individual lives in seemingly insignificant gestures. Populist and urbanist groups had little sympathy or understanding for each other, and the resulting split in intellectual leadership was one of the genuine tragedies of twentieth century Hungary.

The defeat and occupation of Hungary by the Soviet armies brought about major changes in the literary life of the country as well. After the initial postwar years of democratic coalition, during which various voices were allowed to be heard, there followed the subjugation of literature to the often ludicrous political course of the times. Many promising talents fell victim to the war and persecution, and many more to a different brand of barbarism during the subsequent years. The ill-defined principles of Socialist Realism proved to be a straitjacket into which only the writings of a few hacks fit comfortably. The best-known Hungarian socialist writer, Tibor Déry (1894-1977), repeatedly came up against the stone wall of unappreciative official criticism, while many of his best contemporaries were prevented from publishing their works. Although its aftereffects are felt to this day, this period of heavy-handed repression proved to be neither long-lasting nor entirely successful. Hungarian literature did not lose its inherited resilience, and the 1954 "explosion of talent" contributed to raising public consciousness to the level that made the 1956 revolution inevitable. The role of the printed word in the revolution was convincingly affirmed when the Soviet-installed Kádár government imprisoned or silenced a number of writers and disbanded the Writers' Union.

After the end of World War I, millions of Hungarians came under the jurisdiction of the neighboring successor states, and since then they have faced formidable odds in striving to preserve their cultural traditions. Their writers produce some of the most relevant works in contemporary Hungarian prose, most significantly in Transylvania, a land that long nur-

tured its own intellectual heritage. The oppressive policies of the Romanian authorities during later years made this literary activity even more noteworthy. In comparison, the output of Hungarian novelists living in the West, presumably under more favorable conditions, remained by and large unimpressive.

In Hungary, the post-1956 "consolidation" amounted to little more than an admission by the rulers of the country to the effect that writers have the right to be apolitical and mildly experimental. The reorganized Writers' Union was given the task of preserving the position of hegemony that was occupied by Marxist-Leninist aesthetics, while, somewhat ironically, the freedom of non-Marxist but "well-meaning" writers was loudly proclaimed. Within a smoothly running system of self-censorship, a relatively liberal publishing practice was realized, with the result that barely tolerated (or suppressed) pieces of Hungarian prose attracted considerable attention at home and abroad. Many of these works, however, are more correctly classified as sociological reportage, memoirs, or experimental "text." The novel proper, and especially the novel of "socialist content," is in an unenviable position in today's Hungary: It no longer holds monopoly, and even if official lip service grants it preeminence, it makes its appearance infrequently.

András Boros-Kazai

THE SERBIAN NOVEL

Slavic tribes in Southeastern Europe developed their cultures separately beginning in the tenth century. Only in the second decade of the twentieth century were they united in one state called Yugoslavia. Even then, Yugoslav literatures went their own ways despite the ethnic, linguistic, and cultural kinship. For that reason, it is best to discuss fiction of Serbian, Croatian, Slovenian, and Macedonian literatures separately.

Serbian fiction did not fully develop, or show worthwhile results, until the nineteenth century. The main reason is that the Serbs were militarily occupied by the Turks from the end of the fourteenth century almost to the middle of the nineteenth century. Little literature, except for oral epics, was possible. The earlier forms resembling fiction, biographies of saints and kings, the folk epics, and the translations of medieval novels were either not novels or not original creations and therefore belong to the prehistory of the Serbian novel. The Serbs, who had migrated to Austrian lands in the north, slowly began to revive cultural activity in the late eighteenth century. The first novelist of significance was Milovan Vidaković (1780-1841), a writer of limited skill but unlimited ambition. Imitating both the European baroque adventure novel and the Greek love novels of late antiquity, he wrote several of his own that, though of meager artistic value, were very popular with the readers. The ensuing Romanticism, lasting approximately four decades (1830-1870), emphasized poetry and drama and showed little interest in the novel. The Serbian novel came into its own in the second half of the nineteenth century. The writer most responsible for this development was Jakov Ignjatović (1822-1889). He began by writing historical novels but soon turned to the realistic depiction of the life of his people in Austro-Hungary. Even though he wrote most of his novels when Romanticism was still dominating Serbian letters, it was his interest in everyday life and his attention to minute detail (which he acquired during his stay in Paris and through contacts with French realists) that made him the founder of the realist novel in Serbian literature. He possessed sharp observation, keen understanding of the life around him, and boundless energy. His glaring artistic weaknesses prevented him from becoming an outstanding novelist in the mold of Honoré de Balzac. Nevertheless, Ignjatović's works formed the firm basis for further development of the Serbian novel.

It was not until the last decade of the nineteenth century that other realist novelists appeared. For the most part, they depicted the Serbian village, following the lead of the short story. Furthermore, they tended to emphasize their own region, drawing from its rich folklore and thus bringing that region into the limelight. These writers—Janko Veselinović (1862-1905), Simo Matavulj (1852-1908), Stevan Sremac (1855-1906), and Svetolik Ranković (1863-1899)—brought the Serbian novel closer to the European realistic novel, though not to the same artistic level. They were also very much concerned with social problems, which began to preoccupy the Serbian society, and through their psychological probings they revealed the influence of the nineteenth century Russian realists.

In the twentieth century, the fragile realistic tradition continued while new modernistic tendencies began to make inroads, not dramatic at first but increasingly evident. While Borisav Stanković (1876-1927) and Ivo Ćipiko (1869-1923) also wrote about provincial regions, Milutin Uskoković (1884-1915) attempted to write a city novel about Belgrade, in contrast to the existing literature, which was almost entirely about either village or small-town life. The true modernists, however, appeared after World War I, spurred by their traumatic war experiences and keeping in step with the dramatic changes in their country. A noticeably enhanced artistic value of their novels, imbued with a pronounced poetic atmosphere, as manifested in the novels of Rastko Petrović (1898-1949) and Miloš Crnjanski (1893-1977), finally brought the Serbian novel to the level of world fiction after a century of lagging behind.

The culmination of this advance is embodied in the three novels by Ivo Andrić (1892-1975) published in 1945. His *magnum opus*, *Na Drini ćuprija* (1945; *The Bridge on the Drina*, 1959), combines the epic tradition with modern approaches to the novel, notably those of psychological penetration and myth-making. Andrić stands at the watershed of the preceding century and the contemporary period. After World War II, the Serbian novel was characterized by increased output, improved artistic quality, and the tradition adapting to developments in other literatures.

The leading contemporary novelists are Dobrica Ćosić, Meša Selimović, Danilo Kiš, and Milorad Pavić. Dobrica Ćosić (born 1921) deals in *Vreme smrti* (1972-1979; *A Time of Death*, 1978; *Reach to Eternity*, 1980; *South to Destiny*, 1981) with the momentous event in Serbian history, World War I, and with the struggle of the Serbian army against overwhelming enemies. In *Vreme zla* (1985-1990; a time of evil), he dissects the experience of Serbs with communism, tracing the painful road from early idealism of true believers to the internecine fight symptomatic of totalitarian movements. In *Vreme vlasti* (1996; a time of power), he follows that experience to the next, logical step, the inevitable corruption of power and painful betrayal of initial goals. Even though Ćosić bases his novels on historical and political themes, he creates strong, credible characters and builds skillful plots. He represents best the neorealistic trend in contemporary Serbian novels, using the political scene as a background to underscore the need for morality in everyday life. In one of the best contemporary Serbian novels, *Derviš i smrt* (1966; *Death and the Dervish*, 1996), Meša Selimović (1910-1982) grapples with some of the basic ethical problems. Drawing from his personal experience—the loss of his brother at the hands of his communist brethren—he weaves a powerful story of love and loyalty. His semiphilosophical musings and psychological probing lead to a charming fusion of the East and the West and to a thoughtful quest for the meaning of life within a Moslem frame of mind.

Among the younger writers, Danilo Kiš (1935-1989) impressed critics and readers, both at home and abroad, with his novels *Bašta, pepeo* (1965; *Garden, Ashes*, 1975) and *Grobnica za Borisa Davidoviča* (1976; *A Tomb for Boris Davidovich*, 1978). In his early works he dealt with the tragic loss of his Jewish father at the hands of the Nazis, creating in him an almost mythical character. In his later novels he used a modernistic approach to deal with burning political and ideological questions of the time. *A Tomb for Boris Davidovich*, consisting of seven loosely related stories yet with an organic unity, follows the crisscrossing paths of several victims of the totalitarian communist ideology. It was illogical to Kiš to oppose one form of dictatorship—Nazism—while disregarding or even supporting its sibling—communism. In *Enciklopedija mrtvih* (1983; *The Encyclopedia of the Dead*, 1989), which is similarly a collection of nine loosely related stories but is treated also as a novel, he deals mostly with the syndrome of death, intertwining documentary and fictitious material. Kiš's insistence on authenticity of his subject matter, which he achieved by meticulously studying historical documents, led to a peculiar mixture of fact and fiction, transformed by the author's unmis-

takable artistry into internationally acclaimed works of fiction.

Milorad Pavić (born 1929), a leading representative of postmodernism in Serbian fiction, achieved significant international success with his *Hazarski rečnik* (1984; *Dictionary of the Khazars*, 1988), as well as with other novels. In *Hazarski rečnik*, Pavić employs dazzling flights of imagination, spanning centuries and bringing together a colorful array of characters, in order to show that reality and fantasy are constantly interchanged and that their borderlines are therefore deliberately blurred. This pervasive relativity is underscored by the fact that the story is presented in three versions—the Christian, the Islamic, and the Hebrew. Laden with many possible interpretations, the novel is a perfect example of postmodernism, which has taken a strong hold among the Serbian novelists. Pavić continues in a similar vein in *Predeo slikan čajem* (1988; *Landscape Painted with Tea*, 1990), and *Unutrašnja strana vetra ili Roman o Heri i Leandru* (1991; *The Inner Side of the Wind: Or, the Novel of Hero and Leander*, 1993), using striking metaphors, similes, paradoxes, hyperboles, maxims, and other tropes, making the novel just as complex yet delightful to read. Pavić has become most representative of the present trends in Serbian long fiction.

Other significant novelists are Mihailo Lalić (1914-1992), Branko Ćopić (1915-1984), Aleksandar Tišma (born 1924), Miodrag Bulatović (1930-1991), Dragoslav Mihailović (born 1930), Borislav Pekić (1930-1992), Živojin Pavlović (1933-1998), and Slobodan Selenić (1933-1995). Each has contributed at least one memorable novel, such as Lalić's *Lelejska gora* (1952, revised 1962, revised 1990; *The Wailing Mountain*, 1965), Bulatović's *Crveni petao leti prema nebu* (1959; *The Red Cock Flies to Heaven*, 1962), Tišma's *Upotreba čoveka* (1976; *The Use of Man*, 1988), Mihailović's *Kad su cvetale tikve* (1968; *When Pumpkins Blossomed*, 1971), Pekić's *Vreme čuda* (1965; *The Time of Miracles*, 1976), and Selenić's *Ubistvo s predumišljajem* (*Premeditated Murder*, 1996). While following their own paths, they have contributed to a sophisticated, innovative, and lasting brand of fiction. They are not reluctant to explore the formalistic possibilities of the modern novel while having their characters persistently cope with the dilemmas and difficulties of everyday life.

Serbian novelists of a younger generation are pre-occupied with the difficult situation in which Serbs find themselves, especially after the war in Bosnia. Even though writers such as Pavić and Pekić tend to use the extraneous events only as a distant back-ground for their novels, others use the everyday events as direct stimuli. Among the more successful ones are Vladimir Arsenijević and Radoslav Petko-vić. Arsenijević (born 1965) enjoyed great success with his first novel, *U potpalublju* (1995; *In the Hold*, 1996), in which he uses the war between the Serbs and the Croats in 1991 as a background governing the fate of all the characters involved and their efforts to avoid being drawn and destroyed in the war's vor-tex. Arsenijević does not limit himself to the de-piction of the war; he delves into Belgrade's drug culture, blackmarketeering, and crime, along with desperate flights into emigration of the young peo-ple and suicides. The author's control over the sub-ject matter, his subliminal moral messages, and the novel's high literary quality make it not only excel-lent literature but also a harbinger of a new spirit in Serbian fiction. Radoslav Petković (born 1953), in his most successful novel *Sudbina i komentari* (1994; destiny and comments), traces in a wide sweep cov-ering over three hundred years the destinies of sev-eral characters in order to establish the connection between the events in the past and the present. Using a postmodernist technique, he probes the relationship between history and literature, thus lending the mod-ern Serbian novel a much wider and more universal scope.

Vasa D. Mihailovich

THE CROATIAN NOVEL

Croatian fiction had an early beginning in Petar Zoranić's *Planine* (1569; mountains), but that was an isolated case. Like Serbs, the Croats were dominated by a foreign power for centuries, this time Austro-Hungary. The true development began with August Šenoa (1838-1881), who wrote several historical novels during the Romantic period in Croatian litera-ture. Šenoa approached his novels more like a realist, especially when describing social conditions. Histor-ical events and figures from the fourteenth to the eighteenth centuries were used by Šenoa to inspire his people in their struggle for independence and so-cial order. Toward the end of his life, he turned en-tirely to topics from everyday life, foreshadowing several realist novelists concerned almost exclusively with social problems. Ante Kovačić (1854-1889), Eu-gen Kumičić (1850-1904), Josip Kozarac (1858-1906), Vjenceslav Novak (1859-1905), Ksaver Šandor Djalski (1854-1935), and Janko Leskovar (1861-1949) attempted, each in his own way, to cope with the pressing problems besetting their people, while striv-ing to advance the novel. Some novelists reflected a local milieu, while others showed the influence of Balzac, Gustave Flaubert, Ivan Turgenev, and the nat-uralists. Although they were usually successful with one or two novels, they all helped in establishing a tradition in Croatian fiction that was lacking before and that would later bring forth outstanding works.

Around the beginning of the twentieth century, re-alism lost its vitality, and new currents, spurred by developments in West European literatures, espe-cially the French, began to take hold. A movement called Moderna (modern) established itself as the leading literary trend, as it did in Serbian literature on a smaller scale. Leading novelists of this period—Milutin Cihlar Nehajev (1880-1931), Dinko Šimu-nović (1873-1933), and Janko Polić Kamov (1886-1910)—advocated close ties with European litera-tures, considered form as important as content, and demanded full independence for the artist. Their efforts were soon overshadowed by the most domi-nant writer in Croatian literature between the two world wars—indeed, in all of Yugoslav literature in the twentieth century—Miroslav Krleža (1893-1981). His political activism, based on humanitarian com-munism, colored his approach to literature as well, primarily in the topic selection and in his treatment of social problems. His favorite theme, the rise and fall of the bourgeois society in Austro-Hungary, is designed to show the obsequious role of the Croatian upper class in that society as well as the suffering of the lower class. Thanks to his artistic prowess, the author succeeded in keeping his social criticism from slipping into preaching, and a certain long-windedness is compensated by a wealth of pertinent detail, exquisite character sketches, fine nuances, and a sharp eye for shape and color. Krleža is a master of hint and allusion, and he knows how to keep his distance. His pessimism—even nihilism, at times—and his irony, often turning to sarcasm, are tempered with humor and compassion. All of these characteristics, coupled with his enormous erudition and savoir faire steeped in Central European culture and tradition, made Krleža, next to Andrić, a very important writer, not only in Croatian literature but in world literature as well.

Other novelists at this time, though writing in Krleža's shadow, helped create a lively atmosphere and great literary ferment in this period. They were preoccupied with social and political problems much more than writers in other Yugoslav literatures, and the main reasons were Krleža's influence and the specific conditions present in the Croatian part of Yugoslavia after 1918.

The postwar era is characterized by a large number of gifted novelists who are continuing with the tradition of the prewar periods while striking new paths. Versatility is perhaps the most telling feature of the contemporary Croatian novel. Also, for the first time, the novel reached the level of the short story, which had dominated Croatian fiction from the beginning. Although most of the new novelists were under the heavy influence of Krleža, many of them were able to free themselves of this influence in their later development. Petar Šegedin (born 1909), Vladan Desnica (1905-1967), Ranko Marinković (born 1913), Vjekoslav Kaleb (born 1905), Mirko Božić (born 1919), Vojin Jelić (born 1921), and Slobodan Novak (born 1924) have addressed new themes and problems, both artistic and social, with sophistication and verve seldom seen before in Croatian literature. The general growth of the novel, paralleling that of other Yugoslav literatures, reflects maturity and familiarity with world standards of the genre. A newer generation of novelists, led by Ivan Aralica, Pavao Pavličić, Goran Tribuson, and Dubravka Ugrešić, among others, is showing even greater versatility,

maturity, and affinity with modern tendencies in world fiction. Ivan Aralica (born 1930) frequently uses historical themes of his native Dalmatia in order to comment on the present situations, combining the elements of medieval chronicles, oral folklore, and contemporary jargon, as in *Psi u trgovištu* (1979; dogs at the market), *Put bez sna* (*Journey Without Sleep*, 1982), *Duše robova* (*Souls of the Slaves*, 1984), and *Okvir za mržnju* (*Frame for Hatred*, 1987). Pavao Pavličić (born 1946) writes in a light, entertaining style, dwelling on urban, unusual, and sometimes esoteric themes, as in his novel *Večernji akt* (1981; evening act). Goran Tribuson (born 1948), also writes about urban life, often in the form of mystery novels, as in *Povijest pornografije* (1988; history of pornography). Dubravka Ugrešić's (born 1949) novel *Forsiranje romana-reke* (1988; *Fording the Stream of Consciousness*, 1994), is a quasi detective novel about a literary meeting in Zagreb, written in a humorous and ironic vein castigating the self-aggrandizement of the literary world. The so-called fatherland war of the 1990's has become an increasingly favorite subject in all of Croatian contemporary literature, including long fiction, with a varying degree of success. As expected, Croatian novelists are attempting to join the world scene even more than before the war.

Vasa D. Mihailovich

THE SLOVENIAN NOVEL

Like their South Slavic brethren, the Slovenes were suppressed by a foreign power, Austria, for almost ten centuries and were not allowed to develop their self-government, let alone their culture. For that reason, Slovenian fiction made a late appearance; the first novel, *Deseti brat* (the tenth brother), by Josip Jurčič (1844-1881), was published in 1866. Although it lagged somewhat behind other Yugoslav literatures, Slovenian fiction has proved to be a valuable contribution to the genre. The early novels were based mostly on the native folk narratives, but they were much more than imitations; rather, they transformed the folkloric material into genuine works of literature. While the short story was dominant in the nineteenth century, the novel made quick and significant strides. Besides Jurčič, Josip Stritar (1836-1923), Janko Kersnik (1852-1897), and Ivan Tavčar (1851-1923) wrote in a style showing either a mixture of Romanticism and realism or straight realism. The main feature unifying them was a strong preoccupation with social conditions of their people who, unlike other Slavic tribes, did not gain full independence until 1918. Because most of the writers were of peasant origin, they depicted most often the plight of the peasantry oppressed by foreign rule and exploited by domestic upper class.

With Ivan Cankar (1876-1918), one of the greatest of Slovene writers, Slovenian fiction reached its high point in the first two decades of the twentieth century. A leader of the Slovenian Moderna, with his several novels he laid the solid foundation of contemporary Slovene fiction. At first affected by the spirit of Decadence and Symbolism at the beginning of the twentieth century, he later developed his own style without severing ties with the Moderna yet going beyond its purely artistic objectives. On the par with Ivo Andrić and Miroslav Krleža, he ushered in a new spirit and a new era in Slovene literature.

The post-Moderna novelists were neither numerous nor artistically accomplished, but they aided the development of the genre through a great variety of approaches, partaking of almost all literary movements prevalent in world fiction between the two world wars and afterward. While some, such as F. S. Finžgar (1871-1962), were still closely tied to their native soil or, like Prežihov Voranc (1823-1925), were preoccupied with social conditions, others, such as Ivan Pregelj (1883-1960) and Miško Kranjec (1908-1983), were psychologically oriented or imbued with lyricism. The younger, postwar generation—Andrej Hieng (born 1925), Lojze Kovačič (born 1928), Pavle Zidar (1932-1983), Rudi Šeligo (born 1935), and Vitomil Zupan (1914-1987), among others—have made great strides in expanding novelistic horizons and overcoming the staple themes that dominated the Slovenian fiction for almost a century. Their efforts await final judgment.

Vasa D. Mihailovich

THE MACEDONIAN NOVEL

Macedonian literature was officially recognized only after World War II, although it has existed in a subterranean fashion for centuries. Since Macedonian literature bypassed entire literary movements and had no tradition of its own upon which to draw, it is not surprising that the novel would take some time to appear. After the first novel—*Selo zad sedumte jaseni* (1953; the village behind the ash trees), by Slavko Janevski (born 1920)—the Macedonian novelists not only asserted themselves fully but also caught up, to a large degree, with other Yugoslav writers. Understandably, the novelists dealt at first with basic changes in Macedonian society, especially the village, after the war. Soon, however, they began to probe more deeply the inner world of their characters and experiment with more advanced approaches to the novel. While there is no single dominant figure, several novelists, especially among the younger writers, have written promising works that can take their place alongside other achievements in South Slav long fiction.

In retrospect, there are several common features among South Slav novelists. They all started rather late because of the specific developments of their societies. For that reason, they lagged behind the developments in other world literatures and have never been able to fully catch up. They were spurred on, at the beginning, by other literatures, mostly those of Western Europe, but they also tried to express the indigenous narrative tradition rooted in folklore and national epics. In addition, most of them have been preoccupied with the conditions in their respective societies, and this concern has somewhat hampered their development in the pure artistic sense. As a compensation, however, they wrote novels that transcended their artistic value or intent. As they matured and built up their own tradition, they kept looking abroad for improvement, especially toward the German, Russian, and French literatures. Today, the South Slav novelists have, for the most part, made up for the lost ground and have reached the world standard in several excellent accomplishments, some of which have been translated into many languages.

Vasa D. Mihailovich

BIBLIOGRAPHY

Barac, Antun. *A History of Yugoslav Literature*. Ann Arbor: Michigan Slavic Publications, 1973. A solid overview by a leading literary historian that traces the development of the Yugoslav novel.

Bogert, Ralph. *The Writer as Naysayer: Miroslav Krlema and the Aesthetic of Interwar Central Europe*. UCLA Slavic Studies, vol. 20. Columbus, Ohio: Slavica Publishers, 1991. Wide-reaching references to the literature, including long fiction, of Yugoslavia as seen through the analysis of the greatest contemporary Croatian writer.

Eekman, Thomas. *Yugoslav Literature 1945-1975*. Ann Arbor: Michigan Slavic Publications, 1978. A complementary volume to Barac's opus that discusses the main novelists and novels of the three decades after World War II.

Goy, E. D. "The Serbian and Croatian Novel Since 1948." *The Slavonic and East European Review* 40, no. 94 (1961): 58-84. An astute discussion of the Serbian and Croatian novel by one of the best literary critics of Yugoslav literature in England.

Matejić, Mateja. "On the Contemporary Yugoslav Novel." *Canadian Slavic Studies* 5, no. 3 (1971): 362-382. A competent overview of the contemporary Yugoslav novel.

Mihailovich, Vasa, ed. *Dictionary of Literary Biography*. Vol. 147: South Slavic Writers Before World War II; Vol. 181: South Slavic Writers Since World War II. Detroit, Mich.: Gale Research, 1995, 1997. Extensive biographies and expert critical analyses of all important Southeast European novelists written by the best scholars in the field.

_____. "On the Contemporary Serbian Novel." *The International Fiction Review* 2, no. 1 (1975): 18-25. The main achievements of the Serbian novel are discussed both historically and aesthetically.

Norris, David A. *The Novels of Miloš Crnjanski: An Approach Through Time*. Nottingham, England: Astra Press, 1990. One of the best treatments of Crnjanski's novels.

Pogačnik, Jože. *Twentieth Century Slovene Literature*. Ljubljana: Milan Simčič, 1989. A thorough survey of contemporary Slovene literature by a leading Slovene literary historian.

Vucinich, Wayne, ed. *Ivo Andrić Revisited: The Bridge Still Stands*. Berkeley, Calif.: International and Area Studies Publications, 1995. A collection of scholarly essays on various aspects of Andrić's works, emphasizing the novels.

Zorić, Pavle. "The Contemporary Serbian Novel." *Literary Quarterly* 1, no. 2 (1965): 92-103. The best contemporary Serbian novels through 1965 are perused by a leading Serbian literary critic.

CHINESE LONG FICTION

In surveying some six centuries of the Chinese novel, from the first major accomplishment, *Sanguo yanyi* (fourteenth century; *The Romance of the Three Kingdoms*, 1925), to the novels of the present, some important distinctions must be observed.

DEFINITIONS AND TRADITIONS

First, a Chinese novel's style depends on whether it belongs to the tradition of the "old novel" (*jiu xiaoshuo*)—written before the launching of the Literary Revolution in 1917—or to that of the "new novel" (*xin xiaoshuo*), written after 1917. Both kinds of novels are said to be written in the "vernacular," but this term needs to be understood properly; it refers to written style, not to speech, and it covers a broad spectrum in respect to writing. For a written work to be regarded as "literature" in ancient China, it first had to be written in the literary idiom of *wenyan*, a highly formalized style that is commonly known today as "classical Chinese." Because the novel ordinarily contained colloquialisms adopted from common speech, it was considered by nearly all scholars and critics, if not by many of its readers, "impure" in style as well as frivolous in content and hence outside the pale of genuine literature. The vernacular style of the traditional novel, however, despite its use of colloquialisms—actually confined mostly to dialogue—bore little resemblance to informal speech, for classical Chinese remained an essential ingredient of this style.

Indeed, a comparative inspection of the language of the traditional Chinese novel reveals a kind of evolutionary process in respect to the proportion and purpose of colloquialisms embedded in the literary idiom. For example *The Romance of the Three Kingdoms* follows the standard history of the turbulent Three Kingdoms so closely as to quote the state documents verbatim and in full. On the other hand, the sixteenth century *Jin Ping Mei* (*The Golden Lotus*, 1939; also as *Chin P'ing Mei: The Adventurous History of Hsi Men and His Six Wives*, 1940) employs a larger count of colloquial particles than do some of the much earlier short tales called *huaben*, which were based on oral telling and whose heyday was the twelfth and thirteenth centuries. The early eighteenth century *Rulin waishi* (*The Scholars*, 1957) is relatively free of *wenyan*, *guanhua* (official speech), and *liyan* (slang). The late eighteenth century *Honglou meng* (1792; *Dream of the Red Chamber*, 1929; also as *The Story of the Stone*, 1973-1986; also as *A Dream of Red Mansions*, 1978) shows a considerable advance over the previous novels in individual characterization, which is accomplished mostly by idiomatic speech uttered by its principal characters. The new novel of modern times came into being following the launching of the Literary Revolution in 1917 and the introduction of Western novelistic standards. Its leaders, Hu Shi and Chen Duxiu, despised classical Chinese and advocated that the written vernacular, *baihua*, replace it in all writing. Their view eventually obtained general acceptance: The modern Chinese novel is written exclusively in the colloquial language and in terms of Western, not traditional Chinese, literary standards.

Second, the traditional Chinese novel must be viewed in the light of its own history, literary tradition, and narrative standards. The novel in the West emerged during the eighteenth century predominantly out of the epic, collections of novellas, and various modes of the romance—chivalric, classical, pastoral, picaresque, allegorical, gothic, and historical. In China, on the other hand, the traditional novel appeared during the fourteenth century under the dominant influence of historiography and oral techniques of the professional storytellers. The first major Chinese novel, *The Romance of the Three Kingdoms*, adheres closely to standard history and is concerned predominantly with historical characters; few ahistorical figures or fictional episodes appear. Hence the novel is not a historical novel in the Western sense but rather dramatized history produced by skillful narrative architectonics, especially a closely knit internal structuring of incidents, rendered in an elegant style. Thus, the line between historiography and fiction in old China is not easy to draw. If novels after *The Romance of the Three Kingdoms* move further in the direction of fiction, history often serves as a starting point and a baseline.

The strong influence of the technique of oral storytelling is another marked feature of the traditional Chinese novel. This feature is evident in the largely colloquial speech of the characters, which sometimes descends into slang and even into billingsgate. Apart from the colloquial idiom of the dialogue, however, the traditional novel contains other oral conventions: the quoting of popular songs, the adapting of popular tales, and the creating of pseudohistory. An important oral convention is the simulation of the oral storytelling situation by using a single narrative point of view that represents a generalized storyteller speaking to a generalized reader. This method contrasts prominently with that employed in the Western novel, in which a variety of simulacra, limited or unlimited, are used and often individualized. In the dialogue of the novel, the Chinese author provides no hint of the emotion implicit in a speech; he simply uses such terms as *Ta shuo dao* (He said as follows), *Song Jiang jiao dao* (Sung Chiang shouted), or *Ta yue* (He said), and so on, without the "stage directions" often found in the Western novel, particularly in popular fiction: "'I agree,' he said haltingly" or "'I won't,' she angrily replied."

Furthermore, prefixed to each *zhang* (chapter) of the old novel conventionally appears an antithetical couplet of verses whose meaning is related to the contents of the chapter. Also, chapters commonly end on a note of crisis or suspense that is emphasized by a conventional formula amounting to: "If you don't know what happened afterward, then *listen* to the *telling* of the next chapter" (italics added). Finally, the episodic development of the narrative is a feature of the inherited orality of the old novel. Here, the term "episodic" means the intricate interweaving of incident and coincidence throughout the whole narrative without any evident concern that the whole will finally assume some discernible shape identifiable with that unity of structure that Western critics tend to demand of the novel.

In short, whatever social or psychological realism the traditional Chinese novel manages to convey to the Western reader—a mimetic aim never envisioned by the Chinese author—that effect is both restricted and aided by its oral conventions. On the other hand, the new novel in China is a product of the rejection of the previous Chinese literary tradition in favor of Western literary standards and conventions, whether "bourgeois" or "proletarian."

Third, the episodic orientation of the old novel was ultimately a product of the traditional Chinese cosmology shared by most educated people. Rejecting the notion that the cosmos and the humans in it had come about as the result of some ultimate cause, they conceived of the universe as a self-generating, finite, dynamic process—a single, organic whole whose parts interacted in harmony. Humanity was viewed as an intimate part of this holistic, creative process. Employing the "Rule of Three," these educated people abstracted the principal parts of the cosmic organism as Heaven, Earth, and Man, seeing their relationship as triadic and symbolizing it emblematically as an equilateral triangle. If the Chinese rejected the idea of an ultimate cause or external force in terms of the transcendent, the anthropomorphically conceived Jewish Jehovah or Christian God, Heaven (*tian*) was nevertheless regarded as Providence, an immanent force that silently directed both the workings of the physical world and the affairs of humans. Hence, Confucians spoke of the "Mandate of Heaven" (*tianming*); Daoists spoke of "The Way and the Power" (*daode*), referring to the power of nonbeing that "does things without doing them"; and Buddhists spoke of "The Great Void" (*wu*), by which they also meant nonbeing, and "moral retribution" (*baoying*), meaning "present retribution in this life" according to a person's just desserts as dictated by the law of karma.

This sort of worldview accounted for the lack of emphasis on causality in the traditional Chinese novel. Events are presented in a different arrangement and with a different focus from those commonly found in the Western novel. According to Western thinking, an "event" is the consequence of a previous happening: It is an "outcome" and a "result." As such, events in a Western novel are presented in a linear and temporal fashion as a sequence of cause-and-effect occurrences. That is, each event (E) has its proximate cause in some preceding event

(C_1), the occurrence of which, in the circumstances prevailing at the time, necessitated the occurrence of E—that is, made it happen. If traced backward through some intermediary steps, E may also have some remote cause (C_2). Cause and effect are thus considered an event, but the things, substances, or people that affect or are affected by this happening, and thereby undergo some change, are considered agents or receivers. In a narrative, "agents" imply "actors," which in turn imply "action." "Receivers" imply those people, things, and substances that experience the action and may be affected by it. "Things" and "substances" imply "setting" and "atmosphere." A sequence of causally connected events arranged in some meaningful pattern constitutes the plot, or the line of action, of a narrative from the Western standpoint. Additionally, it is the principal factor that structures the story and gives it a shape that is supposed to possess unity. The acceptance of this view of causality has tended to make the Western author choose between two possible foci: His focus will be directed either at character or at action. The former gives rise to the novel of character and the latter to the novel of adventure. Either character or action becomes the principal force imparting motion and momentum to the sequence of cause-and-effect events. Indeed, the Western conception that human experience is a process opposed to stasis eventually placed the emphasis on internal rather than external events; the former were put in the realm of consciousness or subconsciousness.

The traditional Chinese worldview, however, was not wedded to a causal interpretation of events. The universe is a dynamic process, to be sure, whose parts interact with one another, but not in a linear, progressive fashion. Rather, it is a complementary, reciprocal process, a dual interrelation in which the duality remains constant, hence is neither progressive nor dialectical but simply cyclic. Unlike G. W. F. Hegel's philosophy, which proposed that when a thing is negated, a new thing arises at a higher level, traditional Chinese philosophy held that when a thing is negated, it simply repeats the old. The "Great Harmony" initiates the forces of *yin* and *yang*, whose interaction brings all things into form but eventually destroys their forms. Still, because things cannot be dispersed without forming again, their perpetuation is spontaneous, inevitable, and cyclic. Thus, motion (*yang*) becomes rest (*yin*), and rest becomes motion once more. This process continues ad infinitum in a spatiotemporal universe that is a finite whole. Hence, the Chinese did not think of events as causally linked. Furthermore, because motion is opposed to rest, events have their opposite in nonevents, and events are interwoven in the tapestry of the universe with nonevents as woof and warp. Events are connected, not causally linked, merely by succession or coincidence and are juxtaposed to nonevents. In this way, both events and nonevents are spatialized into a pattern of dynamic and static episodes.

This traditional Chinese worldview was responsible for the focus and the structure of the old novel. The traditional novel does not focus on a single character or a single event to the length that one or the other serves to unify the whole. The interest tends to embrace many people in their interrelationships in a variety of social contexts. The principal characters may not change—may neither develop nor decline, as they frequently do in Western novels—but simply remain the same.

In dealing with the fortunes of a series of protagonists, the novelist presents a series of cycles in each of which a different protagonist is featured. First one and then another character or incident takes the lead in forwarding the linear progress of the narrative on the printed page. The novel is developed by a system of linked plots, usually governed by some central issue, and these plots together structure the novel as a whole.

In dealing with an individual protagonist, a conflict-resolution pattern (proceeding through the stages of point of contention, confrontation, conflict, and resolution) is linked to that of the next individual protagonist, but emphasis is placed on nonevents nearly as much as on events. In other words, this "overlapping" of events takes into consideration what has been called "the interstitial spaces between events." In this procedure, the novelist sets his "clearly defined events" into "a thick matrix of nonevents" such as static descriptions, set speeches, formal banquets, and discursive digressions. The effect is to give the reader a sense of the continuity of discrete events that are not causally linked.

This spatial, noncausal, and nonlinear structuring typical of the traditional Chinese novel is in part obscured by the necessarily temporal, line-by-line arrangement of the narrative language. If the novel were a Chinese landscape painting—whose principles of organization stem from the same cosmological theory, in which the iconology is presented to the eye simultaneously within the confines of the picture plane—this kind of structuring would be immediately apperceptible. In painting, Chinese artists do not aim at the realistic representation of surface appearances. They are not interested in presenting an illusion of depth, for instance, by imitating visual phenomena according to certain optical principles. Rather, they follow the "Law of Three Sections": They place the foreground low; depict trees, a pond, and a fisherman in a boat in a middle area; and then sketch the mountains above. Making use of intervals of space and rhythmic lines, Chinese artists seek to induce in the viewer a sense of the "life breath" and the "life motion" of the cosmic organism. Indeed, they regard the lines of their configurations as a vascular network made up of "dragon veins," and they seek to depict the pulse of the universe.

In sum, these discriminations are the first and foremost that the Western-oriented reader must draw in attempting an appraisal of the Chinese novel, whether "old" or "new," from an aesthetic standpoint. It is therefore a mistake to arbitrarily take Western fiction as a standard against which to appraise Chinese traditional fiction. Aesthetic standards and techniques differ in terms of time, place, cultural orientation, and aim. In respect to the Chinese new novel, the critic must distinguish between those novels that have "bourgeois" aesthetic aims and those composed according to the aesthetic principles of the "proletariat" revolutionary movement, especially those laid down by Communist Party chairman Mao Zedong in *Zai Yan'an wenyi zuotanhui shang de jianghua* (1942; *Talks at the Yenan Literary Conference,* 1965), which later became the literary program of the "New China."

ORIGINS AND DEVELOPMENT

In the European tradition, epic verse was an important forerunner of long fiction, but such was not the case in China, where special historical and intellectual conditions precluded the production of folk epics. Chinese fiction originated from its oral traditions of myth, folklore, legend, and history, in ballads to be sung and tales to be told. Hence, Chinese fiction emerged from certain other oral practices and forms as well as from certain rhetorical techniques common to fiction that appeared in written histories, philosophies, and religious texts such as narratives, descriptions, biographies, and dialogues.

The premodern view of fiction in China differed significantly from that held in the Western world. To the ancient Chinese, fiction was termed *hsiao-shuo* (small talk). They regarded it as something trivial and frivolous that had little or no literary merit. To them, orthodox literature consisted of but four genres: classics (the "Four Books" and the "Five Official Classics"), histories, philosophies, and belles lettres (poetry, literary criticism, and miscellaneous essays on sundry subjects). Thus, fiction in China received little respect and less attention from scholars and critics until the twentieth century.

The late Tang Dynasty (618-907 C.E.) scholars who wrote the earliest Chinese fiction, short stories called *chuangi* (tales of the marvelous), did so as practice exercises for the public civil-service examinations. Hence, these stories were also known as *wenquan* (warming-up scrolls). Furthermore, these stories were written in classical Chinese and not in the vernacular favored by later writers of short stories and novels. Those scholars who wrote vernacular stories and novels were not anxious to reveal their true identities and thus tarnish their reputations, so they concealed them by leaving their works anonymous, using a pseudonym or "studio name," or citing an earlier (deceased) writer as the original source. Consequently, many Chinese authors of traditional fiction remain unknown or were identified only in later scholarship.

By the fall of the Han Dynasty in 220 C.E., the scholar class had practically become the exclusive custodian of the Chinese written language. In their hands, the written script broke away from the common speech of the people and went its separate way. The characters were normally given sounds (either imaginatively, in silent reading, or aloud, in recitation) in some dialect because the script had no pronunciation of its own. This style, called *wenyan* (classical or literary Chinese), came to be used exclusively for all serious writing. At the same time, the written script was also used to simulate the vernacular favored by later writers, and the colloquial forms were mixed with the classical. The colloquial style was called *baihua* (plain speech). Thus, Chinese literature as a whole came to have two contrasting prose styles—literary Chinese, or *wenyan*, and colloquial Chinese, or *baihua*. *Wenyan* was also developed in two contrasting styles—*pianwen* (parallel prose) and *guwen* (ancient prose), but the latter replaced the former for most serious writing by the ninth century C.E. Not until the Yuan (Mongol) Dynasty (1279-1367 C.E.) were dictionaries produced giving the Chinese characters in Mandarin pronunciation. At any rate, the history and development of Chinese fiction closely parallel the history and development of both literary and colloquial prose.

Although written records prove that public storytelling in China was a common social institution as early as the Tang Dynasty, such an activity goes much further back into history. The major writings of the Zhou Dynasty (1122-221 B.C.E.), such as the *Shujing* (*The Book of Documents*, 1950), the *Guoyu* (conversations from the states), the *Zhanguo Ce* (fifth to second century B.C.E.; intrigues of the warring states; English translation, 1970), and the *Lun yu* (late sixth or early fifth century B.C.E.; *Analects of Confucius*) are all within the oral tradition. While primitive conventions of narrative form and technique stem from this oral tradition, both traditions—oral and written—continued to influence narrative until the twentieth century. Even when written in classical Chinese, this narrative, especially the novel, continued to reflect the colloquial idiom.

Although the downfall of the Zhou led to the creation of the first Chinese empire under Emperor Shi Huang Di, only two developments took place during the short-lived Qin Dynasty (221-207 B.C.E.). The au-

tocratic Shi Huang Di harshly censored and burned all books of which he disapproved. A more significant development for the future of literature was the standardization of the Chinese script.

The Han Dynasty (207 B.C.E.-220 C.E.), however, was a more fruitful literary period. The Han emperors actively promoted literary scholarship and rewarded worthy scholars with official appointments and promotions. Scholars tried to reconstruct the texts of the burned books, and the "Confucian classics" were edited, redacted, and "fixed." The first etymological dictionary was prepared. The civil-service examination system was firmly established. A reliable and effective historiography was founded through the efforts of Sima Qian (c. 145-c. 85 B.C.E.) and Ban Gu (32-92 C.E.). Two new poetic forms, the *fu* (rhyme-prose) and the *yuefu* (lyrics and ballads), were devised, and Indian Buddhism was introduced in the Former Han (207 B.C.E.-24 C.E.) to compete with the indigenous Confucian and Daoist creeds.

All the developments already described contributed to the later development of Chinese fiction. The examination candidates of the Tang Dynasty were to create the first literary short stories, the *chuangi*, as practice exercises. The essence of history is narrative, and later Chinese fiction would draw heavily upon Chinese historical narrative, particularly the novel. The new poetic *fu* and *yuefu* were narrative forms. Finally, Indian Buddhism was to have a profound impact on the Chinese imagination.

The fall of the Han Dynasty resulted in relative political chaos in China for four centuries, a period known as the Six Dynasties (220-589 C.E.). During this time, the two chief indigenous systems of thought, Confucianism and Daoism, reacted to the introduction of Buddhism, the foreign creed from India, prompting an increased interest in mysticism and metaphysical speculation. This led to a distortion of the heretofore practical system of ethics that Confucianism had espoused. Mystical meanings were interpolated into the Confucian classics, while the more speculative and metaphysical Daoism rose in popularity. Eventually these trends led to a new school of philosophy called *xuanxue* ("dark," or subtle, learning). This philosophy sought to encourage metaphysical speculation by means of dialogues studded with wit and humor called *qingtan* (pure conversations), which were recorded in writing. One such compendium, entitled *Shishuo Xinyu* (fifth century B.C.E.; *A New Account of Tales of the World*, 1976), was made in the fifth century by Liu Yiqing (404-444 B.C.E.). The contribution of the institution of *qingtan* to later fiction was no doubt greater than that made to philosophical speculation. Rooted in speech rather than in *wenyan*, it minimized the importance of the content of the essay and focused on the wit, encouraging a search for choice words and phrases.

Another side effect of the introduction of Buddhism was the revival of the ancient Chinese spiritualist cult of the *wu*. A *wu* was a shaman or priest who acted as a mediator between spirits and humans. The cult's preoccupation with gods and ghosts was enhanced by the teachings of Buddhism. Members of the cult adopted the practice of writing stories about gods and ghosts. These stories became so popular with the people that noncult writers began to compose such stories for entertainment. Even scholars took an interest in them and began to collect and publish them. One such collection was published about the beginning of the third century under the title *Liyizhuan* (c. 220; strange tales); the identity of its author or editor is unknown, though it has been ascribed to Caa Bei. Other collections were brought out by Zhanghua (232-280), Gan Bao (fl. c. 300), and Wu Qun (469-519). The adherents of Buddhism and Daoism also wrote similar tales.

Such "ghost stories" were called *qigui* (tales of the supernatural). Although the scholars of the Six Dynasties period took an interest in them, they did not take them seriously as literature, referring to them as *qigui xiashuo*. Actually, the *qigui* were simply journalistic recordings of folklore or religious propaganda. Nevertheless, they are significant in the history of fiction because they were among the first attempts at imaginative writing and point to the Buddhist and secular *pianwen*, which began to appear near the end of the Six Dynasties period.

The introduction of Buddhism into China resulted in an imaginative expansion of Chinese mythology and legend that later provided stock for fiction. Legendary tales were scattered in various ancient books such as the *Shijing* (c. 500 B.C.E.; *The Book of Odes*, 1950); the *Zuozhuan* (c. 450 B.C.E.), which covered political, social, and military events from 722 to 463 B.C.E.; and the *Shanhai jing* (c. 200 B.C.E.; classic of mountains and seas). The Chinese began learning of Buddhas and bodhisattvas; numberless universes; many heavens and hells; endless cycles of rebirths; Gautama Buddha; Amitabha Buddha, the ruler of the Western Paradise; Vairochana, the primordial eternal Buddha; and Maitreya, the Laughing Buddha, who will come again. There were legends, too, of Siddhartha Gautama sitting under the bo tree, the dream of Emperor Ming Di, and Bodhidharma meditating before a wall at the Shaolin Monastery and then teaching his novices the art of *quanfa* (the law of the fist).

Buddhism also had an impact on the Chinese language and on prose style. With its introduction, there was an urgent demand for translations of the Buddhist sutras (sacred texts). New words and concepts had to be interpreted and translated from Sanskrit into Chinese. The translators saw that Daoist words and concepts could be used to explain Buddhist ideas; this method was called *geyi* (interpretation by analogy). In other cases, if no Chinese words could be substituted for the Sanskrit, transliteration was employed. Thus, the Sanskrit *nirvāna* became the Chinese *nipan*. Truth and comprehension were paramount in the eyes of the translators, and they made every effort to keep their prose style plain and unadorned, perfectly clear, and as faithful to the original as possible.

The Buddhist narrative compositions, the *pianwen* (changed composition), were the products of peripatetic Buddhist monks who recited them before temple audiences. Composed in alternate prose and verse, the *pianwen* were creative popularizations of passages selected from the Buddhist scriptures that were illustrated by stories taken from the life of Gautama Buddha, the founder of Indian Buddhism. Because these "sermons with exempla" were popular adaptations of sacred scriptures, they were regarded as "changed compositions." These changes included an irregular alternation between the use of verse and prose, as well as the "bridging" of the compositional process by means of the episodes taken from the Buddha's life.

The Buddhist *pianwen* became so popular with Chinese audiences that similar types of secular narratives were modeled after their religious prototypes. Specimens of *pianwen*, both religious and secular, were among the numerous manuscripts dating from 406 to 995 recovered at Dunhuang. Among them is a religious *pianwen* of the Five Dynasties period (907-960) referred to as *Mulian pianwen* (the story of Mulian). It is the story of a young man who becomes a Buddhist monk and his effort to rescue his mother from hell. There is also a secular *pianwen* called *Shunzi qi xiao pianwen*, which may be the earliest fictional account of the legendary Emperor Shun, the Chinese model of filial piety. At any rate, the *pianwen* substantially influenced later Chinese fiction.

These first attempts at formal imaginative writing seen in the *qigui* and the *pianwen*, as unsophisticated, crude, and awkward as they were, prepared the ground for the emergence of the first mature Chinese fiction, the literary short prose romances called *chuangi* that reached their greatest vogue in the late Tang Dynasty. Written in *wenyan*, or literary Chinese, in the new prose style called *guwen*, these short stories were written by the literati (*rusheng*) for other literati. As romances, they were longer, more sustained, better organized, and superior in style to previous fictions. Although written in *guwen* classical prose instead of the vernacular, the dialogue portions of the stories showed an attempt to approximate living speech. In terms of the literary tradition, the *chuangi* was the main fictional form of the Tang period. At the same time, the manuscripts of the Denhuang caves show that popular fiction in the form of the *pianwen* was produced throughout the Tang period and well into the Song Dynasty (960-1279).

During the Northern Song period (960-1126), however, the art of the oral storyteller had reached such a state of perfection that the literati turned from the writing of *chuanqi* to the writing of short tales in colloquial Chinese based on the art of the popular oral narrators of fiction. These vernacular stories were called *huaben* (story roots) because the literati

derived them from the promptbooks that the *shuohua ren*, or "speech makers," prepared to jog their memories when they found that necessary. By the Southern Sung period (1127-1279), the vogue of the *chuanqi huaben* had diminished to such an extent that the *huaben* had become the dominant fictional form. Indeed, the greatest *huaben* stories written by literati were produced during the Southern Song period.

During the Ming Dynasty (1368-1644), however, interest in *chuanqi* was revived for a time by the stories of Ch'ü Yu (1347-1433), who had used the Tang *chuanqi* as his models. Most of the extant Tang tales had been preserved in a collection made at the insistence of the Song emperor Taizong. During the Ming Dynasty, at the time of this brief revival of interest, some further collections were made.

A more potent revival of the *chuanqi* form, however, occurred during the Qing (Manchu) Dynasty (1644-1911), which inspired the most famous of all such tales by the masterly hand of Pu Songling (1640-1715) published in 1679 under the title *Liaozhai zhiyi* (*Strange Stories from a Chinese Studio*, 1880). Although his range of subject matter is in line with earlier *chuanqi*, his tales display an unusual command of literary Chinese and the ability to make the improbable, sometimes even the impossible, convincing. His work inspired many imitators. As for the *huaben* stories, there are no extant Song or Yuan collections. Several collections of such stories, however, were made during the Ming Dynasty. The earliest of these stories were printed by Hong Pian, around 1550, in six volumes. Although sixty tales were originally preserved, only twenty-nine of them have survived. In the 1620's, a major anthologist and writer, Feng Menglong (1574-1646), published a three-volume collection known as the *Sanyan* (three words), each volume containing 40 stories, or 120 tales altogether. Most of them are of the *huaben* type written during the Yuan Dynasty or even earlier, but some are Ming pieces. These collections were followed by the inspired writing of Ling Meng-qu (1580-1644) and Li Yu, or Li Liweng (1611-c. 1680), who wrote their own *huaben* fiction. Such tales continued to be written until the twentieth century.

In comparison to the short tale, the novel was long

in coming in China, not emerging until near the close of the fourteenth century. If the term "novel" is used in its general sense to mean "a long prose fiction with a relatively complex plot or pattern of events," then the first major Chinese novel is *The Romance of the Three Kingdoms*, attributed to Luo Guanzhong (c. 1330-1400). This novel was partly inspired by a previous fictional form that originated with the oral storytellers of the Southern Song period and flourished in conjunction with the *huaben*. Some oral storytellers specialized in telling long narratives of fictionalized history that required serial development. Even more than the *huaben* tellers, they needed promptbooks in writing. These serialized stories were called *pinghua* (common talk) because, like the shorter *huaben*, they were written in the vernacular (actually Mandarin mixed with classical Chinese). Their development seems to parallel that of the Southern drama.

Pinghua promptbooks in their original condition, although lost in China, were preserved in Japan, all printed between 1321 and 1323, during the reign of Yuan Yingzong of the Yuan Dynasty. These texts retain the formal properties of their Song predecessors. Beginning with a prologue setting forth a small story analogous to the main tale to be told and suggesting its moral, the *pinghua* is a much longer narrative than the *huaben* type of short story and belongs to a different genre. It is the transitional fictional form between the vernacular short story and the vernacular novel, and it points directly toward the colloquial novel that was to come. The *pinghua* that partly inspired Luo was the *Sanguozhi pinghua* (1321-1323; a *pinghua* of the history of the Three Kingdoms), but he also made use of a reliable official history and a commentary on it.

Following Luo's *The Romance of the Three Kingdoms*, the vernacular novel completely dominated the Chinese tradition. Although the *guwen* style of *wenyan* had proved effective for short narratives, it was not a satisfactory instrument for extended fiction in which dialogue played a prominent part. Sung writers of short fiction had abandoned the literary Chinese of the *chuanqi* in favor of the vernacular of the *huaben*. It was natural, therefore, that Luo should have adopted the *pinghua* as his model.

Although some novels were written in classical Chinese, especially during the Qing Dynasty, none is comparable to the best vernacular novels. A Qing *guwen* novel entitled *Yin shi* (c. 1800; the tale of a silver fish), by Tu Shen (1744-1801), has enough magic to be relatively successful. A more lengthy effort, however, a 300,000-word novel in *pianwen* (parallel prose) written by the eccentric Chen Qiu, entitled *Yan Shan waishi* (c. 1810; the informal history of Yan Shan), and whose style is involved and complex, is virtually unreadable.

At any rate, the vernacular novel tradition brought forth the greatest masterpieces. The next major effort after Luo was *Shuihu zhuan* (fourteenth century; translated by Pearl S. Buck as *All Men Are Brothers*, 1933; also as *Water Margin*, 1937), attributed to Shi Nai'an (c. 1290-1365), about whom nothing is known. Although written in the fourteenth century, the earliest known edition dates from the middle of the sixteenth century. Following this work, novel writing seems to have been eclipsed by the Yuan drama. Two centuries elapsed before another masterpiece appeared, *Xiyuo Ji* (1592; *The Journey to the West*, 1977-1983; abridged by Arthur Waley as *Monkey*, 1943), by Wu Cheng'en (c. 1500-c. 1582). In the late Ming Dynasty, a great novel appeared that was quite different in character from those preceding it. This was the novel of manners called *Jin Ping Mei* (*The Golden Lotus*, 1939; abridged as *Jin Ping Mei: Adventurous History of Hsi Men and His Six Wives*, 1940), traditionally attributed to Wang Shichen (1526-1590), although this attribution has been questioned. A one-hundred-chapter novel, it was circulated in manuscript in the 1590's, and the first printed edition appeared around 1610. The previous masterpieces are of a semihistorical character and have a close alliance with Chinese historiography. Although the *Jin Ping Mei* purports to show the dissolute manner of the time of Emperor Hui Zong of the Song Dynasty, it actually depicts, realistically and with considerable precision, the manners of the author's own time. This Ming novel was followed by perhaps the greatest masterpiece in the history of the Chinese novel, *Dream of the Red Chamber*, by Cao Xuegin (c. 1716-1763). The story of the decline of a wealthy aristocratic family of the author's own time, centering on the romantic love affair of the two teenagers, Jia Baoyu and his cousin and playmate Lin Daiyu, the narrative is infused with Buddhist and Daoist myth.

After the appearance of these five—*The Romance of the Three Kingdoms*, *Water Margin*, *The Journey to the West*, *Chin Ping Mei*, and *Dream of the Red Chamber*—nothing comparable followed in the Chinese novel tradition. There are, however, other novels of considerable value and significance. Two are of special importance: *Rulin waishi* (early eighteenth century; *The Scholars*, 1957), an early Qing work by Wu Jingzi (1701-1754) that satirizes pseudo-scholarship and the civil-service examination system; and a late Qing work, *Lao Can youji* (1909; *The Travels of Lao Can*, 1952), by Liu E (1857-1909; also known as Liu Tieyun), a delightful story of an itinerant Chinese physician concerned about his country's condition and opposed to injustice and harsh government.

Originating in Chinese myth, legend, and folklore, the oral tradition of Chinese literature strongly influenced written literature. Although the Chinese literary language became divorced from common speech, an alliance between writing and speech was maintained from early to modern times. Traditional Chinese fiction, like Western fiction, is divisible into the short story and the novel, but unlike Western fiction it is also divisible into fiction written in the literary as opposed to the vernacular language. This latter distinction is as important as the former.

With the Literary Revolution in 1917, the character of Chinese fiction drastically changed. The acceptance of *baihua* (common speech) for all forms of literature, as well as the acceptance of Western forms and standards, meant the complete rejection of the ancient Chinese literary tradition and the culture that accompanied it. Therefore, modern Chinese literature is a special study in itself. The fiction of the Chinese Renaissance of 1930 to 1937, based on Western literary criteria, showed promise, if not fulfillment. The Sino-Japanese War (1937-1945) and the subsequent civil war, however, stopped this progress.

With the establishment of the People's Republic of China in 1949, Chinese fiction quickly became a propaganda instrument of the state, and the sanctioned literary production was strictly controlled. Although the communist hierarchy prescribed the rejection of Western influences and a return to the Chinese tradition, this meant the tradition of the folk but not of the literary elite. Furthermore, communist fiction turned to formula and dogma, and writers were required to express themselves solely according to the Marxist-Leninist view of the world. No vital and authentic fiction has as yet emerged under these circumstances.

THE TRADITIONAL VERNACULAR NOVEL

The first great vernacular novel produced in China was *The Romance of the Three Kingdoms*, attributed to Luo Guanzhong, a playwright and writer of the late Yuan and early Ming periods. If he modeled his novel on the oral form of the *pinghua*, which he saw recorded in the promptbook *Sanguo zhi pinghua*, which was fictionalized history, Luo also turned to reliable official history to keep his facts straight. Indeed, in his novel he adhered closely to the official history of Chen Shou (233-297 C.E.), the *Sanguo zhi*, *juan* 36, but also consulted the commentary on it made by Pei Songzhi (fl. 400-430 C.E.). He may also have been indebted to Yuan drama for some structural principles.

The story told in *The Romance of the Three Kingdoms* occurs during the Three Kingdoms period (220-265 C.E.), actually extending from 168 to 265 C.E. Following the eclipse of the Han Dynasty, the three states of Wei, Shu, and Wu contended for dominance and the reunification of China. Contrary to Chen, who regarded Wei as the legitimate successor to Han, Luo considered Shu the rightful heir. Presenting his hero, Liu Bei, who becomes the King of Shu, as the legal successor to the Han family, Luo sees the struggle for power as a great historical drama involving opposite moral principles. Consequently, he pits Liu Bei, whom he depicts as the personification of legitimacy, righteousness, and honor, in alliance with Sun Quan, who has inherited the Wu kingdom, against Cao Cao, the founder of the Wei and the embodiment of falsehood, treachery, and cruelty. At Liu

Bei's side is his friend Guan Yu, the ideal feudal Chinese knight, who, though good and pure, is also foolhardy and arrogant. Liu Bei's prime minister and generalissimo, Zhuge Liang, combines loyalty, sagacity, and resourcefulness with amazing examples of military strategy. Another prominent hero-knight is Zhang Fei, who represents physical prowess, reckless bravery, and impetuous temper. Although Luo obviously intends to glorify Liu Bei and his friends and vilify Cao Cao and his supporters, he does not fail to humanize his characters and displays their weaknesses as well as their strengths. They are not stereotypes; rather, they are well-rounded, complex human beings. Although the novel is concerned mainly to show forth the vain ambitions of humans and their inability to control their own destinies, it is also a novel of character.

The term *yanyi* in the Chinese title of the novel has commonly been translated by Westerners as "romance," but it literally means "an expansion of the text in a popular version." In short, it means "popular history." To regard *The Romance of the Three Kingdoms*, however, as nothing more than popularized history, as some critics have, detracts much from the full measure of the author's achievement. Reacting against the superstitions and vulgarities of a cyclic tale told many times over by oral storytellers, Luo sought to create in writing a long narrative of the *zhang-hui* (chapter division) type which would be more artistically designed and more elegant in style than the folk version. Purging the story of most of its vulgar elements, he blended popular legend with authentic history, eliminating or selecting incidents to suit his purposes. He invented incidents to fit the personalities of his characters and changed the nature of historical personages to suit himself. Although the oral version supported the Buddhist theme of *baoying*, or "moral retribution" according to the law of karma, he substituted the Confucian theme of *tian ming*, or the "Mandate of Heaven," by which all events are determined. Working in this manner, Luo stitched together a strong internal pattern of military campaigns, political intrigues, small exciting incidents of various kinds, and vivid human relationships. Out of the multiplicity of characters and

heroes, Zhuge Liang emerges as the principal hero and the model of intelligence, wisdom, competence, resourcefulness, and selfless service to his prince. *The Romance of the Three Kingdoms* was a great pioneering effort and remains an important landmark in the history of Chinese fiction.

Possibly written as early as 1358 and circulated in handwritten manuscript, nothing of which is extant, the first printed edition of *The Romance of the Three Kingdoms* dates from about 1545. During the Qing Dynasty, around 1679, Mao Lun and his son Mao Zonggang edited a revised version of the novel together with a commentary. This Mao edition has been regarded as the standard since 1925, when C. H. Brewitt-Taylor brought out an English translation of the novel in two volumes, which is relatively complete and reads smoothly. A reprint of this translation with an introduction by Roy Andrew Miller appeared in 1959.

If *The Romance of the Three Kingdoms* is a great re-creation of an exciting historical period, which is also relatively authentic history, the next major effort in the history of the Chinese novel, *Water Margin*, is a creation of a historical epoch which is almost wholly fictitious. In seventy chapters in the standard edition, *Water Margin* is the story of 108 heroes who have rebelled, not against the government itself, but against the activities of corrupt officials in the government, and who are living the life of outlaws. The term *shui hu* means "water margin"; in this context, it refers to a region in present-day Shandong Province, Liangshanbo. It is in this area, composed of Mount Liang (Liangshan) and the marshes that surround it, that the brigand-heroes, under the leadership of Song Jiang, have established their headquarters. Although the novel is almost entirely imaginative, this situation had a historical basis. A similar band of outlaws, including the historical Song Jiang, were active at this location in a similar manner from about 1117 to 1121, or immediately prior to the collapse of the Northern Song Dynasty in 1126. The historical Song Jiang and his outlaw band surrendered to the government in 1121. According to some historical sources, the government then enlisted the band in a campaign to quell a much more threatening revolt led by the rebel Fang La.

The story of Song Jiang and his outlaw band was a favorite topic with the oral storytellers of the Southern Song Dynasty; it also became a popular subject with the Yuan Dynasty playwrights. The Mongol historian T'o T'o mentions the activities of Song Jiang and his outlaws in his dynastic history, the *Songshi* (1345). Finally, an early Yuan fiction, apparently based on a Song *pinghua* promptbook, also tells this tale. *Water Margin* must have been inspired by these sources as well as by popular legend.

Unlike *The Romance of the Three Kingdoms*, whose tight internal structure results from the interweaving of narrative strands and interrelated conflict situations, *Water Margin* is composed of a sequence of cycles, each of which features a different hero. Hence, although its internal structure is weaker than that of *The Romance of the Three Kingdoms*, its overall structure is stronger. Jin Shengtan's 1641 redaction in seventy chapters, which has become the standard edition, ends with the brigand-heroes assembled in the Hall of Loyalty and Righteousness. They are assembled to receive the Heavenly Tablet, on which their names are inscribed together with the mottoes "Carry Out the Will of Heaven" and "Fidelity and Loyalty Complete." Although Jin's ending was actually designed to avoid heaping praise on the outlaws, it nevertheless underscores their lofty principles and the grandeur of their mission. It was no wonder that the Jin version of the novel scored such a hit with the Chinese people.

It must be pointed out, however, that the Jin edition is an arbitrary redaction of a 120-chapter version possibly edited by Yang Tingqian in 1614. The ending of the story in this edition differs significantly from the one provided by Jin in 1641. In the Yang edition, the story ends tragically, the heroes dying one by one with their missions unfulfilled. Jin actually retained seventy-one chapters of the Yang version but converted chapter 1 into a prologue. Jin's ending, therefore, was both new and arbitrary. It was motivated not by any aesthetic consideration but by political morality, slanted by Jin's personal dislike for the rebel leader Song Jiang. The Jin edition became the standard simply because of its great popularity. An edition prior to Yang's also once existed.

This was the Guo Xun edition of about 1550, which consisted of one hundred chapters. It is this edition that states that Shi Nai'an was the author and Luo Guanzhong the editor. Although only five chapters of this edition have survived, the whole appeared in a Kangxi reprint of 1589. The problem of the definitive text of the novel, therefore, is complex.

At any rate, *Water Margin* in the Jin edition is perhaps the finest example of *wuxia xiaoshuo* (military knight fiction) in Chinese literature. Pearl S. Buck produced an English translation of the novel in 1933 under the title *All Men Are Brothers*, issued in two volumes, and J. A. Jackson issued an English translation as *Water Margin* in 1937, also in two volumes. Jackson's translation is more condensed and less literal than that of Buck. Although Buck's contains some expurgations, it is faithful to the original text, yet it lacks the spirit of action and movement which Jackson's conveys. There are many inaccuracies in both translations.

With these two masterpieces of the late Yuan period, *The Romance of the Three Kingdoms* and *Water Margin*, the Chinese novel came of age. No doubt because of the popularity of Yuan and Ming drama and other types of theatrical entertainment, however, a hiatus in novel writing set in for nearly two centuries, and it was not until the 1560's that another novelistic masterpiece finally appeared. This work was *The Journey to the West*, by Wu Cheng'en, a writer, poet, scholar, and official of the middle Ming period. The discovery of the novel's true author did not occur, however, until the twentieth century. Previously, its composition had been ascribed to Qiu Zhuqi (1148-1227), a great traveler who was an adviser to Genghis Khan.

On the literal level, *The Journey to the West* is the story of the journey from China to India of a Chinese Buddhist monk named Xuanzang, or Tripitaka, who is accompanied by four animal spirits who serve as his disciples. In fact, it is not the monk who is the hero of the story but one of his disciples, a monkey spirit named Sun Wukong. The other disciples are a pig spirit named Zhu Bajie, a fish spirit named Sha Heshang, and the monk's white horse, who is a dragon prince in disguise and understands human speech. Consisting of one hundred chapters, the novel is divided into four parts. The first deals with the birth and early life of the monkey spirit. Born of an egg-shaped rock, he becomes king of the monkey tribe. Highly intelligent, he studies Buddhism and Daoism, acquires magical powers and superhuman abilities, and becomes an immortal. A resident in Heaven, his ego is so inflated that he seeks to replace the Jade Emperor on the throne. After causing havoc in Heaven, he is subdued by Buddha himself and imprisoned beneath the Mountain of Five Elements. Five hundred years later, he is released to serve Tripitaka. The second division is the story of the early life of Tripitaka and the origin of his quest. The third division relates the adventures of Tripitaka and his disciples on their way to India. After fourteen years, the pilgrims reach their destination, where they collect numerous scriptures. Not until their return to China, however, do they attain enlightenment and Buddhahood. The journey is described in a lively and rapid narrative embracing many episodes and numerous trials, tribulations, and confrontations with demons and monsters. The fourth part presents the conclusion of the journey.

Despite its supernatural cast, the tale had a small basis in fact. There was a historical Chinese Buddhist monk named Xuanzang who was known by the religious name of Tang Sanzang (or Tripitaka—the collection of Buddhist scriptures). He traveled to India and was absent from China for seventeen years (629-645). When he returned to China, he became a national hero and a favorite of the emperor. He spent the rest of his life translating the Indian texts and teaching his disciples. He dictated his account of his journey to a disciple, Pianqi, entitling it *Da Tang xiyu ji* (seventh century; *On Yuan Chwang's Travels in India, 629-645 A.D.*, 1904-1905). Xuanzang and his journey became a popular subject of the oral storytellers. The Tripitaka legend became as popular with the Chinese as the Liangshan legend of Song Jiang and his outlaw band.

Wu Cheng'en's fantastic novel, however, appears designed to suggest much more than its literal level of presentation, as interesting, exciting, and amusing as that is. Although the author good-naturedly pokes fun at the three Chinese religions and the governmental hierarchy and its bureaucracy, underneath or beyond that is a serious thrust, a satire upon the nature of humanity itself and an effort to explain the fundamental process through which any human, regardless of his or her particular religious orientation, comes to enlightenment and consequent peace of mind. It is clear that Tripitaka represents Everyman. An ordinary physical mortal, he is fearful, humorless, not too bright, gullible, preoccupied with his own well-being and safety, yet also filled with love and compassion. All too human, he is a model of unenlightened human behavior, a *ying'er* (a babe in the woods). At the same time, he and his animal spirit friends also clearly represent the various aspects of the human self. He is referred to in the text as "the body of the Law" (*fashen*), "the original nature" (*benxing*), and the "primal spirit" (*yuanshen*).

On the other hand, the monkey spirit obviously represents the human mind at its most efficient and is referred to as the "mind-monkey" (*xinhou*). He is smart, nimble, clever, rampant, courageous, arrogant, and vainglorious. He personifies the genius of humans, and he calls himself "The Great Sage, Equal to Heaven." Yet as Lucifer could not outwit or best God, so Monkey cannot outwit or best Buddha, who is simply the Enlightened One and no divinity. The pig spirit represents humanity's gross nature and sensual appetites; he is lazy, lecherous, gluttonous, jealous, envious, and stupid. The fish spirit, a water monster who lived in the River of Flowing Sands prior to joining Tripitaka, is a coward and a bluffer who seeks to deceive through a ferocious appearance and a bold front; he represents people's self-deceptions, illusions, and fears. The white dragon/horse symbolizes humanity's will and determination, an indomitable spirit and sense of responsibility and a willingness to take on a burden and see it through to the end.

These are but some general observations on the complex range of meaning with which the novel is infused in terms of symbolization and allegory. This range of meaning supports the novel's main concern, which is Wu Cheng'en's explanation of the process of human salvation. This state comes about by self-cultivation of the whole person, mind and body. With discipline and humility, humans can arrive at a mental and physical equilibrium, their minds in tune with the corporeal world, the total human in harmony with himself or herself and the universe. It is only through corporeality that humans can arrive at the necessary perception of nothingness—a realization that completes the process of enlightenment whereby humans reach complete peace of mind. In short, Wu Cheng'en's formula is *yisiwukong*—that is, "to perceive the nature of emptiness through the medium of illusion," for the corporeal world, though real, is not Ultimate Reality, which is Void. *The Journey to the West* is not only an outstanding example of a novel on a supernatural theme but also a polysemous, complex, and seminal book.

Arthur Waley's English translation under the title *Monkey*, though partial, is superb and has long been popular with the general public. Anthony C. Yu, however, has produced the first complete translation, published under the original title in four volumes. Yu's translation is both highly readable and faithful to the original text, and it is supplemented by helpful notes.

Possibly written as early as 1565, the next great masterpiece in the history of the Chinese novel, *Jin Ping Mei* (the title consists of parts of the names of three women characters), is of uncertain authorship. Its composition generally has been attributed to Wang Shizhen, a scholar and writer who is alleged to have written it as an instrument of revenge against an official who had ruined the author's father, another official. This attribution, however, has been questioned, and several other candidates have been proposed, including Xu Wei (1521-1593), a writer and painter, and Li Kaixian (1501-1568), a poet and playwright. At any rate, the problem remains unsolved. At least one handwritten manuscript of the one-hundred-chapter novel was in circulation during the 1590's.

The first printed edition appeared around 1610, but it met with destruction. The earliest extant edition, known as the Wanli edition, was published around 1617 under the title *Jin Ping Mei Cihua* (Jin Ping Mei, a vernacular novel with songs). Sometime between 1666 and 1684, the critic and writer Zhang Zhupo (c. 1654-c. 1694) prepared an edition with a commentary entitled *Zhang Zhupo ping Jin Ping Mei* (Jin Ping Mei commented on by Zhang Zhupo). This edition has been regarded as standard. The important thing as far as Chinese literary history is concerned is that *Jin Ping Mei* was a complete departure in terms of the previous history of the novel. Previous novels had dealt either with people who were of epic proportions or with characters who were different in kind from humans, such as immortals, spirits, demons, and monsters. As specific fictional forms, they are "romances." *Jin Ping Mei*, however, deals with ordinary people in the context of social relations and manners. Indeed, it is a "novel of manners," a "novel" in the specific formal sense, the first such long narrative in China.

Although *Jin Ping Mei* purports to show the dissolute manners of the time of the Song emperor Huizong, it actually depicts those of the author's own time, the first half of the sixteenth century. Set in the town of Quinghe in present-day Shantung Province, the story is primarily concerned with the town's leading citizen and businessman, Ximen Qing, and his six wives. The wealthy owner of an apothecary shop and an underworld figure as well, his principal activities are making money, gaining social prestige, and searching for fresh sexual experience, particularly by seducing married women. The novel delineates representative figures at most levels of Ming society; it was the first Chinese novel to adequately characterize women. Although the title *Jin Ping Mei* may be read literally to mean something like "plum blossoms in a golden vase," it actually refers to three women in Ximen Qing's life: "Jin" to Pan Jinlian (Golden Lotus), the fifth wife; "Ping" to Li Ping'er (Little Vase), the sixth wife; and "Mei" to Chunmei (Spring Plumblossom), Lotus's maid, whom Ximen debauches. The other women of Ximen's household are Yueniang (Moon Lady), who holds the honored position of first wife; Li Qiao'er, the second wife; Meng Yulou, the third wife; and Hsüeh-o, the fourth wife; of these, only Moon Lady is a decent person. It is Golden Lotus, a veritable femme fatale, who is the dominant character of the book. She promotes her husband's financial ruin and contributes to his early death.

Although the novel progresses by episodes, the tension developed between the parts and the whole is, for the first time in Chinese long fiction, satisfactorily resolved. Its explicit descriptions of sexual activity have frequently been termed pornographic, but they are in fact supportive of the novel's individualized characterizations and naturalistic view of life. Its naturalism, however, is not based on the Western notion of the influence of heredity and environment in human makeup but on the Buddhist notion of moral retribution, in which humans are a product of the quality of their deeds throughout their previous states of existence. The personal view of the author, however, appears more Confucian than Buddhist because he has taken pains to show the folly of those men and women who become hopelessly trapped in the net of a hedonistic and materialistic world. He appears to regret the necessity of the novel's religious solution when Moon Lady permits her only son, the fifteen-year-old Hsiaoko, to enter a Buddhist monastery to become a monk to save his father's soul. Although the author derived the opening of his novel from chapter 22 of *Water Margin*, introducing the reader to the famous military knight Wu Song, he quickly shifts the focus from him to Golden Lotus, who murders her husband, Wu Song's brother, in order to marry Ximen, with whom she is having an adulterous affair. On this and other sources, the author shows but little dependence. *Jin Ping Mei* is primarily a work of a single imagination and a unified and effective narrative. Although heavily erotic, the novel is a strong work of social criticism.

In 1939, Clement Egerton issued an English translation of *Jin Ping Mei* in four volumes, reprinted in 1954; the erotic passages, however, are rendered in Latin. A revised version, fairly complete and unexpurgated, was published in 1972 and is readable and fairly accurate. There is also an English translation by Bernard Miall from the German of Franz Kuhn, published in 1940 in two volumes and reprinted in one volume in 1947. It is abridged and expurgated.

Although *Jin Ping Mei* has been highly regarded by some critics, the consensus is that the greatest masterpiece in the history of the Chinese vernacular novel is *Dream of the Red Chamber*, by Cao Xueqin,

the scion of a wealthy family that inherited the office of supervisor of the imperial textile factory at Nanjing but suffered a fall from prosperity to poverty. In 120 chapters altogether, the first eighty chapters were thoroughly completed by Cao about 1763 and circulated in handwritten manuscript. The novel in this form included a commentary prepared by an older cousin of the author, Cao Yufeng, known by his pen name, Zhiyan Zhai. Cao Xueqin died at about this time, leaving behind a forty-chapter conclusion to the novel in a rough draft. Nearly thirty years later, Go E and a contemporary, Cheng Weiyuan, edited the last forty chapters and issued the whole in a printed edition in 1792 under the new title *Dream of the Red Chamber*. The novel is presumed to be at least partly autobiographical because it relates the story of the wealthy Jia family and its decline and fall and thus duplicates to some degree the experience of the author himself.

Actually, *Dream of the Red Chamber* tells what might be called three stories in one, arranged in three insetting frames, the smallest set within the border of a larger and that larger set within the largest. The smallest story is concerned with the tragic love affair between two teenagers, Jia Baoyu (Precious Jade), the hero of the novel, and Lin Daiyu (Black Jade), his cousin and playmate, the heroine. The larger narrative is concerned with the decline and fall of the Jia family, within the context of which the romance takes place, but it features Baoyu's widowed grandmother, Jia Mu (Matriarch), who presides over the Rungquofu household, and Wang Xifeng (Phoenix), the wife of the Matriarch's grandson, Jia Lian, and the crafty manager of the household who, however, contributes to the family's ruin.

The largest narrative, the one that frames the others, utilizes a Chinese creation myth about the goddess Nügua and her efforts to repair the Dome of Heaven with pieces of rock. One such rock being left unused laments its fate to two passersby, a Buddhist monk and a Daoist priest. It expresses the wish to be transported to the earth so that it might experience life in the "red dust" (*hongchen*). While waiting at the court of the Goddess of Disillusionment to be thus transported, the celestial rock cares for a celestial plant by watering it daily with dew. This loving care makes the plant blossom into a fairy who vows that if she may accompany the rock to earth, she will repay his love with tears of gratitude. When Baoyu is born into the Chia family, he is "born with a piece of jade in his mouth" and obviously is the rock incarnate in the earthly setting. He falls in love with his cousin Lin Daiyu, who, sickly and temperamental, is like a sensitive plant and is clearly the plant fairy incarnate on earth. In her romance with Baoyu, she cries many tears, but they are tears of self-pity and jealousy rather than tears of gratitude. After the Jia family requires Baoyu to marry another cousin, Xue Baochai (Precious Clasp), instead of the unsuitable Daiyu, who soon dies, Baoyu begins to undergo a severe disillusionment. He begins to see desire, whether for love, status, wealth, or knowledge, as the root of all suffering. Longing to free himself from suffering, he decides to renounce the world, or life in the "red dust," to become an unattached monk. He is last seen disappearing into the horizon accompanied by a Buddhist monk and a Daoist priest. Thus, through Buddhist wisdom and Daoist grace he has achieved enlightenment after having experienced the sufferings of a man in this life. The myth rounds out the novel.

The autobiographical background of *Dream of the Red Chamber* and its treatment of its subject have prompted various interpretations as to its real meaning. Some of the interpretations are simply silly. It is not easy to decide whether Cao Xuegin intended his novel to be an attack on Confucian ideals and morality and on the feudal system generally, or a vindication of Confucianism and the feudal system (by demonstrating that sensual indulgence, the neglect of the cultivation of Confucian morality, and the irrationality of romantic love can wreck not only the individual but also an entire family), or a compromise with Confucianism and the feudal system (by advocating a Buddhism-Daoist form of escapism). It appears that the novel is actually a complex response to the whole Chinese cultural tradition and that the device of ambiguity is its watchword. This ambiguity is given expression by the author's attitudes of detachment, toleration, and compassion, which foster a subjective interpretation of the novel's meaning at the hands of every reader. To a Confucian, romantic love is disas-

trous, and the ending is a regrettable form of escapism. To a Buddhist or Daoist, romantic love can mean only suffering, and the ending points out the proper solution. To a Chinese taken by Western democratic ideals, Confucianism and the feudal system were cruel anachronisms whose destruction was overdue in the eighteenth century. To a Chinese communist, the novel is a direct attack on Confucianism and the feudal system, and its ending is a regrettable capitulation to superstition. It would seem that Cao Xueqin himself was more concerned with rendering a tragic sense of life than championing any one of these interpretations.

Dream of the Red Chamber is notable for a variety of qualities, some of which mark an important advance over previous Chinese novels. The plot, though complex, is carefully framed and tightly knit in its development to the end. The characterization is outstanding, particularly in respect to older women. The portrait of the widowed grandmother, Jia Mu, is certainly one of the finest characterizations of an elderly woman to be found in any novel, and that of Wang Xifeng is also vivid and forceful. The characters of the young girls, Lin Daiyu and Xue Baochai, are well defined and individualized. Baoyu's character is developed step-by-step through dialogue, through his reactions to various situations and through his dreams until he is well understood by the reader. The novel is outstanding for its psychological analysis and penetration. The author rarely indulges in didacticism or authorial comment but allows the opposition between the attitudes of detachment and compassion to develop the ambiguity necessary for subjective judgment. He also makes subtle use of poetry to guide the reader's feelings. The style he employs is a polished, refined, and highly expressive form of the colloquial that is unusually advanced. Altogether, *Dream of the Red Chamber* is a work that is both realistic and imaginative. It is a close study of the everyday life of a wealthy and aristocratic Chinese family of the eighteenth century, a precise analysis of the ravages of a romantic love affair, and a profound religious and philosophical commentary on the nature of human life.

The standard Chinese text of *Dream of the Red*

Chamber is the Chengqao edition, published in 1792. It was reprinted in Taibei (Taipei) in a two-volume edition under the title *Tsu-pen Hung-lou mêng* (1957). A variorum edition in four volumes, however, was published in Beijing in 1958. This work was prepared by Xu Pingbo and Wang Xishi and issued under the title *Honglou meng bashi wei chao ben*.

There are several English translations of *Dream of the Red Chamber*. One translated from a German version by Franz Kuhn was done by Florence McHugh and Isabel McHugh and published in 1958. Another was done by Wang Qichen and published in the same year. Neither is completely satisfactory, for different reasons. In 1973, however, David Hawkes began a multivolume English translation under the title *The Story of the Stone*, which makes up for what the previous translations lack.

In addition to the five outstanding masterpieces of the Chinese novel already discussed, there are two other traditional vernacular novels of such importance that they deserve mention. They are the eighteenth century *The Scholars*, by Wu Jingzi, and the early twentieth century *The Travels of Lao Can*, by Liu E.

Wu Jingzi's *The Scholars* (the Chinese title literally means "unofficial history of the forest of scholars") is an attack on pseudoscholarship and hypocrisy and an exposure of the ill effects produced by the civil-service examination system, especially after the emphasis put on the writing of the *bagu wen* (eight-legged essay). Wu Jingzi came from a well-to-do family that had produced many scholars and officials. He himself, however, was of a nonconforming temperament. He shunned an official career and took no interest in preparing for the civil-service examinations. Indeed, he preferred the company of poets, painters, writers, monks, prostitutes, and actors rather than that of officials and bureaucrats. Although his novel is satiric, it is also good-humored. It displays his sincere Confucian convictions, the first and last chapters describing paragons of Confucian virtue who are ignored by high officialdom. In the rest of the book, he satirizes both the worst elements produced by the civil-service system and the rest of the social order as well. In addition to being the first ef-

fective novel of exposure, it is also a *roman à clef*, because many of the book's characters are based on either famous historical people or personal acquaintances of the author. Although the novel is composed of episodes that are lacking in unity, the characterization is individualized and well-rounded and is perhaps the most distinguished feature of the novel.

In his epilogue, Wu Jingzi presents his own moral vision. Although still in resistance against corrupt and hypocritical authority, he introduces four humble scholar-artist recluses who represent the Four Noble Pastimes of the Chinese scholar: the playing of the *guqin* (a particular kind of lute); the playing of *weigi* (Chinese checkers; called *go* in Japan); the practice of *shufa* (writing with the brush or calligraphy); and the practice of *wen ru hua* (literary painting, the art that combined painting, calligraphy, and poetry). Through these four figures, Wu suggests that if the world is easily misled by degrees, official rank, and material success, there are in the background genuine scholars and true artists. If they are unknown and in humble circumstances, they practice their scholarship and their noble pastimes with sincerity and moral sensibility. Such men can carry forward the cause of culture and morality in China even if others have failed.

There is an adequate English translation of *The Scholars* by Hsien-i Yang and Gladys Yang, published in Beijing in 1957. The full-scale Chinese text was published in Taibei in a fourth printing under the title *Ju-lin wai-shih* (1957).

Liu E's *The Travels of Lao Can* is the most important Qing novel produced after the end of the nineteenth century. Written between 1904 and 1907, it was given partial publication in a magazine and a newspaper. The first complete version appeared in book form in 1909. Its literary value, however, was not fully appreciated until the publication of the Ya Dong edition of 1925, which included an introduction by the renowned scholar and critic Hu Shi (Shih), who had in 1917 successfully advocated the use of vernacular Chinese (*baihua*) in "respectable" literature. Like *The Scholars*, *The Travels of Lao Can* is a novel of exposure (and also a *roman à clef*). The novel of exposure became particularly fashionable during the declining years of the Qing period. Some critics think that these "muckraking" novels reflect the transition between the traditional and the modern vernacular novel. *The Travels of Lao Can* launches an attack on official corruption and harsh government and shows Liu E's concern over the declining state of China in his time. At the same time, he celebrates in lyric style the pleasures of living and remains optimistic about China's future.

It is generally taken that Lao Can is a self-portrait of the author. Although Liu E was born into a scholar-official family, he declined to prepare for the civil-service examinations and instead devoted himself to a variety of studies: medicine, law, astronomy, engineering, music, poetry, and oracle bone inscriptions. He began his career by practicing medicine. Later, at various times, he operated a tobacco shop, a printing shop, and a mining company, and he tried to organize a railroad company. He also supervised flood-control operations and took an interest in criminal justice. The Lao Can of the novel is an itinerant physician who practices traditional Chinese medicine. He is fond of music and poetry and enjoys the drum-tale recitations of the Fair and the Dark Maids. He is interested in good and just government, flood-control measures, and the criminal justice system. He acts the part of the famous eleventh century judge-detective, Bao Zheng, by intervening in a sensational murder case, thwarting the harsh official, Gang Bi, and saving the lives of thirteen members of the Jia family. Like his creator, he is a man of varied interests, wide learning, practical competence, independent courage, and humanitarian compassion. He is a lover of people, nature, art, and life. Although a spokesman for the author, Lao Can is at the same time a credible character and a real human being in his own right.

The Travels of Lao Can, which in a genuine edition consists of twenty chapters, is mainly concerned with the fate of China and the sufferings of its people in Liu E's time. Quite loosely organized, the book divides itself into three main parts. At the beginning, in the preface and the first chapter, Liu compares the Chinese state to the endgame in chess, the onset of old age, and a leaky ship, which, though floundering in tempestuous seas and on the verge of sinking, refuses any outside assistance. The first part, however, is mainly concerned with the wanderings through Shantung Province of the itinerant physician, Lao Can, and with the reports he hears of a harsh official, Yu Xian. The second part is mainly a philosophical interlude in which a woman philosopher, Yu Gu, and a hermit-sage, Yellow Dragon, offer their views on various philosophical problems. The third part is mainly about Lao Can's investigation of the murder case being prosecuted by another harsh official, Gang Bi, and his exposure.

Despite the novel's loose construction, the entire work has a pattern. The first and last parts constitute a third-person journal of the travels of a highly interesting person and his observations, conversations, and reflections. The middle section gives his responses to what he has seen, heard, and meditated upon—in short, it gives his responses to his own times. The book ends with Lao Can saving thirteen innocent lives and then taking one of the unfortunate singsong girls for a concubine. Thus, the two contrasting sides of his nature are shown—his humanitarian idealism and his capacity to enjoy the pleasures of life. Technically, the novel exhibits several unusual qualities: the effective use of the third-person narrator, the skillful use of the character of Lao Can as a persona for the author, the artistry displayed in the vivid descriptions of scenery, and, finally, the adroit harmonizing of a lyric style with the dissonance of sociopolitical concerns. On the whole, the novel is a delight to read. An excellent, complete English translation of *The Travels of Lao Can* by Harold Shadick was published in 1952.

THE MODERN MOVEMENT

The twentieth century saw the Manchu rulers of the Qing Dynasty enter into their last days. It was evident on every side that drastic reforms were needed if China were to overcome its backwardness and catch up with the progress made in the West. Although the monarchy initiated various reforms, it failed to satisfy the new Chinese revolutionaries led by Sun Yat-sen (Zhongshan). While Sun was abroad, his followers in China rebelled in 1911. With Russian communist support, they overthrew the Manchu monarchy, and China became, at least technically, a republic. Although Sun was chosen the first president, he soon resigned in favor of army commander Yuan Shikai, who possessed sufficient military strength to defeat the republic if he wished.

The new "republic" faced enormous problems on every side: economic distress among the masses, steadily increasing indebtedness to foreign nations, contentions among foreign nations on Chinese soil for railroad concessions, and disunion. Army commanders, or "warlords," in various areas of the country were powers unto themselves and not subject to the control of the central government. China entered World War I on the side of the Allies, hoping to improve its international position. These hopes were frustrated by the growing power of Japan. China stood in desperate need of all sorts of reforms.

In 1917, the Western-educated scholar and critic Hu Shi (Shih) launched the Literary Reform Movement, which was to have widespread effects on Chinese education and the future of Chinese literature. In an article published on January 1 of that year, in a magazine called *Xin Qingnian* (new youth), edited by Chen Duxiu, Hu Shi (Shih) argued that *wenyan*, or literary Chinese, had outlived its usefulness as the language of communication and should be replaced by *baihua*, or vernacular Chinese. His argument proved convincing. Yet, because there were many local dialects of colloquial Chinese, this complication posed a problem. If there were to be a national language, one of these dialects would have to be chosen as the standard. Considering that the Mandarin dialects of the north were understood by ninety percent of the Chinese population, the dialect of Beijing was selected as the standard. It, therefore, received the designation of *guoyu*, or "national language."

In 1920, the Chinese government decreed that standardized *guoyu* be taught in the first two grades of elementary school. By 1928, this decree was extended to the junior middle schools, and textbooks in classical Chinese were banned from these grades. This new attitude toward *baihua* prompted a reevaluation of those old novels, short stories, plays, and folk poems that were written in a style close to the colloquial but had no respectable standing as literature. By this time, also, many translations of Western books had made their appearance, and Chinese intellectuals had begun to read Western literary masterpieces. They were amazed to learn that in the West short stories, novels, plays, and poems written in the vernacular were regarded as great works of art. Therefore, when Chinese authors began to write fiction and other literary forms in *guoyu*, they imitated the Western literary forms that enjoyed such high prestige. They ignored the fact that China had, for centuries, possessed a vernacular literature of its own. Although a few intellectuals insisted that traditional Chinese vernacular literature had artistic merits of its own, they were unable to convince others that this opinion had any validity; it took almost a generation before the idea gained wide currency.

Few Westerners realize the full significance of the Literary Revolution, which may be said to have actually begun with the abolition of the civil-service examination system in 1905 and was completed by the rejection of literary Chinese for modern writing in 1920. It was not merely that the classical language had been replaced by the vernacular of *guoyu*. More important for the future of Chinese literature was the fact that the reading audience that had enjoyed the perusal of literary Chinese and traditional vernacular literature was also dispensed with, together with its entire culture, and replaced with an entirely new audience, a popular audience. At the same time, however, this popular audience was rejected by the new intellectual class. In rejecting the elite audience and its culture, the new intellectuals also rejected the traditional popular culture that was the inheritance of the mass person. The new intellectuals were therefore cultureless in the Chinese sense. Having stripped themselves of their Mandarin robes and insignia and donned plain Western garb, they attempted to graft Western culture to the new mass person whom they had created in the laboratory of their imaginations but who did not yet exist. They set themselves the difficult task of creating not only a new literature but also a new audience.

When Sun Yat-sen (Zhongshan) died in 1925, the former director of the Wangpu Military Academy, Chiang Kai-shek (Jiang Jieshi), emerged as the new leader. His immediate object was the reunification of China through conquest of the northern warlords, and he launched his "northern expedition" against them in 1926. Meanwhile, the communists within the Guomingdang (Kuomintang) attempted to organize the workers and peasants to support their cause. Rightly suspecting that the communists were bent on taking over the Guomindang, Jiang expelled them from that body in 1927. In 1928, he succeeded in overcoming the Beijing government and thus reuniting China more than it had been since 1911, but genuine reunification was never achieved. Some warlords still held out against Jiang's leadership, and the communists, largely driven from the cities, established themselves in the hinterlands under the leadership of Mao Zedong and Zhu De. China was therefore continually engaged in domestic warfare until the Japanese invasion of China in 1937. The modern Literary Reform Movement therefore labored under unusually adverse conditions from 1920 to 1937, when it practically ground to a halt. From 1937 until the Japanese defeat, most Chinese writers believed that it was their patriotic duty to support the war effort to defeat and expel the foreign invader. If they wrote fiction at all, it became an instrument of patriotic propaganda. With the Japanese surrender in 1945, civil war broke out between the communists and the Guomindang; it ended when, in 1949, mainland China fell to the communists and the Nationalist Government fled to Taiwan.

The first writer of the Literary Reform Movement to gain enduring fame was Lu Xun (1881-1936), whose real name was Zhou Shuren. In 1918, he published his first short story in the May, 1918, issue of *Xin Qingnian*, "Kuangren Riji" ("The Diary of a Madman"), an attack on Confucian morality. It is considered the first work of modern Chinese fiction. He is most widely known, however, for his novella *Ah Q zhengzhuan* (anthologized 1923, published separately, 1946; *The True Story of Ah Q*, 1927), which he wrote in 1921 as an illustration of the failure of the revolution of 1911. He did not write many stories, and *The True Story of Ah Q* is the nearest he came to novel length. He devoted himself mainly to writing polemical essays.

The period 1930 to 1937 proved the most productive for the new literature; some critics have dubbed this period the Chinese Renaissance. Many poems,

short stories, and novels were produced during this time, but perhaps the finest work was done in the short story. Several novels, however, have gained considerable fame. They are the work of Mao Dun (pseudonym of Shen Yanping, born 1896), Lao She (pseudonym of Shu Qingchun, 1899-1966), Shen Congwen (born 1902), and Ba Jin (pseudonym of Li Feigan, born 1904). All of these writers also wrote short stories.

Mao Dun's second novel, *Zi ye* (*Midnight*, 1957), published in 1933, is regarded as his finest effort and is considered a masterpiece in the People's Republic of China. Set in Shanghai during the years 1925 through 1927, it concerns the owner of a silk mill, Wu Sun fu, and the struggle between capitalists and workers. The point of view is anti-Trotsky. The novel presents a panorama of the industrial and business activity of the great city of Shanghai and its environs.

Lao She grew up in poverty, a condition that developed in him a philosophy of fatalism. His most famous novel is *Luotuo Xiangzi*, which English-speaking readers know in Evan King's 1945 translation by the title *Rickshaw Boy*. Published in 1938, it is the story of an honest, sensitive, and industrious ricksha boy who fails to survive in the face of destructive socioeconomic forces.

Shen Congwen, hailing from Hunan Province, had a military rather than a conventional academic background. Of the modern writers, he has paid the least attention to Western influences. As a youth, he served in the army and saw many places and many people. His fiction is peopled with garrison soldiers, bandits, peasants, landlords, civil servants, scholars, artisans, sailors, and prostitutes. He wrote many novels and an abundance of stories. His finest novel is generally considered to be *Chang he* (1949; the long river), which he wrote in about 1937. It is a sensitive pastoral story that is realistically and objectively presented. Interwoven with social criticism and Daoist wisdom, it shows a profound understanding of human nature.

Ba Jin grew up in a landowning family in Sichuang Province. As a youth, he absorbed the anarchistic ideas of the Russians Mikhail Bakunin and Pyotr Kropotkin. Having revolted against the Chinese family system and Confucian morality, he dramatized his feelings in his novel *Jia* (1933; *The Family*, 1964). It immediately became popular with radical Chinese youths. While it made its author famous, it is an overrated novel, sentimental and immature.

After the founding of the People's Republic of China, a series of measures was taken by the ruling communist party to make writers faithful tools of the dictatorship of the proletariat. All the writers became members of writers' federations under the control of the party. As *ganbu* (cadres), writers were paid fixed salaries and were required to follow the policy laid down by Mao: Art and literature must serve workers, peasants, soldiers, and the party's political agenda.

Most of the novels published during the period of 1949 to 1966 exemplify what Mao called "revolutionary realism" combined with revolutionary romanticism and glorify Mao or ordinary revolutionaries under his leadership. Among these novels are Wu Qiang's *Hongri* (1957; *Red Sun*, 1961) and Hao Ran's *Jinguang dadao* (1972; *The Golden Road*, 1981). Few works depicting intellectuals and business people were allowed to be printed, and all of them had to reflect the ideological remolding of the intellectuals and the transformation of business people by the party. Yang Mu's *Qingchun zhi ge* (1958; the song of the youth) serves as an example. Almost no novels were written by such writers as Lao She and Bao Jin, who had established themselves before 1949.

Members of writers' federations had to undergo rigid ideological reform by studying Marxism-Leninism and Maoism, undergoing relentless political examinations under the supervision of party organizations, and living and working among factory workers and poor and lower-middle class peasants to become aware of the difference between "the pettiness of their bourgeois thinking" and the admirable qualities of the rank and file revolutionaries. Moreover, they were subjected to repeated and merciless political purges ordered by Mao. Survivors of one major purge might not escape the next one. Among the major purges was the Suppression of the Counter-Revolutionaries in the early 50's, with Hu Feng and his close colleagues being the most famous victims in the literary circle. Dur-

ing the Anti-Rightists Movement in 1957, such famous writers as Ting Lin, Ai Qing, Wang Meng, and Liu Binyan were condemned as antiparty rightists and sent to forced labor camps without a trial. However, all these persecutions of writers and other intellectuals, though already cruel and illegal, were simply dwarfed by the so-called Great Culture Revolution started by Mao in 1966.

Mao's zealous followers publicly humiliated, physically brutalized, psychologically tortured, and in many cases even murdered those they considered to be anti-Mao elements. Such elements included Liu Shaoqi, vice chairman of the party and president of the republic, who died in solitary confinement, and Zhao Shuli, author of *Xiao Erhei jiehun* (1943; Xiao Erhei getting married), who was beaten to death by red guards. To protest the ceaseless, unlawful persecutions of innocent people and preserve their dignity, a large number of artists committed suicide. One of them was a literary giant in modern Chinese history, Lao She, who threw himself into the Weiming Lake at the most prestigious institution of higher learning in China, Beijing University. Those who happened to survive the first waves of vicious assault by Mao's followers were then dispatched to the countryside to do forced labor, all in the name of what Mao called "reeducation" by the workers and peasants.

The rampage of Mao's revolution eventually came to an end with his death and the fall of the Gang of Four headed by his wife in 1976. Then, one by one, almost all the writers victimized by Mao's constant purges were rehabilitated. Literary creation resumed. What first appeared on the scene was *shonghen wenxue* (literature of the wounded), with personal or family tragedies under Mao's tyranny as the only logical and inevitable subject matter. One of its earliest representatives was Lu Yanxio's *Tianyunshan chuanqi* (1980; legend of the Tainyun mountain). In 1979 New Realism emerged with the publication of several important novellas, such as Shen Rong's *Ren dao zhongnian* (1980; *At Middle Age*, 1987) and pieces of reportage literature (*baogao wenxue*), such as Liu binyan's *Ren yao zhijian* (1982; People or Monsters?: and Other Stories and Reportage from China after Mao, 1983).

New Realism differed from the literature of the wounded in that the former endeavored to reveal the disparity between the ideals of socialism and the reality of corruption and bureaucracy, while the latter attempted to recall the historical tragedy. Whatever their difference was, both were daring and successful attempts to break away from the fetters imposed by Mao, thus paving the way for a new generation of writers who could afford to ignore what Mao had said about literature. Among the new writers were Liu Sola, interested in experimental fiction; Mo Yan, author of *Hong gaoliang jiazu* (1987; *Red Sorgan: A Novel of China*, 1993), devoted to depicting life as lived by ordinary people with real strengths and weaknesses, moral aspirations, and sexual desires; and Eryue He, author of *Kangxi dadi* (1985; *Emperor Kangxi*), fascinated by the important lessons people can learn from Emperors Kangxi, Qilong, and Yongzheng instead of from Mao's workers, peasants, and soldiers.

After Mao's death, many taboos were broken, and a degree of freedom emerged. Writers were no longer forced to serve as tools of the party or undergo ideological remolding. Nevertheless, an awareness of the existence of a line that no one was allowed to cross remained; in other words, no one was allowed to challenge the legitimacy or authority of the ruling party. The consequence of breaking this ultimate taboo was unmistakably demonstrated by the massacre of students at Tiananmen Square on June 4, 1989.

Richard P. Benton, updated by Chenliang Sheng

BIBLIOGRAPHY

Hsia, Chih-tsing. *The Classic Chinese Novel: A Critical Introduction*. Reprint. Ithaca, N.Y.: Cornell University East Asia Program, 1996. A good introduction to Chinese long fiction. Includes a bibliography and an index.

Idema, Wilt, and Lloyd Haft. *A Guide to Chinese Literature*. Amsterdam: Amsterdam University Press, 1996. Translation Center for Chinese Studies, University of Michigan, 1997. This book covers Chinese literature up to the early 1990's. It contains a 103-page bibliography and a glossary and index of major works.

Lee Yee, ed. *The New Realism*. New York: Hippocrene Books, 1983. Contains an important introduction entitled "A Reflection of Reality." Provides the background of New Realism, highlights its impact on Chinese society, and outlines the authority's reaction to it.

Leung, Laifong. *Morning Sun: Interview of Chinese Writers of the Lost Generation*. Armonk, N.Y.: M. E. Sharp, 1994. A valuable reference for studies in literary works by writers of the so-called zhiqing generation, namely those who participated in Mao's Cultural Revolution, then went to the countryside to be rusticated, and finally, after Mao's death, came back to cities to face a rapidly changing society driven by materialistic desires.

Link, Perry, ed. *Roses and Thorns: The Second Blooming of the Hundred Flowers in Chinese fiction, 1979-80*. Berkeley: University of California Press, 1983. Useful and important to students interested in some writers' disastrous attempt to challenge the validity of Mao's literary theory in 1956-1957 and their successors' achievements three years after Mao's death.

McDougall, Bonnie S. *Mao Zedong's "Talks at the Yan'an Conference on Literature and Art": A Translation of the 1943 Text with Commentary*. Ann Arbor: Center for Chinese Studies, University of Michigan Press, 1980. The 1943 text is a must for anyone interested in understanding the theory behind the party policy on art and literature and the reason for artists' resistance to the party policy between 1949 and 1976.

Nienhauser, William H., ed. *The Indiana Companion to Traditional Chinese Literature*. Bloomington: Indiana University Press, 1986. An encyclopedic guide to Chinese literature completed by nearly two hundred scholars around the world, it concentrates on important authors, representative individual works, and various genres as well as unique types, including Buddhist and Daoist writings.

Rushton, Peter Halliday. *The "Jin Ping Mei" and the Non-linear Dimensions of the Traditional Chinese Novel*. Lewiston, N.Y.: Mellen University Press, 1994. Examines the important work and its impact on future Chinese literature.

THE ENGLISH NOVEL

To a greater extent than any other literary form, the novel is consistently and directly engaged with the society in which the writer lives and feels compelled to explain, extol, or criticize. The English novel, from its disparate origins to its development in the eighteenth century, from its rise in the nineteenth century to its present state, has been strongly influenced by the social, political, economic, scientific, and cultural history of England. In fact, English writers dominated the novel genre in its earliest stages of development and continued to do so through much of its history. As a realistic form, the novel not only reflects but also helps define and focus society's sense of itself, and as the novel reflects the growth of England first into a United Kingdom, then into an empire, and its decline to its present role in the Commonwealth of Nations, it does so predominantly through the eyes of the middle class.

Indeed, the origins and development of the English novel are most profitably examined in relation to the increasing growth and eventual dominance of the middle class in the course of several hundred years. Typically concerned with middle-class characters in a world largely of their making, the novel sometimes features excursions into the upper reaches of English society; with more frequency, it presents incursions by members of the upper class into the familiar world of the solid middle class. As a form of realistic literature intended primarily for the middle class, often for their instruction and edification (or excoriation), the novel frequently depicts the worlds of the lower orders of society, not only the exotic cultures subjugated by Imperial Britain, but also the familiarly strange domestic worlds of the "criminal classes," a subculture with its own hierarchies, vocabulary, customs, and occupations.

As distinguished from allegory and romance, the English novel has for its primary focus the individual situated in society and his or her emotions, thoughts, actions, choices, and relationships to others in complex and often bewildering environments. Set against backgrounds that realistically reflect all facets of the English experience, the "histories" or "lives" of the novels' protagonists must hold a necessary interest for readers who, in turn, seek to make sense of, master, cope with, escape from, or become fully assimilated into the society in which they, like their heroes and heroines, find themselves. While any attempt to trace with great particularity the multiple relationships between the history of the English novel and the larger patterns of English society remains necessarily imperfect, the general outlines of those relationships can be sketched.

ORIGINS OF THE ENGLISH NOVEL

Although long-standing debates about the origin of the English novel and the first English novel continue, it is both convenient and just to state that it is with the fiction of Daniel Defoe (1660-1731) that the first novel appeared, especially in the sense that term came to have in the late eighteenth century and continues to have today. Without considerable injustice it may be said that the novel first developed out of a series of false starts in the seventeenth century and a series of accidents in the eighteenth. The reading public, having been exposed to large amounts of novelistic material, fictions of various lengths, epics, and prose romances, appears to have been ready to receive a form that went beyond Aphra Behn's *Oroonoko: Or, The History of the Royal Slave* (1688), John Bunyan's *The Pilgrim's Progress from This World to That Which Is to Come* (1678), and the prose works of earlier masters such as Thomas Malory, John Mandeville, Robert Greene, Thomas Dekker, and Thomas Nashe. Such a form would emphasize unified action of some plausibility, individualized and articulate characters, and stories presented with such verisimilitude that the readers could find in them highly wrought illusions of the realities they knew best.

The literary children of the eighteenth century, the novel and its sibling the short story, created a taste for fiction of all varieties in a middle-class readership whose ranks were swollen by a newly literate mercantile class. This readership appears to have wanted and certainly received a literary medium of their own, filled with practically minded characters who spoke the same middle-class English language and prized the same middle-class English goals (financial and familial success) as they themselves did. In general, the novel helped make the position of the individual in new, expanding, and increasingly urban social contexts more intelligible; frequently addressed directly to the "dear reader," the novel presented unified visions of individuals in society, reflected the cultural and social conditions of that society, and the presumed rationalist psychology endemic to the age, which was fostered by Francis Bacon, Thomas Hobbes, and John Locke.

The novel was influenced by historic events and societal developments, especially tidal changes that involved the class structure of English society. The merchant class had existed for centuries and had steadily grown in the Age of Discovery and during colonization in the seventeenth century. In that century, a number of events conspired to begin the disestablishment of the feudal, medieval world, a disestablishment that would become final in the early nineteenth century. The beginning of the English Civil War (1642) marked the most noteworthy outbreak of religious and class strife England had yet seen. The subsequent regicide of Charles I in 1649 and the abolition of monarchy and the House of Lords by the House of Commons in that year signaled the formation of the Puritan Commonwealth (1649-1660) and the first rise to political dominance of the middle class, a much-contested context. In the Glorious Revolution of 1688, Parliament invited William of Orange and his wife, Mary, the Protestant daughter of the Catholic James II, to rule England. James II (the "Old Pretender") fled to France with his son Charles (the "Young Pretender" or "Bonnie Prince Charlie"), established himself in exile, and began plotting a return to power that would eventuate in the Scottish rebellions of 1715, 1719, and 1745-1746 on behalf of the Stuart monarchy. The Glorious Revolution may, in part, be seen as establishing the principle that the English middle class, through Parliament, could choose their own ruler; it may also be seen as another phase in the growth of power of that middle class.

A war with France (1689-1697) saw the beginning of the national debt, but the late seventeenth and early eighteenth centuries (especially during the reign of Queen Anne, 1702-1714) were marked by material progress, increased mercantilism, drastically increased population, and a rapid and irreversible shift of population from the country to the city. Apart from two major trade monopolies (the Hudson Bay Company in Canada and the East India Company in the Indian subcontinent), trade was open to all after 1689. Free enterprise flourished and with it the middle class, as early eighteenth century England became a mercantile society teetering on the brink of the Industrial Revolution and the concurrent scientific revolution that abetted it. While the governance of England still rested with a relatively small number of families, the hereditary landowners of England had to share power with the new merchant princes of the era.

From this milieu of class conflict emerged the earliest English novels. Rooted both in the picaresque tradition stemming from the anonymous Spanish *Lazarillo de Tormes* (1553) and Miguel de Cervantes's *El ingenioso hidalgo don Quixote de la Mancha* (1605, 1615; *The History of the Valorous and Wittie Knight-Errant, Don Quixote of the Mancha*, 1612-1620; better known as *Don Quixote de la Mancha*) and in the pseudohistorical tradition, Daniel Defoe's novels present their fictions as fact, as the "histories" or "lives" of characters such as Robinson Crusoe, Colonel Newport, and Moll Flanders. Defoe's novels are distinguished by a realism that employs minute and concerted observations, as well as a morality that—despite lapses, an occasional blind eye to folly, and some ambiguous presentations of vice—fits well with the morality of the middle class, especially when erstwhile sinners repent and exemplify the Protestant virtues of seriousness, usefulness, social responsibility, and thrift. Like their many literary descendants, Defoe's characters evince a cheerful triumph of person over place and situation, an eventual mastery of the world and its too-familiar snares in the common and the uncommon adventures that form their educative encounters with the world and with themselves.

Even more obviously in line with middle-class

Puritan ethics is the work of Samuel Richardson (1689-1761), whose epistolary novels of personality, sensibility, and moral conflict present the first multi-dimensional characters in English prose fiction. *Pamela: Or, Virtue Rewarded* (1740-1741) began by accident what Walter Allen calls the "first great flowering of the English novel." Commissioned to compose and print *Familiar Letters* as models of correspondence, moral guides, and repositories of advice to "handsome girls," Richardson expanded the project until it became *Pamela*. The particular virtue rewarded is chastity, in the face of assaults from a member of the Squirearchy, Mr. B., who is, ironically, a justice of the peace. One important artistic concern in the novel is the power of the written word to effect the conversion of wayward characters. One could take the view that Pamela's epistles reinforce traditionally Christian, or social, or merely prudential morality and that they also represent the generally desirable triumph of a member of the lower-middle class over representatives of the upper-middle class and the titled upper class. Virtue is, Richardson suggests, its own reward; it is all the better if it brings other rewards prized by the middle class. The novel's themes of moral courage and virtue reaffirmed bourgeois values and thus helped create an avid reading public.

Following Defoe, whose fiction offered a journalistic facticity, and Richardson, who wrote transparent moral sermons, Henry Fielding (1707-1754) was the first to write avowed novels and depict ordinary English life and the panorama of his age. Like Richardson, Fielding's beginning as a novelist was fortuitous. Sir Robert Walpole served George I and George II as prime minister from 1721 to 1742, and for much of that time he was the object of satire at the hands of several playwrights, Fielding among them. With Walpole's successful introduction of the Licensing Act of 1737, Fielding's career as a dramatist ended, and he turned his ironic and satiric vision to the new prose form, the novel, perfecting that form, many argue, in *The History of Tom Jones, a Foundling* (1749). Before that accomplishment, however, Fielding began his prose efforts by writing a broad satire of Richardson's title character, Pamela

Andrews, which he titled *An Apology for the Life of Mrs. Shamela Andrews* (1741). He followed this success with *The History of the Adventures of Joseph Andrews, and of His Friend Mr. Abraham Adams* (1742), concerning Pamela's imagined brother, but took the story in new directions at midnovel. His *Amelia* (1751) is the first novel of social reform and thus was a point of reference for Charles Dickens and the many contributors to the "Newgate novel" in the nineteenth century. In *Amelia*, Fielding clearly exposes social wrongs and provides possible remedies for them. His portrayal of gambling dens, prison life, and the omnipresent Hogarthian gin mills foreshadows the excessive realism (or naturalism) of Honoré de Balzac and Émile Zola in France and George Moore in late Victorian England.

Two other great eighteenth century novelists, Tobias Smollett (1721-1771) and Laurence Sterne (1713-1768), added various dimensions of eighteenth century English life to the novel's inventory. In *The Adventures of Roderick Random* (1748), Smollett brought to the novel the first extended account of one fundament of English trade, prosperity, and adventure: seafaring life. Like Fielding and Defoe, he used English military history as background material for some of the finest English picaresque novels. Sterne, in *The Life and Opinions of Tristram Shandy, Gent.* (1759-1767), departed from the norm that his contemporaries had established, introducing a stream-of-consciousness technique to refract society through the prism of an individual mind, a technique that would not be further developed until the early twentieth century in the novels of James Joyce and Virginia Woolf.

THE GOTHIC NOVEL

By the end of the eighteenth century, both the novel of sentiment and the gothic novel had appeared in *The Vicar of Wakefield* (1766) by Oliver Goldsmith (1728 or 1730-1774) and *The Castle of Otranto* (1765) by Horace Walpole (1717-1797). While Goldsmith's work and others like it continue in prose the situations and characteristics of the highly popular sentimental domestic drama of middle-class life, Walpole's novel exists outside of the conventions of eighteenth century thought and fiction. His is the only novel of those already mentioned that does not take as its premise the world as it exists, society in the country or city, and the generally agreed upon concept of the possible as coextensive with the real. Premised, then, on questions of epistemology and radical uncertainty, one can ascribe to *The Castle of Otranto* the beginnings of gothic traditions in the novel.

An emphasis upon shared, common experience and consensus unified society and its conception of itself intellectually, philosophically, and psychologically. This society, in many respects the first truly modern society, emerged near the end of the seventeenth century into the era of Enlightenment and took for its tenets common sense, secular reason, science, and gentility. One fundamental emphasis of this era was upon the necessity to treat life and its problems in the spirit of reason and scientific empiricism rather than in the traditional spirit of appeal to authority and dogma. In this era, the landed gentry and not a few of the merchant princes regarded themselves as "Augustans" and sought to imitate the values and beliefs of the Roman patricians of the age of Augustus. In so doing, they set the intellectual tone of their times by asserting rationalism (and skepticism) as the primary focus of thought and by insisting upon symmetry in all phases of life as well as of art, artificial ornament and the preference of artifice to "nature," reserved dignity in preference to any form of enthusiasm, and expansive, urbane sophistication instead of narrow, superstitious thought. It comes, then, as an extraordinary incongruity to find not only Walpole's work but also other novels of horror written, avidly read, and widely praised in this neoclassical Age of Reason.

Nevertheless, Walpole's gothic story was immensely successful, quite probably so in reaction to the restraint of the age, the dominion exercised by the Protestant ethic, and the evangelicalism of the century born in the advent of Wesleyanism and Methodism. In his conscious outlandishness, Walpole set a new course for fiction. His horrific pseudomedieval tale was followed by the gothic novels of Clara Reeve (1729-1807), Ann (Ward) Radcliffe (1764-

1823)—especially *The Mysteries of Udolpho* (1794)—Matthew Gregory "Monk" Lewis (1775-1818), and numerous novels of the Romantic period. The success of this kind of imaginative, experimental writing is most probably what allowed for later development of novels based on fantasy, including science fantasy and science fiction. Mary Wollstonecraft Shelley's *Frankenstein* (1818) continued the gothic strain in the nineteenth century and became the preeminent novel of experimental science.

THE LATE EIGHTEENTH CENTURY

The last quarter of the eighteenth century, a period that saw the beginnings of Romanticism, featured the remarkable first ministry of William Pitt, the Younger (1759-1806), a ministry that laid the foundation for much of the reform movement in the nineteenth century. The intellectual tenets of the Augustan Age, already called into question by the gothic novelists and several poets of the age, were about to suffer a sea change in the triumph of individualism that characterized Romanticism. Economically, however, England maintained rather than altered its newfound tradition of progress, legitimatized by the writings of David Ricardo and Adam Smith. The advances of industry and capitalism begun early in the Augustan Age continued and ensured an economic boom that, with few setbacks, was to characterize the nineteenth century and fuel the expansion of the empire. Culturally, the pre-Romantic period was marked by an extraordinary growth in literacy, helped in great part by the growth of charity schools, the drive to regularize and teach English (if only for commercial purposes), the increasing new opportunities for the education of women, and the establishment and development of circulating libraries.

Two writers of this transitional period—the era, roughly speaking, between the outbreak of unrest in the American colonies in the early 1770's and the accession of Queen Victoria (1837)—stand apart from the mainstream of the rapidly changing world in which they lived. One, Jane Austen (1775-1817), epitomized an age that had already passed; the other, Sir Walter Scott (1771-1832), eschewed his own world except to the extent that he could translate some of its characteristics to other times. Austen's works, unpublished until the second decade of the nineteenth century, are the last novels of the Enlightenment. Unlike those of the other great eighteenth century novels, the characters presented by "the great feminine Augustan" are drawn almost exclusively from the landed gentry. In her novels she presents minute descriptions of the members of that class, their characters, beliefs, aspirations, and hopes in a period marked by a strong desire for stability on the part of the gentry despite the fact that they were surrounded by the armies of change. A supremely accomplished novelist, Jane Austen set the pattern for all subsequent novels of manners and family. Her characters interest themselves in issues of importance only to themselves—social position, socially and financially advantageous marriages, and the orderly passage of property from one generation to the next. The portraits that emerge are absolutely dissimilar to those of Fielding and his fellows and are essentially those of the placid, insulated upper class; as such, they present not only highly wrought pictures of the gentry but also invaluable insights into a social stratum that utterly vanished in the twentieth century.

Scott's Romantic novels, unlike Austen's works, deal with the world as it might have been rather than as it then was. His novels transplant nineteenth century heroes of sense, sensibility, and virtue to remote places or historically distant times. Moreover, his pioneer work in shaping the historical consciousness and national identity of Scotland while recounting its seventeenth century and eighteenth century history, and his novels of medieval and Renaissance Britain won him a place as a universally respected novelist of his century.

Both Austen and Scott are anomalies. Austen clearly summarizes the Augustan Age and its concerns, and Scott is surely the spokesman of a movement that grew in the last decades of the eighteenth century and took hold as the dominant intellectual mode of subsequent centuries, Romanticism. Though his novels rarely treat the world in which he lived, Scott's perceptions were conditioned by the growing intellectual and emotional tenets of Romanticism. Although he sought to explore the political and social

conditions of earlier times in English and Scottish history, he consistently chose not to recognize the inescapable facts of the Industrial Revolution, the expensive (both in money and in lives) wars England waged in his own time, and the bloodless social revolution that saw the gentry finally replaced by the middle class as the political and economic rulers of England. The largest element of Scott's Romanticism is a studied medievalism that may be viewed as an escapist alternative (of considerable psychological necessity) to the pervasive and turbulent revolutions in every sector of society and as a reassertion of fundamental and traditional values. One benefit Scott gained by focusing upon Romantic medievalism as his chief fictional concern is that he thereby escaped the social censure and ostracism other Romantics experienced. Not only did he achieve personal respectability as a poet-turned-novelist, but he also created such a large and insatiable reading public for his and others' novels that the novel became the most popular form of literature.

THE VICTORIAN NOVEL

The Victorian novelists—Charles Dickens was arguably the greatest of them—mark a new era in the novel, an era in which the primary middle-class emphasis on its own place in society and the reformation of society in its own image came to the fore. Society itself expanded in the Victorian Age to include not only England and the United Kingdom but also an empire upon which, proverbially, the sun never set. In consequence, novelists, in their characters, backgrounds, and plots, often surveyed an empire that extended geographically to all continents, covering fully one-tenth of the earth's surface, and financially to the entire populated world. Trade and tradesmen literally moved the empire, opened Australia and Canada to colonization, brought India into the fold (first via the East India Company and then, in 1857, under the Crown), and brought about the foundation of the corporate world with the Companies' Act of 1862.

The reform movement, in part attributable to the Romantic rebellion and in larger part to the middle-class redefinition of societal ideals, came to partial fruition in the 1820's and flourished in the 1830's and in subsequent decades. The hated and inflationary measure of 1815 prohibiting grain imports, the Corn Law, was modified in 1828; the Combination Acts of the era illustrate the pronounced middle-class opposition to trade unionism; the repeal of the Test Act (1828) and the passage of the Catholic Emancipation Bill (1829) brought about a liberalization of attitudes toward Roman Catholics and extended political franchise to a large number of men; the Third Reform Bill (1832) abolished slavery in the empire; the Factory Act (1833) regulated working hours and required two hours of schooling daily for children under the age of thirteen; and the New Poor Law (1834) represented another phase of regularizing governmental services and social programs. These reforms typify, without nearly exhausting, the great social legislation of this era. Reform was the byword of the early decades of the nineteenth century and the hallmark of the entire Victorian era as English society evolved. Subsequent reforms in suffrage, for example, seem to have moved at a glacial pace and only included women in 1928, but each new enfranchisement under the ministerial guidance of Benjamin Disraeli and William Gladstone added appreciably to the power of the middle class. It was quite natural, then, for the English novel to add social reform to its repertoire of themes.

Conditions for novelists also improved in nineteenth century England. As the eighteenth century marked the end of patronage as the primary support of artists and writers, so the explosion of periodicals, the multiplication of newspapers, the growth of publishing firms, and the extension of consumerism to literary works in the nineteenth century made it possible for more writers to try to live by and from the pen. "Grub Street" had meant, since the mid-eighteenth century, hard times for writers such as Dr. Samuel Johnson and Oliver Goldsmith, and in the eighteenth century the supply of writers far exceeded the demand. This, too, was the case in the nineteenth century, but less severely so, and it would remain the case despite the paperback, magazine, and other media revolutions of the twentieth century. It has often been suggested that Charles Dickens, William Make-

peace Thackeray, and most popular novelists of the century whose novels were first serialized in journals and magazines wrote at such length because they were paid by the line of print; while padding is one possible consequence of such a method of publication and payment, the leisurely pace of the novel, its descriptiveness and its length, date from the eighteenth century and grew without regard to such payment schedules. Serial publication no doubt influenced how authors arranged their plot developments. Authors provided rising action toward the end of each installment rather than solely toward the end of the entire novel. These suspenseful moments became known as "cliffhangers" for their ability to tease readers into purchasing the next issue.

The Victorian novel as exemplified in the works of Charles Dickens (1812-1870) not only describes life but competes with it as well. Here one finds a verisimilitude so persuasive that the swarming complexities of Victorian life seem fixed in the novels. While carrying on the traditional celebration of middle-class values, Dickens also tried to make sense of the complex variety of choices open to his readers, of the fabric of society (by explaining, exposing, and mythologizing the middle class), of the ills of his society (by exposing them and calling for their reform), and of the patent injustices of capitalist society (by emphasizing their consequences, the plight of the victims of injustice, and the dehumanization of its perpetrators). To all of these concerns Dickens added a sense of comedy that suffused his early and some of his middle work but that changed to ferocity in his last complete novel, arguably his best after *Bleak House* (1852-1853), *Our Mutual Friend* (1864-1865).

Like Scott and many of his own contemporaries, Dickens is not above providing in his fiction a psychological escape from the mechanized world of his readers, as in *Pickwick Papers* (1836-1837), a genteel picaresque work set in the period before the Age of Steam. Little else but artificially contrived escape exists for the reader and the protagonist of *Oliver Twist* (1837-1839), an intense (and in its initial chapters unrelieved) examination of the workhouse system, one of the more depressing phenomena of the reform movement. Similarly, his descriptions of the criminal classes (so severely criticized, especially in regard to his depiction of child criminals and prostitutes, that he felt compelled to document his observations in the preface to the novel's second edition) illustrate the predatory relationship of this class to all other classes and form an indictment of the society that spawned and neglected them, an indictment that Dickens reiterated in *Bleak House* and elsewhere. Dickens the social reformer achieves some of his most enduring effects by indulging in the sentimentalism inherent in the sort of melodrama popular in the Victorian Age and still popular in some sectors today.

The Chancery Court and the legal system are the objects of Dickens's satiric wrath in *Bleak House*, a novel that amply illustrates that "the Law is a Ass," while in few other novels has the middle-class Gospel of Wealth been so soundly condemned as in *Dombey and Son* (1846-1848). It is significant that in this novel the railway appears for the first time in Dickens's works. Dickens cast a cold eye on another English social institution, debtors' prison, in *Little Dorrit* (1855-1857), in which London's Marshalsea Prison is the primary setting. On a smaller canvas in *Hard Times* (1854), he took on the educational abuses favored by the Gradgrinds of British industrial Coketowns, complete with their belief in the dullest of "facts."

Similar social issues and notions of reform appear in the Newgate novels (picaresque tales of crime and punishment by incarceration in Newgate Prison) and in the important work of the novelist Elizabeth Gaskell (1810-1865). Both Gaskell and Charles Kingsley (*Alton Locke*, 1850) did much to introduce the working-class or proletarian figure as a central focus of fiction, a focus Thomas Hardy would further sharpen late in the century.

William Makepeace Thackeray (1811-1863), a contemporary and sometime friend of Dickens, presented the world of the upper-middle class and limited his novels to that sphere. His *Vanity Fair: A Novel Without a Hero* (1847-1848) eschewed the conventional novel of intrigue and focused on the steady social climb of Becky Sharp from the position of governess to the ranks of the leisured gentry, a new class only possible to the England of empire and In-

dustrial Revolution. Thackeray is at pains to glorify the virtues of the upper-middle class and to bolster them through his fiction: Marriage, home, and children constitute the proper society he portrays. Surely it is still possible to see in these ideals the safe harbors they had become for Victorians: It is also possible to view them as indicative of the societal dichotomy present in nearly every aspect of Victorian thought, a dichotomy that, in this case, emphasized an intense desire for security while positing the need for the adventurous life of acquisition. Like many of his predecessors and contemporaries, Thackeray turned his hand to the historical novel to explore from a nineteenth century perspective the social and literary life of the Queen Anne era, the Jacobite plots to return the Stuarts to monarchy, and the campaigns of the Duke of Marlborough.

Anthony Trollope (1815-1882) brought to the novel two new subject areas drawn from Victorian life: In his Barsetshire novels he introduced the first accurate portraits of English clerics; in his political or parliamentary novels he presented accurate descriptions of English politicians and political life rivaled only by those of Benjamin Disraeli (1804-1881), the first Earl of Beaconsfield and twice Prime Minister of England (1867-1868; 1874-1880). In the novels of Trollope and Disraeli the vast and intricate world of ministries and parliaments, political intrigue, and the multifarious activities of empire in relation to the political process achieve a place in the novelistic tradition of England.

The religious controversies of the era, notably the Oxford movement and the Anglo-Catholicism it induced, are present as background to Trollope's Barsetshire novels. The controversies are the concerns of several characters in the works of George Eliot (Mary Ann Evans, 1819-1880), and enter into *Sartor Resartus* (serial 1833-1834; book 1836) by Thomas Carlyle (1795-1881) as well as into numerous other novels of the era, many of which use the historical convention of setting stories in Roman times to explore the religious question. Eliot's explorations of the internal motivations of her characters, in *Middlemarch* (1871-1872), for example, led to a brand of novel sometimes described as "psychological," although the full manifestation of this inside story would be independently delivered by Virginia Woolf (1882-1941) and James Joyce (1882-1941) after the turn of the century. The scientific basis for certain religious controversies, such as the influx of German higher criticism, the use of evidence from the expanding science of geology, and the introduction of the theory of evolution by Charles Darwin (1809-1882), also find their way into the novels of the period. The religious question and its attendant fideist, agnostic, and atheistic responses find novelistic expression in the works of such writers as Trollope; Charles Kingsley (1819-1875), the exponent of "Muscular Christianity"; Edmund Gosse (1849- 1928), especially in *Father and Son* (1907); and Samuel Butler (1835-1902), particularly in *Erewhon* (1872), *Erewhon Revisited* (1901), *The Fair Haven* (1873), and *The Way of All Flesh* (1903).

Both abrupt and gradual changes in the religious climate are reflected in many Victorian novels, particularly in the otherwise quite dissimilar works of George Meredith (1829-1909) and Thomas Hardy (1840-1928). Meredith's championing of "advanced ideas" generally and his particular advocacy of woman suffrage, free thought, political radicalism, and evolutionary theory (optimistically considered) combine to form a vision of the Comic Spirit that suffuses his works. Hardy was differently affected by the multiplicity of Victorian controversies and conflicting claims; in his works one finds not comedy but a tragic vision of human life dominated by an inexorable sense that the evolutionary process has produced in man a kind of alien species against which the permanent forces of nature are constantly arrayed. Nowhere is this more evident than in *Jude the Obscure* (1895), a novel so universally condemned by churchmen and the conservative literary establishment that Hardy turned away from the novel to become a poet of considerable importance.

Another element in the continuing debate which the Victorians carried on with themselves springs from the social reform movements of the era and collides with the positivistic thought of Auguste Comte (1798-1857), who coined the term "sociology." This element surfaced in some of Dickens' work (*Bleak House*; *Martin Chuzzlewit*, 1843-1844; *Our Mutual Friend*; and the unfinished *The Mystery of Edwin Drood*, 1870), rose to a different plane in the novels of Wilkie Collins (*The Woman in White*, 1860; *The Moonstone*, 1868), and formed much of the matter of "yellowback" or pulp novels as "shilling shockers" and "penny dreadfuls." It reached its logical Victorian zenith in the accounts of the world's greatest private consulting detective, Sherlock Holmes, by Arthur Conan Doyle (1859-1930), narratives that range from *A Study in Scarlet* (1887) to *The Case-Book of Sherlock Holmes* (1927).

THE DETECTIVE AND SPY NOVELS

The phenomenon of detective fiction captured the interest and imagination of the Victorian public at all levels of society. Organized police forces were first created in the nineteenth century, the science of criminology was born, and ingenious threats to life and, especially, property from the criminal classes grew apace with the unremitting urbanization of England. The steady progress of the fictional criminal, from the endearing rogues of sentimental fiction to the personification of social evil created by Conan Doyle in his Napoleon of Crime, Professor Moriarty, is directly related to the growth of the propertied middle class, to the swelling population of the "underserving poor" (in George Bernard Shaw's phrase), to the ample opportunities for anonymity which urban centers and clear class divisions afforded, to the inevitable lure of easy money, and to the multiple examples of corrupt politicians on a national scale. Crime fiction kept pace with developments in crime and in criminal investigation, and in some cases the fiction anticipated developments in criminal science. The crime thriller, mystery story, and detective novel are still staple items of English fiction and have been so for more than a century, thanks to the efforts of Conan Doyle and the prodigious work of such writers as Agatha Christie (1890-1976) and John Creasey (1908-1973).

Still another subgenre linked to the detective novel was born of the armies of empire, international political events, and the information and communication explosions of the nineteenth century—the spy novel. Espionage had run through several Romantic and Victorian novels, but the Secret Service—John le Carré's "Circus" in his novels of the 1960's and 1970's—first came to prominence in *Kim* (1901) by Rudyard Kipling (1865-1936), and revolutionary espionage and anarchy came to the fore in *The Secret Agent* (1907) by Joseph Conrad (1857-1924). The spy novel in the twentieth century has had great impetus from the events of World War I and World War II (in *The Third Man: An Entertainment*, 1950, for example, by Graham Greene [1904-1991]), but is most closely associated with the post-1945 Cold War.

Both the detective novel of the Victorian Age and the spy novel born in its last days came to emphasize, of necessity, plot and action over character development and so tended to evolve into forms that do not fully coincide with the mainstream novel as the Victorians established it for themselves and their successors. A primary example of this is Ian Fleming's (1908-1964) character James Bond; a notable exception is John le Carré's (b. 1931) George Smiley: Both writers and their characters face each other across an abyss. Yet the impulse to both sorts of fiction is historically rooted in the Romantic fiction of Scott and in the Romantic revival of the late nineteenth century, a revival sparked by an ever more urgent necessity to seek in fiction an escape from the complexities and difficulties of the present, and to find in fiction the disordered world set right, a finer or more exotic world, an adventurous world providing a chivalrous alternative to and a definite release from mercantile and corporate life.

In the Romantic revival of the late Victorian era, Robert Louis Stevenson (1850-1894) provided the best and most enduring fictional alternatives to the everyday life of Edinburgh, London, and the great industrial cities of the United Kingdom. Stevenson's novels of Scotland (*Kidnapped*, 1886; *The Master of Ballantrae*, 1889; *David Balfour*, 1893; *Weir of Hermiston*, 1896), his *Treasure Island* (1881-1882) and *The Strange Case of Dr. Jekyll and Mr. Hyde* (1886) set a new fashion for tales of adventure and terror with such prime ingredients as soldiers, rebellions, pirates, and a monstrous transmogrification. His example was followed by H. Rider Haggard (1856-1925) in *King Solomon's Mines* (1885), An-

thony Hope (1863-1933) in *The Prisoner of Zenda* (1894), Bram Stoker (1847-1912) in *Dracula* (1897), P. C. Wren (1885-1941) in *Beau Geste* (1924), and by the writers of "best-sellers" in succeeding generations. The novels of Alistair MacLean (b. 1922), Frederick Forsythe (b. 1938), Jack Higgins (Harry Patterson, b. 1929), and the hundreds of novels about World War II continue the Scott-Stevenson tradition, mixing reality with escapism. Further other-world fiction was provided by authors such as H. G. Wells (1866-1946) who, in science fantasies such as *The Time Machine: An Invention* (1895) offered readers hypothetical realities in novels that were sometimes classified as "speculative fiction."

THE TWENTIETH CENTURY NOVEL

The end of Queen Victoria's reign and the accession of Edward VII (1901) truly marked the end of an age and of a century in which the novel rose to literary supremacy. On the eve of the twentieth century, England had passed several relatively peaceful decades since the Napoleonic era. The military excursions of the Crimean War (1854-1856), the Sepoy Rebellion in India (1857), a war with China (1857-1858), and the Boer War in South Africa (1899-1902) in no way prepared the empire for the global struggle that began in 1914 in the reign of George V and lasted as the Great War (now, World War I), until 1918. This and other military conflicts of the twentieth century left clearly discernible marks upon the development of the English novel. World War II (1939-1945), the most cataclysmic for England, is also the most notable of the conflicts but not the longest. Wars, "police actions," and skirmishes in the distant corners of the empire, from Suez (1956) or Palestine (1949) to the Falkland Islands (1982), and extending temporally from the Boer War to the Argentinian conflict, may have matched in sporadic intensity but not in overall bitterness the continuing Anglo-Irish struggle, begun many centuries ago and marked in the twentieth century by the Easter Risings (1918), the partition of Ireland (1922), and the move to Commonwealth status (1937) and to Republic (1949) for the South. World War II, however, justly overshadowed all other military events of the twentieth century and exerted such an influence upon the course of the English novel that the number of fictional works about Britain's "finest hour" has grown astronomically since 1945: World War II may have passed into cultural memory, but it remained, for whole generations, a recent event of personal history that also marks the beginning of the "postmodern" world. Shortly after the war, beginning around 1947, the empire was virtually dismantled, and more than a billion people throughout the world gained political independence.

THE PROLETARIAN NOVEL AND THE NOVEL OF
SOCIAL CRITICISM

The British economy was sapped by expensive modern warfare, the rapid dissolution of the empire, and the immigration of large numbers of the middle class; it was plagued by taxation (marked by the establishment of the first modern social security system, in 1912, and later by the socialistic British welfare state, 1945-1951), devastated by the Great Depression of 1929 and the wholesale destruction of property in the Battle of Britain and the subsequent saturation bombing of London, and eroded by massive unemployment and the steady devaluation of the pound sterling. These events and their economic effects form a background for the rise of the proletarian novel and the novel of social criticism of the 1950's and subsequent decades, including works by Kingsley Amis (1922-1995), John Braine (1922-1986), John Wain (1925-1994), Alan Sillitoe (b. 1928), and others who are now known as the Angry Young Men.

Social issues that occasioned the protests of the Victorian novelists were largely resolved during the last decades of Victoria's reign, ceased to have the same importance in the years when Edward VII was monarch (1901-1910), and, except for the extension of the voting franchise to women (1928), became legally moot in the early years of George V's reign. A divergent set of social issues replaced them for twentieth century novelists such as John Galsworthy (1867-1933), H. G. Wells (1866-1946), Arnold Bennett (1867-1931), and George Moore (1852-1933). Galsworthy, for example, captured the decline and disintegration of Victorian/Edwardian pillars of the mid-

dle class into the "lost generation" of the 1920's, and in so doing raised lapsarian questions that contribute to a "modernist" sensibility. Wells, apart from his socialist propaganda, also examined the possibilities of dehumanization and the inevitable destructiveness of the retrograde evolution of English class, social, and scientific structures. Bennett and Moore, like Galsworthy, pilloried the bourgeoisie and Victorianism generally, and both imported techniques from the French naturalistic novel to do so. Although French and other Continental writers exerted considerable influence on the cultural development of the English novel from roughly the mid-nineteenth century onward (one finds such influences extending from the novels of George Eliot to those of Henry James), it is noteworthy that the anti-Victorian writers should employ the naturalistic technique of Balzac and Zola in their novelistic experiments.

The form of the novel, as established in the eighteenth century, had evolved but had not drastically changed throughout the nineteenth century. With the influx of the French aesthetic, symbolist, and decadent literature in the 1890's, and the experiments of Bennett and Moore, the stage was set for more radical experiments with the English novel, experiments that centered primarily on the traditional focus of the novel, character, and subordinated all else to it. One must look to the Anglicized American, Henry James (1843-1916), as a primary source for the experimental novel, even if James did remain clearly within the confines of the English novelistic tradition. By emphasizing such elements as angle of narration, the capturing of actual experience and the way people are, the primacy of individual psychology, and the disappearance of the traditional hero, James prepared the way for further experiments by Joseph Conrad, James Joyce (1882-1941), Virginia Woolf (1882-1941), D. H. Lawrence (1885-1930), and Lawrence Durrell (1912-1990), among others. In their fiction variations on the "modernist" questions of ultimate meaning, individual responsibility, and elemental issues of guilt, moral alienation and dehumanization, and atonement find enduring expression as each writer searches for individual answers to similar questions. Whether the scope of the search is global, as in Conrad's settings throughout the empire, or intensely local, as in Joyce's Dublin, Lawrence's Nottinghamshire, or the mind of Woolf's Mrs. Dalloway, it is the same inner search. In the light of the experimental novels of the twentieth century, *Tristram Shandy* no longer seems the oddity it once appeared to be.

Differing from the vast quantity of twentieth century English novels written in the authorized veins of bourgeois or antibourgeois traditions, the abundant novels of adventure, detection, mystery, romance (in all senses), espionage and humor—all forms in which society is reflected and sees itself—the experimental novel provided a different sort of novelistic focus, the novel of social criticism and satire in which the protagonist is no longer concerned with a place in society but is, as his or her American cousins have been since the days of Nathaniel Hawthorne and Herman Melville, most frequently an outsider who seeks to preserve and justify alienation from a disordered and dissolving society and culture. Set adrift from intellectual, social, religious, and cultural stability and identity, the interbellum generation (1918-1939) and the postwar or postmodern generations consistently emphasize the futility of human community under the social contract. Not only the Angry Young Men but also their predecessors, successors, and contemporaries such as Ronald Firbank (1886-1926), Aldous Huxley (1894-1963), Evelyn Waugh (1903-1966), George Orwell (1903-1950), William Golding (1911-1993), Graham Greene, and John le Carré, engage in social criticism and satire that ranges from assailing the societal, mechanistic, technocratic trivializing of human dignity to asserting the necessity of a solitary quest for personal ethics in an era that lacks an ethical superstructure and in which organized religion is one among many residual elements of limited use.

MULTICULTURALISM IN THE NOVEL

In the last half of the twentieth century, a reinvigorated strain of fiction came to reflect the growing ethnic diversity of England's people and their multicultural character and global concerns, as many Commonwealth writers and expatriates chose England as their residence and principal forum. Three writers of the 1980's amply illustrate this diversity. Kazuo Ishiguro was born in Nagasaki in 1954; his family moved to England in 1960. Ishiguro's first novel, *A Pale View of Hills* (1982) is narrated by a Japanese widow, a survivor of Nagasaki, who is living in England. *An Artist of the Floating World* (1986) is the story of an old Japanese painter oppressed by guilt over the prostitution of his art in the service of Japanese imperialism. With his universally acclaimed third novel, *The Remains of the Day* (1989), Ishiguro made a bold leap; here his first-person narrator is an English butler in the mid-1950's, a figure at once comic and poignant. *The Unconsoled* (1995) is Ishiguro's exploration of a dreamscape so ambiguous that it thoroughly upsets traditional narrative concepts. The main character, Mr. Ryder, finds that his conflicted past and his insecurities about his future transform everything he encounters into a surreal dream of reality. This defamiliarization from the real is one of the universal themes that Ishiguro gravitated toward in rejection of the earlier emphasis on the lapse between Japanese and English cultural identities. In either case, his fiction cautions that "we tend to think we're in far more control than we are."

Timothy Mo was born in Hong Kong in 1950; his first novel, *The Monkey King* (1978), examines familial relationships in his native city in the 1940's and 1950's. *Sour Sweet* (1982) offers a Dickensian portrayal of the Chinese community in London. Mo's most ambitious work, the wonderfully capacious *An Insular Possession* (1986), concerns cultural, political, and economic conflicts between the Occident and the Orient in Macao and Canton before and during the Opium Wars of the nineteenth century. Mo's *The Redundancy of Courage* (1991) continues to focus on postcolonial issues into a first-person account of warfare from the perspective of a cultural assimilator.

Salman Rushdie, born in Bombay in 1947, was educated in England. His novel *Midnight's Children* (1981) views the partition of India and the creation of the independent Muslim state of Pakistan through the lens of Magical Realism. *Shame* (1983) covers much of the same territory. Rushdie achieved international notoriety with his patently Joycean novel *The Satanic*

Verses (1988), a great wheel of a book that was condemned by Muslim fundamentalists for its handling of religious themes. In *Haroun and the Sea of Stories* (1990), a children's book written for adults as well, Rushdie, threatened with death and forced into hiding, answers his critics with a celebration of storytelling and the unconstrained imagination. His return to the context of improbable reality in *The Moor's Last Sigh* (1995) offers readers a heightened emphasis on storytelling as a theme.

Less emphatically concerned with diversity issues, A. S. Byatt (b. 1936), Julian Barnes (b. 1946), and Martin Amis (b. 1949) seem to have inherited the position of authorial status occupied by the writers of the 1950's through the 1970's. Their novels exhibit such sophisticated strategies that in some cases, such as Barnes's *Flaubert's Parrot* (1984), they are considered post-postmodern. Amis is perhaps more attuned to postmodernist practice, his novels being a conflation of his father, Kingsley Amis; Saul Bellow (b. 1915); and Vladimir Nabokov (1899-1977). They are often self-referential in texture, as in *The Rachel Papers* (1973) and *Money: A Suicide Note* (1984). Byatt's works tend to focus on intellectual problems characteristic of past eras, such as allegorical representation common to the Renaissance, evidenced in her *The Virgin in the Garden* (1978), and deistic wrangling over biblical stories, in *Babel Tower* (1996). She translates these pedantic puzzles into contemporary English life, providing relevance for both the society she writes about and the history of ideas that influence them.

The English novel, then, to paraphrase William Shakespeare's Hamlet, holds the mirror up to society and shows the very age and body of the time, its form and pressure. Even a brief sketch of the varied patterns of societal influences on the development of the English novel demonstrates that the novel is of all literary forms the most responsive to the changing emphases of an evolving society. Whether in overt reaction to the values of a society, in praise of them or in criticism of them, the novel consistently presents the society as the individual must confront it, explains that society to itself, and helps society to define itself.

John J. Conlon, updated by Scott D. Vander Ploeg

BIBLIOGRAPHY

Adams, Percy G. *Travel Literature and the Evolution of the Novel*. Lexington: University of Kentucky Press, 1983. An improvement on the 1962 work *Travelers and Travel-Liars, 1600-1800*, this study suggests a correlation between deception in travel stories and the essential (un)trustworthiness of the narrator.

Aldiss, Brian W. *Billion Year Spree: The True History of Science Fiction*. New York: Doubleday, 1973. The development of science fiction is defined from a British historical focus.

Allen, Walter. *The English Novel: A Short Critical History*. New York: Dutton, 1954. This study focuses attention on the pervasive question of how the novel can speak to its contemporary audience and yet transcend the limits of historical place to appeal to universal concerns.

Altick, Richard. *The Presence of the Present: Topics of the Day in the Victorian Novel*. Columbus: Ohio State University Press, 1991. A copiously researched study.

Baldridge, Cates. *The Dialogics of Dissent in the English Novel.* Hanover, N.H.: Middlebury College Press, 1994. Baldridge's heavily theoretical book analyzes the manner in which such English authors as Charles Dickens and Elizabeth Gaskell used dialogue in their novels to create multiple voices of social dissent.

Bradbury, Malcolm. *The Modern British Novel*. London: Penguin Books, 1994. Bradbury explores the great variety of twentieth century British literature.

Cavaliero, Glen. *The Supernatural and English Fiction: From "The Castle of Otranto" to "Hawksmoor."* Oxford: Oxford University Press, 1995. The main strength of Cavaliero's wide-ranging book on the supernatural in English fiction is that it deals not only with well-known authors such as Ann Radcliffe and Horace Walpole but also with numerous unfamiliar writers and novels.

Horsman, Alan. *The Victorian Novel*. Oxford, England: Clarendon Press, 1990. Both the major and many minor authors are given urbane and comprehensive treatment. Includes a helpful chronology.

Kettle, Arnold. *An Introduction to the English Novel.* 2 vols. 1951. Rev. ed. London: Hutchinson, 1967. This study attempts a thorough history that focuses on both the development of novel structure and the sense of life portrayed in its shifting forms.

Kiely, Robert. *The Romantic Novel in England.* Cambridge, Mass.: Harvard University Press, 1972. Covering the period from 1764 to 1847, this work is an overview of a dozen of the most commonly discussed Romantic and gothic novels.

McKee, Patricia. *Public and Private: Gender, Class, and the British Novel (1764-1878).* Minneapolis: University of Minnesota Press, 1997. Surveys sociological implications of changing roles represented in the novel from the early period through much of the Victorian era.

McKeon, Michael. *The Origins of the English Novel: 1600-1740.* Baltimore, Md.: The Johns Hopkins University Press, 1987. An aggressive exploration of the philosophical and religious underpinnings of the early English novel.

Richetti, John, et al., eds. *The Columbia History of the British Novel.* New York: Columbia University Press, 1994. A good standard of critical opinion on matters pertaining to the novel.

Roberts, Andrew Michael, ed. *The Novel: A Guide to the Novel from Its Origins to the Present Day.* London: Bloomsbury, 1994. Part of the Bloomsbury Guides to English Literature series, this is a handy primer on the novel, which is well versed in contemporary critical trends.

THE EUROPEAN NOVEL

How early was the earliest novel? Critics attempt to establish a beginning for the form in order to make the analytical task manageable. Because the novel, as generally defined, holds many elements in common with drama, epic, folktale, fable, satire, biography, and autobiography, it is impossible to designate one work as the earliest novel. Furthermore, when critics do include certain early works as novels, they are making a distinction that did not exist before the eighteenth century. Thus, literary historians must include as novels many works for which the category did not exist at the time they were written, or that were not considered novels by either their authors or their first readers. For example, Samuel Richardson's *Pamela: Or, Virtue Rewarded* (1740-1741) itself was originally conceived of by its author, a printer by trade, as an illustrative guide to the art of letter writing, not as a work of fiction. Richardson's predecessor, Daniel Defoe, author of *The Life and Strange Surprizing Adventures of Robinson Crusoe, of York, Mariner, Written by Himself* (1719) and *The Fortunes and Misfortunes of the Famous Moll Flanders, Written from Her Own Memorandums* (1722), called his own works histories and specifically wrote against novels, a class of writing that, he said, "invents characters that never were in Nature."

BEGINNINGS OF THE NOVEL IN EUROPE

The canon of the novel, then, should probably include all important works, no matter how early, that are read as novels are read today and that have clearly influenced the shape of European fiction. In this light, it makes sense to trace the origins of the novel back to the origins of Western literature, perhaps to Homer's *Iliad* and *Odyssey* (both c. 800 B.C.E.). Certainly, two of the oldest traditions in fiction, the heroic and the picaresque, maintain these works as prototypes. Among other ancient works, the narratives of the Old Testament have also been of immeasurable influence in shaping the forms and themes of Western fiction. Genesis, for example, can be said to have shown the West how to use character to embody the history and spirit of a people; indeed, the Old Testa-

ment is rich in narratives of many kinds. Perhaps even more influential in Western literary history, however, have been the Gospels of the New Testament, which present the archetypal story of the individual versus society, or, more precisely, of the individual's defining his or her personal relationship with the divine, irrespective of society's definition. Because most critics see the growth of the novel in terms of a movement toward realizing unique individuals and away from reiterating stereotypes, one way to view the history of the novel is in terms of its lesser or greater success in achieving the iconoclastic ideal set by the Gospels. Given the Gospels' pervasive influence on Western culture, it is only to be expected that critics will frequently see Christian parallels in the acts of well-known characters. Similarly, the most important novels have been considered radical, even dangerous, books, though perhaps none so radical and dangerous in its time as were the Gospels at the time of their writing.

Because of their importance in the school curricula of the Middle Ages and the Renaissance, and hence in the growth of some forms of the novel, such Roman writers as Vergil, Horace, Plautus, and Terence must also be mentioned. Plautus and Terence, the comic dramatists, gave to European literature a particular character type, the wily slave, versed in the ways of the street, the market, and the noble household and able to outwit anyone he meets—noble, tradesman, or fellow slave. Through the Italian popular drama, this figure made his way throughout the Western Mediterranean countries and into prose fiction of the sixteenth century in the rogue stories of Spain, France, and England. Horace and the other Roman satirists contributed to this same fictional strain by re-creating the milieu of contemporary Rome and peopling it with types of actual citizens. The realistic novel grew out of these satirists' attention to the things and events of everyday life.

The poetry of Vergil was the most eminent model for the Middle Ages and the Renaissance of the idealization of life through literature. His *Aeneid* (c. 29-19 B.C.E.; English translation, 1553) carried forward the epic tradition from Homer and, in Aeneas, gave Europe a model of heroism in peace and in war. The Arthurian romances of the later Middle Ages take much of their inspiration from the Vergilian hero; the tales of Arthur inspired other chivalric romances (such as *Amadis of Gaul*, 1508) that brought the Vergilian ideal into the Renaissance, these romances remaining popular into the seventeenth century and even, albeit in different form, today. Vergil was also the primary model of the pastoral strand in fiction and poetry through the Renaissance. His *Eclogues* (c. 43-37 B.C.E.; also known as *Bucolics*; English translation, 1575) created Arcadia, an idealized landscape somewhat removed from the turmoil of the city and hospitable to the daylong singing of love songs. In Arcadia, shepherds vie without malice for the love of shepherdesses, regret the coldness of their lovers, and lament the foolish ambitions of city folk, who can never know Arcadian serenity. Based on the Greek myth of the Golden Age and the biblical idea of Eden, this pastoral ideal has exerted great continuing force on the literary imagination, producing among its manifestations the pastoral romances of late sixteenth century England and Spain, the aristocratic love intrigues of seventeenth century France, and the romances and high-society novels that fill the paperback racks in stores today.

The influence of the ancients on both the heroic and the pastoral modes was augmented in the sixteenth century by the rediscovery and translation of the Hellenistic romances (c. 200 B.C.E.) of Longus (*Poimenika ta kata Daphin kai Chloen*; *Daphnis and Chloë*, 1587), Heliodorus, and Achilles Tatius. Considered by some critics to be early novels, these long prose tales combined pastoral episodes with violent adventures: wars, shipwrecks, kidnapings by pirates. These books gave European writers an easily imitable format that has proven immensely successful in succeeding centuries.

THE MIDDLE AGES TO THE RENAISSANCE

During the Middle Ages, verse and prose works in the heroic, realistic/satiric, and pastoral modes continued to be written, thus nourishing the soil that produced the long fictions of the Renaissance that mod-

ern critics most frequently call the first novels. The dominant heroic form of the early Middle Ages, the lives of Christian saints and martyrs, blended the influences of Vergil with those of the Gospels and the letters of Paul to create a Christian heroic type that would flourish in the later Middle Ages in the epics of Roland, the Cid, and Arthur. The saints' lives also carried forward the Roman satiric mode, primarily in the form of tricks played by the saints on the always greedy, pompous, pagan soldiers and magistrates. In the later medieval period, such satire was most often directed at corrupt clerics and wealthy burghers, with pranks being pulled on them by such masterful imps as the German Tyll Eulenspiegel. The French fabliaux of the thirteenth and fourteenth centuries contain many stories of this type, besides satires in which the trick is a sexual one played by a lusty youth with the wife of a rich, gout-ridden old merchant. Geoffrey Chaucer worked marvelous variations on these themes in *The Canterbury Tales* (1387-1400), and Giovanni Boccaccio worked the same vein in his *Decameron: O, Prencipe Galetto* (1349-1351; *The Decameron*, 1620), both collections providing continuing inspiration for later writers of fiction.

Of incalculable effect on the eventual rise of the intellectual novel, or novel of sensibility, was the introspective devotional literature of the Middle Ages, its greatest example being the *Confessiones* (397-400; *Confessions*, 1620) of Saint Augustine. Using autobiographical narrative in the service of ethical and religious speculation, the *Confessions*, like the greatest novels, grant high dignity and importance to the individual life. The *Confessions* also brought to Western literature that intimacy of tone and truthfulness of thought and feeling that are the essence of the modern intellectual novel.

THE INVENTION OF MOVABLE TYPE AND THE INFLUENCE OF THE HUMANISTS

Perhaps the single most important event in the development of the modern novel was Johann Gutenberg's invention of movable type in 1450. Without the technology to produce thousands of copies, each several hundred pages in length, the novel as it is known today, sprawling in scope of time and place, dependent on a diverse reading public, is inconceivable. In terms of the historical development of the genre, this invention also occasioned the amazing speed with which the influence of major works moved from country to country after about 1500, as works written in one vernacular were translated and made available to new publics only a few years after their first printing. As a result, one sees continual enrichment by foreign sources of the distinctive national traditions.

The clearest example of this multicultural influence is that of the Dutch-born Desiderius Erasmus von Rotterdam, whose *Moriae encomium* (1509; *The Praise of Folly*, 1941) and *Colloquia familiaria* (1518) affected satiric fiction throughout Western Europe from as early as the 1530's. *The Praise of Folly* raises to the level of Christian type the anticlerical trickster of the Eulenspiegel tales and the fabliaux. *Colloquia familiaria*, originally intended as a speaking and writing manual for students of Latin, includes clever dialogues and realistic stories that continued to reappear in new garb throughout the century, in such works as those of William Shakespeare and Miguel de Cervantes. The French Humanist François Rabelais was influenced by Erasmus in his writing of the monumental *Gargantua et Pantagruel* (1532-1564; *Gargantua and Pantagruel*, 1653-1694, 1929), which was in turn disseminated widely by mid-century. Through the scatological and gluttonous acts, never subtle and frequently grotesque, of his Gargantua, Rabelais attacked the abuses of church, court, and marketplace, his rambling narrative in some ways a precursor of the picaresque novels that would flourish in Spain for close to a century.

A third Humanist and a friend of Erasmus, Sir Thomas More, made his mark on European fiction with *De Optimo Reipublicae Statu, deque Nova Insula Utopia* (1516; *Utopia*, 1551). Intended as criticism of the unregulated capitalism of English landowners, *Utopia* became a fully detailed picture of an ideal monarchy, related as a travel narrative by one Raphael Hythloday. Though an extended work of fiction, *Utopia* explores ideas rather than characters or events, and it may therefore be regarded as a model of what the novel is not, rather than what it usually

has been. *Utopia* may perhaps be called an example of the pastoral novel, since it presents an idealized society (much nineteenth and twentieth century science fiction fits into this category as well), but it diverges from most pastoral literature, which sees its Arcadia as an escape from worldly affairs rather than an improvement in terms of social planning. True novels in every mode, even the heroic, tend to take a jaded view of human character and interaction. Perhaps part of the definition of the novel is that in it, society is never harmonious.

THE NOVEL IN SPAIN: 1550-1630

Most historians see the Spain of the mid-sixteenth century as the birthplace of the novel, or at least of a form of fiction that they see leading clearly toward the eighteenth century novel of sensibility. The feature that sets these Spanish novels apart from their predecessors is their use of a first-person narrator who relates with unembarrassed candor the degradations of his life. Moreover, this character is a believably real Spaniard of the current time, who vividly depicts the sights, sounds, and, particularly, smells of the actual environment. One way to see this development of the novel is as a combining of the realistic/satiric mode with the confessional mode in Christian devotion, as exemplified by Augustine's *Confessions*. However this form is defined, the anonymous author of *Lazarillo de Tormes* (1553; English translation, 1576), which began this trend, hit upon a formula that changed European fiction and set it on a road it has followed ever since.

Why this phenomenon first occurred in Spain rather than elsewhere in Europe has been much debated. One reason frequently cited involves Spain's position in the sixteenth century as the most religiously and philosophically conservative nation in Europe, the country under the strongest domination by the Catholic Church and with the most rigid socioeconomic stratification. Whereas in England, for example, the satiric impulse produced visions of reform, such as *Utopia* and countless manuals for improvement in education and manners, in Spain the satiric eye looked inward and beneath the skins of other humans, to dwell on corruptions of the soul. In this climate, Renaissance Humanism merely deepened the cynicism, because it kept the observer focused on the imperfections of the here and now by denying the medieval choice of seeing this "vale of tears" as a mere stepping-stone to eternal glory. Whereas Augustine's *Confessions* become a prayer of hope and thanksgiving, *Lazarillo de Tormes* and the works to follow—including the greatest, *El ingenioso hidalgo don Quixote de la Mancha* (1605, 1615; *The History of the Valorous and Wittie Knight-Errant, Don Quixote of the Mancha*, 1612-1620; better known as *Don Quixote de la Mancha*))—end with the hero facing death or in a temporary lull before the next—and certain—disaster. What makes this literature comic and compelling is that the narrators are so resigned to the status quo that they can view the grotesque happenings they relate without anxiety; by contrast, the greedy and ambitious in these novels appear funny fools indeed, because they lack the hero's peace of mind.

In design, *Lazarillo de Tormes* and its followers retain the episodic structure of the medieval satires and the travel motif—the movement from adventure to adventure—of the Pentateuch, the *Odyssey*, and the tales of knighthood, but *Lazarillo de Tormes* departs from this tradition in its exact descriptions of the contemporary milieu and in the confessional candor of the title character. The portraits of Lázaro's masters, in particular the blind man, the squire, and the pardoner, are precisely drawn; one is convinced of the actuality of these men, even as one understands their function as representatives of several classes of Spanish society. Lázaro's self-portrait is the most convincing. He describes his experiences so minutely and accepts his sufferings so humbly that there can be no doubt that the reader is being addressed by the same man who has lived these adventures. One does not question, while reading, how the illiterate son of illiterate parents can so casually allude to the classics during his discourse; one merely enjoys his erudition, his practiced blending of formal address with the minutiae of the streets. The allusions, it is assumed, are convenient phrases he has picked up during a lifetime of surviving by his wits and his tongue. Yet herein lies the romantic illusion of the story and perhaps the

essence of its charm, both in the sixteenth century and now: *Lazarillo de Tormes* simultaneously allows the reader to rub elbows with the oppressed, persevering child of poverty and to be comforted that Lázaro's life of pain does not lead to early death or to a career of villainy, but rather to mental serenity and the material reward of his clever tactics.

Lazarillo de Tormes spawned many imitations; what was fresh at the origins of the Spanish picaresque became, in a period of some seventy-five years, all too predictable. That one could work within the convention created by *Lazarillo de Tormes* and still produce a novel of stunning coherence and originality is shown, however, by the example of Miguel de Cervantes, whose *Don Quixote de la Mancha* was the popular rage of its time. To many modern critics, *Don Quixote de la Mancha* is the first work worthy of being called a true novel. This monumental book, published in two parts ten years apart, was intended by its aging author as a last attempt to gain popular success after a long, futile career as a playwright and pastoralist. He succeeded in fashioning a novel that realized an individual character more profoundly than had anyone since Augustine and that contained the best features of the heroic, pastoral, and realistic/satiric modes. Indeed, one explanation of the novel's power is that in *Don Quixote de la Mancha* the heroic, satiric, and pastoral stereotypes collide, destroying the illusions and pretenses of each mode and leaving their essences. This collision occurs because Cervantes sets the aged landowner Quixote, a man who loves and devoutly believes in the heroes of the medieval tales of knighthood, right in the middle of the same Spain—dry, poor, vicious, and self-deluded—through which Lázaro had been swept. Cervantes endows the old man with a crazy dream of becoming a knight-errant, riding off in search of adventures, chances for triumphs won on behalf of his virtuous lady, a creature of his imagination named Dulcinea del Toboso. The mission is heroic, but as a nostalgic dream its form is pastoral, an attempt to escape the sensible, dull, humiliating final years facing this childless, wifeless owner of a few dusty acres and some scrawny livestock. When these diverse modes come together in this way, an amazing thing occurs: Through nine hundred pages, the old man's dream proves so resilient that a kind of transformation begins to work in the hard-bitten, cynical minds of the other characters. It is not that they come to accept his heroically optimistic perspective on reality, but that they come to appreciate the beautiful alternative his faith and actions offer in an otherwise squalid world. Indeed, it does not take Cervantes many pages to show the reader that each individual, no matter how he may scoff at the illusions of others, has his own comfortingly false views of the world. This is first demonstrated when the priest and the barber of La Mancha, in a parody of the Inquisition, ferret through Don Quixote's library to find and burn those books that have warped his mind. Like the local board of motion-picture censors, the more they search, the more excuses they find to save certain chivalric books because of particularly exciting stories or characters. As the novel proceeds, particularly in part 2, Don Quixote becomes a legend in his own time; even the nobility seek him out, supposedly as entertainment but really because they want to verify his faith in order to find something worth believing in themselves.

The sad countercurrent in the novel is that the absurdly cruel lengths to which characters go to test Quixote's beliefs eventually wear them out of him. On his deathbed, the old "knight," who now calls himself by his given name, Alonso Quixano, says that he "abominates" all the books of knight-errantry that once had guided him. Ironically, none of his hearers—who had so earnestly worked to "cure" him throughout the story—wants to hear this. They are all prepared to accompany him on a new adventure, going out to live like shepherds in idyllic pastoral fashion. They try to encourage him back into his delusion; his sudden sanity suggests that he is indeed about to die, and it is this that they cannot tolerate, for his death means the loss of an imaginative force that has dignified all of their lives.

Cervantes adhered to the framework, conventional in both the picaresque novels and the chivalric romances, of the hero's traveling from place to place, adventure to adventure. He used each episode in this format to refine further the reader's understanding of Quixote and his strange quest. Like the characters who surround the old man, these episodes test Quixote and define him for the reader. For example, the early episode with the windmills shows Quixote as a grave misinterpreter of reality, but later, when he rejects the attentions of a servant girl at an inn on the basis of his loyalty to Dulcinea, one sees the nobility of character that his new identity includes. Such use of the picaresque format is not primarily satiric, even though the contrast between gentle, fair-minded Quixote and the ignorant, equally self-deluded people he meets is clear enough. The satirist goes after more aggressive evils: thievery, seduction, malfeasance in office; Cervantes depicts primarily good-natured folk who sometimes hurt others unwittingly, or out of a sense of duty (as does Quixote himself), or out of fear, usually brought on by the narrowness of their views. *Don Quixote de la Mancha* continues to inspire readers because it is easy for them to see themselves in these people. Readers must admit that they would react to the old knight as do his niece, his housekeeper, the priest, and the barber.

The reader is particularly encouraged to identify with Sancho Panza, Quixote's "squire," an ever-present barometer of the typical reaction to Quixote of a person of good heart, some imagination, and little self-confidence—in short, an average person. Critics have argued about who is the more masterful creation, the knight or the squire. Undertaking Quixote's quest because he naïvely believes the old man's promise that he will one day receive an island as his reward, Sancho stays with him out of an ever-stronger loyalty and compassion, virtues put to painful test at every encounter, with every blow he receives from angry tradesmen and travelers. When, ironically, he eventually is given governorship of an island—if only as part of a large practical joke—he carries off the tasks of ruling with a clarity of judgment that does not surprise the reader but that could not have been predicted at the outset of the quest. Sancho consistently lets the reader judge how he himself has developed as an interpreter of Don Quixote; Sancho Panza's presence is a principal reason for the novel's remarkable coherence and momentum through its many diverse episodes.

THE NOVEL IN FRANCE: 1600-1740

That the early histories of the novel in Spain, France, and England are largely independent phenomena is exemplified by the failure of *Don Quixote de la Mancha* to attract a wide readership in England and France for many decades. In England, *Don Quixote de la Mancha* was "discovered" in the eighteenth century and became an influential work. The most successful French writers of the period from 1600 to 1740, working in a very different fictional tradition in a very different social and philosophical climate, were not at all influenced by this book, though Cervantes and the other picaresque writers did have disciples among the few French satirists and realists of the age.

Aspects of the chivalric romances, particularly their aristocratic heroes and exotic settings, held the French imagination during much of this period. French writers of the late sixteenth and early seventeenth centuries modified the tradition in two important ways, however; first, the violence of the books of knight-errantry was subdued, replaced by greater emphasis on verbal combats conducted under strict rules of manners and decorum; second, the heroic ideal became more and more modified by the pastoral, with its focus on coy debates between lovers. Writers seized on the heroic/pastoral models provided by the rediscovered Greek romances and on more recent pastorals, such as those of the Spanish Jorge de Montemayor (*Los siete libros de la Diana*, 1559; *Diana*, 1598) and the Italians Jacopo Sannazaro and Giovanni Guarini. This literary movement in France was led by a powerful coterie of women within the court of Henry IV, its influence partly explained by a general desire throughout France for a literature of escape from the religious and political upheaval of the preceding half century.

One of the most popular works of this period, indeed throughout the seventeenth century, was Honoré d'Urfé's *L'Astrée* (1607-1628; *Astrea*, 1657-1658), its twelve volumes exploring countless varieties of love conflict and presenting for each a series of Platonic speeches by the impeccably mannered lovers. Set in the fifth century in a society of shepherds and nymphs, the novel is a thinly veiled portrait of an idealized seventeenth century French aristocracy.

So popular was d'Urfé's work that members of the court, and many other aristocratic and bourgeois readers as well, strove to emulate the language and sentiments of Celadon, Astrea, and the many other characters. The course of the novel in France for the next fifty years was set by *Astrea*, as the Marquise de Rambouillet and the other members of literary high society cultivated imitators of d'Urfé.

If the French novel can be said to have developed in this period, it did so by gradually abandoning the pastoral idyll and returning to the more martial heroism of the chivalric tradition. The best-known exemplar of this shift is Madeleine de Scudéry, herself the leader of a literary salon and the author of *Artamène: Ou, Le Grand Cyrus* (1649-1653; *Artamenes: Or, The Grand Cyrus*, 1653-1655) and *Clélie* (1654-1660; *Clelia*, 1656-1661). Critics of the time applauded *Artamenes* for the greater verisimilitude of its pseudohistorical setting in ancient Greece and Persia, though her work was at an idealistic extreme from the earthy realism of the Spanish picaresque. The main concern of Scudéry's fiction is still the verbal intrigues of courtship, no longer of shepherds but of warlike heroes and elegant heroines. Within the episodic design of these novels, each encounter is an occasion for speeches and letters on the vagaries of passion. Another attraction of these novels for their readers was the similarity in description between the characters and actual members of the French court, with readers vying to unmask the "real" identities of Scudéry's figures.

The d'Urfé-Scudéry convention in France was not without its antagonists. Parallel to this trend, but beyond the pale, was a realistic/satiric school based on the medieval fabliaux, the gross satires of Rabelais, translations of the picaresques, and translations of violent tales of love intrigue written by the Italian Matteo Bandello in the sixteenth century. Actually, d'Urfé himself had contributed to this school by including within *Astrea* a cynical shepherd, Hylas, purportedly based on the author's view of himself. The first seventeenth century novelist to build a work around such a character was Prudent Gautier, whose *Mort d'Amour* (1616) mocked *Astrea* by making this same Hylas a seducer/hero; his love affair with

Jeanneton, a real shepherdess, is grossly and realistically portrayed. Following Gautier in this satiric mode was Charles Sorel, an important critic as well as a boldly experimental novelist. His *Histoire comique de Francion* (1623, 1632; *The Comical History of Francion*, 1655) and *Le Berger extravagant: Ou, L'Antiroman* (1627; *The Extravagant Shepherd*, 1653) undercut the pretenses of the pastoral and no doubt hastened its downfall. *The Comical History of Francion* replaces the usual idealized setting with an actual countryside and also leads the reader, in picaresque fashion, through the French counterparts of the criminal districts described by Alemán. Instead of idealized aristocrats, Sorel peoples the book with accurately drawn bourgeois characters, petty nobility, and criminals. *The Extravagant Shepherd* attacks the pastoral by creating a Quixote-like figure, Lysis, a real shepherd, who fills his head with pastoral literature and wants his environment to conform to that of the books. The satire works by showing the impossibility of Lysis's task: Real life is simply not a pastoral. The flaw of Sorel's novel is that the contrivances of satire defeat the sympathetic intent, so the novel appears even more artificial than the convention Sorel is attacking. Ironically, this is the very flaw with which Sorel had charged Cervantes.

The most successful of the attacks on the mainstream French novel of this time was *Le Roman comique* (1651, 1657; English translation, 1651, 1657; also as *The Comical Romance*, 1665), by the novelist and playwright Paul Scarron. His satire was more technical than thematic, directed against the ponderous descriptions of scenery and clothing in the pastorals and heroics, as well as their seemingly endless rhetorical displays. He practiced what he preached, for *The Comical Romance* is remarkably economical, but effective, in its descriptions and conversations. The book also succeeds as realistic fiction because, in the spirit of Cervantes, Scarron is not making fun of the provincial townspeople he presents but is merely trying to recount as accurately as possible their interactions, often ludicrous, with the troupe of actors who are the focus of the story. The book is so authentic, its comedy so natural, that historians have found it a trustworthy guide to the organization and

ambience of actual troupes of the time of Molière. Scarron could achieve this because he was writing out of his experience, rather than out of his fantasies or to emulate a fashion. His dramatic background, particularly the demands of playwriting, also contributed to his ability to economize in prose, to suggest much about personality through salient rather than profuse description.

Where Scarron described people and places in the region surrounding Le Mans, another novelist, Antoine Furetière, contributed to the realistic movement by describing the manners and mores of Paris in his *Roman bourgeois* (1666; *City Romance*, 1671). A Parisian by birth, Furetière depicted a small segment of the capital's middle class, his plot centered on the love affairs of a young coquette, Lucrece, infatuated with the nobility, and of an ingenue, Javotte. Furetière's satire of the Scudéry school is implied in the contrast between Lucrece's expectations of noble behavior and what actually befalls her; nevertheless, as with Scarron, Furetière's intent is not really to attack mainstream fiction but to tell his story as accurately as he can. What keeps *City Romance* from reaching its novelistic potential is a somewhat disjointed second part, a series of Parisian anecdotes in which the unity of the Lucrece story is lost.

The pressure on the heroic novel exerted by Sorel and the realists produced a critical desire in the 1660's for a new kind of novel. The new form would abandon the exotic foreign settings and the rigidly Platonic love stories of the Scudéry novels, while staying clear of the merely entertaining, but morally uninstructive (it was thought), stories of the realists. French settings, recognizably French characters, and plots that would encourage the reader's respect for sound moral judgment were required. Such a novel appeared in 1678—Madame de La Fayette's *La Princesse de Clèves* (1678; *The Princess of Clèves*, 1679), which some critics see as not only the ideal novel for its time but also the first novel of sensibility—some sixty years before Richardson's. Its plot is extremely simple, especially in comparison to the involved tapestries of the heroics; its events are roughly based on French history, while its characters, particularly the heroine and her husband, exhibit believable psychologies, although some critics have been hard put to swallow their almost superhuman ability to reason and act logically.

In outline, the heroine, wife of a nobleman, confesses to her husband that she is in love with another man. Admirably, he sympathizes and thanks her for her candor, though his sympathy is greatly tested when the lover clearly shows himself to be a seducer, totally unworthy of the heroine's love. The tension of the novel lies in the struggle of the husband to overcome jealousy and of the wife to withstand her reckless passion. The ending is tragically ironic: The Prince of Clèves is dying, convinced that his wife has yielded to the seducer; gratefully, he hears the truth just before his death. The tragedy convinces the wife of her grave error and steels her to reject the lover.

Though this novel turned out to be exactly what the critical temper demanded, *The Princess of Clèves* was revolutionary in a number of ways. Unlike the heroic, pastoral, or satiric novels, it was not organized episodically on the resilient model of the chivalric romances. Instead, its focus on a single issue harked back to the short Italian *novelle* of Bandello and even further back to the fabliaux. The fabliaux also provided the stereotype of the adulterous wife, against which *The Princess of Clèves* works. This is actually the book's greatest coup; it asserted two unorthodox hypotheses: one, that a husband could realize that his wife did not love him yet could keep his reason and his dignity, and two, that a wife would dare confide her adulterous desires to her husband. These hypotheses were a strain under which no earlier French writer had dared place his or her characters; La Fayette both dared and succeeded, the spiritual and mental strength of her characters allowing them to perform these highly unorthodox moral feats.

The Princess of Clèves produced numerous imitators over the next few decades. A by-product of La Fayette's success was heightened interest in French history; native settings became the vogue. Imitators of La Fayette did not, however, satisfy the public's undying interest in the grand deeds and noble sentiments of heroes; thus, a new hybrid emerged, the autobiographical novel, which combined history (and quasi history), valorous deeds, a dose of satire from the realist

school, and exciting heroes, blends of the Spanish picaro and the psychologically more interesting figures popularized by La Fayette. Noteworthy among these novels are *Les Mémoires de M. d'Artagnan* (1700), by Gatien de Courtilz de Sandras; *Les Mémoires du Comte de Grammont* (1713), by Anthony Hamilton; and the greatest of this type, *Histoire de Gil Blas de Santillane* (1715-1735; *The History of Gil Blas of Santillane*, 1716, 1735; better known as *Gil Blas*, 1749, 1962), by Alain-René Lesage.

Gil Blas, the work of a deliberate satirist and a fine novelist, accomplished what none of the picaresques or the works of the seventeenth century French realists had: a consistently comic novel of manners in every level of society, as well as a moving study of an individual. Though at times Lesage the satirist strives for comic effects at the expense of Gil's development, not since *Don Quixote de la Mancha* had a novel balanced so many characters and intercalated stories without losing sight of their purpose—to illuminate the central figure. That figure, Gil Blas, is the consummate rogue, and the succeeding stories, set in Spain, show how he learns from his mistakes to grow ever more adept at disguises and verbal ploys. Still, he is not a mere time waster; time and again he puts the interests of others before his own, sometimes leading to disasters for himself. Aware of this tendency in his character, Gil is puzzled because he judges himself a thoroughly worthless fellow. This paradox is one of the book's brightest attractions; frequently victimized, misunderstood, and punished for the evils of smoother hypocrites, Gil is a most sympathetic character.

A more somber, deterministic philosophy pervades the work of the next notable autobiographical writer to follow Lesage. Abbé Prévost, whose eminence spanned three decades beginning in 1730, brought to the French novel the dark foreboding of Jean Racine's tragic style and his own Calvinist theology. In his early *Le Philosophe anglois: Ou, Histoire de Monsieur Cleveland, fils naturel de Cromwell* (1732-1739; *The Life and Entertaining Adventures of Mr. Cleveland, Natural Son of Oliver Cromwell*, 1734, 1735; also as *The English Philosopher: Or, History of Monsieur Cleveland*, 1742), Prévost's hero seems fated to be betrayed and well-nigh destroyed by his violent passions and those of others. The only hedge against passion in this system is reason, which means for Prévost a disciplined detachment and a universal acceptance of Calvinist social principles. The effect of this program on the novel is inevitable: Characterization and plot are manipulated to prove Prévost's thesis, and the pace of the story is painfully slowed by lengthy moralizing discourses. For the sake of his point, Prévost even transports Cleveland to America, so that his hero can make a rationalistic society out of a recalcitrant, but finally malleable, tribe of savages. Nevertheless, Prévost is a worthy successor to La Fayette and Lesage; his Cleveland is a forthcoming, personable narrator, intellectually interesting if not a man of real sensibility. In his post-1740 works, especially the novella-length *Histoire du chevalier des Grieux et de Manon Lescaut* (1731, 1733, 1753; *Manon Lescaut*, 1734, 1786), his masterpiece, Prévost develops his compelling characters according to the logic of their interactions rather than according to his philosophy; thus, they are characters of sensibility, not mere intellectuals.

In two regrettably unfinished novels of Prévost's contemporary Pierre Carlet de Chamblain de Marivaux, the reader encounters an author's commitment to his character's integrity that equals that of Cervantes. The first, *La Vie de Marianne* (1731-1741; *The Life of Marianne*, 1736-1742; also as *The Virtuous Orphan: Or, The Life of Marianne*, 1979), its initial part published nine years before Richardson's *Pamela*, is a collection of letters purportedly by an aging gentlewoman reflectively describing her adventurous life. The second novel, *Le Paysan parvenu* (1734-1735; *The Fortunate Peasant*, 1735), presents Jacob, a sharp-witted peasant, who rises to economic and social success not by roguish ruses but by the marvelous understanding of the desires and temperaments of others, especially women.

One of the ironies of the history of the novel is that *The Life of Marianne*, although it has influenced many novelists in France and England for two centuries, was not popular in its time. A major reason for this fact is that the qualities that make this novel great were not popularly or critically acceptable in the 1730's. Still tied to the status quo, the French would

not accept the rise of an orphan girl (though an orphan, as it turns out, of noble birth) through her intelligence and self-assertion. Indeed, some critics have attributed Marivaux's failure to complete this voluminous novel to his fear of drawing it to its logical conclusion: Marianne's achievement of a secure place in the upper rank of society without having relied on her family connections. Another reason for Marivaux's unpopularity with both critics and the reader may have been that he was as experimental in style as he was in theme; he strained the patience of readers by having his characters exhaustively analyze events from every angle and by having them play with words, coining new ones and giving old ones unaccustomed shades of meaning. As a consequence of this practice, the somewhat pejorative term *marivaudage* entered the literary vocabulary.

Besides the revolutionary conception of Marianne's character, what makes this book a landmark in the history of fiction is Marivaux's philosophy of the novel, as expressed in his preface: "Marianne has no form of a work present in her thoughts. This is not an author, it is a woman who thinks. . . . It is neither, if you wish, the tone of the novel, nor that of history, but it is her own." He warns the reader not to expect the typical chain of events, as if the novel were embodied in plot, but to be prepared to enter into the wonderful complex of Marianne's feelings, her analysis of those feelings, and her subsequent actions.

This emphasis on thought does not make the book a philosophical treatise, like Prévost's *The Life and Entertaining Adventures of Mr. Cleveland*; rather, it makes *The Life of Marianne* precisely what it says it is, the intimate letters of a thoughtful, sensitive woman trying to understand who she has been, who she is now, and how she relates to the worlds through which she has moved. This focus on thought, however, does not keep the novel from also being vividly precise in its descriptions of people and situations. It is a superb novel of manners, neither caricatured nor idealized. Marivaux thus became an important model for Honoré de Balzac and the other realists of the nineteenth century.

Christopher J. Thaiss,
updated by Laurence W. Mazzeno

BIBLIOGRAPHY

Auerbach, Erich. *Mimesis: The Representation of Reality in Western Literature.* Translated by Willard R. Trask. Princeton, N.J.: Princeton University Press, 1953. Examines ways writers from the classical period through the nineteenth century have attempted to portray reality in fiction. Careful explications of individual narratives illuminate the development of the novel as a distinct genre and provide clear demarcations among various historical and literary periods. Compares the development of the novel with other genres, especially the drama.

Bell, Michael. *The Sentiment of Reality: Truth and Feeling in the European Novel.* Boston: Allen & Unwin, 1983. Includes a useful bibliography and index.

Cohen, J. M. *A History of Western Literature.* Baltimore: Penguin Books, 1956. Traces the history of European literature, including that produced in Russia, to show why certain works, including important European novels, have continued to enjoy wide readership for centuries after they were written. Separate chapters explore the development of the genre on the Iberian peninsula, in France, and in Germany.

Curtius, Ernst Robert. *European Literature and the Latin Middle Ages.* Translated by Willard R. Trask. New York: Pantheon Books, 1953. Focuses on works written in Latin from the fifth century until the blossoming of the Renaissance in Europe. Examines the rhetorical, stylistic, and metaphoric techniques used by poets, chroniclers, and romancers that influenced works traditionally considered the earliest novels and novellas.

Dunn, Peter N. *The Spanish Picaresque Novel.* Boston: Twayne, 1979. Traces the development of the picaresque novel in Spain, from sixteenth century versions such as *Lazarillo de Tormes* through seventeenth century tales written by Miguel de Cervantes and others. Explains distinctive qualities of the genre and demonstrates how these are continued in novels as the tradition of realistic fiction develops.

Eriksen, Roy, ed. *Contexts of Pre-Novel Narrative: The European Tradition.* New York: Mouton de Gruyter, 1994. One in a series entitled Approaches to Semiotics, this volume of essays includes bibliographical references and indexes.

Fraser, Theodore P. *The Modern Catholic Novel in Europe.* New York: Twayne, 1994. Geared for the introductory student, this overview of Catholic issues and writers in European fiction considers an important tradition in the history of the European novel. Includes bibliographical references and an index.

Gutiérrez, Helen Turner. *The Reception of the Picaresque in the French, English, and German Traditions.* New York: Peter Lang, 1995. Explores ways a common tradition is adapted in various countries in Europe to meet the needs of individual writers and the expectations of reading publics. Discusses the development of the picaresque in three countries, examining examples from the sixteenth through the twentieth centuries.

Jensen, Katherine Ann. *Writing Love: Letters, Women, and the Novel in France, 1605-1776.* Carbondale: Southern Illinois Press, 1995. Argues that the critical histories of French literature concentrate almost exclusively on male writers. Examines ways women novelists in seventeenth century France used the epistolary tradition as a strategy for constructing novels. Also shows how men adopted this technique, often using female pseudonyms to take advantage of the popularity of this genre.

Lowenthal, Leo. *Literature and the Image of Man: Sociological Studies of the European Drama and Novel, 1600-1900.* 2d ed. Freeport, N.Y.: Books for Libraries Press, 1970. Includes bibliographical references.

Lukács, George. *The Theory of the Novel: A Historico-Philosophical Essay on the Forms of Great Epic Literature.* Translated by Anna Bostock. London: Merlin Press, 1971. Lukács regards the novel as "an expression of the transcendental homelessness" of modern humankind, its development paralleled by the decline of religious myth and the rise of scientific ideology. An early, classic examination of the novel as an expression of historical developments.

Moretti, Franco. *Atlas of the European Novel, 1800-1900*. New York: Verso, 1998. An unusual and fascinating approach to the "geography of literature" in Europe, including chapters such as "Geography of Ideas," "Village, Provinces, Metropolis," and "The Three Europes." Maps, bibliographical references, index.

Nelson, Brian, ed. *Naturalism in the European Novel: New Critical Perspectives*. New York: Berg, 1992. One in a series of European studies by the publisher, this collection of essays examines one of the most important schools of the novel in the nineteenth and early twentieth centuries. Bibliographical references, index.

Reed, Walter L. *An Exemplary History of the Novel: The Quixotic Versus the Picaresque*. Chicago: University of Chicago Press, 1981. This history of the novel in Europe compares the two main traditions in fiction—the heroic and the picaresque—defining each by way of contrast. Bibliographical references and index are included.

Watt, Ian. *The Rise of the Novel: Studies in Defoe, Richardson, and Fielding*. London: Chatto & Windus, 1957. The novel in its modern form is said to have arisen during the eighteenth century and achieved its unique expression in the works of these writers. In this classic, Watt analyzes the novel's development as a separate form during this period of history.

Whitbourn, Christine J., ed. *Knaves and Swindlers: Essays on the Picaresque Novel in Europe*. London: Oxford University Press, 1974. Individual essays examine examples of the picaresque in Spain, Germany, England, France, and Russia. Explains how the popularity of the genre influenced writers across the Continent and served as a forerunner to the realistic novel. Explores the development of the picaresque from the seventeenth through the nineteenth centuries.

Williams, Ioan. *The Idea of the Novel in Europe, 1600-1800*. New York: New York University Press, 1979. Contradicts prevalent theories that the modern novel emerged in England in the eighteenth century. Argues instead that the development of the novel from 1600 until the nineteenth century was evolutionary and that writers from Spain, Germany, and France gradually developed an idea for a form of literature that would represent everyday life and provide a realistic portrait of society.

FRENCH LONG FICTION TO THE 1850's

The roots of French fiction run deep in France's history, from the medieval epic *chansons de geste* and *romans*, or "romances," of the late medieval period to the Renaissance and early modern periods, when the novel in its modern form began to emerge. Storytelling is fundamental to human life, and certainly the French are no exception to this rule. Stories can be told in verse, as in French epic poems and great tragedies and comedies for the stage; prose chronicles and histories also share a storytelling function, but they promise their readers "truth," not fiction, even when employing the technical devices of prose fiction writing. Long fiction in France, as in other Western societies, found its métier in the novel, and it is the story of the novel's rise to prominence and popularity among critics and the reading public alike that necessarily forms the central focus of this survey. While to modern readers the novel's place in literature is beyond dispute, the reasons for its emergence, development, and survival are varied and complex.

In English, the distinction between novel and novella is easier to grasp than in French; short fiction means the short story, and a novella represents some sort of halfway mark between a story and a full-fledged novel. The French word *roman* means simply "novel" to the modern reader, but its original usage conveyed instead the sense of "romance," a literary genre lacking what are now taken to be some of the novel's central features, even if certain conventions can be said to have survived. In the eighteenth century, when the novel was coming increasingly into its own, the philosophe Denis Diderot (1713-1784), in a glowing appreciation of the novels of Samuel Richardson, complained of the unfortunate connotations of *roman* and argued that a different word needed to be found for Richardson's novels.

As for "novella," the French *nouvelle*, which serves today as that word's equivalent, originally meant something other than a short novel. In the sixteenth and seventeenth centuries, *nouvelles* were more akin to short factual reports and were linked to what is now thought of as historical writing. This, in turn, points to a state of confusion concerning the relationship between novels and histories—*chroniques* or *histories*—confusion that occasionally resurfaces when contemporary historians debate the merits of employing novelistic techniques in their writing or perhaps express grudging envy for a best-selling "popular" historian whose books "read like novels."

In addition, both the English "novel" and the French *nouvelle* convey an obvious sense of something new—that is, novel. To eighteenth century French anglophiles, such as Diderot, who no doubt believed that they were witnessing the development of a unique new genre, the English word must have seemed more propitious than the French *roman*.

The novel, then, has evolved in France and elsewhere into a genre marked by certain conventions and formal characteristics. Yet even while pointing to the distinctiveness of the novel, one cannot lose sight of its kinship with earlier forms of storytelling and fictional narrative.

FROM *CHANSONS DE GESTE* TO *ROMANS COMIQUES*

Today, fiction is associated with prose, but the earliest French tales appeared in verse, often in rhyming couplets. One notable thirteenth century exception to this rule was the anonymous *chante-fable* (song-fable) *Aucassin et Nicolette* (c. 1200; *Aucassin and Nicolette*, 1880), with its mixed prose and verse form. The earliest examples of the French verse epics were the tales of the great deeds of warriors and heroes known as the *chansons de geste*; the word *chansons* (songs) is a reminder of their beginnings in the oral tradition. The most famous of them, the *Chanson de Roland* (c. 1100; *The Song of Roland*, 1880), was set down by an anonymous author during the twelfth century, but it recounts deeds of the great French hero Roland from around the year 800. Despite its poetic form and its pretensions to historical accuracy, *The Song of Roland* established the idealized theme of the noble hero that would dominate French fiction until at least the seventeenth century.

The twelfth century was the period of high feudalism in France, characterized by the dominant role of the landholding aristocracy and the central importance of the Roman Catholic faith. The first works to be called *romans* were the so-called *romans courtois* (courtly romances) of the twelfth century. The best-known author of such works was Chrétien de Troyes (c. 1135-c. 1183). His *romans courtois* featured idealized knights and aristocratic figures of court society, much like the personae of Arthurian legend. Similar to the songs of the Provençal troubadours, the *romans courtois* were composed of octosyllabic lines and rhyming couplets.

The most important romance of the thirteenth century was *Le Roman de la rose* (thirteenth century; *The Romance of the Rose*, 1846) of Guillaume de Lorris (c. 1215-c. 1278) and Jean de Meung (c. 1240-1305), a long epic poem that extolled modes of feminine conduct befitting the so-called Cult of the Virgin, the increased preoccupation with the legend of the Virgin Mary in the popular religion of the day, a concern that complemented some of the themes of courtly love. As latter-day feminist scholars and others have been able to appreciate acutely, these idealized literary treatments of women not only masked the reality of their oppression but also participated directly in that oppression.

The late Middle Ages also saw the rise in importance of urban commercial centers on a limited scale. A bourgeois, or merchant, class played a vital cultural role in the towns and served as the audience for a newer form of literature, known as bourgeois or "realistic." *Fabliaux* (the word is of Breton or Norman origin), or "fables," were the chosen form of this new literature in the thirteenth and fourteenth centuries and, by featuring nonaristocratic characters, served to broaden the representational scope of French fiction. If the connotations of words such as "bourgeois" or "realistic" were far from positive, they nevertheless prefigured the later sense of those terms as applied to the novelistic treatment of recognizable figures placed within a familiar social landscape, even if such characters in the *fabliaux* are more often to be found in improbable situations.

Despite the popular trend, there was in the late Middle Ages at least one important aristocratic use of prose in the official chronicles of such beneficiaries

of royal patronage as Jean Froissart (c. 1337-c. 1404), remembered for his *Chroniques de France, d'Engleterre, d'Éscose, de Bretaigne, d'Espaigne, d'Italie, de Flandres et d'Alemaigne* (1373-1410; *Chronicles*, 1523-1525) of the Hundred Years' War. This work serves as a reminder that, as far as the upper classes were concerned, the function of prose narrative was to supply historical chronicles, recording the deeds of actual historical personages in a favorable light. For many centuries to come, notions of "great literature" required the use of verse, as in the more valued genres of epic poetry and drama.

In the fifteenth and sixteenth centuries, French artistic and cultural life shared in the world of the Renaissance, deriving originally from the Humanism of Florence in the age of the Medicis. The aged Leonardo da Vinci spent his last years as the guest of the French king Francis I at the latter's château at Amboise, and this act of hospitality is symbolic of the interest taken in Italian Humanism by the arbiters of French cultural taste. The Renaissance in France was a great age for poetry and for both Neoplatonic and Neo-Aristotelian philosophy. Prose fiction realized a much smaller output. For that matter, the first of the two important French authors of fiction during this period derived her style and subject matter almost exclusively from Italian sources. That author was Marguerite d'Angoulême de Navarre (1492-1549), or Marguerite de Navarre, whose collection of seventy-two stories, known as *L'Heptaméron* (1559; *The Heptameron*, 1959), was heavily modeled on Giovanni Boccaccio's *Decameron: O, Prencipe Galetto* (1349-1351; *The Decameron*, 1620) and shared that work's tendencies toward the ribald. This similarity is worth mentioning, especially as a reminder that for centuries, salacious and erotic details and themes were thought to be the unavoidable tendencies of prose fiction, which thus by definition could never rise to the heights of eloquence and moral example to be gained from the more idealized genres of poetry and drama, especially great tragedy. The mimetic tendency of fiction to represent realities that aristocratic culture depended on literature to obscure was thus suspected early in the history of the novel, although it was not until the nineteenth century that this lifelikeness was to be celebrated as the ultimate goal of fiction.

This observation provides a fitting point at which to take up the achievement and significance of the second great French Renaissance author of fiction, one of the world's most entertaining and outrageous storytellers: François Rabelais (1490-1553). While the original sense of Humanism derived from the effort pioneered in Florence to cull from ancient writings exemplary models of moral and civic conduct to be applied to contemporary life, Rabelais represents the later expanded sense of Humanism as the appreciation of and even delight in all things human, including the coarsest details of bodily activity. It is this latter tendency by which most readers have known Rabelais over the centuries. In 1532, Rabelais, a Benedictine monk and physician, published *Pantagruel* (English translation 1653), following it two years later with *Gargantua* (English translation 1653). It was not until after Rabelais's death that the two were published together as *Gargantua et Pantagruel* (1532-1564; *Gargantua and Pantagruel*, 1653-1694, 1929). Ever since, Rabelais's masterwork has stood as one of the most ambitious, sprawling, and encyclopedic tales in Western literature, rivaling Dante Alighieri's *La divina commedia* (c. 1320; *The Divine Comedy*, 1802) and James Joyce's *Ulysses* (1922) in its will to comprehensiveness. Fusing epochal synthesis with humor, *Gargantua and Pantagruel*, like Dante's and Joyce's works, encapsulates much of the cultural activity and controversy of its age.

"Tall tale" best captures for an American reader the sense of the surface narrative found in this book. Gargantua and Pantagruel are portrayed as giants, with character traits writ equally large. Indeed, the adjective "gargantuan" enshrines the Rabelaisian penchant for exaggeration. The giants, father and son respectively, are given grandiose characteristics, qualities, and appetites. Accordingly, they find themselves in outlandish situations that allow Rabelais to exploit their inherent excessiveness to rich comic effect. The result, for generations of critical readers, has been to rule this book out of bounds in discussions of the novel, one of whose chief characteristics is assumed to be believable characters of everyday proportions.

Alternately, the book has been interpreted as a rich expression of the "carnivalesque" spirit of the folk culture of Rabelais's time. Erich Auerbach, author of perhaps the most authoritative study on the representation of reality in Western literature, treats *Gargantua and Pantagruel* in a manner more typical of a critical reading of a realist novel. In *Mimesis: The Representation of Reality in Western Literature* (1953), Auerbach focuses upon descriptive passages in which Rabelais presents a clearly recognizable world, once the fantastic premises introducing such episodes have been accepted by the reader. Such a reading differs from those that treat *Gargantua and Pantagruel* as an aberration in the French literary canon and places it instead more squarely in the novelistic tradition.

An important common characteristic of the texts mentioned thus far is that these works were not written in the modern French language, whose spelling and punctuation were not standardized until the seventeenth century. That was the achievement of the Académie Française, founded in 1635 by the powerful Cardinal Richelieu and charged with the immediate task of compiling a dictionary of the French language. Today, the Académie Française functions more as a national honorary society for distinguished writers, yet it nevertheless retains something of its role as chief guardian of the treasure that is the national language. Its very existence might be taken as a symptom of the French compulsion toward centralization, a trend whose origins are located in the early seventeenth century period, during which the foundations of monarchical absolutism, of which Richelieu was a principal architect, were erected. Richelieu, regent to the boy king Louis XIII, undertook the establishment of more centralizing political and cultural policies. Analogous to the later national mercantilist projects of Louis XIV's finance minister, Jean-Baptiste Colbert, Richelieu's aim was not only to establish language itself, in an age in which "French" was still unknown in some regions of France, but also to establish a literary use of language on a truly national basis. For that, a learned body, or *académie*, was needed. By the end of the century—by which time Louis XIV had withdrawn, in the Revocation of the

Edict of Nantes in 1685, royal toleration of religions other than Roman Catholicism, a parallel standardization that rigidly proscribed linguistic and aesthetic activity had been imposed.

If absolutism meant the vigorous assertion of hereditary monarchy *and* the imposition of rigid models of linguistic and literary expression, then it is not difficult to understand that the aristocracy would be in a position to dictate rules of literary composition, theme, and style. In Richelieu's day, "preciosity" held sway as the dominant literary aesthetic. Taking shape in the fashionable salons of upper-class aficionados, preciosity complemented the baroque spirit of the early seventeenth century in its emphasis on idealized love and heroism in literature, as well as in its affection for prolixity and highly embellished language. In prose, the most memorable example of a work embracing the aesthetic code of preciosity was the enormously long novel *L'Astrée* (1607-1628, 1925; *Astrea*, 1657-1658), written by Honoré d'Urfé (1568-1625).

Astrea was a tour de force within the novelistic genre of its day, but it was a genre for which even the French authors who worked within it felt the need to apologize; after all, "novels" were not really French but were instead derived from the literary traditions of Spain. French readers had been most impressed with Miguel de Cervantes's *El ingenioso hidalgo don Quixote de la Mancha* (1605, 1615; *The History of the Valorous and Wittie Knight-Errant, Don Quixote of the Mancha*, 1612-1620; better known as *Don Quixote de la Mancha*) and had developed some appreciation for the picaresque tradition in Spanish fiction; many of the French *romans* that followed in the decades after *Astrea* were based heavily on this imported style. They were adventure stories, often wildly comic and improbable—*romans comiques*, as they came to be known in France. Like the picaresque heroes of the Spanish novels from which they derived, such novels featured roguelike protagonists whose misadventures perhaps best qualified them as antiheroes. Leading examples include *Histoire comique de Francion* (1623, 1632; *The Comical History of Francion*, 1655), by Charles Sorel (1597-1674), and *Roman comique* (1651, 1657; English

translation, 1651, 1657; also as *The Comical Romance*, 1665), by Paul Scarron (1610-1660). Members of the French reading public, quite small and by definition elitist in this age, enjoyed these stories but were at the same time almost embarrassed to admit it. If one considers the apologies that intellectuals of today routinely offer for watching television, one can gain some sense of the mixture of bemusement and discomfort with which readers of the seventeenth century confronted this output that they were not quite willing to call "literary."

The legacy of this more or less imported tradition was that the word *roman*, like the word *bourgeois* in this aristocratic age, came to convey a sense of something low or debased, so that when Antoine Furetière (1619-1688) published his somewhat Swiftian parody of the heroic novel called *Le Roman bourgeois* (1666; *City Romance*, 1671), the title must have seemed redundant to his contemporaries. Those who clung to an older notion of *roman* as heroic romance, on the other hand, must have regarded the title as an oxymoron, by definition a contradiction in terms. In a country less prone to elevate questions of literary style and taste to a national focus, these trends might scarcely have been heeded. Yet this was France, and under Louis XIV, its most successful absolute monarch, leading cultural figures could flourish and influence the national aesthetic life only to the degree that the royal sun beamed down upon them.

By appointing the great tragedian Jean Racine (1639-1699) and the poet-critic Nicolas Boileau-Despréaux (1636-1711) to the newly created post of "royal historiographer," Louis XIV vigorously reasserted the dominant positions of classical tragedy and poetry as the genres most capable of lending radiance to his royal splendor. Just as Jacques-Bénigne Bossuet (1627-1704), one of the leading prelates of the French Church, used his sermons and theological writings to unify the nation around its king and chief defender of the faith, so Boileau, steeped in the aesthetics of neoclassicism, joined forces with the Académie Française to clearly spell out the acceptable forms and styles of literary creation, most vividly in his *L'Art poétique* of 1674. Prose fiction was banished from the fold; this cultural policy had the unintended effect, while codifying rules and criteria for the use of verse, of freeing the novel and other prose fiction for experimentation and innovation, constrained only by the threat, applied intermittently, of royal censorship.

THE FRENCH NOVEL IN THE TWILIGHT YEARS OF THE *ANCIEN RÉGIME*

During the hundred years or so that transpired before the great revolution of 1789, France experienced profound cultural, social, economic, and demographic changes. The realities of these changes can be obscured by excessive emphasis on narrowly defined political history or by a tendency to assume from the shock waves of 1789 that France was a dormant country prior to that time. From the artificially sheltered, and therefore distorted, point of view of the absolutist Bourbon monarchs, the social fabric lay largely undisturbed. This was the Age of Enlightenment, the *Siècle des lumières*, when a new class of writers and social critics called philosophes advanced progressive ideas to a rapidly expanding bourgeois readership critical of the Crown and anxious to be rid of the feudal obligations and restrictions that undergirded the edifice of French absolutism. Such philosophes as Voltaire (1694-1778), Montesquieu (1689-1755), and Diderot also lashed out at the Roman Catholic Church for its legacy in France of persecution and bigotry. Here, too, they found ready assent from the middle-class readers to whom they appealed.

The philosophes could count on a burgeoning readership for their tracts and treatises and for the massive multivolume *Encyclopédie: Ou, Dictionnaire raisonné des sciences, des arts, et des métiers* (1751-1772; partial translation *Selected Essays from the Encyclopedy*, 1772; complete translation *Encyclopedia*, 1965) edited by Diderot and Jean le Rond D'Alembert (1717-1783); a steadily increasing literacy rate, an increasing number of outlets and vehicles for literary activity, and a general and dramatic population increase resulting largely from the growth of a middle, or bourgeois, class were perhaps the most significant trends shaping the literary culture of this period. Population growth was itself linked to a sig-

nificant decline in pestilence and other natural disasters and to an impressive expansion of the food supply. Indeed, economic growth was steady throughout the eighteenth century, although England was as yet the only country in which manufacture rather than agriculture largely set the pace.

It is estimated that the percentage of literate (defined as those who could sign their names) French people at the end of the seventeenth century was 21 percent, increasing by the end of the eighteenth century to 37 percent. Unlike England, France had to wait until the revolution to experience a real proliferation in newspapers, but they were increasing, as were broadsides and pamphlets of various kinds. By the mid-eighteenth century, the institution of the café, modeled on the British coffeehouse, had taken hold as the social setting for reading and discussing new books, periodicals, and newspapers. Voltaire and the other philosophes all experienced censorship at one time or another, and several of them, including Voltaire, knew imprisonment and exile, yet they lived to see the ban lifted and experience the sense that their ideas circulated ever more widely. The growing body of readers to whom they appealed, however, were interested in more than political treatises and satires. They read novels eagerly, and occasionally the philosophes themselves accommodated them with *contes philosophiques* (philosophical tales) and didactic novels.

Though it would occupy a more central role in the publishing world of the nineteenth century, the novel's popularity was increasingly noted by French publishers of the *ancien régime*. On the face of it, the "frivolous" novel would seem to have been a safer venture for a publisher than the more overtly political writings of a Voltaire, but the latter were not always more vulnerable to censorship. The world of French publishing was far from standardized in the eighteenth century, and this lack of predictability and routine provided headaches for publisher and author alike. Surely one of the publisher's major headaches was the uneven and unpredictable exercise of royal censorship. In order to operate, a publisher needed a royal license, or *privilège*, which granted him, in some cases, a monopoly in certain types of publishing, but this could easily be withdrawn on a royal whim. Apart from that major uncertainty, publishers could not be sure when they might face censorship. By definition, broad powers of censorship were in the hands of royally sanctioned provincial courts called *parlements*, of which the most important and most active was the Parlement de Paris. The institution of *parlements* reflected the increasing tendency since the age of Louis XIV for publishing to be concentrated in and around Paris itself, whereas regional centers such as Rouen and Lyons had been prominent in earlier centuries. Even the Parlement de Paris, Voltaire's great nemesis, occasionally let a "scandalous" book pass. When censorship came, however, punishment was often harsh. This fact, coupled with the pessimistic tendencies of some publishers to expect the worst from the *parlements*, led to the creation of a thriving underground publishing industry. Diderot is the best-known name associated with this illegal publishing activity.

Authors, too, faced an uncertain existence—and not merely because of the more serious threats of censorship and imprisonment. Authors' relationships with their publishers were often severely strained. To begin with, nothing resembling a modern copyright law existed in the eighteenth century. An author's name would not necessarily appear on the book, and payment was not always guaranteed. Piracy was a common problem; unscrupulous publishers were known to seize manuscripts of authors whose names could be counted upon to sell copies. Royalties were unknown. Today, an author commonly receives a fixed percentage of the price of each copy that is sold. This practice was not, however, adopted until the nineteenth century.

In the age of the philosophes, it was possible for an author to enter into an agreement whereby he would receive a fixed sum for a certain number of copies to be printed, regardless of whether they were actually sold. If the book proved popular and additional printings were run, the author received nothing. Not until nearly the end of the eighteenth century was this practice modified so that the author was paid a fixed amount on a certain quantity of copies that were actually sold, and it was well into the nineteenth

century before the per-copy royalty practice was adopted. As a result of these many uncertainties, most eighteenth century authors were forced to rely on some sort of patronage from wealthy admirers and benefactors. Diderot was one of the few examples of a truly professional writer who attempted to earn a living, albeit a modest one, by his pen, and even he benefited, at least temporarily, from the royal patronage of Russia's czar, Catherine the Great.

Most critics and historians of French literature reserve the adjective "great" for the novels of the nineteenth century, but within the changing eighteenth century milieu, the French novel began to come into its own. To a great extent, this can be attributed to the very exclusion pronounced by Boileau and other guardians of tradition in the preceding century. Not that the sense of shame and apology held toward the novel, even by novelists themselves, was completely dispelled in the eighteenth century, but the novel and other fictional genres were free, in a sense, to develop in an undefined new literary space: a terra incognita unglimpsed by *académiciens* and other traditionalists. The novel's proven popularity with a steadily expanding readership further undermined whatever reservations authors might have.

It has become commonplace in French literary history to assign *La Princesse de Clèves* (1678; *The Princess of Clèves*, 1679), by Madame de La Fayette (1634-1693), the position of "first" in the development of the modern French *roman*, using the argument that it embodies the essential characteristics of the genre in its modern form: recognizable, believable characters; ordinary settings; and attention to the feelings, motivations, and psychological states of the principal characters. Set in the period of the French Renaissance, La Fayette's novel nevertheless offers descriptions of scenes much more recognizable to her late seventeenth century readers. In portraying privileged court society, she adhered to the aesthetic of the more established genres but broke radically with literary tradition by translating this milieu into the novelistic realm.

Much of the interest this novel has held for readers past and present has been its presentation of a woman as the central tragic figure, coupled with the fact of its feminine authorship. The Princess is a woman caught in an intolerable situation, for she is married to a man she does not love. Though she is pursued by a would-be lover, she resists temptation as she remembers the counsel of her beloved mother with regard to the crucial importance of wifely virtue. Even her virtue goes unrecognized and unacknowledged by her husband, who torments and eventually destroys himself through suspicious jealousy. At the end of the novel, the Princess has become widowed, and, shunning the attentions of the man she would then be free to marry, she retires to a convent, remaining true to the memory of the husband she never loved.

Certainly, in one sense, *The Princess of Clèves* reaffirmed the carefully circumscribed social role available to women, even women of the privileged class. Ending her days in the convent, the Princess recalls the much earlier, prototypically tragic, figure of Héloïse. Yet La Fayette was able to portray her protagonist in such a way as to encourage empathy with her on the part of readers both male and female. As an author herself, like her aristocratic predecessor Marguerite d'Angoulême de Navarre, La Fayette provides a case study of the relatively greater degree of freedom enjoyed by an admittedly small group of women of her era. Not merely literate but an accomplished prose stylist, La Fayette has served to illustrate Virginia Woolf's well-known claim that, if women had been permitted incomes and "rooms of their own," they would have been the ones producing the world's literature. Still, the association between a well-to-do woman and a marginally acceptable literary genre would scarcely have posed a threat to the social and sexual order of the French classical age.

While few novels of the eighteenth century in France matched *The Princess of Clèves* in attention to human psychology, most continued to examine central themes of social life, often exposing the contradictions and injustices of the social sphere to the harsh light of irony. This accords well with the project of the philosophes, and, not surprisingly, most leading philosophes tried their hand at the novel. More often, they showed little interest in extensive plot or character development, preferring to exploit

the genre for didactic purposes. The typical novel or novella of the philosophes was what the French call a *roman à thèse*, or "thesis novel," like the *contes philosophiques* of Voltaire, of which *Candide* (1759; English translation, 1759) is the best-known example. In many such novels, the characters are extremely one-dimensional, mere mannequins over which the author has draped the extravagant clothing of his political opinions.

Occasionally, however, the philosophes made real contributions to the evolution of the novel as a genre. *Les Lettres persanes* (1721; *Persian Letters*, 1722), by Charles de Montesquieu (1689-1755), better known for his legal and juridical writings, was one such example. As a specious travel narrative, it was certainly typical of the writings of the philosophes. The text purports to be the discovered letters of a Persian sheikh, written to his homeland during a sojourn in France. He relentlessly dissects the baffling mores of the French people, much as an anthropologist might report on the customs of an isolated tribe. Naturally, this affords Montesquieu the opportunity to unleash his barbed criticism on his own society, under the ruse of claiming that this text is but a translation from the Persian. Suffice it to say that Montesquieu could avoid censorship best and perhaps register his criticism of France most effectively by these indirect means.

Philosophes occasionally availed themselves of the time-honored devices of adventure novels, with their improbable occurrences and their cliff-hanger episodes. It became clear that such novels could accomplish their goals of social criticism more effectively by including entertainment. Voltaire's *Candide* is once again the best-known such example. The earlier picaresque form remained somewhat in vogue during the eighteenth century and was recast most memorably in the novel *Histoire de Gil Blas de Santillane* (1715-1735; *The History of Gil Blas of Santillane*, 1716, 1735, better known as *Gil Blas*, 1749, 1962), by Alain-René Lesage (1668-1747), whose reputation in his own time was established more by his plays. Lesage's debt to Cervantes and the Spanish picaresque tradition was clear. Even though the adventures of Gil Blas might strain the reader's credulity, the settings had become recognizably French. Along with *The Princess of Clèves*, *The History of Gil Blas of Santillane* helped establish the novelistic practice of constructing the plot against a more recognizable backdrop.

Another playwright who, like Lesage, tried his hand at the writing of novels was Pierre Carlet de Chamblain de Marivaux (1688-1763). Despite the fact that he never completed his *La Vie de Marianne* (1731-1741; *The Life of Marianne*, 1736-1742) or *Le Paysan parvenu* (1734-1735; *The Fortunate Peasant*, 1735), these novels have not lacked for readers, as they provide rich and complex insights into the shifting, sometimes contradictory psychological states of their introspective characters. Marivaux's characters are continually expressing confusion and indecision, prompting some contemporary critics and literary historians to cite Marivaux as an example of the kind of eighteenth century novelist who, in this embryonic period of the novel's formation, prefigures the more difficult and ambiguous texts of literary modernism.

A particularly rich evocation of psychological torment is provided by *Histoire du chevalier des Grieux et de Manon Lescaut* (1731, 1733, 1753; *Manon Lescaut*, 1734, 1786), by the Abbé Prévost (1697-1763). *Manon Lescaut* is the story of the doomed love of des Grieux for the young Manon Lescaut, who, unlike the Princess of Clèves, is the embodiment of confusion and contradiction where sexual morality is concerned. Prévost depicts his characters' emotions more vividly and with much less ambiguity than does Marivaux.

Prévost also played a central role in discussions of novelistic form based on the examples being established in England. "Anglomania" was rife in French intellectual life in the eighteenth century. The English were admired for their freedom of the press and much greater religious and social toleration. For that matter, the expression of admiration for England was developed by the philosophes into an effective indirect means of criticizing France. The eighteenth century was the age of great achievement in the English novel; the names of Jonathan Swift, Daniel Defoe, Samuel Richardson, Henry Fielding, and Laurence Sterne spring immediately to mind. Prévost champi-

oned Richardson, one of the more complex, even daunting, English novelists, and translated his *Pamela* (1740-1741) in 1742, *Clarissa* (1747-1748) in 1751, and *Sir Charles Grandison* (1753-1754) between 1755 and 1758.

Prévost opened up a debate over the place of the novel in French letters, a debate joined by a novelist named Claude Crébillon (or Crébillon, *fils*, 1707-1777), who argued for an experimental approach as the one most befitting the genre itself, developing as it was in a sort of aesthetic limbo. Societies have a way of imposing limits on experimentation, however, and Crébillon, by publishing such novels as *Le Sopha* (1740; *The Sofa*, 1742) and *Les Égarements du cœur et de l'esprit* (1736; *The Wanderings of the Heart and Mind*, 1751), was judged by his society to have overstepped those boundaries. His books were condemned, and he served a sentence in that infamous prison of the *ancien régime* known as the Bastille. Crébillon was a member of the scandalous group of writers and wits known as libertines. These libertines argued for the removal of all restrictions on the enjoyment of sexual pleasure, which they saw as indispensable to intellectual freedom. This "forbidden" tradition in French intellectual life resurfaced from time to time during the eighteenth century, most notably in the notorious Marquis de Sade (1740-1814) in the years of the great French Revolution.

The philosophe who contributed most to the ongoing discussion of the novel's aesthetic was Denis Diderot, the great encyclopedist who was himself the author of several works of fiction, including the novel *La Religieuse* (1796; *The Nun*, 1797) and the novella *Le Neveu de Rameau* (1821, 1891; *Rameau's Nephew*, 1897). The latter is thought to have been written around 1773 even though it was not published until 1821. With its frank discussion of sexual morality, including equality of the sexes and the toleration of homosexuality, Diderot judged it unsuitable for publication in his lifetime. Diderot's major intervention in the critical debate over the novel came in the form of a gushing expression of admiration for the novels of the English writer Samuel Richardson. This "Éloge de Richardson" (1762) was symptomatic of the anglomania to which many Frenchmen were prey, yet Diderot went so far as to argue that Richardson's achievement constituted a radical break with earlier traditions in prose fiction. Richardson had ennobled the new genre, Diderot argued, but the connotations of the French word *roman* prevented people from realizing it. Diderot called for a search for a new word in the French language to designate the new "novel." Given Diderot's stature, this essay has had an unfortunate impact on later French criticism and literary history, creating a serious, though recently somewhat corrected, undervaluation of earlier works such as *The Princess of Clèves*.

If Diderot was perhaps the most representative of the philosophes, his contemporary Jean-Jacques Rousseau (1712-1778) was far less typical. While Rousseau joined with other philosophes in criticizing the monarchy and the injustices of the *ancien régime* and, like Diderot and Voltaire, produced a large body of writings of various types and genres, he sharply condemned the artificiality and aridity of the intellectual climate of his day. His one great novel, *Julie: Ou, La Nouvelle Héloïse* (1761; *Eloise: Or, A Series of Original Letters*, 1761; also as *Julie: Or, The New Eloise*, 1968; better known as *The New Héloïse*), exemplified his project of exhorting his contemporaries to abandon "polite" society in order to find true meaning and redemption in the natural world. *The New Héloïse* is suitably steeped in what would come to be called the Romantic attitude toward nature, and the story of Julie is extravagantly sentimental. Julie is presented to the reader as the paragon of feminine virtue, a "new Héloïse," recalling the devotion of Héloïse to Abélard. The source of her virtue, glimpsed through her unaffected personality, is her contact with nature. This heroine's "nature," however, turns out to be most typically expressed in her subservience toward her husband and serves as a reminder that Rousseau, who was widely and enthusiastically read by women as well as men, helped influence the strong reassertion of the patriarchical nuclear family put firmly in place by the later revolutionary and Napoleonic eras. It is one of the tragic ironies of this complicated genius that Rousseau the "apostle of liberty" should have contributed so substantially to the tradition of modern misogyny.

Rousseau was a celebrated iconoclast, but other contemporary writers shared affinities with him, though his reputation has tended to relegate them to the shadows. One writer who should be mentioned in any survey of eighteenth century French fiction is Jacques-Henri Bernardin de Saint-Pierre (1737-1814). He was the author of a long and little-read work called *Études de la nature* (1784; *Studies of Nature*, 1796), which nevertheless contained the influential novella *Paul et Virginie* (1787; *Paul and Mary*, 1789; also as *Paul and Virginia*, 1795). Rousseau-esque in its natural settings and extreme sentimentality, *Paul and Virginia* became an important part of the stream of exoticism in modern French culture. One of the defining characteristics of Romanticism, this taste for the exotic was also manifested in the late nineteenth century novels of Pierre Loti (1850-1923) and paintings by Paul Gauguin (1848-1903) and Henri Rousseau (1844-1910).

The suppressed current of "libertinism" was to surface again in French fiction in the last years of the Bourbon monarchy and the heady early days of the French Revolution, before the austere Maximilien de Robespierre (1758-1794) imposed a Cromwellian "republic of virtue" on the infant French Republic in 1793. Thus, it is perhaps not surprising that one of the most notorious of the libertines, Nicolas Restif de la Bretonne (1734-1806), wrote both semipornographic novels and utopian political tracts. Restif de la Bretonne was a salacious fetishist whose most memorable novel is *Le Paysan perverti* (1776; *The Corrupted Ones*, 1967) and who, like the great utopian socialist Charles Fourier (1772-1837) whom he somewhat resembles, called for the establishment of a utopian community featuring, among other things, gratification of the most minutely specific forms of sexual pleasure.

Restif de la Bretonne's works are seldom read today, but one of the most famous "libertine" novels, *Les Liaisons dangereuses* (1782; *Dangerous Acquaintances*, 1784; also as *Dangerous Liaisons*, 1962), by Pierre Choderlos de Laclos (1741-1803), has gained more and more readers in subsequent centuries. Laclos was a well-known libertine who later served under Napoleon Bonaparte. His contemporaries thought the book pornographic, but *Dangerous Liaisons* has been interpreted according to other criteria by later critics. An important example of the epistolary tradition in French fiction, *Dangerous Liaisons* consists entirely of letters circulated among four principal characters. Like Lovelace in Richardson's *Clarissa* (which may have served as a model for Laclos), the fictional authors of these letters attempt, successfully, to use them as vehicles for actual seduction. With a mixture of candor and dissimulation, they probe their shifting psychological states, attempting to register love's complicated emotional impact. The achievement of Laclos has been likened in this regard to the much later poems of Charles Baudelaire (1821-1867) and the great novel of Marcel Proust (1871-1922) in its contribution to the psychology of love. The aspects of *Dangerous Liaisons* that scandalized the late eighteenth century public would today be far from shocking.

The same cannot be said for the brutally sordid novels of the Marquis de Sade (1740-1814), whose books retain the ability to offend the modern reader. This author, who spent a significant portion of his life as a prisoner of King Louis XVI in the Bastille and, after the destruction of that hated symbol of royal oppression, in the asylum at Charenton (where he died), adhered to a philosophical outlook dominated by the central concept of evil. In such books as *Justine* (1791; English translation, 1889) and *Les 120 Journées de Sodome* (1904; *The 120 Days of Sodom*, 1954), he relentlessly and dispassionately cataloged the varieties of the human capacity for evil, including bestiality and the "sadism" that serves as a constant reminder of Sade's name. Perhaps these preoccupations can be likened to the taxonomic effort of eighteenth century biologists or, as Roland Barthes (1915-1980) suggested, to the massive effort evident in the theological writings of Saint Ignatius Loyola or the utopian writings of Fourier; less justifiable is the facile equation of some sort of Sadean "sexual revolution" with the political and social upheaval of the French Revolution.

Likewise, the relationship between Romanticism and the political events from 1789 through Napoleon's rule (1799-1814) has been exaggerated, at least with regard to French Romantic literature. This error is somewhat akin to the overestimation of the role played by the ideas of the philosophes in the revolutionary era. This is not to say that no link may be demonstrated. Certainly the spirit of Voltaire, Rousseau, and others was invoked by the revolutionaries themselves. Just as certainly, significant Romantic poets, composers, and artists celebrated the coming of the revolution, even if its excesses later prompted some of them to repudiate it. At the time most of the events of the period from 1789 to 1814 took place, however, the Romantics who commented on them were for the most part not French. Romanticism in literature, music, and the visual arts was late in coming to France, partly because of the heroic classicism embraced by the Napoleonic regime and partly because the French identified Romanticism with Germany and England. Only after nearly running its course in those countries did Romanticism enter the main currents of French literature; once Romanticism arrived in France, however, it put down very deep roots.

ROMANTICISM AND EARLY NINETEENTH CENTURY FRENCH NOVELS

The seeds of Romanticism were sown to a great extent within the Enlightenment period that preceded the Romantic age, most obviously in the writings of Rousseau. Rousseau's influence on English and German Romantics was considerable, but the full-blown Romanticism that developed in those traditions reentered France by a circuitous route. Matters were complicated by the political and military upheaval of the quarter of a century, roughly, that transpired from the advent of the French Revolution to the defeat of Napoleon. European Romantics had been divided in their support for the French Revolution and likewise divided into groups expressing either admiration or contempt for Napoleon Bonaparte. Occasionally, this division became manifest within the same person, as in the example of the composer Ludwig van Beethoven (1770-1827), who moved sharply from adoration to hatred for the man he came to see as a tyrant. The story of the growing Romanticism in French literature during the last years of Napoleon's rule is further complicated by its mediation by writers such as Chateaubriand (1768-1848), who enjoyed official approval, as well as by Madame de Staël (1766-1817), denounced by the Bonapartist regime.

Be that as it may, clear distinctions can be made between Romanticism and the Enlightenment outlook that preceded it. The philosophes had stressed universal attributes and qualities, whereas Romantics savored the unique and the particular. Philosophes had championed the rational mind's capabilities, but Romantics asserted the claims of the heart and such alternatives to rational consciousness as dreams and the mysterious processes of the creative imagination. Romantics elevated the role of the suffering creative genius marked by his alienation from others—something of a repudiation of the philosophe's self-appointed role as crusader on behalf of his fellow human beings. The Enlightenment interpretation of history, inseparable from an ongoing propaganda war against the claims of the Church, had demanded the total discrediting of the Middle Ages as a backward age of superstition and hysteria, but many leading Romantics rehabilitated Christianity and celebrated the medieval period as a rich and poetic age of faith and imagination.

The lonely, questing spirit of the troubled Romantic protagonist emerges from the pages of two of the earliest French Romantic novels: *Obermann* (1804; English translation, 1910-1914), by Étienne de Senancour (1770-1846), and *Adolphe* (1816; English translation, 1816), by Benjamin Constant (1767-1830). Indeed, the title *Obermann* is certain to evoke for readers of today the "overman" (*Übermensch*) of Friedrich Nietzsche (1884-1900), a philosopher sometimes viewed as one whose work represents a late nineteenth century revival of Romantic themes. Senancour's novel seems more akin to an early, somewhat pre-Romantic style of German literature known as Sturm und Drang (storm and stress). The great Johann Wolfgang von Goethe (1749-1832) and Friedrich Schiller (1759-1805) had been the leading writers of this movement, and *Obermann* is strikingly similar to Goethe's *Die Leiden des jungen Werthers* (1774; *The Sorrows of Young Werther*, 1779).

Both *Obermann* and *The Sorrows of Young Werther* are notable examples of the epistolary novel. Senancour's work is a compilation of eighty-nine let-

ters that, like the letters of Werther, portray their fictional author's turbulent emotional life. Like Goethe, Senancour presents a protagonist suffering from Romantic *Weltschmerz* combined with a sense of being isolated and overwhelmed by life; *mal du siècle* is the French phrase that was eventually adopted to denote this state of the soul. Constant's *Adolphe* continues this theme as well, and Adolphe's life unfolds in the novel along the lines of what Goethe and others have called a *Bildungsroman* (a "development" novel, the story of the successive stages of a character's life through childhood, education, adolescence, and the entry into the adult world).

While these novelists made no particular issue of their debt to German literature, the French writer who campaigned most tirelessly on behalf of the examples set by German Romantics was perhaps the most famous European woman of the Napoleonic age: Madame de Staël (1766-1817). Acquainted with most of the leading writers of Continental Europe and especially partial to German writers (which is notable for the usually ethnocentric world of French letters), Madame de Staël became deeply interested in differences among national literatures. She avoided, however, the growing tendency in early nineteenth century culture to imagine some separate realm called "literature," divorced from specific historical and social contexts. Her great critical work, *De la littérature considérée dans ses rapports avec les institutions sociales* (1800; *A Treatise on Ancient and Modern Literature*, 1803; also as *The Influence of Literature upon Society*, 1813), anticipated the day when twentieth century critics such as Lucien Goldmann (1913-1970) would call for the establishment of a "sociology of literature." Madame de Staël also argued vigorously for drastic improvement in the status of women, a stance that earned her the detestation of Napoleon Bonaparte, whose repressive *Code Napoléon* (1804) had legitimated a reactionary patriarchal sexual hierarchy. Her novels *Delphine* (1802; English translation, 1803) and *Corinne: Ou, L'Italie* (1807; *Corinne: Or, Italy*, 1807) feature strong, superior women who encounter the idiotic obstacles of sexual discrimination; the autobiographical element in them is pronounced.

If Madame de Staël was the thorn in Bonaparte's side, Chateaubriand (1768-1848), devoutly Roman Catholic and Bonapartist, was almost the Empire's poet laureate. Nobly handsome in a manner reminiscent of the English Romantic poet Lord Byron, with an ego of equally Byronic proportions, Chateaubriand nevertheless irked Bonaparte as something of a rival claimant to his mystique, or charisma. Chateaubriand made his mark with *Le Génie du Christianisme* (1799, 1800, 1802; *The Genius of Christianity*, 1802), the most substantial contribution to the Romantic project of restoring Christianity to its central cultural role. Themes of Christian faith and inspiration continued throughout Chateaubriand's long literary career, from *Les Martyres* (1809; *The Martyrs*, 1812) to *La Vie de Rancé* (1844; the life of Rancé). At the same time, the religious emphasis was worked in with the standard Romantic theme of the isolated creative genius who, by definition, cannot thrive in conventional human society. For example, *La Vie de Rancé* glorifies the extreme solitude of monastic life.

French Romanticism found one of its greatest champions in its most acclaimed writer of the nineteenth century, Victor Hugo (1802-1885), whose early plays and poetry exemplified the more dominant role Romanticism came to play in the years from 1815 to 1848. His celebrated novel *Notre-Dame de Paris* (1831; *The Hunchback of Notre Dame*, 1833) provides perhaps the best example outside the English novels of Sir Walter Scott of the Romantic fascination with the Middle Ages. However, Hugo was to live and write well beyond the limits of Romanticism in France, and his later novels owe more to realism and the increased stature realized by the French novel in the first half of the nineteenth century. Romantic attitudes continued to play a role in French literature but lost ground as the novel came more and more to eclipse other literary genres for the French reading public.

THE GOLDEN AGE OF THE FRENCH NOVEL: BALZAC TO FLAUBERT, 1829-1857

After the downfall of Napoleon, France attempted to reenter the *ancien régime* for a time. The Bourbon monarchy was revived, with Louis XVIII occupying the throne from 1814 to 1824 and Charles X, the last Bourbon king, reigning thereafter until 1830. Prerevolutionary France was a lost world that could not genuinely be revived. The bourgeoisie continued to expand and longed to reclaim the promise of property rights affirmed by the French Republic. France lagged behind England in the Industrial Revolution, but industrialization was underway, adding impetus to the bourgeois drive for recognition and enfranchisement. In 1830, the rebellion in Paris forced Charles X into exile, and Louis-Philippe, the Duc d'Orléans, formed a government that came to be known as the July Monarchy, in honor of the revolutionary events that ended the Bourbon monarchy.

Louis-Philippe originally enjoyed the support of the middle class but continually postponed real reforms and frustrated bourgeois hopes. A more decisive uprising followed in 1848, precipitating a general European rebellion in major capitals that Karl Marx (1818-1883) and Friedrich Engels (1820-1895) were briefly tempted to interpret as the opening chapter of the universal proletarian revolution they envisioned. France became a republic once again, but, after an interlude marked by constitutional wrangling and class division leading at one point to massacres in working-class neighborhoods of Paris, Louis Bonaparte, recapitulating his celebrated uncle's coup of 1799, seized control of the government in December, 1851. Not long afterward, he proclaimed the Second Empire, which lasted until 1870.

France thus experienced, during the first half of the nineteenth century, major episodes of revolution and rebellion, as well as the first wave of changes wrought by industrialization. These memorable and traumatic events, the stuff of heroic paintings by such artists as Eugène Delacroix (1798-1863), awakened the French people to an acute sense of history. Perhaps more than any other European nation, France entered into consciousness of what was to become one of the central preoccupations of nineteenth century culture: historical time and its transformations. The modern study of history was in fact a nineteenth century invention, and among its greatest practitioners was the great French historian Jules Michelet (1798-1874).

Novels, like works of history, depend upon the accumulation of successive stages and episodes in the lives of their characters. Narrative has traditionally been seen as indispensable respectively to long fiction and historical writing. As far back as the seventeenth century, when it was possible for a poet to occupy the post of royal historiographer, confusion had been registered over the possible distinction between a *roman* and an *histoire*. The nineteenth century novel proved to be the literary genre most capable of nurturing, in the century of geology, morphology, and Darwinian evolution, this new consciousness of chronology, bringing to its readers the dramatic sweep of historical transformations.

The transformations visited upon French society by an emergent industrial capitalist economy, if not yet of the magnitude of those transformations observed in Britain in the same period, nevertheless increasingly became the focus of critical social commentary. As in England, the novel came to be regarded as the genre best suited to the demanding task of representing the complexities and contradictions of the society as a whole. The novel's mimetic capabilities were therefore assumed, and the longer the novel, the more comprehensive and supposedly more successful was the feat of representation. Readers demanded long novels, easily assimilable in their customary serialized form. The growth of a literate reading public favored the proliferation of a variety of newspapers (a variety that would astound a reader of today), and, through the practice of serialization, the novel's growth in popularity kept pace with expanded newspaper circulation. Because newspapers were usually willing to pay more for fiction than book publishers were, authors profited from this practice, as long as they were prolific.

Such a novelist was Honoré de Balzac (1799-1850), considered by many to have been the greatest realist of the nineteenth century (realism being defined as the literary or artistic effort to capture in detail the essence of contemporary life). Balzac was an indefatigable writer, capable of writing for fifteen hours at a stretch. The demands of his publishers, to whom he continued to promise new books, kept him almost continually at his task. In all, he produced ninety-one novels and novellas. His first novel was a historical treatment of a chapter in the French Revolution. Then, in 1833, he conceived a plan for a comprehensive series of novels with the collective title *La Comédie humaine* (1829-1848; *The Comedy of Human Life*, 1885-1893, 1896; better known as *The Human Comedy*, 1895-1896, 1911). The echoes of Dante in this title were assuredly deliberate.

Balzac portrayed life as it was in postrevolutionary French society, particularly under the Bourbon Restoration. Out of sympathy with the spirit of the 1830 revolution, he preferred returning to the past in celebrating the promise of the future. In order to, in a sense, "repopulate" this lost world, he hoped to create ten thousand characters, a veritable universe. As it turned out, he managed to create "only" two thousand or so. These novels typically feature ambitious, often unscrupulous arrivistes, characters determined to take advantage of the new world of expanding opportunities afforded by nineteenth century Paris. The novels *Le Père Goriot* (1834-1835; *Daddy Goriot*, 1860; also as *Père Goriot*, 1902) and *Illusions perdues* (1837-1843; *Lost Illusions*, 1893) provide especially memorable examples in the characters of Eugène de Rastignac and Lucien de Rubempré, respectively. The dialectic of the individual in society was thus central to Balzac's fictional project.

A monarchist at heart, Balzac was nevertheless able to portray peasants and urban laborers in a sympathetic light. Because his stated goal was to interject himself as little as possible into his narrative, for which he fashioned a neutral language that allowed him to hold a mirror up to the society of his day, he took pride in his ability to report dispassionately on the facts of life among the social orders he personally did not prefer. Many readers have argued that Balzac portrays the lower classes both more realistically and more sympathetically than those authors who profess much more egalitarian views. As for the other Balzacian boast, close reading of the novels will show that Balzac failed to live up to his credo of impersonal detachment from his narrative. Indeed, he intervenes vigorously and frequently with various rhetorical asides and digressions. Modern critics of fictional realism have grown increasingly distrustful of such claims.

Contemporary critical opinion assigns Marie-Henri Beyle, who is better known as Stendhal (1783-1842), a nearly equally distinguished position alongside Balzac in the history of the early nineteenth century novel. Yet, as Stendhal himself gloomily predicted, he was largely unnoticed and unread during his own time. In part, this fact may have resulted from the greater ambiguity of Stendhal's writing, particularly with regard to his characters' roles and motivations, though he shared with Balzac a fascination for the drama of the individual finding his way within a complex and often corrupt society. Stendhal painted, so to speak, with a softer brush, so that his novelistic canvases appear perhaps less vivid than those of Balzac. Moderately liberal, he was less pronounced in his political opinions and less imbued than the almost messianic Balzac with a grandiose sense of his artistic career. In his greatest novels, *Le Rouge et le noir* (1830; *The Red and the Black*, 1898) and *La Chartreuse de Parme* (1839; *The Charterhouse of Parma*, 1895), however, Stendhal was certainly capable of touching upon the conflicting and often confusing array of political, philosophical, and social trends at work in his time. The shadow of Napoleon haunts Stendhal's work, as does the legacy of the revolution. The novels of both Balzac and Stendhal illustrate the claim frequently made by literary historians that the novel flourishes during times of social or political turmoil.

The long literary career of Amandine-Aurore-Lucile Dupin, or George Sand (1804-1876), unfolded in such times. Known chiefly as a novelist, she moved from an early Romanticism to, after 1848, an increasingly pronounced avowal of a somewhat revolutionary socialism. Having taken by necessity a masculine nom de plume in order to publish her books, she organized her keen political sensibilities around the central theme of the oppression of women. This theme dominates such early novels as *Indiana* (1832; English translation, 1833) and *Lélia* (1833, 1839; English translation, 1978), while later novels, perhaps most notably *François le champi* (1850; *Francis the Waif*, 1889), embody themes of socialism and compassion for the lower classes. In enunciating humanitarian themes, Sand played a role similar to that of Victor Hugo in nineteenth century French culture. In her day, Sand's works were widely read in France and abroad. Even if she attracted more attention in her early years as the lover of Alfred de Musset (1810-1857) and Frédéric Chopin (1810-1849) and as one contemptuous of the opinions of conventional society than as a novelist, she came to be considered one of the most illustrious of French writers, and she received glowing tributes from foreign novelists. From her death until the resurgence of feminist literary scholarship, however, she was consigned to literary oblivion.

Prosper Mérimée (1803-1870) was one of the many fellow writers Sand befriended, and, like her, Mérimée cultivated his own circle of friends among foreign writers. Like Madame de Staël in her endorsement of German literature, Mérimée broke new ground in introducing nineteenth century French readers to the works of some of the greatest names in Russian literature. He befriended Nikolai Gogol and Leo Tolstoy and translated some of their writings. Mérimée was the author of a historical novel, *Chronique du règne de Charles IX* (1829; *A Chronicle of the Times of Charles the Ninth*, 1830; also as *A Chronicle of the Reign of Charles IX*), and, in *Colomba* (1841; English translation, 1853), produced one of the notable examples in the novella genre.

James A. Winders

BIBLIOGRAPHY

DeJean, Joan. *Tender Geographies: Women and the Origins of the Novel in France*. New York: Columbia University Press, 1991. This witty, highly readable study of the role of women writers in the development of the French novel includes analysis of salon life, social class, and the relationship between gender and authorship. Provides a rich bibliography.

Hollier, Denis, ed. *A New History of French Literature*. Cambridge, Mass: Harvard University Press, 1989. The most comprehensive and, for the student or general reader, accessible history of French literature available in English. The arrangement is unusual, approaching French literary history through selected landmark dates. Essays by distinguished scholars reflect up-to-date critical approaches and provide important bibliographical resources. Includes several valuable essays on the history of French fiction.

Russo, Elena. *Skeptical Selves: Empiricism and Modernity in the French Novel*. Stanford, Calif.: Stanford University Press, 1996. The author applies postmodern theoretical debates about the status of the self or subject to authors and narrative voices in French novels. Abbé Prévost and Benjamin Constant, among other important figures, are examined.

Schor, Naomi. *George Sand and Idealism*. New York: Columbia University Press, 1993. One of the most significant critical works in a flood of reexaminations of this beloved nineteenth century novelist. Schor's writing style is both personal and intellectually rigorous, as she seeks to demonstrate the relationship between Sand's idealism

and her long exclusion from the French critical canon.

Showalter, English, Jr. *The Evolution of the French Novel 1641-1782*. Princeton, N.J.: Princeton University Press, 1972. Despite its date of publication, Showalter's book is still a valuable source for its ambitious scope and the clarity of its presentation. Few critics cover such a range of novels, novelists, and themes.

Unwin, Timothy, ed. *The Cambridge Companion to the French Novel: From 1800 to the Present*. New York: Cambridge University Press, 1997. This anthology features important, up-to-date critical essays that provide an overview of the French novel during the nineteenth and twentieth centuries. Topics include women and fiction, romantic and realist fiction, and popular fiction of the nineteenth century.

FRENCH LONG FICTION SINCE THE 1850's

The ascendancy of the novel as the prime literary genre in France was established, by no means accidentally, during the reign of the so-called Bourgeois King, Louis-Philippe. The shifting patterns of population and of economic status had made the middle class dominant, especially in Paris, that cradle of culture; it was perhaps no more than normal that the kind of reading the bourgeoisie preferred—the novel—should in that era have become what the nation as a whole preferred. The key factor in the novel's development to ascendancy, during the years 1830 to 1850, was that Honoré de Balzac, with his visionary ideal of the novel as society's true reflection and record, had imposed on the reading public, by his creative energy and example, his private conception of what a good novel should be: an accurate portrayal of some aspect of the contemporary world. By the start of Napoleon III's Second Empire in 1851, it could be said that, from an exercise in imagination, the serious French novel had become an exercise in observation. The novel had turned decisively realistic. Unhappily, however, the Second Empire, which owed its existence to the violent repression of revolt, was a sternly restrictive regime that alienated writers by its policy of censorship. After the *coup d'état*, artists and intellectuals tended to withdraw into silence, concerning themselves with abstract theory rather than with the concrete, observable world around them.

Not surprisingly, the twenty-year span of the Second Empire was not a richly productive period for the French novel, or indeed for any of the literary arts. Accurate observation of reality was a risky business under such a regime, unless the reality being observed was inconsequential. On the basis of such reasoning, a literary school took shape in the 1850's that called itself Le Réalisme, publishing its own journal and offering readers novels exemplifying the aesthetic. Writers of this school avoided the attention of the state censor simply by defining realism as the art of depicting the ordinary, everyday life of humble citizens, arguing that literature had too long neglected the commonplace activities that were reality for the greatest number of French citizens. The novels produced by this school were, by and large, flat and pedestrian and did not sell; their authors had misunderstood the nature and purpose of Honoré de Balzac's insistence on the principle of realism in the novel.

Only one writer of that period really understood what Balzac meant—Gustave Flaubert (1821-1880), a brilliant recluse and a great admirer of Balzac's work, who managed to revolutionize the course of the modern novel with his first publication, the celebrated *Madame Bovary* (1857; English translation, 1886). Flaubert recognized that Balzac's ingenious notion of the novel as a record of what exists was focused on the need to be accurate, to avoid distorting reality, rather than on a specific definition of which aspect of reality merited attention from the novelist. Balzac was interested not only in the common person but also in all of society, which is why his novel *Le Père Goriot* (1834-1835; *Daddy Goriot*, 1860; also as *Père Goriot*) offered a microcosm of Parisian society, from top to bottom, in the cast of characters associated with Madame Vauquer's boardinghouse. Flaubert's dismissive comment on the theories of the *réalistes* of the 1850's (Champfleury, Louis-Émile-Edmond Duranty, and Ernest Feydeau were the best known) was to note, dryly, that "Henri Monnier [author of a comic novel about a bourgeois who thinks and speaks in clichés] is not more real than Racine." For Flaubert, the term "realism" as used by his contemporaries had no valid literary meaning, since it was restricted to but one corner of the observable world. Accordingly, he always rejected the label of "realist" whenever it was applied to him. Yet Flaubert fully embraced Balzac's insistence on fidelity to the real, for that was a matter of being true to the facts, which to Flaubert was not only a writer's obligation but also an aesthetic necessity; Flaubert was a firm believer in Plato's conception of beauty, according to which the preconditions for any object to be beautiful were that the object be true and good. Since the only worthy objective for a writer, Flaubert thought, was to create something beautiful, he argued that the writer's first task is to render the truth—*faire vrai* was his expression. If the writer's words faithfully render the truth, they will necessarily be morally good, for the truth cannot be evil, and if the words are both true and good, they meet the Platonic standard of beauty. From that reasoning, Flaubert derived the logic of his own practice as a novelist: Research the facts meticulously to be sure that what was written was true. Since the aesthetic value of what he produced depended wholly, according to his theory, on his fidelity to the truth, he took elaborate pains to get everything correct. Documentary research and recorded observations were indeed part of his method, as he readily acknowledged, but he refused to call that effort "realism," for that word distorted his literary purpose. The problem he saw with "reality" was that it can be whatever anyone decides it to be, whereas the truth is never merely a matter of opinion.

There was a good deal more to truth, as Flaubert saw it, than merely rendering the facts. To convey truth, words must be chosen and arranged properly, providing all the necessary nuances and distinctions and bearing the imprint of natural human speech. The mode of expression—which is to say, the style—is an implicit element in the truth of any assertion. A sentence or paragraph that is unnatural or artificial in its rhythm, sound, or vocabulary, Flaubert believed, was ipso facto false. For that reason, Flaubert devoted much of his time to rewriting, recasting his sentences over and over again, in search of the perfect arrangement that would "ring true" and pass the test of being read aloud. A sentence that could not be read aloud comfortably, without forcing the reader to breathe abnormally, was to Flaubert unacceptable and in need of revision. That kind of truth, both factual and stylistic, is a difficult standard to meet and explains why Flaubert took so long to complete each of his compositions and why his correspondence is filled with epic lamentations about the suffering he endured for the sake of his art—what he called *les affres du style*, or the tortures of style. There can indeed have been few writers for whom writing was a slower or more painful process than it was for Flaubert. Yet this strangely excruciating torture to which he subjected himself had a coherent rationale behind it that points clearly to the nature of the revolution that Flaubert effected in the modern novel and

that constitutes his most important contribution to its development.

While still an unpublished aspirant to the literary life, Flaubert meditated often on the art of composition and exchanged thoughts on the subject by means of letters with his friends. In response to a correspondent's question about his addiction to novel writing and his lack of interest in writing verse, Flaubert remarked that the art of poetry had been practiced for so long that every secret of meter, rhyme, rhythm, and sonority was known, and there were consequently no new discoveries to be made in that medium. The great attraction of novel writing for him, he declared, was that the art of prose was still relatively new and unstudied, and the most important discoveries about what it is that makes a sentence artistic were yet to be made. From that observation, Flaubert went on to elaborate a personal conception of the art of the novel that would make the novel as exacting to write as a poem, with each word weighed and selected for its perfect fit in its context, each sentence the perfect expression of its intended thought, and all parts of the novel carefully integrated into a harmonious and coherent whole. It became his ambition to raise the artistic level of the novel in his own lifetime and make it the equal of poetry in every respect. Much as he admired Balzac, he was pained by Balzac's frequent lapses of style and taste—which Flaubert knew to be the product of haste and a lack of concern for beauty. He set out to make his own first publication, *Madame Bovary*, a model of what a novel should be if it is an accomplished work of art. He succeeded, and the novel has never been the same since, anywhere in the Western world. Readers of *Madame Bovary* are still discovering new ways in which Flaubert's fanatic attention to detail gave that novel such a subtle, fine texture. Like a carefully wrought poem, *Madame Bovary* conceals its art beneath a seamless surface and gives up its secrets grudgingly.

It was not, however, the novel's delicate art that attracted attention upon publication but rather what was perceived by the government censor to be its offenses against public morality. It was, after all, the story of a sordid bourgeois adultery occurring in a dull provincial town and was therefore shocking for the times. Because it did not concern heroic or noble people but rather scrutinized in minute detail the tawdry doings of commonplace characters, *Madame Bovary* was hailed—or denounced, according to one's point of view—for its daring realism, much to Flaubert's dismay. In spite of his many disclaimers, Flaubert was forced to watch helplessly as his suddenly notorious novel was avidly bought and read for what he considered to be the wrong reasons. His lovingly created masterpiece gave added impetus to the determinedly realist direction the French novel had taken since Balzac—an irony that Flaubert himself appreciated. Realism was what the age seemed to demand—or at least what the readers of novels in that age wanted—and Flaubert has been classified ever since as one of the masters of realism. Almost a generation passed before it was realized that the abiding importance of *Madame Bovary* was not that it was an example of realism but that it had transformed the novel, raising it to a high literary art and setting a new standard of excellence for the genre.

While the novel continued to be a popular form, published in profusion during the 1850's and 1860's, Flaubert now stands out as the only novelist of his generation to have made a lasting contribution to the genre. Only after the Franco-Prussian War did a new generation of young novelists begin to attract attention. The best of the new generation, it soon became apparent, were admirers and even disciples of Flaubert who understood his artistic principles well enough to apply them to their own work and who had a clearly realistic bent in their preferences of subject matter. What set them apart was that their realism seemed more reasoned and more thoroughly grounded in theory and a sense of system. These novelists saw storytelling as both an art and a badly needed instrument of information gathering and analysis for a world grown too complex for the individual to grasp unaided. The special gift, and responsibility, of the artist, as they conceived it, was a superior sensibility that allowed a more profound perception of reality than most people commanded, as well as the capability of transmitting that perception effectively through the power and attraction of art. Such ideas were repeatedly articulated by novelists in their prefaces,

manifestos, and journal articles during the 1870's and 1880's, presenting a concept of the novel's function that honored Flaubert's artistic idealism while simultaneously accepting a utilitarian role that served deeply felt public needs.

The members of this new generation seemed not to have become writers out of pure instinct or desire but rather as the result of a process of reasoning that would justify their calling in practical terms; they were clearly influenced by their times, for it was an age of growing faith in the inevitability of progress based on the seemingly unlimited power of human reason to penetrate the secrets of nature and to understand—and therefore eventually control—the evolution of humanity's social institutions. It was an age that tended to place all of its hope for the future on the newly developed fields of study and analysis called sociology, psychology, and science. Science especially, with its well-advertised method of investigation that guaranteed objectivity, had attained enormous public prestige by 1870, and writers found an irresistible logic in assimilating their own enterprise to that of the experimental scientists, seeing themselves as equally objective observers and investigators of the human animal.

The novelist who emerged as the clear leader of this new generation, Émile Zola (1840-1902), was also the one who undertook to codify and publicize its new artistic principles. The resulting action in the novel is not the product of the novelist's imagination, he argued, but the carefully observed consequence of the newly discovered laws of heredity, environment, and human physiology and psychology. In other words, Zola agreed with Balzac that the novel records and interprets social reality as it exists, but Zola insisted that the novel was able to be scientifically accurate and objective about many things not known in Balzac's day fifty years before. To underline the close relationship of the novelist's methods to those of the natural sciences, Zola gave the new form of realism the name "naturalism," and in a series of theoretical essays to which he did not hesitate to give the title *Le Roman expérimental* (1880; *The Experimental Novel*, 1894), he suggested that the novelist who chooses a milieu and a set of characters for a novel is actually setting up an experiment in much the same way as the laboratory scientist.

Whether Zola fully believed his published theories—and there is evidence that he did not but was rather exercising his considerable gifts as a publicist—the concept proved popular and influential, and the great majority of the novels published in the 1880's were unmistakably in the naturalist vein, broadly conceived. To be sure, not even Zola's own novels could be plausibly compared to a laboratory experiment in any literal sense, but the naturalist vein was readily identifiable by the tendency to write about a highly specific milieu, to provide the kind of detailed information about that milieu that could come only from direct observation or experience, and to govern all action in the novel by a consistently deterministic view of human nature.

In the heyday of naturalism, running from the mid-1870's to the mid-1880's, the major contributors, in addition to Zola himself, were Edmond and Jules de Goncourt, Joris-Karl Huysmans, Alphonse Daudet, and Guy de Maupassant, all of whom produced work of distinction that was widely read at the time. The novel was naturalism's ideal vehicle, but the movement extended, to an important degree, to the short story as well, and with less, but by no means negligible, impact on drama and even on poetry. Probably in no period in French cultural history has literature been more in consonance with the mood of the surrounding society than was the case during naturalism's hour of triumph, and for that reason, the greatest achievement of the naturalistic novel was that it provided for posterity an extensive, detailed, and quite reliable portrait of French society as it really was in the 1870's and 1880's. Zola alone delved into an impressive array of French social and economic institutions, each of which constituted a unique milieu: the world of banking, the atmosphere of the department store, the demimonde, squalid urban tenements, a coal-mining community, the artist's life, the railroad industry, and so on. One must add that, because the best of the naturalist novelists also wrote with skill and grace and imagination, striving conscientiously to live up to the standards of form and style set by Flaubert, the spiritual godfather of

the movement, their works remain readable and worthy of study today, having the dual attraction of being both informative and aesthetically satisfying.

It was perhaps the very success of the movement, and the exceptional productivity of its members, that caused naturalism's dominance of the novel to wane toward the end of the nineteenth century. By 1890, the public seemed surfeited with so much information about themselves, so solemnly presented, and plainly longed for more inspiriting, or more frivolous, fare. A journalistic survey of 1891 confirmed that both writers and readers agreed that naturalism's moment had passed. With historical hindsight, one can even recognize the telling symptoms of disaffection that had already appeared during the 1880's among some of naturalism's strongest partisans: the publication in 1884 of Huysmans's strange antinaturalist novel, *À rebours* (*Against the Grain*, 1922); the violent antinaturalist manifesto of 1887 signed by five of Zola's young disciples; and the success of Paul Bourget's disturbing antirationalist novel, *Le Disciple*, published in 1889 (*The Disciple*, 1898). Whatever the root causes, there was no mistaking the fact that, in 1890, the French novel, its genius for realistic representation of society confirmed by a half-century of outstanding achievement, had grown tired and was earnestly groping for new directions to take and new worlds to conquer.

NEW REALITIES, NEW TECHNIQUES: 1890-1940

If naturalism in literature had indeed run its course by 1890, as seemed to be the case, it was surely because faith in science, with which naturalism was closely and consciously allied, had proved illusory as the savior of French society. As it became clearer, in the 1880's, that there were too many questions science could not answer, a wave of skepticism, sometimes turning to darkest pessimism, swept over intellectual circles, and it became fashionable to point to those phenomena of the natural order—including human nature—which the rationalism of the scientific method could never hope to explain. The irrational, the supernatural, the metaphysical, in all their variety of forms, once again fascinated those who had been most devastated by the discovery of the limits of science. By the 1890's, a religious revival and an intense curiosity about the human subconscious were in full bloom in France, and no time was lost in incorporating these new interests into the flow of fiction that continued unabated, inundating the reading public with what writers believed the public wanted to read.

Weary of the analysis of the observable data of their society, both writers and readers now directed their attention to what was not observable, though it was just as real: the mysteries of belief and desire; the power over humans of both the will to live and the consciousness of mortality; the exact nature of existence, time, and change—all the intangibles that define and distinguish the human spirit beyond its purely mechanistic components. Novelists began to pursue all the realities that were, by definition, missing in the naturalistic novel. Yet such is the power of custom that the analytical method, which had served the purposes of naturalism so effectively, continued to be the basic approach employed by the novelists of the 1890's and beyond. Though these were quite different realities with which they were now concerned, novelists instinctively recognized that the great strength of the novel was its representational or mimetic power, and they were content to use its analytical process to render these nonphysical realities as well.

A typical expression of this new mood among novelists can be found in the opening chapter of a novel about Satanism, *Là-bas* (1891; *Down There*, 1924; better known as *Là-Bas*, 1972), by Joris-Karl Huysmans (1848-1907), one of the original naturalist group. The protagonist is—who else?—a novelist who has been a practicing naturalist and an admirer of Zola. As the novel opens, the protagonist is discussing naturalism as a literary theory with a physician friend. They agree that Zola and company have served literature well but believe that the theory is now producing dull repetitions of its best work, because there is nowhere else for it to go, given the strict limits of material reality—which is the only reality naturalism recognizes. After the discussion, the protagonist (whose name is Durtal and who is clearly a surrogate for Huysmans himself) meditates regard-ing his next work and decides the naturalistic method itself must be adapted to the task of writing, not about the body exclusively but about the body and the soul, a duality that is far truer to the reality of human nature:

> It is necessary, he said to himself, to retain the veracity of the document, the precision of the detail, the substance and vitality of language in realism—but we must at the same time trace out a parallel path, another road, in order to get at what lies above and beyond the material realm, in a word, a spiritual naturalism.

With such arguments—or rationalizations, as some might say—Huysmans tried to bridge the gap between his past and present outlooks and to apply the methods of naturalism to the evocation of religious ideas, one of the new realities that naturalism had so far not touched.

Huysmans was articulating more than a private, personal mood with his novel *Là-Bas*. Both by using a writer as a protagonist and by stressing the moral and spiritual realm as subject matter, he was unwittingly forecasting the basic characteristics of the novel as it developed among the two generations of novelists whose work appeared between 1890 and World War II. The use of writers and other artists as fictional protagonists was a tradition that had begun with the Romantics and had been memorably represented in the work of Balzac, Flaubert, and Zola, to name only the most important French practitioners. In the original tradition, the focus of attention was on the troubled and often misunderstood personality of the artist, whereas after 1890, the focus tended to be much more on the nature of the art and of the creative process.

It should be noted that this tradition—the novel about artists—was not exclusively French but was European in scope, and because some of the earliest examples were in German, this type of novel has acquired the name *Künstlerroman*. What one may say of the European *Künstlerroman* generally—and it is entirely valid for the French tradition in particular—is that in the nineteenth century, its theme tended to be the sufferings of the artist as a human type. In the twentieth century, its theme shifted to the legitimacy of the art itself and the theoretical basis on which the art could claim to have a valid function in the world. Huysmans's novel *Là-Bas* was thus an early instance of what became a hallmark of so much of twentieth century fiction: self-consciousness about the novel itself and a restless, self-scrutinizing investigation into its right to exist as an art. *Là-Bas* was equally the herald of a second hallmark of twentieth century fiction in France, the impulse to analyze and to probe into new realities not only more immaterial and more elusive than the realities that had preoccupied the naturalists but also more compelling and more urgent as topics of concern: the role of ideas in human conduct and the struggle with the moral and spiritual issues of existence. The twentieth century novel became, in short, a literature of thought and of moral anguish, characteristically centered on the dual themes of the legitimacy of art and of traditional values.

Nothing comparable to the naturalist movement took shape among French novelists as the nineteenth century turned into the twentieth century; no one theory or approach won enough adherents to become the focal center of a school or a movement. Novelists went their separate ways, each anxiously seeking new ground on which to stand, as a replacement for the outworn naturalism. Between 1890 and 1914, the only coherent trends discernible in the torrent of novels being published were those suggested by *Là-Bas*: constant self-questioning about the nature of the novel and anxious exploration of ideas and moral problems. These two trends found a wide variety of modes of expression, however, leaving little in common to connect one novelist with another. Huysmans, for example, after *Là-Bas* seemed to abandon the novel of invention, writing a group of three barely disguised autobiographical narratives in which his novelist-character, Durtal, traverses the stages of Huysmans's own conversion to orthodox Catholicism and to acceptance of the monastic life. These narratives, though published as novels, have neither plot nor cast of characters nor structure; they simply record a writer's inward journey to salvation.

Meanwhile, Huysmans's contemporary Anatole France (1844-1924) also wrote a novel with a writer as a protagonist, *Le Lys rouge* (1894; *The Red Lily*,

1898), but the novel treated the themes of love and jealousy and offered the ruefully ironic spectacle of a worldly and sensitive writer who could not understand a woman's desire for independence—in that way making an indirect comment on the limitations of the naturalistic novel. Thereafter, France turned to the theme of the past and tended to emphasize, in a group of novels, the inability of the historian to recover the past with any accuracy, suggesting, again by indirection, the folly of claiming to represent reality exactly with the written word. Others of that same generation, such as Paul Bourget and Maurice Barrès, wrote in an increasingly dogmatic vein about moral and political ideas in their novels, to overcome the impasse into which they felt the naturalist novel had fallen by its presumed objectivity and determinism.

As for the younger generation of that period—those born around 1870, who began publishing in the 1890's and the early 1900's—they showed by their experiments with form and style, their introspective focus on artistic or intellectual protagonists, and their irresistible gravitation toward the world of ideas and of moral dilemmas that they, too, belonged fully to the postnaturalistic world. They worked in very different ways and had no discernible influence on one another; among these distinctive voices were those of André Gide, Marcel Proust, Romain Rolland, and Colette. The period which the French call *la belle époque* (1890-1914) was, in the novel, a time of ferment, experimentation, and an uneasy search for new, viable directions for fiction, ways to renew and revitalize an art that had known great achievement but had lost its way when it narrowed its sights to the mere reporting of what can be readily observed.

André Gide (1869-1951) and Marcel Proust (1871-1922), unquestionably the finest and most original novelists of their generation, succeeded in giving the novel new direction and new principles during the transitional era which preceded World War I, influencing profoundly not their own contemporaries but the next generation, those who came to prominence in the 1920's and 1930's. Nothing illustrates better, perhaps, the kind of privacy and isolation in which writers of that era seemed to work than the fact that these two innovators, although born only two years apart and schooled in the same Parisian literary milieu during the same years, should have had so little contact with each other and so little apparent appreciation for each other's work. It is even true that in 1913, Gide, acting in his capacity as editor of the journal he helped to found, *La Nouvelle Revue française*, turned down for publication an early segment of Proust's great novel, *À la recherche du temps perdu* (1913-1927; *Remembrance of Things Past*, 1922-1931, 1981), because he failed to recognize its originality. It is also true, however, that Gide made a full and honorable admission of his error in judgment after World War I, when Proust was awarded the prestigious Prix Goncourt. The principal works of both authors were completed before the war, but it was only after the war that each became famous and truly influential, because a younger generation could appreciate the novelty of their separate yet similar concepts of what fiction could accomplish.

For Gide, fiction was always a personal, if not literally autobiographical, vehicle for expressing both the moral conflicts of his private existence and the dilemmas of the novelist's craft. In two early specimens of the first-person confessional novel, *L'Immoraliste* (1902; *The Immoralist*, 1930) and *La Porte étroite* (1909; *Strait Is the Gate*, 1924), Gide examined both sides of the ethical problem created by the coexistence within the same individual of a reasoned rejection of traditional morality and a deeply ingrained puritan outlook. At the same time, both novels demonstrated, in a brilliant display of technique, the dangers of the first-person narrative style by presenting a text whose surface assures the narrator's absolute sincerity but whose subtle undercurrents alert the attentive reader to the narrator's bad faith. The two works, taken together, shake the reader's confidence both in the moral coherence of human behavior and in the truth of narrative discourse.

A few years later, Gide turned to the comic vein, in *Les Caves du Vatican* (1914; *The Vatican Swindle*, 1925; better known as *Lafcadio's Adventures*, 1927), to tell a willfully improbable and convoluted story, featuring wildly unrealistic characters set in very real and carefully described surroundings. The central event of the novel brings together, on a train, by pure chance, two of the main characters, who are strangers to each other; one character throws the other out a window of the speeding train, purely for the pleasure of performing a motiveless crime and observing the confusion of the authorities who try to decipher its meaning afterward. By such devices, Gide contrived to make his comic novel a disturbing challenge both to the reader's preconceptions about the rational basis of human conduct and, even more, to standard notions about order and coherence in the form and structure of novels. Life is never neat or orderly, Gide seems to be saying, and the traditional modes of fiction actually falsify reality, rather than represent it, by imposing an artificial order on events and presenting them as clear instances of cause and effect.

Gide's most daring and innovative challenge to the novel, however, came in 1925, with the publication of his longest and most complex narrative, *Les Faux-monnayeurs* (*The Counterfeiters*, 1927), the only one he chose to identify with the label "novel." There can be no doubt that *The Counterfeiters* is intended as a critique of the novel itself, since its central figure is a novelist who happens to be writing a novel called *The Counterfeiters* and who keeps a diary of his progress and of his artistic dilemmas and decisions as he writes. The title ostensibly refers to the activities of a band of teenagers who defy society by making counterfeit coins and successfully passing them off as real, but Gide is explicit about the title's more important symbolic value, suggesting not only that most individuals are "moral counterfeiters," passing themselves off as other than who they really are, but also that novelists are unwittingly the greatest counterfeiters of all, passing off as the true image of reality the sadly distorted products of their imaginations. What Gide did for the novel was to undermine previous assumptions both about reality and about the fictional techniques appropriate for the rendering of that reality and to offer models of narrative that could deal with the stubborn ambiguity and irrationality of the human world. Gide simply shattered the foundation upon which the naturalist novel of his predecessors had been constructed.

Proust chose a different approach from that of Gide, but he had approximately the same objective:

to refute the validity of the traditional novel of realism and to demonstrate the techniques and concepts by which a novel can engage with a more comprehensive view of reality and still be a work of art. These ideas he embodied in a single monumental novel, in excess of three thousand pages in length, composed over a period of more than a decade and bearing the evocative title *À la recherche du temps perdu*, which C. K. Scott Moncrief rather felicitously rendered into English with a phrase from a Shakespearean sonnet as *Remembrance of Things Past*. The novel was so long that it had to be published broken up into separate volumes, in spite of Proust's reluctance to distort his design in that way. Indeed, the first volume had to be published at the author's own expense, in 1913, because no publisher would undertake the complete work, and its continuation was delayed until after the war. The final volumes appeared posthumously, for Proust raced against a debilitating illness to complete his novel in 1922 but did not live to see all of it published.

Proust's one great novel may stand as the greatest single achievement of the twentieth century in the French novel and one of the most revolutionary works of fiction in the French canon. At the heart of the novel is a philosophical concept, the notion that time has a major role in shaping one's perception of reality and that traditional narrative modes have never given that role its due. Above all, Proust wanted to deal with the problem of the rapid passage of time and the consequent obliteration of the past, unless the memory of that past can somehow be recovered and preserved. Those ideas are implicit in his title for the novel. Two thematic strands make up the armature of that search for lost time that the title promises: One strand is the first-person account that the narrator, Marcel, is able to give of his own growing up, thanks to his involuntary memory, which brings back the past so vividly; the other strand is the careful dissection of the society in which Marcel grew up and the changes in it that he witnessed and finally learned to understand, as memory overcame the effects of time and enabled him to see the truth. When these two strands fuse at the end of the novel, Marcel realizes why he wants to be a writer: If the effects of involuntary memory can suddenly conjure up his own past so completely and in such exact detail, only the power of the written word can fix that past permanently and preserve it for future generations. For that reason, the calling of novelist seems to him both noble and worthy, and, having thus confirmed his vocation, Marcel decides to write the novel that the reader has just finished reading—a novel that demonstrates how art can recapture lost time.

As long, meandering, and formless as the novel must seem to readers making their way through it for the first time, there is a firm guiding hand in control at all times, for Proust planned his novel meticulously, like a piece of architecture, as he was fond of saying. Some have suggested that symphonic form is a better analogy for the way the novel is composed, because of Proust's use of themes that are stated, developed, interwoven with other themes, and returned to in a kind of grand recapitulation at the end. Characters appear and reappear in the novel, always as seen by Marcel at the different stages of his own development, so that they seem to have changed, sometimes startlingly so. In this way, Proust is able to make readers aware of time and allows them to experience the effects of time's passing in the same way they experience it in real life. That was one of the ingenious devices Proust invented to make time a tangible presence in his novel and to convey the quality of one's encounter with it. Perhaps the novel's greatest success is that it really does recapture lost time for the reader: The world in which Proust grew up, and which he frequented during his formative years, springs to life in the witty and brilliant pages of the novel, and the reader comes away grateful that one corner of the past, at least, has been saved from oblivion. It is, moreover, a pleasant paradox of Proust's work that, while the world he describes is, for the most part, snobbish and petty, utterly deserving of the scathing satire he heaps upon it, the reader is nevertheless gladdened by its resuscitation. Even a distasteful image can please when it represents, as does Proust's novel, human victory over time.

Proust's great masterpiece, which combines the values of the *Künstlerroman* with the grand-scale re-creative power of the naturalist novel at its best, proposes a new way to look at reality by adding the dimension of time and demonstrates a new range of possibilities for giving a novel freedom to grow without losing the sense of form. These are capital enrichments of the novel's potential, but Proust's greatest contribution to the genre's development was surely the exalted function he imagined for the art of fiction: to reclaim the past for posterity from the dead hand of time. Proust's vision helped to give new dignity and prestige to the calling of novelist in the twentieth century.

Proust and Gide were not quite alone in laying the groundwork for influential new directions in the novel during the period before World War I. A significant, though lesser, role was also played by their contemporary, Romain Rolland (1866-1944), who published a novel cycle almost as massive as Proust's masterpiece well before the first volume of *Remembrance of Things Past* appeared. This novel was a ten-volume saga of a musician's life called *Jean-Christophe* (*John-Christopher*, 1910-1913; better known as *Jean-Christophe*, 1913), published between 1904 and 1912. While there is no evidence that Rolland's multivolume novel had any direct influence on Proust's, the surface similarities at least are striking, since both have an artist's consciousness at their center and both exhibit a looseness of structure aimed at breaking free of the nineteenth century tradition of the well-made novel. Rolland had no original contribution to make to the definition of reality or to the discovery of new novelistic techniques for the rendering of reality; he was, in fact, taking both Balzac's novel sequence, *La Comédie humaine* (1829-1848; *The Comedy of Human Life*, 1885-1893, 1896; also known as *The Human Comedy*, 1895-1896, 1911), and Zola's *Les Rougon-Macquart* (1871-1893, 20 volumes; *The Rougon-Macquart Family*, 1878-1893) and modernizing the idea by giving it more unity.

Jean-Christophe is organized around a single central character rather than a family of characters or a society, and in relaxing the inclusive realism that would depict a milieu in depth (in order to concentrate on the psychological and moral development of the protagonist), Rolland can be credited with having renewed and modernized the concept of the novel cy-

cle as developed by Balzac and Zola. That his creation proved a fruitful example for others can be seen in the successful cycles published in the 1920's and 1930's by Roger Martin du Gard, Georges Duhamel, and Jules Romains, to say nothing of the 1920's success of Proust's cyclic novel, which probably owed something, at least, to the fact that Rolland had created an audience willing to give its attention to a multivolume composition.

The period between World War I and World War II was dominated, in the novel, by the influences of Gide and Proust and, to a degree, by that of Rolland. Insofar as that period produced fiction that broke with nineteenth century practices and pursued new forms and new themes, it was a vigorous continuation of the trends established during *la belle époque* by those major innovators. It cannot be said, however, that the interwar era changed the direction or the concept of the novel in any fundamental way, as Gide and Proust had done earlier.

Several writers carved out a unique niche for themselves through their work in this period, mainly because of highly individual personal traits rather than because of new ideas about the genre. As a result, those authors generally had no influence on posterity. Each was one of a kind. Typical of the leading novelists of the between-wars generation was Colette (1873-1954), who perfected the small but delicate art of the novel of sensuality. She made the depiction of all the pleasures of the senses her personal domain, evoking the sensations of smell and touch and taste as successfully in prose as Charles Baudelaire had done in verse in the previous century. Colette has had no successor, for hers was almost a private art. Much the same may be said of the Catholic novelist François Mauriac (1885-1970), who analyzed the sinful compulsions of the newly enriched provincial bourgeoisie with fine psychological insight and a remarkable flair for the dramas of the soul but whose art and subject matter were too private to have inspired a trend.

The two outstanding novelists of the 1930's, Antoine de Saint-Exupéry (1900-1944) and André Malraux (1901-1976), are often compared because they are both associated with the novel of adventure and with writing about aviation as a new frontier. On inspection, however, their work, too, can be seen as highly individualized and only superficially similar. Saint-Exupéry romanticizes flying, presenting aviators most engagingly as the heroic pioneers of a new industry, venturing bravely and alone into an alien environment. Malraux, on the other hand, writes obsessively about the adventurer as tragic hero, conscious of his doomed destiny as a mortal and determined to achieve some kind of dignity in his fated encounter with death. Malraux may be credited with inventing a modern technique of narration, eliminating the nineteenth century dependence on passages of physical description to set scenes and on sequential narrative to effect transitions from scene to scene. Instead, he plunges the reader abruptly and without preliminaries into each new scene, doing nothing to connect the scenes in terms of time or even cause and effect. The method forces the reader to participate in the "creation" of the novel as a coherent tale and, at the same time, imparts an extraordinary feeling of rapid action and high tension to the novel. In that technical aspect of his work, Malraux was an innovator and has apparently had some influence on subsequent generations, being one of the likely sources, for example, of the nervous, cinematographic style of rapid scene shifts employed in the novels of Alain Robbe-Grillet (born 1922) and Michel Butor (born 1926) in the 1950's and 1960's. Malraux, however, is a solitary exception in his generation.

The conception of what a novel should be and how it should be composed, as exemplified by the novels published in France in the half-century from 1890 to 1940, was essentially the creation of Gide, Proust, and Rolland, insofar as that conception differed in significant degree from nineteenth century practices in the genre. The outbreak of World War II wrote a forcible end to that era, and what emerged after the war, in the domain of fiction, ushered in a new phase in the history of the novel in France.

THE AGE OF ANXIOUS EXPERIMENT: AFTER 1940

Symptoms of the new phase could have been spotted by discerning readers even before the outbreak of war, in 1938, when Jean-Paul Sartre (1905-1980) published his first novel, *La Nausée* (*Nausea*, 1949),

and Nathalie Sarraute (1900-1999) brought out her first work of fiction, *Tropismes* (*Tropisms*, 1963)—both works now recognized as belonging in spirit to the postwar era. In 1938, however, those works passed almost unnoticed and were not accorded serious attention until a decade later. The war years, mostly years of the Nazi Occupation in France, did not encourage much literary activity, and the production of novels slowed considerably, though one may note that the celebrated novel *L'Étranger* (*The Stranger*, 1946), by Albert Camus (1913-1960), also now associated with the postwar atmosphere, was published in 1942 without causing any stir.

With the bitter experience of World War II and the Occupation behind them, the French were suddenly receptive to philosophies of despair, because what they had witnessed of human nature and the value of life during the war proved to be profoundly demoralizing. The existentialist movement, led by Sartre, the Theater of the Absurd, which dominated the postwar Paris stage, and the first eyewitness accounts of the Holocaust, which began to find their way into print after 1945, all confirmed the postwar French public in their mood of pessimism, for all those phenomena proclaimed the same fundamental perception of life—namely, that it was random and meaningless, the product of pure chance and ungoverned instinct, and that such human-made concepts as virtue, morality, conscience, and belief in a just God had been revealed to be grotesque fantasies by the events the world had recently witnessed. In such an atmosphere, it was obviously difficult for both writers and readers to take the novel, as it had existed before the war, with any degree of seriousness or to believe very readily in the Proustian vision of the novel as the human instrument of victory over time. The urgently felt need in the late 1940's, and indeed throughout the 1950's and 1960's as well, was to devise a new kind of novel capable of giving adequate and truthful expression to this mood of despair and nihilistic outlook.

During the first postwar decade, it was chiefly those novels that reflected the philosophies of despair in their *content* that seemed to meet the public need best, while beginning in the late 1950's, public success went especially to those novels that dramatically shattered tradition in their *form* and *technique*. Both kinds of novel, however, were self-consciously experimental, for their authors were plainly responding to the anxious fear that the novel was a dying genre; they were motivated by the desperate hope that, with the right formula, the novel could be brought back to life and made relevant again. Indeed, since 1940, the French novel can be said to have been passing through an age of anxious experimentation, with both form and content, which has been giving to the genre a hesitant and tentative character suggestive of a period of transition, the outcome of which remains in doubt. Moreover, no durable trends have yet appeared, and few novels or novelists of this period seem likely candidates for lasting fame. There are, however, concepts and innovations associated with the philosophical novels of the 1940's and 1950's and with the New Novel group of the 1950's and 1960's that promise to have an ongoing influence on the way novels will be conceived and written in the future.

The leading innovators of the philosophical novel were Sartre and Camus, both of whom were trained in philosophy and could deal competently and naturally with philosophical ideas in their writing. Sartre's most important novel, *Nausea*, takes the form of an intellectual's diary and is therefore a novel of ideas—at the opposite extreme from a novel of action or adventure. Indeed, nothing happens in *Nausea* except that the diarist, Roquentin, who has been writing a biography of a minor historical figure, decides to abandon his project as pointless. The novel's focus is on the thought process by which Roquentin reaches his decision: He comes to realize that the past has no existence and that it is therefore an act of futility to try to recover it. Moreover, in a kind of strange, visionary experience, he discovers that the mere sight of what does exist, including himself, fills him with the sensation of nausea. His nausea is a symbolic reaction to his discovery that all existence is without inherent value and that no person or object has any significance beyond itself, even though people are constantly contriving specious arguments that would invest the world with transcendent meaning.

Although the novel offers a variety of examples of this incorrigible human need to find meaning in life—

a philosophical idea that Sartre adapted from German philosopher Martin Heidegger (1889-1976)—the real originality of the book lies in the way that philosophical idea is communicated. Rendering the discovery of meaninglessness as a physical sensation, nausea, was a stroke of imaginative genius on Sartre's part. Moreover, he describes the sensation in elaborate clinical detail, including the stomach-turning alien ugliness that familiar objects such as a newspaper page, a tree's roots, or his own hand suddenly take on for Roquentin. The descriptions are as precise and as vivid as any to be found in a realistic novel of the nineteenth century, even though what is being described is an idea in Roquentin's mind rather than a tangible object. Sartre, in other words, had contrived a metaphoric means of rendering a new reality, the "feel" of an idea, thus fusing literature and philosophical thought. It was a device that Sartre himself would use again, effectively, in his plays, and that other writers of his generation would adapt to their own needs. The device added significantly to the expressive capabilities of the novel, once it was fully understood. Paradoxically enough, however, the philosophical idea that Sartre had discovered how to render in literature implied the pointlessness of all literature. It is perhaps because of that underlying contradiction that Sartre's fiction writing reached an impasse soon after the appearance of *Nausea*. During the 1940's he attempted a cyclic novel in four volumes as a portrait of his times, abandoning it after completing three undistinguished volumes.

The innovative contribution to the philosophical novel made by Camus was, like Sartre's, embedded in the first novel he published, *The Stranger*; it was also, as it happens, related to the same philosophical idea of the radical meaninglessness, or absurdity, of life. Camus invented not a metaphor but a character as the means of translating the idea into fictional terms. *The Stranger* is a monologue in written form, the account by a man named Meursault of his chance involvement in a crime and his subsequent trial and conviction. What fascinates the reader is that Meursault, by the indirect evidence of his own choice of words, has a disconcertingly detached and unemotional perception of the events he describes, not because he is pathological but because he is, in the most profound sense, a stranger to the beliefs and values of his society, as though he were a creature from another planet. Meursault's flat, matter-of-fact narrative style dramatizes for the reader the consequences of a confrontation between the philosophical idea that life has no meaning and a social order that attributes significance to life by all its laws, institutions, and customs. The confrontation shocks the reader into recognizing that it is Meursault who sees the world as it really is, while everyone around him invents fictions that give the illusion of meaning to their actions. Camus thus imagines an idea as a person in order to explore the full consequences of that idea when loosed upon the real world. It was a device he found fruitful, refining it with even more impressive results in his next two novels, *La Peste* (1947; *The Plague*, 1948) and *La Chute* (1956; *The Fall*, 1957). All three works constitute a major contribution to the novel of ideas, marrying the discipline of philosophy with the art of the novel.

The phenomenon known as *le nouveau roman* (the New Novel) can best be understood not as something really new in itself but as a systematic assault on the old. No two of the practitioners of that kind of novel actually apply the same principles in their work, so it is hardly accurate to speak of it as a coherent movement or school. Rather, it is a case of a generation of writers who concluded, each independently, that the novel was an outworn form whose conventional devices of plot, characterization, point of view, and time representation distorted the reality of the twentieth century world. Their analyses of the inadequacies of the conventional novel led them to experiment with novels that did without one or more of the devices they found to be so unsatisfactory.

Nathalie Sarraute, suspicious of the neat logic of human psychology as portrayed in the nineteenth century novel, depicted characters whose behavior is enigmatic, erratic, springing from inner impulses—and therefore more authentically human, from her point of view. Marguerite Duras (1914-1996) rejects both plot and psychological coherence in favor of depicting the effects of mood, atmosphere, and chance on events and of showing that people often tend to live their lives vicariously, in fantasy, rather than in coherently motivated actions. Samuel Beckett (1906-1989) reduces plot, character, and time to the most primitive and elemental level conceivable, depicting derelicts who are little more than passive consciousnesses undergoing the brief but meaningless experience of existing in the mud and slime of the material world.

The most abstractly theoretical of the New Novelists, Alain Robbe-Grillet (born 1922), conducted a series of novelistic experiments in which he gradually eliminated all the conventional devices of nineteenth century fiction, leaving only an incoherent sequence of images whose meaning never becomes certain for the reader. His best-known work, *La Jalousie* (1957; *Jealousy* 1959), evokes a suspected love triangle without employing any elements of plot or characterization and without supplying any clarifying circumstantial details of time or place. The narrator remains unidentified, unmotivated, and uninvolved, recording in cameralike fashion only what can be seen at a given time and from a given vantage point. So far as the reader can tell, the drama of the love triangle may be real or only imagined, the fevered fantasy of a jealous husband or a fact.

The reader is deliberately given no way of knowing the truth. By implication, Robbe-Grillet has composed a scathing critique of a thousand conventional novels of jealousy, which analyze in subtle detail the motives of all the characters, describe intimately the actions of sin or folly committed, and so contrive to create the illusion of an eyewitness account of events which no person could know or understand so completely. *Jealousy* illuminates brilliantly the artificialities of the conventional novel, but whether it succeeds as a novel as well as it succeeds as criticism is open to serious question.

The most significant French novelists of the second half of the twentieth century are generally considered to be Marguerite Yourcenar (1903-1987), Michel Butor, and Claude Simon (born 1913). They explored in highly creative ways the human effort to deal with the heavy weight of past events on present lives. Claude Simon received the Nobel Prize in Literature in 1985, and Marguerite Yourcenar became, in 1981, the first woman elected to the French Academy after its creation in 1635. Although these novelists are highly original, their careers have been very different. Yourcenar was born into a wealthy French family. She emigrated to the United States in 1938 and became an American citizen in 1947. Butor was born in France and taught literature for many years at the University of Geneva. Simon was born on Madagascar, an island off the southeastern coast of Africa, which was then a French colony. He was educated in France. During World War II, he was a prisoner of war. As a result of this traumatic experience, he developed a tragic view of the world and came to understand the fragility of human life.

Yourcenar is especially famous for her historical novels, which frequently deal with classical antiquity. Her 1951 book *Mémoires d'Hadrien* (*Memoirs of Hadrian*, 1954; also known as *Hadrian's Memoirs*) is her masterpiece. She presents this novel as autobiographical fiction written by the aging Roman emperor Hadrian to his friend Marcus. Yourcenar carefully re-creates court intrigue and power struggles in Rome: Hadrian reflects on his long reign and his successful efforts to expand the boundaries of the Roman Empire. Although Hadrian considers himself a tolerant and peaceful emperor in comparison with such violent tyrants as Nero and Caligula, it soon becomes clear to the reader that the Roman peace of which Hadrian is so proud was achieved at a terrible human cost. Fear, terror, and exploitation were the foundations of Roman domination in its extensive colonies. Readers come to distrust the first-person narrator in this fictional autobiography. Hadrian is oblivious to the true suffering of the vast majority of his subjects, and he compliments himself on the many beautiful monuments that he constructed throughout the Roman Empire. Hadrian's love for the young man Antinous brought him a great deal of pleasure, but Hadrian fell into profound depression after the death of his lover. In his grief, Hadrian ordered coins, monuments, and statues to honor the memory of Antinous. His obsession with death makes it abundantly clear to readers that Hadrian is a self-centered individual who is indifferent to the real needs of his subjects.

Claude Simon also explored classical antiquity in his 1969 novel *La Bataille de Pharsale* (*The Battle of Pharsalus*, 1971). The Battle of Pharsalus was the decisive battle in the Roman civil war. After the defeat of the republican forces, Julius Caesar succeeded in destroying the Roman Republic, and he established a dictatorship ruled by omnipotent emperors. As the narrator reflects on Caesar's description of this battle, he remembers his own difficulty in translating Caesar's Latin sentences into French and decides to visit the historical site where the battle took place. As he approaches Pharsalus, the narrator comes to realize that the use of military force by Caesar to overthrow an established and relatively democratic government is disturbingly reminiscent of the Nazis' use of military force to occupy countries and enslave citizens. This historical novel includes numerous references to the horrendous crimes against humanity committed by the Nazis and their collaborators. Memories of these traumatic events continue to haunt the narrator long after the liberation of Europe from Nazi domination. Both Simon and Yourcenar show in their novels that thinking about the past can enable people to understand more deeply the meaning of contemporary events.

Michel Butor also eloquently described how the past continues to influence people; his finest novel is generally considered *La Modification* (1957; *Second Thoughts*, 1958; better known as *A Change of Heart*). In this second-person narrative, the narrator is speaking to a French businessman named Léon Delmont, who is traveling by train from Paris to Rome to join his mistress Cécile. For years Léon traveled regularly between these two cities; while in Paris, he stayed with his wife Henriette, and when in Rome he stayed with his mistress. He has a guilty conscience, and as the train slowly moves toward Rome, Léon thinks about his previous train trips between the French and Italian capitals. Readers come to understand Léon's hypocrisy and selfishness. By the end of the novel, readers no longer care whether Léon decides to live with Cécile or Henriette, just as in Yourcenar's *Memoirs of Hadrian*, readers of *A Change of Heart* are profoundly alienated from the major character.

Murray Sachs, updated by Edmund Campion

BIBLIOGRAPHY

Baguley, David. *Naturalist Fiction*. Cambridge, England: Cambridge University Press, 1990. Contains a thoughtful analysis of French naturalist novels written in the late nineteenth century and explains clearly the originality of Émile Zola as a novelist.

Cardy, Michael, George Evans, and Gabriel Jacobs, eds. *Narrative Voices in Modern French Fiction*. Cardiff: University of Wales Press, 1997. This volume of essays includes excellent studies on important French novelists, including Nathalie Sarraute, Gustave Flaubert, and Albert Camus.

Fallaize, Elizabeth. *French Women's Writing: Recent Fiction*. London: Macmillan, 1993. Contains insightful analyses of many important French women writers who were active in the second half of the twentieth century.

Frackman Becker, Lucille. *Twentieth-Century French Women Novelists*. Boston: Twayne, 1989. Good analysis of the contributions of several major twentieth century French women novelists. Includes a solid bibliography of primary and secondary works.

Green, Frederick C. *French Novelists from the Revolution to Proust*. New York: Ungar, 1964. Contains reliable and clear analysis of the evolution of the French novel from the late eighteenth century to the early twentieth century.

Hobbs, Richard. ed. *Impressions of French Modernity: Art and Literature in France, 1850-1900*. Manchester, England: Manchester University Press, 1998. Examines both art, especially Impressionist painting, and novels created during the second half of the nineteenth century.

Houston, John Porter. *Fictional Technique in France: 1802-1927*. Baton Rouge: Louisiana State University Press, 1972. Explores narrative techniques in French novels and explains the significance of Gustave Flaubert.

Pasco, Allan H. *Novel Configurations: A Study of French Fiction*. Birmingham, Ala.: Summa Publications, 1987. Includes a series of well-written studies on such major French novelists as Émile Zola, Marcel Proust, and Joris-Karl Huysmans. This book is a good introduction to the French novel for students.

Peyre, Henri. *French Novelists of Today*. New York: Oxford University Press, 1967. Includes solid analyses of French novels written during the first six decades of the twentieth century. The chapters on Albert Camus and Simone de Beauvoir are especially insightful.

Reid, Roddey. *Families in Jeopardy*. Stanford, Calif.: Stanford University Press, 1993. Examines representations of families in contemporary French novels. Contains a useful bibliography.

Worth-Stylianou, Valerie, ed. *Cassell Guide to French Literature*. London: Cassell, 1996. Includes excellent studies on the general development in French novels in recent centuries. Each essay includes a solid bibliography.

GERMAN LONG FICTION TO WORLD WAR I

Narrative literature written in German had its beginnings in the medieval epics of such poets as Wolfram von Eschenbach and Hartmann von Aue. Although the novels of the Middle Ages were composed in highly stylized verse, conforming to specific metric patterns, they nevertheless exhibit many elements that are characteristic of later prose fiction. Among the significant features shared by these early romances and the productions of modern novelists are divisions of the presentation into chapters, projection of the plot against a broad world background, detailed development of a variety of characters, careful painting of substantial landscapes, and the artistic interweaving of multiple strands of action. The tremendous literary force of major works that were written during the twelfth and thirteenth centuries derives from the effective combination of fullness of life with rhythmic form of exposition. One of the most significant creations of the period was Wolfram's *Parzival* (c. 1200-1210; English translation, 1894), which is, in many respects, a forerunner of the *Bildungsroman*.

Substance for these sophisticated lyric tales came from the common European cultural heritage. Arthurian legend had an especially strong impact on writers of the time, as did Germanic sagas and material pertaining to the world of Charlemagne. Typically, the resulting products were heroic stories of love and adventure that taught carefully calculated lessons about particular chivalrous ideals. In their essence, these components of the courtly ethic are spiritualized and ascetic; at their center is the concept of moderation, which leads to a harmonious life through the exercise of discipline, decency, and decorum. Other advocated virtues include courage, humor, loyalty, constancy, and gentleness. Illustrations of these ideas are offered within the context of portrayals of the problems of the times. The primary focus is knighthood and its attendant phenomena. Courtly love is a key theme, as are the tensions that arise out of certain existential polarities, especially this world and the hereafter, the material and the spiritual aspects of life, and beauty and sin. Heavily pronounced qualities of this medieval fiction are orientation toward the ideal, distance from reality, aristocratic exclusiveness, clarity, and artful simplicity.

During the late Middle Ages, the rise of the middle class and the shifting of the religious-political balance of power in favor of the state had a marked impact upon the evolving literature. As the burghers began to demonstrate increased interest in education, they traveled more and became professionally involved in the arts. One important outgrowth of this situation was the decline of verse and the rise of prose as the new medium of narration.

At the beginning of the fifteenth century, three factors strongly contributed to the expanded use of prose in German fiction. The propagation of expository documents—especially the writings of prominent mystics, including Meister Eckhart, Heinrich Seuse, and Johannes Tauler—served as a stimulus for the refinement of prose style. On another level, the decay of courtly culture fostered the appearance of prose versions of the heroic epics. Perhaps most important of all, German-language writers began to translate stories and novels that had been written in other European languages. These translations from foreign literatures, particularly from the French, Latin, and Italian masters, offered needed models to writers who were interested in genres that were more suited to the real-world bent of the era. Among the most significant accomplishments of this kind were Elisabeth von Nassau-Saarbrücken's renderings of examples of the French *chanson de geste* into German prose and the translation into German of novellas from Giovanni Boccaccio's *Decameron: O, Prencipe Galetto* (1349-1351; *The Decameron*, 1620) by Heinrich Arigo, Niklas von Wyle, and Heinrich Steinhöwe. Many of the so-called *Volksbücher* (folkbooks) that appeared as the Middle Ages waned had their origins in these and other translation efforts.

Narrative prose created during the fourteenth and fifteenth centuries shows little originality in substance or approach. Its tone was dictated to some extent by the melancholy mood of an era subject to famine, pestilence, and disease. An inclination toward concern for things real and useful is manifest in the emergence of social, political, historical, and travel fiction. Didactic stories became increasingly widespread, favoring the employment of allegory and satire.

Aside from the verse epics of the Middle Ages, major achievements in long fiction written prior to the eighteenth century are primarily isolated occurrences that participate in no true continuum of development in point of technical approach or artistic orientation. Nevertheless, individual works and authors did exert significant influence on the later evolution of the novel and the novella in German literature.

Despite the Reformation-inspired Humanistic direction of intellectual life in the sixteenth century, few authors made noteworthy contributions to the prose narrative in German. There were two closely related reasons for that situation. First, the main written language of the Renaissance was Latin; second, much of the energy of creative minds was devoted to religious and technical writings that documented the theological and political controversies of the day. As a result, most of the novels and stories that circulated in German-speaking areas were merely works of popular entertainment with little or no lasting artistic value. The basic tone of these productions was more pedagogical than poetic, and didactic tales were commonly satiric, with religious and political overtones. In addition to novels, various kinds of novellas and *Volksbücher* were widely read.

There are two notable exceptions to the otherwise undistinguished progress of German long fiction during the Renaissance. The first is the early middle-class family story *Fortunatus* (1509). Written by an unknown author, it is unique for its time and certainly the best instructional narrative of the beginning part of the century. The basic account, which describes the life of the title character, whose pursuit of riches rather than wisdom leads to the eventual downfall of his family, is enhanced by fairy-tale elements (a wishing hat and an inexhaustible purse) that contribute to the work's success as literary art. More important within the history of German letters are the books of Jörg Wickram, Germany's earliest successful prose novelist. Wickram moved from tortuously involved novels based on common European themes to clearly organized instructive presentations that combined traditional narrative features with personal experience. Among the characteristic stylistic devices that he introduced into his prose were long monologues and conversations, songs that revealed things that the singer could not say directly, and letters that conveyed information about relationships among characters. With his *Der jungen Knabenspiegel* (1555; mirror of boyhood), based on the then-popular biblical motif of the prodigal son, he became the true founder of the German middle-class novel.

Wickram's creations had little immediate influence on other writers, and after his death, there was a break of many years before significant novels were produced again in German. Much of the popular narrative literature of the last half of the sixteenth century consisted of translations and various free interpretations of material that originally had appeared in other languages.

The first calculated attempts to set up meaningful artistic criteria for German fiction were made by Martin Opitz in the seventeenth century. Opitz worked as a literary organizer, seeking to bring order to belles lettres through the establishment of a well-defined poetics and the generation of paradigms for the various genres. Major authors of the baroque period regarded Opitz as their spiritual father; following his lead, they did away with many of the remains of medieval influences, overcame the dominance of the Latin tradition, and formed the basis for an artistic prose style.

Narratives created under the sway of Opitz's reforms were certainly not uniform in quality and lasting value. What did emerge, however, was a new general orientation toward literary art. It specifically reflected broad cultural developments in other areas. German baroque literature is a part of the art of the Counter-Reformation and documents a definite clash between antiquity and Christianity, with no attempt to find a synthesis of the two. The pessimistic approach to life that was a direct product of the Thirty Years' War (1618-1648) colors many of the novels of the time, with fear of death and hunger for life appearing as characteristic attitudes. Typical productions are heavy with Christian content that focuses on the dualism between extravagant lifestyles and ascet-icism by balancing Christian stoicism against passion and enjoyment of existence. Important themes are the transitoriness of everything earthly, a special aware-ness of death, absolutism in church and state, and the rejection of individualism and subjectivism.

The prevailing style of German baroque fiction is best described as massive and ornate. Overemphasis on form is especially visible in works that incline to-ward accumulation and expansion of substance. A strong tendency to gather, pile up, and vary forms and devices of antiquity is paralleled by a love for af-fectation, ornamentation, the farfetched, and the alle-gorical. Opitz's demand for mastery of technique and aesthetic principles was greeted by a fashion of fas-tidiousness.

During the seventeenth century, epic literature was largely a product of the Protestant regions of northern and eastern Germany. Although occasional novellas appeared, the predominant form was the novel, of which there were three main types: pastoral love sto-ries, historical narratives that were based upon mate-rials from a broad range of sources, and earthy, humorous, picaresque tales, all of which became popular to varying degrees.

Pastoral creations are found in all baroque genres, including poetry and drama. They arose out of a longing for naturalness, for a golden age of peaceful existence, and out of a love for masquerade. Anacre-ontic forms were introduced into German literature by Opitz. Apart from him, only a few authors com-posed successful bucolic prose. Opitz set the pattern for this kind of writing with his slender volume *Die Schäfferey von der Nimphen Hercinie* (1630; the pas-toral life of the nymph Hercinie). Among its para-digmatic characteristics are the setting in an idyllic landscape; employment of verse inserts; use of the narrative as a vehicle for intellectual discussion; ex-position about elements of nature such as mountains, rocks, and water; and the emphasis placed on family history. The Anacreontic novel's predilection for the treatment of problems related to love is perhaps best illustrated in Philipp von Zesen's *Die adriatische Rosemund* (1645; Adriatic Rosemund), the most im-portant pastoral work of the period. Its love conflict is centered on the special German situation of the in-surmountable obstacle that is erected by a difference in religious confessions.

Baroque novelists achieved their greatest breadth and diversity in political and social accounts framed in historical settings. These works are notable for their sheer bulk (multiple volumes involving thou-sands of pages in many instances), proliferation of primary characters, labyrinthine webs of many plots and subplots, vast scope, and richness of detail. Events and situations of immediate local Germanic interest are often clothed in the trappings of Romanic or Asian history. More frequently than not, heteroge-neous masses of material make the presentation un-gainly, while accumulations of figures and relation-ships inhibit the story's progress and contribute to weak epic development. Anton Ulrich von Braun-schweig provided significant models for the compli-cated baroque history in his *Die durchläuchtige Sy-rerin Aramena* (1669-1673; the illuminated Syrian woman Aramena) and the more famous *Die römische Octavia* (1677-1707; Octavia of Rome). One of the more powerful literary monuments of the seventeenth century is Heinrich Anshelm von Ziegler und Klip-hausen's *Die asiatische Banise; Oder, Das blutige, doch muthige Pegu* (1689; Banise of Asia, or the bloody but courageous Pegu), an exotic novel that is peculiar for its extremes of terrifying events coupled with indifference of feeling.

The most important accomplishments in German baroque fiction were made in the picaresque novels of Hans Jakob Christoffel von Grimmelshausen. In-deed, the only seventeenth century prose epic with substantial artistic significance beyond its own time is Grimmelshausen's slice of life from the time of the Thirty Years' War, *Der abenteuerliche Simplicissi-mus* (1669; *The Adventurous Simplicissimus*, 1912). Factors that contribute to its unprecedented narrative success include the humanness of the central charac-ter; the fascinating flow of the story; the inexhaust-ible wisdom that is integrated into the partially auto-biographical account of the hero's life; the vividness and plasticity of individual scenes; the stark portrayal of raw reality in a difficult, tumultuous, confused era; and, above all, the pulsating vitality of the whole.

The Adventurous Simplicissimus is especially noteworthy within the framework of German literary history as the first authentic example of the novel of personal development.

Unlike other writers of his day, Grimmelshausen had profound impact on his contemporaries and immediate successors. There were many imitations of *The Adventurous Simplicissimus*, although none was very successful from an artistic point of view. The only other seventeenth century picaresque novel of any real literary magnitude is Christian Reuter's *Schelmuffskys wahrhafftige curiöse und sehr gefährliche Reisebeschreibung zu Wasser und Lande* (1696, 1697; *Shelmuffsky*, 1962), a mendacious travel novel that presents sharp criticism of the society and times in a guise of comical exaggeration, pointed distortion of material reality, and clever social caricature.

During the early part of the eighteenth century, development of the novel and the novella as artistic literary genres languished. At the same time, substantial amounts of mediocre and low-quality entertainment prose were published. Three kinds of light fiction became popular with middle-class readers: The courtly novel had shallow ties to some forms of baroque literature; so-called gallant narratives satisfied the never-ending public craving for stories about love; and tales of travel and adventure provided escape into exotic realms.

An especially representative example of the courtly novel is Johann Michael Freiherr von Loën's *Der redliche Mann am Hofe: Oder, Die Begebenheiten des Grafen von Rivera* (1740; the honest man at the court). A didactic account of intrigue, its central theme is the realization of the ideal of integrity through personal action. Impressive for its combination of utopian scope with interpretation of reality, the work features a typically involved pattern of episodic situations, tested human relationships, life stories, and social challenges.

Gallant fiction was commonly composed in the manner of the courtly historical novel, but it lacked the elements of heroic adventure and involvement in national political processes. It was smoothly written, characterized by the clever arrangement of many captivating episodes, and presented love as an amusingly frivolous play of confusions and mistakes. The writers who created this kind of fiction were quite prolific but produced nothing of lasting importance. Among them were figures such as August Bohse, who published more than twenty volumes, Christian Friedrich Hunold, whose four novels each appeared in several editions, and Leonhard Rost, the author of at least nine books.

A rather interesting phenomenon was the rapid proliferation of adventure novels patterned after Daniel Defoe's *The Life and Strange Surprizing Adventures of Robinson Crusoe, of York, Mariner, Written by Himself* (1719). Within a few years after the first German translation of Defoe's masterpiece was circulated in 1721, between thirty and forty imitations had appeared in print. Especially attractive to the German reader were the ideas of complete isolation and individual activity outside the constraints of society. The German imitations were generally much weaker than Defoe's original; they usually combined elements of traditional adventure stories with the English author's ideas, but they lacked the component of moral education that characterizes *Robinson Crusoe*. Many of the books were simply tales of travel that capitalized on Defoe's many possibilities for exciting episodes while ignoring the profound psychological development of the central character that had been so important for the Englishman. Of all the German novels of this type, only Johann Gottfried Schnabel's *Insel Felsenburg* (1731-1743, 4 volumes; Felsenburg island) is worthy of note as a minor artistic achievement.

Toward the middle of the century, taste and cultural attitudes changed, leading to far-reaching effects on the artistic evolution of German long prose forms. These modifications were a specific product of the Enlightenment. Classicistic in orientation, the new spiritual-intellectual trend emphasized the ideas of tolerance, cosmopolitanism, and philosophical and general education, thereby fostering the reuniting of religious, social, and political elements of life that had become separated during the seventeenth century. The movement had its theoretical basis in the English empiricism of John Locke and David Hume, as mediated on the Continent by Voltaire.

An important contributor to German Enlightenment thought was the philosopher Gottfried Wilhelm von Leibniz, who sought to devise a complementary union of theological-teleological and physical-mechanical views of the world. Leibniz took the position that body and soul exist in a preestablished harmony with each other, and he argued that the artist imitates God in the creative process. As a reflection of nature, art must be formed according to rules. Production thus becomes subordinate to theory. Christian von Wolff popularized and systematized Leibniz's philosophy, emphasizing its practical application and underscoring the ideals of healthy human understanding and virtue as sources of mortal happiness. In turn, Johann Christoph Gottsched spread Wolff's teachings and established their relationship to literature, advocating German adherence to French classicistic, Roman, and classical Greek styles as the realization of reason and nature. Gottsched's demands were later opposed by Gotthold Ephraim Lessing, who insisted that truly German literature was more closely related to English models.

While coming to grips with Enlightenment ideas, German novelists pursued definite goals in their narrative presentations. One of the most pronounced of these goals was a concerted effort to free people from their traditional ties to the world beyond, in order to bring about a universal independent development of human intellect. Especially visible manifestations of this thrust were attacks against the supernatural aspects of Christian theology by people educated in physical science and the promotion of Deism as a more acceptable natural religion. Absolute rationalistic dogmatism that demanded the achievement of social progress through the advancement of reason was tempered only by a parallel insistence upon humanistic behavior, which promoted an attitude of religious tolerance.

Prose literature that was produced under the influence of these ideas is characteristically optimistic in tone and meticulously precise in style. It was intended to be both useful and entertaining. Leibniz's doctrine of the best of all possible worlds finds reflection in works that affirm the complex realities of mortal experience while expressing both doubts about the validity of revelation and a coincident firm belief that everything can be explained. Humans stand in the foreground as entities in the process of perfecting themselves through the exercise of will and reason. They learn to control their drives by basing their conduct upon purposeful rational action that leads in the direction of beauty and social harmony. The most important key to Enlightenment storytellers' approach to the problem of humans in their world is the perception that ethical and aesthetic values are the same.

At the beginning of the Enlightenment period, a literary art that was dominated by feeling had special meaning for the rise of prose fiction as a major mode of expression, not only during the middle years of the century but also during the Sturm und Drang era. Political and social repression of the middle class found a relief valve in writings that were filled with the rapture of self-satisfied sensitivity and enthusiasm, often connected with patriotism and a more subjectively than objectively encountered hatred of tyranny. In contrast to the strongly rationalistic bent of the mature Enlightenment, many of these works were molded by Pietistic tendencies toward a renewal of mysticism. They document the intensification of emotional life that is based on inner experience of salvation and rebirth. Significant substance is provided by a new sense of communality that has as a side effect the participation in spiritual events that takes place within other individuals. A general tie between the literature of sentimentality and mainstream Enlightenment philosophy exists in the emphasis placed upon piousness of the heart that serves as a basis for practical humanistic discipleship in Christ.

Primary stimuli for German propagation of sentimental fiction came from England. During the 1740's and 1750's, Samuel Richardson's narratives about family and virtue, especially *Pamela: Or, Virtue Rewarded* (1740-1741) and *Sir Charles Grandison* (1753-1754), established patterns that became extremely popular in Germany. Richardson's influence was particularly strong in connection with development of the epistolary novel. The works of Henry Fielding became important as models for a deliberate separation of author and narrator with regard to the focus of presentation. Following Fielding's lead, German novelists began to introduce fictive storytellers who became focal figures in creations that revealed the nature of their inner worlds. Even more significant for their impact upon German writers were Laurence Sterne's *The Life and Opinions of Tristram Shandy, Gent.* (1759-1767) and *A Sentimental Journey Through France and Italy* (1768). Sterne stressed the experiences of thinking and feeling, amplifying the concept of the fictional narrator by styling his novels as conversations between storyteller and reader. Employment of the motif of the journey as a frame for the depiction of humanity's internal life became a definitive characteristic of German emulation of his techniques. One other Englishman whose writing profoundly affected German prose throughout the last one-third of the eighteenth century was Oliver Goldsmith. Through its powerful revelation of the central figure's strength of spirit, his famous book *The Vicar of Wakefield* (1766) reinforced existing tendencies toward intense portrayal of inward experience.

The English preoccupation with artistic analysis of human sensitivities is mirrored in the German creation of three types of the sentimental novel. In the first variety, fictional life stories, often told in the first person, mingle the objective narration of events and circumstances with subjective reflections, explanations, and interpretations. Emotionally charged travel narratives constitute a second type, in which the focus is on the hero's heartfelt responses to external impressions; to some extent, these writings are socially critical, but they also frequently feature displays of empathy for meaningless objects and phenomena. Heavily autobiographical accounts form a third kind of sentimental novel that is related to the other two in its intensity of often religiously based self-examination.

Among the more noteworthy examples of the German "life and opinions" novel are Christian Fürchtegott Gellert's *Leben der schwedischen Gräfin von G . . .* (1747-1748; *The Life of the Swedish Countess of G . . .* , 1752), Sophie von La Roche's *Geschichte des Fräuleins von Sternheim* (1771; *The History of Lady Sophia Sternheim*, 1776), Friedrich Nicolai's *Das Leben und die Meinungen des Herrn Magister*

Sebaldus Nothanker (1773-1776; *The Life and Opinions of Master Sebaldus Nothanker*, 1798), and Johann Karl Wezel's *Lebensgeschichte Tobias Knauts, des Weisen, sonst der Stammler genannt* (1773-1776; the life story of Tobias Knaut the wise, otherwise known as Stammler). Gellert and La Roche were conscious followers of Richardson, while Nicolai and Wezel leaned more toward Sterne. *The Life of the Swedish Countess of G . . .* was the first substantial novel of this type. With its first-person narrative; frequently epistolary form; changing situations, perspective, and mode of expression; alternating compression of narrated time and detailed expansion of specific happenings; and stress on aesthetic beauty and the perfection of sensually perceived experience, it provides a compendium of literary trends of the times. *The History of Lady Sophia Sternheim*, a well-arranged account presented in letters, is the earliest significant German novel by a woman. It is remarkable for its individualization of characters and its representation of the finding of self through social action. The two novels by Nicolai and Wezel, consciously patterned after Sterne's *The Life and Opinions of Tristram Shandy, Gent.*, illuminate specific ethical and moral conflicts in the individual's interactions with society. *The Life and Opinions of Master Sebaldus Nothanker* is a work of special moment in its expression of contemporary middle-class taste and its capturing of the atmosphere of Berlin.

Sentimental travel novels are closely related to the fictional biographies in their epistolary style and their focus on bourgeois social conditions. They especially reflect the increased fascination with Sterne that began with the first German translation of *A Sentimental Journey Through France and Italy* in 1768. Like the life stories, they often represent notable firsts in the history of German narrative prose, although they lack, for the most part, true artistic power. Included in this group are Johann Timotheus Hermes's five-volume creation, *Sophiens Reise von Memel nach Sachsen* (1770-1772; Sophie's journey from Memel to Saxony), the first major German novel to focus in depth on the middle-class situation, and Moritz August von Thümmel's *Reise in die mittäglichen Provinzen von Frankreich im Jahre*

1785 bis 1786 (1791-1805; *Journal of Sentimental Travels in the Southern Provinces of France, Shortly Before the Revolution*, 1821), a narrative of extreme epistolary breadth.

The single most significant representation of the autobiographical novel of sentiment pinpoints the link between the literature of sentimentality and the major productions of the Sturm und Drang movement. Entitled *Heinrich Stillings Jugend* (1777; Henry Stilling's Youth), it was written by Johann Heinrich Jung, who was known to his contemporaries as Stilling. Although it was created in Strasbourg under the influence of Johann Wolfgang von Goethe at the height of Sturm und Drang activity, its intense inwardness and peculiar realism tie it closely to the sentimental novel.

Parallel to sentimental fiction, but informed more by the rationalistic secularization tendencies of the Enlightenment than by the emotion-dominated spiritual demands of Pietism, other authors composed narrative works that at last firmly established the novel and the novella as intellectually valid genres of serious literary expression. These writings exhibit careful structuring, the conscious interdependence of form and central idea, powerful tone of language, and an infinite wealth of personal experience, reflection, and ideas. Like the sentimentalists, their creators were influenced by Richardson, Fielding, and other English novelists, but they were not simply imitators of British trends. Rather, they were concerned with relating German long prose to the totality of European literature. Written for a broad readership that was largely unprepared for them, their productions were poorly received and not understood in their time. Lessing accurately identified the factors that separated these new documents from everything that had gone before when he characterized a representative example as a novel for the thinking person with classical taste. Despite their initial lack of popularity, these creations formed the true beginnings of a new German fiction through their exploration of specifically modern problems, including disillusionment, contradiction between appearance and reality, illusion versus truth, and the freedom of the individual from traditional or psychological blindness. Within

the mainstream of artistic prose, themes and approaches were introduced and new literary avenues were opened that anticipated key developments of the decades to come. Particular examples are the focus on the life and fate of the artist within society, experiments with open-ended form and the elimination of continuous plot, the illumination of fundamental existential questions, the examination of the human condition from psychological perspectives, and the employment of devices such as debate, reflection, and essay in the formulation of the philosophical novel.

The outstanding master of Enlightenment narrative was Christoph Martin Wieland, whose compositions became paradigms for the works of the most influential figures of the literary movements that stirred the late decades of the eighteenth century. His first major novel, *Der Sieg der Natur über die Schwärmerey: Oder, Die Abentheuer des Don Sylvio von Rosalva* (1764; *The Adventures of Don Sylvio of Rosalva*, 1773), a picaresque romance with obvious ties to Miguel de Cervantes's *El ingenioso hidalgo don Quixote de la Mancha* (1605, 1615; *The History of the Valorous and Wittie Knight-Errant, Don Quixote of the Mancha*, 1612-1620; better known as *Don Quixote de la Mancha*), was unique in German literature of the time. It had a profound impact on Goethe and on the German Romantics as a model for their many treatments of youthful, Romantic heroes who wander through the world following ideal concepts. *Geschichte des Agathon* (1766-1767; *The History of Agathon*, 1773), in many respects Wieland's finest work, established significant patterns for psychological and philosophical fiction; it was also the first German historical novel to accurately capture the aura of classical antiquity. The carefully conceived satire *Die Geschichte der Abderiten* (1774; *The Republic of Fools*, 1861), remarkable for its perfection of style and cosmopolitan grace, was the first comprehensive novel of social criticism in eighteenth century Germany. Wieland's last masterpiece, *Aristipp* (1801), exemplifies the preoccupation of the era with themes such as superstition, spiritualism, secret organizations, and problems of faith and deception. It carries the epistolary form in a new direction in which the exchange of ideas and opinions between letter writers unveils a broad social landscape rather than illuminating a single traditional main character.

One other major consequence of Wieland's concerted endeavor to raise the literary level of German prose fiction was the emergence of the novella as a viable artistic form. Earlier eighteenth century specimens of the medium-length narrative, including the folk novellas of Christian Friedrich Daniel Schubart, were pedestrian in style and unsettled in approach. Wieland's cultivation of the genre inspired further experimentation—first by Goethe, later by the Romantics—and was the first critical step toward the ultimate perfection of the form during the nineteenth century.

Beginning shortly before 1770, a rather strong reaction against the spirit of the Enlightenment ignited the relatively brief literary upheaval that was subsequently called Sturm und Drang. The spiritual father of the movement was Johann Gottfried Herder, whose programmatic demand for the subordination of the critic to the creative artist's genius became the basis for writings that defied the restraints of rationalism. Herder and his followers insisted that Enlightenment thought and the resulting literature treated the irrational dimensions of human life improperly and unnaturally. Sturm und Drang writers therefore placed concepts such as heart, feeling, suspicion, and instinct in opposition to reason in generating works that glorify the goal of natural social order for natural humans. In some respects, these creations served to satisfy a longing for action that, under despotism, was otherwise impossible, by concerning themselves with the solution of the primarily moral tasks of politics. There was also a strong tendency to deify a nature that had been robbed of its spiritual essence by the rationalists.

Typical Sturm und Drang productions are dominated by clearly identifiable attitudes. Among the most definitive of these attitudes are cultural pessimism complemented by natural optimism and idealism (that is, a clear perception that natural humans are higher than cultural humans) and strong sympathy for specific human types, including innocent children, naïve women, rural people, artisans, petit bour-geois, primitive people, the ancient Greeks, the old Germanic tribes, and original, earthy power figures. The Sturm und Drang view of life is focused in Faustian duality, a peculiar conflict between a sense of the value of all elements of temporal reality and the opposing feeling for the inner endlessness of nature and life in the face of which all worldly things lose their meaning. Application of these approaches to existence results in a variety of specific characteristic manifestations. Especially visible is an intensification of sensual experience and personal consciousness of individual phenomena. Emphasis on individuality corresponds to a picture of life as a restless changing of forms. A new relationship to history and tradition is created, in which the Bible becomes a parable for the fate of humanity as a whole, and humanity's position within the natural order is defined by a philosophy of dynamic pantheism that identifies the divine aspect not as an incalculable person but rather as the highest cause of all things.

Like sentimental literature, creations of German Sturm und Drang were influenced by intellectual and artistic developments in other parts of Europe. Jean-Jacques Rousseau's *Discours sur les sciences et les arts* (1751; *The Discourse Which Carried the Praemium at the Academy of Dijon*, 1750; also as *A Discourse on the Arts and Sciences*, 1913), with its famous advocation of a return to nature, was especially significant for the philosophical approach of Sturm und Drang novelists. Because of their focus on intimate experiences of feeling, novels such as Sterne's *A Sentimental Journey Through France and Italy* were almost as important as models for the representatives of the genius cult as they were for the sentimentalists. There was, however, one distinctive difference in the results. In productions of the Sturm und Drang movement, intense inner sensitivity is frequently pathological; the deep psychological penetration of characters opens to view a spiritual malaise that becomes symbolic for the inward decay of modern cultural humans.

Despite the energy with which they wrote, representatives of Sturm und Drang produced relatively few prose narratives of consequence. By far the most outstanding work was Goethe's *Die Leiden des jun-*

gen Werthers (1774; *The Sorrows of Young Werther*, 1779), which upon publication became an immediate international sensation and for many years remained the most famous novel in the German language. *The Sorrows of Young Werther* is at once a compendium of Sturm und Drang tendencies and a superb illustration of the eighteenth century German novel in general. Both the idea of sensitivity as a dangerous force and the concept of nature as a model for aesthetic and ethical education receive detailed elaboration in an epistolary presentation that responds perfectly to the demand that the novel portray the inner history of an individual who is subjected to a series of changing conditions. Theme, substance, language, narrative technique, figures, situations, milieu—in short, everything that contributes to the story's progress—is oriented toward the revelation of internal processes that are carefully integrated with external events. The result is a clearly crafted work of art that combines for the first time in German fiction a weighty, deeply personal mirroring of the author's own inner world with a vital, direct representation of contemporary life.

The patterns set by *The Sorrows of Young Werther* were unique in their artistic achievement, making the prose writings of other Sturm und Drang authors appear pale and shallow by comparison Friedrich Heinrich Jacobi's confessional illumination of his own experience and suffering in *Eduard Allwills Papiere* (1775-1776; also as *Allwills Briefsammlung*, 1792) combines a portrayal of Jacobi's innermost concerns with sharp social criticism in pointing out the tragic dangers that exist within a society that submits to the domination of feeling. In *Anton Reiser: Ein psychologischer Roman* (1785-1790; *Anton Reiser: A Psychological Novel*, 1926), Karl Philipp Moritz continued the trend established by Goethe with the description of the hypochondria of a youth who must grow up in totally negative circumstances. Only Wilhelm Heinse's *Ardinghello: Oder, Die glückseligen Inseln* (1787; *Ardinghello: Or, The Artist's Rambles in Sicily*, 1839) attained a measure of freshness and vitality through its utopian interpretation of Rousseau. A cycle of novels by the dramatist Friedrich Maximilian Klinger began to appear in 1791; although primarily

philosophical in direction, they are nevertheless tied to the Sturm und Drang movement through their employment of Faustian motifs.

Beginning with Sturm und Drang and continuing well into the nineteenth century, the general tone of major developments in German belles lettres was set by Goethe's epoch-making writings and by specific artistic responses to them. When Goethe consciously renounced his Sturm und Drang tendencies in the early 1780's, he single-handedly inaugurated the classical era of German literature, which overlapped the final stages of the Enlightenment and the beginnings of German Romanticism. Although only a few key authors can be regarded as authentically representative of classicism, their works made contributions to German fiction that have affected its evolution ever since.

The primary defining characteristic of German classicism is cultural idealism. Goethe and similarly inclined authors sought to create a literature of high artistic value that was devoted to well-defined ideals of Greek and Roman antiquity. Key concepts were balance, order, and the application of aesthetic principles to moral and ethical goals; the ultimate aim was harmonious agreement of spirit and intellect in service to all humanity. Two different approaches to the process of cultural purification reflect the respective influences of Enlightenment and Sturm und Drang thought: Goethe's natural and Friedrich Schiller's rational idealism.

Classical idealism had its philosophical bases in the writings of Immanuel Kant, especially his *Kritik der reinen Vernunft* (1781; *The Critique of Pure Reason*, 1838) and *Kritik der praktischen Vernunft* (1788; *The Critique of Practical Reason*, 1873). In *The Critique of Practical Reason*, he examined the process of action, the morality of which is a function of pure, unconditional will. Arguing that nothing is unequivocally good except goodwill, he arrived at his famous categorical imperative. It advocates that activity be based upon the principle that humanity in self and others be employed always as purpose, never as means. Kant associated the aesthetic element of human experience with moral idealism in his *Kritik der Urteilskraft* (1790; *The Critique of Judgment*,

1892). There he stated that the objects of aesthetics are the beautiful and the sublime and that a central property of beautiful art is humanity as a general feeling of participation. According to Kant, the eternal models for this humanistic art are found in the culture of classical Greece.

In coming to grips with the aesthetic and ethical aspects of their own creations, Schiller and others also employed key defining concepts or refinements thereof that were provided by other thinkers, notably Leibniz; Anthony Ashley Cooper, Third Earl of Shaftesbury; Johann Joachim Winckelmann; and Wilhelm von Humboldt. From Leibniz and Shaftesbury came the principle of harmony that is central to the worldview of classicism. Goethe and Schiller focused on the ideal of a concord in which the physical and moral condition of the individual come into play with each other as a substantial characteristic of the beautiful soul. They perceived harmony as a natural condition that had been broken down by culture and was in need of restoration, a goal that could be realized only through aesthetic education. Specifically applying the idea of harmony to works of art, Winckelmann derived from Greek masterpieces the programmatic notions of noble simplicity and quiet grandeur. In turn, Humboldt related the problem of harmonious education to Kant's humanistic aesthetics by insisting that the ultimate aim of the former is human self-perfection, or the purification of the individual through humanity.

The political and social climate of the final quarter of the eighteenth century also had a significant impact upon both the substance and the tone of German classical prose. The French Revolution of 1789, which affected all of Europe, left a deep mark on German intellectuals and fostered the application of philosophical idealism to practical existence. As a result, novelists and storytellers began to treat such themes as cosmopolitanism, the union of nations, individual self-determination, and freedom from subjection to traditional institutions.

During the classical period, the German novel rose from the status of solid artistic legitimacy that had been achieved by Enlightenment authors to one of new creative mastery. Out of the spirit of idealism,

gifted writers sought to present in their long fiction a kind of integrated summary of human existence. The *Bildungsroman* became the symbolic expression of the times. It was based upon a biological mode of observation within which the concept of organism became fundamental to the realization of classical goals of education. A number of definite manifestations are especially characteristic of the progress of the genre toward its modern identity. Increased concern for poetic language and style augmented the aesthetic power of narrative prose. The humanistic application of philosophical idealism to temporal reality established the broad spectrum of humanity's condition as focus and material for a new kind of didactic literature. Special attention given to the inner lives of characters paved the way for intense psychological exploration of human problems through the use of refined techniques. Expansion of perspective beyond the limitations of customary travel and adventure stories permitted the novel to become a vehicle for the presentation of an entire worldview, while the finely detailed creation of characters as concrete, rounded individuals made possible revelations concerning the true nature of humanity. In this regard, classical authors became particularly concerned with the identification and modeling of the qualities that mark the great soul. At the same time, notably in more humorous works, a concerted effort was made to offer a sharp portrayal of that which is typical in life.

As had been the case with the Sturm und Drang novel, Goethe fashioned the pinnacle masterworks of German classical long fiction. The central prose narratives of the period are *Wilhelm Meisters Lehrjahre* (1795-1796; *Wilhelm Meister's Apprenticeship*, 1824), *Die Wahlverwandtschaften* (1809; *Elective Affinities*, 1849), and *Wilhelm Meisters Wanderjahre: Oder, Die Entsagenden* (1821, 1829; *Wilhelm Meister's Travels*, 1827). Virtually all the literary developments of the eighteenth century lead up to *Wilhelm Meister's Apprenticeship*, which—with its originality, multiple layers of plot, uniformity of presentation, immediacy, careful organization, lucid elaboration, perfection of form, and powerful representation of the atmosphere of the times—had a profound effect upon the German novel from that time forward.

The theme of education, upon which the entire work is built, is treated from a variety of perspectives that allow the author to mix traditional motifs with his own inventions, leave decisions open, and move from ironic expression to symbolic meaning. *Wilhelm Meister's Apprenticeship* is of great import as the direct prototype of the nineteenth century *Bildungsroman* and the primary stimulus for the rise of the open-ended novel, in which resolution of plot is no longer the essence of the artistic presentation. In *Elective Affinities*, Goethe produced the first work in a new trend away from the illumination of the individual's inner world and toward the literary analysis of a topical problem. *Elective Affinities* exhibits the richest development of German classical prose style and is the literary high point of classical humanism. Finally, *Wilhelm Meister's Travels* glorifies the ethic of usefulness in what is regarded by many critics as the first truly significant German social novel.

Three other authors made interesting contributions to the evolution of the novel during the classical period. Although he wrote only a few prose works, Schiller demonstrated in them uncommon facility with the psychological penetration of characters and situations, intense revelation of vital human experience, and the effective handling of background and mood. Johann Paul Friedrich Richter, an extremely popular novelist who wrote under the pen name Jean Paul, emulated Goethe in cultivating the *Bildungsroman* as a portrait of contemporary social conditions. His perception of world history as an endless novel enabled him to capture in his writings a forceful sense of the fragmentary nature of existence. At the same time, a special feeling for the humorous aspects of life lent his creations a unique flavor. The writer whose work best exemplifies the ideal of harmony between modern culture and Greek antiquity is the poet Friedrich Hölderlin (1770-1843). His novel *Hyperion oder der Eremit in Griechenland* (1797, 1799; *Hyperion: Or, The Hermit in Greece*, 1965), an extremely original work, is peculiar for its lyric, open style, its powerful symbolism, its uncommon tone and language, and its carefully perfected integration of form and content.

Meaningful events in German long fiction were certainly not limited to the novel during this period. Various writers consciously cultivated the novella, which won its particular definitive form as a direct result of the classicists' experimentation and theorizing. The most important models for the German novella were provided by Boccaccio and Cervantes, although Goethe also translated examples from French and other literatures. From the efforts of Goethe and his contemporaries, there emerged a formal conception of the novella as a narrative focused on a single incident or theme presented in limited space such that no deviation from the exposition of the central problem is permitted. In spite of explicit structural restrictions, the story was to bring forth the environment in all of its color and mood, while portraying characters as multidimensional individuals. Aside from the limited plot, the most important particular of the German novella is the programmed involvement of symbols and motifs that highlight the singularity of the work's focal situation.

Although Wieland, Schubart, and others had had some success in producing novellas before Goethe, it was once again he who perfected the form and provided the patterns for later emulation. His *Unterhaltungen deutscher Ausgewanderten* (1795; *Conversations of German Emigrants*, 1854), a series of stories framed within the milieu of the French Revolution, is the first cycle of its type in German literature. A separate work, simply entitled *Novelle* (1826; *Novel*, 1837), was intended as a paradigm of the genre and is especially attractive for its lyric elements. Additional writers of the classical period who created medium-length narratives worthy of note were Schiller and Jean Paul.

Near the end of the eighteenth century, the articulators of German idealism separated themselves two distinct groups. Goethe, Schiller, and certain other authors continued to pursue the artistic goals of classicism, while a new generation rejected them in favor of the tendencies that are now most commonly associated with Romanticism.

Within the framework of German literary history, the Romantic movement represents a sharp surge away from traditional ideas about the substance, purposes, and techniques of belles lettres. In many respects, it is the direct opposite of classicism. Specific characteristics of the Romantic approach to literature include a focus on Nordic, Germanic, and southern Romanic culture of the Middle Ages; synthesis of irrational and rational components of life; a picturesque lack of rules; emphasis on a particular feeling for nature that glorifies the beauty of the wild and the mystery of ancient ruins; and infatuation with the unknown and with the notion of giving infinite meaning to things that are finite and common. Of special import is a process of reflection that illuminates the tensions between conscious and unconscious dimensions of experience and places dreams, longings, the abysses of the soul, and the power of the demoniac in vivid perspective as vital existential forces. The typical Romantic author perceived life as an unending process of becoming and stressed accordingly the categories of the elemental and the universal.

Like the classicists, the German Romantics derived their worldview from interpretations of Kant's philosophical idealism. Using Kant's doctrines as his starting point, Johann Gottlieb Fichte promulgated the theory of subjective idealism, according to which the individual is center, creator, and master of the external world. Friedrich Wilhelm Joseph von Schelling amplified Fichte's system and transformed his primarily natural philosophy into a strongly religious one. Several aspects of his teachings had tremendous importance for the literary creations of the Romantics. Schelling believed, for example, that nature and spirit form a unity such that nature is visible spirit and spirit is invisible nature. In that context, nature becomes a progressive revelation of spirit because everything in physical existence has a soul. Based upon his religious renderings of Fichte's philosophy, Schelling came to the conclusions that art is the highest form of everything earthly and that history is the prophetic explanation of absolute reality. As a consequence of Schelling's ideas, the Romantics came to regard knowledge and belief, philosophy and religion as inseparable. Religion became the very soil from which their myth-centered art grew.

Schelling's approach was most productively interpreted by Friedrich Schleiermacher, whose essays fostered a reconciliation between idealism and Chris-

tianity. Schleiermacher contributed to the body of Romantic thought a perception of religion as the connection between man and that which is infinite and eternal, a feeling for that which is beyond the reach of the senses, a means of endless observation of the universe. Among the most significant reflections of this new *Weltanschauung* in Romantic letters are a visible return to mysticism and a focus on death as a central human experience that leads either to destruction or to salvation in Christian, especially Catholic, dogma.

Romantic authors cultivated long fiction as a dominant form of what they called "progressive universal poetry," a literature of total synthesis. Within it, they sought to combine all elements of education and cultural development. In direct contradiction to classical demands for consistency, clarity, and Enlightenment theories such as Lessing's separation of visual and literary arts, they advocated the union of writing, painting, and music and the dissolution of boundaries between art and science. Novels and shorter prose works were informed by the principle that all life should be poetized. Accomplishment of this goal required that the narrative unite all the separate genres. Romantic theoreticians insisted that the perfect novel would combine poetry with philosophy and rhetoric; it would contain dramatic monologues and dialogues, both natural and artistic lyric poetry, various prose forms, including novellas, anecdotes, and short tales, as component cells of the epic whole. The inclusion of criticism, episodes, letters, and reflections would assist in making the work a kind of personal bible, a compendium of the entire spiritual and intellectual life of the genial individual. By definition, Romantic universal poetry was to be infinite and free; its first postulate was that the caprice of the writer is not to be considered subject to any law.

What emerged from the pursuit of these goals was a prose fiction that is rich in fantasy and unfettered creativity. The demand for diversity and imagination fostered the renewal of old forms, particularly fairy tales, *Volksbücher*, and sagas. Because improvisation, experimentation, and lack of strict conception are more characteristic than concern for consistency and perfected structure, many Romantic narratives are unfinished fragments that reflect in a peculiar way the intense relationship between the artists' lives and personalities and their literary utterances. Especially visible are manifestations of these authors' ability to lift themselves above everything else, including their own work. The result is Romantic irony that shatters the illusion that has been created and intensified through the careful selection of word, word form, sentence structure, and rhythm in the telling of the story. Other typically Romantic devices are the use of the archaic chronicle style to invoke a feeling of past time and distant milieu and the tearing down of the logical context of situations as a prelude to entry into the fantastic dimension.

As to the nature of its intellectual and artistic activity, German Romanticism can be separated into two relatively well-defined phases. Early Romanticism was more critically and theoretically oriented. Its representatives leaned toward the formation of closed intellectual communities that concerned themselves not only with the creation of new works but also with various philological endeavors, including translation of William Shakespeare and the collection of folk literature. Notable theorists and writers in this group were Friedrich von Schlegel and his brother August Wilhelm von Schlegel, Ludwig Tieck, and Novalis (Friedrich von Hardenberg). Mature Romanticism was less speculative, although it was often strongly irrationalistic. Excepting a small group in Heidelberg, the later Romantics for the most part worked separately. They were also less antagonistic toward contemporary life and more likely to remain within the framework of reality. Among the more remarkable of the later Romantics were Clemens Brentano, Joseph von Eichendorff, and E. T. A. Hoffmann.

The most important prose genre of the initial period was the novel. With its masterful integration of diverse literary forms and its exemplary portrayal of an artistic quest, Goethe's *Wilhelm Meister's Apprenticeship* was a key model for the Romantic *Bildungsroman*. Heinse's *Ardinghello: Or, The Artist's Rambles in Sicily* and Jean Paul's impulsive, sometimes formless works also exerted considerable influence. All early Romantic novels remained fragmentary tor-

sos characterized by sentimentalism and heavy authorial subjectivism. Intense longing, glorification of the Middle Ages, special sensitivity to nature, and the employment of the narrative as a backdrop for the revelation of the writer's inner world are prominent features of this fiction.

A basic pattern for a work of literature that satisfies both the historical and the philosophical yearnings of a seeker for humanity's lost golden age was set by Novalis (1772-1801) in his famous *Heinrich von Ofterdingen* (1802; *Henry of Ofterdingen*, 1842). Enflamed by *Wilhelm Meister's Apprenticeship*, Novalis sought to surpass Goethe in content, power, variety, and thoughtfulness of presentation while spending his whole life on a single novel that would become the ultimate description of humanity's transition from the finite to the infinite. *Henry of Ofterdingen* is especially typical of the early Romantic novel in its happy mixture of reality and fairy tale, its deliberate poetizing of the world, its insertions of lyrics and shorter stories into the narrative structure, and its use of the narration as both elaboration and example of fundamental principles of literary art. Friedrich von Schlegel, in connection with the writing of his less successful *Lucinde* (1799; *Lucinda*, 1913-1915), had insisted that the Romantic novel be at once a theory of the novel and an illustration of the theory. In *Henry of Ofterdingen*, Novalis achieved early Romanticism's most impressive approximation of that ideal.

Although mature Romanticism produced a substantial number of novels, there were few outstanding accomplishments among them. Many of these works adhered to the synthesis principle of Schlegel's literary theory, as, for example, in Achim von Arnim's *Armut, Reichtum, Schuld und Busse der Gräfin Dolores* (1810; poverty, wealth, guilt, and repentance of the countess Dolores), a social novel that interweaves novellas, poems, and dramatic episodes; and Eichendorff's *Ahnung und Gegenwart* (1815; suspicion and presence), a creation that integrates problems of the times with a typical Romantic quest in vague episodes, moonlit forest scenes, and confused situations. Others experimented with radically new forms and substance. Particularly intriguing in this respect are

Hoffmann's *Die Elixiere des Teufels: Nachgelassene Papiere des Bruders Medardus, eines Kapuziners* (1815-1816; *The Devil's Elixirs: From the Posthumous Papers of Brother Medardus, a Capuchin Friar*, 1824) and *Lebensansichten des Katers Murr, nebst fragmentarischer Biographie des Kapellmeisters Johannes Kreisler in zufälligen Makulaturblättern* (1819-1821; *The Life and Opinions of Kater Murr, with the Fragmentary Biography of Kapellmeister Johannes Kreisler on Random Sheets of Scrap Paper*, 1969; also as *The Educated Cat*). The former is notable for its mixture of horror, crime, and guilt motifs with a profound examination of the psychological basis for events. Its themes of obsession and demoniac possession occupied later writers well into the twentieth century. *The Life and Opinions of Kater Murr* opened new avenues of approach to the problem of narrative presentation of material. In it, Hoffmann totally shattered conventional notions of orderly form. The account offers two stories simultaneously, in a peculiar jumble of fragments that are interspersed with each other without benefit of transitions and clear definition of beginning or end of either tale.

At least as important as the Romantic novel for the history of German long fiction are the unique achievements of this period in narratives of medium length. The dominant type of Romantic novella is the fairy tale, of which there are two kinds. Natural fairy tales were created after models provided by folk literature. Substance and atmosphere were commonly taken from legends and sagas of the Middle Ages, and the orientation of the stories is often didactical. The best examples of natural fairy tales are found among Tieck's early novellas. An especially famous one is *Der blonde Eckbert* (1797; *Fair Eckbert*, 1913-1915, 1969). Mature Romanticism favored the artistic fairy tale, although this form also had its beginnings during the early period, in the writings of Novalis. He patterned his work after *Das Märchen* (1795; *The Tale*, 1823), the enigmatic concluding story in Goethe's *Conversations of German Emigrants*. The artistic fairy tale is characterized by a fantastic setting in a highly symbolic world, carefully crafted personalities, bizarre situations, and substantial philosophical content. Particularly representative

of this sort of production are works such as Hoffmann's "Der goldene Topf" ("The Golden Flower Pot") and Brentano's animal stories.

In addition to fairy tales, the Romantics wrote social and historical novellas that parallel their novels in approach and themes. Pertinent examples include Eichendorff's *Aus dem Leben eines Taugenichts* (1826; *Memoirs of a Good-for-Nothing*, 1866), a charming quest narrative, and Hoffmann's "Das Fräulein von Scudéri" ("Mademoiselle Scudéri"), a story of murder and suspense set in the Paris of Louis XIV. Within their fairy tales and other novellas, the Romantics left a lasting legacy of conquest of new literary material, psychological penetration of portrayed reality, and original treatment of historical figures and basic human problems.

Although German Romantics did foster an identifiably conservative political posture with their patriotic allegiance to country and national tradition, they were relatively uninvolved in practical politics. In 1830, however, the July Revolution in France awakened hope for an end to the reactionary era, and certain representatives of the younger generation began to demand active literary contact with political and social life. Mediated by Ludwig Börne's *Briefe aus Paris* (1832-1834; letters from Paris), the social, political, and philosophical ideas of French liberalism found fertile ground in Germany, notably in the southwest. The result was the birth of a new German political literature, created initially by the loosely connected Young Germans and later by other concerned writers.

Narrowly speaking, the main figures of the Young German movement were Börne, Heinrich Heine, Ludolf Wienbarg, Theodor Mundt, Heinrich Laube, and Karl Gutzkow. In 1835, in response to their open attacks on traditional institutions and values and their revolutionary political stance, the writings of these authors were officially banned in Germany, on the grounds that they were blasphemous and immoral.

The political and social doctrines of the Young Germans, which informed their literary creations, were products of interpretations of Georg Wilhelm Friedrich Hegel's philosophy. Hegel viewed world history as development of the concept of freedom. He insisted that in a reasonable state, laws and ordinances are nothing but the realization of freedom in its basic destiny. As the father of critical idealism, Hegel had a deep influence on political thought throughout Europe. Karl Marx and others followed his lead in the search for a rational system of government. In Germany, adaptation of Hegel's teachings ultimately led to the definition of specific political goals that rapidly became the focus for activist literature. Among these aims were the rise of the middle class to political power, territorial unity of the German states, constitutional freedom, and the removal of prior social, religious, and national political restrictions.

In addition to Hegel, other thinkers contributed to the Young German political philosophy. Henri de Saint-Simon amplified Rousseau's and Voltaire's ideas, basing an individual and social ethic upon reason and nature. Fundamental tenets of his Christian socialism were the emancipation of the individual, women, and the flesh; rejection of the exploitation of humans by humans; and the overcoming of social conflict through brotherly love. In response to this stimulus, Ludwig Feuerbach expanded Hegel's philosophy, replacing God with nature and faith with knowledge and reason. Attacking Christian institutional dogma from a psychological point of view, he dismissed God and traditional religion as the products of wishful thinking. The Young Germans' decidedly negative view of contemporary social conditions was further influenced by David Friedrich Strauss's rejection of Christian theology as myth and allegory and by Lord Byron's *Weltschmerz*.

Influenced by Hegelian philosophy, the Young Germans put forth a theoretical program in which political freedom constituted the primary prerequisite for a German national literature. Its direction was democratic, liberalistic, and consistently materialistic. Moreover, it renounced Romantic escape to an imaginary past world of ideal heroism and love. The new trend was toward a poesy that is tied to practical questions of life—not the life of the individual but that of a new national society unified in its struggle to attain clearly defined political goals. Young German theoreticians, especially Wienbarg, proclaimed the task of literary art to be a representation of beauty in

real life and individual situations. Wienbarg argued that proper depiction of reality requires political, social, and scientific knowledge. Despite the repeated employment of political and social criticism as their point of departure, however, the resulting creations were not realistic in nature. Rather, the Young Germans produced a rationalistic, often utopian literature of critical reflection. There was no longer any true concern for the inner, spiritual life of humans; more significant were revolutionary acts and ideas. Works of epic narrative began to examine tensions arising out of various polarities, including national feeling and cosmopolitanism, Christianity and rationalistic criticism, individualism and socialism, tradition and progress, middle-class morality and the emancipation of the flesh. Emphasis was on the improvement of life through reform and revolution, with special attention to things new and modern in anticipation of the future.

Young German writers considered prose to be the most appropriate medium for timely presentation of reality. Accordingly, they cultivated a variety of forms, ranging from diary-type sketches to weighty novels. The novella was a very popular genre during this era, because it was particularly well suited to the clear exposition of pertinent individual problems and themes. Most of the longer works were either social treatments of contemporary issues or novels of personal development used as a frame for panoramic illumination of the times. Although the Young Germans were quite prolific, they produced very little prose of lasting value. Only Heine's fragmentary historical novels represent a measure of enduring artistic accomplishment.

In spite of the general mediocrity of Young German prose, there did emerge one interesting new approach to the novel that had some significance for the further development of long fiction later in the century. Gutzkow, whose *Wally, die Zweiflerin* (1835; *Wally the Skeptic*, 1974) was the immediate cause of the political ban that was placed upon Young German literature, created two massive, relatively unsuccessful political-social narratives: *Die Ritter vom Geiste* (1850-1851, 9 volumes; knights of the spirit) and *Der Zauberer von Rom* (1858-1861, 9 volumes; the magician of Rome). In these works, the author experimented with presentation based upon a principle of simultaneous rather than sequential organization of substance. That is, the primary concern was not the progressive unfolding of a traditional plot but rather the broad rendering of a many-sided, almost static mural of the age. Unfortunately, Gutzkow seldom achieved the desired effect of simultaneity. The remarkable breadth of his portrait of German life did not have the power to counteract the weakness of plot and make the novels appealing to the reader.

Lowell A. Bangerter

THE MID-NINETEENTH CENTURY TO WORLD WAR I

According to the historian Arnold Toynbee, historical periods and entire civilizations may be likened to lights that shine brightly for a time and then grow dim. German literature in the nineteenth century was such a light. The literary luminescence of German classicism and Romanticism and the dynamic, internationally oriented activism of the Young Germans were followed by decades of darkness, a period in which German writers seem to have lost international attention and recognition. Even a well-read person will draw a blank when asked to name German writers between Heine, who died in 1856, and Gerhart Hauptmann, whose first play was performed in 1889, or Thomas Mann, whose early novellas appeared in the 1890's. From the 1840's to the late 1880's, German literature was out of step with the rest of European literature. Where is the German Honoré de Balzac or Stendhal? The German Charles Dickens or William Makepeace Thackeray? The German Fyodor Dostoevski or Leo Tolstoy? The German Nathaniel Hawthorne or Herman Melville? Yet any history of German literature lists Annette von Droste-Hülshoff, Eduard Mörike, Franz Grillparzer, Adalbert Stifter, Friedrich Hebbel, Jeremias Gotthelf, Gottfried Keller, Theodor Storm, and other major writers of prose, poetry, and plays who were active around the middle of the century.

One reason that most of these writers were only rarely or belatedly translated and thus reached only a limited audience is that they persisted in exemplifying the attitudes and techniques of German idealism and Romanticism, a heritage that kept them out of the mainstream of European realism. When histories of German literature discuss the German variety of realism—which extended roughly from the 1840's to the 1880's—they often modify the word *Realismus* with an adjective such as *poetisch*, *psychologisch*, or *bürgerlich*.

The concept of poetic realism seems like a contradiction in terms and is peculiar to German literature. The term, coined by the philosopher Schelling as early as 1802 and later popularized by Otto Ludwig in his studies of Shakespeare, refers both to a style and to a period. Poetic realism may be regarded as the most characteristic expression of the German *Bürgertum* around the middle of the nineteenth century. It reflected the relatively stable political and social structure of the middle class, a structure that was soon challenged by Heine, Marx, Friedrich Nietzsche, and others. In contrast to the age of Romanticism, when the *Bürger* had been decried as a philistine, *bürgerlich* was now an entirely respectable appellation. The poetic realists strove for an aesthetically transformed depiction of reality; avoiding pathos and passion, their style was craftsmanlike, muted, and sober, reflecting a tension between the objective and the subjective.

Victor Lange has pointed out that "German fiction has . . . been provincial in setting and parochial in its belief," and it should be borne in mind that the German writers of this period lacked the coherence and unity of experience that the writers of other European nations possessed. The abortive revolutions of 1848 fostered a Biedermeier-like mood of resignation among these writers; as the Austrian playwright Johann Nestroy put it, "The noblest nation is resignation." The political structure encouraged provincialism and regionalism, and disillusionment with political and social activism caused these writers to retreat into an idyllic, simplistic world and concern themselves with their writings with morality, humaneness, conciliation, and adaptation. The great advances that were made in the 1850's in the natural sciences, technology, and industrialism, as well as the growing pains attendant upon the transformation of a largely agrarian country into a highly organized industrial society, found little reflection in this literature. Only at a later time were class differences and the contrast (sometimes conflict) between rural and urban life given adequate literary expression. Instead, German fiction focused on the *Innerlichkeit*, the inner development and psychology of its characters. Two great *Bildungsromane*, novels of development in the manner of Goethe's Wilhelm Meister novels, were produced during that period: Keller's *Der grüne Heinrich* (1854-1855, 1879-1880; *Green Henry*, 1960) and Stifter's *Der Nachsommer* (1857; the Indian summer).

Above all, the writers of poetic realism seemed afraid to write about the burgeoning big cities, with their multifarious economic and social problems, and preferred instead to depict country life in the regions they knew best. The anthropological religion of this-worldliness that was preached by Feuerbach influenced writers such as Hebbel and Keller. Arthur Schopenhauer's pessimistic philosophy of suffering and resignation, as expressed in his *magnum opus*, *Die Welt als Wille und Vorstellung* (1819; *The World as Will and Idea*, 1883-1886), became widely known only around the time of the philosopher's death in 1860 and influenced Wilhelm Raabe and Ferdinand von Saar, among others. Such philosophies supplied a modicum of support in an age characterized by rapid industrial, scientific, and technological development—changes that threatened to bring about a loss of religious faith and an unraveling of the social fabric, as well as skepticism and despair at the prospect of increasing dehumanization. The coming decades were to be marked by the polar forces of reaction and rebellion, with entrenched privilege fighting a rearguard action against the forces of change. The last novel of the Swiss writer Keller, *Martin Salander* (1886; English translation, 1964), portrays the struggle of a principled individual against new political and social conditions. As Georg Lukács has pointed out, Keller's basic orientation was toward the idyllic, and thus his world crumbled as he tried to give an unvarnished portrait of the coming age.

The *Gründerzeit*

The Franco-Prussian War of 1870-1871 was followed by several decades of general peace, prosperity, and pride in the (Second) Reich fashioned by Otto von Bismarck, who served as chancellor from 1871 to 1890. The early period after the unification of Germany is known as the *Gründerzeit* or the *Gründerjahre*, the time of the founders, builders, and speculators. Factories, cities, and whole industrial empires were expanded, banks were set up, and the export and import trade flourished. The boom led to the creation of a myth of national greatness and vigor that was hardly affected by financial fluctuations, crashes such as the one of 1873, and other growing pains of the *Gründerzeit*. A line from Emanuel Geibel's 1861 poem "Deutschlands Beruf" (Germany's calling), published in 1871 in the series *Heroldsrufe*, "Und es mag am deutschen Wesen einmal noch die Welt genesen" (someday the German spirit may yet cure the world's ills), became a sort of Pan-German slogan; Wilhelm II quoted it in his Münster speech of 1907.

As great numbers of people moved from the country to the city, an industrial proletariat came into being, and this strengthened the workers' movement. What has been called "the dilemma of the industrialized agrarian state" did not have a salutary effect on literature and culture. As the spirit of 1870-1871 focused attention on Germany's political and geopolitical aims—its quest for a place in culture, its pursuit of material advancement, and its enjoyment of luxurious living—intellectual life was bound to decline. Nietzsche believed that the victory over France was having deleterious effects on Germany: "Deutschland, Deutschland über alles," he said in reference to a line from Hoffmann von Fallersleben's poem, which ultimately served as Germany's national anthem from 1922 to 1945; "I fear that was the end of German philosophy." Political unification and material advancement were placed above the kind of freedom of spirit for which the Young Germans had fought some decades earlier. Philosophers such as Nietzsche, Jacob Burckhardt, and Wilhelm Scherer warned of what would happen to the German spirit and culture if the feverish speculative boom, the expansionism, the unbridled realpolitik, and the self-indulgent philistinism of the *Gründerjahre* were not kept in check. There was increasing tension between those writers who maintained a conservative, nationalistic bent and those who adopted a more progressive, socially conscious, cosmopolitan stance.

Many writers of the 1870's and 1880's were aware of the seamy side of the "economic miracle" and the "social question." Their sensitivity to the decline of the bourgeoisie and the plight of the proletariat made them skeptical of traditional values and solutions. This uncertainty and insecurity could only work to the detriment of creativity. It has become axiomatic to say that political power and success tend to go hand in hand with cultural decline. Literary historian Richard M. Meyer discerned such a decline in the 1870's, and the contemporary critic Henry Hatfield believes that "around 1880 German literature was at the lowest point it had reached in over a century."

REALISM

Before discussing the major writers after the middle or late 1880's, it is necessary to take a brief look backward at the fictional forms of German realism. Paul Heyse not only wrote more than one hundred *Novellen*, issued in two dozen volumes between 1850 and 1914, but also became one of the chief theoreticians of the genre. According to his *Falkentheorie* (derived from the story of the falcon in Boccaccio's *Decameron*), a *Novelle* must have a clearly delineated basic motif and a characteristic that sets it apart from all other stories. In 1871, Heyse wrote that a *Novelle* should present "a significant human fate, a spiritual, intellectual, or ethical conflict, revealing through an uncommon occurrence a new side of human nature." (The "uncommon occurrence" seems to be the same *unerhörte Begebenheit* that Goethe specified as the hallmark of the genre.) Despite the fact that the prolific Heyse was once widely read and, in 1910, became the first German to receive the Nobel Prize in Literature, he is all but forgotten today, possibly as a result of what George Wallis Field called the "sentimental fragrance of old lace and lavender which lingers in most of [his] narratives."

Theodor Storm, another prolific practitioner of the genre, gave his own definition of the *Novelle* in an 1881 letter to Keller:

Today's *Novelle* is a sister of the drama and the most defined form of prose. Like the drama, it deals with the profoundest problems of human life and demands for its perfection a central conflict around which the entire story organizes itself. Consequently it requires the most compact form and the elimination of everything nonessential.

Storm, whose reputation has grown over the years, produced a great variety of *Novellen* and in his last decade favored the forms of the *Chroniknovelle* and the *Problemnovelle*, such as *Ein Bekenntnis* (1888; a confession), which deals with euthanasia. ("How does a person get into the position of killing the person he loves most?" wrote Storm to Keller. "And when it has happened, what becomes of him?") In Storm's last work, *Der Schimmelreiter* (1888; *The Rider on the White Horse*, 1915), the protagonist is presented in conflict with nature. Storm also made masterful use of the *Erinnerungsnovelle*, presenting a character's memories in the form of a *Rahmenerzählung*, the framework technique that anticipates the flashbacks of the cinema.

Another outstanding writer of *Novellen*, some of them long enough to rate as novels, was the Swiss Conrad Ferdinand Meyer. This prim patrician and emotionally unstable man wrote passionately and dramatically about the Italian Renaissance and the religious strife of the sixteenth and seventeenth centuries. Meyer's choice of characters, periods, and themes reflects not only his need for strong, vital figures but also the interest of his contemporaries in the late Middle Ages, the Renaissance, the Reformation, and the Counter-Reformation (though he did not share their fascination with the evolutionary process of history). Famous historical figures such as Thomas à Becket, Dante, Cosimo de' Medici, Lucrezia Borgia, Gustavus Adolphus, Louis XIV, and Montaigne appear in Meyer's work, yet he was not so much concerned with historical personages and events as with the ethical problems of their (and his) age. Meyer was a master of the artistic reactivation of history, though he sometimes reactivated it in rather ambivalent fashion and as though from behind a mask of objectivity and detachment. His response to the spiritual cataclysms of a declining age was the presentation and therapeutic working out of what he regarded as timeless psychological, ethical, and philosophical problems. His eleven *Novellen* are thus primarily *Problemnovellen*, accounts of contending polar forces inherent in events or figures. These chronicles of spiritual and intellectual conflicts typically take the form of *Rahmenerzählungen* with copious use of dialogue and poetically stylized language.

Meyer stood at the end of a line of development. As Field put it, "In his turning away from contemporary life to history and distanced violence, there is also an element of *fin de siècle* aestheticism, reflecting the decay of the *Bürgertum* in which the *Novelle* had developed and flourished." E. K. Bennett adds Heyse to the representatives of the forces disintegrating from within and without—in the case of Meyer, his morbidity and neurotic susceptibility to the spiritual malaise of his age, and in the case of Heyse, his facile individualism and cosmopolitanism—that undermined the *Bürgertum* and its characteristic literary form. While Bennett pays due tribute to the sheer strength of will that enabled Meyer to transmute his chronic depression into the art of a virtuosic storyteller, he sees in his work "weakness masquerading as strength, uncertainty and insecurity disguised by the bold gesture" and points out that in Meyer's work "form and subject matter are nearly always in conflict."

Several minor masters, most of whom did not outlast their age, endeavored to inform, inspire, and entertain their contemporaries with massive, frequently multivolume historical novels that have rightly been deprecated as *Professorenromane*, the kind of tedious novels an academician might produce. Gustav Freytag, whose novel *Soll und Haben* (1855; *Debit and Credit*, 1855) painted a positive picture of the German middle class and its business morality, published a cycle of novels between 1872 and 1880 entitled *Die Ahnen* (the ancestors; first two volumes translated as *Ingo: The First Novel of a Series Entitled "Our Forefathers,"* 1873, and *Ingraban: The Second Novel of a Series Entitled "Our Forefathers,"* 1873), an equally ambitious and ponderous panorama of German life from the fourth century to the author's own time. In 1870, Freytag followed the Prussian armies in their advance across eastern France and averred that he had encountered the type of ancient German hero he had glorified in these novels. The quintessential "professorial novel" is Felix Dahn's *Ein Kampf um Rom* (1876; *A Struggle for Rome*, 1878), about the decline and fall of the Ostrogothic empire in Italy. Dahn's *Kleine Romane aus der Völkerwanderung* (little novels from the great migration) appeared in thirteen volumes between 1883 and 1901, and his work led Bismarck, the "Iron Chancellor" himself, to call his novels appropriate reading for men concerning themselves with serious things.

Not all such historical fiction is uncritically patriotic or chauvinistic, to be sure. In some instances, these novels represent efforts to come to terms with the present by providing parables of contemporary political events. Thus, Georg Ebers wrote about Egypt (*Eine ägyptische Königstochter*, 1864; *The Daughter of an Egyptian King*, 1871), Robert Hamerling about classical Greece (*Aspasia*, 1876; English translation, 1882), and Ernst Eckstein about ancient Rome (*Nero*, 1889; English translation, 1889). Others were undisguised *Zeitromane* with contemporary settings and criticism of many aspects of the present, such as the unsound development of the economy and untrammeled speculation. Heyse also wrote novels of this type. In *Über allen Gipfeln* (1895), he tried to rise to the challenge of Nietzsche by telling the story of a Nietzschean, the Prussian official Erik von Friesen. In *Sturmflut* (1876; *The Breaking of the Storm*, 1877), by Friedrich Spielhagen, a tidal wave in the Baltic that takes the life of a speculator is related to the economic tidal wave, with one catastrophe shedding light on the other.

WILHELM RAABE AND THEODOR FONTANE

The two outstanding German storytellers of the latter part of the nineteenth century were Wilhelm Raabe and Theodor Fontane, writers whose reputations grew during the last several decades of the twentieth century. Since at least some of their work falls in the *fin de siècle* period, a more extended discussion of their contribution is in order here.

Wilhelm Raabe was a curiously isolated figure who had no real successors, although some of his narrative techniques foreshadow those of Thomas Mann. In his quirky ambivalence, wry humor, whimsy, and latterday Romantic irony, this subtle and sophisticated storyteller harks back to Sterne and Jean Paul, but these qualities also bespeak an affinity with Dickens and Thackeray. Raabe grasped the moral dilemmas of his world and portrayed that world honestly and truthfully. His social range was rather narrow, his intellectual penetration not very profound, and he had little passion or reformers' zeal. Yet his admitted philistinism had a gleam of true wisdom that has been called "simply an acknowledgment of the inscrutable fitness of things," and his pessimism is somehow uplifting and cheering as often as it is despairing and depressing. Lange sees Raabe as the continuator of a fertile tradition, that of the German baroque imagination, and concludes that "his work represents the impressive climax of the literature of German bourgeois idealism." Barker Fairley calls Raabe's work "the most richly conceived body of fiction in the German language."

"Look up to the stars! Watch life in the streets!" This admonition reflects what may be termed Raabe's idealistic realism as he foreshadows the coming German (and indeed European) crisis of morals. His best-known novels portray the eventual triumph of inner strength and integrity over the forces of decay and dissolution. The individual must stand inviolate amid all onslaughts: "We want to remain what we must be." There is more tension than action in Raabe's novels; his subjective style and multiple narrative perspective may have been intended to facilitate communication with a wider readership, but in effect, his subtleties were lost on many readers, and his modest, pseudonaïve disclaimers were accepted at face value.

Raabe's basic theme is humanity in an age of social change. After 1870, he remained loyal to the Reich, but he was troubled by the political developments and the social upheavals he witnessed, and his late novels reflect his disillusionment with Bismarck's nationalistic policies. *Pfisters Mühle* (1884) deals with the clash of the old and the new as a rural landscape is rapidly transformed into an industrial one. The novel takes the form of a reminiscence of a young Berlin schoolmaster who is spending his honeymoon in his father's mill, soon to make way for a factory. It turns out that the water of the millstream is polluted by the effluvia of a beet-sugar factory. Even though the father wins a lawsuit against the factory, it is a Pyrrhic victory, for he dies knowing that the old way of life is doomed. The conflict between the old and the new worlds is personified by Dr. Asche, who in his youth enjoyed the mill but as an industrial scientist and founder of a dye business aligns himself with the forces of "progress." Yet the fact that he remains essentially humane shows that the march of time need not drown out the harmonies of tradition. *Im alten Eisen* (1887) is less optimistic; the wheel of history rolls over the human community. *Das Odfeld* (1888), set during the Seven Years' War, is about some uprooted civilians who are guided back to their homesteads to rebuild their lives. *Die Akten des Vogelsangs* (1896) tells the story of three children who experience the breakup of an old-fashioned neighborhood in a town that is being modernized. In an ironic concession to popular taste, Raabe called his novel *Stopfkuchen: Eine See- und Mordgeschichte* (1891; *Tubby Schaumann: A Tale of Murder and the High Seas*, 1983) a "murder and sea story"; he also described it as his best and most subjective book. The title is the nickname of a nibbler named Heinrich Schaumann, a warm and humane Biedermeier type, who tells the story of his life to Eduard, a prosperous settler in Africa who is on his way home after a visit to his native Germany. In its attack on tendencies to idealize the past and its deflation of the materialistic person of action, this wry commentary on a quarter-century of change may be regarded as anti-*Faust*.

Pointing out that Raabe "presents metaphysical problems in a precisely described social and historical milieu," Eda Sagarra formulates some basic, penetrating questions that Raabe posed in his most mature novels: Should life be lived in conformity with changing patterns of society at the cost of spiritual and intellectual values, or should it be lived in self-imposed seclusion? Can one be involved in the process of historical change without sacrificing one's humanity?

Theodor Fontane, a Prussian of French Huguenot

ancestry, had had a career as a pharmacist and journalist and was almost sixty years old when he published his first novel, *Vor dem Sturm* (1878), set in Brandenburg just before Napoleon's defeat in Russia and the Wars of Liberation. In two decades, he followed this novel with fifteen more works of fiction that finally placed the German novel in the European mainstream. Roy Pascal has called him "the first German writer since Goethe to stand in easy contact with the public issues of the European world." Betraying the influence of Jane Austen, George Eliot, Thackeray, and the Russian Realists, Fontane actually belongs more to European realism than to the literary tradition of his own country. Though he never enjoyed the kind of worldwide recognition that has been accorded to such writers as Leo Tolstoy and Gustave Flaubert, Fontane did prepare the ground for Thomas Mann and other literary giants of the twentieth century.

Fontane expressed himself repeatedly about the mission of the novel and his own contributions to the genre. He compared German fiction with the works of Ivan Turgenev, to the detriment of the former: "It lacks veracity, objectivity, reality. People constantly do and say things that, given the way they are, they could never do and say." "The task of the modern novel," he wrote elsewhere,

> seems to me to be the description of a life, a society, a group of people, as the undistorted reflection of the life we lead. . . . The novel should be a picture of the times to which we belong, or at least the reflection of the times adjacent to ours, about which our parents have told us.

In reading a novel, Fontane pointed out, one should feel a congruence between the invented life and real life, the only difference being that which arises from "that intensity, clarity, transparency, roundedness, and, consequently, that intensity of feeling which is the transfiguring task of art." This patriotic but remarkably unchauvinistic Prussian chose to write mainly about the declining Prussian nobility, the Junker class, because of its historical importance in the evolution of modern Germany and because of its embodiment of the essence of the contemporary situation.

A relentless critic of the new Reich and its rigid, antiquated, decadent social order, Fontane satirized the self-satisfaction, smugness, and pretentiousness of the titled and moneyed, particularly the nouveau-riche bourgeoisie. He was less concerned with the proletariat, though lower-class characters do appear in his writings. His social novels highlight three basic problems: liaisons between an upper-class male and a lower-class female, misalliances, and adultery. Fontane was aware that his time was witnessing the end of the *Bürgertum*, its established values and social code. The moral code was becoming relativistic rather than absolute, and Fontane, a worldlywise old man who tended to shrink from scenes of intense passion and action and who was an eminently conciliatory spirit, was content to leave some questions unanswered and certain conflicts unresolved. While he came to believe that the revaluation of all values for which Nietzsche called needed to take place, he also believed that for the sake of preserving inner integrity a moral law was needed to keep order in life, especially where the human passions were concerned. Fontane's style is controversial, allusive in its skillful employment of symbols and leitmotifs, and full of anecdotes and epigrams that illuminate the personality, problems, and behavior of a character. Not infrequently, comic and tragic elements intermingle.

Fontane is particularly noted for his series of "Berlin novels," beginning with *L'Adultera* (1882). The theme of *Irrungen, Wirrungen* (1888; *Trials and Tribulations*, 1917; also as *A Suitable Match*, 1968) can be stated in this question: Can an individual find happiness in the face of a rigid order and an unsympathetic environment that in its social and moral pressures harks back to the past? An illicit liaison must here be dissolved in accordance with the code of honor of the Prussian aristocracy, on the one hand, and that of the petite bourgeoisie, on the other. With his distaste for "noise in feelings," the author comes down on the side of traditional order. In *Stine* (1890; English translation, 1969), however, a count wants to break through the barriers of convention, but a poor seamstress knows her place and rejects him, whereupon he kills himself. *Frau Jenny Treibel* (1893; *Jenny Treibel*, 1976) contains a subtle critique of the anti-intellectualism of the bourgeoisie. The protagonist, who has moved up from poverty, claims to be an idealist, but when her son wishes to marry an impecunious girl, she reveals her materialistic attitude.

Fontane's best-known novel, widely regarded as the German *Madame Bovary*, is *Effi Briest* (1895; English translation, 1914, 1962). The adultery committed by the protagonist out of boredom is discovered years later by her stodgy, older husband, Baron von Instetten, and avenged by him not so much out of passion as out of pedantic "correctness." A divorcée and social outcast, Effi dies an early, lonely death. While Fontane seems to condemn the hollowness of society's code of honor, his message is: "Marriage is order." It is interesting to note, though, that he lets similar instances of marital infidelity in *L'Adultera* and *Effi Briest* be treated differently by society. In *Die Poggenpuhls* (1896), problems of mésalliance in an impoverished aristocratic family are solved by the legacy of a wealthy relative. Fontane designated his last work, *Der Stechlin* (1898; *The Stechlin*, 1996), as a political novel, but the ambiguity of the title, which is the name of a lake, a forest, a village, and a castle in addition to that of its principal character, lifts it to a symbolic-mythical plane. The author's original plan was to show the aristocracy as it ought to be, but he wound up painting an unvarnished portrait of *fin de siècle* Prussian society. This novel points back to Fontane's first, in which the author had concerned himself with the task of the Prussian aristocracy and questioned the nature and limits of patriotism. As he contrasts the worlds of the old and the young Stechlin, Fontane bids an optimistic farewell to an irretrievably lost age. The words spoken by a pastor at Dubslav von Stechlin's funeral also apply to the author: "Nothing human was alien to him, because he thought of himself as a human being and was at all times conscious of his own human weaknesses."

Fontane was a Janus-like figure, both the apogee of nineteenth century bourgeois realism and the anticipator of trends and techniques to come. He was in no way an extremist, an innovator, an activist, a utopian thinker, or a propagandist. Yet it is characteristic of the old man that he became the beloved mentor of a new literary generation, the naturalists (and in particular Gerhart Hauptmann) whom he championed without recoiling at the sordidness and disorder in their work. With his vaunted wit and irony, however, he supplied a critical perspective when he played on one of the buzzwords of the day: "Modern? Sprechen Sie das Wort einmal anders aus!" The meaning of the adjective *modern*, stressed on the second syllable, is obvious; the verb *modern*, stressed on the first syllable, means "to decay." Fontane's pun may be reproduced in English by predicting that today's new mold will have mold on it tomorrow.

THE THEORY OF NATURALISM

"Our world is no longer classical," wrote Arno Holz; "our world is no longer romantic; our world is modern." Terms such as *modern* and *die Moderne* (coined by Eugen Wolff) became battle cries as a new generation of writers strove to modify Germany's feudal and parochial structure sufficiently to admit cultural currents from elsewhere in Europe and to allow a heightened realism finally to take hold in German literature. Marxism became increasingly influential in the 1870's and 1880's, and the doctrines of Charles Darwin as presented by his chief German disciple Ernst Haeckel promoted a more materialistic *Weltanschauung*. Nietzsche's rejection of conventional morality and his call for a "new man" appealed to a younger generation of activists, who described themselves as "Das jüngste Deutschland" in programmatical reference to "Das junge Deutschland" earlier in the century. What has been termed *Hochrealismus* but is generally known as *Naturalismus* depended heavily on foreign prototypes. Émile Zola's twenty-volume cycle of novels, *Les Rougon-Macquart* (1871-1893; *The Rougon-Macquart Family*, 1885-1907), viewed human nature as determined by the all-important factors of heredity and environment. Zola's kind of experimental novel, as described in *Le Roman expérimental* (1880; *The Experimental Novel*, 1893), combined objectivity with personal expression, and from him German writers, who tended, according to Felix Bertaux, to alternate "between microscopic treatments of fact and vast empty structures of thought," derived a broadly humanistic view of life. Other influential Frenchmen were Maurice

Barrès, who enunciated an ego psychology in his trilogy *Le Culte du moi* (1887-1891); Paul Bourget, whose *Cosmopolis* (1893; English translation, 1893) highlights the figure of the dilettante; and the Goncourt brothers, Edmond and Jules, with their family novel *René Mauperin* (1864; English translation, 1888). Turgenev, Tolstoy, and Dostoevski became important models, but the greatest number of mentors and models were supplied by the Scandinavian countries: the critic Georg Brandes, the dramatists August Strindberg and Henrik Ibsen, and the novelists Jens Peter Jacobsen, Hermann Bang, Alexander Kielland, Knut Hamsun, Ola Hansson, Peter Nansen, Henrik Pontoppidan, Björnstjerne Björnson, Holger Drachmann, Jonas Lie, Arne Garborg, Hans Jaeger, and Christian Krogh. The example of these authors enabled the naturalists to reject the works of predecessors such as Heyse as epigonal, false, and effete; to turn away from the princes, knights, and other heroes evoked by Freytag and Dahn; and to shine a spotlight on the lowly, the economically and socially disadvantaged, and the seamy side of life. The modern successor of the traditional hero was the passive hero or the irresolute "half-hero" in the manner of Jacobsen's Niels Lyhne.

The theoretical foundation for naturalism was laid by the Hart brothers, Heinrich and Julius. Their six brochures entitled *Kritische Waffengänge* appeared between 1882 and 1884 and made Berlin one of the centers of the movement, spawning a number of journals and associations, such as the Der Verein "Durch" (1886), the Freie Bühne Verein (1889), and the Friedrichshagener Kreis (founded 1890). The leading figures of the Berlin circle were, in addition to the Harts, Arno Holz, Johannes Schlaf, Hermann Conradi, Gerhart Hauptmann, and Karl Henckell. Munich was the second center, and the chief focus there was Michael Georg Conrad's journal *Die Gesellschaft*. Carl Bleibtreu regarded the Sturm und Drang firebrands of the 1770's as the spiritual ancestors of the young writers; once again, "original genius" was to be given its due.

Holz, who believed that "an art can be revolutionized only by revolutionizing its means," originated the idea of a *konsequenter Naturalismus* (consistent naturalism). To Zola's dictum "Une oeuvre d'art est un coin de la nature, vu à travers un tempérament" (a work of art is a corner of nature seen through a temperament), he opposed his own definition (in *Die Kunst: Ihr Wesen und ihre Gesetze*, 1891-1892): "Die Kunst hat die Tendenz, wieder die Natur zu sein. Sie wird sie nach Massgabe ihrer jeweiligen Reproduktionsbedingungen und deren Handhabung." This can be expressed in a simple formula: Art equals Nature minus X, with X representing the unavoidable limitations of the artist's medium and the way it is used or applied. Nature means strict limitation to factual, empirical reality and the exclusion of imaginative or inventive additions by the artist. Holz wished to completely eliminate the omniscient narrator in order to achieve the illusion of perfect objectivity and complete realism; by grasping and conveying everything a character sees and hears, a "phonographic method" was to overcome "paper language." Holz and his collaborator Schlaf called for the employment of *Sekundenstil*, a kind of staccato style making for unretouched snapshots of life that actually anticipated cinematic techniques, a microscopic precision in registering every nuance of setting and atmosphere as well as every inflection of speech. Conrad came to describe the *konsequenter Naturalismus* as an "asphalt plant of a big-city street without fragrance or seeds—an astonishing wonder of technology."

"No more verses, no more novels," wrote Holz, "only the open, living scene exists for us now." It was neither prose nor poetry but the theater that offered the naturalists the most effective pulpit for their preachings, the best forum for their muckraking, and the best proving ground for their techniques. It should be emphasized that their fiction was no match for the power, brilliance, and international stature achieved by a dramatist such as Hauptmann. While few of the narrative works written under the banner of naturalism are still read today, this fiction and its writers nevertheless bespeak a lively and varied literary scene.

THE FICTION OF NATURALISM

The naturalists favored the novel over the *Novelle* or other forms of short prose, but a few outstanding examples of the latter genre deserve pride of place. In

Hauptmann's symbolistic masterpiece *Bahnwärter Thiel* (1888; *Flagman Thiel*, 1933), a railroad gatekeeper is haunted by his deceased first wife even while he is under the erotic spell of his current one, who mistreats his little son and through carelessness causes the boy to be killed by a train, whereupon the Woyzeck-like Thiel goes mad and murders her. Equally tragic is the prose sketch *Papa Hamlet* by Holz and Schlaf, published in 1889; that year Hauptmann dedicated his first play, *Vor Sonnenaufgang* (1889; *Before Dawn*, 1909), to the fictitious Scandinavian Bjarne P. Holmsen, the pseudonym used by Holz and Schlaf. This prose study tells the story of Niels Thienwiebel, a broken-down, brutish, egotistical actor who chokes his infant son. The grandiloquent quotations from Shakespeare, with their high-flown idealism, provide an ironic counterpoint to the sordid goings-on in the dim-witted actor's reality. The deterministic helplessness of the characters is expressed in their very language, which is choppy, stuttering, and fragmented. "Holz often worked on a sentence for a whole day," wrote Schlaf, "because he found it impossible to go on until it sparkled with color, resonance, and even fragrance."

The early naturalists cultivated the *Grosstadtromane*, novels set in big cities, particularly the capital, Berlin. The most noteworthy among the somewhat melodramatic, Dickensian Berlin novels of Max Kretzer are *Meister Timpe* (1888), about the losing fight of an urban craftsman against encroaching mechanization, and *Das Gesicht Christi* (1897), in which the Savior becomes a symbol for the destitute of Berlin. In his story "Die letzte Pflicht" (the last duty), the Scottish-born John Henry Mackay paints an altogether bleak cityscape as he follows a small- town schoolteacher across Berlin in search of a friend; this "story without a plot" is bound to end tragically and conveys the message that "the sad thing is not death but life." Mackay's novel *Die Anarchisten* (1891; *The Anarchists*, 1891) marks his turning to a sort of anarchistic individualism. The short-lived Hermann Conradi wrote two novels, including *Adam Mensch* (1889), in which he gave such a radical analysis of his time that he was condemned by the courts and his writings were labeled as immoral. Conrad Alberti

(pseudonym of Konrad Sittenfeld), "the swashbuckler of naturalism," published *Plebs* (1887), a collection of stories set among Berlin workers. Peter Hille, the legendary Berlin vagabond poet, wrote *Die Sozialisten* (1886), a novel with such thinly veiled characters as Beber and Triebknecht. Carl Bleibtreu's "pathological novel" *Grössenwahn* (1887) has a Bohemian setting. Its hero retreats from the world to find salvation in Darwin. In *Der Büttnerbauer* (1895; *Farmer Büttner*, 1915), a novel praised by Tolstoy, Wilhelm von Polenz described the destructive force of capitalism in a rustic setting. *Frau Sorge* (1887; *Dame Care*, 1891), by Hermann Sudermann, about an East Prussian peasant who incurs debts but finally manages to free himself from the ghosts of his youth and win the love of people who guide him to a better life, was once widely read and admired, but Lange judges the author harshly when he says that "he merely turned the impartial conscientiousness of Zola and Tolstoy into German sentimentality." In the first decade of the twentieth century, Schlaf published two trilogies in which he attempted to present a typology of people in search of a new lifestyle, a new society, and a new human.

There was no "Munich novel" as such, but M. G. Conrad, the chief German apostle of Zola, attempted a ten-volume German pendant to *Les Rougon-Macquart*, though only three novels appeared, beginning with *Was die Isar rauscht* (1888), set in Schwabing, the artists' district of Munich. The once-popular *Jörn Uhl* (1901; English translation, 1905), by Gustav Frenssen, is also about a farmer who struggles to preserve an encumbered farm. This novel is an example of *Heimatkunst*, both a throwback to the regionalism of poetic realism and a forerunner of the nefarious *Blut- und Bodenliteratur* (blood and soil literature) favored by the Nazis. Other works of this type, imbued with an almost mystic belief in the purity and inviolability of the ancestral soil and those living on it, are the stories *Leute eigner Art* (1904; people of a special kind), by Timm Kröger, and *Der Wehrwolf* (1910; *Harm Wulf*, 1931), by Hermann Löns, a gory chronicle of German peasants during the Thirty Years' War who fight for their homesteads like werewolves.

The autobiographical *Roman aus der Décadence* (1898), by Kurt Martens, is set among troubled Leipzig intellectuals and indicates that by then many naturalists had turned from Marx to Nietzsche, from socialism to individualism and anarchism in the spirit of Max Stirner or Peter Kropotkin. The controversial novel *Werther, der Jude* (1893), by Ludwig Jacobowsky, the Berlin editor of *Die Gesellschaft*, presents an autobiographical portrait of a young Jew who experiences the tragic duality of being inadequately rooted in the Jewish tradition and incompletely integrated into German culture and society, which means discrimination, despair, and death.

A more positive note is struck by Julius Stinde, who wrote a series of novels about the cozily materialistic middle-class Buchholz family; by Heinrich Seidel, who produced a group of novels about the lovable eccentric Leberecht Hühnchen; and by Ludwig Thoma, whose *Lausbubengeschichten* (1905-1907) are delightful and durable Bavarian bad-boy stories. The physicist Kurd Lasswitz anticipated space travel in his novel *Auf zwei Planeten* (1897); giving the Martians a higher form of culture than the earthlings enables the author to criticize contemporary conditions. A new kind of *Professorenroman* was attempted by the noted natural scientist Wilhelm Bölsche: In *Die Mittagsgöttin* (1891), the example of an aristocrat done in by spiritism leads a young man to recapture his belief in a better future based on science and socialism. Carl Hauptmann, Gerhart's brother, is remembered for his *roman à clef Einhart der Lächler* (1907), set among artists. In novels such as *Leonore Griebel* (1900) and *Der begrabene Gott* (1905), by the Silesian Hermann Stehr, a brooding awareness of suffering and a mystic religiosity are in evidence. Otto Julius Bierbaum is mainly remembered for two works: *Stilpe* (1897), "a novel from a frog's perspective," is a *roman à clef* with a Berlin bohemian setting in which a megalomaniacal writer sinks in the social scale and commits suicide. *Prinz Kuckuck* (1907-1908), subtitled *Leben, Taten, Meinungen und Höllenfahrt eines Wollüstlings* (life, deeds, opinions, and descent to hell of a voluptuary), betrays the influence of Joris-Karl Huysmans and Oscar Wilde. This great panorama of the Wilhelmian

Age has been extravagantly praised by Klaus Günther Just as "the first great German novel of contemporary life before *The Magic Mountain*."

Cäsar Flaischlen's autobiographical novel *Jost Seyfried* (1905) chronicles, in the form of letters and diary entries, the development of a young writer of the *jüngstdeutsche* persuasion; this "new man" slips back into comfortable middle-class mediocrity. *Modernus* (1904), by Heinrich Lilienfein, is also autobiographical, a novel of development suffused with the spirit of Richard Wagner, Schopenhauer, and Nietzsche, the three sections of which are headed "How I Lost God," "How I Lost the World," "How I Lost Myself." Its hero, however, moves from irresponsible aestheticism and decadent living to a meaningful life. A portrait of *fin de siècle* aristocracy is given in the trilogy *Deutscher Adel um 1900* (1897-1901), by Georg von Ompteda. The Satanist of German literature was Polish-born Stanislaw Przybyszewski, who was indebted to Nietzsche and Huysmans. His interest in Satanism, occultism, demonology, and nihilism is reflected in such works as *Homo sapiens* (1895-1898; English translation, 1915), *Satans Kinder* (1897), and *Androgyne* (1906). Jethro Bithell believes that Przybyszewski's importance "lies in his preaching of sex as the ineluctable purpose of life and as the creative organ of art and literature."

Gerhart Hauptmann's novel *Der Narr in Christo Emanuel Quint* (1910; *The Fool in Christ: Emanuel Quint*, 1911) is indebted to Dostoevski's figure of the Grand Inquisitor. It is a Tolstoyan tale about a Silesian carpenter who tries to emulate Christ; the world is not ready for this, and the man is banished. *Atlantis* (1912) foreshadows the wreck of the *Titanic* in a symbolic presentation of a prewar culture that seems destined to founder.

The outstanding women writers of the time were Clara Viebig and Ricarda Huch. Although Viebig lived mostly in Berlin, her socially conscious and compassionate fiction is set mainly in her native Rhineland or the Polish borderland. "Das Miseräbelchen" is a touching story about a deformed child, "a cacophony in Creation, a mockery of jubilant Nature." *Die Rheinlandstöchter* (1897) pleads for the emancipation of women, and "Halbtier!" is a story about a "new woman" who rebels against her traditional role. *Das Weiberdorf* (1900) is set in a village populated by sex-starved women whose husbands work in distant mines. A trilogy of (somewhat belatedly) naturalistic Berlin novels appeared between 1910 and 1915. Similar subjects are dealt with in the fiction of Helene Böhlau, Gabriele Reuter, Helene Voigt-Diederichs, and Lulu von Strauss und Torney.

Lou Andreas-Salomé, who occupied an important place in the lives of Nietzsche, Rainer Maria Rilke, and Sigmund Freud, published empathic stories such as "Menschenkinder" and novels such as *Ruth* (1895) and *Im Zwischenland* (1902). Ricarda Huch's *Erinnerungen von Ludolf Ursleu dem Jüngeren* (1893; *Recollections of Ludolf Ursleu the Younger*, 1913-1915, 1969) anticipates Mann's *Buddenbrooks* in its account, from the silence of a cloister, of the decline of a patrician Hamburg merchant family because of a passionate love. In *Aus der Triumphgasse* (1902), an old Trieste mansion serves as the squalid domicile of paupers and other outcasts of society.

COUNTERCURRENTS TO NATURALISM

Various countercurrents to naturalism made themselves felt at an early stage of the movement; as early as 1891, the Austrian critic Hermann Bahr wrote a monograph about its *Überwindung* (transcending). Apart from the fact that "consistent naturalism" and other doctrinaire forms were bound to be limited and short-lived, there was a general tendency to abandon the empirical and "scientific" for the irrational, the intuitive, the psychic, the aesthetic, the mystic, and the mythological—to shift from the problems of the time to the problems of the individual. Remembering Goethe's insight that "Art is called art precisely because it is not Nature," the antinaturalists pointed out that the methods of the laboratory and the photographer's studio were not those of the writer. A "return to living things" and a quest for a "literature of nerves" replaced what Bahr described as the "street clothes of truth" and the "insolent despotism of dead things." A desire to give words their due and a striving for inspired language, however, soon produced a new psychological crisis, the awareness of the insufficiency of words.

The prose writers were slower to free themselves from the traditions of realism and naturalism than were the poets and dramatists. While the novel often retained the *Sekundenstil*, fiction, in general, became more subtle and more lyric, concentrating on a second reality of dreams and visions and showing multifarious interconnections between the rational and the irrational. "Without the binding force of nineteenth century Realism and social consciousness," writes H. M. Waidson, "the novel became open to fragmentation through visionary perception and at the same time exposed to that revaluation of all values which so frequently led to nihilistic amorality." The French Symbolists, Oscar Wilde, Walt Whitman, and the Belgians Émile Verhaeren and Maurice Maeterlinck, as well as Huysmans (particularly his antinaturalist novel *Là-bas*, 1891; *Down There*, 1924; better known as *Là-Bas*, 1972), all became important influences on what was generally a European countermovement. This period of intellectual ferment and multiplicity has been classified under many rubrics: Symbolism, neo-Romanticism, neoidealism, neoclassicism, regionalism, aestheticism, art for art's sake, and even incipient expressionism (which Waidson defines as an "ecstatic radicalism which strove to combine visionary awareness with practical social purpose"). The terms impressionism and expressionism were derived from art, as was *Jugendstil* (*art nouveau*), which refers not to a "youthful style" but to the trend-setting periodical *Jugend*, founded in 1896 and aimed at aesthetic refinement in art and literature. This periodical resisted the notion of *fin de siècle* weariness, decadence, or cultural pessimism of Nietzschean or Schopenhauerian provenance: "We are not living among the last gasps of a dying epoch; we are in the morning of a perfectly healthy age. It is a pleasure to live!"

In novels such as *Beate und Mareile* (1903; *The Curse of the Tarniffs*, 1928), Eduard, Graf von Keyserling—the scion of a noble Baltic family and in some ways a continuator of Fontane—describes a thin upper crust trying to live in style above a less refined but more vital lower social stratum, the only contact between these two levels being an occasional and fleeting amorous relationship. Karl May, an enduring phenomenon as a best-selling author, between 1892 and 1910 published thirty-three volumes of what he modestly called his *Reiseerzählungen* (travel tales), exemplifying Wilhelmian Germany's longing for colorful adventures in faraway places. On a higher literary level are the exotic adventure stories and novels of Maximilian Dauthendey, such as *Lingam* (1909) and *Raubmenschen* (1911), as well as the grotesque narratives of Paul Scheerbart, the antierotic *Tarub, Bagdads berühmte Köchin* (1896), and the "snob novel" *Rakkóx der Billionär* (1900).

The fiction of Frank Wedekind, who challenged society on the basis of Freud's thesis that "civilization is based on the permanent subjugation of the human instincts," often is a pendant to his dramas. *Feuerwerk* (1906), a collection of stories, presents such fireworks of eroticism as "Der Brand von Egliswyl," in which a voluptuary, rendered impotent by a girl's rejection of him, sets the entire village on fire to prove his machismo. Wedekind's novel, *Mine-Haha: Oder, Über die körperliche Erziehung der jungen Mädchen* (1903), is a utopian glorification of physical fitness. The early novels of Waldemar Bonsels, *Mare, die Jugend eines Mädchens* (1907) and *Blut* (1909), fasten on the conflict between passion and conscience. In *Freund Hein: Eine Lebensgeschichte* (1902), Emil Strauss took up a subject repeatedly treated in fiction: the anguish of a student who sees suicide as the only way out of a rigid, uncaring school and social system. Friedrich Huch's first novel, *Peter Michel* (1901), deals with a village boy who vainly tries to break out of a confining environment. Similar themes are found in the early novels of the Swabian Hermann Hesse. *Peter Camenzind* (1904; English translation, 1961) depicts a flight to and from people as a country boy, disappointed at what he finds in the city, returns to a simpler life. The protagonist of *Unterm Rad* (1906; *Prodigy*, 1957; also as *Beneath the Wheel*, 1968) is an ambitious and sensitive student who perishes "under the wheel" of an authoritarian, dehumanizing system.

In 1900, Heinrich Mann published his novel *Im Schlaraffenland* (*In the Land of Cockaigne*, 1925), a scathing indictment of corruption among Berlin's nouveaux riches, which foreshadows the author's later social satires. The trilogy *Die Göttinnen* (1902; *The Goddess*, 1918; also as *Diana*, 1929) deals with the gifted and ambitious Duchess d'Assy, and *Die Jagd nach Liebe* (1903) presents a caricatured panorama of Munich high society. In *Professor Unrat* (1905; *Small Town Tyrant*, 1944), an autocratic schoolmaster falls under the spell of an entertainer at a dubious tavern and then takes revenge for his social ostracism by ensnaring his fellow citizens and ruining their morals and reputations. (Twenty-five years later, this novel formed the basis of the celebrated film *Der blaue Engel*, 1930; *The Blue Angel*.) *Zwischen den Rassen* (1907) highlights the contrast between the Nordic and the Latin, and in *Die kleine Stadt* (1909), submerged passions erupt when a troupe of actors appears in a small Italian town.

The great theme of Thomas Mann, Heinrich's more celebrated brother, is the tenuous position of the artist in society, his unassuaged longing for both full acceptance and the "joys of the commonplace," and his status as an anguished outsider. *Buddenbrooks: Verfall einer Familie* (1901; English translation, 1924), as impressive a first novel as has ever been written, is not really a modern novel but a masterful restatement of, and farewell to, the narrative tradition of the nineteenth century. Replete with both naturalistic and impressionistic elements and techniques, it chronicles the decline of a Hanseatic merchant family (clearly in Mann's native Lübeck). Sensitive young Hanno, of the fourth generation, knows that with his artistic sensibilities he represents the end and willingly, almost incidentally, succumbs to a disease. Mann's second novel, *Königliche Hoheit* (1909; *Royal Highness*, 1916), is a modern fairy tale, complete with a happy ending. An impecunious petty prince leaves his ivory tower and achieves an "austere happiness" through his marriage to the daughter of a German American millionaire. The story "Der kleine Herr Friedemann" ("Little Herr Friedemann") represents the artist as cripple; the emphasis on the physical causation of his "chosenness" suggests Zola. In *Tristan* (1903; English translation, 1925), a rather seedy writer living in a sanatorium for the sake of discipline acts as Tristan to a patient's Isolde, and the price of her spiritual-artistic-erotic awakening is her "parodistic" death estranged from her common-place family. The most mature and enduring among Mann's early *Novellen* is *Tonio Kröger* (1903; English translation, 1914). An escapee from his father's bourgeois world and rejected by the attractively mindless and charming people of this world, the protagonist finds the artistic life unsatisfying and is crushed when a confidante suggests that he may be "a commoner gone astray"; in the end, Tonio realizes that his outsider status may be the very source of his creativity and that his true mission may be ironic mediation between life and art.

STORYTELLERS FROM SWITZERLAND, AUSTRIA, AND CZECHOSLOVAKIA

The foremost Swiss prose writer after Conrad Ferdinand Meyer was Carl Spitteler, the recipient of the Nobel Prize in Literature in 1919. A Symbolistic critic of the materialism and utilitarianism of his age, he expressed many psychological insights in his fiction. The story *Conrad der Leutnant* (1898) deals with a young man and his overbearing family. The title of *Imago* (1906), the story of a sexual obsession sublimated in devotion to art and a love attachment emerging from repression, supplied Freud and his circle with the name of both a significant psychoanalytic concept and a journal. *Die Mädchenfeinde* (1907; *The Little Misogynists*, 1923) is a sensitive and colorful tale about boys and girls on the verge of adolescence. The three novels of Robert Walser, who lived in psychiatric clinics for the last twenty-seven years of his life, are partly autobiographical. The subtly ironic Walser foreshadows Franz Kafka (who appreciated him) in that familiar details of everyday life are used as the stepping-stones to fantasy. In *Jakob von Gunten* (1909; English translation, 1969), the author exposes the moral ambivalence of his age through the diary entries and musings of a boy at a boarding school, a sort of urban "magic mountain," who manages to take an imaginary trip that removes him from European culture. In *Konrad Pilater* (1910), by Jakob Schaffner, a young man is torn between political radicalism and love. Jakob Christoph Heer and Ernst Zahn dealt with aspects of Swiss cantonal life in their novels *Der König der Bernina*

(1900) and *Albin Indergang* (1901), and the priest Heinrich Federer wrote *Lachweiler Geschichten* (1911), Swiss village tales in the tradition of Jeremias Gotthelf and Keller.

The Vienna of the end of the nineteenth century has attracted considerable attention in recent years. In the last decades of the old, moribund Habsburg Empire there was a greater consciousness of decline and dissolution in Austria than in Germany, and this sense of life found expression in impressionistic and Symbolistic terms. Naturalism never took hold in Austria, where industrialization was a much slower process, for writers there did not share the political activism of their German colleagues. Most of the *Jung Wien*, or Young Vienna, writers (Hermann Bahr, Arthur Schnitzler, Hugo von Hofmannsthal, Felix Salten, Richard Beer-Hofmann, Peter Altenberg, Stefan Zweig, and Leopold, Freiherr von Andrian-Werburg) were of an upper-middle-class background and thus tended to be conservators rather than reformers.

The great theme of the older generation of writers was the impact of modernization and early capitalism on the landed gentry and the upwardly mobile bourgeoisie. The melancholy Ferdinand von Saar strove to depict society in the manner of Turgenev; his stance of scientific detachment and sympathy for those defeated by change links him to the naturalists. Saar is particularly remembered for his cycle *Novellen aus Œsterreich* (1877-1897; a literary picturebook of Francisco-Josephinian Austria) and the novel *Schloss Kosternitz* (1892). The dramatist Ludwig Anzengruber wrote the powerful novel *Der Sternsteinhof* (1885). The fiction of Peter Rosegger, including the novel *Jakob der Letzte* (1888), is rooted in his native Styria.

The senior member of Young Vienna, the dramatist and critic Hermann Bahr, has been called a "virtuoso of receptivity." His considerable amount of fiction includes his first novel, *Die gute Schule* (1890), subtitled *Seelenstände* (psychic states), which tells the story of a young painter whose overcoming of a creative crisis in Paris makes him conclude that love is "the good school of true wisdom," and *Theater* (1897), a *roman à clef* set in Viennese theatrical circles. The most striking among the few works of Berlin-born Leopold, Freiherr von Andrian-Werburg, is the *Novelle Der Garten der Erkenntnis* (1895), about a narcissistic young nobleman's education, travels, interpersonal relationships, and early death. In Richard Beer-Hofmann's short novel *Der Tod Georgs* (1900), the decadent Paul experiences the death of his "wife"—ostensibly an extension of himself—in a dream and then suffers the death of his gifted friend Georg. Paul's reveries and stream-of-consciousness reflections on his aesthetic existence lead him to an affirmation of life and of his Jewish heritage.

In his stories and novels, Arthur Schnitzler, a great diagnostician of earthly evanescence, decadence, cultural decay, and moral relativism, "combined the naturalist's devotion to fact with the Impressionist's interest in nuance." Schnitzler's first *Novelle*, *Sterben* (1895; dying), already stamps him as a master of the psychological story. A young man doomed by tuberculosis watches in consternation as his lady's *joie de vivre* breaks their death pact; his death is prefigured in the fading of their love. The epistolary story "Die kleine Komödie" features the role-playing of an egocentric playboy and a former actress who aim for "atmosphere." *Leutnant Gustl* (1901; *None but the Brave*, 1925) takes the form of an inner monologue and brings out the emptiness of the conventional morality, specifically the military code of honor. Schnitzler's *roman à clef Der Weg ins Freie* (1908; *The Road to the Open*, 1923) is a *Diskussionsroman* in which the author presents a typology of Viennese society (including Jews trying to come to terms with anti-Semitism and Zionism) seeking freedom and fulfillment. Robert Musil's *Die Verwirrungen des Zöglings Törless* (1906; *Young Torless*, 1955) is a haunting story of adolescent sexual perversion and brutality in a boarding school. A curiosity of literary history is the pornographic novel *Josefine Mutzenbacher* (1906), purportedly the autobiography of a Viennese prostitute; it appeared anonymously but has been attributed to Felix Salten.

In the works of the German storytellers from Czechoslovakia, most of whom were Jews, a definite undercurrent of mystical ecstasy may be discerned.

Prague, that alchemistic melting pot, was a city of raconteurs and "Magical Realists." After the older generation, which produced a wealth of rural legends and ghetto stories, there was increasing concern with the city. The life span of Moravian-born Marie von Ebner-Eschenbach (Countess Dubsky) coincided with that of Emperor Franz Josef. In her numerous novels and stories, she artistically captured the mellow, slightly decadent atmosphere of her country. In her several volumes of *Dorf- und Schlossgeschichten* (1883; tales of village and castle life), she is critical of her own class, but her realism is always tempered with gentleness. The novel *Das Gemeindekind* (1887) tells the story of a boy of unfortunate parentage who overcomes prejudice and discrimination through strength of character. Auguste Hauschner was influenced by naturalistic trends and interested herself in the social problems of women (*Frauen unter sich*, 1901). *Die Familie Lowositz* (1909) presents a kaleidoscopic view of Prague in the 1870's. Bohemian-born Fritz Mauthner, a major philosopher of language, followed his *Berlin W* trilogy (1886-1890) with depictions of the Bohemian milieu such as *Die böhmische Handschrift* (1897). Moravian-born Jakob Julius David, who was hard-hit by poverty and infirmity and who lived in Vienna from 1891 on, wrote melancholy stories and novels that are marked by a pronounced social consciousness, including *Das Höfe-Recht* (1890); *Das Blut* (1891), about problems of Jews living in rural areas; *Die am Wege sterben* (1900), about the misery of students in Vienna; and *Der Übergang* (1902), about the decline of a Viennese family. David's collection *Die Hanna* (1904) contains stories of Moravian village life. Philip Langmann, who also lived in Vienna from 1900 on, published several volumes of naturalistic stories, including *Arbeiterleben* (1893) and *Realistische Erzählungen* (1895). Hugo von Salus, who practiced medicine in Prague, also published collections of stories (*Novellen des Lyrikers*, 1904). Gustav Meyrink is remembered for his later novel *Der Golem* (1915; *The Golem*, 1928), but his interest in the grotesque, occultism, and spiritism is also reflected in such early tales as *Orchideen* (1904) and *Das Wachsfigurenkabinett* (1907). Prague-born Oskar Wiener is known not only as an anthologist but also for his novel *Im Prager Dunstkreis* (1919). Grete Meisel-Hess is the author of novels (*Fanny Roth*, 1902) and stories (*Suchende Seelen*, 1903) that reflect her interest in social reform, feminism, occultism, and sexual and moral problems. Robert Saudek published the novel *Dämon Berlin* in 1907.

After three early prose works—the autobiographical story *Ewald Tragy* (written in the 1890's but not published until 1929; translated into English in 1958), the Tolstoyan *Vom lieben Gott und Anderes* (1900; republished as *Geschichten vom lieben Gott*, 1904; *Stories of God*, 1931, 1963), and the popular *Die Weise von Liebe und Tod des Cornets Christoph Rilke* (1906; *The Tale of the Love and Death of Cornet Christoph Rilke*, 1932)—the Prague-born poet Rainer Maria Rilke published *Die Aufzeichnungen des Malte Laurids Brigge* (1910; *The Notebooks of Malte Laurids Brigge*, 1930; also known as *The Journal of My Other Self*). In the form of the notebook of a Danish aristocrat who tries to live in Paris as a poet, this is an impressionistic depiction of disintegration and decay, with childhood recollections dredged up as a counterpoint to the distressing urban reality.

Finally, this was the milieu that produced one of the greatest writers of the twentieth century, Franz Kafka, whose impact began to be felt in the 1920's with the posthumous publication of his uncompleted novels *Der Prozess* (1925; *The Trial*, 1937) and *Das Schloss* (1926; *The Castle*, 1930). Appearing only a few years after the *fin de siècle* fiction already discussed, Kafka's masterpieces nevertheless belonged to another world: the world after World War I. In fact, only *The Castle* was written after the war (*The Trial* was begun in 1914 and was abandoned, unfinished, in 1915), yet Kafka's novels, like his stories, which began appearing in book form in 1913, seemed peculiarly suited to the "age of anxiety" ushered in by World War I. Indeed, many readers see in the nightmarish logic and bureaucratic evil of *The Trial* and *The Castle* a prescient vision of the Holocaust and all the other totalitarian horrors of the twentieth century.

Harry Zohn, with additions to the
bibliography by Patricia Bankhead

BIBLIOGRAPHY

Adams, Jeffrey, and Eric Williams, eds. *Mimetic Desire: Essays on Narcissism in German Literature from Romanticism to Post Modernism.* Columbia, S.C.: Camden House, 1995. A collection of scholarly essays on the theme of narcissism in the works of several German writers, including novelists Thomas Mann, Gottfried Benn, Max Frisch, Christa Wolf, and Thomas Bernhard.

Berman, Russell A. *The Rise of the Modern German Novel: Crisis and Charisma.* Cambridge, Mass.: Harvard University Press, 1986. The author explains the rise of the German novel by looking at the social processes and political tensions in modern society.

Beutin, Wolfgang, et al. *A History of German Literature: From the Beginnings to the Present Day.* Translated by Clare Krojzl. 4th ed. New York: Routledge, 1993. A basic historical and critical overview. Bibliographical reference, index.

Craig, Gordon Alexander. *The Politics of the Unpolitical: German Writers and the Problem of Power, 1770-1871.* New York: Oxford University Press, 1995. An examination of the attitudes of German authors toward the issue of national unification in the period leading up to the first Germany. Bibliographical references, index.

Diethe, Carol. *Towards Emancipation: German Women Writers of the Nineteenth Century.* New York: Berghahn Books, 1998. A rare, systematic analysis of the contributions of German women writers, beginning with late Romantics and moving through the 1848 revolutionary period to the late nineteenth century. These writers' attitudes toward women's emancipation are explored in all their variety and range. Bibliographical references, index.

Hardin, James, ed. *German Baroque Writers, 1580-1660.* Detroit: Gale Research, 1996.

_____. *German Baroque Writers, 1661-1730.* Detroit: Gale Research, 1996. These reference works, part of the Dictionary of Literary Biography series, provide brief biographies of German writers of the baroque period. List sources for further study; include indexes.

Hardin, James, and Siegfried Mews, eds. *Nineteenth-Century German Writers to 1840*. Detroit: Gale Research, 1993.

_____. *Nineteenth-Century German Writers, 1841-1900*. Detroit: Gale Research, 1993. Two volumes in the Dictionary of Literary Biography series that provide biographical sketches of the periods' writers. Bibliographical references, indexes.

Kontje, Todd Curtis. *Women, the Novel, and the German Nation, 1771-1871: Domestic Fiction in the Fatherland*. New York: Cambridge University Press, 1998. The lives and works of fourteen women writers are introduced and examined in regard to their role in molding attitudes toward class and gender prior to German unification as a nation. Bibliographical references, index.

Sagarra, Eda. *A Companion to German Literature: From 1500 to the Present*. Oxford: Blackwell, 1997. This readable overview surveys nine eras of German literature—from the Reformation and Renaissance to the late twentieth century—providing cultural and historical context for both traditional and neglected authors, including many women. Maps, index.

Vivian, Kim. *A Concise History of German Literature to 1900*. Columbia, S.C.: Camden House, 1992. Readable essays by various scholars; includes illustrations of German authors. Bibliographical references, index.

Watanabe-O'Kelly, Helen, ed. *The Cambridge History of German Literature*. New York: Cambridge University Press, 1997. A thorough overview from the Carolingian period to the Unification of Germany in 1990, providing historical, political, and cultural context for both the student of German literature and the general reader. Quotations are translated into English; bibliographical references, index.

GERMAN LONG FICTION SINCE WORLD WAR I

The Austrian novelist Stefan Zweig, in his autobiography *Die Welt von Gestern* (1941; *The World of Yesterday*, 1943), reminisces about Europe at the beginning of the twentieth century and the then-prevalent hopes for the future. Social and political security were the foundation for all further developments as the new age dawned: Diplomats provided peace, science was steadily eliminating disease and pain, morality became more liberal and more tolerant, the economy provided a comfortable life for millions and work for most, and prosperity was evident in the attractive modern cities as well as in the individual lives of Europeans. Comfort was no longer a dream but rather a reality for most. Mass production had enriched the daily lives of all citizens, and technology promised the widespread availability of indoor plumbing, telephones, radios, and hundreds of labor-saving devices, not to mention such luxuries as the cinema, the automobile, and the airplane. For Zweig and for millions of his fellow Europeans, this was the onset of the true Golden Age. Yet, despite continued astonishing developments in technology, science, and industry, paradise soon slipped from their grasp.

The post-World War I novel

World War I represented a watershed, marring Zweig's wonderful dream with a horrible reality. By 1920, the social and political security so necessary for equilibrium and progress had disappeared. For some, the new era was to prove exhilarating, a time for new beginnings, but for many others, the chaos resulting from the war caused severe trauma and would lead to a later and greater catastrophe in the ensuing search for stability.

The loss of tradition and continuity was felt in all areas of life and thus in the world of literature, which mirrored these social tremors. Some writers accepted the challenge of revaluing cultural traditions in quest of a new future, while others bemoaned the irretrievable loss of "the good old days." This dichotomy, conspicuous in their works, is responsible for a remarkable variety and vitality of expressions—the hallmark of German fiction since 1920.

With the resounding defeat of the Central Powers in 1918, long-standing problems emerged to confront the German-speaking nations. Within fifty years, Germany had developed from a predominantly agrarian society to a modern, industrialized nation. Consequently, traditional middle-class values of an earlier age were no longer sufficient in an era of metropolitan anonymity, of mass conformity and blind obedience to emperor and state. The change was so drastic and so sudden that Hermann Hesse was to write in his *Der Steppenwolf* (1927; *Steppenwolf*, 1929) of one individual's reaction: "Now there are times when a whole generation is caught . . . between two ages, two modes of life, with the consequence that it loses all power to understand itself and has no standard, no security, no simple acquiescence." The many strikes, revolutions, mutinies, putsches, and related forms of chaos during the 1920's were merely reactions to external events that had become unfathomable. In the German-speaking countries, the shame of defeat was compounded by the humiliating terms of the Treaty of Versailles. Germany and Austria saw long-standing monarchical rule replaced by republican forms of government. All colonies were surrendered, territories were ceded or occupied, and the army was limited to 100,000 soldiers. In addition to the loss of a generation of men, the Central Powers had to accept sole responsibility for the war and then make reparation payments to reimburse the victors.

Within a period of five years, Germany and its allies had gone from world powers to shrunken remnants of once-great nations. The shock, humiliation, and confusion could not have been greater. Since all were treading a foreboding *terra incognita*, it became the task of the writers to understand and clarify their situation, to create new values by which all could live.

Aside from the many problems of modernity, dealing with the immediate past was a necessity. War novels abounded, the most popular being Ernst Jilnger's *In Stahlgewittern* (1920; *The Storm of Steel*, 1929), Ludwig Renn's *Krieg* (1928; *War*, 1929), Walther Flex's *Wanderer zwischen beiden Welten* (1916), Arnold Zweig's *Der Streit um den Sergeanten Grischa* (1927; *The Case of Sergeant Grischa*, 1928), and Ernst Glaeser's *Jahrgang 1902* (1928; *Class of 1902*, 1929). Yet only Erich Maria Remarque, in his controversial *Im Westen nichts Neues* (1929, 1968; *All Quiet on the Western Front*, 1929, 1969), was able to capture the boredom and horror, the naïve enthusiasm and ultimate despair of World War I. Translations immediately communicated the experience to other participants around the globe, and a motion picture with the same title proved equally popular on an international scale. Even for Remarque, a journalist by trade, the gestation of the book took some time—it appeared in 1929, fully ten years after the conclusion of the war. In Austria, Joseph Roth required even more time to contemplate the loss of his beloved Habsburg monarchy. His novel *Radetzkymarsch* (1932; *The Radetzky March*, 1933) and its sequel *Die Kapuzinergruft* (1938) trace the ascent and demise of Emperor Franz Joseph through parallel developments in three generations of one Austrian family. For Roth, the death of Franz Joseph is synonymous with the irreplaceable loss of traditional Habsburg Austria and the simultaneous advent of modern existential uncertainty.

This ambivalence, encouraged in the philosophical and scientific writings of Søren Kierkegaard and Friedrich Nietzsche, of Sigmund Freud and Albert Einstein, was to result in a generation of "outsiders." Four novelists of the time represented the concerns of many in their recognition of such isolation. The first, Hermann Hesse, had become famous and wealthy in the ten years preceding the war through popular romantic novels such as *Peter Camenzind* (1904; English translation, 1961) and *Unterm Rad* (1906; *The Prodigy*, 1957; also known as *Beneath the Wheel*). Yet with the outbreak of war, such tales appeared trivial in the light of world events, and, as suspicion of Hesse's patriotism increased, his popularity rapidly dwindled, causing him to have a nervous breakdown. Following these personal crises (and psychological treatment), Hesse began to examine more thoroughly his life and those of his contemporaries. *Demian* (1919; English translation, 1923), published under a pseudonym, was an instant success, becoming the bible of an entire generation.

For the next ten years, Hesse was to chronicle in ever-changing format the trials and tribulations of the disaffected individual. *Siddhartha* (1922; English translation, 1951), *Steppenwolf*, and *Narziss und Goldmund* (1930; *Death and the Lover*, 1932; also known as *Narcissus and Goldmund*, 1968) were all products of the turbulent 1920's, each a literary solution to the existential despair of its titular heroes. Employing exotic settings or, as in *Demian* and *Steppenwolf*, elements of the fantastic and the occult, Hesse introduced a novelistic alienation effect by which the reader could gain intellectual distance from the fictitious events, all the better to arrive at an objective solution to these pressing problems. It was Hesse's unfortunate fate that youthful readers often ignored this objectivity, transforming him into a cult figure for narcissistic escapists. On a primitive level, Hesse's heroes encourage such identification, for they popularize the outsider in the twentieth century: Split personalities of intellect and sensuality, they grope and suffer near suicide for a meaning to their lives, to the "self." In his mature works, however, Hesse renounced this popular preoccupation, promoting a "selfless" solution; in *Die Morgenlandfahrt* (1932; *The Journey to the East*, 1956) and *Das Glasperlenspiel: Versuch einer Lebensbeschreibung des Magister Ludi Josef Knecht samt Knechts hinterlassenen Schriften* (1943; *Magister Ludi*, 1949; also known as *The Glass Bead Game*, 1969), the protagonists devote their lives unselfishly to higher causes.

Thomas Mann, a friend of Hesse, was also preoccupied with the philosophical problems posed by an existence that often seemed alien and hostile to the individual. Mann's first novel, the two-volume *Buddenbrooks: Verfall einer Familie* (1901; *Buddenbrooks*, 1924), achieved popular success despite its length. Influenced by the ideas of German philosophers Arthur Schopenhauer and Nietzsche, Mann traced the decline of a commercial family over three generations. The story asked whether the artistic temperament might be at odds with the "will to live" that these philosophers argued lay at the core of existence. As younger, sensitive, and aesthetically oriented members of the Buddenbrooks family take control of the business, the firm slides into failure.

Decadence, the opposition between art and life, and the interplay of philosophical ideas continued to dominate Mann's work. The novella *Der Tod in Venedig* (1912; *Death in Venice*, 1925) dealt with the passion of an aging writer for a pretty young boy. Mann's massive novel *Der Zauberberg* (1924; *The Magic Mountain*, 1927) presents the story of the ordinary, middle-class citizen Hans Castorp, who is transported to the rarified atmosphere of a tuberculosis sanatorium in the mountains. Away from everyday concerns, Castorp engages in a seven-year philosophical examination of life. He socializes with characters who represent extremes of emotion and reason, and Castorp learns the value of moderation. The ending of the novel is ambiguous, though, because Castorp leaves the mountaintop and is drafted into the German army during World War I. In the last scene, he faces apparently fatal enemy gunfire.

Later biographers of Mann tended to interpret the novelist's concerns with decadence and conflict as products of his psychological turbulence, rather than as purely philosophical matters. Ronald Hayman, in *Thomas Mann: A Biography* (1995), draws a portrait of a man tormented by fits of depression and frustrated bisexuality, who had difficulty forming close relations with family members. Donald Prater's massive biography, *Thomas Mann: A Life* (1995), describes Mann as a repressed homosexual whose inability to demonstrate feelings for others led to a passion for abstract ideas. Anthony Heilbut, in *Thomas Mann: Eros and Literature* (1996), maintains that an idealized love for a series of young men ran through all of Mann's writing.

The Austrian novelist Robert Musil, in his massive, unfinished magnum opus *Der Mann ohne Eigenschaften* (1930, 1933, 1943; *The Man Without Qualities*, 1953, 1954, 1960), created a new kind of novel reflecting the worldview of modern science and philosophy. Trained as an engineer with a broad scientific background, Musil rejected the reductive positivism of the Vienna Circle yet drew on his scientific and philosophical studies to view his characters in a manner unprecedented in fiction: both analytically, from a great distance, and in sympathy with the most intricate movements of thought and feeling. In

The Man Without Qualities, the collapse of the Austro-Hungarian Empire represents the larger crisis in European culture and, on an even larger scale, the existential dilemma of modern man.

Finally, Alfred Döblin's *Berlin Alexanderplatz* (1929; *Alexanderplatz, Berlin*, 1931; better known as *Berlin Alexanderplatz*), a monumental novel, asserts that even the lower-class workingman can find himself an outsider in his own environment. Döblin's hero, a truck driver, is released from prison into the labyrinthine jungle of modern Berlin. He believes that he can control his own destiny but soon is forced to join a gang of thieves. His personal failure and helplessness culminate in the murder of his beloved, a blow that drives the hero insane. Döblin emphasized the chaos of modern life through the hapless reactions of his hero-victim; stylistically, he employed stream-of-consciousness techniques and other impressionistic qualities to depict the unrelenting bombardment of external stimuli on a vulnerable individual.

The works of these four novelists, of course, do not represent the entire range of attitudes and responses characteristic of the post-World War I era. One writer who deserves mention in this context is the Austrian novelist Hermann Broch. Like his compatriot Musil, Broch came to the novel from an extraliterary background; a successful executive in the textile industry, he also had training in philosophy and mathematics. Like Musil, Broch used the novel as an instrument of philosophical inquiry; his great novel *Die Schlafwandler* (1931-1932; *The Sleepwalkers*, 1932) rivals Musil's *The Man Without Qualities* as an exploration of the malaise of modern European culture. Broch's second masterpiece, *Der Tod des Vergil* (1945; *The Death of Virgil*, 1945), was completed during his exile in the United States, to which he emigrated after being briefly imprisoned by the Nazis in 1938.

THE WORLD WAR II NOVEL

Indeed, in one sense, the existential crisis of German culture in the post-World War I era was resolved not by philosophical treatises or literary masterpieces but by political fiat. With the ascension of the Nazi Party to power in 1933, all facets of culture were to be monitored and manipulated by the state. Membership in the respected Prussian Academy of Arts was soon to require an oath of loyalty to the government; similar organizations experienced a similar fate. Another omen of the proscriptive measures to come could be seen in the spring of 1933, when university professors, students, and Nazi Party members publicly burned books written by "undesirables." The works of Freud were consigned to the flames for their purported immorality; Remarque's famous novel was branded as "pacifistic," while the social satires written by Heinrich Mann, Thomas Mann's older brother, were found to be derogatory. Authors of nonconforming racial background, religious preference, or political taint were blacklisted and banned from publishing on German soil. The list of prominent writers (along with scientists, politicians, and other civilian leaders) grew to include literally thousands of prominent Germans. Some were allowed to stay in the country, though they were forbidden to write except along party lines; most were forced into exile, under the threat of imprisonment or death. Thus, from Sweden to Russia, from Mexico to California, "the real German culture" (as one exile phrased it) struggled to survive.

As a result of the Nazi cultural monopoly, three distinct types of German literature emerged during the twelve years from 1933 to 1945. First, there was the "officially approved" literature by those writers who had remained in the Third Reich or whose works had been appropriated by the Nazis, such as Hans Grimm's *Volk ohne Raum*, published in 1926. This *Blud und Bodenliteratur* (blood and soil literature), extolling the virtues of the Germanic race and its cultural roots, was not a product of National Socialist ideology. As in most things cultural, the Nazis adopted earlier works and traditions that had existed long before Adolf Hitler came to power. Here *Heimatkunst* (or regional art), neo-Romanticism, and expressionism provided powerful, already extant sources from which to draw—novels such as *Der Hitlerjunge Quex* (1932; quest of the Hitler Youth), by Karl Aloys Schenzinger, *Die S.A. erobert Berlin* (1933; the S.A. conquers Berlin), by Wilfrid Bade, and *Die grosse Fahrt* (1934; the great journey), by Hans Friedrich Blunck. Parallel to Hitler's penchant for historical figures, a spate of historical novels appeared after 1933. Although purporting to depict ages and situations past, these works attempted to extol current Nazi values. As J. M. Ritchie postulates in his *German Literature Under National Socialism* (1983), Blunck's *Die grosse Fahrt* is typical in many ways: "Essentially the view presented is undemocratic, nationalistic and irrational. There is no analysis of society: instead the novel directs the reader away from reality towards a mystical, Utopian solution to Germany's problems."

These writers were awarded all the literary prizes at the state's disposal, were granted access to publishing houses and the precious supplies of paper, and were reviewed enthusiastically by critics and scholars sympathetic to the Nazi cause. This group remains problematic for the student of literature today: The backlash after the war branded them all as "brown," or as Nazi hacks who merely churned out propaganda for Hitler. This judgment was based on political prejudice similar to that which the Nazis had exercised only a few years earlier; only in the late twentieth century did scholars begin to evaluate the literature of these writers with a dispassionate eye.

Of those writers not employed by the Nazis, two basic groups must be considered. One body consists of authors who remained in Germany, unable to publish, but who nevertheless insisted on the right to be considered members of an "inner emigration." The second, more distinct body is composed of those countless individuals who were forced to flee their homeland. Their individual tales of hardship, of terror and suffering, of despair and accommodation constitute an entire chapter of literary history. Of the thousands of anecdotes created by their exile, the most uplifting recounts Franz Werfel's escape from the Gestapo. While fleeing through France, Werfel was forced to hide in Lourdes, the site of a shrine of miracles. He prayed for a miraculous escape and vowed to dedicate his next novel to the legendary vision of Lourdes. Upon his safe arrival in New York, he wrote the inspiring best-seller of hope and faith, *Das Lied von Bernadette* (1941; *The Song of Bernadette*, 1942).

Simply to live and write on foreign soil became an arduous task for the exiled writers. Some continued to write in German for small exile presses and for even smaller audiences. A few were fortunate in finding competent translators; the undistinguished Vicki Baum, for example, was the beneficiary of such a luxury through her publisher, Doubleday, and consequently her fiction was widely sold through the Book-of-the-Month Club. Another struggling novelist, Stefan Heym, did not trust his literary fate to luck, learning English so well that he continued to write all of his novels in this second language after the war. These writers all wished that the madness in Germany would soon end, that they could return to German soil as productive and respected writers. Yet as the years dragged on without hope, as Germany attacked Poland and war began, their despair grew. Stefan Zweig emigrated first to England, then to Brazil; though wealthy and cosmopolitan, he could not bear the isolation and committed suicide. Others, such as Thomas Mann, reconciled themselves to their fates and survived as best they could, vowing never to return to a Germany they no longer recognized.

As one would expect, the utopian novel flourished during the war years. From around the globe, writers constructed visions of a new and better society; among the more significant were Hesse's *The Glass Bead Game*, Werfel's *Stern der Ungeborenen* (1946; *Star of the Unborn*, 1946), and Jünger's *Heliopolis* (1949). However, the realities of the first years following the war—the incredible destruction of population and property, starvation and deprivation considerably worse than in the waning years of Nazi domination, and the mandatory occupation by the victorious Allied powers—effectively stifled this genre and its implied hope for the future. Although the Allies introduced policies of denazification and publicly judged individual Germans in Nuremberg for their complicity in war crimes, their decision to rebuild Europe through such instruments as the Marshall Plan created the basis for a new Germany. The postwar years thus brought fundamental changes to the political and cultural structures of the German-speaking countries. The defeated Germany was divided into two separate nations: The Federal Republic of Germany was allied with the North Atlantic Treaty Organization (NATO) and Western Europe, while the German Democratic Republic became a member of the Warsaw Pact under Soviet influence. While Austria ultimately became a neutral republic, Switzerland experienced a unique development as the only German-speaking country not directly involved in World War II. These experiences and those of the war itself provided German writers with abundant material for their novels. With the demise of the Nazi dictatorship, additional literary impulses stimulated cultural life: The works of exiled writers and those previously burned and banned were reintroduced into the occupied lands, along with hundreds of works of world literature previously forbidden by the Nazis as "decadent."

WEST GERMAN FICTION

West German fiction after 1945 was strongly marked by the Nazi years. Gradually, many of the exiled authors returned to Europe, though generally with diminished productivity. Of the major writers of the post-World War I era, Musil was no longer living; Hesse wrote no fiction between 1943 and his death in 1962; Mann lived in Switzerland until his death in 1955, publishing one of his greatest works in the immediate postwar years, the novel *Doktor Faustus* (1947; *Doctor Faustus*, 1948); Döblin returned to Germany and died there in 1957, leaving little impact on the new society; and Broch, who had long since emigrated to America, died there in 1951. This generation of writers had fought the early battles with modern ambivalence, but the changing times would encourage others to continue the struggle. Soldiers who had survived the war, the prison camps, and denazification surveyed a devastated homeland and broken families. Some, like Heinrich Böll, would commit their experiences, feelings, and observations to paper. Civilians were to comment on their own memories, as in the case of Walter Kempowski. More censorious authors instigated critical investigations of the German people during the Nazi era; here, Günter Grass, Siegfried Lenz, and Uwe Johnson come to mind. Indeed, no writer in the postwar years could escape the reality of the Nazi era and especially the genocidal "final solution" that led to the Holocaust.

The Holocaust proved an enormous stumbling block for all sides—for the victims and survivors of the death camps as well as for the perpetrators and their descendants. In purely literary terms, the obstacles appeared almost insurmountable: How could one explain or describe the depth and breadth of this abomination? What literary forms existed to portray this singular horror? What narrative perspective would allow a truthful and accurate presentation of the common fate of thirteen million individuals? How could one convey the inhumanity of this atrocity persuasively, so that it can never happen again? These were but a few of the perplexing literary considerations to have confronted the writer in Germany since 1945.

Scholars often write of an imaginary "zero point" immediately after the war, a starting point where the culture had to be rebuilt from ground zero. This implies that all literary trends from the pre-Nazi years were effectively extinguished by Hitler's rise to power, that there was no continuity between the literature of the Third Reich and that of the new Germany to follow. The emerging literature is frequently designated *Trümmerliteratur* (literature from the ruins), conveying not only the immediate surroundings but also the psychological state of the authors themselves. In the words of Heinrich Böll, this development was the result not of normal organic growth but of the catastrophe of war. To write optimistic literature would be cruel in the face of so much destruction, and there was no time for the luxury of reflection, comparison, and thoughtful objectivity. The result was sober and realistic description, neither heroic nor romantic, often couched in autobiographical reports which signaled a new realism.

A younger generation with different experiences and viewpoints dominated West German literature after 1945. Like all novices, the new writers struggled to master their craft, to attract publishers and an audience. To provide mutual support in their efforts to produce a new literature, these authors banded together at the invitation of Hans Werner Richter to establish a working forum for critical discussions of their art; in commemoration of their first annual meeting, they became known as Gruppe 47, which functioned successfully for fifteen years to promote a new German literature of high standards and of world renown—though the group has often been discussed as much for its political engagement as for the fine literature it produced.

The group's activism may be clearly seen in the fiction of Heinrich Böll, Nobel Prize winner and grand old man of German letters. Böll's early prose depicted World War II in a dispassionate manner, focusing on the senseless destruction and waste of human lives. In later works, such as *Billiard um halbzehn* (1959; *Billiards at Half-Past Nine*, 1961) and *Ansichten eines Clowns* (1963; *The Clown*, 1965), he portrayed civilian corruption and hypocrisy during the Nazi period and during the postwar "economic miracle." Böll's social criticism was often exaggerated to the point of grotesque satire, and the figure of the clown was the perfect medium for such criticism; the clown is an artist who lives and performs in society, magnifying its features through pantomime and monologue while maintaining his independence and distance from social convention. Still, the conclusion of Böll's novel was more realistic than many cared to admit, for the clown's independence and social criticism only cause him personal grief; though irritated by his presence, society is able to maintain the status quo by dint of its sheer size and political influence. Despite the fact that Böll experienced a similar reception in his own artistic career, he continued to criticize the prosperous, consumer-oriented Federal Republic of Germany. His novels of the 1970's, including *Gruppenbild mit Dame* (1971; *Group Portrait with Lady*, 1973), *Die verlorene Ehre der Katharina Blum* (1974; *The Lost Honor of Katharina Blum*, 1975), and *Fürsorgliche Belagerung* (1979; *The Safety Net*, 1982), were thinly veiled exposés of actual living persons and contemporary institutions in the West Germany of the time.

The other major figure in West German fiction, Günter Grass, burst upon the literary scene with his overnight best-seller *Die Blechtrommel* (1959; *The Tin Drum*, 1961). His grotesque and irreverent dwarf offered, literally, a different perspective on the events from 1933 to 1945 and on into the early postwar years. The dwarf may make noise on his drum, shatter glass with his voice, or merely outrage people with his behavior and audacious narration, but the reader cannot ignore him or the controversy that Grass's book caused. Although none of his subsequent novels gained quite the international attention (or national notoriety) accorded *The Tin Drum*, Grass himself became a lightning rod for German political engagement. He participated in election campaigns on behalf of the liberal German Socialist Party (SPD), and his "Heilbronn Declaration" of 1983— challenging the constitutionality of nuclear missiles being stationed in West Germany—indicated a return to political activism after the torpid decade of the 1970's. Grass embodied the artist's political responsibility to his society, a position that caused many West Germans discomfort, especially since Grass was an outspoken liberal.

The social criticism present in the fiction of Böll and Grass became a fixture in much of the literature that appeared in the late 1960's and early 1970's during the student protests. Political demonstrations were mounted against foreign targets, especially during the Vietnam War, and national issues such as the West German laws excluding suspected communists from governmental service came under heavy attack. Other groups, disadvantaged or previously ignored, received special attention during this period of heightened awareness and personal involvement. Both workers' literature and women's literature thrived. Max von der Grün's *Stellenweise Glatteis* (1973) marked a conscious (and successful) attempt to develop a style and narrative stance appropriate to the milieu and problems of today's workers. In addition, the growing body of literature by and about women explored a new dimension. Ingeborg Bachmann's *Malina* (1971) and Karin Struck's *Die Mutter* (1975) attracted public attention and stimulated controversy among the general public, not to mention among their fellow writers—compare Grass's *Der Butt* (1977; *The Flounder*, 1978).

While these writers' provocative contributions reexamined social conventions around 1970, subsequent trends toward apathy and isolation diminished the effect of their criticism. The alternative culture

provided an antidote to realistic and documentary literature of the 1960's, replacing political and social involvement with an increasing concern for the individual. Here more personalized literature was evident: Biographies, reminiscences, and diaries were popular genres for portraying intimacy. It must be emphasized, however, that such intimacy and spontaneity were often artificial; in the "diaries" of Max Frisch, for example, the various entries were carefully crafted literary constructions obviously intended for public consumption.

This "new sensibility" attempted to capture the alienation and isolation in modern life, as exemplified in the works of Botho Strauss. His *Marlenes Schwester* (1975), *Die Widmung* (1977; *Devotion*, 1979), and *Paare, Passanten* (1981) explored the sterility in society and the impossibility of human communication. Basing his fiction on physical and astronomical observations—that the planets are moving inexorably away from one another out into the void— Strauss sought to recognize similar physical phenomena among people. His work is thus characterized by lonely individuals who speak primarily in monologues, underscoring the impossibility of communication and therefore of human contact. This trend was also clearly evident, to a lesser degree, in the works of the popular novelist Martin Walser. His early works—*Ehen in Phillippsburg* (1957; *The Gadarene Club*, 1960; also known as *Marriage in Phillippsburg*), for example—were critical of the conformist striving to succeed in the materialistic world of the economic miracle. Later works, such as the novels *Seelenarbeit* (1979; *The Inner Man*, 1984) and *Das Schwanenhaus* (1980; *The Swan Villa*, 1982), and the classic novella *Ein fliehendes Pferd* (1978; *Runaway Horse*, 1980), explored the problems of middle age. Walser devised an initial Kafkaesque shock to jolt the "hero" from his established routine, then traces the latter's soul-searching through monologue, indirect discourse, and interior monologue. The realistic, informal language and the unerring accuracy of his portraits provided psychic identification and understanding between his troubled protagonists and the reader. These writers were only a few of the many and varied talents on the West German literary scene.

The writers of West Germany made use of a variety of novelistic forms and techniques. While some experimental literature tended to the extreme of *Unkunst*, or nonart, such as the do-it-yourself novel, which required the reader to construct the plot, most novelists struggled earnestly to communicate their individual yet typical concerns. As noted earlier, modern ambiguity or isolation may be transmitted effectively through monologue—that is, a subjective utterance in place of pronouncements by the traditional omniscient narrator. Indeed, the inadequacy of any narrator has resulted in novels that "tell themselves." Techniques borrowed from film and radio sometimes eliminated chronological narration, utilizing techniques such as the flashback, dream sequences, and fades. The most resilient, versatile, and thus popular form for presenting simultaneity and complexity in fiction was that of the montage, an arrangement of elements from several different sources joined so that each distinct element contributed to a new composition or totality. Wolfgang Hildesheimer, for example, allowed his first-person narrators to pile fantasy upon fantasy in an attempt to construct a new reality that they can comprehend and thus master. In *Tynset* (1965) and *Masante* (1973), the main character is an insomniac whose imagination creates a pseudoreality in which he can barely survive.

Günter Grass utilized variations of the montage to create a synthesis of *Vergegenkunft*, of past-present-future, emphasizing their interrelation and importance as a continuous process; from *Örtlich betäubt* (1969; *Local Anaesthetic*, 1969), *Aus dem Tagebuch einer Schnecke* (1972; *From the Diary of a Snail*, 1973), and *The Flounder* to *Kopfgeburten: Oder, Die Deutschen sterben aus* (1980; *Headbirths: Or, The Germans Are Dying Out*, 1982), Grass interspersed historical details from the past, actions from the present, with conjecture relating to future developments in order to illuminate the historical process and educate the reader as to the consequences of his or her individual actions.

Christoph Meckel combined documentary materials, personal recollections, and poetic fiction in a composite *Suchbild: Über meinen Vater* (1980; *Image for Investigation About My Father*, 1987), at once a portrait of his father and an allegory of two gen-

erations of Germans. In *Der Mensch erscheint im Holozän* (1979; *Man in the Holocene*, 1980), Max Frisch inserted encyclopedic excerpts into his text as a sobering counterpoint to his main character's improbable assumptions, offering an austere critique of the modern tendency to confuse information with knowledge. Another Swiss author, Gerold Späth, allowed more than two hundred individual characters to narrate their life stories in *Commedia* (1980), each distinct autobiography contributing to a larger story, the mosaic of an entire community.

As a result of its size and potential audience, its marketing capabilities and critical coverage, West Germany enjoyed a preeminent role in the German-speaking publishing world in the years before reunification. The other German-speaking countries—East Germany, Austria, and Switzerland—were all somewhat dependent upon West Germany for inspiration and stimulation. Though their authors may have a core of faithful readers at home, to be published in West Germany was the ultimate sign of critical and financial success.

East German Fiction

An article by Frank Trommler in the volume *Deutsche Gegenwartsliteratur* (1981) observed that East German literature existed under tenuous circumstances: It was only one of many national literatures among its Soviet bloc neighbors and ranked as only a variant within the literature of German-speaking nations. The result was an inferiority complex and an identity crisis on a national scale, creating a situation in which East German literature was dependent upon that of West Germany for critical resonance, contrast, and thus confirmation of its "otherness." Ironically, West German scholars were the first to recognize East German literature as a cohesive body, and they wrote literary histories in the mid-1970's on its evolution.

The literature of East Germany (after 1949, the German Democratic Republic) was initially created by returning emigrants. Socialists and members of the Communist Party exiled from West Germany moved to the Soviet-occupied zone in the hope of contributing to the establishment of a new society.

Their participation in a proletarian-revolutionary movement was encouraged by the government in the form of conferences, subsidies, and various awards, and through the Literature Institute at the University of Leipzig. The Soviet zone thus attracted many returning exiles, among them Arnold Zweig, Bertolt Brecht, and Johannes R. Becher, whose prestige and productivity lent respectability to the socialist sector.

One of the most prominent authors was Anna Seghers. Her most popular novel, *Das siebte Kreuz* (1942; partial translation as *The Seventh Cross*, 1942), and an earlier novella, *Aufstand der Fischer von St. Barbara* (1928; *The Revolt of the Fishermen*, 1929), had gained critical recognition. *Transit* (1944; English translation, 1944) chronicled the exploits of refugees and their attempts to escape the Nazis in Marseilles during the first years of the war. Two complementary novels, *Die Toten bleiben jung* (1949; *The Dead Stay Young*, 1950) and *Die Entscheidung* (1959), offered a broad portrait of developments in Germany from 1918 to 1945 and from roughly 1945 to 1951, respectively, as seen through the lives of representative characters. For the author, a member of the Communist Party since 1929, these descriptions supported the working class and its struggle for sustained influence in German life. She consciously contrasts capitalist and socialist societies and, while admitting the tensions and difficulties present in the life of the workers, ultimately sides with the latter.

The anti-Fascistic tone of the exiles' works was short-lived. The Third Party Congress in 1950 suggested that literature's function was to depict the accomplishments of socialist renewal—the first of continuing reminders that literature was to be subservient to the needs of the party. In response to the congress, the "positive hero" became the programmatic effort to provide a didactic model of enthusiasm for achievement, especially in an industrial setting such s those found in the so-called factory novels. Not surprisingly, few of these early works could claim even moderate success.

By 1956, several prominent authors discussed the unfortunate absence of confrontation with the recent (that is, Nazi) past, encouraging the younger generation to fictionalize their personal experiences. Dieter

Noll's *Die Abenteuer des Werner Holt* (1960) was a *Bildungsroman* that contrasted the young protagonist's ideals with the reality of the war years. Through an inordinate number of adventures, Noll endeavored to trace the development of a "typical" individual who coincidentally served as the representative of an entire collective society. Christa Wolf, arguably East Germany's finest writer, ventured a thoughtful innovation within this general theme. Most novels that deal with the Third Reich constantly rephrase the question "How could the Holocaust have happened?" In her *Kindheitsmuster* (1976; *A Model Childhood*, 1980; also as *Patterns of Childhood*, 1984), Wolf offered a pedagogical twist, insisting that such a historical past is overcome only through a thorough analysis and present awareness; her new, incisive question was "How have we become the people that we now are?"

Another example of the state's initiatives in the field of literature was the conference in Bitterfeld in 1959, which signaled the official trend toward workers' literature. The Bitterfeld Way further encouraged writers to collect concrete experiences in the factories and fields. Erwin Strittmatter revived the cliché of the 1950's positive hero and transformed it into an admirable tragic figure. In *Ole Bienkopp* (1963; English translation, 1966), the titular hero dedicates himself to the development of a collective farm and must struggle against the entrenched bureaucracy and various Communist Party opportunists. The scholar Marc Silberman has labeled Bienkopp an "anticipatory hero," to account for his individual initiative within a collective society: Though Beinkopp disagrees with established socialist policies and the capricious functionaries behind them, his overriding dedication to others (in the form of the collective) leads him to take actions which are later adopted by the party as new policy. Bienkopp's striving is not against the old policies but merely anticipating the new.

With the construction of the Berlin Wall in 1961, it became necessary to justify East Germany's enforced isolation, if not convince its citizens that they were actually in the better half of Germany. Wolf first tackled this dilemma in her novel *Der geteilte Him-*

mel: Erzählung (1963; *Divided Heaven: A Novel of Germany Today*, 1965), articulating the problems inherent in the mass migrations from East to West Germany before the wall was built. Günter de Bruyn accentuated the importance of individual commitment as a positive step in reaffirming one's allegiance to the socialist ideal; his *Buridans Esel* (1968) was a vivid depiction of an indecisive character whose lack of commitment is paralyzing.

By the 1970's, the new directive was to refocus the novel toward the recognition of the numerous problems within East German society, but from the perspective of their resolution. In this type of fiction, the new heroes were to be the planners and managers—in other words, those individuals in decision-making positions who were actively participating in the advancement of the socialist state. The managers, however, would not inherit this world without a struggle; the student unrest, protest, and celebration of individuality that rocked the West during the late 1960's and early 1970's did not spare East Germany. One *cause célèbre* was the appearance of Ulrich Plenzdorf's *Die neuen Leiden des jungen W.* (1973; *The New Sufferings of Young W.*, 1979). A conscious juxtaposition of Johann Wolfgang von Goethe's classic *Die Leiden des jungen Werthers* (1774; *The Sorrows of Young Werther*, 1779) and J. D. Salinger's *The Catcher in the Rye* (1951), this novel employed pop jargon of the younger generation to undermine the socialist work ethic, extolling instead the virtues of individuality and creativity. The sympathetic young protagonist drops out of the ranks of the loyal workers and attempts to find himself, only to be electrocuted while inventing a better paint sprayer. The work's immediate success and popularity (especially in the West, where it served in some quarters as confirmation of the evils of communism) were more the result of its daring theme than its artistic merit.

Despite the sporadic declaration of "official" guidelines for literature, periods of relative liberalization encouraged East German writers to attempt more original themes, though always at the risk of fines, house arrest, censorship, and even deportation. A case in point is that of Stefan Heym. Disaffected by American politics during his exile in the United

States, Heym returned to the fledgling East German state only to find even greater repression. The shock resulting from the Berlin Revolt in 1953 removed any illusions Heym may have fostered concerning the humanistic ideals of the Communist rulers. His subsequent novels dealt with suppression in historical situations, culminating in his *Fünf Tage im Juni* (1974; *Five Days in June*, 1977), the first literary work in East Germany to deal with the 1953 revolt; as a consequence, Heym was at times forbidden to publish in East Germany (as happened between 1963 and 1973), and several of his works could be published only in the West. Nevertheless, writers less bold (or more ingenious) than Heym managed to package their criticism in seemingly harmless forms; fantastic novels (including science fiction), children's literature, and fairy tales all offered an outlet for social commentary. Manfred Bieler and Günter Kuner, who both settled in the West, employed these genres to call into question commonly accepted practices and casual assumptions.

One direct result of the political repression, especially after the appearance of the Berlin Wall, was the isolation of East German literature from many of the trends, influences, and experiments in the West, with resulting stagnation. Also, because of the programmatic nature of their literature, few East German authors gained international recognition. Those few who were critical of East German society or the socialist bureaucracy were well received in the West; the basis for this recognition was primarily political, however, and often had little to do with the literary merits of the individual works.

GERMAN FICTION AFTER REUNIFICATION

The collapse of socialism in East Germany and the reunification of West and East Germany into a single country in 1990 enabled works to be published in the East that would have been banned previously. Uwe Saeger's partly autobiographical novel *Die Nacht danach und der Morgen* (1991) looked at the issue of the border guards who had been charged with keeping easterners from fleeing to the West. Karl Mickel published *Lachmans Freunde* (1991), a novel set in the 1950's and actually written between

1968 and 1983, which considered the problems of socialist society that had led to East Germany's end. Erich Köhler treated the same subject in a novel that blended elements of realism and fantasy, *Sture und das deutsche Herz* (1990), a history of Germany from the Middle Ages to reunification, told from the point of view of a troll.

Despite the new freedom, the specter of East German communism continued to haunt German literature. In 1992, East German state documents revealed that the renowned East German writer Christa Wolf, along with other intellectual leaders, had collaborated with the communist secret service. After these revelations, Wolf wrote the novel *Medea: Stimmen* (1996; *Medea: A Modern Retelling*, 1998). She portrayed the ancient Greek mythical character Medea, who betrayed her own father and murdered her own children, as a victim caught up in political oppression and complex interpersonal relations. Many critics read the apology for Medea as an apology for Wolf's own past.

The foremost writer of the former West Germany also continued to be active after reunification. *Unkenrufe* (1992; *The Call of the Toad*, 1992), by the literary giant Günter Grass, considered the question of Germany's past and future relations with its neighbors. In this novel, an aging German art historian forms a romantic relation with a Polish woman in the Polish city of Gdańsk, which was formerly German Danzig. The two work out their cultural differences, but their plans to establish a cemetery of reconciliation, in which Poles and Germans will rest together, are complicated when German business enterprises become involved; the German free market land-grabbing in Poland becomes reminiscent of the Nazi invasion. Novelist Frank Werner saw a different sort of similarity between the German past and the German present in his novel *Haus mit Gästen* (1992), which drew parallels between the end of Nazi Germany and the end of the communist regime of East Germany.

AUSTRIAN FICTION

The nearly seven-century-old Habsburg monarchy of Austria dissolved in 1918 with national and global consequences. Gone were the giant empire, the cultural influence and prestige, the political alliances, and the practical administration of everyday affairs. While still grieving over their loss, the Austrians were annexed by Nazi Germany and engulfed by the Third Reich. Only after the war, when occupation forces withdrew and exiles returned to aid in the cultural reconstruction, could one envision a restoration of timeless Austrian values. Certain qualities such as stability and equilibrium, an aversion to extremes, an appreciation for timeless and lasting values, a sense of tradition, and an allegiance to a specific geographical region and national culture have always appealed to the Austrian mentality. These traits had survived for centuries, had provided stability and a sense of security under the Habsburgs, and could be trusted once again to provide a solid foundation in uncertain times.

Older writers such as Heimito von Doderer and the revival or rediscovery of Austrian masters such as Musil and Broch influenced the younger novelists in the 1950's and early 1960's, so that critics were convinced of a timeless continuity. Indeed, older and younger authors alike propagated these values during the twenty years following the war. Their efforts for the rejuvenation of literature in Austria centered on the journal *Plan* after its inception in 1945. Young authors were encouraged to publish in this journal and could gain needed recognition and a receptive audience. The Austrian Ministry for Education began to award subsidies to young authors in 1950, and since that time, Vienna and other provinces have introduced similar incentives. The Austrian Society for Literature, founded in 1960, has also provided international contacts and exposure for native writers, encouraging a broader perspective and higher standards for budding authors.

Critics and writers both agreed that postwar Austrian literature represented a continuation of prewar values and traditions. Novels such as Georg Saiko's *Auf dem Floss* (1948, revised 1954; on the raft) only tended to confirm these suspicions. Superbly crafted, Saiko's subjects move in the present but with attitudes out of the distant past. Society may be adrift, but like his contemporaries, Saiko disdained current issues in favor of a distinctly Austrian melancholy romanticism. With the liberal waves that swept across other industrialized nations, Austria's isolation and innocence too were challenged. New critics appeared, young authors who questioned Austrian society and its influence on the individual, represented by the Wiener Gruppe (1952-1964) and the Forum Stadtpark in Graz. The Viennese pioneered the use of dialect in their works as a conscious commentary on modern language and thus on modern institutions. Provincial novels resurrected the unspoiled, timeless qualities in nature, far from the industrialized metropolis. In its critical phase, however, the novel of the province may also reduce the nation to its lowest common denominator, the village, where all the vices of contemporary life can be exposed.

One of the major representatives of the provincial novel was Franz Innerhofer's *Schöne Tage* (1974; *Beautiful Days*, 1976). Written in a touchingly native, primitive style, the novel chronicles an adolescent's experiences on an isolated farm. The cruelty, brutality, and despair of everyday life eventually drive the youth to the big city, there to overcome the debilitating aspects of his development. Innerhofer's first novel, apparently autobiographical, was successful primarily because his unpolished prose complemented the rustic personality of his protagonist. In subsequent volumes of this trilogy, *Schattseite* (1975) and *Die grossen Wörter* (1977), he affected a more elevated form of language to indicate his hero's intellectual maturation—with painfully mediocre results.

The 1960's brought forth a new generation of novelists who, like Innerhofer after them, were to pose embarrassing and often painful questions. One of Austria's more celebrated writers, in drama as well as in prose, was Thomas Bernhard. From the titles of two representative works, the novel *Frost* (1963) and the memoir *Die Kalte* (1981), one can infer his concern with alienation in modern life. In his presentation of the weak, the sick, and the insane, Bernhard stressed the senselessness of striving; his bucolic settings thus became monstrous traps from which the individual could not escape. *In Verstörung* (1967; *Gargoyles*, 1970), the reader is assaulted by the personal recollections of a young student as he accompanies his father, a country doctor, on his various rounds; here the descriptions of mental and physical illness, of brutality and pain, create an image of an insane world. Further proof, if required, abounds in *Das Kalkwerk* (1970; *The Lime Works*, 1973), the testimony of a mine owner, Konrad, relating his failures in business, in his studies, and in his torturous marriage to his crippled wife, whom he has killed.

Like Bernhard, Peter Handke gained international recognition for his dramatic works and his fiction alike. Handke's initial successes occurred in the theater, where he made dramatic history of a sort by insulting his audiences in the mid-1960's. After 1970, however, he devoted his considerable talents mainly to fiction. Early novels such as *Die Angst des Tormanns beim Elfmeter* (1970; *The Goalie's Anxiety at the Penalty Kick*, 1972), *Der kurze Brief zum langen Abschied* (1972; *Short Letter, Long Farewell*, 1974), and *Die Stunde der wahren Empfindung* (1975; *A Moment of True Feeling*, 1977) project an increasing subjectivity, a sensitivity to external impressions as well as to the innermost feelings of people. While Handke was long considered an avant-gardist interested in structural linguistic problems (and as such became a cult figure among deconstructionist critics), his developing preoccupation with the "New Sensibility" became most obvious in *Wunschloses Unglück* (1972; *A Sorrow Beyond Dreams*, 1975), the reconstruction of his own mother's life and suicide. Despite objections by feminists such as Karin Struck, Handke's sensitive yet objective portrayal of his mother's life—the boredom, the disappointment of unfulfilled expectations, the suffering and despair—is an insightful literary portrait colored by sociological observation and the personal scars the son obviously still bears. Handke's novels of the late 1970's reveal a shift in emphasis, with a positive, almost visionary conception of the writer's role unusual in postwar literature; in this regard, Handke has spoken of the influence of the nineteenth century Austrian novelist Adalbert Stifter.

Perhaps Austria's best-kept secret is the prose of Elias Canetti. This master craftsman wrote and published for more than fifty years, yet until he was awarded the Nobel Prize in Literature in 1981, he attracted little attention. The bulk of his writings were essayistic, aphoristic reflections on his travels and on his experiences during and after the war; here one would include *Masse und Macht* (1960; *Crowds and Power*, 1962), *Die Stimmen von Marrakesch* (1967; *The Voices of Marrakesh*, 1978), *Die gerettete Zunge: Geschichte einer Jugend* (1977; *The Tongue Set Free: Remembrance of a European Childhood*, 1979), and *Die Fackel im Ohr* (1980; *The Torch in My Ear*, 1982). Canetti's only novel, *Die Blendung* (1935; *Auto-da-Fé*, 1946; also known as *The Tower of Babel*), deserves special mention. The main character, Peter Kien, is a scholar unable to cope with the uncertainty of reality. His fear of life becomes paranoia, and he withdraws ever deeper into his library and scholarship. Love is also threatening to Kien, so it is only poetic justice that his wife turns into a vile creature. In his denial of life, Kien destroys himself, both literally and figuratively. Despite Canetti's often humorous and satiric treatment, this is a disturbing novel because of the insights it provides into the modern aversion to life, to change, and to love. An article by Claudio Magris in *Modern Austrian Literature* (1983) reflects that Canetti's depiction of a frightening attraction for death has, in effect, transformed the author into a powerful advocate of life. This, too, is the Austrian legacy.

SWISS FICTION

Although Switzerland is politically neutral, the country and its people are not disinterested in world affairs. They are clearly aligned with the democratic West and have always maintained close cultural ties with the other German-speaking countries in Europe. For this reason, the onset of German Fascism was a blow to Switzerland, and in the area of cultural exchange, many Swiss authors could no longer be published in the larger German market. Direct contact among individual writers was often halted, while many German authors attempted to enter Switzerland so that they could continue writing for a native-language audience during their exile.

Because of its long tradition of neutrality, Switzerland was able to survive the war years intact, indeed as a bulwark of German-language culture. Untarnished by National Socialism's excesses, the Swiss could continue the tradition of European humanism so abruptly interrupted in Germany and Austria. Because of their cosmopolitan outlook, Swiss authors provided an enlightened, objective perspective on the events that corrupted German culture.

Although 1945 was not a crucial year in Swiss history, as in the war-ravaged Germany and Austria—there was no "zero point" from which to recover in Switzerland—the Swiss were not untouched. The country had been on military alert since the beginning of the war, and in an unwritten code of solidarity, rigorous self-examination had been postponed for the duration. Now came the time for introspection: Governmental policies concerning refugees from Nazi Germany, private and official collaboration with Hitler's regime, and military plans for the nation's defense all came under consideration. The economic resurgence following the war (with the accompanying problems of imported foreign workers) made the Swiss even more protective in preserving their miniature paradise. Criticism, though ever-present, was seldom welcome, and the Swiss reluctantly endured the milder forms, such as the intrusion of satire and ironic criticism as a literary corrective. In fact, it seems that Swiss authors have perfected these forms, for with the exception of the *Bildungsromane* of Jakob Schaffner, the most noteworthy Swiss novel between 1920 and 1945 was Meinrad Inglin's *Schweizerspiegel* (1938). It was left to the younger generation to resume a critical appraisal of the relationship between the individual and Swiss society.

The image, or rather the myth, of Switzerland as the "land of Heidi"—of rustic clockmakers, alpine pastures, beauty and serenity, independence and democracy—was propagated for centuries in literature, from the itinerant Hans Jakob Christoffel von Grimmelshausen to the natives Gottfried Keller, Jeremias Gotthelf, and Conrad Meyer. Switzerland, however, was not to be spared the crass realities of modern existence. Typical problems of twentieth century life also invaded paradise. Material success and greed have often spoiled the landscape and the tranquillity of small-town life. Problems of identity and self-worth have plagued the Swiss as well. In addition, distinctly Swiss dilemmas have arisen: A suffocating demand for conformity and order has alienated a sizable portion of the youth who must live in this "golden cage." Hypocrisy and bureaucracy only compound the problem.

The more critical Swiss authors have been engaged for some time in examining their national myth and offering correctives. It is difficult to convey the concern that Swiss authors harbor for their country. Critics often chide (or revile) them as traitors, yet their devotion to their native land is sincere and should not be underestimated. They view with distrust any attempts, either accidental or willful, to ignore or conceal national problems. Typical is the accusatory tone displayed in Walter Matthias Diggelmann's *Die Hinterlassenschaft* (1965), in which criticism focuses on Swiss treatment of refugees during World War II; Diggelmann's exposé of selfish, unchristian behavior is a broad indictment of the Swiss as a people. Such attempts at criticism often fall upon deaf ears, provoking harsher and more exaggerated criticism. One example was the scandalous novel by Fritz Zom, *Mars* (1979; English translation, 1980), in which the author, dying of cancer, accused society of causing such destructive illnesses; repression, anger, and frustration are all carcinogenic agents of a society as stifling as that of the Swiss. If Zom overstated his case, many other Swiss novelists provide a more balanced perspective.

As early as 1949, a young architect and writer explained why he was obligated to concern himself with social developments at home and abroad: "When people who speak the same language as I, who like the same music as I, when they are not immune from becoming inhuman, where can I gain the assurance from now on, that I am immune from similar actions?" This young writer's name was Max Frisch. It was this same Max Frisch who, by the middle of the century, had raised Swiss prose to world prominence; together with the dramatist Friedrich Dürrenmatt, Frisch had brought a previously moribund, provincial literature to world attention. In fact, purists would insist that there is no Swiss fiction beyond Frisch. His *Tagebuch 1946-1949* (1950; *Sketchbook 1946-1949*, 1977) reports and reflects on the issues and events immediately following World War II, but with the second volume, *Tagebuch 1966-1971* (1972; *Sketchbook 1966-1971*, 1974), Frisch began to focus his attention on more personal issues. Two of his early novels, *Stiller* (1954; *I'm Not Stiller*, 1958) and *Mein Name sei Gantenbein* (1964; *A Wilderness of Mirrors*, 1965), explore the questions of personal identity and freedom in regimented Switzerland. After 1975, however, Frisch dealt with the problems of aging, love and human relationships, knowledge and its absence during senility, self-worth and ultimate accountability for the sins of omission and commission during an entire lifetime. In *Montauk* (1975; English translation, 1976), Frisch unflinchingly investigates the personal failings of his (autobiographical?) main character. *Man in the Holocene* portrays the poignant results of senility and self-imposed isolation on the aged. His *Blaubart* (1982; *Bluebeard*, 1983) relies on the background of a courtroom investigation to initiate an unrelenting search for accountability in the public as well as in the private sphere. Ultimately, according to Frisch, each life must be examined in minute detail to discover the extent of one's failings in relation to those of other human beings.

Among the younger Swiss authors, Adolf Muschg also mirrors these crises in Swiss life and, like Frisch, is able to elevate them from the merely provincial to the general, as attested in such prose works as *Im Sommer des Hasen* (1965), *Fremdkörper* (1968), *Albissers Grund* (1974), and *Gegenzauber* (1967). Like Fritz Zom, Muschg was interested in the relationship between illness and society. His own experiences with group therapy encouraged him to delve deeper into the mystery of humans as social animals. Muschg dismissed the argument that literature should serve as a form of therapy, either for the writer or for the reader, positing instead that critical self-evaluation is preferable. Muschg prized in his fiction that moment when the protagonist can differentiate between the person he thought he was or had hoped to be and the person that he is in reality. This frightening moment of recognition, of ultimate isolation and truth, can lead to the process of honest evaluation of the person as a complete human being.

Only in this way can isolation be overcome and spontaneity and life be restored.

To avoid wallowing in self-pity or self-delusion, Muschg expanded the apparently egotistical literature of the New Sensibility, directing it outward into political activism. An interview with Muschg in *Studies in 20th Century Literature* (1984) records these observations:

> Individuals who take their own needs seriously cannot be misused to serve the needs of politicians. It is an immunization process. . . . People who are aware of their real needs tend to be more courageous, more rebellious, even in the public sector. They are less corruptible than the flag wavers of every persuasion, including the left.

Here he defends individuality as a counterbalance to mass (social and political) pressures.

Gerold Späth created an enviable collection of works in little more than ten years—novels and short stories that exhibit an amazing versatility and virtuosity. His first novel, the picaresque *Unschlecht* (1970), delightfully translated as *A Prelude to the Long Happy Life of Maximilian Goodman* (1975), was received with critical acclaim. Here and in *Balzapf: Oder, Als ich auftauchte* (1977), Späth investigated the significance of custom and tradition, the importance of wealth and lineage that provide prestige and freedom within Swiss society. His protagonists are rogues who survive and thrive without the external trappings of a prosperous life, all the while gently mocking those who feverishly pursue "the good life." *Die heile Hölle* (1974) depicts a representative family—father, mother, daughter, son—that has acquired material and social success at the expense of happiness; their desperate attempts to find meaning in their lives climax with the son's suicide, which serves as an end to both his pointless existence and the continuation of this familial folly, since he dies childless. Späth's most ambitious project was the novel *Commedia* (1980). Its two distinct parts correspond to the isolated individuals of a modern community, individuals who have become divorced from the accoutrements and traditions that bring meaning to their environment and thus to their lives.

THE CHALLENGE OF MODERN GERMAN FICTION

For all the notable achievements in poetry and drama, the modern period has been a high point for German fiction. One superficial illustration of this is the fact that four of the five German-language writers who won the Nobel Prize in Literature from the 1920's to the 1990's were novelists: Thomas Mann in 1929, Hermann Hesse in 1946, Heinrich Böll in 1972, and Elias Canetti in 1981. Thanks to an abundance of competent translators and a voracious reading public, readers around the globe are now able to enjoy the works of many German novelists, thus bringing great change to the personal circumstances of the individual writers. With the mass production of books (and the innovation of the paperback book in Germany after 1950), writing and publishing have become big business. Since the eighteenth century, the writer has been accepted as a moral force, as the nation's conscience, not seldom as prophet or guru for an entire generation. Now the writer has become a public figure as well, a creation of the "culture industry" that organizes publicity, prizes, receptions, autograph parties, and, ultimately, a reading public on the writer's behalf. For a writer to ignore or to refuse the benefits of this highly organized machine has proved increasingly difficult. Authors have always been dependent on the reading public. Today, however, the stakes have grown to astronomical proportions: Aside from the material advantages to be gained from a best-seller, critical success has become crucial to the continued existence of the *freischaffender Schriftsteller*, or professional writer.

While books have become more readily available and affordable, their authors would admit that they have not become easier to write. The highly publicized "death of the novel" had a significant effect on German literature, for traditional (that is, nineteenth century) means of narration proved inadequate to express or describe the events of the twentieth century. Writers such as Michael Ende, Johannes Mario Simmel, and Heinz Konsalik will always find a large reading public for their conventional novels told by a third-person narrator in chronological sequence. Indeed, the complaint of the average reader continues to be: "Why don't the famous authors write something I can understand?" Those writers most highly prized by critics are not often readily understandable. Here the reader must exercise a good bit of effort (and goodwill) to decipher the new medium or the new message. A changing world seemingly requires changing forms of expression to capture adequately the significance of the new, and the twentieth century certainly provided a rapid succession of changes, overwhelming events, and bewildering circumstances.

The changing circumstances of German society have caused some German writers and the German reading public to question whether German literature is too ponderous and takes itself too seriously. In 1994, the editor of the S. Fischer publishing house, Uwe Wittstock, publicly posed the question, "Is German literature boring?" Wittstock answered that it was, and he claimed that German writers should follow English and American examples and try to be more entertaining. Other writers and literary critics, however, disagreed with Wittstock's verdict and defended the continued relevance of German literature.

One characteristic of German prose has been the attempt to reflect the upheavals in contemporary society while realizing the inherent complexity of modern life. Writers often produce extremely large novels, thereby hoping to encompass the variety and depth of reality. To reflect the impossibility of comprehension, the absence of order, and the lack of individual control, one can note the virtual disappearance of the omniscient narrator. These considerations represent an evolution in literature and expose the writer's insistent questions: What can and do I know? What can I write? What forms are appropriate? How can I master a language that has become suspect as a result of its abuse in the hands of politicians, advertising-slogan writers, and other mass manipulators?

The ambiguity frequently encountered and so often criticized in the modern novel must also be considered from nonphilosophical perspectives. While critics are often confused by an author's seemingly ambivalent stance—and attribute this indecision or hesitancy to the chaos or the complexity in modern life—the rhetorical effects of such ambiguity must not be overlooked. By refusing to fashion a satisfactory conclusion or happy ending, the novelist encourages the reader to evaluate the circumstances for himself or herself, to become involved in the world of the novel (and thus in its "reality"), prompting the reader to participate actively in the decisions of life. This controversial stance consciously creates provocative situations and events, yet without providing a moral or a related answer. Each reader is aware that writers are not without opinions, that they do, in fact, have beliefs, ideals, and causes. Yet through their literary works readers are challenged to reach their own conclusions in regard to political, social, and cultural issues.

Todd C. Hanlin, updated by Carl L. Bankston III

BIBLIOGRAPHY

Adams, Jeffrey, and Eric Williams, eds. *Mimetic Desire: Essays on Narcissism in German Literature from Romanticism to Post Modernism.* Columbia, S.C.: Camden House, 1995. A collection of scholarly essays on the theme of narcissism in the works of several German writers, including novelists Thomas Mann, Gottfried Benn, Max Frisch, Christa Wolf, and Thomas Bernhard.

Berman, Russell. *The Rise of the Modern German Novel: Crisis and Charisma.* Cambridge, Mass.: Harvard University Press, 1986. The author explains the rise of the German novel by looking at the social processes and political tensions in modern society.

Beutin, Wolfgang, et al. *A History of German Literature: From the Beginnings to the Present Day.* 4th ed., translated by Clare Krojzl. New York: Routledge, 1993. A basic historical and critical overview. Bibliographical reference, index.

Boa, Elizabeth, and J. H. Reid. *Critical Strategies: German Fiction in the Twentieth Century.* Montreal, Canada.: McGill University Press, 1972. Although somewhat technical in character, this book will be useful to those looking for a detailed discussion of the ways in which German writers have approached their art. It is divided into four parts that consider structures, textures, themes, and modes (such as realism, symbolism, and irony) of German fiction.

Böschenstein, Hermann. *A History of Modern Ger-*

man Literature. Edited by Rodney Symington. New York: P. Lang, 1990. Covers nineteenth and twentieth century German writers. Index.

Demetz, Peter. *Postwar German Literature: A Critical Introduction*. New York: Pegasus, 1972. This book is helpful for general readers seeking an overview of literature in the various German-speaking nations of Europe. It provides descriptions of society and literature in Switzerland, Austria, the German Democratic Republic (East Germany), and the Federal Republic of Germany (West Germany). (The chapters on East Germany and West Germany have been made somewhat out of date by reunification.) The book also gives short portraits of modern German poets, playwrights, and fiction writers.

Diethe, Carol. *Towards Emancipation: German Women Writers of the Nineteenth Century*. New York: Berghahn Books, 1998. A rare, systematic analysis of the contributions of German women writers, beginning with late Romantics and moving through the 1848 revolutionary period to late in the century. These writers' attitudes toward women's emancipation are explored in all their variety and range. Bibliographical references, index.

Durrani, Osman. *Fictions of Germany: Images of the German Nation in the Modern Novel*. Edinburgh, Scotland: Edinburgh University Press, 1994. A study of the portrayals of the German nation in works by Alfred Döblin, Hermann Hesse, Thomas Mann, and Günter Grass. The author maintains that novels are historical documents and that the literary value of the works of these authors is enhanced by connections between the novels and social events in Germany.

Gay, Peter. *Weimar Culture*. New York: Harper & Row, 1968. Written by one of America's preeminent historians of modern Europe, this offers a short overview of major cultural figures and insti-tutions in Germany in the troubled but artistically productive period after World War I.

Hatfield, Henry. *Modern German Literature: The Major Figures in Context*. London: Edward Arnold, 1966. Critical study of Swiss, Austrian, and German writers (naturalists, expressionists, and the Neo-Romanticists) in the period from 1890 to 1956.

Ritchie, James M. *German Literature Under National Socialism*. London: C. Helm, 1983. This book is unique for its efforts to take National Socialist literature seriously. It looks both at writers who remained in Germany during the Nazi years and at those who wrote in exile.

Sagarra, Eda. *A Companion to German Literature: From 1500 to the Present*. Oxford: Blackwell, 1997. From the Reformation and Renaissance to the late twentieth century, this readable overview surveys nine eras of German literature, providing cultural and historical context for both traditional and neglected authors, including many women. Maps, index.

Watanabe-O'Kelly, Helen, ed. *The Cambridge History of German Literature*. New York: Cambridge University Press, 1997. A thorough overview from the Carolingian period to the Unification of Germany in 1990, providing historical, political, and cultural context for both the student of German literature and the general reader. Quotations are translated into English; bibliographical references, index.

Ziolkowski, Theodore. *Dimensions of the Modern Novel*. Princeton, N.J.: Princeton University Press, 1969. This critical work attempts to display the diversity of the modern German novel and to suggest common features. In the first part, it looks at works by Rainer Maria Rilke, Kafka, Mann, Döblin, and Broch. In the second part, it looks at several common themes that run through the writings of these authors.

IRISH LONG FICTION

Irish writing falls into two distinct categories. Written in the indigenous Irish language, the first includes bardic poems and Celtic sagas. The second, Irish literature written in English, includes what is often called Anglo-Irish literature because it was created by Protestants of English extraction. This phenomenon can be explained by England's colonization of Ireland and the acceptance of Irish writers within the British literary tradition.

THE EIGHTEENTH CENTURY IRISH NOVEL

Although Irish writers are recognized for their enormous contributions to poetry and drama, during the eighteenth century Irish writers contributed also to the rise of the English novel and played a large role in its evolution throughout the nineteenth and twentieth centuries. While very little Irish eighteenth century fiction deals with Irish subject matter, the humor, the sense of the grotesque and fantasy, the significance of anecdote, and the importance of the storyteller categorize the constructs of the Irish novel.

Irish long fiction took root in the eighteenth century with Jonathan Swift (1667-1745) as the major contributor. His exuberant use of humor and fantasy, as well as his expansive imagination, demonstrates the deep influence of Ireland on his psyche and firmly distinguishes him as an Irish writer. Recognized as the foremost prose satirist in the English language, Swift spent much of his life trying to escape from Ireland, which was seen in those days as a place of exile from England. However, politics dictated that he spend the bulk of his life as dean of St. Patrick's Anglican cathedral in Dublin.

Although Swift penned verse early in his life, his true genius did not surface until he turned to prose satire. His *A Tale of a Tub*, published anonymously in 1704, a satire against religion and education, isolated Swift as a genius of satiric wit. His greatest novel, *Gulliver's Travels* (1726), assured his permanent place in literary history. The ironic tension Swift creates prompts questions about the author's views on humankind. In each of the novel's four books Lemuel Gulliver sets sail on a voyage and ends up in a strange land. In book 1, Gulliver finds himself a giant prisoner of the six-inch-high Lilliputians, whom he saves from invasion from the neighboring Blefuscu. He escapes when he is charged with treason.

In book 2, the hero travels to Brobdingnag, where he finds himself as tiny as a toy in a world of giants. Although loved and pampered as a pet, in fear for his life he manages to escape in the talons of a large bird. In book 3, Gulliver visits the floating island of Laputa, where the islanders are so obsessed with scientific activity, particularly those in the Academy of Lagado (a parody of England's Royal Society), that they are blind to commonplace hazards. Book 4 finds Gulliver in the utopian land of the admirable, enlightened, rational horses, the Houyhnhnms, and the degraded, filthy humans, the Yahoos. Although first accepted as a curiosity by the gentle creatures, Gulliver is soon ousted as despicable because of his human physical characteristics. Although, at the end of his fourth voyage, he returns to England, he finds himself no longer able to tolerate human company and lives out his days in the company of horses.

Swift's ironic novel has no clear-cut explanation. Swift utilizes the various places his hero visits to satirize the folly of humankind. Of the human beings he encounters, the Lilliputians and the Brobdingnagians are impractical and mean-spirited, and the intellectuals in book 3 lack any wisdom, if they are not outright mad. The humanlike Yahoos are contemptible and powerless to express any reason whatsoever, but the Houyhnhnms, the horses, are reasonable and kind.

Swift was certainly not the only esteemed eighteenth century Irish writer. In *The Life and Opinions of Tristram Shandy, Gent.* (1759-1767), humorist Laurence Sterne (1713-1768) made a major contribution to English literature, which secured him the reputation of a major novelist. The book is generally considered the progenitor of the psychological novel and the twentieth century stream-of-consciousness novel popularized by James Joyce and Virginia Woolf. In it, the narrator, Tristram, sets out to do the seemingly impossible: to tell the story of his own life. Beginning at the narrator's moment of conception, Sterne parodies the emerging novelistic form by exploring the relativity of time in human experience. Throughout, the author disorders experiences and mocks the development of narrative by providing no consistent plot or conclusion and by inserting outrageous and lengthy digressions throughout. Ultimately, Tristram realizes the telling of his life's story takes longer than the living of it.

Sterne also penned *A Sentimental Journey Through France and Italy* (1768) in an attempt to teach humans to love their fellow creatures. The novel, which parodies the era's wide range of travel books, had a major impact on the campaign toward sentimentalism prevalent in the second half of the eighteenth century. This movement associated acute sensibility and a sympathetic, tender heart with true virtue. In the novel, the narrator, Parson Yorick, who is frequently moved to tears, sets out to travel through France and Italy in search of "sentimental commerce," or genuine human contact.

In 1761, Frances Sheridan (1724-1766), mother of the famous Irish dramatist Richard Brinsley Sheridan (1751-1816) and much influenced by Samuel Richardson, author of *Pamela: Or, Virtue Rewarded* (1740-1741) and *Clarissa: Or, The History of a Young Lady* (1747-1748), wrote the popular sentimental *Memoirs of Miss Sidney Bidulph* (1761), which considers the effect of extreme suffering on ideal virtue by focusing on the social role assigned to women in eighteenth century society. She also wrote the highly acclaimed and didactic Eastern-themed novel, *The History of Nourjahad* (1767), much in keeping with Samuel Johnson's *Rasselas, Prince of Abyssinia* (1759).

Although Oliver Goldsmith (1728 or 1730-1774) achieved eminence as an essayist (*The Citizen of the World*, 1762), a poet (*The Deserted Village*, 1770), and a dramatist (*She Stoops to Conquer: Or, The Mistakes of a Night*, 1773), he is also well recognized as a novelist for his pastoral novel *The Vicar of Wakefield* (1766). Early in his life, his first calling as a physician was soon submerged by his writing talent, which gained him much literary renown. He was one of the founding members of the famous Literary

Club, which included Samuel Johnson, Sir Joshua Reynolds, David Garrick, Edmund Burke, and James Boswell. The melodramatic *The Vicar of Wakefield* presents a picture of idealized rural village life and the unforgettable vicar, Dr. Charles Primrose. The family's troubles begin when the vicar loses his income and is forced to move the family near the estate of Squire Thornhill, who abducts his daughter Olivia. Next, the vicar's son George is imprisoned after his attempt to avenge his sister. The vicar's troubles continue when his other daughter Sophia is also abducted. After the family's house burns down, the vicar is imprisoned for debt. Despite such hardship, the vicar remains unfailingly charitable throughout. Goldsmith, who had the ability to crystallize the human personality, provides a comic look at the human predicament.

Maria Edgeworth (1767-1849) authentically captures eighteenth and nineteenth century rural Irish life in her popular novels and children's stories. Deeply involved with issues of nationality and cultural identity, Edgeworth is known for presenting the first believable children in the English novel in *The Parent's Assistant: Or, Stories for Children* (1796, 1800). Her actual involvement in running her father's estate in Ireland provided her with the knowledge necessary to authentically characterize rural Irish society in her first novel, *Castle Rackrent* (1800), said to be the first fully developed regional novel and the first true historical novel in English. Edgeworth focused attention on the much-maligned practice of absentee English landowning in *The Absentee* (1812), said to influence Sir Walter Scott to finish his novel *Waverley: Or, 'Tis Sixty Years Since* (1814). *Patronage* (1814) and *Ormond* (1817) explore the relationship between culture and politics and heightened Edgeworth's literary reputation. During the Irish famine in 1846, Edgeworth became a spokesperson for Irish relief.

William Chaigneau (1701-1781) contributed one the earliest Irish novels, *The History of Jack Connor* (1752). A picaresque novel in the tradition of Miguel de Cervantes's *El ingenioso hidalgo don Quixote de la Mancha* (1605, 1615; *Don Quixote de la Mancha*, 1612-1620) and later Henry Fielding's *The History of*

Tom Jones, a Foundling (1749), it concerns the cultural identity of a young Irish man forced to become an English soldier.

THE NINETEENTH CENTURY IRISH NOVEL

The nineteenth century saw progress from sentimentalism to sensationalism with the development of the Irish gothic tradition, which made use of gothic architecture, convoluted plot, emotional intensity, and supernatural agency. The Irish gothic was popularized by Charles Robert Maturin (1780-1824), author of *Melmoth the Wanderer* (1820), which was set inside seventeenth century madhouses, and Joseph Sheridan Le Fanu (1814-1873), author of *The House by the Churchyard* (1863), a tale of a ghostly hand that taps on windows. Undoubtedly, however, the most popular Irish gothic writer is Bram Stoker (1847-1912), the author of the widespread horror tale *Dracula* (1897), the subject of many films. Told principally through multiple diary entries, the tale features the unforgettable undead vampire Count Dracula, who travels to England and there victimizes young Lucy Westerna. Dr. Van Helsing and the young solicitor Jonathan Harker attempt to overpower Dracula and keep him from Mina, Harker's fiancé. After his return to Transylvania, Dracula crumbles to dust after he is beheaded and stabbed through the heart by his captors. Stoker is also the author of the lesser-known *The Snake's Pass* (1890), *The Mystery of the Sea* (1902), *The Jewel of Seven Stars* (1904), and *The Lady of the Shroud* (1909).

Oscar Wilde (1854-1900), another Irish writer better known as a dramatist (*Lady Windermere's Fan*, 1892, and *The Importance of Being Earnest*, 1895) contributed to the Irish gothic tradition by creating one of the most popular nineteenth century novels. *The Picture of Dorian Gray* (serial 1890, expanded 1891) blends supernatural elements with French decadence. The novel caused a great deal of scandal: Wilde declared in the preface that there was no such thing as a moral or immoral book. In the novel, the beautiful youth Dorian Gray has his portrait painted before he turns to a life of vice and corruption. However, the painting has supernatural powers and grows more and more degenerate and corrupted, reflecting the actual appearance of Gray, who maintains his youthful appearance. At the end, Gray kills the artist and stabs the painting; he is discovered as the very image of depravity, a knife through his heart, while the painting depicts an innocent youth. A leader of the aesthetic movement in England and a well-known, flamboyant, social wit, Wilde was greatly influenced by Walter Pater (1839-1894), who advocated art for art's sake.

Although not as popular, George Moore (1852-1933) nevertheless deserves consideration for his innovations in fiction. In his first novels, *A Modern Lover* (1883), set in artistic bohemian society, and *A Mummer's Wife* (1884), he introduced French naturalism into English literature, coming later to utilize the realistic techniques of Gustave Flaubert and Honoré de Balzac. Moore counted among his friends Irish poet and dramatist William Butler Yeats and played a role in the development of the Abbey Theatre. He is best known for his trilogy *Hail and Farewell* (1911-1914) a comic, autobiographical satire in monologue form that features Yeats and Irish dramatist Lady Isabella Augusta Gregory and records the history of the Irish Literary Revival.

THE TWENTIETH CENTURY IRISH NOVEL

While the twentieth century Irish Literary Revival encouraged the publication of poetry, drama, and folklore, Ireland continued producing long-fiction writers. The novelist James Joyce (1882-1941), arguably Ireland's best novelist, is highly celebrated for his experimental use of language. In 1904, in the company of a young girl named Nora Barnacle, Joyce left his native Dublin for the European continent to begin his writing career in earnest. His early stories, and all his later works, feature the city of Dublin—socially frozen and inanimate—and deal almost exclusively with Irish subject matter. Concerned with both the Symbolist and realist literary movements, Joyce integrated both styles, utilizing every word he composed to provide meaning. His autobiographical novel, *A Portrait of the Artist as a Young Man* (serial 1914-1915, book 1916), sketches the development of young Stephen Dedalus, who ultimately leaves Dublin for Paris to dedicate his life to art.

Joyce's best-known novel, *Ulysses* (1922), parallels Homer's *Odyssey* (c. 800 B.C.E.). All the novel's action takes place in Dublin on a single day, June 16, 1904, which has popularly come to be known as Bloomsday. The novel features Stephen Dedalus, the hero of Joyce's earlier novel; Leopold Bloom, an advertising salesman; and his wife Molly Bloom—all modern representations of the mythic Telemachus, Ulysses, and Penelope. Through interior monologue, or the stream-of-consciousness technique, their myriad thoughts, impressions, and feelings—rational and irrational—are revealed as they make their way through the day in Dublin.

Finnegans Wake (1939), written in a unique and extremely difficult but comic style, features the archetypal family, about whom everyone dreams, metaphorically falling and rising. The novel characterizes a Dublin tavern-keeper, Humphrey Chimpden Earwicker; his wife, Mrs. Anna Livia Plurabelle; and their children, Shem, Shaun, and Isabel in a dream sequence throughout the course of one night. In pervasive dreamlike fashion, Joyce utilizes puns throughout, and merges various languages, mythic images, and literary and historical characters to show, albeit obscurely, how history predominates over human experience and relationships.

Although, like Oliver Goldsmith and Oscar Wilde, Samuel Beckett (1906-1989) was more popularly known as a dramatist, he was also widely recognized as a novelist. Strongly influenced by James Joyce (whom he met in Paris), Beckett's popular novel *Murphy* (1938) concerns an Irishman in London who becomes a nurse in a mental institution. While hiding in France during World War II Beckett wrote *Watt* (1953), a highly abstract novel that deals with a servant who continues to work for a master whom he never meets until he is dismissed. Between 1946 and 1949 Beckett wrote *Molloy* (1951; English translation, 1955), *Malone meurt* (1951; *Malone Dies*, 1956), and *L'Innommable* (1953; *The Unnamable*, 1958). Beckett, winner of the Nobel Prize in Literature in 1969, attempts to analyze people's social relationships with one another. His work is thick with literary, historical, and philosophical allusions and draws heavily on the thirteenth century Italian poet

Dante Alighieri, seventeenth century French philosopher René Descartes, and seventeenth century Dutch philosopher Arnold Geulincx, whose philosophy attempts to integrate both the physical and the spiritual sides of men and women. Beckett puzzled continuously over the human condition, considering always who we are and why we are here.

Like Joyce's, Edna O'Brien's (born 1932) work was banned by the Catholic Church in Ireland. Her strict Catholic convent education provided the impetus to write her popular first novel, *The Country Girls* (1960), which concerns solitary women seeking identity and a sense of belonging. This first volume of *The Country Girls Trilogy and Epilogue* (1986) features two Irish girls who leave their strict rural convent school for a more exciting, less curtailed life in Dublin. Their lives are subsequently recorded in *The Lonely Girl* (1962; reprinted in 1964 as *Girl with Green Eyes*) and *Girls in Their Married Bliss* (1964). Disillusioned, both girls leave Dublin for London, finding neither a meaningful connection with men nor happiness in marriage. O'Brien's novels express despair over women's repression and place in contemporary society. Lonely and empty, her female characters, although at times happy, continuously seek fulfillment in doomed erotic relationships.

Although Irish writers are highly recognized for their enormous contributions to poetry and drama, the legacy of Irish long fiction remains splendid and rich. In addition to Joyce, Beckett, and O'Brien, Forrest Reid (1875-1947), Brinsley MacNamara (1890-1963), Peadar O'Donnell (1893-1966), Joyce Cary (1888-1957), Elizabeth Bowen (1899-1973), Francis MacManus (1909-1960), Flann O'Brien (1911-1966), and Mary Lavin (born 1912) carried on the Irish long fiction tradition in the twentieth century.

IRISH LITERATURE INTO THE TWENTY-FIRST CENTURY

Prizewinning novelists Roddy Doyle (born 1958) and Patrick McCabe (born 1955) are two of Ireland's finest contemporary novelists, following in the footprints of earlier Irish literary giants. Roddy Doyle's humorous *Barrytown Trilogy* (1992; includes *The Commitments*, 1987; *The Snapper*, 1990; and *The*

Van, 1991) centers on the irrepressible working-class Rabbitte family in Dublin. His first novel, *The Commitments*, traces the everyday life of the Rabbitte family and their uproarious encounters with a group of working-class Irish teens who form a soul band, the Commitments. *The Snapper* hilariously deals with pregnancy. When nineteen-year-old Sharon Rabbitte becomes pregnant, she refuses to name the father of her "snapper." Her father, Jimmy, Sr., at first feels embarrassed and blames his daughter but eventually takes an active part in Sharon's pregnancy, coming to wonder at the marvels of life and loving. Finally, *The Van* examines male friendship. When Jimmy, Sr., loses his job, what he misses most are his evenings out at the pub with his friends. Although he joins the library and cares for his baby granddaughter, it is not until he and his best pal Bimbo buy a beat-up fish-and-chip van that he gains back his enthusiasm for life. All sections of the trilogy were made into successful films.

In his Booker Prize-winning comic novel *Paddy Clarke, Ha-Ha-Ha* (1993), Doyle captures the wonder and carefree days of youth through the speech patterns of childhood. Ten-year-old Padraic Clarke, or Paddy, runs wild through the streets of Barrytown with his gang of bullying friends, setting fires, playing "Cowboys and Indians," and generally having a good time.

Patrick McCabe has been compared to James Joyce and Samuel Beckett, yet he could easily be classified within the Irish gothic tradition. *The Butcher Boy* (1992), acclaimed as a masterpiece of literary ventriloquism, was short-listed for the 1992 Booker Prize. This finely crafted novel tells the story of a young adolescent's descent into madness and murder. Although Francie Brady, a schoolboy in a small town in 1960's Ireland, has a drunken father and careless mother, his buddy Joe Purcell keeps him on track. When the boys con Philip Nugent out of his comic book collection, Philip's mother calls Francie's family "pigs." Francie the "pig boy" internalizes this insult and comes to hate the socially aspiring Mrs. Nugent. After his mother enters a mental hospital, Francie runs away to Dublin. He discovers upon his return that his mother has committed suicide. Feeling extreme guilt, he breaks into Mrs. Nugent's house

and is then sent to reform school: His best friend Joe at this point befriends his nemesis Philip Nugent, and Francie is lost. He continues his descent into darkness.

McCabe's *Breakfast on Pluto* (1998), another contribution to the author's preferred humorous-macabre genre, is another tale of a youngster not able to come to terms with the conflicts of life in twentieth century Ireland. The emotionally overwrought "Pussy" Braden writes her outrageous memoirs for her psychiatrist, Dr. Terence. A product of the Tyreelin parish priest and his housekeeper, Patrick Braden is abandoned and placed in a foster home with the alcoholic Hairy Braden. The youngster finds deliverance in dreams of stardom and female fashion, winding up with a new name, Pussy, and a new life as a London transvestite hooker. The protagonist soon finds himself in over his head, however, when he starts working for Irish Republican Army (IRA) terrorists. McCabe is also known for his novels *Music on Clinton Street* (1986), *Carn* (1989), and *The Dead School* (1995).

M. Casey Diana

BIBLIOGRAPHY

Augustine, Martin, ed. *The Genius of Irish Prose.* Cork, Ireland: Mercier Press, 1985. Explores the literary constructs that set Irish prose apart from British prose.

Calahan, James M. *Modern Irish Literature and Culture: A Chronology.* New York: G. K. Hall, 1992. Explains events in Irish literature and culture after 1600, connecting historical and political developments with fiction, poetry, and drama.

Deane, Seamus, ed. *The Field Day Anthology of Irish Writing.* New York: W. W. Norton, 1991. Although much anthologized, Irish writing has been concentrated into particular genres. These volumes cover fifteen hundred years of Irish writing, incorporating poetry, prose, short stories, speeches, pamphlets, and longer works.

Hogan, Robert Goode. *Dictionary of Irish Literature.* Westport, Conn.: Greenwood Press, 1996. Focuses primarily on Anglo-Irish writers, specifically essays on major and later Irish writers. Discusses principal themes of Irish writing and the history of Irish writing in English. Provides much critical interpretation.

Leerssen, Joep. *Mere Irish and Fior Ghael: Studies in the Idea of Irish Nationality, Its Development and Literary Expression Prior to the Nineteenth Century.* South Bend, Ind.: Notre Dame University Press, 1997. Examines the idea of Irish national identity, Irish historical background, and how Ireland and the fictional Irish character are represented in English literature.

Mahony, Christina Hunt. *Contemporary Irish Literature: Transforming Tradition.* New York: St. Martin's Press, 1999. Presents the works of contemporary Irish writers of fiction, drama, and poetry, with literary and historical chronologies. Includes contributions from Northern Ireland.

Thuente, Mary Helen. *The Harp Re-Strung: The United Irishmen and the Rise of Irish Literary Nationalism.* Syracuse, N.Y.: Syracuse University Press, 1994. A scholarly work that contends that Irish literary nationalism began as long ago as 1790, rather than in the 1840's, as has been argued.

Welch, Robert, ed. *The Oxford Companion to Irish Literature.* New York: Clarendon Press, 1996. More than two thousand entries cover the major works and writers, literary genres, folklore, and mythology, along with articles on Protestantism, Catholicism, Northern Ireland, the IRA, and the political and cultural background necessary to understand Irish literature.

ITALIAN LONG FICTION

It was argued by no less a figure than Giovanni Papini (1881-1956) that Italians are less suited temperamentally to writing novels than to writing poetry, essays, and biographies. Certainly, the art of storytelling has been long esteemed in Italy; Baldassare Castiglione, in *Il libro del cortegiano* (1528; *The Courtier*, 1561), listed it as one of the attributes of the perfect gentleman. It was simply the length of the fictional narrative that Italians were slow to elaborate. This lack of experimental spirit probably had more to do with historical factors (such as illiteracy, lack of a unified country, and the persistent *questione della lingua* controversy) than with temperament.

THE BEGINNINGS OF THE ITALIAN NOVEL

Besides drawing upon the *novellino* (storybook) tradition of Giovanni Boccaccio, Franco Sacchetti, Matteo Bandello, and many other early Italian writers, would-be Italian novelists of the nineteenth century looked to the narrative-in-verse genre of the eighteenth and nineteenth centuries, such as Johann Wolfgang von Goethe's *Hermann und Dorothea* (1797; *Herman and Dorothea*, 1801), and to the novels and verse of Sir Walter Scott. In Scott, especially, Italians saw the possibility of using adventurous tales of a more substantial length to publicize their cause of political unification.

Giovanni Berchet (1783-1851), whose famous *Lettera semiseria di Crisostomo* (1816; semiserious letter from Crisostomo) was conceived in support of Madame de Staël's recommendation that Italians imitate the new Romantic tendencies of the German writers, himself contributed a major work to the narrative-in-verse genre with his anti-British *I profughi di Parga* (1823; the refugees of Parga). Tommaso Grossi (1790-1853), who wrote Romantic novellas in octaves, bridged the gap between the verse novel and the prose novel in 1834 when he published *Marco Visconti* (1834; *Marco Visconti: A Romance of the Fourteenth Century*, 1907), a historical novel set in Lombardy in the fourteenth century.

The year 1827 was a milestone in the development of the novel in Italy, for during that year were published *Il castello di Trezzo* (the castle of Trezzo), by Giambattista Bazzoni (1803-1850); *Sibilla Odaleta*, by the "Italian Sir Walter Scott," Carlo Varese (1793-1866); *La battaglia di Benevento* (*Manfred: Or, The Battle of Benevento*, 1875), by Francesco Domenico Guerrazzi (1804-1873); and *I promessi sposi* (1827, revised 1840-1842; *The Betrothed*, 1828, revised 1951), by Alessandro Manzoni (1785-1873). The historical novel became so fashionable in subsequent years that Manzoni himself felt compelled, out of his respect for the incontrovertible facts of history, to decry its further cultivation as a genre in his essay "Del romanzo storico" (1845; on the historical novel).

Like most of the other Italian novelists of this period, Manzoni was Milanese; his grandfather was the humanitarian criminologist Cesare Beccaria (1738-1794), whose treatise *Dei delitti e delle pene* (1764; *On Crimes and Punishments*, 1767) is credited with eliminating from European criminal law the use of torture. Manzoni's mother, Giulia Beccaria, separated from his father, and, in 1805, the future novelist went to live with her in Paris, where his friendship with Claude Fauriel brought him under the influence of the Romantic movement. Manzoni's wife's conversion from Calvinism to Catholicism was soon followed by his own, and it was still under the influence of his conversion that he began work on his masterpiece, *The Betrothed*. The impulse to write a historical novel came mainly from his reading of Scott, but his idea for the plot came from a proclamation that he happened to read regarding forced or prevented marriages, issued in October, 1627, by the Spanish governor of Lombardy.

Although Manzoni finished writing the novel in 1823, its publication was not complete until 1827. Displeased with his style, Manzoni began a thorough revision and visited Florence "to wash his rags in the Arno" and thereby increase his sensitivity to the Tuscan literary standard, which would thirty years later become the language of a united Italy. The revised edition, greatly improved in style and in lexical choice but hardly changed at all in content, was published in parts between 1840 and 1842. Writing within a tradition that emphasized the pompous and academic rhetoric of the medieval and Renaissance masters, Manzoni—with a superb ear for dialogue—achieved a remarkable reconciliation between the spoken and the written language as the vehicle for his narrative. Joining the *questione della lingua* controversy that has plagued Italy since the time of Dante, Manzoni argued to the end of his life that Italian writers should conform to the contemporary usage of cultured Florentines.

The Betrothed takes place in Lombardy between 1628 and 1631; the protagonists, the humble silk-weavers Renzo and Lucia, are already betrothed when the story opens. Unfortunately, Lucia has attracted the attention of the unscrupulous Don Rodrigo, who is determined to have her. His henchmen prevent the village priest from performing the marriage, and for their own safety, the two are separated (Renzo is sent to Milan, Lucia to Monza). Throughout the rest of the novel, the reader lives, suffers, and hopes with the ill-starred couple at the mercy of the whims of the rich and powerful and menaced by war, famine, and plague. Manzoni depicts his large cast of characters with a gentle humor that stems from his own delight in the variations of the human personality. As a fictional creation, Renzo is thoroughly convincing; Lucia, however, is more a Romantic period piece than a typical peasant girl.

Although *The Betrothed* was widely read and translated, it failed to win an important place in the gallery of Western literary achievements. Manzoni failed to assimilate fully his historical material; many of his pages are unadulterated history, some encumbered by lengthy quotations from documents and others footnoted with references to actual historical texts.

Manzoni's ever-present Catholicism is perhaps another factor that accounts for his novel's lack of world-wide popularity. The glow of his religious belief, which allows the unfortunate couple to persevere against all odds and serves to counterbalance the dark, cruel world that they must inhabit, does not communicate itself well to many modern readers. Alberto Moravia observed that Manzoni had to choose the seventeenth century as the setting for his novel precisely because that was the last time that Catholic belief was strong, even in Italy. Renzo and Lucia survive because they are sheltered by a magical and encompassing Providence. Providence is what moves the hardened brigand L'Innominato ("The Unnamed") to pity when he hears the supplications of Lucia; Providence is responsible for striking Don Rodrigo dead with plague; and Providence is what makes an eventual reunion of the lovers possible.

Manzoni's son-in-law Massimo D'Azeglio (1798-1866), a member of an aristocratic Piedmontese family who became an important figure in the Risorgimento, wrote historical novels to inspire Italians with pride in their past. *Ettore Fieramosca: O, La sfida di Barletta* (1833; *Ettore Fieramosca: Or, The Challenge of Barletta*, 1854) takes its title from a famous challenge made by thirteen Italian knights at Barletta to a like number of French knights, as recorded by Francesco Guicciardini in his *Storia d'Italia* (1561-1564; *The Historie of Guicciardin*, 1579; better known as *The History of Italy*, 1753-1756), to which plot D'Azeglio added the story of a despondent protagonist who commits suicide. Another of D'Azeglio's novels, *Niccolò dei Lapi* (1841; English translation, 1850), follows the siege of Florence in 1530 and the fortunes of a republican family; this same siege was used in the title of a novel by Guerrazzi, *L'assedio di Firenze* (1836; the siege of Florence).

The novel from the era between Manzoni and Giovanni Verga that is most esteemed today is *Le confessioni di un ottuagenario* (1867; partially translated as *The Castle of Fratta*, 1954), by the Paduan journalist and poet Ippolito Nievo (1831-1861). Nievo's narrator, Carlo Altoviti, is an octogenarian who, though Venetian, wishes to die an Italian. The old man tells his story from before the time of the French Revolution; his youthful love affair with Pisana at the Castle of Fratta is the portion of this very long and sometimes digressive novel that was excerpted and translated into English. Nievo, a colonel in Giuseppe Garibaldi's Thousand fighting against the Bourbons, died the untimely victim of a shipwreck in the Tyrrhenian Sea at the age of thirty.

NATURALISM IN THE ITALIAN NOVEL

The Sicilian Luigi Capuana (1839-1915) did much to incorporate the precepts of French naturalism into Italian literature. Capuana saw the novel as a purely scientific study and as a means to social progress. A man of great versatility, he wrote short stories, children's books, criticism, and plays in Sicilian dialect; he was a bird-watcher, teacher, folklorist, and twice mayor of his native town of Mineo in Sicily. Capuana's novel *Giacinta* (1879), one of the first realistic novels written in Italian, is marred by an incongruous emphasis on the occult. In *Il profumo* (1890; perfume), Capuana explored an abnormal erotic situation. His most lasting work is *Il marchese di Roccaverdina* (1901; the marquis of Roccaverdina), a detective novel of sorts about a Sicilian landowner and his murdered agent. Capuana's characterization of Agrippina Solmi, the landowner's humble peasant mistress, elicited high critical praise, notably from Benedetto Croce. Capuana's influence on Italian fiction, however, stems not from his novels (unfortunately, he never got beyond a dependence on gimmicky, weird effects) but rather from his short stories and from his influence on his friend and fellow Sicilian Giovanni Verga (1840-1922).

Verga, who is accorded the honor of following Manzoni in the hierarchy of Italian novelists, left Sicily and, following the example of Manzoni, went to Florence in 1865 in order to perfect his Italian. In Florence, he acquired instant fame for *Storia di una capinera* (1871; the story of a blackcap), about a young nun in love. There followed four more similarly sentimental novels before he found his true métier, depicting the world of the Sicilian peasant, in the short story "Nedda" (1874). The characters that began to interest Verga in this new, more mature period of his career were poor people, farm workers, or fishermen, and he describes them sparely, without authorial introduction or commentary. Readers of Verga, like readers of William Faulkner, are offered a fictional world that they must interpret for themselves.

While it is true that for Verga the author's lot is to record and not to judge, Verga's fiction nevertheless pulsates with the compassion that he dared not put into words. His attitude toward the precarious existence of his beleaguered peasants, so completely at the mercy of natural forces that remain indifferent to the concerns of humans, is reminiscent of the poetic stance of Giacomo Leopardi (1798-1837). Whereas the ultimate reality had been for Manzoni a boundless Catholic faith, it was for Verga a fatal inevitability, contingent upon circumstances and conditioned somewhat by economic security.

In the six years after his "discovery" of *Verismo* (the Italian literary movement that partakes of both realism and naturalism), Verga wrote short stories and one minor novel but was concerned mainly with the preparation of his greatest work, *I Malavoglia* (1881; *The House by the Medlar Tree*, partial translation 1890, 1953; complete translation 1964). The good-hearted but frugal grandfather, Master 'Ntoni, watches his brood of grandchildren grow up to disappoint his fondest dreams of prosperity for the family. Nature is at its harshest in a storm at sea that destroys a boatload of lupine purchased on credit and in a cholera epidemic that takes its toll on members of his family. To pay for the lost cargo of lupine, the family must give up their beloved house by the medlar tree. When the grandfather hears that his oldest grandson and namesake has been brought to trial for smuggling, he has a stroke and dies. A younger grandson, Alessi, Verga's symbol of faith in traditional hard work, is able to buy back the house by the medlar tree, and the novel ends with the suggestion that, despite the reversals of fortune, once again the Malavoglia may be as "numerous as the stones on the old Trezza road."

Even before the publication of this novel, Verga had conceived the idea—probably inspired by Honoré de Balzac's *La Comédie humaine* (1829-1848; *The Comedy of Human Life*, 1885-1893, 1896; also known as *The Human Comedy*, 1895-1896, 1911) and Émile Zola's *Les Rougon-Macquart* (1871-1893; *The Rougon-Macquart Family*, 1879-1924)—of composing a cycle of five novels entitled "La marea" (the tide) or "I vinti" (the doomed), which would study successive stages in the human struggle for material security. *The House by the Medlar Tree* was to be the first of the cycle, depicting the struggle for minimal needs alone, but unfortunately only one of the four projected novels was finished—*Mastro-don Gesualdo* (1889; English translation, 1893, 1923), the epic of a self-made man who lusts insatiably after greater and greater wealth and who, as a result of his greed, must die alone.

Although it was Capuana who influenced Verga to write in the manner of Zola and Gustave Flaubert, Verga had always been a pessimist and did not require a model on which to base his gloom. Although he is seen as the *verista par excellence* of Italian fiction, he was not dogmatic about his literary ideas. His greatest achievement was to "invent" a language that, while not employing the Sicilian dialect that his peasant characters would naturally speak, echoed their dialect in its phrasing, in its cadences, in its simplicity, and in its repetitions. This echoing of the Sicilian dialect in standard Italian is perceived even in portions of Verga's fiction that are not written in direct discourse. His style is laconic and inherently tragic in its intensity, yet in its selectivity it is also poetic.

One of Verga's closest friends, Federico De Roberto (1861-1927), was born in Naples but grew up in Sicily and considered himself Sicilian. Torn between Verga's regionalism and the emphasis on the psychological analysis of author Paul Bourget (1852-1935), he abandoned the peasant world of his early fiction for a more complex middle- and upper-class cast of characters. De Roberto's masterpiece *I vicerè* (1894; *The Viceroys*, 1962) is a historical and psychological study of three generations of the aristocratic Uzeda family, as well as a bitterly ironic indictment of politicians. According to Sergio Pacifici, there is enough packed into this sweeping novel to satisfy all tastes: a Manzonian taste for miniature biographies that probe psychology, Verga's emphasis on economic causes of people's fate, the psychological approach of Bourget and Capuana, the scientific approach of Zola, the regional approach of *Verismo*, and the stylistic clarity of Flaubert.

Despite its poverty and backward social conditions, Naples during the second half of the nineteenth century was a hotbed of literary creativity, producing significant works of criticism (by Benedetto Croce and Francesco De Sanctis), philosophy (by Croce and Bertrando Spaventa), poetry (by Salvatore Di Giacomo), and theater (by Roberto Bracco). It was in Naples that Greek-born Matilde Serao (1856-1927), of mixed Italian and Greek parentage, chose to make her home, depicting it realistically in her fiction. Fiction for Serao was not so much an art form as a mission, and the effect of Zola's naturalism is evident from her first works. The heroes of her fiction are lowly slum dwellers, and she is at her best describing the hopes and broken dreams of children and the emotions of women who are betrayed in love. Her best work is *Il paese di Cuccagna* (1890; *The Land of Cockayne*, 1901), a study of the lottery and the evil effects that it wreaks on all classes of society. Despite the precision of her Neopolitan settings and her keen powers of empathy for the poverty-stricken masses, her work is marred by excessive sentimentality, a lack of unity, and occasional grammatical carelessness.

Despite the inevitable recognition of Verga's genius, for a quarter of a century following the publication of *Daniele Cortis* (1885; English translation, 1887), it was the Vicenzan Antonio Fogazzaro (1842-1911) who was viewed as the heir presumptive of Manzoni in the line of Italian novelists. He remains today a good example of how desperately the Italian bourgeoisie tried to believe during a time in the post-Risorgimento period when belief was seriously questioned. Since Fogazzaro dealt exclusively with the social class to which he so comfortably belonged and seemed impervious to the socioeconomic problems of his recently unified country and the misery in which the majority of his compatriots lived, his books have less relevance to the majority of readers today than they did to a minority during the time they were written.

Content to perpetuate the traditional prose style of Manzoni, Fogazzaro employed a lofty vocabulary that today smacks of decadence. He was, nevertheless, the first major novelist to incorporate dialect into his literary Italian; this earned for him the censure of many critics. In the manner of Scott's introduction of "braid Scots" into portions of his novels dealing with Scottish life, Fogazzaro availed himself of Lombard, Venetian, Tuscan (with its guttural *gorgia*, or burr), Roman, and Sicilian words and accents in order to render character more faithfully. His forte was characterization rather than plot, and he was noted for the skill with which he captured the natural beauty of the Italian lake region.

Fogazzaro's masterpiece, *Piccolo mondo antico* (1896; *The Patriot*, 1907), depicts the idealized little world of the late Risorgimento and is a love story, as are many of Fogazzaro's plots. Through his protagonists, Franco and Luisa Maironi, the author explores two opposing views of life: the religious view of Franco and the skepticism of Luisa. When their child Obretta is drowned, the disconsolate mother dabbles in Spiritualism; Fogazzaro, like Capuana, was interested in the occult, although not enough to classify him as a decadent author. The novel ends happily as Luisa conceives another child, Piero. Fogazzaro's next two novels concern Piero's development through his worldly stage (*Piccolo mondo Moderno*, 1900; *The Man of the World*, 1907) and on into his spiritual stage (*Il santo*, 1905; *The Saint*, 1906). After Piero becomes a lay brother in the latter novel, he assumes the name Benedetto and ultimately takes on the Pope himself, lecturing the sympathetic but virtually powerless pontiff on the four "evil spirits" that infect the Church—falsehood, greed, immobility, and clericalism.

Leila (1910; English translation, 1910), the last novel of the Piero Maironi tetralogy and Fogazzaro's swan song, addresses the question of what can be done now that all the proposed solutions have been rejected. Like Luisa, Leila represents the skeptical nature of Italian immorality. She eventually marries Massimo Alberti, a favorite disciple of Benedetto "the Saint" who, after his own disillusionment with the Church, takes refuge in the pure altruism of his medical practice. While sadly accepting the official decision of the Church, Fogazzaro can only recommend the diverting solace of humanitarianism.

Fogazzaro was caught in the middle: His ideas about church reform brought charges of Protestantism from the papal contingent, and his novel *The Saint*, soon followed by *Leila*, was placed on the Index; his sympathy with the less radical aspect of socialism, however, was not Marxist enough to please the Marxists. Besides a greater openness within the Church itself, Fogazzaro advocated a stricter application of Christian morality to everyday life. If Italians of subsequent generations were indifferent to the issue of church reform, the issue later regained some of its former immediacy, and the novels of Fogazzaro managed to retain a reading public through the generations. Films and television dramatizations were made from some of his novels, and the future novelist Mario Soldati directed a film of *The Little World of the Past* in 1941.

Another contender for second place in the literary hierarchy after Manzoni, one whose reputation declined even more sharply than Fogazzaro's, is Edmondo De Amicis (1846-1908), born in Oneglia in Liguria on the Italian Riviera. Indeed, in his treatise *L'idioma gentile* (1905; pure language), which reaffirms the superiority of the Florentine dialect, he stands out as a staunch Manzonian, at least in linguistic matters. Educated for the army, De Amicis fought in the Battle of Custozza (1866), which established Italy as a kingdom. His first book of sketches, *La Vita militare* (1868; *Military Life in Italy*, 1882), was based on his military experience. He was a great traveler and a prolific writer of travel books, about foreign countries (Morocco, Spain, Holland), foreign cities (London and Paris), and even remote regions within Italy (Basilicata).

De Amicis's best work, immensely successful but hopelessly sentimental by today's standards, is *Cuore* (1886; *The Heart of a Boy*, 1895), a series of sketches describing the life of a twelve-year-old boy attending the Turin public school system. The book was used in Italian schools until the advent of Fascism and was long a favorite for teaching Italian in the United States. Despite the disrepute into which his sentimentalism fell (even his contemporary Giosuè Carducci dubbed him "Edmondo the Languorous"), one cannot but admire De Amicis's conviction that there is something wondrous and lovable in every child. Nor was De Amicis indifferent to the social ills of his day; in 1891, he became a socialist. His long novel, *Sull'oceano* (1889; *On Blue Water*, 1897), unfortunately no more than a mere string of anecdotes, is devoted to the ordeal of illiterate emigrants as they make their interminable ocean crossing from Italy to a new life in the New World. In a subsequent novel, *Il romanzo d'un maestro* (1890; *The Romance of a Schoolmaster*, 1892), which deals with the idealism of a young schoolteacher pitted against uninspired politicians and supervisors, De Amicis showed the same lack of constructive ability, and in his final years, which were saddened by the suicide of his son, he turned his attention to linguistic matters.

Another novelist noted for his strong moral sense and his compassion for his fellow humans is the Milanese Emilio De Marchi (1851-1901), who has also been compared to Manzoni but who lacks much of the latter's stylistic elegance and religious feeling. Nevertheless, Sergio Pacifici suggests that a reevaluation of De Marchi's contribution to Italian literature is in order, noting with optimism that in modern times a film was made of his detective novel about a murdered priest, *Il cappello del prete* (1888; the priest's hat).

Avoiding all mention of contemporary events, De Marchi was committed to depicting the sad reality of the monotonous bourgeois life led by some Italians, and for this reason, he has been compared to the French naturalists. His most accomplished novel is *Demetrio Pianelli* (1890), about a simple office clerk who is transformed, through a series of reversals, from an unheroic, retiring type of individual into a caring individual who learns to give without thought of reward (for example, he arranges the marriage of his widowed sister-in-law, Beatrice, to a wealthy relative, even though he himself is enamored of Beatrice).

ITALIAN LONG FICTION IN THE TWENTIETH CENTURY

The leading novelist of the first decades of the twentieth century was the Sardinian Grazia Deledda (1871-1936), who won the Nobel Prize in Literature in 1927. By the time of her marriage (1900) and her subsequent removal from Sardinia to Rome, she had already published several collections of essays. Inasmuch as the best of her twenty-five novels are set in Sardinia and depict the primitive conditions of the island, Deledda is classified as a regionalist writer. Her characters struggle against their primitive back-

ground, as in *Elias Portolu* (1903; English translation, 1992), in which the hero, returning from imprisonment for a crime he did not commit, falls in love with his brother's fiancé and, in desperation, is forced to become a priest. *Le colpe altrui* (1914; the faults of others), a novel of tragic perplexities in which good and evil seem to be enmeshed and whose conclusion recognizes the inevitability of evil, is a plea for mutual forgiveness. *La madre* (1920; *The Mother*, 1923, 1974; also known as *The Woman and the Priest*, 1922) is the bitter tale of a mother who strives to make her son—a priest—forget the woman he loves. At the moment of crisis, when the priest seems about to be exposed by his mistress before his congregation, the mother dies, and her son knows instantly that the "shock of that same grief, that same terror which he had been enabled to overcome," was responsible for her death. The entire plot unfolds within the space of two days, and the story is told chiefly in the mother's emotional reactions to the situation.

After 1920, Deledda abandoned the Sardinian background, and her last novels show the influence of Fyodor Dostoevski. Despite her prolonged use of the Sardinian setting, she is more complex than the average regionalistic realist writer; her concerns are, rather, the struggle between good and evil and the temptation of sensual love. In the words of the Swedish Academy, she was honored "for her idealistically inspired writings which with plastic clarity picture the life on her native island and with depth and sympathy deal with human problems in general."

One of the most widely discussed writers of all of Italian literature, Gabriele D'Annunzio (1863-1938), versatile, prolific, and charismatic, is generally dealt with in Italian literary histories more as a poet and as a dramatist than as a novelist, though his fiction was undeniably popular. In fact, D'Annunzio turned from poetry to fiction because he believed that the novel was the genre of the future.

D'Annunzio was a sensualist in the tradition of the Marquis de Sade, Charles Baudelaire, Joris-Karl Huysmans, and Oscar Wilde, and the Romantic novels that he wrote represent a break both with *Verismo* and with the historical novel. The scientific and sociological preoccupations of the *veristi* are replaced in D'Annunzio by a realism of the senses. Pathological psychology, such a noticeable feature of Capuana's short stories, is present in D'Annunzio as well—for example, Tullio, in *L'innocente* (1892; *The Intruder*, 1898), fantasizes about making love to a woman while she is ill—but his novels are weak on plot and characterization. D'Annunzio himself is his own main character, and all of his novels involve a strikingly joyless search for pleasure; his strength lies in his sensitivity to the musical potential of combinations of words.

Il piacere (1889; *The Child of Pleasure*, 1898) is the story of Andrea Spinelli, who is saturated with art, "demanding only experience and more experience of the sharpest kind to feed it," and who moves in a world of duels, fox hunts, and intrigue. D'Annunzio's next attempt at the novel, *The Intruder*, is a psychological study of a Nietzschean Superman, Tullio Hermil, who conspires with his wife to murder her son born of an extramarital indiscretion. Finding this novel "the least D'Annunzian" of D'Annunzio's novels, Luchino Visconti more than eighty years later made a film of *The Intruder* (1975). To accommodate contemporary realism, Visconti felt it necessary to make only one change in his script: Whereas D'Annunzio allowed Tullio to survive the murder "at a level of experience beyond conventional standards of good and evil," Visconti has Tullio commit suicide.

Less pretentious, more unified, and possibly his best novel is *Il trionfo della morte* (1894; *The Triumph of Death*, 1896), in which Giorgio Aurispa loves a woman so intensely that he feels he must destroy her. This novel particularly benefits from its vivid sense of the primitive quality of life in D'Annunzio's native Abruzzi region. *Il fuoco* (1900; *The Flame of Life*, 1900), which baldly details the liaison between a young poet and an older actress, was based on the author's own affair with Eleanora Duse. The descriptions of Venice in this novel are noted by the *Encyclopedia Britannica* (1956) as "perhaps the most ardent glorification of a city existing in any language." A master of embellishment, D'Annunzio is remembered in the annals of Italian fiction primarily for the decorative effect of what he wrote rather than for its content.

Although D'Annunzio fancied himself the mentor and soothsayer of Benito Mussolini, and indeed he contributed to Fascism the famous war cry *Eja, Eja, allala* and was responsible for the militia uniform with the tasseled cap, the thrill of literary creation was always more important to D'Annunzio than groveling for power. In the late twentieth century, there was a minor reassessment of D'Annunzio as a writer, and his influence on Stefan George, Hugo von Hofmannsthal, Heinrich Mann, and Henry de Montherlant was noted; Jackson I. Cope even argued for D'Annunzio's influence upon the young James Joyce (*Joyce's Cities: Archeologies of the Soul*, 1981).

A novelist who wrote in the same vein as D'Annunzio is Alfredo Oriani (1852-1909), a Decadent vulgarian later lionized by the Fascists. Born in Faenza, this tireless writer of novels, plays, and political commentary began as a *verista* and was greatly influenced by French journalism and parliamentary oratory. When he abjured the excesses of Decadence, it was to embrace the excesses of colonial messianism. Many of his ideals are found in what is considered his best novel, *La disfatta* (1896; the defeat), the drama of a scholar and the woman whom he loves and eventually marries. As he sees his son and his friends die and fails to win recognition for his scholarly pursuits, he comes to the disconsolate realization that his life is empty and that his defeat consists in his failure to move onward with life. Oriani's characterizations are effective, and the many ideas that crowd his novels are at least vitally represented, but he stands out more as an intuitive thinker of Hegelian stripe than as a novelist.

As D'Annunzio's novels were being hailed in their French translations as proof of a Latin Renaissance, one writer who found D'Annunzian conventions congenial and faithfully echoed them in her early stories of unhappy heroines is Sibilla Aleramo (1876-1960). Born Rina Faccio in Alessandria of bourgeois parents, she was continuously and irresistibly drawn to men of artistic temperament regardless of physical considerations, and the life she lived is in itself suitable for a novel. When a young poet forty years her junior came to interview the sixty-year-old Aleramo about her liaison with the poet

Dino Campana (1885-1932), the subject of the young poet's university thesis, he himself became involved in a decade-long liaison with the older woman.

Although D'Annunzio dubbed Aleramo his "attentive sister" and she herself was dubbed a female D'Annunzio, her D'Annunzian stance was significantly tempered by her encounter with the sociology of Guglielmo Ferrero (1871-1942), and in 1906, she wrote *Una donna* (1906; *A Woman at Bay*, 1908; also as *A Woman*, 1980), a lightly fictionalized memoir hailed immediately as an international classic and taken as a proclamation that women are human beings entitled to fulfill their ideals. Although she was one of the few courageous intellectuals who dared to sign Benedetto Croce's anti-Fascist manifesto, she eventually supported Mussolini and said she envied D'Annunzio for having been spared the horror of witnessing the outcome of Fascism. Still later, however, she became a militant communist and read from her poetry at proletarian rallies.

Although originally an admirer of D'Annunzio and, like D'Annunzio, sympathetic with Fascism, the Sicilian Luigi Pirandello (1867-1936) managed to break free of D'Annunzian influence. In 1929, before the Italian Academy, Pirandello boldly took his revenge for a full thirty years of fame that D'Annunzio had usurped from him by broadly categorizing human types as either superficial "spinners of words" or more productive "spinners of things." It was the theater in which Pirandello excelled and for which he won the Nobel Prize in 1934, but he was also a master of the novella. He began his literary career as a poet and, at the urging of the ever-influential Capuana, applied himself to long fiction in 1893, the year he returned from his philological studies in Germany.

Pirandello wrote several novels, the third of which is his most acclaimed, *Il fu Mattia Pascal* (1904; *The Late Mattia Pascal*, 1923), a significant influence on the *teatro grottesco* of Luigi Chiarelli (1880-1947). Tired of his marriage and his job as a librarian, Pascal uses a false newspaper report of his suicide as an excuse to flee and assume a new identity. Assuming this new identity, however, is impossible, because he lacks proper identification, and when he decides to return home, he finds that because his wife has re-

married, he has lost his old identity as well. Pirandello's powerful sense of irony, evident here as well as in his drama, derives from Ludovico Ariosto and Niccolò Machiavelli and was tempered by Verga's vision of humanity (although Pirandello abhorred being called a *verista*) as a world of vanquished souls bound together in a religion of compassion. This novel stands thematically at a point midway between Pirandello's early emphasis on humans as a type within society and his later emphasis on the inner nature of humans, and structurally between the novels emphasizing plot and setting and those that abandon external reality to explore the characters' inner reality.

In an age of D'Annunzian rhetoric that followed a period of brutally candid *Verismo*, the uncomplicated storytelling of the conservative Romagnol Alfredo Panzini (1863-1939) must have been welcomed by more than a few readers. Although he had a fine sense of balance, tempering his criticism with humor, Panzini was a thoroughly bourgeois writer, unmoved by the wretchedness of the masses, and while he could represent pathos, he could not depict tragedy. *Io cerco moglie* (1920; *Wanted—A Wife*, 1921), his only novel translated into English, purports to analyze different kinds of women but reveals the author's conviction that there are only two: those a man falls in love with and those a man marries. His best novel, *La madonna di mamá* (1916; the madonna-mother), traditional in every sense, elaborates the theme of a young man's move from the country to the city and turns into a war novel with crepuscular overtones.

Marino Moretti (1885-1979), one of the original three poets to whose work the gifted critic, novelist, and playwright Giuseppe Borgese (1882-1952) first applied the term *crepuscolari* (twilight poets) in 1910, was also a novelist and, like Panzini, from Romagna. Moretti's fiction is meditative, Catholic in the tradition of Manzoni, and particularly effective when dealing with the melancholy nature of the humble characters for whom Moretti cherished a special love. His peasants are from his native Romagna, a region with a long history of violence and sensuality capable of producing within a single generation the likes of Mussolini and Giovanni Pascoli. The gallery of Moretti's characters, who suffer but do not despair, is remarkably large, and he is particularly effective in his portrayal of women characters, as in *Il sole del sabato* (1907; the sun of the Sabbath).

Sometimes classified together as Tuscan storytellers *par excellence* are Enrico Pea (1881-1958), Bruno Cicognani (1879-1971), and Aldo Palazzeschi (1885-1974). As a result of having had little formal education and an early period spent living in Egypt, Pea was freer than most of his contemporaries from hampering literary conventions. He wrote from personal rather than intellectual or literary experience, and his books (for example, *Moscardino*, 1922; English translation, 1956) create a fablelike atmosphere that depends little on structure or chronology.

More intellectual is Cicognani, a Florentine lawyer who used his daily practice for human observation and, like Pea, worked outside the literary mainstream. His first novel, *La crittogama* (1908; the cryptogram), was written under the influence of D'Annunzio, while *La velia* (1923; the shrike) is an Italian version of Gustave Flaubert's *Madame Bovary* (1857). Although his portraits of immoral women place him with the French naturalists and his cultivation of Florence as his setting links him with *Verismo*, the psychological dimension he gives to his characters aspires to universality.

Palazzeschi, born Aldo Giurlani and an only child of bourgeois parents, first turned to poetry and participated in both the Futurist and the crepuscular movements. His first novel, dispensing with plot, dramatic action, and dialogue, was the epistolary *Riflessi* (1908; also as *Allegoria di novembre*, 1944), remarkable for its attempt to represent a homosexual relationship between a Roman prince, Valentino Core, and a young Briton, John More. In order that the relationship remain pure and perfect (and therefore socially acceptable), any depiction of bodily contact is scrupulously avoided; the prince writes Johnny daily letters until one day the prince mysteriously vanishes, apparently a suicide. The decadence of its setting and language is reminiscent of D'Annunzio; this influence persists in the futuristic *Il codice di perelà* (1911; *Perelà, the Man of Smoke*, 1936; also

as *Perelà, uomo di fumo*, 1954) and *La piramide* (1926; the pyramid). There is, however, the flavor of Manzoni in *Sorelle Materassi* (1926; *Materassi Sisters*, 1953), a tableau of Tuscan life during the 1930's depicting the relationship of two lonely women with their orphaned adolescent nephew Remo, who brings warmth into their empty house but takes advantage of them financially. As a narrator, Palazzeschi is sympathetic but aloof, and his gentle laughter is the only judgment that he makes on the all-too-human folly of his characters. The contrast between the misguided dreams of the young and the materially adequate but spiritually deficient ambience that they must inhabit reappears as the theme of his less successful later novels, *I fratelli Cuccoli* (1948; the Cuccoli brothers) and *Roma* (1953; English translation, 1965).

Another Tuscan writer, Federigo Tozzi (1883-1920), whose abrasive genius contrasts with the traditional emphasis on *il bello stile* (beautiful style), underwent a reevaluation during the postwar period and became ranked by Alberto Moravia in fourth place among Italian novelists, after Manzoni, Italo Svevo, and Verga. The product of an unhappy childhood, Tozzi wrote tragic and autobiographical fiction, tempered only by a trace of Dostoevskian compassion. Like his mentor Verga, he was interested in the effect of property on people's lives; material wealth for Tozzi was an obstacle to be overcome if people were to find their way in the woods. In *Il podere* (1921; the farm), remarkable for its suffusion of tragedy rather than for its plot, Remigio returns home to take over the management of a farm from his dying father, a return that for Tozzi betokens a retrogression and a setting forth on the road toward death.

Tre croci (1920; *Three Crosses*, 1921) takes its title from the graves of the three brothers whose lack of moral fortitude leads to their successive catastrophes. The brothers inherit a bookstore from their father. Business is bad, so they borrow money, eventually become involved in fraud, and nevertheless continue to waste money that they do not have on gormandizing. The portraits of the three, with their idiosyncrasies, fears, temper tantrums, and gluttony, are studies of unusual depth. Unfortunately, the author's own untimely death deprived him of seeing either of these novels in print, but today overdue recognition is granted him as a forerunner of Franz Kafka and existentialism.

Farther removed from the mainstream than even Tozzi is Italo Svevo (1861-1928), literally "Italo the Swabian," the pen name of Ettore Schmitz. Born in Trieste of Jewish parents, his father was of German-Italian parentage and his mother a native Triestine. Svevo's father sent him to Germany to perfect his German, which was vital to the boy's future in what was then the Austro-Hungarian port city of Trieste. He was an Italian citizen only for the last decade of his life (1918-1928).

Although he always yearned to be a writer, Svevo's literary success was retarded first by economic necessity and then, after the appearance of *Una vita* (1892; *A Life*, 1963) and *Senilità* (1898; *As a Man Grows Older*, 1932), by public indifference. For the next quarter of a century, Svevo did not publish, although he did continue to write. His friendship with James Joyce led eventually to the publication of his third novel, *La coscienza di Zeno* (1923; *Confessions of Zeno*, 1930), which became popular in France and only later in Italy.

Svevo's antiacademic writing style—dry, too close to the Triestine dialect, and perhaps influenced by the author's greater fluency in German—alienated many critics, although those readers nourished on Verga and Tozzi admired him. His helpless characters are intelligent anomalies, portrayed in the first two novels with the objectivity of the French naturalists. *A Life* is about the insincerity of Alfonso Nitti's love affair with his employer's daughter and his humdrum white-collar life, and it ends with an official communication announcing Nitti's suicide. *As a Man Grows Older*, an improvement in subtlety and psychological penetration, is about Emilio Brentani, who falls in love with a tart and achieves senility at the age of thirty-five when his dying sister tells him the truth about his lover.

After Svevo discovered Sigmund Freud, around 1912, he used the idea of psychoanalysis in the writing of *Confessions of Zeno*. The morbid Zeno Cosini seeks his salvation through psychoanalysis, recounting his life supposedly to find the origin of his smoking habit, as well as his innumerable other psychosomatic diseases, and thereby exposing his contradictory ideas and desires.

As a pro-Italian Austro-Hungarian subject, a Jew, a businessman who liked literature, and a pacifist during World War I, Svevo was naturally an outsider prone to the pleasures of introspection. His novels project an absurdist world where people are prevented by their spinelessness and other foibles from assuming the responsibility for their own weakness and are unable to share happiness or sorrow with others. To probe this sorry state, Svevo analyzes human consciousness (the Italian *coscienza* of his title suggests both "consciousness" and "conscience"), and because his work provides such a detailed look at the contradictions between reality and personality (Zeno habitually says the opposite of what he thinks and does the opposite of what he wants to do), Svevo has a modern flavor for the contemporary reader.

The founding of the journal *La voce* (1908), which provided a much-needed forum for serious writing by many gifted writers, foreshadowed both the Hermetic (obscurantist) tradition in poetry and the journal *La ronda* (1919-1923), which championed a reactionary return to classic tradition, emphasizing clear style, well-constructed syntax, and literary vocabulary. The versatile Riccardo Bacchelli (1891-1985) was the only one of the *rondisti* to make his imprint on the novel, and this he did with his two-thousand-page historical epic, *Il mulino del Po* (1938-1940; *The Mill on the Po*, 1950). It follows successive generations of the Scacerni family, from the time of Napoleon to the end of World War I. Political events are not important to Bacchelli per se, but rather as they affect the lives of his characters. In his many, diverse attempts at the novel and other forms of narrative, in which he was only cautiously experimental, he followed the formalism of Manzoni and, like Fogazzaro, dignified his own robust sensuality under a veil of Catholic unction.

In 1926, the gifted Massimo Bontempelli (1878-1960) and Curzio Malaparte (1898-1957) attacked the aesthetic formalism of the *rondisti* as well as the popular realism (which scored its final triumph in Deledda's Nobel Prize of 1927) by founding the review *'900: Cahiers d'Italie et d'Europe*, also known as *Il novecento* (the twentieth century). Although short-lived, the review attempted, by publishing its material in French, to expose Italians to the influences of French and Continental literature. A critic, playwright, aphorist, novelist, and short-story writer as well as an editor, Bontempelli's literary creed was "to clothe in a smile the most sorrowful things and with wonderment the most common things" in order to evoke the surreal inherent in the real. One of his several novels, *Vita e morte di Adria e dei suoi figli* (1930; the life and death of Adria and her sons), concerns a woman who withdraws from the world in order to preserve the legend of her beauty.

The younger Malaparte, pen name of Curzio Suckert, was the son of a German father and an Italian mother and was born in Prato. Controversial and contradictory, he wrote his best book, *Kaputt* (1944; English translation, 1946, 1948, 1964, 1966), while confined to Finland after he had angered the Nazi command. *Kaputt* is an apocalyptic vision of Europe crumbling under the violence of war. Later in 1944, his experiences as Italian liaison officer with the Allies in Naples offered the material for his most controversial novel, *La pelle* (1950; *The Skin*, 1952, 1954, 1964), whose Surrealism was mistaken for documentary realism. Both novels were international best-sellers. The comparison with D'Annunzio is inescapable, but as Luigi Barzini points out, while D'Annunzio was both admired and loathed by his outstanding contemporaries, Malaparte managed to strike only the obscurest of his contemporaries as irritating or charming.

The founding of the Florentine review *Solaria* in 1926 represented an attempt to reconcile the stylistics-oriented *rondisti* with the current dedicated to modern European trends responsible for Bontempelli's *Il novecento*. *Solaria* was pledged to introducing Italians to such modern figures as Kafka, Marcel Proust, T. S. Eliot, and Joyce and to refurbishing the images of such underrated Italian authors as Svevo and Tozzi, to whom they dedicated special commemorative issues. The *solariani* did not oppose regionalism: It was their successful blend of regional and universal concerns that gave rise to the work of Cesare Pavese, Elio Vittorini, Ignazio Silone, Carlo Levi, Vasco Pratolini, Vitaliano Brancati, Corrado Alvaro, and Giorgio Bassani. *Solaria*, however, had a formidable enemy in Fascism; the *solariani* were called Jew-lovers for their devotion to the likes of Kafka and Svevo, and by 1937, they were forced to close their doors.

Elio Vittorini (1908-1966), from a middle-class Sicilian family of Syracuse, left home in 1928 with his wife, Rosa Maria, the sister of poet Salvatore Quasimodo (1901-1968), to settle in Gorizia in northeastern Italy. His contribution to Italian intellectual life figures more in terms of his work as literary critic and organizer than in his narrative output, and he became a sort of Italian Jean-Paul Sartre, dispensing theories about the necessity of updating literature.

His first short story appeared in *Solaria* in 1929, and soon he began working for the periodical as proofreader and office boy. In 1933, he published his first translation, of D. H. Lawrence's 1925 *St. Mawr: Together with the Princess*, and in February of that year, *Solaria* began serializing his own novel *Il garofano rosso* (wr. 1933, pb. 1948; *The Red Carnation*, 1952). Because the novel explored the fascination that Fascism held for young people, especially emphasizing the sexual-sadistic element, the censors stopped its publication after the third installment, and Vittorini, in the wake of interest in American literature stimulated by the awarding of the Nobel Prize in Literature to Sinclair Lewis in 1930, continued his work on translations of Edgar Allan Poe, Faulkner, William Saroyan, and Erskine Caldwell.

His masterpiece, *Conversazione in Sicilia* (*In Sicily*, 1948; also known as *Conversations in Sicily*, 1949), published in 1941 but confiscated by the censors and reprinted in 1942, was immediately praised for its lyric beauty, its innovative style, and its emotional impact; later, Italo Calvino would call it the basis for modern Italian literature. The story of thirty-year-old Silvestro as he travels from the North back to Sicily to see his mother and the conversations he has with various people are converted by Vittorini into a rare allegory on the need to rekindle hope in freedom and justice. The book circulated in French and German translations in Nazi-governed countries and was a great inspiration in those dark days of oppression.

In 1943, Vittorini joined the Resistance movement, was jailed, and used the experience for *Uomini e no* (1945; *Men and Not Men*, 1985), the story of a Resistance group that was immediately hailed as a wartime classic and the cornerstone of the neorealistic movement (although Vittorini himself denied the neorealism of the book). A few years later, Vittorini wrote *Le donne di Messina* (1949, 1964; *Women of Messina*, 1973), whose first edition was a wordy novel seven hundred pages long. It involves a group of displaced people (many of whom are from the Sicilian city of Messina, which has risen phoenixlike from its ashes many times in its history) who resettle an abandoned village. It is the story of a society that is reborn, but Vittorini was always dissatisfied with the novel.

Vittorini believed that Italians had more in common with Americans than they had with Italian life of Manzoni's era, and he demanded that authors be more responsive to contemporary sensibility than the Italian literary idols of the past, such as D'Annunzio and Croce. He accused authors who persisted in writing from the omniscient point of view of catering to the "mystic enjoyment" of a reactionary reading public, and he rejected his own novel *Women of Messina* because it smacked of the nineteenth century. This explains his disapproval of Verga and why he as an editor rejected Giuseppe Tomasi di Lampedusa's *Il gattopardo* (1958; *The Leopard*, 1960) as typifying an obsolete literature that barred the way for works of more responsible and revolutionary conception. Long novels he felt were passé, and literature as a system of representing relations with the modern world must not fail to incorporate the newest technological changes. He fiercely defended science in the hope that man could someday come to win control over the machines that he understands so little.

Vittorini founded and directed the *I gettoni* (literally "gambling chips") series for Einaudi, which published first works by such budding authors as Mario Tobino, Carlo Cassola, Giovanni Arpino, and Italo Calvino. Vittorini also founded and served as editor of the controversial and short-lived periodical *Il*

politecnico, which he intended to serve as a vehicle for former Fascists to shrive themselves of their wartime complicity. He also established the avant-garde periodical *Il menabò*, and just before he died in 1966, he was trying to organize "Gulliver," an international periodical.

"Neorealism" is the blanket term applied to the socially aware postwar movement in literature, the fine arts, and cinema. It was probably most successful in the great films in the decade following the war when directors such as Roberto Rossellini, Vittorio De Sica, and Visconti were producing some of the most original films in the Western world. Factors contributing to this heightened sensibility were the anti-Fascist struggle, the postwar social and political struggle within Italy, and the spread of Marxism arising from the rediscovery of the works of Antonio Gramsci. In their concern for the condition of the masses, many writers (including some northern Italians such as Pavese and Levi), freed of the bonds of Fascist censorship, came to refocus on the plight of the Italian South in the tradition of Verga, Capuana, Serao, and Di Giacomo. The poverty-stricken South (called the *mezzogiorno*) is a special enigma to the Italian nation. Because southern Italians are admittedly a frugal and hardworking people at the mercy of an inhospitable terrain and the feudal legacy of the latifundium, it would seem reasonable that with proper guidance they could be made into an asset instead of a liability for the country.

At this time, a great number of Italian writers arose to place the urgent problems of the South squarely in view of the Italian reading public. The three southern writers chosen by Pacifici as typical of three different tendencies within the category of the "southern novel" are Corrado Alvaro (1895-1956), Vitaliano Brancati (1907-1954), and Giuseppe Tomasi di Lampedusa (1896-1957).

The Calabrian Alvaro grew up under the style-conscious influence of *La ronda*, which gave to his style a complexity and richness that does not quite qualify as neorealism. His fiction is reminiscent of Verga in its emphasis on a cruel destiny, in his distance from his characters, and in his sense of irony; his masterpiece *Gente in Aspromonte* (1930; *Revolt in Aspromonte*, 1962), which elaborates the difficult life led by a family of Calabrian shepherds and their struggle to survive the reversals that ultimately obliterate their modest dreams, resembles *The House by the Medlar Tree*. By the beginning of World War II, Alvaro had produced twelve volumes of fiction, ten of nonfiction, three of poetry, two plays, and translations from English, Russian, and Greek. After the war, he wrote a trilogy of "Rinaldo Diacono" novels— of which *L'età breve* (1946; the brief age) was the only one published in its finished form—that focus on Italian bourgeois society under Fascism and after the war through the eyes of a young, urbanized, transplanted southerner who longs for his native land, which he has idealized beyond recognition.

Unlike Alvaro, who created a world full of dramatic tension, the Sicilian Brancati employed a more comic approach to portray southern Italian morals and manners. Writing in reaction to D'Annunzio's glorification of sexual freedom, Brancati satirized in *Don Giovanni in Sicilia* (1941; Don Juan in Sicily) *gallismo*, the aggressive eroticism of southern males who are reared in a matriarchal society only ostensibly ruled by men, where honor consists of saving face and morality consists of conformity. Originally a Fascist, Brancati was disabused of his early loyalties when he migrated to the mainland and made the salutary acquaintance of Giuseppe Borgese and Benedetto Croce. Because neither Alvaro nor Brancati proposed any radical solutions to the plight of the *mezzogiorno*, neither received more than a passing recognition from the Marxist-oriented criticism of modern Italy.

A literary anomaly—it is the only frankly decadentistic novel to appear in the postwar period—but undeniably one of the most extraordinary and most written-about books of modern Italian literature is *The Leopard*, by the Sicilian aristocrat Giuseppe Tomasi, Duke of Palma and Prince of Lampedusa. Despite his international education and his love of literatures other than Italian (he especially liked William Shakespeare, Leo Tolstoy, Marcel Proust, and Thomas Mann), Lampedusa felt so thoroughly Sicilian that it was about Sicily that he felt compelled to write.

The odyssey of his manuscript is remarkable; the same year as his death (1957), Lampedusa submitted the manuscript to Mondadori of Milan and to Einaudi of Turin, two of the most prestigious publishing houses in Italy, headed respectively by Vittorio Sereni and Elio Vittorini. The book was rejected by both, and after Lampedusa's death, his widow gave Elena Croce (the daughter of Benedetto Croce) a handwritten copy of the manuscript. She passed it on to Giorgio Bassani, a senior consulting editor at Feltrinelli of Milan; this time the novel was accepted.

Lampedusa's "leopard," named after the proud beast emblazoned on the family coat of arms, is Don Fabrizio, Prince of Salina, modeled on the author's own great grandfather, an enlightened despot who ruled over vast estates on the eve of Garibaldi's landing in Sicily. Too intelligent to resist the inevitable future but reluctant to join the present, he views the fall of the Bourbon monarchy with "historic nausea," as well as a strange equanimity, for in Lampedusa's frankly pessimistic representation of Don Fabrizio's world, despite the appearance of change, nothing really changes.

A forerunner of this trend to enlighten readers about the sorry conditions in the South, which was not even published in Italian (1930, 1933, 1958) or English (1934, revised 1960) until long after its translation into German (1930), is *Fontamara*. Its author, Ignazio Silone (1900-1978), the pen name of Secondo Tranquilli, here undertook to communicate to the free world from his exile in Switzerland the totalitarian repression of Fascism, which served only to compound the misery of the southern Italian *cafoni* (peasants). Nothing is going to change, according to Silone, unless the *cafoni* can unite their forces to create change. *Fontamara*, however, is not quite a realistic novel, for its peasants are idealized and its Fascists are caricatured. *Brot und Wein* (1936; as *Pane e vino*, 1937, revised as *Vino e pane*, 1955; *Bread and Wine*, 1936, revised 1962) and *Der Samen unterm Schnee* (1941; as *Il seme sotto la neve*, 1942; *The Seed Beneath the Snow*, 1942) are set in the same barren land of the Abruzzi and chronicle the life of Pietro Spina, a revolutionary disguised as a priest who rediscovers a renewed way of life tending the soil of his homeland but who eventually dies for another man's crime. Silone invests in his character Spina his own transformation from communist to primitive Christian socialist. Strangely enough, Silone is more widely known in the United States than in Italy.

Like Silone, Carlo Levi (1902-1975) was an intellectual in exile when he wrote about the condition of southern Italian peasants. More for his anti-Fascist sentiments than for being a Jew, Levi, a painter and physician, was sent to a small town twenty miles from the nearest railroad station in remote and impoverished Basilicata in the instep of the Italian boot. Here, for the first time, Levi did not feel the sting of racial prejudice, for "his" peasants, as he came to call them, did not know what a Jew was. The title of his masterpiece, *Cristo si è fermato a Eboli* (1945; *Christ Stopped at Eboli: The Story of a Year*, 1947), refers to the peasants' belief that they were bypassed by Christianity and even by civilization: "Christ never came this far, nor did time, nor the individual soul, nor hope, nor the relation of cause to effect, nor reason nor history." The book, which depicts a people so worn down by the gratuitous insults of life and nature that Mussolini's Fascism is hardly a matter of importance to them, ends when the author is freed by a political amnesty in 1936. It was written eight years later while Levi was living in Florence as a hunted member of the Resistance, published after the war, and immediately became an international best-seller. The spirit of Levi's moving diary-novel set the tone for much of the truth-seeking neorealism that was to follow, and it also marks the beginning of a new vogue for the subgenre of books that combine travel and observation, such as Carlo Bernari's *Il gigante Cina* (1957; gigantic China), Moravia's *La rivoluzione cultural in Cina* (1967; *The Red Book and the Great Wall*, 1968), and Levi's own book on the Soviet Union, *Il futuro ha un cuore antico: Viaggio nell'Unione Sovietica* (1956; the future has an ancient heart).

Francesco Jovine (1902-1950) conjured up his own brand of "poetic realism" describing the peasants of his native Molise region. His best novel, *Le terre del Sacramento* (1950; the estate in Abruzzi), is the epic of a depressed people who succeed in occu-pying uncultivated land. At the center of this peasant insurrection against the privileges of the ruling class is Luca Marano, who was called one of the most felicitous creations of contemporary Italian fiction.

The northerner Giovanni Arpino, born in 1927 in what is now Yugoslavian territory, and who normally depicts the Piedmontese countryside in his fiction, employed a southern setting to expose the absurdity of the practice of the southern vendetta in *Un delitto d'onore* (1961; *A Crime of Honor*, 1963). In a small town south of Naples, a leading citizen murders his wife when a doctor certifies that she was not a virgin at the time of their marriage. The narrative is permeated with black irony but is also remarkable for the author's understanding of the traditions involved.

Leonardo Sciascia (1921-1989), whom Luigi Barzini considers "perhaps one of the best of all" contemporary Italian writers, evokes the Sicilian mentality. The author of a number of scholarly works on Sicilian history, Sciascia is primarily concerned in his fiction with exposing the crimes of the Italian Mafia and the strict primitive adherence of Sicilians to *omertà* (the code of silence). Unfortunately, Sciascia's novels are generally classified as mysteries in the United States; as Herbert Mitgang observes of *A ciascuno il suo* (1966; *A Man's Blessing*, 1968), Sciascia's murder stories exemplify the gemlike difference between a simple mystery and a work of fiction that does not depend upon a tidy solution for its vitality.

Sardinia, which is considered part of the Italian South, is portrayed by Giuseppe Dessí (1909-1977), a follower of *Solaria* and a reader of Proust and Mann with a lyric gift for blending autobiographical detail with regional realism, especially evident in *Michele Boschino* (1942). *Paese d'ombre* (1972; the forests of Norbio), perhaps a little too dependent on the Sardinian ambience for an American audience, is the life story of Angelo Uras and his anger at the wanton destruction of the magnificent forests of Norbio, sacrificed to fuel the insatiable furnaces of technology.

The teeming metropolis of Naples is the preferred subject matter of Neopolitan novelists Carlo Bernari (born 1909), one of the forerunners of neorealism with his *Tre operai* (1934; three factory workers), which deals with the urban proletariat of his native city; Michele Prisco (born 1920); and Domenico Rea (born 1921). Prisco and Rea both write short stories as well as novels; Prisco is fond of describing the aristocracy and the petite bourgeoisie, whereas Rea is more interested in the tragicomic condition of the common people.

Depicting the southernmost province of Calabria are Fortunato Seminara (born 1903), who probes the psychological motives for the archaic social structures of the area, and Saverio Strati (born 1924), who creates a world of day laborers, coal miners, and masons who dream of emigration to more civilized and charitable lands to escape the squalor of their lives and who sometimes return empty-handed to Calabria after an odyssey abroad. Prisco, Rea, Seminara, and Strati are not well-known in the United States, which is lamentable—and ironic, because a majority of Italian Americans have their roots in precisely the areas of Italy that these authors describe.

A northern writer who wrote his first novel while a political exile in Calabria is the Piedmontese Cesare Pavese (1908-1950), whose short novels constitute, according to Calvino, the "most dense, dramatic, and homogeneous narrative cycle" of modern Italian literature. Although his fiction was a major influence upon neorealism, his novels cannot be said to be realistic, for he is not as much interested in the outside world as he is in how his characters come to terms with their world.

Asthmatic, Pavese was judged unfit for military service and for the same reason could not participate in the guerrilla warfare of the Resistance movement. A reading of his diary through the war years reveals only a few offhand references to the war and a lack of involvement for which he would later be criticized. Pavese was a major interpreter of American and English letters for Italians, translating works by Lewis, Gertrude Stein, Herman Melville, Faulkner, Charles Dickens, and Daniel Defoe, among others; he admired F. Scott Fitzgerald and Ernest Hemingway so much that he claimed he did not dare to translate them. He worked as an editor for Einaudi, the publishing house that he had helped to found in Turin.

A sensitive man who believed that life was not worth living unless for the sake of others, Pavese nevertheless found it difficult to relate to other people. Despite his belief that the advance of civilization rested on men overcoming their misogyny, he was obsessed by his love for individual women and ended his life by his own hand, recognizing that he was sexually hopeless. He came to the novel from poetry, which he freed from formal metrical requirements, emphasizing rhythm and synthesis and preoccupied with the problem of solitude.

Like Vittorini, Pavese wished to infuse new vitality into what he perceived as a tired tradition by the introduction of American literature and by making technical innovations, which for Pavese involved mixing local dialect with literary Italian, and experimentation with ungrammatical, unliterary language. (He was fascinated by the American slang in the novels which he translated.)

Using the "return of the wanderer to his homeland" theme elaborated into such a powerful allegory by Vittorini, Pavese wrote *La luna e i falò* (1950; *The Moon and the Bonfire*, 1952), emphasizing memory as a key to understanding past experiences, which can in turn be prodded by a reimmersion in the past (hence, Pavese's realism). His character Anguilla ("eel" in Italian, referring to the eel's characteristic return to its birthplace) returns to his mountain village after an absence of twenty years in America (which he characterizes as an illusory heaven, a land where, like the moon of Pavese's title, there is nothing, no real women and no wine), re-creates his idyllic past and then suffers the anguish of seeing these memories disintegrate in the present. Although he finds that nothing has really changed, he does become reconciled to what he perceives as his own destiny, his own identification with the people of his homeland and with the natural forces (the mountains) that shaped them all.

Pavese's women characters are more convincing than his men; this is particularly evident in *Tra donne sole* (1949; *Among Women Only*, 1953), set in the world of haute couture. The Rosetta of this novel, like Rosalba in *Il diavolo sulle colline* (1949; *The Devil in the Hills*, 1954), finds suicide the only escape—a solution to which Pavese himself resorted on August 27, 1950.

The Resistance novel treats an area of such overwhelming and specialized interest to Italian readers that some critics have attempted to call it a subgenre of the novel. The Resistance novel, however, does not admit of a facile definition, especially considering that for many who use the term, it is generously applied even to those novels of wartime or postwar activity by or about those who were not even sympathetic to the Resistance movement.

British and American critics understandably exclude from the category such novels as *Tiro al piccione* (1953; *The Day of the Lion*, 1954), by Giose Rimanelli (born 1926), or *Il cielo è rosso* (1947; *The Sky Is Red*, 1948), by Giuseppe Berto (1914-1978). The former, a sympathetic presentation of the losing side and based on the author's own experiences, depicts a rebellious adolescent's escape from the boredom of his southern Italian village to join the bedraggled Fascist army and his subsequent emergence from the ruins able to accept the future. The latter, written about four adolescents who come together after their families have been killed and form a nucleus of life amid the ruins of 1943 to 1944, was conceived while the author was in a prison camp in Hereford, Texas; its style was even affected by some of the American authors that Berto read while in prison (for example, John Steinbeck, Melville, Faulkner, Hemingway).

The first of what are unequivocally called Resistance novels by British and American standards is Vittorini's *Uomini e no*, which employs the 1944-1945 struggle of a group of Milanese partisans to suggest that World War II was a conflict between men and nonmen. Vittorini portrays his Nazis and Fascists as either stupid, unfeeling automatons or sadists, and his anti-Fascists as simple people who react with human sensitivity. Vittorini's protagonist is identified only by his code name N2; the other characters are not well drawn, and the dialogue, which reveals the influence but not the skill of Hemingway, is repetitive and banal.

Two years later, Italo Calvino (1923-1985) published *Il sentiero dei nidi di ragno* (1947, 1957, 1965;

The Path to the Nest of Spiders, 1956). It deals with a partisan movement originating in the mountains around Genoa and has as its hero an unloved orphan boy named Pin who finds in the partisans with whom he associates a comaraderie new to him. Although the partisans offer Pin at least the hope of redemption, Calvino is careful not to idealize his characters, who remain ordinary, even shocking in their crudity.

Renata Viganò, born in 1900 in Bologna and a prolific writer of short stories, enshrined the touching heroism of her communist peasant woman protagonist in *L'Agnese va a morire* (1954; Agnese goes to her death). In a narrative unencumbered by speculation and rhetoric, Agnese, whose aged husband has been carried off to a German work camp, where he perishes, performs faithfully the instructions of the partisans with whom she works until she is killed in an encounter with an enraged German soldier.

The Resistance novels of Pavese, Carlo Cassola (1917-1987), and Mario Tobino (born 1910) are more complicated and reflect more on the failures of the movement than do Vittorini, Calvino, or Viganò. In Pavese's *La casa in collina* (1949; *The House on the Hill*, 1956), his introspective and alienated protagonist Corrado cynically observes that all men, unless they throw bombs or otherwise risk their lives in combat, are Fascists. *Fausto e Anna* (1952; *Fausto and Anna*, 1960), by Roman author Cassola, active in the Resistance fighting in Tuscany and later a schoolteacher, spans a period of eight years and of all the Resistance novels portrays most successfully the tension of those years. The joyful disbanding of the partisans of Cassola's novel betokens a return to a normality that does not promise to be better than before. Fausto, previously devoted both to Anna and to the Communist Party, loses both of them by the end of the novel.

Like Pavese's Corrado, the Tuscan Tobino is unstinting in his accusation in his *Il clandestino* (1962; *The Underground*, 1966, 1967) that the vast majority of Italians were Fascists and that it was precisely these people who were responsible for the war. In this novel, Tobino gives a collective character to the Resistance movement and deprives his story of a single protagonist. Despite an overpopulated cast of characters, what emerges from the novel is a remarkably complete picture of the Resistance period. Like Cassola, however, Tobino is not sanguine about a renewal or a restructuring of Italian society.

L'ombra delle colline (1964; shadow on the hills), by Giovanni Arpino, presents a protagonist who returns to the Langhe Hills in Piedmont years after he has worked with the Resistance there as a youth. In this novel, there is the wistfulness about the lost ideals of the Resistance, the sad acceptance of the status quo, and the conflict between myth and history that had tortured Pavese.

Resistance novels continued to be written, most notably by Beppe Fenoglio (1922-1963), who seems to have intended to produce a panoramic cycle of the Italian civil war from September, 1943, through April, 1945. Fenoglio, who was born in Alba and spent his entire life in the Langhe region of the Piedmont, was an Anglophile who made extensive use of English words and phrases in his novels and translated a variety of English works, including Kenneth Grahame's *The Wind in the Willows* (1908). His lightly fictionalized autobiographical hero appears first as an officer cadet in Rome in *Primavera di bellezza* (1959; spring of beauty) and continues through *Il partigiano Johnny* (1968; Johnny the partisan); finally, the former partisan's readjustment to civilian life is examined in *La paga del sabato* (1969; Saturday's wages).

Of the northern Italian writers who partook of the vogue of neorealism, perhaps the Florentine Vasco Pratolini (1913-1991) is the most typical; certainly he is one of the most prolific. His realism, as opposed to the *Verismo* of Verga, does not emphasize folklore and local color per se but rather uses the setting as a backdrop for a drama of ordinary human emotion. Neither does Pratolini strive to be scientifically objective or shrink from intervening to plead the case of one of his characters, if necessary. Pratolini's masterpiece is *Cronache di poveri amanti* (1947; *A Tale of Poor Lovers*, 1949), which Frank Rosengarten considers a Resistance novel because it depicts so graphically a microcosm of the Italian world (in the mid-1920's) on the eve of political tyranny.

The postwar works of the Vicenzan Guido Pio-

vene (1907-1974) are sometimes classed as neorealistic despite their overtones of D'Annunzian decadence. Pier Paolo Pasolini (1922-1975), born in Bologna, came to the novel from poetry and abandoned the novel for film; he also made his mark on literary history as a critic. Because literary language is a reflection of the ruling classes so distasteful to Pasolini's Marxism, he rejected it; with the scholarship of a philologist, he followed the example of Carlo Emilio Gadda (1893-1973) and employed the crude dialect of the Roman riffraff for much of his first two novels, *Ragazzi di vita* (1955; *The Ragazzi*, 1968) and *Una vita violenta* (1959; *A Violent Life*, 1978).

Giorgio Bassani, born in 1916 in Bologna, is a chronicler of Ferrara who creates vulnerable characters such as Jews and homosexuals and examines them in times of stress. *Il giardino dei Finzi-Contini* (1962; *The Garden of the Finzi-Continis*, 1965), made even more popular by De Sica's 1970 film, is a pathetic story of a wealthy Jewish family that lives impervious to the growing turmoil outside their garden walls, which will lead to their own persecution. The novella *Gli occhiali d'oro* (1958; *The Gold-Rimmed Spectacles*; revised as *The Gold-Rimmed Eyeglasses*, 1975) is the no less pathetic story of a homosexual doctor eventually forced to commit suicide; the story is narrated by a sympathetic young Jew who is growing more and more aware of the anti-Semitism that he himself must inevitably face.

Writing during these years with the spirit of an *avant gardista* was Dino Buzzati (1906-1972), who was born in Belluno; best known for his short fiction, Buzzati was a journalist and an editor by profession and a gifted painter as well as a writer. In 1940, he published an allegorical novel reminiscent of Kafka, *Il deserto dei Tartari* (*The Tartar Steppe*, 1952). His more conventional *Un amore* (1963; *A Love Affair*, 1964) is about a dignified middle-aged man in love with a shameless tart. Although Buzzati filled his fiction with historical characters, this was not, in the words of Pacifici, to encourage realism, but "simply to heighten the irony of a world teetering on the brink of madness."

Another author of this period who does not conform to neorealism is Gadda, a civil engineer born in Milan of an Italian father and a German mother; he is the author of the Italian equivalent of Joyce's *Ulysses* (1922). Written in a mixture of standard Italian and Roman dialect with liberal admixtures of Milanese, Venetian, and Neapolitan dialects, *Quer pasticciaccio brutto de via Merulana* (1957; *That Awful Mess on Via Merulana*, 1965) seems to be a detective story, but it soon becomes clear that Gadda is more interested in the welter of possibly sapphic relationships that could have provided the motive than he is in solving the crime itself.

In a separate category are several authors whose works are substantially more popular in the United States than in Italy. Giovanni Guareschi (1908-1968), born near Parma and a prisoner of the Germans from 1943 to 1945, was a sort of James Thurber who illustrated his own works. By confining himself to whimsy, Guareschi managed to publish books under Fascism even before he emerged in his true light as a political satirist with his Don Camillo sketches (*Mondo piccolo: Don Camillo*, 1948; *The Little World of Don Camillo*, 1950, 1967), which satirize extremists of both the Left and the Right.

Another contemporary author less esteemed in Italy than abroad is Carlo Coccioli, born in Leghorn in 1920 and a participant in the Resistance. Influenced by modern French authors, he typifies, according to Thomas F. Staley, the postexistential novelist who tried to integrate existential thought with unorthodox Christian idealism. His *Il cielo e la terra* (1950; *Heaven and Earth*, 1952) is a controversial novel about a priest who gathers strength as he struggles with the many conflicts of life. Beginning in 1955, Coccioli, following an Italian tradition that extends from Marco Polo to Giovanni Papini and Gabriele D'Annunzio, chose to write in French rather than in Italian.

Alberto Moravia (1907-1990), the son of a Jewish agnostic from Venice and a Catholic mother, is without question the dominant figure of postwar fiction. His first novel, *Gli indifferenti* (1929; *The Time of Indifference*, 1953), published at his own expense, was an instant success and rightly interpreted as an indictment of the bourgeoisie and an exposé of the corrupt

social situation that allowed Fascism to develop. This novel, which remains one of his most important works, contains most of the themes seen in his later works and would be his last explicitly ideological novel until *Il conformista* (1951; *The Conformist*, 1952, made into a film by Bernardo Bertolucci in 1969).

While it is often claimed that Moravia is a founder of neorealism (because of his reportorial scrutiny applied to the hypocrisies of the middle classes), such a claim conflicts with his undeniably strong existentialism. If *La ciociara* (1957; *Two Women*, 1958) can be called neorealistic because of setting, characterization, subject, and a certain idealism represented by its protagonist, his next novel *La noia* (1960; *The Empty Canvas*, 1961), must be recognized for its return to a philosophical, almost Sartrean emphasis.

Seeking to avoid Mussolini's censors, Moravia turned to indirect modes of expression, cloaking his stories in satire and Surrealism; nevertheless, *La mascherata* (1941; *The Fancy Dress Party*, 1952) was personally censored by Mussolini, and by 1943, Moravia was forced to flee his home in Rome with his wife, novelist Elsa Morante (born 1918?). The couple spent nine months hiding with peasants and living in a pigsty; the experience strengthened Moravia's tendencies toward Marxism and inspired *Two Women* (made into a film by De Sica in 1960, starring Sophia Loren), about a mother and daughter's struggle to survive wartime violence.

When Moravia's characters seek reality, they usually embark on their search through the medium of sexuality, which, according to Moravia, replaced love in the modern world; because an estranged man can find a moment's solace with a prostitute, some of Moravia's most sympathetic characters are prostitutes. (As a result of his treatment of sexual matters, the Roman Catholic Church, in 1952, placed all of his books on the Index.) This is not to say that this search for sexual satisfaction has even a chance of being successful; the sexual act itself is perceived by Moravia as ugly and unnatural, and the typical Moravian character who is searching for happiness through sex meets with nothing more than failure.

Moravia is not a structural innovator, nor is he

fancy with words, nor does he waste time. Wishing to expose for his readers hidden realities, which he attempts to isolate for them, Moravia's aims as a storyteller are openly didactic. Unlike most Italian novelists of the middle class, who prefer to write about the working class, Moravia is fascinated by the mores of his own class. His clinical method of analyzing character may have been inherited from Svevo, and his works are saturated with passages and situations absorbed from his prodigious reading of the classics of other generations and literatures.

By the late 1950's, most everything that could be said about the wretchedness of the lower classes in Italy had been said, and a literary backlash inevitably occurred. While some awaited the appearance of a second D'Annunzio, there came to the attention of the public the ironic Italo Calvino, with his love of fantasy from earlier centuries. Calvino, born in Cuba of Italian parents and already famous for his somewhat fablelike *The Path to the Nest of Spiders*, turned to the Renaissance and to his favorite poet, Ludovico Ariosto (1474-1533), for inspiration; like the author of *Orlando furioso* (1516, 1521, 1532; English translation, 1591), Calvino uses his fanciful narration to convey an implicit moral. His trilogy comprising *Il visconte dimezzato* (1952; *The Cloven Viscount*, 1962), *Il barone rampante* (1957; *The Baron in the Trees*, 1959), and *Il cavaliere inesistente* (1959; *The Non-Existent Knight*, 1962) was also issued in a single volume as *I nostri atenati* (1960; *Our Ancestors*, 1980). Also a folklorist, Calvino produced a monumental anthology of Italian fairy tales (*Fiabe italiane: Raccolte della tradizione popolare durante gli ultimi cento anni e transcritte in lingua dai vari dialetti*, 1956; *Italian Fables*, 1959) and turned to science fiction in *Le cosmicomiche* (1965; *Cosmicomics*, 1968), a collection of stories depicting a world peopled by ciphers and essences.

Like Calvino, the Sicilian Ercole Patti (1904-1976) worked in a Surrealistic medium. His last novel, *Gli ospiti di quel castello* (1974; the guests of that castle), tells the story of a twenty-three-year-old man who suddenly finds himself forty years older. Also breaking away from realism in a quest for hallucinatory memories of the past is Elsa Morante (1918-

1985). Her masterpiece, *L'isola di Arturo* (1957; *Arturo's Island*, 1959), is the haunting recollection of a lonely adolescence rudely punctuated by the boy's awareness of his infatuation with his young stepmother and of the fact that his father is a homosexual. Morante's language is musical, rich, and allusive, and her imagery is poetic. Morante's long-awaited *La Storia* (1974; *History: A Novel*, 1977) is an allegory with appeal to both Christian and Marxist readers; set in Rome during World War II, it portrays death and violence as dominating human experience.

In addition to Elsa Morante, there is Natalia Ginzburg (1916-1991), the daughter of a Jewish biology professor and a Gentile mother. Married to Russian expatriate Leone Ginzburg, who was murdered by the Nazis after his arrest for editing an anti-Fascist newspaper, Ginzburg writes prose of unsentimental reminiscence, observation, and invention, often autobiographical and exhibiting a Hemingwayesque precision. Her *Lessico famigliare* (1963; *Family Sayings*, 1967) is a recollection of her childhood and early adulthood and a portrait of Italy between the wars.

The periodical *Il menabò*, founded by Vittorini and Calvino in 1959, especially encouraged writers who sought to analyze the phenomenon of Italian industrialization. Depicting the effect of technology upon man is the primary interest of such novelists as the Roman Ottiero Ottieri (born 1924), Paolo Volponi (born 1924), from Urbino, and Luciano Bianciardi (1922-1971), from Grosseto. The latter, who coauthored the social inquiry *I minatori della maremma* (1956; the miners of Maremma), also wrote *La vita agra* (1962; *La vita agra: It's a Hard Life*, 1965), about the anxiety that develops in an idealistic intellectual who comes to the city with a revolutionary mission and is defeated by the daily grind of making a living.

Lucio Mastronardi (1930-1979), born near Milan, wrote in the experimentalist tradition of Gadda and Pasolini, drawing heavily on the Milanese and Neapolitan dialects. He was interested in the southern Italian who goes north for economic reasons and meets with undisguised prejudice from the northerners, especially in *Il meridionale di Vigevano* (1964; the southerner of Vigevano).

Also interested in the plight of the southern Italian who finds himself at the mercy of the northern cities is Giovanni Testori, born in 1923 in a suburb of Milan and who applies his vigorous religious belief to social problems. His five-volume cycle "I segreti di Milano" (the secrets of Milan) contains his novel *Il fabbricone* (1961; *The House in Milan*, 1962), a proletarian version of William Shakespeare's *Romeo and Juliet* (1595-1596), and the stories of *Il ponte della Ghisolfa* (1958; the bridge on the River Ghisolfa), which were the inspiration for Visconti's film *Rocco e suoi fratelli* (1960; *Rocco and His Brothers*, 1960), which portrays the disintegration of a southern family upon contact with the industrial North.

The zeal fostered by neorealism for examining situations with reportorial accuracy persisted into the 1960's—for example, in the social criticism of Sicilian social reformer Danilo Dolci (born 1914) and the controversial theater criticism of *enfant terrible* Alberto Arbasino (born 1930), who is also the author of the best-selling novel *Super Eliogabalo* (1969; super Heliogabalus), which explores self-destructive power. Mario Soldati (born 1906), a journalist, short-story writer, and film director born in Milan, had his first success in long fiction with *Le lettere da Capri* (1954; *The Capri Letters*, 1956), a study of a poorly matched American couple in Allied-occupied Rome. A sort of Henry James in reverse, Soldati was fascinated by Americans; in 1935, he wrote *America primo amore* (America, first love), a novelist's sort of travel book destined to be influential in forming the Italian conception of the United States during those years. In *La confessione* (1955; *The Confession*, 1958), Soldati explores a young man's odyssey from the proscriptions of his Jesuit upbringing to arrant homosexuality, and in *La busta arancione* (1966; *The Orange Envelope*, 1969), he depicts the friction of a destructive mother-son relationship.

In 1960, the most aggressive adherent of neorealism, Pier Paolo Pasolini, took it upon himself to pronounce the demise of neorealism in verse that parodied Marc Antony's funeral oration for Caesar: "Friends, Romans, countrymen, lend me your ears./ I have come to bury Italian realism, not to praise it." Recalling the glorious genesis of neorealism in the

light of the Resistance, he proceeds to blame Lampedusa, the neo-experimentalists, and his own erstwhile friend Carlo Cassola for dealing the deathblows. The term "neo-experimentalist"—which, in the words of Olga Ragusa, refers here to the expressionistic rather than the mimetic subversive use of language in the creation of poetry—was sanctified to use by Pasolini himself and was the term adopted by the avant-garde writers who riotously convened in Palermo in 1963 and subsequently called themselves the Gruppo 63.

These writers argued that literature is essentially antirational, and they heartily rejected literary works which imitated or mirrored reality. Thus, while they accepted Gadda, Svevo, and Pirandello, they rejected Moravia, Pasolini, Bassani, Cassola, and most of the other Italian authors. Nevertheless, many of the writers belonging to the Gruppo 63 had different responses to and personal ways of experiencing the criticism they were transferring to Italy's recent narrative past. Most of the discussions took place in the monthly journal *Quindici*, which appeared in Rome in 1967. Very soon the Gruppo 63 was declared finished, and the focus became the political activity surrounding the 1968 movement. *Quindici* itself was short-lived, and the critic and writer Umberto Eco (born 1932), a member of the Gruppo 63, defined the question of whether literature should be devoted to direct political action. He proposed the criticism of culture as the only direction to take. The lively debate created a variety of literary productions that followed different routes: Some authors continued to follow the neorealistic modules, while others preferred a more experimental technique. Individual creativity offered various solutions, generating a profusion of interesting novels that are difficult to situate in precise categories.

Among those who pursued neorealistic models was Carlo Cassola, who was able to combine that vein with an existential motif that distinguishes his works from neorealism. After his most important novel, *La ragazza di Bube* (1960; *Bebo's Girl*, 1962), he wrote *L'antagonista* (1976; the antagonist), *La disavventura* (1977; the misfortune), and *Un uomo solo* (1978; a lonely man). Despite the criticism of him by the Gruppo 63, who considered him the "Liala of 1963," his novels achieved a distinct public success.

Writers often mixed the realistic flavor and the description of everyday life with an emphasis on universal human values and feelings. This was the case, for example, with Giorgio Saviane (born 1916), who devoted most of his books to an attentive analysis of peasant culture in the Veneto region and to the values that surrounded it, particularly its religion and sense of sin. These reverberate in many of his books: *Il papa* (1963; *The Finger in the Candle*, 1964), the famous *Eutanasìa di un amore* (1976; euthanasia of a love affair), and *Getsèmani* (1980; Gethsemane). More part of "subaltern" culture is Gavino Ledda, whose widely read *Padre Padrone* (1975; my father, my master) recounts the narrative autobiography of a shepherd in Sardinia and who grew up under the care of a traditionally authoritarian father, the last surviving example of the disappearing patriarchal culture of the island.

Writers such as the Neapolitan Michele Prisco, on the other hand, although starting in the area of neorealistic regionalism and later analyzing the static cultural situation, arrive at a novel centered on psychological analysis and introspection of characters, as in *Una spirale di nebbia* (1966; *A Spiral of Mist*, 1969), which reveals the decay of a bourgeois marriage; *I cieli della sera* (1970; evening skies); *Gli ermellini neri* (1975; black ermines); and the later *Le parole del silenzio* (1981; the words of silence). Another novelist who cannot be neglected is Primo Levi (1919-1987), who became immediately famous with the publication of the nonfiction work *Se questo è un uomo* (1947; *If This Is a Man*, 1959; revised as *Survival in Auschwitz: The Nazi Assault on Humanity*, 1961) after World War II. Levi's autobiographical first novel, *La Tregua* (1963; *The Reawakening*, 1965), narrates the adventures and the return home of a group of young men after they are liberated from a Nazi concentration camp. *Se non ora, quando?* (1982; *If Not Now, When?*, 1985) is also based on the postwar chronicles of Jewish partisans fighting for the rediscovery of their dignity, while Jewish characters are also at the center of his last novel, *I sommersi*

e i salvati (1986; *The Drowned and the Saved*, 1988).

Among the women writers who in the 1970's and 1980's made everyday life and everyday people the centers of their narratives was Lalla Romano (born 1906), who won the Strega Prize in 1969 with *Le parole tra noi leggere* (light words between us). Written like a journal, this novel analyzes with psychological detail the relationship between mother and son. It began a series of narratives, which from *L'ospite* (1973; the guest) to *Ho sognato l'ospedale* (1995; I dreamt about the hospital) became increasingly dramatic.

Quite different is the writing of Piero Chiara (1913-1986), who instead of simply describing the quiet bourgeois life of the Lago Maggiore, especially that of Luino, reverses narrative traditions with his highly sarcastic tone, sometimes reaching the grotesque. This is evident in *Il piatto piange* (1962; the kitty is short), *Il balordo* (1967; the fool), *La stanza del vescovo* (1976; the bishop's room), *Il cappotto di astrakan* (1978; the Astrakhan coat), and *Una spina nel cuore* (1979; a thorn in the heart).

Although the description of ordinary life seems to be at the center of the Italian novels of the 1970's, the ideological novel was not completely abandoned; some writers who pursued it found international fame. Oriana Fallaci (born 1930), for example, in her more successful stories chooses a mixture of journalistic narrative and polemical prose to engage either in the abortion issue, in *Lettera a un bambino mai nato* (1975; *Letter to a Child Never Born*, 1976), or in the biography of young Greek dissident Alexandros Panagulis, in *Un Uomo* (1979; *A Man*, 1980). *Niente e così sia* (1969; *Nothing, and So Be It*, 1972) engages in the political events connected with the Vietnam War, while *Insciallah* (1990; *Inshallah*, 1992) translates into fiction stories surrounding oppression in Beirut.

Another genre, the detective novel, seems to have grown during the 1960's and 1970's in a very peculiar way. In these years the detective novel assumed characteristic national forms and themes in the so-called *giallo all'italiana*. It is important to study its evolution in this period in order to understand its future implications in the novels of Umberto Eco. Following the tradition of Sciascia, Giorgio Scerbanenco (1911-1969) puts a fragile and sentimental detective in charge of investigating the mediocre criminality of Milan (*I milanesi ammazzano di sabato*, 1969; the Milanese kill on Saturday). What is at stake in Scerbanenco's novels is not the aristocratic murder of Arthur Conan Doyle's stories, but the violence and the frustration of crime among the lower class. The team of Carlo Fruttero and Franco Lucentini was able to exploit literary consumerism by creating novels that would easily attract the public. In novels such as *La donna della domenica* (1972; *The Sunday Woman*, 1973), *A che punto é la notte* (1979; at what stage is the night?), and *Enigma in luogo di mare* (1991; *An Enigma by the Sea*, 1994), murder is at the center of the stories, but the detective novel plot is enriched by a number of characters with peculiarities and problems.

This genre reached one of its most interesting peaks with Umberto Eco's best-seller *Il nome della rosa* (1980; *The Name of the Rose*, 1983), which sold about five million copies around the world. Eco explained the formidable success of the book by attributing it to the formula he used, that of the detective novel imbued with historical information and erudite citations, creating a very postmodern mixture that attracted readers of every nationality. William of Baskerville, the astute detective and semiotician of *The Name of the Rose*, in the end fails to solve the murders he was hired to investigate, while the murderer kills himself and burns the building that had been at the center of the diabolic plot, the library.

Eco demonstrated with his two following novels that *The Name of the Rose* had not been a fluke. With *Il pendolo di Foucault* (1988; *Foucault's Pendulum*, 1989), Eco returns to the detective novel, but this time he sets the action in the Italian cultural sphere of the 1980's and surrounds the murders with the aura of conspiracy inherent in the actions of secret orders such as those of the Templars and the Rosicrucians. In *L'isola del giorno prima* (1994; *The Island of the Day Before*, 1995), Eco abandons the detective genre in favor of historical fiction, following Manzoni's legacy but portraying the state of mind, memories, and hallucinations of a young man shipwrecked on a deserted ship during the seventeenth century. Long-

ing to reach the island that stretches in front of him but unable to swim, Roberto, the main character of the novel, dreams and creates a proliferation of possible worlds in which all his fantasies and fears are played out, including his desperate love for the beautiful Signora.

None of the writers contemporary to Eco equaled his international success, but the productions of different kinds of novels in the late twentieth century enriched the Italian literary sphere. Gesualdo Bufalino's *Diceria dell'untore* (1981; *The Plague-Sower*, 1988) achieved much popular and critical success. Bufalino (1920-1996) was unknown at the time the book was published and already past sixty, but the way in which his book narrates the events surrounding war victims who are enmeshed in the degradation of a sanatorium in Sicily is fresh. Bufalino's admirable style, sometimes elaborate, sometimes crystal clear, always has the effect of a personal and precious testimony of human debasement. Although still admirable, his following books, *Museo d'ombre* (1982; the museum of shadows), *Argo il cieco, ovvero, I sogni della memoria* (1984; *Blind Argus*, 1989), and *Tommaso e il fotografo cieco* (1996; Thomas and the blind photographer), did not enjoy the same level of success .

Another writer and film director who was extremely popular in Italy in the second half of the twentieth century, although his writing style was often under attack, is Alberto Bevilacqua (born 1934). He became famous in the 1960's with the novels *La Califfa* (1964; *Califfa*, 1969) and the Campiello Prize-winning *Questa specie d'amore* (1966; this type of love). Enriched by flashbacks, memories, anticipations, and dreamlike events, Bevilacqua's novels appear sometimes verbose and excessive, but when he writes about his hometown, Parma, he achieves his most sincere results, as in *La festa parmigiana* (1980; celebration in Parma), *Il curioso delle donne* (1983; curious about women), or *La donna delle meraviglie* (1984; the woman of wonders).

Born in the same year as Bevilacqua are two interesting, although different, novelists, Giuseppe Pontiggia (born 1934) and Ferdinando Camon (born 1935). The first relates a journalistic account of the events of contemporary times in a clean and readable style, but not without interpreting and situating them in a dreamlike zone, as in *Il raggio d'ombra* (1983; ray of shadow) and *La grande sera* (1989; the great night), winner of the prestigious Campiello Prize. Camon, on the other hand, began by writing about the people of his own area, the Veneto region, linguistically reproducing the musicality of their way of speaking, in *Il quinto stato*, (1970; *The Fifth Estate*, 1987) and *Un altare per la madre* (1978; *Memorial*, 1983). He later moved to the realistic novel, turning his analysis to introspective and psychological aspects of relationships, as in *La malattia chiamata uomo* (1981; *The Sickness Called Man*, 1992), *La donna dei fili* (1986; the woman of threads), and *Il canto delle balene* (1989; the whales' song).

Women writers also became prominent in the last decades of the twentieth century. Many, following the legacy of Sibilla Aleramo, chose to promote women's rights through the heroines of their novels. One of the most interesting of these figures is Dacia Maraini (born 1936), whose scholarship allowed her to resort to the historical past as a means for her critique of the feminine condition. Maraini made her debut in the 1960's with the novels *La vacanza* (1962, *The Holiday*, 1966), *L'età del malessere* (1963, *The Age of Malaise*, 1963), and *A memoria* (1967; by heart), but she became more famous with *Storia di Piera* (1980; story of Piera) and especially with *La lunga vita di Marianna Ucrìa* (1990; *The Silent Duchess*, 1993), which won the Campiello Prize and enjoyed a large public success.

Another writer who made feminism one of the most important aspects of her works is Gina Lagorio (born 1922). After *La spiaggia del lupo* (1977; the wolf beach), in which she followed the itinerary of a young woman toward emancipation, she published *Tosca dei gatti* (1983; Tosca of the cats). In this novel Lagorio portrays the loneliness of a common middle-aged widow, whose heroism consists of her being able to evoke the best qualities in the people that surround her; she is similar to Michele, the main character of Lagorio's following novel, entitled *Golfo del paradiso* (1987; the gulf of paradise). Like Maraini, Lagorio turned to history in search of exemplary heroines. In *Tra le mura stellate* (1991; within starred walls), for example, she remembers the writer Countess Lara, and in *Il bastardo* (1996; the bastard), she relates the love affairs and the vicissitudes of Don Emanuel of Savoy.

Isabella Bossi Fedrigotti (born 1948) found in her family house interesting historical documents referring to the Italian Risorgimento and made them sources for a few of her novels. *Amore mio uccidi Garibaldi* (1980; my love, kill Garibaldi) and *Casa di guerra* (1983; house of war) are the direct outcomes of her interest in historiography, but she achieved national fame with *Di buona famiglia* (1991; of a good family), winner of the Campiello Prize, in which two sisters from high society spend their time imagining opposite lives. Other popular women novelists include Francesca Duranti (1935-1988), also winner of the Campiello Prize with *Effetti Personali* (1988; *Personal Effects*, 1993); Paola Capriolo (born 1962), who wrote *Vissi d'amore* (1992; *Floria Tosca*, 1997) and *La spettatrice* (1995; *The Woman Watching*, 1998); and Susanna Tamaro (born 1957), whose *Va'dove ti porta il cuore* (*Follow Your Heart*, 1994) was a national best-seller in 1994.

Many Italian novelists devoted their writing to the criticism of contemporary society, mostly achieved with a nostalgia for a lost age. In the novels of Carlo Sgorlon (born 1930), the message is that in a computer age, human beings need to narrate and listen to stories. In *Il trono di legno* (1973; *The Wooden Throne*, 1988), Sgorlon explores the value of writing and his writing vocation through the stories of an old carpenter, while in *Gli dèi torneranno* (1977; the gods will come back) he reinstates his belonging to a courageous people, the population of the Friuli region in northern Italy, who reacted to natural disasters with a peculiar strength. In his novels of the 1980's—*La conchiglia di Anataj* (1983; Anataj's seashell), *L'armata dei fiumi perduti* (1985; the army of the lost rivers), and *Il caldèras* (1988; the coppersmith)—the focus is on the victims of history who have been cheated and beguiled by society. In *Il regno dell'uomo* (1994; the kingdom of man) and *La malga di Sîr* (1997; the "malga" of Sîr), he returns to the everyday life of the common people of Friuli. The same belief in the capacity of literature to restore lost values is shared by Raffaele Crovi (born 1934). Crovi passes from the political interests manifested in his first novel, *Il franco tiratore* (1968; the sniper), to the denunciation of technology in *Il mondo nudo* (1975; the naked world) and finally arrives at the description of his own personal experience and at the formulation of his creed in his two following novels, *La convivenza* (1985; living together) and *Le parole del padre* (1991; the words of the father).

Another important writer is Giorgio Montefoschi (born 1946), who prefers to transfigure reality in a dreamlike atmosphere. In *La terza donna* (1984; the third woman) and *La felicità coniugale* (1982; happiness in marriage), although he deals with interpersonal relations, especially the relationship between husband and wife, he tackles the fundamental abstract concepts of love and time and the reasons for existence.

In her study of contemporary Italian novels published in the collection *Da Verga a Eco* (1989; from Verga to Eco), Angela Ferraro identifies a group of writers whose fiction implicitly manifests the impossibility of narration. Wishing to deconstruct the novel, these writers choose to reveal secret narrative mechanisms by showing the contradictions and the inconsistencies of stories. Among the writers is Luigi Malerba (born 1927), who in *Salto mortale* (1968; *What Is This Buzzing, Do You Hear It Too?*, 1969) chooses the detective novel format but subverts it by manifesting different points of view and multiple narrators: The detective, the murderer, and all the suspects are named Giuseppe. Similarly, in *Il pianeta azzurro* (1986; blue planet), three different narrators recount the same story, but they continuously contradict themselves. The younger Antonio Tabucchi (born 1943) seems to belong to this same tradition of metafiction. *Notturno Indiano* (1984; *Indian Nocturne*, 1988) presents a narrator occupied in his search for a lost (or nonexistent) friend, but two discourses are revealed in which the roles are inverted, and it becomes the friend who is searching for the narrator. This disrupts all literary conventions, resulting in the disenchantment of the reader. The same is valid for Tabucchi's following novel, *Il filo dell'*

orizzonte (1986; *The Edge of the Horizon*, 1990), in which the linear narration becomes circular as the detective strongly resembles the murdered victim discovered in the beginning of the book.

The reflection on the text and the implicit deconstruction of the subject seem to be common aspects of the Italian novels of the late twentieth century. The dialogue with the narrative structures and the fragmentation of the individual do not seem to impair the proliferation of themes. On the contrary, modern authors reveal an optimistic view of the subject's possibilities and a creative way of approaching the loss of traditional conventions and ideologies.

Jack Shreve, updated by Cristina Farronato

BIBLIOGRAPHY

Amoia, Alba della Fazia. *Women on the Italian Literary Scene: A Panorama*. Troy, N.Y.: Whitston, 1992. Introduces the major women writers present in Italian culture in the nineteenth and twentieth centuries.

Arico, Santo L., ed. *Contemporary Women Writers in Italy: A Modern Renaissance*. Amherst: University of Massachusetts Press, 1990. A collection of essays dedicated to Italian contemporary women writers, including Elsa Morante, Natalia Ginzburg, Lalla Romano, Gina Lagorio, Dacia Maraini, and Oriana Fallaci.

Brand, Peter, and Lino Pertile, eds. *The Cambridge History of Italian Literature*. Cambridge, N.Y.: Cambridge University Press, 1996. Similar to other Cambridge histories, this volume presents an excellent overview of Italian literature. This first substantial history of Italian literature written in English provides a comprehensive survey from the beginnings to the 1980's.

Capozzi, Rocco, and Massimo Ciavolella, eds. *Scrittori, tendenze letterarie e conflitto delle poetiche in Italia (1960-1990)*. Ravenna: Longo, 1993. Most of the essays contained in this volume are in Italian, but two interesting essays—one on Umberto Eco and one on Alberto Moravia and Pier Paolo Pasolini—are written in English, by Linda Hutcheon and Patrick Rumble, respectively.

Cervigni, Dino S., ed. *Italy 1991: The Modern and*

the Postmodern. Chapel Hill, N.C.: Annali d'Italianistica, 1991. Contains an analysis of Italian contemporary literature, with particular references to what characterizes the modern and postmodern in contemporary authors.

Gordon, Robert S. C. *Pasolini: Forms of Subjectivity.* New York: Oxford University Press, 1996. Gordon analyzes the public works of Pier Paolo Pasolini, including his poetry and his films.

Haywood, Eric, and Cormac O' Cuilleanain. *Italian Storytellers: Essays on Italian Narrative Literature.* Dublin: Irish Academy Press, 1989. Growing out of a series of public lectures given at the University of Dublin, this volume contains essays on Verga and Italian fiction from Manzoni to Gadda, Eco, and Calvino.

Marcus, Millicent Joy. *Filmmaking by the Book: Italian Cinema and Literary Adaptation.* Baltimore, Md.: The Johns Hopkins University Press, 1993. Marcus proposes a series of studies dedicated to the negotiations between literary text and film adaptation in Italian literature and cinema.

Marotti, Maria Ornella, ed. *Italian Women Writers from the Renaissance to the Present: Revising the Canon.* University Park: Pennsylvania State University Press, 1996. This collection of essays, written by eminent scholars of Italian, revolves around the twin themes of canon formation and canon revision in Italian literature.

Pickering-Iazzi, Robin. *Politics of the Visible: Writing Women, Culture, and Fascism.* Minneapolis: University of Minnesota Press, 1997. Presents an analysis of interesting figures of Italian women writers during the Fascist period.

Russell, Rinaldina, ed. *Italian Women Writers: A Bio-bibliographical Sourcebook.* Westport, Conn.: Greenwood Press, 1994. Analytic studies of the most significant Italian women writers from the fourteenth century to the end of the twentieth.

Testaferri, Ada, ed. *Donna: Women in Italian Culture.* Ottawa, Ontario: Dovenhouse Editions, 1989. A selection of papers presented at a symposium on women in Italian studies. Contains essays on Italian women writers such as Elsa Morante and Maria Corti, as well as essays on images of women in Italian literature, such as Lucia Mondella.

Wood, Sharon. *Italian Women's Writing 1860-1994.* Atlantic Highlands, N.J.: Athlone Press, 1995. The aim of this book is to present a survey of Italian women from 1860 to 1994 as the subjects and objects of literary analysis, including figures such as Matilda Serao, Grazia Deledda, Anna Banti, Natalia Ginzburg, Elsa Morante, and Dacia Maraini.

JAPANESE LONG FICTION

In Japan, the earliest text that shows essential characteristics of long fiction is the *Kojiki* (712 C.E.; *Records of Ancient Matters*, 1882, 1968). Presented to the Japanese imperial court shortly after the establishment of the first permanent capital in 710 C.E., in what is now called the city of Nara, *Records of Ancient Matters* was compiled from narratives that traditional storytellers had handed down. The text combined history and myth. The graphemes, or written characters, used to record the text were Chinese. Because there was as yet no independent Japanese writing system, the Chinese characters used to transcribe *Records of Ancient Matters* were employed sometimes to project the semantic sense of their Chinese meaning and sometimes to convey the phonetic value of Japanese proper nouns, elements of song, and passages of incantation.

EARLY JAPANESE LONG FICTION

Japanese long fiction in its formative aspects and for much of its tradition of nearly thirteen centuries may be treated basically as a recitative form, derived from the human impulse to tell a story, sing a song, do a dance, or paint a picture. As such, it may be readily related to the development of narrative prose elsewhere. In Japan, as in China, India, and Persia, however, the narrative, or recitative, mode became interpenetrated with both lyric and dramatic modes of projection. Thus, fiction and poetry, story and song, drama and recitation were frequently mixed. This was already true of the earliest texts, *Records of Ancient Matters* as well as the *Nihon shoki*, or *Nihongi* (720 C.E.; *Chronicles of Japan*, 1896), which was also presented to the court early in the Nara period; and the early eleventh century court romance *Genji monogatari* (c. 1004; *The Tale of Genji*, 1925-1933), by Murasaki Shikibu (c. 978-c. 1030), all of which combined narrative and lyric modes of representation. Poetic elements were harnessed to augment the narrative, as in long Chinese fiction and as discussed by the translator of *Hsi-yu chi* (1592; *The Journey to the West*, 1977-1983), Anthony C. Yu, in his introduction to volume 1.

Typically, the lyric element in traditional Japanese long fiction served to project a character or person's state of mind or emotion, and the narrative element provided description, something like a pattern inscribed on a vase or embroidered on a cloth background. A sense of drama and immediacy came from dialogue, which is found in the earliest examples of Japanese narrative prose. Narration and dialogue in *Records of Ancient Matters* and in the Bible, for instance, afford a useful comparison. Both texts are third-person narratives. In the preface to *Records of Ancient Matters*, however, the storyteller is identified as "O no Yasumaro" (I, Yasumaro), whereas in the Bible, the reportorial voice remains anonymous. Although such a view is admittedly speculative, these two widely separated traditions from eastern and western Asia may conceivably be linked by oral traditions that span the entire Eurasian landmass, which from prehistoric times was inhabited by various nomadic peoples. Indeed, such oral traditions may even have been transmitted into the New World with the migrations of people across what is now the Bering Strait and down the land corridors of North America.

Accordingly, concepts such as specificity and universality may be employed in analyzing Japanese long fiction: The first of these concepts makes Japanese long fiction uniquely Japanese; the second guarantees general intelligibility and translatability. For example, the personal names of the procreative deities that appear in *Records of Ancient Matters*, Izanagi and Izanami, the male and female figures of the land-creating myth in the text, require familiarity with the Japanese cultural code in order to take on meaning, but their function allows readers everywhere to understand their role in a theogonic story of creation.

Although *Records of Ancient Matters* may be discussed in terms of its mythological, historical, or religious significance, both it and the companion work, *Chronicles of Japan*, deserve close attention as the earliest recorded texts that allow readers to investigate the roots of Japanese long fiction. In terms of physical size, they make up generous one-volume editions in modern movable-type format, whether in the original Chinese script, modern Japanese, or English. The question of fictionality, however, needs some qualification. A reader who expects fully rounded characters and a sense of individual growth will surely be disappointed. Other fictional elements, nevertheless, can readily be identified. These may be classified as structural, on the one hand, or semantic, on the other. For example, putative conversations, which are embedded in a narrative framework, may be treated as a fictional element of a structural nature. The following passage provides an example:

> "This bird's cry is ominous. It must be shot to death."
>
> As soon as she thus advised him, Ame-no-waka-hiko took the bow of hagi wood and the deer-slaying arrows and shot the pheasant to death.

The narrative voice and the storyteller's, or reciter's, frame may be defined as structural rather than semantic; they provide shape and form rather than referential meaning to the narrative.

By contrast, many episodic units in *Records of Ancient Matters* involve adventures, interpersonal relationships, human activities as well as their consequences, the passage of time, descriptions of settings, and the attribution of feeling to characters. Such units may be analyzed as fictional elements of a semantic nature; the sequence in book 1, chapters 17 to 37, known as the Izumo sequence, which tells how a new land was subdued and pacified, represents a case in point.

THE TALE OF GENJI

Thus, both myth and folklore may be seen as sources of long fiction in Japan. Later, in *The Tale of Genji*, for example, which describes the career of Prince Genji and two generations of his progeny as well as the society in which they lived, examples abound. To mention only one, in the last ten chapters of *The Tale of Genji*, water spirits derived from Japanese mythology appear to be personified as female characters. Indeed, this most widely admired part of the text acclaimed as the supreme masterpiece of Japanese literature may be read as an extended allegory of female water spirits that invite the love of human

men and that pass away like water flowing swiftly in its course from mountain springs to the salty sea, leaving behind sad memories.

The lyric, or poetic, element in Japanese long fiction, which virtually every critic recognizes, is exemplified by its function in *The Tale of Genji*. Distributed throughout the narrative are nearly eight hundred examples of thirty-one-syllable poems known as *waka* or *tanka*. Sometimes these poems furnish the germ for a situation or mood that is then developed in the text; at other times, a verse recapitulates emotions that a character experiences, summarizing a situation and serving as a distillation of human feeling. More of these short poems appear in *The Tale of Genji* than in the shortest of the imperial anthologies of such verses, which were compiled between the tenth and fifteenth centuries under court auspices.

It is no wonder, then, that by the twelfth century in Japan, poets and critics expressed great admiration for *The Tale of Genji*, not so much because of the story and plot as because of the role of the poetry in the tissue of the text. The poet and critic Fujiwara Shunzei (1114-1204), for example, taught that familiarity with the tale was essential to every poet's education. To him, the individual episodes together with the verses with which they were integrated conveyed the essence of various aspects of love, of the human response to the beauty of nature, and of the poignancy of human situations such as suffering, old age, and death. All of these features may be subsumed under the classical Japanese exclamatory word *aware*, which in a nominative sense became *mono-no-aware*, a term used in the vocabulary of criticism and aesthetics to suggest great sensitivity and a range of powerful human feeling.

Besides its sensitivity, *The Tale of Genji* came to exemplify another classical Japanese aesthetic quality, *miyabi* (courtly elegance), which exerts a soothing and civilizing influence. In large measure because *The Tale of Genji* survived through centuries of social upheaval and civil war, literary and artistic culture became irrevocably embedded in the fabric of Japanese culture. To Shunzei and successive generations of critics, *The Tale of Genji* remained a handbook for poets.

In yet another way, *The Tale of Genji* manifests a characteristic of traditional Japanese long fiction. This relates to connections between what may be termed "icon" and "logos"—picture and word. Unlike in England, where as late as the eighteenth century there existed a great tradition of literature with virtually nothing "that could be called a native tradition of painting," as Ronald Paulson observed in *Book and Painting* (1982), Japan, as *The Tale of Genji* reveals, saw word and picture develop hand in hand.

Within the text itself, word descriptions could be projected by means of visual terms: When a young boy, as if especially dressed for the occasion, walked out among flowers early on a misty summer day, his trousers wet with dew, and picked a morning glory, the narrative relates, "He made a picture that called out to be painted." Already by the time *The Tale of Genji* was written, there existed a pictorial tradition that accompanied such fictional narratives. Chapter 17 of the tale, "A Picture Contest," describes in fictional terms how word and picture were connected. In fact, *The Tale of Genji* may be seen as a confluence of literary and iconographic systems, in which iconocentric and logocentric aspects of the human imagination are combined and integrated in a fresh and appealing way. The tradition of combining picture and word continued virtually until the present day. Successive editions of *The Tale of Genji* were marvelously illustrated, and other novels and romances were similarly illuminated. Even now, in long fiction published serially in newspapers, illustrations retain a prominent place.

By way of contrast, early English novels had little connection with illustrations. As Paulson points out, in the European tradition, word came first and image followed, whereas in Japan, picture and story emerged together; icon might even take primacy over logos. In the twelfth century, an edition of *The Tale of Genji* already existed in the form of *e-maki* (illustrated scrolls) that combined literary text and painted scenes in a harmonious way. Later, a system of complex iconographic conventions developed, as Miyeko Murase describes in her book *Iconography of "The Tale of Genji"* (1983). The illustrator's pictorial imagination was often regarded as deserving credit equal to that of the author, especially in a kind of short Japanese chapbook that foreshadowed modern comic books.

Long or short, any fictional configuration that employs language as its principal medium needs two basic elements. The first of these is structural, involving narrative techniques and devices. The second is semantic and involves the extended units or episodes that relate to human feeling. In *The Tale of Genji*, much of the sense of universality and psychological realism that amazes many modern readers may be traced to episodes that depict basic human relationships in terms of dyads and triads.

As the basis for all simple and complex relationships between two people, various sorts of dyads may be analyzed. One common kind is a competitive dyad. This is best characterized by Genji and his long-standing companion Tō no Chūjō. Similar in age as well as social station and growing up together, the two men are fond of each other and resemble each other in many ways, sometimes being virtually indistinguishable. As the people around them make incessant comparisons between them, rivalry develops, leading in time to animosity. Eventually, in chapter 33, a degree of reconciliation takes place, as if to suggest restoration of a pristine harmony. Other dyads, too numerous to mention in a brief survey, figure in the tale. The dyadic unit may be traced throughout the course of Japanese long fiction, exemplifying the type of semantic configuration that guarantees translatability.

A further example may be drawn from *Nansō Satomi hakkenden* (1814-1842; Satomi and the eight dogs), by Takizawa Bakin (1767-1848). In this long, historical romance of several thousand pages, one male dyadic relationship is especially reminiscent of that between Genji and Tō no Chūjō. Two of the eight heroes (all of whom have emblematic and symbolic canine connections), Shino and Gakuzō, grow up together and develop a lifelong friendship, reflecting a universal literary phenomenon known variously as doubling, twinning, and splitting, as R. Rogers describes in *A Psychoanalytical Study of the Double in Literature* (1970). Similarly, the two women Yōko and Komako in the highly acclaimed novel, *Yukiguni*

(1937, 1947; *Snow Country*, 1957), by Yasunari Kawabata (1899-1972), form a female dyadic relationship.

In *The Tale of Genji*, certain dyads involving women are characterized by rancor or jealousy. Two characters, the Rokujō lady and Lady Aoi, one loved by Prince Genji and the other married to him, came to be celebrated in drama and painting as well as in prose fiction as archetypes of destructive female jealousy. Other women in *The Tale of Genji*, such as Murasaki and the Akashi lady, to mention the most exemplary case, barely avoid falling into such a destructive and futile relationship.

Another kind of dyad in *The Tale of Genji* touches on incest. Bonds between men and women that would normally be considered taboo are treated in various ways in *The Tale of Genji*. The boldest exploration of the incest theme involves Prince Genji and his stepmother, Fujitsubo. Prince Genji's later marriage to one of his nieces, the Third Princess, would be regarded in the West as incest, as would that of Genji's son, Yūgiri, to his cousin, Kumoinokari. Modern Japanese writers of fiction, whether short or long, from time to time continue to construct situations that remind Western readers of the ancient Greek story of Oedipus and Jocasta. The presence of incest in the literature of virtually all societies suggests a universal recognition of its existence and of the emotional strain to which such relationships give rise.

Another extended semantic confrontation skillfully treated in Japanese long fiction and particularly in *The Tale of Genji* involves triads. Surely the relationship most often depicted in world literature, such triangles may be broken down into three component dyads, each of which overlays the other two. In a relationship of this sort, people experience a mixture of joyous and painful emotions. Negative feelings and tragic consequences may come from the need, as in Ukifune's case toward the end of *The Tale of Genji*, to decide to which of two rival lovers a woman ought to grant her affections. Unable to make the decision, Ukifune first attempts suicide and then becomes a nun.

Turning one's back on the world of love gives rise to an independent theme, that of renunciation. Especially during the Middle Ages, under the influence of Buddhism, the idea of renouncing the world and taking religious orders was often treated in long Japanese fiction.

Within the Japanese tradition, *The Tale of Genji* stands out as a compendium of themes that give life to the extended episodes and sequences serving to make up narrative structures. One that reflects universal appeal is a man's search for a perfect woman or, conversely, a woman's quest for a dependable and loving mate. In Prince Genji's case, such a search stems from the early loss of his own mother and his admiration for Fujitsubo, his father's later consort and in effect his own stepmother. This admiration leads to a secretive love affair and to the birth of a son believed by the world to be the Emperor's but who in reality is Genji's.

Love in *The Tale of Genji* and elsewhere in Japanese long fiction involves the idea of substitution. Genji's father, the Emperor, finds Fujitsubo as a substitute for his lost love, Genji's departed mother. Genji, in turn, takes Murasaki as a replacement for the unattainable Fujitsubo, and so on. Tamakazura, a woman who appears in chapter 22, emerges as a substitute for the Lady of the Evening Faces, whose life was snuffed out in chapter 5 under mysterious circumstances.

In the last part of the tale, one of the main characters is Kaoru, Genji's putative son, who is in fact the offspring of a clandestine affair between Genji's young wife of his later years, the Third Princess, and the son of Tō no Chūjō, Genji's best friend. For Kaoru, two women, Nakanokimi and then Ukifune, become substitutes for Oigimi, who prefers death to the uncertainty of a love commitment. Behind such complex interconnections lies a relatively simple repertory of basic patterns and situations. In Kawabata's modern novel *Snow Country*, for example, the hero, Shimomura, and two women, Yōko and Komako, form such a triangle.

Long fiction would be tedious if narrative situations were always limited to people interacting in twos and threes. As in the orchestration of musical instruments in symphonic productions, long fiction often involves scenes of mass action, festive occasions, or public mourning when many people come together. Japanese long fiction is no different in this regard from that of other traditions. By virtue of the irony and contradictions that life involves, effective portrayal of human feeling and emotion may result from juxtaposing a collective atmosphere of gaiety, auspiciousness, or victory to a private mood of sadness, distress, or death. In Western literature, for example, Ulysses' victory at Troy is counterpointed by Achilles' defeat and death.

Often, *The Tale of Genji* involves a similar kind of irony. In chapter 9, the Kamo festival, a gala religious and social event something like the Mardi Gras, with a grand procession of people vying to display their finery, represents a case in point. Against this backdrop of collective joy, the tragic rivalry between the Rokujō lady and Lady Aoi reaches its climax, resulting in Aoi's death by the ghostly possession of the Rokujō lady's living spirit as Aoi is giving birth to Genji's son, Yōgiri. That such techniques are exploited in the tale stands as a tribute to the author's artistic mastery and as a testimony that Japanese long fiction from early times attained a high degree of subtlety and sophistication.

By the eleventh century, a broad repertory of literary ideas and themes was available. A literary language, albeit with a relatively narrow vocabulary, and a writing system that combined a phonetic syllabary of Japanese invention with the semantic resources of Chinese characters allowed compositions to be recorded, disseminated, and preserved. All of these and other developments enriched literary culture, remaining part of the tradition down to the present day, as J. Thomas Rimer pointed out in *Modern Japanese Fiction and Its Traditions* (1978).

THE HEIKE MONOGATARI

About one hundred and fifty years after the appearance of *The Tale of Genji*, Japanese society entered a period of turmoil that ushered in cataclysmic social and political change. One of the works of long fiction that grew out of the collective experience of the age was the epic chronicle known as the *Heike monogatari* (*The Heike Monogatari*, 1918; also as *The Tale of the Heiki*, 1975, 1988). As an account of

the rise and fall of the Taira family in the late twelfth century, *The Heike Monogatari* took form gradually in the following century. Originally intended for recitation to the musical accompaniment of the Japanese lute, it stands out in form and impact over the centuries since as the nearest equivalent in Japan to a great epic. Written in a heightened style and dotted with about one hundred short lyric verses, the text, like *The Tale of Genji*, has much of the tone of narrative poetry. Although *The Heike Monogatari* is now admired chiefly for its literary qualities, it was formerly read for its historical content; the same was true with *Records of Ancient Matters*. This point suggests that in the tradition of Japanese long fiction, certain texts exemplify the idea of telling a tale that combines elements of both make-believe and truth.

Above all, the unifying force in *The Heike Monogatari* is the passage of time; various transitional segments and expressions suggest the temporal flow of events. In turn, this theme is related to the philosophical concerns of Buddhism. In the epic, both lyric descriptions and the development of character are subordinated to Karma, or the concept of fate, the vanity and transitoriness of life, and the value of abandoning ordinary pursuits in favor of monasticism. A profound moralistic bent also runs through *The Heike Monogatari*, which can be traced to the Chinese influence of Confucianism. Confucian moralism appears in the form of an emphasis on intense personal loyalty; an unstinting spirit of service that links master and retainer, husband and wife, parent and child in *The Heike Monogatari* is also a product of Confucian values. The interplay of the Buddhist and Confucian worldviews imparts a sense of poignancy and a tone of tragedy to *The Heike Monogatari*, lending it an elegiac quality. Modern Japanese critics have observed that, in a text which superficially focuses on armed conflict, the reader finds surprisingly few descriptions of actual bloodshed.

Narrative techniques and conventions that came to maturity in *The Tale of Genji* are found in *The Heike Monogatari*. This partly explains why it has endured as a sourcebook for long Japanese fiction down to the present day. Approximately two hundred episodes make up the epic's twelve numbered books and the culminating book known as the *Kanjf-no maki*. Each book is divided into twenty or more episodes, suggesting units suitable for oral reading or recitation to the accompaniment of the Japanese lute.

Matsumura Gekkei (1752-1811; also known as Goshun), a prominent haiku poet and painter, chose the image of a spotted fawn with a humped back, a furry tail like that of a rabbit, and a face as meek as that of a mouse to illustrate a famous and representative passage of *The Heike Monogatari*. The episode tells of an emotionally charged moment in the life of a former empress who lost her child in the conflict between the two rival clans that figure in the book. The former empress is forced to take refuge in a lonely mountain temple amid the fallen leaves of the surrounding oak trees. Hearing a rustling sound, as if someone were approaching her retreat, she asks her companion to see who is coming and to signal her if she should hide. Discovering that the sound was only that of a deer passing by, the lady, her eyes filled with tears, recites a poem:

> "What visitor dares/ Tread this rocky mountain path/ To see my lady?/ It was only a young stag/ That rustled the fallen oak leaves,/ Only a deer is stirring,/ As it passes on its way."

More than episodes involving heroic action in battle or tragic and untimely death, the description of the frightened empress's forlorn existence as a nun in a remote temple among moss-covered rocks, frost-laden bushes, and withered chrysanthemums characterizes the mood of the text and the tone of the best Japanese long fiction.

The Heike Monogatari was composed in a noble style that mixes Chinese characters with Japanese phonetic symbols, in contrast to *Records of Ancient Matters*, which was written completely in Chinese characters. Stylistically, the language of *The Heike Monogatari* represents a literary forerunner of the modern mixed colloquial style of Japanese narrative prose.

Recognition that beauty is related to frailty and perishability lends an aesthetic coherence to the tale, making the text more than merely a series of episodes describing the fall of the Taira clan. Read and reread,

The Heike Monogatari still functions as part of the living culture of Japan. In early modern times, popular authors such as Bakin drew on it for inspiration. More recently, several novelists have reworked it, the most notable being Eiji Yoshikawa (1892-1962), author of *Shin-The Heike Monogatari* (1950-1957; *The Heike Story*, 1956). Films and television shows based on it continue to appear, and every year thousands of young people still visit places made famous by the tale.

THE THIRTEENTH THROUGH THE SEVENTEENTH CENTURIES

About two hundred works of narrative prose fiction produced in Japan between the thirteenth and the seventeenth centuries are extant today. Besides those that have survived, some two hundred other titles remain in name only, being mentioned in anthologies, catalogs, and the like, largely from the Middle Ages. Most of these titles, however, are short fiction, retold versions or elaborations of parts of *The Tale of Genji* and *The Heike Monogatari*. In time, the best of these became *yfkyoku* (librettos) for Japanese theatrical performances known as Nō, or *mai-no-hon* (literally, dance books), as texts for singing and chanting a form of medieval ballad were called. James T. Araki, in *The Ballad Drama of Medieval Japan* (1964), discussed this aspect of Japanese literature, which combines the art of narration or recitation with that of performance.

Similarly, a tradition of historical and literary texts analogous to *The Heike Monogatari* developed. Accounts of events organized in chronological fashion and composed of narrative units with partly fictional material were compiled by monks and scribes. One such title is the *Taiheiki* (1318-1367; English translation, 1959, 1961). Now valued primarily as a historical sourcebook, it is also praised for its narrative technique and rhetorical excellence.

In addition to such chronicles, there were also literary tales, consisting mostly of short fiction typically preserved in illustrated manuscripts. A third kind of compilation also deserves attention. From the ninth century on, there appeared collections of anecdotal tales and narratives called *setsuwa* (explained stories), the earliest of which were written in Chinese. Around the beginning of the twelfth century, one such work was recorded in a mixed style of Chinese characters and Japanese syllabary foreshadowing that of *The Heike Monogatari*: This was the *Konjaku monogatari* (*Tales of Times Now Past*, 1979, partial translation). W. Michael Kelsey's *Konjaku monogatari-shū* (1982) discusses this massive collection of thirty sections and 1,039 titled items, which in total length exceeds *The Tale of Genji*.

Quite different from elegant court literature, the *Konjaku monogatari* and its successors reflect a primitive oral impulse. In later Japanese long fiction, whenever a suggestion of salaciousness, a strain of ribald humor, or a flight of farfetched fantasy occurs, the influence of anecdotal tales and narratives is usually at work. Modern authors such as Ryūnosuke Akutagawa (1892-1927), best known for his short stories about fantastic, grotesque, and macabre topics, turned to such sources for inspiration, as Beongcheon Yu pointed out in *Akutagawa: An Introduction* (1972).

JAPANESE LONG FICTION AFTER THE SEVENTEENTH CENTURY

With the reestablishment of an era of peace in the early seventeenth century following a period of civil war, conditions became conducive to literary production. The total number of titles of narrative prose preserved from the seventeenth to the mid-nineteenth centuries amounts to more than ten times as many as those dating from the eighth through the sixteenth centuries. In the twentieth century, Japanese literary historians developed a complex generic terminology for narrative prose. As authorship of long fiction gradually proliferated, the distinction between practical, historical, philosophical, dramatic, and poetic compositions, on the one hand, and works of narrative prose, on the other hand, became somewhat more clear-cut.

Moreover, new titles of long fiction—as distinct from newly printed editions of old titles previously available only in manuscript—increased in number. Three essential conditions were met: First, authors had the leisure to write; second, readers had time to read; and third, a system of dissemination evolved

with the spread of woodblock printing and illustration. By the end of the early modern, or Edo, period (1600-1868), Japanese long fiction was read and admired not only in urban centers such as Edo (modern-day Tokyo), Kyoto, and Osaka but also in the remote countryside, as Bakin pointed out, wherever small boats could pass or people would walk the mountain pathways between distant villages.

By the late eighteenth century, new titles of long and short fiction alike were appearing every year in woodblock printed editions. Typically, these editions were sold in soft paper covers in sets of as many as five or more thin volumes. Only the longer items deserve to be classified in the category of fiction discussed here. Besides the connections with court romances, literary tales, chronicles, and anecdotal narratives (including permutations and pastiches), one new influence deserves to be pinpointed. Literary and colloquial fiction from China had a fresh impact on Japanese long fiction.

Such an influence can be traced to the publication of a collection of short tales, *Otogi bōko* (1666; the storyteller's servant). The compiler, Ryōi Asai (c. 1610-c. 1691), acknowledged indebtedness to a collection of Chinese tales, *Ch'ien teng hsin hua* (late fourteenth and early fifteenth centuries; new tales for lamplight). Thereafter, Chinese fiction had a growing impact on literary and intellectual life in Japan, extending to virtually every author of long fiction. The influence of Chinese fiction in early modern Japan foreshadowed the impact of Western literature on Japanese long fiction after the late nineteenth century. Without the attention that Japanese authors of the Edo period paid to Chinese literature, especially literary and colloquial fiction, Japanese authors and readers could hardly have been as receptive to new literary currents from the West.

Publication of *Kfshoku ichidai otoko* (1682; *The Life of an Amorous Man*, 1964), by Ihara Saikaku (1642-1693), marked a significant event in the history of Japanese long fiction. First, the idea of engaging dialogue and lively conversation amid a realistic urban setting imparted a fresh impulse to long fiction in Japan. For decades afterward, other authors emulated Saikaku, as Howard Hibbett observed in *The*

Floating World in Japanese Fiction (1959) and as Blake Morgan Young discussed in *Ueda Akinari* (1982). While seeming to break with traditions and conventions of the past, Saikaku actually extended them in new and original directions.

The very title of *The Life of an Amorous Man* evokes the world of *The Tale of Genji* and other texts of the courtly tradition. More obvious, the fifty-four episodes in *The Life of an Amorous Man* match the number of chapters of *The Tale of Genji*. Finally, just as Prince Genji gathered around him a large number of female companions, Saikaku's hero, Yonosuke, during the fifty-four years of his life, enjoys 3,742 women.

Instead of the world of the aristocrat or the warrior, however, *The Life of an Amorous Man* deals with the newly prosperous townspeople. By writing of their life in a realistic vein, Saikaku broke with the traditions of earlier narrative prose. Nevertheless, epoch-making though *The Life of an Amorous Man* was, the influence of the past should not be overlooked. Besides allusions to *The Tale of Genji*, examples of indebtedness to the rhetoric and conventions of traditional poetry abound. Not so much a direct response to the aristocratic *waka*, the text is derived from the more popular and plebeian haiku. Although a number of Saikaku's titles have been translated into English, there is no successful and complete version of either of Saikaku's most widely acclaimed works of long fiction. The second of these, *Kōshoku ichidai onna* (1686), was translated by Ivan Morris in *The Life of an Amorous Woman and Other Writings* (1963). As Bakin appreciatively commented in 1811, "Writing about daily things that people see with their own eyes and moreover to do this in an amusing manner began with Saikaku."

In its day, *The Life of an Amorous Man* struck readers as a shocking and salacious book, especially emerging as it did from the milieu of the townsperson. Its plebeian origins in a class-structured society prevented its consideration on a par with titles in the aristocratic tradition, such as *The Tale of Genji*. Until almost the middle of the twentieth century, even in modern, movable-type editions, certain passages of Saikaku's works were regarded as inappro-

priate for study in schools and universities, mainly because free love between men and women in the context of a neo-Confucian code of morality was held to be a threat to the social fabric. Wine, women, and wealth were regarded as the three temptations that men must resist.

The hero of *The Life of an Amorous Man*, Yonosuke (whose name suggests an allegorical meaning, "man-of-the-world" or "worldly man"), far from eschewing contact with women, has an insatiable craving for female companionship and for sexual intercourse. Exactly as young Prince Genji in his seventh year is described as having been taken to visit the women's quarters in the imperial palace and presumably initiated to sexual experience, young Yonosuke in his seventh year is also introduced to coitus, his partner being an older and experienced maidservant. The choice of such an improbably young age may stem from the traditional Confucian injunction that by the age of seven, boys and girls should begin to lead segregated lives.

Until the modern era and the transformation of Japanese literature under influence from the West, long fiction continued to be integrated with lyric modes of expression, and Saikaku's case was no exception. His training and apprenticeship as an author were in *haikai* (amusing) poetry, a popular, plebeian, and comparatively light form of *renga* (linked verse), which was a communal variety of chain poetry that developed in aristocratic circles and gradually spread during the Middle Ages to all classes of society. It was from such circles that haiku emerged.

No wonder, then, that each of the fifty-four short chapters, or sections, of *The Life of an Amorous Man* begins with a rhetorical flourish reminiscent of the all-important opening verse of a chain poem. In terms of structure, each segment of the text in a cryptic and anecdotal manner describes scenes from stages of the hero's life. Depiction of the manners and customs of people that Yonosuke meets enriches the texture. Human foibles and contradictions are exaggerated in a dry and humorous manner. Each part ends in a witticism, paralleling the conventions that govern linked verse. Thus, Saikaku's text, like earlier representative examples of Japanese long prose, amounts to a composite form with rhetorical elements common to both prose and poetry. Not until the late nineteenth century was this pattern broken.

The weakness of Saikaku's style, as well as that of his successors and imitators, lies in excessive abbreviation of an underlying expository narrative; the result is something like rice without enough gluten to hold the grains together. Initiated readers can exercise their imaginations and complete the tale as they please, but outsiders often experience frustration at trying to discern the basic outline. Thus, Saikaku's prose has a relatively low level of translatability. To the present day, certain kinds of Japanese long fiction still have the same weakness, creating difficulties for translator and reader alike.

Japanese long fiction of the traditional epoch culminated in Bakin's *Nansō Satomi hakkenden*. An illustrated historical romance in nine sections and 181 chapters, *Nansō Satomi hakkenden* describes the fortunes of a warrior family. Falling in defeat during the fifteenth century, the Satomi family's fortunes are revived with the aid of eight "dog" warriors and a host of other loyal retainers and dedicated citizens. Such a restoration may be seen as a paradigm both for the Meiji Restoration of 1868 and for Japan's dramatic revival following World War II. Literary themes both reflect and feed social ideals. Art both follows and shapes nature.

Nansō Satomi hakkenden, which was the longest literary work hitherto written in Japan, reflected Bakin's personal outlook and particularly his deeply moral sensibility, tempered by compassion and a belief in human dignity. Loyalty, filial piety, and the restoration of hard-pressed or destitute samurai families like his own were Bakin's main themes. In *Nansf Satomi hakkenden*, as well as his other full-length historical romances, special attention to Chinese and Buddhist philosophy was tempered by belief in the efficacy of the Japanese gods and a concern for language and style. Bakin's work represents a culmination of a Japanese literary response to nearly fifteen centuries of Chinese cultural influence, dating from the introduction of the Chinese writing system in about the fifth century.

As a pivotal work in the tradition of Japanese long fiction, *Nansō Satomi hakkenden* illustrates Japanese transformation of Chinese literary conventions into a rich and distinctive body of long fiction (to say nothing of the other literary forms, such as poetry and drama). With this precedent, Japanese long fiction of the modern era could accommodate powerful outside influences from the West without losing a sense of its own identity.

Structurally, *Nansō Satomi hakkenden* may be divided into three parts. Chapters 1 through 14 describe the establishment of the Satomi clan in what is today the Chiba area near modern Tokyo; chapters 15 to 131 tell how the eight "dog" warriors assemble under the Satomi banner; and finally, chapters 131 to 181 relate the struggle of the Satomi clan against the combined forces of other powerful clans and opponents, who contest their right to live in peace and enjoy prosperity.

After the Satomi victory, the eight "dog" warriors accompany a clan embassy to the traditional capital of Kyoto to pay respects to the Emperor as well as the Shogun and to ask that Fusehime (the daughter of the Satomi patriarch and a kind of sacrificial victim who offered herself to the cause of familial restoration) be recognized as a goddess. A shrine is built in her honor, because of the many miracles she performed. At the end, each of the eight "dogs" is married to one of the patriarch's eight daughters. The Satomi clan then flourishes in peace for generation after generation until the virtue of the founding patriarch of the clan is seemingly exhausted. Like that of the Taira clan in *The Heike Monogatari*, the Satomi glory becomes but an evanescent dream.

"When people control their desires, govern their passions, store up good and not work evil," Bakin wrote in his didactic voice as narrator near the end of *Nansō Satomi hakkenden*, "and when they show discretion in their acts, while alive they need feel no shame on earth, and after death their descendants will continue to flourish." Owing to the great virtue of the first two generations of Satomi lords, Bakin records with a flourish at the end, "The citizens of the domain remembered them and responded to their profound influence." Bakin concludes with three verses, one in Chinese and two in Japanese, the last of these reflecting a conventional gesture of self-deprecation: "Like a floating weed/ Passing countless dreary hours,/ I've tried hard to write,/ But my brush may seldom touch/ Elusive words that have no roots."

Even today, when compared with their Western counterparts, most Japanese novels lack an architectonic sense of plot, tending to be episodic and notoriously lacking in overall shape and structure. This characteristic partially stems from the legacy of medieval linked verse. The early conventions of narrative recitation and the rhetorical techniques of court poetry have also played their part. Structural coherence in Japanese long fiction derives more from associations of idea and image than from well-wrought unity in a classical Western sense.

Nevertheless, *Nansō Satomi hakkenden* stands as an exception. Indeed, Bakin's long historical romances, known as *yomihon* (reading books), belong in a class of their own, distinguished by the author's close attention to plot construction and conscious technique, for both of which he was much indebted to Chinese influences. In *Nansō Satomi hakkenden*, the action includes an escape from the flaming ruins of a besieged castle (which bears comparison to a parable about a burning house found in the *Lotus Sutra*, the most widely read Buddhist holy book in East Asia). A death curse of a usurper's malicious concubine evokes ideas and imagery found in an early Chinese classic that warns against women sharing in the highest affairs of state. These are but two of the motifs from which the overall structure is generated.

Eight lost jewels from a charmed rosary—the same number as the *Lotus Sutra* has parts—foretell how eight heroes will break the sinister curse and help institute a benevolent rule. The name of the Satomi daughter, Fusehime, is written with Chinese characters suggesting "Princess of Man and Dog," the morpheme "Fuse-" (from a verb meaning to submit, to lie in wait, or to be hidden) employing a character with the "man radical" and "dog." Fusehime's fate is linked to that of a wolflike dog, Yatsufusa (Eight Patches). This canine beast, in turn, is a reincarnation of the malicious concubine of the usurper already mentioned.

Retiring into the mountains with the dog, the girl seems to become pregnant (a phenomenon inspired by Chinese accounts of a woman's miraculous conception through a beast). Fusehime thereby becomes the godmother of eight warriors who mysteriously possess eight jewels from her rosary. She serves as their protective deity as well as that of the Satomi house.

Farfetched as such a plot might sound, within the overall form and structure of a historical romance of an allegorical nature, fantastic elements help to sustain reader interest over several thousand pages of text and add to the suggestive power of the narrative. On the one hand, a literal meaning unfolds. Scenes and situations describe an imaginative likeness of what happened in history. On the other hand, a complex allegory is revealed. Good and evil are imagined as persons who serve as emblems as well as human characters in their own right. History and make-believe are combined in an aesthetic structure that bears special comparison with texts of long Chinese fiction such as *Shui-hu chuan* (fourteenth century; translated by Pearl S. Buck as *All Men Are Brothers*, 1933; also as *Water Margin*, 1933) and *The Journey to the West*.

Restoration of a family that has unjustly fallen on hard times is the basic theme of *Nansō Satomi hakkenden*. Morality is described as the foundation for such a restoration. Fate in a Buddhist sense is a force ensuring that morality prevails. Good and evil are interwoven "like tangled strands of thread." Religious and ethical beliefs that people's behavior may influence fate are expressed in literary terms. Good is seen to benefit one's progeny more than oneself. Evil deeds meet punishment in one's own lifetime. Good and evil may both activate supernatural forces. Bakin accordingly expounds Confucian and Buddhist ideas that fate is linked to morality and embodies this concept in the imaginative structure of his lengthy romance.

Even in modern times, long Japanese fiction—especially in its popular manifestations—shows a strong didactic bent. Fictionalized history remains a common form of reading matter. *Nansō Satomi hakkenden* exemplifies the interpenetration of history and fiction in Japan and marks the high point of the didactic function of literature. A modern version appeared serially in one of the mass circulation daily newspapers, *Asahi shimbun*, and a critical exposition of Bakin's text by Takada Mamoru, *Hakkenden-no sekai* (1980; the world of Satomi and the eight dogs), sold an impressive number of copies in a paperback edition.

About twenty years after the Meiji Restoration, Japanese authors of long fiction began to respond to Western literary influences. The period of modern literature began. Like that of other nations, Japanese literature, in response to various new modes of communication and cross-cultural intercourse, has increasingly converged with the currents of its world counterpart. By the time the twentieth century began, the chief impetus in Japanese long fiction involved a concerted effort to break with older traditions. This force has had both a positive and a negative side. In a positive sense, Japanese writers embraced Western literary movements and theories, trying to model their works on particular European or American examples.

Although the result of turning to Europe and America was imitative in many cases, the impulse to reach out and adapt Western literature to native needs was basically constructive. Western literature brought fresh vitality to traditions and conventions that reached back a millennium and a half. On the negative side, writers turned away from their own heritage, rejecting many native myths, archetypes, and conventions.

Tradition, however, dies hard in Japan. The conservative impulse remains strong. Albeit undergoing transformation, classical modes of long fiction and various conventions that developed alongside them have survived. Old texts regularly appear in new editions or in fresh garb, as the serial version of *Nansō Satomi hakkenden* suggests. Indeed, long fiction together with its short counterpart has emerged as the principal literary genre. Enriched by new examples introduced from the outside world and having overshadowed lyric and dramatic forms, Japanese long fiction remains indebted to an indigenous lineage of narrative prose that goes back to *Records of Ancient Matters*, *The Tale of Genji*, and many other predecessors.

THE TWENTIETH CENTURY JAPANESE NOVEL

By the beginning of the twentieth century, the modern counterpart of older forms of Japanese long fiction proved to be a medium capable of dealing with the main theme of twentieth century Japanese literature—awareness of the self. Japanese writers espoused the ideology of individualism. A characteristically Japanese form of long fiction, the *shishfsetsu* (literally, "I novel"), emerged. Concurrently, Japanese authors capitalized on newfound personal freedom to deal with topics that indicated heightened social and political awareness. One of the most famous "I novels" is *An'ya kfro* (1921-1937; *A Dark Night's Passing*, 1976), by Naoya Shiga (1883-1971); it was described by Edwin McClellan, the translator, as "an intensely private and self-centered novel," in which the "identification of the author with his hero is complete."

A widely acclaimed early twentieth century title that dealt with social problems is *Hakai* (1906; *The Broken Commandment*, 1974), by Shimazaki Tōson (1872-1943). According to Natsume Sōseki (1867-1916), a critic and widely translated author of long fiction, *The Broken Commandment* was "the first [genuine] novel of the Meiji era."

Although the "I novel" deserves to be seen as a manifestation of a newfound sense of individual identity, reflecting the process of Westernization, it also has connections with earlier Japanese literary genres. In addition to forms discussed previously, the *nikki* (diary) and the *zuihitsu* (miscellaneous essay) involved the concept of a private self, as distinct from that of a group, or corporate, self. Certain situations in *A Dark Night's Passing* call to mind parallels with *The Tale of Genji*. Likewise, the idea of socially engaged literature predates *The Broken Commandment*. Bakin's tales and romances, as well as the works to which they are indebted, presaged Tōson's morally committed novel. Thus, older Confucian views of literature, which stressed a didactic function, found a new direction in modern literary movements that emphasized an ideological reference.

Besides such dichotomies as old and new, native and Western, self and other, which permeate twentieth century Japanese literature, other dualities also deserve mention. For example, a split between the so-called *jun-bungaku* (pure literature) and *taishn bungaku* (literally, "mass literature" or, by extension, "popular literature") unavoidably implies class differences of high and low. Similar distinctions such as *gabun* (elegant writings) and *zokubun* (common writings) existed in earlier times. *The Tale of Genji* exemplifies the former. Compilations of anecdotal tales and narratives such as *Konjaku monogatari* led to the latter. Nowadays, the literature of court salons and of plebeian groups has been replaced by modern overtones of social or educational class. Pure literature is thought to belong to an elite level of society and mass literature to the ordinary people. Certain critics dismiss mass literature as being beneath contempt.

To be sure, most critical attention in modern Japan has been on a succession of elite writers who have dominated the literary scene. Popular writers, whose work has a strong emotional appeal and continues to capture the Japanese imagination, have been ignored if not scorned by literary scholars. One such author is Kaizan Nakazato (1885-1944), whose *Daibosatsu tfge* (1951-1953; *Dai-bosatsu Toge: Great Bodisattva Pass*, 1929) is a saga about a nihilistic master of Japanese swordsmanship. This novel combines elements of the Japanese narrative tradition with the humanism of Western literature.

Yet another example is Eiji Yoshikawa's *Miyamoto Musashi* (1936; *Musashi*, 1981). A historical romance of travel and adventure about a late sixteenth and early seventeenth century warrior, the novel has been widely read in North America. Many business people believe that the book reveals important cultural and organizational traits that have helped Japan achieve its dramatic success as a leading economic power in the contemporary world.

A younger popular author, Hisashi Inoue (born 1934), is a leading exponent of the Japanese tradition of satire and parody. Debunking orthodoxy and exploiting the seamy and ribald side of human life goes back to the very beginnings of Japanese long fiction; even in *The Tale of Genji*, comic scenes appear. The Akashi Lay Monk, father of the Akashi Lady, for example, is presented as a garrulous, tiresome, and eccentric person who "seemed ridiculous as he bustled

around seeing to Genji's needs." Hisashi Inoue's proud Gallic priest, a French teacher at "S. University" in Tokyo, in the best-selling novel *Mokkimpotto-shi-no ato-shimatsu* (1974, originally serialized in the *Mainichi Daily News; The Fortunes of Father Mokinpott*, 1976), represents a modern counterpart. Father Mokinpott, incidentally, has been called perhaps "the first living, breathing, fully realized non-Japanese character in Japanese literature."

One twentieth century author who was adept at creating both "pure" and "popular" literature was Yukio Mishima (1925-1970). His bucolic novel *Shiosai* (1954; *The Sound of Waves*, 1956), belongs to the latter category, and *Kinkakuji* (1956; *The Temple of the Golden Pavilion*, 1959) belongs in the former. His tetralogy, *Hfjf no umi* (1969-1971; *The Sea of Fertility: A Cycle of Four Novels*, 1972-1974), represents an attempt to create a hybrid form of long fiction in a dazzling richness of style that might appeal to both classes of readers in Japan.

Other general points that relate to Japanese long fiction of the twentieth century include the centralization of literary activity in the capital city of Tokyo. This, too, had its earlier counterpart in literary history; the names of Japanese literary periods, such as Nara, Heian, Kamakura, Muromachi, and Edo, come from centers of political power. In this sense the modern age may be called the Tokyo period. One of the first authors to write about Tokyo and describe its people in long fiction was Nagai Kafū (1879-1959). A native of the city, he was heir to the older traditions of Edo, the former name of Tokyo. Most modern Japanese authors live and work in Tokyo or nearby cities and towns and depend upon the communications and distribution system that is centered in Tokyo.

Newspapers and serials published in Tokyo serve as a primary medium of disseminating novels. Formerly, woodblock editions of long fiction were published in serial form; for example, Bakin took twenty-eight years to finish *Nansō Satomi hakkenden*. At first, installments appeared every two or three years; later, they were issued annually. Even today, the book version of a novel often follows serialized publication in the daily, weekly, or monthly press. More than in English-speaking countries, authors are public personalities, giving them added reason for living and working in the Tokyo area. Izumi Kyōka (1873-1939), whose reputation enjoyed a revival in Japan, was one of many early twentieth century authors of long fiction whose works first appeared serially.

Another characteristic of modern Japanese long fiction involves style. Today, the colloquial language is the main medium of expression; a larger gap formerly existed between the style of literary texts and ordinary discourse. This change took place gradually and needs to be seen in the context of the entire tradition. Two stages, however, may be singled out. First, late in the nineteenth century, people searched for a suitable idiom for translating Western literature into Japanese. Futabatei Shimei (1864-1909) dominates as the author of long fiction who brought literary composition into line with everyday speech.

The second stage dates from after World War II. Between 1948 and 1952, a number of reforms in language and education took place. Meanwhile, the use of Chinese (the earliest literary language in Japan and the writing system of *Records of Ancient Matters*) declined. Study and translation of literature flourished. Virtually all the famous European and American works of long fiction became available as models for would-be writers and as a reference for readers and critics. Nowhere is there a more world-oriented literary culture than in Japan. So complex has the Japanese literary code become that any given work of long fiction may at least hypothetically involve allusions to Homer's *Odyssey* (c. 800 B.C.E.), Murasaki Shikibu's *The Tale of Genji*, and Hermann Hesse's *Siddhartha* (1922; English translation, 1951) in the same text. Critics of Mishima's *The Sound of Waves* have compared it to Longus's *Daphnis and Chloë*, a second century Greek pastoral romance.

Modern world literature took root in Japan primarily after the Russo-Japanese War (1904-1905). A new era in Japanese long fiction brought fame and popularity to young writers. When Japan forced Russia to sue for peace, authors, including several who remained active into the 1940's and 1950's, felt a surge of inspiration and confidence. Innovations by young writers still in their thirties hastened the break with tradition. Novelists such as Shimazaki Tōson,

whose goal was to depict life as it is, without glossing over the seamier side, established the naturalistic novel.

Meanwhile, authors such as Natsume Sōseki (1867-1916) opposed the naturalists' excesses of lurid sensationalism and thinly disguised autobiographical exhibitionism. Sōseki, especially, still holds a firm place in the Japanese reader's affections; his crisp conversational style continues to influence young writers. In *Kusamakura* (1906; *The Three-Cornered World*, 1965), he taught that the leisurely moments one devotes to art and letters offer relief from the unavoidable suffering of existence. This belief contrasted with the unrelieved gloom and despair of naturalists such as Tōson. In spite of a period of study in England, Sōseki's philosophy and theory of literature show an affinity for those of an earlier poet, diarist, and critic, Matsuo Bashō (1644-1694). Yet, in *Kokoro* (1914; English translation, 1941), written toward the end of his life, Sōseki, whose thought combined "art for art's sake" and pronounced Buddhist tenets, granted humans only three equally dreary choices: death, madness, or religion. Actually, the intellectual differences between Japanese naturalists and antinaturalists often seem small or even nonexistent.

Toward the end of the Meiji period (1868-1912) and into the Taishō era (1912-1926), a group of writers who shared criticism of the naturalists' excesses published a periodical called *Shirakaba* (1910-1923; white birch) with serialized works of long fiction as well as other forms of literature and criticism. Humanitarian in outlook and aristocratic in temperament, the group's members included Naoya Shiga and Takeo Arishima (1878-1923). Curiously enough, the outspoken and emotional tone of Arishima's best-remembered novel, *Aru onna* (1919; *A Certain Woman*, 1978), stands at variance with his prevailing image as a quiescent, scholarly humanist of strong ethical bent.

Although the boundary between naturalist and antinaturalist now seems vague, such distinctions at least show how modern writers in Japan have tended to band together into small, independent groups and how critics, at least in Japan, continue to follow such categories. One of the leading modern writers of long fiction was Jun'ichirō Tanizaki (1886-1965). Tanizaki explored human life with daring, sensitivity, and psychological acumen; his long fiction appeals readily to Western readers, and his work has achieved worldwide recognition. His most ambitious novel, *Sasameyuki* (1949; *The Makioka Sisters*, 1957), published in three volumes in Japanese, deals with such matters as the conflict between traditional ways of life and superficial Westernization. Other titles include *Kagi* (1956; *The Key*, 1960) and *Fnten rfjin nikki* (1962; *Diary of a Mad Old Man*, 1965), which date from the productive last years of his life.

Taishō literature usually takes in several years of Meiji and the early part of the Shōwa era (1926 to the present). Although Japanese commentators have criticized Taishō authors for failing to transcend traditional, feudal, or nationalistic concepts, during the 1910's and 1920's a number of novels with delicately wrought detail were produced. Some writers, whether despite or because of their acute perception of life, shirked social responsibility and feigned moral decadence. Western readers may readily discover untranslated literary works that are at once original and part of the twentieth century *Zeitgeist*. Reevaluation of the contribution Taishō authors have made to the creation of a distinctly modern sensibility is comparatively recent.

Among writers whose careers began in the 1920's, Yasunari Kawabata (1899-1972) was one of those who advanced such European causes as Futurism, expressionism, and Dadaism. Kawabata, however, developed an intuitive, subjective, sensual, and faintly decadent tone that owed as much to classical Japanese texts as to modern European "isms." Among his works of long fiction, three titles in particular stand out. In addition to *Snow Country*, mentioned previously, *Sembazuru* (1952; *Thousand Cranes*, 1958) and *Yama no oto* (1954; *The Sound of the Mountain*, 1970) best convey the atmosphere of Kawabata's long fiction. Kawabata was the first Japanese writer to win the Nobel Prize in Literature.

For a time in the 1920's, it seemed that leftist literature might overshadow the efforts of avant-garde writers and modernists such as Tanizaki and Kawabata. Despite the support of many established writers,

however, the proletarian movement was suppressed. Some prominent leftist authors failed to survive World War II; others lived through government repression and the hardships of war, resuming literary activity after Japan's defeat in 1945.

Nonleftist writers active during the 1930's include Ibuse Masuji (born 1898), one of the most underrated of modern Japanese novelists. His fictitious journal of the atomic bombing of Hiroshima in August, 1945, brought him well-deserved fame. A make-believe diary of a Hiroshima resident at the time of the bombing, *Kuroi ame* (1966; *Black Rain*, 1969) strikes the reader as an extraordinary interpretation of the event. *Black Rain* relates how Japanese society carried on in the wake of the atomic holocaust. The author's deep belief in the futility of war and a tone of gentle irony toward the militaristic and bureaucratic mentality permeate the book.

Best typifying the immediate postwar period, the autobiographical novels of Osamu Dazai (1909-1948) describe a time of excruciating self-examination and extreme nihilism in Japan. In some respects, they anticipated Beat literature. *Shayf* (1947; *The Setting Sun*, 1956), about the privation and despair that an aristocratic family endures, gave birth to a new expression in the Japanese language, "setting sun people," which referred to anyone who fell from a position of comfort and prosperity to one of abject misery, much like the Heike clan at the end of the twelfth century. *Ningen shikkaku* (1948; *No Longer Human*, 1958) particularizes the gloomy postwar years in Japan.

Many other writers emerged after World War II. Paradoxically, in the same way as victory over Russia in 1905 stimulated literary activity, defeat by the Allies in 1945 led to a renaissance in literature and art as well as to economic revival. The most notable postwar author of long fiction was Yukio Mishima. Mishima may be best remembered for focusing on individuals who groped—often without success—for new directions in a fragmented, dislocated society. His characters suffer from the aftereffects of the most disastrous war in the nation's history. In microcosm, they represent a country still struggling to transform itself from an isolated and ingrown local society in

East Asia to an economic and political power on the world stage. Mishima's characters' wild, bizarre, and perverse behavior contrasts with the collective ideals, restraints, and discipline that held the desperate nation to its course. In 1970, he committed seppuku in the manner of the Edo-period samurai; Mishima's highly theatrical suicide was followed by Kawabata's self-asphyxiation in 1971.

While Mishima was making his reputation as a fiery young author, Fumiko Enchi (1905-1986), twenty years his senior, was exploring the experience of betrayal and sensuality with keen insight and haunting beauty. Her novel *Onna men* (1958; *Masks*, 1983) unfolds against a background that involves the medieval Japanese theatrical form, Nō, which is still widely patronized in Japan today. She published a well-received and highly praised new translation into modern Japanese of *The Tale of Genji*. Shūsaku Endō (born 1923), one of the few Christian writers in Japan, has been compared by Western critics to Graham Greene; among Endō's many novels translated into English are *Umi to dokuyaku* (1957; *The Sea and Poison*, 1972), *Chimmoku* (1966; *Silence*, 1969), and *Kuchibue o fuku toki* (1974; *When I Whistle*, 1979).

An author representative of the immediate postwar years is Inoue Yasushi (born 1907). Two of his historical novels have been translated into English: *Tempyf no iraka* (1957; *The Roof Tile of Tempyf*, 1975), which is set in eighth century Japan, and *Tonkf* (1959; *Tun-huang: A Novel*, 1978). The setting for the latter is a Central Asian oasis community astride the ancient Silk Road, over which desert caravans kept up intercourse between the East and the West until navigational techniques allowed for more dependable use of sea routes.

In the 1960's, new writers continued to appear, and postwar authors such as Kōbō Abe (1924-1993) extended their reputation. Abe's long fiction has been widely translated and read outside Japan. He combines a scrupulous attention to the individual's emotional state, characteristic of the best traditional Japanese long fiction, with a deft appreciation of the present human situation, in which, as Arthur Kimball wrote in *Crisis in Identity* (1973), "the outlines of one's identity may become an unreadable confusion."

Kenzaburō Ōe (born 1935), in *Kojinteki na taiken* (1964; *A Personal Matter*, 1968), probed into modern youth's confrontation with sex and society. His feisty and diminutive hero, Bird, despite appearances, demonstrates that right will prevail over might, light over darkness, and order over chaos. The hero's abrupt about-face at the end has led critics to complain that the conclusion is unconvincing.

During the 1970's, other fresh authors contributed to the vibrant state of Japanese long fiction. For example, a controversial, best-selling fantasy of sex, drugs, and violence by Ryū Murakami (born 1952), *Kagirinaku tōmeini chikai burū* (1976; *Almost Transparent Blue*, 1977), won a coveted literary prize. By means of rich imagery and often crude language, a repellent world in an advanced state of disintegration, decay, and corruption is projected. Such works fairly represent one facet of Japanese long fiction today.

THE LATE TWENTIETH CENTURY

After the early 1980's, a number of shifts occurred in the attempts by younger authors in Japan to reveal in their novels a broader representation of the complexities of contemporary Japanese life. Older distinctions between "high" and "popular" fiction have been steadily breaking down. Some critics see parallels between the situation in contemporary Japan and the United States, where postmodern concerns often preempt attention from older forms of modernism.

In some ways, this trend began as early as the 1960's in Japan, when the work of two important writers attracted and sustained widespread attention. The first of these was Kita Morio (born 1927), whose lengthy novel *Nireke no hitobito* (1964; *The House of Nire*, 1984-1985) helped characterize, often with trenchant humor, the life of his family, spanning the often tumultuous years between the two world wars. Morio's father, Saitô Mokichi, was a noted poet and a psychiatrist, and the son's disguised portrait of his father is as vivid as it is compelling. Morio was one of the first to introduce elements of humor into this kind of family chronicle, although the work harbors shadows. The success of this novel helped launch the author's subsequent career as a humorist.

The second of these writers, Maruya Saiichi (born 1925), also introduced humor into his delineation of the contemporary social scene, notably in his novel *Tatta hitori no hanran* (1972; *Singular Rebellion*, 1986). While dealing with such volatile issues as the antiwar demonstrations current at the time and other potentially disturbing topics, the tonality of the book (particularly because of the delightful old lady, who, straight from prison, enters the narrator's family to become the book's main character) is surprisingly successful in creating a relaxed, even droll atmosphere.

In this context, the tonality of Saiichi's writing is at considerable variance with that of, say, Kenzaburō Ōe. Ōe, who was awarded the Nobel Prize in Literature in 1994, may well represent the last of the significant writers in Japan to maintain this stance. Younger novelists, on the whole, tend to either withdraw into themselves to compose highly introspective fiction or turn to writing in a more hedonistic, often fanciful way, which they are happy to define as postmodern or cutting edge. At the end of the twentieth century a spectrum of important writers were at work, ranging from these modernistic writers to those who still made at least some use of the long heritage of Japanese culture and tradition. In this sense, these writers may be said to mirror the variegated, sometimes contradictory nature of contemporary Japanese culture itself.

The cutting-edge writers in particular have taken an interest in international popular culture. The characters in their novels often live abroad, or at the least have foreign friends. Video, film, animation, and computer games also figure in their aesthetic. Perhaps the most widely read of these authors is Ryū Murakami, who wrote a number of best-sellers, in particular *Koin rokka beibizu* (1980; *Coin Locker Babies*, 1995), with deals with the surprising, often grotesque adventures of two boys in the Tokyo labyrinths, abandoned and originally brought up in an orphanage. Another writer in somewhat the same vein is Eimi Yamada (born 1959; also known as Amy Yamada), who often sets her stories abroad. Her novel *Torasshu* (1991; *Trash*, 1994), set in New York, is both ironic and harrowing as it explores the com-

plex relationship between the heroine, her African American boyfriend, and his son Jesse. Another popular woman writer, Banana Yoshimoto (born 1964), became well known abroad after the publication of her novel *Kitchin* (1988; *Kitchen*, 1993), in which she first displayed the kind of heroine—at the same time both vulnerable and optimistic—which made her works so popular around the world.

Among those who make use of some of the kinds of larger concerns found in earlier modern Japanese literature is Yūko Tsushima (born 1947), the daughter of the famous novelist Osamu Dazai. Among her many compelling novels, *Yama o hashiru onna* (1980; *Woman Running the Mountains*, 1991), which chronicles the travails of an unwed mother, is breathtaking for both its powerful human insights and its lack of sentimentality. Even more popular is Haruki Murakami (born 1949), who developed a large readership around the world. His many novels often possess the kind of laid-back characters that may seem somewhat familiar to those who know the works of the American crime novelist Raymond Carver, some of whose works Murakami translated into Japanese. In one of his later novels, however, *Nejimaki-dori kuronikuru* (1994-1995; *The Wind-up Bird Chronicle*, 1997), he does touch for the first time upon Japan's role in Asia during the Pacific War. Then too, some of his writing shows a leaning toward creation of a kind of science-fiction universe. His successful *Sekai no owari to hādo-boirudo wandārando* (1985; *The Hard-Boiled Wonderland and the End of the World*, 1991) creates parallel worlds that reveal an eerie dimension to our commonsense understandings of contemporary urban society.

Finally, two other late twentieth century writers reveal still closer ties to the great traditions of Japanese literature. The first of them, Yoshikichi Furui (born 1937), a student of German literature, translated works by such significant modern writers as Hermann Broch and Robert Musil into Japanese. His compelling novella *Yōko* (1971; *Child of Darkness*, 1997), which involves the discovery by the narrator of a mysterious woman sitting in a ravine, reveals his ability to question the very structures of human identity. These and other works give ample evidence to the claim that Furui is one of the most powerful writers of the entire postwar period.

The second writer, another acknowledged master of postwar prose, is Kenji Nakagami (1946-1992), whose relatively early death ended the career of one of the most powerful postwar voices. Born in a poor, wild area of Japan known as Shingû, a port at the edge of the mountainous peninsula south of Osaka, Nakagami used the legends and history of his region, plus his own early experiences as a day laborer, to express his belief in the basic instabilities of human nature. One of the most important themes in his various works is the shifting, usually unarticulated relationships between humans and nature.

Despite the fame of the nation's poetry and drama, Japanese works of long fiction have probably made that country's greatest contribution to world literature. Japanese fiction of all eras commands the attention of students of literature worldwide, not because of its supposedly exotic qualities but because of its technical artistry and its attention to problems common to human life everywhere.

The theme that dominates much of modern Japanese long fiction is the search for the self in society. That which best characterizes traditional forms is the sadness of ephemerality—the recognition that all creatures who live must die and that worldly attachment leads people to cling, however vainly, to whatever fleeting happiness, glory, or prosperity becomes their lot. Toward the end of the Edo period and the early Meiji period, traditional Japanese society collapsed. Old morals, religion, and loyalties proved inadequate. Using all the resources of a rich language with a literary tradition extending from the eighth century, modern Japanese authors describe nature and life with verve and imagination. At times, some accept Western ideology, religion, or literary forms. Others seek original answers to the questions of life, literature, and art. Young authors still seek a place for the individual in mass society. They grope to find a substitute for an accepted system of duties and obligations that gave structure to traditional society in a transient world.

The ultimate origins of fiction in Japan, as elsewhere, can be found in the human need to form inter-personal relationships and to share common experience by the use of language. Japanese long fiction reflects the continuing vitality of a prosperous nation of more than one hundred million people. For celebrated writers, the rewards are enormous, in terms of both wealth and public acclaim. Nevertheless, the current educational system places little emphasis on creative writing, which as an occupation is generally discouraged, making it all the more of a marvel that so much energy and attention are devoted to this particular human activity.

Leon Zolbrod, updated by J. Thomas Rimer

BIBLIOGRAPHY

Bowring, Richard. *The Tale of Genji*. Cambridge, England: Cambridge University Press, 1988. The most lucid and thoughtful guide in English to Japan's greatest classic novel.

Gessel, Van C. *Three Modern Novelists: Soseki, Tanizaki, Kawabata*. New York: Kodansha International, 1993. Three brief but balanced accounts of the lives and works of three modern masters of Japanese fiction.

Inouye, Charles Shiro. *The Similitude of Blossoms: A Critical Biography of Izumi Kyoka*. Cambridge, Mass.: Harvard University Press, 1999. The first thorough study in English of one of Japan's most evocative modern romantic writers.

Keene, Donald. *Dawn to the West: Japanese Literature in the Modern Era*. New York: Columbia University Press, 1999.

_____. *Seeds in the Heart: Japanese Literature from the Earliest Times to the Late Sixteenth Century*. New York: Henry Holt, 1993. With the following two books, a three-volume history of Japanese literature from its origins through the 1970's, this is clearest and most persuasive treatment of all forms of Japanese literature. The basis for any collection of writing on Japanese fiction.

_____. *World Within Walls: Japanese Literature of the Pre-Modern Era*. New York: Holt, Rinehart and Winston, 1976.

Lewell, John. *Modern Japanese Novelists: A Biographical Dictionary*. New York: Kodansha International, 1993. An excellent reference work, with plot summaries, useful critical opinion, and bibliographies of works available in English translation.

Napier, Susan. *Escape from the Wasteland: Romanticism and Realism in the Fiction of Mishima Yukio and* Ōe Kenzaburō. Cambridge, Mass.: Harvard University Press, 1991. Evocative treatments of two major postwar writers in their cultural and literary contexts.

Rimer, J. Thomas. *A Reader's Guide to Japanese Literature*. Rev. ed. New York: Kodansha International, 1999. A guide to all periods of Japanese literature, which extended discussions of more than fifty works, the bulk of them works of long fiction. Bibliographies of translations and secondary works are included.

LATIN AMERICAN LONG FICTION

Inherent in the ideology underlying the conquest and colonization of Latin America were certain factors that severely retarded the development of the novel there. Notable among them was the Church's view that the novel form was harmful to morals, coupled with the vision of Latin America as a mission field, from which such negative influences could and should be excluded. Thus, in 1531, it was forbidden for books such as *Amadís de Gaula* (1508; *Amadis of Gaul*, partial translation, 1567, 1803; better known as *Amadís*) to be imported. While it is true that from 1580 on, all sorts of fiction did enter the region—and it even appears that a sizable portion of the first edition of Miguel de Cervantes's *El ingenioso hidalgo don Quixote de la Mancha* (1605, 1615; *The History of the Valorous and Wittie Knight-Errant, Don Quixote of the Mancha*, 1612-1620; better known as *Don Quixote de la Mancha*) came to the New World—the law is indicative of an attitude that, in the Spanish-speaking regions, successfully prevented the production of anything that might properly be called a novel until 1816.

In Brazil, in contrast, the attempt to exclude the form was not so successful. It was, in fact, a churchman who produced the first novel there. Four years after the publication of John Bunyan's *The Pilgrim's Progress from This World to That Which Is to Come* (1678, 1684; more commonly known as *The Pilgrim's Progress*), the Jesuit Alexandre de Gusmão (1628-1724) published *História do predestinado peregrino e seu irmão Precito* (1682). Also in the allegorical mode is the *Compêndio narrativo do peregrino da América* (1728), by Nuno Marques Pereira (1652-1728), and in 1752, Teresa Margarida da Silva e Orta published *Aventuras de Diófanes*. These attempts to turn the form to the service of morality left no progeny, and when the Brazilian novel returned, it was in the fullness of the Romantic movement.

The outstanding Brazilian novelist of the Romantic period was José de Alencar (1829-1877), whose early work consists of a series of sentimental novels of adventure, dealing particularly with the idealized Indian, modeled on Chateaubriand's noble savage, who predominated throughout Latin American literature in this era. Alencar's more mature works, including *Lucíola* (1862), *Iracema* (1865; *Iracema, the Honey-Lips: A Legend of Brazil*, 1886), and *Senhora* (1875; *Senhora: Profile of a Woman*, 1994), are more concerned with the portrayal of urban society, as is the notable *Memórias de um sargento de milícias* (1854; *Memoirs of a Militia Sergeant*, 1959), by Manuel Antônio de Almeida (1831-1861), which concentrates on Rio de Janeiro. At the same time, Bernardo Guimarães (1825-1884) was dealing with nationalistic themes.

THE NINETEENTH CENTURY

The first novel of Spanish America, as well, appeared within the politically liberal orientation of nascent Romanticism. With the accession of the Bourbons to the Spanish throne in 1700, considerable French influence began entering the colonies, and the Enlightenment left its mark on their literature. José Joaquín Fernández de Lizardi (1776-1827), known as "The Mexican Thinker," was fundamentally a pamphleteer and essayist who traveled with a portable printing press, turning out material in support of the war of independence. His first novel, *El periquillo sarniento* (1816; *The Itching Parrot*, 1942), was, appropriately, a statement of reason at the same time that it led to a current of Romantic novels in the region. Although the picaresque genre in Spain had been an instrument of the Church, useful in the preaching of morality, Lizardi's picaresque novel is brutally anticlerical even while its entertaining narrative is marred by lengthy sermons. This tendency toward essay in the novel perhaps had its roots in the missionary traditions of the colonies and has continued to the present day, particularly in the fiction of the Mexican Carlos Fuentes. In the Mexican novel, there is also a tendency to employ circular structures, which are already visible in Lizardi's work. Each episode presents the reader with a turn of the Wheel of Fortune, as the protagonist becomes successful only to end in desperate straits again.

The vast majority of Latin America's nineteenth

century novels appeared in the second half of that century, although one notable work spans nearly a half century in itself: *Cecilia Valdés* (first part 1839, completed 1882; *Cecilia Valdés: A Novel of Cuban Customs*, 1962), by the Cuban author Cirilo Villaverde (1812-1894). Like nearly all fiction following the attainment of independence by most of Latin America (although not yet by Cuba), *Cecilia Valdés* is Romantic in character; following the example set by Lizardi, Villaverde's is a political Romanticism, relatively unconcerned with nature.

The Latin American short story has its roots in the celebrated narrative "El matadero," by Esteban Echeverría (1805-1851). Another work of doubtful genre in the same era, *Vida de Juan Facundo Quiroga* (1845; *Facundo: Life in the Argentine Republic in the Days of the Tyrants: Or, Civilization and Barbarism*, 1868), by Domingo Faustino Sarmiento (1811-1888), exercised considerable influence on the course of the novel for decades to come. A combination of biography, novel, and essay, it establishes with its subtitle, *Civilización y barbarie*, the theme of the struggle between the relatively sophisticated, often Europeanized, cities of Latin America and the more barbaric outlying areas, be they the Argentine pampas or the Venezuelan llanos. In general terms, the novel of the nineteenth century tends to contrast the refinement of Europe with the crudeness of the New World. The sons of Brazilian planters, for example, received the finest education that Europe could offer, often returning to bewail their homeland's lack of culture.

The most prominent of a number of novels written in opposition to the Argentine dictator Juan Manuel de Rosas was *Amalia* (first part 1851, second part 1855; *Amalia: A Romance of the Argentine*, 1919), by José Mármol (1817-1871), who learned his craft from Sir Walter Scott and Alexandre Dumas, *père*. In his struggle against injustice, Mármol's Daniel Bello is the prototype of the Romantic hero, while the heroine Amalia is representative of European refinement surrounded by New World vulgarity. In this era, many novels were serialized in newspapers, among them *Amalia*, which exhibits the episodic character of this type of composition.

Probably the most widely read Latin American novel of the nineteenth century was *María* (1867; *María: A South American Romance*, 1890), by Jorge Isaacs (1837-1895). At this stage, the Romantics were generally more concerned with nature, and the heroine of Isaacs's novel appears to be almost a projection of the landscape of Colombia's Cauca Valley. The tale is typical of the novels of its day, involving an encounter of soul mates who are separated and then reunited at the conclusion, only to learn that fate has made their marriage impossible. In this case, the couple are brother and sister by adoption, and her death prevents their marriage. A variation on the theme appears in *Cumandá* (1879), by the Ecuadoran Juan León Mera (1832-1894): After the lovers have overcome many obstacles, the proposed marriage is prevented by the revelation that the couple are brother and sister, separated in infancy. In *Cumandá*, Mera lays the foundations for the modern novel of protest against the inhuman treatment of Indians, concerning whom he has solid documentary knowledge. In 1889, the same type of novel, overlaid with European sentimentalism and full of fateful coincidences and melodramatic surprises, including the usual impossible marriage of siblings, appeared in Peru under the title *Aves sin nido* (*Birds without a Nest: A Story of Indian Life and Priestly Oppression in Peru*, 1904). The author, Clorinda Matto de Turner (1854-1909), wrote a preface within the tradition of the moralistic essay, declaring that her purpose in writing was to exhibit the unjust treatment of the Peruvian Indian and argue for the marriage of priests. It is a prime example of the nineteenth century Romantic novel in that it is far more concerned with theme than with technique. Nevertheless, it exercised a powerful influence in Latin America.

Cuban-born Gertrudis Gómez de Avellaneda (1814-1873) published her novel *Sab* (English translation, 1993) in 1841, with a black slave as protagonist, anticipating by nearly a century the handful of novels that would attempt to set black people's situation in relief. More significant is her *Guatimozín* (1846; *Cuauhtemoc, the Last Aztec Emperor: An Historical Novel*, 1898), a well-researched historical novel dealing with the conquest of Mexico and one of the two most important of that genre in the century, the other being *Durante la reconquista* (1897), by Alberto Blest Gana (1831-1920).

French literary influences gradually gained momentum throughout Latin America in the nineteenth century, and critics are often hard-pressed to identify the tendency to which a given writer or work belongs. It is preferable to point out that while Romantic tendencies underlie nearly all the novelistic production of the region until 1880 or so, writers were beginning to feel the influence first of Honoré de Balzac and Émile Zola and then of the Parnassian and Symbolist movements, and to experiment with them. In Brazil, *Inocência* (1872; *Innocencia: A Story of the Prairie Regions of Brazil*, 1889), by Alfredo de Escragnolle Tarmay (1843-1899), represents something of a transition from the dominance of Romanticism to realism in that country. The well-known *Martín Rivas* (1862; English translation, 1916), by Blest Gana, is illustrative of his desire to become the Balzac of Chile, although at its base it is still a Romantic work rather than a realistic one. It has, in fact, been termed the best example of "Romantic realism" in Latin America, and it exhibits the typical polarity that is so evident in the novels of this period: city against country, reality against appearances, good characters against evil ones.

The Mexican writer Ignacio Manuel Altamirano (1834-1893) attempted to raise the quality of the Latin American novel by urging his fellow authors to read widely in order to gain a more universal literary vision, something that Lizardi and others had already been doing. Although an Indian himself, and desirous of making the novel more realistic, he tended to produce romantically stereotyped characters, Indian or otherwise, and failed to plead the Indian's case strongly. His *Clemencia* (1869) and *La Navidad en las Montañas* (1871; *Christmas in the Mountains*, 1961) are worthy novels, but his considerable ability to tell a good adventure story is best displayed in *El Zarco: Episodios de la vida Mexicana en 1861-1863* (1901; *El Zarco, the Bandit*, 1957), in which he attempts to break with Romanticism yet employs as an omen an owl in the tree where his title character is to be hanged. There are two couples, one positive and the other negative, the one illustrating what is good

for Mexico and the other illustrating what threatens to destroy it.

About 1880, the call of writers such as Altamirano bore fruit, for there was at that time a considerable increase in both the quantity and the quality of Latin American fiction, corresponding, perhaps coincidentally, to the emergence of naturalistic tendencies. These were mixed with what remained of Romanticism and realism, the best of which led to the regionalist novel as the writer became increasingly preoccupied with accurately describing the circumstances on the land. *Costumbrismo*, as the term indicates, involves the more or less superficial portrayal of types and customs in a given region. The term *criollismo* is related, but the *criollista* writer is more deeply involved in the subject of study. In the last two decades of the century, these tendencies became mixed with the emerging *Modernismo*, whose most powerful impetus was provided by the publication in 1888 of *Azul*, a collection of short stories and poems by Rubén Darío (1867-1916). *Modernismo* in the Spanish-speaking countries (in contrast to the modernism of Brazil) was a truly indigenous movement, the roots of which, however, were in French Parnassianism and Symbolism. *Modernismo* is a movement characterized by refined sensibilities, even hyperaestheticism, and in contrast to *criollismo*'s desire to come to grips with Latin American reality, its aim in general was to rise above it in a manner of escape. It left its mark on prose fiction in a greater concern on the part of the writer for sound artistic accomplishment and in an increase in the use of imagery in prose style, issuing ultimately in some novels that must be read almost as poetry on account of the intensity of their language.

In the Spanish-speaking countries, the leading exponent of naturalism is probably Eugenio Cambacérès (1843-1890), whose *Música sentimental* (1884), while clearly influenced by Zola, still exhibits realistic tendencies. In Mexico, the most prominent of those deeply influenced by naturalism was Federico Gamboa (1864-1939), a careful artist whose most important works are *Suprema ley* (1896) and *Santa* (1903). The latter was more successful than any Mexican book up to its time and strongly influenced the later prominent Mexican novelist Mariano Azuela (1873-1952). Gamboa's principles are drawn from French naturalism, but his work serves as a bridge between the Romantic realism of the nineteenth century and the regionalism of the twentieth. Another Mexican novelist, Emilio Rabasa (1856-1930), was the first to come to grips with the social issues leading to the Mexican Revolution of 1910, and as such anticipates the novel of that revolution. The Cuban Carlos Loveira (1882-1928) produced a late example of the naturalist novel, *Juan Criollo* (1927), whose protagonist, reared in a family of higher social class, is nevertheless condemned to a life of misery by his lower-class birth.

In Brazil, the most prominent writers in the realist-naturalist camp were Aluísio Azevedo (1857-1913), whose best works are *Casa de Pensão* (1884) and *O cortiço* (1890; *A Brazilian Tenement*, 1926; also as *The Slum*, 1999), and Adolfo Caminha (1867-1897), whose *Bom crioulo* (1895; *Bom-Crioula: The Black Man and the Cabin Boy*, 1982), concerning homosexuality in the Brazilian navy, produced a national scandal. Among the Brazilian writers whose novels defy classification are Euclydes da Cunha (1886-1909), whose *Os sertões* (1902; *Rebellion in the Backlands*, 1944), regarded as one of the masterpieces of Brazilian literature, deals with war in the backlands and is similar to Sarmiento's *Facundo* in its mixture of genres, and Raul Pompéia (1863-1895), whose *O Ateneu* (1888) employs a boys' boarding school as a microcosm of society.

Equally difficult to classify is the man generally considered to be Brazil's greatest writer, Joaquim Maria Machado de Assis (1839-1908), whose principal model was Laurence Sterne. Machado de Assis ignored naturalism to explore the psychological dimensions of alienation. Although he is considered a pioneer of psychological realism, his major concern is not with character development but with novelistic technique, so that his work both fits into the emerging aestheticist tendencies of the Spanish-speaking countries and anticipates the later Latin American novel's preoccupation with language as such, in the handling of which he is an acknowledged master. His first work of excellence is *Memórias póstumas de*

Brás Cubas (1881; *The Posthumous Memoirs of Brás Cubas*, 1951; better known as *Epitaph of a Small Winner*, 1952), but it was only with *Quincas Borba* (1891; *Philosopher or Dog?*, 1954; also as *The Heritage of Quincas Borba*, 1954) and *Dom Casmurro* (1899; English translation, 1953) that his greatness was generally recognized.

A significant novel later retrieved from critical oblivion was important in the development of technical excellence in the late nineteenth century: *Mi tío el empleado* (1887), by the Cuban Ramón Meza (1861-1911), is characterized by what has been described as a picaresque *costumbrismo* similar to that of Emilio Rabasa. It exhibits a Wheel of Fortune structure somewhat similar to that of *The Itching Parrot*, as the hero experiences a rise, a fall, and finally what is presumably a permanent rise in Mexico. The work's picaresque qualities, rooted in the Cuban *choteo*—the Trickster-like practice of mocking everything—anticipates a persistent humorism in the modern Spanish American novel.

Known as one of the foremost *Modernista* poets, the Colombian José Asunción Silva (1865-1896) produced *De sobremesa* (1896), a lesser-known novel of some importance for the understanding of the direction the genre was taking around the end of the nineteenth century. Rooted in the aesthetic decadentism that was one of the primary characteristics of urban Latin American culture at that time, it presents a protagonist whose values are emphatically those of the *Modernistas*, just as the earlier Colombian writer Jorge Isaacs's Efraín (in Isaacs's novel *María*) is the quintessential Spanish American Romantic hero. The *Modernista* concern for aesthetic values as opposed to those of pragmatism is delineated in an essay by the Uruguayan José Enrique Rodó (1871-1917), *Ariel* (1900; English translation, 1922), a work perfectly placed for psychological impact at the opening of the new century. In it, Rodó insists that the developing culture of Latin America, while taking advantage of the admirable advances of technology in North America, reject its materialistic values in favor of those of the spirit. *Ariel* profoundly influenced an entire generation of Latin American intellectuals.

THE EARLY TWENTIETH CENTURY

In the novel at this time, there is an increasing commitment to technical quality, along with an attempt at a more skillful analysis of the regions in which the authors lived. Regionalist tendencies were accentuated in the first decades of the twentieth century by the relative isolation of national capitals from one another, and added to the geographical isolation was the almost worshipful attention paid by authors in each region to what was taking place in Europe, so that a writer in Lima and one in Santiago might each be far more aware of the literary scene in Paris than in the other's city. Therefore, the regionalist tendency became strong within a general *criollista* current.

One of the most skillful of the regionalist writers was Tomás Carrasquilla (1858-1940), whose novels, including *Frutos de mi tierra* (1896), *Grandeza* (1910), *La marquesa de Yolombó* (1928), and *Hace tiempos* (1935), are set in the city and countryside of Colombia's Antioquia, a region of difficult access before the advent of air travel. Correspondingly, the circumstances of Carrasquilla's characters are static, as is generally the case in the early regionalist novels of Latin America. Characterization for Carrasquilla is largely by way of regionalistic speech.

In Chile, Blest Gana had a successor in Luis Orrego Luco (1866-1949), whose *Casa grande* (1908) was the first novel to analyze in depth the life of the Chilean upper classes. Orrego Luco's concern, that of the psychological penetration of a social sphere that interests him, using a calm, controlled, polished language, is typical of Chilean fiction, from its inception to the present day, and is especially evident in the work of José Donoso. Orrego Luco is something of a transitional figure, standing between nineteenth century realism and twentieth century *criollismo*. Another transitional figure is Manuel Gálvez (1882-1962), who straddled the gap between Romanticism and *Modernismo*, producing books of unbridled subjectivism, a quality associated with both schools. As typically Argentine as Orrego Luco was Chilean, Gálvez sought to analyze his nation's reality in terms of his own ongoing spiritual crisis, to produce an opus illustrative of his and Argentina's anxiety and hope for the future. His *La maestra normal* (1914) is a prime example of the *costumbrista* novel, but in its agonized introspection it anticipates the novels of Eduardo Mallea as well as the call for social reform and women's rights.

Among the Brazilian regionalists, the most prominent was Lima Barreto (1881-1922), who, like Machado de Assis, was black. Unlike Machado de Assis, however, Barreto reacted violently against the racism that he felt even in his relatively easygoing country, becoming a militant anarchist. His bitter parodies of the Brazilian mainstream caused the critics of his day to ignore him.

Out of the wave-interference pattern of sometimes contradictory literary movements, there emerged some novels of clearly definable *Modernista* character, while others whose *Modernista* aesthetic is discernible, such as *El embrujo de Sevilla* (1922; *Castanets*, 1929) and *El gaucho florido* (1932), by the Uruguayan Carlos Reyles (1868-1938), betray the melodramatic character of the old Romanticism. Among the better *Modernista* novelists was the Chilean Augusto d'Halmar (1882-1950). In 1902, Manuel Díaz Rodríguez (1868-1927) published *Sangre patricia* (English translation, 1946), in which he struggled to force psychological penetration beyond the limits of *Modernismo*'s usual superficiality. In it, however, even the protagonist's suicide becomes a positive aesthetic event. Another tour de force is *La gloria de don Ramiro* (1908; *The Glory of Don Ramiro*, 1924), by Enrique Larreta (1865-1961), which employs a historical setting in Toledo as the basis for a transformation of that reality into a sensorial experience—a process betraying *Modernismo*'s roots in Symbolism, in which the object perceived is gradually metamorphosed into a representation of the observer's psychic state. Some critics have mistakenly placed Rafael Arévalo Martínez (born 1884) and his works, such as *El hombre que parecía un caballo* (1916), in the naturalist camp because his characters are often compared to animals. In fact, this process in his stories is also an example of Symbolist transformation.

The advent of modern communications eventually began unifying Latin America to the extent that authors came to have freer access to one another. There are some modern authors who have commented that, as their centuries-long insularity finally gave way, they became aware of their common goals, and several have even spoken of "the novel that we are all writing," which has issued in Carlos Fuentes's attempt, in *Terra nostra* (1975; English translation, 1976), to pick up the quests of the heroes of several novels written by his peers and complete them, even bringing a number of those heroes together at the conclusion of his novel. This attitude stands in contrast to that of many nationalistic leaders of the individual countries, who at times insist that there is no real Latin America—that each individual nation is an entity in itself and impossible to classify with others.

As the authors of Latin America came to an increasing awareness of their common experience and concerns, regionalist tendencies gradually became less important, and the focus came to be upon America as a problem. While European literary currents continued to exercise a strong influence, a complex series of events moved the Latin American novel into the channels it was to follow. Rodó's plea for a continuing stress on Latin American cultural identity was very much in the minds of these writers, as they wrote in the *costumbrista* and *criollista* modes. This Latin American identity was reinforced in 1910 by the centennial of the outbreak of the wars for independence from Spain. Intellectuals became preoccupied with what Latin America had become in those hundred years, and their stress on America as a viable, powerful entity in itself, rather than a stepchild of Europe, became known as *mundonovismo*.

Because little had changed with independence save the replacement of Spanish-born political leaders by governors of Spanish descent born in the New World, in many cases government had deteriorated into dictatorship. One of the worst of these governments in terms of its emphasis on progress at the expense of the cynical exploitation of the poor was that of Porfirio Díaz in Mexico, and in another instance of timing with considerable symbolic value, in the centennial year of 1910, a true revolution (as opposed to the typical Latin American replacement of one dictator by another) broke out there. Latin Americans, already profoundly concerned with the direction to be taken by their region, watched closely as, in the midst of the Mexican Revolution, World War I broke out, and then, before either war was concluded, the Russian Revolution took place. Sociopolitical upheaval was clearly the order of the day, and Latin America already had a well-established tradition of writers influencing the course of such events.

This confluence of currents produced, among other effects, a subgenre of the regionalist novel, that of the Mexican Revolution, the first example of which appeared in the course of the fighting. *Los de abajo* (1916; *The Underdogs*, 1929) is most notable for the ability of its author, Mariano Azuela (1873-1952), to transform living experience into fiction as it occurred. The work has the typically Mexican circular structure, the protagonist dying at the same location at which he begins his successful career in the revolution. While this has been termed an epic structure, it may also be viewed as another turn of the Wheel of Fortune, indicative not only of the nature of one revolutionary's fortunes but also of the lot of the nation as a whole as its revolution was to lead to new forms of death-dealing oppression. *The Underdogs* was largely ignored until 1925, when journalists discovered it and brought it to the public's attention.

Martín Luis Guzmán (1887-1976) also published a work linked to journalism, *El águila y la serpiente* (1928; *The Eagle and the Serpent*, 1930), which is a novel of the sort that a war correspondent might be expected to write; it nevertheless contains some of the best prose of its day. The next year, he produced *La sombra del caudillo* (1929), in which he, like Azuela, views the Mexican people as being swept inexorably along by the revolution. For him, its story is one of *caudillos*, the petty regional dictators whose story was to emerge in its most powerful form in a work by Juan Rulfo (1918-1986), *Pedro Páramo* (1955; English translation, 1959). Gregorio López y Fuentes (1897-1966), in his *El indio* (1935; English translation, 1961), bridges the gap between the novel of the Mexican Revolution and the Indianist novel, examining the role played by Indians in the conflict and questioning their treatment since that time. In doing so, he moves away from the traditional narrative technique of Mexico's novel involving the common people, treating them as masses rather than as individuals. Many other authors turned to a portrayal of the Indian plight during the 1920's and 1930's. If America was a problem, then at its roots was the situation of its aboriginal peoples, who had been raped, slaughtered, enslaved, and generally exploited throughout the centuries since the conquest.

John S. Brushwood pointed out that three stages should be recognized in the development of Indian-oriented fiction in Latin America. The first has its roots in some of the earliest writings of the region, in works such as *Arauco domado* (1596; *Arauco Tamed*, 1948), by Pedro de Oña (1570- c. 1643). In this epic poem, the aboriginal American is glorified and made to conform to European ideals of language, behavior, and even physical appearance. Later, under the influence of French writers such as Chateaubriand, these conceptions were reinforced in the "noble savage" mode, as in Avellaneda's *Guatimozín* or Mera's *Cumandá*. The second stage involves a view of Indians as a problem, describing and protesting against social injustice and dealing with them in terms of what has been called social realism, as in *El indio*. Finally, there are novels such as *Los ríos profundos* (1958; *Deep Rivers*, 1978), by José María Arguedas (1911-1969), and *Oficio de tinieblas* (1966; *The Book of Lamentations*, 1996), by Rosario Castellanos (1915-1974), in which the author actually writes from the Indians' viewpoint, revealing their vital experience from within. These works belong to a period of more universal concerns in the novel in general.

In the regionalist mode of the second stage, one of the important novels is that of the poet César Vallejo (1892-1938), *El tungsteno* (1931; *Tungsten*, 1988), dealing with the agelong problems of Indians in the mines of Latin America. In other Indianist novels, the stress is on the unjust distribution of land, not merely for the purpose of pointing out the problem of economic exploitation but because of the Indians' need for a sense of belonging. In this connection, it should be stressed that to the extent that Marxist concepts entered Latin American thinking in this area, they tended to be received in terms not so much of their economic import as of their cultural import, which is in part the result of the fact that these writers derived their Marxist ideals from Nikolay Berdyaev rather than the more economically oriented theoreticians.

Thus, while the Indians in these second-stage novels are generally portrayed as masses, they are never simple adjuncts to an economic theory, but rather a people in quest of ethnic wholeness. An early example by Alcides Arguedas (1879-1946), *Raza de bronce* (1919), deals with the impossible position in which Indians find themselves, even while the author fails to call for any radical change. Jorge Icaza (1906-1978), in his *Huasipungo* (1934; *The Villagers*, 1964), chose to employ scenes of unspeakable atrocity to shock the reader into indignation, while the Mexican Mauricio Magdaleno (born 1906) makes use of astronomical metaphors to depict the Indians' situation in *El resplandor* (1937; *Sunburst*, 1944), reflecting the preconquest belief of the people in a destiny set in the heavens. The last significant novel in this stage, by the Peruvian Ciro Alegría (1909-1967), was *El mundo es ancho y ajeno* (1941; *Broad and Alien Is the World*, 1941), in which the Indians are dispossessed by the greed of white people. The novel is most notable for its creation of a powerful individual, the chief Rosendo Maqui, a sign of hope as in his human qualities he towers over his oppressors in their venality.

One of the issues that greatly intrigued the regionalists was the response of Americans to a nature that was often perceived as overwhelming. During the 1920's, this concern resulted in a series of landmark novels, each dealing with the issue in a different manner. The novelist of the Colombian jungle, José Eustacio Rivera (1889-1928), wrote of how "men disintegrate like worms and nature closes implacably over them." His *La vorágine* (1924; *The Vortex*, 1935) treats the jungle as an irresistible destructive force, reducing human beings to pitiful shells and then swallowing them. Sarmiento's civilization-versus-barbarism theme was transferred to the plains of Venezuela by Rómulo Gallegos (1884-1969), who later was to become president of his country. His *Doña Bárbara* (1929; English translation, 1931), complete with allegorical names, portrays the victory of city-based enlightenment over superstition and the raw lust for power found in the outlying regions.

In Sarmiento's Argentina, however, what appeared in *Facundo* as an ambivalent Romantic attitude toward the gaucho is transformed into a *Modernista* presentation of him as, paradoxically, the Romantic ideal of humans in harmony with nature in both suffering and triumph: *Don Segundo Sombra* (1926; English translation, 1935), by Ricardo Güiraldes (1886-1927), is a sort of *Bildungsroman* for Argentine youth, in which the hero is drawn from his effeminate civilized surroundings into the gaucho world, eventually to return as a landowner. The cycle of major novels dealing with humans and nature is completed, as humans have been viewed as dominated by nature, dominant over it, and in harmony with it. Each of the novels deals with the problems of a specific region, even while creating an experience to which all Latin Americans can relate. The fact that the three can be seen almost as a loose sort of unwitting trilogy on humans and nature is indicative of the growing tendency of Latin American writers to write on the same topics in ways that indicate shared experiences and concerns.

THE 1920'S AND 1930'S

There has been an unfortunate critical tendency to treat the situation of prose fiction in the 1920's and 1930's as if the only significant works were of the regionalist variety, whether they dealt with the Mexican Revolution, social issues of some other sort, or more general Latin American themes. For this reason, many have viewed later Latin American novels as if they had been created *ex nihilo* or pieced together from foreign sources. The fact is that there had been a more or less steady and consistent development of the vanguardist novel, parallel to those works preoccupied with sociopolitical issues. The most important link between the two lay in the profound rejection of existing social values in virtually all the novels of this period. From that point on, there was a divergence, some writers, as in the nineteenth century, being more concerned with their message than with the language in which it was couched, while others were primarily concerned with their novels as works of art. In the mid-1910's, the Chilean poet Vicente Huidobro (1893-1948) produced his "Creation-

ist Manifesto," in which he rejected the demand that the artist reproduce external reality to make mimetic art, asserting instead the right to invent new realities, in an art involving genetic processes. Huidobro's view is that the poet is "a little god," so that each literary work is a new creation in the world. In the full flush of social commitment, his cries were ignored by a considerable percentage of writers, but many more followed his lead and those of other influential writers, among whom Marcel Proust, James Joyce, and the Peninsular author Benjamín Jarnés are the most frequently mentioned. In the 1920's, these theories were displayed most prominently in a series of often short-lived literary magazines.

At this time, vanguardist writers experimented with such techniques as antichronological development and interior monologue. In the fiction of this period, characterization is radically interiorized, and there are often variations in the narrative point of view. There is an increasing concern with visual effects and the use of startling imagery, along with an interest in playing with typography. Underlying it all, there is the conviction that the author is under no obligation to reproduce visible reality. *El café de nadie* (1926), by Arqueles Vela (born 1899), is heavy with radical innovations, including the concept of a fictional space within which the plot develops, and some early experiments with Surrealism.

Even when a novel of this time bears a regional cast, the increasing interest in a psychological penetration of the characters often places the universal orientation of an author in bold relief. The best examples in this period are two works of the Chilean Eduardo Barrios (1884-1963): *El niño que enloqueció de amor* (1915; *The Little Boy Driven Mad by Love*, 1967), in which a young boy falls in love with his mother's friend, and *El hermano asno* (1922; *Brother Asno*, 1969), a study of the emotional torment of a saintly monk. In the same decade, *La educación sentimental* (1929), by Jaime Torres Bodet (1902-1974), focuses on interior experience to such a degree that there is virtually no action. In the Argentine tradition of novels dealing with anguished characters obsessed with questions concerning the meaning of an alienated existence is *Los siete locos* (1929; *Seven Mad-*

men, 1984), by Roberto Arlt (1900-1942), in which the revolutionary impulse has motives solely of personal gain. The Nietzschean will to power figures largely, as does Joycean interior monologue. In Chile, what Fernando Alegría terms the "deathblow to *criollismo*" was produced in two stages. In 1934, María Luisa Bombal (1910-1980) published *La última niebla* (*The Final Mist*, 1982; previously published as *The House of Mist*, 1947), which deals in a cool and elegant style with both the universal human condition and specifically feminine psychology. It was not until 1951, however, that Manuel Rojas (1896-1972) completed the process with *Hijo de ladrón* (*Born Guilty*, 1955), a completely secular novel—something virtually unknown before this time in Latin America—that examines the life of a modern people in the cosmopolitan vein.

MODERNISM

In Brazil, the regionalist tendency was first challenged by that country's version of modernism, which represents a combination of vanguardist currents. Modernism suddenly appeared on the scene in 1922 and had the effect of making poetry dominant until 1930, when a series of neorealistic novels of a social orientation began appearing, among them *Vidas sêcas* (1938; *Barren Lives*, 1965), by Graciliano Ramos (1892-1953), a novel of psychological realism in the tradition of Machado de Assis focusing on character development rather than plot.

Still another major contribution to the complex set of influences on the Latin American novel was made by Jorge Luis Borges (1899-1986), who never wrote a novel himself but whose short stories serve as the primary impetus of what Seymour Menton calls *cosmopolitismo*. In the work of Borges, who wrote in Buenos Aires, prose fiction tends to move away from rural, regional concerns and into more urbane, universal settings, with the result that in the last several decades of the twentieth century there was a curious split in the best Latin American novels, some, such as *Rayuela* (1963; *Hopscotch*, 1966), by Julio Cortázar (1914-1984), with settings in the great cities of Europe and America, and others, most notably *Cien años de soledad* (1967; *One Hundred Years of Soli-*

tude, 1970), by Gabriel García Márquez (born 1928), set in remote rural areas but nevertheless universal for it. Borges's major scholarly interests lie in medieval Northern Europe and England, and Nordic mythology therefore plays a role in his stories. He is known for his play with mythic and philosophical concepts, and his stories are rife with paranormal events, which differ from those of writers interested in the African and indigenous traditions mainly in having their roots in European mythologies and philosophies.

In Borges, the author's demand for the right to invent his or her own reality comes to full fruition. His *Ficciones, 1935-1944* (1944; English translation, 1962) and *El aleph* (1949, 1952; translated in *The Aleph and Other Stories, 1933-1969*, 1970) appeared at exactly the right moment, as the Latin American novel was ready to move into a new phase and take its place as one of the most creative and active in the world. Even before Borges's landmark works, however, Juan Filloy (born 1894) had produced a radical piece of fiction entitled *Op Oloop* (1934, 1967) in the Joycean tradition, particularly in its innovative language. In 1941, Macedonio Fernández (1874-1952) published *Una novela que comienza*, insisting in the text that if he can locate a certain woman he has seen and incorporate her into the work, the novel can get under way. In this period, throughout Latin America, the general inclination to express dissatisfaction with social values was giving way to a cultural internationalism on the one hand and political liberalism on the other. *Adán Buenosayres* (1948), by Leopoldo Marechal (1898-1970), presents a character attempting to re-create Buenos Aires through language in order to make it conform to such ideals.

The Surrealists took a deep interest in inner landscapes. As painters, they portrayed visions supposedly arisen from the unconscious mind, while the poets, following André Breton's model of "the chance occurrence, upon a dissecting table, of a sewing machine and an umbrella," wanted to be the first to join two words together. Such a preoccupation with the unconscious and the seemingly irrational involves a flight from normal, supposedly logical, visions of reality that merge with several other concerns of the

Latin American novelists of this era, among them an interest in penetrating beneath the surface of the Indians' world into their often radically different vision of the cosmos. The word "primitive" began to lose its negative connotations as archaeologists and anthropologists revealed that the pre-Columbian civilizations had been vastly superior in many aspects to that of the Europeans who conquered them. Latin American writers came to the realization that the myths, folktales, and rituals of even the modern descendants of the Mayas and Incas could not be dismissed as inferior, childish attempts to be civilized in the European sense.

Contributing to this change in attitude was the decreasing influence of the Church, which had condemned such myths and rituals as pagan and therefore satanic. Furthermore, Europe was experiencing yet another resurgence of interest in its own ancient mythologies, which were proving to be fascinatingly similar to those that anthropologists were collecting around the world. One result, in a world in which it appeared that the values of Western civilization were leading only to war and chaos, was a sense that the concepts that had aided in structuring the ancient societies of a region should be examined in search of their possible values for the same region in the twentieth century. Writers such as Joyce appeared to be searching for significance in their characters' acts by relating them to the archetypal deeds of the heroes of the past. Joyce, whose influence has been considerable in the Latin American novel, early went to Odysseus as a model and later seemed to allude to the Irish hero Finn MacCool and the expectation of his return to life in *Finnegans Wake* (1939).

Much of Latin America had placed its hope in European values. Sarmiento, having reluctantly rejected the gauchos (who were mainly *mestizos*) as a viable social force, called for European immigration as the salvation of Argentina. Civilization must prevail over the barbarity of the plains, and Gallegos echoed the cry from Venezuela eight decades later. Yet by 1929, with Arlt's *Seven Madmen*, it was becoming evident that Sarmiento's theories were not working in the most important area, that of the human spirit.

Other voices had been heard, although they had been overwhelmed for a considerable length of time. Eugenio María de Hostos (1839-1903), active in education in the Caribbean, declared in an essay entitled "El cholo" that the hope of America lay in the fusion of the three major racial groups: Caucasian, African, and Indian. Later, in *La raza cósmica* (1925; *The Cosmic Race*, 1979), José Vasconcelos (1882-1959), a Mexican writer, expressed the theory that Latin America had the unique opportunity to reunite those racial groups, drawing on the strengths of each to build a great new society.

In order to do so, the intelligentsia would have to examine and come to a comprehension of the roots of the thinking of those groups, as expressed in Latin America. One early attempt was made by the brilliant Cuban Alejo Carpentier (1904-1980), in *¡Ecué-Yamba-O! Historia Afro-Cubana* (1933), an attempt to penetrate the experience of the Afro-Cuban religious cults. Later, the author was to repudiate the work, having realized that he had been far from any true understanding of the premodern thought of the people involved. The Nobel Prize winner from Guatemala, Miguel Ángel Asturias (1899-1974), was the first to make a serious attempt to deal adequately with Indian mythology, with his *Leyendas de Guatemala* (1930), in which he recovers as much as possible of the thought of the Mayas as it survived in their descendants. Asturias serves as something of a transitional figure, for his social commitment is abundantly clear in his attacks on Latin American dictatorship and the United Fruit Company in works such as *El Señor Presidente* (1946; *The President*, 1963) and *Hombres de maíz* (1949; *Men of Maize*, 1975), while at the same time he laid the foundation for what was to become known as Magical Realism in Latin American prose fiction (not to be confused with the movement of the same name in North American painting). In *Men of Maize*, he revealed the continued effect of the *Popol Vuh* on the life of the Central American Indian.

MAGICAL REALISM

The term "Magical Realism" is nebulous, and many authors and critics prefer *lo real maravilloso*, which is based loosely on the French Surrealists' concept of *le merveilleux*. Magical Realism is fundamentally a reflection of the twentieth century's departure from what has been perceived as bourgeois categories. Psychology and sociology have shown that rational categories are not necessarily dominant in determining the course of the life of a person or society, and even physics has departed from the Newtonian model, with its more or less mechanistic bias. While the nineteenth century realist wanted to show life as it was actually lived, the Magical Realist believes that true reality is that which underlies the ordinary events of daily life. In this sense, the term "realism" is accurate, for writers in this vein believe that, once found, reality will always prove to have a paranormal, magical cast to it. Typically, in this type of fiction, supernatural occurrences are narrated in a matter-of-fact manner, as if they formed a part of normal daily life.

Demetrio Aguilera Malta (1909-1981) had been experimenting with such alternative realities in the early 1930's, along with writers such as Carpentier and Asturias. His *Don Goyo* (1933; English translation, 1942, 1980) reveals an early animistic tendency to personify nature that was to contrast sharply with the views of Alain Robbe-Grillet, whose *Pour un nouveau roman* (1963; *For a New Novel: Essays on Fiction*, 1965) contains a fierce repudiation of the pathetic fallacy of the Romantics. Aguilera Malta commented that if the works that he and others were writing in this vein during the 1930's had been received more enthusiastically, they would have continued writing them, but the Social Realist tendency nearly swamped the other. Only in 1970 did he return with one of the best examples of the novel of Magical Realism, *Siete lunas y siete serpientes* (*Seven Serpents and Seven Moons*, 1979), with its eerie, brooding evocation of the Ecuadoran jungle. People are transformed into animals or appear to be manifestations of otherworldly beings, and even the narrator is unsure of whether to believe what he has recounted. By the time he provides the reader with a rational explanation, the reader is not persuaded that it is valid.

In the context of the same great pre-Columbian culture, the Peruvian José María Arguedas, while, like most of these authors, not an Indian himself, lamented the inadequacy of the Spanish language to express the realities experienced by the descendants of the Incas, for his native language was the Quechua of the Indian household servants among whom he spent his first few years. His powerful *Yawar fiesta* (English translation, 1985) was published in 1941.

In the same period, however, there was another current in Latin American fiction, based in the Río de la Plata (often referred to as River Plate) region, which has experienced little influence from indigenous groups. The Argentine Eduardo Mallea (1903-1983) was extremely influential in the years between 1934 and 1940, and in 1941, his *Todo verdor perecerá* (*All Green Shall Perish*, 1966) was published. It is a vaguely existentialist work of human alienation, angst, and the impossibility of meaningful communication between people, yet it lacks the existentialist's concept of self-affirmation through struggle. The works of the Uruguayan Juan Carlos Onetti (born 1909) are in much the same vein. His *Tierra de nadie* also appeared in 1941, and his later works, such as *El astillero* (1961; *The Shipyard*, 1968), present the same dismal atmosphere of hopelessness. The Argentine Ernesto Sabato (born 1911) deals with psychological and sociological issues. In *El túnel* (1948; *The Outsider*, 1950; also known as *The Tunnel*) he, too, presents the case of people together physically but spiritually isolated from one another. Later, in *Sobre héroes y tumbas* (1961; *On Heroes and Tombs*, 1981), he makes use of the Borgesian labyrinth as his hero descends to the network of sewers underlying Buenos Aires. His *Abaddón, el exterminador* (1974; *The Angel of Darkness*, 1991) focuses on the Argentine apocalyptic motif, seen earlier in Arlt's short story "La luna roja" and in Mallea's work.

There appeared a number of novels that might be considered transitional between the older regionalist and vanguard tendencies and the explosive "New Novel." In them, there is what Fernando Alegría calls a thirst for universality, along with a further development of the long-standing movement to move from mimetic to genetic forms. If the Impressionist artist had demanded the right to portray his or her subjective reactions to the perceived, and Huidobro had insisted that the poet is a creator rather than an imitator,

Borges would absorb such theory and delight in creating a mixture of philosophy, fantasy, and play elements. The novelists accepted his spirit of inventiveness, using language to draw the reader into a new sort of participatory experience. Among the important transitional novels is *Al filo del agua* (1947; *The Edge of the Storm*, 1963), by Agustín Yáñez (born 1904), a work regional in its setting but more concerned with the interpersonal and intrapersonal conflicts of the characters and with the use of whatever narrative techniques the author believes are most effective in presenting them. Another experimenter is the aforementioned Asturias, whose *The President* uses vanguard techniques to re-create the atmosphere of dread that characterizes the Latin American dictatorship. In 1949, Carpentier published *El reino de este mundo* (*The Kingdom of This World*, 1957), introducing in it his preoccupation with the cyclical nature of tyranny and revolution, employing a highly cerebral style. In *Los pasos perdidos* (1953; *The Lost Steps*, 1956), Carpentier experimented with time, at the same time laying hold of the ongoing American fascination with the marvelous qualities of the land. In it, the protagonist is able to travel backward in time by departing from a modern city into the ever more primitive wilderness. Ten years later, Carpentier's masterful *El siglo de las luces* (1962; *Explosion in a Cathedral*, 1963) was to ring the historical novel firmly into the stream of the new fiction.

The Mexican novel, with its rich tradition leading from *The Itching Parrot* through the works of its revolution and those of Yáñez, began to come to full maturity in Rulfo's *Pedro Páramo*. Like much of Mexican fiction, it is preoccupied with death, and the reader eventually learns that all the characters, including the narrator, are dead. In a sense, this, too, is a transitional work, in that its setting is regional and it deals with the *caudillo* system and the revolution, but in it the act of making art is the controlling factor, and the predominant impression gained by the reader is one of the magical atmosphere into which the protagonist descends as he visits the town of his birth, an atmosphere made up of classical mythology, pre-Columbian ideologies, and even voodoo.

In his first novel, *La región más transparente*

(1958; *Where the Air Is Clear*, 1960), Carlos Fuentes (born 1928) deals with the betrayal of the Mexican Revolution in a generally realistic manner, while frankly admitting the influence of Joyce, John Dos Passos, and several other foreign writers where technique is concerned. He attempts to incorporate an element of *lo real maravilloso* in the form of a character known as Ixca Cienfuegos, a sort of incarnation of Mexico's indigenous heritage, who, as a quasi-mythic being, is not very well integrated with the other characters. In his later novels, Fuentes moved more fully into the mythic mode, with the exception of *Las buenas conciencias* (1959; *The Good Conscience*, 1961) and *La muerte de Artemio Cruz* (1962; *The Death of Artemio Cruz*, 1964); in them and his short stories, he was refining the themes and techniques he was to use in his massive *Terra nostra*, which represents an attempt to mythologize the history of the West for the past two thousand years. In its extremely free handling of time, multiple reincarnations, appearances of supernatural beings such as Satan, and other features, it represents a manifestation of Magical Realism carried to the limit. While *Terra nostra* is his most important novel, his best technical achievement remains *The Death of Artemio Cruz*, a masterpiece of novelistic construction in which another character guilty of betraying the Mexican Revolution is viewed at the time of his death. Narration is variously in the first, second, and third persons, and in the present, future, and past tenses, respectively.

THE NEW LATIN AMERICAN NOVEL

Fuentes's works are central to the related but separate phenomena known as the "New Latin American Novel" and the "Boom." The former refers to what most critics would call the coming of age of the Latin American novel, a gradual process that was accelerated in the 1950's. At that time, the prose fiction of the area was worthy of moving into the realm of world literature and exercising a good deal of influence of its own. On the other hand, the Boom, somewhat difficult to define at best, is fundamentally a phenomenon of the 1960's and early 1970's involving a more general recognition of the quality of the novels of a limited group of authors, some of whom believe that the Boom was essentially a phenomenon of public relations and economics, in that a few authors became celebrities and were at last able to make a living from their writing and closely related activities: Fuentes, García Márquez, Cortázar, Rulfo, Carpentier, Guillermo Cabrera Infante, Donoso, and Mario Vargas Llosa, among others. Donoso (1924-1996) wrote its story in his *Historia personal del "boom"* (1972; *The Boom in Spanish American Literature: A Personal History*, 1977), while Fuentes produced an excellent analysis of the larger movement, entitled *La nueva novela hispanoamericana*, in 1969.

The Chilean Donoso's novelistic production represents an advance in the novelist's art in his country at the same time that it continues that country's tradition of examining a segment of society by the use of carefully controlled language. His *Este domingo* (1965; *This Sunday*, 1967) dissects the wealthy class of Santiago, while the shorter *El lugar sin límites* (1966; *Hell Has No Limits*, 1972) deals with the underclass. His best novel, *El obsceno pájaro de la noche* (1970; *The Obscene Bird of Night*, 1973), employs more radical techniques.

The work of Julio Cortázar presents a major example of the movement of the Latin American novel into the universal sphere. The novel that first attracted the world's attention to him was *Hopscotch*. Moving from the sterile atmosphere of most of the Argentine novels of his generation, he presents a far more authentic existentialist hero in Horacio Oliveira (although author and character would deny the latter's adherence to the existentialist philosophy), who converses with others in Buenos Aires and Paris and almost reaches them. The essential point is that Oliveira is a person in motion, creating a persona, however defective, as he moves. There is humor in the work, the title of which presents the reader with a child's-play version of Borges's characteristic labyrinth. The chapters are not presented in any prescribed order; Cortázar only suggests a hopscotch order in which the reader might approach them. One of his important contributions to the New Novel is his insistence that the reader participate in the creative act with him. Five years after *Hopscotch*, speculating

on the possibility of constructing a novel on the basis of "found" materials, including chapter 62 of the earlier novel, he produced *62: Modelo para armar* (1968; *62: A Model Kit*, 1972). Among Cortázar's other novels is *Libro de Manuel* (1973; *A Manual for Manuel*, 1978), a handbook for a child growing up in a world of radical change.

The Cuban exile Guillermo Cabrera Infante (born 1929) has produced two novels based on humor—especially puns and other forms of wordplay—and, as in *Hopscotch*, the frenetic search for creativity in chaotic language. *Tres tristes tigres* (1967, 1990; *Three Trapped Tigers*, 1971) challenges its reader to discover a meaningful structure, which emerges only on the level of a nebulous mythology created by language as it disintegrates. After a series of books of essays and short stories, in 1979 Cabrera Infante brought forth *La Habana para un infante difunto* (*Infante's Inferno*, 1984), a *Bildungsroman* dealing with the sexual initiation of a young would-be Don Juan in pre-Castro Havana.

Another explosive experiment with language and mythology in Cuba was *Paradiso* (1966; English translation, 1974), the only novel of the premier poet of that country, José Lezama Lima (1910-1976), a work that in a sense constitutes his poetics. A dense atmosphere is created as the author overlays his characters' words and deeds with metaphor, in one expression of what the critics have termed the Cuban neobaroque. Lezama Lima, too, appears to be attempting to lend significance to his characters' acts by comparing them to the archetypal deeds of heroes.

Another major writer of the Cuban baroque tendency is Severo Sarduy (1937-1993), who has written a number of novels characterized by an explosive language and humor, among them *De donde son los cantantes* (1967; *From Cuba with a Song*, 1972) and *Cobra* (1972; English translation, 1975). Reinaldo Arenas (born 1943), forced to leave Cuba in 1980 as one of the boat people, combined features of Magical Realism with a baroque style in *El mundo alucinante* (1969; *Hallucinations: Being an Account of the Life and Adventures of Friar Servando Teresa de Mier*, 1971) but generally withdrew from both in his more important *El palacio de las blanquísimas mofetas*

(1975; *The Palace of the White Skunks*, 1990).

Carpentier, who had done much to provoke the baroque movement in Cuba by his use of a self-consciously erudite style, in 1974 published *El recurso del método* (*Reasons of State*, 1976), which is one of a number of Latin American novels appearing in various countries in the space of a few years to deal with the subject of dictatorship. One of the persistent themes of the Latin American novel for more than a century had been the "shadow" of the dictator, the man depersonalized and viewed more as a malevolent force, as in *Amalia* or, a century later, in *The President*, but in some of the new novels of dictatorship there is a tendency analogous to the new presentation of Indians from their own perspective, as the reader now finds himself or herself inside the dictator's palace and, in some cases, inside his mind. Carpentier creates a powerful effect by the use of interior monologue to characterize his *Primer Magistrado*. In *Hijo de hombre* (1960; *Son of Man*, 1965), by the Paraguayan Augusto Roa Bastos (born 1917), the emphasis is still on the action of the people against tyranny as exemplified by the individual dictator, while Aguilera Malta had moved into a radically mythic vision with *Seven Serpents and Seven Moons* in 1970 only to descend to an often ludicrous level through an excess of Magical Realism in *El secuestro del general* (*Babelandia*, 1985) in 1973. The novel of this tendency that has received the most attention is *El otoño del patriarca* (1975; *The Autumn of the Patriarch*, 1975), by Gabriel García Márquez, a personal view of the perennial dictator in decline. Exaggerating the already incredible events typical of such a dictator's rule, he attempts to re-create the stifling atmosphere of tyranny, an atmosphere that unfortunately is communicated to the text itself.

García Márquez had previously dealt with the towns of the Caribbean coast of Colombia, in that often seemingly regional focus of the New Novel that nevertheless takes on universal appeal in the nature of the experience created in the text. His *La hojarasca* (1955; *Leaf Storm and Other Stories*, 1972) and *El coronel no tiene quien le escriba* (1961; *No One Writes to the Colonel and Other Stories*, 1968) had already established his reputation when he published

One Hundred Years of Solitude in 1967. This is the Latin American novel that has had the greatest impact worldwide, and it won for García Márquez the Nobel Prize in Literature in 1982. The novel is the history of a fictional town called Macondo and of the Buendía family within it. Reversing normal values so that the commonplace appears marvelous and vice versa, and exercising the storyteller's right to exaggerate and embellish, García Márquez has created another prime example of Magical Realism, one in which the atmosphere is the private property of author and reader, bearing little relationship to reality outside the text.

It subsequently became difficult to establish trends and tendencies in other Latin American fiction. There has been a wide variety of subjects and treatments, ranging from the Argentine Manuel Puig's tongue-in-cheek satires on pop culture in such works as *La traición de Rita Hayworth* (1968; *Betrayed by Rita Hayworth*, 1971) and *Pubis angelical*, 1979 (English translation, 1986) to the dense, brooding works of José María Arguedas, most notably his *Deep Rivers*. One of the foremost novelists of the newer generation is the Peruvian Mario Vargas Llosa (born 1936), much of whose work has to do with the military establishment, prostitution, or a combination of the two. With *La ciudad y los perros* (1962; *The Time of the Hero*, 1966), his credentials were established, and *La casa verde* (1965; *The Green House*, 1968) and *Conversación en la catedral* (1969; *Conversation in the Cathedral*, 1975) continued in the vein of almost bitter analyses of Peruvian society. With *Pantaleón y las visitadoras* (1973; *Captain Pantoja and the Special Service*, 1978), however, he was drawn in spite of himself into a humorous treatment of the military and prostitution themes, and this approach continued in *La tía Julia y el escribidor* (1977; *Aunt Julia and the Scriptwriter*, 1982), a masterful example of the New Novelist's concern with revealing in his or her work the process involved in its composition. His *La guerra del fin del mundo* (1981; *The War of the End of the World*, 1984) is a long, difficult, and powerful novel based on the same historical incident that inspired Euclydes da Cunha's *Os sertões*.

In Brazil, around 1960, there came about a rejection of the emphasis on the social message of the novel in favor of a concentration on the craft of the writer. The most prominent novelists of this generation have been João Guimarães Rosa (1908-1968) and Clarice Lispector (1925-1977). The former's interest in universalizing local experience leads to a concentration on the mythic and folkloric traditions of the Brazilian outback, expressed in a Joycean language rich in neologisms and regional speech. His work culminates in *Grande sertão: Veredas* (1956; *The Devil to Pay in the Backlands*, 1963). Lispector's mentor was Lúcio Cardoso (1912-1962), whose *Crônica da casa assassinada* (1959) is considered one of the best of modern Brazilian novels. Lispector herself departs from Guimarães Rosa in emphasizing thematic development over technique, in works such as *A maçã no escuro* (1961; *The Apple in the Dark*, 1967). One of Brazil's most popular novelists is Jorge Amado (born 1912), whose works contain some of the finest treatments of the feminine experience in Latin American literature.

THE LATE TWENTIETH CENTURY

The decade of the 1980's was the era of the post-Boom novel in Latin America, and it signaled a new era in which women, gays, and Afro-Hispanics were finally allowed into the literary canon. While a Boom novel typically portrayed the earnest search of the protagonist for the meaning of life, the post-Boom novel was more likely to describe a journey of this kind with parodic humor; pastiche was its favored trope. It is true that the Boom writers continued to publish during the 1980's—García Márquez wrote *Crónica de una muerte anunciada* (1981; *Chronicle of a Death Foretold*, 1982); Fuentes, *Gringo viejo* (1985; *The Old Gringo*, 1985); and Vargas Llosa, *¿Quién mató a Palomino Molero?* (1987; *Who Killed Palomino Molero?*, 1987)—but this era was especially characterized by a group of new writers.

Luna caliente (1983; *Sultry Moon*, 1998), by the Argentine Mempo Giardinelli (born 1947), tells the story of a young man, Ramiro Bermúdez, recently returned to Buenos Aires from Paris, who has a distinguished career before him but whose life swiftly disintegrates once he becomes fascinated with Araceli, the thirteen-year-old daughter of a doctor friend, whom he

rapes and kills (or so he thinks). The novel parodies the genre of the *novela negra* (hard-boiled crime novel) to produce a gripping plot, combined with a Cortazarian sense of the uncanny that unexpectedly explodes that world from within. *Ardiente paciencia* (1985; *Burning Patience*, 1987), by the Chilean Antonio Skármeta (born 1940), centers on the love affair and eventual marriage of Mario Jiménez and Beatriz González. In order to win Beatriz's heart, Mario seeks the help of the famous Chilean poet, Pablo Neruda, for whom he works as the postman. In a playfully parodic way, literature is depicted in the novel as a cultural reservoir which plays a direct formative role in the everyday lives of ordinary people. *Gazapo* (1985), by the Mexican Gustavo Sainz (born 1940), tells the story of a group of adolescent boys living in Mexico City who share their tales of sexual and criminal exploits with each other. The novel suggests that the telling of the stories is more important than the events that they supposedly relate, all of which gives the novel a playful feel.

It was the novels of the female authors of the post-Boom that caught the public's attention. While there were earnest political novels written by women during this period—*Conversación al sur* (1981; *Mothers and Shadows*, 1986) by Marta Traba (1930-1983) was the prototype—it was the way in which *La casa de los espíritus* (1982; *The House of the Spirits*, 1985) by Isabel Allende (born 1942) mixed politics with Magical Realism that captured the readers' imagination in Latin America and Europe. The novel traces the political struggle in twentieth century Chile between the Left (symbolized by Pedro García; his son, Pedro Segundo; and his grandson, Pedro Tercero) and the Right (personified by Esteban Trueba). Whereas the Left is presented in terms of continuity through family lineage, the Right is shown finally to be issueless, since Esteban Trueba's male progeny either become Marxists (Jaime) or dropouts (Nicolás) and his female progeny fall in love with revolutionaries. Allende's novel is ultimately a positive—as well as playful—affirmation of the value of solidarity in the face of evil and political oppression. *Como agua para chocolate: Novela de entregas mensuales con recetas, amores, y remedios caseros* (1989;

*Like Water for Chocolate: A Novel in Monthly In-
stallments with Recipes, Romances, and Home Remedies*, 1992) by the Mexican novelist Laura Esquivel
(born 1950), redolent of the television soap (a great
favorite in Mexico), is, in essence, a feminist coun-
terversion of the Mexican Revolution, offering a
kitchen's-eye view of those turbulent years that is
at odds with the masculinist rhetoric of the history
books. This novel was one of the best to emerge in
the post-Boom era, and its humor and metaphoric
flair were successfully carried over into the 1985
movie version, which was a box-office hit in the
United States as well as Mexico.

The most significant Hispanic gay writer, the Argentine Manuel Puig (1932-1989), had published his
major works in the 1970's—his masterpiece *El beso
de la mujer araña* (*Kiss of the Spider Woman*, 1979)
came out in 1976—and these set the scene for the acceptance of gay writing in the following decade. *Otra
vez el mar* (1982; *Farewell to the Sea*, 1986) by the
Cuban Reinaldo Arenas (1943-1992) is written from
the perspective of a young Cuban couple who are
spending a holiday on the beach. There is a plot of
sorts (a woman moves with her son into the cabin
next door, and the latter, mysteriously, is found dead
later on that day), but more striking is the novel's
Joycean rejection of the limitations of Euclidean
space and time and its playful use of language. *La
nave de los locos* (1984; *The Ship of Fools*, 1989)
by the Uruguayan-Spanish writer Cristina Peri Rossi
(born 1941) is a postmodern, gay text that rewrites
the alphabet of Christian culture. It describes the misadventures of a character, whose name is simply a
letter of the alphabet, equis (that is, *X*), in a variety of
urban settings; the novel includes episodes describing sordid sexual encounters, far-fetched dream sequences, and Equis's philosophizing about life and
the universe with his companions, Vercingetorix and
Graciela. Like gay writing, Afro-Hispanic literature
also created space for itself in the new literary canon
of the 1980's, and here the major work is *Changó, el
gran putas* (1983) by the Colombian Manuel Zapata
Olivella (born 1920), which has five parts, each of
which traces successive historical eras in which the
Africans struggled against oppression in the New

World. Zapata Olivella's novel expresses a wake-up
call for all Americans of African descent to take up
the fight for the right to own their own culture.

William L. Siemens, updated by Stephen Hart

BIBLIOGRAPHY
Boland, Roy C., and Sally Harvey, eds. *Magical Real-
ism and Beyond: The Contemporary Spanish and
Latin American Novel.* Madrid: Vox/AHS, 1991.
Explores Latin American authors' use of Magical
Realism in modern long fiction.
King, John, ed. *Modern Latin American Fiction: A
Survey.* London: Faber and Faber, 1987. An excel-
lent collection of first-rate, readable essays on all
the major novelists of the Boom, including Gabriel
García Márquez, Carlos Fuentes, Mario Vargas
Llosa, and Julio Cortázar.
Martin, Gerald. *Journeys Through the Labyrinth: Latin
American Fiction in the Twentieth Century.* London:
Routledge, 1989. An elegantly written overview of
the development of the Latin American novel in
the twentieth century. Highly recommended.
Shaw, Donald. *The Post-Boom in Spanish-American
Fiction.* Saratoga Springs: State University of New
York Press, 1998. An authoritative, hard-hitting sur-
vey of the main figures of the post-Boom novel
written by an acknowledged expert.
Sommer, Doris. *Foundational Fictions: The National
Romances of Latin America.* Berkeley: University
of California Press, 1991. The best study of the
Latin American nineteenth century novel. Sepa-
rate chapters treat *Amalia, Sab,* and *Iracema,* ex-
amining the interplay between the path toward na-
tionhood and the journey of love in those novels.
Swanson, Philip. *The New Novel in Latin America:
Politics and Popular Culture After the Boom.* Man-
chester: Manchester University Press, 1995. Au-
thoritative overview of the work of the post-Boom
novelists. Contains separate chapters on Manuel
Puig and Isabel Allende, among others.
Williams, Raymond L. *The Modern Latin American
Novel.* New York: Twayne, 1998. Part of
Twayne's Critical History of the Novel series, this
is an excellent introduction to long fiction in Latin
America.

THE MIDDLE EASTERN NOVEL

The novel did not begin to take root in the Middle East until after World War I and did not develop into a serious genre until after World War II. Although Arabic, Kurdish, Persian, and Turkish literatures have a long and rich assortment of oral narrative forms, it seems that none of them has become a major narrative type in the way that the European novel has. Lacking a native tradition of their own, Middle Eastern novelists thus had to turn to Western models for inspiration and guidance. Prior to the outbreak of World War I, there was some contact between the West and the Middle East. Napoleon invaded Egypt in 1798; following the French withdrawal, the country's ruler, Muhammad Ali, began to send missions to Italy and France to study military tactics and new weaponry. In 1882, the British occupied Egypt. However, serious contact with the West, as far as literature was concerned, did not really occur until after the whole region came under French and British domination following the collapse of the Ottoman Empire around 1915.

Many Western editors complain that the trouble with the literatures of the Middle East is that they are always about politics. That is indeed the case. However, this should not be surprising. The Middle East, after all, is a volatile region. The widely publicized Arab-Israeli conflict is only one of several conflicts in the area. Iraq invaded Kuwait in 1991 and was at war with Iran from 1980 to 1988. Syria and Jordan have been cool toward each other and on several occasions have threatened war. The Sudan has suffered through a bitter civil war involving the Muslim-led government in the north and the Christian rebel group in the south. Turkey, which adamantly refused to give its ten million Kurds cultural rights, began a war with the military wing of the Kurdistan Workers Party and maintained frosty relations with most Arab countries over its military alliance with Israel. In addition, regional secularism and freedom of expression have faced ongoing challenges from orthodox Islam and undemocratic systems of government. Under these circumstances, it is difficult to imagine literature not entering political life.

THE EGYPTIAN NOVEL

Egypt has long been the region's undisputed cultural capital. In 1927 Muhammad al-Muwaylihī's 1907 novel *Fatra min al-zaman* (a period of time), better known as *Ḥadīth ʿĪsā ibn Hishām* (the story of ʿIsa ibn Hishām), was adopted as a school text. Two years later, Muhammad Ḥusayn Haykal's novel *Zaynab*, completed in 1911 and published in 1913, went into its second printing. These two literary events generated so much interest in the novel that in 1930 a competition in novel writing was announced. The winner was Ibrāhīm al-Māzinī's 1931 novel *Ibrāhīm al-kātib* (*Ibrahim, the Writer*, 1976).

Muwaylihī's novel proved quite popular, largely because of the way it juxtaposed two very different ways of life, one Egyptian, the other European. Many Egyptians found it fascinating to read about the inventions and technological marvels displayed at the Great Paris Exhibition of 1899. This came to be known as the "European Visit" theme and became the focus of a good number of novels that were published during the 1940's and 1950's, a period during which there was a serious and prolonged debate concerning the advantages and disadvantages of contact with the Europeans. Even when Europe is not directly the theme, its impact on the thinking of ordinary people can be easily felt. In Haykal's novel, for example, Zaynab is prevented by tradition from marrying the man she loves. In Māzinī's novel, Shushu's marriage cannot take place until after her older sister is married off. Exposure to European ways turns both protagonists against tradition, which they see as confining and outdated. Forces of change—government bureaucracy, the justice system, and secularism—also seem to be the source of conflict in Tawfiq al-Ḥakim's 1937 *Yawmiyyāt naʾib fi al-aryāf* (*Maze of Justice*, 1947).

These novelists played an important role in the development of the novel in the Middle East. However, the writer who contributed the most to the genre and has been the most influential is Naguib Mahfouz. Born in Cairo and educated at King Fuad I (now Cairo) University, Mahfouz worked as a civil servant for a number of years; he did all his writing at night. His first novel, *ʿAbath al-aqd* (the game of fate), appeared in 1939, but it was his later novels that won him international recognition and the 1988 Nobel Prize in Literature. These include *Zuqāq al-Midaqq* (1947; *Midaq Alley*, 1966), *Bayn al-qaṣrayn* (1956; *Palace Walk*, 1990), *Qaṣr al-shawq*, 1957 (*Palace of Desire*, 1991), and *Al-Sukkariya* (1957; *Sugar Street*, 1992). The last three are also known as *Al- Thulāthiya*, or *The Trilogy*.

The Trilogy, some fifteen hundred pages long, is in the great novelistic traditions of Leo Tolstoy, John Galsworthy, Anthony Trollope, and Victor Hugo. In tracing the life, beliefs, tragedies, and difficulties of Abd al-Jawwad and his family in the years leading up to World War II, this massive work serves as a vast historical study of a society in transition. The first volume centers on the father, who, following tradition, rules the family with an iron fist. No one dares to oppose him. In volume two, his son, now attending Teachers' College and sick of tradition, begins to challenge his father. In volume three, the father, now weak and old, has relinquished most of his authority to his son. It is a changed world: Boys and girls attend school together, people talk about communism and the impossibility of belief in God, the young rebel against tradition and openly embrace European ways, fathers are the subject of ridicule and hate, and the old constantly complain about change but are powerless to stop it.

Although Mahfouz never joined any political party, he said that politics were "the very axes" of his thinking. He once credited George Bernard Shaw and Karl Marx for his development into a socialist and a believer in science. He strongly supported the 1952 revolution that brought Colonel Gamal Abdel Nasser to power in Egypt, hoping that Nasser would create a "true socialism and true democracy." When that did not happen and Nasser grew increasingly autocratic, Mahfouz responded with a series of critical novels: *Ḥikāyāt Ḥāratinā* (1975; *The Fountain and the Tomb*, 1988), *Al-Liṣṣ wa-al-kilāb* (1961; *The Thief and the Dogs*, 1984), *Al-Shaḥḥādh* (1965; *The Beggar*, 1986), and *Al-Karnak* (1974; *Karnak*, 1979).

Of these, *The Beggar* is the bleakest. It is the story of Omar, a former poet, revolutionary, and socialist who is now a wealthy, middle-aged lawyer. He is married and has two daughters, but he has lost all interest in living. He has become alienated from everyone around him, but what appalls him the most is the government's intolerance of any form of dissent and the terrible economic mess it has created in the name of socialism. All this proves too much for Omar. He tries one diversion after another—travel, drink, sex—but to no avail. As the novel comes to a close, he goes mad.

Mahfouz also criticized his country's Muslim fundamentalists after they assassinated President Anwar Sadat in 1981 for making peace with Israel. Mahfouz responded with the novella *Yawm Qutila al-Zaʿīm* (1985; *The Day the Leader Was Killed*, 1989), which underlined his belief that society, in order to overcome violence, intolerance, and poverty, must grow out of its need for religion. When Muslim fundamentalists assassinated author Farag Foda in 1992, Mahfouz accused the group of "intellectual terrorism." On October 14, 1994, Mahfouz himself became the target: A young militant Muslim stabbed the author in the neck while he was waiting for a ride. He was hospitalized for two weeks.

Mahfouz is well versed in Western philosophy and literature and has been greatly influenced by such important authors as William Shakespeare, James Joyce, Franz Kafka, Thomas Mann, Eugene O'Neill, Henrik Ibsen, and George Bernard Shaw. Some Arab nationalists have accused Mahfouz of going too far in embracing Western ideas and traditions.

THE QUESTION OF PALESTINE

A good number of Arab and Israeli novelists came into prominence after the creation of Israel in 1948. Arab novelists seem to focus mostly on the plight of the Palestinians and the ongoing Arab-Israeli conflict. Among these, Ghassan Kanafani, who was assassinated in Beirut, Lebanon, in 1972, at the age of thirty-six, gained a wide readership after the publication of *Rijal fil al-shams* (*Men in the Sun, and Other Palestinian Stories*, 1978) in 1963 and *Mā tabaqqā lakum* (*All That's Left to You*, 1990) in 1966. Both focus on the horrendous difficulties that Palestinians face as they try to find a home. In the first book, three young men brave the scorching heat of the Jordanian desert trying to make it to the Kuwaiti border on foot, where a truck driver agrees to smuggle them into the country for an exorbitant fee. After a long delay, the driver manages to make the crossing with his hidden human cargo undetected. By the time he crosses the border, however, the men have all suffocated inside the water tank. The driver throws the bodies into a garbage dump. Out of this tragic event, Kanafani creates a tale that carries with it, from beginning to end, the pain of national dispossession and its consequences for ordinary people.

As another novel of dispossession, *All That's Left to You* is the moving story of a brother, Hamid, and a sister, Maryam, who get separated from each other and their mother. Hamid, on his way to Jordan in search of his mother, must cross the desert at night so that he will not be detected by the border guards. His sister, made pregnant by Zakariyya, already married and the father of five, has no choice but to marry the man, a Palestinian paid by the Israeli to spy on his fellow Palestinians. The end is bloody: Maryam stabs her husband to death in self-defense, and Hamid kills an Israeli border guard. Both end up in prison for life.

Like Kanafani, Syrian writer Halīm Barakāt deals exclusively with the question of Palestine. *Sittat Ayyām* (1961; *Six Days*, 1990) is an eerie anticipation of the Arab-Israeli Six-Day War of 1967, while *'Awdat al-ṭā'ir ilā al-baḥr* (1969; *Days of Dust*, 1974) is a response to it. In the latter, Ramzi Safadi is a Western-educated professor at the American University in Beirut, Lebanon. As a displaced Palestinian, he cannot call Lebanon home. His dream is to one day return to Palestine; he and his students are led by the national media to believe that this might actually happen. However, the war turns out to be a crushing defeat for the Arabs. With their illusions shattered, Ramzi and his students find themselves in a state of shock and disbelief. For Ramzi this is a turning point. Enraged by American and British support for Israel, he turns against everything Western. Apart from its vividness of character and description, the novel is popular because it succeeds in demolishing the myths of Arab invincibility and the West's neutrality

in the Arab-Israeli conflict. It forces Arab readers to ask themselves whether they too are implicated, in one way or another, in this national defeat, and whether they need to revise their attitude toward the West.

OTHER ARAB NOVELISTS

The appearance of Ṭayyib Ṣāliḥ's *Mawsim al-hijra ilā al-shamāl* (1967; *Season of Migration to the North*, 1969) was a major literary event in the Middle East. Ṣāliḥ, who earned degrees in education from Exeter and London Universities and served for twelve years as head of drama for the British Broadcasting Corporation's (BBC) Arabic Service, created the first truly postcolonial Middle Eastern novel. Told by two British-educated narrators, one unnamed and the other a father of three named Mustafa, this novel moves back and forth between a small village in the Sudan and a London slowly emerging from the devastation caused by World War I. Just like the author, Mustafa has been sent on a scholarship to London. As a student, he frequents the bars and clubs of the Chelsea and Hampstead districts, attends gatherings of the Bloomsbury Group, and develops a strong affinity for Bernard Shaw and other Fabian socialists. He marries an English woman and acquires the nickname "the Black Englishman." He earns a Ph.D. in economics from the world famous London School of Economics. As he becomes increasingly critical of capitalism and colonialism, however, Mustafa begins to refer to himself as "a lie" and sets out to erase it. He turns his back on everything English and European and returns to his native village, where he marries a local woman and begins farming. He seems to blend in easily. Mustafa is attempting what postcolonial critics call the process of resistance and reconstruction: confronting the past in order to purge it of colonial influence and domination. However, this is an impossible task to accomplish. For one thing, the English language has taken him further and further away from his roots. For another, he declares war on hybridity at a time when the world is becoming increasingly hybridized. His suicide, as the other narrator makes clear, is meant to underline the futility of his undertaking. The novel seems to conclude that although hybridity might be painful, it should, as Chinua Achebe and Edward Said have said, be appropriated rather than discarded.

At the time, what was most surprising about Ṣāliḥ was that, while the region's other novelists seemed unable or unwilling to disengage from all the troubling political upheavals sweeping the region, Ṣāliḥ offered a novel that seemed to be oblivious to all that, focusing instead on such postcolonial themes as identity, sexuality, spirituality, materialism, modernity, change, and the problematics of belonging and not belonging to East and West. What is more, unlike his earlier work ʿUrs az-Zen (1966; *The Wedding of Zein and Other Stories*, 1968), *Season of Migration* appropriated the techniques and forms of the European novel to create a stunning narrative of displacement that is rich in imagery and tone, and multiple and fragmentary in scope.

Abdelrahman Munif, another gifted contemporary Arab novelist, favors themes that deal with Arab nationalism and the impact that the discovery of oil has had on Middle Eastern societies. Because of his involvement in Arab nationalism, an ideology highly critical of the role of the United States in the Middle East, Munif was stripped of his Saudi citizenship in 1963, after which he moved to Damascus, Syria. Munif's 1975 novel *Sharq al-Mutawassit* (the Mediterranean) is a bitter denunciation of the Arab governments that fought Israel in 1976. Despite their crushing defeat, these governments continued to talk about victory and the near annihilation of Israel, and they severely punished anyone who dared to speak out against government policy. To underline the significance of the issue, the novel starts out with a quote from the Universal Declaration of Human Rights.

In later works, Munif focused on the way that the discovery of oil changed age-old traditions and led to an increase in the region's domination by the West. His novel *Sibāq al-masāfāt al-zawtlah: Rihlah ila al-Sharq* (1979; the long competition) is generally understood to be an allegorical study of Iran in the early 1950's. The United States, represented by the protagonist, cannot allow a popularly elected government to pursue independent oil policies. The Central Intelligence Agency (CIA) therefore overthrows the

government and installs a puppet prime minister.

Al-Tīh (1984; *Cities of Salt*, 1987) dwells on a similar theme in a country resembling modern Saudi Arabia, perhaps one reason why the novel has been banned there. Americans arrive with equipment to look for oil. They bring with them prefabricated houses and air conditioning, and they start building roads and recreational facilities, all of which seem to be quite at odds with a nomadic way of life centered on the desert. Some of the natives try to resist, but they are unsuccessful as the powerful clan leaders, with American support and supervision, transform the region into a modern police state. Such rivalries and disagreements about the United States and the forces of modernization are also the subject of Munif's *Taqāsīm al-layl wa-al-nahār* (1989; *Variations on Night and Day*, 1993), also banned in Saudi Arabia.

ISRAELI NOVELISTS

Other significant contributions to the Middle Eastern novel have come from Israel. Since its creation in 1948, Israel has produced many highly gifted novelists who explore in a variety of forms and techniques what it means to be Jewish in a land where identity and nationality are so problematic. One of the most distinguished is the Romanian-born Holocaust survivor Aharon Appelfeld. Although he moved to Palestine in 1947, Appelfeld seems like an exile writing for a public that has lost all interest in the past. His early works—ʿAshan (1962; smoke), *Ba-gai ha-poreh* (1963; in the fertile valley), and others—are collected in the English translation *In the Wilderness* (1965); they consist of a series of dream sequences involving his Holocaust experience. The novels have a feeling of allegory to them, dark and philosophical, poetic and sometimes obscure. The novel *Badenheim, ʿir nofesh* (1975; *Badenheim 1939*, 1980) portrays a Europe where to be labeled a Jew is tantamount to a death sentence. The protagonists were all born in Badenheim, but the Austrian authorities refuse to accept them as citizens and have no qualms about sending them to a concentration camp in Germany. The Jews live a life of isolation, uncertainty, fear, and denial. This is also the case with the protagonist of *Bartfus ben ha-almavet* (1988; *The Immoral Bartfuss*, 1988), who, in Appelfeld's words, "has swallowed the Holocaust whole." To survive, he must remain silent and distant himself from all those around him.

In *To the Land of the Cattails* (1986; also known as *To the Land of the Reeds*), Appelfeld takes readers once again to a Europe dominated by Adolf Hitler. It is the summer of 1939. A woman insists on going back to the land of her childhood, "the land of the cattails," not far from Appelfeld's own birthplace. She is accompanied by her son, Tony. The mother is caught by the Nazis and is shipped by a mysterious train to an unknown destination. In desperation, Tony turns to alcohol and begins to negotiate an identity for himself based on his Jewish and Gentile heritage. In the end, suffering gives him no choice but to reject everything that is not Jewish.

Another distinguished Israeli novelist is Abraham Yehoshua, who, in addition to novels, has written a number of short stories, plays, and screenplays. In his novels, Yehoshua tends to focus on issues that became central to the Israeli experience after the Six-Day War of 1967: the relationship between Jews and Arabs, the fight over territory, Israeli national borders, the large-scale displacement of Palestinians, and the conflict between orthodox and secular Jews. His novella *Bithilat Kayits 1970* (1972; *Early in the Summer of 1970*, 1977) takes readers to a postwar Israel. A father is still mourning a son killed in the Six-Day War. Midway through the novel, however, the father learns that the reported death was a case of mistaken identity; the corpse discovered was not that of his son. Although he receives proof that his son is still alive, the father cannot stop grieving. The story is constructed in a circular pattern: The final chapter repeats the first with only a slight variation.

Yehoshua uses a similar technique in his first novel, *Me'ahev* (1977; *The Lover*, 1977). It is a series of monologues told by separate people, and it intentionally leaves things murky. Readers do not know exactly who the lover of the title is or, for that matter, why he has been adopted by the couple Asya and Adam. Also, readers do not know what bearing these personal events have on the national situation, such

as the ongoing war with the Arabs, and what to make of the Arab Naim, who plays an important part in the novel.

Things are less murky in *Molkho* (1987; *Five Seasons*, 1989), *Mar Mani* (1990; *Mr. Mani*, 1992), and *Gerushim me'uharim* (1982; *A Late Divorce*, 1984). The latter concerns an American Jew who travels to Israel to divorce his Israeli-born wife. The story is meant to parallel the national debate on the relationship between Israel and the Diaspora. After the divorce, in a clearly symbolic act meant to stress the inextricable linkage between the personal and the national, the man starts wearing his ex-wife's clothes.

No contemporary Israeli novelist matches Amos Oz's innovative writing about the problematics of the Jewish experience in the Holy Land. Born in Jerusalem in 1939 and educated at Hebrew University, Oz became Israel's best-known novelist. After working as a visiting professor at a number of prestigious schools in the United States and Europe, he became a professor of Hebrew literature at Ben Gurion University in 1987. In addition to novels, Oz's output includes short stories, novellas, literary criticism, and political essays. His first novel, *Ma'kom a'her* (1966; *Elsewhere, Perhaps*, 1973), juxtaposes two realities that seem to be at odds with each other. On the surface, the kibbutz life seems orderly, rational, peaceful, and fulfilling. Beneath there seems to lurk a different reality, eleven times alluded to as the "other place." The place, however, remains mysterious throughout the novel; it is at once the source of yearning and revulsion, pain and gaiety. The upright father, Reuben, and his beautiful daughter, Noga, have come to the kibbutz to build a society that will presumably know no discrimination, no injustice, and no economic disparity. However, the daughter finds herself drawn to the sinister visitor from Germany, Siegfried; much to Reuben's surprise and revulsion, Noga needs little persuading to give up her life on the kibbutz for a new one in Germany.

Oz's highly popular novel *Mikha'el sheli* (1968; *My Michael*, 1972) also takes place in a world in which the personal always seems to be a much stronger force in shaping people's lives than national considerations. Told in the form of a memoir, the story is built around the mind of the leading female figure and narrator, Hannah, who remembers in vivid detail how she and Michael met, became engaged, and married in 1950. Within this personal narrative, readers also know that the national scene in the country is peaceful, prosperous, and optimistic. This world of conformity and stability is juxtaposed with the private world of Hannah's fantasies, which involves Arab twins, rape, terror, surrender, domination, and suicide. While Israel happily celebrates its first decade of independence, Hannah's mind begins to disintegrate, creating a sharp contrast between two seemingly irreconcilable realities.

Oz's writing is easily accessible, and his stories take place in recognizable Israeli settings. However, an element of mystery often surrounds his characters' private lives. *La-da'at ishah* (1989; *To Know a Woman*, 1991) and *Matsav ha-shelishi* (1991; *Fima*, 1993) present characters that seem to be on one level quite ordinary but on another mysterious and perplexing.

Israeli novelist David Grossman's stature rose considerably after he received the Israel Publishers Association prize for 1985. Like Oz, Grossman welds the political with the personal in a writing style that mixes stream-of-consciousness technique and journalistic reporting. A good example is Grossman's first novel, *Hiyvkh ha-gedi* (1983; *The Smile of the Lamb*, 1990), a vivid representation of life in the West Bank under Israeli occupation. The story is told by both Arab and Israeli protagonists, the governors and the governed, and is a conflicting account of personal and political considerations. Although the novel seems to cast doubt on certainties, it nevertheless can be interpreted as making a case against the Israeli occupation of the West Bank and in favor of Arab self-determination, a position he restates more unequivocally in his documentary piece *Ha-zeman ha-tsahov* (1987; *The Yellow Wind*, 1988).

His novel *'Ayen 'erech: Ahavah* (1986; *See Under: Love*, 1989) also uses multiple voices and modes. The first section, "Momik," reconstructs the Holocaust through the mind of a nine-year-old boy who relies more on his imagination than on his surviving relatives' accounts to understand exactly what hap-

pened at the concentration camps. The next three sections challenge chronology and traditional narrative techniques even further by making the boy rely entirely on fantasy in order to understand Bruno Schulz's death and Anshel Wasserman's experience in Auschwitz. *Sefer ha-dikduk ha-penimi* (1991; *The Book of Intimate Grammar*, 1994) does away with the adult narrator by making the child the fictionalized memoir's only voice.

WOMEN NOVELISTS

During the late 1950's, a good number of women novelists began emerging in the Middle East, most famous among them Nawāl al-Sa'dāwī, Hanan al-Shaykh, and Ghādah al-Sammān. These writers saw a pressing need to use the fictionality of the novel to address the one issue that affected them the most: the status of women.

Though Nawāl al-Sa'dāwī became a gynecologist in 1956, she achieved fame through her many novels, short stories, plays, and critical essays as a passionate crusader for women's rights. Her first novel, *Mudhakkirāt Tabība* (1958; *Memoirs of a Woman Doctor*, 1988), which has been translated into many languages, is the story of a woman doctor who remains nameless throughout the novel. As a child, the narrator quickly becomes aware of the limitations imposed on her by a male-dominated culture. Unlike her brother, she cannot go out and play in the street, cannot wear what she likes, cannot have short hair, and cannot go anywhere without her parents' permission. Out of frustration, she first turns against herself: "The first real tears I shed in my life weren't because I'd done badly at school or broken something but because I was a girl." She then begins questioning God's fairness as her period starts. Later, as a physician trying to dissect a male body, she is astounded by its unattractiveness; in a fit of anger and in an obvious act of revenge against men for oppressing women, she violently and repeatedly stabs the body. Her most shocking realization about what it means to be a woman in a sexist society comes when, in order to get married, she is forced to give up her "human rights." Predictably, the marriage soon ends in a divorce.

As can be seen from this brief summary, Sa'dāwī has quite a few axes to grind; hers is a fight against the entire society. In agreeing to perform an abortion on a rape victim, her narrator seems to speak for the author: "How could I punish her alone when I knew that her society as a whole had participated in the act?" Her 1987 novel, *Suqūt al-Imām* (*The Fall of the Imam*, 1988), aims at undermining the patriarchal order by taking on the very system upon which it is based. The Imam, a religious and political figure of enormous authority, represents patriarchy. To protect his authority, he must hide the fact that his own daughter is illegitimate. The novel then becomes a test of will between a father who is the ultimate symbol of power and his young daughter, who is determined to challenge that power. In the end the father is assassinated by an enraged public, and the daughter is hailed as a female Christ.

Sa'dāwī's writing seems to demonstrate how difficult it is for a woman writer living under a patriarchal order to keep her struggle against that order separate from her writing. That also seems to be the case with the Lebanese novelist Hanan al-Shaykh, who, like Sa'dāwī, is both admired and vilified in the Middle East because of her feminism. Her first novel, *Hikayat Zahra* (1980; *The Story of Zahra*, 1986), was banned in several Middle Eastern countries because of its vivid discussion of female sexuality. As a child, Zahra quickly learns that to be a girl is to be condemned to lifelong servitude. Her brother, Ahmad, gets the best of everything and has the freedom to talk, play, and bring home friends. As she grows up, Zahra realizes that to be a woman is even worse; she is repeatedly raped by a cousin and later by a family friend, as a result of which she must undergo two abortions before reaching adulthood. In her helplessness, Zahra turns against herself and inflicts severe scars on her own face in the hope that men would no longer find her attractive. Her ordeal continues even in marriage, as she has to deal with an extremely abusive husband. The novel was hailed as a hallmark in Arab feminism for its challenge to patriarchy.

Shaykh's 1988 novel, *Misk al-ghazal* (*Women of Sand and Myrrh*, 1989), is equally daring in its attack on patriarchy, which is why it, too, was banned in most Middle Eastern countries. It is the story of four women living in an unnamed desert kingdom closely resembling modern Saudi Arabia. Their lives consist of series of unfulfilling events and activities that center on the home. What angers some Middle Eastern readers is the novel's portrayal of the private side of these women: At home they wear tight jeans and makeup, take pleasure in one another's bodies, and talk openly about their sexual problems. Two of them even start a passionate lesbian affair. Another woman, a young widow by the name of Tamar, struggles to start a sewing business of her own. Since her father is dead, she is required to get her brother's permission. After he refuses, Tamar goes on a hunger strike, forcing the brother to give his consent. Then she must go to an office to get permission from the government, where she is told that women are not allowed to enter the building. In the end, and against all odds, she gets the state's permission. Shaykh's novel is not just a dry narrative of social criticism. In sharp contrast to Sa'dāwī's novels, *Women of Sand and Myrrh* is a highly readable book, full of tension and nastiness, but also joy, beauty, and laughter.

The status of women in the Middle East is also an important theme in the works of Syrian-born Lebanese resident Ghādah al-Sammān. For her, women's problems cannot be solved until both men and women are liberated from dogma and repressive traditions. Sammān studied English literature at the American University in Beirut, and, after a short career in teaching, she became a full-time writer in 1966, turning out four collections of short stories before writing her first novel in 1975. The novel, *Bayrūt 75* (*Beirut '75*, 1995), whose events coincide with the 1975 Lebanese civil war, begins with a taxi ride from Damascus to Beirut, a place where the characters hope their dreams will come true. Farah wants to become a successful businessman, while Yasimina, a young woman who is fed up with her society's insistence that women belong in the home, hopes to find romance and a more fulfilling career than teaching at a convent. The taxi is black, the driver is mute, and the three women passengers in the back are all dressed in black—details clearly designed to foreshadow the novel's bleak outcome.

In Beirut, success eludes Farah. For a while, Yasimina seems to be doing well. She spends her time in the company of a rich boyfriend sunbathing nude on his yacht. After years of seeing her body as "a burden, a corpse," she begins to discover it "as a world of pleasure." The pleasure, however, is short-lived. The daily bombing by Israeli planes of Palestinian targets in and around Beirut puts a stop to the normal flow of life. Yasimina's boyfriend breaks up with her. In desperation, she turns to her brother, a longtime Beirut resident, who takes her money and, after accusing her of tarnishing the family honor through her sexual transgressions, stabs her to death. Sammān clearly intends the novel to be an exposé of horrific forms of social and political oppression, the responsibility for which must lie with both men and women. As she herself has said, "We should demand rights for women and men together—that is, demand rights for the repressed human race of which women form such a large part."

Sammān returns to this theme in her next novel, *Kawabis Bayrūt* (1976; *Beirut Nightmares*, 1997), which is in the form of a series of nightmares involving a nameless female narrator's many struggles in a patriarchal society amid civil war. A stray bullet from a sniper goes through the narrator's apartment window, grazing her ear. She puts the bullet next to her pen, then comments, "this particular bullet . . . seemed to me at first sight as long as my pen. Then it grew and became a pillar of fire, while my pen trembled and shrank." Another bullet scores a direct hit at her university diploma. Later, a missile pierces her apartment, destroying her entire library. Through these images, Sammān is trying to determine if violence can be justified to bring about a revolution. The narrator herself has been trying to start some sort of a peaceful revolution against society: "My library was not merely books. It was a dialogue. Every book was a man with whom I had argued." She soon realizes that a peaceful revolution will have little chance of success in a war-torn country. At the end of the book, the narrator, despite serious misgivings ("I need it, but I still detest it"), begins to carry a pistol along with her pen.

TURKEY

In its early days, the Turkish novel, especially those of Ahmet Mithat (1844-1912), Halit Ziya Usakligil (1866-1945), and Peyami Safa (1899- 1961), extolled the virtues of Turkish society while at the same time stressing the importance of Western know-how for material success. Safa's *Fatih-Harbiye* (1931) is a naturalistic portrayal of life in Fatih, an old Istanbul district where age-old traditions give men and women contrasting gender roles, and in Harbiye, a sprawling suburb of European-style homes and businesses where women work outside the home and do not have to cover their faces. Other early novelists, most notably Refik Halit Karay (1888- 1965) and Resat Nuri Guntekin (1889-1956), found inspiration in the country's heartland, the Anatolia region, where the peasantry's seemingly harmonious relationship with nature proved alluring to them. This gradually developed into what came to be known as the peasant novel, and Yashar Kemal, who emerged as Turkey's most famous novelist during the 1950's, was its undisputed perfecter.

Kemal's many novels have been translated into some thirty languages, and he has been a frequent candidate for the Nobel Prize in Literature. The recipient of numerous awards, including the 1997 German Book Trade Peace Prize, Kemal was born in 1923 in Turkey's southeast to the only Kurdish family in the poverty-stricken village of Hemite. Although Kemal moved to Istanbul in the early 1950's, the region of his birth and its poor peasantry continued to dominate his novels. Like William Faulkner, who was a strong influence on Kemal, the Turkish writer returned time and time again to his birthplace, weaving out of its people, their songs and legends, their lyrical ways with language, their many struggles, and their age-old traditions stories of epic proportions. His 1955 novel, *İnce Memed* (*Memed, My Hawk*, 1961), is the story of Memed, a fatherless peasant boy who must work long hours in the field in order to support himself and his mother. Unusually mature for his age, Memed puts up with an abusive, tyrannical landowner and scorching summer heat; the only bright spot in his life is his sweetheart, Hatche. However, the landlord, Abdi Agha, tries to force Hatche to marry his nephew, Veli. Hatche and

Memed elope. In a shootout with the Agha and his men, Memed kills Veli, wounds the landlord, and escapes to the mountains. Hatche is eventually captured, charged with Veli's death, and thrown into prison. The story, however, is the stuff of legend: Memed returns, rescues his sweetheart, gives chase to the Agha, and divides his fields among the peasantry. As can be seen from this brief sketch, the novel is action-packed, cinematic, and quite lyrical in its rendering of the peasant imagination.

These are also the qualities that characterize other Kemal novels that have been translated into English, especially *Ölmez otu* (1968; *The Undying Grass*, 1977), and *Yılanı öldürseler* (1976; *To Crush the Serpent*, 1991). Though the latter is much shorter than *Memed, My Hawk*, its scope and style are easily recognizable. Esme is forced to marry a man, Halil, she does not love. A son, Hasan, is born. Esme's lover murders Halil, but most everyone in the village blames Esme for it. Killing a woman in revenge, however, is out of the question. According to popular belief, however, failure to avenge the murder would result in the community being terrorized by Halil's spirit, which would return in the form of a poisonous snake. The burden is now on the young Hasan to avenge his father's death, but he decides to leave for the city rather than stay and become trapped in and possibly destroyed by violence. This plot twist reflects Kemal's outspoken criticism of feudalism.

Like most Middle Eastern writers, Kemal is intensely political. In a 1997 essay, "Literature, Democracy, and Peace," Kemal makes it clear that his intention has always been to use "the word" to expose and oppose social and political oppression. He hopes his novels will make his readers more accepting of other people and more willing to speak out against injustice, especially that committed by national governments. As a case in point, Kemal cites the Turkish government's refusal to grant the Kurdish minority cultural and political rights.

Orhan Pamuk's novels, highly acclaimed for their technical innovation and mesmerizing prose, have been translated into some fifteen languages. Appropriating the techniques of such European writers as James Joyce, Marcel Proust, and Thomas Mann, Pamuk has created stories that explore Turkey's Ottoman past, its troubled present, and its uncertain future.

Pamuk's international fame came with his third novel, *Beyaz kale* (1985; *The White Castle*, 1990). Set in the 1690's, the time when the Ottoman Empire began to decline, it tells the story of a Venetian aristocrat and a Turkish inventor known only as Hoja. Hoja sees the West as the source of all scientific knowledge. He invents a war machine with which he helps the sultan's army lay siege to a white castle in southern Poland. Hoja settles in Europe, while the Venetian retires to Anatolian exile. The identities of the two men remain unclear: Despite the fact that one is from the East and the other is from the West, they are interchangeable. The novel seems to call into question the notions of cultural and racial purity. The Venetian character is created out of all the fictions that the narrator has read and appropriated. There is also nothing real about the Ottoman character, for he, too, is created out of myths and stories that the Turkish state requires schoolchildren to learn as facts. The novel's theme is clearly postmodern: Where do the Turkish people living on the margins of Europe belong? East or West? Such questions are complicated by the fact that modern Turkey was founded on secular and Western, rather than religious and Eastern, principles. After the Ottoman defeat in World War I, modern Turkey was created in the West's image. Religion was banned as something backward and outdated, the Latin alphabet was introduced, the Turkish language was purged of its Arabic and Persian words, and the dervish sects were outlawed. As a result, most Turks today cannot read their own classical texts. Another complication comes from the fact that Turkey became a member of the North Atlantic Treaty Organization (NATO) in 1954, yet its attempts to join the European Union were repeatedly rebuffed.

Pamuk challenged himself to explore this enduring identity crisis, revisit the past rejected by the postwar government, and study the lines of filiation between East and West. His novel *Yeni hayat* (1994; *The New Life*, 1997) is the story of a student who is greatly influenced by a mysterious book he has been reading. His country is big and sparsely populated; some of it is modernized and Westernized, but most of it remains tribal and traditional. The more the student tries to find out where he belongs, the more troubling and confusing the notion of identity becomes for him. Pamuk's view is that all Turks, being in the "provinces of world culture," suffer from "this feeling of being off the track" and "forgotten."

IRAQ

The novel had a promising start in Iraq, a country with a long, rich literary tradition. Mohamud al-Sayyid and Dhū al-nūn Ayyūb began writing in the late 1930's, and Ayyūb's 1939 *Duktur Ibrahim* (Dr. Ibrahim), which deals with the moral bankruptcy of a Western-educated physician, became a best-seller in the nation. The establishment of Saddam Hussein's dictatorship in 1968 dealt a heavy blow to the novel as the state incorporated all forms of artistic and literary production into its massive propaganda machine in support of the leader. The policy forced many to quit writing altogether, but some chose to collaborate with the state. Typical of such work is Abd al-amir Mu'allah's massive *Al-Ayyam al-tawila* (1978-1981; *The Long Days*, 1982-   ), a novel that transforms Saddam Hussein into a heroic figure of mythic proportions. It is mandatory reading for soldiers, students, and government employees.

Sabah A. Salih

BIBLIOGRAPHY

Allen, Roger. *The Arabic Novel: An Historical and Critical Introduction.* Syracuse, N.Y.: Syracuse University Press, 1982. Organized chronologically, this readable study discusses the circumstances that led to the development of the Arabic novel into a serious genre after World War II and provides detailed analysis of a good number of novelists, including those whose works have yet to be translated into English.

Chertok, Chaim. *We Are All Close: Conversations with Israeli Writers.* New York: Fordham University Press, 1989. A thorough and detailed discussion of themes, techniques, and ideological positions that have become the hallmark of such Israeli writers as David Grossman, Amos Oz, Abraham Yehoshua, Aharon Appelfeld, and others.

Dino, Guzine. "The Turkish Peasant Novel, or the Anatolian Theme." *World Literature Today* 66, no. 2 (1986): 200-206. Traces the development of the Turkish peasant novel and discusses in detail Yeshar Kemal's contribution to it.

el-Enany, Rasheed. *Naguib Mahfouz: The Pursuit of Meaning.* London: Routledge, 1993. Intended for the nonspecialist, this thematically organized study covers the literary and nonliterary aspects of Naguib Mahfouz and his writing.

Fuchs, Esther. *Israeli Mythogynies: Women in Contemporary Hebrew Fiction.* Albany: State University of New York Press, 1987. This thought-provoking, gender-oriented study covers all the Israeli writers discussed in this overview.

Guneli, Gun. "Orhan Pamuk." *World Literature Today* 80, no. 3 (1992): 30-38. An accessible discussion of Orhan Pamuk's literary accomplishments, including themes, techniques, and influences.

Mehrez, Samia. *Egyptian Writers Between History and Fiction: Essays on Naguib Mahfouz, Sonallah Ibrahim, and Gamal al-Ghitani.* Cairo, Egypt: The American University in Cairo Press, 1994. A thorough study of these three influential Egyptian novelists.

Ramras-Rauch, Gila. *The Arab in Israeli Literature.* Bloomington: Indiana University Press, 1989. A useful and accessible discussion of how the Arab-Israeli encounter has been portrayed in the novels of David Grossman, Abraham Yehoshua, Amoz Oz, Aharon Appelfeld, and others.

Silberschlag, Eisig. *From Renaissance to Renaissance: Hebrew Literature in the Land of Israel.* New York: KTAV, 1977. A solid and thorough discussion of the origins, developments, themes, and circumstances of early Israeli literature, with a long chapter on the novel.

Zeidan, Joseph T. *Arab Women Novelists: The Formative Years and Beyond.* Albany: State University of New York Press, 1995. Intended for the general reader, this is a comprehensive study of almost all the Arab women novelists who have been published. Provides a bibliography and a historical overview of the status of women in Arab societies.

RUSSIAN LONG FICTION

The eighteenth century is generally considered the beginning of modern Russian literature for several reasons. The most important is that a clear break occurred with the Age of Faith, as Serge Zenkovsky calls it in the introduction to his anthology, *Medieval Russia's Epics, Chronicles and Tales* (1974). The acceptance of Christianity in 988-989 C.E. by Vladimir the Great (who ruled Kievan Rus from 980 to 1015) from culturally superior Byzantium established the authority of the Orthodox Church and enabled it to determine the nature of literature, such as it was, for several centuries. Written by clergy and monks in Old Church Slavonic, a language elaborated for the Slavs in the ninth century by Saints Cyril and Methodius, the literature ("writings" would perhaps be a better term) consisted of the Bible, liturgical texts, Church books, sermons, saints' lives, chronicles and annals, military tales, and some translated literature. The latter included popular works of a secular nature, such as the historical heroic romances *Aleksandriya* (c. twelfth century; the story of Alexander the Great) and *Troyanskoe deyanie* (c. eleventh century; Trojan deeds), which, however, often contained religious motifs. Didactic stories offering instruction in the form of a fable or homily, such as "Varlaam i Yosafat" (c. thirteenth century; Barlaam and Yosaphat), a Christian version of the story of Buddha, were also common. It is important to note that the great classical Greek and Roman heritage was not transmitted to Rus: The Byzantines regarded the Russians as culturally inferior, unworthy of this heritage, while the Orthodox Church considered such writings pagan literature.

The destruction of Kievan Rus by the Mongols from 1238 to 1240 was followed by more than 150 years of Tatar domination (the Tatar Yoke, as it is called), which ended with the rise of Muscovy as the new center of power. Religious literature continued to dominate throughout the fifteenth and sixteenth centuries, although secular themes, realistic details, and the vernacular gradually became more widespread. This is particularly evident in the gradual changes in the canonical form of the saint's life, which by the seventeenth century was supplanted by secular biography, autobiography, and first-person confession. A good example of this is "Povest o Yulianii Lazarevskoy" (c. 1620; the life of Juliania Lazarevsky), which, although written in the traditional form of a saint's life, is, in fact, a secular biography in conception.

There was also a gradual shift from Church Slavonic, a language that virtually none but clergy spoke, toward the vernacular, a shift that was closely linked to the rise of secular literature. Consequently, an account of a Tver merchant's journey to India, "Khozhdeniye za tri morya Afanasiya Nikitina 1466-1472 gg" (c. 1475; "The Travels of Athanasius Nikitin"), describing its exotic animals, lush landscapes, and strange customs, is written in a language almost entirely free of Church Slavonicisms. The vernacular was also dispersed by numerous stories satirizing corruption, irreligious practices among the clergy and monks, and a host of other common abuses, as seventeenth century literature moved to a closer portrayal of everyday life.

MODERN RUSSIAN LITERATURE

The passage from the Age of Faith into modern Russian literature is strikingly illustrated by the story "Povest o Frole Skobeyeve" (late seventeenth century; "Frol Skobeev, the Rogue," 1963). The story introduced a new type for Russian literature, the rogue, the social outsider who managed through his scheming to rise in station. Sharply satiric in its portrayal of the relationships between the rich and the poor, the story also contains erotic scenes and realistic details of Moscow life. Written in the vernacular, it is devoid of any religious features and is an excellent example of native Russian literature of the Petrine period (1682-1725).

In addition to the secularization of literature, there are other reasons for considering the eighteenth century as the beginning of modern Russian literature. The efforts of Peter the Great (1682-1725) to westernize Russia increased contacts with Western Europe and freed Russia from its relative isolation. This led to a large influx of foreign literature, which served as a model for Russian authors and stimulated their own literary efforts; it also prepared the ground for the acceptance of French classicism—which was, however, modified by native Russian traditions.

French classicism exerted its greatest influence on Russian poetry, which was the dominant genre of the eighteenth century. Prose, which was not regarded as on an equal footing with serious art such as poetry or drama, had to struggle for recognition and legitimacy, and rose to prominence only in the last quarter of the century, after the demise of classicism in the early 1770's. In keeping with the distinction made by classicism between high and low genres, Russian prose fiction of the eighteenth century tended primarily toward the low genres—the picaresque, the satire, the adventure story, and the romance—rather than the high genres—the tragedy or the *Staatsroman*, the novel concerned with how the ideal state should be governed. The latter was influenced by the Enlightenment belief in reason and centered on the discussion of the correct way a monarch was to rule his or her subjects; it was considered, therefore, to have a serious purpose. The former, the lower genres, were considered mere amusement and diversion. These popular forms were, however, much more widely read, and as a result, they furthered the penetration of the vernacular into literature.

The eighteenth century also saw the first conscious efforts made to fix the standard of the Russian literary language, which to that time consisted of an incongruous mixture of Church Slavonic, the vernacular, chancellery terms, and foreign borrowings. Under the influence of classicism, Mikhail Lomonosov (1711-1765), a prominent poet and scholar, established the doctrine of three styles—high, middle, and low—which were distinguished by the relative abundance of Church Slavonicisms. The high style, with its predominance of archaisms and Church Slavonicisms, was deemed appropriate for heroic poems, odes, and prose orations on important matters; the middle style, for epistles in verse, satires, eclogues, theatrical productions, and elegies; and the low style, for comedies, songs, humorous epigrams, and prose letters to friends. As one can see, prose fiction was

not an art form recognized by Lomonosov, although he accepted the satiric novel as a tool for edification. In the ongoing debate concerning the novel, the principle of usefulness was, in fact, often invoked by its defenders, who pointed out that the novel conformed to Horace's doctrine of *dulce et utile* and therefore deserved to be recognized. The expectation that literature should serve as a force for social change, a notion upheld throughout the nineteenth century as well, was fostered by the Russian satiric tradition and the hostile reaction of the nativists to the flood of popular French literature entering Russia.

Translations of European novels, primarily French but later German and English, played a crucial role in the development of Russian prose fiction of the eighteenth century. They provided models for Russian authors and were themselves very popular. Handmade copies of novels circulated extensively among the aristocracy—which, by and large, spoke French, as did nearly every educated Russian of the eighteenth century. The French novels generally provided entertaining reading, especially the popular adventure novel, which described travels to strange countries, exotic landscapes, fantastic encounters, and amorous adventures. Consisting of loosely connected episodes, the popular novels emphasized melodramatic action rather than character development. They first appeared in large numbers in the early 1760's; in fact, only one novel was published in Russian between 1725 and 1741, and that was a translation of Paul de Tallemant's *Voyage à l'isle d'amour* (1663; Russian translation, 1730).

The influence of French literature is evident in the works of Russia's first novelist, Fyodor Emin (c. 1735-1770). He wrote six original novels between 1763 and 1769, intertwining melodramatic plots characteristic of the adventure novel with verbose digressions on politics, society, geography, and love. He made extensive use of clichés in his portrayal of character and wrote in a pathetic-emotional style, but he was also among the first to voice sympathy with the plight of the peasants. His first novel, *Nepostoyannaya fortuna ili pokhozhdenie Miramonda* (1763; fortune inconstant, or the voyage of Miramond), is a typical adventure novel in which the hero travels through Europe and offers a commentary on geography, political systems, the relationship between rich and poor, and so on. Similar topics appear in his *Priklyucheniya Femistokla* (1763; the adventures of Themistocles), which is set in the Athenian age and consists of conversations between a father and son about politics and society—in particular, the way an enlightened monarch should govern. In this regard, Emin was influenced by François Fénelon's popular novel *Les Aventures de Télémaque* (1699; *The Adventures of Telemach*, 1720; Russian translation, 1766), the translation of which went through eight editions in Russia by 1800, and by his wish to flatter Catherine the Great (reigned 1762-1796), who fancied herself an enlightened monarch. Emin's most noted work is his four-volume novel *Pisma Ernesta i Dovravry* (1766; the letters of Ernest and Dovravra), the first Russian epistolary novel. Influenced by *Julie: Ou, La Nouvelle Héloïse* (1761; *Eloise: Or, A Series of Original Letters*, 1761; also as *Julie: Or, The New Eloise*, 1968; better known as *The New Héloïse*), by Jean-Jacques Rousseau (1712-1778)—but without its social conflict—it is the story of the unhappy love of the socially equal but poor nobleman Ernest for the wealthy Dovravra. Its weaknesses are its style, too clumsy and awkward for depicting the fine sentiments of the two lovers; its overly melodramatic and emotional tone; and its numerous digressions. It was through these digressions, however, that Emin expressed his criticism of the aristocracy, corruption, and political inequality, and his sympathy for the plight of the peasants. The novel also foreshadowed the rise of a later literary movement, sentimentalism, by some twenty years.

PICARESQUE LITERATURE

Along with the adventure novel, another popular genre of the eighteenth century was the picaresque. Although the picaro had appeared in earlier works of Russian literature, the popularity of the genre was primarily the result of the translations of the works of Alain-René Lesage (1668-1747). The Russian translation of Lesage's *Histoire de Gil Blas de Santillane* (1715-1735; *The History of Gil Blas of Santillane*, 1716, 1735; better known as *Gil Blas*, 1749, 1962),

for example, went through eight editions from 1754 to 1800, while Lesage's *Le Diable boiteux* (1707, revised 1726; *The Devil upon Two Sticks*, 1708, 1726) went through five editions from 1763 to 1800, quite an achievement when one considers that in eighteenth century Russia, only twenty works of belletristic prose went through more than four editions. The popularity of the picaresque novels prompted Russian authors to try their hand at the genre.

Although itself not a picaresque novel, *Peresmeshnik: Ili, Slavyanskie skazki* (1766-1768; the mocker, or Slavic tales), by Mikhail Chulkov (1743-1792), combined elements of the picaresque with those of the fairy tale and knightly romance. Influenced by Giovanni Boccaccio's *Decameron: O, Prencipe Galetto*, 1349-1351 (*The Decameron*, 1620) and *The Arabian Nights' Entertainments* (fifteenth century; Russian translation, 1763), Chulkov's novel consists of separate stories told by three narrators, and, in comparison to other works of fiction of its time, it stands out for its native Russian character. His second work, *Prigozhaia povarikha: Ili, Pokhozhdenie razvratnoy zhenschiny* (1770; *The Comely Cook: Or, The Adventures of a Depraved Woman*, 1962), was the first Russian work to present a picara: It is the story of a young widow's trials and amorous adventures told in the form of a confession and limited to her naïve perspective. There is, however, very little that is genuinely Russian—the characters' names are foreign, the places and events are typical of the genre rather than specifically Russian, and virtually no Russian customs or traits are mentioned.

The most frequently published work influenced by the picaresque (as well as by the Russian satiric tradition) was "O Vanke Kaine, slavnom vore i moshennike kratkaya povest" (1775; a short tale about the famous thief and swindler Vanka Kain). The story of a real Moscow thief and police informer, it went through three versions and sixteen editions, thus surpassing all other single works of belletristic prose published in the eighteenth century. Strongly influenced by the Russian folktale, it describes real Russian types and the actual setting of Moscow; it contains few foreign words and many folk sayings and expressions, and even includes thieves' jargon, with translations provided in the footnotes by the unknown author, who maintains the first-person narration and the satiric intent characteristic of the genre. In 1779, it was reworked by Matvey Komarov (eight of the sixteen editions are of his version), who included witnesses' statements, police reports, and folk songs about Kain. He also added a moralistic, sentimental tone and stressed the value of education in turning evil into good, points uncharacteristic of the picaresque.

Works containing picaros or tricksters continued to appear throughout the century and maintained their popularity until the early 1830's, but by the 1780's a gradual shift in literary taste had occurred. Once again, translations of European works—Rousseau's *Émile* (1762; Russian translation, 1779), Johann Wolfgang von Goethe's *Die Leiden des jungen Werthers* (1774; Russian translation, 1781), Oliver Goldsmith's *The Vicar of Wakefield* (1766; Russian translation, 1787), Samuel Richardson's *Pamela* (1740-1741; Russian translation, 1787), and the idylls of Thomas Gray, Edward Young, and Goethe—played a crucial role in shaping the movement called sentimentalism. Sentimentalism (also referred to as pre-Romanticism) asserted the primacy of the individual and the emotions (instead of reason) as the source of moral virtue and developed the cult of friendship and sensibility. It emphasized the virtues of the countryside as opposed to the corrupt city and the honest simplicity of the peasant as opposed to the worldly veneer of the aristocrat.

The transition to sentimentalism can be seen in the works of the minor writer Nikolay Emin (died 1814), son of Fyodor Emin. His *Roza* (1786; Rosa) and *Igra sudby* (1789; the play of fate) combine the classicist conflict of duty versus feelings with the melodramatic plot of the adventure novel and attempt, unsuccessfully, to incorporate the new sensibility in describing fine emotions. The influence of foreign works can also be seen in the absence of real Russian characters. The same is true of another minor writer, Pavel Lvov (1770-1825), in his novel *Rossiyskaya Pamela: Ili, Istoriya dobrodetelnoy poselyanki* (1789; the Russian Pamela, or the history of a virtuous peasant girl). Influenced by the idyll and

the adventure novel as well as by Richardson's *Pamela*, it, too, contained very few Russian elements.

SENTIMENTALISM

Critics of the time were quick to point out that few of the numerous stories written in the sentimental vein described Russian reality and characters. Striving for grace and pleasantness (*priyatnost*) in literature, sentimentalist writers offered idyllic images of Russia and its society that occasionally ended in absurdity, especially in the portrayal of peasants, who were often shown speaking in the high style and occasionally even singing songs from French operas. The influence of the French rococo, with its emphasis on playfulness and lightness, was also evident in the predilection for short fiction of various types, designated by a number of sometimes overlapping terms: *skazka*, *rasskaz*, *romanets*, *novost* (from the French *nouvelle*), or *povest* (which could refer to a short story but more often designated a long tale, a novella, or a short novel). The absence of clearly defined generic features merely reflected the nascent stage of Russian prose fiction.

One of the leading writers of the sentimental *povest* was Nikolay Karamzin (1766-1826). Among his most important contributions was the development of a smooth, readable literary style, achieved by forgoing the heavy syntax of Lomonosov's German model and approximating the lightness and elegance of French. This Karamzin accomplished by shortening the syntactic period, avoiding Slavonicisms, and establishing a middle style of educated speech. Although criticized by Admiral Aleksandr Shishkov (1754-1841) and the conservatives (*Arkhaisty*) for his rejection of native Slavonic words and his introduction of Gallicisms, Karamzin's reform shaped the language in which the poetry of Russia's Golden Age was written and established an elegance that was imitated but unsurpassed in the eighteenth century. His most famous tale was "Bednaya Liza" (1792; "Poor Liza," 1803), with its theme of seduced innocence. Contemporaries praised his artistic rendition of the two lovers, the weak nobleman Erast and the poor country girl Liza, and their emotional and psychological portrayal. The story's great success was also a result of the absence of exaggeration, the careful use of detail, and the native Russian elements, such as the character types and the setting (Moscow and its environs). The story's immense popularity led to numerous literary imitations and even to pilgrimages to the pond near Simonov Monastery, where, in the story, Liza drowned herself. Karamzin also wrote one of the first Russian gothic tales, "Ostrov Borngolm" (1793; "The Island of Bornholm," 1821). A gloomy, Romantic atmosphere is evoked by features typical of the genre—a subterranean dungeon, vaults, a gothic castle, nocturnal settings, storms, fogs, and the suggestion of a terrible sin (incest) that has doomed the hero.

In addition to his stories, Karamzin left a fragment of a novel (thirteen chapters were published), *Rytsar nashego vremeni* (1803-1804; a knight of our time), in which he focused not on plot or incident but on the psychological portrait of his hero, the young boy Leon. Influenced by Rousseau's *Les Confessions* (1782; *The Confessions of J. J. Rousseau*, 1783-1790; Russian translation, 1797), which also deals with childhood, and by Laurence Sterne's *Tristram Shandy* (1759-1767; partial Russian translation, 1791-1792), with its whimsical play with narration, the fragment remains an interesting if incomplete document. Another of Karamzin's contributions to long fiction was his popular travelogue *Pisma russkogo puteshestvennika* (part 1, 1791-1792; part 2, 1794-1795; *Letters of a Russian Traveler*, 1957). The epistolary form enabled him to combine personal expression and commentary with factual description of his journey through Europe. The later entries, however, resembled essays, as Karamzin shifted his attention from his surroundings to general philosophical topics. The success of Karamzin's work was a result of his moderate use of facts and statistics, the absence of pronounced sermonizing, and his elegant literary style.

THE TRAVELOGUE

The travelogue was the most popular genre at the end of the eighteenth century and the start of the nineteenth century. One of the first Russian authors in this genre was Denis Fonvizin (1745-1792), with his "Pisma iz vtorogo i tretego puteshestvij po Evrope"

(written 1777-1778, 1784-1785, and published in his complete works of 1959; letters from the second and third journeys abroad). Addressed to his sister and his friend Count Peter Panin, these letters were written in colloquial Russian and were not necessarily intended as a finished literary work. The patriotic Fonvizin wished, however, to point out that social and economic conditions were not better in France than in Russia. By exposing sham, corruption, hypocrisy, and immorality in European countries, Fonvizin wished to show that human vices and frailties were universal and that Russian imitation of European culture was, therefore, pointless.

Because of its political significance, the best-known Russian work in this genre is *Puteshestvie iz Peterburga v Moskvu* (1790; *A Journey from St. Petersburg to Moscow*, 1958), by Aleksandr Radishchev (1749-1802). Without undertaking an actual journey, Radishchev utilized the form of the travelogue to launch an attack against Catherine II and the Russian nobility, arguing for a constitutional monarchy and the abolition of serfdom. In spite of the illusion of a real journey, there is little description of the countryside or local customs. Instead, Radishchev discusses law, the individual's rights in relation to the state, new concepts of morality, and a variety of other subjects. Often relying on allegory to convey his didactic message, Radishchev wrote in a ponderous, uneven style incorporating Church Slavonic syntax, Latinisms, archaisms, and grammatical forms of his own creation in order to approximate the elevated high style established by Lomonosov. While the work has its faults, Radishchev was admired (and is today) for his courageous protest, for which he was sentenced to death for sedition, a sentence commuted by Catherine II to ten years exile in Siberia.

Censorship was a problem facing literature throughout the eighteenth century (and it continues to be a problem in modern times). During Catherine II's reign, the struggle between the autocracy and literature was graphically played out in the satiric journals. Publishing her own rather harmless satiric journal, *Vsyakaya vsyachina* (1769; all kinds of things), Catherine encouraged others to follow suit, and several leading literary figures did so, only to have the censors close the journals for their hostile attitudes toward the government: Nikolay Novikov (1744-1818) published *Truten* (1769-1770; the drone); Chulkov published *I to i se* (1769; this and that); and Emin published *Adskaya pochta* (1769-1774; hell's post). In addition to the political significance of the satiric journals, which were sharply critical of the autocracy, the nobility, and serfdom, they sustained native Russian traditions by presenting Russian reality and characters, folk sayings, and customs, serving as a counterbalance to the influx of European literature. They were closely watched and were frequently shut down by the censors, particularly following the Pugachov Rebellion (1772-1774), after which not a single satiric journal appeared until the end of the 1780's. Censorship was again vigorously enforced by Catherine as news and reports of the French Revolution (1789) became known in Russia; her fear of radical ideas and political unrest led to Radishchev's arrest in 1790. It also led to Novikov's arrest in 1792 and the burning of twenty thousand books published by him, as well as the burning of Karamzin's translation of William Shakespeare's *Julius Caesar* (1599-1600) as seditious. As a means of increasing government control over literature, Catherine closed down all private publishing houses in 1796, the last year of her reign. Matters did not improve under Paul I (reigned 1796-1801), who well understood the potential political danger inherent in literature. This point was also grasped by many of the leading political and social thinkers of the nineteenth century, who wished to make literature a tool for edification and social criticism, an issue that remained hotly debated throughout the nineteenth century.

THE NINETEENTH CENTURY

The first three decades of the nineteenth century are appropriately referred to as Russia's Golden Age of Poetry, an age that was dominated by Russia's greatest poet, Alexander Sergeyevich Pushkin (1799-1837). Unable to rival the achievements of poetry, prose fiction continued to struggle for acceptance as a serious art form. Many of the issues facing prose fiction in the eighteenth century remained unresolved by the relatively minor authors who wrote in the pop-

ular prose genres of the previous century. Minor contributions to the travelogue, which continued to enjoy popular success, were made by Vasily Zhukovsky (1783-1852), with *Puteshestvie po Saksonskoy Shveytsarii* (1821; journey to Saxon Switzerland); Konstantin Batyushkov (1787-1855), with "Puteshestvie v Zamok Sirey" (1814; journey to the Chateau Sirey), an essay describing his visit to Voltaire's château at the conclusion of the Napoleonic War; and Aleksandr Bestuzhev-Marlinski (1797-1837), with *Poezdka v Revel* (1821; journey to Revel).

Translations of picaresque novels also enjoyed continued success, as evidenced by the four editions of *Gil Blas* and the two editions of *The Devil upon Two Sticks* that appeared between 1800 and 1821. The influence of Lesage is seen in *Russkiy Zhil Blas: Ili, Priklyucheniya knyazya Gavrila Simonovicha Chistakova* (1814; the Russian Gil Blas, or the adventures of Prince Gavrilo Simonovich Chistakov), by Vasiliy Narezhny (1780-1826), the last three parts of which were forbidden by the censor. The novel was immensely popular for its Russian character and spawned numerous imitations. One of the most famous of these was *Ivan Vyzhigin: Ili, Russkiy Zhil Blas* (1825; Ivan Vyzhigin, or the Russian Gil Blas), by Fadey Bulgarin (1789-1859), excerpts of which appeared in the journal *Severny arxiv* (the northern archive). In the final version, it was called *Ivan Vyzhigin, nravstvenno-satiricheskiy roman* (1829; *Ivan Vejeeghen: Or, Life in Russia*, 1831); the novel went through three editions by 1830 and was translated into French, German, Polish, English, Swedish, and Spanish. Its popularity resulted from Bulgarin's successful adaptation of the picaresque novel to Russian conditions. Modifying the traditional worldview of the picaro, Bulgarin focused on descriptions of the Russian countryside, villages, and customs, and on the life of the middle class. In this respect, Bulgarin shrewdly assessed the literary tastes of the newly established average reader, who was primarily interested in entertaining books about Russian life.

The major task of forming a readership, shaping public opinion, and introducing Russian authors and European literary and philosophical movements to the public was carried out by the journals and newspapers. As in the eighteenth century, their significance extended to the political arena as well. Often advocating a particular literary tendency, they were carefully scrutinized by the censors, and many were suppressed—*Moskovskiy Telegraf* (1825-1834), *Literaturnaya gazeta* (1830-1831), *Evropeets* (1832), and the monthly *Teleskop* (1830-1836), to name but a few. Survival depended less on the literary qualities of the publications than on coming to terms with the authorities and successfully catering to the public, a point not lost on publishers and editors scrambling to increase circulation.

Fueled by the defeat of the French in the Napoleonic War (1814), new demands were being placed on prose fiction—namely, that it represent Russian reality. The current genres were considered inadequate: The travelogue, while interesting, focused on foreign countries and had no specific form; the picaresque form, in spite of adapting to Russian conditions, lacked the dignity appropriate for high art; and the sentimental novel of manners, although presenting scenes from everyday life, was unable to express the new sense of national pride.

THE HISTORICAL NOVEL

In the 1820's, the Russian sense of national pride found expression in the historical novel, which combined everyday reality (*byt*) with the heroic fate of the nation. Elements of the historical novel could already be found in Bestuzhev-Marlinski's early works, *Zamok Neygauzen* (1824; the castle of Neuhausen) and *Revelskiy turnir* (1825; the tournament at Revel), which were influenced by Sir Walter Scott's Waverley novels. It was not until 1829, however, that the historical novel proper made its presence felt with the appearance of the popular *Yuri Miloslavsky: Ili, Russkie v 1612 godu* (1829; Yuriy Miloslavskiy, or the Russians in the year 1612), by Mikhail Zagoskin (1789-1852), which he followed with *Roslavlev: Ili, Russkie v 1812 godu* (1831; Roslavlev, or the Russians in the year 1812). So successful was the historical novel that it soon outpaced all other genres of prose fiction of the time; numerous authors, among them the popular Ivan Lazhechnikov (1792-1869) and even the great writers Pushkin and Nikolai Gogol (1809-1852), turned to

this Romantic genre. Its success was, however, short-lived, and by the mid-1830's it had lost its appeal to a public demanding that fiction reflect contemporary life.

The late development of the historical novel is indicative of the delayed influence of Romanticism on Russian literature. Reacting against classicism, with its distinct genres, rules, and emphasis on clarity, Romanticism sought to fuse disparate elements into new forms by combining reality with fantasy and the rational with the irrational. It introduced the folk and folklore as subjects worthy of attention; it championed the individual's sincerity and passion over society's hypocrisy and constraints. In Russia, the influence of Romanticism was spread through the works of Scott, Lord Byron, the English and German balladeers, and the German Romantics, particularly Goethe, Friedrich Schiller, Ludwig Tieck, and E. T. A. Hoffmann. The full development of Russian Romantic long fiction was slowed by peculiarly Russian conditions. First, the novel was still in its early stages of development, and therefore there were no models of successful novels; second, the readership demanded a Russian national literature representing Russian reality; and third, by the time the Romantic influence affected Russian prose, Western European literature was already turning to realism. Nevertheless, a limited impact of Romanticism can be seen among both major and minor writers and both short and long fiction in nineteenth century Russia.

In addition to the historical novel, the influence of Romanticism on prose is evident in the current theme of the alienated hero in conflict with his surroundings, a conflict already expressed in Russian poetry of the 1820's, particularly in Pushkin's so-called southern poems and in the poetry of Mikhail Lermontov (1814-1841). Several popular writers of the Russian novel of the 1830's incorporated this theme into their works. Nikolay Polevoy (1796-1846), in his *Mechty i Zhizn* (1834; dreams and life), presented the theme as a conflict between the alienated artist-genius and his society, a popular interpretation. Bestuzhev-Marlinski treated it in his *Frigat 'Nadezhda'* (1833; the frigate "Hope") as a conflict between the hero's code (being true to himself) and society's code, but in his *Mulla-Nur* (1836), it received a new twist: The mountain tribesman Mulla-Nur overcomes his alienation and returns to society. Similar themes and variations thereof were widespread in the literature of the 1830's as prose fiction supplanted poetry as the dominant form.

In spite of the steady rise of prose fiction, several major problems remained. The language of prose fiction still had to be elaborated, for neither the rhetorical bookish style nor the measured precision of poetry was appropriate for depicting everyday reality. Writers also faced the problem of defining the form of the novel, their readership, and themselves as writers of Russian literature. In the 1830's, the novel was still an eclectic genre characterized by narrative digressions, fragmentation, lyric pathos, and episodic plots. There were as yet no brilliant successes that could have served as models for the large form. A transitional step appeared in the guise of the story cycle, a form that provided the justification for unifying separate stories into a larger whole. Fairly common in the 1830's, this form also appeared among the major precursors of Russian realism—Pushkin, Gogol, and Lermontov.

THE STORY CYCLE

Pushkin's first attempt at prose fiction resulted in a fragment of a planned historical novel, *Arap Petra velikogo* (1828-1841; *Peter the Great's Negro*, 1896). Although he made several attempts at long fiction, he had only limited success, leaving several prose fragments and only one completed novella, *Kapitanskaya dochka* (1836; *The Captain's Daughter*, 1846), a historical romance about the Pugachov Rebellion, influenced by Scott. Pushkin's most famous work, the long narrative poem *Evgeny Onegin* (1825-1832, 1833; *Eugene Onegin*, 1881), subtitled *A Novel in Verse*, is of interest because of its subsequent influence on long fiction. The work is remarkable for its fine portraiture, its factual description of Moscow and Saint Petersburg, and its details of everyday life (it has been called an encyclopedia of Russian life), all of which produced an accurate description of the period and milieu and served to individuate the characters. In prose, Pushkin was more successful with

short forms; in 1831 he published *Povesti Belkina* (*Russian Romance*, 1875; better known as *The Tales of Belkin*, 1947), a collection of five stories parodying current genres and styles.

Pushkin's lack of success with long fiction and his turning to the story cycle, a form then in vogue, are indicative of the ongoing efforts to master the large form. Although he reformed and shaped the language of poetry, he did not choose to take up this issue in regard to prose. His prose language, influenced by the constraint, precision, and simplicity of his poetry, gave the impression of artificiality and was not well suited to bridging the gap between the normal spoken language and the bookish style. This step in the development of prose language was successfully carried out by his younger contemporary, Nikolai Gogol.

Gogol's importance for Russian prose rests on several notable achievements. He was able to develop a middle prose style that raised the spoken idiom to an acceptable literary standard, which he achieved by blending Russian and Ukrainian, a language (to many Russians a dialect) in which the stylistic distinction between the literary language and the spoken language was not as pronounced as in Russian. This fusion arose quite naturally out of his cycle of stories about the Ukraine: *Vechera na khutore bliz Dikanki* (volume 1, 1831; volume 2, 1832; *Evenings on a Farm near Dikanka*, 1926) and *Mirgorod* (1835; English translation, 1928). The latter collection included Gogol's historical romance *Taras Bulba* (expanded 1842), an exaggerated heroic account of the Polish-Cossack conflict. The stories were well received by the reading public, which perceived the Ukraine, with its bountiful landscape, colorful peasants, and former Cossacks, as exotic and foreign yet still within the Russian sphere. In spite of presenting an abundance of realistic details of everyday life, Gogol did not fall into ethnographic realism. Contemporaries were misled by the details and considered him a realist, often overlooking the comic devices and the presence of the mysterious and supernatural—the latter influenced by the German Romantics Tieck and Hoffmann.

Stories about the Ukraine, often referred to as Little Russia (Malorossiya), had appeared earlier, in the works of the minor Romantic writers Aleksey Perovsky (the pseudonym of Antoni Pogorelsky, 1787-1836) and Evgeny Grebenka (1812-1848), and for a time rivaled the exotic Caucasus as a literary subject. Gogol's treatment of the subject spurred interest in folklore and in the folk (*narod*), as well as demands for their portrayal in works about Russian life. Not surprisingly, Russia turned to Gogol after Pushkin's death in 1837, expecting him to create the national literature, and was not disappointed by his two fine novels *Myortvye dushi* (1842, 1855; *Dead Souls*, 1887) and *Taras Bulba* (1842; English translation, 1886), the latter an expanded version of a short story published in 1835. Influenced by Henry Fielding, Sterne, Lesage, and Narezhny, Gogol's novel is full of stylistic devices—non sequiturs, hyperboles, illogicalities, obfuscations, and lyric digressions. Contemporaries, however, attracted by the wealth of accurate details from Russian life, the Russian types, and the passages concerning Russia's destiny, proclaimed Gogol a realist. Only a fragment remains of part 2 of the novel, the bulk of which Gogol burned in 1852 under the influence of the mystical religious orientation that dominated the last decade of his life. Gogol's influence on Russian literature has been immense; many of his characters have served as prototypes, and many of his stylistic devices have been imitated by later writers. He developed the theme of the abused little man (usually a government clerk) and of Saint Petersburg (the artificial city created by the will of Peter the Great), themes introduced by Pushkin in his poem *Medniy vsadnik* (1837; *The Bronze Horseman*, 1899). Gogol's Petersburg tales brought forth a host of stories about poor clerks and prompted Fyodor Dostoevski (1821-1881) to offer his own interpretation of those two themes. Gogol's influence extends into the twentieth century, when he was rediscovered and reinterpreted by the Symbolists, and is still vital today.

Gogol's contemporary, Mikhail Yuryevich Lermontov, was, like Pushkin, a poet who later turned to prose, and his prose work was of great importance to the development of the Russian novel. Lermontov's first two attempts at prose produced the fragment *Vadim* (written 1832-1834, serialized 1873, book

1935-1937) and the unsuccessful novel *Knyaginya Ligovskaya* (written 1835-1838, book 1935-1937; *Princess Ligovskaya*, 1965). His third attempt was the remarkably successful novel *Geroy nashego vremeni* (1840; *A Hero of Our Time*, 1854). Influenced by Benjamin Constant's *Adolphe* (1816; Russian translation, 1831) and the Byronic tradition of the alienated hero who despises society for its hypocrisy and corruption, the novel is set in the Caucasus—an exotic region popular in the literature of the time, as evidenced by Bestuzhev-Marlinski's popular tale *Ammalat Bek* (1832; English translation, 1843). Using the travelogue and diary forms, Lermontov's book consists of five stories set within a frame narrative. Although he avoided many of the shortcomings typical of the novel in the 1830's, Lermontov was unable to show character developing over time and had to rely on the form of the story cycle to illustrate different aspects of his hero's character. The static portrayal of the hero does not, however, detract from the novel's significant achievements—Lermontov's ability to create atmosphere and his excellent psychological study of the hero, the ironic, analytical Pechorin.

REALISM

The psychological study of the individual was a significant step in the development of realism, as was the focus on details of everyday life. The latter point was the hallmark of the so-called natural school (*naturalnaya shkola*) that appeared in the 1840's. Paying careful attention to details, they presented the unpleasant, harsh side of reality commonly found among the poor and the peasants. This aspect was dealt with by the minor writer Dmitri Grigorovich (1822-1899), in his two novels *Derevnya* (1846; the village) and *Anton Goremyka* (1847), in which he attempted to describe peasant and village life from the peasant's point of view. The striving for verisimilitude and accurate detail was also apparent in the physiological sketch (*fisiologichesky ocherk*) popularized by the writers of the natural school. Influenced by the French *feuilleton*, the sketches described social types and milieus, city quarters, and nature in minute detail.

The demand for verisimilitude was not, however,

the only expectation placed upon literature in the 1840's. The influential literary critic Vissarion Belinsky (1811-1848) also insisted that literature should be inspired by socially significant ideas, and similar views were to be heard throughout the nineteenth century. First attracted to the German Idealists Friedrich Schelling (1775-1854), Johann Fichte (1762-1814), and Georg Wilhelm Friedrich Hegel (1770-1831), Belinsky later adopted a materialistic position that judged literature not in aesthetic terms but in terms of its utilitarian social function. Oriented toward Europe, Belinsky and the Westernizers were sharply attacked by the Slavophiles, who stressed the superiority of native Russian traditions, institutions, and laws and championed the Russian soul. For both parties, the question concerned Russia's relationship to Europe, an issue frequently found in the novels of Russia's great realists, Ivan Sergeyevich Turgenev (1818-1883), Dostoevski, and Leo Tolstoy (1828-1910).

The late 1840's witnessed the development of a remarkable range of novelistic talents. While the novel *Dvoynaya zhizn* (1848; *A Double Life*, 1978), by Karolina Pavlova (1807-1893), reflects the passing of the Romantic era by contrasting a young society woman's stifling daytime experiences with the rich dream world that opens up to her at night, other works display the pronounced shift toward realism urged by Belinsky. For example, Dostoevski's first novel, *Bednye lyudi* (1846; *Poor Folk*, 1887), was enthusiastically reviewed by Belinsky himself and was soon followed by *Dvoynik* (1846; *The Double*, 1917) and "Gospodin Prokharchin" (1846; "Mr. Prokharchin," 1918). Polemicizing with but not parodying Gogol in these three works, Dostoevski gave his own interpretation to the themes of the little man and St. Petersburg. The stories also reflected the influence of the natural school, as evidenced by his focus on ugliness, poverty, and the dull, dirty milieu of the city. The Petersburg theme surfaced in a very different guise, as a dreamer's city, in his "Khozyayka" (1847; "The Landlady," 1917) and "Belye nochi" (1848; "White Nights," 1918), the latter published in the year in which Dostoevski was arrested for being a member of the Petrashevsky Circle, a group that dis-

cussed socialist ideas and criticized existing conditions in Russia. His four years of penal service in Siberia and subsequent military service interrupted his literary activity; he did not return to St. Petersburg until 1859.

From 1850 to 1880, Russian literature was dominated by three writers—Turgenev, Dostoevski, and Tolstoy—whose works defined the form of the novel as well as the broad literary movement called "realism." Their focus on details of everyday life, on the surroundings, on the social milieu, on individuals and their psychology, and their narrative technique of staging scenes rather than commenting through narrative intrusion, became the hallmarks by which realism was defined.

Although the 1850's were dominated by Turgenev, several writers made significant contributions to the novel in this period, among them Tolstoy, who published his first major work, a nonautobiographical trilogy about a young boy growing up: *Detstvo* (1852; *Childhood*, 1862), *Otrochestvo* (1854; *Boyhood*, 1886), and *Yunost'* (1857; *Youth*, 1886). Influenced by Sterne, Charles Dickens, Rousseau, and Rodolphe Töpfler, Tolstoy utilized a child's own peculiar angle of perception to present familiar objects and experiences in a new and unusual manner an example of the device, frequent in Tolstoy's works, which the Russian Formalist critic Viktor Shklovsky calls *ostranenie* ("making strange," or "defamiliarization"). A similar subject was treated by Sergey Aksakov (1791-1859) in his trilogy of family generations and a young boy's development: *Semeynaya khronika* (1856; *Chronicles of a Russian Family*, 1924), *Vospominaniya* (1856; *A Russian Schoolboy*, 1917), and the most well known volume, *Detskiye gody Bagrova-vnuka* (1858; *Years of Childhood*, 1916). The latter volume, an example of an *Entwicklungsroman*, is a captivating study of a child's psychology as he begins to understand the conflicts and tension among members of his own family; it is also remarkable as a realistic narrative of ordinary life.

Another author known for a realistic narrative of ordinary life was Ivan Goncharov (1812-1891), whose first novel, *Obyknovennaya istoriya* (1847; *A Common Story*, 1890), was hailed by Belinsky as an example of realistic fiction second only to Dostoevski's *Poor Folk*. His novel *Oblomov* (1859; English translation, 1915) is best known for its phlegmatic eponymous hero, whose philosophy of resignation and inactivity aroused the ire of many activists—including the radical socialist critic Nikolay Dobrolyubov (1836-1861), who wrote an article, "Chto takoye Oblomovshchina?" (1859-1860; "What Is Oblomovism?," 1903), in which he denounced the gentry for being an obstacle to progress.

These relatively minor achievements of the 1850's were overshadowed by Turgenev's success, which was readily acknowledged by critics and the public. Turgenev began his literary career writing poetry, but by the late 1840's, he had turned to writing the stories that he later incorporated into his collection *Zapiski okhotnika* (1852; *Russian Life in the Interior*, 1855; better known as *A Sportsman's Sketches*, 1932), which made him an overnight success. The volume was noted for its lyric mood and atmosphere evoked by the detailed nature descriptions and for its sympathetic portrayal of the serfs. In addition to this volume, Turgenev wrote many stories, several plays, and six novels. In the novels, plot is secondary to character, which is skillfully revealed through polished dialogue and social milieu. Turgenev's novels are generally structured around a romance between a morally superior woman and a weak, irresolute man, a theme made famous by Pushkin in *Eugene Onegin*, and at the same time, around a current political issue. Although he was a civil-minded liberal Westernizer, Turgenev avoided becoming tendentious in his depiction of the ideological struggle between the generations (between the fathers and the sons). He supported the cause of the young radicals but failed to portray a positive Russian political activist. Stung by the radicals' criticism of his portrayal of Bazarov, the nihilistic hero of *Ottsy i deti* (1862; *Fathers and Sons*, 1867), Turgenev decided to remain abroad and settled in France for most of the remainder of his life. In his last two novels, *Dym* (1867; *Smoke*, 1868) and *Nov* (1877; *Virgin Soil*, 1877), he gave vent to his bitterness toward Russia, but although it was clear that he had lost touch with Russian life, he remained a popular writer. Pushkin's influence is evident in Turgenev's poetic prose, masterfully shaped for expressing nuance, atmosphere, and character. Turgenev was the first Russian author to achieve fame in Western Europe, particularly in France, where he died in 1883.

While Turgenev was a member of the nobility and a Westernizer, Dostoevski was a *raznochinets* (educated plebeian). His experience in prison, which he chronicled in his novel *Zapiski iz myortvogo doma* (1861-1862; *Buried Alive: Or, Ten Years of Penal Servitude in Siberia*, 1881; also as *The House of the Dead*, 1915), produced a profound change in his personal and political views. Arrested for his socialist and Western views, Dostoevski returned from exile having rejected them along with Rousseauism, utopianism, rationalism, and Schillerian Romanticism and having embraced Christ, a belief in Russia and its elect status, and the human need for freedom. He was the first in world literature to find a literary medium for the metaphysical novel, which he combined with the crime story, a combination found in varying degrees in all five of his major novels but particularly evident in his famous *Prestupleniye i nakazaniye* (1866; *Crime and Punishment*, 1886). Plumbing the depths of his characters' souls, Dostoevski presents the dialectic struggle of good and evil. His characters are shown testing the strength of their rational position against their emotions. Salvation for the proud, the guilty (murders are committed in four of the major novels), and the "supermen" (those who assume that they are beyond good and evil) can be achieved, according to Dostoevski, only through suffering and humility, which will lead to faith in Christ, an issue masterfully illustrated in his *Bratya Karamazovy* (1879-1880; *The Brothers Karamazov*, 1912). Dostoevski also assigned to God a crucial role in Russia's salvation and messianic mission. In perhaps his best novel, *Besy* (1871-1872; *The Possessed*, 1913; also as *The Devils*, 1953), he attacked the atheistic ideological offspring of the liberals of the 1840's (the novel included a vicious satire of Turgenev). *The Possessed* is an excellent example of polyphony, in which each character's voice is given equal weight in the frequent metaphysical arguments. Aspiring to a "higher realism," Dostoevski sought to penetrate to the essence of his characters, avoiding narrative intrusion, and this remains one of his major achievements.

The literary activity of Count Leo Nikolayevich Tolstoy, one of the greatest figures in world literature, falls into two distinct periods, divided by his spiritual crisis in 1879, after which Tolstoy the moral philosopher took precedence over Tolstoy the artist. In his early long fiction, written in the 1850's—the childhood trilogy, the Sevastopol stories, *Kazaki* (1863; *The Cossacks*, 1872), and *Semeynoye schast'ye* (1859; *Family Happiness*, 1888)—he introduced many of the themes he developed further in his two great novels, *Voyna i mir* (1865-1869; *War and Peace*, 1886) and *Anna Karenina* (1875-1877; English translation, 1886): the morality of killing, the enigmatic question of death and the meaning of life, and the question of how one should live, to mention but a few. In his pursuit of truth, he debunked many popular myths concerning war, patriotism, and romantic heroism, particularly in *War and Peace*. In form, *War and Peace* resembles a classic epic, charting the collective experience of the Russian nation during the Napoleonic era; at the same time, it is a modern novel in which the individual searches for meaning and his or her relation to the collective, to society. While Tolstoy's heroes often serve as subjective centers, their individual perceptions revealed through the devices of estrangement (*ostranenie*) and interior monologue, the objectivity of outside reality is not challenged. Tolstoy's interest in the development of character and society over time (and in the question of causation) led him to focus on the individual's changing relationship to family and society. Through this self-reflection within a social setting, an influence of sentimentalism, his characters learn the obligations of responsibility and responsiveness.

This theme also appears in Tolstoy's *Anna Karenina*, a novel about upper-class society of the 1870's. Structured around two contrasting love relationships, the novel focuses on the moral and personal dilemma of transgressing society's ethical code for the sake of love. Through the introduction of stream of consciousness, Tolstoy gives an excellent rendition of the heroine's psychological and emotional turmoil, adding a consummate truth to an already memorable portrait of an individual human being.

Carefully differentiating even minor characters by specific details or traits, even in his large works, Tolstoy was not content with remaining only an observer; he felt the need to guide the reader to the truth by means of direct appeals, narrative intrusions, and digressions. Tolstoy's tendency to instruct, a characteristic feature of his fiction, and his personal search for faith and the meaning of life led to a spiritual crisis that culminated in his work *Ispoved'* (1884; *A Confession*, 1885). Thereafter, his long fiction took on an increasingly moralizing tone, attacking the state, the church, and society as he turned literature into a vehicle for his views. He still produced several great works, such as the novellas *Smert' Ivana Il'icha* (1886; *The Death of Ivan Ilyich*, 1887) and *Khadzi-Murat* (1911; *Hadji Murad*, 1911), but in the last two decades of his life his fame rested not on his fiction, but on his moral teachings.

The thirty years from 1850 to 1880 were also a period of activity among socialist critics whose articles and novels were of literary and political significance. Among them was the influential critic Aleksandr Herzen (1812-1870), the author of the *povest Kto vinovat?* (1847; *Who Is to Blame?*, 1978) and publisher of the enormously influential weekly *Kolokol* (1857-1867), which was frequently smuggled into Russia, where it had a wide readership. He advocated a positivist, national socialism and was close to the Slavophiles. Much more radical were N. G. Chernyshevsky (1828-1889), who wrote the famous and tendentious radical novel *Chto delat?* (1863; *What Is to Be Done?*, 1886) and who was arrested in 1862 and later exiled to Siberia, and Dobrolyubov, who was the most influential critic after Belinsky. They both advocated a scientific rationalism as a means to achieve progress, and they professed great faith in the Russian peasant, whose emancipation from serfdom (granted in 1861) they ardently championed. Dobrolyubov also served as the literary critic of the successful journal *Sovremennik* (1836-1866) and had a great impact on succeeding generations.

In addition to the great realists, numerous writers of varying caliber also appeared, among them Aleksey Pisemsky (1820-1881). His novels were known for their unadorned, unidealized view of humankind and for their portrayal of Russian characters not of noble birth, whose dialect Pisemsky expertly rendered. Another notable writer of this period was Mikhail Saltykov-Shchedrin (1826-1889), acclaimed for his many satiric novels, some excessively topical and written in Aesopian language. His crowning achievement, which established his place among the realists, was *Gospoda Golovlyovy* (1872-1876; *The Golovlyov Family*, 1955), a gloomy depiction of the materialistic provincial gentry. Other so-called civic or plebeian writers include Nikolay Pomyalovskiy (1835-1863), Gleb Uspenskiy (1843-1902), and Ivan Kushchevsky (1847-1876). Populist novels celebrating the virtues of the peasants also appeared, generally written by minor authors, such as Nikolay Zlatovratsky (1845-1911) and Pavel Zasodimsky (1843-1912).

A writer of considerable talent was Nikolai Leskov (1831-1895), known for his excellent rendition of speech, which he often expressed through *skaz*, a narrative form in which the narrator's presence is marked by his or her individualized language and tone. Leskov, who excelled in short fiction, was contemptuously treated by the critics for his portrayal of the radicals and for his works on ecclesiastical life, which he sympathetically described in his popular novel *Soboriane* (1872; *The Cathedral Folk*, 1924).

THE 1880'S AND 1890'S

The early 1880's are generally taken as a watershed in the history of the Russian novel. Two of the great realists had passed from the scene, Dostoevski in 1881 and Turgenev in 1883, and Tolstoy, after his crisis, produced no major novels. There was also a change in the political climate following the assassination of Alexander II (reigned 1855-1881), an event that ended the period of political reforms and introduced the repressive measures of Alexander III (reigned 1881-1894). In the prose fiction of the 1880's and 1890's, there was a movement away from long fiction, from the globalism (the philosophical questions of existence and the thorough representation of everyday life) of the nineteenth century novel,

toward shorter forms with a narrower field of vision.

Several minor but popular writers of this period continued, however, to make use of the novel. One such writer was Aleksandr Ertel (1855-1908), known for his popular novel *Gardeniny, ikh dvornya, priverzhentsy i vragi* (1888; the Gardenins, their retainers, their friends, and their enemies), the second edition of which was prefaced by Tolstoy himself. The novel presents a vast panorama of contemporary life on a provincial gentry estate in southern Russia. Another popular author of the time was Vladimir Korolenko (1853-1921), known for his romantic though rather shallow *povesti* with nature descriptions reminiscent of Turgenev, whose works enjoyed a revival at that time. Also popular was N. Garin (the pseudonym of Nikolay Georgievich Mikhaylovskiy, 1852-1906), whose trilogy about a young boy's education was immensely successful.

In addition to the short form of prose, poetry flourished once again, dominated by the Symbolists, who heralded in Russia's Silver Age of Poetry. The Russian Symbolists, influenced by their French counterparts, spoke of a higher reality existing beneath the surface of everyday life. Defending the aesthetic value of literature, one of the leading Symbolist critics, Dmitry Sergeyevich Merezhkovsky (1865-1941), who also wrote a trilogy of novels in the 1890's, blamed the social tendentiousness of the civic critics for the decline of Russian literature. This new critical position, which denied the basic tenets of the nineteenth century, is indicative of the social crisis experienced by the intelligentsia and the writers. It forced a reevaluation of their relationship to literature and society, as well as a reconsideration of the role of literature itself. These issues, raised at the close of the nineteenth century, became even more pertinent in the twentieth century.

THE EARLY TWENTIETH CENTURY

Russian literature of the twentieth century began like the literature of the nineteenth century, with the dominance of poetry and under the influence of Western European writers, among them Henrik Ibsen (1828-1906), August Strindberg (1849-1912), the French Symbolist poets, and the German philosopher

Friedrich Nietzsche (1844-1900). There was, however, a distinct break with the commonality of issues and viewpoints characteristic of the nineteenth century. Instead of consensus, division prevailed among schools of poetry, whose positions were provocatively stated in literary manifestos, an entirely new phenomenon in Russian literature.

The Symbolists, the leading school of poetry in the first decade of the twentieth century, also produced several interesting novels. They believed that the visible world is symbolic of a higher reality behind it and that the poet, as a superior being (a Romantic conception of the artist), is able to articulate this truth, which can only be alluded to, through art. Their writing is, therefore, intentionally vague and ambiguous. They question the identity of objects and only hint at the essence hidden beneath the surface. These traits are clearly evident in *Melkiy bes* (1907; *The Little Demon*, 1916; also as *The Petty Demon*, 1962), written by Fyodor Sologub (the pseudonym of Fyodor Terternikov, 1863-1927), a work strongly influenced by Gogol, whom the Symbolists reinterpreted. Similar qualities inform the works of another Symbolist novelist, Valery Bryosov (1873-1924), whose best-known novel was *Ognenny angel* (1908; *The Fiery Angel*, 1930). Both were surpassed by Andrey Bely (the pseudonym of Boris Bugayev, 1880-1934), a Symbolist poet and a disciple of Rudolph Steiner's Anthroposophy. Although best known for his poetry, Bely wrote several novels, the most remarkable of which was *Petersburg* (serial 1913-1914, book 1916, revised 1922; *St. Petersburg*, 1959; better known as *Petersburg*), considered by the renowned novelist and critic Vladimir Nabokov (1899-1977) to be one of the best novels of the twentieth century. Revised several times, it offers a philosophical and metaphysical interpretation of Russian history in terms of two opposing forces—Western rationalism and a destructive Asiatic-Tatar element of irrationalism. Complex in style and structure, and full of literary allusions, it continues the great tradition of the Petersburg theme, portraying the city's malevolent atmosphere and artificial existence.

There were few identifiable schools of prose fiction prior to the Russian Revolution (1917); one

small group of writers, however, did appear. Centered on the journal *Znanie*, from which it took its name, this group was led by the internationally renowned Maxim Gorky (the pen name of Aleksey Maksimovich Peshkov, 1868-1936). The group consisted of Aleksandr Kuprin (1870-1938), known for his realistic novels of military life and his compassionate novel about prostitutes, *Yama* (1909-1915; *Yama: The Pit*, 1929); the minor writer Mikhail Artsybashev (1878-1927), whose popularity rested on his sensational novel *Sanin* (1907; *Sanine*, 1917), with its violence, erotic scenes, and empty metaphysical discussions; Leonid Andreyev (1871-1919), an extremely popular writer of stories focusing on the pathos of the soul; and Ivan Bunin (1870-1953). Bunin was a direct descendant of the nineteenth century realist tradition, as is evident from his short novel *Derevnya* (1910; *The Village*, 1923) and its companion piece *Sukhodol* (1912; *Dry Valley*, 1935). After the Russian Revolution, he emigrated to Paris, where he continued to write on Russian subjects. In 1933, he was awarded the Nobel Prize in Literature, the first Russian to receive the award.

The most significant member of the *Znanie* group, which soon dissolved, was Gorky, who in the Soviet Union became the center of a personality cult, although he himself was critical of the revolution and suspicious of the masses. Having developed from an early Nietzschean Romanticism, Gorky turned from the principle that literature should beautify life to the depiction of current political issues. His novel *Mat* (1906; *Mother*, 1906), based on the events of a May Day demonstration in Sormovo in 1902, gave the first comprehensive portrait of the Russian revolutionary movement. Influenced by Tolstoy, whom he knew personally, Gorky wrote an autobiographical trilogy depicting the hard life of the lower classes in the provinces, of which the first volume, *Detstvo* (1913; *My Childhood*, 1915), is the best. Living in Italy for many years because of poor health, Gorky did not return to Russia for good until the early 1930's. Up to the time of his death, a suspicious affair, he worked on his four-volume "novel-chronicle" *Zhizn Klima Samgina* (1927-1936; *The Life of Klim Samgin*, 1930-1938). It has something of the scope of Tolstoy's *War and Peace*, offering a vast panorama of historical events and social change seen through the eyes of a developing intellectual. Often rhetorical, uneven, and heavy-handed in his fiction, Gorky the publicist outweighed Gorky the artist. While serving as a bridge between the two centuries, he continued the nineteenth century tradition of the Russian writer acting as a public figure. He had an immense influence on the progress of literature and the arts in the Soviet Union and has been called the father of Soviet literature.

THE BOLSHEVIK REVOLUTION

The most decisive event in twentieth century Russian history was the revolution that brought the Bolsheviks to power. It had a profound impact on all spheres of life, including literature. Control over literature was only gradually asserted, however, and as a result, the 1920's were years of relative artistic freedom. Although a radical break with the past political system had occurred, that was not so with regard to culture; the nineteenth century literary tradition continued to exist alongside modernist experiments. Intellectuals, writers of the intelligentsia, often derogatorily referred to as "fellow travelers," had not yet been displaced by the proletarian writers who swarmed to the metropolis to establish the new literature, to reflect the new morality.

The issue facing the writers of the 1920's was how the novel should depict the new reality. World War I, the revolution, and the bitter Russian Civil War (1918-1921) had shattered the belief in the wholeness of the world, in the collective experience so frequently reflected in the nineteenth century novel. In the West, this experience led to the sense of alienation, epitomized by the "lost generation." While the same was true for some Russians, in particular for the intellectuals and those who emigrated, the strong sense of an ending was countered by a firm belief that a new and better time was at hand. The sense of fragmentation did indeed lead to a reassessment of the individual's relationship to society, to the new collective, but the 1920's were still a period of optimism. These issues surfaced in various forms in the prose fiction of nearly every literary school or

movement of the time, which made the 1920's a variegated and productive literary period.

The intellectual exuberance of the early 1920's is particularly evident in the works of the Formalist critic Viktor Shklovsky (1893-1984). The Formalists—whose influence on modern criticism, both direct and via French Structuralism, has been enormous—emphasized the internal dynamics of literary works, the devices by which they are "made." (Thus, in a characteristic passage, Shklovsky boasts: "I know how Don Quixote is made.") Shklovsky's *Sentimental' noye puteshestviye: Vospominaniya, 1917-1922* (1923; *A Sentimental Journey: Memoirs, 1917-1922*, 1970), *Zoo: Ili, Pis'ma ne o lyubvi* (1923; *Zoo: Or, Letters Not About Love*, 1971), and *Tret'ya fabrika* (1926; *Third Factory*, 1977) combine a sophisticated awareness of literary forms with a strikingly original tone; part novel, part memoir, part literary criticism, these works are marked by the spirit of artistic freedom for which Shklovsky and others were to be attacked in the late 1920's.

Shklovsky's language, fresh and colloquial yet able to accommodate technical literary terms, reflects in part the influence of Aleksey Remizov (1877-1957). Remizov, who emigrated from Soviet Russia to Berlin in 1921, settling in 1923 in Paris, where he remained for the rest of his life, sought to invigorate the Russian literary language with a return to its native resources. In his novels, which resist translation, Remizov forged a style at once racy and ornate, drawing heavily on colloquial speech, proverbs, and folktales, mixing many different levels of diction and different genres within a single work.

One loosely organized group of nonproletarian writers active in the 1920's was the Serapion Brotherhood. Vaguely influenced by E. T. A. Hoffmann but also by Shklovsky and the Formalists, they combined reality and social criticism with fantasy and action plots. Not unsympathetic to the revolution, they resisted pressure to write works praising the new society and focused instead on the individual consciousness in an alienated world. An excellent illustration of this theme appears in *Zavist'* (1927; *Envy*, 1936), a novel that made Yury Olesha (1899-1960) an overnight success. The historical background of the

1920's is present in the novel but on a reduced scale, and reality becomes subject to the laws of fantasy. Olesha creates this fantasy through his method of "magic photography," whereby he transforms reality into images of an alternative world for his superfluous, imaginative little man, estranged from the materialistic, pedestrian new world he envies.

The theme of alienation is also expressed by Konstantin Fedin (1892-1977) in his novel *Goroda i gody* (1924; *Cities and Years*, 1962). Using the technique of montage to convey the fragmentation of reality, Fedin traces the demise of a superfluous man, an intellectual, not able to fully accept the revolution and the new regime. His second novel of the 1920's, *Bratya* (1928; brothers), also portrays a sensitive intellectual out of step with the times.

One of the most interesting novels to appear in the 1920's was *My* (corrupt text published 1927, reissued 1952; *We*, 1924), written in 1920-1921 by Yevgeny Zamyatin (1884-1937), a member of the Serapion Brotherhood. The novel was first published in English and was not published in the Soviet Union for several decades for the obvious reason that it is an antiutopian novel. Combining two genres, the diary and the utopian novel, it denies the possibility of utopian happiness and, by implication, the possibility of a future communist paradise. Zamyatin's novel appeared before the rise to power of Joseph Stalin (1879-1953) and is not, therefore, merely a satire on totalitarianism; it is also a novel about communication and language. The conflict between the individual and the state is expressed through the hero's discovery of many languages—the languages of love, poetry, and the past—that create a threatening polyphony that the authorities suppress in the name of collective happiness. After the publication of *We*, Zamyatin served as head of the Leningrad section of the Union of Writers until 1929, when the Stalinist crackdown on literature began. He was fortunate to be allowed to emigrate in 1931.

Utopias and the future were topics widely discussed in the 1920's. Another novel that raises interesting questions in this regard is *Chevengur* (1972, written 1928-1930; English translation, 1978), an idiosyncratic novel with an unusual history of publica-

tion. Written by the unorthodox Andrey Platonov (1899-1951), the novel is constructed as a pilgrimage through the steppe, as a search for utopian solutions. Full of literary allusions to Dostoevski, Novalis (1772-1801), and Miguel de Cervantes's *El ingenioso hidalgo don Quixote de la Mancha*, 1605, 1615 (*The History of the Valorous and Wittie Knight-Errant, Don Quixote of the Mancha*, 1612-1620; better known as *Don Quixote de la Mancha*), it ironically focuses on the inherent contradiction of the revolution as a dynamic, ongoing force and utopia as a static state of collective happiness.

A critical appraisal of the revolution also appears in *Goly god* (1922; *The Naked Year*, 1928), written by an influential writer of the 1920's, Boris Pilnyak, also a member of the Serapion Brotherhood. Influenced by Andrey Bely's prose style, the novel is composed of episodes and fragments that intentionally disrupt and obscure the chronology and logical sequence of events in order to convey the disruptive force of the revolution itself. The revolution is represented as an elemental deed of blind biological forces and organized, machinelike movement. Pilnyak wrote several other novels, and his style and manner were widely imitated during the 1920's.

In contrast to the critical attitude of many intellectuals, the proletarian writers widely acclaimed the revolution, glorifying its heroes and achievements. Forming their own groups, such as Proletcult, Pereval, and the Smithy, they were quite conservative as writers and continued the literary traditions of the nineteenth century. Their novels are simple and straightforward rather than experimental and convey a social message that usually takes precedence over artistic and technical considerations. Their heroes are portrayed as individual representatives of the collective, for which they make personal sacrifices in combat or on the industrial front. The relationship of the individual to the collective created problems that became the center of considerable debate in the 1920's and that remained an unresolved issue in Soviet literature.

Among the works glorifying the revolution and the revolutionary hero was the novel *Chapayev* (1923; English translation, 1935), by Dmitri Furmanov (1891-1926). Basing the novel on events from Vasily Chapayev's life, Furmanov subordinated this charismatic figure (an actual leader of Red partisans) to the historical context and produced a kind of documentary, not a photographic realism, but a "literature of fact" (*literatura fakta*), a literary phenomenon of the 1920's. Not as well known, Furmanov's second novel, *Myatezh* (1925; the uprising), was also about the partisan movement in the southeastern steppe.

In the enthusiasm for glorifying the revolution, many early works of the proletarian writers portrayed the revolution as a historical movement and overemphasized the role of the collective. A case in point is the popular epic *Zhelezny potok* (1924; *The Iron Flood*, 1935), by Aleksandr Serafimovich (the pen name of Aleksandr Popov, 1863-1949). The novel describes the transformation of an anarchic mass into an organized fighting force that overcomes the Whites. Although ideologically sound, the novel was criticized for its abstractness, its undistinguished characters, and the absence of an individuated revolutionary hero.

The novel that successfully struck a balance between portraying the hero as an individual yet representative of the collective, as resolute and disciplined but with human weaknesses, was the popularly acclaimed *Razgrom* (1927; *The Nineteen*, 1929), by Aleksandr Fadeyev (1901-1956). Fadeyev adequately presented the Marxist notion of historical processes (the revolution) finding expression through concrete individuals. The novel was later praised as a paragon of Socialist Realism, and Fadeyev was proclaimed the "Red Leo Tolstoy." Tolstoy's influence on Fadeyev and the proletarian writers in general was pronounced: Attempting to establish the legitimacy of the new literature, the proletarian writers turned to the classic author of Russian realism, Tolstoy, with whose concept and portrayal of reality they could identify.

Tolstoy's influence is particularly apparent in *Tikhii Don* (1928-1940; partial translation *And Quiet Flows the Don*, 1934; also as *The Don Flows Home to the Sea*, 1940; complete translation *The Silent Don*, 1942; also as *And Quiet Flows the Don*, 1967), an extremely popular novel in four volumes that has

often been compared to *War and Peace*. Written by Mikhail Sholokhov (1905-1984), the novel focused on the turbulent and brutal events among the Don Cossacks from World War I to the end of the civil war. Controversy arose concerning both authorship (charges of plagiarism were made, revived in the 1970's by Aleksandr Solzhenitsyn) and the portrayal of the reflective hero, who questions the legitimacy of the revolution and thus suggests the possibility of a third way, the existence of which is denied by communism. Avoiding simplistic oppositions and taking a critical attitude toward the communists, Sholokhov achieved a complexity and verisimilitude that was immediately acknowledged by readers and critics alike.

Few works written by the proletarian writers went so far as to suggest the possibility of a third way between communism and capitalism. Even when presenting the shortcomings of the revolution or the defeat of the communist forces, such setbacks were presented as temporary, as heroic sacrifices necessary to achieve the goals of the revolution. Such a position is taken by Yury Libedinsky (1898-1959) in his novel *Nedelya* (1922; *A Week*, 1923), in which a small detachment of communists is sacrificed for the general good. Libedinsky also wrote two novels on a subject current in the 1920's—the reappearance of bourgeois influences during the period of the New Economic Policy (NEP), a particularly disturbing phenomenon for orthodox communists and one sharply attacked in the novel *Shokolad* (1922; *Chocolate*, 1932), by Aleksandr Tarasov-Rodionov (1885-1938).

Anecdotes, stories, and novels satirizing the return of philistinism, the ineptness of the bureaucracy, and the mundane concerns of everyday life during the NEP were a welcome relief from the steady stream of novels about the revolution. Particularly popular were the satiric novels of Ilya Ilf (1897-1937) and Evgeni Petrov (1903-1942), such as their *Dvenadtsat stuliev* (1928; *The Twelve Chairs*, 1961) and *Zolotoy telyonok* (1931; *The Little Golden Calf*, 1932). Another author of interest was Ilya Ehrenburg (1891-1967), who had been allowed to travel to the West and later wrote several works critical of Western culture and the capitalist economic system. Some of the first Russian science fiction also appeared during the NEP. One writer of Wellsian fantasies was Aleksey Tolstoy (1883-1945), who is better known for his unfinished historical novel *Pyotr Pervy* (1929-1945; *Peter the First*, 1959). Although of aristocratic background, he was a willing apologist for the Stalin regime.

The conditions under which literature developed during the NEP did not continue for long. In 1928, the First Five-Year Plan was adopted, and the Communist Party decided that literature was to be harnessed to the needs of the state. By 1932, all autonomous literary organizations were disbanded by a party directive, and all writers were exhorted to follow the precepts of Socialist Realism. Socialist Realism remained an intentionally vague term, to be defined as the authorities wished; novelists were to avoid psychological realism focusing on the individual and objective realism revealing negative aspects of Soviet life, concentrating instead on the positive, inspiring aspects of Soviet life. In 1934, the First Congress of Soviet Writers was held, and the Union of Writers was launched; membership was virtually obligatory. During the 1930's, many writers were forced to publicly admit their errors and "heresies"; arrests were frequent, and many writers and poets perished in the charged atmosphere of the infamous Stalinist purges from 1936 to 1938. Those who survived were forced to be silent or accept a role as an instrument of education and propaganda within the Soviet apparatus.

The novels of the 1930's primarily focused on the subject of industrialization, a topic that had already replaced revolutionary romanticism in the 1920's. The model for the writers of the 1930's was *Tsement* (1925; *Cement*, 1929), by Fyodor Gladkov (1883-1958), which downplayed the hero's family tragedy and emphasized his constructive role in rebuilding a local factory. Virtually all the major writers responded with novels on the theme of industrialization: Sholokhov wrote about collectivization, as did Fyodor Panferov (1896-1960); Pilnyak wrote about the construction of a great dam and hydroelectric station; Valentin Katayev (1897-1986) wrote about the

construction of a huge metallurgical plant in the Ural Mountains in *Vremya vperyod!* (1932; *Time Forward!*, 1933); Ehrenburg also contributed to the subject, as did many others.

The 1930's also saw the appearance of autobiographical educational novels such as *Kak zakalyalas stal* (1932-1934; *The Making of a Hero*, 1937; also as *How the Steel Was Tempered*, 1952), by Nikolay Ostrovsky (1904-1936), and *Pedagogicheskaya poema* (1935; *The Road to Life*, 1954), by Anton Makarenko (1888-1939). Such novels depicted the development of exemplary communists in the face of great obstacles and the process of disciplining the dynamic forces of the revolution. They were clearly intended to inspire the reader with appreciation for the sacrifices made and to provide the proper ideological orientation.

The literature of the 1940's (such as there was) was concerned with the patriotic efforts of the Red Army, the party, and the *narod* (the folk) in the defense of the motherland, a theme that remained a staple of popular Soviet literature. Again, writers responded to social demand and produced novels of varying quality. Among the more interesting are Gladkov's *Klyatva* (1944; the vow), Fadeyev's *Molodaya gvardiya* (1946; *The Young Guard*, 1958), and *V okopakh Stalingrada* (1946; *Front-Line Stalingrad*, 1962), by Viktor Nekrasov (1911-1987). In spite of the emphasis on the role of the collective in the war effort, several works "rediscovered" the individual. One such novel was *Sputniki* (1946; *The Train*, 1948), by Vera Panova (1905-1973). In her presentation of the members of a medical team during World War II, she focused on their personal lives and portrayed the collective as a group of individuals with a common goal: a new conception of the collective. The 1940's were also saturated with memoirs relating to the war experience.

THE POST-STALIN NOVEL

A significant change in Soviet literature occurred after the death of Stalin in 1953. Commonly referred to as the "thaw," after the title of Ehrenburg's novel *Ottepel* (part 1, 1954; part 2, 1956; *The Thaw*, 1955; also as *A Change of Season*, 1962), it led to the revival of the novel genre and reasserted the individual's role within the collective. Mild criticism of the system, evident in *Vremena goda* (1953; *The Span of the Year*, 1956), by Panova, and *Russkii les* (1953; *The Russian Forest*, 1966), by Leonid Leonov (1899-1988), was not, however, a departure from the tradition of the Russian novel (as one can see from the novels of the nineteenth century), but it was an attempt to break away from the dogmatic treatment of political and social issues. Such works were indicative of the paradoxical relationship between literature and politics. The demand by authorities that literature reflect the goals and needs of the state allowed a realistic (convincing) portrayal of characters in conflict, but it introduced contradictions and ambiguities that obscured the simplistic Communist Party point of view. At such moments of crisis, as in 1954, the party periodically stepped in to reassert its control over literature.

It is not surprising, therefore, that the famous poetic novel of Boris Pasternak (1890-1960), *Doktor Zhivago* (1957; *Doctor Zhivago*, 1958), which was announced in the journal *Znamya* as forthcoming, was rejected when submitted in 1956 and had to be published abroad. Concerned with symbolic truth, Pasternak gave a metonymic representation of the revolution and the civil war, as witnessed by the passive but receptive poet, Yuri Zhivago. The novel provides a remarkable portrait of an individual in the nineteenth century tradition and opens a critical dialogue with the past.

This dialogue was continued by the publication of the rediscovered works of Mikhail Bulgakov (1891-1940), written some thirty years earlier. Among his novels satirizing Soviet life and deflating Soviet institutions was his masterpiece *Master i Margarita* (written 1940; censored version 1966-1967; uncensored version 1973; *The Master and Margarita*, 1967). A modern treatment of the Faust theme with a fantastic, dreamlike atmosphere, it is a metaphysical inquiry into the evil of Stalin and the "cult of personality"; it is also a novel about the creative process, about the writing of a novel about Christ and Pilate. The appearance of the novel created a sensation in Russia, and in the context of Soviet literature, it was indeed a magnificent achievement.

Another author whose works were rediscovered was Platonov. His *Chevengur* (mentioned earlier) and his novel *Kotlovan* (1968; *The Foundation Pit*, 1973, 1975) were not originally published in the Soviet Union, though *samizdat* (underground) copies of both circulated widely. Full of symbolic images and folklore and written in a peculiar style, *The Foundation Pit* is a dark, ironic satire of early Soviet industrialization and education.

A work that focused on a relatively unexplored side of the Soviet past was *Odin den' Ivana Denisovicha* (1962; *One Day in the Life of Ivan Denisovich*, 1963), by Aleksandr Solzhenitsyn (born 1918). Its appearance was made possible by a change in the political climate following a speech by Nikita Khrushchev at the Twentieth Congress of the Communist Party in 1956, in which he acknowledged Stalin's "mistakes" (that is, his crimes). In the same year, Vladimir Dudintsev (born 1918) published his novel *Ne khlebom edinym* (1956; *Not by Bread Alone*, 1957), in which he defended the individual's rights against the vulgar careerists wielding power. Dudintsev was sharply attacked by the Communist Party, which quickly moved to curb the liberal tendencies appearing after Khrushchev's speech. Three years later, however, controls were eased again, and with Khrushchev's personal intervention, Solzhenitsyn's novel was published.

One Day in the Life of Ivan Denisovich is a stunning indictment of the camp experience of the Stalin era. Describing life in reduced situations, a characteristic of nearly all of his fiction, Solzhenitsyn illustrates the struggle of the *zeks* (prisoners) to survive with dignity. He portrays the harshness of the prison but points out that, paradoxically, freedom is possible only within the camp. Introducing a wide range of characters in his novels *V kruge pervom* (1968; *The First Circle*, 1968) and *Rakovy korpus* (1968; *Cancer Ward*, 1968), Solzhenitsyn skillfully renders their speech and creates a polyphony of views that constitute a complete picture of Soviet society. Solzhenitsyn's position as a moral conscience and a voice for those not able to speak out is well in evidence in his monumental *Arkhipelag GULag, 1918-1956: Opyt khudozhestvennogo issledovaniya*

(1973-1975; *The Gulag Archipelago, 1918-1956: An Experiment in Literary Investigation*, 1974-1978), which exposed the magnitude of the evil of Stalin's camps. It is a historical document shaped by an artist into a powerful and profound epic.

Of the many works written about the camps and the purges, most are a mixture of history, biography, confession, and memoir, emphasizing the factual nature of the content, its truth value. Many courageous people did leave accounts: Varlam Shalamov (1907-1981), who wrote of his experiences in Kolyma; Evgenia Ginzburg (c. 1906-1977), who wrote of her arrest in the purges; and Anatoly Marchenko (born 1938), who was arrested several times for his defiance of the state, are but a few.

Three major waves of emigration from Russia occurred in the twentieth century: after the revolution, after World War II, and during the 1960's and 1970's. A number of Russian novelists found themselves cut off from their homeland and confronted with a new reality, a new freedom that affected their creativity in various ways. Among the more prominent Russian writers outside the Soviet Union were Bunin, Merezhkovsky, Remizov, Zamyatin, the minor novelists Boris Zaitsev (1881-1972) and Ivan Shmelyov (1873-1950), both of whom wrote about the émigré experience, and Mark Aldanov—the pen name of Mark Landau (1886-1957), a prolific and serious writer of novels on Russian history. One of the most accomplished writers to have emigrated was Vladimir Nabokov, who, before turning to English, wrote eight novels in Russian, only two of which are not about émigrés. An exquisite craftsman influenced by Gogol and Bely as well as by Marcel Proust (1871-1922), Franz Kafka (1883-1924), and the German expressionists, Nabokov enjoyed great success with his English-language novels such as *Lolita* (1955) and *Ada or Ardor: A Family Chronicle* (1969). Several other émigré writers of note are Andrei Donatevich Sinyavsky (1925-1997), who often wrote under the pen name Abram Tertz, the author of surreal novels and tales in the tradition of Gogol, as well as of brilliant, idiosyncratic critical studies; Vasily Aksyonov (born 1932), a prolific and original novelist; Vladimir Voinovich (born 1932), best known for his satiric

Chonkin trilogy; and Vladimir Maximov (1932-1995), whose novels exhibit a pronounced hostility both to communism and to Western liberalism—views similar to those of Solzhenitsyn, who was himself forced into exile and only allowed to return to Russia in the mid-1990's. Two younger émigrés who also created distinctive works of fiction were Sergey Dovlatov (1941-1990) and Sasha Sokolov (born 1945), whose novel *Shkola dlia durakov* (1976; *A School for Fools*, 1977) offered a unique vision of the lyric freedom found in mental illness.

Many of the émigré writers had published in the Soviet Union before arriving in the West. Aksyonov and Voinovich both represented the young generation, critical of the stale abstractions, political slogans, and dullness of Soviet life. Others had to rely on *samizdat* to circulate their work; among these was Venedikt Erofeev (1938-1990), whose novel *Moskva-Petushki* (1973; *Moscow to the End of the Line*, 1980), about alcoholism as an escape from the banality of Soviet life, had no chance of being officially published. While not officially sanctioned, the literature of protest was tolerated to a certain degree, the limits of which fluctuated with the political climate. When necessary, the authorities simply reasserted their control.

A significant trend in Soviet literature appeared in the late 1950's. Writers of the same generation as the writers of protest turned to village and rural themes. Surprisingly, the nineteenth century did not produce a single significant work about peasant life, while in the twentieth century, the Marxists have found little more in the peasant than an obstacle to progress, to socialism. The village writers were the first to show a reverence for peasants, describe their traditions, present their uneven struggle with the bureaucracy, and portray them as individual human beings. Many of the novels on peasant life espouse such conservative and traditional Russian values as love of nature and pride in one's work. They are critical of collectivization, often seeing it as the reason for the poor state of Russian agriculture, and of the treatment that the peasants have received at the hands of government officials. These themes can be found throughout the works of some of the leading village writers: Fyodor

Abramov (1920-1983), Vasily Belov (born 1932), Valentin Rasputin (born 1937), and the popular and talented Vasily Shukshin (1929-1974).

THE LATE TWENTIETH CENTURY

Also widespread in the 1960's and the 1970's were novels dealing with urban themes. They focused on problems in the workplace, the harried life of women in Soviet urban society, careerism, and the mundane concerns of everyday life. Novels returning to the subject of the revolution and World War II also continued to appear, focusing primarily on the individual's private experience. The major writers on such themes were Yury Trifonov (1925-1981), I. Grekova (the pseudonym of Elena Ventzel, born 1907), Yury Kazakov (1927-1982), Andrey Bitov (born 1937), Vasily Bykov (born 1924), and Viktoria Tokareva (born 1937).

The elevation of Mikhail Gorbachev to the post of general secretary of the Communist Party in 1985 opened a fresh era for Russia's writers. Eager to reform the stagnant economy, Gorbachev encouraged a new openness (*glasnost*) in Soviet society. During the last few years of the Soviet Union, from the mid-1980's to 1991, many works that had hitherto been prohibited from publication were allowed to appear in print for the first time. The year 1988, for example, saw the first Soviet publication of Pasternak's *Doctor Zhivago*, Zamyatin's *We*, several works by Nabokov, and the controversial novel by Vasily Grossman (1905-1964), *Zhizn i sudba* (finished in 1960, published in the West in 1980; *Life and Fate*, 1985). Many of the newly published works, including Grossman's novel and the novel *Deti Arbata* (written in 1966, published in 1987; *Children of the Arbat*, 1988), by Anatoly Rybakov (1911-1998), countered official views of Soviet society and politics, and they generated considerable debate among the reading public. Yet while much attention was focused on works previously unavailable for general consumption, other developments in literature also triggered excited discussion. New writers appeared in print, along with some older writers whose work had not been readily accessible. Among the most celebrated of the new or recently discovered writers were Lyud-

mila Petrushevskaya (born 1938), Vladimir Makanin (born 1937), Yevgeny Popov (born 1946), Vyacheslav Pyetsukh (born 1946), Tatyana Tolstaya (born 1951), and Viktor Erofeev (born 1947). These writers were willing to depict the seamier side of Soviet life, and their writing ranged from the farcical to the grotesque. Although they often preferred shorter genres, they also produced longer works of haunting intensity, such as Petrushevskaya's *Vremya noch* (1992; *The Time: Night*, 1994), which challenged the myth of the nurturing mother in Russia.

The swirling currents of change came to a head in 1991, when the failed coup attempt by a group of hard-line Communists led to the final dissolution of the Soviet Union. This breakdown of traditional state authority had major consequences in the literary sphere as well. Writers and publishers could no longer count on hefty state subsidies to support their work; publishing houses had to adapt to the pressures of a free market economy. For a year or two, Russian intellectuals fretted about a crisis in literature. In their rush to make a profit, publishing houses had begun turning out an enormous quantity of pulp fiction, from detective stories to erotic thrillers. Demand for "serious" literature diminished considerably. What is more, now that there were no longer any official constraints on what could appear in print, literature was deprived of its traditional role as the prophetic voice or moral conscience of the nation. Within a few years, however, the sense of crisis died down, and Russian literature saw a new flowering of individual talents. The creation of the Russian Booker Prize in 1992 helped provide a focus for the literary establishment, and signs of renewed growth soon became evident. In addition to the original publication of long-suppressed or buried works, such as the memoir-novel *Vremena* (1994; *How It All Began*, 1998), written by the Bolshevik Nikolay Bukharin in prison in 1937-1938 before his execution at Stalin's behest, fresh writers appeared in print. Many of the authors who came to prominence in the 1990's were distinguished by their innovative approach to fiction writing, and several seemed to reflect a particularly Russian brand of European postmodernism. Among the most interesting of these were Vladimir Sorokin (born 1955) and Victor Pelevin (born 1962). Their work, including Pelevin's *Zhizn nasekomykh* (1993; *The Life of Insects*, 1996), raised existential questions through extraordinary forms of pastiche and parody. With the arrival of this new generation of writers, the prospects for the future development of Russian literature once again looked bright.

George Mihaychuk, updated by Julian W. Connolly

BIBLIOGRAPHY

Brown, Deming. *The Last Years of Soviet Russian Literature*. Cambridge, England: Cambridge University Press, 1993. Designed to follow the author's previous book, *Soviet Russian Literature Since Stalin*, this text examines currents in Russian literature that surfaced within the Soviet Union between 1975 and 1991.

_____. *Soviet Russian Literature Since Stalin*. Cambridge, England: Cambridge University Press, 1978. A detailed study of literary developments from Joseph Stalin's death into the 1970's. Contains individual chapters on Aleksandr Solzhenitsyn, Andrei Sinyavsky, and village prose.

Brown, Edward J. *Russian Literature Since the Revolution*. Cambridge, Mass.: Harvard University Press, 1982. A bracing survey of the evolution of literature and its relationship to political winds of change in the Soviet Union from 1917 through the 1970's.

Cornwell, Neil. *Reference Guide to Russian Literature*. Chicago: Fitzroy-Dearborn, 1998. This extremely useful reference work contains introductory essays to major topics in Russian literature, biographical essays, and articles on numerous individual works.

Freeborn, Richard. *The Rise of the Russian Novel*. Cambridge, England: Cambridge University Press, 1973. A stimulating study of some of the most famous works of nineteenth century Russian literature, including *Eugene Onegin*, *Dead Souls*, *A Hero of Our Time*, *Crime and Punishment*, and *War and Peace*.

Jones, Malcom V., and Robin Feuer Miller, eds. *The Cambridge Companion to the Classic Russian Novel*. Cambridge, England: Cambridge University Press, 1998. Fourteen essays by prominent scholars cover a wide range of subjects reflected in the Russian novel, from politics and religion to psychology and gender issues.

Kelly, Catriona. *A History of Russian Women's Writing, 1820-1992*. Oxford, England: Oxford University Press, 1994. This comprehensive study of the evolution of women's writing in Russia combines sociohistorical analysis with close readings of individual works.

Ledkovsky, Marina, Charlotte Rosenthal, and Mary Zirin, eds. *Dictionary of Russian Women Writers*. Westport, Conn.: Greenwood Press, 1994. Contains a wealth of information on a broad range of literary figures.

Moser, Charles A., ed. *The Cambridge History of Russian Literature*. Cambridge, England: Cambridge University Press, 1989. Ten chapters, each by a noted scholar, trace the evolution of Russian literature from the medieval period to 1980.

Terras, Victor. *A History of Russian Literature*. New Haven, Conn.: Yale University Press, 1991. The most comprehensive single-author survey of Russian literature from its beginnings through the Soviet period.

SCANDINAVIAN LONG FICTION

The earliest prose in Scandinavia consists of medieval law collections, chronicles, legends of saints, and other didactic literature; fictional prose came later, with the emergence of the Icelandic sagas. The so-called kings' sagas and family sagas are set in the period from 850 to 1200; the contemporary sagas are set in the authors' own time, from 1180 to 1350; and a special group, the *fornaldar* sagas, remove the action to a distant past before the discovery of Iceland.

BEFORE 1800

Apart from a number of the kings' sagas, most of the sagas are anonymous. No original manuscripts exist; the sagas are preserved only in a number of widely varying copies. They are based partly on oral, partly on written tradition, and the sources—often anecdotal or legendary—are used with great freedom. Their composition was guided primarily by artistic considerations rather than by principles of historical accuracy.

The sagas reached their zenith in the thirteenth century. In the following century, they were superseded by translations of an ecclesiastic character (for example, sagas about the Virgin Mary and about saints) and of European romances. The earliest written are the kings' sagas, which to a larger extent than the others can be conjectured to contain historical facts. Even in the kings' sagas, however, these facts are subordinate to purely artistic principles of composition, as in the oldest, from about 1180, *Olafs saga helga* (Saint Olaf's saga). In approximately 1230-1235, Snorri Sturluson (1178 or 1179-1241) wrote his version of the saga, which he later included in his major work, *Heimskringla* (English translation, 1844), a history of Norway until 1177. Sturluson proceeds as a modern, critical historian, but, despite his striving for historical truth, he does not neglect the artistic rendition, the colorful, significant detail, and the pithy dialogue. Many episodes from Old Norse history, regardless of their authenticity, achieved their classic form in Sturluson's vivid prose.

The family sagas, the climax of the genre, are somewhat younger. They resemble historical novels, often following several generations. The scene is primarily local, but voyages are frequent. In these passages, the narration shifts from the factual and realistic to the fantastic in intricate stories of the Icelanders' deeds in exotic lands and their success with foreign kings and chiefs as a result of their physical courage and skaldic art. About 1220, the family saga reached full maturity with *Egils saga* (*Egil's Saga*, 1893). Especially fine is its portrait of the tenth century skald, Viking, and farmer Egil Skallagrímsson (c. 910-990), a historical figure and a prolific and innovative poet. His life in Iceland, as well as on exciting trips abroad, is followed from the time when, at three years of age, he composes his first poetry to the day when, as a blind and helpless old man, he tricks his heirs by burying his life's fortune in a secret place.

While Egil still reveals elements of barbaric savagery in his character—as when, for instance, he bites through the throat of an adversary—and while he worships the old gods, an atmosphere of European chivalry permeates *Laxdæla saga* (English translation, 1899). In this somewhat later saga from about 1250, the main protagonists, Bolli and Kjartan, have been baptized in Norway, and the woman whom they both love, Gudrun, the source of their rivalry and ruin, lives out the remainder of her life as the first nun in Iceland. Pagan fatalism persists, however, in another saga written around the same time, *Gísla saga* (*The Story of Gísli the Outlaw*, 1866), a story of unprovoked criminality and death. Even here, however, fatalism is tempered by the psychological nuances of the hero's relationships with those closest to him. Gísli vacillates between hope and fear when faced with his destiny via two phantasms, the good and evil women of a dream, who in turn offer him consoling and ghastly omens. The saga moves inexorably toward Gísli's destruction, a reflection of the author's own disillusionment.

The masterpiece of the family sagas, *Njál's Saga* (English translation, 1861), from the end of the thirteenth century, is pure tragedy. Its center is the friendship between Gunnar and Njál, a friendship that survives the vicious designs of their wives. Despite Gunnar's placidity and Njál's wisdom, however, destiny takes its course. Njál's good advice leads to catastrophe; finally, with bitter acceptance, he relinquishes his hopeless fight against fate and allows himself to die in the fire that destroys his home. The author excels in characterization, penetrating and multifaceted to a degree unique in saga literature. Even though the story ends weakly in the reconciliation of the survivors, *Njál's Saga* stands out as one of the great prose tragedies of world literature.

Among the contemporary sagas are a number of accounts of the Icelandic bishops, but more important are the secular sagas—which, teeming with people and events, constitute a unique source for knowledge of life in Iceland. The main work is *Íslandingasögur* (saga of the Icelanders) from the 1270's, written by Sturla Þorðarson (1214-1284), a nephew of Snorri Sturluson. This saga makes up one-third of the somewhat later *Sturlunga saga* (saga of the Sturlungs), compiled by Þorðr Narfason (died 1308), which describes the history of Iceland during the twelfth and thirteenth centuries. Þorðarson's masterful narration clearly anticipates the twentieth century documentary novel. He took an active role in political life and often steps forth as a direct eyewitness of or participant in the dramatic events he describes: violence, arson, family feuds, and revenge.

Elements of the fairy tale and folk legend dominate the *fornaldar* sagas. Their characters are stereotyped, and the authors concentrate on describing dramatic Viking raids, trolls, giants, and fabulous animals, far from any realism. They often paraphrase Germanic heroic poetry, such as the *Volsunga saga* (c. 1270; English translation, 1870) and Old Norse lays, occasionally preserving a few stanzas. There has been a tendency to regard these sagas as a degeneration of the more realistic family sagas, but both types probably existed simultaneously; the family sagas might even have taken some of their more imaginative traits from the *fornaldar* sagas. Undoubtedly somewhat later—from the fourteenth century—is the purely romantic *Frithiofs saga* (1825) and the fairy-tale saga *Örvar-Odds saga* (*Arrow-Odd: A Medieval Novel*, 1970), with its magic tools and unimpeded

shift of scenery from Iceland to Palestine. The *fornaldar* sagas, with their dramatic plots and easy prose, gained immense popularity; thus, they became a favorite source for later Scandinavian writers.

In artistic quality, however, they cannot compare with the family sagas and kings' sagas. Here one finds components that elevate these Icelandic novels to the level of world literature. The narration's objectivity—perhaps sometimes more formal than real—renders characters' feelings and thoughts through their physical reactions and particularly through their own speech. Powerfully understated dialogue is unusually frequent and contributes to the drama of the sagas' moods. The protagonists are complex and passionate personalities, often compelled by warring impulses: falseness and loyalty, love and hate. Always apparent, however, is the admiration for courage in catastrophe. The saga authors fully recognize that sudden death strikes even the most innocent—fate disregards moral justice—and their works affirm spiritual grandeur in the face of abysmal tragedy.

Icelandic literature's predominance declined during the fifteenth century as new Continental trends gained a footing in the Nordic countries. The historiography of the early Middle Ages found its climax with the *Gesta Danorum* (twelfth century) of Saxo Grammaticus (fl. mid-twelfth century-early thirteenth century), a history of Denmark from the first legends of the country's foundation to contemporary events. The leading genre of this period was the anonymous folk ballad, especially in Denmark and Sweden. A more pronouncedly epic genre, the chivalric verse novel, emerged in the early fourteenth century—again following Central European models. In Sweden, the didactic religious writing that dominated the era produced only one figure of lasting importance, the Holy Birgitta (1301-1373), whose *Revelationes* (published in 1492) is a distinguished example of the period's mysticism.

In all the Nordic countries, the Reformation brought a rupture with the European cultural tradition. In this period, Scandinavian literature was dominated by hymns, Bible translations, anti-Catholic satires, and prayer books, and strong theological orthodoxy suppressed free artistic expression. Not until the end of the sixteenth century were the ideas of Humanism and the Renaissance accepted; they dominated the first half of the seventeenth century, demanding the creation of a national literature based on the classic traditions of genre, style, and meter. Poetry was enthroned in Sweden with Lars Wivallius (1605-1669) and Georg Stjernhielm (1598-1672), and in Denmark with Anders Arrebo (1587-1637); the predominant genres were the didactic epic and occasional poetry.

This development betokened the secular consolidation that followed the ecclesiastical one in Denmark and Sweden. At this time, Iceland was under Denmark's trade monopoly and was falling into economic dependency and cultural isolation. Norway was completely under Danish control, while Finland was under Swedish control; Sweden thus evolved to become a European superpower in bellicose rivalry with Denmark. This led to a strengthening of both monarchies, which—in Denmark in 1660 and in Sweden after 1680—established them as autocratic. Under absolutism—and under the impact of the Thirty Years' War—baroque literature, with its mixture of stately commendation, ornamentation, and strong consciousness of death, flourished. The greatest prose work of the period is *Jammersminde* (1869) (*Memoirs of Leonora Christina*, 1872), the autobiography of the Danish princess Leonora Christina (1621-1698). She describes her imprisonment in Copenhagen Castle from 1663 to 1685 with rare sensitivity to situations and people and with natural dialogue, which was, for that time, unique.

Early in the eighteenth century, French classicism reached Scandinavia and merged with the ideas of the Enlightenment. Central in this development was the Dano-Norwegian Ludvig Holberg (1684-1754), whose thirty-three plays are both bitingly comical and realistic. Holberg was also the master of this period's prose, with his *Moralske Tanker* (1744; moral thoughts); *Epistler I-IV* (1748-1750; *Epistles I-IV*, 1955) and *Epistler V* (1754; *Epistles V*, 1955); and the novel *Nicolai Klimii iter subterraneum* (1741; *Journey to the World Underground*, 1742). In Latin, Holberg tells of Klim's journey through the interior of the earth. First he visits the ideal Potu ("utop[ia]"

backward), based on absolutism and Deism; then Martinia, a caricature of France, its citizens pleasure-seeking monkeys; and finally Quama, an underdeveloped country that slavishly proclaims Klim emperor. Pride in one's cultural superiority goes before a fall, however, and Klim has to escape, returning to the surface of the earth. The novel is both a satiric travelogue in the style of Jonathan Swift and a moralizing *Bildungsroman* recommending moderation and tolerance.

In Sweden, these ideas were promoted in a periodical of Olaf von Dalin (1708-1763), *Them Swänska Argus* (1732-1734), modeled after the English *Spectator*. This periodical, together with von Dalin's political fable *Sagan om hästen* (1740; the tale about the horse), became the foundation for modern Swedish prose. To von Dalin's model was added further precision and lucidity with Emanuel Swedenborg's (1688-1772) mystical and philosophical writings, while the travelogues of Carl von Linné (better known as Linnaeus, 1707-1778), contributed stylistic elegance.

Throughout the eighteenth century, to counterbalance the Enlightenment, a lyric and sentimental undercurrent—often connected with Pietistic religiosity—led to pre-Romanticism. In Denmark, a major exemplar was the lyric poet Johannes Ewald (1743-1781), whose autobiography, *Levnet og meninger* (1804-1808; life and opinions), broke sharply with the more academic prose style. *Levnet og meninger* resembles eighteenth century English author Laurence Sterne's novels; the action is only a pretext for digressions in which—through dialogue, lyric sketches, and penetrating self-analysis—Ewald describes the ecstasy he finds in wine and love. This strategy is continued by the travelogue *Labyrinten* (1792-1793; the labyrinth), by Jens Baggesen (1764-1826). With Sterne and French philosopher Jean-Jacques Rousseau as models, Baggesen places the capricious self of the poet in the center, and from that vantage he describes the surrounding world: a journey through Germany, Switzerland, and France, transformed by the artist's impulsive temperament.

In Sweden, the eighteenth century was dominated by King Gustav III and his brilliant, French-oriented court. The greatest writer of the period was the bohemian lyric poet Carl Michael Bellman (1740-1795); indeed, poetry, drama, and opera were the predominant artistic modes. The prose of this period was mainly nonfictional and retains only historical interest. Two travelogues, however, are noteworthy: *Min son på galejan* (1781; my son on the galley), by Jacob Wallenberg (1746-1778), is a humorous account of a voyage to East India in an agile but nevertheless precisely descriptive style; by contrast, *Resa till Italien* (1786; travel to Italy), written and illustrated by C. A. Ehrensvärd (1745-1800), forgoes description for laconic, aphoristic reflections on the author's encounter with nature and art.

The few Danish and Swedish plagiarisms of foreign novels are negligible. Periodical literature, on the other hand, includes several fictional discursive accounts of contemporary life. These efforts culminated in Sweden with two picaresque novels by Fredrik Cederborgh (1784-1835), *Uno von Trasenberg* (1809-1811) and *Ottar Trallings leftnadsmålning* (1811-1818). Like Voltaire's Candide, the title characters are inexperienced young men confronted with the folly of the world and finally taught by experience. Cederborgh's rather kindhearted satire partly ridicules the haughtiness of the nobility and the greediness of the petite bourgeoisie and partly attacks the defects of the judicial and prison system. Thus, Cederborgh provides a connection among the Enlightenment, Romanticism, and the bourgeois realism characteristic of the mid-nineteenth century.

ROMANTICISM AND POETIC REALISM

During the first decades of the nineteenth century, Danish and Swedish literature alike were dominated by a pantheistic, universal Romanticism. In Sweden's Erik Johan Stagnelius (1793-1823), this trend manifested itself in Platonic nature and love poems, while Denmark's Adam Oehlenschläger (1779-1850) based his works, often dramas, on Nordic mythology or history. Oehlenschläger led Romanticism into its second phase, national Romanticism. Following Sir Walter Scott, Bernhard Severin Ingemann (1789-1862) wrote historical novels based on Denmark's Middle Ages, among which *Valdemar Seier* (1826; *Waldemar, Sur-*

named *Seir: Or, The Victorious*, 1841) stands out with its perfect composition and exciting plot. All of Ingemann's works—so typical of Danish national Romanticism—combine nationalism with religion: The spirit of the people, and thus the power of the country, blossoms only when church and state ally. Ingemann's contemporary novel *Landsbybørnene* (1852; the village children) is an optimistic *Entwicklungsroman* (novel of development) that intersperses elements of Hans Christian Andersen's life with the story of the poet-protagonist. Despite its realistic milieu, the novel idealistically champions simple ethics over personal and social egotism.

Johannes Carsten Hauch (1790-1872), also familiar with Scott, was less concerned with historical accuracy than was Ingemann. After two novels set in previous centuries, he wrote *En polsk familie* (1839; a Polish family), a love story set against the Polish rebellion of 1830-1831. Structurally, the novel recalls German writer Johann Wolfgang von Goethe's Wilhelm Meister tales in its alternation between epic, lyric, and dramatic strategies. The fragmentary novel *En dansk students eventyr* (1843, written 1824; the adventures of a Danish student), by Poul Martin Møller (1794-1838), is more single-mindedly directed toward character delineation; its straightforward attack on sentimentality introduced critical realism to Denmark. The trend's finest representative is Steen Steenson Blicher (1782-1848), but better known are the novels of Hans Christian Andersen (1805-1875). All view life as a fairy tale that might just as easily end catastrophically as happily. *Improvisatoren* (1835; *The Improvisatore*, 1845) describes a poor young poet's road to success—recalling Andersen's own stay in Italy and forecasting his own career. *O.T.* (1836; English translation, 1845) is likewise optimistic, although darkened by the main character's having been born in a prison and the consequent speculations about fate. The protagonist of *Kun en spillemand* (1837; *Only a Fiddler*, 1845) also grows up in a poverty that overrules his artistic talent. This work is episodic, like the philosophical novel *At være eller ikke være* (1857; *To Be, or Not to Be?*, 1857), an indictment of nineteenth century materialism. Indeed, Andersen's novels live in single episodes and a host of acutely realized secondary characters. Andersen's novels indicate how descriptions of contemporary society gradually gained recognition, especially after the social analyses of Honoré de Balzac and Charles Dickens replaced Scott's historical novels as models in all Nordic countries. The Danish novel, however, retained its ties to the *Entwicklungsroman*. While Andersen's characters pursue artistic and social recognition, those of Mär Aron Goldschmidt (1819-1887) strive for ethical triumph, searching for an ideal that is not reached because of an old guilt. This concept of nemesis is not fully developed in Goldschmidt's first work, *En jøde* (1845; *The Jew of Denmark*, 1852), about a disappointed idealist who, like a Byronic hero, participates in European freedom struggles but ends up as a Copenhagen usurer. Less negative is *Hjemløs* (serialized 1853-1857; *Homeless: Or, A Poet's Inner Life*, 1861), in which the hero realizes on his deathbed that life is not something to be demanded but a debt to be paid. Another *Bildungsroman*, by Hans Egede Schack (1820-1859), *Phantasterne* (1857; the phantasts), follows three young men to show that a good life must subordinate fantasy to reality. With its brilliant psychology and its attack on sentimentality in the period's idealistic literature, Schack's work prefigures naturalism.

In Sweden, naturalism had been anticipated in 1839 with a novel by Carl Jonas Love Almqvist (1793-1866), *Det går an* (*Sara Videbeck*, 1919), which both questions the institution of marriage and defends a woman's right to choose her own profession. Besides August Strindberg, Almqvist is the most complex figure in Swedish literature. From 1832 to 1851, he published *Törnrosens bok* (the book of the briar rose), a diverse mix of novels and tales, plays and essays, and lyric and epic poems, held together by a frame story, "Jagtslottet" (the hunting seat). His *Drottningens juvelsmycke* (1834; the queen's jewel) is also unique—cryptic and inaccessible. The external action takes place at the Rococo court of Gustav III, where the androgynous Tintomara appears; she embodies both Almqvist's dream of a new human being and elements of his own personality.

The realistic trend seen in *Sara Videbeck* continued with Fredrika Bremer (1801-1865), who in 1828 had made her debut with the first part of *Teckningar utur hvardagslifvet* (*The Novels of Fredrika Bremer*, 1844-1849, 11 volumes)—the collective title she gave her novels through the 1830's—the epistolary novel *Axel och Anna* (1836; *Axel and Anna*, 1844), which depicts a confined and restrained woman. During these years, Bremer created the Swedish family novel, a genre that, in only slightly idealized detail, describes life in the well-to-do bourgeois homes and manor houses. A stay in the United States from 1849 to 1851 prompted her to work out her thoughts on women's liberation, culminating in *Hertha* (1856), which passionately discusses social equality between the sexes.

Overall, Swedish literature in the mid-nineteenth century was characterized by an insipid academic idealism, especially prevalent in a number of justly forgotten poets; not until Viktor Rydberg (1828-1895) was there a significant writer. Rydberg's historical adventure novel *Fribytaren på Östersjön* (1857; the freebooter in the Baltic Sea) also propagandizes against the tyrannical nobility and the religious intolerance of the seventeenth century. Its detailed description of a witch-hunt evidences Rydberg's cultural and historical concerns, but his style and characterization are still immature. Nor is his best-known novel, *Den siste Athenaren* (1859; *The Last Athenian*, 1869), artistically polished, marred as it is by the complicated intrigues common to popular novels. As an argument for spiritual freedom, however, it is significant, its picture of fanaticism in third century Greece exposing that of Rydberg's own time. The novel *Singoalla* (1857; *Singoalla, a Medieval Legend*, 1903), about the love of a young knight for a Gypsy girl, set in the legendary Middle Ages, includes mystical and Platonic elements that make it a beautiful and stately culmination of Swedish Romanticism.

In Norway, early nineteenth century literature was shaped by the decisive events of 1814, when Denmark was forced to cede the country to Sweden. Not until the work of Henrik Wergeland (1808-1845) did Norwegian literature become original. Wergeland is regarded as his country's greatest lyric poet. His bold imagination highlighted the breakthrough of Romanticism, which did not actually take place until the 1840's, when the young nation revived its national history, harking back to the epoch before its union with Denmark in 1397. The center of gravity was the lyric poem, and the novel was almost neglected. The first modern Norwegian novel, *Amtmandens døttre* (1855; the governor's daughters), was written by Wergeland's sister, Camilla Collett (1813-1895). With this artistically rather insignificant book, she not only paved the way for realistic problem fiction but also introduced the subject of the social position of women, which was carried further by Henrik Ibsen and Jonas Lie and ended in the tendentious works of Alexander Lange Kielland and Arne Garborg of the 1880's.

NATURALISM

The ideas of naturalism had been heralded in Scandinavia since the 1830's, but their sudden and definite breakthrough in the early 1870's should be credited to the Danish critic Georg Brandes (1842-1927). His dictum "That a literature exists in our time is shown by the fact that it sets up problems for debate" focused anew on social, sexual, and religious problems.

In Denmark, the major names in this new literary generation were Jens Peter Jacobsen (1847-1885) and Holger Drachmann (1846-1908). Jacobsen was by nature a dreamer, and his essential motif is the ongoing struggle between dream and reality. His artistic maturity was established with his story *Mogens* (1872; included in *Mogens og andre Novellen*, 1882; *Mogens and Other Stories*, 1921), the first naturalistic Scandinavian novella, containing precise impressions from nature and a perception of humans as physiological as well as spiritual beings. Jacobsen's *Fru Marie Grubbe* (1876; *Marie Grubbe*, 1917) signals a renewal of the historical novel. Realism was the goal; the means to that goal was an exhaustive study of sources in archives and libraries; and the result was a magnificently executed period piece. Marie's story—her fall through the social strata into the depths—from castle to hut to the primitive and strong man who can dominate her—is unrelievedly naturalistic. *Niels Lyhne* (1880; English translation, 1896),

on the other hand, is more contemporary. It portrays the development of a man ill-suited for life, escaping into dreams because he expects too much from reality; it is also a problem novel about a freethinker whose heart cannot keep pace with his brain and who longs for "a god to accuse and to worship." Jacobsen had learned much about psychological portrayal from French writers such as Stendhal and Gustave Flaubert, but he was no French naturalist. In his acute understanding of human beings and his melancholy tone, he more closely resembles the Russian novelist Ivan Turgenev, whose books were very popular at that time in all the Nordic countries. Thus, Drachmann, in his novel *En Overkomplet* (1876; a supernumerary), employs Turgenev's favorite motif of a strong woman versus a weak man. Drachmann was primarily a lyric poet; nevertheless, he wrote one of the most remarkable novels of the nineteenth century, *Forskrevet* (1890; signed away). Its characterization of men as unpredictable beings whose existence is paradoxically determined by dark fate is so mature and intense that it far surpasses the realistic works of the period.

Outside the Brandes camp stood the two greatest figures of the 1880's, Herman Bang (1857-1912) and Henrik Pontoppidan (1857-1943). Bang, a critical realist, emphasized that realism ought to be founded in aesthetics, not partisanism. His first novel, *Haabløse Slægter* (1880; generations without hope), is a naturalistic novel of inheritance and degeneration, a theme basic to Bang and derived from the French naturalists Balzac and Émile Zola. During his peak as a writer, from 1885 to 1890 (thereafter he devoted his efforts to stage direction), Bang wrote *Tine* (1889), which, against a historical backdrop—the Dano-Prussian war of 1864—plays the tragic love story of a servant girl. Tenderness, desire, and destruction are likewise stages of development in *Ludvígsbakke* (1896; *Ida Brandt*, 1928). Here, Bang portrays the relationship between husband and wife as a torture leading to life's destruction. His last novel, *De uden fædreland* (1906; *Denied a Country*, 1927), though marred by a mannered style and a hysterical tone, best shows Bang's style: The main action occurs in one afternoon, exposition having been given in a prologue. As in Bang's other impressionistic works, the novel is a drama: Everything happens before the eye of the reader; everything is situation, action, and direct speech.

The pessimism of the late decades of the nineteenth century, which determined Bang's view of life, found even more powerful expression in the works of Pontoppidan. He was a confirmed realist, an opponent of complacency, but he also sharply criticized naturalism. Scorn and biting irony lift his writing to an irrational sphere of passion and fantasy. His trilogy *Det forjættede land: Et tidsbillede*, 1892 (*The Promised Land*, 1896) is at once a satire on the times, a penetrating study of the soul of a religious dreamer, and a tragedy of an idealist. Like the main protagonist, Emanuel, the title character of Pontoppidan's next cycle, *Lykke-Per* (1898-1904; lucky Per), also searches for happiness, but whereas Emanuel pursues altruistic goals and perishes as a result, Per is interested only in his own happiness and finally finds it by losing everything except himself under the influence of medieval mysticism. At the beginning of the twentieth century, in *De dødes rige* (1912-1916; the realm of the dead), Pontoppidan condemns his own epoch by showing how the characters, in their conflict with moral and political conditions, demean themselves or are even destroyed. The basic theme of the cycle is the emptiness of human existence owing to the absence of love; this religious experience of the nothingness of life, combined with the moral experience of its valuelessness, makes it unique in Nordic literature.

In Sweden, the new intellectual and literary movement of naturalism was not established until around 1880, with the ground-breaking novel *Röda rummet* (1879; *The Red Room*, 1913), by August Strindberg (1849-1912). What makes the work a breakthrough is the sharp criticism of economic and political conditions in Sweden, of the early rise of capitalism. Yet in spite of the indignation, the mood is not bitter. Strindberg's style sparkles with subtle observations and impressionistic technique—an example is the famous panorama of Stockholm in the early pages of the book. After a number of strictly naturalistic dramas, Strindberg returned to fiction with a novel about people and nature in the archipelago, *Hemsöborna* (1887; *The Natives of Hemsö*, 1959). A foreman from the mainland, Carlsson, comes to reorder a neglected farm—and to win financial security by marrying the owner's widow—but throws away his chances because of his desire for a younger woman. Carlsson, although he belongs to the lower class, represents a superior type of human being. Strindberg was, therefore, ready when Brandes, in 1888, called his attention to the writings of Friedrich Nietzsche, whose homage to strong personalities is clearly reflected in Strindberg's novel *I havsbandet* (1890; *By the Open Sea*, 1913). The novel has an explicit antidemocratic prejudice. Its Nietzschean superman is Borg, an inspector of fisheries and Strindberg's alter ego, an absolute individualist of superior intelligence, battling a world of mediocrities.

Strindberg became a model for a group of writers called "Young Sweden," which emerged during the 1880's, wanting to mirror reality in all its everyday banality and tragedy. In the spirit of Brandes they took passionate positions on current problems and thus brought the social realism of the 1840's to a sharper and more insistent naturalism. The driving force behind Young Sweden, the prolific Gustaf af Geijerstam (1852-1909), illustrates the period's pessimism, suggested by the title of his first volume of novellas, *Gråkallt* (1882; gray cold).

In Norway in the 1880's, naturalism took a much more bellicose character than it did elsewhere, and doctrinaire writing became a force in society. Kristian Elster (1841-1881), strongly influenced by Turgenev, wrote *Farlige folk* (1881; dangerous people), contrasting modern ideas of progress with their reception in a small Norwegian provincial town. To Amalie Skram (1846-1905), Brandes's program gave the courage to break up an unhappy marriage in 1877 and to choose a career as a writer. She became the most consistent representative of naturalism in Scandinavia. The lives of many of her heroines were based on personal experience; in the cycle of novels *Hellemyrsfolket* (1887-1898; the people from Hellemyr), she penetratingly portrays a woman's unsatisfied desire for love in a deterministic, desolate world.

While Elster and Skram openly expressed their

hopeless view of life, Alexander Kielland (1849-1906) concealed it behind the elegance of his style. His novels *Garman og Worse* (1880; *Garman and Worse*, 1885) and *Skiper Worse* (1882; English translation, 1885) portray with warmth and humor the members of an old trading firm in a plot interspersed with critical comments on social injustice, stifled conventions, and religious hypocrisy. More direct in attacking social dishonesty are *Gift* (1883; poison) and *Fortuna* (1884), translated together as *Professor Lovdahl* (1904), while Kielland's last novel, *Jacob* (1891), satirizing the vulgar careerist in a democracy, marks him as the most acerbic ironist of his generation. Despite this emphasis on day-to-day problems and the topicality of his themes, Kielland's best novels are masterpieces of vivid psychology, completely transgressing the ideology of naturalism.

More typically transitional is Arne Garborg (1851-1924), whose entire work is informed by a dread of life and by religious longing. As a Christian journalist for a conservative newspaper, he at first opposed Brandes, but after an intensive study of the Danish critic—and of Charles Darwin—he changed his mind. In 1878, Garborg published the novel *Ein fritenkjar* (a freethinker), which clearly shows this shift in opinion, describing a radical theologian's disappointment in orthodox Christianity, which is for him a caricature of true faith. The novel, however, like Garborg's later ones, suffers from excessive theorizing and tendentiousness. In 1891 came a clear renunciation of Garborg's belief in naturalism as an ideology which can solve all social and individual problems. In *Trætte mænd* (weary men), he repudiated the materialism and dogmatic atheism of the time. In diary form, he portrays the spiritual despair and self-criticism, and finally the conversion to Christianity, of the main protagonist—a development which clearly anticipates the changing ideological climate of the 1890's.

Completely outside the dogmatic naturalistic school was Jonas Lie (1883-1908), whose visionary fantasies were expressed in essentially realistic writing. His first novel, *Den fremsynte* (1870; *The Visionary*, 1984), embodies the mysticism of northern Norway, a world in which the borders between the real and the unreal are strangely blurred by powerful nature. *Livsslaven* (1883; *One of Life's Slaves*, 1895), which treats the problem of poverty and social disparities, shows that Lie had developed into a writer of modern realistic novels, whose partisanship, however, never interfered with his art. In the same year, Lie's *Familien paa Gilje* (1883; *The Family at Gilje*, 1894), was published—a major Norwegian work. Protesting a marriage of convenience, Inger-Johanna breaks her engagement, thus sacrificing an advantageous match, but does not get the man she really loves. In *Kommandørens Døttre* (1886; *The Commodore's Daughters*, 1892), the title of which refers to Camilla Collett's earlier novel, the question of the emancipation of women, already touched upon in *The Family at Gilje*, is treated in a similarly undogmatic way. In the 1890's, Lie abandoned contemporary topics, publishing two volumes of tales entitled *Trold* (1891-1892; partial translation *Trolls* in *Weird Tales from Northern Seas*, 1893). The concept of a demoniac lower stratum in the soul dominated Lie's next works, giving a symbolic character to many of them. He creates a delicate impressionistic style from allusions and characteristic details that appeal to the imagination of the reader.

A national Finnish literature did not arise until the nineteenth century. The cultural language was primarily Swedish, the scholarly language Latin. The publication of the medieval epic *Kalevala* in 1835 (English translation, 1888), by Elias Løhnrot (1802-1884), laid the foundation for an independent Finnish literature and a national revival. Johan Ludvig Runeberg (1804-1877) and Zacharias Topelius (1818-1898) also attempted to promote Finnish nationalism through literature. Topelius found the material for his long series of novellas, *Faltskärns berättelser* (1853-1867; *The Surgeon's Stories*, 1883-1887), in historical events in Sweden and Finland during the seventeenth and eighteenth centuries. Influenced by Sir Walter Scott and Edward Bulwer-Lytton, he added excitement and adventure to his skillful narratives.

Both Runeberg and Topelius wrote in Swedish. A Finnish literary language was not created until Aleksis Kivi (1834-1872). Thereafter, Finnish and Finno-Swedish literature diverged. Kivi's novel *Seitsemän veljestä* (1870; *Seven Brothers*, 1929) tells how seven brothers leave their ancestral farm to settle in the wilderness, mature through hardship into social-minded citizens, and return to civilization. It is a novel that fluctuates between Romanticism and realism, baroque humor and seriousness; at the same time, it offers a symbolic history of Finnish culture.

After Kivi's death, literary activity stagnated for almost a decade, until 1880. At that time, Finnish literature became strongly influenced first by French and Scandinavian naturalism and later by Leo Tolstoy's doctrines of altruism, self-denial, and social responsibility. Common people, everyday life, and the socially oppressed were increasingly treated by young writers, who in 1885 formed a group called Nuori Suomi (Young Finland), led by Minna Canth (1844-1897) and Juhani Aho (1861-1921). *Papin tytär* (1885; the daughter of a clergyman), Aho's first attempt at a tendentious depiction of the middle class, stresses the experience of Elli, a passive being, doomed to tragic resignation in unsympathetic surroundings—a typical motif in Nordic literature of the 1880's, found, for example, in the novels of Lie and Bang. The tone became sharper in Aho's depiction of student life in *Helsinkiin* (1889; to Helsinki), but around 1900 he moved from Zola-influenced realism toward a more impressionistic lyricism. This shift is clearly reflected in his masterpiece, *Papin rouva* (1893; the wife of a clergyman), a sequel to his novel of 1885. Here, description and epic elements are secondary; instead, the emphasis is on the psychological analysis of the minister's wife and of her brief passion, doomed from the outset, for a blasé, cosmopolitan houseguest.

Iceland's contact with European cultural life was not very extensive until the eighteenth century, and it is impossible to speak of a Romantic movement there before 1830. The country finally achieved political and financial autonomy in 1874. Because Iceland did not have its own university until 1911, Icelanders had to study in Copenhagen. There, around 1880, Icelandic realism and naturalism developed, under the influence of Georg Brandes. These currents, however, were not as influential in Iceland as they were in other Nordic countries, primarily as a result of the lack of urban centers and an industrial proletariat. The 1870's and 1880's were years of great hardship in Iceland; one-fourth of the nation's people emigrated to North America during this period.

Radical views were proclaimed in the periodical *Verðandi* (1882). Promoting a new realistic prose were Gestur Pálsson (1852-1891) and Einar Hjörleifsson Kvaran (1859-1938). Their pessimistic short stories analyze injustice and hypocrisy in contemporary society. Kvaran's attacks on conservatism give way in his later writings to psychological portrayal of the oppressed, not the oppressors, but they are devoid of any propagandistic tendency. This development, influenced by William James's theories of the subconscious, is also manifest in Kvaran's novels. *Ofurefli* (1908; overwhelming odds) and *Gull* (1911; gold) offer the first realistic depictions of the Reykjavík bourgeoisie, the main theme being the victory of liberal theology against orthodoxy. Yet in *Sálin vaknar* (1916; the soul awakens), a murder story, Kvaran supports immortality and spiritualism; the novel's optimistic tone also permeates Kvaran's later writings.

To WORLD WAR I

Nordic literature in the 1890's generally departed from past traditions—in Sweden, Finland, and Iceland perhaps less than in Norway and Denmark. Even in these countries, however, neo-Romanticism and Symbolism clashed with naturalism and realism. The ethical demand for truth was succeeded by the aesthetic demand for beauty, and rationalism was met by a new metaphysics and a mystically colored religiosity. Nature and history became favored subjects, and lyric poetry, which had been totally neglected, was revived.

In Sweden, this change was evident in the novel *Hans Alienus* (1892), by Verner von Heidenstam (1859-1940), which treats antiquity both historically and imaginatively. A strong bond to the homeland, based on an ideal conception of heroic death, raises Heidenstam's historical novellas *Karolinerna* (1897-1898; *A Kind and His Campaigners*, 1902; better known as *The Charles Men*, 1920) to the level of tragic national epic. *Folkungaträdet* (1905-1907; *The*

Tree of the Folkungs, 1925), a two-volume novel, is Heidenstam's greatest historical work. Composed as a unit, it was based on extensive studies of Swedish society and language.

Swedish history and folklore form the basis for the works of Selma Lagerlöf (1858-1940). Her best-known novel—a true masterpiece—the two-volume *Gösta Berlings saga* (1891; *The Story of Gösta Berling*, 1898; also as *Gösta Berling's Saga*, 1918) is a modern lyric and dramatic epic. In place of the coherent plot characteristic of the naturalistic novel, Lagerlöf favored episodic narratives; here, diverse episodes are joined by unity of place: an old estate and its surroundings in the author's home province of Värmland, the domain of adventurers, drunks, and artists who live unreflectively for the passion of the moment. Though Lagerlöf renders their dealings in a lyric style influenced by Thomas Carlyle, she morally condemns them. In 1896, she visited a colony of Swedish farmers in Jerusalem who had experienced a religious awakening in the province of Dalecarlia. Leaving farms and families, they had emigrated to practice works of mercy and to await the second coming. Lagerlöf describes them in the two-volume novel *Jerusalem* (1901-1902; in English in two volumes as *Jerusalem*, 1915, and *The Holy City*, 1918); the first volume is the most significant with its brilliant psychological portrayal of an old farming family and the world of their thoughts.

Lagerlöf was in total agreement with the national movements of her time when, in 1906 and 1907, she published her next major work, *Nils Holgerssons underbara resa genom Sverige* (*The Wonderful Adventures of Nils*, 1907, and *The Further Adventures of Nils*, 1911), written as a geography reader for the elementary schools. Nils, an ill-mannered farm boy, is changed into a Tom Thumb and carried off by a wild goose, in a situation reminiscent of Rudyard Kipling's *The Jungle Book* (1894). Not content with this main plot, Lagerlöf incorporates numerous fairy tales, legends, and short stories, all designed to spur Nils's progress toward honesty and duty. Not until 1925 did Lagerlöf again publish a major work, the first volume of the Löwensköld trilogy, *Löwenskölds ringen* (*The General's Ring*, 1928), followed by

Charlotte Löwensköld (1925; English translation, 1928) and *Anna Svärd* (1928; English translation, 1928); a translation of the three volumes of the trilogy appeared in English as *The Ring of the Löwenskölds: A Trilogy* (1928). The trilogy suggests Lagerlöf's frequent inability to differentiate between the original and the banal; nevertheless, she possesses a great talent for epic construction, for vivid characterization, for rich fantasy, and for other neo-Romantic features, which can also be found among the works of many writers of the next generation.

Most of these writers, however, turned toward realism, especially in a newly vigorous precision in the treatment of social classes. Having lost faith in evolution's implied optimism, they maintained their belief in its determinism. The influence of the 1890's persisted in the disillusioned skepticism—expressed earlier in European literature in the works of Oscar Wilde, Anatole France, and Herman Bang, among others, and finding a significant representative in Hjalmar Söderberg (1869-1941). The protagonist of his novel *Martin Bircks ungdom* (1901; *Martin Birck's Youth*, 1930), unstable and melancholy, is typical of the period. Plot is subordinated to feeling and thought; especially distinctive are the shattering of Martin's illusions about his vocation and love and his role as an ironic observer of existence.

Among the writers of the first decade, Hjalmar Bergman (1883-1931) had the most expansive imagination. About 1900, he, too, progressed from neo-Romanticism to realism, never, however, abandoning a symbolic treatment of his subjects. Thus, in the trilogy *Komedier i Bergslagen* (1914-1916; comedies in Bergslagen), the mixture of fairy-tale world and colorful and realistic description elevates the episodic portrayal of human suffering and spiritual ailments, reminiscent of Dostoevski, to an inspired expression of Bergman's pessimism. The violent, brutal quarrels between father and son, the tormenting jealousy and unhappy love, all unmask life's demoniac forces.

Bergman's succeeding novels, *Markurells i Wadköping* (1919; *God's Orchid*, 1924) and *Farmor och vår Herre* (1921; *Thy Rod and Thy Staff*, 1937), describe, with elements of comic relief, a tragic narrative—the theft of illusions. By contrast, epic plot gives way to the psychology of the subconscious life of a businesswoman—an approach influenced more by Dostoevski than by Sigmund Freud—in Bergman's last great prose work, *Chef en fru Ingeborg* (1924; *The Head of the Firm*, 1936). Bergman's work is an attempt to compensate for the blind game of fate with humor and satire—learned from Balzac and Dickens—and to overcome disharmony and destruction through art.

The reorientation in the Norwegian literature of the 1890's is perceptible in the works of many older authors, such as Jonas Lie and Arne Garborg. The fruitless debates and analyses had grown wearisome, and disappointment over the inconclusiveness of radical ideas led to a skeptical attitude toward democracy, as in the works of Hans Ernst Kinck (1865-1926) and Knut Hamsun (1859-1952).

Most outstanding among the nationalistic neo-Romantics was Kinck. Half poet, half cultural philosopher, well-read in history and psychology, Kinck describes periods of transition in which two cultures combat each other or an individual combats society. Thus, in *Herman Ek* (1923), Kinck portrays the clash between the old peasant culture and the modern urban culture. The trilogy *Sneskavlen brast* (1918-1919; the avalanche broke) gathers all of Kinck's essential themes: inhibited eroticism, rejected tenderness, and the relationship of the farmer to the estate holder. Kinck's figures are always shown in the context of their cultural milieu; yet he always emphasizes the subconscious mind's interaction with nature. External events are for him only unfocused and counterfeit images of the private psyche.

Hamsun also searched for the primitive and the natural. His novel *Sult* (1890; *Hunger*, 1899) introduced a new epoch in Norwegian literature. It portrays the hopeless struggle of a poverty-stricken writer. Tormenting hunger is scientifically analyzed as it slowly destroys his nervous system and self-control, strictly omitting all social and political perspectives. In Hamsun's next book, *Mysterier* (1892; *Mysteries*, 1927), the main character, Johan Nagel, who suddenly appears one day in a small Norwegian town, is, like the poet in *Hunger*, a stranger in life. Hamsun, however, makes no attempt to explain his

behavior, wanting to demonstrate the mysterious depths of the human soul. The Nagel type appears again in the lyric, first-person narrative *Pan* (1894; English translation, 1920); Lieutenant Glahn is also a maverick, a hunter and a man of nature, rejecting modern civilization.

In the twentieth century, Hamsun moved from subjective to more objective narration, unfolding fully in *Børn av tiden* (1913; *Children of the Age*, 1924) and its sequel *Segelfoss by* (1915; *Segelfoss Town*, 1925). Hamsun, whose interest had been limited to his protagonists, here created a wide-ranging realistic picture of the social range of northern Norway, especially the clash between the old, patriarchal feudal system and material progress. The epic novel *Markens grøde* (1917; *Growth of the Soil*, 1920), instrumental in Hamsun's winning the Nobel Prize in Literature, tells the story of the settler Isak, who stubbornly makes the wilderness arable and establishes his own farm. As Isak's estate grows, other settlers move into the woods and establish a new self-supporting community. Such optimism yielded to social bitterness and criticism in Hamsun's novels *Konerne ved vandposten* (1920; *The Women at the Pump*, 1928) and *Ringen sluttet* (1936; *The Ring Is Closed*, 1937); in the latter, once again, a maverick figure shuns, with aristocratic contempt, bourgeois society.

The Finnish neo-Romantics were deeply influenced by Hamsun's cult of nature and Lagerlöf's imaginative narrative art, and they found their motifs not only in Finnish history and folklore but also in distant countries, antiquity, mythology, and the Bible. Most were lyric poets, such as Eino Leino (1878-1926) and Otto Manninen (1872-1950); Leino also wrote several rather superficial novels on contemporary life in Helsinki. The only prolific prose writer of the neo-Romantic period was Johannes Linnankoski (the pseudonym of Vihtori Peltonen, 1869-1913). His novel *Laulu tulipunaisesta kukasta* (1905; *The Song of the Blood-Red Flower*, 1920) is uneven but was tremendously successful; it sets the Don Juan motif in contemporary Finland among lumberjacks and timber floaters. With *Pakolaiset* (1908; the refugees), Linnankoski created a masterpiece. Descriptions of nature are subordinated to dramatic suspense in the story of a young wife's faithlessness to her older husband and his hard-won inner development when he discovers her deception.

The Finnish Civil War of 1918 brought about a skeptical and apocalyptic mood; melancholy and hedonism became popular. In *Onni Kokko* (1920), by Jarl Hemmer (1893-1944), the civil war forms an ominous backdrop to the complex ethical question of suffering in a presumably just world order. Christianity colors Hemmer's major work, the Dostoevski-like novel *En man och hans samvete* (1931; *A Fool of Faith*, 1936). With existential commitment, Hemmer analyzes suffering and death, the quest for consolation in religion, and, finally, the belief in sacrificial death as a possible means of salvation.

As in Finland, the foremost writers of the 1890's in Iceland were lyric poets. Home rule in 1904, however, encouraged nationalism and the revival of traditions that precluded introversion and ennui. The novels of Guðmundur Kamban (1888-1945) deal mainly with Iceland's history from the Middle Ages into the twentieth century. The monumental *Skálholt* (1930-1935; parts 1 and 2 as *The Virgin of Skalholt*, 1935) analyzes the psychology of love set against a panorama of everyday seventeenth century life, based on extensive historical study. In *30. Generation* (1933; thirtieth generation), Kamban returned to a portrayal of contemporary Reykjavík, while his last novel, *Jeg ser et stort, skønt land* (1936; *I See a Wondrous Land*, 1938), retells the discovery of Greenland and Vineland (America).

Writers of the new literary generation in Denmark were not, as in Sweden and Iceland, rediscoverers of the national past, but rediscoverers of the soul. The primary Danish Symbolists were all lyric poets, with the exception of Johannes Jørgensen (1866-1956), whose five short novels from 1888 to 1894 describe uprooted students from the provinces being confronted with the modern metropolis. After his conversion to Catholicism in 1896, Jørgensen achieved a place as an international Catholic author with his extensive, knowledgeable biographies, *Den hellige Frans af Assisi* (1907; *Saint Francis of Assisi*, 1912) and *Den hillige Katerina af Siena* (1915; *Saint Catherine of Siena*, 1938).

The lyric introverted literature of the 1890's was followed in Denmark by a new realistic and rationalistic wave, different from the naturalism of the 1870's and 1880's in its decided materialism and occasional socialism. Two directions can be distinguished in the literature of this period: regionalism and social agitation. Regional literature was dominated by two vastly different writers, Johannes V. Jensen (1873-1950) and Jakob Knudsen (1858-1917).

The first major work of Knudsen, the novel *Den gamle Præst* (1899; the old pastor), concerns the clash between social convention and the individual's conscience. Knudsen's partially autobiographical two-volume novel *Gjæring-Afklaring* (1902; fermentation-clarification) portrays with both satire and empathy the spiritual situation of Knudsen's own generation. Until this point, peasants had been merely secondary figures in Knudsen's works. In his artistically most significant novel, *Sind* (1903; temper), nature and the rural population are primary. In *Fremskridt* (1907; progress), Knudsen confronts the old peasant community's social, political, and spiritual development with modern reform politics.

One of the most influential figures in modern Danish literature was Jensen. Influenced by Jørgensen and Hamsun, Jensen's early novels *Danskere* (1896; Danes) and *Einar Elkær* (1898), in the decadent mood of the 1890's, have as protagonists introverted, self-centered students from the provinces. Fresher is Jensen's first masterpiece, the collection of stories *Himmerlandsfolk* (1898; Himmerland people), immortalizing his home region, its traditions and its people. In its regional setting, the novel *Kongens fald* (1900-1901; *The Fall of the King*, 1933) is linked to *Himmerlandsfolk*. It focuses on the figure of the sixteenth century king Christian II. The king's character is secondary, but his skepticism, which leads to the dissolution of all plans and energy into reflection and dream, symbolizes the paralysis Jensen perceived as a major flaw in the Danish character. Scenes of harsh naturalism alternate with passages of exquisite lyricism. *The Fall of the King* is a historical novel—the most significant in Danish literature—but Jensen broke decisively with the historical naturalism of Flaubert and J. P. Jacobsen. The apparently accidental juxtaposition of tableaux and situations creates a myth of loneliness, transitoriness, and death.

A journey to the United States in 1902 and 1903 resulted in two novels, *Madame d'Ora* (1904) and *Hjulet* (1905; the wheel), both of which reveal Jensen's confrontation with the modern United States. Their brilliant descriptions of New York and Chicago coexist, however, with shopworn attempts at suspense. At the same time, they turn against all speculations concerning immortality. Jensen's finest narrative art—aside from *The Fall of the King*—is in the smaller prose pieces of *Myter* (myths), which appeared in eleven volumes between 1907 and 1944. The "myths" elevate visionary existentialism over conventional plot. Several are studies for the great series of novels *Den lange rejse* (1908-1922; *The Long Journey*, 1922-1924, 1933, 1945). This history of the world begins before the Ice Age in the tropical Danish forests and encompasses the epochs of the tribal migrations and Viking raids to the discovery of America. It tells of the progenitors of the "Gothic race," of their longing for distant places, and finally of their departure from their northern homeland toward the lost land before the Ice Age. Influenced by Darwin's evolutionary theories, Jensen attempts to explain universal human symbols and conceptions, purely on the basis of practical experience.

Martin Andersen Nexø (1869-1954) was the first significant writer of the Danish workers' movement, the first to make the proletariat central. In his novel *Pelle Erobreren* (1906-1910; *Pelle the Conqueror*, 1913-1916), Nexø traces the growth of the Danish workers' movement in the last decades of the nineteenth century. The novel contains many agitatory passages, and the later parts of the novel are frequently utopian and naïve without the artistic merit of earlier parts. *Pelle the Conqueror* is nevertheless carried along by the epic power of the narrative and by Nexø's social commitment. His second major work, *Ditte Menneskebarn* (1917-1921; in three volumes as *Ditte: Girl Alive, Ditte: Daughter of Man, Ditte: Toward the Stars*, 1920-1923), is based on the same human and social concerns as *Pelle the Conqueror*. Like Pelle, Ditte begins at the very bottom,

ambitious and hungry for life, but her fate is different. Whereas Pelle becomes involved in politics in order to build a new social order, Ditte fights alone against poverty and finally succumbs. Nexø was the only Danish Marxist writer of his generation, but he obviously differed from the socialist authors of the 1930's; he still adhered to an idealistic belief in human goodness that, cutting across all social and economic relationships, asserts itself despite everything.

BETWEEN THE WORLD WARS

The democratization of Sweden after World War I clearly shows in its literature. Around 1910, several writers emerged from the working class to portray the lowest social strata, a dominant feature of twentieth century Swedish literature, yet their realistic material and naturalistic techniques posed new aesthetic problems. For many, Zola was the master; above all, the proletarian writers were strongly influenced by Maxim Gorky, Upton Sinclair, and the Scandinavian pioneer of proletarian writing, Nexø.

The satiric novels of Jan Fridegård (1897-1968) describe the conflicts of the poor with society—as in his major work, the autobiographical "Lars Hård" cycle (1935-1951). Ivar Lo-Johansson (born 1901) was the first of the proletarian novelists of the 1930's to depict poor farmhands collectively, in *Godnatt, jord* (1933; good night, earth). In a number of social novels, Lo-Johansson continued his treatment of working-class problems; *Analfabeten* (1951; the illiterate) is the first of an eight-volume autobiographical series, concluding with *Proletärförfattaren* (1960; the proletarian writer).

The first novel of Vilhelm Moberg (1898-1973), *Raskens* (1927), introduced the character type of the exploited farmhand in an unsentimental story of a peasant soldier, his large family, and their fight against misery and poverty. Moberg's major work is his partly documentary prose epic about the nineteenth century emigration of Swedish farmers to the United States, the multivolume *Romanen om utvandrarna* (1949-1959; includes *Utvandrarna*, 1949 [*The Emigrants*, 1951]; *Invandrarna*, 1952 [*Unto a Good Land*, 1954]; *Nybyggarna*, 1956, and *Sista brevet till Sveriga*, 1959 [*The Last Letter Home*, 1961, an abridged version of the last two volumes]). It is at once a social chronicle, a myth about the search for happiness, and a satire of Swedish bureaucracy and social hierarchy.

The postwar mentality, familiar from world literature, shattered all illusions; any belief in moral order seemed ludicrous. The nihilism of the "lost generation" was eventually evident in all countries, in the works of Ernest Hemingway, André Malraux, and Erich Maria Remarque—in Denmark in the work of Tom Kristensen and in Iceland in that of Halldór Laxness.

In Swedish prose, next to Pär Lagerkvist, Eyvind Johnson (1900-1976) probably most accurately expresses this postwar attitude. Whereas Lagerkvist's angst is primarily metaphysical, Johnson's is more pragmatic. The expressionism of his early works gives way to more humanistic democratism, as in the trilogy *Krilon* (1941-1943), which attacks fascism and Sweden's neutrality during World War II. After the war, Johnson wrote two historical novels that depict his essential theme—the hopeless battle of the right and good for a better world. *Strändernas svall* (1946; *Return to Ithaca*, 1952) reworks Homer's *Odyssey* (c. 800 B.C.E.) from a modern point of view, fragmenting the firmness of the classical figures. *Drömmar om rosor och eld* (1949; dreams of roses and fire) expresses Johnson's pessimism, treated in *Molnen över Metapontion* (1957; clouds over Metapontion) on three time levels: ancient Syracuse, World War II, and the 1950's, suggesting that freedom and love are always threatened and that history is unpredictable and senseless. His most successful treatment of this theme is *Hans nådes tid* (1960; *The Days of His Grace*, 1968), set in Charlemagne's France, describing how several young rebels become either tools of imperial power or sink into paralysis. The narrative experiments are continued in *Livsdagen lång* (1964; life's long day), which combines several stories from different epochs, held together by the narrator. In *Några steg mot tystnaden* (1973; a few steps toward silence), the action again shifts between different periods to illustrate the futile effort of Western humanism to retain integrity when threatened by injustice and violence.

The central figure of the 1920's was Pär Lager-

kvist (1891-1974). His early pessimism is overcome in *Det eviga leendet* (1920; *The Eternal Smile*, 1934), the setting of which is the realm of the dead, where the dead philosophize about the meaning of life and alternately decide to seek out God, to demand an explanation. The political crises of the 1930's are clearly reflected in Lagerkvist's works. The first part of the novella *Bödeln* (1933; *The Hangman*, 1936) is set in a medieval village inn, the second part in a dance hall in the Fascist present. The medieval hangman, Lagerkvist suggests, was watched with anxious fascination; his counterpart in the Fascist era is celebrated. In 1944, in the novel *Dvärgen* (*The Dwarf*, 1945), Lagerkvist again investigated the psychology of evil, this time through the diary of a dwarf at the court of an Italian Renaissance prince. A kind of Antichrist, the dwarf comprehends only inhumanity, gruesomeness, and the struggle for power. This work brought Lagerkvist to the reading public, leading up to his international breakthrough with the novel *Barabbas* (1950; English translation, 1951), about the liberated robber who, though incapable of love or sacrifice, is filled with a vague metaphysical yearning for something beyond himself.

With *Barabbas*, Lagerkvist began to express a new longing for a distant God. In *Sibyllan* (1956; *The Sibyl*, 1958), which brings together a seeress from Delphi and the wandering Jew Ahasuerus, the theme is the human encounter with God. Only at the end of *Ahasverus död* (1960; *The Death of Ahasuerus*, 1960) does the restless wanderer find quiet in a monastery, where he experiences Christ not as the Son of God but as an unhappy fellow man. This novel and the following two, *Pilgrim på havet* (1962; *Pilgrim at Sea*, 1964) and *Det heliga landet* (1964; *The Holy Land*, 1966), all set in the European Middle Ages, describe restless pilgrims who find peace through love. Lagerkvist's last book, *Mariamne* (1967; *Herod and Mariamne*, 1968), carries the same message, expressed, as in his other mature works, through the greatest possible stylistic simplicity and lucidity.

Two significant—and very different—interwar novels were written by lyric poets. Karin Boye (1900-1941) wrote the utopian *Kallocain* (1940; English translation, 1966), based on her travels in Germany and the Soviet Union, which is stylistically indebted to Aldous Huxley's *Brave New World* (1932) and to Franz Kafka's novels. It depicts a totalitarian state that has eliminated all personal freedom, without, however, completely denying the survival of humanity. This humanism found an outstanding representative in Harry Martinson (1904-1978), particularly in his poem cycle *Passad* (1945; trade winds). In his novel *Vägen till Klockrike* (1948; *The Road*, 1955), Martinson shapes the theme of humanism's clash with science in the portrayal of a vagabond who renounces society to find spiritual poise in meditation and nature.

Knut Hamsun's development after 1900 into a social critic after 1900 accorded with the increasing preoccupation of Norway's younger generation with social issues. The working class grew at a pace unknown in the other Nordic countries, and the population shift from country to city and factories led inevitably to political radicalization, expressed most clearly in works by Johan Falkberget (1879-1967) and Kristofer Uppdal (1878-1961). In Falkberget's trilogy *Christianus Sextus* (1927-1935), set in the 1720's, the miner appears for the first time in Norwegian literature. In the tetralogy *Nattens brød* (1940-1959; bread of night), Falkberget unforgettably pictures the upheaval in the life of the late seventeenth century peasants who gave up their property to work in the foundries. Falkberget's work is not only realistic but also has a Romantic vein, as his religiously colored optimism remains victorious over the described misery. It fell to Uppdal to depict the workers as a class and to found the modern Norwegian social novel. His uneven ten-volume novel cycle, *Dansen gjenom skuggeheimen* (1911-1924; the dance through the shadow land), is based on the clash between the feudal structures of the villages and those of modern industry.

Two Norwegian writers, the world-renowned Sigrid Undset (1882-1949) and the less well-known Olav Duun (1876-1939), stand above most of the Nordic writers of the epic in the twentieth century. In his main work, the six-volume family saga *Juvikfolke* (1918-1923; *The People of Juvik*, 1930-1935), Duun chronicles a peasant family over a one-hundred-year period to the end of World War I. He explores the relationship between individual and environment in a collective portrait of the spiritual life of the Norwegian people as they develop from feudalism to a society of high ethical standards. Duun's last book, *Menneskene og maktene* (1938; *Floodtide of Fate*, 1960), which embodies all of his essential ideas and motifs, envisions apocalypse in the story of the inhabitants of a small island and their dread of being swallowed up by the sea. In modern point-of-view technique, each scene is told from more than one character's perspective.

The work of Undset was more traditional. Her historical novels of the Middle Ages—including two trilogies, *Kristin Lavransdatter* (1920-1922; English translation, 1923-1927) and *Olav Audunssøn i Hestviken* and *Olav Audunssøn og hans børn* (1925-1927; *The Master of Hestviken*, 1928-1930, 1934)—constitute a significant contribution to world literature. *Kristin Lavransdatter*, set in the fourteenth century, begins with the struggle of the title figure for the man she loves. After her husband's death, Kristin's life becomes a humble pilgrimage toward final peace in service to God and her fellow humans. Undset's conversion to Catholicism in 1925 shaped *The Master of Hestviken*, a thirteenth century tragedy of love and marriage that glorifies religion. As in *Kristin Lavransdatter*, the major motif is the struggle between willfulness and obedience to God. Undset returned to the twentieth century in the two-volume novel *Gymnadenia* (1929; *The Wild Orchid*, 1931) and *Den brændende busk* (1930; *The Burning Bush*, 1932), portraying a young man's harrowing progress from humanism to Catholicism. Contemporary settings also characterize Undset's two novels of marriage, *Ida Elisabeth* (1932; *Ida Elizabeth*, 1933) and *Den trofaste husfru* (1933; *The Faithful Wife*, 1937), strongly attacking modern materialism.

Although Norway was neutral in World War I, many younger authors felt the unsettling events of the period. Several embraced socialism, on the one hand, and Freud's theories, on the other. Outside all political groups stands Cora Sandel (the pseudonym of Sara Fabricius, 1880-1974), whose works analyze women's inhibitions and feelings of inferiority. Her trilogy comprising *Alberte og Jacob* (1926; *Alberta and Jacob*, 1962), *Alberte og friheten* (1931; *Alberta and Freedom*, 1963), and *Bare Alberte* (1939; *Alberta Alone*, 1965) follows a woman's hard-won independence in a narrow petit bourgeois milieu, finally leading to her personal and artistic liberation.

Sigurd Hoel (1890-1960) was, in contrast to Sandel, a cool and ironic commentator. His first significant work, and the first attempt by a Norwegian to write a collective novel, was *En dag i oktober* (1931; *One Day in October*, 1932)—modeled on Elmer Rice's play *Street Scene* (1929)—concerning an Oslo apartment house and its inhabitants. Hoel's most penetrating psychological work of the interwar period, *Fjorten dager før frostnettene* (1935; fourteen days before the frosty nights), focuses on a man who deserts his beloved because he is incapable of love. In 1943, during the German Occupation, Hoel fled to Sweden. There he began *Møte ved milipælen* (1947; *Meeting at the Milestone*, 1951), which asks the crucial questions: Why did so many Norwegians become traitors to their country? To what degree is everyone responsible? The novel contains superb descriptions of the Occupation years, but it is more absorbing in its sophisticated structure, constantly shifting between time planes, a technique that one finds even in Hoel's prewar novels. In his last novel, *Trollringen* (1958; the magic ring), possibly Hoel's greatest artistic achievement, fantasy can again unfold freely, unburdened by the satiric comments on the period that pervade so many of his works.

Around 1930, Tarjei Vesaas, Aksel Sandemose, and Johan Borgen made their appearance. Their work was influenced by the period's growing political tension, but the excesses of totalitarianism also challenged these writers to a psychological investigation of human nature. This group was much influenced by translations from other modern literatures, particularly from American literature.

Tarjei Vesaas (1897-1970) was the Norwegian novelist who broke most consistently with realism. In the novel *Kimen* (1940; *The Seed*, 1964), the forces of destruction haunt a peaceful island community, symbolized in a merciless hunt for a mentally disturbed man who has killed a girl. Vesaas's next novel,

Huset i mørkret (1945; *The House in the Dark*, 1976) likewise portrays the present in its depiction of the occupation of Norway, yet the plot is elevated to an allegory concerning the essence of evil. In *Bleikeplassen* (1946; the bleaching place), realism and Symbolism are blended in a suggestive world, and the process of spiritual purification and salvation through death is analyzed. *Fuglane* (1957; *The Birds*, 1968) follows the same development: When Mattis discovers the love between his sister and another man, he knows he is standing in their way; his death upon the water is viewed as a sacrifice for his sister and her love. Vesaas's last novel, suggestively entitled *Båten om kvelden* (1968; *The Boat in the Evening*, 1971), gathers sixteen semiautobiographical sketches into a symbolic pattern that suggests the miraculous and enigmatically ominous elements in nature and human existence.

Aksel Sandemose (1899-1965), on the other hand, was fascinated by the struggle between the individual and the masses. Though he insisted that environment inevitably overcomes free will, he remained critical of dogmatic materialism. In Sandemose's novel *En sjømann går i land* (1931; a sailor goes to shore), Espen Arnakke escapes off Newfoundland from the ship on which he has fought to be accepted by his comrades. He murders a friend in a crime of passion; in the sequel, the episodic *En flyktning krysser sitt spor* (1933; *A Fugitive Crosses His Tracks*, 1936), set seventeen years later, Espen comes to understand that the murder was rooted in his childhood. The atmosphere of death dominates *Vi pynter oss med horn* (1936; *Horns for Our Adornment*, 1938), a novel in which Sandemose depicts the relationships among the crew members of a schooner bound for Newfoundland. *Det svundne er en drøm* (1946; the vanished is a dream) offers the journal entries of a Norwegian American's visit to his homeland, from 1938 to 1940, in order to reexperience the past. Another novel dealing with traumas rooted in the past is Sandemose's last significant work, *Varulven* (1958; *The Werewolf*, 1966), a sequel to which, *Felicias bryllup* (Felicia's wedding), appeared in 1961. The werewolf symbolizes the repression that precludes happiness; typically, Sandemose weds love to murder and lust to death in his attempt to track down the elusive, self-destructive, irrational mind.

Johan Borgen (1902-1979) was the most innovative stylist of the period. The question of identity is central to his work: Is it merely created by societal expectation and the private need for concealment? His major work, the trilogy *Lillelord* (1955-1957; little lord), describes a shattered, middle-class Oslo boy just before World War I, who grows into a lonely man, masking his destructive amorality with good upbringing. *Den røde tåken* (1967; *The Red Mist*, 1973) shapes Borgen's most characteristic themes into a single inner monologue. Through the entire volume, the reader follows one person's consciousness, behind whose search for harmony is concealed a lost self, who has committed a crime. In *Eksempler* (1974; examples), about a dissolving marriage, Borgen is skeptical about the possibilities for personal integrity, as a result of the inability of language to serve as a medium of communication.

World War I's impact was stronger in Danish literature than in that of the other Nordic countries. A new generation of lyricists emerged spontaneously, affirming life amid the threat of war. The two most prominent were Emil Bønnelycke (1893-1953) and Tom Kristensen (1893-1974). One year after his poetic debut, Kristensen published a novel, *Livets arabesk* (1921; arabesque of life), conveying a desperate view of life as absurd, rendered in a colorful, expressionistic style. Kristensen's major novel, *Hærværk* (1930; *Havoc*, 1968), can be read as an autobiography, a *roman à clef*, or a case study of psychological decline. The main motif is the paralyzing fear of the major character, Ole Jastrau, that he cannot realize himself. In his decline, Jastrau ironically experiences not only joy in his self-destruction but also a sense of infinity. Formally, *Havoc* is indebted to James Joyce's *Ulysses* (1922), and Jastrau's search for identity is reminiscent of the characters in Aldous Huxley's *Point Counter Point* (1928). As an unsentimental examination of the postwar character, however, *Havoc* stands forth as one of the most significant and independent expressions of the "lost generation" in world literature.

Next to Kristensen, Jacob Paludan (1896-1975) is most typical of his generation. Both writers occupied themselves with postwar crises, but whereas Kristensen felt the chaos within himself, Paludan critically observed and condemned it from a conservative standpoint. The interwar period's dehumanizing technological concentration is dramatized in the social novel *Fugle omkring fyret* (1925; *Birds Around the Fire*, 1928). The victim's revenge comes when the sea destroys the new harbor, which had been built as a financial speculation. This pessimism is somewhat alleviated in Paludan's major work and the most significant *Entwicklungsroman* in modern Danish literature, *Jørgen Stein* (1932-1933; English translation, 1966). Paludan demonstrates the changes that occur because of the outbreak of World War I—in the countryside, the provinces, and in Copenhagen—especially for the young generation. The main themes are cultural decline and the futile attempt to bring oneself into harmony with a fast-changing world, another significant expression in Danish literature of the mood of the lost generation.

Nis Petersen (1897-1943) most convincingly expresses the period's nihilism. In 1931, his major work *Sandalmagernes gade* (*The Street of the Sandalmakers*, 1933) broadly portrayed the uprootedness and uncertainty of Marcus Aurelius's Rome. Superficially a historical novel, the work actually suggests modern Copenhagen, and its author shows how it, like Rome, stands in a negative relationship to the Gospels' message of love. The thoroughly realized setting and society are rendered through the use of ironic anachronisms and a modern, subjective style.

Another significant prose work of the period is the collective novel *Fiskerne* (1928; *The Fishermen*, 1951), by Hans Kirk (1898-1962). In the naturalistic tradition of Pontoppidan and Nexø, it tells of a group of families who leave a barren coastal area for a milder environment. Though clearly separate from the inhabitants of the new region, their cohesiveness and their strong faith conquer the community's strong resistance from within. The basic viewpoint of the novel is sociological and Marxist, but this bias is somewhat offset by credible characterization.

Kirk influenced a number of collective novels by the Faroese writer William Heinesen (born 1900).

The first, *Blæsende gry* (1934; stormy daybreak), offers a cross section of a small island's struggle between old and new and the exploitation of the poor by the wealthy merchants and ship owners. *Noatun* (1938; *Niels Peter*, 1940) adds to these themes the individual's battle with harsh Faroese nature. In this novel, as well as in his masterpiece, *De fortabte spillemænd* (1950; *The Lost Musicians*, 1971), Heinesen's imagination is freed and combined—in the latter, with a grotesquely humorous portrayal of eccentric musicians and poets threatened by the material world. Comedy and tragedy are also ingeniously mixed in *Det gode Håb* (1964; the good hope), an epistolary novel set in the seventeenth century, while Heinesen's childhood provided the material for *Tårnet ved verdens ende* (1976; the tower at the end of the world). In about seventy brief chapters made up of a young boy's dreams and fantasies, the novel provides a vehicle for the aging author's magnificent farewell to life, its lyric, occasionally humorous, language masking a deep sadness and resignation.

Hans Christian Branner (1903-1966) was skeptical of his time's ideological and social systems. As an early influence of psychoanalysis on Branner diminished, that of existential philosophy—its concepts of angst, responsibility, and loneliness—increased. *Drømmen om en kvinde* (1941; dream about a woman) deals with human isolation, in particular with the two situations in life in which men and women stand completely alone, birth and death. Branner uses a complex inner monologue which gives way in *Rytteren* (1949; *The Riding Master*, 1951; also as *The Mistress*, 1953) to brief dialogues in a story about four people whose lives are dominated from beyond the grave by the riding master of the title. World War II darkened almost everything Branner wrote after 1939, but not until 1955 did he use the war itself as material. In the novel *Ingen kender natten* (1955; *No Man Knows the Night*, 1958), he portrays members of the Resistance as well as collaborators, though his main concern is with the personal dispossession of a man dominated by nihilism and Freudianism.

Martin Alfred Hansen (1909-1955), who began as a realistic social critic, became by the late 1940's a major advocate of religious and antinaturalistic trends. The picaresque novel *Jonatans rejse* (1941; *Jonatan's journey*) builds on the old fable of the blacksmith who lures the devil into a bottle and thus is able to acquire all the world's riches. In Jonatan and his analytical comrade, Askelad, the modern and the more harmonious medieval worldviews clash. Similarly, Hansen's next book, *Lykkelige Kristoffer* (1945; *Lucky Kristoffer*, 1974), combines picaresque form and historical material, with Miguel de Cervantes's *El ingenioso hidalgo don Quixote de la Mancha* (1605, 1615; *Don Quixote de la Mancha*, 1612-1620) as the model. The novel depicts the collapse of the Middle Ages itself and calls into question its universal figures, the knight and the priest. Hansen's last fictional work, the novel *Løgneren* (1950; *The Liar*, 1954), tells of a sexton and teacher, Johannes Vig, the liar of the title, who sketches his life in his diary for a confidant, Nathanael, whose name is meant to evoke that of the biblical prophet who was "without deceit." Johannes is a dilettante of faith who finally confronts and conquers evil; in the terms of Søren Kierkegaard, whose philosophy inspired the novel, Johannes advances from the ethical to the religious stage.

Prose literature in interwar Finland was dominated by several authors writing in Finnish, who, during the years of the 1918 civil War between the Right and the Left, rejected neo-Romanticism and addressed themselves to social themes—in contrast to the Finno-Swedish lyric poets' sophisticated modernism. Realistic prose flourished, sharply contrasting with earlier idealizations of Finnish folk life but offering no clear political program.

Thus Joel Lehtonen (1881-1934) expected no substantial political change to result from the social criticism of his novels and short stories. In his major work, *Putkinotko* (1919-1920), naturalistic characterization and dialogue are framed with impressionistic, colorful descriptions, alleviating the poverty and misery of the family described. More negative is Lehtonen's last novel, *Henkien taistelu* (1933; the struggle of the spirits), a series of loosely connected scenes from everyday life, framed by a philosophical discussion between God and Satan about good and evil in human beings.

The interwar author most connected with his native soil was Frans Eemil Sillanpää (1888-1964). The merger of the self and nature in his first novel, *Elämä ja aurinko* (1916; life and the sun), inspired by Hamsun, proved to be a successful novelty in Finnish literature. *Nuorena nukkunut* (1931; *The Maid Silja*, 1933; also as *Fallen Asleep While Young*, 1939), which brought Sillanpää international recognition, tells the story of the destruction of an old peasant family, interwoven with sensitive descriptions of the Finnish summer. The poverty and illness of the protagonists recedes before their inner strength as they face death—showing the spirit's victory over matter. The atmosphere of Sillanpää's first novel was resumed in his novels of the 1930's, *Miehen tie* (1932; the way of man) and *Ihmiset syviyössä* (1934; *People in the Summer Night*, 1966). The first is a love story, accompanied by seasonal changes; the second offers a cross section of human destinies during a few days and nights.

With the novel *Alastalon salissa* (1933; in the living room of Alastalo), Volter Kilpi (1874-1939) created the most interesting Finnish prose experiment of the period. On the surface, the novel is a didactic story in the manner of Kivi's *Seven Brothers*. The external action takes place in only six hours, but Kilpi adds a mystical dimension; the characters function not only in the present but also in the past and in the future. *Kirkolle* (1937; on the road to the church)—concerning the gathering of some churchgoers, their journey in a boat, and their arrival—takes place in only three hours. Again, thoughts and feelings are primary, and the narrative moves between past and present.

As the most original talent in Finnish prose, Kilpi's audience has been limited. More traditional is Mika Waltari (1908-1979). His best work was written in the 1930's: the trilogy comprising *Mies ja haave* (1933; a man and a dream), *Sielu ja liekki* (1934; the soul and the flame), and *Palava nuoruus* (1935; burning youth), published in one volume as *Isästä poikaan* (1942; from father to son), about a family that settles in Helsinki, and *Vieras mies tuli taloon* (1937; *A Stranger Came to the Farm*, 1952), a novel with a rural setting. In the postwar years up to 1964,

Waltari wrote six historical novels that made him the best-known Finnish author of all time. These works were translated into most major languages, and the first, *Sinuhe, egyptiläinen* (1945; *The Egyptian*, 1949), was filmed in Hollywood. Behind the historical façade, Waltari here analyzes the disillusionment after Finland's defeat by Russia in 1944.

Icelandic literature after 1920 moved toward greater realism and receptiveness to foreign influences. An intense cult of the self, the present, and sexuality emerged, together with a greater political consciousness. Gunnar Gunnarsson, Kristmann Guðmundsson, and Halldór Laxness brought prose to a high level of perfection during the late 1920's. Gunnar Gunnarsson (1889-1975), though he wrote in Danish during his residence in Denmark from 1897 to 1939, deals exclusively with Icelandic topics in his more than forty volumes. His first success, the tetralogy *Af Borgslægtens Historie* (1912-1914; partial translation *Guest the One-Eyed*, 1920), re-creates Iceland in a family saga whose protagonist is a legendary saint. Of the philosophical middle-class problem novels which Gunnarsson began during World War I, the most important is the contemporary story *Salige er de Enfoldige* (1920; *Seven Days' Darkness*, 1930), about the struggle between a humanitarian doctor and his cynical opponent, ending with the doctor's defeat and internment in an insane asylum.

Gunnarsson eventually found faith in humankind through recognition of the past. With *Jón Arason* (1930), the story of the last Catholic bishop in Iceland, Gunnarsson resumed work on a monumental cycle of twelve novels on Iceland's history, begun in 1918 with a description of the early saga period in *Edbrødre* (*The Sworn Brothers*, 1920). The masterpiece of the series is *Svartfugl* (1929; *The Black Cliffs*, 1967), a story of eighteenth century crime and punishment. As a whole, the series tells of the founding of a nation, its unification, then its decline and disintegration caused by egotism and aggression.

Kristmann Guðmundsson (1902-1983) became the most frequently translated Icelandic novelist—into thirty-six languages in all. His best works, such as *Den første vår* (1933; the first spring), describe youthful love, sometimes resulting in disillusionment, sometimes ending on an optimistic note. *Bru-dekjolen* (1927; *The Bridal Gown*, 1931) and *Livets morgen* (1929; *Morning of Life*, 1936) are well-constructed family chronicles. Guðmundsson also wrote historical works. *Gyðjan og uxinn* (1937; *Winged Citadel*, 1940), for example, is a romance set in Mycenaean Crete yet clearly alluding to World War II politics.

After writing his first work, a romantic story influenced by Hamsun, entitled *Barn náttúrrunnar* (1919; child of nature), Halldór Laxness (1902-1998) visited Denmark and Sweden and stayed in Germany and Austria between 1921 and 1922; in 1923, he converted to Catholicism. The autobiographical *Vefarinn mikli frá Kasmír* (1927; the great weaver from Kashmir) comes to terms with the conflicts of the postwar times from a Catholic viewpoint, making Laxness the Icelandic representative of the lost generation. During a stay in the United States from 1927 to 1929, Laxness turned to the socialistic views that would shape his work in the following decade. The first result was the two-volume novel comprising *Þu vínviður hreini* (1931; O thou pure vine) and *Fuglinn í fjörunni* (1932; the bird on the beach), published together in English as *Salka Valka: A Novel of Iceland* (1936). In a small fishing village, the first trade union is established, a strike breaks out, and the domination of the local capitalist merchant is threatened. *Sjálfstætt fólk* (1934-1935; *Independent People*, 1946) is the story of the impoverished farmer Bjartur at the threshold of modernity, a physical giant betrayed by his traditions and stubborn individualism. The protagonist of the four-volume *Heimsljós* (1937-1940; *World Light*, 1969), on the other hand, is a poet whose genius is cramped by his surroundings; the novel is an analysis of the artist's eternal problem, rendered as social criticism.

After World War II, Laxness's distinct individualism led him far from his socialist views. In *Brekkukotsannáll* (1957; *The Fish Can Sing*, 1966), the narrator recalls the life of his grandparents in Reykjavík, who honored simple, traditional values but also allowed themselves to be deceived by them. Similarly, the farmer in *Paradísarheimt* (1960; *Paradise Reclaimed*, 1962) leaves his homestead and family to travel to Utah, the promised land of the Mormons; realizing his mistake, he returns, only to find the ruins of his old farm. This revolt against ideology continues in Laxness's humorous fable *Kristnihald undir Jökli* (1968; *Christianity at Glacier*, 1972). Laxness never stagnated; he had the courage to give up accepted viewpoints, just as he continuously chose new artistic directions—he was also an excellent lyric poet and a productive dramatist.

POSTWAR DEVELOPMENTS

The turbulent years after the outbreak of World War II began with Finland's Winter War against Russia (1939-1940) and continued with German aid to Finland (1941-1944), the occupation of Denmark and Norway by German troops (1940-1945), the occupation of the Faeroe Islands and Iceland by the British (1940-1945), and Sweden's armed neutrality. Approaching the 1960's, Nordic literature became increasingly political. The modern welfare state and growing materialism were sharply attacked, as was the ivory-tower attitude, defended by some writers as the means of artistic survival. In addition, the 1960's led to a radical questioning of women's role in society. Consequently, a fierce debate arose about the artist's position and responsibility, as well as speculations on the relationship of language to reality.

The first of the Swedish prose writers of the 1940's, Lars Ahlin (born 1915) belonged to the generation of young people who suffered from the economic crisis of the 1930's; the resulting sense of disenfranchisement stayed with him. Ahlin's first book, *Tåbb med manifester* (1943; Tåbb with the manifesto), lays down his program: The young proletarian Tåbb is a "zero being" and seeks a worldview corresponding to his life. He finds communism existentially inadequate, but he is attracted to the Lutheran view that the human being is essentially a sinner, to be judged according to his or her deeds.

Next to Ahlin, Stig Dagerman (1923-1954) is the most significant prose writer of the postwar years in Sweden. For him, too, point zero was the necessary point of departure, but, unlike Ahlin's characters, Dagerman's never find a solution to contemporary anxiety. In his first novel, *Ormen* (1945; the serpent),

Dagerman symbolically writes of the terror that spreads among the soldiers in a barracks as they realize that an escaped snake is loose among them. The novel *De dömdas ö* (1946; island of the condemned) also deals with the stresses of the time in its picture of seven people who, shipwrecked on an uninhabited island, face an agonizing death.

The writing of the 1940's had been informed by a common, pessimistic worldview; this was not true in the 1950's. Certain common traits, however, can be noted—particularly an inclination toward aestheticism and optimism. Lars Gyllensten (born 1921) is an exception. His first two prose works, *Moderna myter* (1949; modern myths) and *Det blå skeppet* (1950; the blue ship), stand in a dialectical relationship to each other. The first is aphoristic and ironic. The second, a complex story of a youth growing up on a ship, employs rituals and myths in a romantic manner. Both modes—the intellectual/analytical and the romantic/naïve—are combined in Gyllensten's masterpiece, *Barnabok* (1952; children's book). This psychologically intense and verbally precise work follows the progressive ruination of a marriage and of a human being. Both *Sokrates död* (1960; the death of Socrates), questioning the value of the philosopher's death, and *Kains memoarer* (1963; *The Testament of Cain*, 1967), defending Cain in a number of aphorisms, suggest that truth is relative. A similar tack is taken in *Grottan i öknen* (1973; the cave in the desert), based on the Orpheus and Eurydice myth, and in *I skuggan av Don Juan* (1975; in the shadow of Don Juan).

Two authors of the 1950's, Sara Lidman (born 1923) and Per Wästberg (born 1933), treat the problems of the developing countries, a theme which several other authors were to treat during the next decade. Lidman's novels *Tjärdalen* (1953; the tar valley) and *Hjortronlandet* (1955; the land of cloud-berries) introduce modern Swedish neoprovincialism. Here one finds her recurrent outcast figure and the topics of guilt and responsibility, a moralistic approach that becomes even more pronounced in her two-volume novel *Regnspiran* (1958; *The Rain Bird*, 1962) and *Bära mistel* (1960; to carry mistletoe). In the 1960's, Lidman's stay in Africa resulted in the novels *Jag*

och min son (1961; I and my son) and *Med fem diamanter* (1964; with five diamonds), sharply attacking apartheid and neutrality. In 1968, she returned to a Swedish setting with *Gruva* (mine), a mixture of fiction and social reportage which strongly advocates a strike among the miners of northern Sweden.

Per Wästberg's early writings are deft but somewhat disinterested portrayals of a dreamy childhood world. In *Arvtagaren* (1958; the heir), Wästberg's hero leaves the Swedish idyll to learn about postwar Europe. In the trilogy comprising *Vattenslottet* (1968; the water castle), *Luftburen* (1969; *The Air Cage*, 1972), and *Jordmånen* (1972; *Love's Gravity*, 1977), the author returns to a Stockholm setting to synthesize his earlier explorations of freedom and to exemplify the shift from provincialism to internationalism.

Swedish fiction of the 1960's was strongly influenced by the New Novel, especially the work of Alain Robbe-Grillet. His disciple, Torsten Ekbom (born 1938), like Robbe-Grillet's Danish contemporary Svend Åge Madsen, insisted that an author should interest himself not in *what* his characters perceive but in *how* they perceive. Thus, *Signalspelet* (1965; the signal game) is a work composed from a popular boys' book, cut into pieces and reassembled, picturing the haphazardness of existence.

One implication of Ekbom's theories is the preoccupation with the relationship of the author to objective reality. This question culminated in the extensive use of a documentary and journalistic style. In *Ekspeditionen* (1962; *The Expedition*, 1962), Per Olof Sundman (born 1922) uses Sir Henry Morton Stanley's jungle expedition to investigate relationships among a group of people isolated by their surroundings. *Ingenjör Andrées luftfärd* (1967; *The Flight of the Eagle*, 1970) is an account of an actual balloon trip, in 1897, from Spitzbergen to the North Pole, which failed as a result of poor planning. The reader learns nothing of the physical and psychological burdens of the characters, and their fate is presented without melodrama. On the contrary, Sundman created a double documentary by publishing his preliminary research for the novel as *Ingen fruktan, intet hopp: Ett collage om Salomon August Andrée, hans medresenärer och hans polarexpedition* (1968: no fear, no hope: a collage on S. A. Andrée, his fellow travelers, and his polar expedition).

The question of subjectivity versus objectivity is also the topic of a novel by Per Olov Enquist (born 1934), *Färdvägen* (1963; the direction of travel), a picaresque journey through life's alternatives. Enquist gained international recognition with *Legionänerna* (1968; *The Legionnaires*, 1973). The point of departure of this documentary novel was the Swedish government's turning over to the Russians, in 1946, Baltic prisoners of war who had served in the German army—an action undertaken by the government against a storm of public protest. Enquist weaves his own personality into the presentation, and with constant revision and discussion, it becomes an example of how one's understanding of a political situation can be altered when one works one's way into it more deeply.

An alternative to the objectivity inspired by the New Novel is offered by Sven Delblanc (1931-1992) and Per Christian Jersild (born 1935), who tell fantastic stories, partly burlesque, partly serious. Delblanc's *Åsnabrygga* (1969; the donkey's bridge) is an extreme example of the Swedish semidocumentary novel. Whereas Sundman sets forth historical material about Andrée's balloon trip and Enquist and Lidman attempt to present actual circumstances objectively, Delblanc's book—his own diary—shows how subjectively he relates to traditional objectivity, implicating himself to such a degree that he crosses the line between fiction and autobiography, thus again questioning the role of the artist—a theme also discussed in his novel *Kastrater* (1975; *The Castrati*, 1979).

In the work of Jersild, there is a sharper satiric interest in society than one finds in the novels of Delblanc or Sundman. Jersild's major novel, *Grisjakten* (1968; the pig hunt), deals with the perfect civil servant, who loyally and unthinkingly follows orders. Jersild again warns against such manipulation in *Djurdoktorn* (1973; *The Animal Doctor*, 1975), a satiric novel envisioning a repressive system which absorbs its few revolts with appeals to solidarity and tolerance. The human compassion underlying this work

also permeates *Babels hus* (1978; the house of Babel), a penetrating satiric analysis of Swedish health policy.

Lars Gustafsson (born 1936) stands outside all the literary trends in contemporary Sweden. His works—which range across many genres, including fiction and nonfiction, poetry and prose—explore questions of human identity and the relations between the self and objects with acuity and nearly mystical imagination. His novel *Poeten Brumbergs sista dagar och död* (1959; the last days and death of the poet Brumberg) is a mosaic from the literary legacy of the title character, including quotations from his Renaissance novel and recollections from his friends. In the allegorical novel *Bröderna* (1960; the brothers), Gustafsson discusses how environment shapes personality and perception. Whereas Gustafsson's earlier works were marked by defeatism and bewilderment, his novel cycle "Sprickorna i muren" (the cracks in the wall) is more extroverted, more pragmatic, and more hopeful. It begins with *Herr Gustafsson själv* (1971; Mr. Gustafsson himself), a presentation of the narrator and his confrontation with political reality, and concludes with *En biodlares död* (1978; the death of a beekeeper), the tragic but heartwarming story of a man dying of cancer.

Swedish writers of the 1970's were increasingly skeptical about the value of fiction; they attempted to establish new connections with reality, often forsaking fiction to encourage solidarity and a growing political awareness of oppression outside and inside Sweden. A work by Jan Myrdal (born 1927), *Rapport från kinesisk by* (1963; *Report from a Chinese Village*, 1965), typical of this trend, is a detailed description of everyday life in China after the revolution; the results of the Cultural Revolution are analyzed in *Kina: Revolutionen går vidare* (1970; *China: The Revolution Continued*, 1970).

The form of the pseudodocumentary, employing the diary of a fictitious hero, was taken up by Per Gunnar Evander (born 1933). Many of his novels are reconstructions of actual events. *Sista dagen i Valle Hedmans liv* (1971; the last day in Valle Hedman's life) deals with the accidental death of the title character through evidence and police reports actually fabricated by the author, while *Judas Iskariots knutna händer* (1978; the fists of Judas Ischariot) matter-of-factly describes the last days of Jesus through the eyes of Judas.

The more experimental trend is represented by Lars Norén (born 1944), inspired by French surrealism. In 1970, he published the first part of a trilogy, *Biskötarna* (the beekeepers), followed in 1972 by *I den underjordiska himlen* (in the underworld heaven), an autobiographical, semidocumentary, dealing with human evil and cruelty, replete with symbolic structures interrupted by realistic dialogue.

After the first coming to terms with war and occupation, Norwegian literature suddenly shifted to lyric poetry after 1945. There were few dramas; prose, with the exception of Paal Brekke's novels, did not break with psychological realism until the 1960's, when it joined the currents of European modernism. Thematically, ethics dominated Norwegian postwar prose, which rejected the arbitrary divisions of the courageous and cowardly, the active and passive for the hard-won conviction that all are equally responsible for crime and war. Sigurd Hoel attempts in his novel *Meeting at the Milestone* to explain the Nazi motivation of the Norwegian traitors during the German Occupation. Younger authors also attacked this problem, such as Sigurd Evensmo (1912-1978) in his *Oppbrudd etter midnatt* (1946; departure after midnight), the somewhat glossy tale of a Fascist farmer whose patriotic feelings bring him into conflict with the Germans. This novel is surpassed by Evensmo's best book, *Englandsfarere* (1945; *Boat for England*, 1947), which deals with the capture and execution of a group of Resistance fighters.

A strong ethical commitment characterizes the prose of poet and playwright Jens Bjørneboe (1920-1976). His first novel, *Før hanen galer* (1952; before the cock crows), depicts the medical experiments in the German concentration camps. Bjørneboe, however, does not seek the specific causes of Nazism but investigates evil as a schism between feeling and intellect. Human cruelty is likewise analyzed in his trilogy comprising *Frihetens øyeblikk* (1966; *Moment of Freedom*, 1975), *Kruttårnet* (1969; the gunpowder tower), and *Stillheten* (1973; the silence), one of the most significant works of postwar Norwegian prose, a running chronicle of violence and torture.

In 1951, in his wordy Joycean novel *Aldrende Orfeus* (aging Orpheus), Paal Brekke (born 1923) analyzed the generation gap before and after the war, strongly attacking conventional mores. *Og hekken vokste kjempehøy* (1953; and the hedge grew enormous) is clearer. Here the theme of human isolation is interwoven with an exciting murder plot, revealing that all the characters in the book could be guilty of the crime.

A more traditional approach is taken by Terje Stigen (born 1922), whose lyric novels are strongly influenced by Hamsun. Like Hamsun's *Hunger*, Stigen's *Nøkkel til ukjent rom* (1953; key to the unknown room) tells of a hypersensitive man who fluctuates between an ironic view of his misfortune and anarchy. In his succeeding novels, Stigen employed a more epic treatment of extroverted men of action. With *Det flyktige hjerte* (1967; the fickle heart), perhaps Stigen's best work, he turned to the period around 1800. The main character is a student of theology who becomes a pastor north of the Arctic Circle. His travel experiences are linked to the idea of love as erotic perversion, as he exploits love for his own artistic development and falsifies the life of feeling.

Stigen's realism contrasts sharply with the symbolic prose of Finn Carling (born 1925), especially in Carling's novels, such as *Arenaen* (1951; the arena) and *Piken og fuglen* (1952; the girl and the bird). All treat the same theme despairingly: The artist betrays life by removing himself from it. The documentary technique is used in *Resten er taushet* (1973; the rest is silence), about death and humanity's relationship to it. *Fiendene* (1974; the enemies) contains prose sketches and poems about violence, fear, and isolation, posted against a glimmer of hope.

Foremost among contemporary Norwegian prose authors stands Finn Alnæs (born 1932). Including the entire cosmos in his thinking, he shows human insignificance in a demoralized and inhilistic world. His novel *Gemini* (1968) is a polemical argument against the times, treating the ethical and aesthetic position of the artist in a modern welfare society from the vantage of a conservative worldview. This individualism also permeates *Musica* (1978), the first part of a cycle in eight volumes entitled *Ildfesten* (the fire feast), a family chronicle of disintegration and adherence to tradition.

Many of the most interesting writers of contemporary Norwegian literature contributed to *Profil* (established in 1943), originally a philological journal, which became an organ of Marxist theory in the early 1970's. Tor Obrestad (born 1938), the oldest of the *Profil* rebels, was for a long time regarded as this group's central force. Marxism is conspicuous in his most important work, the novel *Sauda! Streik!* (1972; Sauda! Strike!), a semidocumentary based on an illegal strike at an ironworks.

The most controversial revolutionary Norwegian author is Dag Solstad (born 1943). The title character in his *Arild Asnes 1970* (1971) seeks to escape from his limited milieu and finally finds an answer in Marxist-Leninist ideology. Solstad's *25. september-plassen* (1974; the twenty-fifth of September square) chronicles the working class of postwar Norway. Less convincing are the first two parts of a projected trilogy: *Svik: Førkrigsår* (1977; betrayal: prewar years) and *Krig: 1940* (1978; war: 1940), social, realistic works marked by superficial characterization.

Several others of the *Profil* group turned from the individualistic to the social but refused to enter the political arena. Einar Økland (born 1940) combines prose, poetry, and drama in *Gull-alder* (1972; golden age), in which he makes startling associative leaps to reflect on his childhood and his role as a writer. In *Anne* (1968), by Paal-Helge Haugen (born 1945), the documentary approach is sustained for the first time in Norwegian literature. The story of a girl who dies of tuberculosis at an early age is commented on with excerpts from medical books, a reader, and the Bible, interspersed with lyric fragments. Haugen's anti-ideological viewpoint is shared by Kjartan Fløgstad (born 1944), whose novel *Rasmus* (1974) matter-of-factly levels strong attacks at fashionable trends. The picaresque *Dalen Portland* (1977; the valley Portland) mirrors contemporary Norwegian society, portrayed in both comic and tragic, fantastic and realistic ways, a technique characteristic of the general antidogmatic trend in contemporary Norwegian literature.

Among the contemporary Norwegian novelists not associated with the *Profil* group, one of the most significant is the prolific Tor Edvin Dahl (born 1943), who is known for short stories, detective novels (under the pseudonym David Torjussen), cultural criticism, studies of true crime, and a variety of other works in addition to mainstream novels. Reared in a family that was active in Norway's Pentecostal Church, Dahl explores issues of sin and guilt, responsibility, and spiritual striving. His first novel, *Den andre* (1972; the other), indicts materialistic modern society for the amorality that permits a student to remorselessly murder a friend. The trilogy comprising *Den første sommeren* (1980; the first summer), *Renate* (1981), and *Abrahams barn* (1982; Abraham's children) reveals the pervasiveness of evil, both individual and social, with little explicit hope for redemption.

Most prose writers in Danish literature after World War II followed the traditions of the 1930's, whereas the poets were more innovative. Many of them contributed to the journal *Heretica* (1948-1953)—"heretical" in relation to the dominant rationalism and materialism. The common ground was a recognition of the "cultural crisis," analyzed by Ole Sarvig (born 1921), his generation's leading poet and the major representative of a modern metaphysical trend. His first novel, *Stenrosen* (1955; the rose of stone), is set in postwar Berlin, a city that was destroyed because it was a manifestation of demoniac modernism. In *Limbo* (1963), lyricism predominates at the expense of more traditional structure in its description of a woman's waiting and her dead husband's continued life in her soul. Sarvig's most significant novel is *De rejsende* (1978; the travelers). On one level, it tells the story of a middle-aged Danish American and his attempt to settle accounts with his childhood myths; on a more philosophical level, it deals with finding oneself in today's world.

Typical of several prose writers of the 1950's is the atmosphere of myth and fairy tale; also characteristic is a renewed interest in the work of Isak Dinesen (pseudonym of Karen Blixen, 1885-1962), particularly noticeable in the novels of Willy-August Linnemann (born 1914). Along with fantasy, Danish prose of the 1950's evinces experimentation in the short stories of Villy Sørensen (born 1929) and Peter Seeberg (born 1925), the latter also a noted novelist. His first novel, *Bipersonerne* (1956; secondary characters), breaks consistently with realism. It portrays the shadowy existence of foreign laborers in a German film studio during World War II. In *Fugls føde* (1957; bird pickings), Seeberg deals with deliberate escapism. Tom, a writer, is a dreamer whose plans miscarry; at the same time, he is sharply aware of human follies and ruthlessly exploits them. *Hyrder* (1970; shepherds) is an apparently realistic story that suggests that people must be one another's shepherds in order to survive catastrophe. Such confidence is less apparent in Seeberg's last novel, *Ved havet* (1978; at the sea), but in his entire authorship it places him among the great humanists of recent Nordic literature.

Less exclusive is Leif Panduro (1923-1977), whose work primarily revolves around a person divided by his or her ties to the past. In this theme, Panduro, like many other Danish writers, was influenced by Villy Sørensen's treatment of humankind's psychological and social inadequacies. *Rend mig i traditionerne* (1958; *Kick Me in the Traditions*, 1961) is based on Panduro's favorite subject: the trials of puberty, when one capitulates to the seemingly ordered and normal adult world. Both the action-filled *Daniels anden verden* (1970; the other world of Daniel) and Panduro's last novel, *Høfeber* (1975; hay fever), are variations on the normal/abnormal theme as well as fascinating psychological analyses of love and responsibility.

The political climate of the years immediately after the war had favored a quest for the cosmic or metaphysical. In the mid-1950's, however, a gradual shift to a lyric rendering of social reality was perceptible. This lyric blossoming was largely attributable to Klaus Rifbjerg (born 1931), who, in addition to poetry, wrote film scripts, plays, and numerous short stories and novels. Like Panduro's *Kick Me in the Traditions*, Rifbjerg's first novel, *Den kroniske uskyld* (1958; chronic innocence), portrays the mystery of unprotected and vulnerable puberty. The problems of insecure youth are also explored in the novels *Arkivet* (1967; archives) and *Lonni og Karl* (1968; Lonni and

Karl). In a series of novels, Rifbjerg also treats the psychology of the adult world. *Operaelskeren* (1966; *The Opera Lover*, 1970) portrays the love of a mathematician for an opera singer, which eventually ends in catastrophe as the cool rationalist discovers that his well-ordered world is undercut by irrational powers. The full consequences of such a situation are experienced by the principal character of *Anna(jeg)Anna* (1969; *Anna(I)Anna*, 1982), a diplomat's neurotic wife who escapes from her luxurious life to travel with a young criminal hippie across Europe. In the complex *R.R.* (1972), Rifbjerg again criticizes the crippling effects of rationalism to which the main character, a Faust-like figure, has sold his soul. The broad chronicle *De beskedne* (1976; the modest ones), on the other hand, which tells of Danish everyday life during the 1950's and 1960's, is more accessible. Along with the subsequent novels *Tango* (1978) and *Joker* (1979), *De beskedne* confirms Rifbjerg's position as an exceptionally sensitive writer.

Around 1960, Danish prose modernism became the focus of topical debate. Authors now turned from the experiences of the war, and the novel form was transformed under the influence of the New Novel, subordinating traditional plot and sharply distinguishing a novel's narrator from its characters.

Clearly influenced by the New Novel is one by Svend Åge Madsen (born 1939), *Besøget* (1963; the visit), which contrasts different narrative perspectives. In *Otte gange orphan* (1965; eight times orphan), seven independent stories are told in the first person in a monotonous and image-free language, suggesting that literature does not describe but rather creates reality according to the author's notions of it. In *Dage med Diam* (1972; days with Diam), readers must combine characters and events to create not the story they want to read but the reality they want to experience. A renewal in Madsen's writing is evident in the pseudodocumentary novel *Tugt og utugt i mellemtiden* (1976; decency and indecency in the meanwhile), a political and social analysis of Denmark in the 1970's.

Myth predominates in the writings of Ulla Ryum (born 1937); her attempt to create an ambiguous and associative dream-language is reminiscent of the work of the American writer Djuna Barnes. Ryum's main interest revolves around those tragic figures who find meaning only in death. Such a person is the protagonist of *Natsangersken* (1963; the night singer), a psychological and symbolic portrait of a woman abandoned by life and love.

The neorealistic trend that emerged in the mid-1960's had a forerunner in Thorkild Hansen (born 1927), who achieved great success with *Det lykkelige Arabien* (1962; *Arabia Felix*, 1964), based on two archaeological expeditions to Kuwait and the Nubian desert and focusing on scientists torn from their cultural milieu. *Jens Munk* (1965; *The Way to Hudson Bay*, 1970) deals with a sailor's bold but unsuccessful attempt to find the Northwest Passage to India and China. The theme of Hansen's "Slave Trilogy" (comprising *Slavernes Kyst*, 1967; *Slavernes skibe*, 1968; and *Slavernes øer*, 1970) is the slave trade practiced by the Danes between the Gold Coast of Africa and the West Indies. Hansen, however, oversteps the bounds of objective reporting through his subjective style, the use of inner monologue and literary leitmotifs, turning the trilogy into a masterful literary achievement.

The most popular of the neorealists is Anders Bodelsen (born 1937). His novels of 1968, *Hændeligt uheld* (*Hit and Run, Run, Run*, 1970) and *Tænk på et tal* (*Think of a Number*, 1969), cleverly combine the realistic novel with the thriller. *Frysepunktet* (1969; *Freezing Point*, 1971) approaches science fiction. In Bodelsen's writing—as in most of the realistic Danish authors—the close of the 1960's brought increased interest in the social mechanisms of the modern welfare state. *Bevisets stilling* (1973; *Consider the Verdict*, 1976), based on a much-debated contemporary criminal case, describes a taxi driver falsely accused of murder, concluding in a violent accusation of judicial inhumanity. Things as they are, however, predominate in *De gode tider* (1977; the good times) and its sequel *År for år* (1979; year by year), which deal with the economic boom of the 1960's and the growing political awareness of the period.

Christian Kampmann (born 1939) is also critical of middle-class mores, but his analyses have a wider psychological perspective. Thus, in *Nærved og næsten* (1969; near and nearly), social problems give

way to existential ones in the picture of six married couples' attitudes toward love, isolation, and death. Kampmann's most significant achievement is the cycle, begun in 1973 with *Visse hensyn* (certain considerations), about the Copenhagen bourgeoisie after World War II, which reflects the Cold War of the 1950's, the prosperity that followed, and finally the economic crisis of the 1970's.

The dogmatic demand of the 1960's for social and political commitment in Denmark is also evident in so-called reportorial writing, especially feminist novels. Documentary literature is represented in a number of studies of the work environment done by collectives, students, and the workers themselves; it has also influenced fictional writing, as in the novels of Jette Drewsen (born 1943) and Jytte Borberg (born 1917). A more traditional neorealism, however, is practiced with great talent by Ole Hyltoft (born 1940) and Henrik Stangerup (born 1937).

In the work of Ebbe Kløvedal Reich (born 1940), Thorkild Hansen's historical documentary is combined with undogmatic political awareness. In 1977, Reich published his story of the Cimbrian march against Rome (c. 100 B.C.E.), *Fæ og frænde* (cattle and kinsman). Clearly referring to the European Economic Community, Reich has Rome represent everything evil: economic, political, and cultural imperialism.

Often the demand for a new society is expressed as a romantic, revolutionary dream. This dream is realized in *Smukke tabere* (1970), by Vagn Lundbye (born 1933); the title is a direct translation of Leonard Cohen's *Beautiful Losers* (1970). The narrator's diary records the feelings of a religious relationship with a partisan group on its way to blow up a nuclear reactor. In the novels *Tilbage til Anholt* (1978; back to Anholt) and *Hvalfisken* (1980; the whale), Lundbye calls for a return to "the original condition—a life-style between light and darkness, cold and warmth, closeness and cosmos."

During World War II, almost all literary activity ceased in Finland. Finnish literature of the 1950's was self-critical, nationalism gave way to disillusionment, and, on the whole, authors shunned any participation in the debates on current political and social issues.

Paavo Haavikko (born 1931), Finland's great modernistic poet, also wrote a number of plays and novels. Whereas Haavikko's plays are nearly absurdist, his prose treats social and political events pessimistically as the meaningless actions of insignificant individuals. Hence, the protagonist of *Yksityisiä asioita* (1960; private matters) experiences the political events of 1918 only as an occasion for profitable business deals. Likewise pessimistic is the novel *Tohtori Finckelman* (1952; Doctor Finckelman), by Jorma Korpela (1910-1964), which represents one of the earliest postwar breaks with traditional Finnish prose style.

The remaining prose of the 1950's is primarily distinguished by its factual style. War is generally seen as a personal, relativistic experience. Even when the narration is realistic, as in the popular war novel by Väinö Linna (1920-1992), *Tuntematon sotilas* (1954; *The Unknown Soldier*, 1957), such relativity is present. Linna's description of the destiny of a single platoon's actions at the front is free of nationalistic myth-making and permeated with a redeeming sense of humor. Realism and humor are also foremost elements in the trilogy *Täälä pohjantähden alla* (1959-1962; here under the polar star), which tells of the civil war of 1918 from the perspective of the vanquished, confirming Linna's position as a great epic narrator in the tradition of Kivi and Sillanpää.

Whereas Linna represents a more traditional trend within modern Finnish prose, Veijo Meri (born 1928), more experimental, follows in the steps of Korpela. Meri's basic themes are also the war; he often contrasts war's irrationality with the soldiers' discipline in a way that exposes the absurdity of the military events themselves. This is demonstrated in *Manillaköysi* (1957; *The Manila Rope*, 1967). The hero, Joose, smuggles home a piece of rope on his leave, thus risking his life without understanding his motives. A deserter is the main character in *Sujut* (1961; quits), about the Russian military breakthrough in 1944, but Meri's soldiers lack the inner stability that makes Linna's soldiers act correctly.

Meri pursues objective reporting. The most typical representative of such a purely factual approach, however, is Antti Hyry (born 1931), whose work forms a Finnish parallel to the French *nouveau roman*. Thus, *Maailman laita* (1967; the edge of the world) simply describes a fishing trip in which a boat drifts away but is recovered the next day. Hyry's religious view of life is expressed in the novel *Kevättä ja syksyä* (1958; spring and fall) through the character Niilo, who experiences childhood as a paradise, a spontaneous realization of God and the world, which is lost in the materialistic world of adults.

Standing outside all literary groups is Paavo Rintala (born 1929), whose novels blend all the trends of the 1950's in their treatment of religious and ethical issues. Rintala shares with Hyry the northern Finnish milieu and the view that urban life is spiritually alienating. In his trilogy *Mummoni ja Mannerheim* (1960-1962; Grandmother and Mannerheim), Hyry attempts to dismiss the myths about Finland's national heroes during the civil war and World War II. Even more controversial is *Sissiluutnatti* (1963; *The Long Distance Patrol*, 1967), an unvarnished picture of the horrors of war. During the 1960's, Rintala assembled a documentary on the siege of Leningrad, followed by other accounts of major twentieth century crises, including the first Nordic novel to deal exclusively with the Vietnam War, *Vietnamin kurjet* (1971; the cranes from Vietnam). This documentary trend, of which Rintala is the most talented Finnish representative, continues in *Nahkapeitturien linjalla* (1976; the tanner's line), which reevaluates the events at the Finnish-Russian front during World War II.

The wave of report and debate literature reached its crest around 1970, most convincingly represented by an accusatory report on the textile industry by Marja-Leena Mikkola (born 1939), *Raskas puuvilla* (1971; heavy cotton). Less radical than Mikkola, who is also one of the few Finnish contributors to Nordic feminist literature, is Samuli Paronen (1917-1974), whose novels depict social needs rendered in traditional prose. The foremost representative of this style is Hannu Salama (born 1936), whose novel *Juhannustanssit* (1964; the midsummer night dance) aroused strong public debate with its alleged blasphemy. Less controversial and characterized by a more objective approach is the first volume of a planned series about contemporary Finland, *Kosti Herhiläisen perunkirjoitus* (1976; Kosti Herhiläisen's inventory). With pessimism Salama portrays a man who searches his past for something with which to face a present that is threatened by decay and catastrophe.

In the 1970's, the provincial narrative returned in a rediscovery of long-forgotten cultural traditions. The novels of Eeva Kilpi (born 1928), such as *Häätanhu* (1973; summer dance), reflecting a Rousseau-inspired dream, depict the village as a place of security and redemption, whereas the city, with its impersonal efficiency, is strongly attacked—as, for example, in a novel by Eina Säisä (1935-1988), *Kukkivat roudan maat* (1971; the lands of flowering frost).

The major representative of modern Finnish and Swedish prose is Tito Colliander (1904-1989). The strong influence of Dostoevski is especially noticeable in *Förbarma dig* (1939; have mercy), a study of the psychology of suffering, guilt, and atonement. A longing for salvation recurs in *Bliv till* (1945; come into being) and likewise in a work by Göran Stenius (born 1909), *Klockorna i Rom* (1955; *The Bells of Rome*, 1961), which relates the author's conversion to Catholicism. It is acknowledged as the best religious novel in Finland after World War II.

Political commitment, on the other hand, characterizes the novels of Christer Kihlman (born 1930), among them *Se upp salige!* (1960; pay heed, O blest!), which satirizes a small town and its self-centered Finno-Swedish bourgeoisie, and *Den blå modern* (1963; the blue mother), which follows two brothers through childhood, revealing what is hidden beneath their superficial respectability. A true masterpiece is *Dyre prins* (1975; *Sweet Prince*, 1983), both a humorous satire on the Finnish nouveau riche after the war and a penetrating Dostoevskian psychological study. The same intensity and commitment to his subjects characterizes Anders Cleve (born 1937); however, in his novels such as *Vit eld* (1962; white fire), he employs a much more diffuse and occasionally fragmentary language to express the chaos from which the narrator tries to escape.

The two most significant Finno-Swedish prose writers of the 1970's were the married couple Märta and Henrik Tikkanen. Märta Tikkanen (born 1935) speaks for the oppressed, focusing on the situation of modern woman, as in *Män kan inte våltas* (1975; men cannot be raped). Henrik Tikkanen (born 1924) achieved his literary breakthrough in 1975 when he published the first part of his confessions, *Brändövägen 8 Brändö. Tel. 35* (*A Winter's Day*, 1980), followed by *Bävervägen 11 Hertonäs* (1976) and *Mariegatan 26 Kronohagen* (1977)—the titles refer to three important addresses in his life. Rather than exposing the corruption of Tikkanen's environment and within his own family in particular, the three volumes primarily attack hypocrisy and taboos in the Finno-Swedish upper class in general.

After World War II, Icelandic writers became less insular. Numerous translations were published, especially of English and American writers, including Aldous Huxley, D. H. Lawrence, Ernest Hemingway, John Steinbeck, and Sinclair Lewis. Halldór Laxness's development was typical of the postwar period. After writing a dramatic account of Iceland's materialistic decadence, he turned to historical novels and increasingly occupied himself with questions of literary form. In spite of the political optimism of 1944, when the final dissolution of the union with Denmark was proclaimed, a pessimistic, almost nihilistic note was sounded among the younger writers—inspired by the Swedish modernistic poetry of the 1940's.

A return to preindustrial Icelandic tradition and history as a remedy for existential anguish is evident in poetry as well as in prose, dominated into the 1960's by an epic, realistic narration. Thus, the setting of the novel *A bökkum Bolafljots* (1940; on the banks of the Bola River), by Guðmundur Daníelsson (born 1910), is his native southern lowlands, but the time is the past. Ólafur Jóhann Sigurðsson (born 1913) is a more sophisticated stylist, employing a richly nuanced, lyric language. His most convincing novel, *Fjallið og draumurinn* (1944; the mountain and the dream), is set in the provinces and contains overtones of social criticism. After many years of near silence, Sigurðsson published the novel *Hreiðrið* (1972; the bird's nest), a bitter critique of modern welfare society.

Sigurðsson's distaste for the contemporary scene is also characteristic of the work of Indriði G. Þorsteinsson (born 1926), whose books focus on those who have moved to the city from the country, the only source of permanent value, and who no longer belong anywhere. This motif recurs in the novels *Land og synir* (1963; land and sons) and *Norðan við strið* (1971; north of the war), dealing with the Allied occupation of Iceland during World War II and its negative consequences for the old peasant society.

The most significant stylistic renewal of Icelandic prose occurred in the work of Thor Vilhjálmsson (born 1925), who was influenced by Kafka and—following a stay in postwar Paris—by existentialism. In Vilhjálmsson's first novel, *Fljótt, fljótt sagð i fuglinn* (1968; fast, fast said the bird), which deals with death and erotic love, the dimensions of personality, time, and space are absent. In *Fuglaskottís* (1975; bird dance), the action unfolds during a twenty-four-hour stay in Rome and depicts two Icelanders' search for two missing girls, which at the same time is a search for their own identity in an absurd world. A similar search is the main theme of *Mánasigð* (1976; crescent moon), executed with such artistic sophistication that Vilhjálmsson stands out as his generation's most distinguished prose writer.

In the late 1960's, there was a considerable upsurge of leftist literature, turning in particular against foreign political and economic influences. Thus, for example, *Astir samlyndra hjóna* (1967; the love of a harmoniously married couple), by Guðbergur Bergsson (born 1932), depicts the threatening conformity of modern Iceland and attacks the United States and its relation to Icelanders. Reality merges with absurdity and takes on mythic dimensions in the two-volume novel *Það sefur í djúpinu* (1973; it sleeps in the depths) and its sequel *Það rís úr djúpinu* (1976; it rises from the depths). In surpassing reality to disclose the extreme, grotesque, and negative in everyday life, Bergsson became the leading experimenter in Icelandic prose. The diversity of his work is an excellent example of the universal perspective that characterizes the principal writers of the five Nordic countries.

THE MODERN WELFARE STATE

The 1980's brought a reevaluation of Scandinavia's political and literary position. The radical politicizing of large segments of the population, increasing interdependence on the global market, financial burden of government services, and ever-growing immigrant populations all served to fragment what had been a homogeneous society. In Sweden, government support of literature aimed to preserve a diversity of national literatures while taking a negligible role in the quality of literature. Political novels remained popular, including those by Per Wästberg, who wrote extensively about Swedish colonialism in Africa. Stockholm was the setting for *Vindens låga* (1993; the flame of the wind) in which he explored dark, love relationships. Documentary novelist Per Olov Enquist turned to psychological themes in *Nedstortad ängel* (1985; *Downfall: A Love Story*, 1986), an intense tale of altruistic love, and *Kapten Nemos bibliotek* (1991; *Captain Nemo's Library*, 1992), which explores how the power of imagination can shape reality. Per Gunnar Evander examined the psychological theory that life achieves meaning only through relationships in such novels as *Mörkrets leende* (1987; smile of darkness).

Sven Delblanc's family saga explored the recent past in *Samuels bok* (1981; Samuel's book), *Samuels döttrar* (1982; Samuel's daughter), *Kanaans land* (1984; the land of Canaan), and *Maria ensam* (1985; Maria alone). Delblanc's recurring theme of the overbearing father is personalized in his terrifying autobiographical novels *Livets ax* (1991; gleanings from life) and *Agnar* (1992; chaff). Kerstin Ekman (born 1933) brought a balancing feminist perspective to the historical novel in *Rövarna i Skuleskogen* (1988; *The Forest of Hours*, 1998). In the acclaimed *Händelser vid vatten* (1993; *Blackwater*, 1995), Ekman combined aspects of the detective story with a rich portrayal of northern Sweden. Göran Tunström (born 1937) placed his novels in the province of Värmland, including *Juloratoriet* (1983; *The Christmas Oratorio*, 1995), which resembles a musical composition, and *Tjuven* (1986; the thief), which explores betrayal and the human cost of artistic endeavor.

The biting social satire of Per Christian Jersild

used science and technology to manipulate individuals in *En levande själ* (1980; *A Living Soul*, 1988) and speculated on the nature of being human in *Efter floden* (1982; *After the Flood*, 1986). He returned to bureaucratic satire with *En lysande marknad* (1992; a wide-open market). The writings of Stig Claesson (born 1928) concern people whom the welfare state has forgotten in *Min vän Charlie* (1973; my friend, Charlie) and *Utsikt från ett staffli* (1983; view from an easel). The most important of the social satirists is Lars Gustafsson, whose reputation was well established by the 1980's. His masterpiece of international intrigue *Bernard Foys tredje rockad* (1986; *Bernard Foy's third castling*, 1988) demonstrates that nothing is as it seems. Gustafsson examined personal isolation in the workers' novel *En kakelsättares eftermiddag* (1991; *A Tiler's Afternoon*, 1993) and a Texan bankruptcy judge in *Historien med hunden* (1993; *The Tale of a Dog: From the Diaries and Letters of a Texan Bankruptcy Judge*, 1998).

Bunny Ragnerstam (born 1944) wrote about the Swedish labor movement in *Uppkomlingen* (1980; the upstart) and *Ett prima liv* (1983; a first-rate life), known collectively as *En svensk tagedi* (a Swedish tragedy). Reidar Jönsson (born 1944) achieved international recognition when his autobiographical novel *Mitt liv som hund* (1983; *My Life as a Dog*, 1989) was made into an award-winning film in 1987.

Literary feminism gained prominence through the novels of such writers as Inger Alfvén (born 1940), who wrote about female discontent. In *Ur kackerlackors levnad* (1984; from the lives of cockroaches) and *Lyckans galosch* (1986; lucky dog) she examines relationships involving more than two people, and in *Judiths teater* (1989; Judith's theater) she explores the relationship between a mother and a daughter who love the same man. The poet Sun Axelsson (born 1935) interprets her own life from a feminist perspective in the trilogy *Drommen om ett liv* (1978; *A Dreamed Life*, 1983), *Honungsvargar* (1984; honey wolves), and *Nattens årstid* (1989; night's season). The work of Heidi von Born (born 1936) concerns material deprivation in *Månens vita blod* (1988; white blood of the moon) and the devastating effect of childhood neglect in *Tiden år en tjuv* (1989; time is a thief).

As the Cold War drew to a close and the economic problems facing the modern welfare state developed, Norwegian literature increasingly reflected an ironic postmodernism that examined the contradictory paradoxes of existence. Two writers emerged during the 1980's as prototypic Norwegian postmodernists: Kjartan Fløgstad (born 1944) and Jan Kjærstad (born 1953), both of whom wrote in Nynorsk (new Norwegian). Fløgstad began the new decade with *Fyr og flamme* (1980; fire and flame), an amalgam of different styles that both tells a story and comments upon its themes. In *U3* (1983), Fløgstad fabricates devices as part of the narrative in order to interpret information that otherwise would not be available to his characters. Using the "retrospectroscope," the protagonist, Alf Hellot, interprets how the downing of the American U2 spy plane affects Norwegian defense policy. Fløgstad's controversial *Det 7. klima: Salim Mahmood i Media Thule* (1986; the seventh climate) is a social commentary on the effect of thousands of immigrants on Norwegian culture and intellectual life. *Det 7. klima* was written in a perplexing style that purposefully obscured its meaning and caused such extensive reader frustration that Fløgstad published a debate about the novel, entitled *Tyrannosaurus text* (1988).

Kjærstad achieved prominence as editor of the literary journal *Vinduet* (the window). He conducts a search for love amongst the remnants of a Norwegian society grounded on writing in *Det store eventyret* (1987; the great adventure). Taken with *Det 7. klima*, Fløgstad and Kjærstad defend a traditional Norwegian culture being replaced by the transitory images of the popular media.

Modern feminism is advocated in the novels of Cecilie Løveid (born 1951) and Karin Moe (born 1945), both of whom utilize language in an expressionistic manner. Løveid combines poetry and prose to examine nurturing in *Sug* (1979; *Sea Swell*, 1986), while Moe mirthfully plays on the fact that the title can mean either "mother-daughter" or "murder again," depending upon how the word is divided in *Mordatter* (1985). Popular poet-novelist Eva Jensen (born 1955) speculates that life can best be interpreted through language in *Teori nok for eit kort liv:*

Roman-roman (1987; theory enough for a short life: novel-novel).

Although generally considered to be of minimal quality, postmodernist thinking in Danish literature challenged social humanism during the 1980's, examining the relationship between the individual's life and society. Martha Christensen (1926-1995) can be singled out as the most popular of these writers, particularly for *Dansen med Regitze* (1987; dancing with Regitze), with its message of petty-bourgeois humanness. Dagny Joensen (born 1944) emerged as the preeminent feminist writer by depicting the destructive nature of marriage for three women, *Gerandislangnur* (1981; everyday fates).

Just as Danish literature seemed to be sinking into a quagmire of mediocrity, Peter Høeg (born 1957) published his first novel, *Forestilling om det tyvende århundrede* (1988; *The History of Danish Dreams*, 1995), a saga covering 450 years of history interpreted through the eyes of everyday people. Høeg's second novel, *Frøken Smillas fornemmelse for sne* (1992; *Smilla's Sense of Snow*, 1993), tells a tale of international intrigue, whose protagonist is a remarkable half-Dane, half-Greenland Inuit glaciologist. Smilla's innate knowledge of snow allows her to recognize that a child's death was not accidental, but murder. The novel has been translated into more than a dozen languages, and it established Høeg as the first internationally renowned Danish writer after Isak Dinesen. *Da måske egnede* (1993; *Borderliners*, 1994) is the harrowing tale of three orphaned youths at the center of a social experiment that shows the real consequences of a so-called enlightened social policy. *Kvinden og aben* (1996; *The Woman and the Ape*, 1996), an experiment in evolutionary theory, continues Høeg's investigation of Danish social issues in a manner that appeals to an international audience. Høeg single-handedly raised standards for Danish and Scandinavian literature with his artistic freshness, love of language, depth of learning, characterization, and intensity of storytelling.

Sven H. Rossel, updated by Gerald S. Argetsinger

BIBLIOGRAPHY

Bredsdorff, Elias, Brita Mortensen, and Ronald Popperwell. *An Introduction to Scandinavian Literature from the Earliest Time to Our Day.* Cambridge, Mass.: Harvard University Press, 1951. An excellent single-volume history beginning with Old Norse and extending through the early postwar period.

Einarsson, Stefan. *A History of Icelandic Literature.* New York: John Hopkins Press for the American-Scandinavian Foundation, 1957. A single-volume history beginning with Old Norse writings and continuing through the early 1950's.

Naess, Harold S., ed. *A History of Norwegian Literature.* Lincoln: University of Nebraska Press, 1993. The second volume of a Scandinavian literature series. It begins with Viking literature, extends through the 1980's, and includes chapters on women's and children's literature.

Rossel, Sven H., ed. *A History of Danish Literature.* Lincoln: University of Nebraska Press, 1992. The first volume of a Scandinavian literature series (see above) that provides greater depth analysis of Danish writings than is available in single-volume histories. Leading scholars examine topics extending from Runic literature through the early 1990's. Separate chapters discuss Faroese and women's and children's literature.

_____. *A History of Scandinavian Literature, 1870-1980.* Minneapolis: University of Minnesota Press, 1982. An excellent history of modern Scandinavian literature.

Schoolfield, George C. *A History of Finland's Literature.* Lincoln: University of Nebraska Press, 1998. The fourth volume of a Scandinavian literature series. It begins with the sixteenth century and extends through the mid-1990's.

Warme, Lars G., ed. *A History of Swedish Literature.* Lincoln: University of Nebraska Press, 1996. The third volume of a Scandinavian literature series. It begins with the Middle Ages and extends through the early 1990's.

SOUTH ASIAN LONG FICTION

The Indian subcontinent, or what geographers call South Asia, includes India, Pakistan, Bangladesh, Sri Lanka, Nepal, and Bhutan. Though world leaders can change borders and create new political entities, they cannot persuade men and women of letters to observe such artificial boundaries. Thus, even though she is not an Indian in the narrow sense of the word but "technically Pakistani," Bapsi Sidhwa is included in *Mirrorwork: 50 Years of Indian Writing, 1947-1997* (1997). As coeditor Salman Rushdie explains, "this anthology has no need of Partitions"; indeed, he recognizes Sidhwa's *Ice-Candy-Man* (1988), published in the United States as *Cracking India* (1991), as a valuable re-creation of "the horror of the division of the subcontinent."

Even if political divisions are disregarded, however, there are other issues confronting any student of South Asian long fiction. One is how to deal with the many worthwhile novels and short stories written in the vernacular. Since there are fourteen major languages in the state of India alone, it is obvious that if these works are to receive the general recognition they deserve, they must be translated into English. Though there are objections to the use of a colonial language for such purposes, they are outweighed by practical considerations and even broad social benefits. In their introduction to *The Penguin New Writing in India* (1995), Aditya Behl and David Nicholls express their belief that such translations will enable people long separated by language to come to a better understanding of other cultures, thus enabling them to interact more successfully in what has always been a multicultural and multilingual society.

The fact that so many South Asians are choosing English as the language in which they express themselves has also dismayed some critics. However, these writers evidently feel more comfortable in English than in the vernacular, and they are well aware that works written in English will be more likely to reach readers throughout the world. They may also point out literary precedents early in the nineteenth century.

ENGLISH IN INDIA

Two years before Thomas Babington Macaulay introduced his famous "Minute" on English education in India (1835), Raja Rammohan Ray, one of several Indian writers who were using the English language successfully even before compulsory English education was officially introduced to India, died in Bristol. It was Macaulay who insisted that all funds appropriated for education in India be set aside for English education alone. In insisting on English education in India, Macaulay was recognizing that Indians could use English advantageously. In fact, he praised the linguistic competence of the people he knew, describing the town natives as "quite competent to discuss political or scientific questions with fluency and precision in the English language." Macaulay also recognized that the use of English opened up a vast information source and audience to the Indians. Thus, an empire was built not only for the British but also for modern Indian writers, providing them with both a form and an audience.

Before Macaulay, Christian missionaries had been teaching English in schools and colleges around the country. Indians, for their part, were eager to obtain a Western education and link people in their nation with the changing world. By the early part of the nineteenth century, Indian literary activity in English had already begun. Henry Louis Vivian Derozio (1807-1831), Kasiprasad Ghose (1809-1873), Michael Madhusudhan Dutt (1824-1873), and Bankim Chandra Chatterjee (1838-1894) were some of the early Indians to use English for their creative and social purposes. By the latter half of the nineteenth century, educated Indians were using English for all purposes, from mundane government work to poetry.

Today, English has become a naturalized member of the citizenry of Indian languages. Along with Hindi, it is used throughout India, unlike other Indian languages. Jawaharlal Nehru, in dealing with the question of a national language for India, noted that English, like Sanskrit and Persian before it, was the language of invaders but had become totally assimilated into Indian life.

The introduction of English to India brought with it an introduction to English literature. The reading public in India soon discovered the novel form and took it over. While India has a long, indigenous tradition of fiction in the form of the oral tale, the short morality story, and the *Pañcatantra* (between 100 B.C.E. and 500 C.E.; *The Morall Philosophie of Doni*, 1570; the Indian equivalent of *Aesop's Fables*) it was to the current British forms that nineteenth century Indian writers turned. Nick Wilkinson, writing about the modern Indian novel, notes that the novel was imported from England and patterned after the popular works of Sir Walter Scott and Charles Dickens. The genre as it has developed in India is a product of the two cultures.

Two major habits that were thus inculcated in Indian authors were the forcing of Indian subject matter into European forms and the imitation of the trendiest of these European forms. In addition, the audience was seen as a European audience hungry for an Asian element in their lives. The exoticism of Indian myth and culture was soon to be exploited even further. As they met with critical acclaim abroad, Indian writers seemed to be writing for the Western critics, who were amazed at and patronizing of their achievements, expressing wonder at the ability of Indian writers to write in English, a second language, and at their ability to use the European form of the novel. At the same time, Indian writers themselves manifested an ambiguity toward their Indian roots. This ambiguity was primarily manifested in the overwhelming choice of English as the medium for their creativity. Questions of nationalism or alienation became inextricably linked with both the development of Indian literature and its criticism. Even the "father of the Indian novel," Rabindranath Tagore, felt compelled to translate his work into English and then even to compose in English. This turn to English drew from William Butler Yeats the following disclaimer. In a letter to William Rothenstein in 1935, Yeats lamented:

> Damn Tagore, we got three good books and because he thought it more important to see and know English than to be a great poet he brought off sentimental rubbish. No Indian knows English. Nobody can write music and style in a language which is not their own.

This dictum became a significant issue both in the formulation of Indian literature and in its criticism. To this day, critics wrangle over whether English or one of the many Indian vernaculars is an appropriate medium for the development of a literature in India's multilingual, multicultural setting. This is not to imply, however, that any literary development in Indian fiction can be attributed entirely to the influence of English.

THE INDIAN TRADITION

Ancient Indian manuscripts written on *bhurjapatra*, or palm leaves, are for the most part lost, extant only in Chinese and Tibetan translations that testify to their previous existence. Excluding well-known works—such as the epic poetry of the *Rāmāyana* (c. 350 B.C.E.), *Mahābhārata* (c. fifth century B.C.E.), and *Bhagavad Gītā* (c. fifth century B.C.E.); and the Sanskrit drama of Kalidasa and the critical work on drama *Nātya-śāstra* (c. 100 C.E.)—a whole body of short works of fiction exists. Their origins can be dated to the *Jātakas* (birth stories), the Buddhist tales that describe the cultural encounter between the indigenous Dravidians and the Aryans. In the popular Sanskrit literature, drama reigned supreme.

The tales from the epics were dramatized on festival days. This was so until the Muslim invasion of the twelfth century C.E., and under the Moguls, Persian literature was dominant. An Indian critical tradition, however, remained significant in the shaping of the literary tradition. Drawing upon the critical theory in the *Nātya-śāstra* of the concepts of *rasa* (meaning) and *dhwani* (undertones or poetic language), Indian literature has always been preoccupied with poetic expression to the detriment of the development of prose and prose fiction. Tracing the growth of Indian literature from the Middle Ages to the Renaissance, Nehru noted in his *Discovery of India* (1946) that popular literatures in Hindi, Gujarati, Marathi, Urdu, Tamil, and Telugu were developing an oral tradition. With the use of the printing press, some of these orally transmitted epics and collections were documented. Nehru notes, however, that these works were in the form of memorizable songs and collections of poems. Hence, it was not until the early Christian missionaries brought English and English education to India that a canon of fiction developed.

THE INDIAN NOVEL

By the 1920's, English education in India was all-pervasive, and by the end of the nineteenth century, English literature held sway over the Indian imagination. Nevertheless, the Indians trained under Rammohan Ray's system of English education in India were not simply to remain Baboos and clerks in British government offices. Their newly acquired language found expression in creativity in a newly learned form. The ancient traditions of the oral epic tales came together with Scott's serialized, romantic *Waverly: Or, 'Tis Sixty Years Since* (1814) to found the annals of a new *Rama Katha* (epic of Rama). The traditional story of the adventures of the Hindu deity Rama, told night after night by the village elder at the local temple, was transformed, in the nineteenth century Indian literary tradition, into nationalist Indian novels written sometimes in English and sometimes in the vernacular, largely about the oppression of the poor by the middle class and the British. These novels sometimes described situations related to tyrannical customs, sati, arranged marriages, and child marriages, sometimes, however, as in the work of Tagore, they merely evoked sentimentality for Indian mysticism.

Because Bengal was the first geographic region to come in contact with the British, the first Indian novel was written in Bengali—a distinction customarily granted to Bhudeva Chandra Mukherjee's *Anguriya Binimoy* (1857). Chatterjee's *Raj Mohan's Wife* was serialized in 1864 in the fashion of Scott's novels. Lal Behari Day's *Govinda Samantha* (1874) is a documentary of peasant life in Bengal. The zamindar professed interest in the lives of the peasants; Day described his novel as a "plain and unvarnished tale of a plain peasant living in the plain country of Bengal . . . told in a plain manner." The story of the peasant Govinda and his exploits with a moneylender, *Govinda Samantha* is the first in a long tradition, culminating in Munshi Prem Chand's social-realist *Godān* (1936; *Gift of a Cow*, 1968), to describe the oppression of peasants by feudal lords. Govinda and

his relative Kalamanik attempt to pay off a debt to the zamindar, who responds by levying a new tax against them and falsely charging them with having borrowed money, in order to keep them indebted to him. When they refuse to pay him, their homes are burned. In the midst of this story of oppression, Day describes the famine of 1873, thus depicting the poverty and the uncertainty that characterize Indian agriculture to this day.

In *fin de siècle* Indian fiction, a need to explore the Indian in relation to the Westerner, including an attempt to educate the West about Indian customs and mores, shaped the themes. Sochee Chunder Dutt's *The Young Zemindar* (1885) presents the crosscultural encounter, the weighing of Eastern and Western traditions, and the question of whether East and West can in fact meet as a major theme in the development of any Anglo-Indian or Indo-Anglian literary tradition. Indian traditions are outlined, and the effect of the British on these traditions is analyzed. In the novel, a sannyasi leads the main character, Monohur, to places of religious importance and describes the customs of those places. Legends connected with the major subcontinental rivers—the Ganges, the Indus, and the Brahmaputra—are retold, as are the stories of the *Mahabharata* and the *Rāmāyana*. Even the Muslim festival of the martyrdom of Mohammed, Moharrum, is pictured. All of this is an effort to show that the British government was attempting to interfere with Indian customs.

The vernacular novel continued to be developed under the shadow of Scott, but the themes tended to be nationalist, emphasizing the importance of traditional Indianness or describing the oppression of the people by feudal lords and the British government. In Hindi, Kishorilal Goswami's *Labangalata* (1891) and Devki Nandan Khatri's *Chandrakāntā* (1892) established themes that lasted into the 1920's and were picked up by the Progressive Writers' Union; such themes were definitely nationalist and, if the term may be used, socialist. Hari Narayan Apte's first novel in Marathi, *Maisorcha Wagh* (1890), is a translation of Meadows Taylor's *Tippoo Sultan* (1840) and refers to him as the Lion of Mysore. *Maisorcha Wagh* brought the celebration of Tippoo Sultan, the great nationalist Indian guerrilla fighter, to the people of his region. In Malayalam, Raman Pillai wrote *Martanda Varma* (1891). At the same time, the retelling and documenting of Indian sacred tales continued: Dwijendranath Neogi published *Sacred Tales of India* (1916), *True Tales of Indian Life* (1917), and *Anecdotes of Indian Life* (1920).

In all of this diverse activity in the writing of fiction, Rabindranath Tagore (1861-1941) stands out. For his prose translations of lyrics composed in Bengali, entitled *Gitānjali* (1910; *Gitanjali (Song Offerings)*, 1912), Tagore was awarded the Nobel Prize in Literature in 1913. With the encouragement of Macmillan, his English publisher, Tagore translated several collections of his own poetry and fiction. His best-known work of fiction is *Gora* (1910), the English translation of which was published by Macmillan in 1924. Tagore's next novel, *Ghare bāire* (1916; *Home and the World*, 1919), reflects the changing politics of Bengali society. Both novels again have nationalist themes. Gora, meaning "white," is a foundling reared as an orthodox Hindu who learns that his mother was Irish. This brings to the forefront questions of caste and religion, leading to an eventual preference for Indianness. Nationalism returns even more aggressively in *Home and the World*. The concept of *Swadeshi*, or Indian, which was to become a key element of the Gandhian movement, is a central concept in this novel about revolutionary Bengal in 1905. Even the conservative Indian wife is drawn by the call of the outside world. Sandip, another character in the novel, would like to move toward Western modernization. Hence the novel portrays the traditional clash between the Western and the Indian.

What constituted the modern, the new, the Western? Was it sociological or technological advancement into the modern era? Was it a recognition of one's roots as reflected through the prism of Westernization? Was it a breaking from the acquiescence that kept Indians under oppressive rulers, whether Muslim or British? These are the questions that were forced to the forefront during the first four decades of the twentieth century, and, whether in English or in one of the vernaculars, these were the questions that were articulated in Indian fiction. With the documen-

tation of a social milieu and with the changing feelings of the moment, the literature of the Indian people seemed to turn toward the novel of social realism.

THE DEVELOPMENT OF THE INDO-ENGLISH NOVEL

The tradition of the Indo-English novel took deep roots during the early twentieth century. K. S. Venkatramani, whose long poem *On the Sand Dunes* (1923) was highly derivative of Tagore's *Gitānjali (Song Offerings)*, was more original as a novelist. His *Murugan, the Tiller* (1927) and *Kandan, the Patriot* (1932) were harbingers of the realism that was to mark Indian literature during what in Indian history is called the Gandhian era (1920-1947). World War I had replaced *fin de siècle* Romanticism and Georgian effusions with a new idiom and new role models that the Indian writers were soon to imitate. The war also brought to India an awareness of socioeconomic problems and of the British exploitation of India's human and economic resources, a feeling that was to be enhanced later in World War II and embodied in Mahatma Gandhi's call for noncooperation with the Stafford proposal of cooperation with the Allies and postponement of the Quit India movement. The impact of Marxism and an accompanying attraction to socialism are also apparent in the Indian novel of this period.

Venkatramani's two novels are notable chiefly as works marking the general turn away from poetry toward the novel. With the appearance of Mulk Raj Anand (born 1905), Indian writing gained its first major fiction writer; his first novel, *Untouchable* (1935), established social realism as a rich vein for the Indian novel. British-educated and a member of the intellectual Bloomsbury group in the early 1920's, Anand began his writing career with a Joycean stream-of-consciousness "tract" about an untouchable. It was not until his conversion to Gandhism that he was able to move past his interest in stylistic imitation to a primary interest in subject matter. *Untouchable* became the first of a trilogy of novels. Various options to the tyrannical caste system are discussed as the plot develops around the incidents of maltreatment of the main character, Bakha, and his sister. As E. M. Forster pointed out in his foreword to the book, it is another story of the difference between tradition and modernity, the Mahatma and the machine, in Indian fiction. The same theme runs through the other two novels of the trilogy, *Coolie* (1936) and *Two Leaves and a Bud* (1937): The poor remain poor, exploited, and Indian.

In "Why I Write?" (in *Indo English Literature*, 1977), Anand describes his first attempt at "Tagorean singsong rubbish." Anand got the same reaction from his Bloomsbury friends when he read them his confessional narrative-turned-novel about Bakha, the untouchable:

> I had borrowed the technique of word coinage from James Joyce's *Ulysses* and made the narrative rather literary, and that the novel was a prose form not an epic poem like [John] Milton's *Paradise Lost*. Only one thing they liked about my fictional narrative: that it faced the poverty, the dirt and squalor of the "lower depths" even more than Gorky had done. And I was confirmed in my hunch that, unlike Virginia Woolf, the novelist must confront the total reality, including its sordidness, if one was to survive in the world of tragic contrasts between the "exalted and noble" vision of the blind bard Milton and the eyes dimmed with tears of the many mute Miltons.

Realism had become Anand's hallmark, and he steadfastly espoused it. In *The Sword and the Sickle* (1942), he portrayed the horrors resulting from the independence movement and the subsequent partition. In a succession of works—*The Village* (1939), *Across the Black Waters* (1940), *The Barber's Trade Union and Other Stories* (1944), *The Big Heart* (1945), *Seven Summers* (1951), *The Old Woman and the Cow* (1963), *The Road* (1962), and *Morning Face* (1968)—he remained steadfast in his depiction of the wronged poor.

In espousing realism, Anand had in fact taken up the cause of the 1920's British intellectuals; to that extent he was imitative. He made no apologies for this formative influence on his writing and was singularly forthright in his admissions. In "The Story of My Experiment with a White Lie" (in *Critical Essays on Indian Writing in English*, 1972), he acknowledged all the intellectual influences on him:

> I had become conscious, after the suppression of the general strike of the South Wales miners by [Winston] Churchill, of the kind of defiance which, under democratic conditions, the better off untouchables of Europe could indulge in. . . . I am not sure whether the *Confessions* of Rousseau, which I had just then read, or some of the books of the Russian writers like [Nikolai] Gogol, [Leo] Tolstoy and [Maxim] Gorky . . . were not then forcing me to acknowledge what most Indian writers of the modern period, like Bankim Chandra Chatterjee, Ratanath Sarshar and Rabindranath Tagore, had not accepted in their novels that even the so-called lowest dregs of humanity, living in utmost poverty, squalor and degradation, could become the heroes of fiction.

Pursuing the cause of realism and Indianization, Anand moved beyond word coinage by incorporating in his fiction English as spoken in the Indian streets, generously sprinkled with Indian words.

"INDIANIZING" ENGLISH

At the same time, mindful of the nationalism at home and of the general call to abandon English from their daily lives, most Indian writers, whose only medium of expression in some cases may have been English, responded with efforts to Indianize the English language.

In 1938, Raja Rao's preface to *Kanthapura* expressed the problem of conveying through English the speech and thought patterns of a people whose language was not English. In *Kanthapura*, an oral tale of the coming of Gandhism told by an old crone to her village, Rao attempted to capture the rhythms of Indian speech in English. Told in the lyric, lilting voice of the village crone, *Kanthapura* gave the English language a new meter and a new rhythm, so skillfully developed that it seems to have been a unique achievement both for the writer and for other writers. Rao's other novels, including *The Serpent and the Rope* (1960) and *The Cat and Shakespeare: A Tale of India* (1965), resort to conventional English, varied only for dialogue.

G. V. Desani's *All About H. Hatterr* (1948), written as a deliberate attempt to capture Indian English, is much less successful than *Kanthapura* and appears as mumbo jumbo, almost impossible for most readers to comprehend. In part, the language is meant to fit the character of H. Hatterr, who is of mixed blood and mixed cultural background. Yet as Anthony Burgess wrote in his introduction to the 1970 Bodley Head edition, "it is the language that makes the book a sort of creative chaos that grumbles at the restraining banks." Burgess compares Desani's language with that of Joyce; indeed, in the language and the rambling stream-of-consciousness technique of the novel, the influence of Joyce is evident and ultimately fails to transcend stylistic imitation. It is no puzzle that the book went underground and became a "coterie pleasure," as Burgess observed. The language itself is an obstacle for readers both in India and abroad.

While other Indian writers in English were focusing on imitations or language experimentation, R. K. Narayan (born 1906) was creating a style of his own. Various labels have been used to describe him—the Indian Jane Austen or the Indian Anton Chekhov— but Narayan is in a class all his own, combining the skills of those two literary giants and at the same time creating his own fictional world. In a career of more than fifty years, he has won for his imaginary South Indian town of Malgudi a permanent place on the literary map, along with William Faulkner's Yoknapatawpha County. From *Swami and Friends* (1935) to *The Painter of Signs* (1976), readers around the world have lived with the characters from Malgudi, felt with them, and seen the history of India evolve from the coming of Gandhism (*Waiting for the Mahatma*, 1955) to the coming of "American ways" (*The Sweet-Vendor*, 1967; also known as *The Vendor of Sweets*). Narayan's best-known work, *The Guide* (1958), was made into both a film and an unsuccessful Broadway production—both versions disliked by Narayan himself. Narayan focuses in a Malrauxian manner on the disparity between humanity's hope and humanity's fate, yet he does not spend time musing on large philosophical questions. There is in his work no Indian religiosity, nor is there an attempt to describe exotic India for the Westerners; there is simply the presentation of situations and moments of character revelation and awareness.

Narayan's language is straightforward, traditional English. English, for him, is a tool for the person who can use it. Contrary to other Indian writers, Narayan has always believed that English is a very adaptable language. In his descriptions of South Indian life, Narayan makes a deliberate effort to incorporate the Indianized English heard in the Indian streets and households. It is because of the Indian English that his descriptions and vignettes come through with an effectiveness that would make any effort to convey such an essence through language variations superfluous, for they are simply descriptions of life, of universal moments.

Thus, Narayan's portrayal realistically captures a distinct variety of English as spoken by a sizable body of Indians. His style includes all the features formed in English through a process of hybridization—collocations of English words with Indian words (for example, "marriage pandal" or "lathi charge") or compounding of words ("high caste" or "low caste") or expressions of Indian English speech ("your good self"). Another example comes from *The Dark Room* (1938): "If you can't cook properly do the work yourself, what have you to you to do better than that?" The last phrase is not a mistake but a nativized idiom. So is this continuous participial construction: "Ramani would keep calling the servant Ranga in order to tell him what he was and where he ought to be, for not polishing his boots properly." In using Indian English quite straightforwardly, Narayan is the Indian writer writing in English who has most successfully avoided the self-consciousness implicit in the situation of being an Indian writer writing in English. He has successfully resisted the attempt to shape his writing according to current literary trends.

Some Indian critics bemoan the fact that Narayan has been guided primarily by his desire to be an entertaining storyteller. Such criticism reveals some of the prejudices that have been inherent in the Indian critical response to a literature written in English: The literature cannot be any good if it does not imitate what is produced abroad; it cannot be any good if it is written in English by someone who has not been abroad (implicit in this attitude is the judgment that

Indians cannot use English effectively without Western guidance); writers cannot produce great literature if they are not concerned with the "profound" issues, which can range from Indianizing English to expressing Indian philosophical problems to dealing with the current nationalistic issues; and writers are suspect if they have received acclaim abroad.

In such a response to Narayan, one can see recapitulated the conflicts that have beset Indian literature in English since its birth. Against these odds, those writers who have had the courage to pursue their own course have endured, while those who have shaped their writing to suit either Western or Indian ideals have failed.

Dual perspectives

The same prejudices that motivated the attacks on Narayan and other writers of his generation are evident in the critical response to later writers. Typical is the case of Kamala Markandaya (born 1924), who writes with a solid command of the English language. Could this be a sign of alienation? Markandaya's situation is particularly disconcerting to the critics. Married to an Englishman, she has written about India from abroad, particularly with a perspective identified as Western. Her fiction often depicts the difference between the Eastern and Western views of life, as in *Nectar in a Sieve* (1954), *Some Inner Fury* (1955), *A Handful of Rice* (1966), *The Coffer Dams* (1969), *Two Virgins* (1973), and *Pleasure City* (1982; published in the United States as *Shalimar*, 1983), which incorporate descriptions of India through Western eyes, while they remain essentially accurate portrayals of urban and rural poverty. The plight of Rukhmani, the peasant woman in *Nectar in a Sieve*, reflects the poignant and passive acceptance of poverty in India. It also juxtaposes the traditional and the modern as the peasants are displaced by a leather factory and neglected by their modernized sons in the city. When Rukhmani and her husband move to the city in search of their son, they find themselves singularly unequipped to deal with it and are able to find employment only as stone breakers. While they are living on handouts at a temple, Rukhmani's husband dies, leaving Rukhmani to re-

turn to the village. The only voice of reason in the novel is that of the English doctor Kenny. *A Handful of Rice* again reflects poverty in the city; here, however, the emphasis is on the rich taking advantage of the poor. Both the conflict between the city and the country and the issue of exploitation are explored in *Shalimar*. However, while the author recognizes that there will be a certain loss of innocence when a luxury resort, Shalimar, is built in a coastal area up to now inhabited only by simple fishermen, she also knows that there is nothing admirable about being hungry. As a realist, Markandaya will not wax sentimental about poverty, just as she refuses to romanticize the colonial past, as represented in this novel by the beautiful, decaying house called Avalon.

Ironically, Markandaya's very honesty has brought her works under attack. Her sympathy for the poor and her poignant descriptions of their often desperate lives have been perceived by nationalists as evidence of Markandaya's alienation from her native land. If she still had any feeling for India, they argue, she would show it at its best, rather than at its worst. In contrast to the critical perspective of her as an alienated writer, as the Commonwealth writer overseas, Markandaya sees herself as having "the blessing and the bane of duality." The strength of Markandaya's ties to India is demonstrated by her use of language. In her early works, she generally kept to standard English. However, she later modified this view, believing that Indian writers can use their own dialect forms or localisms with the same brio that American counterparts use Americanisms.

A writer who uses her double perspective as an arch, Ruth Prawer Jhabvala (born 1927), though born in Germany and reared in England, has been acclaimed by some critics as truly Indian. In a career that began while she was living in India, Jhabvala has explored and described upper-middle-class Indian life—particularly as she saw it in New Delhi. Her *Esmond in India* (1958) is almost an allegory of contemporary Indian civilization. Gulab, the Indian girl married to the Englishman Esmond, is an embodiment of traditional India. Shakuntala, the young college girl with whom Esmond later develops a relationship, is the personification of the new India—

modernized, sprightly, and yearning for achievement—embarrassed by her slower and more traditional counterpart. Despite his knowledge of Indian culture, civilization, and languages, Esmond remains the foreigner, unable to understand the simultaneous existence of the modern and the traditional, attracted only to exoticism and unable to fit in. Jhabvala seems to concede that such is the position of the foreigner in the mixed, pell-mell Indian society.

Jhabvala's later novels are both broader in scope and more complex in structure than her earlier ones, but their themes are the same: the conflict between East and West, old ways and new, alienation, and the search for meaning. Jhabvala won a Booker Prize for *Heat and Dust* (1975), a brilliant juxtaposition of two stories about young British women in India. Letters written by the narrator's step-grandmother, who deserted her husband for an Indian prince in 1923, mark the way for her descendent a half century later, as she, too, succumbs to India. Jhabvala's Westerners like to believe that either the East or Eastern practices can assuage their pain. If they do not travel to India, they look for a guru to follow, like the Jewish refugee who takes charge of a group of German Jewish immigrants in Jhabvala's *In Search of Love and Beauty* (1983). The wealthy innocents in *Three Continents* (1987) turn over their lives and their fortunes to an Indian known as the Rawul. In both novels, the gurus are revealed as self-serving and dangerous people, who deprive their followers of their wills and of whatever good sense they may at one time have had.

Three Continents is set in New York, London, and Delhi. *Poet and Dancer* (1993) takes place in Manhattan, but it has two important Indian characters. *Shards of Memory* (1995) moves from place to place as easily as *Three Continents*, chronicling the adventures and misadventures of a mixed Indian-American-British family over the course of four generations. Again, an Indian guru is important to the plot, though he never appears and leaves no record of his teachings. The "shards" of the title are the random recollections of family members, all of whom are affected in one way or another by this unprincipled, charismatic figure.

From the beginning of her literary career, when she wrote what were termed novelistic comedies of manners, Jhabvala has satirized fools, and she often seems as unsympathetic to the Westerners duped by these gurus as she is sympathetic to some of her Indian characters—like the wise, compassionate patriarch in *Shards of Memory*. It is not Indians, but India itself, that Jhabvala finds so perilous. Her tales of gurus and disciples remind Westerners drawn to India that they will have a difficult choice to make. If they do not renounce their Western identity and become totally Indian, they must live with a sense of alienation. In "Introduction: Myself in India," which prefaces her volume *Out of India: Selected Stories* (1986), Jhabvala comments that Europeans and many modern Indians sometimes find India, "the idea, the sensation of it," so overwhelming, so "intolerable," that they either leave or retreat into themselves, and even those who leave will eventually have to return. Jhabvala has concluded that the primary subject of her fiction is, as she states it, "myself in India." Certainly India, or the "idea" of India, is somehow present in everything she writes.

STYLE AND SUBJECT

Because of the critical emphasis on theme and subject matter, the question among the new generation of Indian novelists of the 1960's and the 1970's was not "Should we use English?" or "How can we Indianize English?" but rather "How best can we use the English language to reflect our society and culture?" Manohar Malgonkar (born 1913) and Nayantara Sahgal (born 1927), for example, both experimented in form and structure, but they did not do so at the expense of their subject matter. Malgonkar's novels, *Distant Drum* (1960), *Combat of Shadows* (1962), *The Princes* (1963), and *A Bend in the Ganges* (1964), deal with the transition from British colonialism to Indian nationalism. Life in the Indian army, the tea estates, the princely states, and the role of wars in India's recent history are the subjects of his novels. Sahgal's novels, beginning with *A Time to Be Happy* (1958), reflect the changing political history of India that began with the independence movement. The conflict between modernity and tradition is one of the major themes in Sahgal's novels. In his

This Time of Morning (1965) and *Storm over Chandigarh* (1969), symbols control structure. The dawning of the Indian nation is seen in the functioning of politicians' lives and ethics; it is still morning for a new nation, yet innocence has no place in the political world.

Both of these novels by Sahgal show that a changing order is taking over postindependence India. India is strike-ridden; the nonviolent movement of Gandhi's day has given way to stone-throwing, factory-burning mobs. In *Storm over Chandigarh*, the city of Chandigarh, designed and built by Le Corbusier, and commissioned by Nehru to be built with starkly simple lines, is a symbol of Westernization and represents the imposition of the strange, Westernized ways of an alien political order on Indian lives. For men such as Harpal Singh, one of the older politicians in the novel, the starkly simple lines become symbolic of a terrifying, angular coldness in the new order. "It's a revolution in architecture and what's more a revolution in people's thinking . . . but revolutions are sudden and have peculiar results." The gray starkness of the architecture, one of the women in the novel reflects, is opposed to the Indian warmth and effusiveness embodied in the traditional Indian woman.

One of the most highly acclaimed Indian novels in English, Salman Rushdie's *Midnight's Children* (1981), in expressing an alienation from contemporary, political India, concentrates heavily on stylistic innovation. *Midnight's Children*, perhaps more clearly than any other postwar Indian novel, highlights the failure of criticism—a criticism that continuously calls for stylistic imitation and pushes Indian writers in the direction of imitating modern British writers. The clue to the theme of *Midnight's Children* lies in the individual's connection to history and in the individual's power to make history. With the gift of extrasensory perception, Saleem Sinai, the narrator, attempts to reconstruct and remake Indian history. The metaphorical manifestation of his attempts finds him cutting up newspaper headlines and rearranging them to make scandal notes that incite trouble. Rushdie's novel reflects the communal feelings of a Muslim family as it experiences the history of India. The communal fighting and killing that pervaded the in-

dependence movement and later the "Widow's Rule" is described as graphically in Rushdie's novel as it is in Richard Attenborough's film *Gandhi* (1982). *Midnight's Children* actually reflects regret at the departure of the British. The narrator assesses the end of the second five-year plan in 1961: "The number of landless and unemployed masses actually increased, so that it was greater than had ever been under the British Raj . . . illiteracy survived unscathed; the population continued to mushroom." "Maybe I am wrong. Maybe we are not ready yet," Gandhi had said after the first general strike after which Adam Aziz, the narrator's grandfather, had felt so optimistic about India. Perhaps the lack of readiness, particularly to give up on individual needs and their accommodation, continues to be the root of India's problems; this is the theme of *Midnight's Children*.

FICTION IN THE VERNACULAR

The development of fiction in the vernacular most clearly demonstrates the imitative tendency among Indian writers. There has been a continual imitation of European trends from the social realism of the 1930's in Munshi Prem Chand's writing to the self-consciously modernist idiom, not only in English but also in its translated forms in the vernacular and the self-consciously experimental forms of fiction such as that published in *Matrubhumi* (Malayalam), *Dharmayug* (Hindi), and similar literary magazines.

Like Anand, Prem Chand (1880-1936), the best-known and most well-respected Hindi writer, began with the romanticized socialist themes of the previous generation of European writers. His *Gift of a Cow* is a prose epic of the peasants' battle with the moneylender and the zamindar. Other themes of social concern in his work are early marriage and widowhood in *Nirmalā* (1928), the dowry system and prostitution in *Sevā Sadan* (1918), and the rise of capitalism in *Rangabhūmi* (1925). The same themes of social reform mushroomed in the other vernaculars with few variations: in *Palli Samaj* (1916), by Sarat Chandra Chatterjee (Bengali); *Rantitangazhi* (1949; *Two Measures of Rice*, 1967), by Thakazhi Pillai (Malayalam); and works by Rajendra Singh Bedi, Pannalal Patel, and Jaswant Singh "Kaneval." In this period, from the

1930's to independence in 1947, Bengal remained the most prolific source of fiction. Novels written in Bengali include Bibhutibhusan Bannerjee's *Pather Panchali* (1929; English translation, 1968), filmed by Satyajit Ray as part of his Apu Trilogy, and Manik Bandopadhyaya's well-known *Putul nacher itikath* (1936; dance of the dolls); several anthologies of short stories in Bengali have also appeared. Social realism was quickly developing into a nationalist consciousness, and Indian literature began to reflect the move toward independence.

GANDHI AND GANDHISM

Ironically, the best and perhaps the only Indian nationalist fiction, appeared in English. Rao celebrated Gandhi in *Kanthapura*, while Narayan dealt with him in the lighthearted, humorous *Waiting for the Mahatma*. Anand's trilogy *The Sword and the Sickle* depicts the turbulence of the Quit India movement, and Khushwant Singh's *Train to Pakistan* (1955) documents the immense violence of the partition of India and Pakistan. A well-known Marathi writer, Prabhakar Machwe, however, notes that Gandhi seems to have failed to provide inspiration for those writing in the vernacular. In his *Four Decades of Indian Literature: A Critical Evaluation* (1976), he recalls, "Gandhi's non-violent and non-cooperation movement found still less place in fiction published in the Indian languages. In the celebrations of Gandhi's centenary in 1969, it was difficult to locate even one literary classic which was a reflection of contemporary events, or which documented the impacts of the movements. . . ." This fact, however, is not at all surprising. Astute politician that he was, Gandhi recognized the usefulness of English in uniting the country; the great nationalist debates and arguments, even the one for Hindustani as a national language, were made in English. The irony of this situation was heightened when a noted Bengali writer and nationalist critic, Buddhadeva Bose, claimed in the 1963 edition of *The Concise Encyclopedia of English and American Poetry* (edited by Stephen Spender and Donald Hall) that "Indo-Anglican literature" (by which he means literature written in English by Indians) is "a blind alley lined with curio shops."

VERNACULAR FICTION AFTER INDEPENDENCE

It was after independence and the call to abandon the "imperialist" yoke of English that fiction in the vernaculars began to struggle to make some advancements. In its nationalist impulse, however, it quickly turned to European models. P. Lal, in his review entitled "Contemporary Hindi Fiction" (in *The Concept of an Indian Literature*, 1968), notes the influences of Jean-Paul Sartre, Søren Kierkegaard, and particularly Sigmund Freud. Freudian themes, symbols, and impulses permeate Hindi fiction, particularly of the magazines—Lal recalls the celebration of the sesquicentennial of Kierkegaard's birth by a popular Hindi literary magazine. The impulse toward European modernism rather than toward an experimental idiom that turned to folk and indigenous roots has been demonstrated in the plastic arts. While experimental artists pursue what is new in the West, the more individualistic artists, such as Narayan, work in their own distinctive style. A similar precedent has not been established in the vernacular fiction.

Among the vernacular novels since independence, there are, however, some landmark achievements. Sivasankara Pillai's *Chemmeen* (1956; English translation, 1962) deals with the superstitions and lives of the tribal fisherfolk who live along the Malabar coast. Karuthamma, the heroine, believes that the dishonesty of her parents will make the sea go dry. In her own dishonesty in taking a lover, she darkens Arundhati, the star that guides fishermen, thus killing her husband Palanni in a storm at sea as he attempts to bait a shark. The novel has something of the fablelike quality of Ernest Hemingway's *The Old Man and the Sea* (1952).

Amrita Pritam's *A Line in Water* (1975) is reminiscent of Kate Chopin's *The Awakening* (1899) in that it deals with a woman's feelings, often not communicable to a male sensibility. Her characters, too, are caught in the whirlwind of tradition and change, and such concepts as "widowhood without even a wedding," while revolutionary in Indian fiction, underscore the permanent and universal in her work. *Jalavatan* (1969) contains two short novellas, "Jalavatan" (the exile) and "Kala Gulab" (the black rose). The latter is autobiographical, with descriptions of symbolic dreams leaning toward the Freudian tendency in Hindi modernism.

In Punjabi, the work of Kartar Singh Duggal, as well as Rajendra Singh Bedi's *I Take This Woman* (1967), also reflects the changing social scene in India. Bedi's novel was translated into English by Khushwant Singh, himself an Indian novelist in English. Other Indian writers who belonged to the generation of novelists of independence and deserve mention include Ka Naa Subramanyam, who wrote in Tamil; Khwaja Ahmad Abbas, who wrote *Inquilab* (1945; revolution) and who writes both in Urdu and in English; Chaman Nahal, who wrote *Azadi* (1975; independence) in English; K. M. Munshi, who is considered the father of Gujarati fiction; and Aditya Sen, a modern Bengali writer.

U. R. Anantha Murthy, the Kannada writer and scholar, is best known as a theorist who has questioned the turning to Western models: "Why do we import even our radicalism via [Allen] Ginsberg, [John] Osborne or [Jean-Paul] Sartre?" In several speeches and essays, he urges a "search for identity." He, too, has recognized that while Indian writers cannot return to their roots per se, they must take into consideration the race, moment, and milieu of their own writing—the interaction of the current idiom of the contemporary scene in India with its ancient roots. Bose, also a theorist of Indian literature, has attempted this cultural merger by creating the dramatic novel in Bengali, wherein an Indian consciousness is cast in a dramatic monologue. His novels include *Lal Megh* (1934), *Kalo Haoa* (1942), and *Tithidor* (1949).

Among translations into English recommended by the Authors' Guild of India are Jainendra Kumar's *The Resignation* (1946; originally in Hindi as *Tyaga patra*, 1937); Kalinidi Charan Panigrahi's *A House Undivided* (1973; originally in Oriya as *Matiro manisha*, 1930), Neela Padmanaban's *The Generations* (1972; originally in Tamil as *Talaimnraikal*, 1968), M. T. Vasudevan Nair's *The Legacy* (1975; originally in Malayalam as *Kalam*, 1969), S. H. Vatsyayan's *To Each His Stranger* (1967; originally in Hindi as *Apane apane ajanabi*, 1961), and Lokenath Bhattacharya's *Virgin Fish from Babughat* (1975;

originally in Bengali as *Babughatera kumari macha*, 1972). This list demonstrates that literary activity in vernacular remained healthy as the century progressed. However, few critics can overcome the barriers presented by at least fourteen languages, many in different linguistic families and alphabets. Therefore they remain dependent upon translators and interpreters for an understanding of works written in languages beyond the two, or at most three, with which they are familiar.

TRENDS AT THE END OF THE TWENTIETH CENTURY

At the end of the twentieth century, the fiction of the Indian subcontinent had not yet found a voice and a method of its own. Critics and authors alike seemed uncertain as to how they might rekindle the techniques and values of India's ancient tradition, how to come to terms with its mixture of cultures and languages without allowing one of them to become dominant, and how to move away from Eurocentric models and criticism while still aiming at high standards and at the communication of universal values. One fact was obvious: The only literary works that could reach an audience throughout the entire subcontinent were those either written in English or translated into English. It was also evident that the English language alone could make possible the worldwide recognition and the impressive sales figures for which South Asian writers hoped. By the end of the century, practical considerations had effectively stifled the nationalists' protests, and to all intents and purposes English had become the literary language of the Indian subcontinent.

As long as India was striving for independence, it was difficult for Indian writers to view the colonial past or the British with any objectivity. One of the first to do so was Kamala Markandaya, who in *The Golden Honeycomb* (1977) demonstrated how entrenched traditions and the colonial system prevented decent people—such as the maharajah, his son, and the British resident—from fully understanding each other, much less the people for whose welfare they were responsible. Gita Mehta's novel *Raj* (1989) reveals the frustration of a capable maharajah's daughter, prevented from assuming a position of leadership simply because of her gender. In *Olivia and Jai* (1990) and its sequel *The Veil of Illusion* (1995), both of which are set in the middle of the nineteenth century, the pseudonymous Rebecca Ryman emphasizes how difficult it was to ignore the ethnic distinctions on which the colonial system depended.

In the final decades of the century, writers also reexamined the tumultuous period immediately after independence, when India was torn apart by religious and ethnic differences. Like Rushdie's *Midnight's Children*, most of the novels about this terrible era focused less on actual events than on the way the atmosphere of fear and distrust affected individuals. In *Cracking India*, Sidhwa incorporated horrifying details about the riots in and around Lahore into a comic account of daily life in a prosperous Parsee family, seen through the eyes of the young protagonist. Like *Cracking India*, *Funny Boy* (1994), by the Sri Lankan writer Shyam Selvadurai, is a story about coming of age, made doubly difficult by the enmity between neighbors and former friends. The protagonist of *Funny Boy* has to come to terms with his own identity as a homosexual and as a member of the Tamil minority in a largely Sinhalese community; he learns first-hand how cruel human beings can be.

WOMEN WRITERS, WOMEN'S LIVES

Intolerance and injustice based on ethnic and religious differences were not the only targets of postindependence South Asian fiction. There had been hints of a demand for women's rights in Indian literature as early as the 1930's. For example, in his atypical novel *The Dark Room*, R. K. Narayan told the story of a devoted Hindu wife driven into rebellion by her husband's infidelity but helpless to make good her escape. In the second half of the twentieth century, the drive for Indian independence, the worldwide feminist movement, and the proliferation of women writers combined to make women's issues one of the dominant subjects in South Asian fiction. It is significant that the protagonists of five of the novels written by Nayantara Sahgal between 1966 and 1985 were women and that in three instances they walked out on their husbands.

Like *Midnight's Children*, Anita Desai's *Clear Light of Day* (1980) is set in 1947. However, her focus is not on India's success in gaining independence from Great Britain, but on the need for India's women to be freed from a stifling, patriarchal society. In novels such as *That Long Silence* (1988), Shashi Deshpande asks questions to which there are no easy answers, including whether an arranged marriage is safer than one based on love; if there is no prior emotional involvement, one is less likely to be hurt. Deshpande is enough of a realist to understand how difficult it is for Indian women to become assertive when for centuries they have been taught that submissiveness is a virtue; she also shows how hard it is for modern daughters to feel close to their traditional mothers, who so often feel inadequate and are possessed by despair. Deshpande also decries the obsession with female purity, which can cause rape victims to commit suicide rather than live on in shame. The women in *Listening Now* (1998), by Anjana Appachana, may seem contented, but the purpose of the novel is to show how angry they are at being denied both passion and a sense of self-worth. Appachana shares the conviction of feminists throughout the world that the political upheavals and social changes of the twentieth century did not suddenly cause women to become dissatisfied with their lot but instead brought forth women writers who could voice their feelings and protest against centuries of systematic oppression.

THE DIASPORA

Twentieth century fiction also reflected the effects of the diaspora from the Indian subcontinent, usually motivated by the hope of a better life but often resulting in a profound sense of alienation. In an early novel, *Wife* (1975), Bharati Mukherjee shows the tragic results when a young Indian woman is married to a stranger and transported to the United States, where she is supposed to act the part of an obedient Indian wife, ignoring the fascinating world around her. It is hardly surprising that she retreats into a fantasy world and eventually explodes into madness. The complexity of the American immigrant experience is also explored in *The Mistress of Spices* (1997) and *Sister of My Heart* (1999), by Chitra Banerjee

Divakaruni. In the first of these novels, a shopkeeper in Oakland, California, uses her magical powers for the benefit of confused new immigrants; in the second, it is only the sisterly love two cousins feel for each other that enables them to survive.

In some novels, the immigration experience leads to a rejection of the past. The recently widowed title character in Bharati Mukherjee's novel *Jasmine* (1989) plans to commit "sati," or ritual immolation, as soon as she gets to the United States; instead, she kills a rapist, settles down in Iowa with one man, then leaves him for another and heads toward California. Jasmine seems to have become an American. The Pakistani Parsee student in Sidhwa's *An American Brat* (1993) may be appalled by the violence and immorality she sees in the United States, but she decides to remain there rather than returning to Pakistan, with its repressive policies toward women.

Sometimes writers explore the differences between East and West by having a South Asian return home. This device is utilized by Indira Ganesan in *The Journey* (1990), Arundhati Roy in *The God of Small Things* (1997), and Vikram Chandra in *Red Earth and Pouring Rain* (1995), a brilliant novel in which a returning student's lapse from custom prompts the intervention of the gods a nd enables the author to recapitulate Indian history. The theme of East versus West also underlies novels in which the major characters are Europeans or Americans in India, perhaps seeking spiritual fulfillment, as in Jhabvala's Three Continents and Anita Desai's Journey to Ithaca (1995), or perhaps, like the displaced Jew in Anita Desai's poignant Baumgartner's Bombay (1988), wishing for nothing more than a safe place to live.

A NEW COSMOPOLITANISM

South Asian writers, too, are involved in the diaspora from their subcontinent. For years, promising students have attended universities in Great Britain or the United States, but late in the century more and more writers were either making their homes outside of the subcontinent or dividing their time among various countries. Bharati Mukherjee, Chitra Banerjee Divakaruni, Anjana Appachana, and Bapsi Sidhwa moved to the United States, while Kamala Markan-

daya and Salman Rushdie relocated to Great Britain. Gita Mehta and Ruth Prawer Jhabvala were described as living in the United States, England, and India, Anita Desai as moving between the United States and the United Kingdom, and Vikram Seth, author of the monumental work *A Suitable Boy* (1993), as equally at home in Bombay and Washington, D. C.

Admittedly, the diaspora may sometimes lead to a diminished use of South Asian subject matter, as with Ruth Prawer Jhabvala. Meira Chand's first four novels were set in Japan, where she lives; not until *House of the Sun* (1989) did she write a story about Indians in India. On the other hand, though Kiran Desai's home is in New York City, her hilarious *Hullaballoo in the Guava Orchard* (1998) is as convincing a story of Indian village life as one finds in the fiction of R. K. Narayan, who spent his life in Madras. If it is true that only by observing other cultures can one arrive at a real understanding of one's own, the diaspora may do far more good than harm. Indeed, the new cosmopolitanism may well account for the technical complexity, thematic density, and amazing variety that had become the salient characteristics of South Asian long fiction by the end of the twentieth century.

Feroza Jussawalla,
updated by Rosemary M. Canfield Reisman

BIBLIOGRAPHY

Behl, Aditya, and David Nicholls, eds. *The Penguin New Writing in India.* London: Penguin, 1995. Published in 1992 as a special issue of the *Chicago Review* and revised for Penguin Books India, 1994, this anthology features new or relatively unknown writers. Includes poetry and prose originally written in thirteen different languages, including English.

Clark, T. W., ed. *The Novel in India: Its Birth and Development.* Berkeley: University of California Press, 1970. Traces the evolution of prose fiction in the six major languages of India and Pakistan, devoting a chapter to each. Indexed.

Gupta, R. K. "Trends in Modern Indian Fiction." *World Literature Today* 68 (Spring, 1994): 299-307. The author identifies six major themes in contemporary Indian fiction. Although he sometimes finds the writers' thinking simplistic, Gupta praises their technical skill and their "boundless creative energy."

Hogan, Patrick Colm, and Lalita Pandit, eds. *Literary India: Comparative Studies in Aesthetics, Colonialism, and Culture*. Albany: State University of New York Press, 1995. Essays by various scholars compare works from very different literary traditions, considering such topics as caste and race, home and exile, political and social change, and language. An interview with Anita Desai is also included. Indexed.

Modern Fiction Studies 39 (Spring, 1993). This special issue, "Fiction on the Indian Subcontinent," contains an introductory essay by guest editor Aparajita Sagar, articles, reviews, and a photo essay. Several articles deal with gender issues.

Mukherjee, Meenakshi. *Realism and Reality: The Novel and Society in India*. Delhi: Oxford University Press, 1985. An eminent scholar demonstrates how the conflict of value systems in colonial society was reflected in the form and content of novels written before the twentieth century. Appendices, notes, bibliography, and index.

_____. *The Twice Born Fiction: Themes and Techniques of the Indian Novel in English*. New Delhi: Heinemann, 1971. Insisting that Indo-Anglian literature must be viewed as "the product of two parent traditions," Mukherjee looks at language and style, the use of myth, and the theme of renunciation. Bibliography and index.

The New Yorker 73 (June 23/June 30, 1997). These issues include essays on the novel, an article about R. K. Narayan, and short stories by Rushdie, Kiran Desai, Vikram Chandra, and Ruth Prawer Jhabvala.

Rushdie, Salman, and Elizabeth West, eds. *Mirrorwork: 50 Years of Indian Writing, 1947-1997*. New York: Henry Holt, 1997. Includes fiction and nonfiction, translations and works written in English. Rushdie's introduction is excellent. Brief biographical notes.

Tharu, Susie, and Lalita, K., eds. *Women Writing in India: 600 B.C. to the Present*. Vol. I: *600 B.C. to the Early 20th Century*. New York: Feminist Press, 1991. Vol. II: *The 20th Century*. New York: Feminist Press, 1993. Introductory essays provide a feminist context for the works in this monumental anthology, which unfortunately does not include works by authors from Pakistan, Bangladesh, and Sri Lanka. Contains guide to pronunciation, bibliography, and index.

SPANISH LONG FICTION

The prose form that eventually came to be called the novel has always been the least precisely defined of literary genres. For that reason, it is difficult to assign a beginning to the history of the novel in Spanish literature. Most of the prose of the Middle Ages and much of that written during the eighteenth century does not fit very well into the category of long fiction of which the nineteenth century realistic novel is the synthesis. Poetry could be defined—at least until the advent of the experimental poetry of the twentieth century—as a literary form in which the language is ordered through rhyme and meter, and drama is identified by the fact that it is intended for live presentation on a stage. The characteristics that make a work of prose "novelistic," however, have eluded most attempts at precise identification.

The history of the novel in Spain is the history of a form that is constantly new, or "novel." The shape of that history is determined to some extent by a concern for the purpose of the novel, which is really a concern for the effect of the novel on the reader. Throughout the development of long fiction in Spain, as in many other Western cultures, reading for pleasure was considered an idle and potentially dangerous pursuit and reading for edification an admirable pastime. The novel was subjected to a process of more or less subtle censorship by the official institutions of society, which tended to make it justify itself as something other than pure entertainment, as something useful. This social phenomenon is most obvious in the case of the masterpiece of Spanish fiction, Miguel de Cervantes's *El ingenioso hidalgo don Quixote de la Mancha*, 1605, 1615 (*The History of the Valorous and Wittie Knight-Errant, Don Quixote of the Mancha*, 1612-1620; better known as *Don Quixote de la Mancha*), but it is manifest even in the earliest extant imaginative prose writing in Spain, the exemplum literature of the thirteenth century.

EARLY DIDACTIC FICTION

The first examples of exemplum prose fiction—probably translations or adaptations of Arabic works—include *Calila e Dimna* (c. 1251; Calila and Dimna) and the *Libro de los engaños e los asayamientos de las mujeres* (c. 1253; *Book of Women's Wiles and Deceits*, 1882). The propagation of these early didactic works was facilitated by the increase in the manufacturing of paper in Spain during the thirteenth century and the invention of eyeglasses toward the end of it. This exemplum literature belongs to the tradition of short fiction because of its form—collections of brief prose pieces, each serving as an example of appropriate or inappropriate social conduct—but it presages some of the characteristics of the longer prose forms that eventually evolved into the novelistic form of the seventeenth century and after. As the titles of some of these collections indicate—the anonymous *Libro del consejo e de los consejeros* (early 1200's; book of advice and advisers) and the *Libro de los exemplos del Conde Lucanor y de Patronio* (1328-1335; *Count Lucanor: Or, The Fifty Pleasant Stories of Patronio*, 1868) of Juan Manuel (1282-1348)—the exempla are linked together by a fictional device involving the relationship of central characters: usually an older, wiser counselor who tells the stories to a naïve, inexperienced person for whom the counselor is in some way responsible. Although the "short stories" that form the text may be unrelated to one another, they are unified by the presence and concerns of the teacher and the student.

The collections of exemplary literature were important antecedents of the novel in that the history of long fiction is replete with examples of a great diversity of experience portrayed in a single work, synthesized into a unified narrative through some point of reference, such as one character, locale, or theme. The obviously didactic intent, which often seems to be only a necessary justification for the "idle pleasure" of reading ingenious, sometimes satiric stories, is another characteristic that the novel inherited from medieval prose literature. The tendency toward a more imaginative fictional representation was evident throughout the fourteenth and early fifteenth centuries, culminating in *El Arcipreste de Talavera*, commonly known as *El corbacho* (1498, written 1438; first three parts as *Little Sermons on Sin*,

1959), of Alfonso Martínez de Toledo (1398-c. 1482), who held the position of Archpriest of Talavera, and in the work of Diego de San Pedro, a late fifteenth century writer about whom almost nothing is known. His sentimental novels of courtly love, which include the *Tratado de amores de Arnalte y Lucinda* (c. 1481; *Arnalte and Lucenda: A Certayne Treatye Most Wyttely Devysed Orygynally Written in the Spaynysshe*, 1543) and the *Cárcel de amor* (1492; *The Castell of Love*, c. 1549), were precursors of the pastoral and chivalric fiction of the sixteenth century.

CHIVALRIC AND PASTORAL ROMANCES

The advent of a long fictional form that resembled in some ways the modern novel occurred only after the invention of movable type in the late fifteenth century. Although there are two significant examples of adventure fiction in the early 1300's—the *Libro del caballero Zifar* (book of the knight Zifar) and the *Gran conquista de Ultramar* (the great overseas conquest)—the sixteenth century was the first period of extensive dissemination of long prose works. Some of this fiction was from the late fifteenth century, but the large, diverse audience that was the prerequisite for the development of the modern novel did not exist until the advent of printing made books accessible to less than wealthy readers.

The most popular works of fiction were, unquestionably, the romances of chivalry. The primary source of the Spanish version of the Arthurian legend was *Amadís de Gaula* (*Amadis of Gaul*, partial translation, 1567, 1803), originally in Portuguese and widely circulated in manuscript during the fourteenth century, then revised about 1492 by Garci Rodriguez de Montalvo (c. 1480-c. 1550), who published it in 1508. It was so popular that it had been reprinted thirty times by 1587. In the sixteenth century, there appeared a total of twelve books about Amadis and his descendants, including Montalvo's *Las sergas de Esplandián* (c. 1510; *The Sergas of Esplandián*, 1664), *Amadís de Grecia* (sixteenth century; *Amadis of Greece*, 1694), *Lisuarte de Grecia* (1514; *Lisuarte of Greece*, 1652) by Feliciano de Silva (c. 1492-1558), *Palmerín de Oliva* (1511; *Palmerín d'Oliva*, 1588), and *Primaleón* (1512; *Primaleon of Greece*, 1595-

1596). The great popularity of the romances of chivalry is evident in the records of the number published and the frequent attempts by the government to ban their publication. The histories of the perfect knights and the rigid codes of honor and courtly love were evidently out of touch with the actual experiences of the readers but surely embodied some important aspiration or truth for the sixteenth century. The romances of chivalry presented an ideal world of absolutes that surely seemed to be more manageable than the vagaries of actual everyday experience.

The pastoral romances, which achieved a popularity almost equal to that of the romances of chivalry, presented an equally ideal world, one based on the Neoplatonic concept of cosmic love as the controlling force of the universe. The reflection of this universal love in the chaste relationship of perfect lovers and the vicissitudes of those who love unwisely dominated novels such as *Los siete libros de la Diana* (c. 1559; *The Seven Books of Diana*, 1596), by Jorge de Montemayor (1520-1561), and *Primera parte de Diana enamorada* (1564; *First Part of Enamored Diana*, 1598), by Gaspar Gil Polo (c. 1519-1585). The pastoral novels were not only representations of shepherds stricken by love but also somewhat polemical as they expounded various humanistic theories about the nature and effects of true love. Miguel de Cervantes (1547-1616) contributed to the genre with *La Galatea* (1585; *Galatea: A Pastoral Romance*, 1833) and continued until his death to promise that he would produce a second part of this successful story. The first two novels of the most important and prolific dramatist of the time, Lope de Vega Carpio (1562-1635), were in the pastoral mode: *La Arcadia* (1598) and *Los pastores de Belén* (1612; the shepherds of Bethlehem).

Chivalric and pastoral fiction represented an evasion of reality, in that their portrayal of experience was based on an idealized concept of the world. Their appeal was in part a result of the fact that, even though they were not what could be called realistic, they did deal in some way with the real concerns of the reading public—honor, love, and suffering—and in part because those concerns were portrayed in the exotic contexts of heroic exploits and peaceful, bucolic settings.

Even more exotic was the subject matter of the Byzantine novel, which often took the form of a Moorish novel and experienced a period of popularity in the sixteenth century. The most successful was the anonymous *Historia de Abindarráez y Xarifa*, more commonly known as the *Historia del Abencerraje y la hermosa Jarifa* (three versions, in 1561, 1562, and 1565; history of the Abencerraje and the beautiful Jarifa) or simply the *Abencerraje*, which narrates a story of love and chivalry in the context of Christian-Moorish conflicts along the Andalusian frontier during the retaking of Spain from the Moors. Another significant example of this genre was the widely read historical novel by Ginés Pérez de Hita (c. 1544-c. 1619), *Las guerras civiles de Granada* (1619, written 1595-1597; *The Civil Wars of Granada*, 1803).

LA CELESTINA AND THE PICARESQUE

Throughout the sixteenth century, the development of long fiction took two directions. Paralleling the novelistic prose that portrayed the world in the idealistic terms of the chivalric, pastoral, and Byzantine modes was a type of fiction more firmly based on the truth of sixteenth century experience. The earliest example is one of the masterpieces of Spanish literature, first published anonymously in 1499 as the *Comedia de Calisto y Melibea* (comedy of Calisto and Melibea). It reappeared several years later in a series of expanded versions entitled *Tragicomedia de Calisto y Melibea* (1502; *Celestina*, 1631), in which there was textual evidence that the author of at least the major part of the work was Fernando de Rojas (c. 1465-1541). Because of the popularity of the main character, an earthy old woman who uses her skills of witchcraft to further her professional reputation as a go-between, the printers changed the title to *La Celestina*, by which title the work is now known. It is a story of the passionate love of Calisto and Melibea, doomed to failure by the circumstances of their birth. Some critics have called *La Celestina* the first novel in Spanish, because it portrayed characters from all social classes in a more realistic manner than did the romances, which tended to idealize and perfect the world that they created.

La Celestina became a very popular work, and the name of the old witch, Celestina, entered the lexicon of Spanish as the generic term for a go-between or pimp. Throughout the sixteenth century, there were imitations of *La Celestina* and examples of prose fiction influenced by Rojas's work that presented a fairly realistic portrayal of certain baser aspects of sixteenth century life. A surprisingly frank and erotic account of the life of a prostitute appeared in the *Retrato de la lozana andaluza* (1528; *Portrait of Lozana, the Lusty Andalusian Woman*, 1987), by Francisco Delicado (c. 1480-c. 1534), a priest who published in the following year a treatise on a supposed cure for syphilis, a disease from which he himself suffered.

The sixteenth century work of fiction that had perhaps the greatest impact on the development of the European novel was *La vida de Lazarillo de Tormes y de sus fortunas y adversidades*, published anonymously in 1554 and translated into English as *The Pleasant Historie of Lazarillo de Tormes* (1586; commonly known as *Lazarillo de Tormes*). His work was the first example of what later was called the picaresque novel, the fictional biography (or often, as in this case, autobiography) of a parasitic delinquent. Lazaro, the picaro who narrates his own story, rises above his miserable surroundings by serving a series of masters, using all of his cunning and wit to survive in a cruel society. As he changes from a child to an adult, he accumulates the experience of sustained contact with a deceptive world and becomes as cynical and dishonest as the people who have exploited and mistreated him. *Lazarillo de Tormes* is extraordinary for its brutal satire and comic narrative, particularly in the context of the prevailing literary vogue of heroic chivalric adventures, courtly conduct, and pastoral love.

Lazarillo de Tormes continued the tradition of social realism established by *La Celestina*, and part of that realistic portrayal of society was its consideration of the nature of honor—whether it is something intrinsic or something acquired through conduct. In the later manifestations of the picaresque genre, the theme of honor became more important and often was related to the more specific question of *limpieza de sangre* (purity of blood), a concern central to the plot of *La Celestina*. Particularly after the expulsion or forced conversion of the Jews in 1492 and the Muslims in 1502, purity of blood became a significant question. To be a *converso* (convert, or New Christian) was to be a second-class citizen, barred from positions of public prominence and respect and often harassed and mistreated. Because of the implication that, if honor was inherited and dependent on the purity of Christian blood, a *converso* was not honorable, the theme of intrinsic or acquired honor represented an actual, socially conditioned anxiety of the time.

The concern over discovery of questionable ancestry and the pursuit of recognition of one's honor pervades the satiric exposure of society's hypocrisy that emerges from the texts of the picaresque novel. *La vida y hechos del pícaro Guzmán de Alfarache* (part 1, 1599, part 2, 1604; *The Rogue: Or, The Life of Guzman de Alfarache*, 1622; also known as *The Life and Adventures of Guzman d'Alfarache: Or, The Spanish Rogue*; best known as *Guzmán de Alfarache*), by Mateo Alemán (1547-c. 1614), is the fictional autobiography of a reformed delinquent who, because he has established himself as a respectable citizen, can moralize about Original Sin and redemption as he narrates his devilish escapades. Significant examples of the picaresque novel with innovative variations appeared well into the seventeenth century. The *Libro de entretenimiento de la pícara Justina* (1605; *The Life of Justina, the Country Jilt*, 1707) of Francisco López de Úbeda (died 1620) uses the picaresque form as a thinly veiled satire of the Spanish court. *La hija de Celestina* (1612; *The Hypocrites*, 1657), by Alonso Jerónimo de Salas Barbadillo (1581-1635), was primarily an exploitation of the genre, an entertainment without the moralizing overtones.

In 1618, Vicente Espinel (1550-1624) published a pseudo-picaresque novel, the *Relaciones de la vida del escudero Marcos de Obregón* (*The History of the Life of the Squire Marcos de Obregón*, 1816), which tells the episodic adventures not of a delinquent, but of a respectable man. In the *Segunda parte de la vida de Lazarillo de Tormes, sacada de las crónicas antiguas de Toledo* (1620; *The Pursuit of the Historie of Lazarillo de Tormes*, 1622), Juan de Luna (c. 1590-c. 1650) used the picaresque genre as an attack on the clergy and the Inquisition. The most enduring of the genre, after *The Pursuit of the Historie of Lazarillo de Tormes*, was the *Historia de la vida del Buscón llamado don Pablos* (1626; *The Life and Adventures of Buscón, the Witty Spaniard*, 1657), written by one of the most extraordinary poets of the seventeenth century, Francisco Gómez de Quevedo y Villegas (1580-1645). The history of Don Pablos, a disadvantaged young man who longs to be a gentleman, is an example of the picaresque returning to the witty, humorous narrative of grotesque brutality that characterized *Lazarillo de Tormes*. There is an implicit didacticism in the constant punishment that Don Pablos suffers for trying to move from his lower social class to the more respectable station of the nobility. The tradition of the picaresque novel is, in fact, a continuation of the tradition of the early didactic prose, the exemplum literature of the thirteenth century, another manifestation of the tendency to justify literature as something other than pure entertainment or art.

The motifs of satire and social criticism of the picaresque novel were also evident in other forms of fiction during the sixteenth and seventeenth centuries. *El crotalón* was a satiric dialogue in the style of Lucian (second century C.E.), written and circulated in 1553 (though not published until 1871), which bore the pseudonym Christóphoro Gnósopho and has been attributed to the Erasmian writer Cristóbal de Villalón (c. 1500-1558). Quevedo published a series of *Sueños* (1607-1622; *The Visions of Dom Francisco de Quevedo Villega*, 1667), witty, conceit-filled satires of social types in the form of extravagant hallucinations, and Baltasar Gracián (1601-1658) created a monumental allegorical narrative of prudence, optimism, and pessimistic disenchantment with the world in *El criticón* (1651-1657; *The Critick*, 1681). *El diablo cojuelo* (1641; the lame devil, published in English as *Le Diable Boiteux: Or, The Devil upon Two Sticks*, 1741) of Luis Vélez de Guevara (1579-1644) was an extensive panorama of Spanish society, as were the less successful but more satiric works of the prolific novelist Francisco Santos (c. 1617-c. 1697), which include *Día y noche de Madrid*

(1663; day and night in Madrid) and *El arca de Noé y campana de Belilla* (1697; Noah's ark and Belilla's bell). In 1632, Lope de Vega Carpio produced *La Dorotea* (the story of Dorotea), an autobiographical novel in dialogue influenced by the realistic portrayal of characters in *La Celestina* that deals with the illusions and disillusionment of love and the emptiness of a life restricted to the pursuit of sensual pleasures.

Miguel de Cervantes

The life of Cervantes fell in the two centuries of the Spanish Golden Age, the sixteenth and seventeenth. The publication of his monumental *Don Quixote de la Mancha* was a culmination of the previous trends of prose fiction in Spanish and a point of departure for the novelistic works not only of the remaining years of the Golden Age but also of the prose literature of the eighteenth century. Examples of all the significant forms of fiction that had developed by 1600 are found in Cervantes's writing. His *Galatea* is a pastoral romance. The picaresque as well as reflections of the early didactic tales appear in the collection of his short novels, the *Novelas ejemplares* (1613; *Exemplary Novels*, 1846), while *Los trabajos de Persiles y Sigismunda* (1617; *The Travels of Persiles and Sigismunda: A Northern History*, 1619) is a Byzantine novel. The chivalric tradition is the foundation of *Don Quixote de la Mancha*, but this vast panorama of Spanish life and literary tradition contains interpolated, self-contained stories that represent all of these styles of literature. *Don Quixote de la Mancha*, in fact, is a work of fictional literature that deals directly with fictional literature and its relationship to real, historical experience. It is a culmination of the tendency to regard literature as serving some motive other than pleasurable entertainment, yet it is as much a satire of that tendency as a restatement of the conviction that literature does—and perhaps should—influence its audience in an edifying manner.

The emphasis on literature and its audience is clear in the basic presuppositions of the history of Don Quixote—that his insanity is the result of reading too many chivalric romances and that his assuming the role of a knight errant is the result of his interpreting the romances as history rather than fiction. The episodes with moralizing commentary of Don Quixote and his squire Sancho Panza are reminiscent of the early exemplum literature but are rendered ironic by the insanity of the counselor and the shifting of roles of the knight and the squire as teacher and student. This vast and complex novel seems to be concentrated on a theme of the fickleness of human perception, but it is in fact an exploration of the nature of reality and the various illusions to which humans succumb in the course of their ambitious quest for respectability, honor, or mere survival.

The history of Don Quixote is, above all, the narrative of a continual process of experiencing the world as it really is, a slow disintegration of idealistic visions, both optimistic and pessimistic, of the world. *Don Quixote de la Mancha* is unquestionably what it has been called by numerous critics, the first modern novel. The astounding diversity of motifs and perspectives present in the narrative signify a radical departure from all the previous forms of prose fiction. While the pastoral, the chivalric, the picaresque, the Byzantine, and the sentimental novel begin with presuppositions or postulates about the nature of reality and are developed, for the most part, according to those a priori convictions, Cervantes's novel is an exploratory text that develops independent of any fixed notion about the nature of reality or the strictures of a particular literary genre.

Although *Don Quixote de la Mancha* has often been described as a satire of the romances of chivalry, it is more accurate to interpret the novel as a satire of the tendency to regard an idealistic concept of reality as a valid model for human conduct. Don Quixote believes that the codes and rituals of chivalry are viable in his historical reality. The humorous satire of the text derives from the futility of transferring that fictional vision to his real experience. In his prologues and his novel, Cervantes creates characters who proclaim that *Don Quixote de la Mancha* was written with the intent of destroying the influence of the romances of chivalry. Throughout the seventeenth and eighteenth centuries, that claim of authorial intent was repeated in hundreds of critiques, imitations, and adaptations of Cervantes's novel. It is more likely that the popularity of the literature of chivalry and the fact that there were many nobles who actually performed chivalric rituals as a form of entertaining, idle pastime provided Cervantes with a theme that would be at once ridiculous and credible, and provide an incomparable opportunity to develop the dichotomy of appearance and reality that forms the unifying concept of his novel. As he proclaimed the efficacious intent of his work, Cervantes was also exploiting the commonplace notion of the potentially pernicious effect of idle reading and participating in the tendency to justify literary art by its usefulness.

Because of the widespread success of *Don Quixote de la Mancha*, there were many imitations. One of the most interesting and significant cases occurred before Cervantes had completed the second part, which was published in 1615. In 1614, someone published the *Segundo tomo del ingenioso hidalgo Don Quixote de la Mancha* (*A Continuation of the Comical History of the Most Ingenious Knight, Don Quixote de la Mancha*, 1705) under the pseudonym Alonso Fernández de Avellaneda. Most critics have judged this spurious second part, commonly referred to as the "false Quixote," to be inferior to Cervantes's work and to be a ridiculous, unimaginative attempt at Cervantine satire. Understandably, Cervantes was furious and even included a critique of the false Quixote in his own second part.

THE EIGHTEENTH CENTURY

Although *Don Quixote de la Mancha* had considerable influence in the seventeenth century, the most significant manifestations of the impact of Cervantes's work on Spanish literature appeared during the Enlightenment, along with evidence of the influence of Quevedo and Gracián. That these three writers were emulated during the eighteenth century is understandable, for it was the supreme age of social criticism and the last great attempt in European culture to renovate society according to rational principles. It was a time of supreme optimism, in which intellectuals were convinced that, through judgment, insight, and good taste, a perfect world could be established. Thus, Quevedo and Gracián, as social satirists, were appealing enough to be imitated by Diego de Torres

Villarroel (1693-1770) in his satiric fantasy of life in Madrid, the *Visiones y visitas de Torres con Don Francisco de Quevedo por la corte* (1727-1728; visions and visits of Torres with Don Francisco de Quevedo in the court). Cervantes was also attractive as the writer who, according to the generally accepted critical judgment of the century, had single-handedly driven out a contemporary social evil, the romances of chivalry.

Many writers prefaced their works with comments about Cervantes's accomplishment and the promise that they would do the same—eradicate some flaw of society through a judicious satire. The most notable examples were Francisco de Isla (1703-1781) and José Cadalso (1741-1782). Isla's voluminous *Historia del famoso predicador Fray Gerundio de Campazas, Alias Zotes* (part 1, 1758, part 2, 1770; *The History of the Famous Preacher Friar Gerund de Campazas, Alias Zotes*, 1772) is a satiric attack on the extravagant preachers of the day, whose sermons were so filled with ingenious conceits and convoluted language that no one understood much of what they said. Cadalso's major work was the *Cartas marruecas* (1789; Moroccan letters), a collection of letters exchanged among a young Moor living in a Christian household in Spain, his Moorish mentor in Morocco, and the Christian host. The epistolary work has no significant evidence of Cervantine influence, but Cadalso's preface compares his attempt to improve society through social criticism to Cervantes's intent.

There is a paucity of significant eighteenth century Spanish novels, for the Spanish Enlightenment was primarily an age of the essay, didactic poetry, and exemplary drama. The most interesting form of prose literature was a hybrid form, a type of essayistic prose work that made use of novelistic devices such as the portrayal of imaginary characters who represented more or less obviously real people or fictional characters from the Spanish literary tradition. It was an age of polemics, and much of the "essayistic fiction" was pointedly didactic and argumentative, often witty and ingenious in its direct attacks on certain individuals. Most of the major writers of the second half of the century engaged in the literary exchanges, though most did so through poetry or short prose pieces. The two most significant examples of works that can be termed novelistic in the context of the literary values of the period are *Los literatos en cuaresma* (1773; writers during Lent), by the poet and fabulist Tomás de Iriarte (1750-1791), and *Los gramáticos: Historia chinesca* (c. 1783; the grammarians: a Chinese history), a fierce attack on Iriarte and his entire family, by Juan Pablo Forner (1756-1797).

Of the more traditional novelists, the notable examples were Pedro de Montengón y Paret (1745-1824), who wrote sentimental historical novels, and José Mor de Fuentes (1762-1848), whose epistolary novel *El cariño perfecto: O, Los amores de Alfonso y Serafina* (c. 1795; perfect affection, or the love of Alfonso and Serafina) continued the Renaissance literary tradition of praise of country life and scorn of the court.

ROMANTICISM AND *COSTUMBRISMA*

During the early years of the nineteenth century, few novels were published in Spain; in part, this was a consequence of a particularly strong expression of the recurring idea that prose fiction is immoral and detrimental to its readers. Indeed, the government attempted, with some success, to suppress the publication of novels. In spite of an official ban on translated fiction, a Valencia publishing house began in 1816 to publish a collection of novels that introduced foreign novelists to the ever-growing Spanish reading public.

The Romantic influences prevalent during the 1820's and 1830's resulted in a spate of historical novels, some written by the outstanding literary figures of the Spanish Romantic movement. The dramatist Francisco Martínez de la Rosa (1787-1862) published his historical novel *Doña Isabel de Solís, Reyna de Granada* in parts from 1837 to 1846. One of the finest Romantic poets, José de Espronceda (1808-1842), developed the typical Romantic themes of spiritual vacuity and despair over the failure of love in *Sancho Saldaña* (1834). Mariano José de Larra (1809-1837), the satiric essayist whose suicide and funeral rallied the Romantic writers to a proclamation of unity against a disapproving Establishment, published *El doncel de don Enrique el doliente* (1834; the squire of Sir Henry the Sufferer). The best of the historical novels appeared several years after a strong ideological reaction to Romanticism had set in. *El Señor de Bembibre* (1844; *The Mystery of Bierzo Valley: A Tale of the Knights Templars*, 1938), by Enrique Gil y Carrasco (1815-1846), is unusual because of its strong evocation of a regional Leonese setting and its development of the conflict between traditional values and the Romantic despair that results from a loss of faith in the moral, religious, and intellectual beliefs that formed those values. There were also hundreds of historical novels published by lesser writers such as Wenceslao Ayguals de Izco (1801-1873), Francisco Navarro Villoslada (1818-1895), and Manuel Fernández y González (1821-1888), who, in spite of their popularity, never gained the attention of literary scholarship.

Particularly popular during the Romantic period and the remainder of the nineteenth century were the *novelas por entregas* or *folletines*, serialized novels that appeared either in magazines or separate installments that were sold a chapter at a time. The most striking feature of early nineteenth century historical fiction and the serial novels was the apparent indifference to a careful, convincing portrayal of physical reality; this is the feature that also distinguished this fiction from the literary tradition of works such as *La Celestina, Lazarillo de Tormes*, and *Don Quixote de la Mancha*, as well as from post-1850 fiction. More in the tradition of fiction based on preconceived notions about the nature of reality and experience—the tradition of the pastoral and the chivalric romance—the nineteenth century historical novel did not contribute significantly to the development of the novel as an artistic form until the advent of the most notable novelist of the century, Benito Pérez Galdós (1843-1920).

A major influence on the novel at mid-century was the importation of the French novels of Eugène Sue (1804-1857), six of which were translated and published in 1844 alone. Sue's novels inspired in Spanish writers an interest in a different type of historical novel, one that dealt with recent events and propagated social and political ideas. Significant examples were Ayguals's *María: O, La hija de un jornalero* (1845-1846; Mary, or the daughter of a day laborer) and *Misterios de las sectas secretas: O, El francmasón proscrito* (1847-1852; mysteries of secret sects, or the proscribed Freemason) by José M. Riera y Comas (1827-1858).

The more careful observation of recent historical reality evident in these novels had a parallel in another type of fiction that pervaded the middle years of the century—the *costumbrista* literature. The popular *costumbrista* sketches portrayed specific "authentic" aspects of everyday life in Spain in precise detail and often with a nostalgic attitude toward the quaint, typical customs that were disappearing with the advance of the modern world. The *costumbrista* tradition influenced two important novelists who began publishing in the mid-nineteenth century, Fernán Caballero (pseudonym of Cecilia Böhl von Faber, 1796-1877) and Pedro Antonio de Alarcón (1833-1891). Fernán Caballero is an unusual case in the history of Spanish fiction. Usually credited with preparing the way for the important realistic novelists of the second half of the century, she wrote her novels in German or French and had them translated for publication by her agent. She was best known for *La gaviota* (1849; *The Sea-Gull: Or, The Lost Beauty*, 1867), which is typical of all of her novels, moralizing and somewhat sentimental, superficially descriptive in the tradition of the *costumbrista* sketches.

Alarcón was an aggressive proponent of the conservative Catholic point of view. Except for his delightful, whimsical *El sombrero de tres picos* (1874; *The Three-Cornered Hat*, 1886), which inspired the ballet by the Spanish composer Manuel de Falla (1876-1946) and is reminiscent of the exemplum literature of the Middle Ages and the *Exemplary Novels of Cervantes*, his novels are rather severely ideological. *El final de Norma* (1855, written 1850; *Brunhilde: Or, The Last Act of Norma*, 1891), *El escándalo* (1875; *The Scandal*, 1945), and *El niño de la bola* (1880; *The Child of the Ball*, 1892; also as *The Infant with the Globe*, 1959) are attacks on irreligion, immorality, and the liberal ideas that were prevalent during Alarcón's career. *La pródiga* (1882; *True to Her Oath: A Tale of Love and Misfortune*, 1899) is a more interesting novel; it narrates the story of a woman's illicit sexual behavior and suicide, stimulated by an idealized Romantic attitude toward love.

REALISM

The triumph of the nineteenth century "liberal" movement in Spain, the September Revolution of 1868, which dethroned the Bourbon monarchy and led to the establishment of the short-lived republic in 1873, was a turning point in the history of the novel. The aspirations, problems, and anxieties of Spanish society were, rather suddenly, appropriate material for narrative fiction, and the decade of the 1870's was fertile ground for the thesis novel, a type of fiction in which the theme seems to unduly determine the structure, characterization, and plot development. It was also the decade of intense interest in the idealism of the German philosopher Karl Christian Friedrich Krause (1781-1832). The intellectual movement appropriately called Krausism, which emphasized a harmony of the spiritual and the rational and stressed principles of liberal education, led to the establishment in 1876 of the Institución Libre de la Enseñanza (Free Institute of Teaching) by Francisco Giner de los Ríos (1839-1915), a disciple of the Spanish intellectual leader Julian Sanz del Río (1814-1869), who was in turn a student and disciple of Krause. Krausism had a considerable, if temporally limited, effect on the novelists of the period, such as Juan Valera (1824-1905) and Pérez Galdós, whose novel *El amigo Manso* (1882; *Our Friend Manso*, 1987) is a disenchanted portrayal of a Krausist professor. During the 1870's, Pérez Galdós established himself as a significant novelist with the thesis novels that would bring him extensive recognition as an enemy of religious and social intolerance—*Doña Perfecta* (1876; English translation, 1880), *Gloria* (1876-1877; English translation, 1879), and *La familia de León Roch* (1878; *The Family of León Roch*, 1888).

In contrast to Pérez Galdós's liberalism, which was moderate but impressive for its contrast to prevailing social attitudes, the regional novels of Jose María de Pereda (1833-1906), published during the 1870's, are characterized by a reinforcement of traditional values and institutions, as in *Los hombres de pro* (1872; the supporters), *El buey suelto* (1877; the freed ox), and *Don Gonzalo González de la Gonzalera* (1878). Pereda went on to write the most widely read novelistic accounts of provincial life in Spain, characterized by a *costumbrista* nostalgia and idealism about rural society—*El sabor de la tierruca* (1881; the smell of the land), *Sotileza* (1884; English translation, 1959), and *Peñas arriba* (1895; atop the mountain). Pereda's fiction had an enormous appeal for its own kind of exoticism, the life of the simple country people, but his lack of detached, objective narrative rendered his fiction less significant to the development of the dominant trend of nineteenth century fiction—realism—in spite of the astounding wealth of descriptive details in his novels.

A more significant novelist was Juan Valera, who began his career with *Pepita Jiménez* (1874; *Pepita Ximenez*, 1886), an elegant, refined, and subtle work that in less judicious hands would have been a blatant thesis novel. His later works, which include *Las ilusiones del doctor Faustino* (1875; the illusions of Doctor Faustino), *Juanita la larga* (1896; Juanita the longsuffering), and *Genio y figura* (1897; spirit and form), presented idealized studies of the difficulties of love and the emotional frustrations resulting from the conflict between worldliness and spirituality.

The other novelist of the time who, with Valera, Alarcón, and Pérez Galdós—for *Pepita Ximenez, The Three-Cornered Hat*, and *Doña Perfecta*—gained considerable recognition in Europe and the United States was Armando Palacio Valdés (1853-1938). The less familiar novels of Palacio Valdés were more significant to the development of nineteenth century fiction than the immensely popular *Marta y María* (1883; *The Marquis of Peñalta*, 1886), *José* (1885; English translation, 1901), and *La hermana San Sulpicio* (1889; *Sister Saint Sulpice*, 1890). *La espuma* (1891; *The Froth*, 1891) and *La fé* (1892; *Faith*, 1892) are innovative novels of social and religious protest with fantastic elements that imply political symbolism.

The most significant novelists of the century were, unquestionably, Emilia Pardo Bazán (1851-1921), Clarín (pseudonym of Leopoldo Alas, 1852-1901), and Benito Pérez Galdós. Pérez Galdós was the literary giant of the century, for the quantity and sustained quality of his fiction, while Clarín's reputation and importance as a major novelist rested on a single, monumental work, *La regenta* (1884; English translation, 1984). Although Emilia Pardo Bazán produced many novels that were widely read and continues to gain the somewhat qualified respect of literary scholarship, she was most influential for her activities as a literary critic and her rather outrageous public image. An enormous, robust woman who smoked cigars in public and alienated many with her feminist ideas and outspoken manner, Pardo Bazán was the first writer in Spain to publish commentaries on French naturalism—*La cuestión palpitante* (1883; the burning question)—and was instrumental in creating widespread interest in the nineteenth century Russian novelists. While she praised the literary talent of Émile Zola (1840-1902), she condemned the impersonal, scientific observation characteristic of his naturalistic fiction. She proposed instead a balance of naturalistic and idealistic fictional motifs, a sort of hybrid ideological approach that was the perspective, if not the theory, of the realists.

Pardo Bazán's pronouncements were considered rather scandalous, and her novels were equally offensive to the conservative establishment. *La tribuna* (1883; the tribune) portrays the struggles of a young woman caught in the unpleasantries of urban working-class life. *Los pazos de Ulloa* (1886; *The Son of the Bondwoman*, 1908; also as *The House of Ulloa*, 1992) and *La madre naturaleza* (1887; mother nature), her best-known novels, are somewhat idealized portraits of lusty, earthy conflicts between the idle aristocracy and the greedy, rural working class. The themes of sometimes illicit sexual behavior and class conflicts dominate *Insolación* (1889; *Midsummer Madness*, 1907) and *Morriña* (1889; *Morriña: Homesickness*, 1891), but in the later novels, such as *La quimera* (1905; the chimera) and *La sirena negra* (1908; the black siren), Pardo Bazán's perspective shifted to one of more conservative and religious ideology.

The career of Clarín was also established primarily through his activities as a literary critic, but his personality was more serene and his public image more that of an intellectual, humanistic spokesman for the liberal consciousness. Except for his elegant and moving narrative *Su único hijo* (1890; *His Only Son*, 1970), Clarín's only novel was *La regenta*, a vast panorama of life in a provincial capital developed around the interior conflict of Ana Ozores, a young woman married to a much older man and tempted by her sexual attraction to her priest and the local playboy. Clarín's judicious and subtly satiric portrait of the manners and mores of Spanish society is rivaled in excellence and perceptivity only by the *novelas contemporáneas* of Pérez Galdós.

BENITO PÉREZ GALDÓS

Since the death of Pérez Galdós in 1920, the general reading public of Spain has been more familiar with his historical novels, the *Episodios nacionales* (1873-1912; national episodes), than with his realistic novels of contemporary urban society, the *novelas españolas contemporáneas* (contemporary Spanish novels), although these have always received more serious attention from scholars. The forty-six *episodios* form a fictionalized history of Spain's recent past, from the Battle of Trafalgar in 1805 to the Restoration of the Bourbon monarchy in 1874. While these are historical novels, they are somewhat unusual in that all the principal characters are fictional personages whose lives are intertwined with historical figures and events to a greater or lesser degree, depending on the particular novel. Throughout the *episodios*, which Pérez Galdós published at the amazing rate of from one to five per year from 1873 to 1879 and again from 1898 to 1912, the recent past is revealed as primarily a struggle between two opposing ideologies, the traditional Carlist point of view and the progressive, liberal ideas that led to the revolution of 1868 and the establishment of the First Republic in 1873. In contrast to the development of the historical novel in Spain and elsewhere, Pérez Galdós's *episodios* are very much a part of the realistic fictional mode that dominated the second half of the nineteenth century. While they are somewhat more ideologically directed than the *novelas españolas contemporáneas*, they lack the nostalgic idealization of the past evident in most historical fiction before Pérez Galdós.

After the thesis novels of the 1870's, which usu-

ally are referred to as Pérez Galdós's *novelas de la primera época* (novels of the first period), the novelistic development of Pérez Galdós changed dramatically. With *La desheredada* (1881; *The Disinherited Lady*, 1957), Pérez Galdós began what eventually became an all-encompassing portrait of urban middle-class life in Madrid. The twenty-eighth novel, *Casandra* (1905), is usually considered the end of the series, because Pérez Galdós's last two novels—*El caballero encantado* (1909; the enchanted knight) and *La razón de la sinrazón* (1915; the reason of nonreason)—are markedly different and so peculiar that they are often disregarded as unfortunate postscripts to a remarkable career.

Pérez Galdós was known for his liberal tendencies, as indicated by the title of the first biography published in English, H. Chonon Berkowitz's *Benito Pérez Galdós: Spanish Liberal Crusader* (1948). The label of liberal, however, must be understood in the context of the last decades of the nineteenth century. Pérez Galdós's novels are not primarily political, and they certainly are not radical in their treatment of middle-class society. They are, rather, fairly objective representations of the established institutions of urban Spain and the amazing variety of human experience that one might expect in such a diversified society. The censure of morally aberrant behavior that is evident in the work of many novelists of the century is replaced by a sympathetic understanding in novels such as *Tormento* (1884; *Torment*, 1952), *Ángel Guerra* (1890-1891), and *Tristana* (1892; English translation, 1961), which was the source of a 1970 film version by the Spanish director Luis Buñuel (1900-1982), who also made a film version of Pérez Galdós's *Nazarín* (1895; the Nazarene) in 1958. In novel after novel, Pérez Galdós exposed with masterfully subtle irony the hypocrisies and foibles of the middle class. Whether he was portraying the unfortunate plight of a mediocre bureaucrat fired from his job with only months to go before acquiring a retirement pension in *Miau* (1888; English translation, 1963) or the excruciating task of a pretentious housewife trying to solve the riddle of bourgeois society—how to get away with spending ten times what one earns—in *La de Bringas* (1884; *The Spendthrifts*,

1951), Pérez Galdós maintained a congenial and benevolent narrative voice. Through his consummate ability for giving the impression that his narrative is more objective than it in fact is, Pérez Galdós creates characters who reveal themselves as they really are. The variety and complexity of their aspirations, of their admirable spirit or deplorable lack of it, of their naïveté or cynical wisdom are evident in all of Pérez Galdós's contemporary novels, but more so in his two longest works, *Fortunata y Jacinta* (1886-1887; *Fortunata and Jacinta: Two Stories of Married Women*, 1973) and the Torquemada cycle (published in English translation as *Torquemada* in 1986)—*Torquemada en la hoguera* (1889; *Torquemada in the Flames*, 1956), *Torquemada en la cruz* (1893; *Torquemada's Cross*, 1973), *Torquemada en el purgatorio* (1894; Torquemada in purgatory), and *Torquemada y San Pedro* (1895; Torquemada and Saint Peter). The epic history of Fortunata, an earthy, uneducated young woman from the slums of Madrid, and Jacinta, a respectable, middle-class woman, both in love with the same errant playboy, is one of the most extraordinary novels of the European realist tradition. The story of Francisco Torquemada, a moneylender of questionable social origin who establishes himself as a prominent member of the new upper-middle class through his financial dexterity and his marriage to an impoverished aristocrat, is in some ways the most important fictional work of Pérez Galdós. At no other point did he explore so thoroughly the essence of the nineteenth century social phenomenon of the dependence of respectability on the acquisition of material wealth. It is significant that Pérez Galdós dominated the development of the realistic novel in the last decades of the nineteenth century, for he created a vast body of fiction that exemplifies all that the realistic tradition in fiction has, in retrospect, been judged to represent—an artistic creation through which the varied truths of nineteenth century urban existence are revealed.

GENERATION OF 1898

At the beginning of the twentieth century, several nineteenth century novelists, such as Pérez Galdós, Pardo Bazán, and Palacio Valdés, were still active,

and there were others whose principal work retained the tone and the concerns of the late nineteenth century. Vicente Blasco Ibáñez (1867-1928), after the enormous success of naturalistic novels such as *La barraca* (1898; *The Cabin*, 1917) and *Cañas y barro* (1902; *Reeds and Mud*, 1928), turned to the anti-German wartime novels that became popular in Spain and abroad—*Los cuatro jinetes del Apocalipsis* (1916; *The Four Horsemen of the Apocalypse*, 1918) and *Mare Nostrum* (1918; English translation, 1919). The ultraconservative Catholic novelist Ricardo León (1877-1943) continued the tradition of the thesis novel with *Casta de hidalgos* (1908; *A Son of the Hidalgos*, 1921) and *El amore de los amores* (1917; *The Wisdom of Sorrow*, 1951), and Concha Espina de la Serna (1877-1955) published *La esfinge maragata* (1914; *Mariflor*, 1924) and *El metal de los muertos* (1920; the metal of the dead), novels characterized by an unusual combination of subjective sentimentality and social protest in response to the deplorable conditions of the life of working-class people.

While these and other novelists cultivated a wide reading public, the prose fiction that is recognized as of extraordinary importance was produced by another group of writers, many of whom formed a sort of informal literary alliance that came to be called the Generation of 1898. These novelists, poets, dramatists, and essayists held two things in common—their attempts at innovation in their literary work and a concern for the regeneration of Spain after the humiliating defeat suffered in the Spanish-American War in 1898. The second of these concerns—the quest for a rebirth through a spiritual awakening and an affirmation of authentic, individual values—was the subject of much essayistic and journalistic writing, and it passed into the fiction of the period, usually as a subtle ideological base rather than as an overt expression. A concurrent movement in Spanish-American literature that cultivated a conscious aestheticism through radical innovations in prose and poetry, *Modernismo*, was related to the artistic concerns of the writers of the Generation of 1898 and had considerable influence on their search for innovative expressive forms.

Certain novelists of the period, such as Miguel de Unamuno y Jugo (1864-1936), Pío Baroja (1872-1956), Azorín (pseudonym of José Martínez Ruiz, 1873-1967), and Ramón Pérez de Ayala (1880-1962), were clearly participants in the ideological and artistic Generation of 1898, according to the three prerequisites aptly defined by the British Hispanist Donald L. Shaw:

> participation in a personal quest for renewed ideals and beliefs; interpretation of the problem of Spain in related terms, i.e., as a problem of mentality, rather than as political or economic and social; and acceptance of the role of creative writing primarily as an instrument for the examination of these problems.

The other major novelist of the time, Ramón María del Valle-Inclán (1866-1936), seemed disinterested in the "Spanish problem," although the satiric observation of Spanish society in many of his works indicates that his interest was greater than suggested by the lack of direct, soul-searching statements that characterize the novels, plays, poems, and essays of other writers of the Generation of 1898. Valle-Inclán's interest was primarily aesthetic, however, and his first important novels, the four exotic *Sonatas*—*Sonata de primavera* (1904; spring sonata), *Sonata de estío* (1903; summer sonata), *Sonata de otoño* (1902; autumn sonata), and *Sonata de invierno* (1905; winter sonata), which were published together in English as *The Pleasant Memoirs of the Marquis de Bradomín: Four Sonatas* (1924)—show a marked influence of *Modernismo* in their apparent indifference to questions of morality and their emphasis on the development of pure aesthetic artifice. Valle-Inclán's later novels, notably *Tirano Banderas: Novela de tierra caliente* (1926; *The Tyrant: A Novel of Warm Lands*, 1929) and *El ruedo ibérico* (1927-1958; the Iberian arena)—*La corte de los milagros* (1927; the court of miracles), *Viva mi dueño* (1928; long live my master), and *Baza de espadas* (serialized 1932, published 1958; spade trick)—present a bitter censure of all levels of Spanish society, both rural and urban, through an aesthetic distortion achieved by a systematic deformation of the characters and the milieu. This type of fictional narrative,

which Valle-Inclán called earlier in his career the *esperpento* (distorted mirage), anticipated the *tremendismo* of the post-Spanish Civil War novel initiated by Camilo José Cela (born 1916).

Azorín, who adopted his pseudonym from the name of the protagonist of his early novel *La voluntad* (1902; the will), was obsessed for a short period with the problem of the struggle between thought and action, a major preoccupation of the Generation of 1898. *La voluntad* develops the alternatives of acceptance of nihilism or resignation to the Nietzschean doctrine of eternal recurrence. The anguish of *La voluntad* became a quiet resignation mixed with nostalgia for the past in *Antonio Azorín* (1903) and *Las confesiones de un pequeño filósofo* (1904; confessions of a little philosopher). In later novels, such as *Don Juan* (1922; English translation, 1923) and *Doña Ines* (1925), the emphasis remained on a frustrated resignation in the face of time and its destructive power. The last novels of Azorín, written after 1927, were experimental departures from the traditions of realism, but they are generally regarded by critics as being more ambitious than successful.

The most astounding novelist of the early twentieth century, for the sheer volume of his work if not for its artistic accomplishment, was Pío Baroja, whose more than fifty novels form a fictional document of modern Spanish society equaled only by the novels of Pérez Galdós. Baroja is indeed a curious case. From 1901, the year of his first significant novel, *La casa de Aizgorri* (the house of Aizgorri), to his last novels in the 1950's, his novelistic technique and the ideological bases of his work remained essentially unchanged. The style is simple, direct, and unadorned by the aesthetic mannerisms that characterize at least some of the work of almost every major twentieth century novelist. The ideological vision is clear throughout his work, and on it is founded his early trilogy *La lucha por la vida* (1904; *The Struggle for Life*, 1922-1924)—*La busca* (1904; *The Quest*, 1922), *Mala hierba* (1904; *Weeds*, 1923), and *Aurora roja* (1904; *Red Dawn*, 1924). Life is a struggle for survival, and only the fittest survive through the only remedy that exists for the inevitable *abulia*, or lack of will—individual action, action without aim, finality, or social implications of any kind. Any hint of meaning in life, any emotion—love, for example—is simply a *mentira vital* (vital lie) that enables the individual to bear the truth of the lack of meaning in the world. The intellect destroys illusions, as Sacha realizes in *El mundo es ansí* (1912; the world is thus), and action is the only alternative to the paralysis of the will that leads to the disillusionment and suicide of Andrés Hurtado in *El árbol de la ciencia* (1911; *The Tree of Knowledge*, 1928).

Baroja wrote what at first seems to be a variety of fiction—adventure novels, historical novels, biographical and autobiographical fiction—but his approach scarcely changed as he moved from one to the other. Some are dominated by narrated action, and some are made up almost entirely of conversations in which his characters reveal their own manifestations of the conflict of the intellect and the emotions. Baroja's strongest trait is his ability to evoke a sense of the physical atmosphere through a careful choice of details. It is perhaps not surprising that Baroja had many admirers, including Cela, who asserted that the entire twentieth century Spanish novel stems from Baroja, and Ernest Hemingway (1899-1961), who declined the invitation to serve as a pallbearer at Baroja's funeral, claiming to be unworthy of the honor.

The truly monumental figure of the Generation of 1898 was Miguel de Unamuno y Jugo, essayist, poet, dramatist, philosopher, philologist, and novelist. Partly because of the enormous prestige that he had acquired by the first years of the twentieth century, he was unofficially designated as the father of the Generation of 1898. After his first attempt at fiction, *Paz en la guerra* (1897; *Peace in War*, 1983), his novels represented an extraordinary break with the realist tradition of the nineteenth century and embodied the spiritual and ontological anguish that characterized much of the work of the early twentieth century Spanish writers, as well as the existentialist writings of French authors such as Jean-Paul Sartre (1905-1980) and Albert Camus (1913-1960). The scene in *Niebla* (1914; *Mist*, 1929) in which the despairing hero Augusto Pérez confronts the author Unamuno and asserts his independence from him is frequently cited as an important precursor of the techniques of

the Italian playwright Luigi Pirandello (1867-1936). This scene is equaled in its fantastic and ridiculous but serious implications only by the novel's prologue, written by another character in the novel, Víctor Goti, who calls Unamuno a liar, and by the epilogue, written by Augusto Pérez's dog.

This "game of fiction," as Unamuno's narrative tricks have been called, has serious existentialist implications that Unamuno continued to explore in *Abel Sánchez: Una historia de pasión* (1917; *Abel Sánchez*, 1947), a fascinating version of the Cain and Abel story. It is a complex history of ontological envy, developed through a simple, straightforward narrative interspersed with fragments of Joaquín's (Cain's) confessional journal and a suggestion that the entire story is a novelistic text written by Abel's son. Unamuno further questioned existence and its relationship to fictional characters in the strange, autobiographical *Cómo se hace una novela* (1927; *How to Make a Novel*, 1976) and *La novela de don Sandalio, jugador de ajedrez* (1930; the novel of Don Sandalio, chess player). Unamuno's last novel, which is in a sense a fictionalization of *Del sentimiento trágico de la vida en los hombres y en los pueblos* (1913; *The Tragic Sense of Life in Men and Peoples*, 1921), his famous treatise on the conflict of faith and reason, was *San Manuel Bueno, mártir* (1931; *Saint Manuel Bueno, Martyr*, 1956). Again Unamuno plays with fiction in a Cervantine fashion, as the novel, which is the confessional memoir of a young woman who suspects that her priest does not believe in eternal life, turns out to be a manuscript found by a fictionalized Unamuno who claims to have only edited it for publication. Unamuno's fiction was a radical departure from the realist tradition, for at almost no point did it attempt to objectively portray contemporary historical reality. It did, however, transform the novel into what it would be throughout much of the twentieth century, a means of investigating and reflecting on the question of human existence.

Ramón Pérez de Ayala, like Unamuno, began his career with a novel in the realist tradition, *Troteras y danzaderas* (1913; trotting and dancing around), and then began to experiment with more innovative narrative devices. His *Prometeo, Luz de domingo, La caída de los Limones: Tres novelas poemáticas de la vida española* (1916; *Prometheus, Sunday Sunlight, The Fall of the House of Limón: Three Poematic Novels of Spanish Life*, 1920) are not poetic in the usual sense, but grotesque, brutal distortions of the literary legends of Prometheus and Odysseus (*Prometheus*), of the daughters of the Spanish epic hero El Cid (*Sunday Sunlight*), and of the Spanish *conquistadores* (*The Fall of the House of Limón*). *La pata de la raposa* (1912; *The Fox's Paw*, 1924), *Belarmino y Apolonio* (1921; *Belarmino and Apolonio*, 1931) and, to a lesser extent, the 1923 novel published in two parts, *Luna de miel, luna de hiel* and *Los trabajos de Urbano y Simona* (published together in English translation as *Honeymoon, Bittermoon*, 1972), create complex situations of varied perspectives on single realities. The two final novels of Pérez de Ayala, published in 1926, *Tigre Juan* and *El curandero de su honra* (combined in English translation as *Tiger Juan*, 1933), are generally considered to be his finest accomplishments. As a restatement in Freudian terms of the story of Don Juan and the theme of honor and sexual fidelity so pervasive during the Golden Age, these novels are further manifestations of Pérez de Ayala's penchant for creating fiction from the legends and classics of early Spanish literature.

Three other novelists, contemporaries of the writers of the Generation of 1898 but lacking achievements as substantial as those of Unamuno, Baroja, and Azorín, were Gabriel Miró (1879-1949), Ramón Gómez de la Serna (1888-1963), and Benjamín Jarnés (1888-1949). Miró's reputation among literary scholars has grown over the years, but his refined aestheticism and his refusal to turn his novels into topical studies of the "Spanish problem" limited the popular appeal of his work in the early part of the twentieth century. Much of his prose work consisted of collections of short pieces, and his novelistic production was limited to four penetrating psychological novels about the complexities of human behavior, *Las cerezas del cementerio* (1910; the cherries of the cemetery), *El abuelo del rey* (1915; the king's grandfather), *Nuestro Padre San Daniel* (1921; *Our Father San Daniel*, 1930), and *El obispo leproso* (1926; the leprous bishop), in which Miró evoked the experience of provincial life in Spain in an elegant narrative style.

Gómez de la Serna, quite in contrast to Miró, created for himself a significant reputation as the creator of the *greguería*, a form of epigrammatic statement made up of witty, surprising, and often trivial metaphors. Some of his novels, such as *El doctor inverosímil* (1914; the unbelievable doctor), seem to be little more than collections of *greguerías*, and only his novel about the relationship of the game of fiction to human existence, *El novelista* (1923; the novelist), is of particular interest. Jarnés was a much more substantial novelist, with an ideological perspective that recalls Unamuno and an elegant, elaborately cultivated style similar to Miró's. There is much introspective concern in his texts for the creative act of narrative observation and for the meaning of existence. Jarnés's unconventional narrative techniques in novels such as *Locura y muerte de nadie* (1929; madness and death of a nobody) and *Teoría del zumbel* (1930; theory of the top-string) made his work too esoteric for a general audience. His later work— *Lo rojo y lo azul: Homenaje a Stendhal* (1932; the red and the blue: homage to Stendhal) and *Venus dinámica* (1943; dynamic Venus)—is more conventional, with a more traditional approach to plot and characterization.

The Civil War and the Franco era

The Spanish Civil War (1936-1939), a bloody conflict between the conservative Nationalists and the liberal Republican forces that led to the establishment of the dictatorship of Francisco Franco (1892-1975), had an extraordinary effect on the history of the twentieth century Spanish novel. Many of the outstanding literary figures went into exile and produced their most important novels in countries other than Spain. Also, the war experience became the material with which the novel dealt, in much the same way that the social malaise resulting from the disaster of 1898 had become the subject matter for novels in the early part of the century.

The two novelists who established themselves most successfully as representatives of postwar fiction are Camilo José Cela and Juan Goytisolo (born 1931). Cela's *La familia de Pascual Duarte* (1942; *The Family of Pascual Duarte*, 1946, 1964) initiated the literary vogue of *tremendismo*, a pessimistic cultivation of the shocking, grotesque aspects of human experience. A later novel, *La colmena* (1951; *The Hive*, 1953), portrays the wretchedness of life in postwar Madrid through multiple narrative perspectives. Goytisolo's early novels, *Juego de manos* (1954; *The Young Assassins*, 1959) and *Fiestas* (1958; English translation, 1960), attacked the repression and psychological deprivation of Franco's Spain in a conventional narrative style typical of social realism. His principal contribution to the innovative postwar novel is his trilogy of exile—*Señas de identidad* (1966; *Marks of Identity*, 1969), *Reinvindicación del conde Don Julián* (1970; *Count Julian*, 1974), and *Juan sin tierra* (1975; *John the Landless*, 1975). The first of the trilogy is a fictionalized autobiographical account of the exile's return to Barcelona that makes use of diverse narrative techniques and multiple points of view but remains a rather conventional novel for its time. The second and third novels of the trilogy, however, are bitter, grotesque experimental narratives that attempt to convey an overwhelming repulsion and an obsession with the destruction of every traditional value of society.

Other postwar novelists experimented with narrative techniques, conveying an equally pessimistic view of Spanish society in a less shocking way than Goytisolo. *El Jarama* (1956; *The One Day of the Week*, 1962), by Rafael Sánchez Ferlosio (born 1927), and *Tiempo de silencio* (1962; *Time of Silence*, 1964), by Luis Martín-Santos (1924-1964), are portraits of Spanish society that are made up of fragmented, anecdotal mosaics, examples of a kind of social realist subject matter transformed through experimental narrative devices.

Luis Goytisolo (born 1935), the brother of Juan Goytisolo, first attracted critical attention with *Las afueras* (1958; the suburbs), a novel that portrays postwar Catalonia in terms of the contradictory forces at work in the economic and class structures of society. Gonzálo Torrente Ballester (1910-1999), a professor of history and literature and well-known drama critic, produced an impressive series of successful novels beginning with *El señor llega* (1957; the master comes), many of which are unusual narratives about the process of novelistic invention. For his most ambitious and successful work, *La saga/fuga de J. B.* (1972; the legend/flight of J. B.), Torrente Ballester won the coveted Crítica Prize, only one of many literary awards that he received during his career.

José María Gironella (born 1917) and Miguel Delibes (born 1920), two novelists who remained in Spain during and after the wartime experience, represent two very different trends in fiction. Gironella's epic war trilogy—*Los cipreses creen en Dios* (1953; *The Cypresses Believe in God*, 1955), *Un millón de muertos* (1961; *One Million Dead*, 1963), and *Ha estallado la paz* (1966; *Peace After War*, 1969)—is among the most widely read accounts of the Spanish Civil War. Delibes is a less popular novelist, but he is respected for his elegant style, his sympathetic portrayal of the simple, natural life of the country, and the gradual evolution of his work. *El camino* (1950; *The Path*, 1961) is a charming story of rural society. *Mi idolatrado hijo Sisí* (1953; my beloved son Sisí) is a cynical but delicate satire of middle-class aspirations. *Cinco horas con Mario* (1966; five hours with Mario) is an experiment in interior monologue, and *Parábola del náufrago* (1969; *The Hedge*, 1983), a technically innovative allegorical fantasy.

Some of the best postwar fiction was produced by a group of novelists who were adults at the time of the war and remained in exile after 1939. Ramón José Sender (1902-1982), the only one of these to achieve wide recognition, produced a vast amount of fiction beginning with the appearance of his first successful novel, *Imán* (1930; *Earmarked for Hell*, 1934; also as *Pro Patria*, 1935). Sender's work is characterized by an Unamunian preoccupation with the meaning of human existence. In novels such as *Crónica del alba* (1942-1966, 3 volumes; *Before Noon*, volume 1, 1957) and *La esfera* (1947, 1969; *The Sphere*, 1949), published first in 1939 as *Proverbio de la muerte* (proverb of death) and subsequently published in an expanded version with the new title, he achieved a distinctive fusion of realistic and fantastic techniques.

Antonio Barea (1897-1957), Francisco Ayala (born 1906), and Max Aub (1903-1972), the other exiled novelists of considerable significance, did not match the volume of work that Sender produced nor did they enjoy his success. Barea's *La forja de un rebelde* (1941-1944; *The Forging of a Rebel*, 1941-1946) is a fictionalized autobiographical memoir of the prewar and war years in Spain. Ayala, a prolific novelist as well as a short-story writer, created a brutal, cruel portrait of life in a fictional Spanish-American republic in *Muertes de perro* (1958; *Death as a Way of Life*, 1964) and its sequel, *El fondo del vaso* (1962; the bottom of the glass). Ayala's *El jardín de las delicias* (1971; the garden of delights), the source of the 1970 film by the Spanish director Carlos Saura (born 1932), is a dazzling display of novelistic art, a mosaic of references to the painting by Hieronymus Bosch (1450-1516) that forms the narrative of the psychic suffering of a twentieth century industrialist left paralyzed after an automobile accident.

The most esoteric of these novelists was the avant-garde writer Max Aub. His cycle of novels about the war experience, *El laberinto mágico* (1943-1968; the magic labyrinth), is a complex tapestry of fragmented characterizations and conversations that together form an interpretation and analysis of the psychological manifestations of wartime experience. Aub's most unusual work is *Jusep Torres Campalans* (1958; English translation, 1962), a painstakingly detailed biography of a fictitious artist and friend of Picasso. As if following the tradition of Unamuno, Aub evoked through this "biography" questions of the relationship between art and life.

During the late 1940's and the 1950's, a new generation of novelists began to emerge who were dedicated to a neorealist fictional mode as a means of exploring the nature of the human condition, particularly as it is manifested in a repressive society. Ignacio Aldecoa (1925-1969), author of *El fulgor y la sangre* (1954; lightning and blood), was an active stimulus to this revival of the novel through his journalistic criticism and his association with other writers such as Sánchez Ferlosio, Jesús Fernández Santos (1926-1988), Juan Goytisolo, José Luis Castillo

Puche (born 1919), and Carmen Martín Gaite (born 1928).

A striking feature of the period after the Spanish Civil War was the unusual number of women who established themselves as successful novelists. In 1944, Carmen Laforet (born 1921) won the prestigious Nadal Prize for her neorealist novel of tedium and repression, *Nada* (English translation, 1958). The prominence achieved by Laforet, Martín Gaite, Dolores Medio (born 1914), and Ana María Matute (born 1926), whose *Primera memoria* (1960; *School of the Sun*, 1963) also was awarded the Nadal Prize, is a significant phenomenon, given the disadvantaged position of women during the Franco era. Of these writers, Martín Gaite has received the most lasting and serious attention from critics for works such as *El balneario* (1954; the spa), *Ritmo lento* (1963; slow rhythm), and *El cuarto de atrás* (1978; *The Back Room*, 1983).

While this group of women novelists enjoyed considerable success, the Spanish novel of the 1970's and 1980's was dominated by men, particularly Juan Goytisolo, Juan Marsé (born 1933), and Juan Benet (1927-1993)—the novelist who, according to some critics, established the new direction in fiction evident in Goytisolo's *Count Julian* and in Delibes's *The Hedge*. Benet's trilogy, consisting of *Volverás a Región* (1967; *Return to Región*, 1985), *Una meditación* (1970; *A Meditation*, 1982), and *Una tumba* (1971; a tomb), is the complete antithesis of the realist tradition of Pérez Galdós and the neorealist tradition of the postwar novel. The narrative style is so difficult that the work seems almost unintelligible at first, though the identity of the characters and the details of the plot begin to emerge toward the end of the first novel through various techniques that reveal the text as an exaggerated evocation of memory. Marsé's first success was *Últimas tardes con Teresa* (1966; last afternoons with Teresa), a kind of "suburban" novel characterized by a blend of psychological and objective realism. The irony of Marsé's tone, however, limits the novel's tendency toward social realism. Marsé also attracted considerable critical attention for *Si te dicen que caí* (1973; *The Fallen*, 1976), a narrative of ambiguous accounts of the war years woven into the details of social existence in postwar Spain.

As the dictatorship ended with the death of Francisco Franco in 1975, the Spanish novel gradually ceased to be a discourse concentrated on a response to the circumstances of life under the existing totalitarian regime. It became, rather, primarily a consideration of the various forces at work in society as the post-Franco struggle for power began to take shape.

THE NOVEL AFTER FRANCO

The Spanish novel from 1950 to the end of the Franco regime in 1975 was dominated by two significantly different trends that have characterized the novel throughout its history. The neorealist mode is a continuation of the attempt of prose fiction to create an aesthetic experience that parallels the varied experiences of historical, "real" human existence. The other trend, represented by the diverse textual experimentation of the more innovative novelists such as Juan Goytisolo and Benet, represents the attempt to portray the authentic nature of human experience more effectively through a nontraditional narrative.

These two tendencies in prose fiction continued to be apparent in the novel after 1975, but there is evidence of a preference for a less complex narrative style. One of the manifestations of this trend is the emergence of a significant number of novelists working in the genre of detective or crime fiction. The first novel of Eduardo Mendoza (born 1943), *La verdad sobre el caso Savolta* (1975; *The Truth About the Savolta Case*, 1992), is an example of the genre, as are many of the novels of Lourdes Ortiz (born 1943), Benet's *El aire de un crimen* (1980; scent of a crime), and *Visión del ahogado* (1977; a drowned man's vision), by Juan José Millás (born 1946). Manuel Vázquez Montalbán (born 1939) cultivated the genre with a series of novels about his fictional hero, Pepe Carvalho, a bodyguard for President John F. Kennedy turned detective. Among his many novels of this type, all characterized by a perverse sense of humor unusual in the Spanish fiction of the period, are *Yo maté a Kennedy* (1972; I killed Kennedy), *Los mares del sur* (1979; *Southern Seas*, 1986), and *El delantero centro fue asesinado al atardecer* (1988; *Offside*, 1996).

Many of the novelists who established themselves before and during the Franco era continued to publish in the period after 1975. Cela's *Mazurka para dos muertos* (1983; polka for two dead people) and Delibes's *Los santos inocentes* (1981; the innocent saints) are evidence of the continued vitality of the older writers. The principal novelists of the 1960's and 1970's, such as Juan and Luis Goytisolo, Benet, Marsé, and Martín Gaite, continued to enjoy considerable success and enhanced their reputations as significant figures in the history of the twentieth century Spanish novel.

In the last decade of the century, decisive changes were occurring in the novel, not so much in terms of narrative form as in ideology. After the end of the Franco era, the principal discourse of the novel gradually ceased to be a dialogue with the social forms that thrived under the totalitarian regime. It became instead a response to the emerging ideological factions of the new democratic society. The younger novelists, such as Lourdes Ortiz, Rosa Montero (born 1951), Antonio Muñoz Molina (born 1956), Ester Tusquets (born 1936), and Terenci Moix (born 1943), produced numerous novels that explore the influences of popular culture and the various conflicting ideologies (sexist, fascist, communist, capitalist) that shaped Spanish society in the late twentieth century.

From its beginning, Spanish prose fiction has portrayed the circumstances of human existence in terms of the surrounding reality and the predominant ideological perspectives of the period in which it was created. The novelistic narrative of the late twentieth century period was characterized by considerations of issues that were suppressed either by official governmental actions or societal taboos during the earlier years of the century. The novel of this era posed questions about concepts of gender, homosexuality, psychoanalysis, and the dominant power structures of society, questions that often were presented in terms of the conflict between the prevailing ideologies of Francoist Spain and those gaining prominence in the Spain of the new democracy. Prose fiction continues to be marked by the opposing tendencies that have characterized the genre from its beginning, the struggle between a realist representation and various experimental, innovative modes of portraying the world. In its diversity of form and its singularity of purpose—the representation of human experience—the complex genre of linguistic and literary art that is the novel in Spain is heir to the tradition of Cervantes.

Gilbert Smith

BIBLIOGRAPHY

Charnon-Deutsch, Lou. *Gender and Representation: Women in Spanish Realist Fiction.* Amsterdam: John Benjamins, 1990. A significant study of the sexual polarization of nineteenth century Spanish society and the patriarchal values and ideologies of gender inscribed in the fictional discourses of the major novelists, including José María de Pereda, Juan Valera, Clarín, and Benito Pérez Galdós.

Close, Anthony. *The Romantic Approach to Don Quixote.* Cambridge, England: Cambridge University Press, 1978. A critical overview that had considerable repercussions in Hispanic studies. A general discussion of the Romantic interpretation of *Don Quixote de la Mancha*, from the time of the Romantic movement through the realist period, the Generation of 1898, and twentieth century criticism.

Dunn, Peter N. *Spanish Picaresque Fiction: A New Literary History.* Ithaca, N.Y.: Cornell University Press, 1993. An interesting study by a prominent Hispanist of the reading public and the cultural implications of the picaresque form of fiction.

Eoff, Sherman. *The Modern Spanish Novel: Comparative Essays Examining the Philosophical Impact of Science on Fiction.* New York: New York University Press, 1961. Excellent essays on José María de Pereda, Clarín, Vicente Blasco Ibáñez, Benito Pérez Galdós, Pio Baroja, Miguel de Unamuno, and Ramón José Sender, with considerations of their relationship to philosophical trends and works of British and other European novelists of the period.

Gold, Hazel. *The Reframing of Realism: Galdós and the Discourses of the Nineteenth Century Novel.* Durham, N.C.: Duke University Press, 1993. An effective study of the novels of Pérez Galdós from the perspective of narrative frame theory. Discusses his work in the context of the nineteenth century novel.

Ilie, Paul. *Literature and Inner Exile: Authoritarian Spain, 1939-1975.* Baltimore: The Johns Hopkins University Press, 1980. A discussion of the novels of Marsé, Sanchez Felosio, Castillo Puche, and others by an eminent Hispanic scholar. Relates the internal novelistic structures of exile to the sense of exile felt by the expatriate novelists and the phenomenon of the Jewish diaspora.

Johnson, Carroll B. *Don Quixote: The Quest for Modern Fiction.* Boston: Twayne, 1990. A general introduction to the historical context of Cervantes's novel and the characteristics of the book-reading public of the seventeenth century.

Landeira, Ricardo. *The Modern Spanish Novel, 1898-1936.* Boston: Twayne, 1985. An introductory study of the novel from the Generation of 1898 to the beginning of the Spanish Civil War in 1936, including studies of Vicente Blasco Ibáñez, Miguel de Unamuno, Pio Baroja, Ramón María del Valle-Inclán, and Ramón Pérez de Ayala.

Pérez, Janet. *Contemporary Women Writers of Spain.* Boston: Twayne, 1988. An interesting study of the situation of women in Spanish society during the reign of Francisco Franco and the changes that occurred after his death. Includes a preliminary consideration of the position of women in nineteenth century Spain and the work of Fernán Caballero and Emilia Pardo Bazán.

Sieburth, Stephanie. *Inventing High and Low: Literature, Mass Culture and Uneven Modernity in Spain.* Durham, N.C.: Duke University Press, 1994. An enlightening discussion of the representation of the technological, social, and cultural transformations of the modern period in the mass cultural novels of Benito Pérez Galdós, Juan Goytisolo, and Martín Gaité.

Solé-Leris, Amadeu. *The Spanish Pastoral Novel.* Boston: Twayne, 1980. A general introduction to the pastoral novel and the literary tradition of which it is a product, with considerations of the novels of Montemayor, Gil Polo, and Cervantes.

Spires, Robert C. *Post Totalitarian Spanish Fiction.*

Columbia: University of Missouri Press, 1996. Based on Michel Foucault's concept of the *epistème* (the totality of relationships between the sciences in a given period as they are expressed in discourse), a thorough discussion of self-referential novelistic texts.

Thomas, Gareth. *The Novel of the Spanish Civil War (1936-1975)*. Cambridge, England: Cambridge University Press, 1990. Discussions of the portrayal of the Spanish Civil War and the conditions of exile in the novels of José María Gironella, Max Aub, Francisco Ayala, Antonio Barea, Castillo Puche, and Ana María Matute. Interesting considerations of the propagandistic Republican novel and the process of myth creation in Nationalist fiction.

NORTH AMERICAN LONG FICTION

AFRICAN AMERICAN LONG FICTION

Nineteenth century American fiction influenced the form and content of many of the slave narratives, while nineteenth and twentieth century African American fiction owes a great debt, in form and content, to the slave narrative. Thus the development of African American fiction can be traced to nineteenth century American fiction only by way of the slave narrative.

Just as Africans arriving in the Americas staked their claims to humanity on the basis of the cultural models available to them—European Enlightenment and Christian values– so too did the first "authors" of the slave narrative model their testimonies on the Christian confessionals of Jonathan Edwards and the sentimental fiction of Harriet Beecher Stowe. Yet despite these debts to Puritanism and sentimentality, the best and most influential narratives transcended their origins to create an entirely new prose genre. Thus an achievement such as *Narrative of the Life of Frederick Douglass, an American Slave, Written by Himself* (1845) is instructive, if rare. Because the slave narrative was, by definition, a collaborative effort between white and free black abolitionists, political or social supporters and the slave, a great number of reputed slave narratives were outright frauds concocted by abolitionists to fan the flames of the antislavery movement or, occasionally, by proslavery forces determined to demonstrate the slaves' satisfaction with their lives. Yet even in those slave narratives that have been generally authenticated by meticulous historical research, the voice of the slave is often muffled under letters of support, prefaces, introductions, reproductions of bills of sale, and appendices, all deployed to assure the reader of the truthfulness of the tale about to be, or already, told. Indeed, insofar as many of the slave narratives are careful to depict the slave's freedom as having been the result of the aid of sympathetic white people, the narrative moral reinforces its collage format: The story of a slave's flight to freedom is inconceivable without the support and aid of northern and, occasionally, southern whites.

Narrative of the Life of Frederick Douglass, an American Slave, Written by Himself is distinguished, however, by both its literary elan and political independence. This well-known narrative boldly rises above its encumbering supplementary materials to depict one man, one slave, fighting his way to freedom. Of course luck, as well as friendly white hands, play a role in Douglass's flight to freedom, just as they do in every other slave narrative. However, the thrust of Douglass's narrative is that he, and he alone, took his life into his hands and forged for himself a new destiny. This theme was also evident in Olaudah Equiano's *The Interesting Narrative of the Life of Olaudah Equiano: Or, Gustavus Vassa, the African* (1789).

Such independence and bravado was not always available for enslaved African American women, as demonstrated in Harriet Jacobs's narrative, written under the pseudonym Linda Brent. *Incidents in the Life of a Slave Girl* (1861) has many parallels with Harriet E. Wilson's novel, *Our Nig: Or, Sketches from the Life of a Free Black, in a Two-Story White House, North. Showing That Slavery's Shadow Falls Even There* (1859). Wilson's protagonist, Alfrado, submits to a marriage with a fugitive slave who abandons her while she is pregnant, forcing her to work for an abusive white female employer. For Jacobs, affirming her gender means that she will be forced to submit to her sexual identity as an African American woman in order to escape sexual exploitation by her white master. The central psychological crisis for Jacob occurs when she decides to take a white man as a lover in order to block the predatory sexual advances of her master. For Jacobs, the submission to sexuality as a form of power over her circumstances is humiliating, but it is a humiliation redeemed, if only in part, by her choice to decide with whom she will have illicit sexual relations. Having learned that literacy is not enough to affirm and defend her humanity (her freedom), she must affirm her racial and sexual difference—her status as a black woman—by a decision that ironically insures her identity as both a woman and a human.

The narratives escape the limitations of their origins and their utility as propaganda for the antislavery cause precisely because they emphasize specific individuality rather than a vague "humanity." That they differ in terms of gender stereotypes— physical prowess for the men, sexual wiliness for the woman—only underscores the narrow band of options available for those attempting to escape slavery. More important, Douglass and Equiano can demonstrate their humanity with a number of virile activities, while Jacobs has only one way to demonstrate her humanity: sexuality. This imbalance in the range of choices, along with the stereotypical, sentimental, and fiction-derived narrative of flight, disguise, concealment, near discovery, and final freedom orients the trajectory of the African American novel along lines that consistently wed identity to gender, which then orient the positions authors take on issues such as class, caste, and skin-color distinctions; individualism and integration; and cultural nationalism.

Before these themes are considered, however, it is necessary to examine a subgenre of the slave narrative known as the narrative of revolt. *The Confessions of Nat Turner* (1832) is a peculiar document of some twenty pages, a reputed record of Nat Turner's descriptions of the revolt he launched against white Virginian men, women, and children in 1831. Augmented with the usual preface attesting the truthfulness of what follows, *The Confessions of Nat Turner* resembles in form the stereotypical slave narrative. However, the witnesses in question are proslavery white men, and the content of the narrative is indeed a "confession" of the conception, planning, and execution of the revolt. This slave narrative is thus not an attempt to affirm the humanity of the "author." Instead there is only the justification of righteous violence, the inspired zealot wreaking judgement upon the sinners—that is, the slave owners. Thus, just as white abolitionists created the format of the slave narrative to depict the horrors of slavery, so too was *The Confessions of Nat Turner* created to justify not only the continuation of slavery but also the ruthless suppression of the few privileges permitted selected slaves.

The Confessions of Nat Turner may well have benefitted the proslavery cause, but it also inspired other slave revolts, as well as the first "protest" novel

in the African American literary tradition, *Blake: Or, The Huts of America* (1859), by William Delany, himself an African American. *Blake* did not appear as a book until 1970, but it ran serially in a black abolitionist newspaper between 1861 and 1862. *Blake* is a call to arms, an explicit justification for open slave revolt and the establishment of a black sovereignty. It is, in some respects, the novelistic version of David Walker's *Appeal in Four Articles* (1830), judged to be so inflammatory that a large number of people called for its suppression; it also allegedly cost the author his life a short time after its publication. Like *Appeal in Four Articles*, *Blake* rejects the possibility of slaves integrating into American society. Instead, Delany imagines a black-ruled Cuba as the only viable option for the enslaved Africans. Both *The Confessions of Nat Turner* and *Blake* imagine violence as the only solution to slavery and link this violence to masculinity.

POST-RECONSTRUCTION

Francis E. W. Harper's *Iola Leroy: Or, Shadows Uplifted* (1892), Charles Waddell Chesnutt's *The Marrow of Tradition* (1901), and Paul Laurence Dunbar's *The Sport of the Gods* (1902) represent three different reactions in the African American novel to the post-Reconstruction United States, although Harper's idealized treatment of injustice, suffering, and redemption stands in marked contrast to the bitterness evident in the works by Chesnutt and Dunbar.

Iola Leroy is the story of a woman who is, unbeknownst to herself and others, a mulatto. Iola Leroy believes she is white until the unexpected death of her father spurs her uncle, who has long resented his brother's interracial marriage, to sell Iola and her mother separately into slavery. Aside from the search for her mother and abolitionist arguments that function as subplots, the novel focuses on Iola's courtship by two men, one a white abolitionist doctor, the other a mulatto like Iola herself. Though tempted by the doctor's offer to "pass" into white society, Iola steadfastly rejects the opportunity. Instead, she weds herself to the cause of abolition by agreeing to marry the mulatto. The novel's happy ending suggests that Jacobs preferred to invoke the nineteenth century sentimental novel of manners rather than the "tragic mulatta," a figure that had already appeared in William Wells Brown's *Clotel: Or, The President's Daughter* (1853; revised as *Miralda: Or, The Beautiful Quadroon*, 1860-1861; *Clotelle: A Tale of the Southern States*, 1864; and *Clotelle: Or, The Colored Heroine*, 1867).

On the other hand, Chesnutt's *The Marrow of Tradition* and Dunbar's *The Sport of the Gods* are much darker assessments of African American life during the so-called decades of disappointment. Based loosely on the Wilmington, North Carolina, riot of 1898, Chesnutt's novel follows the lives of several white and black characters whose unacknowledged but intertwined lives culminate in a literal "revelation" amid a murderous riot. Ostensibly a depiction of the end of Reconstruction—the riot is fomented by white people who want to "take back" their town—*The Marrow of Tradition* is also a morality tale concerning the futility of hate and violence, themes that Chesnutt links to the obsession with racial purity. For Chesnutt, miscegenation is the only viable solution to the race problem.

If Chesnutt offers some hope to his audience, Dunbar's vision of the destiny of the newly freed slaves is relentlessly desolate. *The Sport of the Gods* concerns the dissolution of a postslavery African American family forced to flee to New York City after the father is jailed on trumped-up burglary charges. Every family member ends up losing his or her moral integrity in the urban landscape; even when the parents are reunited near the end of the novel, it is clear that their lives will be cheap imitations of their shattered dreams. Dunbar's dismal vision of the urban landscape, already anticipated by *Our Nig*, looks forward to those novelists of the Harlem Renaissance whose portraits of city life effectively undermine any romantic notions of what it might mean to have come "up from slavery."

THE HARLEM RENAISSANCE

The concern with skin color, particularly with miscegenation, became particularly urgent during the Harlem Renaissance (1919-1929) as the possibility of an "authentic" African American culture began,

however tentatively, to take shape. Insofar as the fledgling culture had to partake of the culture of its former oppressors, the tensions and arguments over who and what was, in fact, "Negro" took on a certain urgency. Yet not every African American writer treated this issue with morbid seriousness. Wallace Thurman's *Infants of the Spring* (1932) is an excoriating *roman à clef* about the central figures of the Harlem Renaissance. Its vicious attacks on the petty prejudices of the leading personages of the day echo themes developed in his first and most popular novel, *The Blacker the Berry* (1929), which concerns skin-color prejudice within African American culture.

Less well known but in many respects a better work, George Schuyler's *Black No More: Being an Account of the Strange and Wonderful Workings of Science in the Land of the Free,* A.D. 1933-1940 (1931) is a hilarious send-up of the obsession with "race advancement" by newly formed organizations such as the National Association for the Advancement of Colored People (NAACP) and the obsession with "racial purity" by the Ku Klux Klan. Thurman's and Schuyler's satires on race, class, and gender, published during the Great Depression shortly after the Harlem Renaissance, mock the absurdities often paraded out by politicians and artists identified with the Harlem Renaissance.

For example, James Weldon Johnson's *The Autobiography of an Ex-Coloured Man* (1912) represents a logical extension of the reconciliation themes evident in the novels of Frances Harper and Charles Chesnutt. If, in their works, the mulatto/mulatta appears to embody the race's best chance for advancement, then "passing"—mulattos and mulattas "disappearing" into white society—would obviously be the next logical step. Johnson's novel idealizes the passing motif even as it rehearses its tragedy: the mulatto as a wanderer between separate cultures, never at home in either.

At the opposite end of the spectrum is Nella Larsen. Her two novels, *Quicksand* (1928) and *Passing* (1929), contain depictions of the tragic mulatta. In *Quicksand*, Helga Crane, a mulatta never at ease among African Americans or Caucasians, winds up marrying and having children. In *Passing*, Clare

Kendry is a mulatta passing for Caucasian while her friend, Irene Redfield, is both disgusted and envious of her freedom. Kendry's sudden death offers her escape from the humiliation of being unveiled as a "nigger" by her white, racist husband.

Larsen's analyses of middle-class mulattas represents an extension of Jean Toomer's *Cane* (1923), a collage of poetry and fiction centered on multiple themes in early twentieth century African American life: the juxtaposition of urban and rural lifestyles, tensions between the North and the South, and "pure-bred"/mixed blood characteristics. As with Harper, Chesnutt and others, Toomer links the resolution of these oppositions to the mulatto. Like Larsen, however, Toomer is not optimistic about this figure, who is shunned and scorned by both African American and white cultures.

Between Johnson's idealism and Larsen's cynicism lie authors such as Claude McKay and Zora Neale Hurston on the one hand and Jessie Redmon Fauset on the other hand. McKay's novel *Home to Harlem* (1928) was a commercial success, which some critics, including W. E. B. Du Bois, attributed to its exotic treatment of Harlem nightlife. Richard Wright made similar criticisms of Zora Neale Hurston's novel *Their Eyes Were Watching God* (1937), charging Hurston with creating laughable caricatures of African Americans.

Like the novels of Larsen, Jessie Redmon Fauset's three best novels, *There Is Confusion* (1924), *Plum Bun: A Novel Without a Moral* (1929), and *The Chinaberry Tree: A Novel of American Life* (1931), concern the plight of middle- and upper-class African American women struggling with racial passing, material possessions, marital prospects and self-worth. Unlike Larsen, and in some respects more like Johnson, Fauset delineates the pitfalls of racial confusion without the melodrama of tragedy. At the same time, Fauset's protagonists are clearly more sensitive to, and more psychologically damaged by, the perplexing anxieties of the color caste system in African American culture.

POST-RENAISSANCE REALISM

If the problem of the color caste system dominated African American fiction as a concern before and during the Great Depression, perhaps it was because of the effects of post-Reconstruction migrations of African Americans from the South to the North. Although writers such as Dunbar attempted to unmask the urban dreamscape, the struggle by so many writers to confront color prejudice within the race is linked to the social problems associated with mass migrations: poverty, joblessness, overcrowding, and, in the case of African Americans, accelerated class distinctions tied to the presence or absence of "white" blood. Underlying the tendency to privilege or castigate on the basis of miscegenation was a belief that becoming "white" was either a way to escape the stigma attached to African blood or a way to delude oneself that white America would accept African Americans if they acted less "African."

Richard Wright's groundbreaking first novel, *Native Son* (1940), changed the terms of the debate, dramatizing the conflict between race and class. Wright's portraits of the communists—the naïve Mary, the careless Jan, and the rough-house Max—were augmented by his negative portraits of both "liberal" Caucasians, such as the Daltons, and African American women, such as Bigger's mother, sister, and girlfriend. Wright's realist novel was widely criticized, and in this respect Dunbar's equally desolate, if less brutal, *The Sport of the Gods* can be seen as its most immediate ancestor. A similar combination of gritty realism and broad criticism can be seen in two relatively minor writers of the period, Chester Himes and Ann Petry.

Of the two, Himes is the most significant as his postwar work is an effective combination of the hard-boiled detective fiction of Raymond Chandler and the protest fiction of Wright. His best novel, *If He Hollers Let Him Go* (1945), is a masterful hybrid of these two genres. On the one hand, like *Native Son*, Himes compresses his story into a short time frame (four days) that allows him to explore the effects of unrelenting racism on the consciousness of his narrator-protagonist, Bob Jones. At the same time, Himes pays tribute to the detective story as Jones struggles to figure out why a Caucasian coworker has fabricated a rape charge against him. Later novels, such as

Retour en Afrique (1964; *Cotton Comes to Harlem*, 1965), owe more to the detective genre than the protest novel, perhaps because Himes wrote them after his expatriation to France.

Ann Petry's fame rests primarily on the basis of *The Street* (1946), the first novel by an African American woman to sell over one million copies. While some critics have compared the novel to Wright's *Native Son* because of its intense focus on urban decay and squalor, a case could also be made for linking it to Dunbar's *The Sport of the Gods* and Hurston's pioneering *Their Eyes Were Watching God*. Just as Hurston's novel concerns Janie's triumph over the patriarchal traditions of white male racism and black male chauvinism, so too does Petry's novel focus on Lutie Johnson's attempts to eke out a meager living away from the brutality of her father. Like those of the mother in Dunbar's novel, Lutie's dreams to provide for herself and her son are driven by a naïveté that drags her even further down the social ladder. If Hurston's Janie seems like an idealized role model for all women to emulate, Petry's Lutie is a grim reminder of what so many black women actually go through in their daily lives.

Compared to the grim urban realism of Wright, Himes, and Petry, the fiction of Ralph Ellison offers a way out of the morass of frustration, rebellion, defeat, and despair. Ellison's only novel published during his lifetime, *Invisible Man* (1952), has been heralded as one of the great, if not the greatest, American novels ever written, and it is precisely the role of "Americanism" in the work that has made it a lightning rod for political debates since its appearance.

Told in a flashback by an unnamed narrator, *Invisible Man* chronicles the misadventures of a naïve high school graduate in the grand tradition of the episodic, picaresque novel. Boiled down to its essential themes, the novel traces the gradual awakening of a potential leader who believes that the key to the salvation of his community is organized group action, the most notorious of which turns out to be the Brotherhood, a political organization loosely based on the Communist Party of America. In the epilogue, however, the narrator realizes that individualism is the answer to his, and his community's, problems, that all groups are, to one degree or another, straitjackets of intolerance.

Ellison's novel was thus read as a direct rebuke to *Native Son*, though Wright himself saw more affinities than differences between the two works. Nevertheless, Ellison was heralded as the successor to Wright, whose commitment to the communist cause, if not the Communist Party, isolated him and his later work in the context of, and fallout from, McCarthyism. Moreover, a chorus of new voices began to declaim their relevancy and militancy, a phenomenon that had the effect of elevating Wright while demoting Ellison.

The writer who not only functions as a transitional figure between the 1950's and 1960's but also inherited all the contradictions and conflicts between the two decades, represented by the trajectories of Wright's and Ellison's careers, is James Baldwin. Baldwin authored six novels, but his fame rests almost entirely on his provocative essays, especially "Everybody's Protest Novel," which signalled his aesthetic break from his mentor, Richard Wright. Just as Baldwin slays his literary father in the essay, so too does his first novel, *Go Tell It on the Mountain* (1953), a depiction of the Oedipal struggle between a religious father and unconventional son, seem to be directed at his real-life stepfather, David Baldwin. Baldwin's next two novels, *Giovanni's Room* (1956) and *Another Country* (1962), explore homosexuality and black pride as avenues toward individualism. More ominous, the tone of these novels is a little more high-strung than that of the first novel, and in his subsequent novels—*Tell Me How Long the Train's Been Gone* (1968), *If Beale Street Could Talk* (1974), and *Just Above My Head* (1979)—the pitch is strident, a development reflected in the essays. In one of those ironies that permeate African American literary history, Baldwin wound up writing the same kind of protest novels, articles, and essays for which he criticized Wright and others.

How did this happen? To answer this question, it is necessary to examine the effects that the developing Civil Rights Movement, the black power spin-offs, the antiwar protests, and the Black Arts movement had on Baldwin's growth as an artist. That is, it is necessary to examine the cultural, social, and political upheavals of the 1960's and 1970's through the lenses of the African American writers who would emerge as distinctive literary voices.

SONS OF THE 1960'S, 1970'S, AND 1980'S

The counterculture movements of the 1960's and 1970's affected all American artists, and African American novelists were no exception. Though his first two novels and various essays had gained him some notoriety, Baldwin had written himself into an aesthetic corner not unlike that inhabited by Ellison. Just as Ellison's post-*Invisible Man* essays would put distance between his nineteenth century genteel aesthetics and the politicized aesthetics of the new African American writers, so too would Baldwin's criticism of Wright's *Native Son* as mere "protest" fiction alienate Baldwin from a new generation of African American writers anxious to relate literature to social concerns. For writers attempting to forge a black aesthetic based on the values of working-class African Americans, Baldwin was aesthetically and politically irrelevant. Worse, Baldwin's avowed homosexuality only confirmed the suspicions of the largely homophobic Black Arts movement.

In 1967, one of the few novelists of the Black Arts movement, John A. Williams, penned *The Man Who Cried I Am*, a kind of *roman à clef* of African American literary history, featuring Langston Hughes, Richard Wright, and James Baldwin under pseudonyms. Williams's novel, about a semifamous African American male writer who struggles with illness, the envy of his peers, conniving women, and rampant racism, is composed with the crude urban realism of Himes and Wright, but its value is primarily archival.

It was during the same year, 1967, that John Edgar Wideman's first novel, *A Glance Away*, first appeared, presenting Wideman as a transitional figure between Ellison and Baldwin on the one hand and the Black Arts movement on the other. Perhaps influenced by Baldwin's interest in the contingencies of sexuality and race, *A Glance Away* is a concentrated study—the narrative covers a single day—in the lives of an African American drug addict and a gay Cauca-

sian professor. *Hurry Home* (1970), Wideman's second novel, focuses on the attempt of an African American to unite his European and African cultural heritages. Both novels are less concerned with racial issues per se than philosophical ones. However, by the publication of his third novel, *The Lynchers* (1973), Wideman was under the influence of the Black Arts movement, though aesthetically the book remains outside their camp, a stance evident in subsequent work such as *Damballah* (1981) and *Sent for You Yesterday* (1983).

Finally, 1967 saw yet a third auspicious debut. The most important male African American novelist to follow Ellison appeared in the person of Ishmael Reed. Eschewing the simplistic posturing of many of the Black Arts movement products, *The Free-Lance Pallbearers* (1967) was a remarkable first novel as Reed laid claim to being the best African American satirist since George Schuyler. The form of his avantgarde novel was inspired as much by experimental jazz and film as James Joyce and Ellison. *Yellow Back Radio Broke-Down* (1969), his second novel, was an even greater triumph, a full-blown parody of the American Western as portrayed in dime-store novels and black-and-white films. Subsequent novels during the 1970's—such as *Mumbo Jumbo* (1972), *The Last Days of Louisiana Red* (1974), and *Flight to Canada* (1976)—reinforced Reed's reputation as one of the most innovative comic spirits of his generation.

Ernest J. Gaines inaugurated the 1970's as the first major African American regional novelist since Jean Toomer, though he was soon followed by the equally talented Leon Forrest. Like Toomer, Gaines situates his novels in the complicated racial, sexual, and class mixtures of Cajun culture in Louisiana, Gaines's birth place. His first novel, *The Autobiography of Miss Jane Pittman* (1971), was a major literary and, later, television event as its 108-year-old narrator interweaves her personal history with that of the United States, allowing her to witness and comment on American history from nineteenth century slavery to the Civil Rights movement. Other significant novels would follow, including *In My Father's House* (1978), *A Gathering of Old Men* (1983), which was also made into a television movie, and *A Lesson Before Dying* (1993).

Leon Forrest has staked a claim as the most important regional novelist of the North as his four historical novels are all set in Forrest's native home, "Forest County"—that is, Cook County, Illinois. Focusing on the life and development of one central character, Nathaniel Turner Witherspoon, *There Is a Tree More Ancient than Eden* (1973), *The Bloodworth Orphans* (1977), *Two Wings to Veil My Face* (1984), and *Divine Days* (1992) trace the interrelated histories of two families by way of collage as Forrest draws on traditional oral storytelling, dream sequences, and mythological allusions to dramatize the intrinsic uncertainties of knowledge.

Forrest's redeployment of the serial novel—interrelated novels that follow a central theme, character, or family (for example, the Snopeses and Compsons in William Faulkner's fiction)—was mimicked by a number of other novelists, including Albert Murray. Unlike Faulkner, who used the serial novel to trace the disintegration of southern gentility, African American novelists such Forrest and Murray used its epic possibilities to depict male heroism. Thus Murray's trilogy of novels—*Train Whistle Guitar* (1974), *The Spyglass Tree* (1991), and *The Seven League Boots* (1996)—celebrate the spirit of adventure by linking the travels of an African American musician to those of the Greek hero Odysseus. The serial novel has even been used by avant-garde writers such as the poet and novelist Nathaniel Mackey. His ongoing fiction series, *From a Broken Bottle Traces of Perfume Still Emanate*, has manifested itself in two epistolary novels, *Bedouin Hornbook* (1986) and *Djbot Baghostus's Run* (1993). Focusing on an ensemble of experimental jazz musicians, Mackey plays with polar oppositions usually taken for granted, especially those that supposedly define cultural borders, gender differences, racial and class biases, and natural and supernatural events.

Yet the traditional novel has hardly lost its viability among African American male writers. Yoking together the sophistication of northern urbanity with the penetrating eccentricity of southern folklore, David Bradley published *The Chaneysville Incident* (1981), a tour de force of historical guilt, murder, and atonement very much in the tradition of Dante's *La divina commedia* (c. 1320; *The Divine Comedy*, 1802).

Myth plays a fundamental role in the fiction of Charles Johnson. Like the early Wideman, Johnson was and remains essentially a philosophical writer. Johnson's first novel, *Faith and the Good Thing* (1974), is a good but unremarkable effort, though it already intimates the philosophical and theological concerns that would become more central to the next novel. *Oxherding Tale* (1982) could not be more different from the first book. Written under the influence of Zen Buddhism, *Oxherding Tale* revisits the slave narrative from an Asian philosophical perspective. Though not as pronounced in subsequent novels such as *The Sorcerer's Apprentice* (1986) and the award-winning *Middle Passage* (1990), Johnson's Buddhist perspective tempers all his writings, both fiction and nonfiction. Oddly enough, Johnson's use of myth and philosophy has more in common with the experimental work of Mackey than it does with the mainstream novels of Toni Morrison, whose unique blend of myth, philosophy, folklore, and political outrage is unique, not only among African American women writers but also among all African American novelists.

AFRICAN AMERICAN WOMEN WRITERS

No African American woman novelist has plumbed the depths of African American history with as much insight, eloquence, and passion as Toni Morrison. Along with Alice Walker, she takes seriously the feminist aphorism that "the personal is the political" and redefines the relationship between African American women and their culture.

Morrison's and Walker's most immediate predecessor, Paule Marshall, labored in relative obscurity, perhaps, in part, because of her ethnicity. Born in New York City to Caribbean parents, Marshall's work draws on myriad cultural influences. Independent girls and women dominate her fiction, and when they are not strong, Marshall's narratives lead them back to healing sources, which are invariably African (as opposed to "American") or pan-African (in other words, Caribbean) in nature. Her novels—including *Brown Girl, Brownstones* (1959), *The Chosen Place, the Timeless People* (1969), *Praisesong for the Widow* (1983), and *Daughters* (1991)—counterpoise, to varying degrees, American materialism and individualism to African American, Caribbean, and African spiritual ideals; these themes are also present in the writing of Marshall's literary descendant, Jamaica Kincaid.

Still, when all is said and done, Toni Morrison was the most important African American novelist between the 1970's and 1990's. Like Alice Walker, Gloria Naylor, Gayl Jones, and Toni Cade Bambara, Morrison's fiction focuses on the relationships between African American women and Caucasian women, African American women and African American men, and African American women and white America in general from a gendered and politically engaged perspective.

Morrison's novels—including *The Bluest Eye* (1970), *Sula* (1973), *Song of Solomon* (1977), *Tar Baby* (1981), *Beloved* (1987), *Jazz* (1992), and *Paradise* (1998)—range across the landscape of African American culture. For example, while all the novels—with the lone exception of *Song of Solomon*—feature women as central protagonists, none of the novels is "feminist" in any sort of predetermined, hackneyed way. Morrison's work is primarily concerned with class and caste distinctions and divisions within African American culture; while slavery and racism, along with sexism, frame all the novels, Morrison's work cannot be reduced to protest fiction since it is not addressed primarily to either male or Caucasian readers. Nevertheless, it certainly can be said that the novels have become increasingly political insofar as slavery, sexism, and racism loom larger in each succeeding novel. Although this process has been gradual, many critics, both detractors and proponents, cite *Beloved*, Morrison's best-known work and most controversial novel, as the linchpin text.

Beloved, like *Jazz*, is based on a true story. It centers on Sethe, an ex-slave and mother who attempts to escape from the South but pays a tremendous personal price. Trapped by slave hunters, she tries to kill both of her baby daughters rather than see them re-

turned to slavery, succeeding only with the youngest, unnamed one. Years later, free in Ohio but ostracized from the African American community because of the murder, Sethe and Denver, her surviving daughter, are visited by the ghost of Sethe's dead daughter, Beloved, as well as Paul D., Sethe's lover who wants to start a new life with her. Thus the novel centers on the tug-of-war Sethe endures as she is alternately pulled back by the past (Beloved's claim of birthright) and toward the future (Paul D.'s claim on her as his wife).

The controversy over the novel centered on the question of the murder of Beloved. Was it indeed better to kill oneself or one's children than submit to the horrors of slavery? Or was it better to live, knowing that those who survived the ordeal would pass their indomitable genes and traditions on to a hoped-for, but unforeseeable, future of freedom? Morrison herself never directly addressed the issue, and readers are not helped by the ambivalence of the novel's last pages, which assert that the "story" was one "to pass on" and "not pass on."

This ambivalence, a feature of all Morrison's novels, tempers the heightened political profiles of the stories. None of Morrison's contemporaries has achieved this precarious balance between political outrage and human complexity. For example, Alice Walker, whose first novel, *The Third Life of Grange Copeland* (1970), appeared in the same year as Morrison's *The Bluest Eye*, is more an important cultural figure than a significant writer. *The Third Life of Grange Copeland* is, however, a well-written, harrowing account of women that are not only physically and psychologically abused but also driven to madness by men. To this extent, Walker is much more a feminist than Morrison. However, *The Third Life of Grange Copeland* is also about racism and class bias, as well as their relationship to violence against women. In that respect, Walker's first novel was quite promising.

Walker is best known, however, for her second novel, the controversial *The Color Purple* (1982). An epistolary novel, *The Color Purple* explores the gradual sexual and feminist awakening of a young teenager, Celie, who has been abused by both her family and her husband, whom she designates "Mister." Although she writes letters addressed to God, Celie is actually saved by Mister's mistress, Shug. The narrative of the novel implies that Shug's lesbian relationship with Celie is sparked, in part, by the oppression both undergo from Mister, a connection that understandably upset lesbians since it reduced female same-sex relationships to reactions against misogyny and sexism. At the same time, the portrait of Mister angered writers such as Ishmael Reed and Amiri Baraka, who believed that Walker and other African American feminists were unwittingly playing into the hands of a culture that had long demonized African American male sexuality. Walker's attempt to remind readers on all sides of the debate that Celie is complicit in her own abuse and oppression and that Mister is transformed by the novel's end into a humane father and friend to Celie went largely unheard. When Walker sold the screen rights of the novel to director Steven Spielberg, who produced a movie that essentially deleted the sexual politics and romanticized the South, supporters and critics of the book were dismayed. Although she continued to produce readable novels such as *The Temple of My Familiar* (1989) and *Possessing the Secret of Joy* (1992), Walker's growing interest in African American lesbianism made her a marginal figure in African American culture, a fate not unlike that suffered by Baldwin, poet Audre Lorde, and others.

Next to Morrison and Walker, other African American women novelists have shown sporadic, inconsistent promise. Toni Cade Bambara was a brilliant short story writer and a promising novelist. *The Salt Eaters* (1980) showcased complex narrative textures and jazz influences similar to those in Ishmael Reed's early novels. However, Bambara's career was shortened by her premature death in 1995.

Gloria Naylor's first novel, *The Women of Brewster Place: A Novel in Seven Stories* (1982), was a major success that was made into an even more successful television movie. However, it was published in the same year as *The Color Purple*, and, worse, its similar themes of African American lesbianism and African American male cruelty echoed the inferior but more controversial book by Walker. Naylor re-

wrote and updated Baraka's *The System of Dante's Hell* (1965) with her second novel, *Linden Hills* (1985), revived the novel of manners in the vein of Jesse Redmon Fauset in *Mama Day* (1988), and, in *Bailey's Café* (1992), echoed the improvisational experiments of Morrison's *Jazz*.

Finally, Gayl Jones's first two novels, *Corregidora* (1975) and *Eva's Man* (1976), despite their familiar themes of misogyny, sexism, and abuse, showed promise. In many ways the most interesting of the new writers, Jones's interest in the abnormalities of psychological profiles and their link to linguistic modes suggests an intelligence only partially realized in the first two novels. Jones, however, suffered a series of personal and professional traumas, and it was more than two decades before a third novel, *The Healing* (1998), appeared. This novel, along with her fourth, *Mosquito* (1999), suggested a return to creative and psychological health for Jones, which augured well for the continued development of African American fiction.

Tyrone Williams

BIBLIOGRAPHY

Beaulieu, Elizabeth Ann. *Black Women Writers and the American Neo-Slave Narrative: Femininity Unfettered.* Westport, Conn.: Greenwood Press, 1999. Beaulieu discusses the efforts of African American women writers to redefine the slave narrative in the twentieth century. Among the novels discussed are Sherley Anne Williams's *Dessa Rose* and Toni Morrison's *Beloved.*

Braxton, Joanne M., and Andree Nicola McLaughlin. *Wild Women in the Whirlwind: Afra-American Culture and the Contemporary Literary Renaissance.* New Brunswick, N.J.: Rutgers University Press, 1990. This is the best anthology of critical writings on African American women writers, past and present. The range of writers covered is impressive, and the language is free of jargon.

Butler, Robert. *Contemporary African American Fiction: The Open Journey.* Madison, Wis.: Fairleigh Dickinson University Press, 1998. Butler's book, as the subtitle suggests, covers a wide range of subject matter, from a study of the picaresque in the fiction of Zora Neale Hurston and Richard Wright to a discussion of Octavia E. Butler's vision of the twenty-first century.

Callahan, John F. *In the African-American Grain: Call-and-Response in Twentieth-Century Black Fiction*. Middletown, Conn.: Wesleyan University Press, 1988. Callahan examines the way novelists and short story writers from Charles Chesnutt to Alice Walker have insisted on the importance of call-and-response in the creation of a personal identity that remains bound to larger ideals of African American culture.

Christian, Barbara. *Black Feminist Criticism: Perspectives on Black Women Writers*. New York: Pergamon Press, 1985. Although these brief essays read like journalistic reviews, Christian's book is valuable for the range of African American women writers she covers, as well as the influential ideas she uses to assess sexuality and empowerment in African American women's fiction.

Davis, Charles, and Henry Louis Gates, Jr., eds. *The Slave's Narrative*. Oxford, England: Oxford University Press, 1985. This valuable addition to the growing commentary on slave narrative provides an introduction to three modes of interpreting the slave narrative: journalistic, historical, and literary.

Gates, Henry Louis, Jr. *The Signifying Monkey: A Theory of African-American Literary Criticism.* New York: Oxford University Press, 1988. This ambitious but concise text argues for the importance of the trickster figure in African American literature and its link to the problem of literacy and identity.

Greene, J. Lee. *Blacks in Eden: The African American Novel's First Century*. Charlottesville: University Press of Virginia, 1996. Greene traces the development of the African American novel through the twentieth century.

Joyce, Joyce Ann. *Warriors, Conjurers and Priests: Defining African-centered Literary Criticism*. Chicago: Third World Press, 1994. Joyce examines the work of neglected African American writers such as Ann Petry and Sonia Sanchez while taking on antifeminist critics such as Ishmael Reed. Joyce also provides the first tentative assessments of emerging writers such as Terry McMillan and E. Ethelbert Miller.

Kostelanetz, Richard. *Politics in the African-American Novel: James Weldon Johnson, W. E. B. Du Bois, Richard Wright, and Ralph Ellison*. New York: Greenwood Press, 1991. This investigation of the development of the African American novel charts the movement from the protest fiction of Johnson and Du Bois to the more complex and thus "better" work of Wright and Ellison.

THE AMERICAN NOVEL

American literature turned to the subject of America after the Revolutionary War, when American authors began the exploration of themes and motifs distinctly American. Continuing the Puritan belief in America as the New Eden, American authors stressed the millennial nature of settlement and progress. Each milestone in improvement and enlargement marked a national movement toward spiritually sanctioned political dominion. Geographic, industrial, and social changes found justification in America's mythic vision of itself independent of England and free of European hierarchy.

A complex and often contradictory ethos emerged based on tensions in American dualities: Calvinistic sin and predestination opposed to romantic optimism; determinism opposed to free will; idealism versus materialism; European aristocracy opposed to democracy; capitalistic prosperity versus economic struggles. As the country expanded, such dichotomies were complicated by tensions between long-settled areas in New England, the genteel South, the expansive plains states, and the wide open West. These contrary and interlocking forces created variety and crosscurrents in American fiction.

PURITAN INFLUENCE

The original Puritan experiment lasted less than one hundred years but indelibly marked American thought and expression. Emphasis on a godly life and personal motives shapes the diaries of colonial governors William Bradford (1590-1649) and John Winthrop (1588-1694). Their documents reveal harsh dealings with merchandisers who invaded the colonies only to reap the wealth of the New World. The diaries of Judge Samuel Sewall (1652-1730) and Puritan cleric Jonathan Edwards (1703-1758) endorsed the same catalog of virtues Benjamin Franklin listed in his *Autobiography* (1791). Puritan temperance, order, frugality, industry, and justice also suited the rational, moral sensibility of Franklin's Enlightenment God, the deistic Watchmaker-Creator who let the world tick on unhindered.

Though Edwards's harsh God had been replaced by a nearly indifferent craftsman, America's habit of thought was focused on the quest for personal identity and spiritual journeys central to Puritan self-examination. The search for identity and meaning articulated in Puritan journals appears in many guises in America's long-fiction tradition. Herman Melville's (1819-1891) Ishmael (*Moby Dick*, 1851), Kate Chopin's (1851-1904) Edna Pontillier (*The Awakening*, 1899), F. Scott Fitzgerald's (1896-1940) Amory Blaine (*This Side of Paradise*, 1920), and Toni Morrison's (born 1931) Milkman (*Song of Solomon*, 1977) all struggle with the context and significance of their lives.

Puritan practice shaped American novels metaphorically long after the Spartan spiritual regimen weakened. Puritan preachers reveled in comparisons between the biblical world and their own. Pairing events across time created a deeper sense of significance for American life. Moses's prophetic leadership made him a model for Puritan patriarchs. As men of God, their calling and authority mimicked Moses's. Puritans were encouraged to see life's events as spiritual lessons designed to increase piety and faith or express God's nurturing. Persistent comparison made the nature of life metaphoric. Events in real time were seen as images of biblical experiences and were symbolically interpreted

Overt transference of symbolism to fiction is clear in Nathaniel Hawthorne's (1804-1864) *The Scarlet Letter* (1850), in which protagonist Hester Prynne's scarlet letter *A* marks her as a symbol of fallen womanhood. The whale in *Moby Dick*, a massive symbol of evil, exhibits a subtle turn by making the evil force white rather than black. Modernists, following in the wake of late nineteenth century realists and naturalists, capitalized on this penchant for symbols, but their main figures were literary, not biblical. Ernest Hemingway's (1899-1961) code heroes rely on knowledge of traditional heroes to be effective. Jake Barnes's depressed wandering in *The Sun Also Rises* (1926) makes a hollow warrior's quest. He is an Odysseus without honorable men to lead or a homeland to reclaim. Moving beyond storytelling to the theory of narrative, Gertrude Stein's (1874-1946) experiments with repetition of words and phrases invite skepticism about language and its reliability as an interpretive tool. In "Melanctha" (*Three Lives*, 1909), her use of the word "love" causes readers to constantly redefine it. Stein moved beyond the Puritan equation, comparing two objects or people to question the process and means of comparison. Contemporary use of metaphoric construction influenced E. Annie Proulx's (born 1935) *The Shipping News* (1993), in which chapters are headed by the names of particular nautical knots, and the sea around Nova Scotia is ever-present as a force and locus of possibility in the character Quoyle's life. The ties for Proulx are elliptical and suggestive; readers must decide for themselves what the significance and the connections are. Unlike the Puritans, contemporary American novelists draw no absolute lines between symbols and moral values or truths. The reader, not a minister, defines the significance of events. The novel itself, rather than Puritan beliefs or biblical passages, provides codes for translation. Yet the search for meaning still requires cross-references between text and life—a Puritan strategy of interpretation.

Material prosperity fueled by the Industrial Revolution increased after the Civil War, and the effect of money on American moral fiber became a dominant theme in fiction. Mark Twain (1835-1910) satirized the greed and hypocrisy of *The Gilded Age* (1873). William Dean Howells (1837-1920), one of the creators and promoters of American realism, reflected on acquisition and class structure in *The Rise of Silas Lapham* (1885), about a man who inherits and exploits a paint factory in New England. The Laphams attempt to enter Boston society, but, being nouveau riche, they know none of the behavior codes that signal breeding; they are never accepted by the upper class. Silas's moral compass is corrupted by market forces, as he wins material rewards through speculation and investment, not by his own labor. Only renunciation of wealth restores his moral stature.

THE TWENTIETH CENTURY NOVEL IN AMERICA

The effects of speculation and class aspirations on American moral character persisted into early twenti-

eth century novels. Edith Wharton (1862-1937) portrayed the painful significance of class and wealth in a woman's life in *The House of Mirth* (1905). Her work explores the dislocation and struggle of people caught in social forces beyond their control. The post-Civil War transition to industrial strength and expansion left New England's shipping industry and economy weakened, signaling the end of America's cycle of origination and settlement. Writers Mary Eleanor Freeman (1852-1930) and Sarah Orne Jewett (1849-1909) recorded the details of village life and change in *Pembroke* (1894) and *The Country of the Pointed Firs* (1896) respectively, detailing the lives of those who remained when those such as Howells's Silas Lapham migrated to the city. Unlike Silas, Jewett's Mrs. Todd Maine is not liable to be corrupted. Freeman's characters do not fare as well. Although Freeman's novel's central dilemma seems romantic, the sources of tension and tragedy for the inhabitants of Pembroke are the versions of Puritan theology and moral strategies that control village households. Unlike later critics who marginalized the women as quaint, regional authors, Howells lauded their veracity in depicting American life, publishing them as his peers when he was editor of *The Atlantic Monthly*. Their frank look at economic and social changes makes them authoritative American voices.

The focus on capitalism's affect on American life was not always negative, however. Horatio Alger exploited the "rags-to-riches" myth in more than one hundred novels in which material success was, paradoxically, both the cause of and reward for moral virtue. Edwards's and Franklin's programs, now expunged entirely of sectarian doctrine, became a new "way to wealth." Alger's vastly popular novel *Ragged Dick* (1867), modeled in part on the life of American industrialist Andrew Carnegie, offered hope to thousands of trapped stock boys, shop girls, and factory workers. Many of them were part of the waves of immigration that began in the late 1800's. Their stories came into view when early twentieth century America's authors mined their own lives for writing material. In *The Bread Givers* (1925), Polish Russian Anzia Yezierska's (1885-1970) narrator, Sara, relates the poverty and need for education that urban Jewish immigrants felt so keenly in New York ghettoes. Yezierska used a phonetic facsimile of Yiddish dialect to heighten the pathos of the immigrant struggle.

Willa Cather's (1873-1947) stories of frontier life recorded the American Dream unfolding in the West. Alexandra of *O Pioneers!* (1913) and the immigrants cast in *My Ántonia* (1918) foreground the frontier's freedom for women and the opportunity Europeans experienced in America's western territories. Other immigrant groups found voices. O. E. Rölvaag's (1876-1931) *Giants in the Earth: A Saga of the Prairie* (1927; translated from *I de dage*, 1924, and *Riket grundlægges*, 1925) tells an eloquent saga of isolation, back-breaking labor, and temporary madness set in the Dakotas. Dutch truck farmers pursue their chance to rise socially through hard work on their farms south of Chicago in Edna Ferber's (1887-1968) Pulitzer Prize-winning novel *So Big* (1924).

THE HARLEM RENAISSANCE

The flowering of culture and identity known as the Harlem Renaissance was in full bloom during the 1920's, at the same time the novels of immigrant experience were appearing. Langston Hughes's (1902-1967) stories, poetry, and plays, along with Claude McKay's (1889-1948) *Home to Harlem* (1928), presented all aspects of African American life. McKay's work introduced the urban experience of working-class blacks that many black intellectuals chose to downplay. Later, Ann Petry's (1908-1997) *The Street* (1946) took another hard look at black urban life, portraying the pressures on a single mother trying to raise her son in Harlem, their lives beset by poverty and the temptations of the street.

Immigrant and African American experiences narrated in novels of the 1920's showed aspects of the American Dream Horatio Alger overlooked in his optimistic portrayal of opportunity for most whites. Yet McKay's cynical Ray and Cather's optimistic Alexandra still strove to enter the mainstream. They aspired to knowledge or property as a measure of success, adopting a version of the Puritan work ethic, even with backgrounds far from New England. Insistence on personal independence and the ability to affect one's destiny is a primary theme in early twentieth century novels.

MORALITY IN AMERICAN FICTION

The theme of testing moral formulas for material success was present in the stories of mainstream white America as well. *The Great Gatsby* (1925), by F. Scott Fitzgerald, illustrates the ironic coexistence of great wealth and moral carelessness. Like Silas Lapham, Jay Gatsby cannot rise in old-money society. The two characters replace the unifying moral framework of Ben Franklin's schema with faith in a tangible world of goods. For Fitzgerald, relational morality and context changes are emblems of modern society.

Sherwood Anderson (1876-1941) dealt overtly with appearance and reality in *Winesburg, Ohio* (1919). Sinclair Lewis's (1885-1951) *Elmer Gantry* (1927) combines several American strains in the adventure of a rogue evangelist whose commodity is religion. E. L. Doctorow's (born 1931) *Ragtime* (1975) explores the interplay of public events and private lives as characters grapple with restless shifts in the American way of life. John Updike's (born 1932) Rabbit series (1960-1990) chronicles American striving in the span of one man's life and milieu. *That Night* (1987), by Alice McDermott (born 1953), measures love, loss, and success in post-World War II suburban neighborhood life. Finally, Wallace Stegner's (1909-1993) *The Spectator Bird* (1976) offers a retrospective on how one man's professional and private lives coincide in contemporary times. American characters ceaselessly question who they are and how they have arrived at their particular dilemmas and epiphanies.

The conflict between free will and determinism that informs American fiction can also be traced to the Puritan era. Ralph Waldo Emerson's (1803-1882) early defection from Puritanism's angry God to transcendental "self-reliance" (in *Essays: First Series*, 1841) set the stage for America's doctrine of manifest destiny. Emerson's themes fed a harmonic vision of America's purpose, as Americans set out to dominate a new continent and succeeded in a remarkably short time. In the latter half of the nineteenth century, personal, political, and religious activity devoted to progress and westward expansion had a redemptive purpose. All effort and experience took on spiritual significance for white Americans, which encouraged expansion as it provided the philosophic rationale for abuses of power leveled against the environment and American Indian cultures. By the close of the nineteenth century America's central paradoxes also included the increasing duality of urban and rural lifestyles and the impact of Darwinism on the moral philosophies at the basis of human society. William James's (1842-1910) *The Principles of Psychology* (1890) and Henry Adams's (1838-1918) *The Education of Henry Adams* (1907, 1918) explored the spiritual, educational, and behavioral bases on which modern life was founded. Adams particularly worried about how moral sensibility would keep pace with technological advances.

Naturalism

In fiction, Stephen Crane's (1871-1900) *Maggie: A Girl of the Streets* (1893), Theodore Dreiser's (1871-1945) *Sister Carrie* (1900), and Frank Norris's (1870-1902) *The Octopus* (1901) exemplified the naturalist movement. Their novels, like those of Émile Zola (1840-1902), stressed that the forces at work in nature worked in man as well. Transcendence was a myth. The relentless effect of portraying life as a process controlled by indifferent natural forces put an end to the sentimental romantic tradition that had begun with Washington Irving (1783-1859). The fantastic quality of *The Legend of Sleepy Hollow* and his folk figure in "Rip Van Winkle" (both from *The Sketch Book of Geoffrey Crayon, Gent.*, 1819-1820) featured American landscape and the phenomenal effects of the Hudson River Valley light but had no relationship to real events. James Fenimore Cooper's (1789-1851) work was an amalgam of American democratic ideas, Rousseau-like philosophy, and Cooper's fascination with aristocratic England. His Leatherstocking Tales, produced between 1823 and 1841, romanticized Natty Bumppo as a "knight-like" figure who righted wrongs and was aided by the noble savage Chingachgook. Despite his aristocratic tendencies and the foolishness of some of

his scenarios, Cooper's work remained popular because it promoted the mythic belief Americans had in individual determination, as well as their romantic vision of the American wilderness as a place that could engender the highest ideals in people.

Local colorists

The pervasive optimism of American devotion to personal success accounts for other bridging novels of the late nineteenth and early twentieth centuries. Novels of local color or of the regional movement capture the essence of different geographic areas of American life, which were beginning to erode as America was bound together by transportation and communication. Critics tend to group all local-color writers in a quaint or nostalgic subgenre. In fact, there are distinct differences among the work of men and women local colorists. The stories of Bret Harte (1836-1902) in the West, George Washington Cable (1844-1925) in Creole Louisiana, Joel Chandler Harris (1848-1908) in the South, and Mark Twain in the Midwest capture the rambunctious character of life in their regions with dialect and flamboyance. New England's local-color female writers, discussed previously, pay serious attention to social structure and the business of daily life. Their use of parochial dialect and event portrays one area's character without claiming superiority. Their work also tends to avoid the irony and satire that pervade most literature produced by men in this school.

Willa Cather's fiction embodies the serious attention to local detail these women engendered in their view of New England's rapidly shifting economic landscape. Although written later, her novels *O Pioneers!*, *The Song of the Lark* (1915), and *My Ántonia* chronicle events of an earlier time which all depend on the character of frontier life. Even later, Eudora Welty (born 1909) and William Faulkner (1897-1962) molded their southern heritage into stories and novels that captured the gothic quality of southern life, which had seeped into the twentieth century. Faulkner created his mythic Yoknapatawpha County as an archetypal southern context. Contemporary African American writers Alice Walker (born 1944) and Toni Morrison, in *The Color Purple* (1982) and *Be-*

loved (1987) respectively, focus on African American southern life with clarity and compassion, bringing local color's emphasis on region and cultural diversity into later twentieth century fiction.

MUCKRAKERS

Authors known as muckrakers are known for their crusading vision, as typified by Upton Sinclair's (1878-1968) *The Jungle* (1906), an exposé of the Chicago meat-packing industry that prompted enactment of the first pure food and drug laws. Such effort is a version of the Puritan quest for a new Eden. Although not preoccupied with social change per se, other American novelists called attention to America's problems and their costs. Ellen Glasgow (1873-1945) wrote *Vein of Iron* (1935), about an Appalachian woman's struggle during the Great Depression. Character Ada Fincastle's Scotch-Irish immigrant history and gritty determination enabled her to survive as she molded a new working identity for herself. John Steinbeck's (1902-1968) Pulitzer Prize-winning *The Grapes of Wrath* (1939) laid bare the vulnerability of the Joad family, caught, like a sea of other Americans, in the grip of big money and farmers who exploited migrant workers. Tillie Olsen's (born 1913) heart-wrenching *Yonnondio: From the Thirties* (1974) was begun in the 1930's and tells the story of illiterate Anna and Jim Holbrook, who barely survive with their children. Hanging on to hope by the merest thread, they finally settle in a shack near slaughterhouses, where the stench and heat overwhelm them. These two books deal with the desperate plight of workers denied the basic requirements of food and decent living conditions, as well as education for their children.

UTOPIAN NOVELS

Utopian novels offered another alternative to naturalism's grim paradigms between 1889 and 1900. The most famous, *Looking Backward: 2000-1887* (1888) by Edward Bellamy (1850-1898), influenced social philosophers such as John Dewey. Charlotte Perkins Gilman (1860-1935), an author and lecturer for social reform, wrote three utopian novels. *Herland* (1915 serial, 1979 book) posits a society free of

men that functions perfectly, even on the reproductive level. Her use of humor and the plight of three men stranded in the strange land show how gender-driven life is in Western society. All the utopian novels explore the interaction of context and culture. Far from the rigid Puritan dogmas, they investigate how to fashion a better world for oneself and society, a dilemma that has plagued Americans since their appearance on the continent.

From the earliest days of derivative sentimental and gothic novels, the creators of American literature sought an indigenous art and culture. They sought to establish aesthetic standards of their own on a par with the standards set by European and English masters. This often led to consideration of the European preoccupation with hereditary class distinction and how Americans fit into such society, a theme raised to its highest form by Henry James (1843-1916). In *The American* (1876-1877), *Daisy Miller* (1878), and *The Ambassadors* (1903), he showed the dangers inherent in New World sensibilities braving European society, where moral superiority cannot measure up to European style and cultural sophistication. James's narrative style gave rise to an introspective novel that paved the way for later interior monologues.

THE LOST GENERATION

In the 1920's European and American values collided in the works of the lost generation, a group of expatriate artists, including Ernest Hemingway, F. Scott Fitzgerald, Henry Miller (1891-1980), and Gertrude Stein. These writers fled America for the openness and sophistication of the old world, though the Spanish Civil War (1936-1939) corrupted their idealistic beliefs.

Hemingway produced novels that explored individual male quests for masculinity and identity via the odd amalgam of free love, decadent travel, self-indulgence, and foreign civil wars. He filled the epic novel form with American expatriates looking for ultimate reality and self-expression among societies their immigrant forebears and settlers had abandoned, some more than a century ago. Jake Barnes in *The Sun Also Rises* (1926) finds no way to exert himself for his own or anyone else's happiness. In 1925, while F. Scott Fitzgerald and Zelda Fitzgerald lived in Europe, *The Great Gatsby* appeared, detailing, again, the sad hero's tragic search for meaning in the material world. In exile, these writers expressed a hopelessness and a cynicism that replaced the faith and vision that had propelled earlier Americans across the Atlantic. Ironically, their works asked more questions about individual worth and possibilities than they answered. The chief values of a European sojourn were cheaper living costs and proximity to new aesthetic trends.

The effect of European forms on American experience can also be seen in the development of the gothic genre in America. Edgar Allan Poe's legacy lived on in the southern traditions fed by genteel aristocratic customs that exploited slaves, where graceful manners coexisted with the violence of lynchings and the Ku Klux Klan. Faulkner's broken perspective in *The Sound and the Fury* (1929) creates dislocation in reader and narrative progression. Carson McCullers's (1917-1967) novels furnish a cast of nonconventional characters who long for safety. Flannery O'Connor's (1925-1964) tortured Catholics clutch at a faith that offers only torment. Harper Lee's (born 1926) protagonist, Atticus, in *To Kill a Mockingbird* (1960), as well as plain-spoken characters from Eudora Welty's southern novels, counteract the gothic mutations. Their compassionate portrayals offer a South tolerant of eccentricity, a region trying to comprehend the effect of changing times on tradition and decorum.

MODERNISM IN THE AMERICAN NOVEL

American modernism, launched by the 1913 Armory Show in New York, prefigured the collapse of spirit after World War I that led to the cynicism and materialism of the Jazz Age. Modernism's emphasis on the unpredictability of narrative time and voice echoed uncertainties about the permanence of values and life's possibilities. Doubt altered the form and emphasis of modern American novels. The search for identity became acutely personal in J. D. Salinger's (born 1919) *The Catcher in the Rye* (1951), as well as in Jack Kerouac's (1922-1969) Beat classic, *On the Road* (1957). The protagonists of Saul Bellow's (born 1915) *Herzog* (1964) and John Irving's (born

1942) *The World According to Garp* (1978) search endlessly for meaning in a jumbled context. No underlying dogma but the certainty of change supports contemporary American expectations and the vision of society set in motion by pre-World War I modernist writers. John Barth's (born 1930) experiments in discontinuity and narrative games that began in *The Sot-Weed Factor* (1960) are examples of contemporary fiction's exploration of its own form. Barth strips away conventional plot lines and chronology. Readers are forced to accept his books on terms dictated by form, not expectation. More and more, novel form began to echo the fragmented perspectives of contemporary life, with chapters or sections offering competing views of the same events and people.

A vibrant mix of ethnicity and place dominate contemporary fiction. Leslie Marmon Silko's (born 1948) *Ceremony* (1977) occurs after World War II, when disillusioned Native American veterans return to their reservation and encounter discrimination from white America. Toni Morrison's *Song of Solomon* considers the conflict between races during the 1960's, as well as the conflicting annals of two black families. Her cautionary tale warns of the dangers of forgetting one's past and the risk of worshipping commercial success. Alice McDermott's Irish American Brooklyn family seen through the eyes of a child in *At Weddings and Wakes* (1992) evokes the urban neighborhood of the 1940's and 1950's, along with the suffocating closeness that is the legacy of immigrant communities.

Characters in all these novels search for meaning and identity within their cultural traditions, similar to Puritan introspection. However, they have no homogenous social or religious codes like those that unified early Americans. Cormac McCarthy's (born 1933) John Grady Cole in *All the Pretty Horses* (1992) may head for unknown lands, but he returns unsatisfied. Partial and very personal answers are merely implied. Ultimately, the vision of American identities is shaped by landscapes—literal, political, and social— but the contemporary sense of the field is more fluid and strives to be more inclusive than in times past. American novels continue to reveal people as they are.

David Sadkin, updated by Karen Arnold

BIBLIOGRAPHY

Bradbury, Malcolm. *The Modern American Novel.* New York: Oxford University Press, 1992. Provides interesting insight into the modern novel in America.

Donaldson, Susan Van D'Elden. *Competing Voices: The American Novel, 1865-1914.* New York: Twayne, 1998. Part of Twayne's Critical History of the Novel series, this book covers major works from 1865 to 1914.

Elliott, Emory, et al. *The Columbia History of the American Novel.* New York: Columbia University Press, 1991. Contains a good overview of long fiction in America.

Faulkner, Donald, ed. *New England Writers and Writing.* Hanover, N.H.: University Press of New England, 1996. A collection of articles and reviews, many previously uncollected, that gives a good overview of all genres of literature and major writers of the region, from Ralph Waldo Emerson to John Cheever. Contains an interesting essay on Nathaniel Hawthorne's writing habit as well as commentary on the less often featured Horatio Alger.

Kazin, Alfred. *An American Procession: The Major American Writers from 1830 to 1930, the Crucial Century.* New York: Alfred A. Knopf, 1984. Chapters comment on Ralph Waldo Emerson, Henry Thoreau, Edgar Allan Poe, Mark Twain, Henry James, Theodore Drieser, Stephen Crane, Henry Adams, William Faulkner, and Ernest Hemingway. Kazin weaves connections between the writers, their works, and times throughout the book. His wide knowledge of criticism and historical trends makes this a good source for understanding literary movements in the widest possible context.

Ruas, Charles. *Conversations with American Writers.* New York: Alfred A. Knopf, 1985. Contains interviews with fourteen modern and contemporary American writers, including several women. A good collection of commentary on American literature from writers' perspectives. Includes their ideas about American identity, writing, and the politics and preoccupations of American life in their times and regions.

Wagner-Martin, Linda. *The Mid-century American Novel, 1935-1965.* New York: Twayne, 1997. Another volume in Twayne's Critical History of the Novel series, this book covers long fiction published in the middle of the twentieth century. Examines works by minority writers in America, popular literature, and postwar novels.

Wright, George Thaddeus, ed. *Seven American Stylists from Poe to Mailer: An Introduction.* Minneapolis: University of Minnesota Press, 1973. A book of eight introductory essays compiled from pamphlets in the American Authors series. A good general introduction to each author includes a biography and interpretations of the author's work. Chronologically covers the early nineteenth century to the late twentieth century.

ASIAN AMERICAN LONG FICTION

In the study of Asian American literature, the issue of authenticity is as problematic as the definition of the term Asian American itself. While the racial boundary of the Asian American community is historically and geographically delineated by the origins of its immigrants and ontologically dictated by the communality in people's struggle for dignity and social justice, Asian American literature's cultural configuration is a subject of controversy. For example, *The Big Aiiieeeee! An Anthology of Chinese and Japanese American Literature*, edited by Chinese American writer and critic Frank Chin et al., was published in 1991. The selections chosen for the anthology are as controversial as Chin's introductory article, "Come All Ye Asian American Writers of the Real and the Fake," in which he divides Chinese and Japanese American writers into two groups: Asian American authors and Americanized Asian authors.

Chin posits that only those Asian American writers who are not susceptible to Christian conversion and who uphold traditional Chinese and Japanese values such as Confucianism, the Japanese sense of honor, and the samurai sense of nobility can be considered the "real" voice in Asian American literature. This group includes Chinese American writer Louis Chu (*Eat a Bowl of Tea*, 1961) and Japanese American writers Toshio Mori (*Yokohama, California*, 1949) and John Okada (*No-No Boy*, 1957). Chinese American writers such as Pardee Lowe (*Father and Glorious Descendant*, 1943), Jade Snow Wong (*Fifth Chinese Daughter*, 1950), Maxine Hong Kingston (*The Woman Warrior*, 1976; *China Men*, 1980, and *Tripmaster Monkey: His Fake Book*, 1989), and Amy Tan (*The Joy Luck Club*, 1989; *The Kitchen God's Wife*, 1991; *The Hundred Secret Senses*, 1995), Japanese American writers Mike Masaru Masaoka and Bill Hosokawa (*NISEI: The Quiet Americans*, 1969), and Asian American writers who, Chin argues, use the exclusively Christian form of autobiography and revise Asian history, culture, and childhood literature and myth are the "fake." In their depictions of dual personality and identity crises, these writers, according to Chin, not only misrepresent their own cultural heritage but also betray its values.

In the foreword to *Reading the Literatures of Asian America* (1992), Korean American scholar Elaine H. Kim acknowledges that the pioneering work of the members of the Combined Asian-American Resources Project (CARP)—Frank Chin, Jeffery Paul Chan, Lawson Fusao Inada, Nathan Lee, Benjamin R. Tong, and Shawn Hsu Wong—played an important role in helping to define the identity of the Asian American community and to establish Asian American literary voices. However, Kim points out that the terms of Asian Americans' cultural negotiations have changed, and are changing, over time because of differences in historical circumstances and needs. As the body of Asian American literature grows, it reflects desires to traverse the boundaries of unity and diversity, to make Asian American rootedness enable the individual to take flight, and to claim infinite layers of self and community. Chinese American Amy Ling agrees with Kim. In the article "Creating One's Self: The Eaton Sisters," Ling reiterates what has become almost a truism—that the self is not a fixed entity but a fluid, changing construct or creation determined by context or historical conditions and particularly by power relationships. By using the example of the Eaton sisters, who were Amerasians but in creative writing had adopted identities of their choice, one Chinese and one Japanese, Ling convincingly reveals the dialectical relationship between creation and re-creation and between the permeability of the boundaries of the self and the influence of historical conditions. In *Articulate Silence* (1993), Chinese American scholar King-Kok Cheung suggests that it is a distrust of inherited language and of traditional myth with a patriarchal ethos that brings Asian American writers, especially Asian American female writers, to the conclusion that they must cross cultural borders. They seek ways not only to revise history but also to transfigure ethnicity; the point is not to return to the original but to tell it with a difference. The "two-toned language" thus concretely objectifies the attempt of a large group of Asian American writers to negotiate a ground on which they can establish their own identity.

Many Asian American writers are trying to identify a voice that can describe the Asian American experience; they are not in search of a mouthpiece that can only echo what has already been expressed and described in Asian literatures. Given the fact that a person cannot achieve self-actualization without first identifying his or her relationship with her or his own cultural heritage, to be a hyphenated American means that a person is blessed with two cultures and can have the freedom and luxury to be selective. As Brave Orchid, the dynamic mother in Maxine Hong Kingston's *The Woman Warrior*, puts it: "When you come to America, it's a chance to forget some of the bad Chinese habits."

HISTORY OF ASIAN AMERICAN LITERATURE

The development of Asian American literature can be divided into two periods. The first period lasted for almost a century. It started with journals, diaries, and poems written by new Asian immigrants in their native languages and culminated with semiautobiographical novels in the early 1980's. This period was marked by Asian American writers' interest in using the autobiographical approach to describe their experience and to define their relationship with mainstream American culture. Chinese American writers Pardee Lowe, in *Father and Glorious Descendant*, and Jade Snow Wong, in *Fifth Chinese Daughter*, Japanese American writers Daniel Inouye, in *Journey to Washington* (1967), and Monica Sone, in *Nisei Daughter* (1953), and Filipino American writer Carlos Bulosan, in *America Is in the Heart* (1943), use autobiography to describe the authors' struggles with both intercultural and intracultural conflict.

Asian American long fiction was born in the autobiographical tradition and born of Asian American writers' sharpened sensitivities built on an increased awareness of their own cultural heritage. From the mid-1960's to the early 1980's, Asian American literature was rich with fictionalized memoirs that can be read as semiautobiographies. Virginia Lee's *The House That Tai Ming Built* (1963), Chuang Hua's *Crossings* (1968), Maxine Hong Kingston's *The Woman Warrior* and *China Men*, Shawn Wong's

Homebase (1979), and Kazuo Miyamoto's *Hawaii: End of the Rainbow* (1964) could be (and often are) categorized as creative nonfiction rather than fiction. The authors follow the autobiographical tradition in portraying the Asian American experience, in celebrating their cultural heritage, and in reclaiming their sense of history and identity.

The late 1980's and early 1990's were a busy period in the development of Asian American literature. Established Asian American creative writers were able to continue their successful writing careers, while new Asian American novelists launched theirs. During this period Asian American long fiction came of age. In 1989, Japanese American writer Cynthia Kadohata and Chinese American writer Amy Tan published their critically acclaimed novels *The Floating World* and *The Joy Luck Club*. Both heralded the Asian American renaissance of the early and mid-1990's. In 1991 alone, novels by four Chinese American writers appeared: Amy Tan published her second novel, *The Kitchen God's Wife*; Gish Jen's first novel, *Typical American*, received strongly positive reviews; Frank Chin published his first long work, *Donald Duk*; and Gus Lee, a lawyer from California, released an autobiographical novel, *China Boy*.

During the same period, Asian American novelists of Filipino, Korean, and South and Southeast Asian descent were ready to meet the challenge of diversifying the portrayal of the Asian American experience. Filipino American writers Cecilia Manguerra Brainard's *When the Rainbow Goddess Wept* (1994) and Jessica Hagedorn's *The Gangster of Love* (1996), Korean American writers Kim Ronyoung's *Clay Walls* (1987) and Chang-Rae Lee's *Native Speaker* (1995), Asian Indian American writer Bharati Mukherjee's *Jasmine* (1989), and Vietnamese American writer Jade Ngoc Quang Huynh's *South Wind Changing* (1994) enriched the voice and spectrum of Asian American long fiction and brought readers' attention to the diverse nature of the Asian American community.

CHINESE AMERICAN LONG FICTION

Maxine Hong Kingston's *The Woman Warrior* and *China Men* and Amy Tan's *The Joy Luck Club* represent two distinctive periods in the development of Asian American literature to the end of the twentieth century. *The Woman Warrior* and *China Men* are representative of the early development and achievement of Asian American literature. Both use the autobiographical approach to describe their characters' struggles with their identities and their search for voice. Both use memories, oral stories, and traditional Chinese legends, and both interweave the past and the present, fact and fiction, reality and imagination, and traditional Chinese and modern American culture. As Frank Chin, in "Come All Ye Asian American Writers of the Real and the Fake" observes, in *The Woman Warrior* Kingston mixes two famous Chinese legendary characters, Fa Mulan and Yue Fei, from two different stories. The attempt, contrary to what Chin argues, is not to rewrite Fa Mulan according to "the specs of the stereotype of the Chinese woman as a pathological white supremacist victimized and trapped in a hideous Chinese civilization" but to reveal the richness of the Asian American experience in general and of Asian American literature in particular. Kingston attempts to destroy both the traditional Chinese gender line, which places women at the bottom of the social totem, and the line that separates imagination and reality. (The latter approach explains why both *The Woman Warrior* and *China Men* are often categorized as nonfiction.)

Amy Tan's *The Joy Luck Club* intermingles the thematic treatment of intercultural conflict with that of intergenerational conflict. The mothers who immigrated to the United States from China still have strong cultural ties to their old home, and they want to rear their children in the traditional way. Their Chinese American daughters, however, believe that they are trapped in the conflict between traditional Chinese culture and mainstream American society, between their aspirations for individual freedom and their sense of familial and social obligations, and between their false and their true identities. The conflict is both frustrating and constructive. The daughters are eventually led to conclude that they must embrace what they cannot culturally reject and to realize that they are as American as they are Chinese.

Filipino American long fiction

Filipino Americans occupy a unique place in the history of the United States. From the end of the Spanish-American War (1898) to the independence of the Philippines (1946), Filipinos were considered subjects of the United States, and there was no restriction on their immigration. For many years, therefore, Filipino Americans were the largest ethnic group in the Asian American community. This unique historical phenomenon created ambivalent feelings among Filipino Americans toward the United States. Whereas many appreciate the economic opportunities, Filipino American writers such as Joaquin Legaspi, José Garcia Villa, Alfred A. Robles, Bayani L. Mariano, N. V. M. Gonzalez, Samuel Tagatac, J. C. Dionisio, and Bienvenido N. Santos also aspire to reconnect with the native Filipino culture, literature, and art. Filipino American long fiction is largely built on this aspiration; it grows out of the fear of losing what Mariano, in his poem "What We Know," calls the "best of ourselves."

Cecilia Manguerra Brainard and Jessica Hagedorn are two leading Filipino American novelists. The main event of Brainard's *When the Rainbow Goddess Wept* occurs in Asia during World War II. The novel is narrated from a nine-year-old's perspective. With her family, Yvonne Macaraig flees the Japanese invasion of the Philippines to join the resistance effort. In the jungle she is nourished by the legends of Bongkatolan, the Woman Warrior, and the merciful rainbow goddess. Jessica Hagedorn is a novelist, critic, and anthologist. Her novel *Dogeaters* (1990) was nominated for a National Book Award. In her 1996 novel *The Gangster of Love*, she portrays a new immigrant from the Philippines who, while excited about his new life in the United States, is haunted by the memory of the homeland he left behind. Both Brainard's *When the Rainbow Goddess Wept* and Hagedorn's *The Gangster of Love* represent Filipino Americans' effort to reclaim their sense of history and identity by making connections with their homeland and with the Filipino culture.

Japanese American long fiction

Japanese American literature started with logs, diaries, journals, and chronicles written in Japanese. Many Issei (first-generation Japanese immigrants to the United States) did not feel the need to learn English. They were not allowed to become U.S. citizens, and many had come to the United States with the intention of returning to Japan when they had saved enough money. Japanese American literature began to take shape with the emergence of Nisei (second-generation) writers. Some of these writers spoke fluent Japanese as well as English. Besides serving as a bridge between their parents' Japanese culture and American culture, many Nisei writers assumed the responsibility of making the Japanese American voice heard in what Japanese American poet and critic Lawson Fusao Inada calls "the Occidental world of mainstream American literature."

Japanese American novelist John Okada was one of the first Nisei writers to bring readers' attention to the traumatic experience suffered by many Japanese Americans during and after World War II. During the war, 120,000 Japanese Americans were evacuated from the West Coast and put in relocation camps. The experience left an indelible impact on the Japanese American community and its literature. Okada's *No-No Boy* (1957) depicts a second-generation Japanese American's struggle to balance his loyalty to the Japanese culture, to his parents, and to his country, the United States. The protagonist, Ichiro Yamada, interned during World War II, is put in jail for refusing to forswear allegiance to Japan and join the U.S. Army. After he is released from prison, Ichiro moves back to Seattle and is caught between two seemingly irreconcilable worlds. On one side are his parents, very proud of being Japanese. On the other side is the United States, a country to which he still feels he belongs. During his search for his identity, Ichiro meets several people who help shape his perspective of himself and of his relationship with America. After witnessing the tragic deaths of several of his friends, Ichiro starts to think about his own future. He begins to chase the faint insinuation of promise that takes shape in his mind and heart.

In the second period of Japanese American literature, Sansei (third-generation) female writers started to make significant contributions. Cynthia Kadohata

and Holly Uyemoto are two leading voices in the development of Japanese American long fiction. The narrator of Cynthia Kadohata's *The Floating World* (1989), Olivia Ann, is a Sansei. As Olivia is growing up in the 1950's, her family is always on the move from job to job. Having to live in *ukiyo*, the floating world—"the gas station attendants, restaurants, and jobs," "the motel towns floating in the middle of fields and mountains"—the narrator learns early in her life that she and her family must rely on what is stable while traveling through an unstable world. What is stable is the secret of the family's history, the strong role models in Olivia's mother and her grandmother (*obasan*), and the closeness of the family.

Holly Uyemoto's *Go* (1996) also describes a Sansei's search for connectedness, for her identity, and for her spiritual home. Wil is a burned-out college student. After having an abortion and separating from her politically correct boyfriend, she returns to her family in search of support. Through the disentanglement of her family history, Wil learns about her grandparents' past, the experiences of Issei and Nisei in World War II internment camps, and a cultural heritage deeply embedded in her emotional and spiritual being. If *The Floating World* is exquisitely elegant, picaresque, and observant, *Go* is amusing, zany, and engaging. Both works celebrate Japanese American culture, both portray strong Japanese American female characters, and both suggest strong ties in characters' relationships with their family history and with that of the community.

KOREAN AMERICAN LONG FICTION

Korean American long fiction came into its own in the 1980's and 1990's. Because of the Korean War, Korean immigration to the United States had dramatically increased in the 1950's and 1960's. Children of first-generation Korean immigrants graduated from college in the late 1970's and early 1980's and began to contribute to the flourishing of Asian American literature. Kim Ronyoung was one of the pioneers in Korean American long fiction. Her novel *Clay Walls* (1987) fictionally chronicles the journey of a newly married Korean couple, Haesu and Chun, to the United States and their struggle to take root in the new land. The novel experiments with narrative points of view. Events are seen through the eyes of three characters: Haesu, Chun, and Faye, the couple's American-born daughter.

Like the literary works produced by writers from other ethnic groups in the United States, Asian American long fiction includes an important component which is frequently neglected in the study of Asian American literature. Asian American popular novels occupy a special place in Asian American literature and often introduce the culture to the reading public. Amerasian writer Ruthanne Lum McCunn's *Thousand Pieces of Gold* (1981), Chinese American writer Bette Bao Lord's *Spring Moon* (1981) and *The Middle Heart* (1996), Evelina Chao's *Gates of Grace* (1985), and Gus Lee's *China Boy* (1991) and *Tiger's Tail* (1996) all fit into this category. In Korean American literature, Chang-rae Lee's *Native Speaker*, a detective story, also belongs in this company. The narrator of the novel, Henry Park, is a spy for a private business. His ethnicity provides him with an expedient cover for his work. This amusing and intriguing novel vividly and accurately introduces the customs and traditions of the Korean American community to the reader.

SOUTH AND SOUTHEAST ASIAN AMERICAN LONG FICTION

In the late 1980's and the 1990's, the spectrum of contemporary Asian American long fiction witnessed two major changes from its earlier period. First, autobiographical novels and fictional memoirs were replaced as the predominant voice in the description of the Asian American experience. Asian American writers became more interested in experimenting with different literary genres and in searching for literary forms that can accurately depict the Asian American experience. Second, Asian American writers other than Chinese, Japanese, Filipino, and Korean Americans began to attract attention.

One pioneer South and Southeast Asian American novelist is Asian Indian American writer Bharati Mukherjee. Mukherjee is a first-generation immigrant from India. Her novel *Jasmine* (1989) depicts a new immigrant's journey from her native country to the United States. The narrator, Jasmine Vijh, was born in Hasnapur, India, and given the name Jyoti. She is her parents' fifth daughter and the seventh of nine children; as such, she was somewhat unwanted. An astrologer predicted that she was doomed to widowhood and exile. Determined to chart the course of her own life, Jasmine married Prakash Vijh at the age of fourteen, and he renamed her Jasmine as a means of breaking her from her past.

After her husband is murdered by a Muslim fanatic, Jasmine fulfills Prakash's wish and goes to the United States. She first works as a caregiver for Taylor Hayes, a college professor in New York City. She then flees from Sukhwinder, the man who killed her husband, and moves to Baden, Iowa, where she falls in love with Bud Ripplemeyer and becomes his common-law wife, living as Jane Ripplemeyer. Taylor eventually finds Jasmine, and the two decide to move to California. In the novel, Jasmine has several identities; she is a different person to different people. To Prakash, she is Jasmine; to Half-Face, a man who rapes her, she is the goddess Kali; to Lilian Gordon, who helps her find a job in New York City, she is Jazzy; to Taylor, she is Jase; to Bud, she is Jane. Her various identities finally make Jasmine realize that she can be whoever she wants to make herself. At the end of the book, she is ready to take control of her own destiny.

Vietnamese American writer Jade Ngoc Quang Huynh is also a first-generation immigrant. Huynh was a college student in Vietnam, but he was sent to labor camps for "education in communist ideology, psychological and physical retraining, and lessons on how to become a happy and productive member in their new society." Huynh escaped Vietnam in 1977, a few years after the end of the Vietnam War, and went to the United States. His *South Wind Changing* (1994) follows the traditions established by Vietnamese American writers such as Le Ly Hayslip, whose two powerful autobiographies, *When Heaven and Earth Changed Places* (1990) and *Child of War, Woman of Peace* (1993), touched readers' hearts and were later made into a film (*Heaven and Earth*, 1993) directed by Oliver Stone. *South Wind Changing* is about family, traditions, and the stark contrast between the beauty of nature and the cruelty of war and ideological battles. The novel traces the narrator's footsteps from Vietnam to the United States. Its first-person narrative is believable, patient, and moving.

Qun Wang

BIBLIOGRAPHY

Chan, Jeffery Paul, Frank Chin, Lawson Fusao Inada, and Shawn Wong, eds. *The Big Aiiieeeee! An Anthology of Chinese American and Japanese American Literature*. New York: Meridian, 1991. The anthology includes Frank Chin's article "Come All Ye Asian American Writers of the Real and the Fake," which not only discusses literary histories of Chinese and Japanese American literature but also criticizes the development of contemporary Asian American literature from a cultural nationalist point of view.

Cheung, King-Kok. *Articulate Silences*. Ithaca, N.Y.: Cornell University Press, 1993. The book uses Japanese American writer Hisaye Yamamoto, Japanese Canadian writer Joy Kogawa, and Chinese American writer Maxine Hong Kingston as examples to discuss Asian American and Asian Canadian female writers' contributions to the development of Asian American and Canadian literature.

_____, ed. *An Interethnic Companion to Asian American Literature*. New York: Cambridge University Press, 1997. A collection of essays that surveys North American writers of Asian descent in terms of both national origins (Chinese, Filipino, Japanese, Korean, South Asian, Vietnamese) and shared concerns.

Hune, Shirley, Hyung-chan Kim, Stephen S. Fugita, and Amy Ling. *Asian Americans: Comparative and Global Perspectives*. Pullman: Washington State University Press, 1991. An interdisciplinary study of Asian American political movements, history, cultures, and literature.

Kim, Elaine H. *Asian American Literature: An Introduction to the Writings and Their Social Context*. Philadelphia: Temple University Press, 1982. One of the pioneer works in the study of Asian American literature. It includes discussions of first-generation and second-generation Asian American writers and of their portraits of Chinatown, the Japanese American community, and the search for a new self-image. An invaluable resource.

Lim, Shirley Geok-lin, and Amy Ling, eds. *Reading the Literatures of Asian America*. Philadelphia: Temple University Press, 1992. A collection of essays by leading scholars in the study of Asian American literature and cultures.

Ling, Amy. *Between Worlds: Women Writers of Chinese Ancestry*. New York: Pergamon Press, 1990. Another early attempt by a Chinese American scholar to evaluate Chinese American female writers' contributions to the development of Asian American literature.

Takaki, Ronald. *Strangers from a Different Shore: A History of Asian Americans*. New York: Penguin Books, 1989. Critically acclaimed study of Asian American immigration to the United States. One of the first comprehensive examinations of the history of Asian American immigration from a multicultural perspective. Provides excellent background information for those who are interested in Asian American history, literature, and cultures.

Wong, Sau-ling Cynthia. *Reading Asian American Literature: From Necessity to Extravagance*. Princeton, N.J.: Princeton University Press, 1993. A thematic and theoretical study of Asian American literature and cultures.

CANADIAN LONG FICTION

Given the geographical and historical proximity of Canada and the United States, it stands to reason that their national literatures would reflect similar concerns. Early Canadian settlers traveled from Europe, with the majority emigrating from Great Britain and France. They were faced with a wilderness that seemed almost infinite—that would not be completely settled even into the twentieth century—inhabited by people whose appearance, beliefs, and customs were different from their own. Their national economy was closely linked to natural resources, dominated by such industries as farming, fishing, mining, logging, and milling. Little in their previous experience had prepared them for such an encounter, and few of the artistic models they had brought from Europe allowed them to completely express the reality of their relation to this "new" world. Like their cousins to the south, Canadians were continually renegotiating their identity relative to the surrounding landscape, and early Canadian writers sought to raise this daily phenomenon of encounter and compromise to an expression of national selfhood.

As such, it is strange to note how differently Canada and the United States developed, in both literary and historical senses. Where Americans were driven by their "manifest" directive to settle the continent, Canadian settlement was less rapid and headlong. Official groups such as the Royal Canadian Mounted Police often preceded settlers into the wilderness, carving out a habitable and "known" space for pioneers who followed. The emphasis was usually on order, which prevented the frenzied land rushes and cultural clashes occurring to the south. Where American settlement was often violent, punctuated by slavery and wars with American Indians, Canadian movements across the landscape were deliberate and, at some level, introspective. Relations with Indians, though not perfect, were enhanced by the Canadian government's simple willingness to adhere to its treaties. Other interchange between cultures, despite friction, infrequently rose to the level of martial conflict that punctuated U.S. history. Indeed, the high premium that Canadians have historically placed on cultural dialogue continues to be exemplified by the coexistence of anglophone and francophone cultures.

EARLY CANADIAN NOVELS, 1769-1852

The complexities of cultural interchange and of comprehending the landscape beyond simple conquest have epitomized Canadian long fiction from its inception. Chief among such works is Frances Brooke's *The History of Emily Montague* (1769), arguably the first North American novel. Written by an Englishwoman who had lived for five years in Canada and adhering closely to a standard romance plot, *The History of Emily Montague* nevertheless invokes the sense of dichotomy that would characterize later Canadian novels. The matrices that form the novel's thematic base—civilization versus savagery, urban versus rural, feminine versus masculine, and domestic order versus natural law—challenged the assumption that European society could be instantly transplanted to North America. While the lead characters Emily Montague and Colonel Rivers marry at the novel's end—per the genre's conventions—the negotiations that occur during their courtship in Canada suggest how Brooke's writing subtly undermines the moral, sexual, and political expectations of her English audience. Though no great upheaval occurs within the book's social order, the mere suggestion of necessary compromise (between characters of various backgrounds and between humans and the wilderness) creates a sense of cultural dialogue uncommon in works of the time.

Such dialogues are stressed in John Richardson's *Wacousta: Or, The Prophecy, a Tale of the Canadas* (1832), the next seminal novel in Canadian literary history. Similar to James Fenimore Cooper's Leatherstocking Tales in its depiction of a white army facing an Indian foe, *Wacousta* eschews the easy valorization of "civilization" over "savagery" implicit in Cooper's works. From the novel's start, Richardson refuses to uphold any character type as absolutely worthy or moral, and even the notion of identity itself—who people are, what qualifies them as good or evil, how rapidly they change—is negotiated at a frenetic pace. The title character is not even an Indian but a British gentleman whose unrequited love for Clara Beverly has caused him to masquerade as a Scottish renegade, a French officer under Montcalm, and finally a lieutenant to Pontiac among the Ottawa. In this last capacity, he helps lead the Indians against Fort Detroit, home to Colonel De Haldimar (the widower of Clara Beverly) and his three children. The relationships formed by Haldimar's family with military personnel, Indians, and finally Wacousta himself weave an intricate cultural tableau in which Richardson presents his readers with a seemingly fixed version of the world only to invert the relationships in ensuing chapters. The novel is finally presided over by the schizophrenic figure of Wacousta, whose negotiation of cultural borders suggests an ironic ability to alter his identity even as his ongoing psychological torment over Clara suggests his inability to elude the singular essence of what he is as a man. This metaphor could serve for most of the novel's characters, whose mores cannot keep pace with their rapidly changing situations in the novel, forcing them and their audience to reconsider the values they believe to be "permanent."

Wacousta is the most complex novel of early Canadian literature, outlining the thematic and cultural core of many works to follow, especially novels about the Canadian wilderness and cross-cultural contact. If Richardson is concerned with the way human identity both shapes and is shaped by the natural landscape, Susanna Moodie's *Roughing It in the Bush: Or, Life in Canada* (1852) offers an interesting thematic supplement, a chronicle of settlers attempting to deal with their environment after the "wilderness" has been largely tamed. Of particular importance is the way that the novel serves both as a precursor to the "farm" or prairie novels of the early twentieth century and as a blueprint, with its vocal female protagonist, for the strong tradition of women's writing in Canadian letters. The book is narrated by a woman named Susanna Moodie (not to be completely taken for the author herself) who recounts her failure, along with her husband Dunbar, at farming in southern Ontario. Members of the gentry, the Moodies find themselves physically unprepared

for the rigors of farm life and overly romantic about the promise of the land (unlike their poor neighbors, who are more accustomed to the labor that farming requires). Offering a series of realistic sketches depicting the frontier in early Canada, the novel, like its predecessors, pits various opposites against one another: European versus North American, wealthy versus poor, urban versus rural. Again, it refuses to completely valorize any set of cultural mores; readers are disappointed by the literal failure of the optimistic Moodies yet skeptical of the unadorned, often menial physicality implicit in the lives of the more successful farmers. This ambivalence breaks down the absolute nature of the binaries that the author originally constructs, suggesting the inadequacy of using the Moodies, their neighbors, or any individuals as templates for a representative national identity.

THE INTERIM PERIOD, 1852-1920

Despite the impressive novels of the early nineteenth century, Canadians did not produce many long literary works from 1852 to 1920, and those that were produced did not rival the complexity of their predecessors; the best-known work from this period is a children's book, L. M. Montgomery's 1908 *Anne of Green Gables*. Indeed, a quick look at the number of Canadian titles produced throughout the nineteenth century would be enough to demonstrate that Canada was not developing the sizable literary tradition of the United States at the time. In part, this situation was the result of demographics: A small Canadian population spread over a broad area did not have the resources to support an indigenous publishing industry. The disparity was also the result of American history. Obsessed with becoming a world power, the United States engaged in not only a quick march across the continent but also a furious drive to place before the world a literature that could be considered emblematically American. Success against Britain in gaining independence, as well as the attention of European philosophers and a growing industrial economy, had made Americans keenly aware of their need for an intellectual apparatus to match their imperial aspirations. The novels they produced out of this sensibility were largely future oriented, singular in their belief in the eventual greatness of the United States, and philosophically rooted in a tradition that generally—if ironically—raised individual liberties, the spirit of revolution, and a proclivity for violence to the level of national-cultural persona.

Canadians, by contrast, often viewed the "chaos" of U.S. imperial designs with skepticism and dismay; many British loyalists had, in fact, fled north during the America Revolution. Canada, more than the United States, was forced to deal with crises of identity at an early stage of nationhood. Despite strong ties to the British crown, Canada was made up of a variety of cultural groups: loyalist English in Ontario, Maritime Scots sympathetic to the United States, French-speaking Catholics in Quebec, not to mention numerous Indian tribes. Lacking the central (if dubious) myth of a unified predestined empire, Canada operated under a sometimes fragile sense of shared geography and cultural balance-of-power until confederation in 1867. Even after confederation, various groups continued to agitate for greater recognition, such as the Québécois independence movements that continued to occur throughout the twentieth century. Moreover, Canadian history and literature suffered from a kind of neocolonial complex, a sense of "inadequacy" in the face of both British tradition and the United States' burgeoning—if self-proclaimed—historic and artistic greatness.

Responding to this situation, Canadian writers in the early twentieth century worked to embrace their nation's "median" status, exploring the cultural borders on which Canadians found themselves and adopting analogues from British and American culture that represented their experience even as they rejected the idea of Canada as a mirror image of either foreign culture. Their job, as always, was to find in their multifarious history what was distinct about them as a people, a more introspective process than either British or American models probably allowed. This focus on "discovering" the past rather than pushing toward the future evolved into a quintessential feature of the Canadian novel, a direct outgrowth of the cultural exploration and self-analysis implicit in the earliest works of Brooke, Richardson, and Moodie. What became important to Canadian intellectuals late in this period—and remained important through the twentieth century—was the idea of "process" by which a person or a nation comes to articulate an identity. Without a central cultural myth to which all others must refer, Canadian authors found themselves in the unique position of being able to write their own history well after it had unfolded—that is, to probe the past in an attempt not only to recount events but also to investigate how and why such events are told, to recognize the many viewpoints inherent in "making history," and to acknowledge the past not as a single set of incidents but as a more fluid series of interpretations constantly subject to review.

THE PRAIRIE AND THE WEST

During the 1920's and 1930's, a common metaphor for this process of discovering history recurred in novels about the Great Plains and the Western interior. Unlike the American frontier novel—where white pioneer-cowboys contended against American Indians, villains, and the forces of industry to settle the continent—Canadian Western novels dealt with settlers coming to terms with the "vast absence" around them. If violent contests did occur in the Canadian West, they more often took the shape of humans versus the landscape or versus their own demons than a contest against those external forces struggling to prevent the advance of "civilization." Thus while most American Westerns resolved themselves quite neatly—the defeat of the savage cleared the way for the nation's progress—Canadian writers were troubled both by the absolute moral oppositions of the American system and by the way that system failed to address their own historical experience. Implicitly aware of the multiple viewpoints shaping their past, these writers struggled with the concept of how to build "history" out of many voices—or, more to the point, how to articulate Canadian identity when no one cultural voice told the nation's full story and history became a kind of "surrounding silence" incapable of revealing itself. Canadian experiences with both the prairie and the Western interior served as apt metaphors for this struggle, though for different reasons. The prairie—flat, empty, even desolate—

offered a vacant site where the task of self-creation seemed simultaneously imminent and impossible, a blank slate on which to inscribe both personal and national identity that contained no external signposts to suggest exactly what that identity should be. The Western interior, by contrast, offered a mountainous landscape filled with spectacular topography and various cultures, a place full of external stimuli yet also filled with different people who encountered those stimuli through vastly divergent historical, economic, and personal contexts.

Of the prairie novels, the most notable are Frederick Philip Grove's *Settlers of the Marsh* (1925), Martha Ostenso's *Wild Geese* (1925), Robert J. C. Stead's *Grain* (1926), and Sinclair Ross's *As For Me and My House* (1941). While all have been called works of realism, depicting the harsh nature of prairie life, later critics recognized them as psychological quests for self-understanding. *Grain* follows the attempts of a slow-witted man, Gander Stake, to come to terms with his own social and sexual identity even as the farm life to which he is accustomed slowly gives way to a post-World War I industrial economy. *Settlers of the Marsh* and *Wild Geese* explore the worlds of egomaniacal patriarchs trying to found personal dynasties on the plains, as well as the oppressed characters (often female) attempting to break free from their single-minded imperatives. *As for Me and My House* analyzes the process by which characters construct their identities away from civilization, isolated in a small prairie town.

Of these works, *As for Me and My House* is the most interesting because of the way it explores identity construction as more than a reaction to another's demagoguery; Ross's work excludes dominant, if detestable, central figures (such as Grove's Neils Lindstedt or Ostenso's Caleb Gare) in order to avoid amoral touchstones through which the actions of others can be measured and understood. Instead, he offers only the town of Horizon—a mere spot on the Saskatchewan map—during the Great Depression, where characters come to understand themselves through interactions with the community. The novel is rendered in journal format by the wife of Philip Bentley, Horizon's minister. Mrs. Bentley is a proud

and stand-offish woman, a former musician who claims to detest everything about the small, isolated place to which her husband has been sent. Philip Bentley is an agnostic, a failed artist, and a man who has assumed his religious post more out of his sense of duty than belief or desire. Together the Bentleys struggle to understand themselves against the backdrop of the desolate prairie, Philip's extramarital affair, an illegitimate child and constant rancor. Despite her desperate need to be loved, Mrs. Bentley refuses to turn to Philip because of the many betrayals which she believes he has heaped upon her. Despite his desperate need for artistic stimulation and his overwhelming self-doubt, Philip refuses to leave Horizon, motivated by the same pride that motivates his wife. In both cases, the prairie becomes a symbol of the isolation and emptiness that both characters feel. Even the one person who seems capable of escaping the oppressive psychological weight of Horizon—Philip's lover Judith—dies by the novel's end, and the Bentleys subsequently move back east.

Amid the despair, though, Ross's novel offers an ironic glimmer of hope in the figure of the prairie itself. Unending and oppressive, the prairie is ultimately the psychological catalyst that erases the characters' faulty self-conceptions and lets them see themselves for what they truly are. Mrs. Bentley regularly walks down the train tracks away from Horizon and into the prairie, an act that suggests her figurative desire to embrace the landscape's blankness and create a psychological space in which she can discover her true nature or even reinvent herself according to her deepest desires. Their insistence that the prairie stifles self-expression notwithstanding, both Bentleys explore various sides of their personalities while in Horizon and, while making critical mistakes, seem more self-satisfied by the novel's end. Their final move east can thus be read either negatively (as a retreat from that version of themselves that Horizon has revealed) or positively (as a redemptive shift toward grace following the Purgatory in which their souls have been laid bare). In either event, it is the process of identity discovery and even construction central to Canadian fiction that leads one Bentley family into Horizon and another away from it one year later.

Published almost concurrently with *As for Me and My House*, Howard O'Hagan's *Tay John* (1939) was the first work set in the Western interior to raise the prairie novel's quest for personal identity to the overt level of cultural politics and national myth. The protagonist of *Tay John* is a mixed-blood Shuswap Indian navigating the margins of both Indian and white society. A failed messiah to his people and an enigmatic hunter-tracker among white people, Tay John is labeled time and again by the novel's other characters only to disregard their expectations. Even his name, which changes several times, is evidence of the way that words fail to tell his story. He goes from being Kumkan Kleseem, to Kumkleseem, to Tête Jaune, to Tay John—all very different names but each offering no more than a rudimentary assessment of his uncommonly yellow hair. Identity after identity is subverted until it becomes clear that no one—neither the Shuswap into whose tribe he was born nor the white people in whose camps he works—can begin to define him. His demise is equally enigmatic: Pulling a sled bearing his dead white wife, he appears merely to descend into a snow drift, dying but not dying, defying explanation again.

If one point of *As for Me and My House* is to demonstrate how difficult it can be to tell one's own story, then the point of *Tay John* is to demonstrate how impossible it must be to tell someone else's. In this sense, the ubiquitous Tay John—despite his mythic aspect—is one of the least compelling characters in the work. Rather, the book asks its audience to identify with those people who try, yet fail, to tell the protagonist's story: the Shuswap, who want Tay John to lead them to their promised land; Alf Dobble, the failed land developer who sees Tay John as a fixture in his mountain empire; and even Blackie, who tries to narrate Tay John's death as simply as possible, yet relegates him to myth again. These characters, O'Hagan suggests, are emblematic of the book's readers—people for whom names order the world, yet for whom names completely misidentify that world. As Jack Denham, the narrator of most of the book, observes, "naming is unnaming," tacitly admitting the way that a name ascribed by one person or culture necessarily undoes the name assigned by an-

other. Interpersonal misunderstandings are raised to the level of cross-class, cross-race, and cross-gender miscommunication, underscoring a near complete futility to the notion of productive interchange among different people and cultures. Yet Tay John, both the man and the idea, remains indelibly fixed at the core of the tale—a story that cannot necessarily be told but one that undeniably exists.

These seemingly dichotomous elements—the need to tell the story despite skepticism that any one story can account for all the necessary viewpoints—has remained a feature of the Canadian Western since *Tay John*'s publication. Latter-day practitioners of the form have focused more specifically on the problems of cross-cultural interchange, keenly aware of historical frictions between Caucasians and Indians. For example, Peter Such's *Riverrun* (1973) inverts the "conventional" version of history by exploring the extinction of the Beothuck Indians of Newfoundland from the Indians' point-of-view. Rudy Wiebe's *The Temptations of Big Bear* (1973) challenges the idea of history proper by noting that any recorded version of the past marginalizes the Indian culture in whose language that history is not written. The story revolves around the Cree chief Big Bear—who refuses to select a reservation site for his people—and the numerous failed attempts of surrounding characters, Caucasians and non-Cree Indians alike, to understand him. Other novels offer an occasionally humorous, if no less poignant, angle on this subject. Robert Kroetsch's *Gone Indian* (1973) tracks the attempts of an American graduate student to discover his "real" life as a mock Canadian Indian; George Bowering's *Caprice* (1987) comically inverts the normal order of the American Western by having two dry-witted, semi-omniscient Indians narrate the story of a whip-wielding cowgirl-heroine; and Philip Kreiner's *Contact Prints* (1987) follows the misadventures of a white teacher at an Indian school who makes a living covertly selling her art as "authentically" native.

Such an environment has also helped to foster a vibrant native literature in Canada. Despite hard-edged fiction that explores the brutal reality of some Indian lives—such as Beatrice Culleton's *In Search* of *April Raintree* (1983)—most Native Canadian novelists have echoed their white counterparts in adopting a sympathetic, even humorous, tone relative to Indian characters. As in the United States, the Native Canadian novel does not have a long tradition in itself, but many of its themes and devices derive from oral narratives that have existed since before first contact. In addition, Indian writers have been strongly influenced by the expansive tradition of the Canadian novel, especially the experimental styles of writers such as Kroetsch and Bowering. In fact, the Indians in Thomas King's *Medicine River* (1990) more closely resemble *Caprice*'s sardonic Indian narrators than more polemical protagonists, while his *Green Grass, Running Water* (1993) offers a multi-layered postmodern tale in which members of one Indian family, several spirits, and an "omniscient" trickster figure are set on a course that brings them (and their immediate surroundings) to a farcical apocalyptic end. In addition, as scholars have noted, later Indian novels focused as much on the similarities between white and Native lives as on the differences. King's work—along with books by Maurice Kenny, Ruby Slipperjack, and Jeanette Armstrong—provides a version of everyday Indian life that seems quite similar to everyday white life even as it partakes of a lyricism and mysticism echoing its specific past. This duality, which acknowledges cultural similarities while being able to embrace differences, continues the careful balancing act of personal and cultural identity so precious to Canadian novelists. Nowhere is that process of national identity construction more evident than in Western Canadian fiction, from Richardson and Moodie through Ross and O'Hagan to Wiebe and King.

CANADIAN NOVELS AFTER 1960

While Native Canadians comprise the most prominent minority group writing in Canada, other races and ethnicities have found room for themselves within the nation's pluralistic literary tradition. Mordecai Richler has charted the Canadian Jewish experience in books such as *The Apprenticeship of Duddy Kravitz* (1959), *St. Urbain's Horsemen* (1971), and *Joshua Then and Now* (1980). Sky Lee's *Disap-*

pearing Moon Café (1990) and Joy Kogawa's *Obasan* (1981) recount the sometimes tragic histories of Chinese and Japanese immigrants, respectively. Beginning around 1980, novelists of Asian-Indian and Sri Lankan descent also assumed a prominent place in Canadian letters. Before *The English Patient* (1992) won the Booker Prize, Michael Ondaatje was quite famous within Canada for experimental fiction such as *The Collected Works of Billy the Kid* (1970) and *Coming Through Slaughter* (1976). His success has been echoed by such writers as Rohinton Mistry, who won the 1991 Governor General's Award for *Such a Long Journey* (1991), and Bharati Mukherjee. Even Caribbean writers have found their way to a northern home: Neil Bissoondath's *A Casual Brutality* (1988) recounts the moral devolution of a Caribbean island and one ordinary man's inability to cope with such changes.

Such inclusions do not mean that latter-day Canadian novels have completely lost a sense of their British "origins." The works of Robertson Davies, Canada's best-known writer, demonstrate a stylistic and thematic affinity for the Old World. Davies, who died in 1995, is best known for his trilogies—the Salterton trilogy, the Cornish trilogy, and the Deptford trilogy; his erudite language, fascination with psychology, and use of European mysticism and arcane lore make his sweeping sagas of Canadian families closely akin to John Galsworthy or Henry James. Of his work, the Deptford trilogy is probably the most famous. Following the lives of three men from the small town of Deptford, Ontario, the trilogy addresses the Jungian issues of how closely all human lives are interrelated, how issues of the spirit impact issues of the flesh, and how even the smallest actions can have profound effects on the future. The narrative begins when Percy "Boy" Staunton throws a stone-filled snowball at Dunstable Ramsay, who dodges, allowing the snowball to strike Mary Dempster instead. Mary gives birth prematurely to a son, Paul, before going insane. The rest of the trilogy follows the lives of Staunton, Ramsay, and Paul, never letting its audience forget the profound impact of a single snowball on all three characters and the people around them. On the surface, such connections seem only marginally related to the issues of historical investigation, revision, and self-creation typical of contemporaneous Canadian novels. Yet at the same time, each novel in the trilogy is imbued with deep senses of guilt and responsibility. In particular, *Fifth Business* (1970), the opening work in the series, emphasizes the Canadian impulse to understand the past, revolving around an autobiographical letter in which Dunstable Ramsay attempts to make sense of his place in the chain of events that led to Paul's birth and Mary Dempster's dementia. Such uncertainty—Ramsay's quest for the original definitive moment in his life—is what ultimately reinscribes Davies as a prototypical Canadian writer. The search for identity that many of his characters undergo echoes the larger quest of Canadians defining themselves both within and against Anglo-American ideas. Accused sometimes of being too urbanely English himself, Davies writes with the polish of British predecessors but always about characters whose lives undermine the historical sense of certainty often associated with the Anglo-American culture.

Beyond culture, Canadian novels have accommodated difference in various senses. Most important is the strong tradition of women's writing present from the genre's inception by Brooke and sustained by writers such as Julia Catherine Hart, Moodie, Rosanna Leprohon, Nellie L. McClung, Laura Goodman Salverson, and Ostenso through the early 1920's. The second half of the twentieth century produced women novelists writing on every theme and in every style imaginable. Margaret Laurence's five Manawaka novels—especially *The Stone Angel* (1964) and *The Diviners* (1974)—bear the distinct imprint of Ostenso and even Willa Cather in their epic record of women protagonists struggling to assert their identity after small-town beginnings. Aritha Van Herk's *The Tent Peg* (1981) and Anne Cameron's *The Journey* (1982) revise conventional Western plots, placing women in male roles and even having women masquerade as men in an attempt to undermine the rigid gender inscription of the American West. Sheila Watson's *The Double Hook* (1959), an experimental novel relying on modified stream-of-consciousness to navigate between characters' thoughts, anticipates the postmodern style of Alice

Munro's *Who Do You Think You Are?* (1978; published in United States as *The Beggar Maid: Stories of Flo and Rose*, 1979), in which parallel episodes, flashbacks, seemingly random images, and nonlinear events piece together to delineate the complex relationship between a mother and daughter. Carol Shields's *The Stone Diaries* (1993) offers readers a graceful and straightforward depiction of a middle-class female protagonist, Daisy Stone Goodwill, whose "Everywoman" qualities resonate one of Laurence's realist portraits or even narratives from one century earlier.

One feminist writer deserves special consideration. Margaret Atwood—a novelist, poet, and literary critic—has had such a profound effect on world literature since the late 1960's that it is impossible to discuss Canadian long fiction without her. More than her contemporaries, Atwood's novels exploit ideas of duality and multiplicity, bringing together cultural binaries in ways that not only articulate the complexity of individual oppositions but also illustrate their relation to each other. From early novels such as *Surfacing* (1972)—where a character's exploration of sexual identity leads her to question the meaning of her life generally—to later ones such as *The Robber Bride* (1993)—which inverts the sexual mechanics of a Grimm's fairy tale to illustrate the influence of gender on larger cultural issues—Atwood's novels demonstrate an uncanny ability to find the links among various kinds of identity and to balance those within single narratives. *The Handmaid's Tale* (1985)—an apocalyptic future narrative about an American theological revolution in which women become slaves—epitomizes this ability, demonstrating the links among gender and other identities but never allowing any one of these identities to predominate. For Atwood, identity is a matter of worldly forces in constant flux, with relationships changing daily. As such, she might be viewed as the consummate Canadian writer, a woman fundamentally concerned with how people define themselves but recognizing such definitions as a matter of ongoing process never to be articulated finitely.

MULTIPLICITY AND THE ISSUE OF A CANADIAN SELF

At its most basic level, Atwood's writing reminds audiences of the differences that have existed and continue to exist within Canada. With its diverse geography and cultural history, Canada frequently produces writers who seem more influenced by localized forces than national ones. Certainly this is true in the case of Quebec, where early novels such as *Les Anciens Canadiens* (1863; *The Canadians of Old*, 1864) by Philippe-Joseph Aubert de Gaspe and *Jean Rivard* (1874; English translation, 1977) by Antoine Gerin-Lajoie emphasize Québécois individuality and differences from anglophone Canada. English-language writers also have their regional traditions; one has only to consider Alistair MacLeod's Nova Scotia (*The Lost Salt Gift of Blood*, 1988; revised 1991), Matt Cohen's southern Ontario (*The Disinherited*, 1974), or Jack Hodgins's British Columbia (*The Invention of the World*, 1977) to recognize the indelible mark that such small places have left on the Canadian literary world.

Yet such differences, always a part of Canada, have never quite overwhelmed the similarities. If one trend within the Canadian novel has been to emphasize separation, it has not been without some recognition of a larger geographical, social, and historical shared experience. Thus, a francophone farm novel such as Ringuet's *Trente Arpents* (1938; *Thirty Acres*, 1940) or a work of psychological naturalism such as Gabrielle Roy's *Bonheur d'occasion* (1945; *The Tin Flute*, 1947) can address many of the same issues as works by Grove or Ostenso. Atwood's *Bodily Harm* (1981), a novel about a white Canadian woman witnessing a Caribbean revolt, can anticipate by several years the postcolonial fictions of Neil Bissoondath. Jack Hodgins and Thomas King can use Irish and American Indian myth respectively to arrive at similarly satiric versions of the rise and fall of "civilization" in western Canada.

These incidental similarities, however, are less important than the process Canadian novelists have developed to discuss Canadian identity—a process ironically begun with the admission that pinpointing such an identity is impossible. Arnold E. Davidson has written that "the Canadian novel is especially Ca-

nadian in the very way in which it persistently unwrites and rewrites that problematic adjective, *Canadian*." In other words, it is their common belief in the absence of a single national identity that draws Canadian novelists from all eras and backgrounds together. Such a belief could be produced only by a country precariously united at times by the sheer fact of its common nationality. Then again, such a national literature thrives on ironies, oppositions, borders, and continual negotiations of selfhood. In refusing to stake out its exact parameters, the Canadian novel affirms its identity. Its pluralistic sensibility, its skill at balancing many cultural voices, and its belief in identity formation as an ongoing process continue to make it one of the most progressive and intriguing traditions in the literary world.

J. David Stevens

BIBLIOGRAPHY

Atwood, Margaret. *Survival: A Thematic Guide to Canadian Literature*. Toronto: Anansi, 1972. A thematic analysis of the chief issues in Canadian literature. Atwood writes in prose that is clear, witty, and accessible to a broad audience. A classic work of Canadian criticism.

Benson, Eugene, and William Toye, eds. *The Oxford Companion to Canadian Literature*. Toronto: Oxford University Press, 1998. Like Oxford's other "Companion" volumes, this work offers insightful introductions to a broad range of Canadian writers and literary issues. Entries range from one-quarter of a page to over ten pages in length and are as uniformly well-written as they are diverse in subject matter. A thorough set of cross-references accompanies most entries.

Davidson, Arnold E., ed. *Studies on Canadian Literature: Introductory and Critical Essays*. New York: Modern Language Association of America, 1991. A collection of essays on both anglophone and francophone writers that explores Canadian literature from numerous critical perspectives. A fine overview of Canadian cultural issues, and a must-read for beginning scholars of Canadian work.

Harrison, Dick. *Unnamed Country: The Struggle for*

a Canadian Prairie Fiction. Edmonton: University of Alberta Press, 1971. The preeminent work on the historical circumstances and cultural imperatives that precipitated the strong, if complex, tradition of Canadian Western writing.

Hutcheon, Linda. *The Canadian Postmodern: A Study of Contemporary English-Canadian Fiction*. Toronto: Oxford University Press, 1988. An analysis of late twentieth century Canadian literature from one of North America's foremost postmodern critics. Hutcheon makes the convincing case that Canadian literature—in its historic negotiation of borders and balancing of different cultural voices—has been "postmodern" for much of its history.

Moses, Daniel D., and Terry Goldie, eds. *An Anthology of Canadian Native Literature in English*. 2d ed. Toronto: Oxford University Press, 1998. A comprehensive selection of Native Canadian writing. Entries are representative, if not always ex-

tensive, and offer readers a solid sense of both the differences and the similarities between the concerns of American Indians and Canadian Indians.

New, W. H. *A History of Canadian Literature*. London: Macmillan, 1989. A critical reading of Canadian literature from its Inuit-Indian origins through 1989. While not the most recent history, New's book is the most critically astute and succinct. A sixty-page chronological table provides a useful overview to new and experienced scholars alike.

Vautier, Marie. *New World Myth: Postmodernism and Postcolonialism in Canadian Fiction*. Montreal: McGill-Queens University Press, 1998. Explores the way in which late twentieth century Canadian novels undermine the kind of New World myths that were central to settling the continent. This book also extends the discussion (prominent in Canadian letters) of the multiple meanings of "postcolonial" in Canadian cultural history.

THE CARIBBEAN NOVEL

Critic Roberto González Echevarría asserted that it was "in the Caribbean that Latin American literature 'began,' for it is in fifteenth century explorer Christopher Columbus's diary that we first encounter what will become the most persistent theme of Latin American literature: how to write in a European language about realities never seen in Europe before." Caribbean writers find before them the tools of four European languages, imported by the imperial aspirations of the Dutch, English, French, and Spanish nations. Writers from Dutch Caribbean regions, such as Frank Martinus Arion and Astrid H. Roemer, have been translated into other languages, making their work available to non-Dutch-speaking audiences, but the Dutch Caribbean tradition stands largely unexplored.

Caribbean literature unites literary works that have been studied not only in terms of national traditions (Haitian, Cuban, and so on) but also under other, more broad-ranging classifications, such as West Indian (meaning from the English-speaking Caribbean), francophone (French outside of France), and Latin American literatures, as well as African diaspora and postcolonial literature. Caribbean literature designates literature not only from the island nations but also from Central and South American continental territories such as Belize, Guyana, Suriname, and French Guiana, which share a common experience of slavery and sugar-plantation economies with the island territories. Because the indigenous populations of Arawaks, Tainos, and Caribs of the Caribbean basin were almost wholly exterminated through violence and disease, Caribbean peoples primarily descend from settlers exogenous to the region, most notably the large number of African slaves brought to toil on the plantations and the indentured Asian laborers brought to replace African labor after emancipation. Consequently, Caribbean writers must negotiate a relationship with both a colonial metropolitan culture and the memory of the other African and Asian cultures from elsewhere.

EARLY FLOURISHINGS

If Caribbean literature began with Columbus's diary, the Caribbean novel, by contrast, was largely a product of the twentieth century. Nineteenth century Cuban antislavery novels, such as Anselmo Suárez y Romero's *Francisco* (1880), Cirilo Villaverde's *Cecilia Valdés* (first part 1839, completed 1882; *Cecilia Valdés: A Novel of Cuban Customs*, 1962), and Gertrudis Gómez de Avellaneda's *Sab* (1841; English translation, 1993), offered early intimations that nationalist, anticolonial thought in the Caribbean was inextricably bound to the legacies of slavery. For the most part, however, novelistic interrogations of Caribbean identities waited until the first decade of the twentieth century, when Haitian writers began their realist experiments and thus provided the seeds for the later, great genre of Haitian literature, the peasant novel.

In this early period, the novels of a writer claimed by the Harlem Renaissance proved paradigmatic. The Jamaican Claude McKay (1889-1948) was the first black anglophone Caribbean novelist. His first novel, *Home to Harlem* (1928), depicts Jake, an African American returned from World War I to the streets and nightlife of Harlem, and Ray, an exiled Haitian intellectual and aspiring writer, who instructs Jake in pan-Africanism and awareness of a global proletariat. Notably, Ray finds himself in the United States working alongside Jake as a Pullman Car porter because he has fled the U.S. occupation of his island. McKay's second novel, *Banjo* (1929), revisits Ray, this time as he pronounces on culture, world politics, and racial roots with an international assembly of drifters living on the Marseilles waterfront. Through Ray's debates with Banjo, McKay comments on colonialism and its racial manifestations while honing his portrait of the alienated intellectual. His final novel, *Banana Bottom* (1933), signals precisely the kind of nativist sentiment that his Haitian contemporary Jean Price-Mars advocated in his seminal study of Haitian folk culture, *Ainsi parla l'oncle* (1928; *So Spoke the Uncle*, 1983). McKay's novel depicts the return of Bita Plant to the Jamaican rural community of Banana Bottom after her education in England (arranged by her white missionary guardians) and charts her rejection of both the stilted middle-class pruderies that her guardians expect from her and the mate they would choose for her. In returning to the "folk," Bita negotiates a more natural, integrated identity that takes what it can from the European intellectual tradition but is still most comfortable happily ensconced in the lush setting and rituals of rural black culture.

McKay's figure of the alienated, Western-educated intellectual returns countless times in Caribbean novels of the twentieth century, as does his appreciation of the folk culture. The effects of a colonial education—African Guadeloupians taught about "their ancestors the Gauls," Jamaican children taught to recite poems about daffodils and snow they have never seen—are a common touchstone in the Caribbean novel's depiction of childhood, particularly the popular *Bildungsroman* genre, as epitomized by Michael Anthony's *The Year in San Fernando* (1965), Merle Hodge's *Crick, Crack, Monkey* (1970), Zee Edgell's *Beka Lamb* (1982), Jamaica Kincaid's *Annie John* (1985), Michelle Cliff's *Abeng* (1984), and Myriam Warner Vieyra's *As the Sorcerer Said* (1982). The perils of colonial education are treated with particular emphasis in Austin Clarke's pointedly titled *Growing Up Stupid Under the Union Jack: A Memoir* (1980). McKay's pan-Africanism predated the negritude movement spearheaded by the Martiniquan poet Aimé Césaire, and his privileging of rural folk culture resonated with the emphases of the peasant novel in Haiti, most notably Jacques Roumain's *Gouverneurs de la rosée* (1944; *Masters of the Dew*, 1946).

By contrast, the Trinidadians Alfred Mendes and C. L. R. James added an early urban spin to the Caribbean novel. James is primarily known for his studies of Caribbean history and culture—for instance, his study of the Haitian Revolution, *The Black Jacobins: Toussaint Louverture and the San Domingo Revolution* (1938), and his meditation on cricket, *Beyond a Boundary* (1963)—but he also authored one novel, *Minty Alley* (1936). *Minty Alley* joined Mendes's *Pitch Lake* (1934) and *Black Fauns* (1935) in inaugurating a tradition of social realism and protest that focused on the oppression of "yard," or slum, life. Later, Roger Mais's *The Hills Were Joyful Together* (1953) and Orlando Patterson's *The Children of Sisyphus* (1964) revisited this theme.

ALEJO CARPENTIER

The Cuban writer Alejo Carpentier (1904-1980) shares the baroque style of the Cuban novel with José Lezama Lima, Severo Sarduy, Reinaldo Arenas, and Guillermo Cabrera Infante. Carpentier began his novelistic career under the influence of the *Afro-Cubanismo* of the 1920's and 1930's. His first novel *¡Ecué-Yamba-O! Historia Afro-Cubana* (1933; Lord praised be thou) reflected the anthropological bent of the period by drawing on Carpentier's observations of the syncretic African Cuban *santería* ritual. Influenced by the avant-garde, particularly the Surrealists, Carpentier's idea of the "marvelous real" of Caribbean life was transformed into the literary style of Magical Realism synonymous with the Colombian writer Gabriel García Márquez. A 1943 trip to Haiti, during which Carpentier came face-to-face with the magical presence of *vodun* (or Voodoo) in everyday life, led him to theorize that this commonplace "marvelous" quality was far superior to the contrived attempts by the European Surrealists to achieve similar effects. In his prologue to *El reino de este mundo* (1949; *The Kingdom of This World*, 1957), Carpentier introduced his idea of *lo real maravilloso* produced by the hybrid nature of New World culture. Set in Haiti, the novel traces an arc from a slave insurrection to the establishment of a postcolonial state, from 1751 to 1831, depicting real historical figures and drawing on the mythical traditions associated with the revolt. Haitian Voodoo figures prominently as a factor in the quest for independence, and religion and music appear as two mediums for New World cultural mixture. The Haitian novelist Jacques Stephen Alexis would later elaborate his own theories on Haiti's marvelous realism, reflected in his novels *Compère Général Soleil* (1955; *General Sun, My Brother* (1999) and *Les arbres musiciens* (1957). The late eighteenth century setting of *The Kingdom of This World* proved fertile ground for Carpentier's exploration of emerging New World identities; he returned to it in his novels *El siglo de las luces* (1962; *Explosion in a Cathedral*, 1963) and *Concierto barroco* (1974; *Concert Baroque*, 1976).

Carpentier is notable for his recognition of the centrality of African culture to New World cultural forms, as well as for an emphasis not on pure origins but on examples of cultural mixture, such as syncretic religious practice and Caribbean music forms. He also stands at the forefront of thought that began to envision a pan-Caribbean or inter-Antillian commonality, which began to take stronger hold at the end of the twentieth century. Finally, his preoccupation with elaborating a Caribbean history not fully accounted for by European intellectual traditions, an emphasis that offers a window on contemporary Caribbean life, is a common strategy of the Caribbean novel. For example, V. S. Reid's *New Day* (1949) links the granting of the 1944 Jamaican constitution to the 1865 Morant Bay Rebellion; Jean Rhys's *Wide Sargasso Sea* (1966) offers a perspective on 1830's post-emancipation life in the British territories of Jamaica and Dominica; Pedro Mir's *Cuando amaban las tierras communeras* (1978) spans the years 1916 to 1965 and chronicles the dismantling of communal land ownership in the aftermath of the U.S. occupation of the Dominican Republic; and Caryl Phillips's *Cambridge* (1991) and *Crossing the River* (1993) return to Caribbean life of the eighteenth and nineteenth centuries. Michelle Cliff's *Abeng* and Maryse Condé's *La vie scélérate* (1987; *The Tree of Life*, 1992) also demonstrate a historiographic impulse by linking a young protagonist's investigations of her familial history to obscured features of Caribbean history.

WILSON HARRIS

In its emphasis on history and mythology, the work of Guyanese writer Wilson Harris (born 1921) has much in common with that of Carpentier. Harris's novels, however, leave all trappings of realism behind. His nonlinear, hallucinatory style is by far the most challenging of contemporary Caribbean novelists, although his experimental approach is shared by the fragmented and polyphonic novels *Jane and Louisa Will Soon Come Home* (1980), *Myal* (1988), and *Louisiana* (1994), by the Jamaican Edna Brodber. While Carpentier, too, plays with time, particularly in his best-known novel *Los pasos perdidos* (1953; *The Lost Steps*, 1956), in Wilson's hands, it becomes even more fluid, looping in and out of itself in ways

that defy any straightforward chronology. In an excellent metaphor for what it means to live with the history of the Caribbean, Harris's explorers in *Palace of the Peacock* (1960) encounter their dead selves and then die again. *Palace of the Peacock* is the first of the four novels known as *The Guyana Quartet* (1985), Harris's best-known work; the other three are *The Far Journey of Oudin* (1961), *The Whole Armour* (1962), and *The Secret Ladder* (1963). Harris's novels are distinctive in their emphasis on the American Indian presence in the New World and for their evocation and symbolic use of the rivers and jungles of the Guyanese territory. His *The Eye of the Scarecrow* (1965), *The Waiting Room* (1967), *Tumatumari* (1968), and *Ascent to Omai* (1970) deploy a symbolic Guyanese landscape, and they "remember" perspectives of endangered communities, stretching back to before Columbus. Harris identifies a flute made by Carib Indians from the bone of an enemy as a symbol for what occurs in his work:

> Flesh was plucked and consumed and in the process secrets were digested. Spectres arose from or reposed in, the flute . . . the flute became the home or curiously *mutual* fortress of spirit between enemy and other, an organ of self-knowledge suffused with enemy bias so close to native greed for victory.

In Harris's fiction, natives and European, African, East Indian, and Chinese settlers do commune, but with an unblushing acknowledgment of the violence of their mutual history. In this way, Harris's work both consumes what he terms "dilemmas of history" and becomes an "organ of self-knowledge," the bone flute that harmonizes the multihued peoples of Guyana with their historical struggles and conflicts.

GEORGE LAMMING AND V. S. NAIPAUL

Unlike Harris, Barbadian George Lamming (born 1927) and Trinidadian V. S. Naipaul (born 1932) embrace realism. These authors stood at the forefront of the anglophone literary boom in the 1950's. This decade was marked by an exodus of British West Indians to England to seek work and the burgeoning of independence movements that would come to fruition in the 1960's and 1970's, when British Caribbean territories began to gain their independence. Whereas Carpentier praises the "marvelous," in the sense of magical realities of Caribbean hybridity, Lamming and Naipaul focus rather unflinchingly on grim Caribbean realities. Both take a critical view of colonial status and its legacies in the West Indies and explore themes of alienation and exile in their depiction of West Indian life. Beyond this, however, their intentions and conclusions wholly differ.

In his collection of essays *The Pleasures of Exile* (1960), Lamming represents the voyage to London as initiating a mutual recognition between people of the various West Indian islands, related to but distinct from the homogenizing imperial gaze of the "mother country." At home, these voyagers are Trinidadian, Jamaican, and Barbadian, but in England (on the way there, even), they become West Indian. Migration enables pan-Caribbean identification and community, a possibility also proposed in Samuel Selvon's trilogy *The Lonely Londoners* (1956), *Moses Ascending* (1975), and *Moses Migrating* (1983). In refusing to read "exile" as tantamount to a flight from identity, but rather as constitutive of it, in refusing to see migration as deracination, Lamming predates later studies of African diaspora culture, such as Paul Gilroy's *The Black Atlantic* (1993) and Carol Boyce Davies's *Black Women, Writing, and Identity: Migrations of the Subject* (1994), which see international flows as producing, rather than diluting, culture. As Gilroy suggests, "routes" are as important as "roots."

For Lamming, the voyage to England is also a voyage of enlightenment, a journey into the heart of colonialism that permits one to emerge from its darkness. London is one symbolic stop along the journey to independence. Lamming's *The Emigrants* (1954) brings black workers to London, and *Of Age an Innocence* (1958) returns them to the Caribbean and its growing independence movements. Approaching the themes of voyage and colonialism from another angle, his *Natives of My Person* (1972) charts the travels of a white crew of would-be settlers as they sail from the Guinea coast to the island of San Cristobal during the sixteenth century. The crew's shipboard interactions, particularly the male-female relationships, reveal ingrained patterns of conquest and dom-

ination and serve as an allegory for the society they will find in the New World. Lamming's voyagers were succeeded by other novelistic travelers: Maryse Condé's Veronica in *Hérémakhonon: On doit attendre le bonheur* (1976; *Hérémakhonon*, 1982) and Michelle Cliff's Clare Savage in *No Telephone to Heaven* (1987) also undergo migrations that help them reflect on their personal identities and Caribbean heritage.

Lamming's later novel *Water with Berries* (1972) takes its title from a speech in William Shakespeare's *The Tempest* (1611) and presents guilt-ridden West Indian artists, the sons of Caliban, in London. This journey to London also involves an appropriation of the national bard. Both *Water with Berries* and *The Pleasures of Exile* develop the idea of Caliban as the colonial writer who has been taught the master Prospero's language and has learned to curse in it, a recurrent figure in the literature of the Caribbean, most notably in Aimé Césaire's play *Une Tempête, d'après "La Tempête" de Shakespeare: Adaptation pour un théâtre nègre* (1969; *The Tempest*, 1974). This figure also epitomizes Caribbean writers' ongoing dialogue with Western literary tradition, as demonstrated by Jean Rhys's appropriation of Charlotte Brontë's *Jane Eyre* (1847) in her *Wide Sargasso Sea* and Derek Walcott's Odyssean transformations in his Caribbean epic *Omeros* (1990).

Booker Prize-winner V. S. Naipaul became particularly invested in this Western tradition. Naipaul is largely regarded as the leading novelist in the anglophone tradition and among the region's most widely acclaimed writers. Ironically, however, he repeatedly demonstrated disgust with his Caribbean homeland, as evidenced in his nonfiction work *The Middle Passage: Impressions of Five Societies—British, French, and Dutch—in the West Indies and South America* (1962). Drawing on an education in nineteenth century realism, Naipaul gives his readers modern, alienated, West Indian protagonists who are trapped in claustrophobic, inauthentic, and ineffectual lives. In his deft hands, apparently trivial elements—a yellowed, filthy pillowcase; cooking odors; the ugly sound of an in-law's chewing—convey the hopelessness and degradation of his characters. Unlike Lamming, who critiques colonial Caribbean social organizations as a spur toward envisioning true political and ideological independence, Naipaul regards the faults of incompetent and corrupt government, poverty, poor educational opportunities, and general cultural provincialism as impediments to the full expression of individual Caribbean selves. Particularly adept at conveying the cultural conflicts within the East Indian communities of Trinidad, as well as their place within the mosaic of Trinidadian society, Naipaul's art is one of supreme vividness, humor, and despair.

Naipaul's first three novels are both comic tributes to and ironic commentaries on the place of his childhood. *Miguel Street* (1959) depicts the residents of the eponymous Port of Spain Street, a slum to outsiders, through the wide eyes of a young artist who departs for England at the book's conclusion, never to return. The other two novels—*The Mystic Masseur* (1957) and *The Suffrage of Elvira* (1958)—establish Naipaul's distinctive critique of island politics. The first details the career of a lowly masseur who exploits his status as a mystic in order to rise in island politics, sacrificing his personal integrity along the way; the second depicts islanders who are ill prepared for universal suffrage and whose petty feuds and superstitions are exploited by self-interested politicians. Naipaul's two best-known Caribbean novels are *A House for Mr. Biswas* (1961) and *The Mimic Men* (1967). The former book richly but pessimistically depicts the struggles for autonomy of its sensitive, ineffectual title character. *The Mimic Men* represents Naipaul's most pointed exposure of the fraudulence of Caribbean political rhetoric, the pomposity and mimicry of the Caribbean's would-be leaders. Naipaul's ousted Caribbean politician, the self-loathing cynic Ralph Singh, flees his native Isabella and embraces the possibilities of exile, later recalling his participation in island politics as a "period in parenthesis." Ultimately, for Naipaul, exile is a strategy of survival, a preservation from the derivative mediocrity of Caribbean culture, a cultural "mimicry" that is the enduring legacy of colonialism.

ÉDOUARD GLISSANT

One response to this sense of Caribbean derivativeness has been a search for roots—not European ones, as in Naipaul's case, but African ones. The appreciation of "blackness" and the connection to Africa was epitomized by the highly influential negritude movement associated with the poet Aimé Césaire and his seminal *Cahier d'un retour au pays natal* (1939, 1947, 1956; *Memorandum on My Martinique*, 1947; better known as *Return to My Native Land*, 1968), but the movement's positing of a historical black identity that serves as a prelapsarian preserve against the "fall" of the Middle Passage and enslavement came under fire for its essentialism and romanticized view of Africa. The Martiniquan poet, essayist, and novelist Édouard Glissant (born 1928) critiqued this craving for pure, stable origins. Glissant's theoretical work *Discours antillais* (1981; *Caribbean Discourse*, 1989) poses models of *métissage* (mixture and miscegenation) and *créolité* (creoleness) that destabilize notions of a fixed or permanent identity. These concepts are modeled on Creole, the mixed language that was born in the Americas. For Glissant, Creole is not a degraded cultural form, but the epitome of Caribbean cultural formations. From this perspective, other sites of hybridity, such as Caribbean music and the carnival ritual, prove valuable forms of Caribbean expression.

Glissant's theories inspired novelists who choose to write in Creole, among them Raphaël Confiant and Patrick Chamoiseau. Chamoiseau's writing is increasingly available in English translation, particularly his Prix Goncourt-winning novel *Texaco* (1992; English translation, 1997). Puerto Rican writers Ana Lydia Vega and Luis Rafael Sánchez similarly embraced investigations of inter-Antillian traffic and commonalities, such as those posed in Glissant's *Poétique de la relation* (1990; *Poetics of Relation* (1997). Sánchez's *La guaracha del Macho Camacho* (1976; *Macho Camacho's Beat*, 1980) and Guillermo Cabrera Infante's *Tres tristes tigres* (1967, 1990; *Three Trapped Tigers*, 1971) employ a regional Spanish strongly evocative of the French Creoles of Haiti, Martinique, and Guadeloupe. These writers also exhibit a preoccupation with popular culture and an ironic postmodern style that link them to other postmodern Caribbean novelists, such as Marie Chauvet, Dany Laferrière, and Willie Scott.

Glissant's own novel, *La Lézarde* (1958; *The Ripening*, 1985), recounts a series of voyages down the Lézarde river, using the Martinique landscape to meditate on the island's history. The titles of his later novels, such as *Tout-Monde* (1993), particularly reflect his theoretical interests.

MARYSE CONDÉ

Like Glissant, the Gaudeloupian writer Maryse Condé (born 1937) also strained against the return to African origins embraced by negritude thinkers, and her work displays a healthy postmodern irreverence. She leaves no sacred cows standing. Her first novel, *Hérémakhonon* (the title means "welcome house" in Mandingo), records the internal monologue of the cynical, Sorbonne-educated Veronica, who travels to Africa to teach at a university. Confronted with a postcolonial Africa torn by internecine violence, an Africa that has moved on since her ancestors' removal from it to Guadeloupe, Veronica concludes her visit by reflecting, "My ancestors led me on. What more can I say? I looked for myself in the wrong place." The role of intellectuals and women's sexuality likewise emerge as legitimate means for exploring larger social and political issues. Her own critical study of French Caribbean women novelists, *La parole des femmes* (1979), reflects her insistence on the importance of women's perspectives in understanding Caribbean art and societies.

Condé stands among the most prolific and well-established women writers of the Caribbean, with many of her novels available in English translation. She played a major role in debating the theoretical merits of creolization as a construct for understanding Caribbean culture. After *Hérémakhonon*, her novels dealt with contemporary life in modern Africa—*Une Saison à Rihata* (1981; *A Season in Rihata*, 1988)—as well as the epic sweep of its history, in *Ségou: Les murailles de terre* (1984; *Segu*, 1987) and *Ségou II: La Terre en miettes* (1985; *The Children of Segu*, 1989). Her novella *Pays mêlé* (1985), translated as *Land of Many Colors* (1999), marked a return to Guadeloupe. Her subsequent novels *Moi, Tituba, sorcière noire de Salem* (1985; *I, Tituba, Black Witch of Salem*, 1992); *La Vie scélérate* (1987, *Tree of Life*, 1992);

Traversée de la mangrove (1989; *Crossing the Mangrove*, 1995); *Les Derniers Rois Mages* (1992; *The Last of the African Kings*, 1997); and *La migration des coeurs* (1995; *Windward Heights*, 1998) all deal with Caribbean and more broadly American settings.

Along with Merle Hodge, Marie Chauvet, Paule Marshall, and Simone Schwarz-Bart, Condé's novelistic career predates the explosion of writing by Caribbean women that began in the 1980's. The Antiguan Jamaica Kincaid is perhaps the best-known anglophone writer to emerge during this boom. Condé's later work nonetheless reflects the trends and attitudes in both the literature and scholarship of the Caribbean at the end of the twentieth century.

Throughout their century-long meditations on Caribbean identity, history, and culture, Caribbean novels have often explored connections to Europe, Africa, and Asia. Beginning in the 1980's, increasing attention was paid to both regional Caribbean and inter-American relationships, in particular with the United States. This focus was especially evident in the work of women novelists, presaged by Paule Marshall's *The Chosen Place, the Timeless People* (1969). In the 1990's, Michelle Cliff's *Free Enterprise* (1993), Edna Brodber's *Louisiana*, and Evangeline Blanco's *Caribe: A Novel of Puerto Rico* (1998) paralleled Condé's *I, Tituba, Black Witch of Salem*, *The Last of the African Kings*, and *The Tree of Life* in representing intersections between U.S. and Caribbean history and culture. These joined novels of Caribbean nationals' migrations to the United States, such as Jamaica Kincaid's *Lucy* (1990), Julia Alvarez's *How the García Girls Lost Their Accents* (1991), Judith Ortiz Cofer's *The Line of the Sun* (1989), and Edwige Danticat's *Breath, Eyes, Memory* (1994) in reorienting the transcontinental perspectives of Caribbean writing (Europe, Africa) to treat inter-American routes as well. A similar type of hemispheric intercalation appears in the Puerto Rican writer Rosario Ferré's choice to compose her novels of Puerto Rico, *The House on the Lagoon* (1995) and *Eccentric Neighborhoods* (1998), in English. Caribbean writing at the end of the twentieth century reflected not only new patterns of migration and the Caribbean diaspora but also the century-long presence of the United States in the Caribbean region.

CARIBBEAN TRANSIT

The idea of migration features prominently in the literature of the Caribbean region. Interestingly, other novelists not from the Caribbean region have also seen fit to "migrate" there for fictive purposes: Ernest Hemingway's much-acclaimed novella *The Old Man and the Sea* (1952) pits humanity against nature in the ocean off Cuban shores; war correspondent Martha Gellhorne's novelistic skills matured in *Liana* (1944), her tale of a powerless mulatto living on a Caribbean island; Graham Greene chose Cuba on the eve of revolution as the backdrop for his satirical reflection on Cold War paranoia in his *Our Man in Havana: An Entertainment* (1958); and Toni Morrison created a fictional Caribbean island as the primary setting for *Tar Baby* (1981) and its meditation on racial identity and race relations. As in the work of its more "native" authors, these novels mark the Caribbean as a vital hub in the traffic of global literature, a place of import and export, migration and exile, the origin, endpoint, and transit zone of many cultural passages.

Nancy E. Castro

BIBLIOGRAPHY

Arnold, A. James, ed. *Hispanic and Francophone Regions.* Vol. 1 in *A History of Literature in the Caribbean.* Philadelphia: John Benjamins, 1994. An excellent overview of all genres of Caribbean literature from the Spanish- and French-speaking Caribbean.

Balutanksy, Kathleen M., and Marie-Agnès Sourieau. *Caribbean Creolization: Reflections on the Cultural Dynamics of Language Literature, and Identity.* Gainsville: University Presses of Florida, 1998. Critics and writers, among them Maryse Condé and Wilson Harris, provide an introduction to theories of Caribbean creolization.

Cudjoe, Selwyn R, ed. *Caribbean Women Writers: Essays from the First International Conference.* Wellesley, Mass.: Callaloux Publications, 1990. Many anthologies on Caribbean women's writing were later produced, but with its depth of critical essays, author interviews, and pan-Caribbean bibliographic overviews, this collection continues to offer a valuable survey of the field.

Dance, Daryl C. *Fifty Caribbean Writers: A Bio-Bibliographical Critical Sourcebook.* Westport, Conn.: Greenwood Press, 1986. A quick and informative guide to the works and careers of writers from the anglophone Caribbean.

Dash, J. Michael. *The Other America: Caribbean Literature in a New World Context.* Charlottesville: University Press of Virginia, 1998. Arguing that broad critical categories, such as postcolonial and postmodern, elide the particularities of Caribbean literature, Dash provides a thematic and formal overview of Caribbean literature as a "New World" expression.

Ormerod, Beverley. *An Introduction to the French Caribbean Novel.* London: Heinemann, 1985. Novels by Jacques Roumain, Édouard Glissant, Jacques Stéphen Alexis, and Simone Schwarz-Bart, among others, are interpreted. Ormerod's is still regarded as the best available introduction to the French Caribbean novel.

Ramchand, Kenneth. *The West Indian Novel and Its Background.* 2d ed. London: Heinemann, 1983. This important early study of the anglophone Caribbean novel remains useful for its discussion of the factors, such as illiteracy, affecting the production of novels in the Caribbean.

Torres-Saillant, Silvio. *Caribbean Poetics: Towards an Aesthetic of West Indian Literature.* London: Cambridge University Press, 1997. Taking Kamau Brathwaite, René Depestre, and Pedro Mir as the primary subjects, Torres-Saillant's study provides a comprehensive overview of the literature of the Caribbean region in arguing for the existence and integrity of a regional literary tradition. He joins Dash in elaborating a pan-Caribbean approach.

Webb, Barbara J. *Myth and History in Caribbean Fiction: Alejo Carpentier, Wilson Harris, and Edouard Glissant.* Amherst: University of Massachusetts Press, 1992. Webb's insightful comparative study addresses how these authors challenge the opposition of myth to history and the alignment of history with literary realism.

THE EURO-AMERICAN IMMIGRANT EXPERIENCE IN LONG FICTION

Before the middle of the twentieth century, most immigrants to the United States were Europeans or involuntary immigrants from Africa who arrived in America as slaves. The first U.S. census, in 1790, reveals that most free Americans were of English or other Northern European ancestry. That first census reported that 60 percent of white Americans described themselves as English, 14 percent as Scottish or Scotch Irish, 9 percent as German, 4 percent as Catholic Irish, and 13 percent as other. Because of the English predominance, the earliest American fiction tended to follow English models. The Pennsylvanian Hugh Henry Brackenridge published *Modern Chivalry*, a satirical novel about American frontier life, in installments from 1792 to 1815. Although *Modern Chivalry* dealt with American subjects, it was heavily influenced by English satirical novelists such as Jonathan Swift and Henry Fielding. Even James Fenimore Cooper, often celebrated as the first great American writer of long fiction, showed the influence of the English author Sir Walter Scott.

Although early American novelists such as Nathaniel Hawthorne and Herman Melville distanced themselves from English models, American literature throughout the nineteenth century continued to develop out of the English tradition and to be written by people of English ancestry. For this reason, "immigrant literature" or "ethnic literature" in the United States has generally referred to writing that reflected the experiences of the non-English groups that arrived over the course of the nation's history.

The "old immigrants"

After 1820, European immigration to the United States began to increase greatly. Those who arrived between 1820 and the Civil War (1861-1865) are often referred to as the "old immigrants," in contrast to the "new immigrants," who began to arrive in the decades between the Civil War and World War I. Many of these immigrants came either from Germany, already the main country of origin for Americans who spoke a language other than English, or from Ireland. Germany, in particular, continued to supply the greatest number of immigrants to the United States, so that nearly one-fourth of Americans of European origin in 1990 reported that they were primarily of German ancestry. German was widely spoken in the United States until World War I, and many German American communities had their own newspapers and schools. Some of the earliest literary expressions of the Euro-American immigrant experience, therefore, were produced by Germans. One of the most important early immigrant writers from the German-speaking area of Europe was the Austrian Karl Postl, who changed his name to Charles Sealsfield after his arrival in New Orleans in 1823. Among his other writings, Sealsfield published a widely read historical novel, *Tokeah: Or, The White Rose* (1828), set in the Neches River area of Texas. Later in the nineteenth century, another major German American writer, August Siemering, also wrote about Texas Germans in his novel *Ein Verfeihtes Leben* (1876; the failure), which dealt with the experiences of Texas Germans during the Civil War.

By the twentieth century, authors of German descent were frequently regarded as native-born American writers rather than as immigrant writers. Nevertheless, some continued to deal with the ethnic German or immigrant German experience. Theodore Dreiser's *Jennie Gerhardt* (1911) is notable as a work of long fiction about the German experience by a major American author. Other twentieth century works concerned with the German immigrant experience include George Hummel's *Heritage* (1935), Conrad Richter's *The Free Man* (1943), and George Freitag's *Lost Land* (1947).

The United States saw one of its greatest waves of immigration during the late nineteenth and early twentieth centuries. While most of the older immigrants had come from northern and Western Europe, many of these new immigrants came from southern and Eastern European nations, such as Italy, Greece, Poland, and parts of the Russian Empire. Although some of the immigrants during this time became farmers, many settled in cities, so that much of the new immigrant literature was urban. The immigrants who arrived after the Civil War also frequently met with prejudice from Americans of older stock. The great wave of immigration around the beginning of the twentieth century gave rise to a literature that was often self-consciously ethnic and was concerned with the problems of fitting into a new society; it took immigration and the consequences of immigration as a central subject.

SCANDINAVIAN IMMIGRANTS

Although Swedes and Finns settled in North America as early as 1638, when colonists established New Sweden at the mouth of the Delaware River, people from the countries of Sweden, Norway, Denmark, and Finland did not begin to arrive in American in large numbers until after the Civil War. Driven by political troubles and crop failures in their homelands, these immigrants were exceptions to the general trends in immigration in two respects. First, they came from northern Europe, while most other immigrants at the time came from southern and Eastern Europe; second, many of the Scandinavians settled in rural areas of the Midwest and became farmers, while immigrants from elsewhere generally settled in cities.

Establishing their own ethnic communities in isolated regions, Scandinavians were often able to resist Americanization and cling to their languages and traditions. They often wrote in languages other than English. The best-known Scandinavian American novelist, Ole Edvart Rölvaag (1876-1931), wrote the two volumes of his masterpiece, *I de Dage* (1924) and *Riket Grundlægges* (1925), entirely in Norwegian. These two volumes became best-sellers in Norway. They were put together in a single book in the English translation called *Giants in the Earth: A Saga of the Prairie* (1927). The English version became a Book-of-the-Month Club selection and also became a best-seller in the United States, making the author a celebrity in both Norway and America. Rölvaag's novel, and its two sequels, dealt with the struggle to wrest a living from the American wilderness, and it exhibited nostalgia for the old country. These themes were embodied in the book's main characters, Per Hansa, possessed by the urge to conquer the wilder-

ness, and Beret Holm, a woman homesick for the land and traditions of Norway.

The best-known Scandinavian writer who worked in English was the Danish American Sophus Keith Winther, who arrived in the United States as a small child and grew up on a Nebraska farm. Winther, like Rölvaag, wrote about the difficult lives of immigrant farmers in novels that included *Take All to Nebraska* (1936), *Mortgage Your Heart* (1937), and *This Passion Never Dies* (1938). Ironically, while Rölvaag is still considered a classic American author and is widely read in courses on American literature, Winther's work has been almost forgotten.

THE "NEW IMMIGRANTS"

Most of the "new immigrants," those who arrived after the Civil War, settled in cities. The United States industrialized rapidly at the end of the nineteenth century, creating jobs in urban areas. New York City, in particular, became a center for Italians and Jews from Eastern Europe. Unfamiliar with American ways and frequently impoverished, immigrants settled in some of the poorest neighborhoods of American cities. The term "ghetto," an Italian word that referred to Jewish areas in Italian cities, came to mean an urban concentration of minority group members of any ethnicity. The earliest novels about immigrants, then, concerned life in the ghetto.

Abraham Cahan spent his childhood in a Lithuanian Jewish village and arrived in the United States without a cent in 1882. Cahan worked in New York sweatshops, became active in labor unions, educated himself, and became known as a cultural leader in the ghetto of the Lower East Side. He published his first novel, *Yekl: A Tale of the New York Ghetto*, in 1896. Published just three years after Stephen Crane's *Maggie: A Girl of the Streets*, Cahan's novel is frequently compared to Crane's, because both writers were dedicated to realism in the portrayal of the hard facts of urban life. Among other novels in the "tenement fiction" genre—writing concerned with the social problems of the urban immigrant ghetto—were James Sullivan's *Tenement Tales of New York* (1895), about the Irish of New York's West Side; Julian Ralph's *People We Pass* (1896), about German and

Irish youth in a New York tenement; and Isaac Kahn Friedman's *The Lucky Number* (1896), about an immigrant community in Chicago.

One of the recurrent themes of immigrant fiction in the years before World War I was the struggle of immigrant laborers for social justice. David M. Fine, author of *The City, the Immigrant, and American Fiction, 1880-1920* (1977), argued that the proletarian novel of the 1930's grew out of the immigrant labor novel. One of the greatest immigrant labor novels, *The Jungle* (1906), about immigrant workers in the meat-packing industry, was written by the nonimmigrant Upton Sinclair (1878-1968). Isaac Kahn Friedman produced another notable novel about immigrant labor in *By Bread Alone* (1901), a dramatic story of strikes in a steel mill.

The predominant theme among urban immigrant writers of the early twentieth century was the struggle to fit into American society. The Jewish Russian immigrant Elias Tobenkin treated this subject in *Witte Arrives* (1916), which tells the story of Emile Witte. Tobenkin's hero had left Russia for America as a boy and managed to enter a university and become a journalist. Although Witte is successfully Americanized, his adaptation to the new country involves conflict with his father, who clings to the traditions of the old country. Tobenkin's second novel, *The House of Conrad* (1918), deals with the same topics of assimilation into American society and intergenerational conflict. These topics became common in immigrant novels, many of which were heavily autobiographical.

The best-known and most highly praised novel of immigrant assimilation and upward mobility in the early twentieth century was Abraham Cahan's *The Rise of David Levinsky* (1917). Many other early immigrant novels, such as those of Tobenkin, wholeheartedly embraced the idea of assimilation into American society. Cahan, however, presented the immigrant success story as one of loss as well as gain. David Levinsky, Cahan's protagonist, arrives in America in 1885, a penniless young Jewish refugee from persecution in czarist Russia. He becomes a peddler, selling goods on the street, and also becomes familiar with crime, political corruption, and prostitution. He dreams of attending New York's City Col-

lege, but poverty forces him to become a manufacturer. Through hard work, ruthlessness, and the willingness to take advantage of his own workers, Levinsky achieves material success. He manages to overcome his accent and his Russian Jewish ways. In the end, though, the millionaire Levinsky feels that he has lost his own identity, and all his achievements seem empty to him.

By the 1930's, many of those writing about the European immigrant experience had either arrived in the United States as young children during the great wave of immigration before World War I or were born in the United States to immigrant parents. Growing up in an ethnic ghetto and youthful conflicts with the foreign ways of parents became recurrent topics in the writings of these authors. Mike Gold's *Jews Without Money* (1930) looked back at a boyhood in the ghetto. Henry Roth's *Call It Sleep* (1934) may have been the best young immigrant novel of the 1930's. Roth (1906-1995) was born in an area of the Austro-Hungarian Empire that later became part of Ukraine and arrived in New York City with his parents as a small child. He was educated in New York public schools and graduated from New York's City College in 1928. Like so many other immigrant works of fiction, *Call It Sleep* was fictionalized autobiography. It told the story of a young Jewish immigrant boy growing up in the Lower East Side of New York in the years prior to World War I. The novel was highly praised by critics, who compared Roth to Irish writer James Joyce. However, sales of new books were slow during the Depression years, and Roth's first novel quickly went out of print. Roth was rediscovered by literary critics in the early 1960's, and *Call It Sleep* acquired a large, if belated, readership.

Roth did not publish another work of long fiction for many years, until the multivolume autobiographical work *Mercy of a Rude Stream*, which included *A Star Shines over Mt. Morris Park* (1994), *A Diving Rock on the Hudson* (1995), *From Bondage* (1996), and *Requiem for Harlem* (1998). Even though these books were published long after other works by authors of Roth's generation, they tell the story of Roth's younger years and provide a literary portrait of early twentieth century immigrant life.

Pietro di Donato, born in 1911 to an Italian immigrant family in New Jersey, presented the Italian immigrant experience. His autobiographical novel *Christ in Concrete* (1938) told the story of Italian immigrant workers in the United States. The book's protagonist, Paulino, is the son of an Italian bricklayer. After his father dies when a building collapses, the twelve-year-old Pietro must take up the responsibility of supporting his mother and seven younger brothers and sisters. *Christ in Concrete* achieved wide popular recognition, and it was a Book-of-the-Month Club selection in 1939. Di Donato's second novel, *Three Circles of Light* (1960) was the story of Paulino's family before the father's death. This second novel did not achieve the critical or popular success of the first, and it was criticized as a loose assembly of impressionistic stories, rather than a coherent narrative.

LATER EUROPEAN IMMIGRANTS

The United States Congress passed legislation limiting immigration to the United States in 1924. As a result, immigration dropped drastically in the following years. In 1965, Congress changed the law to allow more people to enter the country, but the largest numbers of immigrants after 1965 came from Latin America and Asia, rather than from Europe. This meant that the immigrant experience in America largely ceased to be a European one. With the exception of older writers such as Henry Roth, most American authors of European Jewish, Italian, Scandinavian, or German ancestry in the 1960's and after had grown up in English-speaking families who had planted roots in the New World.

Some native-born American writers did look back at the immigration experiences of their families. For example, in *Unto the Sons* (1992), the Italian American Gay Talese looked at his own family's immigrant background. Among Jewish Americans, the mass murder of European Jews by the Nazis led to an intensified awareness of European Jewish heritage. American writers such as Philip Roth (born 1933), Bernard Malamud (1914-1986), and Saul Bellow (born 1915) presented portraits of Jewish immigrants in the United States. Isaac Bashevis Singer (1904-

1991) was one of the few Jewish American writers working in the second half of the twentieth century who was himself an immigrant. Born in Poland, Singer fled Europe for the United States in 1935, when he was thirty-one years old. He was a prolific author, and he composed many of his works in Yiddish, despite his fluency in English. Most of Singer's novels are set in Jewish villages before World War II, but he did sometimes write about immigrant life in the United States. In *Meshugah* (1994; crazy), Singer described the encounters of Polish immigrant Aaron Greidinger with Holocaust survivors in New York during the 1950's.

Carl L. Bankston III

BIBLIOGRAPHY

Bilik, Dorothy S. *Immigrant Survivors: Post-Holocaust Consciousness in Recent Jewish-American Fiction*. Middletown, Conn.: Wesleyan University Press, 1981. Bilik examines "the new immigrant novel": Jewish immigrant novels after the 1950's. She argues that the Jewish immigrant, largely missing from American fiction after the 1930's, began to reappear around 1957. While older works about immigrants had been concerned largely with the efforts of Jews to fit into American society, the new writing was haunted by memories of the mass murder of Jews in Europe during World War II.

DiPietro, Robert J., and Edward Ifkovic, eds. *Ethnic Perspectives in American Literature: Selected Essays on the European Contribution*. New York: The Modern Languages Association of America, 1983. A collection of twelve essays, each devoted to the literature of a European immigrant group in America. The essays describe writings both in English and in other languages.

Fine, David M. *The City, the Immigrant, and American Fiction: 1880-1920*. Metuchen, N.J.: Scarecrow Press, 1977. This book is one of the best studies of American immigrant fiction in the late nineteenth and early twentieth centuries. It places this writing in the context of American immigration history. It offers a particularly useful chapter on the writing of Abraham Cahan.

Hada, Janet. *Isaac Bashevis Singer: A Life*. New York:

Oxford University Press, 1997. This may be the best available biography of the great Jewish American writer.

Haugen, Einar. *Ole Edvart Rölvaag*. Boston: Twayne, 1983. A study of the life and art of the Norwegian American author. It contains a useful chronology of Rölvaag's life.

Howe, Irving. *World of Our Fathers*. New York: Harcourt, 1976. Howe tells the history of the immigration of more than two million Jews from East Europe from the 1880's to the 1920's. He describes their efforts to maintain a Yiddish culture while establishing themselves in the new country.

Lyons, Bonnie. *Henry Roth: The Man and His Work*. New York: Cooper Square, 1977. This book is somewhat dated, since it was written before Roth returned to long fiction in his final years. Nevertheless, it is a helpful study of *Call It Sleep*.

Napolitano, Louise. *An American Story: Pietro di Donato's Christ in Concrete*. New York: Peter Lang, 1995. The fourth volume in the series Studies in Southern Italian and Italian/American Culture, it examines di Donato's work in the context of American society.

JEWISH AMERICAN LONG FICTION

Approximately five hundred Jews lived in the United States in 1700. The majority lived in the Newport, Rhode Island, area, while the rest settled primarily in New York City, Savannah, Charleston, and Philadelphia. Newport was particularly attractive because of the relatively liberal political administration of Roger Williams, who vied for a strict separation of Puritan church and political state. There is little evidence to indicate a concentrated persecution of the Jews in any of the original American colonies. Many of the cultural values with which Jews were identified, such as thrift, industry, and a devout adherence to the word of God, were also values of a Puritan America; by the time of the First Continental Congress in 1774, when the chafe of British oversight had become intolerable, the colonists may well have felt an immediate kinship with the Jews in their midst. After all, Jews personified the Protestant work ethic, and many colonists believed that they, like the Jews, were God's chosen people, badly abused by a powerful nation.

EARLY JEWISH AMERICAN LITERATURE

The earliest Jewish American writers to produce widely recognized fictional narratives were journalists who also wrote for the popular stage, such as the early nineteenth century melodramatists Mordecai Manuel Noah and Samuel B. H. Judah. An editor of the *National Advocate* and the founder of the *New York Inquirer*, Noah avoided including Jews in his most popular melodrama, *Siege of Tripoli* (1820), as did Judah in his most popular work, *A Tale of Lexington: A National Comedy, Founded on the Opening of the Revolution in Three Acts* (1823). As such, there is nothing identifiably Jewish American about their writing.

The first Jewish American writers to speak from a decidedly Jewish perspective were women poets. Taking the ancient Jew as its subject matter, *Fancy's Sketch Book*, published in 1833 by Penina Moise, was one of the few such collections to reach a large audience in its day. However, Emma Lazarus's *The New Colossus* (1883) is by far the more familiar now,

if for no other reason than that one of its passages, "Give me your tired, your poor/ Your huddled masses," became the Statue of Liberty's invitation—and by extension, America's as well—to the disenfranchised of the world.

Lazarus's enthusiasm for America as a "melting pot" was shared by a number of early Jewish American novelists, Israel Zangwill to name but one. In *The Melting-Pot*, the 1908 drama that coined the phrase, Zangwill envisions a land where Jew and Gentile can live and labor in harmony, if only they are willing to become, first and foremost, "Americans":

> There she lies, the great Melting Pot—Listen! Can't you hear the roaring and the bubbling? . . . There gapes her mouth—the harbor where a thousand mammoth feeders come from the ends of the world to pour in their human freight . . . Celt and Latin, Slav and Teuton, Greek and Syrian—black and yellow— Yes, East and West, North and South, the palm and the pine, the pole and the equator, the crescent and the cross—how the great alchemist melts and fuses them with his purging flame! . . . Ah, Vera, what is the glory of Rome and Jerusalem and all nations and races that come to worship and look back, compared with the glory of America, where all races and nations come to labor and look forward!

The possibility for inclusion must have been appealing to Jewish immigrants in particular. The history of Jews was one of persecution and homelessness; it is no wonder then that the possibility that the United States could provide a place where the Wandering Jew could finally put down roots became perhaps the single most persistent concern of the Jewish American novel. However, a second overriding theme surfaced more or less concurrently with this one. Henry Harland's *Mrs. Peixada* (1886) and *The Yoke of the Thorah* (1887) deal with Jewish Americans who, while coming of age in the ghetto, are willing to marry outside their faith against the wishes of their elders. Such story lines anticipate the generational concerns of much later novels, such as Henry Roth's *Call It Sleep* (1934) and Albert Halper's *Sons of the Fathers* (1940), and later still the novels of

Philip Roth and Saul Bellow, in which children come to feel estranged from their parents' way of life, yet have no meaningful alternative of their own. Hebrew, both literally and metaphorically, becomes the language of the father, a distant, often foreign tongue that speaks of restraint, denial, and suffering in a world of possibility and plenty. As Halper describes the relationship between the generations cited in the title of *Sons of the Fathers*,

> From his naturalized American lips issued Hebrew, an old world language, somberizing the room with its rich and mournful cadences. And though none of the children understood a word their father had said, they had the feeling they were in the synagogue. Every year their father sat upon a pillow during this service and every year, though enticing food lay within hands' reach, they forgot for a moment the prospect of eating as a feeling of solemnity stole into the room.

A related concern of early Jewish American novels is perhaps more daunting—namely, the fear that Jews may be able to find a proper place in mainstream, mercantile, American culture only by sacrificing what is most sacred to the Jew's human experience: being a Jew. This dilemma is first addressed seriously in Abraham Cahan's *The Rise of David Levinsky* (1917). Like Noah and Judah before him, Cahan was primarily a journalist, making his mark as an editor of the *Jewish Daily Forward*, a Jewish socialist newspaper. Unlike Noah and Judah, however, Cahan was more an artist than a popular entertainer. His novel deals with a young Russian Talmudic student who travels to the United States, enters the garment industry, educates himself, and begins his rise to the top of American society. If the American Dream is a dream of success, he achieves it. He becomes rich and powerful. He discovers, however, that the American Dream is most of all a secular dream; paradoxically, having found his place in America, he feels spiritually lost and without a home.

THE EARLY TWENTIETH CENTURY

Novels published immediately after World War I, such as Samuel B. Ornitz's *Haunch, Paunch, and Jowl* (1923), voiced some of the same concerns as

Cahan, but only in passing. Most of these books were issued amid a great burst of postwar prosperity and therefore seem naïvely optimistic. Generally, these novels chronicled the ascent of their protagonists from the ghettos of New York City's Lower East Side to the heights of American prosperity, for the sky, apparently, was the limit for any Jew who appreciated the value of personal initiative paired with formal education; however, such a vision of upward mobility was as short-lived as it was trusting in the promise of the United States, and these works were soon replaced by the "proletariat" novels written in response to the Great Depression.

Although novels such as John Steinbeck's account of Oklahoma sharecroppers, *The Grapes of Wrath* (1939), are classified as "proletariat" writing, the proletariat novel was an urban, Jewish American phenomenon. It signalled a new generation of Jewish American novelists, the American-born children of Jewish immigrants who were coming of age during a period when American capitalism was being challenged more seriously than ever before in the twentieth century. It also signaled the first time that Jewish American novelists as a group defined a place for themselves in American literature.

Their work reflects the left-of-center politics that became attractive to so many out-of-work Americans during the depths of the Depression. Michael Gold was surely the most doctrinaire of the group. Gold was the editor of *The New Masses*, the American Communist Party's influential literary magazine; in his *Jews Without Money* (1930), it is communism that promises a better future. So great was Gold's impact that a hard-line Marxist-Leninist agenda is often attributed to the other proletariat novelists as well, though Nelson Algren (*Somebody in Boots*, 1935), Meyer Levin (*The Old Bunch*, 1937), Albert Halper (*The Foundry*, 1934), Isidor Schneider, and Daniel Fuchs demonstrated more faith in collective bargaining and trade unionism than in communist doctrine. Even at their most dogmatic they seemed to be utopian writers as much as anything else. They envisioned a way to bring the compassion and values of Jewish orthodoxy to the factory and the mill, a compromise between the sacred and the profane. To paraphrase Algren, theirs was a utopian socialism, a vision of "the New Jerusalem being built on the ashes of failure of American capitalism." The writing often has an almost religious fervor about it. In Isidor Schneider's *From the Kingdom of Necessity* (1935), for instance, readers are told that the protagonist

> had set out from the kingdom of necessity; he had found a way out, the escape from his class, only to find that, outside, he was homeless. He was to learn that no one enters the kingdom of freedom alone. He would return to his class. With it, he would march, taking his place in the advancing lines, in the irresistible movement of the masses of mankind from the kingdom of necessity to the Kingdom of Freedom.

The work of Daniel Fuchs should be of particular interest to anyone studying the development of the Jewish American novel. Fuchs is better remembered for his Hollywood screenplays (*The Human Jungle*, 1954; *Interlude*, 1957; *Jeanne Eagels*, 1957) than for his novels, yet his Williamsburg trilogy (*Summer in Williamsburg*, 1934; *Homage to Blenholt*, 1936; and *Low Company*, 1937; published in one volume as *Three Novels*, 1961; also as *Williamsburg Trilogy*, 1972) remains an important literary achievement. The trilogy takes its name from the Williamsburg section of Brooklyn in New York City. At the height of Jewish immigration to the United States, the Lower East Side of Manhattan in New York City was more densely populated than Calcutta, India, and Jews gradually had to make their way across the Williamsburg Bridge to the outskirts of Brooklyn to find space in which to live. Fuchs's characters, who live in Williamsburg, begin to cast their eyes back toward Manhattan's Madison Avenue. In this regard their longings are reminiscent of those Ornitz characters who wished to leave their ghetto tenements and better themselves. However, there is a difference in how Fuchs treats such material: Unlike his predecessors, Fuchs infuses humor into his work. He is as much a satirist of human nature as he is a chronicler of upward mobility, and much that will be attributed to later Jewish American novelists such as Philip Roth—caricaturing the Jewish mother for comic effect, for instance—was pioneered by Fuchs.

THE HOLOCAUST AND POSTWAR FICTION

World War II and the Holocaust had a tremendous impact on Jewish literature, particularly in Europe. Holocaust survivors such as the Italian novelist Primo Levi and the Romanian Aharon Appelfeld offer unique perspectives on what it meant to be a Jew in the twentieth century by virtue of the ordeals they suffered. Levi addressed his experiences during the Holocaust in two autobiographies, *Se questo è un uomo* (1947; *If This Is a Man*, 1959; revised as *Survival in Auschwitz: The Nazi Assault on Humanity*, 1961) and *La tregua* (1963; *The Reawakening*, 1965), then drew from them obliquely in his novel *Se non ora, quando?* (1982; *If Not Now, When?*, 1985). Appelfeld directed his attentions to the writing of fiction. His first novel was *Badenheim, 'ir nofesh* (1975; *Badenheim 1939*, 1980), and though he continued to publish after its translation, *Badenheim 1939* remains his best-known work. None of these chronicle the realities of his own internment and eventual escape, but the death camps are seldom far removed from the hearts and minds of his characters. They are often unwary Jews, well-respected in their communities, whose lives are overtaken by the Nazis in the early years of the war, as in *Badenheim 1939*, *Tor-ha-pela'ot* (1978; *The Age of Wonders*, 1981), *Kutonet veha-pasim* (1983; *Tzili: The Story of a Life*, 1983), *To the Land of Cattails* (1986; also known as *To the Land of the Reeds*), *Be-'et uve'onah ahat* (1985; *The Healer*, 1990), *Unto the Soul* (1994). Other novels depict Jews who are struggling after the war to reclaim their place in the world, as is the case in *Bartfus ben ha-almavet* (1988; *The Immortal Bartfuss*, 1988) and *Al kol hapesha'im* (n.d.; *For Every Sin*, 1989).

Jewish American fiction flowered after 1945. To offer even the slightest list of Jewish American authors who rose to prominence after World War II is to list some of the most influential writers in the canon of contemporary American literature: E. L. Doctorow, Joseph Heller, Bernard Malamud, Stanley Elkin, Bruce Jay Friedman, Cynthia Ozick, Isaac Bashevis Singer, Tillie Olsen, Grace Paley, Norman Mailer, Philip Roth, Saul Bellow, and Chaim Potok. Mailer's *The Naked and the Dead* (1948) was a debut that had a great impact following the war, earning its twenty-five-year-old author a berth at the forefront of American letters. The novel recounts a long and lethal patrol by a U.S. Army platoon on an isolated island in the Pacific Ocean. Two of these soldiers, Herman Roth and Joey Goldstein, are Jewish. Roth, the better assimilated of the two, is more quickly accepted by the other men, but he is without the moral compass necessary to internalize what he is going through. Goldstein, by contrast, is devout. His worldview is that of an ancient Hebrew, and he is one of the few characters in the novel for whom the patrol has any meaning. Goldstein is paired in the novel's final chapters with Ossie Ridges, a Southern fundamentalist Christian, as they carry a wounded soldier on a litter through the jungle. Theirs is a Sisyphean chore that ends in failure, but it serves to unite them. Both Goldstein and Ridges have what the other men lack, a sense of a well-ordered universe in which humankind is in the hands of a punishing God, and such understanding stirs in each a compassion for the suffering of the other.

Philip Roth's first novel-length work, *Goodbye, Columbus* (1959), takes its title from the dream of its protagonist, Neil Klugman. Klugman's dream puts him aboard a masted sailing ship moored in the harbor of a paradisal island. An undertow begins to draw the ship out to sea. Powerless to stop the ship's departure, Klugman watches as beautiful native goddesses on the shore bid him farewell, chanting "Goodbye, Columbus, Goodbye," while the paradise before him grows more distant by the minute. The book's title and dream images befit much that Roth has written and certainly represent an experience shared by Roth protagonists as otherwise diverse as Alexander Portnoy, David Kepesh, Peter Tarnopol, and Roth's recurring alter ego, Nathan Zuckerman: The nearer one comes to the America of one's dreams, the more certain one can be that it will never be discovered.

Roth's work has at its core several additional consistencies. His novels often deal with Jewish American writers who are at or near the top of their public lives, rich and famous novelists with no shortage of creature comforts or sensuous and willing women in their lives; yet they live in the depths of personal de-

spair, at odds with their current wives or ex-wives and haunted by their parents. Sooner or later this estrangement manifests itself in psychic and physical pain. The greater the suffering they experience, the more self-obsessed they become; the more self-obsessed they become, the more estranged they become from others and the greater their pains. It is a vicious cycle, but a comic one as well.

Roth gets much comic mileage out of psychosomatic—or at least undiagnosable—afflictions, including Alexander Portnoy's trips to his analyst in *Portnoy's Complaint* (1969) and Nathan Zuckerman's wrenching back pains in *The Anatomy Lesson* (1983). His protagonists lack the spiritual wherewithal required to negotiate the problems they face; their complaints have more to do with their souls than with their minds and bodies. This harkens back to matters Roth dealt with first in his depiction of Klugman, who is from a working class Newark, New Jersey, Jewish household. Shortly after his discharge from the U.S. Army, Klugman falls in love with Brenda Patimkin, a Smith College student who is home for the summer and whose family lives in a fashionable and religiously mixed Newark suburb called Short Hills. Klugman resents Patimkin for the countless ways in which her life has been made easier than his own because of her parents' money, but he is envious as well. Is it Patimkin he loves, or is it Short Hills and all the material pleasures it represents? Late in the novel, Klugman uncharacteristically tries his hand at a prayer:

> If we meet You at all, God, it's that we're carnal and acquisitive, and thereby partake of you. . . . Where do we meet? Which prize is You?" Within moments, Neil thinks he has his answer: "Which prize do you think, *schmuck*? Gold dinnerware, sporting-goods trees, nectarines, garbage disposals, bumpless noses . . .

Klugman suspects that happiness is to be found not in physical pleasures or material possessions but rather in what in European *shtetl* tales of the nineteenth century would have been called being a "good and virtuous man." Still, virtue is a slippery concept. A ritzy department store and the goods available within it are not.

Roth's characters come to a situation with a much better grasp of secular matters than they have of their spirits, and something of the same thing is true of Saul Bellow's protagonists as well. Like those of Roth, Bellow's protagonists are second- and third-generation American Jews who are several times removed from their deepest spiritual roots and who have much clearer knowledge of themselves as consumers and Americans than they have of themselves as Jews. Therein rests their dilemma. They are often seasoned literary men, or at least highly successful in their chosen careers, and, like Bellow himself—who won the Nobel Prize in Literature, a Pulitzer Prize, and two National Book Awards—have been handsomely rewarded by the world at large. In the course of the novel they go through a spiritual crisis. The dimensions of the crisis change from book to book, yet it is fundamentally the same in each work. Something is awakened in their souls that will not let them rest. Something, they sense, is amiss in how they have lived their lives, and the comedy begins as their attempts to set things right only make matters worse. Having accompanied his astrophysicist wife Minna to Eastern Europe, for instance, Albert Corde, the university dean of *The Dean's December* (1982), senses that the court case in which he has been involved back in Chicago speaks of an evil that neither his wife's capacity for science nor his own capacity for logic and reason can comprehend. It is an amazing moment of recognition for a high intellectual such as Corde, yet it serves only to paralyze him rather than move him to act.

Bereft by personal and financial problems, Charlie Citrine, the artist protagonist of *Humboldt's Gift* (1975), turns to meditation and Rudolph Steiner's quasi-mystical Theosophy. The title character of *Herzog* (1964) tries to restore order to his life by writing letters and reconstructing his personal history for any and all who are willing to listen. The novel ends with Herzog in the Berkshire Hills of western Massachusetts, having left the big city behind. He lies on his couch in the novel's final pages and speaks aloud with no one there to hear him; though he thinks this will help him resolve his problems, he only succeeds in talking himself into further confusion. It is

surely more than an autobiographical impulse that leads Bellow to make so many of his protagonists famous writers and fervent talkers, for the task he is putting before them is nothing short of articulating the unspeakable, and they fare no better than one might expect. Each protagonist has had a fleeting glimpse of some ultimate cosmic order in the universe. Each has experienced some longing of the spirit that defies translation into words.

Chaim Potok is the American novelist whose temperament and interests seem to be nearest to what readers expect of European authors. His earliest novels are his most formidable and perhaps still his most frequently read. Potok is at once a religious scholar and a creative artist, and his *The Chosen* (1967) and *The Promise* (1969) deal with the Jews' search for meaning, not only through prayer and study but also through the protagonists' encounters with the diversity to be found in modern Judaism itself, such as Hasidism, Orthodox Judaism, and Conservative Judaism. Subsequent novels, such as *In the Beginning* (1975) and *The Book of Lights* (1981), cast a wider net in an attempt to locate the place of Jews in twentieth century history. His protagonists discover that the defining moments of the twentieth century were horrors of staggering dimension, such as the nuclear bombing of Hiroshima, but they avoid the alienation and despair to be found in so much of contemporary writing. They discover in these horrors the fruits of a spiritual quest that affirms rather than denies their most deeply felt religious beliefs.

LATE TWENTIETH CENTURY

The 1990's witnessed the emergence of several talented Jewish American writers, particularly Lev Raphael, Melvin Bukiet, Steve Stern, and Allegra Goodman. Crime novelist Raphael (*Winter Eyes: A Novel About Secrets*, 1992; *Let's Get Criminal: An Academic Mystery*, 1996; *The Death of a Constant Lover: A Nick Hoffman Mystery*, 1999;) offers Nick Hoffman as his protagonist, an English professor at the State University of Michigan who finds himself solving murder mysteries between teaching classes and grading papers. These crimes inevitably shake him free of the ivory tower of academia in which he is trying to live his life, but they do more than that. In the process of investigating crimes, he is apt to be reminded that he is twice removed from the mainstream American experience he has sought in becoming a professor, first because he is a Jew, second because he is gay.

Bukiet, the child of Holocaust survivors, writes with the charming spirit of a fabulist in his short story collection *While the Messiah Tarries* (1995). This dose of charm is somewhat deceptive, however, as he proves in *After* (1996) and *Signs and Wonders* (1999), both of which are laced with comic acid. *Signs and Wonders*, set at the end of the twentieth century, follows Snakes Hammurabi, a burlesque version of Christ-like savior, as it explores a modern world that is well beyond any chance of salvation. *After*, written in the picaresque tradition, is set in the final days of World War II as the Nazi concentration camps are being liberated by the Allies. Bukiet's picaro protagonist is nineteen-year-old Isaac Kaufman, a concentration camp survivor who emerges from his experience a rogue, a nihilist, and a victim who has learned to savor the pleasures of the victimizer. The novel follows Kaufman and two comrades across Europe in a scheme to liberate a fortune in Nazi gold and virtually anything else that might strike their fancy.

Steve Stern has published short stories (*Lazar Malkin Enters Heaven*, 1986), novellas (*A Plague of Dreamers*, 1994), and novels (*Harry Kaplan's Adventures Underground*, 1991), but perhaps his greatest achievement is his creation of Pinch, a backwater Jewish immigrant community in Memphis, Tennessee, in which much of his fiction is set. Ignored by upwardly mobile Memphis, Pinch is an enclave where magic is still possible, and, in Stern's quite competent hands, even probable. Stern has all the skills of *shtetl* storytelling at his disposal, but he has a distinctly modern sensibility that prevents his fiction from becoming an imitative homage to a literature that no longer seems to speak of contemporary times.

Many critics believe that Goodman has established herself as the Jewish American writer who is most clearly the heir of Grace Paley, Cynthia Ozick,

Bellow, and Roth. In 1989, she published a novel titled *Total Immersion*, followed by two short story collections—*The Family Markovitz* (1996) and *Kaaterskill Falls* (1998). A number of the stories in the collections first appeared in *The New Yorker*, and they benefit from collecting, if only because seeing them together makes one conscious of how consistent are her authorial concerns. The former deals with three generations of one Jewish American family; Rose, the grandmother, tries to make sense of two grown sons and a world that defy her understanding. The irony is that Rose is closer to her granddaughter Miriam than she is to either of her own children, not only because Rose and Miriam share a generational enemy in common but also because Miriam is willing to embrace a Judaic tradition that neither of Rose's sons can fathom. *Kaaterskill Falls* takes its name from an upstate New York town in which Jews are a minority. The stories follow several Orthodox Jews of the baby-boomer generation who have traveled to Kaaterskill for the summer. At the center of this community are the Shulmans, who have opened a general store in the area. The Shulman elders are much less able to embrace Judaism wholeheartedly than are their grown children, who are ultimately more comfortable being Jews than are their parents.

Jewish American literature continues to ponder whether assimilation into the fabric of American life is tonic or toxic to the Jewish experience. Is it possible to be a Jew in a meaningful sense and also take one's place within American culture? Whether written by Jews or Gentiles, American novels are no more sure today than they have ever been. Jay McInerney's *Bright Lights, Big City* (1984) is narrated by a yuppie whose ventures into the fashionable night life of New York City have resulted in a powerful cocaine addiction. This has cost him an enviable job, the woman he loves, his family, and his future. In one scene, he gets on the subway and sits beside a Hasidic Jew who is studying the Talmud. Says the narrator,

This man has a God and a History, a Community. He has a perfect economy of belief in which pain and loss are explained in terms of a transcendental balance sheet, in which everything works out in the end and death is not really death. Wearing black wool all summer must seem a small price to pay. He believes he is one of God's chosen, whereas you feel like an integer in a random series of numbers.

Jay Boyer

BIBLIOGRAPHY

Fiedler, Leslie. *To the Gentiles*. New York: Stein & Day, 1972. A collection of readable articles that first appeared in the magazine *American Judaism* that focus on the Jewish experience in America.

Furman, Andrew. *Israel Through the Jewish American Imagination*. Purchase: State University of New York Press, 1997. Issued as part of the State University of New York's Modern Jewish Literature series, this study deals with fiction published between 1928 and 1995, specifically focusing on the place Israel occupies in twentieth century American letters as setting, myth, and metaphor.

Mersand, Joseph. *Traditions in American Literature: A Study of Jewish Characters and Authors*. Port Washington, N.Y.: Kennikat Press, 1968. A solid and accessible consideration of the development of Jewish American fiction, with a broader focus and understanding of literature than its title would announce.

Neusner, Jacob. *Studying Classical Judaism*. Louisville, Ky.: Westminster, 1991. Neusner's book, originally published during the 1960's, is still the best introduction to the study of Judaism.

Potok, Chaim. *Wanderings: Chaim Potok's History of the Jews*. New York: Knopf, 1978. Potok's scholarship is handsomely presented in this historical study, and, unlike other histories of the Jews to be found in public and college libraries, it can be appreciated by readers with little or no background in Judaism.

Shapiro, Ann R., ed. *Jewish American Women Writers*. Westport, Conn.: Greenwood Press, 1994. Offers biographical, bibliographical, critical, and reference material on a wide range of Jewish American women fiction writers, from the relatively obscure (Rhoda Lerman-Sniderman, Nessa Rapoport, Ilona Karmel) to those with a high popular readership, among them Erica Jong, Francine Prose, and Lynne Sharon Schwartz.

Shapiro, Gerald, ed. *American-Jewish Fiction: A Century of Stories*. New York: Brown Books, 1998. This excellent collection of Jewish American fiction spans the twentieth century, beginning with pioneers such as Abraham Cahan and concluding with such writers as Francine Prose, Robin Hemley, and Allegra Goodman.

Shatsky, Joel, and Michael Taub, eds. *Contemporary Jewish American Novelists*. Westport, Conn.: Greenwood Press, 1997. A collection of about sixty-five brief essays alphabetically arranged by novelist, from Walter Abish through Leon Uris, offering brief biographies, a discussion of major works and themes, and critical reception for each.

Tenenbaum, David, and Shelly Tenenbaum, eds. *Feminist Perspectives on Jewish Studies*. New Haven, Conn.: Yale University Press, 1994. The title is misleading insofar as it suggests one political agenda, for the central focus of this collection of polished essays is gender. Particularly useful is Joyce Antler's "Sleeping with the Other: The Problem of Gender in American-Jewish Literature."

LATINO LONG FICTION

Latino fiction presents the experience and multiplicity of perspectives unique to Latinos—residents of the United States whose cultural, ethnic, and linguistic ties to Latin America connect them as members of a distinct yet multiethnic community. The principal Latino ethnic or cultural groups include Chicanos, or Mexican Americans; Puerto Rican Americans; Cuban Americans; and residents or citizens of the United States who trace their origins to other countries in Central or South America. Each of these constituent groups is distinct in its own right, with its own history, folklore, and traditions. However, they all share commonalities of language, culture, religion, experience, and values; these attributes distinguish Latino culture both from the dominant Anglo culture of the United States and from those of other immigrant populations. Much Latino long fiction is characterized by a sense of ethnicity and by the portrayal of ethnic experience.

MEXICAN AMERICAN/CHICANO LONG FICTION

In 1848 the Treaty of Guadalupe Hidalgo ceded all Mexican territories north of the Rio Grande to the United States. One year later, all former citizens of Mexico who still resided in the area automatically became U.S. citizens. These people were a diverse group engendered principally from a mixture of European, Aztec, and Native North Americans; from each ethnocultural wellspring the group derived myths, values, religious and cultural traditions, laws, and literary models. In the ensuing years the overlay of Anglo influence enriched the mixture. The resulting culture came to call itself Chicano, a term used to designate the distinct history, culture, and literature of the American Southwest.

Chicano long fiction, like Chicano language and culture generally, derives from three distinct sociohistorical sources: Mexican Indian, predominant prior to 1519; Spanish Mexican, predominant from 1519 to 1848; and Anglo, emergent after the signing of the Treaty of Guadalupe Hidalgo in 1848. These sources provide a richness of myth, legend, history, and literary models and techniques, both oral and written, from which Chicano writers have drawn inspiration and material, the reactions to which have constituted the conflicts and tensions that drive all forms of Chicano literary expression.

Chicano long fiction is multilingual, employing Spanish, English, and Pocho, a hybrid blend of linguistic elements. Used together, these language options allow the Chicano novelist to express the full range of his or her experience, encompassing the dominant Anglo culture, the culture of origin, and the culture of the home and the *barrio*. Chicano novelists are conscious of their linguistic and ethnic heritage and depict a people proud of their history and culture, aware of their uniqueness, and committed to preserving their familial, social, and literary traditions. Their novels portrays men and women who accept themselves as they are and resist pressures to become more closely aligned with the mainstream Anglo culture that threatens to Americanize them. Proximity to Mexico and movement both north and south across the border continually reinforce the Hispanic and mestizo ways, creating a cultural dynamic, unique to Chicano literature, which continues to influence the Chicano novel's vital, energetic, and creative momentum.

The first significant Chicano novelist was José Antonio Villarreal. His *Pocho* (1959) was the first Latino novel issued by a major publishing firm, and it is frequently regarded as the first work of real literary or historical value to reflect the Chicano experience. The protagonist is a boy who seeks self-discovery, but as a Chicano he also must decide which of the ideals, traditions, and attitudes of his parents to reject in favor of Anglo ones he likes. Though sometimes criticized for not placing appropriate emphasis on racial and cultural issues, *Pocho* remains an important work in Latino fiction. Richard Vásquez's *Chicano* (1970), like *Pocho*, has been criticized for its failure to depict the Chicano experience realistically, but in its portrayal of Chicano themes, the novel constitutes a seminal work. Raymond Barrio's *The Plum Pickers* (1969) exposes the harshness of social and economic life for migrant Mexican and Chicano farmworkers in Southern California. Its literary excellence, the richness of its narrative technique, and its realistic depiction of the difficulties faced by Chicano laborers have earned it an important place in the evolution of Chicano fiction.

The novelists who represent the emergence into maturity and international acknowledgment of the Chicano novel include Rudolfo Anaya, Rolando Hinojosa, Ron Arias, and Sandra Cisneros. The critical acclaim accorded these novelists has established them as major twentieth century artists and has drawn attention to the genre of Latino fiction.

Rudolfo Anaya's *Bless Me, Última* (1972) uses dream sequences, Magical Realism, and mythological echoes to approach the fantastic. The novel's protagonist, through the agency of a folk healer named Última, achieves a level of spiritual and perceptual experience that awakens his awareness of the mythological figures of his Chicano heritage, teaching him respect for folk wisdom and custom and leading him to an alternate reality which, by extension, becomes available to the reader as well. The novel, widely read and critically acclaimed, established Anaya as a major force in American letters.

Rolando Hinojosa was the first Chicano writer to win an important international literary award. He was also the first U.S. citizen to be honored by the Casa de las Américas panel. His novel *Klail City y sus alrededores* (1976; *Klail City: A Novel*, 1987) was the second book in a trilogy that re-creates the reality, beliefs, and vision shared by generations of members of the Spanish-speaking community in south Texas, where Hinojosa was born. The other two volumes of the trilogy are *Estampas del valle y otras obras/ Sketches of the Valley* (1973; English revision, *The Valley*, 1983) and *Claros varones de Belken* (1981; *Fair Gentlemen of Belken County*, 1986). Hinojosa creates a collage of points of view, personalities, landscape snapshots, spots of time, and events both trivial and sublime that establish a palpable, vital fictional world through which a powerful sense of identity and continuity surges. Hinojosa suggested that he wrote the trilogy to help himself keep alive a past that grew in importance as it became more remote; in doing so, he has also made the Latino experience immediate and accessible to a broad spectrum of readers.

Ron Arias's *The Road to Tamazunchale* (1975) reveals the influence of contemporary international literary currents. The emphasis on the subjective, internal reality of his protagonist, rather than on the exterior world of objects, is consistent with the emphases of many other modern novelists. The effect of this emphasis on alternative reality is to diminish the narrative distance between writer and reader by smearing the distinctions within the novel between illusion and reality. Arias's mastery of contemporary literary technique and his emphasis in the novel on the *barrio* experience, the problems of illegal Mexican immigrants in the United States, and the rejection of victimhood in favor of empowerment make *The Road to Tamazunchale* unique in the body of Latino fiction, perhaps setting a new standard for the Chicano novel.

Sandra Cisneros is one of an emerging group of Chicano writers who have graduated from a creative writing program; her novel *The House on Mango Street* (1984) was completed during her tenure as a National Foundation of the Arts Fellow, and it received the Before Columbus American Book Award in 1985. Employing fragmentation and montage, she depicts not only the Chicano experience from the unusual perspective of growing up in the Midwest among predominantly Puerto Rican Americans but also the emergence of her self-awareness as a writer and creator. Like Hinojosa, Cisneros admits a need to recapture the past in order to fulfill the needs of the present.

PUERTO RICAN LONG FICTION

The population of Puerto Rico is a blend of the cultures and races of Europe, Africa, and the Americas. From 1493 until 1898, Puerto Rico was a Spanish colony. Puerto Rican fiction assumed a mestizo identity, in opposition to Spanish pressures to assimilate; this emphasis evolved to reflect a more Latin American character in the twentieth century, when Puerto Rico became a U.S. territory. After World War II, almost a third of the island's population immigrated to the United States, dispersed to points as far apart as Hawaii and New York. This distribution complicated the process whereby Puerto Ricans sought to define and protect their cultural and literary identity. Furthermore, by physically separating family and community members, the immigration reduced the efficacy of the oral tradition as a means of propagating values and traditions, making long fiction the culture's principal mechanism for articulating its vision of its own reality.

The language of the Puerto Rican American novel reflects the diversity of Puerto Rican ethnic and linguistic origins, a product of the melding of European (Spanish, French), African, and Native American cultures overlaid with an American patina. Puerto Rican American fiction has retained diverse elements of myth, culture, and value structures. Most Puerto Rican American fiction is bilingual, and it employs grammatical elements and vocabulary of the Caribbean patois and the Native American elements of its linguistic heritage.

The development of Puerto Rican literature has been constituted in part by a series of reactions. The reaction of nineteenth century Puerto Rican artists to Spanish dominance was to create a sense of identity that emphasized the values and linguistic elements of the indigenous, African, and mestizo aspects of its cultural heritage. From 1898 to about 1940, Americanizing pressures prompted Puerto Rican writers to emphasize the Spanish language itself and to use Latin American models in their efforts to define and protect their identity as a separate culture. Finally, since the end of World War II and in reaction to the new assimilating forces following the surge in emigration of the 1940's and 1950's, the efforts to preserve their cultural autonomy have increasingly led Puerto Ricans away from idealized depictions of the island and toward settings in New York, Chicago, and other enclaves of Puerto Rican American cultural influence.

The long fiction of the late twentieth century, written by the children of first-generation working-class immigrants, criticizes the complacency of an Americanized middle class as well as the oppressive dominance of Anglo culture. Typical of this class is Pedro Juan Soto's novel *Spiks* (1956), which emphasizes the anguish of the impoverished immigrants

and looks wistfully back to an idyllic past. Another novelist who focused on the oppression and alienation of the Puerto Rican American in New York was José Luis González, with *En Nueva York y otras desgracias* (1973; in New York and other disgraces). Critics have come to regard these novels as reactionary, creating a distorted, idealized view of the reality that existed before American involvement in Puerto Rico and reflecting a skewed, one-dimensional image of Puerto Rican American life, focusing only on the tragedy, alienation, and exploitation of immigrants at the mercy of a cold and greedy America.

New York Puerto Rican writers of the late twentieth century were writing mostly in English and had inherited a popular tradition heavily influenced by Hispanic folklore and the multifaceted culture of one of the world's largest cities. Thematically and structurally their work has much in common with African American, Third World, and other Latino writers seeking identity through recognition of their multiethnicity rather than through acquiescence to pressures to assimilate. Nicholasa Mohr, one of the most productive and critically acclaimed Puerto Rican American novelists, deemphasizes the theme of alienation, creating characters who are not overly conscious of cultural conflict or crises of identity. *Felita* (1981) and *Rituals of Survival: A Woman's Portfolio* (1985) are examples of this fiction of self-determination.

CUBAN AMERICAN LONG FICTION

Cuban literary influence in the United States can be traced to the early 1800's, when José Martí and other patriots worked from the United States for Cuban independence. After Fidel Castro's 1959 victory in the Cuban Revolution and the large-scale emigration that followed, however, Cuban Americans emerge as a major contributing force to Latino culture and literature. Unlike Puerto Ricans, Cubans came as refugees rather than immigrants. Furthermore, although Cuba had been a U.S. protectorate since 1898, it was never a political colony of the United States in the same sense as Puerto Rico. At the time of the Cuban Revolution, then, Cuban writers, having felt no assimilationist pressure, had developed no literary expressions of defiance or protection against the imposition of mainstream American culture onto Cuban American identity. In fact, because it was sparked by a political and social revolution, the emigration involved a cross-section of Cuban society: workers, middle-class service personnel, professionals, intellectuals, and the wealthy. Many subsequently adapted to and became a part of U.S. and Hispanic mainstream culture.

The fiction of Cuban Americans in the 1960's was primarily written in Spanish. One reason may be that the audience targeted by these first-generation exiles was primarily Spanish-speaking, either Cuban or Latin American. Another reason may be found in the essentially political, often propagandistic nature of the material. The themes were less concerned with discovery and preservation of an ethnic, cultural, or literary identity than with criticizing Cuba's communist economic and political system. Therefore, the Cuban American novel of the 1960's was almost devoid of the kinds of ethnic and linguistic self-consciousness that marked Chicano, Puerto Rican, and other minority ethnic fiction.

Fiction written by Cuban American novelists of the 1970's was less preoccupied with exile and looking back to the island past than with meeting the demands of the Cuban American communities then flourishing in the United States. Their novels were dominated by English, although code-switching (changing languages when expression in one seems richer or clearer than in the other) became more frequent, as did representation of a Cuban dialect heavily influenced by American idioms. Cuban American novelists of the late twentieth century have more in common with other Latino writers than did their forerunners of the 1950's and 1960's, having sought solidarity with the Latino community of writers and thinkers rather than returning to another, or remaining distinct as exiles. Immigration from Cuba continues to reinforce the dynamic nature of this evolution, however, and to provide an impetus resisting assimilation.

The first Cuban American novels, which began to be published in 1960, almost exclusively attacked Marxist doctrine in general and the political manifestation of it in the Cuban Revolution in particular. The

first such novel, *Enterrado Vivo* (1960; buried alive), written by Andrés Rivera Collado, was published in Mexico; the ensuing decade saw similar novels, published in the United States and abroad. At worst, these works were openly propagandistic and inflammatory, while at best they were unrealistically and ineffectively nostalgic in their idealization of prerevolutionary Cuba.

A change in direction for Cuban American fiction was initiated by Celedonio González, whose focus in *Los primos* (1971) was on Cuban life and culture in the United States. The thematic emphasis in González's subsequent novels, *Los cuatro embajadores* (1973; the four ambassadors) and *El espesor del pellejo de un gato ya cadáver* (1978; the thickness of the skin of a cat that's is already a cadaver), is on the cultural and social conflicts experienced by Cuban Americans in a predatory economic system that keeps immigrants disadvantaged and alienated in order to exploit them. Like other Latino fiction, these novels depict a people not fully Americanized but clearly unable to return to or participate fully in their land or culture of origin.

Cristina Garcia's work seeks resolution of the tensions between first and subsequent generations of Cuban Americans; born in 1958 in Havana, she grew up in New York City and was educated at Barnard College and The Johns Hopkins School of Advanced International Studies. Her first novel, *Dreaming in Cuban* (1992), earned favorable critical reception and became widely popular. Neither strident nor nostalgic, the novel avoids romantic excess, depicting a search for cultural and personal identity.

In the novels of Oscar Hijuelos, the evolution of Cuban American fiction moved even closer to integration in the American mainstream. He was born in New York in 1951, and neither Hijuelos nor his parents were exiles. Their experience, and his, is more consistent with that of Chicano and Puerto Rican American writers who lack the political agenda of writers in exile and whose thematic emphasis is on discovery and preservation of the integrity of their cultural and linguistic legacy. His first novel, *Our House in the Last World* (1983), is autobiographical, though often classified as a novel. He won the 1990

Pulitzer Prize for fiction; further evidence of his acceptance by mainstream America was the adaptation of his second novel, *The Mambo Kings Play Songs of Love* (1989), for film by Warner Bros.

Andrew B. Preslar

BIBLIOGRAPHY

Baker, Houston A., Jr., ed. *Three American Literatures: Essays in Chicano, Native American, and Asian American Literature for Teachers of American Literature*. New York: Modern Language Association of America, 1982. A collection of critical essays for students and general readers, offering historical and traditional critical perspectives. Overview essays direct students to subjects of further study. Chapters include notes and references.

Behar, Ruth, ed. *Bridges to Cuba/Puentes a Cuba*. Ann Arbor: University of Michigan Press, 1995. For students and general readers with literary interests, this collection of essays, poems, drawings and stories by Cuban and Cuban American writers and scholars explores issues of culture, language, and national identity. Excellent resource for understanding the Latino search for ideological solidarity.

Christie, John S. *Latino Fiction and the Modernist Imagination: Literature of the Borderlands*. New York: Garland, 1998. Examines the works of Cuban Americans, Mexican Americans, and Puerto Ricans, among others. Includes thirteen pages of bibliographical references, as well as an index.

Gish, Robert Franklin. *Beyond Bounds: Cross-Cultural Essays on Anglo, American Indian, and Chicano Literature*. Albuquerque: University of New Mexico Press, 1996. An insightful exploration of the interrelationships of myth, language, and literary traditions of the overlapping cultures of the American Southwest.

Horno-Delgado, Anunción, et al., eds. *Breaking Boundaries: Latina Writings and Critical Readings*. Amherst: University of Massachusetts Press, 1989. Focusing on the experience of Hispanic female writers from all ethnic and cultural backgrounds, this collection of critical essays on fiction, poetry, and linguistics offers explanatory, introductory, and analytical studies of issues relating to all aspects and genres of Latina literary production. Scholarly but accessible, with notes and a bibliography.

Marqués, René. *The Docile Puerto Rican*. Translated with an introduction by Barbara Bockus Aponte. Philadelphia: Temple University Press, 1976. Essays written for young Puerto Ricans to help them understand their cultural, ideological, and historical legacy. Treats issues of national identity directly and clearly, focusing on language, art, and literature. Endnotes offer explanation but are not intrusive or obscure; index and bibliography direct the student to further reading.

Robinson, Cecil. *Mexico and the Hispanic Southwest in American Literature*. Tucson: University of Arizona Press, 1977. Appropriate for a general audience, this book offers an excellent historical perspective on the evolution of culture and literature in the American Southwest. An introduction and prologue provide context and focus. Contains illustrations, an epilogue, unobtrusive references by chapter and page, a bibliography, and an index.

Shirley, Carl R., and Paula W. Shirley. *Understanding Chicano Literature*. Columbia: University of South Carolina Press, 1988. An introduction helps focus the material of the chapters following: poetry, theater, the novel, short fiction, and more, with notes, bibliography, index, and a list of suggested readings. Dense with information; appropriate for high school seniors and above.

Steele, Cynthia. *Politics, Gender, and the Mexican Novel, 1968-1988: Beyond the Pyramid*. Austin: University of Texas Press, 1992. A thoughtful study of contemporary Mexican long fiction. Discusses politics, social problems, sex roles, and female characters.

NATIVE AMERICAN LONG FICTION

Although Native Americans, also known as American Indians, are an ancient people, much of their written literature is fairly recent. It was only in the twentieth century that Native American authors began to produce long fiction and that Native American ethnicity became a central theme in novels and other forms of writing. Nevertheless, the literature of America's oldest minority group does have deep cultural roots.

ROOTS OF NATIVE AMERICAN LONG FICTION

Long before the arrival of Europeans in America, the tribes and nations that inhabited North America passed stories from generation to generation. These stories were intended for education of the young and for perpetuation of cultural traditions, as well as for entertainment. They told of the origins of the earth and of the human race, of the order of the universe and of the human place in it, and of bawdy tricksters who are mischievous but creative. Modern Native American fiction writers have frequently woven traditional narratives into their works.

Many of the earliest works of Native American written literature were autobiographies, intended for communication with the written culture of the invading Euro-Americans. In 1829, the Pequod William Apes published his life story in *A Son of the Forest: The Experience of William Apes, A Native of the Forest*, in order to tell the story of the defeated and beleaguered Pequod people. The Sauk Black Hawk published *Black Hawk: An Autobiography* in 1833, after being defeated by Euro-American forces. The most famous of all Native American autobiographies was *Black Elk Speaks* (1932), the memoirs of the Oglala Sioux medicine man Black Elk, as told to poet John G. Neihardt. Although these autobiographies were generally intended for Euro-American audiences, they also influenced Native American writers. Much of contemporary Native American literature is heavily autobiographical.

The oral narratives and even the early autobiographies were works of people who saw themselves as parts of small communities, such as Pequod, Sauk, or Oglala. Over the course of the late nineteenth and early twentieth centuries, as anthropologist Peter Nabokov pointed out, Native Americans developed a sense of belonging to a wider group. By the mid-twentieth century, when Native American written fiction began to flourish, writers such as N. Scott Momaday and James Welch were writing self-consciously as people with an ethnic or racial identity and members of specific tribes or nations. The sense of belonging to a single group, the autobiographical written tradition, and oral narratives may be identified as the primary cultural roots of modern Native American fiction.

EARLY NATIVE AMERICAN FICTION

The early twentieth century saw the first written works of fiction by Native American authors. In 1927, Mourning Dove published the romance *Cogewea, the Half-Blood*. During the same decade, the Oklahoma Cherokee John Milton Oskison became widely known as a short-story writer and novelist. His novels, which dealt with life in and around the Indian Territory—which became Oklahoma—include *Wild Harvest* (1925), *Black Jack Davey* (1926), and *Brothers Three* (1935). Both Mourning Dove and Oskison are frequently criticized for their stock characters and their adherence to the conventions of popular fiction.

Literary critics generally regard the mixed-blood Osage Indian John Joseph Matthews as a more sophisticated author than Mourning Dove or Oskison. Matthews wrote mainly history and autobiography, but he did publish one highly regarded novel, *Sundown* (1934). He set the story in the Osage country of Oklahoma, where the Osage are divided into the full-bloods and the mixed-bloods and into those who have money from oil leases and those who do not. The novel's hero goes away to college and then returns to struggle with his emotions about tribal life. Many of the themes, such as the tensions between tribal life and the modern economy and the struggle between assimilation and cultural traditionalism, became dominant in later Native American fiction.

D'Arcy McNickle (1904-1977), a member of the Confederation of Salish and Kutenai Tribes of Montana, is often regarded as one of the best of the early Native American authors. Educated at the University of Montana and Oxford University, McNickle went to work for the Bureau of Indian Affairs in 1936, where he served as assistant to commissioner John Collier. McNickle dedicated himself to Collier's attempts to reverse the efforts of the U.S. government to force Native Americans to give up their cultural and political identities. McNickle gave passionate expression to the struggles of Native Americans in his novel *The Surrounded* (1936), which tells the story of a young man who returns from a government Indian school to his reservation.

THE NATIVE AMERICAN RENAISSANCE

By the 1960's and 1970's, a new generation of university-educated Native Americans, many of whom were influenced by the Civil Rights movement, began to produce novels that met with wide popular acceptance. The Kiowa Indian N. Scott Momaday (born 1934) was one of the first of this generation to be recognized as a major American author. A professor of literature, Momaday explored his Kiowa heritage in both poetry and prose. In 1968, he published the novel *House Made of Dawn*, which won the Pulitzer Prize in literature in 1969. The protagonist of Momaday's novel, Abel, returns to his reservation after serving in the military in World War II. He kills an albino, whom he believes to have been an evil sorcerer, and serves a prison term. After his release, Abel settles in Los Angeles, where he meets with hardship and brutality from white society and the corruption of traditional ways by other Native Americans. At the end, he returns to the reservation and runs a ritual race against death and evil at dawn.

Gerald Vizenor (born 1934), whose father was Ojibwa, also became both a professor and a writer. A prolific author, Vizenor wrote poetry, history, ethnography, and literary criticism, in addition to novels. His first novel, *Darkness in Saint Louis Bearheart* (1978; revised as *Bearheart: The Heirship Chronicles*, 1990), is an autobiographical work that examines Vizenor's own experience as a Native American. Another of Vizenor's novels, *Dead Voices: Natural Agonies in the New World* (1992), draws on Native American tradi-

tions of oral narrative. This difficult, experimental novel looks at the trickster figure of Native American myth in the context of contemporary society.

Poet and novelist James Welch, part Blackfoot and part Gros Ventre Indian, looked at the Native American experience in works set in both contemporary and historical settings. Welch's first novel, *Winter in the Blood* (1974), is a story with some autobiographical basis, about a young Indian on a Montana reservation. The reservation and its social problems were also at the center of Welch's second long work of fiction, *The Death of Jim Loney* (1979), which deals with alcoholism and the confusion of a man of mixed race. His third novel, *Fools Crow* (1986), tells of a band of Blackfoot Indians in Montana in the 1870's. A fourth novel, *The Indian Lawyer* (1990), returns to the modern reservation in a tale of a successful Native American's struggles with the temptations of political corruption.

Leslie Marmon Silko (born 1948) achieved critical acclaim with her first novel, *Ceremony* (1977), which deals with a mixed-race Navajo veteran's struggles against insanity after returning from World War II. Under the guidance of a wise, elderly, mixed-race man, the protagonist finds peace and cosmic order through participation in traditional ceremony. Marmon's second novel, *Almanac of the Dead* (1991), is an epic that took the author ten years to complete. It covers five hundred years of the struggle between Native Americans and settlers from Europe.

THE NEW GENERATION

By the 1980's, the Native American novel was well established, and works of fiction on Native American themes were popular with a large readership. Louise Erdrich (born 1954), daughter of a Chippewa mother and a German American father, was one of the most successful Native American authors of the decade. In 1984, after having published a volume of poetry, Erdrich published her first novel, *Love Medicine* (revised and expanded, 1993). She followed this with a series of related novels: *The Beet Queen* (1986), *Tracks* (1988), *The Bingo Palace* (1994), and *Tales of Burning Love* (1996). The novels in this series tell the stories of three related Native

American families living in North Dakota from 1912 through the 1980's. Sometimes compared to William Faulkner, Erdrich is concerned with universal patterns of family life, as well as with contemporary Native American issues. She collaborated with her late husband, Michael Dorris, on both fiction and nonfiction works.

New, young Native American novelists emerged during the last decade of the twentieth century. Ray A. Young Bear's *Black Eagle Child: The Facepaint Narratives* (1992) is an autobiographical novel in the form of a long blank verse poem. It tells the story of Edgar Bearchild, a member of the Black Eagle Child settlement of the Mesquakie tribe. A dominant theme of the novel, one found in many Native American works, is the perplexing relationship between an individual who is part of modern American culture and the individual's ancient tribal heritage.

Sherman Alexie (born 1966) was the most widely praised new Native American author of the 1990's. A Spokane/Coeur d'Alene Indian, Alexie grew up on the Wellpinit Indian reservation and continued to live on the reservation after achieving literary renown. Most of Alexie's poetry and fiction focuses on contemporary reservation life, mixing portrayals of alcoholism and poverty with bitter but sympathetic humor and flashes of fantasy. *Reservation Blues* (1995) is set on a Spokane reservation. Its main characters are young Native Americans who have been out of high school for several years and face despair and a bleak future. After legendary blues guitarist Robert Johnson shows up, looking for a way to undo his deal with the devil, the young friends form a rock-and-roll band and reach fame after making their own deal with the devil, who happens to be a white man. Written after Alexie himself had achieved success, the story treats the problem of the threat to American Indian identity posed by succeeding in the white world, as well as with the frustrations and dangers of Native American life. Alexie's 1996 novel *Indian Killer* is one of the few works not set on the reservation. The novel features a serial killer in Seattle who scalps his white victims, and it deals with issues of racial violence and loss of culture.

Carl L. Bankston III

BIBLIOGRAPHY

Blaeser, Kimberly M. *Gerald Vizenor: Writing in Oral Tradition*. Norman: University of Oklahoma Press, 1996. In her study of Vizenor's work, Blaeser looks at how the writer expresses traditional Native American themes and characters in the form of the contemporary novel.

Lincoln, Kenneth. *Native American Renaissance*. Berkeley: University of California Press, 1983. This is probably the most influential critical work on the Native American renaissance. It traces the writings of modern authors back to their roots in oral narrative and autobiography. The book contains chapters devoted to N. Scott Momaday, James Welch, and Leslie Marmon Silko.

Nabokov, Peter, ed. *Native American Testimony: A Chronicle of Indian-White Relations from Prophecy to the Present, 1492-1992*. New York: Penguin, 1991. In one of the best introductions to Native American history from the Indian perspective, anthropologist Peter Nabokov presents the recorded responses of Native Americans to the European and Euro-American incursion over a five-hundred-year period. He also introduces each historical period with a summary and commentary.

Velie, Alan R., ed. *American Indian Literature: An Anthology*. Rev. ed. Norman: University of Oklahoma Press, 1991. This anthology contains a wide range of literature, including traditional tales and modern poetry and fiction, by Native Americans on Native American subjects. It contains useful commentaries on the different forms of literature.

_____. *Four American Indian Literary Masters: N. Scott Momaday, James Welch, Leslie Marmon Silko, and Gerald Vizenor*. Norman: University of Oklahoma Press, 1982. An examination of the writings of the major figures of the Native American renaissance.

Vizenor, Gerald, ed. *Native American Literature: A Brief Introduction and Anthology*. New York: HarperCollins, 1995. A collection of Native American writings assembled by an acclaimed Native American author.

Wiget, Andrew. *Native American Literature*. Boston: Twayne, 1985. An overview of Native American writing, from the earliest oral narratives to the writers of the Native American renaissance. Contains a chronology of Native American literary history from the approximate time of the development of agricultural myths to the publication of Silko's *Ceremony*.

THE SOUTHERN NOVEL

The South can be defined historically, as an area consisting of the states south of the Mason-Dixon line or of the states that made up the Confederacy. It can also be defined topographically, as a region made up of three sections, one coastal, another hilly, and a third mountainous. However, from a cultural perspective, neither of these classifications is accurate. Coastal Savannah, Georgia, is totally unlike coastal Panama City, Florida, and there are few similarities between Birmingham, Alabama; New Orleans, Louisiana; and Dallas, Texas, except that they are all large cities. It might seem that the South is not a cohesive entity, or that, if it once was, it vanished after the Civil War or perhaps with desegregation. Nothing could be further from the truth. The elements that make up the common heritage of the South are courtesy and honor; dedication to family, home, and home cooking; a love of slow talk and storytelling; a sense of humor, deeply rooted in rural life; a tendency toward nostalgia; a distrust of outsiders, especially those who are rude and arrogant; a willingness to tolerate eccentrics, at least those of known origins; and the conviction that good and evil forces are constantly at war, both in the outside world and in the soul of every human being. These elements are basic in southern literature. Where southern writers differ is not in how they define the South, but in how they define life, whether they look at it from the perspective of a romanticist or that of a realist, whether they see it as a tragedy, a comedy, or a farce.

NINETEENTH CENTURY FICTION

The romantic perspective pervaded nineteenth century southern fiction, whether in the form of historical romances or in ostensibly realistic works that presented an idyllic picture of plantation life, such as John Pendleton Kennedy's *Swallow Barn* (1832). Though "serious" fiction was considered the province of upper-class white men, sentimental, domestic novels by women writers such as Caroline Lee Hentz and Augusta Jane Evans Wilson, who, like Kennedy, romanticized the South, were immensely popular not only in the South but also in the North, even during the Civil War. One of the novels in which Wilson defended the Confederate cause, *Macaria, or Altars of Sacrifice* (1864), was adjudged so dangerous that a Yankee commander in Tennessee banned his men from reading it.

However, these romantic novels did not have a lasting impact on southern fiction. By contrast, the realistic, earthy sketches classified as "southwestern" humor because they were set in the frontier states—Alabama, Georgia, Arkansas, Mississippi, Tennessee, and Kentucky—directly influenced later writers, including Mark Twain (1835-1910). Like those earlier sketches, Twain's *Adventures of Huckleberry Finn* (1884) was funny, farcical, and irreverent. It even satirized some of the most cherished beliefs of white southerners, including their assumptions about class and race. Other nineteenth century southern writers also attacked the prevailing romantic vision. In *Margret Howth* (1862), Rebecca Harding Davis wrote about the exploitation of workers in the iron mills, while in *The Awakening* (1899), Kate Chopin described the subjugation of women in a patriarchal society.

THE RICHMOND REVIVAL

At the beginning of the twentieth century, Richmond, Virginia, became the center of rebellion against the literary and social conventions of the Victorian South. Richmond had long been a center of journalistic activity and book publishing, but until the works of Amélie Rives (Princess Troubetzkoy; 1863-1945), Mary Johnston (1870-1936), Ellen Glasgow (1873-1945), and James Branch Cabell (1879-1958) began to appear, the onetime capital of the Confederacy was associated with a romanticized version of the past. None of the writers of the Richmond Revival could be accused of having a nineteenth century sensibility. For example, although earlier writers would have been overly sentimental about a woman's obsession with her dead husband, in *The Quick or the Dead?* (1888), Rives approached her heroine with the detachment of a twentieth century psychologist. Rives's conclusion, that it is both unhealthy and impractical to be in love with loss, was not an idea that would have been advanced in a Victorian novel, much less in a Richmond drawing room. It has been suggested that the gothic ending of *The Quick or the Dead?* owes something to another Richmond writer, Edgar Allan Poe, but Rives's gothicism really anticipates that of William Faulkner and Flannery O'Connor.

Like Rives, Mary Johnston insisted on thinking for herself. Although she was sympathetic to the Confederacy, as is evident in her early novels, Johnston defied convention with *Hagar* (1913), a demand for women's suffrage; *The Witch* (1914), an attack on intolerance; and *Croatan* (1923), her version of what happened to the Lost Colony, which shows the settlers and the Native Americans retreating into the interior of the country, intermarrying, and establishing a utopian society.

Ellen Glasgow was also a feminist. Her southern heroines routinely rejected the protection of chivalric southern males and fled to New York City and freedom. Though, like Johnston, she was loyal to her own people, in her Civil War novel *The Battle-Ground* (1902) Glasgow opted for a realistic version of history. Instead of portraying all southern men as heroes and all Yankees as villains, as southern tradition dictated, Glasgow placed good and bad characters on each side.

Glasgow's friend James Branch Cabell shared her passion for honesty. *The Cords of Vanity* (1909) was a satirical novel intended to expose the hypocritical nature of Richmond society. In his later fiction, Cabell continued to attack pretense, which he saw as the basis of southern life. The title character in *Jurgen* (1919) was a typical Cabell protagonist, an unashamedly hypocritical southerner. Cabell himself was finally rewarded for his uncompromising honesty; after *Jurgen* was banned in New York because of its sexual content, the author became a popular success and an international celebrity.

THE SOUTHERN RENAISSANCE

Shortly after World War I, a group of faculty members and students at Vanderbilt University in Nashville, Tennessee, began publishing a magazine called *The Fugitive*, a literary and critical journal that focused on the South and on its traditions. Most of these "Fugitives," including Andrew Lytle (1902-1995), Allen Tate (1899-1979), and Robert Penn Warren (1905-1989), later became Agrarians, opposing the inroads of industrialism into the South and urging a return to an agricultural economy. Some Fugitives and Agrarians, among them Tate, Warren, and Cleanth Brooks (1906-1994), also spearheaded the movement known as New Criticism. They taught their students to examine texts closely, rather than merely looking at them from a biographical standpoint or assigning them a place in literary history.

While the Nashvilleans were all important figures in the Southern Renaissance (1920-1950), that movement had no single geographical center; rather, it encompassed the entire South. Andrew Lytle's connection with Tennessee went back for generations, but Warren was born in Kentucky, and his best-known novel, *All the King's Men* (1946), evolved out of his stay in Louisiana during the Huey Long governorate. Other natives of Kentucky were the poet Allen Tate, who wrote a Civil War novel, *The Fathers* (1938), and his first wife, the fiction writer Caroline Gordon (1895-1981).

Among the fiction writers of the Southern Renaissance were William Faulkner (1897-1962) and Eudora Welty (born 1909) of Mississippi; Thomas Wolfe (1900-1938) of North Carolina; Flannery O'Connor (1925-1964), Carson McCullers (1917-1967), and Erskine Caldwell (1903-1987) of Georgia; Peter Taylor (1917-1994) of Tennessee; and Katherine Anne Porter (1890-1980) of Texas. Probably the most famous African American writer of the period is Mississippi's Richard Wright (1908-1960), but James Weldon Johnson (1871-1938) and Zora Neale Hurston (1891-1960), both of whom were Floridians, are also important.

The writers of the Southern Renaissance resembled each other only in that they recognized a common heritage. In emphasis and outlook, they could be as different as Erskine Caldwell, who in *Tobacco Road* (1932) and *God's Little Acre* (1933) blamed society for the misery and moral degradation of his sharecroppers, and Flannery O'Connor, whose novels, like her short stories, revealed her commitment to the Christian faith. Each writer had a distinctive style as well. Wolfe's poetic prose was markedly different from the colloquial narratives and dialogues of Welty and Hurston.

WILLIAM FAULKNER AND SOUTHERN LITERATURE

William Faulkner's continuing preeminence among southern writers is due in part to his amazing scope. His novels recapitulate southern history, and the characters in his fictional Yoknatapawpha County are drawn from every social class and represent various ethnic and racial groups. Moreover, the moral dilemmas and spiritual uncertainties that trouble all of his characters, except for the ones who are incapable of reflection or are resolutely amoral, are those that must be faced not just by southerners, but by every human being.

Faulkner's stature in the international community was recognized formally in 1950, when he was awarded a Nobel Prize. Though his fiction has a universal appeal, however, it is profoundly southern. Faulkner was fascinated with families of all sorts: the Sutpens, the Compsons, the despicable Snopeses, and the poor, ignorant Bundrens, who in *As I Lay Dying* (1930) make a valiant effort to have a dead wife and mother properly buried. Faulkner liked to tell a good story, and he enjoyed comic exaggeration. Many of his accounts of the Snopeses' doings and his last novel, *The Reivers* (1962), are reminiscent of southwestern humor.

If Faulkner was sometimes nostalgic about the past, it was because, like Quentin Compson in *The Sound and the Fury* (1929), he saw such spiritual emptiness in the present. The contrast between the old world and the new is made explicit in the Civil War novel *The Unvanquished* (1938), in which the southerners try to live by a code of honor, while the Yankee invaders are merely rapacious. Faulkner knew that the southern distrust of outsiders and change was not just a long-lasting reaction to the Civil War and Reconstruction. As Isaac McCaslin pointed out in *Go Down, Moses* (1942), though the Old South was cursed by slavery and torn apart by racial prejudice, many southerners felt that the industrial, technological New South, with its gospel of greed, denied moral and spiritual values and might well end by destroying the natural world.

A CONTINUING RENAISSANCE

Although the Southern Renaissance is customarily described as lasting from 1920 to 1950, the continuing vitality of southern literature may prompt future literary historians to extend that second date at least to the end of the twentieth century. In the 1990's, at least seventy southern fiction writers appeared in almost every bibliographical listing, and new names were being added almost constantly.

Another sign of vitality is the fact that instead of imitating Faulkner in theme and content, as many critics had expected, later southern writers proved to be highly original. Madison Smartt Bell's dark historical novel *All Souls' Rising* (1995) could hardly be more different from Robert Morgan's gentle Appalachian love story *The Truest Pleasure* (1995), nor could the poor white people in the fiction of James Dickey, Bobbie Ann Mason, and Lewis Nordan have less in common with the upper-class Atlantans in Anne Rivers Siddons's *Peachtree Road* (1988). Moreover, instead of imitating Faulkner's convoluted style, southern writers invented or developed their own. William Styron's prose, for example, is complex but less elaborate than that of Faulkner, while Reynolds Price and Fred Chappell are known for classical simplicity, and Mason is considered minimalistic.

Though the common heritage is the basis of all southern literature, evident even in the works of writers who have left the South or abandoned southern settings, one cannot generalize as to how life is defined in southern fiction. A southern novel can be comic or tragic, Romantic or realistic, gothic or satirical. It can exhibit stark pessimism, alienation and uncertainty, or profound religious faith. Cormac McCarthy emphasizes human depravity, Walker Percy believes love can provide relief from the modern malaise, and Reynolds Price holds to his belief in divine grace and ultimate salvation.

The final decades of the twentieth century brought one very important change to southern literature: The southern experience was no longer the province of white males alone. New kinds of voices began to be heard—voices of African Americans, such as Margaret Walker, Ernest J. Gaines, Alice Walker, Bebe Moore Campbell, and Dori Sanders; voices of women, including Kaye Gibbons, Anne Tyler, Josephine Humphreys, Jill McCorkle, Jayne Anne Phillips, Lee Smith, and Mary Hood; and voices of gays and lesbians, such as Allan Gurganus and Rita Mae Brown. In the fiction of these authors, the essential elements of the southern heritage are still apparent; however, because they had experienced alienation in ways that their white, male, or heterosexual contemporaries had not, these writers saw the South quite differently and thus added new dimensions to an already rich literary tradition.

Rosemary M. Canfield Reisman

BIBLIOGRAPHY

Bassett, John E., ed. *Defining Southern Literature: Perspectives and Assessments, 1831-1952*. Madison, Wis.: Fairleigh Dickinson University Press, 1997. Selections arranged in chronological order reflect diverse views of the South and its literature.

Booker-Canfield, Suzanne. Introduction to *Contemporary Southern Men Fiction Writers: An Annotated Bibliography*, edited by Rosemary M. Canfield Reisman and Suzanne Booker-Canfield. Lanham, Md.: Scarecrow Press, 1998. In an introductory essay addressed to students and general readers, Booker-Canfield points out the salient characteristics of southern literature in the final decades of the twentieth century. An excellent starting point for the study of contemporary writers.

Brooks, Cleanth. *Community, Religion, and Literature: Essays*. Columbia: University of Missouri Press, 1995. Contains previously uncollected essays by this important New Critic, some about major southern writers, others on such topics as "The Crisis in Culture as Reflected in Southern Literature" and "The Past Alive in the Present."

Folks, Jeffrey J., and James A. Perkins, eds. *Southern Writers at Century's End*. Lexington: University Press of Kentucky, 1997. An attempt to survey southern writing during the final quarter of the twentieth century. In the section entitled "New Faces" are the popular but critically neglected James Lee Burke and John Grisham, as well as some relatively unknown novelists. Contains a foreword by James H. Justus, an introduction by the editors, bibliography, and index.

Inge, Tonette Bond, ed. *Southern Women Writers: The New Generation*. Tuscaloosa: University of Alabama Press, 1990. Includes essays about fifteen southern authors. In her introduction, Doris Betts points out how female authors redefined their art as they reevaluated their society.

Ketchin, Susan. *The Christ-Haunted Landscape: Faith and Doubt in Southern Fiction*. Jackson: University Press of Mississippi, 1994. An attempt to determine whether religion plays as important a role in the lives of southern writers as in the society at large. Each of twelve sections consists of an interview with a writer, a selection from his or her works, and Ketchin's comments.

Rubin, Louis D., Jr., ed. *The History of Southern Literature*. Baton Rouge: Louisiana State University Press, 1985. A good comprehensive study of southern literature. Contains critical analysis and valuable background information, bibliographical essay, and index.

Simpson, Lewis P. *The Fable of the Southern Writer*. Baton Rouge: Louisiana State University Press, 1994. One of many volumes by a major literary historian. Simpson believes that ever since the Civil War, the literary imagination has been a vehicle for self-examination.

THE WESTERN NOVEL

The "formula" Western genre is rooted in the fertile soil of nineteenth century popular American literature. Among its antecedents were the Leatherstocking Tales of James Fenimore Cooper, a series of five novels of the American frontier featuring a self-sufficient and morally incorruptible backwoods character named Natty Bumppo, who is considered America's first literary hero. Though Cooper was ultimately ambiguous about the meaning of the frontier in American life, he clearly demonstrated that frontier materials could sustain serious literary consideration and that the frontier's pristine beauty, the savagery of its conflicts, and its colorful inhabitants could have immense popular appeal.

Hard upon Cooper's heels came the House of Beadle and other dime-novel publishers, all ignoring the serious cultural questions that Cooper could at least identify, if not resolve. For the most part, the dime novels were cynically commercial in intention, with scant regard for all but the most lurid themes, episodes, and personalities in frontier history.

In addition, the Western was indebted to the "local-color" movement of the late nineteenth century, of which the works of Bret Harte are among the most familiar examples. Although the local colorists, by definition, failed to find in their materials matters of general cultural importance, they demonstrated the popular appeal and the literary validity of close attention to local and regional folkways, the distinctive personalities, dialect, and daily experience of common people, at times developing into the American tall tale.

OWEN WISTER AND ZANE GREY

Owen Wister (1860-1938), creator of the first genuine Western, *The Virginian: A Horseman of the Plains* (1902), is not the kind of person one would ordinarily think of as the author of cowboy novels. Born into a wealthy Philadelphia family, Wister received the best education his day could offer, culminating in a degree from Harvard. Culturally sophisticated, Wister enjoyed close friendships with Henry James, William Dean Howells, and Theodore Roose-velt, and his abilities as a pianist impressed even the aged Franz Liszt, for whom he played at Bayreuth. Talent and family connections, unfortunately, did not bring happiness: Unable to find a satisfying career in either the arts or the tawdry business world recommended by his father, Wister suffered a nervous breakdown in 1885, for which his doctor prescribed a recuperative trip to Wyoming. During this vacation on the cattle ranch of a family friend, he became impressed with the fictional potential of the American cowboy and began the literary experimentation that would lead to creation of the Western novel.

The Virginian was not the first appearance of the cowboy in American literature. The local colorist Alfred Henry Lewis, several dime novelists, Wister himself as early as 1891, and others had featured cowboy heroes in novels and stories. However, it was Wister's nameless Virginian who first provided just the right combination of colorful dress and speech, violent environment, and romantic potential to set the pattern for a new literary genre's success.

The critical novelist Henry James expressed admiration for *The Virginian*, and many readers with more simplistic preconceptions regarding Westerns are surprised at the sophistication of the novel. Although the novel is somewhat episodic because it grew in part from short stories, *The Virginian*'s two main plots—the corruption of Trampas from an honest cowhand to a rustler, which results in the lynching of the Virginian's friend Steve and Trampas's death at the Virginian's hands in the famous walkdown; and the Virginian's courtship of the eastern schoolmarm, Molly Wood—are complex and skillfully narrated. Critics have observed that, although a cowboy novel, *The Virginian* contains not a single scene in which cowboys actually work with cows, but such facile judgments do scant justice to the social and historical realism of the novel. The cowboy's dress, his language, his customs, his ethics, his humor, and the environmental imperatives within which he operates are carefully depicted and assessed.

Wister's literary output was not great, for he was not a prolific writer, and the West was only one of his concerns. Moreover, *The Virginian* is marred by much of the same confusion over the meaning of the West that had haunted Cooper: How can one relate the morally innocent—yet savage and violent—tenor of Western life to the culturally sophisticated, yet corrupt, East? The marriage of the Virginian and Molly indicates some sort of cultural accommodation, but in his final collection of Western stories, *When West Was West* (1928), Wister concludes that no such accommodation is possible.

As important as *The Virginian* was in the creation of the Western, no single work can create a genre, and it remained for Wister's innumerable successors and imitators to develop, out of the materials provided by *The Virginian*, the Western formula. By far the most prominent of Wister's early successors was Zane Grey (1872-1939). Grey's family had figured with some significance in the history of the Ohio River frontier, and he was reared on tales of ancestral exploits to compensate for the painful reality of the family's more recent decline from wealth and influence. Like Wister, Grey was unable to adjust idealistic youthful dreams and aspirations to the realistic necessities of earning a living. After undistinguished completion of a dental course at the University of Pennsylvania, Grey attempted to open a dental practice in New York City. He soon abandoned dentistry in favor of writing, but his early efforts, a trilogy recounting the exploits of his pioneer ancestors, sold poorly.

After a summer in Arizona and Utah in 1906, Grey discovered characters, settings, and themes that he was confident he could turn into literature, and his first Western, *The Heritage of the Desert* (1910), a story of Mormons, rustlers, and the rejuvenative, indeed redemptive, qualities of the West, sold well enough to encourage him. Grey's phenomenal literary success began in 1912 with the publication of *Riders of the Purple Sage*, surely the most famous Western ever written. In that novel, Grey introduces a black-clad gunfighter hero, Lassiter, whose bloody encounters with the Mormons in the dramatic canyonlands of southern Utah established important literary precedents. Grey exhibited, in that and in many later novels, a much greater debt to the dime novels

than did Wister: There is much less subtlety in Grey's violent scenes, much less complexity in his characters' emotions and motives, and much less restraint in his descriptions of setting.

Nevertheless, Grey shared with Wister an unfeigned love for the West and its history and culture, and he took pains to try to portray it realistically. Grey chose a wide variety of western settings for his novels and an even wider variety of character types, including ethnic minorities that had interested few other authors. Furthermore, he invested his books with a philosophical burden often missing in popular writing: The West alone, in his view, offered free scope for development of complete human beings, including those primitive virtues and self-reliant skills that the overcivilization of the East had submerged.

Most of Grey's best work appeared during the decade between *Riders of the Purple Sage* and *Under the Tonto Rim* (1926). Thereafter (and occasionally during that decade as well), the urgency of his message, the originality of his characters, and the carefulness of his descriptions are much less poignant. Much of Grey's unevenness probably results from the sheer quantity of his work. During a career of some thirty years, Grey wrote nearly one hundred novels and stories and dozens of magazine articles.

Even at that, Grey's output is dwarfed by the production of perhaps the most prolific creator of Western literature since the dime novelists, a would-be epic poet named Frederick Schiller Faust (1892-1944), who supported both his literary aspirations and his sybaritic life in an Italian villa by producing more than six hundred Western novels and stories under some twenty pseudonyms, the best known of which was Max Brand. Though Faust, who was reared in California, knew the West well, there is little of the actual West in his books; he preferred instead to borrow his plots from the Greek and Roman classics, garbing Oedipus and Agamemnon in chaps and six-guns but cynically dismissing his Western works as "cowboy junk."

It is tempting to take Faust's cynicism at face value and disdain to consider seriously his Western works. However, in spite of his scornful attitude and rapid composition (during one thirteen-week period in 1920, he turned out 190,000 publishable words), Faust wrote some fine novels. *The Untamed* (1919), his first Western novel, features a memorable hero, Dan Barry, who lives an isolated, wild life in the desert, tames a wild horse and a wolf, and holds out against making an accommodation with civilization. *Destry Rides Again* (1930), later made into a popular motion picture, is a revenge story recounting the way a framed man gets even with the jury members. Unlike Grey's Lassiter, Harry Destry prevails more through guile and cleverness than through violence.

Faust's work, then, represents a considerable retreat from the realism of Wister and Grey, demonstrating that good novels need only be believable, not necessarily authentic. The career of Clarence Edward Mulford (1883-1956) followed Faust's in that respect and also called to mind the dime-novel tradition in his love of violence. Reared in Illinois, Mulford was working in a minor civil service position in Brooklyn when he began to write Westerns, but he did not visit the West until eighteen years after beginning to write about it. He was unimpressed and discovered that western reality interfered with his imaginary conception of the West, so he never again left his eastern home. His first Western, *Bar-20* (1907), and many thereafter featured an actual working cowboy named Hopalong Cassidy, whose proletarian speech and bloodthirsty love for fighting made him a far cry from the character of the same name played on film by William Boyd.

Bertha M. Bower (1871-1940), by contrast, was as deeply rooted as a cottonwood tree in the real West. One of her four husbands, Clayton Bower, was a Montana cattleman, and she spent her entire life in the region about which she wrote. In *Chip, of the Flying U* (1906), which was illustrated by her friend, the cowboy artist Charles M. Russell, Bower established her trademark, the unglamorous cowboy character. Though Chip himself is extraordinary—he occasionally quotes William Shakespeare, and he is a gifted, untutored artist—Bower chose to make literature out of the smaller human dramas that occurred in the cowboy's daily work routine, forgoing any great universal truth.

ERNEST HAYCOX AND LOUIS L'AMOUR

Ernest Haycox (1899-1950), whom many critics consider the finest literary craftsman to emerge from the popular Western tradition, was one of a younger generation of writers who became popular during the heyday of Western fiction, 1930 to 1950. Like many of the older writers, he completed his apprenticeship in the pulp magazines, writing fast-moving Western romances with shallow characters and plenty of action. Like Faust, Haycox had serious literary aspirations, but unlike Faust, he wished to realize those aspirations through the use of Western materials. In several mature novels toward the end of his career, beginning with *Bugles in the Afternoon* (1944) and culminating in his posthumously published masterpiece, *The Earthbreakers* (1952), Haycox demonstrated the resilience of the Western formula.

Bugles in the Afternoon, a fictional account of General George Custer's Seventh Cavalry and the events leading up to its annihilation at the Battle of the Little Big Horn, is marred for many contemporary readers by its unabashed love for the military life. In spite of that, its main theme, how much the individual owes to the group, is extensively explored, and the depth of its realism, as seen in Haycox's poignant descriptions of bleak North Dakota towns and of the Seventh Cavalry soldiers and their equipment, is memorable.

Haycox was born, reared, and educated in Oregon, and it was of Oregon, with its mouldy, misty forests, succulent soils, and salty, windy estuary towns that he wrote most effectively. The three great novels of Haycox's maturity, *Long Storm* (1946), *The Adventurers* (1954), and *The Earthbreakers*, are all set in Oregon's lower Willamette Valley. The main theme of each of the novels is the endurance and gradual victory of idealism over forces of savagery and cynicism. The great peril of such a theme is sentimentalism, and one must acknowledge that Haycox is occasionally ensnared by it, particularly in the two earlier novels. Haycox, like Grey, never learned to make sin attractive enough to make victories over it appear genuine; his villains, such as the Southern sympathizer Floyd Ringrose in *Long Storm*, who clumsily tries to subvert Oregon's strong Union commitment during the Civil War, are too often melodramatic caricatures. Ringrose abuses women and children, drinks too much, brags ridiculously, conspires ineptly, and fights poorly.

At his best, though, Haycox escapes the perils of sentimentalism. In *The Earthbreakers*, he places his hero, an ex-mountain man named Rice Burnett who has chosen to guide a wagon train to the Willamette Valley where he will stay and settle, in the midst of several characters representing various degrees of commitment to civilization and forces him to make genuine, often painful, choices concerning with whom and to what degree he will ally himself. Burnett has a yearning for civilization, though his love for the wild, free life of a trapper will not die easily or completely; still, defining what that civilization is, among the various choices available, is no easy matter. Burnett is an appealing hero, but he is a far cry from the superhuman gunslingers of much popular Western fiction and even from the overly idealistic characters of Haycox's earlier books.

Haycox's craftsmanship had a profound influence on popular Western literature. In 1952, a group of novelists, many of them Haycox disciples, founded the Western Writers of America (WWA). The WWA, which has grown steadily in size and sophistication, began publishing *The Roundup*, a monthly magazine with news, reviews, and articles on writing and the publishing business. The association also began making awards at each annual meeting for the best writing of the previous year in several categories of Western writing. The effect of the organization has been to establish higher literary standards and assist aspiring writers in meeting those standards.

Although Haycox's influence on younger writers was undeniable, none of his direct disciples or imitators climbed to the master's level. One of his leading competitors in sales, if not in literary quality, was Frederick Dilley Glidden (1908-1975), who wrote under the name of the Kansas gunfighter Luke Short. If many journalists are frustrated novelists, Glidden the novelist was a frustrated journalist. Born in Illinois, he graduated with a journalism degree from the University of Missouri. Though Glidden worked in various locations for brief periods on newspapers, the

onset of the Great Depression cost him one job after another. Finally, in 1935, he began writing Westerns to support himself.

Like many writers of Westerns, Glidden was capable of massive production: During the 1940's alone, he wrote fourteen novels. His success enabled him to move to Aspen, Colorado, where he spent most of the rest of his life. At about that time, he began to lose interest in Western writing; during the 1950's, he wrote only six novels and began trying, with little success, to break into other genres.

Glidden admired Haycox and successfully competed with him for a time in the high-paying "slick" magazines such as *Collier's*; in literary quality, however, he was no match for Haycox. In fact, most of his novels could be regarded as throwbacks to the pre-Haycox days when characterization and setting were not as important as action. Unlike most literary chroniclers of the masculine world of the frontier, Glidden knew how to develop convincing heroines. Both *Hard Money* (1940) and *Paper Sheriff* (1966), perhaps his best novel, feature at least one believably complex female character.

Undoubtedly the best-known modern Western writer is Louis L'Amour (1908-1988). From the age of fifteen, when he left his North Dakota home to ease the financial burden on his family, L'Amour lived a colorful life not unworthy of some of his characters. His travels throughout the country working at a multitude of occupations inspired him with a clear vision of the diversity of American culture and the sturdy masculine virtues required to settle the American continent. L'Amour began writing for magazines during the 1930's. Soon he conceived a plan for a massive fictional saga of the westward movement based on the stories of three families: the Sacketts, the Talons, and the Chantrys. Even with 101 books at the time of his death, not all of which were part of the saga, the project remained incomplete.

On the covers of his books and in his frequent television appearances, L'Amour was much more interested in discussing Western history than writing techniques and literary theory. He was convinced that his strongest suit as a writer was the authenticity of his novels, some of which even contain historical footnotes. Critics have argued that L'Amour confused authenticity with believability and that, like the works of Zane Grey, his novels often suffer from their heavy burden of undigested historical data.

L'Amour's *Hondo* (1953) expresses the opinion, well in advance of the current ecological movement, that humans are responsible for the use they make of their natural environment. Perhaps even more prevalent in L'Amour's fiction is the disillusioned, hard-bitten hero for whom survival is the only goal: *Shalako* (1962) is a notable example. Such novels were only the beginning of vast changes in values in the Western literature of the 1960's and 1970's, which paralleled changes in American culture as a whole. Several publishers widened the chink opened by Doubleday's Double-D Western series, which featured, to the astonishment of readers of traditional Westerns, graphic descriptions of sex and violence and other formerly taboo material. Perhaps it is appropriate that the lead in establishing the subgenre of the "sex Western" was taken by Playboy Press. With its series written by staff writers under the collective name of Jake Logan, Playboy introduced graphic and lengthy sex scenes alongside more traditional Western elements. The trend caught on; as the Jake Logan series grew, other series, such as the Longarm series published by Jove Publications, appeared. One can choose among several such series, each boasting several dozen titles. The assembly-line nature of those series, incidentally, is revealed in their packaging by number as much as by title. During its burgeoning years, the sex Western was a controversial issue: Much of *The Roundup* during 1982 was taken up by a heated debate regarding the validity of the sex Western, many writers haughtily disdaining its economic temptations. In response to the unprecedented openness of sexual discussion and expression in American life, often to the point of unabashed hedonism, the sex Western seems to have attained a solid place in the Western literary canon.

Equally noteworthy is the rise of the "violence Western," the leading proponent of which is an Englishman named Terry Harknett, creator of the Edge series under the name George Gilman. The depiction of extreme violence in Westerns clearly parallels larger cultural developments, yet the Edge series and the novels of another Englishman, J. T. Edson, are often revolting by any standard. Gilman's *The Living, the Dying and the Dead* (1978), for example, after an assortment of shootings, stabbings, dismemberments, and disfigurements, culminates with a scene in which the rotting corpse of a dead prostitute is dissected.

Fortunately, not all trends in popular Western literature pandered to the most ignoble human instincts. Stephen D. Overholser's Molly series, for example, attempts to reach those touched by the call for greater freedom and equality for women. The series contains sex, which the author says he tries to make a plausible and integral part of the story, but it also recounts the activities of an independent, resourceful woman on the frontier.

LARRY MCMURTRY AND CORMAC MCCARTHY

To some extent the Western novel has come into its own with its acceptance in the realm of real literature. Perhaps no contemporary writer of importance is more directly associated with the Western novel than Larry McMurtry. Born in 1936 in Wichita Falls, Texas, McMurtry earned degrees from North Texas State University and Rice University and did graduate work at Stanford University as a Wallace Stegner Fellow. He entered the teaching profession as creative writing teacher at Rice University but eventually turned to writing on as full-time a basis as possible, residing in such diverse areas as Virginia, California, and Arizona before returning to his native Texas and settling in rural Archer City in 1986.

Although his earlier works, including *Horseman, Pass By* (1961; better known to many by the title of its film adaptation, *Hud*), *The Last Picture Show* (1966), and *Terms of Endearment* (1975), brought consistent, favorable attention to McMurtry and his work, it was not until *Lonesome Dove* (1985), which won the 1986 Pulitzer Prize, that McMurtry's fame moved into many diverse areas. The film versions of these works brought even more attention and acclaim to McMurtry.

Thematically, one can pigeonhole each of McMurtry's works into any one of four major concepts: initiation of the young man, the negative effect of modern civilization, a strong need to belong to a particular place, and the durability of the western American myth. For instance, in *Horseman, Pass By*, the first novel in his Thalia trilogy, McMurtry places two value systems into conflict, much like James Fenimore Cooper does in his Leatherstocking novels. Homer Bannon represents the old values based upon belonging to the land and hard work, while his stepson Hud represents the change to a get-all-you-can-as-soon-as-you-can attitude that had engulfed much of the younger population of the West as it had the remainder of the country.

Leaving Cheyenne (1963) and *The Last Picture Show*, the concluding two parts of the Thalia trilogy, continue to portray the deteriorating life in the small-town West. In each, the reader is constantly told that the modern West must come to terms with changing times that often do not permit values long a part of western lore to go unchallenged, most often shown in these three novels by the life-changing decisions that young characters must make.

Although McMurtry's earlier works deal almost entirely with the modern American West, he turned a new artistic corner in 1985 with the publication of *Lonesome Dove*, the first installment of the adventures of aging Texas Rangers Woodrow Call and Augustus McCrae. These two western archetype characters continue McMurtry's depiction of diametric opposites: Call fails to express any degree of emotion, and McCrae lives with his emotions just below the surface. After the work earned the Pulitzer Prize and spawned a successful television miniseries, McMurtry published such books as *Texasville* (1987), *Buffalo Girls* (1990), *The Evening Star* (1992), *Streets of Laredo* (1993), *Dead Man's Walk* (1995), and *Comanche Moon* (1997), among others. From the beginning of his career, McMurtry has fulfilled his reading audience's need for further installments of the continuing saga of America's mythical West. Although the names may change and situations may undergo major alterations, the story of the West looms large in the American imagination. The changes that McMurtry's characters undergo mirror the changes that America, itself, has undergone.

Another writer who tries to tell a portion of the West's story is Cormac McCarthy (born 1933). Like Owen Wister, McCarthy was not born in the West, and his writing career did not begin with novels about the western United States. McCarthy was born in Rhode Island but moved with his family to Knoxville, Tennessee, in 1947 so that the father could accept a position as an engineer. McCarthy attended Knoxville's Catholic High School, graduating in 1951. He then entered the University of Tennessee but left in 1952. McCarthy entered the United States Air Force, after which he returned to Knoxville to pick up on the writing career of which he had dreamed.

McCarthy's early fiction was replete with the violence and the grotesque that ensconced him in the world of modern gothic writers. However, in 1992 McCarthy moved to another realm of fiction when he produced the first installment of his Border trilogy. Although the locale changed from the American South to the American West, McCarthy continued to incorporate the violent and the strange into his fiction. The works of which McCarthy's Border trilogy consists, *All the Pretty Horses* (1992), *The Crossing* (1994), and *Cities of the Plain* (1998), continue the saga of the modern American West but with a McCarthy slant.

These three novels allow the reader to witness the initiation of two young cowboys, John Grady Cole in *All the Pretty Horses*, Billy Parham in *The Crossing*, and both in *Cities of the Plain*. As happened in many earlier Western novels, McCarthy's protagonists are thrown into situations that challenge all that they have been taught. The lesson that each learns is that the evil against which people must fight is most often found within themselves, echoing the quintessential American tragic hero, Captain Ahab of Melville's *Moby Dick* (1851). They find that under the right circumstances they are able to kill other human beings with only minimal remorse, a lesson reminiscent of Natty Bumppo in Cooper's Leatherstocking novels. Cole and Parham are often forced to realize that they cannot meet their quests and that they must salvage whatever remains of their lives when their attempts are thwarted. In this manner, McCarthy contributes to moving Western novels further into the realm of realism and, to some extent, experimentalism through his less-than-positive endings and his use of the gothic techniques that characterized his earlier fiction about Knoxville and eastern Tennessee.

One of the most significant developments in popular Western literature during the 1970's, 1980's, and 1990's was the increasing acceptance of the Western among literary critics and intellectual historians as an object of serious study. Some of this is certainly a result of the general democratization of American life after the 1960's and the rise of New Left historiography, with its emphasis on the life of common people. One may view this trend most graphically, perhaps, by comparing the two editions, ten years apart, of Richard W. Etulain's bibliography of Western literary studies. In *Western American Literature: A Bibliography of Interpretive Books and Articles* (1972), the entries on even such famous popular writers as Zane Grey often included some fairly flawed and fugitive articles and reviews, and even those appeared in limited numbers. By the time his *Bibliographical Guide to the Study of Western American Literature* appeared in 1982, Etulain could choose from a fertile field of books and articles from major presses and journals, and in much greater quantities than the previous decade. Etulain's book and Fred Erisman's *Fifty Western Writers: A Bio-Bibliographical Sourcebook* (1982) featured essays on Zane Grey, Luke Short, and Louis L'Amour alongside the likes of Frank Waters, John Steinbeck, and Jack London. The massive *Literary History of the American West*, sponsored in 1987 by the Western Literary Association, gave ample space to the development of the popular Western. Finally, the WWA began to take a more searching look at their craft through substantive articles in their revamped journal, *The Roundup*. Before 1988 *The Roundup* was little more than a trade journal that appeared ten times each year. Beginning in September of 1988, it changed to a much larger and intellectually substantial quarterly format.

The popular Western, then, gives every sign of remaining a living part of American literary legacy. Far from becoming ossified in outworn romantic horse opera clichés, the Western remains largely abreast with ongoing developments in the culture at large, while keeping in touch with important elements in American history and traditional values.

Gary Topping, updated by Tom Frazier

BIBLIOGRAPHY

Braun, Matt. *How to Write Western Novels.* Cincinnati: Writer's Digest Books, 1988. This work fits well into any study of the history of the Western novel. Braun, a Western novelist himself, discusses the different formulas utilized in creating the various types of fiction gathered under the umbrella title of Western fiction.

Brown, Bill. *Reading the West: An Anthology of Dime Novels.* New York: Bedford, 1997. Probably the most readily available introduction to the dime novel. However, it is the extensive introduction to the dime novel that is most important to any student. The works themselves merely put everything into perspective.

Busby, Mark. *Larry McMurtry and the West: An Ambivalent Relationship.* Denton: University of North Texas Press, 1955. This work demonstrates how a writer must come to terms with the foundation of his subject matter.

Simonson, Harold P. *Beyond the Frontier: Writers, Western Regionalism, and a Sense of Place.* Fort Worth: Texas Christian University Press, 1989. Simonson delves into the myth of the West and how it is presented in the fiction of the American West.

Sonnichsen, C. L. *From Hopalong to Hud: Thoughts on Western Fiction.* College Station: Texas A&M University Press, 1978. Sonnichsen places the development of the Western fiction genre into perspective with the development of the myth of the American West.

GENRE
OVERVIEWS

THE *BILDUNGSROMAN*

Who has not been told that one learns more about oneself from failures than from successes? Is there a more reliable theme to draw readers than success following chronic failure? Literature's undying story line is the determined progress of an unlikely hero against the odds.

Traditional fiction has no more crucial mandate than that by the end the protagonist exhibit major change: Proud Oedipus the king becomes blind Oedipus the exile. Although audiences in the golden age of Greek drama may have undergone catharsis in witnessing Sophocles' play concerning the tragic hero Oedipus's recognition of the losing hand that fate has dealt him, the audience may sometimes wish that even tragic destiny might just once be foiled. We are more receptive to a hero like Joseph Conrad's Lord Jim, who seizes the main chance and is redeemed, than to Thomas Hardy's Jude, who gives in to an indifferent universe.

Everyone begins in the infantlike state portrayed by James Joyce in the opening lines of *A Portrait of the Artist as a Young Man* (1914-1915), proceeds as uncertainly as Ernest Hemingway's returning soldier in "Big Two-Hearted River," faces life-changing decisions like the heroines in Kate Chopin's stories, and ends as knowing as Theodore Dreiser's Carrie or as defeated as James T. Farrell's Studs Lonigan. The universal story is what happens when innocence confronts forces, human or cosmic, that are not innocent. For the playing out of that progress, literature has found an eighteenth century German word, *Bildungsroman*, that has transcended italics and become international.

ORIGIN OF THE *BILDUNGSROMAN*

It is far more difficult to locate the source of the *Bildungsroman*—a term combining the German words *Bildung*, personal growth, with *roman*, novel—than it is to credit the book that is its exemplar. The *Encyclopedia of German Literary History* claims that the philosopher and literary historian Wilhelm Dilthey famously defined the term in an analysis in 1870 of Johann Wolfgang von Goethe's *Wilhelm Meisters*

Lehrjahre (1795-1796, 4 vols.; *Wilhelm Meister's Apprenticeship*, 1825), almost eighty years after the publication of Goethe's masterpiece. In the *Bildungsroman*, Dilthey wrote,

> [a] regulated development within the life of the individual is observed, each of its stages has its own intrinsic value and is at the same time the basis for a higher stage. The dissonances and conflicts of life appear as the necessary growth points through which the individual must pass on his way to maturity and harmony.

In 1942, in his comprehensive *English Novel in Transition, 1885-1940*, William Frierson applied the terms "life-novel" and "spiritual autobiography" to many of the novels that can be categorized as *Bildungsromane*. As if unwilling to get bogged down by the Germanic *Bildungsroman* and its cognates, Frierson never mentions the word or the novel by Goethe that exemplifies it. Other scholars prefer "education novel" or "apprentice novel." Thousands of novels—from Samuel Richardson's *Pamela: Or, Virtue Rewarded* (1740-1741) to J. D. Salinger's *The Catcher in the Rye* (1951), from Henry Fielding's *The History of Tom Jones, a Foundling* (1749) to F. Scott Fitzgerald's *The Great Gatsby* (1925)—could lay claim, if barely, to being chronicles of passage. This survey discusses only a select few that both follow Dilthey's lead and meet the main criterion for any classic—endurance—concentrating on landmark works, most of them originally written in English. American literature is notable for writers whose oeuvres—career-long or in a sequence—have moved from innocence to experience but whose heroes, especially in contemporary novels (notably those of John Updike), are unchanging.

In the closing third of the twentieth century, the *Bildungsroman* was given new vitality by novels dramatizing alternative patterns, especially women's strivings toward commensurate status with men. The feminist *Bildungsroman*, given scant attention earlier, has become a major force in the revival of the form.

WILHELM MEISTER'S APPRENTICESHIP

The paragon for the nineteenth century novel of education was Johann Wolfgang von Goethe's *Wilhelm Meisters Lehrjahre* (1795-1796, 4 vols.), translated by Thomas Carlyle as *Wilhelm Meister's Apprenticeship* (1825), published as a reworking of *Wilhelm Meisters theatralische Sedung* (or mission), of which only a fragment survives. The earlier work introduces a hero whose object is to seek self-realization in the service of art: As actor and later manager of a stage company, he will make the German theater a primary agent of cultural change. In *Wilhelm Meister's Apprenticeship*, this aim must compete with many other intentions and values.

Scattered throughout are many details and impressions adapted from Goethe's own experience: a childhood delight in puppets, the tension between visionary son and hard-headed practical father, efforts at amateur acting and firsthand observations of the vagaries of fellow-players, responses to the esoteric rituals of freemasonry, even Wilhelm's lovesick wandering of the streets. In most scenes Wilhelm appears, sometimes as protagonist, more often as spectator or auditor, a young man whom Goethe viewed with marked ambivalence. Wilhelm's involvement with the theater makes possible an exploration and broadening of his personality. It offers him an adventurous life, a chance to broaden the self by accepting various roles, but it is life without direction. Following "Confessions," which closes the first half, Wilhelm gradually quits the theater for new rites, literal and figurative: those of passage and those of the secret Society of the Tower. Characteristically for the *Bildungsroman*, entry is achieved only after many missteps.

THE NINETEENTH CENTURY ENGLISH BILDUNGSROMAN

William Makepeace Thackeray's *The History of Pendennis: His Fortunes and Misfortunes, His Friends and His Greatest Enemy* (1848-1850) is called by Thackeray's biographer Gordon N. Ray "the first true *Bildungsroman* in English fiction." Jerome Buckley rejects it as too conventional, perhaps because its hero comes to maturity more by accident than by design.

George Meredith's major *Bildungsromane* derive from Charles Dickens, whom he dismissed as "a caricaturist who aped the moralist." Still, as Buckley avers, the later Victorian was indebted to the earlier, especially in *The Adventures of Harry Richmond* (1871) and in *The Ordeal of Richard Feverel* (1859). The method of narration and even the plotting of *The Adventures of Harry Richmond* recall Dickens's character David Copperfield, and the theme, the shattering of false illusions, resembles that of *Great Expectations* (1860-1861). The frequent caricatures in *The Ordeal of Richard Feverel* are suggestive, according to Buckley, of "Dickensian shorthand."

Dorothea Brooke's two marriages in George Eliot's *Middlemarch* (1871-1872) symbolize a journey from naïve impressionability to practical wisdom and humane sympathy. Samuel Butler's *The Way of All Flesh* (1903) is the most directly autobiographical *Bildungsroman* in English before D. H. Lawrence's *Sons and Lovers* (1913) and James Joyce's *A Portrait of the Artist as a Young Man* (1914-1915). *The Way of All Flesh* remains, in Buckley's view, a "scientific" *Bildungsroman*. Overloaded by digressions—its author's hatred of the middle-class evangelism in which he had been brought up and his disavowal of Charles Darwin's evolutionary theories, which were rampant during the 1870's, when he wrote the novel—*The Way of All Flesh* has gone virtually unread since World War II. The theme of Ernest Pontifex's childhood (the book's main link to the *Bildungsroman*) is not developed with any dramatic immediacy. In Thomas Hardy's *Jude the Obscure* (1895), Jude Fawley's life appears to have been doomed from the day of his birth. As the protagonist of a novel of education, Jude pays much attention to the hero's private study and none to formal schooling. A university education, however, is his great objective. The lure of learning fights an unequal battle with the appeals of sex as embodied in Arabella, the swine girl, who swats Jude with a pig's bladder at their meeting—an obvious symbol of the dismantling of Jude's illusions. Sue Bridehead, a truly interesting woman, becomes his mistress and mentor, but he buckles under her teaching.

Because it affirms the classic *Bildungsroman*,

Dickens's *Great Expectations* bears a closer look than any of the novels previously mentioned. The story of Pip falls into three phases that clearly display a progression. The reader first sees the boy in his natural condition in the country, responding and being instinctively virtuous. The second stage involves a negation of childlike simplicity; Pip acquires his "expectations," renounces his origins, and moves to the city. He rises in society, but because he acts through calculation rather than instinctive charity, his moral values deteriorate as his social graces improve. This middle phase culminates in a sudden fall, the beginning of a redemptive suffering that is dramatically concluded by an attack of brain fever leading to a long coma. Pip rises from it regenerate. In the final stage of growth he returns to his birthplace, abandons his false expectations, and achieves a partial synthesis of the virtue of his innocent youth. Critic G. Robert Strange views *Great Expectations* as a moral fable in the tradition of stories of education. Like Stendhal's Julien Sorel and Honoré de Balzac's Eugène de Rastignac, Pip belongs in the nineteenth century gallery of children of the century.

THE LATER ENGLISH *BILDUNGSROMAN*

In 1948, literary critic and historian Mark Schorer wrote a famous essay, "Technique as Discovery," in which he declared that literary technique is nearly everything:

> [It is] the means by which the writer's experience, which is his subject matter, compels him to attend to it; technique is the only means he has of discovering, exploring, developing his subject, of conveying its meaning, and, finally, of evaluating it.

Without explicitly citing it as the high point in English of the *Bildungsroman*, Schorer extols James Joyce's *A Portrait of the Artist as a Young Man* as the crowning fictional study of passage in an especially rich period, the first quarter of the twentieth century. There is another reason to apply Schorer's strictures in the present context: He not only sets up Joyce's work as a classic in the *Bildungsroman* tradition but also creates a literary rogues' gallery from other famous *Bildungsromane*, including H. G. Wells's *Tono-*

Bungay (1908), D. H. Lawrence's *Sons and Lovers* (1913), Thomas Wolfe's *Of Time and the River* (1935), and James T. Farrell's *Studs Lonigan* trilogy (1935).

As the *Bildungsroman*'s poet, James Joyce in *A Portrait of the Artist as a Young Man* made the intuited destiny of Stephen Dedalus an attainment nonpareil. He utilized the subliminal so convincingly that it rendered the intrusive author in the long biographical novels of Goethe, Dickens, and Stendhal unnecessary. No writers of *Bildungsromane* until Joyce had succeeded in making narrative serve theme contrapuntally. As a famous essay by poet and critic Hugh Kenner puts it:

> Each of the [five] chapters begins with a multitude of warring impressions, and each develops toward an emotionally apprehended unity; each succeeding chapter liquidates the previous synthesis and subjects its elements to more adult scrutiny in a constantly enlarging field of perception, and develops toward its own synthesis and affirmation.

Joyce presents a variety of styles, each appropriate to the movement of Stephen from childhood through boyhood into maturity. Flow of consciousness delineates the mind of the child not yet amenable to selection or judgment. Evocation of the world of sensual and bodily detail is rendered by internal and external emotional bursts—moments rescued from flux that Joyce called epiphanies—that mark Stephen's rejection of domestic and religious values. Gradually Joyce conveys the intellectually assured Dedalus by dialectic as he asserts to himself his soul's call to be a poet.

OTHER ENGLISH *BILDUNGSROMANE*

Working from opposite directions, fiction's two principal figures in modernism between the two world wars were James Joyce and D. H. Lawrence. The former, as noted, internalized fiction by evoking consciousness. The latter, who pioneered few technical innovations, broke down any notion that ego was stable. Books such as Lawrence's *Sons and Lovers* (1913), *The Rainbow* (1915), and *Women in Love* (1920) blurred the usual partitions between and within genders and installed the primitive and savage emotions of "blood" over civilization's crippling decrees of "mind."

Neither the voluntarily exiled, hard-drinking Dubliner nor the Midlands coal miner's son who in his brief span would roam the world in a vain search for transcendence had anything good to say about the other. When *Lady Chatterley's Lover* (1928) began to vie with *Ulysses* (1922) as a book for tourists in Paris, the nearly blind Joyce asked a friend to read to him from it. He listened carefully, then pronounced only one word: "Lush!" To Lawrence's puritan mind, *Ulysses* was a "dirty" book, a reduction of Sex (uppercase)—to him an icon in the merging of consciousnesses— to sex (lowercase)—a mechanical act for prurient readers.

A more fruitful pairing links Lawrence's *Sons and Lovers* with W. Somerset Maugham's *Of Human Bondage* (1915). In their sexual *Bildungsromane*, the introspective hero the reader met in Joyce's *Künstlerroman*, the artist-protagonist, gives way to lovers under siege. Paul Morel and Philip Carey spoke with candor to beleaguered young men everywhere. Lawrence's *Bildungsromane* provided what Patricia Alden calls "the basis for a new, classless elite of the initiate [in which] sexual relationships recapitulate the fundamental conflict between bourgeois individualism and working-class communalism." More simply, his novels always turn on crucial "splits." In *Sons and Lovers*, the conflict between Paul and his mother Gertrude vies with the conflict between kinds of love, physical and spiritual, which draw the son away and are represented by two young women, Miriam and Clara.

Critic V. S. Pritchett, whose short stories and autobiography celebrate his own emergence from late-Victorian squalor, demonstrates in a memorable essay how *Sons and Lovers* bears the defects of its virtues. Galvanic as he is in revealing Paul's drift into spiritual quandary, Lawrence "cheats" too: He almost entirely omits the story of Paul's education, his early teaching, and his gradual separation from the mining village of his birth. Patricia Alden agrees with Pritchett. For her, Lawrence isolates Paul's drive to become an individual from any social context. The story of how Lawrence left the Midlands becomes the story of how Paul leaves his mother; he is seen as the passive victim of three women who embody unmet social ambitions they seek to realize through him.

Joyce and Lawrence represent contrasting traditions with regard to the relationship in literary art between the creator and the created. Joyce, like Henry James and Gustave Flaubert, held that the artist must remain detached from life, producing narratives of experience somehow finished, exhausted, controllable, and manipulable. Lawrence confessed "one sheds one's sicknesses in books, repeats and repeats again one's emotions—to be master of them." Lawrence lives his experiences in the process of writing about them. Both Joycean and Lawrencean traditions have served *Bildungsromane* well.

As a study of a youth's search for meaning and truth in a world of cruelty and deceit, *Of Human Bondage* stands apart from the remainder of Maugham's works. No one is spared, least of all its hero, Philip Carey. In a variation on Lawrence's confession that the writer "sheds his sicknesses" in books, Maugham said he wrote *Of Human Bondage* to rid himself of his obsessions.

Although written in characteristically spare prose, in contrast to the tropes of Joyce, *Of Human Bondage* joins *A Portrait of the Artist as a Young Man* in conveying the hero's life in stages. However, unlike the decisive Stephen, Philip matures in agonizing waltztime, his steps advancing and retreating methodically. His ambivalence mirrors the way of troubled innocence.

Maugham titled the 1915 published version of his novel after the name of the fourth book of seventeenth century philosopher Baruch Spinoza's *Ethica*, 1677 (*Ethics*, 1870): "Of Human Bondage: Or, Of the Strengths of the Affects"—whose preface glosses perfectly the novel's theme:

> The impotence of man to govern or restrain the affects
> I call Bondage, for a man who is under their control is
> not his own master, but is mastered by fortune . . . so
> that he is forced to follow the worst, although he sees
> the better before him.

Philip Carey's *Bildung*, or apprenticeship, can best be told as a series of releases whose permanency depends on his being able to understand a riddle. Critic Forrest Burt notes that the author's placement of the puzzle at the heart of the novel reflects the aging Maugham's "greatest drive," namely, to reshape his life into a pattern that would enable him to overcome a lifelong stammer, a desperate childhood, and rejection by an actress named Sue Jones, daughter of the playwright Henry Arthur Jones. Philip, following the lead of his creator, must free himself from a clubfoot, social restrictions, religious and moral hypocrisy, delusions, unrequited passion, and fear.

Of Human Bondage opens with the death of Philip's mother. Like the young Willie Maugham, the orphaned Philip is forced to move from his French home to England. There he lives with his uncle, the vicar of Blackstable, and kindly Aunt Louisa. They are childless and live a life quite unsuitable for their nine-year-old nephew, who speaks French more fluently than English and has a clubfoot. These early pages comprise a Victorian deprived-child paradigm. Unhappy school days with bullying masters and cruel classmates are reversed by an extraordinary year studying in Heidelberg, Germany, where Philip comes intuitively to the same conclusion he reached emotionally when his prayers to be delivered of his clubfoot went unanswered: There is no God. The intuition of a kind of nihilism brings Philip not despair but joy. He will fail in a journeyman bid to study art in Paris but finds himself as a medical intern in London delivering babies. Philip will have his first sexual experience—brief and unsatisfying—before encountering a London waitress, Mildred Rogers, who, although ordinary in every way, holds him in near-fatal thrall.

Philip deludes himself about Mildred, suffers her brutal insults, rejects her and repeatedly takes her back, hates and adores her, and increasingly curses "the fate which [has] chained him to such a woman." It can be noted that Maugham, whose works are frequently adapted for film, lived to see three film versions of the novel, between 1933 and 1964—none of which reached beyond the theme of bondage to Mildred to explore the book as *Bildungsroman*. As Jerome Buckley notes, "The novel is ultimately concerned with Philip's development and not just with his obsession."

It is easy for Philip to assume that he is fated to suffer and fail—that regret or blame is useless. He is also, however, eager to discover a pattern in his destiny. A drunken minor poet named Cronshaw tells him that he will find the answer to his questions in the pattern of a Persian carpet. One day, depressed by word of his close friend Hayward's useless death in the Boer War, he contemplates Greek funerary sculptures in the British Museum. Something reminiscent of Stephen Dedalus's vision of a maiden on the strand—an epiphany—comes to Philip: Life has no objective meaning; the design is in the mind of the individual.

THE *BILDUNGSROMAN* AND TIME

Shortly before beginning *Sons and Lovers*, the novel that launched his career, D. H. Lawrence revealed to his lover Jessie Chambers his despair upon reading H. G. Wells's *Tono-Bungay* (1908): "Most authors write out of their own personality," Lawrence, then twenty-three, averred. "Wells does, of course. But I'm not sure that I've got a big enough personality to write out of."

Thus Lawrence is awed by the same quality in *Tono-Bungay* that critic Mark Schorer, quoted earlier, deplores: a richness of vision, both retrospectively and futuristically, able to embrace at once the death of Victorianism and the emergence of the new spirit of advertising. For Schorer, in his manifesto favoring Henry James and formalism, Wells's best book proves to be not a novel but a hypothesis. Nearly a century later the issues between fiction and journalism still seethe.

What cannot be denied is that *Tono-Bungay*'s George Ponderevo—like Stephen Dedalus, Paul Morel, and Philip Carey—is the personification of a consciousness that seeks a secure handhold on life. Again and again this kind of hero proves a human test-site for every level and phase of society, with life always crowding in. As a boy living belowstairs in an estate called Bladesover, George becomes secularized early, inclined to follow the liberating force of scientific discovery late, and a survivor of the charlatanry of a bogus patent medicine called tono-bungay in between. The novel pursues a vertical—a futuristic—course. It presents a rocketlike macrocosm that allows Ponderevo to survive the wreckage of a marriage and a love affair, to withstand the "woosh" and sputter of tono-bungay, and, at last, to be the embodiment of a life-force whose ambiguous symbol is a battleship forging ahead into the limitless sea. The purveyor of tono-bungay quackery—the catalyst for George's fall and rise—is a bubbling sprite of an uncle, Teddy Ponderevo. He, like the early Wells having escaped from pill dispensing, storms the bastions of society. Yet for this arriviste, to the manor born too late, the wages are corruption, defeat, and death.

It is curious that John Fowles has never mentioned Wells. In *The French Lieutenant's Woman* (1969), Charles Smithson, marooned in the midst of the Victorian era a generation before George Ponderevo, is also viewed as the man between. Each has lifted one leg out of one time frame and is about to put it down in another of whose substance he is uncertain. Like *Tono-Bungay*, Fowles's novel ends in a dramatizing of "postcultural man" through imagery of the sea. In Fowles's case, it is borrowed from Matthew Arnold's poem "To Marguerite":

> [L]ife . . . is not a symbol . . . not one riddle and one failure to guess it, is not to inhabit one face alone or to be given up after one losing throw of the dice; but is to be, however inadequately, emptily, hopelessly into the city's iron heart, endured. And out again, upon the unplumb'd, salt, estranging sea.

Written three quarters of a century apart, these novels apply bildungsromanic strategies of passage to time itself. They instruct their audience imaginatively in the ways nineteenth century man became twentieth.

The American *Bildungsroman*

Writing his doctoral dissertation in 1948, Philip Young mounted a convincing wound-and-bow theory on Ernest Hemingway, man and writer. The so-called Hemingway hero, as Young defined him, was Hemingway himself. For any real understanding of either the heroes of the novels or their creator, a Hemingway aficionado must take into account the young Er-

nest's severe injuries in the Italian campaign of World War I, which, according to Young, left permanent scars, visible and invisible. Over Hemingway's initial protests—he told Young that to try to psychoanalyze a writer is tantamount to destroying him—Young published the first literary study of his man in 1952, and in 1965, four years after Hemingway's suicide, applied his "wound" thesis to all of Hemingway's books.

Young's ideas gave rise to the term "code hero," whose notion is that in a world dominated by violence and evil a decent young man, placed in testing situations, will maintain his "purity of Line" (a phrase applied to the matador Romero in Hemingway's 1926 novel *The Sun Also Rises*). Grace under pressure requires an earned style of conduct, a code that is a variation on the *Bildungsroman*'s conventional rites of passage. In his first book, *In Our Time* (1924, 1925), Hemingway combined stories and sketches that introduced Nick Adams, the young man who would grow up to be Jake Barnes, Lieutenant Frederic Henry, and all Hemingway's other war-born heroes. Young Nick is the outdoor man whose bliss is hunting and fishing. Even as an adolescent he reveals, always understatedly, a quality contemporary detractors call macho but which forces on Nick a "reckoning with his nerves" that leads to the ritual shut-off of mind necessary to ward off the demons. Young aligns Nick Adams and Huckleberry Finn as exemplars of "a great American story because [theirs] is based not only on the experience of every man as he grows up but also on the particular and peculiar experience of this nation." The Huck-Nick stories tell what happens when a spontaneous virtue meets something alien.

After the appearance of J. D. Salinger's *The Catcher in the Rye* (1951), critics throughout the 1950's extended Young's Huck-to-Nick line to Holden Caulfield. Huck and Holden speak in the first person and in boyish vernacular. Both heroes, in established bildungsromanic custom, long to escape corrupting adult forces for a state of natural innocence. The unfunny Nick Adams lacks Huck and Holden's comedy, but his pattern is the same as theirs: improvisation.

A 1990's version of the *Bildungsroman* is Frank

Conroy's *Body and Soul* (1993). When this novel appeared, it was taken as either an anachronism or a refreshing return to the classic *Bildungsroman*. The first novel of the fifty-seven-year-old Conroy (author of a distinguished memoir published in 1967, *Stop-Time*, and a short-story collection), *Body and Soul* records the romantic history of a musical prodigy's development from humble beginnings to concert fame as a piano virtuoso. It offers a chance for young readers to experience a genuinely happy novel, in which virtue and fidelity are rewarded and joy is made as plausible as divorce or nuclear meltdown. This is Dickens, updated and undistorted.

AMERICAN CHRONICLES AS *BILDUNGSROMANE*

Harry "Rabbit" Angstrom is a decent, unintelligent man who finds that the momentum that sustained him as a high school basketball star has slowed to a crawl in a dingy apartment where the dinner is always late and the wife has stopped being pretty. John Updike takes this common domestic tableau and turns it into a subtle expose of the frailty of the American Dream.

Written entirely in the present tense—in 1960, a virtually unheard-of technique in American fiction—to stress the immediacy of Rabbit's crisis, *Rabbit, Run* (1960) details the sterility of a society that offers television sets and cars but ignores spiritual loss and belief. As critic Donald J. Greiner puts it, "All [Harry's wife Janice] wants is for him to be like other husbands, to give in to the nine-to-five routine of selling Magi-peelers in the local dimestore, but Rabbit senses that loss of life's momentum means loss of life itself. So he runs."

Updike's quester is suggestive of Huck, Nick, and Holden, but Rabbit is neither as improvisatory as they nor as articulate—inside or outside. When asked to explain what he wants, all the uncomprehending Rabbit can do is hit a perfect tee shot, point to the grace of the soaring ball, and shout, "That's It!"

A decade later, in 1971, Updike reintroduced Harry, age thirty-six, in *Rabbit Redux* (Rabbit led back). The junk of ashtrays and closets from which Harry has run earlier is replaced by national events that promise to overwhelm him: Vietnam, the Civil Rights movement, the drug culture. For Rabbit, these

"disasters" are redeemed by the first moon shot, but, try as he might to turn the space flight into a metaphor for his own need to soar gracefully and far, he can see in it only depersonalized technology making contact with a dead rock. In *Rabbit Redux*, any "lighting out for the territory" (Huck's solution) is negated by Rabbit's futility. He returns to his dingy house in the plastic suburb. The last words of the novel—"Sleeps. O.K.?"—are a long way from "Runs."

Rabbit Is Rich (1981) is about the 1970's. Now forty-six, Rabbit does not blame anyone for shopping malls or overflowing garbage cans beside failing restaurants. When he thinks of himself as "the star and spear point of the flourishing car dealership his family owns," readers know that he remains unreconstructed, his value system still defined in terms of athletic prowess. His youthful running has been slowed to gliding in golf carts. He acknowledges neither his son's drug addiction nor his own failing heart.

For *Rabbit at Rest* (1991), Updike combined reprise with sputtering evidence that passage for an unresponsive oldster like Harry merely repeats unalterable patterns. Rabbit runs one final time. He returns to the basketball court despite his weight, his age, and his heart. In short, he tries. His fear, however, presages the final stillness. Rabbit Angstrom has forged entry into the terrain of the modern *Bildungsroman*'s losers. Yet, as Greiner sums up the Rabbit tetralogy, "Harry has [also] joined the pantheon of American literary heroes like Natty Bumppo, Ahab, Huck Finn, Gatsby, Ike McCaslin, Holden Caulfield [in having learned] that no matter how far he runs in space, he cannot outrace time."

THE FEMINIST *BILDUNGSROMAN*

Ellen Morgan ("Humanbecoming: Form and Focus in the Neo-Feminist Novel") identifies the *Bildungsroman* as "the most salient form for literature influenced by [the feminist movement of the 1960's and 1970's]." The female *Bildungsroman* is a "recasting" of the old genre by modern women authors to meet their particular needs. The traditional *Bildungsroman* is often an autobiographical novel depicting adolescent self-development and the educative experiences of youth. Endings to novels such as *Wilhelm Meister's Apprenticeship*, *Sons and Lovers*, *Of Human Bondage*, and *Tono-Bungay* become the beginnings for the protagonists, who either merge into their societies, like Philip Carey, or escape into the promise of a new world, like George Ponderevo.

The modern feminist *Bildungsroman* concentrates on crises in which the female protagonist finds herself facing problematical dilemmas with no assurance, if they persist, of safe passage. A woman awakens in her late twenties or early thirties to what Bonnie Hoover Braedlin calls "the stultification and fragmentation of a personality devoted not to self-fulfillment and awareness, but to a culturally determined, self-sacrificing, self-effacing existence." These crises and concomitant struggles for oneness in cultures that fragment women into accepted roles provide the central themes of the feminist *Bildungsroman*.

Scholars have divided feminist *Bildungsromane* into those that convey a "social quest" and those that focus on a "spiritual quest." The distinguishing factors are, with the former, a search for identity in the socioeconomic sphere and, with the latter, a journey involving a "transcendent deity."

Some structural features of female *Bildingsromane* often stem from their confessional nature. The prevalence of first-person narration follows cause and effect. The recollection and reconstruction of memories and the utilizing of flashback are central strategies. Vivid recollections dominate—of girlhoods haunted by images of deadly mothers and absent fathers, demanding friends, first loves. Later, these heroines find themselves torn apart by the conflicting demands of marriage and motherhood on one hand and the longing for personal freedom and self-actualization on the other. Though the women in *Bildungsromane* arrive at self-awareness through recalling, retelling, and analyzing their lives, they finally achieve the wholeness of selfhood by exploring their inner natures to unite the conscious elements of personality with the unconscious.

Included in an expanding list of authors of feminist *Bildungsromane* cited frequently by scholars are Lisa Alther (*Kinflicks*, 1975), Margaret Atwood (*Surfacing*, 1972, and *Lady Oracle*, 1976), Sheila Ballan-

tyne (*Norma Jean the Termite Queen*, 1975), Francine du Plessix Gray (*Lovers and Tyrants*, 1976), Doris Lessing (*The Golden Notebook*, 1962, and the five novels of the Children of Violence series, 1952-1969), and Madge Piercy (*Small Change*, 1973).

CONTEMPORARY VERSIONS

During the nineteenth and twentieth centuries there was never a shortage of novels concerned with an adolescent's battle for an adequate extension of personality, a quest that brings the initiate into conflict with the constraining factors of parental wishes, first love, and economic and social sanctions. Many landmarks of world literature belong to this distinguished subgenre. In its classic form, the *Bildungsroman* reached its peak in the nineteenth century. The twentieth century added more direct autobiography, an increasingly depersonalized society, and the battle between the sexes.

Writers such as Edmund White (born 1940), author of an honored biography of French writer and iconoclast Jean Genet, has set the stage, with fictions such as *A Boy's Own Story* (1982) and *The Beautiful Room Is Empty* (1988), for *Bildungsromane* of alternative patterns of living as compelling as D. H. Lawrence's works of nearly a century ago. A "coming-out" novel such as *A Boy's Own Story*, besides depicting rites of initiation as the *Bildungsroman* has always done, reveals the harm psychotherapy can do to homosexuals and the self-hatred forced on a young man by society when it conceives of homosexuality only as a sickness, sin, or crime. Also not detailed here (although treated elsewhere in separate essays in this volume) is the blossoming of novels, worldwide and especially in North America, that conflate the *Bildungsroman* with the quest for ethnic and cultural identity in postcolonial, disfranchised, oppressed, immigrant, and other marginalized peoples. Such reinvigoration of the *Bildungsroman* is not surprising: Since Dickens, one of the extraliterary roles of the *Bildungsroman* has been its rage to redress injustice.

Richard Hauer Costa

BIBLIOGRAPHY

Alden, Patricia. *Social Mobility in the English Bildungsroman.* Ann Arbor, Mich.: UMI Research Press, 1979, 1986. This 132-page survey, especially good on Lawrence, confirms the difficulty of economically vulnerable youths, uncertain about aspiration and talent, and under no illusions that the provincial world of their childhood offers an alternative to their effort to escape. The book's morale: Experience unteaches.

Buckley, Jerome H. *Season of Youth: The Bildungsroman from Dickens to Golding.* Cambridge, Mass.: Harvard University Press, 1974. Although scholarly, this survey of more than a century of the English *Bildungsroman* is engagingly written. Buckley demonstrates that gradual imaginative enlightenment has been vital to the hero's initiation and endurance. An indispensable book.

Frierson, William C. *The English Novel in Transition, 1885-1940.* Norman: University of Oklahoma Press, 1942. Decades after it was written, this classic remains fresh, displaying Frierson's deep commitment to what he calls "life" novels on every page. He is especially sensitive to the relative darkness of "passage" novels of the 1930's, compared with those of the 1920's. No commentator improves on Frierson in detecting the influences on lesser writers of the masters. He eschews everything Germanic.

Gohlman, Susan Ashley. *Starting Over: The Task of the Protagonist in the Contemporary Bildungsroman.* New York: Garland, 1990. Protagonists are considered here in terms of their roles in the *Bildungsroman.* Includes bibliographical references.

Hardin, James, ed. *Reflection and Action: Essays on the Bildungsroman.* Columbia: University of South Caroina Press, 1991. A thoughtful collection of essays.

Kontjc, Todd Curtis. *The German Bildungsroman: History of a National Genre.* Columbia, S.C.: Camden House, 1993. Part of the Studies in German Literature, Linguistics, and Culture series, this is a good look at the *Bildungsroman* in German literature. Provides bibliographical references and an index.

Swales, Martin. *The German Bildungsroman from Wieland to Hesse.* Princeton: Princeton University Press, 1978. For a compact linkup between Goethe and other early German practitioners of the *Bildungsroman* with twentieth century novelists such as Thomas Mann and Hermann Hesse, this is one of the best resources.

THE DETECTIVE NOVEL

The detective story is a special branch of crime fiction that focuses attention on the examination of evidence that will lead to the solution of the mystery. *The Oxford English Dictionary* records the first printed use of the noun "detective" in the year 1843. The term had become established in the language because of the formation of the first detective bureaus, the original of which was the Bow Street Runners, a group of detective-policemen organized by Henry Fielding and John Fielding in their capacities as magistrates in London. The Runners operated out of the Fielding residence on Bow Street and were the precursors of the detective branch of Scotland Yard. Some time later, early in the nineteenth century, the Sûreté Générale, the first modern police force, was formed in Paris with a detective bureau. With the establishment of such bureaus, the way was open for the detective story to be developed out of existing literary sources.

EIGHTEENTH AND NINETEENTH CENTURIES

In the eighteenth century, the chaplain of Newgate Prison in London was authorized to publish the stories of notorious criminals in *The Newgate Calendar.* From this practice sprang the often wholly fictional Newgate novels, accounts of sensational crimes. In France, François Vidocq, a criminal himself, became head of the Sûreté and later published his memoirs recounting his exploits in capturing criminals. It is also likely that some of the ambience of the early detective story was derived from the gothic novel. William Godwin's *Things as They Are: Or, The Adventures of Caleb Williams* (1794; also known as *The Adventures of Caleb Williams: Or, Things as They Are*; best known as *Caleb Williams*), for example, although not a detective novel, is a story of a crime solved in order to free an innocent man.

From these beginnings, it remained for Edgar Allan Poe to devise the detective story in its now familiar form. Poe wrote three short works that are certainly detective stories, as well as others that are sometimes included in the genre. The first of these was "The Murders in the Rue Morgue" (1841), which was followed by "The Mystery of Marie Rogêt" (1842) and "The Purloined Letter" (1845). Poe initiated the device of establishing the character of the detective and then using him for several stories. Poe's detective, M. Dupin, is a recluse, an eccentric, aristocratic young man with a keen analytical mind. He has an unnamed but admiring friend who marvels at Dupin's mental prowess and is willing to be his chronicler. Dupin examines the evidence in a given case and solves the crime after the regular police have exhausted their methods—a circumstance that was to become one of the commonplaces of detective fiction.

Apparently impressed by *Mémoires de Vidocq, chef de la police de Sûreté jusqu'en 1827* (1828-1829; *Memoirs of Vidocq, Principal Agent of the French Police Until 1827*, 1828-1829; revised as *Histoire de Vodocq, chef de la police de Sûreté: Écrite d'après lui-même*, 1829), by François Vidocq, Poe set his stories in Paris and borrowed his policemen from the Sûreté. Meanwhile, in France itself, Émile Gaboriau began to produce detective stories that also owed much to Vidocq. His detective, M. Lecoq, a representative of the official police, became the chief figure in a number of tales of detection. The detective short story was thus established and enjoyed great popularity in the century to follow.

Probably the first full-length novel of detection was *The Notting Hill Mystery* (1865) by Charles Felix, but it was quickly followed by Wilkie Collins's *The Moonstone* (1868), which critics consider to be the first important detective novel. Collins introduced Sergeant Cuff of Scotland Yard, who, with the help of amateurs, was able to solve the mystery. The first detective in English fiction, however, antedated Sergeant Cuff by fifteen years: Inspector Bucket of Charles Dickens's *Bleak House* (1852-1853). Detective novels were published at a slow, sporadic pace until the advent of Sherlock Holmes, the most famous of all fictional detectives, in Arthur Conan Doyle's *A Study in Scarlet* (1887).

Holmes starred in four novels and fifty-six short stories and eventually came to have a life independent of his creator, Doyle, who even killed him off in one tale only to bring him back for further adventures. A house on Baker Street in London has been identified as the place where Holmes occupied a flat and is now a tourist attraction. Clubs honor his memory with birthday parties, and a biography has been written based on incidental remarks and inferences about his "life" in the works in which he appeared. The Sherlock Holmes stories follow the pattern established by Poe's Dupin: Holmes is a bachelor given to esoteric studies, an eccentric who plays the violin and occasionally takes cocaine. A keen observer with amazing talents for analysis and deduction, an amateur boxer who performs astonishing feats of physical strength, Holmes is a virtual superman, while the commonsensical Dr. John Watson, the narrator of his exploits, provides a perfect foil.

The success of the Sherlock Holmes stories resulted in an outpouring of detective fiction; many authors adopted the basic technique of establishing the character of the detective and then recounting a series of his "cases." R. Austin Freeman introduced Dr. John Thorndyke, who based his solutions on more strictly scientific evidence rather than the deductions favored by Holmes. An American writer, Jacques Futrelle, introduced Professor S. F. X. Van Dusen, who was called "the thinking machine" and who became one of the early omniscient detectives in the tradition of Sherlock Holmes.

DETECTIVE FICTION'S GOLDEN AGE

With *Trent's Last Case* (1913, revised 1929; also as *The Woman in Black*), by E. C. Bentley, the modern era of the detective story began. Mary Roberts Rinehart modified the pattern of the detective novel by providing a female amateur as a first-person narrator who worked with the official police and who provided the key to the solution almost by accident. Another prolific writer was Carolyn Wells, who wrote seventy-four mystery novels, most of which starred Fleming Stone as the detective. She also made an important contribution to the theory of the detective story with *The Technique of the Mystery Story* (1913).

As the detective story moved closer to its "classi-

cal" stage, it became more realistic and was written with more literary skill. The detectives became less bizarre and less inclined to become involved in physical danger or in personally grappling with the criminal in the manner of the great Holmes. The adventure-mystery involving a sleuth who was proficient both physically and mentally was given over to thrillers such as the Nick Carter stories, while the strict detective tale became purely analytical. In this form, the detective story featured the detective as its chief character and the solution to an interesting mystery as its chief interest. There was generally a narrator in the Watson tradition, and absence of any love interest, and neither characterization nor the tangential demands of the plot interfered with the central business of unraveling the puzzle. With these characteristics established, the detective story moved into its golden age.

The period of 1920 to 1940 represented the golden age of the novel of detection. It included the work of Dorothy L. Sayers, Agatha Christie, Earl Derr Biggers, and S. S. Van Dine (Willard Huntington Wright). Hundreds of novels were written during this period and were enjoyed by people at all levels of literary sophistication. The expectation of the reader was that a clever detective would be faced with a puzzling crime, almost always a murder or a series of murders, that had not been committed by a professional criminal; the solution of this mystery would come about by the examination of clues presented in the novel.

Dorothy L. Sayers was perhaps the most literary writer of the practitioners of the detective novel; she attempted a combination of the detective story and the "legitimate" novel. *The Nine Tailors* (1934) is a good example of the work of her detective, Lord Peter Wimsey, and of her careful research into background material. She is considered to be one of the finest of the mystery writers of this period. Lord Peter Wimsey is a snobbish man given to airy commentary and a languid manner, but he has the analytical skills necessary to solve the mysteries.

Although she may not have had the skill in characterization or the literary quality of Sayers, Agatha Christie surpassed her rivals in the sheer ingenuity of her plots and her manipulation of the evidence that her detective, Hercule Poirot, had to evaluate. Christie used such traditional ploys as the somewhat dense associate (in this instance, Captain Hastings), the least likely person as the murderer, the unexpected turn of the plot, and an exotic manner of committing the crime. Poirot, who became the most popular fictional detective since Sherlock Holmes, appears in thirty-three of Christie's novels. Christie invented yet another fictional detective who became almost as beloved as Poirot: Miss Jane Marple is a quiet Victorian lady who figures in eleven novels and a collection of short stories. Her solutions come about from a shrewd knowledge of human behavior, keen observation, a remarkable memory, and the ability to make startling deductions from the evidence. Despite the popularity of Hercule Poirot and Miss Marple, neither stars in the book that is widely considered to be Christie's best: *Ten Little Niggers* (1939; published in the United States as *And Then There Were None*, 1940; also known as *Ten Little Indians*).

Rivaling M. Poirot and Miss Marple for the affections of detective novel fans was the Chinese-Hawaiian-American detective, Charlie Chan, created by Earl Derr Biggers. Charlie Chan's widespread popularity was especially enhanced by the fact that his stories were turned into some forty-five motion pictures. Chan's characterization includes the frequent use of Chinese aphorisms, an extremely polite manner, and his generally human qualities. Chan is especially interesting in that he was the first example, in this kind of fiction, of an Asian who was a sympathetic character rather than a villain.

S. S. Van Dine is the author of twelve novels starring the detective Philo Vance, who, like Lord Peter Wimsey, is an English aristocrat, although all of his cases have an American urban setting. An extremely erudite man with a world-weary air, Vance was the best-educated and most refined detective of this era. Van Dine, under his real name of Wright, was a literary critic who made the detective story an object of research and study. The result was the publication of the "twenty rules for detective stories," only one of several efforts to define the exact characteristics of the form. Both readers and writers of this period had

definite expectations and resented efforts in the field that did not follow certain specifications. The idea of fair play with the reader was essential; that is, the game must be played with all the evidence needed to solve the crime. There must be no love interest to detract from the business of solving the mystery, the detective could not be the criminal, and the solution could not come about as a result of accident or wild coincidence. During the detective novel's golden age, these rules were taken quite seriously by those who believed that a permanent form of popular fiction had been established.

While the classic detective story was being established in England and the United States, an American development turned the detective novel in a new direction. Manfred B. Lee and Frederic Dannay collaborated to create a detective who would achieve worldwide fame. Ellery Queen, ostensibly the author of the novels that describe his cases, is an amateur detective and professional writer who works with his father, Inspector Richard Queen of the New York Police Department. Inspector Queen provides the clues and investigative techniques while his son, Ellery, puts the evidence together. They are not supermen, after Sherlock Holmes, nor are they all-knowing in the manner of Philo Vance, but professionals dealing with a more realistic crime scene than that of their predecessors. Ellery Queen was thus a crossover figure leading to the police procedural story and to the kind of detective fiction that came to reflect the actual criminal class, as well as the working of the criminal justice system, in the United States.

HARD-BOILED DETECTIVE FICTION

In the 1930's, while the classic detective story was thriving, another kind of mystery story came into being—the hard-boiled detective novel. The preeminent writers of this school were Dashiell Hammett, Raymond Chandler, and—in the next generation—Ross Macdonald. Some of these writers began writing for *Black Mask*, a pulp magazine, in the 1920's. Dashiell Hammett's Sam Spade, who appeared in *The Maltese Falcon* (serial 1929-1930, book 1930), is characteristic of the new detective: a private eye in a not-very-successful office who solves crimes by following people around in unsavory neighborhoods, having fights in alleys, and dealing with informers. He is cynical regarding the political dealings that go on behind the scenes and is aware of the connections between criminals and the outwardly respectable. He trusts no one, while he himself follows the dictates of a personal code. Hammett's *The Thin Man* (1934), which became the basis for a series of motion pictures, was a return to the more traditional form of detective fiction.

Another member of the hard-boiled school was Raymond Chandler, who wrote seven novels about his sleuth Philip Marlowe. Chandler, describing the ideal detective hero, said, "Down these mean streets a man must go who is not himself mean, who is neither tarnished nor afraid." Such a man is aware of the corruption he will find, but he is governed by a code that includes faithfulness to the client and an abhorrence of crime without an avenging or sadistic bent. Chandler specialized in complex plots, realistic settings, and snappy dialogue in novels such as *The Big Sleep* (1939), *Farewell, My Lovely* (1940), and *The Lady in the Lake* (1943). He was also a theoretician of the detective story, and his essay "The Simple Art of Murder" (1944) is an important document in the annals of crime literature.

After the introduction of the hard-boiled detective and the many stories involving the routine investigations of official law enforcement agencies, the tradition of the superman detective declined. Fictional detectives lost their aristocratic manners and eccentricities, while the crimes being investigated gained interest not because they involved yet another bizarre or ingenious way to commit murder, but because of the influence of the psychological makeup or the social status of the criminal. The criminal was also less likely to be an amateur than a habitual malefactor. Limiting the suspects by setting the story in confined quarters—such as a country house or an ocean liner—gave way to a story that took the reader into the mean streets referred to by Chandler. These stories often involved the brutality of the police, more violence on the part of the detective, frankness in matters of sex, and the use of formerly taboo language. Mickey Spillane's Mike Hammer typified a new breed of private

detectives, one who is given to acts of sadistic violence.

This often brutal social realism is also reflected in the work of Erle Stanley Gardner, best known for his creation of the lawyer-detective Perry Mason. The hero of more than eighty novels, Mason was first characterized in the hard-boiled tradition; early novels such as *The Case of the Velvet Claws* (1933) and *The Case of the Curious Bride* (1934) emphasize the fast-paced action and involuted plots that superseded the literary quality typical of Sayers's work. While retaining his early penchant for extralegal tactics, Mason gradually developed into a courtroom hero, allowing his assistant detective Paul Drake to do the research while Mason excelled in the spectacular oral combat of the cross-examination. Many of Gardner's plots were drawn from his own legal experiences as an attorney; having founded the Court of Last Resort, Gardner demonstrated a concern for the helpless. In keeping with this concern, he modified the detective genre by introducing the state as the villain and attacking the urban evils of capitalistic greed for wealth and power.

In championing the defenseless, Gardner was the voice of a modern "Everyman" during the decades between 1930 and 1960. Viewing themselves as vulnerable to the dictates of the state (such as the establishment of Prohibition and income tax), readers achieved vicarious satisfaction in seeing the problems of average people solved. The mass popularity of Mason's cases was the result not only of their victories over the "system" but also of the medium they employed. Gardner was, by his own admission, a "product of the paperback revolution," and he further lowered the literary standards of classical detective fiction by dictating his novels. He was also the script supervisor for the Perry Mason television series (starring Raymond Burr and running from 1957 to 1966), which furthered the personal appeal and accessibility of the detective. Unlike the superhuman Lord Peter Wimsey and Philo Vance, whose intellectual and aristocratic qualities are extraordinary and intimidating, Perry Mason is a successful but common professional, combining the wit of the golden age sleuth with the cynical pertinacity of the hard-boiled detective.

POLICE PROCEDURAL NOVEL

While the hard-boiled mystery developed one element of the classic detective novel—the appeal of a recurring hero with yet another case to solve—in a strikingly new direction, the sheer fascination of deduction that characterized the golden age of the detective novel was developed in a new subgenre: the police procedural, a kind of fictional "documentary" often purporting to be taken from actual police files. These stories detail the routines of investigative agencies, taking the reader into forensic laboratories and describing complex chemical testing of the evidence. Hardworking policemen interview suspects, conduct stakeouts, shadow people, and investigate bank accounts. Even if there is a major figure who is in charge of the case, the investigation clearly is a matter of teamwork, with standard areas of expertise and responsibility: in short, a realistic depiction of actual police methods. These stories date from World War II and are typified by the television series *Dragnet* and Sidney Kingsley's Broadway play *Detective Story* (1949). One of the major writers of the police procedural is Ed McBain, who wrote more than thirty novels about the "87th precinct" in a fictional urban setting that closely resembles New York City. The police procedural has proved to be a versatile form that can be used as the basis for a symbolic story with intentions far beyond that of crime solving, as in Lawrence Sanders's *The First Deadly Sin* (1973). Similarly, Tom Sharpe's *Riotous Assembly* (1971) is a police procedural set in South Africa that uses the form in order to ridicule apartheid, hypocrisy, and racial stereotyping.

Ostensibly, the psychological crime novels of Georges Simenon should also belong in the police procedural category; however, Inspector Jules Maigret of the Paris Police Department uses neither scientific nor rational methods to identify murderers. Similar to Perry Mason in his bourgeois appeal (Maigret is heavyset, smokes a pipe, and is fond of domesticity) and in his delegation of research responsibilities to subordinates, Maigret solves crimes by absorbing the ambience of the place in which they were committed. By familiarizing himself with social customs, geography, and personalities, Maigret "be-comes" the suspect and uses psychology and intuition to discern the criminal's identity. Patience rather than flamboyance characterizes Maigret; he relies on the hunches of his sympathetic imagination instead of on factual clues. While Maigret inhabits the sordid world of the hard-boiled detective, he sees himself as a "repairer of destinies" and acts more like a humble priest eliciting confessions than a vindictive policeman triumphing over evil.

In addition to departing from convention in Maigret's unique style of detection, Simenon also defies genre restrictions in the style of his work. *Pietr-le-Letton* (1931; *Maigret and the Enigmatic Lett*, 1963) was written in 1929, but it has little in common with the analytical works of the golden age. Accused of being too literary in his early psychological novels, Simenon probes the ambiguity of human behavior, acknowledging the capacity of people to sin while maintaining a sympathetic understanding of their actions. Readers of the Maigret novels are unable to see evil in terms of black and white, as readers of Gardner's works do, and come away with as much compassion for the murderer as for the victim. Simenon denies both the mental action of the classical period of detective fiction and the physical action of the hard-boiled period, promoting instead the action of the heart. In so doing, he demonstrates the versatility of the detective fiction genre.

NEW SUBGENRES

While retaining many of its traditional core characteristics, detective fiction in the last decades of the twentieth century became increasingly varied, with many new subgenres emerging. Among the most popular and highly regarded writers that became prominent during this time were P. D. James and Dick Francis of England and Elmore Leonard of the United States. James writes in the so-called golden age tradition of such authors as Agatha Christie and Ngaio Marsh (both of whom are still widely read). Her novels, longer and denser than most in the genre, have series detectives (Scotland Yard inspector Adam Dalgliesh and private eye Cordelia Gray) who are neither stereotypical nor two-dimensional but rather singular people whose private lives directly affect their professional activities. Dalgliesh, for example, is a poet whose wife died giving birth to their first child, a double tragedy that continues to haunt him. The cases he pursues are multifaceted, James develops complex milieus and characters, and there is always a thematic element (sometimes religious). Close to her in method is Ruth Rendell, whose Inspector Wexford novels also feature psychological probing and have equally complex puzzles but lack a thematic dimension. Both women's novels generally fall into the police procedural subgenre, as do Colin Dexter's Inspector Morse novels, which have an introspective, intellectual protagonist who is quite similar in temperament and method to Dalgliesh. Set in and around Oxford University in England, a Dexter novel usually has a religious element and a dollop of social criticism. Younger than James, Rendell, and Dexter, but also a writer of procedurals, is Peter Robinson, a Yorkshire native turned Canadian, whose increasingly popular mysteries are set in his native northern England. His detective is the gruff but sensitive Inspector Banks (closer to Wexford than to Dalgliesh or Morse), and each novel concurrently tracks several separate crimes at once, much as Ed McBain and J. J. Marric do in their police procedurals.

The annual novels of former British steeplechase jockey Dick Francis have been best-sellers on both sides of the Atlantic for decades. Each is a fast-paced thriller, but at its heart is a narrative in the golden age manner, a standard whodunit in which the nonprofessional sleuth exposes industrial corruption, a racing scandal, or some other crime. The admirable, even exemplary, hero inevitably finds himself in an unfamiliar situation, and in a predictable Francis set piece has a life-threatening encounter with an adversary at some late point in the book. Having overcome a variety of physical, intellectual, and emotional challenges, he restores a measure of normality to the society and returns to his normal pursuits. In a departure from the norm, the hero is not an outsider dealing with a case that just came his way, but rather is part of a group into which criminality has intruded. Holmes, Wolfe, Archer, Maigret, and Dalgliesh may never again come into contact the principals in their cases; Francis's detectives, however, continue to live with their erstwhile clients, seeing them regularly at the Jockey Club and other familiar spots. The novels are formulaic, but Francis has maintained a freshness over the years by eschewing the series detective, although his heroes are basically alike. Another Francis standard is the first-person narrative, through which he gains immediacy as well as greater reader empathy with the hero.

Anything but formulaic are Elmore Leonard's best-sellers, which are written in the hard-boiled tradition of Chandler, Hammett, and Macdonald. Like Francis, Leonard shies away from a series detective, but he revisits characters (law enforcers and law breakers), and though his milieus range far and wide, he also returns to such places as Detroit and south Florida. While he fills his varied novels with social misfits and assorted grotesques, many of his characters are ordinary people who find themselves in extraordinary situations. Readers can also expect a spare style in the Ernest Hemingway manner, dialogue that rings true to life, and a fast-paced narrative with a chase as a central element. Leonard began his career as a writer of Westerns, and this background is evident in his plotting and style. Another hallmark is his shifting point of view. His characters, good and bad, tell their own stories, thus avoiding an omniscient narrator. Further, he changes the narrative point of view several times within a book, carrying the practice to an extreme in *Maximum Bob* (1991), in which part of an episode is told from an alligator's point of view. Shifts in time between the past and present are another Leonard commonplace, and this characteristic and the others may reflect his experience as a writer of screenplays. Leonard is less predictable than most of his peers, for his subjects, settings, and plots run the gamut of possibilities. Leonard's books are full of surprises, from a midwestern couple confined in the federal witness protection program to a loan shark turned music producer to an Arizona cowboy caught up in the Spanish-American War. Before he writes, he or a surrogate visits potential milieus and does on-the-spot research to ensure verisimilitude. This process, coupled with his imagination, narrative skills, and incredible ear for dialogue, has led to critical and popular acclaim for Leonard.

Another popular crime novelist who engages in extensive prewriting research is Patricia Cornwell, who, before becoming an author, worked as a police reporter and for the Richmond, Virginia, chief medical examiner as a keeper of forensic records. She also studied forensic science and rode with homicide detectives as a first responder to crime scenes. This background and the preparation she does for each project have allowed Cornwell to produce graphically realistic novels that are almost case studies in such areas as forensic anthropology (*All That Remains*, 1992) or deoxyribonucleic acid (DNA) testing (*Postmortem*, 1990). Her series detective is Kay Scarpetta, a physician who is Richmond's chief medical examiner. Talented scientist though she is, Scarpetta is a woman with a personal life that occasionally intrudes upon her professional activities. Despite these problems and her confrontations with grisly inhumanity and irrationality, Scarpetta remains a decent person who copes and ultimately triumphs, sometimes over a local, state, or federal bureaucracy, but always over criminals. Since the boundaries separating crime writing categories are often indistinct, Cornwell sometimes is placed with the hard-boiled group of writers and other times is placed in the police procedural genre. The latter flourished during the 1980's and 1990's, not only because of new Ed McBain books but also because of such varied series as Tony Hillerman's New Mexico Navajo Indian mysteries, featuring Jim Chee and Joe Leghorn; James Lee Burke's Dave Robicheaux novels set in Louisiana; Archer Mayor's Joe Gunther books, which take place primarily in Brattleboro, Vermont; Reginald Hill's Dalziel and Pascoe Yorkshire whodunits; and Stuart Kaminsky's and Martin Cruz Smith's Soviet Union books.

The traditional mystery, increasingly called the "cozy," experienced a renaissance at the end of the twentieth century. Originally pejorative, the term "cozy" refers to novels in which the setting is noncriminal and in which the detective (usually not a full-time sleuth, but rather a college professor, bookstore proprietor, or English nobleman) engages in an intellectual chess match with the reader and faces a variety of suspects. The seriousness may be tempered with some humor, and the stories shy away from graphic violence, overt sex, and crude, lowlife characters. The cozy is often associated with British writers, with whom the form originated, but Americans such as Amanda Cross, Martha Grimes, Carolyn G. Hart, and Joyce Porter are popular practitioners of the form. The private-eye subgenre also experienced a renaissance toward the end of the century, with a major change being that the stories were set in places other than New York, San Francisco, Chicago, or Los Angeles: Cedar Rapids (Ed Gorman's Jack Dwyer), Cincinnati (Jonathan Valin's Harry Stoner), and Detroit (Loren D. Estleman's Amos Walker). Female private eyes, perhaps influenced by the successes of P. D. James's Cordelia Gray, also started to come to the fore. Liza Cody's London agency operative Anna Lee first appeared in *Dupe* (1980). Two years later came two important American debuts: Sue Grafton's Kinsey Milhone in *A Is for Alibi* (1982) and Sara Paretsky's V. I. Warshawski in *Indemnity Only* (1982). Noteworthy, too, is Linda Barnes's Boston private eye Carlotta Carlyle, whose first appearance in a novel is in *A Trouble of Fools* (1987).

Several detective novel subgenres either emerged or gained in popularity during the 1980's and 1990's. Series with religious themes and clerics as detectives include William X. Kienzle's Father Robert Koesler books, Joseph Telushkin's Rabbi Daniel Winter mysteries, and Ellis Peters's medieval Brother Cadfael novels. The Amanda Cross mysteries starring Professor Kate Fansler, M. D. Lake's campus cop Peggy O'Neill novels, and Edith Skom's literature lecturer Beth Austin books are academic whodunits, mysteries set on college or university campuses. New authors began featuring African American, Native American, or gay or lesbian detectives. Historical detective fiction, in which the action is set in the past, was a rarity until the 1970's, when it became a major subgenre, as practiced not only by Ellis Peters, but also by such authors as Peter Lovesey (whose Victorian mysteries feature Sergeant Cribb) and Edward Marston, the latter of whom authored both medieval and Elizabethan novels. His eleventh century Domesday Book series developed around the device of William the Conqueror's men traveling the countryside to review problems stemming from the ruler's census and property survey. Spurred by sibling rivalry, the desire for material gain, and the determination to purge suppressed grievances, people murder and cause havoc in a society that remains insecure two decades after the upheavals of the Norman conquest. By the time they leave an area, the king's men have adjudicated land claims and have exorcised real and imagined evils. Another Marston series, set in England at the end of the sixteenth century, centers on a London theater group whose stage manager turns to detection when deaths occur offstage.

The several plots that Marston typically orchestrates in each of his medieval and Elizabethan mysteries exemplify such subjects as unrequited love, political and social ambition, sibling rivalry, the intrusion of the past upon the present, and questions of personal identity. They are very much like the subjects of most other detective novels, whatever their category or subgenre. In other words, however much detective fiction changes, it retains fundamentals of early and golden age crime stories, which traditionally used a murder as a dramatic means of focusing upon a wide variety of human issues.

F. William Nelson, updated by Gerald H. Strauss

BIBLIOGRAPHY

Barzun, Jacques, and Wendell Hertig Taylor. *A Catalogue of Crime*. New York: Harper & Row, 1989. A highly personal compilation by two voracious readers of crime fiction, this 952-page volume contains more than five thousand brief descriptions and judgments of works in most categories of the genre as well as a variety of critical studies.

DeAndrea, William L., ed. *Encyclopedia Mysteriosa*. New York: Prentice Hall, 1994. Written by a mystery novel writer and critic, the book comprises alphabetically arranged entries about authors, books, characters, actors, films, and television and radio programs. Includes ample cross-references and occasional longer entries (such as dime novels and the hard-boiled detective) by experts other than DeAndrea.

Gorman, Ed, Martin H. Greenberg, Larry Segriff, and John Breen, eds. *The Fine Art of Murder*. New York: Carroll & Graf, 1993. Not intended as a definitive study of the genre, this collection of articles by crime fiction writers and critics serves as an introduction for the reader. Categories into which the volume is divided tend to overlap, and some important writers are ignored; however, this is a useful and entertaining volume.

Keating, H. R. F. *Murder Must Appetize*. New York: Mysterious Press, 1981. Crime fiction writer and critic Keating engages in a nostalgic, affectionate look at some of his favorite creators of traditional British mysteries, including Nicholas Blake, Agatha Christie, Anthony Gilbert, Gladys Mitchell, and Dorothy L. Sayers.

_____, ed. *Whodunit? A Guide to Crime, Suspense, and Spy Fiction*. New York: Van Nostrand Reinhold, 1982. The contributors to this eclectic volume include many of the luminaries of crime fiction, who not only discuss aspects of the genre but also explain how they go about their own creative tasks. Most useful is the "consumer's guide," 138 pages devoted to brief comments about writers plus ratings of their works by Keating and three other crime novelists.

Steinbrunner, Chris, and Otto Penzler, eds. *Encyclopedia of Mystery and Detection*. New York: McGraw-Hill, 1976. Profusely illustrated, this readable reference contains about six hundred articles that mainly deal with authors but also consider genres, detectives, and other matters. Gothic romances and some other literature not normally considered under the rubric of mystery fiction are also included. Somewhat superseded by later compilations, the volume is still useful for the compilers' opinions and for facts.

Symons, Julian. *Bloody Murder: From the Detective Story to the Crime Novel*. New York: Mysterious Press, 1993. The third and final revision of a classic study by a major writer of crime novels and stories, this book is an appreciation as well as a sound critical and historical analysis. Inclusive in its coverage, the book naturally reflects Symons's biases, but he remained conscious of his commitment to present a balanced overview of the genre. Though he favors his fellow English writers, Symons gives Americans their due.

THE EPISTOLARY NOVEL

The epistolary novel, a prominent form among modern fictions, is defined as a novel presented wholly, or nearly so, in familiar letter form. Its history reaches far back into classical literature, taking special inspiration from the separate traditions of the Roman letter writers Cicero and Pliny, and of Ovid's *Heroides* (before 8 C.E.; English translation, 1567), a series of verse letters celebrating famous heroines of myth. Familiar letters, as such, developed slowly in a world where literacy was rare; but the epistle, a classic rhetorical form, defined by the rules of oratory, was a favorite means of expression for many scholars of the European Middle Ages and Renaissance, yielding learned letters in both prose and verse, most common at first in Latin, then in the vernacular.

Origins

The sixteenth century saw the first dated translation of Ovid's *Heroides* into French, in 1500. The mid-century welcomed with great enthusiasm the first "pure" epistolary novels: Juan de Segura's *Processo de cartas* (1548) and Alvise Pasqualigo's *Delle Lettere amorose* (1563). Letters were used as tools in the earliest modern novels and romances, for they answered the frequent problem of communication between separated lovers, as well as giving the opportunity to multiply complications and mischances by having letters discovered by enemies, lost and intercepted, misinterpreted, or received out of time and season. For example, within the five-volume bulk of Honoré d'Urfé's pastoral novel *L'Astrée* (1610), there are 129 letters that are hidden in hats, stolen, found floating down rivers, or recited from memory.

The seventeenth century in France saw the development of a climate in which letters were one of the most popular forms of written material. The first printed edition of the letters of Abélard and Héloïse came in 1616, and the verse translation published in 1678 by Bussy-Rabutin (himself a celebrated social épistolier) was greeted with great enthusiasm. The collected epistles of Guez de Balzac, first published in 1624, had a great vogue, with many reprintings and new collections. His popular successor, Victor Voiture, was praised still more highly for the light tone and grace of his letters. Within the aristocratic salons of the day, the reading of letters within a circle of friends was a frequent social pastime, and many famous people of the day wrote their letters in the certainty of their being read to a group rather than kept private. Madame de Sévigné wrote to such correspondents as her cousin Bussy-Rabutin in the expectation that they would circulate and increase her reputation as a graceful wit.

Within the salons, expertise in letter writing grew through mutual compliment and criticism, but the appearance of popular letter manuals offered models to a wider circle of literate people. Jean Puget de la Serre published his enormously successful *Secrétaire de la Cour* in 1623 and followed it in 1641 with the *Secrétaire à la Mode*. These manuals were translated and reissued through countless numbers of printings, became very popular in England, inspired a great number of imitations, and had an untold effect on developing popular epistolary style and thematics. The letter writers, as they offered epistolary models on varied subjects and occasions, often offered responses as well and built up a series of letters that told the germ of a story. Samuel Richardson wrote a letter handbook, *The Complete Letter-Writer* (1741), in which can be found the prototype for his epistolary novel *Pamela: Or, Virtue Rewarded* (1740-1741).

Familiar letters were regarded as direct transcriptions of events seen or experienced by their writers, and although the epistles of writers such as Guez de Balzac were acknowledged to be polished productions, letters in general carried the cachet of truth and spontaneity. Thus, arising out of the ferment of epistolary literature, the early epistolary novelists claimed for their works, as a matter of course, the privilege of historical truth. The most frequent *topos* of epistolary novels is the statement that they are a collection of real letters, not literary fabrications, and that the author is only an editor of material from other hands. The first great French epistolary novel, *Lettres portugaises* (1669, *Portuguese Letters*), now recognized as the work of Gabriel Guilleragues, was long believed to be a translation from the Portuguese of genuine letters written by a nun to her French lover. Letters offered a freedom of style, being rhetorically defined as written transcriptions of oral communication. Letters could deal with a variety of subjects, using a light touch, and were not forced to follow any subject through all its logical ramifications. Charles de Montesquieu, the author of *Lettres Persanes* (1721; *Persian Letters*, 1722), refers to these advantages of epistolary form in his "Réflections," which were added to the 1754 edition. Letters carried the atmosphere of lived experience, which gave credence and popularity to the memoir but had the added fillip of retelling stories whose ends were unknown. A memorialist has safely arrived at a point from which he or she can reflect on the past. Letters are written within the flow of present experience, looking back to the last letter written, forward to the next.

THE SEVENTEENTH AND EIGHTEENTH CENTURIES

Love themes are given a special privilege in the epistolary fiction derived from the tradition of Ovid, Abélard, and Héloïse, while the tradition descending from Cicero and Pliny to Guez de Balzac encourages the use of letters to treat a variety of topics of more general interest with the familiar touch of friends in social conversation. The seventeenth and eighteenth centuries saw the rise of the epistolary novel to a dominant prose form throughout Europe, first in France and England, then in Germany and Eastern Europe. Three of the most influential novels of the eighteenth century, Richardson's *Pamela*, Jean-Jacques Rousseau's *Julie: Ou, La Nouvelle Héloïse* (1761; *Eloise: Or, A Series of Original Letters*, 1761; also as *Julie: Or, The New Eloise*, 1968; better known as *The New Héloïse*), and Johann Wolfgang von Goethe's *Die Leiden des jungen Werthers* (1774, *The Sorrows of Young Werther*, 1779), were all in letter form. It was certainly the exploitation by the writers of the epistolary form itself that gave their novels their immense impact.

In *Portuguese Letters*, the epistolary novel is given an emotionally concentrated model, inspiring numerous translations, "completions," and imitations. The French edition of 1669, for example, was translated into English in 1678, 1681, 1693, 1694, and 1716. With its five letters, Guilleragues's work is extremely brief, especially considered in the context of novels such as the five-volume *L'Astrée*. Presented by the author, in his guise as editor, as "a correct copy of the translation of five Portuguese Letters which were written to a noble gentleman who served in Portugal," the letters are univocal; that is, the reader hears only the voice of one correspondent. Every attempt is made to establish the credibility of the letters, which are said to have been circulating in private hands. Publication is resorted to only to ensure that a "correct copy" rather than a spurious compilation is in public circulation. The nun's voice cries in genuine pain, expressed through a correspondence whose failure destroys the romantic ties with her French lover. The expectation of a response is inherent in the nun's use of the letter and in the I-you couple that defines the alternate composers of a correspondence. Direct address calls for direct response. The nun's letters begin in answer to a letter from the absent lover, and a two-sided exchange is expected. In fact, while requesting frequent letters, the nun also tries to set the tone and admonishes her lover not to talk of useless things, nor ask her to remember him. The correspondence, and the romance, have run their course by the fifth and final letter, because the Frenchman does not respond within the expectations of the nun. At first he does not write at all; then his letters are inadequate to feed her passion.

Sentimental analysis, so important in this novel, is doubled by the analysis of the specific written form involved, by the problem of maintaining a satisfactory exchange of letters between parted lovers. The wounded heart of the nun is expressed in complaints of the lack of proper response in the letter chain, as well as of the lack of love. The author exploits the value of the letter as a tool for immediate access to his heroine's emotions, setting the tone for many later epistolary novels in the impassioned style of the nun's effusions. Even Madame de Sévigné joked that if she responded in like tone to a tender note from a gentleman friend, she would have to write a "portugaise."

In 1721, *Persian Letters* was published anonymously by Charles Louis de Secondat, Baron de Montesquieu. The introduction once again insists that the letters are a collection chosen from a great number written and received by Persians lodging with the author, letters copied and kept sometimes without the knowledge of the foreign travelers. The editor has "translated" the letters and adjusted them to European tastes, leaving out the flowery language, "sublime expressions," and long complimentary formulas of the originals. In choosing Persians for the chief characters of his novel, Montesquieu gave his novel an exotic background; in professing to adapt this exoticism to European tastes, he could add just as much as he liked for seasoning, without worrying about authentic Asian style. The choice of Persians also greatly emphasizes the theme of absence inherent in epistolary form; it is the chief difficulty facing Usbek in the administration of his distant harem and the reason for his ultimate downfall as a domestic tyrant. This exotic flavor also allows for comic exploitation in the naïve reactions of the Persians as their letters recount the manners and morals of Montesquieu's world.

Persian Letters includes letters attributed to numerous pens, although the chief correspondents are Usbek and his younger companion Rica. Usbek's exchange with the members of his harem and their keepers provides the story without which this would be no true novel, but this story is only one of the two major strains in the novel. There are a great many letters that serve as discussions of current events in France or deal with moral and philosophical questions. In all the letters, the name of the writer is given, in many of them a definite correspondent. All are dated according to the Persian calendar, covering a span of eight years. There are several complete letter circuits, letters given with their direct response, and subsequent letters to and from that same correspondent. There are also letter exchanges between secondary characters, such as that between the chief eunuch of Usbek's harem and a young protégé destined to replace him. The lapse of time indicated in the complete circuit of response is given great weight, especially at the denouement of the harem in-

trigue, when Usbek helplessly rages at the distances which make his own responses inadequate.

In letter 155, Usbek announces his return to Ispahan. His letters have often been received as much as six months late, and it is abundantly clear that he will not return to his harem until well after the horrible events chronicled in subsequent letters. Letter 148, Usbek's reply to letter 147, giving the chief eunuch universal power over the harem, arrives after the death of the addressee and is kept by his elderly successor as a sealed relic (noted in letter 149). Letter 150, from Usbek, seeking to "reactivate" the sealed letter, is either intercepted by harem rebels (version given in letter 151) or lost during a robbery (letter 152). The last letter of the novel, 161, written by Usbek's favorite, Roxane, is composed after a self-administered dose of poison, noted in the text, and the process of death defines the compass of the letter. In this letter, the writer details the end of the harem world in her own death and ends the novel's text and her life when the pen falls from her hand and she dies.

The varied stylistic possibilities of letters are explored in the harem series; different writers are given different tones in which to express their characters, and the tones of the correspondents change as they address different people. Usbek does not write in the same manner to two different wives, and his tone and subject matter change again in addressing the chief eunuch or his own friend Nessir. The means of transmission of letters across the great distances is noted; letter 150 is to be delivered by some Armenian merchants traveling to Ispahan, but since the harem has moved to Usbek's country house, a servant is sent to fetch it; it disappears during a robbery on the servant's return trip. Letters are objects subject to many strange fates.

Letters serve a different function in the parallel series devoted to the exploration of various themes of French society and thought through the eyes of the Persian visitors. Here the epistolary form is used much as Voltaire later used it in his *Lettres philosophiques* (1734; originally published in English as *Letters Concerning the English Nation*, 1733; also as *Philosophical Letters*, 1961), where no story line is imposed within the letter framework to produce a true epistolary novel. In this use of the letter form, the epistolary license to touch on any subject with a light and familiar tone is the desired feature. The necessary epistolary use of the first person and direct address to the fictional correspondent gives the opportunity for the epistolary writer to build an automatic bridge of sympathy with the reader. In general, the formal fiction of the letter is given less weight as more is given to thematic development of the individual argument. In the Troglodyte series of letters (10 through 14), Usbek writes to his young friend Mirza, with the correspondence acting as a simple frame, an excuse for thematic development. Within the series, there are only the most perfunctory references to the correspondence, none to the letters themselves. Several texts succeed one another with no transition or attempt to explain differing circumstances of composition for different dates. Although written as a "response" to Mirza's letter, this series is a finished whole and requires no answer to complete it.

Persian Letters was followed by many epistolary novels set in exotic locales or using foreign characters for added interest and a pretext for letters. Laurent Versini, in his *Roman épistolaire* (1979), notes that half of the French epistolary novels between Montesquieu's success and 1750 were exotics. The great novels of the eighteenth century, however, concentrate on domestic situations, set within the countries of origin of their authors: *Pamela* in England, *The New Héloïse* in French Switzerland, and *The Sorrows of Young Werther* in Germany. These three works had enormous influence on the European reading public. All were translated into many tongues and inspired many imitators, both in literary terms and within the realm of everyday life. *The Sorrows of Young Werther*, said to have taken inspiration from *The New Héloïse*, in its turn supposed a direct descendant of Richardson's *Pamela* and *Clarissa: Or, The History of a Young Lady* (1747-1748), was not only one of the great propulsive works of German Romanticism but was said to have inspired a rash of suicides on its publication as well.

Pamela appeared in print one year before *The Complete Letter-Writer*, begun earlier, in which Rich-

ardson had set down the novel's premise: a series of letters telling a true story of a virtuous servant girl who defends herself from her employer's advances and eventually is rewarded by his hand in marriage. What is a skeleton in the letter manual is fleshed out to great length in the highly detailed development of the novel. Translated by no less a light than the Abbé Prévost, and succeeded by Richardson's own *Clarissa* and *Sir Charles Grandison* (1753-1754), *Pamela* was parodied, reportedly, by Henry Fielding in *An Apology for the Life of Mrs. Shamela Andrews* (1741), and definitely by Fielding's *The History of the Adventures of Joseph Andrews, and of His Friend Mr. Abraham Adams* (1742). *Pamela* continues to arouse debate. Critics have often seen prurience in Richardson's theme and hypocrisy in his happy ending. Pamela's letters chronicle successive scenes of attempted seduction and rape in panting detail, while steadfastly defending the strictest principles of female chastity. Were Pamela's sufferings in some way a calculated "come-on" to a dupe due to be seduced into marriage? Although psychological credibility may be strained by the union of so much innocence and vulnerability with such a ferocious determination to resist and to recount every evidence of Mr. B.'s passion, the use of the letter form argues for Richardson's insistence on Pamela's candor. Richardson's first great epistolary novel is predicated on the assumption that the familiar letter is a direct window on the soul. Pamela may be taken at face value, and every letter carries what is supposed to be the free expression of the state of her soul.

Pamela is presented by the author as a collection of genuine letters, and he intrudes in his guise as editor to explain and provide transitions as well as to point out the moral at the end. In the opening pages, one finds complete letter circuits between Pamela Andrews and her aged, impoverished parents. These early letters introduce several of the major characters and establish the family's virtuous character, as well as a critical facet of Pamela's behavior. The favorable notice she had received from the lady whose death occasions the first letter had led her to take an inordinate interest in reading and writing, though yet very young (letter 4 gives her age as fifteen), and in general had raised her above her station in education and behavior. The first letter speaks explicitly of itself, drawing attention to rather than leaving in the background the epistolary pretext of the fiction: Pamela's tears are blotting her paper. The means by which the letter is to be sent are discussed, and a postscript opens the theme of letters hidden from and discovered by Mr. B.

As the novel progresses and Pamela passes through a series of harrowing experiences, including lengthy captivity by Mr. B., the letter exchange with her parents cannot continue, and Pamela writes to them in the hope that one day they will read her words and understand the trials through which she has come. Even her early letters are written in the anticipation of preservation and rereading by her entire family. The letters become a sort of journal, although an outward-turning one, in which the destined readers are often mentioned, and their reactions to a particular scene or reflection are imagined. The entries in this letter-journal are dated according to the day of the week, at times even with the time of day. All circumstances of composition are referred to, including the supply source of the paper, pen, and ink, as well as their places of concealment. Some letters from Mr. B. are included in the form of copies, and any communication received by Pamela is closely analyzed in her subsequent writing. First-person narration and direct address are used throughout. Pamela comments constantly on her style, the effect of her circumstances on her composition, and her intention to set down each event as it happens.

The status of the growing body of manuscript is very important indeed and is given a large place in the consideration of the epistolary text. Pamela's early letters are often intercepted and read by Mr. B. Her later journal is kept hidden from him by various expedients, sewn in Pamela's petticoats or, on threat of physical search, buried in the garden. In an attempt to have letters carried to her parents by the parson Mr. Williams, Pamela compromises that gentleman and brings him into disgrace with his patron. As a consequence, she has the piquant experience of reading a misdirected letter meant for Mrs. Jewkes, her keeper, and may contrast the style with the letter meant for herself and sent mistakenly to Jewkes. The recopying of Jewkes's letter serves a double purpose: to illustrate the severity of Mr. B. and to enter the text into the secret letter-journal. At last, when Pamela is dismissed from Mr. B.'s sight and is en route to her parents in disgrace, it is the story told by her letters, surrendered to him, which persuades him to change his resolution and marry her. The marriage restores epistolary commerce between Pamela and the elder Andrewses, and they learn the course of their daughter's acceptance into noble society, ending in their reunion on Mr. B.'s estates. The collection of Pamela's letters is left circulating among the family and friends of Mr. B. at the close of the novel, reconciling all to his choice of a wife.

While *Pamela* includes occasional letters from Mr. B. and other characters, the text is essentially univocal. *Clarissa*, Richardson's next novel, employs correspondence of several different characters in presenting and maintaining a multivocal epistolary narration. In Jean-Jacques Rousseau's *The New Héloïse*, it is the love duet of Julie and her Saint-Preux that holds the central position. The letters are presented by the author as a collection of genuine letters, as the title of the 1761 translation announces: *Eloise: Or, A Series of Original Letters*. Letters are exchanged between inhabitants of a small town at the foot of the Alps and are collected and published by Rousseau. By linking his novel with the long-standing epistolary tradition of Abélard and Héloïse, Rousseau stresses the importance of letters as letters, as well as their aura of historic truth (since the first Héloïse was real, so is Julie), and the importance of the love intrigue, with its implication of suffering and sacrifice.

Letter form is given special weight in the first half of the novel, where, as the letters introduce the characters and lay the foundations for later narration, individual texts respond point-by-point to their predecessors. It is in answering Saint-Preux's letters, written while the lovers are in close daily contact, that Julie enters into a romantic relationship with him. It is in a letter that she first receives his expression of affection and through the letters that they are bound together, even over long absences. The letters are written in the first person, directed to a very definite correspondent, and the mode of communication between the lovers is discussed at length. Themes treated within the letters vary widely and include philosophical discussions, in which cases Rousseau uses the prerogative of the epistolary form to digress from his plot much as Montesquieu did. Within the line of the main narration, letters are important as physical testimony of the loved "other," substitutes for the loved one in absence, and as such they are kissed, caressed, preserved, and reread. Saint-Preux's handling of Julie's letters forces him to recopy them, since the originals are wearing out. This recopying in a certain sense establishes a prototext of the final letter collection represented in the novel. The time lapse between the letters is important, as is their method of transmission.

Letter 21 presents a highly dramatic scene in which Saint-Preux awaits and receives one of Julie's letters from the hand of the mail carrier. This passage highlights all the details of transmission: the necessity of naming oneself in claiming the letter, the opening of the outer packet in which the letter has traveled with the correspondence of others, the confirmation that there is indeed a letter for the narrator, and finally the confirmation of the letter itself as a physical object carrying the imprint of the loved one's hand in the superscription. Saint-Preux continues to recount in his own letter, in response to this one received with so much ceremony, the emotion he felt when he held the paper in his trembling hand and the conditions under which he finally opened and read it. The emphasis lies not only on the single letter so dramatized but also on the entire correspondence. In a text such as Voltaire's *Lettres philosophiques*, no attention is given to building or embroidering the fiction of the epistolary text as a physical reality. In *The New Héloïse*, the highly charged, emotional intimacy between Julie and her Saint-Preux is served by the attention lavished on the mechanics of a letter exchange through which the narration may proceed and by which it is colored. The identification of the reader is sought through the attempt to engage belief in the reality of the characters involved. Again, as in *Pamela*, letters serve as a "hot" medium, transparent to the emotions of the individual writers and immediate to the events which affect them.

The Sorrows of Young Werther, the first major work of Johann Wolfgang von Goethe, is brief and concentrated in its impact, in contrast to the voluminous works of Rousseau and Richardson. Again, the book is presented by the editor as a collection of "all I could find" of Werther's letters. Almost all are addressed to Werther's intimate friend, Wilhelm, with a small number written for the beloved Lotte and her husband Albert. The personality of the correspondent is seldom given much weight within the individual texts, although there are very few letters in which Werther does not use direct address or in which the intended reader is not clearly designated. Wilhelm is almost always the intimate *du* (the intimate, informal form of the pronoun "you"), infrequently *ihr* (plural form of "you") when in the company of Werther's mother. Lotte alone is *Sie* (formal "you"), until the last letter, while Lotte and Albert together are *ihr*, combining formal address for Lotte with familiar form for her husband. Significantly, as in *Persian Letters*, each epistolary text is dated, and the rhythm of the narration speeds or slows with the ebb and flow of the fictional correspondence. When Werther is overcome by the flux of his emotions during time spent with Lotte, the letters to Wilhelm are dated every two or three days, sometimes daily. When bored and depressed by exterior circumstances, such as his position on an ambassador's staff, the letters come only once a week or so. The infrequent letters may be seen as an attempt at verisimilitude, since, although there is no break in the narration during these periods, the editor notes that certain letters of this period have been withheld as indiscreet.

Unlike Rousseau and Richardson, Goethe devotes little attention to the technical aspects of the epistolary commerce. One knows exactly where and how Pamela gets her pen and paper, and how Saint-Preux receives and treats Julie's letters, but there is no indication of how Werther's letters are written or exchanged with Wilhelm. The references to epistolary style are few, but there are some direct responses to Wilhelm's letters, with passages cited as they are answered. Beyond the faithful use of dates, which serves a dramatic purpose in emphasizing the speed with which Werther's passion enfolds and destroys him, there are very few uses of set letter forms. The letters vary greatly in length, some quite long and others reduced to the briefest of paragraphs. No opening formulas are used, and the formal closings are sparse, with at most a simple *Leb wohl* (farewell) inserted at the end. This manner of closing, however, can be effectively dramatized, as in Werther's closing to his suicide letter: "*Lotte! Lotte leb wohl! Leb wohl!*"

Goethe uses the letter form as a painfully intimate reflection of the state of mind of his suffering hero. The fragmentary sentences (which would be out of place in another narrative form), the stringing together of dated paragraphs that gain weight from their status as letters addressed to an outer eye, the license to speak in the first person about all the secret movements of the soul—these are all possibilities inherent in the epistolary form. That Werther makes what amounts to an aberrant use of the form in his emphasis on one pole of the correspondence, his own, is in a way a facet of the characterization of the tragic hero, so locked in on his own suffering that suicide becomes his only escape. The letter form is also open to the many descriptions of Werther's impressions of the people and things around him, yet even his sweeping pictures of the natural beauty he meets are transmuted into personal reflections. This is not the same use that Montesquieu, or even Rousseau, makes of the possibility of including material exterior to the story line within the narrative of a letter. The emotional impact of *The Sorrows of Young Werther* is concentrated and focused through this use of univocal, inward-turning letter form.

The last days of Werther's life are chronicled by the anonymous editor's voice in a curious text formed by the third-person reminiscences of Lotte, Albert, Werther's servant, and other people who met or talked with Werther in that time. These bits of testimony are woven through by fragments of a last, undated letter addressed to Lotte and shorter bits directed to Wilhelm. This last attempt at writing anticipates the reactions of Werther's loved ones after his death, and frequent reference is made to their reading the text after the writer's burial. In it, Lotte changes from the formal *Sie* to *du* and is addressed in the most intimate and intense tones. The last words, addressed to her, are written immediately before the fatal shot. The impersonal editorial voice informs the reader that "From the blood on the back of the seat, one can determine, that he did the deed sitting before the writing desk." The contrast between Werther's own heated voice and the cold style of the editor is devastating, producing an impression of the "truth" of the fatal events and the finality of Werther's death.

The Sorrows of Young Werther, *The New Héloïse*, and *Pamela* all depend heavily on the convention that personal letters are the vehicles of personal truth, open and immediate to the individuals who write them. This understanding plays a part in the characterization of the fictional protagonists and in the emotional effects elicited by their letters. In contrast to these novels, *Les Liaisons dangereuses* (1782, *Dangerous Acquaintances*, 1784; also known as *Dangerous Liaisons*) of Pierre Choderlos de Laclos takes much of its impact from the use made by the libertine protagonists, the Marquise de Merteuil and the Vicomte de Valmont, of this same convention to conceal their emotions and intentions and to seduce and destroy their correspondents. The author plays with several correspondences exchanged within a small social circle, changing styles with each writer and according to each addressee. The totality of the letters is revealed, through various stratagems, to Madame de Merteuil and her sometime ally Valmont, and each letter becomes the object of discussion and analysis between them. If the progress of the seductions by Merteuil and Valmont is one interest of the narrative, the change in their relationship through the course of the novel is another, a chance brought about in part through Valmont's own surrender to love for his victim Madame de Tourvel. The terms of his letters to Merteuil are held as a contract, forcing him to the destruction of the loved object and himself.

Dangerous Liaisons is preceded by a double preface, the first by the "editor," the second by the "writer." Together they form an ironic gem. The editor writes a bit of social commentary, saying that in spite of the author's attempts to make his work seem genuine, it must be a novel because the contemporary age is too moral for such events to take place. The writer produces the image of a pedantic hired hack who has pieced together the letters of the novel, chosen from a great body of possible correspondence, as the smallest number of texts necessary to tell the story. The writer complains that the third party, who commissioned him, did not allow him to change the grammar or style of the letters or to cut the chosen texts, "of which several deal separately, and almost without transition, with subjects altogether unconnected with one another." His employers maintain that a variety of styles, even errors, and a diversity of themes arc expected of personal letters. Such features, the writer thinks, may both attract and repel the public, and since all the sentiments, or nearly so, are pretended, the identification of the public with the characters will be impaired. The reader of both the prefaces will find himself in a position of ironic suspension, where neither introductory voice can be believed or wholly rejected, and thus he must approach the novel with suspended judgment.

The complexity of *Dangerous Liaisons* and the literary virtuosity with which it was composed have attracted a great deal of critical attention. One of the most interesting of such studies, both in regard to this individual work and in its general overview of the epistolary genre, is Jean Rousset's "Le Roman par lettres," included in his collected essays, *Forme et Signification* (1962). Rousset discusses the important factors that enlist the reader's identification with the characters of the epistolary novel: the atmosphere of intimacy provided by the familiar letter form, the fact that the action of the novel is contemporary with the life and voice of the characters, and the seductiveness of the bipolar I-you structure that almost forces a reader to identify with the voices of the letters. Rousset further points out that, in the case of *Dangerous Liaisons*, the reader is, like Merteuil and Valmont, in possession of an entire epistolary text, thus knowing the stratagems employed by the libertines in the composition of their letters. In Rousset's view, this knowledge renders the reader an accomplice of the libertines in their work of seduction.

What are the techniques used by Laclos to write these compromising letters that catch the reader in a dangerous liaison? Great importance is given to the individual letter and its ties with other letters. The names of writer and addressee are given, the dates of composition, and often the place. Frequent reference is made to letters received from the correspondent and other letters written or received by the writers. When Cécile de Volanges runs out of writing materials, Valmont smuggles some to her (letter 123). The mode of transmission of letters and where and how they are kept is a major motif, since so many of the exchanges are clandestine, and the various ruses of delivery and concealment are continuously under discussion.

In addition to the primary series of letters between pairs of correspondents, there is a secondary exchange within the letters of Madame de Merteuil and Valmont, of copies of letters to and from third parties, with detailed commentary and analysis of motivation and circumstances of character and composition. This commentary often completely changes the interpretation that must be given to individual passages or entire letters. One particularly titillating example is letter 48, written by Valmont to Madame de Tourvel. A naïve reader, such as Madame de Tourvel, sees in it nothing but Valmont's agitated state of mind, owing to his professed passion for his correspondent. In letter 47, however, Valmont sends the letter to Madame de Merteuil, who will post it for him from Paris, to preserve a pretense of his remaining in that city. Merteuil and the outside reader are informed that the letter was written on the back of a prostitute, the composition interrupted for intercourse, and that it gives an exact accounting of Valmont's situation and conduct in ambiguous terms. Thus when Valmont says, "The very table on which I write to you, consecrated for the first time to this use, becomes for me the sacred altar of love," the meaning is changed beyond recognition by the added information.

The reading and answering of letters are stressed as acts of self-engagement in the relations of the characters. Valmont sees the future success of his seduction in Madame de Tourvel's first reply to one of his letters; he sees its near accomplishment in the discovery that all his letters have been saved, even while the lady virtuously denies him any other sign of weakening. Several letters are dictated by one character to another, and the final letter with which Valmont must break Madame de Tourvel's heart, in order to fulfill his agreements with Merteuil, is copied verbatim from a model supplied in Merteuil's letter 141.

The chain of events by which all the letters are united in the hands of Madame de Rosemonde, thereby creating the novel text, is a chain of catastrophe. The production of the novel is the destruction of its chief characters. Of the victims, Cécile de Volanges enters a convent, the Chevalier Danceny goes into exile, and Madame de Tourvel dies of humiliation and a broken heart. Valmont is fatally wounded in a duel with Danceny, but as his last act he confides to the young man the packet of letters detailing his own relations with Madame de Merteuil, thus revealing the character of his beautiful and outwardly virtuous confederate. Danceny, after circulating some of these letters, passes the entire packet on to Valmont's elderly aunt, Madame de Rosemonde, the close friend of Madame de Volanges (Cécile's mother) and Madame de Tourvel. Madame de Merteuil herself is cast out of polite society, loses a court case that robs her of her entire fortune, suffers a severe case of smallpox that leaves her horribly disfigured, and finally flees the country, ill and utterly alone but carrying her diamonds with her. Laclos leaves no thread untied, as his bundle of letters is bound into a book.

Dangerous Liaisons opens with a quotation drawn from *The New Héloïse*. In its cynical use of letters as instruments of seduction and betrayal, it destroys the premise of emotional immediacy used to such advantage by Rousseau in his novel. For Saint-Preux, letters are a self-generating system by whose intervention he may always be in the presence of his beloved: "I can no longer separate myself from you, the least absence is unbearable to me, and it is necessary that I either see you or write to you in order to occupy myself with you without ceasing" (letter 11). For Madame de Merteuil, the letter is a tool to be used for definite ends: "What good would it do you to soften hearts with Letters, since you would not be there to profit from it?" (letter 33). Yet in the final analysis, it

is through the letters united in the novel that Laclos paints compelling portraits of his characters, not in direct revelations but through the reflections and combinations of the continuing chain of correspondence. Valmont's inner truth finally does correspond with the appearance of love in his first letters to Madame de Tourvel, and it is Madame de Merteuil's letters that convince society of the evil character she had always before been able to conceal.

THE TWENTIETH CENTURY

Epistolary novels passed into comparative disuse in the nineteenth and early twentieth centuries. Late in the twentieth century, however, writers of experimental and avant-garde fiction and criticism found the letter form, with its constant self-reflection and accepted freedom from certain formal structures, a tempting medium. Certain writers still used the letter as a form suited for naïve confidences, but, in general, its innocence was lost. In fact, even French deconstructionist critic and philosopher Jacques Derrida toyed with epistolary form in *La Carte postale: De Socrate à Freud et au-delà* (1980; *The Post Card: From Socrates to Freud and Beyond*, 1987), a series of letter texts with dates, direct address, and personal tone—sometimes fiction, sometimes criticism, but never a simple story.

John Barth's monumental work *Letters* (1979) uses seven epistolary voices, one of them "John Barth," to simultaneously explore personal letters: Letters in the sense of literature and letters of the alphabet. *Letters* opens with a formal invitation to "John Barth" to accept the honorary degree of doctor of letters from Marshyhope State University. This formal text from the provost is accompanied by a rambling personal postscript; the provost is also Germaine Pitt, the only female voice of the novel. "Barth" declines the honor but nonetheless launches into a dizzying interweaving of texts, stories, and wordplays. The first six letters introduce the separate narrative voices; the seventh (from "John Barth" to "the Reader") belatedly announces the beginning of the novel.

The interrelations of the characters are complex, and this complication is mirrored by the complexity of their letter exchanges. Twice-married Germaine Pitt has been the mistress of a wealthy patron of Marshyhope. Her first husband, André de Castine, may be the alter ego of A. B. Cook VI or may simply be his cousin. A. B. Cook VI may be an extreme political conservative and the poet laureate of Maryland, or he may be André, the father of Germaine's missing son, born to a family of underground revolutionaries. He presents a series of letters that may have been written in the early nineteenth century by his ancestor A. B. Cook IV, a similarly enigmatic character, who may have died in the War of 1812. Germaine is caught up in a passionate affair with Ambrose Mensch, professor at Marshyhope, friend of "John Barth" and adapter of "Barth's" works for a motion picture. The film offers a stage for the novel's actions and reactions, as well as a frame for a debate on the viability of the written word in contrast to cinema.

Letters are written from "John Barth" to all his characters and vice versa, from one character to himself, from Ambrose to an unknown correspondent reached by placing letters in bottles and setting them adrift, from A. B. Cook IV to his unborn children and, after his supposed death, to his "widow," from a son to his dead father, and from "John Barth" to the reader. Letter conventions are scrupulously preserved in the date, salutation, direct address, and frequent reference to composition, means of transmission, and the physical particulars of each letter. One long, revealing letter from Germaine to "John Barth" tells about her affair with Ambrose. Later Germaine writes that a carbon copy of this letter has fallen into the hands of her college president. A digest is made from this carbon copy, and multiple copies are distributed to the trustees of Marshyhope. This doctored document is the pretext on which Germaine and Ambrose are fired from the university; Germaine is displaced for using the techniques of a professional writer on an all-too-personal letter.

In many cases readers are explicitly warned to distrust the identity of the letter writer. In no case are they encouraged to take anything at face value, not even the dates heading the letters or the names at their end. "John Barth" announces that he is writing a novel in which each of the characters is invited to participate; by this ambiguous invitation, he announces that those varied voices are all simultaneously imaginary constructs and separate "real" people. All the letter writers except Germaine are drawn from other works by the actual Barth, a theme that recurs explicitly in their letters. Each of the seven correspondents has a recognizable style and set of issues, and most events are told and retold through more than one narrator. The reader is never allowed to fully identify with the characters, for there is no consistent attempt to foster the illusion that these are "real" people. Few of the letters that form this novel are ever answered by other characters; in a work designed to test whether the epistolary novel can survive in the late twentieth century, the chain of direct response is lost.

The letters in *Letters* are built within an elaborate alphabetical and mathematical framework; value in advancing plot or revealing character is countered by arbitrary number and letter value. This relationship is emphasized by the comments of several characters about recurring events, number structures, and the "anniversary theory of history." Ambrose writes program texts, letters that offer plans for romance to Germaine. His propositions are based on esoteric number and letter puzzles. The film in which the characters are participating, based on the writings of "John Barth," in which they may or may not also have already appeared, repeats and distorts their lives. Letters from Germaine, for example, recount events in her affair with Ambrose that are reenacted for inclusion in the film. Their wedding day and costumes are planned to accommodate the filming of scenes in the motion picture, but Ambrose also enforces a strict schedule of copulation based on the number seven.

As the film spins out of control, the lives of the characters accelerate toward individual crises. In the traditional epistolary novel, the plot is knit together by the final letters; the collection of texts to and from the characters is enough to outline their fate. In *Letters*, the text ends while the most crucial questions remain unanswered. If the pregnant Germaine serves in some ways as a personification of *Letters*, her pregnancy and its outcome are important. However, the reader never learns the outcome of the pregnancy or even if Germaine is really pregnant or if the father is Ambrose or an ambiguous possible rapist. The only part of *Letters* that is satisfactorily brought to completion is the anagram of the title and subtitle built from the alphabetical letters that identify the individual letter texts. In the end, Barth's *Letters* refuses to give an authoritative answer to its own question: Is the epistolary novel still a viable literary form? However, the exuberant complexity of the text, the extravagant experimentation with letter form, and its ambiguities make Barth's work a convincing argument that there is still a long future for the novel of letters.

Anne W. Sienkewicz

BIBLIOGRAPHY

Altman, Janet Gurkin. *Epistolarity: Approaches to a Form*. Columbus: Ohio State University Press, 1982. This sophisticated critical work focuses on the nature of the letter text and the manner in which it is exploited in epistolary fiction. Altman's work chiefly deals with novels drawn from the English and French tradition. Many key citations are in French only. Bibliography includes both epistolary works and critical studies.

Beebee, Thomas O. *Epistolary Fiction in Europe, 1500-1850*. Cambridge, England: Cambridge University Press, 1999. Beebee covers the history of the epistolary novel from the Renaissance to the mid-nineteenth century, with a bibliography on major European epistolary fiction to 1850.

Bower, Anne. *Epistolary Responses: The Letter in Twentieth Century American Fiction and Criticism*. Tuscaloosa: University of Alabama Press, 1997. This innovative, framed feminist study of letter form in novels and criticism of the twentieth century explores the paradoxical quality of letters. Ten chapters are devoted to particular facets of letter texts seen through individual works, such as Alice Walker's *The Color Purple* (1982) and John Barth's *Letters*. The tenth and final chapter is devoted to literary criticism presented in letter form, including "Envois" in Jacques Derrida's *The Post Card*. Letters from the authors studied or their friends enrich several chapters. Bower herself frames one section as a letter to her readers.

Derrida, Jacques. *The Post Card: From Socrates to Freud and Beyond*. Translated by Alan Bass. Chicago: University of Chicago Press, 1980. This collection of many-faceted deconstructionist meditations on letter form is both a novel and a critical genre study, with texts using date, salutation, and signature in letter style.

Goldsmith, Elizabeth C., ed. *Writing the Female Voice: Essays on Epistolary Literature*. Boston: Northeastern University Press, 1989. A critical look at female authors' usage of the epistolary novel.

Howland, John W. *The Letter Form and the French Enlightenment: The Epistolary Paradox*. New York: Peter Lang, 1991. Examines the French epistolary style. Includes bibliographical references.

Kauffman, Linda S.. *Special Delivery: Epistolary Modes in Modern Fiction*. Chicago: University of Chicago Press, 1982. Speaking from a postmodernist and feminist perspective, Kauffman dedicates her six chapters to seven writers, four men (Viktor Shklovsky, Vladimir Nabokov, Roland Barthes, and Jacques Derrida) in part 1—"Producing Woman"—and three women (Doris Lessing, Alice Walker, and Margaret Atwood) in part 2—"Women's Productions." They chronicle the study and dismantling of epistolary form at the hands of powerful scholars and novelists, projecting beyond their own time and into the future. Notes and index.

Singer, Godfrey Frank. *The Epistolary Novel: Its Origin, Development, Decline, and Residuary Influence*. New York: Russell & Russell, 1963. Explains the beginnings of the epistolary novel. A good source for beginners.

EXPERIMENTAL LONG FICTION

Literature is always involved in a process of transformation. A new age is new precisely because its important writers do things differently from the way their predecessors worked. Thus, it could be said that almost all important literature is in one sense or another innovative or experimental at its inception but inevitably becomes, over time, conventional.

At least in reference to long fiction, however, the situation is a bit more complex. It is apparent that, four centuries after Miguel de Cervantes wrote what is generally recognized as the first important novel, *El ingenioso hidalgo don Quixote de la Mancha* (1605, 1615; *The History of the Valorous and Wittie Knight-Errant, Don Quixote of the Mancha*, 1612-1620; better known as *Don Quixote de la Mancha*), readers have come to accept a certain type of long fiction as most conventional and to regard significant departures from this type as in one degree or another experimental. This most conventional variety is the novel of realism as practiced by nineteenth century giants such as Gustave Flaubert, Leo Tolstoy, Charles Dickens, and George Eliot.

The first task in surveying contemporary experiments in long fiction, therefore, is to determine what "conventional" means in reference to the novel of realism. Most nineteenth century novelists apparently considered fiction to be an imitative form; that is, it presents in words a representation of reality. The underlying assumption of these writers and their readers was that there is a single reality shared by everyone that they all—unless they are mad, ill, or hallucinatory—perceive in about the same way. This reality is largely external and objectively verifiable. Time is orderly, moving from earlier to later. The novel that reflects this view of reality is equally orderly and accountable. The point of view is frequently, though not always, omniscient (all-knowing): The narrators understand all, and, although they may take their time in doing so, they eventually tell their readers all they need to know to understand the situation. The virtues of this variety of fiction are clarity of description and comprehensiveness of analysis. By the time readers finish Flaubert's *Madame Bovary* (1856;

English translation, 1886), they are confident they know something about Emma Bovary's home, village, and manner of dress; they know her history, her motivations, and the way she thought; they know what others thought of her; and so on. Not to know any of these things would be a gap in the record—would comprise, according to standards against which readers have judged "conventional" novels, a failure of the author.

MODERNISM AND ITS FOLLOWERS

Early in the twentieth century, a disparate group of novelists now generally referred to as modernist novelists—James Joyce, Virginia Woolf, William Faulkner, Franz Kafka, Marcel Proust, and many others – experimented with or even abandoned many of the most hallowed conventions of the novel of realism. These experiments were motivated by an altered perception of reality. Whereas the nineteenth century assumption was that reality is external, objective, and measurable, the modernists acknowledged that reality is also internal, subjective, and dependent upon context—it is perceived. Reflecting these changing assumptions about reality, point of view in the modernist novel becomes less often omniscient and more often limited, frequently shifting, and even unreliable. This subjectivity reached its apogee in one of the great innovations of modernism, the point-of-view technique dubbed "stream of consciousness," which plunges the reader into a chaos of thoughts arrayed on the most tenuous of organizing principles—or so it must have seemed to the early twentieth century audience accustomed to the orderly fictional worlds presented by the nineteenth century masters.

Once reality is acknowledged to be inner and subjective, all rules are off as to how a novel must be structured. Hence, the most consistent structuring principle of premodernist novelists—the "orderly" progression of time—was rejected by many modernists, in whose works the structure does not follow the conventional earlier-to-later flow of time so much as time, and hence the structure, follows the inner, subjective, shifting logic of the point-of-view character's thoughts. Indeed, the two great innovations of modernist fiction—stream of consciousness and non-chronological structure—go hand in hand.

Among the most famous and earliest practitioners of these techniques were James Joyce (especially in *Ulysses*, 1922, and *Finnegans Wake*, 1939), Virginia Woolf (in many novels, such as *Jacob's Room*, 1922; *Mrs. Dalloway*, 1925; and *To the Lighthouse*, 1927), and William Faulkner (in *The Sound and the Fury*, 1929; *As I Lay Dying*, 1930; and others). Many of the experimental works of post-World War II long fiction extended these techniques, offering intensely subjective narrative voices and often extreme forms of stream of consciousness, including disruptions of orderly time sequences, as their principal innovations.

In *La traición de Rita Hayworth* (1968; *Betrayed by Rita Hayworth*, 1971), for example, Manuel Puig employs (among other techniques) the words of several sets of characters in different rooms of a house without furnishing any identification of the speakers or even transitions to indicate when he has moved from one set of speakers to another. The effect may be experienced by the reader as a strange solipsistic cacophony, or something like a disjointed choral voice; in fact, the technique is a variation on stream of consciousness and not so very different from the tangle of interior monologues in Faulkner's novels.

Tim O'Brien's novel of the Vietnam War, *Going After Cacciato* (1978, revised 1989), is another example of a work that makes fresh use of a modernist strategy. Here, reality at first seems more external and hence clearer than in *Betrayed by Rita Hayworth*. The bulk of the action concerns a rifle squad that follows a deserter, Cacciato, out of Vietnam and across Asia and Europe until he is finally surrounded in Paris, where he once again escapes. The chapters that compose this plot, however, are interspersed with generally shorter chapters recounting the experiences of the point-of-view character, Paul Berlin, at home and in Vietnam. In another set of short chapters, Berlin waits out a six-hour guard shift in an observation post by the sea. The most orderly part of the novel is the pursuit of Cacciato, which moves with chronological and geographic logic. The perceptive reader eventually realizes, however, that the pursuit of Cacciato is a fantasy conjured up by Berlin, whose "real" reality is the six hours in the observation post, where his thoughts skip randomly from his time present to past memories to his fantasy world. As in the best modernist tradition, then, the structure of *Going After Cacciato* reflects an inner, subjective reality.

The post-World War II writer who most famously and provocatively continued the modernist program in long fiction was Samuel Beckett, especially in his trilogy comprising *Molloy* (1951; English translation, 1955), *Malone meurt* (1951; *Malone Dies*, 1956), and *L'Innommable* (1953; *The Unnamable*, 1958). In each successive novel, external reality recedes as the narrative voice becomes more inward-looking. In *Molloy*, for example, the title character searches for his mother, but he is lost from the beginning. He can find neither her (if she truly exists) nor his way back home, wherever that is—nor can he be sure even of the objective reality of recent experience. In one passage Molloy notes that he stayed in several rooms with several windows, but then he immediately conjectures that perhaps the several windows were really only one, or perhaps they were all in his head. The novel is filled with "perhapses" and "I don't knows," undermining the reader's confidence in whatever Beckett tells readers. The subjectivity and uncertainty are intensified in *Malone Dies*. At least in *Molloy* the protagonist was out in the world, lost in a countryside that appears to be realistic, even if it is more a mindscape that a convincing geographic location. In *Malone Dies*, the protagonist spends most of his days immobile in what he thinks is a hospital, but beyond this nothing—certainly not space or time—is clear. As uncertain of their surroundings as Molloy and Malone are, they are at least fairly certain of their own reality; the unnamed protagonist of the final volume of the trilogy, *The Unnamable*, does not have even that consolation. His entire labyrinthine interior monologue is an attempt to find an identity for himself and a definition of his world, the one depending upon the other. In those attempts, however, he fails, and at no time does the reader have a confident sense of time and place in reference to the protagonist and his world.

THE NEW NOVEL

With *The Unnamable*, long fiction may seem to have come a great distance from the modernist novel, but in fact Beckett was continuing the modernist practice of locating reality inside a limited and increasingly unreliable consciousness. Eventually voices cried out against the entire modernist enterprise. Among the earliest and most vocal of those calling for a new fiction was a group of French writers who became known as the New Novelists. Ironically, however—as startlingly innovative as their fiction may at first appear—much of the time they were following in the footsteps of the very modernists they rejected.

Among the many and varied writers frequently labeled New Novelists (sometimes to their dismay) are Michel Butor, Nathalie Sarraute, and Claude Simon. Even though the latter won the Nobel Prize in Literature, probably the most famous (or "infamous") New Novelist is Alain Robbe-Grillet.

Robbe-Grillet decried what he regarded as outmoded realism and set forth the program for a new fiction in *Pour un nouveau roman* (1963; *For a New Novel: Essays on Fiction*, 1965), and his own career might offer the best demonstration of the movement from old to new. His first published novel, *Les Gommes* (1953; *The Erasers*, 1964), while hardly Dickensian, was not radically innovative. With *Le Voyeur* (1955; *The Voyeur*, 1958), however, his work took a marked turn toward the experimental, and with *Jalousie* (1957; *Jealousy*, 1959) and *Dans le labyrinthe* (1959; *In the Labyrinth*, 1960), the New Novel came to full flower.

The most famous technical innovation of the New Novelists was the protracted and obsessive descriptions of objects often apparently unrelated to theme or plot: a tomato slice or box on the table or picture on the wall. The use of this device caused some critics to speak of the "objective" nature of the New Novel, as if the technique offered the reader a sort of photographic clarity. On the contrary, in the New Novel little is clear in a conventional sense. Robbe-Grillet fills his descriptions with "perhapses" and "apparentlys" along with other qualifiers, and the objects become altered or metamorphosed over time, which, after Robbe-Grillet's early novels, is rarely

of the conventional earlier-to-later variety but jumps and loops and returns. One example of the transforming nature of objects occurs in *The Voyeur*, when a man on a boat peers obsessively at the figure-eight scar left by an iron ring flapping against a sea wall. Over the course of the novel the figure-eight pattern becomes a cord in the salesman's suitcase, then two knotholes side by side on a door, then a bicycle, a highway sign, two stacks of plates, and so on—in more than a dozen incarnations.

Moreover, Robbe-Grillet's objects are not always as "solid" as the foregoing list would seem to indicate. A painting on a wall (*In the Labyrinth*) or a photograph in a newspaper lying in the gutter (*La Maison de rendez-vous*, 1965; English translation, 1966) may become "animated" as the narrative eye enters it, and the action will transpire in what was, a paragraph before, only ink on paper or paint on canvas.

Such techniques indeed seemed radically new, far afield of the novels of Joyce and Faulkner. However, it is generally the case with the New Novelists, especially with Robbe-Grillet, that this obsessive looking, these distortions and uncertainties and transformations imposed on what might otherwise be conventionally realistic surfaces, have their origins in a narrative consciousness that warps reality according to its idiosyncratic way of seeing. The point-of-view character of *In the Labyrinth* is a soldier quite likely feverish and dying; in *The Voyeur*, a psychotic murderer; in *Jealousy*, a jealous husband who quite possibly has committed an act of violence or contemplates doing so. In all cases the reader has even more trouble arriving at definitive conclusions than is the case with the supposedly forbiddingly difficult novels written by Joyce and Faulkner. Ultimately the New Novelists' program differs in degree more than kind from the modernist assumption that reality is subjective and that fictional structures should reflect that subjectivity. As famous and frequently discussed as the New Novelists have been, their fiction has had relatively little influence beyond France, and when literary theorists define "postmodernism" (that is, the literary expression that has emerged after, and is truly different from, modernism), they rarely claim the New Novel to be that expression.

METAFICTION

A far more significant departure from modernism occurred when writers began to reject the notion that had been dominant among novelists since Miguel de Cervantes: that it is the chief duty of the novelist to be realistic, and the more realistic the fiction the worthier it is. This breakthrough realization—that realism of whatever variety is no more than a preference for a certain set of conventions—manifests itself in different ways in fiction. In one variety of this new fiction, variously labeled metafiction, self-mimesis, and self-referential fiction, the author (or his persona), rather than trying to cause the reader to suspend disbelief, deliberately reminds the reader that the book is a written entity.

Often the metafictive impulse appears as little more than an intensification of the first-person-omniscient narrator, the "intrusive author" disparaged by Henry James but favored by many nineteenth century writers. Rather than the identitiless "I" employed by William Thackeray in *Vanity Fair* (1847-1848), for example, José Donoso comments under his own name in his novel *Casa de campo* (1978; *A House in the Country*, 1984), as does Luisa Valenzuela in *Cola de lagartija* (1983; *The Lizard's Tail*, 1983) and as do many other post-World War II writers. The difference between commenting on the narrative as an "I" as opposed to the author identifying himself or herself may seem a small one, but it is the difference between trying to maintain the illusion that the novel's world is a "real" world and acknowledging that the novel is a thing, written by an author.

In other novels, the metafictive impulse is more radical and transforming. When Donald Barthelme stops the action halfway through *Snow White* (1967), for example, and requires the reader to answer a fifteen-question quiz on the foregoing, the readers' ability to "lose themselves" in the novel's virtual world is hopelessly and hilariously destroyed. Another witty but vastly different metafictive novel is Italo Calvino's *Se una notte d'inverno un viaggiatore* (1979; *If on a Winter's Night a Traveler*, 1981), in which the central character, Cavedagna, purchases a novel called *If on a Winter's Night a Traveler* by an author named Italo Calvino. Unfortunately, Cavedagna finds that his copy is defective: The first thirty-two pages are repeated again and again, and the text is not even "Calvino's"; it is instead the opening of a Polish spy novel. The remainder of the book concerns Cavedagna's attempts to find the rest of the spy novel, his blossoming romance with a woman on the same mission, and a rambling intrigue Calvino would surely love to parody had he not invented it, all constructed around a number of openings of other novels that never, for a variety of reasons, progress past the first few pages.

FICTION-AS-ARTIFICE

One might well ask, is not metafiction, strictly defined—that is, fiction about the writing of fiction—too narrow an endeavor to define an age (postmodernism)? The answer, surely, is yes. Even *If on a Winter's Night a Traveler* might more properly be described as a novel whose subject is reading a novel rather than writing one. Metafiction is probably best seen as but one variation of a broader, more pervasive impulse in post-World War II long fiction: fiction-as-artifice. Here, rather than narrowly focusing on the process of writing fiction (metafiction), the author through various strategies either directly attacks the conventions of realism or at least acknowledges that all writing is a verbal construct bearing the most tenuous relationship to actuality.

One of the "purest" and earliest examples of fiction-as-artifice in the post-World War II canon is Raymond Queneau's *Exercices de style* (1947; *Exercises in Style*, 1958). The title states quite clearly where Queneau's interests lie: in technique, the manipulation of language, rather than in creating an illusion of reality. The book is composed of ninety-nine variations on a brief scene between two strangers on a Parisian bus. In each retelling of the incident, Queneau uses a different dialect or style ("Notation," "Litotes," and so on). The almost endless replication of the single scene forces the reader to see it all as a verbal construct rather than an approximation of reality. Such "pure" manifestations of fiction-as-artifice as *Exercises in Style* are relatively rare. More often, fiction-as-artifice is a gesture employed intermittently, side by side with realist techniques, the interplay of the two opposing strategies creating a delightful aesthetic friction.

One of the most famous and provocative examples is Vladimir Nabokov's *Pale Fire* (1962). The structure of the work belies all traditional conventions of the novel. *Pale Fire* opens with an "editor's" introduction, followed by a long poem, followed by hundreds of pages of annotations, and ending with an index. The reader discovers, however, that all this apparatus tells a hilarious and finally moving story of political intrigue, murder, and madness. Does *Pale Fire*, ultimately, underscore the artifices of fiction or, instead, demonstrate how resilient is the writer's need to tell a story and the reader's need to read one? Either way, *Pale Fire* is one of the most inventive and fascinating novels ever written.

The same question could be asked of Julio Cortázar's *Rayuela* (1963; *Hopscotch*, 1966), a long novel composed of scores of brief, numbered sections, which, the reader is advised in the introductory "Instructions," can be read in the order presented, in a different numbered sequence suggested by the author, or perhaps, if the reader prefers, by "hopscotching" through the novel.

A similar strategy is employed in Milorad Pavic's *Hazarski recnik* (1984; *Dictionary of the Khazars*, 1988). As the title suggests, the work is constructed as a dictionary with many brief sections, alphabetized by heading and richly cross-referenced. The reader may read the work from beginning to end, alphabetically, or may follow the cross-references. An added inventive complication arises from the fact that *Dictionary of the Kazars* is published in two volumes, a "male" and a "female" version, identical except for one brief passage, which may alter the reader's interpretation of the whole.

Although the fiction-as-artifice impulse is European in origin—indeed, it is as old as Laurence Sterne's *The Life and Opinions of Tristram Shandy, Gent.* (1759-1767)—its most inventive and varied practitioner is the American writer John Barth. In work after work, Barth employs, parodies, and lays bare for the reader's contemplation the artifices of fiction. In his unified collection *Lost in the Funhouse* (1968), for example, Barth narrates the history from

conception through maturity and decline of a man, of humankind, and of fiction itself; the story, however, is told in such a way as to highlight the artificiality of writing. The first selection (it cannot be called a "story"), titled "Frame Tale," is a single, incomplete sentence, "Once upon a time there was a story that began," designed to be cut out and pasted together to form a Möbius strip that, when assembled, leads to the complete yet infinite and never-ending sentence: "Once upon a time there was a story that began Once upon a time . . ." The title story, "Lost in the Funhouse," contains graphs illustrating the story's structure. "Title" is as purely a metafictive piece of fiction as exists. "Glossolalia" is formed from six brief sections all written in the rhythms of the Lord's Prayer. In "Menelaid" the dialogue is presented in a dizzying succession of quotation marks within quotation marks within quotation marks. Barth's experiments in *Lost in the Funhouse* are continued and intensified in later novels, especially *Chimera* (1972) and *Letters* (1979).

FICTION OR NONFICTION?

Even at his most experimental, however, Barth never abandons his delight in storytelling. Indeed, virtually all the long fictions addressed thus far show innovations in certain technical strategies but do not substantially challenge the reader's concept of what is "fictional." A number of other writers, however, while not always seeming so boldly experimental in technique, have blurred the distinctions between fiction and nonfiction and thus perhaps represent a more fundamental departure from the conventional novel.

The "new journalists"—such as Truman Capote in *In Cold Blood* (1966), Norman Mailer in *The Armies of the Night: History as Novel, the Novel as History* (1968), Tom Wolfe in *The Electric Kool-Aid Acid Test* (1968), and Hunter S. Thompson in his Fear and Loathing series (beginning in 1972)—use novelistic techniques in what purports to be factual reporting. The subtitle of Mailer's work notwithstanding, however, the reader rarely is uncertain which side of the fiction-nonfiction line these authors occupy.

The same cannot be said for Don DeLillo's *Libra* (1988). For his interpretation of the Kennedy assassination, DeLillo spent countless hours researching the voluminous reports of the Warren Commission and other historical documents. With this factual material as the basis and Lee Harvey Oswald as the central character, to what degree can *Libra* be considered fictional as opposed to nonfictional?

The question is even more problematical in reference to Maxine Hong Kingston's *The Woman Warrior: Memoir of a Girlhood Among Ghosts* (1976). Kingston conducted her research for her memoir not in library stacks but by plumbing her own memory, especially of stories told her by her mother. At times Kingston not only is imaginatively enhancing reconstructed scenes but also is clearly inventing details. Is this autobiography or a kind of fiction?

One can point to the facts that *Libra* was marketed as a novel but *The Woman Warrior* as a memoir (hence nonfiction); even publishers, however, do not truly know what to make of Nicholson Baker's *The Mezzanine* (1988) or W. G. Sebald's *The Immigrants* (1992). The reader is fairly certain that the point-of-view character in *The Mezzanine* is fictional, but in what sense is his experience fictional? The work is composed of essaylike contemplations of whatever the persona's eye falls on as he goes about his business on the mezzanine, recalling in some ways the intensely detailed descriptions of the New Novelists but with even less of an apparent conflict or movement toward climax one expects in fiction. Sebald's work is in some ways even odder. His short "biographies" of a selection of dislocated Europeans have a documentary surface—complete with photographs. The photographs, however, have a vagueness about them that makes them seem almost irrelevant to their subjects, and the reader has the uneasy impression that the entirety may well be a fabrication.

Just as Baker and Sebald call into question what earlier generations would have thought too obvious to debate—the difference between fiction and nonfiction—the one consistent impulse among experimenters in long fiction has been to ask, what is necessary in fiction and what is merely conventional? Their efforts to test this question resulted in the most provocative and entertaining fiction of the twentieth century.

Dennis Vannatta

BIBLIOGRAPHY

Chénetier, Marc. *Beyond Suspicion: New American Fiction Since 1960.* Philadelphia: University of Pennsylvania, 1996. Chénetier's study is especially useful because he recognizes that the post-World War II years constitute too long a period to comprise a homogeneous whole. Instead, he discusses authors who continue the modernist program from early in the century to 1960, then explores at greater length more recent fiction by Barth, DeLillo, and others.

Currie, Mark, ed. *Metafiction.* London: Longman, 1995. This collection consists of articles previously published in other sources. Experimental themes and techniques are discussed.

McHale, Brian. *Postmodernist Fiction.* New York: Methuen, 1987. McHale discusses what postmodernism means in reference to the fiction of many of the most important experimenters since World War II: Beckett, Robbe-Grillet, Nabokov, and Robert Coover, among many others.

Robbe-Grillet, Alain. *For a New Novel: Essays on Fiction.* New York: Grove, 1965. These essays constitute the single best statement on the aesthetic and philosophical assumptions underlying the New Novel movement, by that movement's most famous author.

Scholes, Robert. *Fabulation and Metafiction.* Urbana: University of Illinois Press, 1979. Scholes addresses two phenomena in post-World War II fiction that distinguish it from innovative fiction from before the war. One, "fabulation" (essentially, romance, allegory, mythmaking), is not necessarily experimental but often is; the other, metafiction, is one of the most important varieties of experimental fiction.

Seltzer, Alvin J. *Chaos in the Novel: The Novel in Chaos.* New York: Schocken, 1974. Seltzer addressees the chaos that seems to lie at the end of so many novelists' search for truth. This chaos is most often reflected aesthetically in experimental forms. Seltzer's book is especially interesting because he traces the roots of contemporary experimentation back not only to the modernists but also to nineteenth and even eighteenth century writers.

THE FANTASY NOVEL

Contemporary publishers use the heading "fantasy" in a narrow sense that distinguishes the works bearing that label from those billed as "horror" or "science fiction," but this distinction is a matter of marketing strategy that should not be taken too seriously. For the purposes of this essay, the term "fantasy" will be taken to refer to all works of fiction that attempt neither the realism of the realistic novel nor the "conditional realism" of science fiction.

Among modern critics, the primacy of the realistic novel is taken for granted. In their eyes, realistic novels not only describe normality but also constitute the normal kind of fiction; fantasy, in dealing with the supernatural, seems itself to be almost perverse.

Prior to the rise of the novel in the eighteenth century, however, this was far from being the case. Prose forms such as the imaginary voyage, the dialogue, and satire blurred even the basic distinction between fiction and nonfiction, let alone that between "realistic" and "fantastic" subject matter. The separation of realistic and fantastic began not with the casting out of fantastic genres from the literary mainstream, but rather with the withdrawal of a realistic genre—the novel—from a mainstream that had easily accommodated fantastic motifs.

EIGHTEENTH AND NINETEENTH CENTURIES

To speak of the "fantasy novel" in the context of the eighteenth century comes close to committing a contradiction in terms: Novels were about life as it was lived and had left behind the conventions of allegory and fable along with the decorations of the marvelous and the magical. It is arguable, though, that the withdrawal left behind a connecting spectrum of ambiguous works, and—more important—that it soon led to some important reconnections. Jonathan Swift's use of the techniques of narrative realism in his chronicling of the imaginary voyages of Lemuel Gulliver gave to his work a crucial modernity that is responsible for its still being widely read and enjoyed today.

The rise of the gothic novel in the last decades of the eighteenth century, in connection with the emergence of the Romantic movement that spread from Germany to France, England, and the United States, represents a definite reaction against the advancement of literary realism. The gothic novel, indeed, is almost an "antinovel" of its day, substituting a fascination with the ancient for a preoccupation with the modern, an interest in the outré for an obsession with the everyday, an exaltation of the mysterious for a concern with the intelligible, a celebration of the barbaric for a smug appreciation of the civilized. From the standpoint of today, the gothic can be seen to have been subversive in several different ways. It was subversive in a literary context because it opposed the dominant trend toward the development of the modern realistic novel. It was subversive in a sociological context because it reflected the fact that the values of the ancien régime were under stress and that the decadence of that regime was symptomatic of its imminent dissolution. It was subversive in a psychological context because it provided a parable of the impotence of the conscious mind to complete its oppressive victory over the forces of the unconscious, whose imprisonment could never be total.

Gothic novels dealt with strange events in strange environments, organized around the passions of the protagonists. The passions were frequently illicit in a perfectly straightforward sense, often involving incest and the breaking of sacred vows, but the more careful and controlled gothics—the archetypal example is *The Mysteries of Udolpho* (1794) by Ann Radcliffe—emphasized the extent to which the trend toward a less permissive morality would eventually rule, especially in England.

With the exception of the gothic novels, few of the products of the Romantic rebellion were cast in the form of long prose narratives. Short stories were produced in much greater quantity, and the evolution of the short story in Europe and America is closely intertwined with the Romantic reaction against realism and classicism. Poetry, too, was affected very dramatically. Even the gothic novel underwent a rapid decline—not into nonexistence but into inconsequential crudeness. After the appearance, in 1824, of

James Hogg's *The Private Memoirs and Confessions of a Justified Sinner*—a masterpiece of psychological terror involving paranoid delusions—there followed a long period in which gothic romance was primarily associated with the lowest stratum of the literary marketplace: with the partworks and "penny dreadfuls" marketed for the newly literate inhabitants of the industrial towns. Such interminable narratives as *Varney the Vampyre* (1847) by James Malcolm Rymer and *Wagner the Wehr-Wolf* (1846-1847) by G. M. W. Reynolds achieved considerable success in their own time but have little to offer modern readers.

Although the gothic novel was primarily a species of horror story, its supernatural trappings did overflow into moralistic fantasies that might be comic extravaganzas, such as James Dalton's *The Gentleman in Black* (1831) and *The Invisible Gentleman* (1833), or earnest parables, such as John Sterling's *The Onyx Ring* (1839). The themes of these novels—tricky deals with the devil, invisibility, wish-granting rings, and personality exchange—were to become the staples of what Nathan Drake had called "sportive gothic," while curses, ghosts, vampires, and madness remained the characteristic motifs of "gloomy gothic."

The writers who produced the most notable works of fantasy in the middle of the nineteenth century—including Edgar Allan Poe and Nathaniel Hawthorne in the United States, George MacDonald and William Gilbert in England, and Théophile Gautier and Charles Nodier in France—primarily worked in the short-story medium. The novels written by these authors often have fantastic embellishments, but for the most part they pay far more heed to the restraints of conventional realism than do these authors' short stories.

VICTORIAN ERA

The revival of the fantasy novel in the last two decades of the nineteenth century was associated with several trends that can be traced through the fiction of the twentieth century. The partial eclipse of substantial work in fantastic fiction in the mid-nineteenth century is clearly related to the repressive morality of that period—it is notable that in France, where the repression was less effective than in Great Britain, the

United States, and Germany, the Romantic heritage was more effectively conserved. It is possible, in consequence, to see the various threads of the revival in terms of reactions against and attempts to escape from that repression.

During this repressive period, indulgence in fantasy came to be seen as a kind of laxity: It was in the Victorian era that the notion of "escapism" was born. An exception was made in the case of children's literature (though even here there was a period when fantasy was frowned upon), and there eventually arose in Britain a curious convention whereby fantasies were considered suitable reading for Christmas, when a little token indulgence might be overlooked, an idea that led to the emphasis on fantasy in the Christmas annuals to which Charles Dickens and William Makepeace Thackeray contributed. Such writers as Thackeray, George MacDonald, and Lewis Carroll brought to the writing of books nominally aimed at children an artistry and seriousness that commended them to the attention of adults and helped to open a space for the production of fantastic novels within the British literary marketplace.

Another form of fantastic fiction that became to some extent associated with the British Christmas annuals was the ghost story, which became extremely popular in the 1880's and remained so for half a century, during which virtually all the classic British work in that genre was done. There is, however, something intrinsically anecdotal about ghost stories that keeps them more or less confined to short fiction. Though there have been some excellent novellas, there have never been more than half a dozen outstanding ghost novels. J. Sheridan Le Fanu, who stands at the head of the line of British ghost-story writers, produced several neogothic novels, but almost all of them are so ponderous as to be nearly unreadable. M. R. James wrote only short stories, and Algernon Blackwood's novels have not worn nearly as well as his shorter pieces.

The Victorian interest in ghosts, however, went far beyond the traffic in thrilling anecdotes. The influence of such contemporary fads as Spiritualism and Theosophy sparked a new interest in the occult that began to be reflected quite prolifically in literary production.

The great majority of the spiritualist fantasies of communication with the dead and accounts of the afterlife supposedly dictated by the dead through mediums are wholly inconsequential in literary terms, despite the eventual involvement in such movements of writers of ability, such as Arthur Conan Doyle. They did, however, lay important groundwork for those authors who followed. The fevered Rosicrucian romances of Edward Bulwer-Lytton, Marie Corelli's exercises in unorthodox theology, and commercially successful accounts of life "on the other side" by such writers as Coulson Kernahan and Elizabeth Stuart Phelps paved the way for much more substantial posthumous fantasies by Wyndham Lewis (*The Childermass*, 1928) and C. S. Lewis (*The Great Divorce*, 1945) and for the theological romances of Charles Williams and David Lindsay. Williams's *All Hallows' Eve* (1945) is possibly the best of the ghost novels, while Lindsay's *A Voyage to Arcturus* (1920) is a masterpiece of creative metaphysics.

The 1880's also saw a renaissance of comic fantasy, exemplified in Britain by the novels of F. Anstey and in the United States by Mark Twain's *A Connecticut Yankee in King Arthur's Court* (1889). The calculated irreverence of these stories reflects a self-confident rationalism that stands in opposition to the mystical movements inspiring most posthumous fantasy. The primary target held up for ridicule in these stories, however, is not the vocabulary of fantastic ideas itself but rather the moral pretensions of the contemporary middle classes. Anstey's stories use fantastic premises in order to expose the limitations of the attitudes that were rigidified within closed Victorian minds.

In the twentieth century, this tradition of humorous fantasy thrived more in the United States than in Britain—the leading American exponent of the species has been Thorne Smith—and this reflects, in part, the fact that as Britain has become somewhat less obsessed with the protocols of middle-class culture, the United States has become gradually more so. It was in the United States also that the absurd logical consequences of fantastic premises began to be exploited for pure amusement, largely in connection with the short-lived magazine *Unknown*, whose

leading contributors were L. Sprague de Camp and Fletcher Pratt, who produced, in collaboration, a series of excellent comic fantasies.

A third species of fantastic fiction that first became clearly delineated in the last decades of the nineteenth century is the kind of story that translocates contemporary men into fabulous imaginary worlds. Stories of this kind are among the oldest that are told. The mundane world has always had its fantastic parallels: its earthly paradises, the land of Cokaygne, and the land of Faerie. In the mid-nineteenth century these alternate worlds were retired into juvenile fiction, except for a few desert islands populated in a relatively mundane fashion. Victorian romances of exploration, however, celebrating the journeys of white men into the heart of the dark continent of Africa, reopened imaginative spaces for more exotic traveler's tales.

Numerous "lost race" stories and a few "hollow earth" romances were published before 1880, but the writer who first made a considerable popular impact with exotic romances of exploration was H. Rider Haggard, first in *King Solomon's Mines* (1885), and later in *She* (1887) and *The Ghost Kings* (1908). The example that he set was rapidly taken up by others, and the fantasization of the lands where adventurers went exploring proceeded rapidly. Because this was also the period when interplanetary stories were beginning to appear among early scientific romances, it was perhaps inevitable that writers began to displace their more exotic imaginary worlds to the surfaces of other planets. The example set by Edwin Lester Arnold in *Lieut. Gullivar Jones: His Vacation* (1905) was rapidly followed by Edgar Rice Burroughs and many others. In *The Lost World* (1912), Arthur Conan Doyle revitalized remote earthly locations with survivals from prehistory, and this too was an example enthusiastically followed. A new vocabulary borrowed from scientific romance allowed later writers to send heroes through "dimensional gateways" of one kind or another into magical fantasy worlds as exotic as could be imagined: The most determined of all writers of this kind of escapist fantasy was the American Abraham Merritt, author of *The Moon Pool* (1919) and *The Face in the Abyss* (1932).

Though the lost-land story set on the earth's surface was gradually destroyed by news of real explorations—the last classic example was James Hilton's *Lost Horizon* (1933)—the borrowing of conventions from science fiction has allowed the basic story framework to be retained to the present day. Contemporary humans can still be precipitated into magical imaginary worlds with the aid of a little fake technology or even a light sprinkling of jargon. The removal of imaginary worlds from darkest Africa to other planets and other dimensions, however, coincided with another and possibly more important innovation in the use of the theme, which was to dispense with the protagonist from the familiar world.

FAIRY TALES AND HEROIC FANTASY

Although traditional fairy tales had, at the time of their origin, been set in the believed-in world, their remote printed descendants could not help but seem to their consumers to be set in an entirely imaginary milieu. The magicalized medieval milieu of such stories became a stereotype useful to modern writers, who began to repopulate it with complex characters whose adventures were filled with allegorical significance. The pioneers of this kind of enterprise were the German Romantic Fouqué, in his novel *The Magic Ring* (1813), and George MacDonald, in *Phantastes* (1958), but their example was followed in far more prolific fashion by William Morris, whose several romances of this kind include *The Wood Beyond the World* (1894) and *The Water of the Wondrous Isles* (1897). The form gathered further momentum in the work of Lord Dunsany, most notably in *The King of Elfland's Daughter* (1924) and *The Charwoman's Shadow* (1926); other contemporary examples include Margaret Irwin in *These Mortals* (1925) and Hope Mirrlees in *Lud-in-the-Mist* (1926). These sophisticated but slightly effete fairy tales then began to give way to a more active brand of heroic fantasy, first featured to extravagant extent in E. R. Eddison's *The Worm Ourobouros* (1922).

Modified fairy-tale fantasy reached new heights of popularity in the fantastic volumes included in James Branch Cabell's "Biography of Manuel," set in the imaginary magical European kingdom of Poic-

tesme. It was also developed in a much more extravagant way by several of the contributors to the magazine *Weird Tales*, who used imaginary lands set in remote eras of prehistory in order to develop the subgenre commonly known as "sword-and-sorcery" fiction. Because it was initially restricted to the pages of a pulp magazine, this subgenre was developed primarily in the short-story form, although it is actually better adapted to novel length. Its most famous progenitor, Robert E. Howard, wrote only one novel featuring his archetypal hero Conan: *Conan the Conqueror* (1950; originally "Hour of the Dragon," 1935-1936). The first important novel of this kind to be published initially in book form was *The Well of the Unicorn* (1948) by "George U. Fletcher" (Fletcher Pratt), but since the advent of the paperback book the species has become established as a successful brand of pulp fiction.

The most notable modern novels set entirely in imaginary worlds tend to give the appearance of being hybrids of sophisticated fairy romance and a variety of heroic fantasy not too far removed from American sword-and-sorcery fiction. The masterpieces of the genre are *The Once and Future King* by T. H. White—published in its entirety in 1958 but absorbing three earlier novels—and *The Lord of the Rings* by J. R. R. Tolkien, published in three volumes between 1954 and 1955.

One of the most striking side effects of the development of fantasy novels of this kind for adults was the revitalization of work done primarily for the juvenile market, which is often remarkably sophisticated in both technical and ideative terms. Tolkien's juvenile novel *The Hobbit* (1937) is an old example; later ones include Ursula K. Le Guin's trilogy of novels set in the world of Earthsea and various works by Alan Garner, Susan Cooper, and Lloyd Alexander.

The paperback publication of Tolkien's *Lord of the Rings* in the 1960's sparked countless exercises in imitation, which proved popular enough to make the trilogy the basic form of modern fantasy fiction. The reborn genre went from strength to strength in commercial terms, making best-sellers out of dozens of writers, many of them direly mediocre in terms of the quality of their prose. Nor is it simply oral fairy tales that were rehabilitated within modern commercial fiction; following the success of Richard Adams's *Watership Down* (1972), animal fables—which were also popular in medieval times—were similarly produced in some quantity.

This exploitation of imaginary worlds is the most striking aspect of the evolution of fantasy novels during the twentieth century, and it is not entirely surprising that the "fantasy" label is now retained for such novels by publishers. There has, however, been a parallel evolution of occult and horrific fantasy. The Decadent movements at the end of the nineteenth century saw the emergence of a kind of fiction that reveled in the "unnatural," and though most of the fantastic fiction of this kind was cast in short-story form, there were a few notable novels, including Oscar Wilde's *The Picture of Dorian Gray* (serial 1890, expanded 1891) and Hanns Heinz Ewers's *The Sorcerer's Apprentice* (1907) and its sequels.

TWENTIETH CENTURY GOTHIC FANTASY

In parallel with these works appeared a new wave of stories that developed the gothic images of fear into new archetypes, treating them with a determined quasi-scientific seriousness. The great success in this line was Bram Stoker's *Dracula* (1897), which has never been out of print since publication and which surely stands as the most heavily plundered fantasy of all time, being the sourcebook for literally hundreds of vampire stories and films.

This resurgence of fiction that deals with the supernatural in a deadly earnest fashion may seem rather paradoxical. It was possible for nineteenth century rationalists to imagine that their victory over superstitious belief was almost won and to look forward to a day when the irrational might be banished from human affairs. If anything, the reverse is true: Superstition, mysticism, and irrationality now thrive to a greater extent than ever before, and modern fiction reflects that fact.

Fantasy novels intended to evoke horror and unease are more prolifically produced and consumed today than they were in the heyday of the gothic, and one of the world's best-selling novelists, Stephen King, is primarily a horror writer. In addition, the

role played by occult forces within the neogothic novel is crucially different; in gothic novels, normality was usually restored, and when the forces of the supernatural *did* break free, they usually did so in order to punish the guilty and liberate the innocent. In later neogothic fantasies, however—whether one looks at the respectable middlebrow tradition that extends from Mervyn Peake's Gormenghast trilogy to the works of Angela Carter or the lowbrow tradition that extends from Dennis Wheatley to James Herbert and Clive Barker—the gothic elements were superimposed in a wholesale manner upon the mundane world, subjecting it to a surrealization from which there could be no possibility of redemption.

This situation has been complicated by a marked tendency among writers of "dark fantasy" to subject the traditional monsters of gothic fiction to moral reappraisal. In modern vampire fiction, particularly the lush historical romances of Anne Rice, Chelsea Quinn Yarbro, and S. P. Somtow, the male vampire is more hero than villain, and his unusual existential plight is subject to a sympathetically fascinated scrutiny. Modern awareness of the extent to which such figures as the vampire and the werewolf embodied and exaggerated the sexual anxieties of the nineteenth century has enabled writers to redeploy them in fictions that champion the cause of liberalism, although the question of whether understanding automatically paves the way to forgiveness remains interestingly and sometimes achingly open. The psychoanalytical sophistication of much modern horror fiction has moved so far beyond traditional considerations of good and evil that it seems to some critics to have turned from stigmatization to glamorization—an argument supported by the strangely reverent tone adopted toward their all-too-human monsters by such writers as Poppy Z. Brite and Thomas Harris.

The concerted attempt made by many modern writers of supernatural fiction to redeem the Byronic literary vampire from the negative image foisted on him by John Polidori and Bram Stoker extends beyond the limits of literary fantasy into lifestyle fantasy. Similarly intricate relationships between literary and lifestyle fantasies, aided and abetted by extravagant scholarly fantasies—a process that began with the modern reformulation of the idea of witch-craft—have developed across the entire spectrum of New Age philosophies, pretenses, and practices. The relationship between fiction and action has been further complicated by virtue of the spectacular success of fantasy role-playing games, pioneered by Dungeons and Dragons, and fantasy-based computer games. Although play has always been a significant medium of fantasy, it has never been the case before that so much play (involving adults as well as adolescents) has drawn so extensively upon a vocabulary of ideas established and embodied by literary and cinematic fantasies.

POSTMODERNISM

While the contents of popular fantasy fiction have overspilled in this remarkable fashion, fantastic motifs and literary methods have been reimported into the literary mainstream on a considerable scale. The mid-1960's and early 1970's saw the beginnings of a significant break with the American realist tradition in novels by such fabulists as John Barth, Thomas Berger, Richard Brautigan, Thomas Pynchon, and Robert Coover, which eventually expanded in the 1980's into an entire field of postmodern fiction closely connected—at least in the eyes of critics—with a series of formal challenges to the very ideas of "realism" and "reality." British writers of a broadly similar stripe whose work spanned the same period included Angela Carter, Peter Ackroyd, Alasdair Gray, Robert Irwin, and Russell Hoban, although the notion of postmodern British fiction never took hold to the extent that their work began to be aggregated into a symptom of some crucial cultural transition.

Although postmodern fiction borrowed a good deal of imagery from science fiction—and postmodern critics happily conscripted such science fiction writers as Philip K. Dick, William Gibson, and Bruce Sterling into the field—its mainstream practitioners usually deployed such imagery as a set of metaphors commenting surreally and satirically on contemporary society, in the manner of Kurt Vonnegut and Don DeLillo. The typical materials of commercial fiction bearing the "fantasy" label are far less diverse, but their potential in this regard has been demonstrated

by such works as Samuel R. Delany's Nevèrÿon series and Steven Millhauser's *Martin Dressler: The Tale of an American Dreamer* (1996).

The translation into English during this allegedly postmodern period of several highly esteemed Latin American novels that productively and provocatively mingled mundane and supernatural materials, including key examples by Gabriel García Márquez and Jorge Amado, introduced the concept of Magical Realism to contemporary literary criticism. The style was widely, and perhaps rather promiscuously, applied to works that owed some allegiance to alternative cultural traditions, whether or not it required translation. Key examples can be found among the works of Ben Okri, Milorad Pavic, and Salman Rushdie. The increasing interest of African American and Native American writers in elements of their traditional cultures that had previously been obscured by the dominant Euro-American culture and increasing curiosity about the folkways of Asiatic and African cultures have sustained a steady flow of exotica into the American arena, much of which is advertised as Magical Realism for want of any other convenient label.

The relaxation of the realist norm allowed several varieties of fantasy that had long been dormant to resurface in the 1970's and 1980's. Although the classical models of the *conte philosophique* established by Voltaire were mostly novellas, their modern equivalents frequently take the form of novels. Significant examples include Umberto Eco's *Il pendolo di Foucault* (1988; *Foucault's Pendulum*, 1989) and *L'isola del giorno prima* (1994; *The Island of the Day Before*, 1995) and the series of theological fantasies by James Morrow begun with *Towing Jehovah* (1994). The classical *Kunstmärchen* (art fairy tale) was also confined to shorter lengths, but its modern variants are similarly making increasing use of the novel form; key examples include John Crowley's *Little, Big* (1981) and Robert Coover's *Briar Rose* (1996). Comic fantasy has been resuscitated with great success by such writers as Terry Pratchett, who was the best-selling novelist of the 1990's in Britain (he made much less impact in the United States because wit tends not to travel very well across cultures).

Although the bulk of the commercial fiction published under the fantasy label has become extraordinarily stereotyped and repetitive, with heavily promoted best-sellers religiously following dumbed-down formulas derived from Tolkien, the fringes of the marketing category continue to play host to a number of highly imaginative and accomplished writers. These include Peter S. Beagle, Tim Powers, and James Blaylock. It is now commonplace for writers who produce excellent fantasy for children to extend their endeavors into adult fantasy; writers working with great facility on both sides of this increasingly ill-defined boundary include Jane Yolen, Patricia McKillip, and Nancy Willard.

The simultaneous extension of all these trends gives contemporary fantastic fiction such an extraordinary variety that it is becoming difficult to attach much meaning to the overarching notion of the fantasy novel—a difficulty clearly reflected in the comprehensive yearly summations of novel production offered by Terri Windling in her introductions to the annual *Year's Best Fantasy and Horror* anthologies that she coedits with Ellen Datlow. Windling routinely employs such categories as imaginary world fantasy, contemporary or urban fantasy, Arthurian fantasy, dark fantasy, religious fantasy, humorous fantasy, fantasy mysteries, historical fantasy, and literary fairy tales but still requires such residual headings as "fantasy in the mainstream," "young adult fantasies," and "oddities" to mop up the remainder. The priority traditionally awarded by critics to realistic fiction seems to be in the process of breaking down, and it may well be that a more elaborate literary taxonomy will have to be developed for the new millennium.

Brian Stableford

BIBLIOGRAPHY

Attebery, Brian. *The Fantasy Tradition in American Literature: From Irving to Le Guin*. Bloomington: Indiana University Press, 1990. A comprehensive and intelligent study of the development of American fantasy.

Barron, Neil. *Fantasy Literature: A Reader's Guide*. New York: Garland, 1990.

_____. *Horror Literature: A Readers's Guide*. New York: Garland, 1990. A matched pair of library guides whose chapters are supplemented by extensively annotated bibliographies of key texts. The sections dealing with fiction include four-part histories, and the former volume also has a chapter on modern fantasy for young adults. The sections entitled Research Aids include chapters on general reference works, history and criticism, author studies, and other sources for further study.

Bleiler, Everett F. *The Guide to Supernatural Fiction*. Kent, Ohio: Kent State University Press, 1983. A huge collection of plot synopses and critical judgments of 1,775 books published between 1750 and 1960. A useful and near-comprehensive guide to the development and key themes of modern fantastic fiction.

_____, ed. *Supernatural Fiction Writers: Fantasy and Horror*. 2 vols. New York: Scribner's, 1985. An extensive collection of critical and biographical essays. The first volume deals with continental European and early British writers, the second with American and modern British writers.

Clute, John, and John Grant. *The Encyclopedia of Fantasy*. London: Orbit, 1997. Although less comprehensive and less well organized than its science-fiction companion, this remains the best general reference book on the part of the fantasy genre that excludes horror and occult fiction.

Hume, Kathryn. *Fantasy and Mimesis: Responses to Reality in Western Literature*. London: Methuen, 1984. One of the best theoretical studies of the aesthetics of fantasy and its significance in postmodern fiction.

Pringle, David, ed. *The St. James Guide to Fantasy Writers*. Detroit: St. James Press, 1996.

_____, ed. *The St. James Guide to Horror, Ghost, and Gothic Writers*. Detroit: St. James Press, 1998. A matched pair of reference works on individual authors, with supportive bibliographies of their relevant books and biographical notes. These volumes cover more authors than Bleiler's *Supernatural Fiction Writers* and take in a good deal of ground untouched by the encyclopedia by Clute and Grant.

FEMINIST LONG FICTION

The term "feminism" refers to a political ideology that demands the same economic and political rights for women that men enjoy. Feminist concerns also include social conditions based on tradition, such as prescribed gender roles. An example would be that all females must be homemakers, concerning themselves with domestic duties. Such confining roles work to prevent women from achieving emotionally satisfying lives. The political campaign for equal rights for women came to be known in the mid-twentieth century as the "women's movement." Thus, feminist long fiction features female characters whose quest for self-satisfaction causes conflict with a traditionally male-centered (patriarchal) society. The authors of feminist long fiction may receive harsh criticism for their shaping of nontraditional female characters.

HISTORY OF FEMINIST IDEOLOGY

The feminist ideology traces its roots to 1792, when English writer Mary Wollstonecraft (1759-1797) published *A Vindication of the Rights of Woman, with Strictures on Political and Moral Subjects*. This piece is recognized as a seminal feminist work in the English language because of its emphasis in print of women's concerns, particularly a desire on the part of women for an education. Not until the twentieth century would women reap the benefits of a long political campaign. Their demands not only for the right to vote but also for property rights, legal recourse against spousal abuse, and custodial rights of children aroused the anger of many men provoked by outspoken women. All aspects of Western culture, including religion, politics, and the workplace, experienced the impact of the feminist revolution. Popular literature also felt the effect of women who took up the pen as a way to make their previously silenced voices heard.

THE EIGHTEENTH CENTURY

Fiction, a genre that did not fully develop until the eighteenth century, provided a perfect vehicle for women who sought support through writing. The first long fiction in England consisted of what may generally be termed "romances." Until the second half of the twentieth century, white males received credit for developing long fiction and, eventually, the novel form. Examples include Samuel Richardson's epistolary novel, *Pamela: Or, Virtue Rewarded* (1740-1741) and Samuel Fielding's *The History of Tom Jones, a Foundling* (1749). In the twentieth century, however, it became known that as early as the end of the seventeenth century, female writers had arrived on the publishing scene. Aphra Behn (1640-1689), likely the first Englishwoman to support herself through writing, published the highly popular *Oroonoko: Or, The History of the Royal Slave* (1688), a prose romance, the first in English expressing sympathy for the plight of slaves. In the next century, female writers enjoyed a popularity equal to that of Richardson and Fielding. Mary de la Rivière Manley wrote *The Secret History of Queen Zarah and the Zarazians* (1705 and 1711), a version of the *roman à clef*. This type of fiction featured real-life personalities thinly disguised as its characters. Eliza Haywood, a highly political figure, also wrote romances, such as *The History of Jemmy and Jenny Jessamy* (1753).

THE NINETEENTH CENTURY

The nineteenth century became a golden age of writing for women, who could now claim their own tradition in writing, thanks to female writers of the previous century. Jane Austen's seven novels, often called novels of manners, parodied the sometimes ludicrous activities of genteel society and served to criticize inequitable social rules applied to women. Wildly popular, *Sense and Sensibility* (1811), *Pride and Prejudice* (1813), *Mansfield Park* (1814), *Emma* (1815), *Persuasion* (1818), and *Sanditon* (1871) did much to advance concerns of women, including their confining environments, shameful lack of education, and pitiful dependence upon male relatives for survival. Austen's *Northanger Abby* (1818) satirizes as sentimental its heroine's love for the gothic genre, fiction that offered readers mysterious castles or mansions with secret passages, dark shadowy beings, a damsel threatened by death, a hero with an obscure past, and visions and ghosts. Mary Wollstonecraft Shelley would rejuvenate the public's appreciation for the gothic in her 1818 novel *Frankenstein*. Rather than emphasize the traditional elements of the gothic, Shelley produced a complex psychological study of her characters, imbuing her horror and science-fiction story with disturbing imagery of aborted creations and multiple deaths. Feminist critics link these factors to Shelley's real-life experiences.

By mid-century, Charlotte Brontë (1816-1855) and Emily Brontë (1818-1848) were producing novels featuring a new hero based on the Romantic ideals of the English poet George Gordon, Lord Byron. Named for the poet and the heroes of his poetry, the Byronic hero most generally had a brooding, dark, independent, and sometimes abusive personality. Charlotte Brontë's *Jane Eyre* (1847) included a Byronic hero in the form of Edward Rochester. More important, however, the novel introduced a never-before-seen heroine in the shape of a plain small governess, whose values for truth and justice caused her rejection of the romantic attentions of Rochester, her master. The character of Jane served to undercut the popular female stereotypes of fiction: the angel of the house, the invalid, or the whore. While Charlotte Brontë's novel was well received by her contemporaries, Emily Brontë's masterpiece, *Wuthering Heights*, also published in 1847, was not. With its metaphysical suggestions that bordered on the gruesome and an abusive, vengeful Byronic hero, its messages proved too strong for its time, particularly to have been written by a woman. By the next century, however, this novel took its rightful place in the evolving canon of feminist long fiction.

THE TWENTIETH CENTURY

Just shy of the twentieth century, the United States produced a feminist fiction writer named Kate Chopin (1851-1904). In 1899, Chopin published *The Awakening*, a novel that many libraries refused to stock, despite Chopin's earlier popularity as a writer of traditional fiction. Her book shocked readers with its heroine who took pleasure in sexual relations and its suggestion of the connections between the imagi-

nation, the artist, and sex. The hostile criticism it received centered on its heroine's rejection of the traditional oppressive role of wife and mother, causing even Chopin's hometown library in St. Louis to ban the book. In 1920, the year women were at last granted the vote, Edith Wharton (1862-1937) became the first woman to win a Pulitzer Prize for fiction for her novel *The Age of Innocence* (1920), despite its emphasis on inequitable treatment of women.

As Wharton's career flourished in the United States, Virginia Woolf (1882-1941), the great English novelist, essayist, editor, and feminist, also enjoyed popularity. She began her publishing career in 1915 with the novel *The Voyage Out*, which required seven years of work. In early adulthood, Woolf studied Greek, an unusual subject for a young woman of her time, taught at a college for working women, performed menial chores for the suffrage movement, and wrote for the *Times Literary Supplement*, a prestigious publication. All these experiences influenced her feminist leanings. In *Night and Day* (1919), Woolf shaped a heroine not unlike herself, who experienced the trials of a young female writer. After *Jacob's Room* (1922), Woolf produced a highly influential novel, *Mrs. Dalloway* (1925). Departing from traditional novel structure, Woolf designed an analysis of post-World War I London society by moving, over a twenty-four-hour period, from her heroine's point of view to that of Septimus Warren Smith, a kind of insane alter ego for Mrs. Dalloway. Woolf's *To the Lighthouse* (1927), often studied by feminist critics, serves to critique the Victorian social mores that could create an environment at once suffocating and stimulating for young women. Woolf's involvement with self-proclaimed lesbian Vita Sackville-West likely inspired her 1928 novel *Orlando: A Biography*. *Orlando* claims to be a biography of a character who lives more than four hundred years, during which time her gender evolves from male to female. The novel represents the history of the aristocratic Sackville-West family and also the development of English literature. In 1929, Woolf produced a long essay published as *A Room of One's Own*, which focuses on the writing life of women; historians agree it represents the first major work in English of feminist criticism. Her most experimental novel, *The Waves* (1931), was labeled by Woolf herself a "poem-play." Made up of a number of monologues, the novel presents six characters, all lamenting the death of a young man named Percival, supposedly fashioned on Woolf's own brother, Thoby, who died many years before. Additional works include the nonfiction *Three Guineas* (1938), considered the most radical of her feminist writings in its examination of social oppression. Her final novel, *Between the Acts*, would appear posthumously in 1941, following Woolf's suicide in the same year.

Woolf's contemporary, English writer Rebecca West (1892-1983), was an actress and a journalist who joined the suffrage movement. Born Cicily Isabel Fairfield, West adopted as her name that of a radically feminist character from Henrik Ibsen's play *Rosmersholm* (1886; English translation, 1889). Although much of her work is in journalism and nonfiction, she published several important fictional works, despite some negative reactions to her writings and to her as an individual. Accounting for a portion of the negative feeling toward West was her love affair with the famous English novelist H. G. Wells, which produced an illegitimate son. The two writers' relationship challenged the conservative values of their society, which believed women should not enjoy physical relations out of wedlock. After West gave birth to her son in 1914, she took a great interest in the situation of unwed mothers, leading her to write *The Judge* (1922). This novel featured the suffragist struggle with additional consideration of issues such as rape, illegitimacy, and motherhood. In 1930, West married and produced more novels as she expressed an enthusiasm for writings by Woolf. *The Harsh Voice* (1935), a collection of novellas, featured as its subject economic and financial matters and focused on the 1929 economic crisis. Many reviewers of the book declared its subject too harsh and its tone too pessimistic for a female writer. Others, however, noted with interest that West shaped female characters who differed from those in her earlier works. These heroines were strong, taking an active part in the determination of their own fates, something women were not encouraged to do in real life. This same strength of character informed West's most

popular novel, *The Thinking Reed* (1936). Although some found the novel's heroine, Isabelle, ruthless, the book garnered much critical acclaim. In her novel, West criticized French, English, and American societies in a manner that some found offensive but that most declared to be accurate. By the 1950's, West departed from her feminist-socialist view to take up a conservative anticommunist stance. Her political reversal earned her the title of dame commander of the British Empire, a somewhat ironic circumstance for a writer who earlier had blasted imperialism in print.

DEVELOPMENT OF A FEMALE AESTHETIC

With the exodus of male workers to participate in the world wars in the first half of the twentieth century, American and English women entered the work force in record numbers to occupy positions other than that of the traditional nurse, teacher, or secretary. As women's roles in the world changed, so did the characterizations of women in novels. Female writers began to connect their work and their lives. They discovered a number of disparities between their own ambitions, ingenuity, and creativity on one hand and the limited, often secondary, roles assumed by the majority of traditional female fictional characters on the other hand. This was easily explained, as the majority of novelists were white males outside the female experience. By the mid-twentieth century, a plethora of long fiction by women with a feminine agenda began to appear, and realistic images of female characters emerged. Women's fiction transformed from products of imitation of a male aesthetic to protests against that aesthetic, eventually becoming self-defining works of literature.

Their success was propelled by the work of feminist literary critics—those who analyzed literature, usually within academia. These critics had begun in the 1960's to declare the characterizations of women as angels or monsters as false. They also identified the textual harassment of women in popular male literature and, most important, refused to except the exclusion of women from literary history. Their diligence in rediscovering female novelists from previous centuries and decades helped propel authors such as Virginia Woolf, George Sand (1804-1876), George Eliot (1819-1880), and Rebecca West to their proper stature. They traced historical connections of recurring images, themes, and plots in women's writing that reflected their social and psychological experience in a culture dominated by males. For example, the caged bird repeatedly appears as an image representing the suppression of female creativity or the physical and emotional "imprisonment" of women in general. These efforts helped convince not only the classroom but also the marketplace of the worthiness of writings by women. Virago Press, which publishes women's writings, reprinted West's novels in affordable editions. While her work in its own day was deemed too intellectual, feminist critics led a reconsideration of those books. West's voice remains popular because of the efforts of such groups.

As the women's liberation movement gained ground, it promoted an increased social sensitivity to conflicts caused by sexism and gender bias, a sensitivity that would lead to legal developments protecting the civil rights of women. Besides resulting in the appearance of a greatly altered type of fiction, the movement also empowered women to question the aesthetic values that appeared in many of the novels that had long been considered classics; from this new perspective, many of these novels were regarded in a disfavorable manner.

Closely related to such questionings was the continuing development of a black aesthetic. Novels by African American women from the early twentieth century, such as anthropologist Zora Neale Hurston's *Their Eyes Were Watching God* (1937), were reissued after decades of neglect. Hurston's novel—which tells the story of a young black woman involved in three abusive marriages who eventually finds redemption through her own strength and beliefs and through the support of her female friend—gained an important place among feminist fiction. Hurston's work prefigured that of Toni Morrison (born 1931), an African American Pulitzer Prize winner (1988) and the first black woman to receive the Nobel Prize in Literature (1993). One of America's foremost novelists, Morrison is celebrated for her acute analyses of the dynamics of race and gender. Often framing

her fiction in the fantastic and the mystical, Morrison is known for *The Bluest Eye* (1970), *Sula* (1973), *Song of Solomon* (1977), *Tar Baby* (1981), *Beloved* (1987), *Jazz* (1992), and *Paradise* (1998). Like Morrison, Alice Walker (born 1944) explores the cultural inheritance of African Americans by examining universal moral issues and by celebrating supportive communities of women. In her critically acclaimed Pulitzer Prize-winning novel *The Color Purple* (1982), Walker presents her story in epistolary form, emphasizing her characters' struggles with articulation of their feelings regarding identity from the complicated perspective of African American experience.

By the 1950's, writers such as Iranian-born Doris Lessing (born 1919) were publishing works that feminists claimed as supportive of their cause. Lessing's *The Golden Notebook* (1962) was one such work. The novel's heroine, Anna Wulf, represents a theme that would be repeated in many of Lessing's books: the struggle of the creative woman against solitude, self-destructive impulses, and the manner by which women practice self-censorship in order to conform to society. Lessing is known for her vision of the writer as a morally responsible person, criticizing capitalist inequities through her socialist philosophy.

Erica Jong (born 1942) is another novelist who has been labeled a feminist. Her popular *Fear of Flying* (1973) sold more than five million copies by 1977 and prompted an avalanche of letters to Jong from women responding to the work as a revelation of emotions they had never seen before in fiction. The book caused a flurry of mixed critical response, partly in reaction to its provocative cover images and to its content, which some labeled pornographic. Expressing in no uncertain terms the anger and energy of the women's liberation movement, it garnered both praise for its frankness and criticism for what some called a banal tone and weak writing style.

In the latter part of the twentieth century, many women who combined ethnic concerns with those of gender arrived on the fiction scene. Maxine Hong Kingston (born 1940), an American daughter of Chinese immigrants, published *The Woman Warrior: Memoirs of a Girlhood Among Ghosts* (1976), combining autobiography with fiction to write of "a girl-hood among ghosts." These ghosts emerged from Chinese myth to show how the definition of "feminine" is shaped in that culture. Frankly oppressive for women, the ancient Chinese culture allows Kingston to investigate challenges to female physical and emotional survival. Louise Erdrich (born 1954) uses her Native American background to interrogate in her National Book Critics Circle Award-winning novel *Love Medicine* (1984; revised and expanded 1993) the social, economic, and emotional pressures suffered by dislocated women.

Virginia Brackett

BIBLIOGRAPHY

Blain, Virginia, Patricia Clements, and Isobel Grundy, eds. *The Feminist Companion to Literature in English: Women Writers from the Middle Ages to the Present*. London: Batsford, 1990. An informative guide to feminist writers of long fiction.

_____. *The Madwoman in the Attic: The Woman Writer and the Nineteenth-Century Literary Imagination*. New Haven, Conn.: Yale University Press, 1979. This seminal text considers nineteenth century stereotypes of female fictional characters and of the writers who created them, framing its discussion with ideas governing restrictive social mores.

Gilbert, Sandra M., and Susan Gubar, eds. *The Norton Anthology of Literature by Women: The Traditions in English*. 2d ed. New York: W. W. Norton, 1996. With two of the best-known feminist critics as its editors, this work represents the most comprehensive anthology available of women's writing, featuring writers from medieval times through the twentieth century. Biographies, works, and excerpts are presented chronologically, with each era preceded by in-depth introductions by the editors that examine the culture in which the women wrote.

Lauret, Maria. *Liberating Literature: Feminist Fiction in America*. New York: Routledge, 1994. Lauret explores the writing of American feminists.

Moers, Ellen. *Literary Women: The Great Writers*. Garden City, N.J.: Doubleday, 1976. Moers makes visible a "subtext" in the writings of women containing messages unrecognized in their own times due to gender discrimination.

Showalter, Elaine. *A Literature of Their Own: British Women Novelists from Brontë to Lessing*. Princeton, N.J.: Princeton University Press, 1977. Revered feminist critic Elaine Showalter works to "rediscover" British women writers by reconstructing the texts in the light of feminist ideology.

Woolf, Virginia. *A Room of One's Own*. 1929. Reprint. New York: Harcourt Brace Jovanovich, 1989. Woolf's work consists of two lectures she delivered on the value of education and income to those confronting the special challenges inherent to the careers of women writers.

GAY AND LESBIAN LONG FICTION

Homosexuality was, for much of history, generally regarded as a disease or perversion that was rigorously denounced or even censored; therefore, there was a long delay in its appearance as an explicit theme in long fiction. English-language novelists resorted to writing gay novels under pseudonyms and publishing them either privately or in foreign countries.

NINETEENTH CENTURY CAMOUFLAGE

Gay characters and sensibility were introduced only by arch subterfuge, with writers following society's unwritten decree to end such fiction with the death, destruction, or extraordinary "conversion" of the characters. In Bayard Taylor's *Joseph and His Friend* (1870), a disastrous marriage causes Joseph to drift toward Philip, a young, golden-haired man; the novel ends, however, with Joseph's sudden, almost inexplicable interest in Philip's look-alike sister. This was presumably meant to save him from a fate worse than death. Henry James's *Roderick Hudson* (1876) sketches wealthy Rowland Mallet's infatuation with a young sculptor, but after a rift between them, the eponymous character sinks into a decadent languor from which he is rescued only by Christina Light, a beautiful, bored girl. Once again, homoerotic love yields to the heterosexual imperative.

In Europe, there were many clandestine erotic novels—such as the lurid *Gamiani* (1833; *Gamiani: Or, Two Nights of Excess*, 1923), attributed to Alfred de Musset and featuring lesbianism—but none of these was a major work. Honoré de Balzac masked homosexuality by artifice. In his vast sequence of interrelated novels about French society, *La Comédie humaine* (1829-1848; *The Comedy of Human Life*, 1885-1893, 1896; also as *The Human Comedy*, 1895-1896, 1911), the exuberantly masculine Vautrin is imprisoned after taking the blame for a crime committed by Lucien, the gentle, handsome young man he loves. Vautrin dreams of owning a plantation in the American South, where he can have absolute power over his slaves, especially their bodies. Only by living outside hypocritical French society can

Vautrin have insight into its excesses and his own nature. In England, Oscar Wilde defied Victorian hypocrisy, but he paid a mortal price. *The Picture of Dorian Gray* (serial 1890; expanded 1891) represents a Faustian pact between young Dorian and the forces of evil. Wilde defiantly embraces and gilds what his society deems evil. Society enjoyed the ultimate revenge by destroying Wilde's reputation and life: He was jailed for homosexual "offences" and went bankrupt while in prison.

If gay fiction wished to vividly portray homosexuality, it had to balance sensuality with social determinism—as in the case of Adolpho Caminha's Brazilian novel, *Bom crioulo* (1895; *Bom-Crioula: The Black Man and the Cabin Boy*, 1982), the first explicitly gay Latin American fiction. The violent Amaro, often described in animal imagery, escapes from slavery and sexual strictures, but his "animal" nature drives him to kill his male lover in a jealous fit. Caminha uses laws of heredity to justify slavery and exploitation, and his novel is flawed by contradictions: Homosexuality is unnatural, yet heroic; it is against nature, yet it is natural for Bom Crioulu. Nevertheless, his novel is an example of the manner in which homosexuality haunts the "normal" world.

EARLY TWENTIETH CENTURY OBLIQUENESS

Lesbianism was a major theme in Colette's novels about teenagers who were infatuated with older women, and male love figured in Robert Musil's *Die Verwirrungen des Zöglings Törless* (1906; *Young Törless*, 1955), set in a military school, and Thomas Mann's *Der Tod in Venedig* (1912; *Death in Venice*, 1925) which narrates the story of Gustav von Aschenbach's fatal infatuation with Tadzio, a fourteen-year-old Polish boy of Apollonian beauty and stillness.

Gay novelists in England and the United States resorted to setting love stories in faraway lands or using other techniques of evasion. Warren Stoddard's *For the Pleasure of His Company: An Affair of the Misty City* (1903), the story of Paul Clitheroe's love affair with two darkly handsome men, runs sour until Paul ends up in the company of three South Sea islanders. Edward Prime-Stevenson's *Imre: A Memorandum* (1906), privately published abroad in a tiny run of 125 copies, ends with a young Englishman, Oswald, in the arms of Imre, a twenty-five-year-old Hungarian army officer, but this "openness" is undercut by the novelist's pretense to be no more than the editor of a manuscript sent to him by a British friend. The guardedness of gay novelists continued for decades, even when the theme was a "coming out" of sorts. Henry Blake Fuller's *Bertram Cope's Year* (1919), set near Chicago, is about the ruined love affair between Randolph and Bertram Cope, but Fuller pretends that the rupture is based on age rather than on rival love.

The 1920's, an age of reckless, fast living and thrills, did not end gay fiction's camouflage. Sophisticates knew of Sigmund Freud's radical sex theories and D. H. Lawrence's carnal characters, but there was no progress in sexual attitudes toward gays. Camouflage through euphuism became the mode, as in Ronald Firbank's high-camp affectation in his novellas or Carl Van Vechten's frothy tone in *The Blind Bow-Boy* (1923), where the notorious Duke of Middlebottom dresses as a sailor and has stationery printed with the motto: "A thing of beauty is a boy forever." The spirit of the times did not welcome serious novels of social protest or self-disclosure, as Radclyffe Hall discovered when she published her semiautobiographical lesbian novel, *The Well of Loneliness* (1928). Virginia Woolf masked her love affair with Vita Sackville-West with the fantastical, androgynous world of *Orlando: A Biography* (1928).

Through the 1930's and 1940's, the "tough guy" novels of Ernest Hemingway and Raymond Chandler, as well as the war novels of Norman Mailer and James Jones, depicted gay characters with contempt, as if they were weak "pansies" and the antitheses of masculine heroes. Although black people and Jews were also maligned by society during this period, their writers resorted to proletarian novels of social protest, whereas gays tried to remain "invisible" for the most part. Consequently, gay fiction was left to hacks, with a few outstanding exceptions. Parker Tyler's *The Young and Evil* (1933), a slice-of-life story about the art set in Greenwich Village, and Frederick Rolfe's

The Desire and the Pursuit of the Whole (1934), whose male protagonist can entertain desire only when his beloved adopts male attire and behavior, revealed gains in the realistic mode. However, Frederic Prokosch used numerous filters to conceal gayness. His novels, such as *The Asiatics* (1935) and *The Seven Who Fled* (1937), were lyrical tales of handsome bachelors in extreme circumstances and exotic places (such as Aden, Turkey, Iraq, or Tibet). Prokosch allowed his heroes, ostensibly straight males, to be placed in sexually charged situations, but his filtrations and dilutions of homosexuality were concessions to establishment society. Djuna Barnes's *Nightwood* (1936) expressed the intensity of lesbian love, but its world was a broodingly gothic Parisian one.

Alfred Kinsey's *Sexual Behavior in the Human Male* (1948) rebuked certain antigay biases, while the horrors of World War II prompted Americans to question traditionally accepted morals and values. Nevertheless, although the "open" homosexual in long fiction became increasingly frequent, literary camouflage and subterfuge were still necessary. Although she herself was gay, Carson McCullers did not concern herself principally with the subject of gayness. Each of her novels contains a male with a crush on another male, but her fictions are really about abnormality and yearning. Despite the fact that Singer's homocrotic love is his only joy and reason for living in *The Heart Is a Lonely Hunter* (1940), homosexuality is one of the few things not attributed to him by other characters. Despite writing of a young man's love for a handsome prize-fighter in *Other Voices, Other Rooms* (1948), Truman Capote also skirted the issue of homosexuality by simply affirming that any love could be beautiful as long as it belonged to a person's intrinsic nature. William Maxwell's *The Folded Leaf* (1945) camouflages Lymie Peters's homosexual interest as an aesthetic one; what is worse, the athletic Spud Latham never realizes his friend's sexual desire for him. John Horne Burns, who thought it necessary to be gay in order to be a good writer, created a gay bar and a vivid set of rapacious, spontaneous, erotic characters in *The Gallery* (1947); however, his story is really not about sex or love per se, but rather human nature in its various vagaries. In *Lucifer with a Book* (1949), Burns acts almost apologetic about his erotic male characters by designing last-minute conversions to heterosexuality for them.

BREAKING THE PATTERN

Gay writers were pressured by society to deny the naturalness of homosexuality. The protagonist in Fritz Peters's *The World Next Door* (1949) admits that he loves a man while denying that he is gay. Helped by new trends in Europe, Patricia Highsmith and Gore Vidal dared to break the pattern. Highsmith's *The Price of Salt* (1952, as Claire Morgan; also published as *Carol*) was overtly lesbian, while Vidal's *The City and the Pillar* (1948; revised 1965) depicts males undressing and kissing. In seeking to show the naturalness of homosexual relations, Vidal used Jim Willard as a reproach to society's censors who wish to bring down retribution on homosexuals: When he is vilely denounced by the man in whom he tries to rekindle their boyhood homoeroticism, Willard strangles the object of his affection. In a revised edition of the book, Vidal goes one step further: Willard rapes his would-be lover.

Vidal's all-male Eden was shocking to American literary critics who expected inverts to be punished or criticized for aberrations of personality. Vidal, however, was hardly in the league of Jean Genet, whose dark, decadent fiction—*Notre-Dame des Fleurs* (1944, 1951; *Our Lady of the Flowers*, 1949), *Miracle de la rose* (1946, 1951; *Miracle of the Rose* 1966), *Querelle de Brest* (1947, 1953; *Querelle of Brest*, 1966), and the semiautobiographical *Journal du voleur* (1948, 1949; *The Thief's Journal*, 1954)— never flinches from portraying the emotional and psychological depths of gay male relations. Sex and violence are mixed with lurid and salacious density, and Genet often creates an extremely perverse but original perspective on theft, rape, and even murder.

Genet's deliberate idealization of outlawed desire was reflected in Yukio Mishima's Japanese fiction. A martial artist and sexual outlaw, Mishima resorted to metaphor for deception. The narrator of *Kamen no kokuhaku* (1949; *Confessions of a Mask*, 1958) enters into anonymous relationships with women, for whom he harbors secret distaste, simply to appear to fit into conventional society.

THE 1950'S AND EARLY 1960'S

The 1950's were rife with McCarthyism and purges of anything deemed anti-American. Homophobia was rampant. Fearing critical drubbing, gay writers were forced to become grotesque, parasitic, or clownish. Capote embraced Manhattan whimsy and capriciousness; Burns wrote a weak, straight novel shortly before he died; and Vidal put his energy into nonfiction and politics. Many versions of the "apprenticeship" gay novel appeared, with themes of a problematic childhood. Basically, gay fiction divided itself into two categories: traditional realism (James Baldwin and J. R. Ackerley) and counterculture writing (William Burroughs), though there were fascinating exceptions to the rule—as in James Purdy's *Malcolm* (1959), an allegorical story about a teenager befriended by a possible pedophile; Fritz Peters's *Finisterre* (1951), which is set in France, where the Europeans are more accepting of the adolescent protagonist's burgeoning gayness than are his parents; James Barr's *Quatrefoil* (1950), a male love story told in a lofty, intellectual manner; and William Talsman's playfully witty and stylish *The Gaudy Image* (1958).

Most of these novels, however, ended in wistfulness or death for the protagonist. Young Matt in *Finisterre* drowns himself; Baldwin's *Giovanni's Room* (1956) ends on a bridge, where David tries to discard his lover's letter, only to have the wind blow the fragments back to him; and in *Quatrefoil*, Phillip, after his lover is killed in an aircrash, contemplates suicide, only to decide that love has made him strong. During this time, no American or British writer had the creative courage of France's Marguerite Yourcenar, whose books defy classification because they mix modes as they tackle different kinds of love to show society's effects on those with homosexual leanings. However, this began to change during the 1960's as gay writers became increasingly overt about their sexuality. In *Another Country* (1962), Baldwin depicts a sleazy New York hell where individuals are caught up in the general malaise of American society. However, Baldwin's gay characters have a greater awareness of their misery than does society at large, which remains ignorant. Christopher Isherwood's *A Single Man* (1964) affirms the value of an aging gay who, in a departure from custom, is not a doomed homosexual with neurotic self-loathing or sexual guilt but a bachelor who entertains a fantasy of killing or torturing bigots unless they agree to end homophobic practices.

Isherwood's quiet prose contrasts with the louder brutality of Charles Wright's *The Messenger* (1963), where New York is a hell filled with junkies and gays, or Hubert Selby's *Last Exit to Brooklyn* (1964), replete with pimps, whores, thugs, and queers. The most controversial novels were John Rechy's *City of Night* (1963) and *Numbers* (1967). In the first, Rechy takes a hard look at the joyless and dangerous side of male prostitution, based on his own raw experiences, but his writing is not primarily confessional. It has a gritty realism that exposes its central character's refusal to express emotion for fear of revealing his sexual identity. *Numbers* is also a horror story with dark imagery, as its protagonist sets off on a journey of self-discovery, literally counting sexual experiences as if numbers could themselves ward off age and death.

New taxonomy

Gayness became iconic after the Stonewall Inn riots in New York City in 1969, which resulted in the emergence of the gay rights movement. Gay writers felt emancipated to the point of full self-disclosure. By the end of the 1960's, gay fiction was able to exercise various subgenres. In Europe, Pier Paolo Pasolini and Jean Genet reveled in picaresque novels. Marie Claire-Blais brought French-Canadian lesbianism to English readers, and Ursula Le Guin wrote science-fiction in which fantasy planets enjoyed gender equality. The 1970's were rich in gay inventiveness. Anne Rice and Marion Zimmer Bradley also wrote in the science fantasy genre, with Bradley becoming one of the first science fiction writers to use independent female characters to explore gender roles. Guy Hocquenghem, a gay rights activist, explored the connections between the body and tech-

nology. Mary Renault used classical history (especially in *The Persian Boy*, 1972) to show how bisexuality was once a cultural norm before it was destroyed by people who refused to understand anything alien to their sensibility.

During the 1970's and 1980's, the new taxonomy of gay writing was consolidated. The rise of small presses specializing in gay writing ensured the publication of diverse writers and genres. The "coming out" and semiautobiographical novels of Andrew Holleran, David Leavitt, Rita Mae Brown, and Jeanette Winterson explored a wide range of experience, including parental disgust and rejection, dispossession of home and the death of innocence, and various discourses on love. The "colonialist" tradition of upper-class men seeking erotic adventure with foreigners or working-class people—already encountered in nineteenth century and early twentieth century writers—continued, most notably in Alan Hollinghurst's *The Swimming-Pool Library* (1988).

The confluence of the gay rights movement and the rise of feminism ensured that lesbian writers could tell their stories from a lesbian-feminist perspective, as in novels by June Arnold (who had a unique vision of women taking control of their own destinies) and the Dutch writer Anna Blaman (who turned language and social stereotypes on their heads). Feminist and postmodernist literary theorists helped shape and direct lesbian writing. Canadian theorist Nicole Brossard associated the lesbian body with an intelligent body, thereby pointing to utopianism. In France, Monique Wittig suggested that women could liberate themselves only by using language in radical ways, and Helene Cixous responded by developing a theory and style called "writing from the body." Cixous's bold celebration of lesbianism as a lever to take apart social structure helped clear a path for writers such as Dorothy Allison and Blanche Boyd. While Allison won acclaim with *Bastard Out of Carolina* (1992), which explored domestic, personal, and psychic violence from a lesbian-feminist viewpoint, Boyd ensured that each of her own novels was female centered, with young women (each of whom becomes a lesbian) learning to overcome obstacles to existential and sexual autonomy.

The new consciousness enhanced gay writers' gambits into social and political themes, even to the point of criticizing their own subculture—as with Larry Kramer's *Faggots* (1978), whose antipromiscuity theme aroused a backlash from the gay community. Lisa Alther incorporated cultural satire into such works as *Kinflicks* (1975), *Original Sins* (1981), and *Five Minutes in Heaven* (1995). The preeminent gay writer of the era, however, was Sarah Schulman, who examined inherent tensions between the nature of art and the reality of politics. Beginning with *The Sophie Horowitz Story* (1984), which reads like a detective story but is really a meditation on lesbian politics and sexuality, and continuing with *Girls, Visions and Everything* (1986), *People in Trouble* (1990), and *Empathy* (1992), Schulman dealt with the individual's responsibility to the world. The author's involvement with various gay and lesbian activist groups served as a major influence on her writing.

Schulman's playful experimentation with the detective genre, especially in *After Delores* (1988), a hard-boiled detective story in the style of James M. Cain and Dashiell Hammett, displays the modern gay writer's literary freedom. English-language writers were no longer forced to envy foreign-language gay writers—such as Manuel Puig (*El beso de la mujer araña*, 1976; *Kiss of the Spider Woman*, 1979), Mutsuo Takahashi (*Zen no henreki*, 1974; Zen's pilgrimmage), or Michel Tournier (*Gilles et Jeanne*, 1983; *Gilles and Jeanne*, 1987)—for their ability to take risks. The achievements of Paul Monette, Armistead Maupin, and Kitty Tsui during the acquired immunodeficiency syndrome (AIDS) era are notable, as are the more experimental and ambitious works of Dale Peck, Edmund White, and Samuel Steward.

Reacting to the subtle and pervasive censorship inherent in political correctness, Peck, White, and Steward began experimenting with mixed styles and modes. Steward's detective and modernist parodies examine the position of the artist in modern society, while promoting erotica as pure entertainment. Peck's *Martin and John* (1993) is an absorbing patchwork of conflicting stories, all with characters named Martin and John, but death is its driving force. However, neither writer matches Edmund White's mainstream success, especially with *A Boy's Own Story* (1982), a mature example of the elegant sensitivity of modern gay fiction.

Keith Garebian

BIBLIOGRAPHY

Austen, Roger. *Playing the Game: The Homosexual Novel in America.* Indianapolis: Bobbs-Merrill, 1977. A literate history of the homosexual novel from its murky beginnings into the 1960's. Covers two hundred novels. Selected bibliography and index.

Lilly, Mark. *Gay Men's Literature in the Twentieth Century.* Washington Square: New York University Press, 1993. A reintroduction to famous texts and an entry into less well known work from the standpoint of gay experience, sensibility, and sexual desire.

Malinowski, Sharon, ed. *Gay and Lesbian Literature.* Vol. 1. Detroit: St. James Press, 1994. Extensive compilation of more than two hundred authors since 1900. Inclusion is based on thematic content, not sexual identity.

Nelson, Emmanuel S., ed. *Contemporary Gay American Novelists: A Bio-Bibliographical Critical Sourcebook.* Westport, Conn.: Greenwood Press, 1993. Fifty-seven articles on such writers as Burroughs, Capote, Isherwood, Kramer, Maupin, Monette, and others.

Pendergast, Tom, and Sara Pendergast, eds. *Gay and Lesbian Literature.* Vol. 2. Detroit: St. James Press, 1998. An invaluable companion to the first volume. Follows the same criteria as volume 1.

Pollack, Sandra, and Denise D. Knight, eds. *Contemporary Lesbian Writers of the United States: A Bio-Bibliographical Critical Sourcebook.* Westport, Conn.: Greenwood Press, 1993. Contains one hundred articles, a bibliography, and appendices of selected periodicals and journals. Articles on Donna Allegra, Beth Brant, Dorothy Allison, Jane Rule, Mary Sarton, and others.

THE GOTHIC NOVEL

The gothic novel is a living tradition, a form that has enjoyed great popular appeal while provoking harsh critical judgments. It began with Horace Walpole's *The Castle of Otranto* (1765), then traveled through Ann Radcliffe, Matthew Gregory Lewis, Charles Robert Maturin, Mary Wollstonecraft Shelley, Edgar Allan Poe, the Brontës, Nathaniel Hawthorne, Charles Brockden Brown, Bram Stoker, Charles Dickens, Thomas Hardy, Henry James, and many others into the twentieth century, where it surfaced, much altered and yet spiritually continuous, in the work of writers such as William Faulkner, D. H. Lawrence, Iris Murdoch, John Gardner, Joyce Carol Oates, and Doris Lessing and in the popular genres of horror fiction and some women's romances.

The externals of the gothic, especially early in its history, are characterized by sublime but terrifying mountain scenery, bandits and outlaws, ruined, ancient seats of power, morbid death imagery, and virgins and charismatic villains, as well as hyperbolic physical states of agitation and lurid images of physical degradation. Its spirit is characterized by a tone of high agitation, unresolved or almost-impossible-to-resolve anxiety, fear, unnatural elation, and desperation.

The first gothic novel is identifiable with a precision unusual in genre study. Horace Walpole began writing *The Castle of Otranto* in June, 1764, finished it in August, 1764, and published it in an edition of five hundred copies on Christmas Eve, 1764. Walpole (1717-1797), the earl of Orford, was a historian and essayist whose vivid and massive personal correspondence remains essential reading for the eighteenth century background. Before writing *The Castle of Otranto*, his only connection with the gothic was his estate in Twickenham, which he called Strawberry Hill. It was built in the gothic style and set an architectural trend, as his novel would later set a literary trend.

Walpole did not dream of what he was about to initiate with *The Castle of Otranto*; he published his first edition anonymously, revealing his identity, only after the novel's great success, in his second edition of April, 1765. At that point, he no longer feared mockery of his tale of a statue with a bleeding nose, mammoth, peregrinating armor, and an ancient castle complete with ancient family curse. With his second edition, he was obliged to add a preface explaining why he had hidden behind the guise of a preface proclaiming the book to be a "found manuscript," printed originally "in Naples in the black letter in 1529." The reader of the first edition was told that *The Castle of Otranto* was the long-lost history of an ancient Catholic family in the north of England. The greater reading public loved it, and it was reprinted in many editions. By 1796, it had been translated into French and Spanish and had been repeatedly rendered into dramatic form. In 1848, the novel was still active as the basis for successful theatrical presentations, although the original gothic vogue had passed.

Close upon Walpole's heels followed Radcliffe, Lewis, and Maturin. These, of course, were not the only imitators ready to take advantage of the contemporary trend (there were literally hundreds of those), but they are among the few who are still read, for they made their own distinctive contributions to the genre's evolution.

Ann Radcliffe (1764-1823) was born just as Walpole's *The Castle of Otranto* was being published. She was reared and continued to live life in a middle-class milieu, acquainted with merchants and professionals; her husband was the editor of *The English Chronicle* and a Fellow of the Society of Antiquaries. She lived a quiet life, is believed to have been asthmatic, and seems to have stayed close to her hearth. Although she never became a habitué of literary circles and in her lifetime only published a handful of works, she is considered the grande dame of the gothic novelists and enjoyed a stunning commercial success in her day; she is the only female novelist of the period whose work is still read.

Radcliffe's works include *The Castles of Athlin and Dunbayne* (1789); *A Sicilian Romance* (1790); *The Romance of the Forest* (1791); *The Mysteries of Udolpho* (1794), her greatest success; *The Italian: Or, The Confessional of the Black Penitents* (1797); and, published after her death, *Gaston de Blondeville*

(1826). She also wrote an account of a trip she made with her husband, *A Journey Made in the Summer of 1794 Through Holland and the Western Frontier of Germany* (1795). Her remarkably sedate life contrasts strikingly with the melodramatic flamboyance of her works. Her experiences also fail to account for her dazzling, fictional accounts of the scenery of Southern Europe, which she had never seen.

Matthew Gregory Lewis, called "Monk" Lewis in honor of his major work, conformed in his life more closely to the stereotype of the gothic masters. Lewis (1775-1818) was a child of the upper classes, the spoiled son of a frivolous beauty, whom he adored. His parents' unhappy marriage broke up when he was at Westminster Preparatory School. There was a continual struggle between his parents to manage his life, his father stern and aloof, his mother extravagant and possessive.

Lewis actually spent his childhood treading the halls of large, old manses belonging both to family and to friends. He paced long, gloomy corridors—a staple of the gothic—and peered up at ancient portraits in dark galleries, another permanent fixture in gothic convention. Homosexual, flamboyant, and deeply involved with the literati of his day, Lewis found an equivocal public reception, but *The Monk: A Romance* (1796), an international sensation, had an enormous effect on the gothic productions of his day. Lewis died on board ship, a casualty of a yellow-fever epidemic, in the arms of his valet, Baptista, and was buried at sea.

Lewis's bibliography is as frenetic as his biography. Although his only gothic novel is the infamous *The Monk*, he spent most of his career writing plays heavily influenced by gothic conventions; he also translated many gothic works into English and wrote scandalous poetry. Among his plays are *Village Virtues* (1796), *The Castle Spectre* (1797), *The East Indian* (1799), *Adelmorn the Outlaw* (1801), and *The Captive* (1803). He was responsible for the translations of Friedrich Schiller's *The Minister* (1797) and August von Kotzebue's *Rolla: Or, The Peruvian Hero* (1799). He was notorious for an imitation of Juvenal's thirteenth satire, *The Love of Gain: A Poem Initiated from Juvenal* (1799).

The Reverend Charles Robert Maturin is the final major gothic artist of the period. Maturin (1780-1824) was Irish, a Protestant clergyman from Dublin, and a spiritual brother of the Marquis de Sade. He was a protégé of Sir Walter Scott and an admirer of Lord Byron. His major gothic novel is *Melmoth the Wanderer* (1820), as shocking to its public as was Lewis's *The Monk*. An earlier gothic was *Fatal Revenge: Or, The Family of Montorio* (1807). He also wrote *The Milesian Chief* (1812); a theological treatise, *Women: Or, Pour et Contre* (1818); a tragedy, *Bertram: Or The Castle of St. Aldobrand* (1816), produced by Edmund Kean; and *The Albigenses* (1824).

Among the legions of other gothic novelists, a few writers, no longer generally read, have made a place for themselves in literary history. These include Harriet Lee, known for *The Canterbury Tales* (1797-1805, 5 volumes); her sister Sophia Lee, known for *The Recess* (1785, 3 volumes); Clara Reeve, known for *The Olde English Baron* (1778); Mrs. Regina Maria Roche, known for *The Children of the Abbey* (1796); Mrs. Charlotte Smith, known for *Emmeline, the Orphan of the Castle* (1788); Charlotte Dacre, known for *Zofloya: Or, The Moor* (1806); and Mary-Anne Radcliffe, known for *Manfroné: Or, The One Handed Monk* (1809).

Critics generally agree that the period gothics, while having much in common, divide into relatively clear subclassifications: the historical gothic, the school of terror, and the *Schauer-Romantik* school of horror. All gothics of the period return to the past, are flushed with suggestions of the supernatural, and tend to be set amid ruined architecture, particularly a great estate house gone to ruin or a decaying abbey. All make use of stock characters. These will generally include one or more young and innocent virgins of both sexes; monks and nuns, particularly of sinister aspect; and towering male and female characters of overpowering will whose charismatic egotism knows no bounds. Frequently the novels are set in the rugged mountains of Italy and contain an evil Italian character. Tumultuous weather often accompanies tumultuous passions. The gothic genre specializes in making external conditions metaphors of human emotions, a convention thought to have been derived in part from the works of William Shakespeare. Brigands are frequently employed in the plot, and most gothics of the period employ morbid, lurid imagery, such as a body riddled with worms behind a moldy black veil.

The various subdivisions of the gothic may feature any or all of these conventions, being distinguished by relative emphasis. The historical gothic, for example, revealed the supernatural against a genuinely historical background, best exemplified by the works of the Lee sisters, who, although their own novels are infrequently read today, played a part in the evolution of the historical novel through their influence on Sir Walter Scott. The school of terror provided safe emotional titillation—safe, because the morbidity such novels portrayed took place not in a genuine, historical setting, but in some fantasy of the past, and because the fearful effects tended to be explained away rationally at the end of the work. Radcliffe is the major paradigm of this subgroup. The *Schauer-Romantik* school of horror, best represented by Lewis and Maturin, did not offer the reassurance of a moral, rational order. These works tend to evoke history but stir anxiety without resolving or relieving it. They are perverse and sadistic, marked by the amoral use of thrill.

There are very few traditional gothic plots and conventions; a discrete set of such paradigms was recycled and refurbished many times. Walpole's *The Castle of Otranto*, Radcliffe's *The Mysteries of Udolpho*, Lewis's *The Monk*, and Maturin's *Melmoth the Wanderer* represent the basic models of the genre.

The Castle of Otranto

Walpole's *The Castle of Otranto*, emphatically not historical gothic, takes place in a fantasy past. It is not of the school of terror either; although it resolves its dilemmas in a human fashion, it does not rationally explain away the supernatural events it has recounted. This earliest of the gothics trembles between horror and terror.

The story opens with Manfred, Prince of Otranto, ready to marry his sickly son, Conrad, to the beautiful Isabella. Manfred, the pattern for future gothic villains of towering egotism and pride, is startled when his son is killed in a bizarre fashion. The gigantic statuary helmet of a marble figure of Alphonse the Good has been mysteriously transported to Manfred's castle, where it has fallen on and crushed Conrad.

Manfred precipitously reveals that he is tired of his virtuous wife, Hippolita, and, disdaining both her and their virtuous daughter, Mathilda, attempts to force himself on the exquisite, virginal Isabella, his erstwhile daughter-in-law elect. At the same time, he attempts to blame his son's death on an individual named Theodore, who appears to be a virtuous peasant lad and bears an uncanny resemblance to the now helmetless statue of Alfonso the Good. Theodore is incarcerated in the palace but manages to escape.

Theodore and Isabella, both traversing the maze-like halls of Otranto to escape Manfred, find each other, and Theodore manages to set Isabella free. She finds asylum in the Church of St. Nicholas, site of the statue of Alfonso the Good, under the protection of Father Jerome, a virtuous friar. In the process of persuading Jerome to bring Isabella to him, Manfred discovers that Theodore is actually Jerome's long-lost son. Manfred threatens Theodore in order to maneuver Jerome into delivering Isabella. The long-lost relative later became a popular feature of the gothic.

Both Isabella and Theodore are temporarily saved by the appearance of a mysterious Black Knight, who turns out to be Isabella's father and joins the forces against Manfred. A round of comings and goings through tunnels, hallways, and churches ensues. This flight through dark corridors also became almost mandatory in gothic fiction. In the course of his flight, Theodore falls in love with Mathilda. As the two lovers meet in a church, Manfred, "flushed with love and wine," mistakes Mathilda for Isabella. Wishing to prevent Theodore from possessing the woman he thinks is his own beloved, Manfred mistakenly stabs his daughter. Her dying words prevent Theodore from revenging her: "Stop thy impious hand . . . it is my father!"

Manfred must now forfeit his kingdom for his bloody deed. The final revelation is that Theodore is actually the true Prince of Otranto, the direct descendant of Alfonso the Good. The statuary helmet flies back to the statue; Isabella is given to Theodore in marriage, but only after he has completed a period of mourning for Mathilda; and order is restored. The flight of the helmet remains beyond the pale of reason, as does the extraordinary, rigid virtue of the sympathetic characters, but Manfred's threat to the kingdom is ended. Here is the master plot for the gothic of the Kingdom.

THE MYSTERIES OF UDOLPHO

Radcliffe's *The Mysteries of Udolpho* presents apparently unnatural behavior and events but ultimately explains them all away. Not only will the sins of the past be nullified, but also human understanding will penetrate all the mysteries. In *The Mysteries of Udolpho*, the obligatory gothic virgin is Emily St. Aubert; she is complemented by a virginal male named Valancourt, whom Emily meets while still in the bosom of her family. When her parents die, she is left at the mercy of her uncle, the villainous Montoni, dark, compelling, and savage in pursuit of his own interests. Montoni whisks Emily away to Udolpho, his great house in the Apennines, where, desperate for money, he exerts himself on Emily in hopes of taking her patrimony while his more lustful, equally brutal friends scheme against her virtue. Emily resists, fainting and palpitating frequently. Emily's propensity to swoon is very much entrenched in the character of the gothic heroine.

Emily escapes and, sequestered in a convent, makes the acquaintance of a dying nun, whose past is revealed to contain a murder inspired by lust and greed. Her past also contains Montoni, who acquired Udolpho through her evil deeds. Now repenting, the nun (née Laurentini de Udolpho) reveals all. The innocent victim of Laurentini's stratagems was Emily's long-lost, virtuous aunt, and Udolpho should have been hers. Ultimately, it will belong to Emily and Valancourt.

This novel contains the obligatory gothic flights up and down dimly lit staircases and halls and into dark turrets; there are also fabulous vistas of soul-elevating charm in the Apennines, which became a hallmark of gothic, and blood-chilling vistas of banditti by torch and moonlight. There is also mysterious music that seems to issue from some supernatural source and a mysterious disappearance of Emily's bracelet, both later revealed to be the work of Valancourt. A miniature picture of the first marchioness of Udolpho, who looks unaccountably like Emily, threatens to reveal some irregularity about pure Emily's birth but in the end reveals only that the poor, victimized marchioness was Emily's aunt. In Udolpho, in a distant turret, Emily finds a body being devoured by worms. Emily is thrown into a frenzy, fearing that this is the corpse of her deluded aunt, Montoni's wife, but it is revealed to be merely a wax effigy placed there long ago for the contemplation of some sinning cleric, as a penance. The dark night of the soul lifts, and terror yields to the paradise that Emily and Valancourt will engender. This is the master plot for personal gothic: the gothic of the family.

Radcliffe was known to distinguish between horror and terror and would have none of the former. Terror was a blood-tingling experience of which she approved because it would ultimately yield to better things. Horror she identified with decadence, a distemper in the blood that could not be discharged but rendered men and women inactive with fright. Lewis's *The Monk* demonstrates Radcliffe's distinction.

THE MONK

The Monk concerns a Capuchin friar named Ambrosio, famed for his beauty and virtue throughout Madrid. He is fervent in his devotion to his calling and is wholly enchanted by a picture of the Virgin, to which he prays. A young novice of the order named Rosario becomes Ambrosio's favorite. Rosario is a beautiful, virtuous youth, as Ambrosio thinks, but one night Ambrosio perceives that Rosario has a female breast, and that "he" is in fact "she": Mathilda, a daughter of a noble house, so enthralled by Ambrosio that she has disguised herself to be near him. Mathilda is the very image of the picture of the Virgin to which Ambrosio is so devoted, and, through her virginal beauty, seduces Ambrosio into a degrading sexual entanglement that is fully described. As Mathilda grows more obsessed with Ambrosio, his ardor cools. To secure him to her, she offers help in seducing Antonia, another virginal beauty, Ambrosio's newest passion. Mathilda, the madonna-faced enchantress, now reveals that she is actually a female demon. She puts her supernatural powers at Ambrosio's disposal, and together they successfully abduct Antonia, although only after killing Antonia's mother. Ambrosio then rapes Antonia in the foul, suffocating stench of a charnel house in the cathedral catacombs. In this scene of heavy breathing and sadism, the monk is incited to his deed by the virginal Antonia's softness and her moist pleas for her virtue. Each tear excites him further into a frenzy, which he climaxes by strangling the girl.

Ambrosio's deeds are discovered, and he is tried by an inquisitorial panel. Mathilda reveals his union with Satan through her. The novel ends with Satan's liberation of Ambrosio from the dungeon into which the inquisitors have thrown him. Satan mangles Ambrosio's body by throwing him into an abyss but does not let him die for seven days (the de-creation of the world?). During this time, Ambrosio must suffer the physical and psychological torments of his situation, and the reader along with him. The devil triumphs at the end of this novel. All means of redressing virtue are abandoned, and the reader is left in the abyss with Ambrosio.

MELMOTH THE WANDERER

The same may be said of Maturin's *Melmoth the Wanderer*, a tale of agony and the failure of redemption. The book may be called a novel only if one employs the concept of the picaresque in its broadest sense. It is a collection of short stories, each centering on Melmoth, a damned, Faust-like character. Each tale concerns Melmoth's attempt to find someone to change places with him, a trade he would gladly make, as he has sold his soul to the devil and now wishes to be released.

The book rubs the reader's nerves raw with obsessive suffering, detailing scenes from the Spanish Inquisition which include the popping of bones and the melting of eyeballs. The book also minutely details the degradation of a beautiful, virginal island maiden named Immalee, who is utterly destroyed by the idolatrous love of Melmoth.

The last scene of the book ticks the seconds of the clock as Melmoth, unable to find a surrogate, awaits his fall into Satan's clutches. The denouement is an almost unbearable agony that the reader is forced to endure with the protagonist. Again the horror is eternal. There will never be any quietus for either Ambrosio or Melmoth, or for the reader haunted by them. These are the molds for the gothic of damnation.

THE MODERNIZATION OF THE GOTHIC

The reading public of the late eighteenth and early nineteenth centuries was avid for both horror and terror, as well as for supernatural history. Such works were gobbled greedily as they rolled off the presses. Indeed, the gothic reading public may have begun the mass marketing of literature by ensuring the fortunes of the private lending libraries that opened in response to the gothic binge. Although the libraries continued after the gothic wave had crested, it was this craze that gave the libraries their impetus. Such private lending libraries purchased numerous copies of long lists of gothic works and furnished subscribers with a list from which they might choose. Like contemporary book clubs, the libraries vied for the most appetizing authors. Unlike the modern clubs, books circulated back and forth, not to be kept by subscribers.

William Lane's Minerva Public Library was the most famous and most successful of all these libraries. Lane went after the works of independent gothic authors but formed the basis of his list by maintaining his own stable of hacks. The names of most of the "stable authors" are gone, and so are their books, but the titles linger on in the library records, echoing one another and the titles of the more prominent authors: *The Romance Castle* (1791), *The Black Forest: Or, The Cavern of Horrors* (1802), *The Mysterious Omen: Or, Awful Retribution* (1812).

By the time *Melmoth the Wanderer* had appeared, most of this had run its course. Only hacks continued to mine the old pits for monks, nuns, fainting innocents, Apennine banditti, and Satanic quests, but critics agree that if the conventions of the gothic period from Walpole to Maturin have dried out and fossilized, the spirit is very much alive. Many modern novels set miles from an abbey and containing not one shrieking, orphaned virgin or worm-ridden corpse may be considered gothic. If the sophisticated cannot repress a snicker at the obvious and well-worn gothic conventions, they cannot dismiss the power and attraction of its spirit, which lives today in serious literature.

Modern thinking about gothic literature has gravitated toward the psychological aspects of the gothic. The castle or ruined abbey has become the interior of the mind, racked with anxiety and unbridled surges of emotion, melodramatically governed by polarities. The traditional gothic is now identified as the beginning of neurotic literature. In a perceptive study of the genre, *Love, Misery, and Mystery* (1978), Coral Ann Howells points out that the gothic literature of the eighteenth century was willing to deal with the syntax of hysteria, which the more prestigious literature, controlled by classical influences, simply denied or avoided. Hysteria is no stranger to all kinds of literature, it is true, but current thinking seeks to discriminate between the literary presentation of hysteria or neuroticism as an aberration from a rational norm and the gothic presentation of neuroticism as equally normative with rational control, or even as the dominant mode.

The evolution of the modern gothic began close to the original seedbed, in the works of Edgar Allan Poe. In "The Fall of the House of Usher," for example, the traditional sins of the gothic past cavort in a mansion of ancient and noble lineage. A young virgin is subjected to the tortures of the charnel house; the tomb and the catacombs descend directly from Lewis. So too do the hyperbolic physical states of pallor and sensory excitement. This tale is also marked, however, by the new relationship it seeks to demonstrate between reason and hysterical anxiety.

Roderick Usher's boyhood friend, the story's narrator, is a representative of the normative rational world. He is forced to encounter a reality in which anxiety and dread are the norm and in which the passions know no rational bounds. Reason is forced to confront the reality of hysteria, its horror, terror, and power. This new psychological development of the gothic is stripped of the traditional gothic appurtenances in Poe's "The Tell-Tale Heart," where there are neither swooning virgins nor charnel houses, nor ruined, once-great edifices, save the ruin of the narrator's mind. The narrator's uncontrollable obsessions both to murder and to confess are presented to stun the reader with the overwhelming force of anxiety unconditioned by rational analysis.

Thus, a more modern gothic focuses on the overturning of rational limits as the source of horror and dread, without necessarily using the conventional apparatus. More examples of what may be considered modern gothic can be found in the works of Nathaniel Hawthorne. Although Hawthorne was perfectly capable of using the conventional machinery of the gothic, as in *The House of the Seven Gables* (1851), he was one of the architects of the modern gothic. In Hawthorne's forward-looking tales, certain combinations of personalities bond, as if they were chemical compounds, to form anxiety systems that cannot be resolved save by the destruction of all or part of the human configuration. In *The Scarlet Letter* (1850), for example, the configuration of Hester, Chillingsworth, and Dimmesdale forms an interlocking system of emotional destruction that is its own Otranto. The needs and social positions of each character in this trio impinge on one another in ways that disintegrate "normal" considerations of loyalty, courage, sympathy, consideration, and judgment. Hester's vivacity is answered in Dimmesdale, whose violently clashing aloofness and responsiveness create for her a vicious cycle of fulfillment and rejection. Chillingsworth introduces further complications through another vicious cycle of confidence and betrayal. These are the catacombs of the modern gothic.

Another strand of the modern gothic can be traced to Mary Wollstonecraft Shelley's *Frankenstein*, published in 1818, just as the gothic was on the wane. Her story represents an important alternative for the gothic imagination. The setting in this work shifts from the castle to the laboratory, forming the gothic tributary of science fiction. Frankenstein reverses the anxiety system of the gothic from the past to the future. Instead of the sins of the fathers—old actions, old human instincts rising to blight the present—

man's creativity is called into question as the blight of the future. Frankenstein's mind and laboratory are the gothic locus of "future fear," a horror of the dark side of originality and birth, which may, as the story shows, be locked into a vicious cycle with death and sterility. A dread of the whole future of human endeavor pursues the reader in and out of the dark corridors of *Frankenstein*.

Bram Stoker *Dracula* (1897) may be considered an example of a further evolution of the gothic. Here one finds a strong resurgence of the traditional gothic: the ruined castle, bandits ranging over craggy hills, swooning, morbidly detailed accounts of deaths, the sins of the past attacking the life of the present. The attendant supernatural horror and the bloodletting of the vampires, their repulsive stench, and the unearthly attractiveness of Dracula's vampire brides come right out of the original school of *Schauer-Romantik* horror. The utterly debilitating effect of the vampire on human will is, however, strong evidence for those critics who see the gothic tradition as an exploration of neurosis.

Stoker synthesizes two major gothic subclassifications in his work, thereby producing an interesting affirmation. Unlike the works of Radcliffe and her terror school, *Dracula* does not ultimately affirm the power of human reason, for it never explains away the supernatural. On the other hand, Stoker does not invoke his vampires as totally overwhelming forces, as in the horror school. *Dracula* does not present a fatalistic course of events through which the truth will not win out. Humankind is the agency of its salvation, but only through its affirmation of the power of faith. Reason is indeed powerless before Dracula, but Dr. Van Helsing's enormous faith and the faith he inspires in others are ultimately sufficient to resolve gothic anxiety, without denying its terrifying power and reality.

THE GOTHIC IN THE TWENTIETH CENTURY

Significantly, in the contemporary gothic, reason never achieves the triumph it briefly found through the terror school. Twentieth century gothic tends toward the *Schauer-Romantik* school of horror. Either it pessimistically portrays an inescapable, mind-forged squirrel cage, or it optimistically envisions an apocalyptic release through faith, instinct, or imagination, the nonrational human faculties. For examples of both twentieth century gothic trends, it may be instructive to consider briefly William Faulkner (1897-1962), whose works are frequently listed at the head of what is called the southern gothic tradition, and Doris Lessing (born 1919), whose later works took a turn that brought them into the fold of the science-fiction branch of gothic.

Faulkner's fictions have all the characteristic elements of the southern gothic: the traditional iconography; decaying mansions and graveyards; morbid, death-oriented actions and images; sins of the past; and virgins. *The Sound and the Fury* (1929) is concerned with the decaying Compson house and family, the implications of past actions, and Quentin's morbid preoccupation with death and virginity; it features Benjy's graveyard and important scenes in a cemetery. *As I Lay Dying* (1930) is structured around a long march to the cemetery with a stinking corpse. *Absalom, Absalom!* (1936) is full of decaying houses and lurid death scenes and features prominently three strange virgins—Rosa Coldfield, Judith Sutpen, and Clytie—or five if Quentin and Shreve are to be counted. In this work, the past eats the present up alive and the central figure, Thomas Sutpen, is much in the tradition of the charismatic, but boundlessly appropriating, gothic villain.

These cold gothic externals are only superficial images that betray the presence of the steaming psychological modern gothic centers of these works. Like Hawthorne, Faulkner creates interfacing human systems of neurosis whose inextricable coils lock each character into endless anxiety, producing hysteria, obsession, and utter loss of will and freedom. The violence and physical hyperbole in Faulkner reveal the truly gothic dilemmas of the characters, inaccessible to the mediations of active reason. As in Hawthorne, the combinations of characters form the catacombs of an inescapable though invisible castle or charnel house. Through these catacombs Faulkner's characters run, but they cannot extricate themselves and thus simply revolve in a maze of involuted thought. The Compsons bind one another to tragedy, as do the Sutpens and their spiritual and psychological descendants.

There is, however, an alternative in the modern gothic impulse. In her insightful, imaginative study of the modern evolution of the gothic, *Ghosts of the Gothic: Austen, Eliot, and Lawrence* (1980), Judith Wilt assigns Doris Lessing a place as the ultimate inheritor of the tradition. Lessing does portray exotic states of anxiety, variously descending into the netherworld (*Briefing for a Descent into Hell*, 1971) and plunging into outer space (the Canopus in Argos series), but Wilt focuses on *The Four-Gated City* (1969). This novel has both the trappings and the spirit of the gothic. The book centers on a doomed old house and an old, traditional family succumbing to the sins of the past. These Lessing portrays as no less than the debilitating sins of Western culture, racist, sexist, and exploitative in character. Lessing does indeed bring down this house. Several of the major characters are released from doom, however, by an apocalyptic World War III that wipes away the old sins, freeing some characters for a new, fruitful, nonanxious life. Significantly, this new world will be structured not on the principles of reason and logic, which Lessing excoriates as the heart of the old sins, but on the basis of something innately nonrational and hard to identify. It is not instinct and not faith, but seems closest to imagination. Lessing's ultimately hopeful vision, it must be conceded, is not shared by most contemporary practitioners of the genre.

While never exhausted, the gothic enjoyed a resurgence in the 1980's that was sustained into the 1990's, which critics have identified as a significant literary trend. Typical of the diversity of writers mentioned under this rubric are those represented in a special section on "The New Gothic," edited by Patrick McGrath in the literary magazine *Conjunctions* 14 (1989). McGrath, himself a writer of much-praised gothic fictions, assembled work by veteran novelists such as Robert Coover and John Hawkes as well as younger writers such as Jamaica Kincaid and William T. Vollmann; the group includes both the bestselling novelist Peter Straub and the assaultive experimental novelist Kathy Acker. McGrath contributes

an essay in which he seeks to outline some of the characteristics of the new gothic. While resisting any attempt at rigid definition (the gothic, he says, is "an air, a tone, a tendency"; it is "not a monolith"), McGrath acknowledges that all the writers whom he places in this group "concern themselves variously with extremes of sexual experience, with disease and social power, with murder and terror and death." That much might be said about most gothic novelists from the beginnings of the genre. What perhaps differentiates many of the writers whom McGrath discusses from their predecessors—what makes the new gothic new—is a more self-consciously transgressive stance, evident in McGrath's summation of the vision which he and his fellow writers share: "Common to all is an idea of evil, transgression of natural and social law, and the gothic, in all its suppleness, is the literature that permits that mad dream to be dreamt in a thousand forms."

Among popular-fiction writers, the gothic split into two main genres, one based on supernatural or psychological horror and the other based on women's fiction, featuring romance and, often, historical settings. Moreover, combinations of the two traditions most approach the hyperreal intensity and blend of fear and passion seen in the original gothic: for example, the saga of the Dollanganger family by V. C. Andrews (c. 1936-1986), or Tanith Lee's *Personal Darkness* (1993) and its sequels.

While horror writers often substitute the suburbs or small town for the isolated castle—and sometimes psychic abilities, deranged computers, or psychotic killers for ghostly nuns and predatory villain-heroes—they continue to explore the intense feeling, perilous world, tense social situations, and alluring but corrupt sexuality of the original gothic. Unlike the romantic gothic, which has seen periods of quiescence and revival, an unbroken line of the horror gothic persists, from *The Castle of Otranto* through *Dracula* and into the twentieth century with books such as M. R. James's *Ghost Stories of an Antiquary* (1904) and the works of Walter de la Mare (1873-1956) and H. P. Lovecraft (1890-1937).

These works continue the trend—seen in Poe, Hawthorne, Faulkner, and others—of maintaining morbid and sensational gothic elements while rooting the terror in psychology and even epistemology. Often, hauntings reveal, or are even replaced by, obsession and paranoia. Before the burgeoning of the modern commercial horror novel, Shirley Jackson's two eerie and lyrical novels *The Haunting of Hill House* (1959) and *We Have Always Lived in the Castle* (1962) used the traditional gothic form and many of its motifs, with both psychological sophistication and true terror. Robert Bloch's novel *Psycho* (1959) also updates and psychologizes gothic conventions, substituting an out-of-the-way motel for a castle and explicitly invoking Sigmund Freud.

The horror genre grew from William Peter Blatty's *The Exorcist* (1971), arguably a gothic novel, and Ira Levin's *Rosemary's Baby* (1967), which transplants to a New York City apartment building the hidden secret, supernatural menace, and conspiracies against the heroine of early gothics. Although the horror market withered in the 1990's, four best-selling authors continued in the gothic-horror vein: Dean R. Koontz (born 1945), Peter Straub (born 1943), Stephen King (born 1947), and Anne Rice (born 1941).

While much of Koontz's horror is better classified as horror-adventure, lacking the brooding neuroses and doubts about rationality prevalent in gothic fiction, gothic aspects do dominate books such as *Whispers* (1980) and *Shadowfires* (1987). Koontz's *Demon Seed* (1973) exemplifies the techno-gothic: A threatening setting and pursuing lover combine in a robot intelligence, which runs the house and wants to impregnate the heroine. Anne Rice explores the gothic's lush, dangerous sexuality and burden of the past in the Vampire Chronicles: *Interview with the Vampire* (1976), *The Vampire Lestat* (1985), *The Queen of the Damned* (1988), *The Tale of the Body Thief* (1992), and *Memnoch the Devil* (1995).

Julia (1976), by Straub, is a drawing-room gothic novel, focusing on the haunting—supernatural, mentally pathological, or both— of a woman dominated by her husband and his disturbing, enmeshed family. In *Ghost Story* (1979), *Shadowland* (1980), and others, Straub widens the focus, exploring and critiquing the small town, boys' school, or suburban setting while developing gothic themes, including dangerous

secrets, guilt, ambivalent eroticism, and a threat from the past. Straub explores other genres as well, especially the mystery, but maintains a gothic tone and intensity. Similarly, King's early work is more strictly gothic, such as *'Salem's Lot* (1975), in which vampires spread through a small town in Maine, and *The Shining* (1977), a story of madness and terror in an isolated, empty hotel. However, later works, even mimetic ones such as *Gerald's Game* (1992) and *Dolores Claiborne* (1993), continue gothic themes and often a gothic tone.

Along with terror and horror, sentimental and romantic elements were established in the original gothic, in the works of Ann Radcliffe, Clara M. Reeve, Susanna Rowson, and the Brontë sisters. In 1938, *Rebecca*, by Daphne du Maurier, the story of a young woman's marriage to a wealthy English widower with a secret, conveyed many gothic conventions to a new audience, paving the way for the genre of gothic romance. Combining mystery, danger, and romantic fantasy, such books tend to feature innocent but admirable heroines, a powerful male love interest and his isolated estate, ominous secrets (often linked to a woman from the love interest's past, as in *Rebecca*), and exotic settings that are remote in place and time. In the early 1960's, editor Gerald Gross at Ace Books used the term gothic for a line of paperbacks aimed at women readers, featuring primarily British authors such as Victoria Holt, Phyllis A. Whitney, Dorothy Eden, and Anne Maybury. The mystery and love plots are inextricable, and the novels feature many gothic elements, including besieged heroines; strong, enigmatic men; settings that evoke an atmosphere of tension and justified paranoia; heightened emotional states; doubled characters (including impersonation); and lurid, sometimes cruel, sexuality. In the 1970's and later, erotic elements flourished and became more explicit, resulting in the new category of the erotic gothic.

Martha Nochimson,
updated by Bernadette Lynn Bosky

BIBLIOGRAPHY

Frank, Frederick S. *Guide to the Gothic*. Lanham, Md.: Scarecrow Press, 1984. With entry below, this set consists of annotated bibliographies of criticism and other bibliographies. Impressively complete and helpful.

_____. *Guide to the Gothic II*. Lanham, Md.: Scarecrow Press, 1995.

Geary, Robert F. *The Supernatural in Gothic Fiction: Horror, Belief, and Literary Change*. Lewiston, N.Y.: E. Mellen Press, 1992. Gothic fiction often contains elements of the supernatural. Geary discusses the most common here.

Hennessy, Brendan. *The Gothic Novel*. New York: Scribner's, 1980. Examines foreign influences as well as English works. Contains a useful bibliography.

Kendrick, Walter. *The Thrill of Fear*. New York: Grove Press, 1991. Entertaining, insightful, and well researched, this volume covers gothic and horror books, plays, and film from *The Castle of Otranto* to the film *The Texas Chainsaw Massacre*, with neither undue praise nor condescension.

Kilgour, Maggie. *The Rise of the Gothic Novel*. London: Routledge, 1995. The beginnings and growth in popularity of the gothic novel. Includes bibliographical references and an index.

MacAndrew, Elizabeth. *The Gothic Tradition in Fiction*. New York: Columbia University Press, 1979. Both solid and innovative, this book examines traditional gothic elements in terms of psychological processes and sociohistorical context, from Horace Walpole to contemporary authors.

Mussell, Kay. *Women's Gothic and Romantic Fiction*. Westport, Conn.: Greenwood Press, 1981. Concise and insightful overviews and lengthy bibliographies concerning the woman's gothic from Ann Radcliffe to commercial gothic romances.

Punter, David. *The Literature of Terror: A History of Gothic Fictions from 1765 to the Present Day*. New York: Longman, 1996. Excellent and clear, including lesser-known writers and schools as well as bigger names.

Varma, Devendra P. *The Gothic Flame*. Metuchen, N.J.: Scarecrow Press, 1987. Originally published in 1957, this groundbreaking study of the early gothic (1764-1826) provides description, analysis, classification, and detailed history.

THE HISTORICAL NOVEL

Popular legend records that the historical novel was born out of frustration—specifically out of Sir Walter Scott's frustration at having been displaced by Lord Byron as the most popular poetic romancer of his day. Scott's early narrative poems, such as *Marmion: A Tale of Flodden Field* (1808) and *The Lady of the Lake* (1810), had established him as the premier storyteller in verse in the first decade of the nineteenth century, but when Byron began publishing his Eastern tales (*The Giaour*, 1813; *The Bride of Abydos*, 1813; and so on), Scott saw his public turning away. Not one to acquiesce easily, Scott resurrected the manuscript of a prose work he had begun almost ten years earlier. In it Scott told of the climactic struggles of the Scottish barons to restore the House of Stuart to the throne, culminating in their final defeat in 1745, some fifty years before Scott had originally written the tale. Since an additional decade had now passed, Scott altered his subtitle and sent off to his publishers the manuscript of *Waverley: Or, 'Tis Sixty Years Since* (1814), thus creating what was to become one of the most popular forms of fiction.

The first edition of *Waverley* was published anonymously, presumably so that Scott would not suffer embarrassment if this experiment in prose were a failure. It was not; the reading public made *Waverley* a best-seller, and a similar reception awaited the novels that followed its prolific author. Before he died in 1832, the father of the historical novel had brought to life the stories of Scotland, England, and, to a lesser extent, France during the Middle Ages, the Renaissance, and the eighteenth century. Historians may well claim that Scott's history is faulty, or that it is told from a slanted point of view; and literary critics may fault him for letting his penchant for adventure override concerns for character development, coherence of plot, and thematic exposition. Whatever faults scholars may find, though, none can deny the immediate success these novels had nor belittle the impact of this new literary venture on the development of fiction. The popularity of the historical novel has, in fact, never abated, and it has consistently ranked with the detective story and the thriller as one of the forms of literature with the widest audience appeal.

The educated reader may well wonder, however, why certain novels have been singled out under the appellation "historical." The fact that all novels are set in some period links them to history; even novels set in the future share that link, however tenuously. What makes a particular novel "historical"? This problem of definition has plagued critics, and virtually everyone who has written of the historical novel has evolved a standard that allows some novels to be included in this category while others are excluded. Most critics agree, however, that certain characteristics identify the historical novel. Writers of historical fiction have certain aims and limitations that mark their works as distinct from other forms of prose narratives and that form a general set of criteria by which their works may be judged.

Since Aristotle, critics have generally contrasted the writings of the historian and the poet (or writer of imaginative literature), seeing their approaches to recording human events as essentially dichotomous. For Aristotle, the historian dealt with the particular, the imaginative writer with the universal; the former wrote of what actually happened, the latter of what was probable in consonance with the verities of human character (*De poetica*, c. 334-323 B.C.E.; *Poetics*, 1705). While modern students of classical and medieval history have come to recognize that not all history is as factual as Aristotle would have liked to believe, the distinction is still useful. The historian is responsible for representing as accurately as possible past events as they really happened. Because the facts of the past do not of themselves speak to people in the present, historians must discern the significance of the data they collect. For most historians, however, any interpretation of the significance of those facts is clearly distinguished from the account of the facts themselves.

The notion of interpretation provides the key to understanding the relationship between historians and historical novelists. Like historians, historical novelists examine the facts of history, but rather than interpreting them analytically, they attempt to bring the past to life and interpret the significance of historical events through the conventions of literature: characterization, plot, and thematic development. They use the tools of their trade—image, symbol, juxtaposition, parallelism, and a host of other rhetorical devices—to provide their interpretation. Their aim is to transport the reader imaginatively to a period removed from the present. The best historical novelists accomplish their aims without violating the spirit of the historical process; they invent only when the chronicles are silent, and they rearrange only sparsely, or more often not at all. Thus, a main characteristic that sets apart the historical novel from other forms of fiction is the novelist's ability to present events of the past without remaining rigidly tied to historical documents (which themselves may be inaccurate). Coupled with the skill to delineate the interaction of human characters in the context of the historical period, their interest in recapturing the past distinguishes truly successful historical novelists from proponents of mere costume romance.

A large number of novels set in the past are indeed no more than costume romances, attempts to disguise modern situations or fantasies (usually involving sex or violence) in the garb of former times. Often, too, the use of history becomes a means of providing an *apologia* for present conditions or of producing a lament for times past without a serious attempt to examine the actualities of those times. Southern American fiction (which includes some of the best historical novels) contains numerous examples of this kind of writing, the most notable being Margaret Mitchell's *Gone with the Wind* (1936). A best-seller in the year of its publication and for years afterward, Mitchell's novel remains the most popular novel ever written by a southerner. Unfortunately, the characters in the novel are stereotypes of the Old South: the gallant plantation youth (Ashley Wilkes), the demure southern belle (Melanie), the rebellious vixen (Scarlett O'Hara), the hardened, aristocratic outcast (Rhett Butler)—the list could be extended considerably. For all its popular success, the novel presents only a superficial view of the real conflicts that engulfed the South as it moved through this traumatic period of transition. For the majority of the

American public, though, the portrait of the South that Mitchell creates has become the accepted one, largely because the work achieved wide readership among the general public and almost simultaneously provided the script for one of Hollywood's most successful motion pictures.

THE APPROACH TO THE HISTORICAL NOVEL

Generally, regardless of their intent, writers of historical novels have followed one of two approaches toward historical events and characters. By far the larger group has written works in which their major characters are fictional personages who live during periods in which great events occur: the glorious years of the Roman Empire; the age of the Crusades; the time of the English, American, French, or Russian Revolutions; the Hundred Years' War; the Napoleonic wars; the American Civil War; or the two world wars. More often than not, the historical novel is set in a time of crisis. The fictional characters often, though not always, interact with real personages in some way. This technique of placing fictional characters on the fringe of great events, used by Scott in his novels and adopted by many others, can provide an effective sense of the period without violating (except, perhaps, for the purist) the sense of history that the reader brings to the work.

In novels that attempt to retain a high degree of verisimilitude, the contact between real and fictional characters generally remains slight; in works better termed "historical romances," such contact is often magnified, sometimes to the point of suggesting that the fictional character has had an impact on real-life events. Examples of this approach can be found in the World War II novels of Herman Wouk, *The Winds of War* (1971) and *War and Remembrance* (1978). Wouk's fictional hero, Victor "Pug" Henry, a U.S. Navy captain, becomes the confidant of President Franklin D. Roosevelt and his emissary to various foreign capitals, where he meets with world leaders Winston Churchill, Adolf Hitler, Benito Mussolini, and Joseph Stalin. Henry's influence in shaping Roosevelt's opinion about the war and his other exploits with foreign leaders is purely fictional and accounts in part for Wouk's own admission in the preface to

War and Remembrance that he is writing a "historical romance."

Linking history to the narrative tradition of the romance has been a common practice for many writers who have chosen to focus on fictional characters living during a period of crisis. Among the more famous practitioners of this method is the French novelist Alexandre Dumas, *père*, who, through his loose weaving of historical fact and fancy, provided the worldwide reading public with figures and stories that have become part of the cultural heritage of the West: Porthos, Athos, and Aramis, the Three Musketeers, and idealistic young D'Artagnan, the real hero of several of Dumas's novels of the reign of Louis XIV. *Les Trois Mousquetaires* (1844; *The Three Musketeers*, 1846) is only one of many, however, that Dumas wrote about that period and about other episodes in French history, including explorations of the age of Henri IV, the Franco-Spanish War of the sixteenth century, the reign of Louis XV, and the French Revolution.

The methodology employed by artists who focus on fictional characters in real-life times of crisis can be seen most vividly in Charles Dickens's *A Tale of Two Cities* (1859). This chilling look at the impact of the French Revolution has given many generations of readers a feeling for that event that even Thomas Carlyle's history of the revolution fails to evoke. In this novel, Dickens re-creates the horrors of the revolution by detailing the effects of the Reign of Terror on the lives of fictional characters whose destinies take them between Paris and London. Few major figures of history appear in Dickens's book, and those who do are given subordinate roles. The historicity of the novel lies in Dickens's graphic portrayal of the masses and of the individuals affected by the actions of the "citizens" of the revolution. The fictional Madame DeFarge, whose insatiable appetite for the blood of aristocrats is motivated as much by a desire for personal vengeance as by any desire for liberty and equality, reinforces the notion that the exploits of the real-life Robespierre and his henchmen were neither anomalous nor necessarily high-minded.

Similarly, the frustrations of the Manette family, as well as the heroism of both Sidney Carton and Charles Darnay, become representative of thousands whose stories are unnoted by the historian, whose personal tragedies and triumphs have been reduced to mere statistics. Thus, history is not violated but rather is vivified by the presentation of characters and incidents that, though unrecorded in chronicles of the period, might have easily occurred. In the best historical novels, the reader senses that, had these events occurred, they would have done so with the same consequences that the novelist has presented.

A second, less common approach to historical fiction is that of choosing as a main character a person who really did live and whose history is recorded in some form. Such an approach is in many ways more difficult; those who choose this method are limited to a great degree by the facts of history in structuring plot, delineating character, providing motivation, and even in developing themes. Usually, the greater the figure chosen, the more restricted the novelist is in exploring the subject through the medium of fiction. Some have done so and been fairly successful. Howard Fast achieved popular acclaim for his portraits of George Washington (*The Unvanquished*, 1942) and Thomas Paine (*Citizen Tom Paine*, 1943). Robert Graves's *I, Claudius* (1934) is a daring attempt to present the decadent life of the emperor's court in post-Augustan Rome through the eyes of one of the major figures of that period.

Another highly successful examination of historical forces seen through the eyes of a major historical figure is found in Russian novelist Aleksandr Solzhenitsyn's *Avgust chetyrnadtsatogo* (1971; *August 1914*, 1972). In the novel, Solzhenitsyn is actually following the example set for him by his predecessor Leo Tolstoy, whose *Voyna i mir* (1865-1869; *War and Peace*, 1886) has been called by some critics the greatest historical novel ever written. Chronicling events in Russia during the Napoleonic era, Tolstoy concentrates on the lives of fictional characters to reveal the nature of personal relationships as they are influenced by the forces of history. Looming large over the novel is the figure of General Kutozov, the commander of the Russian army who defeated Napoleon at Moscow. Also worthy of note is Gore Vidal's fictional chronicle of American history. In *Washing-*

ton, D.C. (1967), *Burr* (1973), *1876* (1976), *Lincoln* (1984), *Empire* (1987), and *Hollywood: A Novel of America in the 1920's* (1990), Vidal skillfully interweaves his fictional characters into the lives of Presidents Martin Van Buren, Abraham Lincoln, and Theodore Roosevelt, as well as luminaries such as John Hay, Henry Adams, and others easily recognizable by students of American history.

An even greater cast of historical personages comes to life in *Freedom* (1987), a novel by American journalist and critic William Safire. This long book (nearly one thousand pages of text and more than two hundred pages of notes and commentary that Safire calls his "Underbook") details life in Washington, D.C., and northern Virginia following the announcement of secession by the Confederate states and the momentous decision by Abraham Lincoln to issue the Emancipation Proclamation. The daily lives—both public and private—of more than two dozen key figures involved on both sides of the Civil War are chronicled in Safire's lively and insightful account. Relying heavily on the historical record, Safire represents his figures with exceptional psychological sensitivity. His decision to steer clear of lengthy analyses of battles and concentrate instead on the political arena—in which decisions were often affected by personality clashes among men and women with oversized egos—makes this study of the causes and consequences of war particularly distinctive. For the student of historical fiction, Safire offers a perceptive observation about his process of composition: "The reader of any historical novel asks, 'How much of this is true?'" Safire's answer is to provide an "Underbook" citing the many sources from which he has drawn his portraits. This historical dimension "is close to the way it happened," reconstructed from "firsthand sources" such as letters and diaries. The rest, he reminds his readers, "is fiction, a device that overrides the facts to keep the reader awake or—when it works best—to get at the truth." Safire's novel gives the reader a sense of peering over the shoulder of real people whose lives seem a bit more dramatic than one might have imagined they could ever have been. The same can be said of another fine historical novel about the American Civil War, Mi-

chael Shaara's *The Killer Angels* (1974). Focusing on the Battle of Gettysburg, Shaara mines the historical record for data about the principal generals and their chief lieutenants, bringing them to life as individuals and revealing some of the complexities of personality that shaped their decisions and, hence, the course of the war.

Writing about real people, however, is not without its dangers. One need only review the controversy surrounding the publication of William Styron's *The Confessions of Nat Turner* (1967). This Pulitzer-Prize-winning novel is a fictional account of the leader of a slave revolt in the Tidewater region of Virginia in 1831. Historical records detailing Turner's revolt are sparse; the primary documentary evidence is contained in a twenty-page pamphlet written by the prosecuting attorney at Turner's trial and ostensibly dictated by Turner himself shortly before he was executed. Contemporary newspaper accounts offer some corroboration, but they are biased. From these slim historical sources, Styron creates what he calls "a meditation on history," a musing, first-person, reflective account of the motivation for Nat's actions.

In addition to taking the daring step of telling his hero's story in the first person, Styron also modifies the available facts to make his character more interesting psychologically. Omitting Nat's wife and father from the story, Styron attributes his hero's education to the efforts of good white masters and emphasizes the thin line between religious fanaticism and repressed sexual desire. Styron's Nat, believing that he is being driven by an Old Testament God who has made him the instrument of vengeance on the white community for their treatment of blacks, puts to use the education he received from whites to incite other slaves to revolt.

Effusive praise from white critics has been far overshadowed by the condemnations issued by African Americans. *William Styron's Nat Turner: Ten Black Writers Respond* (1968), a collection of essays by noted black intellectuals, systematically attacks the novel on grounds both literary and historical. These critics assert that Styron's hero's meditations are a white man's thoughts, that his hero's aspirations are those that white men think black men have, and that his hero's rationale for acting is actually a reflection of the white community's rationalization for the institution of slavery. Social historians have criticized the novel for not presenting a portrait of the real Nat Turner; they charge Styron with avoiding the real issues that led to Turner's revolt. In their view, the book simply does not fulfill one of the main criteria for good historical fiction: It is not sufficiently true to the historical record.

Despite these pitfalls, there is clear evidence that the best historical novels can rank with the finest novels of any kind. One need only look to the works of America's foremost novelist of the twentieth century: William Faulkner. In many ways, the entire corpus of Faulkner's work is an extended study of the history of his region, the American South. Faulkner tries to make sense of what happened there in a society that contained, side by side, aspects of feudal or baronial European culture and the individualizing tenets of the American Dream. As one might expect, Faulkner focuses on the great crime of slavery; that dehumanizing institution on which southern society was based bred racial hatred that continued long after slavery was officially abolished as a result of the Civil War. That catastrophe plays a central role in Faulkner's fiction, either as a subject itself or as an event that looms in the consciousness of those who populate Faulkner's mythical Yoknapatawpha County. Among his novels, *Absalom, Absalom!* (1936) is possibly the best example of a novel intensely concerned with the way people come to understand the past and the way they try to make sense of it so that the present becomes explicable. In the novel, a young southerner, Quentin Compson, and his Canadian roommate at college, Shreve McCannon, attempt to piece together the family history of Thomas Sutpen, a self-styled southern aristocrat whose grand design for establishing a dynasty in the wilds of northern Mississippi is ruined when his son kills the fiancé of Sutpen's only daughter, then flees the country. Quentin must piece together Sutpen's story from oral narratives and meager written accounts, none of which reveals the whole truth about the past. *Absalom, Absalom!* has been described as a kind of detective story, in which Quentin and Shreve make a "persistent at-

tempt to understand the past from partially perceived fragments surviving about it" (Hugh Holman, *The Immoderate Past*, 1977). Because he is a son of the South, Quentin sees in the story of Sutpen the tragedy of his heritage. The novel reveals to the reader the impossibility of ever knowing the past completely; it is to humankind's credit, however, that it tries to do so, because in the past, one may find an explanation for the present, and thereby develop some hope for the future.

Absalom, Absalom! is, in the final analysis, a novel about the historical process itself, a story of the way one comes to understand one's own past. Ironically, these discoveries about the tenuousness and fragility of the historical method appear in a novel that contains almost no references to real personages; yet the reader senses that what is being read is as real as any historical account of the South. The saga of life in Faulkner's fictional Jefferson, Mississippi, and surrounding countryside may be far removed from places where great events have occurred, but the impact of history on the lives of men and women in this rural southern community is transformed by Faulkner into a statement of the way events mold the human race. In Yoknapatawpha County, one finds the engagement with the living past that continues to inspire the best historical novelists.

The evolution of the historical novel

The appetite of the reading public for historical sagas has given several British and American novelists opportunities to write extensively about life in previous centuries. Among the more popular sagas is Patrick O'Brian's series of novels about the career of Jack Aubrey, a naval officer whose exploits at sea occur during the late eighteenth and early nineteenth centuries. Beginning in *Master and Commander* (1969) and extending through twenty volumes, O'Brian uses Aubrey's rise from midshipman to admiral as a fictional platform from which he is able to launch detailed accounts of naval life from the rebellion of the American colonists through the Napoleonic wars. Aubrey's constant companion at sea, Dr. Stephen Maturin, is not only a physician but also an employee of the state sent abroad to collect intelligence about foreign countries. Through him O'Brian is able to describe the political intrigues among nations and rogue groups whose actions influence international conflicts.

By carefully crafting plots that include significant naval engagements and a series of adventures on land, O'Brian creates for readers a sense of what life was like for both sailors and the land-bound populace during these turbulent decades. For example, in *The Hundred Days* (1998), Aubrey is assigned to intercept a shipment of gold intended to support Napoleon's efforts to recapture the French throne after he returns to the European continent from exile. Although few historical figures play a major role in the novel, readers nevertheless gain a sense of the impending European crisis by following Aubrey and Maturin across the Mediterranean as they negotiate with various leaders in the Arab world to block the transfer of gold that would allow Napoleon to equip a fighting force.

The same kind of historical ambience is created with exceptional skill by Charles Frazier in *Cold Mountain* (1997). In this Civil War tale, Frazier uses the conflagration between North and South as a backdrop to tell a story of love, courage, and endurance. His principal characters, the disillusioned soldier Inman and the southern belle Ada, find their lives disrupted and forever altered by the war. Inman is forced to behave brutally in his effort to return to Cold Mountain, where he hopes to rebuild his life with Ada. She, in the meantime, learns to fend for herself in a land where the social skills required for young women in antebellum North Carolina are of little value once the very necessities of life can no longer be obtained without succumbing to hard labor. Frazier's study in the adaptability of human nature and the power of strong emotions is made more poignant by the historical setting, a time of brutality and disdain for the norms of civil behavior.

More traditional historical novels that follow with greater fidelity the techniques used by Sir Walter Scott also found a large audience throughout the final decades of the twentieth century. Typical among the hundreds of historical fictions that populated best-seller lists is Steven Pressfield's *Gates of Fire* (1998). Subtitled *An Epic Tale of the Battle of Thermopylae*, Pressfield's novel recounts the heroism of the three hundred Spartans who stopped the advance of the Persian army at Thermopylae in the fifth century B.C.E. Through the story of Xeones, a fictional character who fights with the Spartans as squire to one of the nobles engaged in the battle, Pressfield not only relates a detailed account of the battle but also offers readers a glimpse into the lives of the Spartans and an analysis of their national character. Much as Scott employs historical personages to interact with his fictional heroes and heroines, in *Gates of Fire* figures such as the Spartan king Leonidas and the Persian emperor Xerxes are given prominence in the novel. Accounts of daily life in Sparta and of the battle itself are based on meticulous research. Characterization, imagery, and the use of literary devices such as similes bear strong resemblance to techniques used by the Greek epic poet Homer in *The Iliad* (c. 800 B.C.E.). Pressfield's novel offers modern readers a lesson in courage and sacrifice drawn from history.

There is a certain irony present in *Gates of Fire*, however, that highlights one of the basic tensions of the historical novel as a genre. Modern historians came to realize that "histories" by classical writers such as Herodotus and Thucydides must be read not as literal records but as creative attempts to paint one country or city-state in a favorable light, often at the expense of other societies—and even at the expense of historical accuracy. For decades, historiographers have demonstrated that the writer of history is more often than not a partisan chronicler. Hence, the line between fact and fiction is blurred not only in historical novels but also in the historical accounts on which they are based. Nevertheless, novels such as *Gates of Fire* attest to the continuing vitality of the genre, as readers find the blend of fact and fiction a particularly enjoyable way to learn about the past through the lives of characters who actually experience events that have become important in the historical record. The historical novel continues to live up to Dr. Samuel Johnson's dictum that literature should teach by delighting.

Laurence W. Mazzeno

BIBLIOGRAPHY

Burt, Daniel S., ed. *What Historical Novel Do I Read Next?* 2 vols. Detroit: Gale Research, 1997. A reference book cataloguing more than seven thousand titles by three thousand authors. Describes novels from the nineteenth and twentieth centuries and provides biographical summaries of authors, brief plot synopses, and bibliographical information. Multiple indexes allow for quick identification of specific works, authors, or subjects treated in these novels.

Fleishman, Avrom. *The English Historical Novel: Walter Scott to Virginia Woolf.* Baltimore, Md.: The Johns Hopkins University Press, 1971. Surveys the development of the English historical novel, outlining ways novelists use history to create fiction and employ fictional techniques to reveal historical truths. Traces formal trends in the historical novel that place it at odds with modern experimental fiction.

Hughes, Helen. *The Historical Romance.* London: Routledge, 1993. Studies more than forty romances to explain how the writer's choice to ground a narrative in the historical past affords opportunities to create plausible fantasies. Examines formal qualities of historical romances and characteristics of readers who appreciate them. Also discusses characterization and typical themes in this genre.

Lukács, Georg. *The Historical Novel.* Translated by Hamma Mitchell and Stanley Mitchell. London: Merlin Press, 1962. The pioneering study of the genre, this book praises writers who value the historical process. Detailed, laudatory critiques of Scott. Heavily biased by Lukács's Marxist views.

McEwan, Neil. *Perspectives in British Historical Fiction Today.* Wolfeboro, N.H.: Academic Press, 1987. Explains how modern attitudes about the nature of fiction and history shaped historical novels written in Great Britain during the twentieth century. Examines ways Mary Renault, Anthony Burgess, Robert Nye, J. C. Farrell, John Fowles, and William Golding continued traditions from realistic fiction or adapt experimental techniques to transform the historical novel into a medium suitable for modern readers.

Orel, Harold. *The Historical Novel from Scott to Sabatini: Changing Attitudes Toward a Literary Genre, 1814-1920.* London: Macmillan, 1995. Explores changes in the concept of historical fiction between Scott's novels and those published at the end of World War I. Concentrates on nine novels by British and Continental writers, and shows the divergent paths taken by writers of historical fiction and historical romance.

Sanders, Andrew. *The Victorian Historical Novel, 1840-1880.* New York: St. Martin's Press, 1979. Discusses more than a dozen novels written by major and minor Victorian figures. Traces trends in historical fiction in the half-century after Scott's death. Explains how Dickens, George Eliot, Thomas Hardy, and others transformed historical events into art.

Shaw, Harry E. *The Forms of Historical Fiction.* Ithaca, N.Y.: Cornell University Press, 1983. Defines the historical novel and explains how Scott created the genre. Provides criteria for evaluating historical fiction on its own terms and as part of the tradition of fiction in the nineteenth and twentieth centuries.

Wesseling, Elisabeth. *Writing History as a Prophet: Postmodernist Innovations of the Historical Novel.* Philadelphia: John Benjamins Publishing, 1991. Highly specialized study describing ways twentieth century novelists transform the traditional historical novel to explore the past and simultaneously explain how it can be apprehended. Traces relationships between historical fiction and several other genres: fantasy literature, detective fiction, and science fiction.

Zimmerman, Everett. *The Boundaries of Fiction: History and the Eighteenth Century British Novel.* Ithaca, N.Y.: Cornell University Press, 1996. Examines eighteenth century notions of history that influenced major precursors of Sir Walter Scott. Explains how the necessity these novelists felt to ground their work in the historical record led to Scott's development of the historical novel.

THE HORROR NOVEL

By the end of the nineteenth century, writers interested in exploring supernatural themes had abandoned the mode of gothic fiction pioneered by eighteenth century English novelist Horace Walpole. Walpole and his imitators had exploited such props as medieval ruins and gloomy manor houses riddled with secret passages, while later gothic novelists had accentuated madness and excessive violence. Newer writers emphasized character, practiced a more sophisticated narrative technique, and displayed an intuitive grasp of the workings of the human psyche. Yet horror fiction continued to do what gothic fiction had done before it. In an era of growing emphasis upon science and reason, it explored humankind's darker and more irrational impulses.

HORROR'S GOLDEN AGE: 1872-1912

The four decades from 1872 to 1912 represent one of the two richest periods of horror fiction in the English language. Because such moods as dread and anxiety are easier to maintain in shorter forms, many of the most successful works from this period are stories and novellas.

The year 1872 saw the publication of *In a Glass Darkly*, by Irish writer Joseph Sheridan Le Fanu. Le Fanu also wrote novels in which the supernatural played some part, but he is remembered for his shorter works, among which is the novella "Carmilla" from this collection. Although not the first work in English to deal with vampires, "Carmilla" is one of the most sophisticated. It is not clear whether Carmilla is "really" a vampire or her feelings for the novella's young narrator are sexual. Nor is it clear what ultimate spiritual fate awaits the narrator herself, who is dead when the story begins.

The same air of ambiguity hangs over *The Turn of the Screw* (1898), by Anglo-American writer Henry James. In this famous novella a governess charged with protecting two young children either battles malignant ghosts or projects onto imaginary ghosts her own destructive feelings toward the children—it is not clear which. Another writer who found the novella especially useful for exploring ambiguous psy-

chological states was Oliver Onions. In "The Beckoning Fair One" (1911), Onions described the disintegration of a writer whose sanity is sapped by his own ghostly creation.

Equally astute psychological analysis characterizes short novels produced by two writers famous for works in a variety of forms. Robert Louis Stevenson wrote the classic fictional treatment of the split personality in *The Strange Case of Dr. Jekyll and Mr. Hyde* (1886). Dr. Jekyll is a paragon of virtue, but the alter ego he releases by chemical means is a monster of murderous desire. In *The Picture of Dorian Gray* (serial 1890, expanded 1891), Oscar Wilde described a bon vivant whose portrait registers the ravages of sin while he himself retains his youthful appearance.

During this same period several British writers produced what American writer H. P. Lovecraft was to describe as "cosmic horror." These included Arthur Machen and William Hope Hodgson. Rather than embodying evil in stock figures such as ghosts, these writers located malignity in the universe itself. Machen's *The Great God Pan* (1894) is an early example. This novella describes a union between a young woman and Pan, ostensibly a minor classical deity but in this case a figure emblematic of a greater and far more frightening "reality" lurking beyond the everyday world. The experience drives the woman mad, and the daughter she subsequently bears instigates a cycle of destruction years later.

Unlike many talented supernatural writers of his time, William Hope Hodgson wrote effectively in longer forms, and his novels constitute a high-water mark of horror fiction. In *The Boats of the "Glen Carrig"* (1907), Hodgson drew upon his years at sea to describe the fate of a ship imprisoned in the weeds of a phantasmagoric Sargasso Sea. The tightly constructed short novel *The Ghost Pirates* (1909) utilized another sea setting to describe a ship "taken over" by sailors from another dimension.

In his masterpiece, *The House on the Borderland* (1908), Hodgson resuscitated the familiar gothic prop of the ruined manor—in this case a deserted stone house in the west of Ireland. Travelers recover from this ruin a manuscript describing an eruption of swinelike creatures from a nearby pit as well as an existentially chilling vision of the fate of the universe. Hodgson's enormous final novel, *The Night Land* (1912), is written in a trying eighteenth century style but describes a world millions of years in the future. The remnants of humankind have gathered in a great pyramid known as the Last Redoubt, outside of which wait a horrifying assembly of malignant deities.

The best literary works often transcend apparent trends or categories. This is true of Bram Stoker's *Dracula* (1897), a melodramatic adventure novel that eschewed the sophistication characteristic of much supernatural fiction of the period. Irish writer Stoker mixed eastern European myths of the *nosferatu* (or vampire) with legends of Vlad the Impaler, a bewilderingly bloodthirsty tyrant of the fifteenth century. Told in the form of letters and journal entries, the novel carries its now-famous central character, Count Dracula, from Transylvania to England and back again. *Dracula* is a compelling and irresistibly readable account of the struggle between good and evil, and it has proven inestimably influential.

BETWEEN THE WARS

The major development in horror fiction between World War I and World War II took place in the United States. American writers such as Nathaniel Hawthorne and Edgar Allan Poe had written prolifically in the gothic tradition, and drawing upon them and such British figures as Machen and Hodgson, H. P. Lovecraft created a highly influential body of work.

Lovecraft's major achievement was the creation of the Cthulhu mythos. The stories written within this framework suggest that earth was once the realm of a host of malignant entities or Old Ones—among them the dreadful Cthulhu—forever striving to regain their foothold. In addition to his many stories, Lovecraft wrote two novels. The more important of them is *At the Mountains of Madness* (1936, collected 1964), a thoughtful adventure novel concerning a scientific expedition to Antarctica that uncovers a dwelling place of the Old Ones. Lovecraft was a conscientious

writer, but his work is often vitiated by a labored, mock-archaic style. For this reason and because of their bizarre subject matter, his stories appeared exclusively in amateur publications and garishly illustrated "pulp" magazines. Lovecraft's many followers and imitators published in the same markets, and as a result horror fiction in the United States was cut off from the mainstream of literary development for decades.

AMERICAN BOOM

After World War II, several American horror writers challenged the sometimes stultifying complacency of a society intent upon preserving the status quo. In *I Am Legend* (1954), Richard Matheson imagined a world in which almost everyone has become a vampire. In *The Body Snatchers* (1955), Jack Finney tapped a similar vein of paranoia by imagining aliens that have "taken over" a small town's seemingly normal residents. Ray Bradbury would go on to describe another small town visited by a sinister carnival in *Something Wicked This Way Comes* (1962).

Most strikingly, noted writer Shirley Jackson challenged the era's normality with *The Haunting of Hill House* (1959), a coolly understated short novel in which the evil personality of a haunted house undermines the sanity of one of the group that comes to investigate its alleged supernatural nature.

In the late 1960's and early 1970's, several horror novels became best-sellers, propelling the genre into public awareness. In *Rosemary's Baby* (1967) Ira Levin transferred the central situation of Machen's *The Great God Pan* to contemporary New York City, while in *The Exorcist* (1971) William Peter Blatty described a case of demoniac possession. Both novels were rapidly paced and appealed to audiences unfamiliar with horror fiction. More poetic was Thomas Tryon's *The Other* (1971), an atmospheric tale of twins and their dark secret. Tryon's next novel, *Harvest Home* (1973), described a New England fertility cult. Robert Marasco's *Burnt Offerings* (1973) posited a haunted house even more malignant than Jackson's Hill House.

These works set the stage for a writer who would transform horror fiction into a staple of contemporary culture. He was Stephen King, whose stories and novels have earned for him not only an enormous readership but also grudging literary respect. King's many works range from treatments of traditional themes to more original creations. *'Salem's Lot* (1975) is a straightforward but vividly realized vampire novel, while *The Shining* (1977) is an equally vivid haunted house novel, the "house" in this case being a snowbound lodge in the Rocky Mountains.

King's lengthy novels *The Stand* (1978, unabridged 1990) and *It* (1986) show his considerable talents stretched to their limits. In *The Stand* a plague has wiped out most of humanity, setting the stage for the ultimate confrontation between good and evil. In *It*, perhaps King's masterpiece, a handful of characters must battle an unimaginably malevolent being buried far beneath earth's surface—as both innocent children and less-than innocent adults.

King has been so prolific that he has written under more than one name. In an original twist on this situation, he simultaneously published a novel, *Desperation* (1996), under his own name, and another, related novel, *The Regulators* (1996), under the pseudonym Richard Bachman. The books deal, appropriately enough, with a shift in the nature of reality and, like all King's best works, exhibit a grasp of realistic detail and an imaginative reach seldom equaled in the genre.

King's contemporaries have profited from his popularity, and some, such as Dean Koontz, have equalled him in production. Others include David C. Morrell, who provided a natural (if harrowing) explanation for supposedly supernatural phenomena in *The Totem* (1979). Anne Rice initiated a series of richly imagined if ultimately repetitive novels with *Interview with the Vampire* (1976), while Suzy McKee Charnas produced a more restrained treatment in *The Vampire Tapestry* (1980).

King's most talented contemporaries include Peter Straub, T. E. D. Klein, and Jonathan Carroll. Straub's *Ghost Story* (1979) and Klein's *The Ceremonies* (1984) both recapitulate the history of the horror genre, and Straub in *Shadowland* (1980) investigates the realm of a modern magician. Carroll's *The Land of Laughs* (1980) looks back to Matheson,

Finney, and Bradbury as it exposes the dismaying reality behind a seemingly idyllic midwestern town.

CONTINUING BRITISH TRADITION

The most enduring British horror fiction of the post-World War II period has been produced by writers working in the mainstream. Sarban (John William Wall) produced a haunting dark fantasy in *The Sound of His Horn* (1952), a short novel that combines time travel with a sadomasochistic fantasy positing Nazi triumph in World War II. In *The Feasting Dead* (1954) and *The Vampire of Mons* (1976), John Metcalfe and Desmond Stewart respectively spun psychologically compelling variations on the vampire theme. Richard Adams wrote a leisurely but grim ghost story in *The Girl in a Swing* (1980).

Noted biographer Peter Ackroyd has written a series of erudite horror novels, of which the best are *Hawksmoor* (1985) and *The House of Doctor Dee* (1994). The former deals with an eighteenth century satanist and architect of churches, while the latter concerns a young man who discovers that he is living in the former abode of a famous alchemist. The most accomplished postwar horror novel in Britain came from an unlikely source: famous comic novelist Kingsley Amis. In *The Green Man* (1969), Amis wrote of a libidinous and alcoholic innkeeper whose establishment is haunted by the ghost of a seventeenth century magician and terrorized by the magician's murderous creation.

Two other British novelists have written consciously within the horror and fantasy genres, and while they have gone on to explore a variety of themes and forms, their first novels remain their best. Ramsey Campbell's short novel *The Doll Who Ate His Mother* (1976) is as ghoulishly unsettling as its title suggests. Clive Barker's lengthy and ambitious *The Damnation Game* (1985) retells in contemporary terms the story of Faust, the sixteenth century figure said to have sold his soul to the Devil.

Grove Koger

BIBLIOGRAPHY

Barron, Neil, ed. *Horror Literature: A Reader's Guide*. New York: Garland, 1990. Arranged alphabetically by author within broad chronological periods, this survey discusses most of the major works of the horror genre as well as many other, more obscure, authors and books.

Bleiler, E. F., ed. *Supernatural Fiction Writers: Fantasy and Horror.* New York: Scribner, 1985. A two-volume collection of accessible essays dealing with every major figure in the field.

Bloom, Harold, ed. *Classic Horror Writers.* New York: Chelsea House, 1994. Bloom's book collects criticism of the works of major gothic and early horror writers.

_____, ed. *Modern Horror Writers.* New York: Chelsea House, 1995. A continuation of *Classic Horror Writers,* covering late nineteenth century and contemporary figures.

Docherty, Brian, ed. *American Horror Fiction: From Brockden Brown to Stephen King.* Basingstoke, England: Macmillan, 1990. A thoughtful look at horror fiction from the eighteenth through the twentieth centuries.

Sullivan, Jack, ed. *The Penguin Encyclopedia of Horror and the Supernatural.* New York: Viking, 1986. An alphabetical treatment of horror and the supernatural in literature, art, music, and film.

NATURALISTIC LONG FICTION

Naturalism is the application of scientific principles to literature, the examination of human life under the influence of heredity and environment. Although the movement flourished in the latter part of the nineteenth century through the early decades of the twentieth century, the term "naturalism" has far-reaching roots. In ancient philosophy, naturalism was used to refer to materialistic philosophies. During the eighteenth century naturalism referred to both a materialistic and a mechanistic view of the universe devoid of metaphysical principles. Denis Diderot considered the naturalists as atheists who viewed the world only as material and not spiritual. Naturalism entered the aesthetic field to describe painting that avoided the prescribed historical, mythological, and allegorical subject matter in order to convey a true depiction of nature. Its aim was to reproduce nature in all its grandeur. The term was later imported into literature by French writer Émile Zola to describe a literary style.

Literary naturalism is often confused with realism, and sometimes the terms are used synonymously. Both are based on the idea that art is mimetic (representational, aiming to mimic reality); each term suggests that fiction should deal with the ordinary and the contemporary and should use an objective methodology. Naturalism, however, has a more specific meaning than realism: Naturalistic fiction deals with more shocking subjects, uses stronger vocabulary, and employs photographic detail. Naturalism also espouses a view of life, in contrast to realism's relative neutrality.

THE RISE OF THE NATURALIST MOVEMENT

Before focusing on the characteristics of naturalism, one must look at the historical and philosophical influences on the movement. Three such influences are the Industrial Revolution, the rise of venture capitalism, and the scientific age.

By the mid-nineteenth century, the effects of the Industrial Revolution were manifest. The agricultural workforce had migrated to the cities, and thousands of large, new factories had been built. New technologies soon began to bring more efficient power sources, such as gas and electricity, to homes and businesses in urban areas. The steam locomotive, the telegraph, and underground cables increased the speed of travel and communication. The new technologies opened new opportunities for entrepreneurs, and those few with access to capital began to build vast industrial empires. Increased wealth came into the hands of these businesspeople, and, for them, the standard of living rose dramatically.

The new industrialization had significant side effects. Factory workers were poor and underpaid, and they worked long hours in unsafe conditions. They had flocked to the cities from the country and found industrial jobs in which they were jammed together in squalid and overcrowded conditions. They lived a mean and brutish existence. The Industrial Revolution replaced romantic idealism with a new and harsh reality that focused on the accumulation of external goods—a new materialism.

Not only were material conditions changing, but also new ideas were attacking the complacent Victorian order. In 1859 and again in 1871, a scientist named Charles Darwin published his theory of evolution: Species are in constant warfare to maintain their existence, he observed. Those that survive are better adapted to the environment and stronger. Thus, through a process he called natural selection, new species evolve. Darwin also held that humans had evolved from the lower forms of animal life. Darwin had struck a blow to the metaphysical order and to most people's religious beliefs. No longer were humans privileged creatures created by a benign God in his own image: They were connected to the animal kingdom. The naturalists were influenced by Darwin and in their fiction would depict humans in a bestial state caught in the struggle for survival.

Although Darwin disapproved of the application of his theories to societies of human beings (the process of natural selection required thousands, even millions, of years, not a few generations), a philosopher named Herbert Spencer applied the process of evolution to the economic and social order with his "social Darwinism." Because social beings are evolving toward a higher order, he reasoned, nothing should tamper with that competitive system. The fittest will survive, prosper, and evolve. Those who do not prosper and survive—the poor and the lower classes—should perish because they are not strong enough to survive. The suffering and hardships of the unsuccessful, Spencer thought, are merely incidental conditions in humanity's evolution toward a perfect state. Social Darwinism allowed people in power to rationalize the exploitation of the working class as part of a grand design of nature. The economic system was not to be tampered with, since attempts to ameliorate the circumstances of the poor, immigrants, and children would encourage the propagation of weakness and ultimately work against society. Social Darwinism's element of natural determinism was reflected by the naturalist writers, who often depicted the struggle for survival.

Determinism also plays a role in the philosophy of Karl Marx. For Marx, economic conditions determine the highest goals of civilization. Individuals are caught in class warfare between the working proletariat and the capitalist class. The proletariat can escape their oppression under the wheels of determinism through revolution and the formation of a socialist state. Unlike social Darwinism, Marxism sees the workers, not the capitalists, as triumphant. Some naturalist writers moved toward a socialist solution to the constant struggle for survival.

Another thinker, Frenchman Hippolyte Taine, also influenced the naturalists. Taine made the Darwinian argument that the human animal is a continuation of the primitive animal, but he looked at three influences on human behavior. First, he said, humans are controlled by their heredity, which is passed on in their genes. The second influence is the environment in which the person is immersed. To these biological factors Taine added a third: the precise moment or circumstances that control a human's action. The naturalists used Taine's ideas concerning the controlling factors of heredity and environment. As a result, much naturalistic literature may seem fatalistic—the outcomes of events are less influenced by the characters' free will than dictated by deterministic factors.

Characteristics of naturalistic fiction

In naturalistic fiction, humans are observed as though they are specimens in a laboratory; the naturalist records their lives much the way an anatomist performs a dissection. The purpose of the naturalistic novel is to expose the truth, not to create an entertaining or sentimental fiction based on an inventive story driven by the rules of plot. Instead, the naturalistic novel is the life story of a person or a group of people whose actions are faithfully depicted. The novelist depends heavily on documentation of facts. For example, Upton Sinclair wrote a series of journalistic exposés on the meatpacking industry before writing his novel *The Jungle* (1906). Émile Zola rode a railway engine, descended into a mine, and measured the dimensions of a prostitute's bedroom before incorporating these locales into his novels. The method espoused by Zola was to take copious notes and observations and let the observations shape the story. Naturalistic novelists had to remain impersonal about their observations and not comment on the story. Zola, however, took the liberty of stating that observations should be filtered through a temperament (the author's) so that there would be latitude for the imagination and the perceptions of the observer. In some of his writings Zola went further, mentioning the creation of the grandeur of the spectacle of nature, referring to the method by which writers reshape their observations in order to make an imprint of genius. Therefore, naturalistic novels are more than journalistic records.

In the romantic and melodramatic novel, which preceded naturalism, great emphasis was placed on abstract virtues. In the naturalistic novel, moral absolutes are of no more importance than chemical products. Taine noted that virtue and vice were treated the same as vitriol and vinegar. Thus, naturalistic fiction was condemned by many readers and critics for its immorality or its amorality. The romantic novel created idealistic women, models of purity, and lovers who were admirably loyal. Often they were pitted against a stock villain. The naturalistic novel depicts both rogues and honest people without taking sides. It goes down into the gutters and reveals the seamy side of life.

Another trait of naturalism is its focus on the lower classes and on class struggle. Although Zola held that all subjects were open to the novelist, many naturalists focused on the squalid life of the lower-class poor and their reduction to bestial conditions. The naturalist was less interested in human beings living under ordinary conditions than in how people behaved in crisis. The naturalistic novelist creates a world in which humans are caught in the clutches of heredity and environment. Terrible things generally happen to the characters. Such a world is deterministic and has been viewed as pessimistic. Many criticized naturalism, equating it with fatalism or deterministic pessimism. Although some naturalistic fiction is indeed pessimistic, not all is. Zola himself believed that deterministic thinking is not necessarily fatalistic. If the novelist can expose the cause of a deterministic cycle, there is room for reformers to change conditions and break the cycle.

Therefore, many naturalistic novels reveal a need for societal reform. The naturalists, like their muckraking counterparts among journalists of the day, often used their writing to report facts that they hoped would open the eyes of their readers and encourage justice for working people victimized by ruthless capitalists and large economic forces beyond their control. Especially in American naturalism, labor strife became a pointed issue with both naturalists and the muckrakers. The naturalistic novel is often critical of social institutions such as church and government, viewing them as corrupt and in need of reform.

One consistent theme in most naturalistic novels is the struggle for survival. Whether on natural terrain or in the social sphere, the characters in naturalistic novels are struggling to survive in an often ruthless world. There are no larger-than-life heroes who come to the rescue of those undergoing life-or-death struggles. Those who are weak and flawed are often destitute or dead by the end of the novel. The prose style of a naturalistic novel, in keeping with the philosophy that engendered naturalism, is often flat, bare of imagery, and lacking in rich ambiguity, yet stuffed with details. If imagery is used, it is often animal imagery. There is little room for the poetical and lyrical in naturalism.

NATURALISM'S ROOTS: ÉMILE ZOLA

Although there were precursors, the naturalistic novel emanated primarily from the works of the French writer Émile Zola. He collected a group of French writers around him, but Zola did not see naturalism as a school. One model for the naturalistic novel is Zola's *Thérèse Raquin* (1867; English translation, 1881). The plot is far from original. Thérèse and Laurent are driven to adultery by their passions, and they murder Camille, her husband, disguising the murder as an accidental drowning. Driven by remorse, they both commit suicide. The two lovers are not presented as characters with intellects and consciences but as creatures driven by blood and nerves. Zola states in his preface to the novel that they are animals devoid of soul. They are products of instinctual drives that pull them together, then, after the murder, drive them apart. Their behavior is the result of their natural, inherited constitutions. Thérèse's background is one of sexual repression, which explains the outpouring of her drives. Temperamentally, Laurent is sanguine and Thérèse is nervous. Thérèse lives in a cramped apartment with an overpowering mother-in-law, which further explains the chemical attraction between the two lovers. Zola is not particularly successful in establishing that their guilt is part of a physiological condition in which the woman's nervous temperament has driven the man to hysterical action. The chemical and physical attraction of two human beings is easily understood, but the organic underpinnings of moral conscience are not.

Throughout his lifetime, Zola assumed the monumental task of writing *Les Rougon-Macquart* (1871-1893; *The Rougon-Macquart Family*, 1878-1893), which includes some twenty novels. The novels are connected in the tracing of the branches of two families throughout five generations. Zola traces the role of heredity through a series of stories of mental and physical diseases. He also explores society from all angles and from a variety of occupations. Each of these fields is thoroughly documented, providing the reader with a vivid picture of French society during the Second Empire.

NATURALISM IN ENGLAND: THOMAS HARDY

In England, naturalism did not take root as firmly as it did in France, and it expressed itself somewhat differently. Thomas Hardy is one English novelist who is usually grouped with the naturalists. *Jude the Obscure* (1895) was his last novel. Because of the controversy over the novel's view of sex and marriage, Hardy ended his career as a novelist. Jude Fawley, who aspires to study divinity at Christminster, is trapped into marriage with a vulgar woman who deserts him. His marriage ties make it impossible for him to court Sue Bridehead, whom he meets later and with whom he falls in love. Jude is unsuccessful in attaining admission to the university, and Sue becomes engaged to Philotson, Jude's old tutor. During the engagement, Jude and Sue are thrown together, which expedites Sue's marriage to Philotson. However, Sue is repulsed by Philotson physically and goes to live with Jude in a nonconjugal relationship. Arabella, Jude's wife, returns, leading to Sue's capitulation to a sexual relationship with Jude. Jude and Sue drift from town to town with Arabella's child and eventually have two more children. Arabella's child kills all the children and himself. Stricken with remorse, Sue returns to Philotson. Jude, in a drunken stupor, remarries Arabella. Jude, who has been ill, finally dies of consumption. The pull of physical attraction is seen in Jude's relationship with Arabella. Physical repulsion is seen in Sue's rejection of Philotson. Fatalism is shown as Sue accuses external forces of preventing Jude and her from working and loving. Jude spouts Greek philosophy as he blames all their miseries on a foreordained destiny. However, Hardy differs from other naturalists in that he sees the universe governed by some malign metaphysical force that toys with human destiny.

AMERICAN NATURALISM: CRANE, NORRIS, DREISER

Although naturalism did not flourish in England, it did take root in the United States. In *Maggie: A Girl of the Streets* (1893), Stephen Crane explores life in the New York slums. Maggie is part of a poor family living in the tenements of the East Side of Manhattan. Maggie is an attractive girl who "blossomed in a mud puddle," a life filled with drunken rows. Trying to avoid the demeaning circumstances of her family, she seeks work in a collar and cuff factory, but life there is a monotonous routine filled with corruption. She meets a bartender, Pete, who takes her to beer gardens and theaters, giving her a romantic escape from drudgery and brutality. Seduced and abandoned by her lover and rejected by her family on moral grounds, Maggie is forced into prostitution and eventually drowns herself in the East River.

With no other choices, Maggie's fall into prostitution is inevitable: Her crippling environment, her work, and her romantic temperament have all ordained the outcome. No one cares about her, and she is consumed by degradation. Her crude brother and drunken mother survive in the human jungle of vice and hypocrisy. The influential critic and novelist William Dean Howells wrote that Maggie's story had the quality of a Greek tragedy.

Frank Norris, another naturalistic novelist, showed how an ordinary working man can turn into a brute. *McTeague* (1899) has the plot line of a typical naturalist novel: All the data are provided, and the action flows from these facts. The protagonist, McTeague, thinks that he has taken a step upward from his working-class background by learning dentistry from a traveling quack. McTeague establishes a practice in San Francisco; he falls in love with and marries Trina, one of his patients. However, he makes an enemy of a rival, Marcus Schouler, who reports him for practicing without a license. When he is shut down, McTeague declines into drunkenness and brutality. He tortures his wife to find out where the greedy woman has hoarded five thousand dollars that she won in a lottery. Eventually he kills her and flees to the mining country in the Sierras whence he came.

The story was suggested by a brutal murder in the poor section of San Francisco. Norris paints working-class life as he recorded it on Polk Street. The story takes the reader through eateries, bars, and the living quarters of the poor and middle classes. The world is violent: Beatings, two murders, torture, and mayhem typify the action. The story ends in Death Valley as two men fight to the death. Unlike Crane, Norris depicts the violence in vivid detail. Though they are controlled, there are also scenes of sexuality:

In one scene, McTeague grossly kisses Trina's mouth when she is anesthetized in his dental chair; in another, Trina lies naked in a bed of money as the instincts of greed and lust are combined.

Norris also shows reverse evolution. He displays how the latent beast inside a man emerges under certain circumstances, as shown in McTeague's biting through Marcus's ear: "It was something no longer human; it was rather an echo from the jungle." McTeague is described as an animal with enormous hands and the mind of a dumb brute. Slowly the animal reveals itself and turns into a ruthless killer.

Perhaps the most famous American naturalist, Theodore Dreiser, created a masterpiece of naturalist fiction in *Sister Carrie* (1900), the story of Carrie Meeber, who finds life harsh in the city, where everything is a commodity for sale. She becomes the mistress first of a cad named Drouet (who has no trouble seducing the girl, predisposed to being seduced), and then of Hurstwood, a restaurant manager and a married man. As his fortunes decline, she rises as an actress. Carrie takes on and drops men as her needs determine. She knows that she has something that is valuable, her physical attractiveness, and she is able to deaden what little conscience she has.

Hurstwood is a creature of circumstances. He has a shaky marriage to a dominant wife and is looking for the first woman who will help him recapture his youth. He robs his boss. He opens the safe and takes out some money to fondle it; then, just as his conscience is telling him not to take it, the safe closes. Chance therefore plays a part in the deterministic outcome of the story, but Dreiser has shown that his character is predisposed to steal. Hurstwood sinks into illness and finally commits suicide. Inevitability is a major part of the pattern of life in this as in other naturalistic novels—as Dreiser warns in the first chapter. Carrie, at novel's end, is a successful stage actress. There is no punishment for her sins; her success grows naturally out of her instinctive ability to cope with the corrupt world of the big city. For that reason, the novel shocked audiences when it was published, all the more so because Dreiser implied that Carrie's story was simply one of many that resembled it.

Although naturalism as a movement was fading by the 1920's, naturalistic techniques have found their way into the novels of Ernest Hemingway, William Faulkner, Norman Mailer, Truman Capote, Joyce Carol Oates, and many others. Many novelists have been influenced by the naturalist call for close observation of the environment and the need for documentation.

Paul Rosefeldt

BIBLIOGRAPHY

Baguley, David. *Naturalistic Fiction*. New York: Cambridge University Press, 1990. Covers the French naturalists, providing background to and theories of naturalism.

Civello, Paul. *American Literary Naturalism and Its Twentieth Century Transformations*. Athens: University of Georgia Press, 1994. Shows how naturalism arose and how it influenced later authors such as Ernest Hemingway and Don DeLillo.

Furst, Lilian, and Peter Skrine. *Naturalism*. London: Methuen, 1971. An excellent, brief introduction to naturalism that covers naturalism in France, Germany, England, and the United States.

Stone, Edward, ed. *What Was Naturalism?* New York: Appleton Century Crofts, 1959. A good collection of primary material related to the rise of naturalism, including excerpts from Darwin, Marx, Spencer, and Zola.

Walcott, Charles Child, ed. *Seven Novelists in the American Naturalist Tradition*. Minneapolis: University of Minnesota Press, 1974. A survey of the major American naturalists—Crane, Norris, Dreiser, and Jack London—as well as later writers influenced by naturalism, such as Sherwood Anderson, John Steinbeck, and James T. Farrell.

THE NOVELLA

The word "novella" comes from the Latin word *novellus*, a diminutive of the word *novus*, which means "new." It first became associated with the telling of stories in the thirteenth century with collections of "new" versions of old saints' tales, exempla, chivalric tales, and ribald stories. Eventually, the term became associated with tales that were fresh, strange, unusual—stories, in short, that were worth the telling.

BEGINNINGS OF THE NOVELLA

The most decisive historical event to establish the term "novella" as a designation for a "new" kind of fiction was Giovanni Boccaccio's decision to give the name "novella" to the tales included in *Decameron: O, Prencipe Galetto* (1349-1351; *The Decameron*, 1620) in the fourteenth century. What made Boccaccio's stories "new" was the fact that they marked a shift from the sacred world of Dante's "divine" comedy to the profane world of Boccaccio's "human" comedy. The resulting realism of *The Decameron* should not be confused, however, with the realism developed by the eighteenth century novel. The focus in Boccaccio's tales is not on a character presented in a similitude of everyday life, but on the traditional world of story, in which characters serve primarily as "functions" of the tale.

With Miguel de Cervantes, in the sixteenth century, as with Boccaccio before him, something "new" also characterized the novella. First, Cervantes in his *Novelas ejemplares* (1613; *Exemplary Novels*, 1846) did not present himself as a collector of traditional tales but as an inventor of original stories. As a result, he became an observer and recorder of concrete details in the external world and a student of the psychology of individual characters. Although plot was still important, character became more developed than it was in *The Decameron*, and thus psychological motivation rather than story motivation was emphasized. Characters existed not solely for the roles they played in the stories but also for their own sake, as if they were real.

In Germany, in the first quarter of the nineteenth century, the novella began to detach itself from the notion of the form inspired by Boccaccio and Cervantes and to be supported by a theory of its own. Friedrich von Schlegel agreed with the Renaissance idea that a novella was an anecdote that must be capable of arousing interest, but he noted that the modern retelling of already known traditional stories necessarily focuses the reader's attention away from mythic authority and toward the authority of the subjective point of view of the narrator. Johann Wolfgang von Goethe added an important new element to the definition of the novella form by arguing that it depicted an unheard-of event that actually took place; thus, although the event can be accounted for by the laws of nature, it must be strange and unusual.

In addition to this theorizing about the novella during the nineteenth century in Germany, numerous examples of the form contributed to its development. The first such example is Goethe's story entitled simply *Novelle* (1826; *Novel*, 1837), an exemplary story that dramatically changed the nature of the genre by shifting the focus from simple events to events that took on a symbolic meaning and form. After Goethe, the novella developed as a most self-conscious genre, a sophisticated literary narrative that deals with the most basic metaphysical and aesthetic issues.

Whereas the logic of Goethe's *Novelle* is governed by the narrative demands of the story and by aesthetic artifice, the logic of the most famous novella of Ludwig Tieck, *Der Blonde Eckbert* (in *Volksmärchen*, 1797), follows the convention of the fairy tale as an externalization of unconscious processes. This act of grounding the supernatural in the psychological is taken to further extremes in the novellas of E. T. A. Hoffmann, whose stories are often self-conscious manipulations of the relationship between fantasy and the everyday that had previously been developed in the fairy tale form. In Hoffmann's best-known novella, *Der Sandman* (1816; *The Sandman*, 1844), the protagonist is caught between fantasy and reality, a dichotomy that Hoffmann makes more explicit than does Goethe or Tieck. The advance of Hoffmann's tale over those of his predecessors lies in its ironic tone, which parodies the romantic view of reality. Hoffmann has the ironic sensibility of Franz Kafka in perceiving that the supernatural world is serious and sardonic at the same time.

Although the term "novella" is used to refer to both the short pieces of fourteenth century fiction best exemplified by *The Decameron* and the highly developed nineteenth century German form, it was more often used in the twentieth century to refer to a number of works of mid-range length, somewhat longer than the short story and somewhat shorter than the novel. The modern novella derives from various preexisting types. It began in the nineteenth century with a quasi-realistic normalizing of the old romance and parable forms and has maintained these romance conventions in such gothic novellas as Horace Walpole's *The Castle of Otranto* (1765) and Henry James's *The Turn of the Screw* (1898) and in such parabolic novellas as Gustave Flaubert's *La Légende de Saint Julien l'Hospitalier*, published in *Trois Contes* (1877; *Three Tales*, 1903), and Flannery O'Connor's *Wise Blood* (1952).

ROMANCE AND REALISM

It is not simply the gothic trappings and decorations that constitute the gothic novel, but rather the placing of characters into traditional romance tales and the resulting transformation of those characters into archetypes of the mythic story. The transformation of "real" people into parabolic figures by the latent thrust of the traditional romance story is characteristic of the novella form and can be seen in an explicit way in *The Castle of Otranto*, in which, even as characters act out their desires on the surface of the plot, desire becomes objectified and totally embodied in the latent and underlying plot.

In *The Turn of the Screw*, this basic combination is focused in a particularly explicit way, becoming the crux and central theme of the story. The issue of whether the ghosts in the story are real or are projections of the governess's imagination is reflective of the basic problem of the novella form—that is, whether a given story features characters who are presented as if they are real or as embodiments of psychological archetypes. This ambiguity is so thorough in James's novella that every detail can be read as evidence for both interpretations of reality at once.

Just as Walpole returned to the medieval romance for a model for his gothic tale, Flaubert returned to the medieval saint's legend or folktale for the exemplar for *La Légende de Saint Julien l'Hospitalier*. Furthermore, just as Walpole's romance differs from the medieval form by combining traditional story with psychologically real characters, so does Flaubert's moral fable differ from its medieval source by self-consciously foregrounding the static and frozen nature of the medieval story itself. The subject matter of Flaubert's story, although it has a moral issue at its center, is more particularly the generic means by which the medieval tale is moral and representative. The movement from the parable of Flaubert to the modern parables of the American writer Flannery O'Connor is a movement from a relatively simple story to a more complex and ironic form. Just as the narrative and symbolic aim of Flaubert's story is the spiritual transformation of its central characters, so also is the central aim of O'Connor's *Wise Blood* to lead its central character to a vision of his own fragmentation so he can be reborn.

Perhaps the two best-known modern parable forms of the novella are William Faulkner's *The Bear* (1942) and Ernest Hemingway's *The Old Man and the Sea* (1952). These two stories differ from the parables of Flaubert and O'Connor in that they both seem to be less illustrations of moral issues than reenactments of primitive rituals that enforce the moral issue. Although they are quite different in their individual syntactical rhythms, both stories are characterized by a highly formal structure and style in which moral values evolve ritually from the hero's encounter with the natural world. Of the two stories, *The Old Man and the Sea* seems closer to the parable form than does *The Bear*, primarily because of the conventional expectation that the parable is a relatively clean structural form, functional and bare in style and point of view.

One of the most common narrative devices of the novella is the convention of the double or *Doppelgänger*. There are both historical and aesthetic reasons for the predominance of this motif in the form.

Because the novella is a combination of the old romance form, in which characters are projections of psychic states, and the new realistic novel form, in which characters are presented as if they were real people with their own psychological life, novellas often present both types of characters, especially in such works as Herman Melville's "Bartleby the Scrivener" (1853) and Joseph Conrad's *Heart of Darkness* (serial 1899, book 1902), in which the narrators seem to be realistic characters with individual psyches, while the central characters Bartleby and Kurtz seem to be manifested as psychological archetypes.

Perceiving reality to be a function more of mind than of external reality, nineteenth century fiction writers could present inner life by means of dreamlike romance projections. If, however, they wished to reveal the inner life in a realistic manner, yet avoid getting lost in a quagmire of introspection, the only answer was to present that subjective and often-forbidden side of the self in terms of external projections—as characters who, although the reader could respond to them as if they were separate external figures, were really projections of the mind of the protagonist. The most obvious means by which such an inner state could be projected as if it were outer reality was to present the projection as a figure somehow very much like the protagonist, not an identical double, but rather an embodiment of some hidden or neglected aspect of the self that had to be confronted and dealt with.

Robert Louis Stevenson's *The Strange Case of Dr. Jekyll and Mr. Hyde* (1886) is perhaps the purest example of this use of the convention; that Dr. Jekyll represents the conventional and socially acceptable personality and Mr. Hyde the uninhibited and criminal self is the most obvious aspect of Stevenson's novella. A more accomplished and subtle treatment of the convention can be seen in Conrad's "The Secret Sharer" (1910), for here the double is not merely a manifested hidden self or a figure imagined to be outside the protagonist, but rather an actual self whose crime is at the core of the moral issue facing the protagonist. Although it can be said that the double in "The Secret Sharer" represents some aspect of the

captain's personality that he must integrate, it is more probable that he is brought on board to make explicit and dramatically concrete the dual workings of the captain's mind: He is distracted and split between his external responsibilities and his concealed secret.

Because of its moderate length, its highly formalized structure, and its focus on the ultimate metaphysical limitations of humanity, the novella has often been compared to classical tragedy. The central character of the novella often seems to be caught in the inevitability of fate or the story, being doomed at the same time as a victim of some limitation within the self. The essential issue is that the "tragic novella" creates the illusion that the characters are responsible for their own defeat, even though readers realize that they are witnessing the fatality demanded by the fable itself. The two most emphatic examples of this tragic form are Stephen Crane's "The Blue Hotel" (1898) and Katherine Anne Porter's *Noon Wine* (1937).

The three basic devices in "The Blue Hotel" that give it a sense of classical tragedy are its formalized structure, which suggests a classical five-act tragedy; a central character neither eminently good nor evil, whose misfortune results not from vice or depravity but from some error, frailty, or limitation; and the creation through metaphor and allusion of the sense that the events and characters are not contemporary and real but archetypal and ritualistic. The most essential requirement is that the protagonist is made to seem responsible for his own downfall, even though his downfall is governed by the rules of the ritual or fable itself.

Whereas the tragedy in "The Blue Hotel" is brought on by the protagonist's mistake about the nature of the world around him, in Porter's *Noon Wine* the downfall is brought on by a limitation in the protagonist's ability to perceive himself. The tragic figure is Royal Earl Thompson; the other two figures, Helton and Hatch, are projections of two aspects of Thompson's personality and situation. Helton makes it possible for him to live a lie about himself, and Hatch forces him to confront that lie.

One of the narrative forms that serves as an important antecedent to the modern novella is the fairy tale, for fairy-tale devices appear in the novella in various self-conscious ways: as a dreamlike state of being that is laid bare, as a structural device to develop a parabolic story, as the means to create the sense of metaphysical mystery in external reality, and as a way to suggest traditional character types and story situations. The fairy-tale conventions in the modern novella are never allowed to lapse into the marvelous and the supernatural; rather, they reflect the extraordinary nature of ordinary life, in which extreme situations seem to transform the world into a kind of reality akin to that found in fairy tales. Carson McCullers's *The Ballad of the Sad Café* (serial 1943, book 1951) and Franz Kafka's *Die Verwandlung* (1915; *The Metamorphosis*, 1936) are two typical examples. McCullers's story seems to take place in the realm of dreams rather than in external reality, for it is a story turned inward on itself, narcissistic and grotesque just as the central figure Miss Amelia's eyes are crossed, peering inward—sealed off from the ordinary world by the obsessions of the story itself. The effect of the work depends primarily on the poetic voice of the storyteller, which lyrically transforms the grotesque external reality into the inner story of the lover; the details of the story are thus transmuted by the teller until they bear no connection to the external world.

Perhaps the most successful example of this combination of fantasy and reality in the modern novella is Kafka's *The Metamorphosis*. The extreme step Kafka takes is to make the transformation of the psychic into the physical the precipitating premise from which the rest of the story follows. The only suspension of disbelief required in the story is that the reader accept the premise that Gregor Samsa awakes one morning from uneasy dreams to find himself transformed into a giant insect. Once the reader accepts this event, the rest of the story is quite prosaic and detailed, fully externalized in a realistic fashion. *The Metamorphosis* is an exemplar of the typical novella effort to present an inner state of reality as a fantastic but real outer event.

METAFICTION

The most common theme and technique in the contemporary novella is metafictional self-reflexivity,

embodied in stories that have to do with the nature of storytelling itself. Philip Roth's *The Ghost Writer* (1979), in which external reality and fictional reality become inextricably blurred as the central character tells a story about the almost mythical figure Anne Frank, is one example. Perhaps the most commercially successful attempt at this kind of self-reflexive fiction, however, is Kurt Vonnegut, Jr.'s *Slaughterhouse-Five: Or, The Children's Crusade, a Duty-Dance with Death* (1969), which uses the popular science-fiction genre as a vehicle to explore methods of storytelling.

More sophisticated than *Slaughterhouse-Five* are the metafictional works of John Barth, Robert Coover, and William H. Gass. *Dunyazadiad* (in *Chimera*, 1972) reflects Barth's fascination with the notion of characters in fiction becoming readers or authors of the very fiction they inhabit. *Dunyazadiad* takes its premise and its situation from the Scheherazade story, as told by her younger sister Dunyazade on the final night of the famous 1,001 nights. Barth transports a modern storyteller (himself) back to "Sherry's" aid to supply her with the stories from the future that she has told in the fictional past.

Just as Barth takes his inspiration from the origins of storytelling in *The Arabian Nights' Entertainments*, Coover traces his debts back to Cervantes, who created a synthesis between poetic analogy and literal history and thus gave birth to the modern novel. Coover's most popular novella, *The Babysitter* (in *Pricksongs & Descants*, 1969), is his most forthright example of this mixture of fantasy and reality. The story is a confused combination of the two realms in which, as is usual in the novella, unreality predominates over external reality. The story presents the fantasy reality in the same mode as external reality, so that in trying to unravel the two, the reader gets hopelessly lost in the mix. Gass carries the self-reflexive mode to even further extremes. The primary premise of his novella *Willie Masters' Lonesome Wife* (1968) is that the book the reader holds in his hands is the wife herself. This trope is carried out by such devices as varying the typography and the texture of the book pages and by using graphics and other purely physical devices to give readers the sense that they are not simply seeing through the medium of the book but are dealing with the medium itself.

The novella was not a popular form during the renaissance of the American short story in the 1980's, stimulated by writers, such as Raymond Carver and Anne Beattie, who practiced a cryptic and abbreviated narrative style notoriously known as "minimalism" or "hyperrealism," the ultimate extreme of which was the short-short story, sometimes dubbed "sudden fiction" or "flash fiction." So many writers tried to cash in on the popularity of the trend that reviewers began to criticize the form for lacking any moral or social content. The backlash spawned a return to a more expansive, discursive writing style in the 1990's, closer to the classic realism of the novel form.

Typical of this reaction against minimalism by a younger generation is Christopher Tilghman, whose debut collection, *In a Father's Place* (1990), featured stories that affirmed such novelistic middle-class values as family, the land, and tradition. The novella-length title piece casually meanders through a story about a traditional patriarch who sends his son's girlfriend packing when she tries to convince her boyfriend to write a novel that "deconstructs" the family. Ethan Canin, first introduced to the public with his short-story collection *Emperor of the Air* (1988), turned to the novella form in 1994 with *The Palace Thief.* Canin centers his title story on a teacher of ancient history who retires from a private school after many years of teaching and tries to expose one of his former students, a powerful businessman and politician who has reached his pinnacle of success through cheating.

John Updike, one of the best-known practitioners of the often highly stylized stories that appeared in *New Yorker* magazine, began, in his later years, to write longer, more leisurely stories. "The Sandstone Farmhouse," the longest story in his 1994 collection *The Afterlife and Other Stories,* is an understated, elegiac story about a fifty-four-year-old man who must dispose of his dead mother's possessions. As he goes through her things, comparing his own transitory life in Manhattan to the solidity of the stone house where his mother lived, he discovers that although he moved to New York City to be where the action is, the real action has occurred in the farmhouse.

The stories of Andre Dubus, a writer who refused to follow the minimalists, are based on the conviction that most human beings are seeking love rather than sex, relationships rather than one-night stands, and family rather than thrills. In the long title story of *Dancing After Hours* (1996), a forty-year-old female bartender who lives alone finds new hope when she meets a wheelchair-bound man who lives life with gusto in spite of his disability.

The novella-length title story of Andrea Barrett's 1996 collection, *Ship Fever and Other Stories,* takes place in the 1840's when thousands of poor Irish fled the potato famine, only to land on harsh Nova Scotia shores plagued by typhus and other diseases. The protagonist is a young doctor from Quebec who volunteers to work at a quarantine station on Grosse Island. A powerful abbreviated historical novel, "Ship Fever" creates a fully realized world focused on a social disaster.

A number of writers who were part of the minimalist or hyperrealism trend of the 1980's also published novellas during the 1990's. Richard Ford's *Women with Men: Three Stories* (1997) includes a novella told from the point of view of seventeen-year-old Montana boy who travels with his aunt to visit his mother. In contrast to her earlier minimalist narratives, Ann Beattie's later short fictions made more use of novelistic techniques of expanded character exploration and realistic, nonmetaphoric detail. In the novella-length title story of *Park City: New and Selected Stories* (1998), the central character spends a week at a Utah ski resort during the off-season looking after her half-sister's daughter, trying to find new meaning in her life.

Alice Munro, a respected writer of short fiction who began publishing in the 1960's, also focused more on novella-length stories in the 1990's. The long title story of her collection *The Love of a Good Woman* (1998) begins in Wally, Ontario, a familiar Munro location, with three boys finding the body of the town's optometrist in his car in the river. Although one might expect the plot to immediately focus on the mystery of the drowned man, Munro is in absolutely no hurry to satisfy the reader's curiosity. She follows the three boys into their individual homes and leisurely explores their ordinary secrets.

Other collections of stories that featured novellas in the 1990's include Cynthia Ozick's *The Puttermesser Papers* (1997), which contains three novellas about her character Ruth Puttermesser; Amy Hempel's *Tumble Home* (1997), which contains seven stories and one novella; and Saul Bellow's *The Actual*, which was published separately as a novella in 1997. Story collections by Robert Stone—*Bear and His Daughter* (1997)—and Charles Baxter—*Believers* (1997)—each feature a novella as its title story. Other 1990's novellas by established writers include Stephen Dixon's *Gould* (1997), Richard Bausch's *Rare and Endangered Species: A Novella and Stories* (1994), and Antonya Nelson's *Family Terrorists: A Novella and Seven Stories* (1994).

David Leavitt, one of the best-known spokesmen for the life of young gay males, also tried his hand at the novella form in 1997 with *Arkansas: Three Novellas*, the most controversial of which is "The Term Paper Artist," in which a character named David Leavitt writes a term paper for a young heterosexual male in return for a sex act, after which he is pursued by a number of other straight male students with similar offers. In a short article on the novella, Leavitt wrote that if a novel is a marriage and the short story an affair, the novella is a "prolonged infatuation."

Charles E. May

BIBLIOGRAPHY

Clements, Robert J., and Joseph Gibaldi. *Anatomy of the Novella*. New York: New York University Press, 1977. Historical survey and analysis of theory and practice of the Renaissance novella from Giovanni Boccaccio to Miguel de Cervantes. Concludes that because the form was middle-class in orientation, most novellas are ironic, dealing with characters inferior in power or intelligence to the reader.

Good, Graham. "Notes on the Novella." In *The New Short Story Theories*, edited by Charles E. May. Athens: Ohio University Press, 1994. A concise historical survey of the generic debate about the novella's basic characteristics and its adjacency to the short story and the novel. Focuses on the implications of the form being an imitation of a live telling in which the end of the story is known by the teller at the beginning.

Lee, A. Robert, ed. *The Modern American Novella*. New York: St. Martin's Press, 1989. A collection of essays by various critics on American novellas from the nineteenth and twentieth centuries, including essays on Stephen Crane's *The Red Badge of Courage*, Kate Chopin's *The Awakening*, Ernest Hemingway's *The Old Man and the Sea*, and the novellas of J. D. Salinger and Saul Bellow.

Leibowitz, Judith. *Narrative Purpose in the Novella*. The Hague: Mouton, 1974. Focusing on the European and American novella from the mid-nineteenth century to the 1970's, Leibowitz argues that the generically distinct nature of the novella is its double effect of intensity and expansion. She contends that although the repetitive structure and theme complex of the novella may also be found in the short story and the novel, they do not operate in those forms as mutually dependent devices, as they do in the novella.

LoCicero, Donald. *Novellentheorie: The Practicality of the Theoretical*. The Hague: Mouton, 1970. An analysis and critique of the three most important nineteenth century theories of the German *Novelle*: Johann Wolfgang von Goethe's theory of "the unheard-of event," Ludwig Tieck's theory of the "turning point," and Paul Heyse's "falcon theory." Urges a descriptive rather than a prescriptive approach to genre theory of the novella.

Plouffe, Bruce. *The Post-war Novella in German Language Literature: An Analysis*. New York: AMS Press, 1998. Discusses developments in the novella in Germnay in the second half of the twentieth century. Includes bibliographical references and an index.

Remak, Henry H. H. *Structural Elements of the German Novella from Goethe to Thomas Mann*. New York: Peter Lang, 1996. A look at the German novella, from the eighteenth century through the twentieth.

Rodax, Yvonne. *The Real and the Ideal in the Novella of Italy, France, and England.* Chapel Hill: University of North Carolina Press, 1968. Analysis of the renaissance novella form, with chapters on *The Decameron*, *The Canterbury Tales*, *The Heptaméron*, and such sixteenth century English collections as William Painter's *Palace of Pleasure*.

Springer, Mary Doyle. *Forms of the Modern Novella.* Chicago: University of Chicago Press, 1975. Using the rhetorical approach of the so-called Chicago school of criticism, Springer discusses five types of novella plots: serious plot of character, degenerative tragedy, satire, apologue, and the example.

THE PICARESQUE NOVEL

The words *picaresque* and *picaro* achieved currency in Spain shortly after 1600; today they are current terms in literary criticism, sometimes misused because of the vague meaning attached to them. The revival of the genre in the twentieth century was accompanied by an increased critical interest in this type of novel, with the result that some critics try to stretch the definition of the picaresque while others attempt to restrict it. Still, some features are generally accepted as distinct characteristics of the picaresque, including a loose, episodic structure; a rogue-hero (the *picaro*) who is on the move and goes through a series of encounters with representatives of a hostile and corrupt world; a first-person narrative; and finally, a satirical approach to the society in which the adventures occur. The typical social background of the picaresque involves a disordered, disintegrating world in which traditional values are breaking down. The instability of the social structure permits the emergence of the *picaro*, a resilient rogue but not a criminal, a person of low birth or uncertain parentage, an outsider whose adventures take him from innocence to experience. In this sense, the picaresque novel has affinities with the *Bildungsroman*, but unlike the protagonist of the latter, the *picaro* is a fixed character. While he learns survival techniques from his adventures, he does not change inwardly; he remains faithful to his healthy instincts without questioning the larger order of things. Pressured by circumstances to choose between integrity and survival, the *picaro* makes the pragmatic choice and learns to adjust to the corrupt values of his environment.

Origins

The picaresque genre emerged in sixteenth century Spain, an age of turmoil and upheaval when medieval homogeneity and social stability were giving way to Renaissance mobility and a greater emphasis on the importance of the individual. All Spanish picaresque novels present a low-life character passing from master to master in search of some financial stability, thus providing a splendid occasion for the author to give an overall picture of Spain in an age of disintegrating values. The differences between the two first examples of the genre, however, already indicate its protean nature.

Lazarillo de Tormes, published anonymously in 1553, presents a *picaro*, a victim of tricksters who by necessity becomes a trickster himself. The novel's anonymous author was the first to employ a realistic first-person narrator, creating a countergenre to the fastidious courtly literature of the period. Some critics suggest that both the anonymous author of *Lazarillo de Tormes* and Mateo Alemán, the writer of the second Spanish picaresque, were Jews or converted Jews, outsiders to the mainstream of Spanish society; in any case, the picaresque view of life is an outsider's point of view as far as protagonist and author are concerned.

Fear of starvation and anger are Lazarillo's true masters. The lesson he draws from his experience of privation and exploitation is not one of resistance or revolt; on the contrary, it is one of conformity. His is a kind of success story because, at the end of the novel, he finds a secure job as a town crier, but this is qualified success, since he pays for it with his honor, marrying the archpriest's mistress. He accepts the archpriest's advice to concern himself only with his own advantage. The advice, of course, reflects the hypocritical standards of Spanish society. Lazarillo is more than ready to heed the counsel; his bitter adventures have taught him to be content with low expectations. The feeling of being defenseless and unprotected against the wickedness of the world lends a tragic note to the story of his childhood and adolescence. Though most of his adventures make the reader laugh, anguish and despair prevail throughout the novel. The comic and the serious exist side by side, adding a note of ambiguity. *Lazarillo de Tormes* is a mixture of childish immaturity, innocence, and bitter cynicism; it excels in a fusion of modes and attitudes. At the end, Lazarillo compares his rising fortunes to Spain's rising political power; consequently, the unknown author not only puts his *picaro*'s story in an ambiguous light but also extends that ambiguity to the whole empire of Charles V.

A DIFFERENT PICARO

Charles V was succeeded by Philip II and Philip III; disillusionment followed triumph in the history of the empire. The picaresque novel, from the beginning a protean genre, adjusted to the new demands. Despair and anguish are present already in Lazarillo's story, but the *picaro* protagonist in Mateo Alemán's *Guzmán de Alfarache* (1599, 1604) is first of all a tormented soul. As an investigator of the prison system, Alemán was well acquainted with prison life. In Guzmán he presents a repentant sinner. The confessions reveal a lower-class character whom a dehumanizing society has forced to adjust to its corrupt values; the emphasis is not on Guzmán's adventures, however, but rather on his tormented soul. He is a kind of psychological *picaro*, one very much concerned with his soul. Guzmán compares the human predicament to warfare: an existence without any certainty or truth, a life full of hypocrisy and instability.

In spite of the many hilarious tricks played by the rogues on their masters, the Spanish picaresque novels were not intended to be amusing. There is a subtle balance of comedy and seriousness in *Lazarillo de Tormes* and *Guzmán de Alfarache*; at the same time, however, through the encounters of the rogue-hero with various masters—all of them representing the hypocritical, materialistic standards of contemporary Spanish society—these picaresque novels give a fragmented but valid and realistic picture of a society in change.

FRANCE AND GERMANY

The protean nature of the picaresque novel made it easy for the genre to spread rapidly all over Europe. Adaptations of *Lazarillo de Tormes* appeared in 1561 in France and in 1568 in England. *Guzmán de Alfarache* appeared in 1615 in Germany. The Spanish original blended in each country with the native tradition, and the Spanish *picaro* turned into the English rogue, later a foundling; into the German *Schelm*; and in France, into a *gentilhomme*. Despite differences in each of these countries, the picaresque consistently performed the function of a countergenre, making legitimate the serious attention given to low-life characters. With the advance of capitalism, the middle class grew in size and influence, and its members found pleasure in a genre that centered on the plight of a low-life character seeking upward mobility. At the same time, printing techniques improved, and booksellers, in order to boost their profits, encouraged more and more printings of picaresque fiction because of its appeal to the taste of the bourgeoisie. As a matter of fact, in the following centuries the genre came to be adopted to reflect a bourgeois world view rather than a truly picaresque outlook. With the optimistic attitudes of the Enlightenment, the picaresque novel lost its quality of despair; the former *picaro*, though in different degrees and in different ways, came to be integrated into the mainstream of society.

In Germany, the Spanish picaresque merged with the native tradition of tales about false beggars. The most significant German novel of the picaresque type is Hans Jakob Christoffel von Grimmelshausen's *Der abenteuerliche Simplicissimus* (1669; *The Adventurous Simplicissimus*, 1912). The background of the book fits the requirements of the picaresque atmosphere: The Thirty Years' War was certainly a period of disorder and disintegration in German history. Simplicius Simplicissimus, as his name implies, is a naïve, simple, ignorant boy; his peasant background emphasizes this feature. He is almost another Parzival, a "pure fool," but the war destroys his pastoral life. His picaresque wanderings eventually lead him to live the life of a hermit. Compared to what is considered normal and sane in the gambling, warring, drinking, whoring society of contemporary Germany, the seemingly foolish idealism of the hermit is perhaps the only truly sane attitude amid universal madness. While society may consider Simplicissimus mad, his madness makes more sense than the reality created by the so-called respectable people. The German *picaro*, by tearing off the masks, shows the real face of society behind the facade.

In France, the Spanish picaresque merged with the tradition of criminal biographies and books on vagabonds; in the seventeenth century the genre came to be exploited by writers such as Charles Sorel and Paul Scarron, whose comic, realistic novels functioned as a countergenre to the improbable romances that flooded the market. The French *picaro*, born into the middle class, uses his tricks to unmask the society to which he belongs by birth; in consequence, the social criticism always implicit in the genre becomes more obvious. By far the most famous French picaresque novel is Alain-René Lesage's *Histoire de Gil Blas de Santillane* (1715-1735; 4 vols.; *The History of Gil Blas of Santillane*, 1716, 1735; better known as *Gil Blas*, 1749, 1962). Though the adventures of this son of humble parents take place in Spain, Gil Blas is different from the original Spanish *picaro*. Influenced by Molière and La Bruyère, satirists of morals and manners, Lesage turned his Gil Blas into an observer of rogues rather than a participant in roguery. Indeed, Gil Blas is a noble-hearted adventurer who, in view of his virtuous behavior, deserves the success he achieves in the end.

ENGLAND

In England, the first translation of *Lazarillo de Tormes* appeared in 1586, the work of David Rowland; the first English *Guzmán de Alfarache* appeared in 1622. Soon thereafter, the Spanish picaresque merged with the native tradition of anatomies of roguery. The best early English picaresque is Thomas Nashe's *The Unfortunate Traveller: Or, The Life of Jack Wilton* (1594). *Guzmán de Alfarache* was very popular with translators; Richard Head's and Frances Kirkman's *The English Rogue* (1665, 1668) is the best among English adaptations of the original *Guzmán de Alfarache*.

In the eighteenth century, a kind of picaresque enjoyed a boom in English literature. Most of Tobias Smollett's fiction is in the picaresque vein. In his outstanding novel *The Adventures of Roderick Random* (1748), the protagonist, an orphan, foreshadows the English *picaro* as a foundling. He is a decent young person, and his inherent virtues contrast sharply with the cruelty and viciousness of most of the other characters in the novel. They stand for the attitudes of a dehumanized society that subjects the young protagonist to all kinds of hardships and misfortunes on land and on sea. Resilient, in the true picaresque spirit, Roderick Random bounces back after each misadventure. Although his personal fortunes are

straightened out in the end when he finds his father and is happily married, on the whole, Smollett presents a rather gloomy view of the human condition.

Daniel Defoe's *The Fortunes and Misfortunes of the Famous Moll Flanders, Written from Her Own Memorandums* (1722) is an episodic fictional autobiography of a *picara*, a female rogue. She is a true criminal whose crimes are rooted in capitalistic attitudes. Indeed, Moll is a bourgeois *picara*; inspired by the spirit of profit and investment, she acquires the fortune necessary for investment in the New World by the only means available to her: thievery and prostitution. Her behavior and standards reflect on the materialistic values of the society to which she wants to conform.

Henry Fielding's *The History of Tom Jones, a Foundling* (1749) illustrates better than any other novel of the eighteenth century the transformation of the *picaro* from a roguish outsider to a belonger. Tom Jones is a foundling and thus an outsider, as a true *picaro* is expected to be, and in the course of the novel he must take to the road, where he undergoes various adventures. Never for a minute, however, is there any real doubt that by the end of his journey he will be integrated into society. As a matter of fact, Tom Jones is a kind of vanishing *picaro* on his way to becoming the traditional English fictional hero. This hero always ultimately conforms to accepted norms. Tom Jones's place in the world of Allworthy is only being questioned in order to provide adventures for the amusement of the reader. The element of economic necessity is entirely lacking; in consequence, ambiguity and despair vanish and the adventures provoke wholehearted, easy laughter.

The next step on the path of the vanishing English *picaro* falls in the nineteenth century. In Charles Dickens's *Pickwick Papers* (1836-1837), the picaresque structure is nothing more than a form of convenience. The rogue is Jingle, yet the hero of the adventure-series is the most respectable Mr. Pickwick. He is the *picaro* turned respectable, in an age when respectability, exemplified by Queen Victoria and the Prince Consort, dominated British society. Mr. Pickwick goes through a series of hilariously comic adventures, gains experience, and even goes to prison, but in the end he returns to society. Integration, so important in British fiction, is achieved at the end of the adventures.

America

The American development of the picaresque followed a radically different course. American black humor, born on the pioneer frontier, recalls in its mixture of laughter and terror the atmosphere of the early Spanish picaresque. The early American himself, a lonely figure on a vast, unknown, and possibly hostile continent, is a distant cousin of Lazarillo and Guzmán. It is not surprising, then, that the novel from which, according to Ernest Hemingway, all American literature derives, Mark Twain's *Adventures of Huckleberry Finn* (1884), is an American picaresque story not only in the obvious picaresque pattern of Huck's adventures but also in the elements of loneliness and terror that fill up the frame.

Huck is an outsider, belonging to the lowest rank of whites in his society; he recognizes that society pays only lip service to ideals and decides to stay true to his own conscience. While the adventures of his trip down the Mississippi match Lazarillo's experiences of near starvation, the haunting experience with his own conscience over the case of Jim, the runaway black slave, makes Huck a relative of Guzmán, tortured about his soul. Huck, the American *picaro*, is a rogue with a conscience who chooses to listen to his own heart rather than follow the sham values of society.

The picaro in modern fiction

Many features of the original Spanish picaresque pattern and of its *picaro*-rogue hero correspond to trends in modern fiction and to the concept of the modern limited hero or antihero. The episodic, open-ended plot is an appropriate device for the modern writer, who knows "only broken images" for presenting the fragmented reality of a disorderly, chaotic universe. The *picaro* is not unlike the modern alienated individual, born into a world turned upside down. Many critics, therefore, consider the picaresque mode to be one of the most characteristic in twentieth century fiction, while others speak of a picaresque renaissance.

Irish writer James Joyce's *Ulysses* (1922), the archetype of modern fiction, shows striking similarities with the picaresque. Joyce's "joco-serious" recalls the unbalanced Spanish picaresque atmosphere of half-comical and half-serious attitudes. Leopold Bloom, a Jew in Ireland, is an outsider in society; a betrayed husband, he is also an outsider in his family. Both *Ulysses* and the Spanish picaresque present a series of experiences rather than a coherent narrative. They present a roguelike hero, who is no criminal but still less than an example of virtue and whose life is a hard-luck story. Leopold Bloom experiences a despair and anxiety which was alien to the more respectable *picaros* of the eighteenth and nineteenth centuries but which recalls the mood of *Lazarillo de Tormes*.

The English writer Joyce Cary also used the picaresque genre for his First Trilogy, which concerns the life of the artist Gulley Jimson, a rascally but appealing *picaro*. Interestingly, only the first and third volumes can qualify as picaresque novels, for the narrator of the second book, *To Be a Pilgrim* (1942), is Thomas Wilcher, who does not fit the definition of a *picaro*. Wilcher is a member of the establishment, a rich, respectable lawyer who believes himself to be on the way to the Heavenly City. However, the first novel in the trilogy, *Herself Surprised* (1941), is narrated by a *picara* worthy to be classed with Moll Flanders; she not only habitually disregards the moral laws but also has no difficulty justifying even the most flagrant betrayal of trust—for instance, systematically stealing from Mr. Wilcher while she pretends to be the perfect housekeeper. Like Moll, Sara is eventually caught; *Herself Surprised* is written from prison. Gulley, who was probably the most important man in Sara's life, also falls victim to the law. *The Horse's Mouth* (1944, 1957), which he narrates, begins with his release from prison, an old man, but still adept at lying, cheating, stealing, and justifying his sins as necessitated by his art. Nevertheless, Gulley's zest for life and his ability to laugh both at the world and at himself make him a particularly appealing *picaro*.

The picaresque pattern also emerged in the novels of Britain's "Angry Young Men" in the 1950's. The angry picaresque novel of postwar Great Britain resulted from serious discontent with the welfare state. The decade found England in unsettled conditions, with the empire falling to pieces and the class system only slowly weakening in its traditional rigidity. Just as the Spanish picaresque novel arose in part as an expression of the social resentment of the underdog against the privileged classes, so Kingsley Amis's *Lucky Jim* (1954), John Wain's *Hurry on Down* (1953), and Alan Sillitoe's *Saturday Night and Sunday Morning* (1958) reject the values of the phony middle class. Yet their protagonists share Lazarillo's dream of belonging; in consequence, the angry picaresque stays within the pattern of integration characteristic of British fiction.

The American picaresque novel of the twentieth century may describe a restless small-town youth, as in John Updike's *Rabbit, Run* (1960), or a wild drive across the continent, as in Jack Kerouac's *On the Road* (1957). The present-day American rogues display an old American attitude; they try to recapture the heroic spirit of the frontier and confront the nature of humanity, of the self. The modern American *picaro* is an outsider; he may be a sensitive adolescent shunning the phony world, like Holden Caulfield in J. D. Salinger's *The Catcher in the Rye* (1951), or a man fighting the military in order to survive, like Yossarian in Joseph Heller's *Catch-22* (1961); he may be a member of a minority group—African American, like Ralph Ellison's *Invisible Man* (1952); Irish, like Ken Kesey's McMurphy in *One Flew over the Cuckoo's Nest* (1962); or Jewish, like Saul Bellow's Augie March in *The Adventures of Augie March* (1953).

Augie March is the product of the Chicago ghetto environment, the son of Jewish immigrants forced by his dehumanizing environment into a *picaro* attitude. A servant to many masters, resilient and ready to adjust, Augie ultimately refuses any attempt to be adopted and preserves his outsider status. Practical and pragmatic, he is able to do almost anything. While he is open to any new experience, he remains faithful to his own self, considering all his adventures as means to find his true identity. The Invisible Man, an African American, learns to accept his invisibility

in white America; his picaresque experiences take him through a series of rejections at the end of which he emerges as a truly protean individual and even a trickster.

A PICARESQUE RENAISSANCE

Despite the protests of purists, who felt that the term "picaresque" was being applied too loosely, in the last three decades of the twentieth century novels thus described appeared in ever-increasing numbers, as did scholarly articles about specific works and books in which the genre was discussed more generally. Not surprisingly, much of the scholarship focused on the literature of Spain and Latin America, where the tradition has always flourished, and to a lesser degree on fiction from England and America. Occurrences of the picaresque novel were also found in some unexpected places, such as Morocco and Japan.

If the latter part of the twentieth century did see not only the preservation of the genre but also a very real picaresque renaissance, it can be explained by the fact that the form is so adaptable. Danny Deck, the successful writer-protagonist in Larry McMurtry's *All My Friends Are Going to Be Strangers* (1972), has little in common with the drug-dependent drifter in Jay McInerny's *Bright Lights, Big City* (1984), which is one of the few picaresque novels written in the second person. In *All My Friends Are Going to Be Strangers*, Danny travels from Texas to California and back to Texas, sometimes stopping for a time but always moving on, until at the end of the book he comes to a halt in the borderland between Texas and Mexico, his future uncertain. By contrast, all the adventures of McInerny's *picaro* take place in Manhattan over the course of one week, with frequent flashbacks into the past, and his story ends with his realizing that he must reclaim the values he was taught in childhood. The quest of the *picaro*-narrator in Paul Auster's *Moon Palace* (1989) is also successful, though it takes some time for the aptly named Marco Stanley Fogg to realize that his own lack of purpose is rooted in his knowing nothing about his father and little about his mother, who is now dead. The scope of the novel is broadened geographically, temporally, and thematically by an interpolated narrative, a story told by the elderly man for whom Fogg works, which with the customary picaresque dependence upon happy coincidence enables the hero to identify his father and propels the hero westward across the continent to his own rebirth.

THE HISTORICAL PICARESQUE

Interjected narratives, letters, and diaries have sometimes extended the time frame of picaresque novels a short distance into the past, but as long as one aim of the genre was to satirize a corrupt society, it did not occur to writers to set such works in the distant past. Late in the twentieth century, however, a new form appeared, in which a fictional *picaro* operates within a historical setting. In his introduction to *Flashman* (1969), the British writer George MacDonald Fraser pretended to have discovered the papers of a minor character in Thomas Hughes's *Tom Brown's School Days* (1857). In this novel and in those that followed it over the next three decades, Harry Paget Flashman exposed himself as an unprincipled rogue, a lecher, and a coward who not only seduced every woman who caught his eye but also survived such episodes as the Indian Mutiny, the Charge of the Light Brigade, China's Taiping Rebellion, John Brown's raid on Harper's Ferry, and Little Big Horn, winning a reputation as a hero and eventually rising to the rank of brigadier general. Fraser's plots are exciting, but the secret of his popularity is the character of Flashman, perhaps because no matter how much he deceives others, he is always honest with himself.

In other picaresque novels, however, the *picaro* is very different from Lazarillo de Tormes or Flashman. A first-person narrator with a need to survive, the *picaro* candidly relates his adventures, while also serving as an observer. Having attached himself to a historical figure, the *picaro* talks with and observes him or her, thus presenting the author's interpretation of history. In E. L. Doctorow's *Billy Bathgate* (1989), for example, the title character is involved with the Depression-era gangster Dutch Schultz, and in Larry McMurtry's *Anything for Billy* (1988), the inept train robber Ben Sippy develops a real affection for Billy

Bone, or Billy the Kid, the legendary outlaw of the Old West. The primary goal of both narrators is to survive, Billy by finding a way out of the slums, Ben by fleeing from a household of females and the stifling life of a Philadelphia gentleman. However, they also have a boundless curiosity, and they knowingly risk their lives in order to satisfy it.

THE FEMINIST PICARESQUE

Another new development in the late twentieth century picaresque renaissance was the novel with a feminist slant. Though *picaras* had appeared in earlier works, such as *Moll Flanders*, now picaresque novels written by women and about women began to proliferate. They varied widely in content and in tone. Rita Mae Brown's semiautobiographical *Rubyfruit Jungle* (1973) was both a moving description of what it is like to be rejected by society and a defiant celebration of lesbianism. Margaret Atwood's *Lady Oracle* (1976) was about another kind of rebel, one who would be seen more and more frequently in fiction during the years that followed: a mature woman who becomes a runaway. Atwood's heroine, Joan Foster, a writer, is so tired of her marriage, her ongoing affair, and her fans that she decides to fake her own death and run off to Italy. By the time she is found out and forced to return, this picaresque heroine has made some important decisions about the direction her life will take.

In the 1980's, picaresque novels by female writers took many different shapes. There are dozens of fantasies by writers such as Marion Zimmer Bradley, Jo Clayton, Sharon Green, Tanith Lee, Anne Maxwell, Anne McCaffrey, and Janet Morris, all of which are feminist in philosophy and picaresque in form. The picaresque is also allied with Magical Realism, as in Isabel Allende's *Eva Luna* (1987; English translation, 1988), in which the title character survives one crisis after another with the aid of unseen powers and the force of her own imagination. Erica Jong's *Fanny: Being the True History of Fanny Hackabout-Jones* (1980) is much more like the picaresque novels of the eighteenth century, the period in which it is set. The author uses not only the language, capitalization, and punctuation of novels written in that era but also a huge cast of characters and a plot dependent on mistaken identities, chance meetings, and improbable coincidences. As in the historical novels already mentioned, the fictional Fanny meets and comments on real people; among her customers in a brothel are Dean Swift, William Hogarth, and John Cleland, whose *Fanny Hill: Or, Memoirs of a Woman of Pleasure* (1748-1749) she insists was an inaccurate account of her life. *Fanny* could well have been written in the eighteenth century, as it appears to be, were it not for the fact that the author's twentieth century sensibility and, specifically, her feminism are evident in every one of Fanny's pronouncements.

A GENRE OF LASTING VALUE

One of the reasons for the widespread use of the picaresque form at the end of the twentieth century was obviously its flexibility. It has been utilized by writers from very different cultures, representing a wide range of literary traditions, from the historical novel to Magical Realism and fantasy. Picaresque works can be confessional, autobiographical, philosophical, or savagely satirical, and their protagonists can range from the unfortunate to thoroughgoing scoundrels. Some *picaros* and *picaras* even reform. What they all share with their Spanish originals is an exuberant love of life and a determination to survive in order to enjoy it.

The picaresque renaissance in the final years of the twentieth century can also be attributed to the times themselves. The disorder, instability, and chaotic nature of the age may remind one of the transitional character of the sixteenth century. Modern men and women, dwarfed by an awareness of their lack of control over events in the outside world as well as over their own behavior, cannot hope for heroism; the best they can achieve is a kind of *picaro* status—an unwilling conformist, a rebel-victim, a picaresque saint. In the protean genre of the picaresque, sixteenth century Spanish writers created a fictional form appropriate for presenting the human predicament in an age of turmoil and instability.

Anna B. Katona,
updated by Rosemary M. Canfield Reisman

BIBLIOGRAPHY

Benito-Vessels, Carmen, and Michael Zappala, eds. *The Picaresque: A Symposium on the Rogue's Tale.* Newark, N.J.: University of Delaware Press, 1994. Specific picaresque works are discussed in most of these essays, while others deal with more general topics, such as translation. In their preface, written with a general audience in mind, the editors explain the disagreement about what constitutes picaresque literature.

Bjornson, Richard. *The Picaresque Hero in European Fiction.* Madison: University of Wisconsin Press, 1977. A history of the picaresque through the eighteenth century, presented through the examination of major works, such as *Moll Flanders* and *The Adventures of Roderick Random.* Illustrated, with copious notes and an extensive index.

Dunn, Peter N. *The Spanish Picaresque Novel.* Boston: Twayne, 1979. Traces the development of the picaresque novel in Spain, from sixteenth century versions such as *Lazarillo de Tormes* through seventeenth century tales written by Miguel de Cervantes and others. Explains distinctive qualities of the genre and demonstrates how these are continued in novels as the tradition of realistic fiction develops.

Friedman, Edward H. *The Antiheroine's Voice: Narrative Discourse and Transformations of the Picaresque.* Columbia: University of Missouri Press, 1987. Utilizing feminist assumptions and deconstructive methodology, the writer considers the effect of the author's gender and outlook on a novel with a *picara* as first-person narrator. Highly theoretical but thought-provoking. Notes, bibliography, and index.

Gutiérrez, Helen Turner. *The Reception of the Picaresque in the French, English, and German Traditions.* New York: Peter Lang, 1995. Explores ways a common tradition is adapted in various countries in Europe to meet the needs of individual writers and the expectations of the reading public. Discusses the development of the picaresque in three countries, examining examples from the sixteenth through the twentieth century.

Kaler, Anne K. *The Picara: From Hera to Fantasy*

Heroine. Bowling Green, Ohio: Bowling Green State University Popular Press, 1991. After outlining the relationship among the *picara*, the *picaro*, and picaresque literature, the author considers the six characteristics that differentiate a *picara* from a *picaro*. Kaler points to many *picaras* in contemporary literature, notably in fantasies. Bibliography and index.

Miller, Stuart. *The Picaresque Novel*. Cleveland, Ohio: Press of Case Western Reserve University, 1967. Miller scrutinizes six works in order to arrive at a definition of the genre. The book is still valuable, not only because of Miller's comments about technical matters but also because of its accessibility. Notes, bibliography, and index.

Monteser, Frederick. *The Picaresque Element in Western Literature*. University: University of Alabama Press, 1975. Traces the picaresque novel from its Spanish beginnings into France, Germany, Britain, Latin America, and the United States but concludes that American society is now constituted so as to make the existence of a *picaro* impossible. Includes chronological list of works, notes, bibliography, and index.

Parker, Alexander Augustine. *Literature and the Delinquent: The Picaresque Novel in Spain and Europe, 1599-1753* Edinburgh: Edinburgh University Press, 1967. A compilation of lectures given on an important expression of the long-fiction form. Includes bibliographical references and illustrations.

Reed, Walter L. *An Exemplary History of the Novel: The Quixotic Versus the Picaresque*. Chicago: University of Chicago Press, 1981. This history of the novel in Europe compares the two traditions, helping to define the picaresque by way of contrast. Bibliographical references and index are included.

Whitbourn, Christine J., ed. *Knaves and Swindlers: Essays on the Picaresque Novel in Europe*. London: Oxford University Press, 1974. Issues addressed by various scholars range from "Moral Ambiguity in the Spanish Picaresque Tradition" to arguments for the inclusion in the picaresque canon of Denis Diderot's *Le Neveu de Rameau* (1821, 1891; *Rameau's Nephew*, 1897) and Nikolai Gogol's *Myortvye dushi* (1842, 1855; *Dead Souls*, 1887). Each essay is footnoted and followed by a brief bibliography. Indexed.

Wicks, Ulrich. *Picaresque Narrative, Picaresque Fictions: A Theory and Research Guide*. New York: Greenwood Press, 1989. In the first part of this important volume, the author examines the picaresque from a theoretical standpoint and also provides a comprehensive list of secondary sources. In the second section, Wicks analyzes more than sixty picaresque fictions, films as well as novels, in alphabetical order. Each analysis includes a short bibliography as well as information on editions, if applicable. Chronology and index.

PSYCHOLOGICAL LONG FICTION

From the ancient belief in humors to the twentieth century's psychoanalytic and pharmacological methodologies, diverse theories about the mind have affected the literary production of novelists. Categorization according to these is difficult, because authors tend to mix them and use more than they admit. Hermann Hesse's works, for example, began to overflow with the analytical psychology of C. G. Jung after the latter treated him, yet Hesse tended to belittle that influence and spoke of being closer to Sigmund Freud. Consequently, psychological long fiction is most easily categorized not according to medical theories but according to four literary techniques: playful etiology, unrepentant confession, stream of consciousness, and Kafkaesque fantasy.

PLAYFUL ETIOLOGY

Charles Baudelaire's novella *La Fanfarlo* (1847; the flaunter) attributes the idiosyncrasies of the protagonist, Samuel Cramer, to his mixed parentage (German and Chilean), French education, and heaven-bestowed partial genius. Baudelaire is thus practicing etiology—diagnosing the causes of a condition—but not with the seriousness a physician would adopt. Instead, he explains a condition through a whimsical mixture of rationales based on nature, nurture, and God. Such jocular syncretism (or, indeed, any extensive etiology) is common in fiction only from the eighteenth century onward. In Ovid's *Metamorphoses* (c. 8 C.E.; English translation, 1567), for example, although Myrrha's incestuous passion for her father creates the kind of situation that later fascinated psychologists, the narrator simply comments on it as criminal and disgusting without investigating why she should have such an unusual craving. Presumably, fate or the gods are somehow responsible. With the rise of science in the eighteenth century, however, tacit reference to supernatural influence was not enough to explain personality differences. Before the Romanticism of the early nineteenth century, the characters to be diagnosed seldom deviated far from normality and thus were little in need of lavish elucidation. Thereafter, however, neurotics and psychotics

began multiplying through a growing interest in extreme expressions of individuality.

To demonstrate this individuality, authors must at some point diagnose characters' deviance from the norm; paradoxically, since what can be thus cataloged is not uniquely individual, the authors must also show a distaste for diagnosis itself. In *Washington Square* (1880), for example, Henry James's narrator details the characters' psychological quirks quite directly, yet the story turns against such insights. The shrewd Doctor Sloper, known for diagnosing in too much detail, ruins his daughter's life by exposing her fiancé's temperament. In later works, James continues to provide etiological information, but it is filtered through points of view that render it ambiguous, as in his novella *The Turn of the Screw* (1898), which never establishes whether its ghosts are real or symptoms of a governess's hysteria. Even more complexly, the narrator of Thomas Mann's *Doktor Faustus* (1947; *Doctor Faustus*, 1948) tries to demonstrate that the genius and mental illness of the composer Adrian Leverkühn are symptoms of both Germany's brilliance and its degeneration. Moreover, the narrator's mannered prose undercuts faith in his judgments. As Mann's essays also demonstrate, he considered the complexity of life to transcend simple categories. On a somewhat less sophisticated level, his method (obsessive use of etiology, yet skepticism about its conclusions) also appears in many thrillers, including Thomas Harris's *Red Dragon* (1981) and *Silence of the Lambs* (1988). In these, both a psychoanalyst turned cannibal and the investigating detectives employ psychological profiling. To this guesswork (which is not always accurate), Harris counterpoints pervasive religious imagery, meant to give the evil an apocalyptic quality, but without reducing it to any single theory, either psychological or theological.

In *Against Interpretation and Other Essays* (1966), Susan Sontag combats the psychological and particularly the biographical study of literature. Accordingly, she peoples her novels with misfits on whom she comments in a manner that is more a parody of psychology than a reliance on it. Comparably,

Thomas Pynchon took imagery from C. G. Jung's psychological introduction to the Tibetan Book of the Dead and travestied it in his comic novel *The Crying of Lot 49* (1966). As do other of his fictions, it treats all analysis as itself a form of paranoia. Causing controversy, the "New Novelist" Alain Robbe-Grillet placed obvious allusions to Oedipus (a basic pattern in the Freudian system) throughout *Les Gommes* (1953; *The Erasers*, 1964); then he denied publicly that they were there. In her essays, Nathalie Sarraute, another New Novelist, has explained that her characterization describes "tropisms" (behaviors with which people try to control one another), but she believes that no depths lie beneath these. Citations of psychological diagnoses merely to deny or ridicule them occur on a popular level in such novels as Ken Kesey's *One Flew over the Cuckoo's Nest* (1962), in which the character Big Nurse embodies a health care system eager to label patients as a way of demeaning and bullying them.

UNREPENTANT CONFESSION

In classic psychoanalysis, discovering etiology is largely the doctor's role. The patient engages in a secular form of confession, as a result of which (unlike the religious version) no one is required to repent. Literature has followed a similar path. In Fyodor Dostoevski's *Zapiski iz podpolya* (1864; *Letters from the Underworld*, 1913; also known as *Notes from the Underground*), the narrator's almost gloating self-exposure, without purgation or salvation, broke with Christian contrition and set a model for twentieth century confessional fiction. According to literary theorist Mikhail Bakhtin, Dostoevski's later novels, at their best, consist of a dialogue of voices presented without a commenting narrator. This would make Dostoevski's works confessional throughout, but, as Bakhtin admits, Dostoevski sometimes resorts to diagnosis and etiology, as in the epilogue to *Prestupleniye i nakazaniye* (1866; *Crime and Punishment*, 1886), with an obtrusive psychology based on Christianity.

At the beginning of the twentieth century, André Gide's *L'Immoraliste* (1902; *The Immoralist*, 1930) took the confessional mode further toward secularity.

Until near the book's conclusion, its protagonist, Michel, is unaware of his homosexuality, so he cannot divulge it, except by reporting behavior he understands less than do the readers. Furthermore, since homosexuality is not an action but a latent tendency, it is not, in Christian terms, a sin; despite the guilt it instills, it does not seem susceptible to purgation. By persuasively associating the human condition with embarrassing impulses, *The Immoralist* sets a despairing tone for French fiction. This continued at least as late as Albert Camus's *La Chute* (1956; *The Fall*, 1957). Its protagonist, Clamence, is unwilling to risk his life to save a drowning man. Disillusioned by his own cowardice, Clamence abandons conventional behavior and slips into cruelty, intent on convincing everyone that his imperfection springs from an ineradicable strain within humanity itself: a fall for which there is no savior. Like Michel's homosexuality, Clamence's sadism is one of the sexual orientations that the first half of the twentieth century brought to psychological attention. That age, shocked by the repressed, appears again in Kazuo Ishiguro's nostalgic first three novels. They show how reluctant people were to discover their own destructiveness, as shown in the disguised sadomasochistic relationship between Sachiko and Mariko in *A Pale View of Hills* (1982). Although Freud argued that aggressive and sensual drives might be sublimated into cultural achievements, novelists, along with the public, tended to be dismayed at psychology's disclosure of an unconscious prone to irrationality.

With the exception of such nostalgic works as Ishiguro's, confessional fictions in the twentieth century's second half were not as easily dismayed by implacable instincts. In Anthony Burgess's *A Clockwork Orange* (1962), for example, the narrator, Alex, is a young rapist and murderer who is treated with aversion therapy so that he becomes nauseated at the thought of sex or violence. In other words, he has been coerced into being as repressed as a stereotypical Victorian. Readers are expected to condemn his psychological castration. In a victory of free will, however, he overthrows the conditioning and returns to committing mayhem. Comparably, in Orson Scott

Card and Kathryn H. Kidd's *Lovelock* (1994), the narrator is an artificially enhanced capuchin monkey, who, like Alex, must overcome his conditioning to be capable of sex and violence. Here, even more clearly than in *A Clockwork Orange*, evil is an animal side of the mind to be freed. Liberation of the bestial permeates many first-person works that were popular in the 1960's, such as Jack Kerouac's *The Dharma Bums* (1958) and John Barth's *Giles Goat-Boy* (1966). Although more conscious of evil than Kerouac, Barth makes psychological liberation sound relatively innocent compared with Burgess, whose acute awareness of human destructiveness is more typical of British fiction, such as J. G. Ballard's *Crash* (1973), which is about taking sadomasochistic joy in automobile accidents.

Perhaps because the nature of drama predisposes it to public rituals, in such plays as Peter Shaffer's *Equus* (1973) and in countless movies, psychoanalysis itself forms a setting for confession. In first-person fiction, however, the closest analogy to it is the relationship between narrator and reader. When psychoanalyst-like figures are present in fiction, they are often disguised to emphasize either the negative or positive associations of psychiatry. Thus, fresh from a productive therapy with Jung, Hesse made the rebellious, precocious title character of *Demian* (1919; English translation, 1923) into its narrator's unofficial analyst. Similarly, in J. D. Salinger's Glass family saga (such as in "Seymour: An Introduction," 1963), although family members sometimes find themselves on a psychiatrist's couch, the older brothers, one of whom commits suicide. combine the functions of guru and therapist. Whether the analyst is a cannibal or a friend who helps people live with their sins, the process has less to do with penitence and forgiveness than with providing the readers entertainingly shocking revelations about what Joseph Conrad, in his 1902 novel of the same name, termed humanity's heart of darkness.

STREAM OF CONSCIOUSNESS

According to Keith M. May's *Out of the Maelstrom: Psychology and the Novel in the Twentieth Century* (1977), stream of consciousness—an attempt to represent barely conscious thinking—belongs to a relatively brief period when the two world wars forced people to recognize human irrationality. Significantly, May omits the fact that Édouard Dujardin's stream-of-consciousness novel *Les Lauriers sont coupés* (1888; *We'll to the Woods No More*, 1938) was published long before World War I. More perceptively, Dorrit Cohn contends that ungrammatical fragments in stream of consciousness approximate a deep stratum of the mind, since the psycholinguist Lev Semenovich Vygotsky has demonstrated such incoherence to be its nature.

According to Shiv Kumar, psychologist William James originated the phrase "stream of consciousness" in 1890, but its introduction to literary criticism occurred in a 1918 article on Dorothy Richardson. In her *Pilgrimage* (1938, 1967), Richardson confines herself to her protagonist's consciousness, without providing the customary information readers expect early in a book. For example, only after fifty pages does one learn that the character is a teenager. As Katherine Mansfield did for the short story, Richardson brought the stream of consciousness into the English novel, but she is far less important than its major practitioners: Virginia Woolf, James Joyce, and William Faulkner.

The first of Woolf's novels to employ the technique is *Jacob's Room* (1922), about the life of an Englishman who dies in World War I. It repeatedly marks characters' inattention to traditional religion even when church bells chime in the background. (Her generation associated stream of consciousness with a world that was replacing theology with psychology.) By focusing on a single day, her next novel, *Mrs. Dalloway* (1925), achieves greater intensity in the depiction of relatively plotless mental flux. A unifying element, though, is repeated reference to Septimus Smith, who consults a psychiatrist and kills himself to avoid another physician. On an extreme level, his suicide parallels the importance internal events have for the other characters.

Although "stream of consciousness" means something slightly different in each novelist's works, Joyce shows the greatest range of techniques. In his *A Portrait of the Artist as a Young Man* (serial 1914-1915, book 1916), most sections are in third person, but they are so attuned to their protagonist's developing mind that they range from baby talk (in the earlier ones) to the erudition of an educated young man (in the concluding ones). His *Ulysses* (1922), however, unifies each section by parodying some genre or style, such as journalistic prose or expressionist drama. The last section, rendering the mind of Molly Bloom as she falls asleep, is an unpunctuated flow of words that particularly suits the term "stream of consciousness." Her monologue should not be confused with works whose authors simply provide their own musings. In the first draft of *On the Road* (1957), for example, Jack Kerouac, at maximum speed, wrote the whole as a single, unedited sentence to achieve spontaneous self-revelation. In contrast, Joyce is distancing himself from Molly's irrationality and somnolence. If "stream of consciousness" means representation of one mind at a time, then Joyce's monumental last work, *Finnegans Wake* (1939), has moved beyond it to a very nonlucid dream that takes incoherence almost to unintelligibility. Its readers enter something like C. G. Jung's collective unconscious: the whole human race's heritage of symbols.

After treating Joyce's daughter, Jung misunderstood even *Ulysses*, which he considered the spontaneous outpourings of hereditary madness, exacerbated by alcohol. Although no proof of its authors' insanity, the incoherence of stream of consciousness can well portray characters' mental aberrations. The first section of William Faulkner's *The Sound and the Fury* (1929), for example, records the barely comprehended sensory impressions occurring to Benjy, an idiot. Readers then encounter the mental contents of other witnesses to the same story, including a young man who killed himself because of incestuous feelings for his sister. Similarly, in Faulkner's next novel, *As I Lay Dying* (1930), Darl, a clairvoyant headed toward madness, is the character whose mind is most often sampled.

Although interest in stream of consciousness was fostered by the rise of psychology, the technique itself implies that a mind is being observed not clinically but telepathically; thus, Darl's clairvoyance has much in common with those who author or read stream of consciousness, which thus seems to be a composite of science and New Age concepts. Another inherent problem with stream of consciousness is that, even more than first-person confession, it diverts attention from the action to the manner of its telling. There is, though, another literary form that brings psychology and action together: Kafkaesque fantasy. This approach has become more popular than stream of consciousness as a narrative technique.

KAFKAESQUE FANTASY

Stream of consciousness views characters' minds as if the author were separate from them. In Kafkaesque literature, however, characters and their authors converge. Indeed, Kafkaesque writers tend to place images of themselves within their works. Franz Kafka calls the protagonist of *Das Schloss* (1926; *The Castle*, 1930) by Kafka's own initial, K., while the main character of *Der Prozess* (1925; *The Trial*, 1937) is Joseph K. (Kafka was named Franz after the emperor Franz-Joseph). Kurt Vonnegut puts himself in *Slaughterhouse-Five* (1969) as a minor character who describes the book's composition and thereby tells the readers that the action is imaginary. Billy Pilgrim slips back and forth through time because of an association of ideas in Vonnegut's mind. Milan Kundera makes his part in composition even more explicit by interrupting action with essays explaining how he created one character or another. In *L'Insoutenable Légèreté de l'être* (1984; *The Unbearable Lightness of Being*, 1984; in Czech as *Nesnesitelná lehkost bytí*, 1985), for example, he shapes the protagonist through meditations on living in truth as this idea is expressed by Kafka and Václav Havel. Although Kafka himself was subtler, examination of his works demonstrates that he structured events in quite as artificial a way as Kundera, with almost no attempt at verisimilitude. Rather, Kafkaesque fiction is like a lucid dream or nightmare in which the action, however exciting, is never quite real.

In non-Kafkaesque fiction, the work is a buffer between author and reader, so that they lose sight of each other. The Kafkaesque creates at least the illusion of transparency, where author and reader may glimpse one another as if they were characters. In Italo Calvino's *Se una notte d'inverno un viaggiatore* (1979; *If on a Winter's Night a Traveler*, 1981), for example, the readers take an active part in the plot; indeed, a male reader of Calvino's book is described as having a romance with a female one. This is one of the most elaborate attempts to make "you" a character, but other notable ones include Michel Butor's *La Modification* (1957; *Second Thoughts*, 1958; better known as *A Change of Heart*) and Carlos Fuentes's novella *Aura* (1962; English translation, 1965). Kafka's fragmentary *Beim Bau der Chinesischen Mauer* (1931; *The Great Wall of China*, 1933) has both a first-person narrator, related complexly to Kafka himself, and a "you" as protagonist. Like characters in nightmares, Kafkaesque protagonists may sometimes lack individual depth. Nonetheless, in its detailed probing of the authorial mind's dreaming its fictions, the Kafkaesque mode is at least as introverted and self-reflexive as are the other forms of psychological narrative.

James Whitlark

BIBLIOGRAPHY

Axthelm, Peter M. *The Modern Confessional Novel.* New Haven, Conn.: Yale University Press, 1967. Axthelm contrasts Christian confession with confessional fictions by Fyodor Dostoevski, André Gide, Jean-Paul Sartre, Albert Camus, Arthur Koestler, William Golding, and Saul Bellow.

Cohn, Dorrit. *Transparent Minds: Narrative Modes for Presenting Consciousness in Fiction.* Princeton, N.J.: Princeton University Press, 1978. Cohn divides the fictional rendering of consciousness into three modes: psycho-narration, which is both diagnosis and summary of mental contents; quoted (interior) monologue; and narrated monologue, a third-person narration that adopts the style of the character described.

Edel, Leon. *The Modern Psychological Novel.* New York: Grosset & Dunlap, 1964. This revision of Edel's *The Psychological Novel, 1900–1950* (1955) concerns modes of subjectivity in early twentieth century fiction, particularly stream of consciousness.

Kumar, Shiv K. *Bergson and the Stream of Consciousness Novel.* New York: New York University Press, 1963. Although it overemphasizes the importance of Henri Bergson on Dorothy Richardson, Virginia Woolf, and James Joyce, this book is a valuable guide to stream-of-consciousness techniques.

May, Keith M. *Out of the Maelstrom: Psychology and the Novel in the Twentieth Century.* New York: St. Martin's Press, 1977. Ranging from the beginning of the twentieth century to Jean-Paul Sartre in the 1960's, this study suggests analogies between psychology in novels and in the writings of psychologists contemporary with them.

Meurs, Jos van, ed. *Jungian Literary Criticism, 1920–1980: An Annotated Critical Bibliography of Works in English.* Metuchen, N.J.: Scarecrow Press, 1988. Along with Scarecrow's previously published *Psychoanalysis, Psychology, and Literature, a Bibliography* (1982), a good source for locating additional studies.

Whitlark, James. *Behind the Great Wall: A Post-Jungian Approach to Kafkaesque Literature.* Rutherford, N.J.: Fairleigh Dickinson University Press, 1991. Whitlark analyzes the psychological implications of Franz Kafka's fictions and of works by thirty-six authors influenced by him.

THE SCIENCE-FICTION NOVEL

The emergence of the "modern" novel in the eighteenth century, with its emphasis on narrative realism and its intimate involvement with the affairs of everyday life, is correlated with a gradual separation between mundane and imaginative fiction, a crucial breaking of categories that was later to be represented by such distinctions as that between "realism" and "romance." There have always been problems in defining the boundary that marks this categorical break, as there have always been problems in defining exactly what is meant by the term "novel," but from the end of the eighteenth century onward writers and critics have been aware of some such fundamental distinction and convinced of its propriety.

ROOTS OF SCIENCE FICTION

Many individual works lie within the borderland between mundane and imaginative fiction, but there is one entire genre that occupies a curiously ambiguous position, a genre that depends on the use of the imagination to a considerable degree but that tries to make its imaginative products responsible in some way to a realistic outlook. The names given to this genre all have a somewhat oxymoronic flavor in common: "scientific romance," "realistic romance," and "science fiction."

There are, as might be expected, two conflicting traditions in science-fiction criticism. One of these traditions stresses the close alliance between science fiction and other kinds of fantasy, and values the genre for its venturesome qualities. The other tradition emphasizes the responsibilities of the conscientious science-fiction writer in maintaining a firm base within scientific possibility and in the avoidance of any traffic with the occult. Brian Aldiss, in *The Billion Year Spree* (1973; revised as *The Trillion Year Spree*, 1986), suggests that science fiction is "characteristically cast in the Gothic or post-Gothic mode" and traces its ancestry from Mary Shelley's *Frankenstein* (1818). Robert Heinlein, by contrast, contributes to a symposium on *The Science Fiction Novel* (1959), introduced by Basil Davenport, a spirited defense of science fiction as a species of realistic fiction, likening the method of science-fiction writers to the scientific method itself.

Not unnaturally, adherents of these two views differ markedly on the issue of which texts should be labeled "science fiction" and which ought to be cast out as pretenders. Everyone agrees, though, that publishers and critics tend to use the label irresponsibly—on one hand, extending it promiscuously to cover stories that are "really" fantasy, and on the other hand, refraining from its use in respect of many prestigious works that, though "really" science fiction, might somehow be stigmatized or devalued if they were so named in open court.

Despite the fact that several different histories of science fiction have been compiled by adherents of different definitions, it is to the history and development of the genre that one is inclined to turn in the hope of discovering a reasonable analysis of the genre's characteristics and relationships with other literary traditions.

There is, in fact, no evidence whatsoever of a coherent tradition of literary endeavor extending from *Frankenstein* to more recent science fiction. Although there were echoes of gothic freneticism in a few of the works produced in the last decades of the nineteenth century, when fiction recognizably akin to what today bears the label began to proliferate, most of it was very different in character.

One can recognize four main stimuli that encouraged writers in the late nineteenth century to produce more-or-less careful and conscientious works about imaginary inventions, future societies, and alien worlds. The first was the revolution in transportation, which brought the products of the Industrial Revolution into the everyday world of the middle classes in the shape of steam locomotives and steamships. This stimulated the growth of the novel of imaginary tourism, the greatest and most popular exponent of which was Jules Verne, author of *Voyage au centre de la terre* (1864; *A Journey to the Centre of the Earth*, 1872), *De la terre à la lune* (1865; *From the Earth to the Moon*, 1873), and *Vingt mille lieues sous les mers* (1869-1870; *Twenty Thousand Leagues Under the*

Sea, 1873). Most of the early novels of space travel have a distinctively Vernian flavor and represent the more ambitious extreme of this particular subspecies. Examples include *Across the Zodiac* (1880), by Percy Greg, and *A Columbus of Space* (1909), by Garrett P. Serviss.

A second important stimulus was the discussion provoked by the publication of Charles Darwin's *On the Origin of Species by Means of Natural Selection* (1859) and *The Descent of Man, and Selection in Relation to Sex* (1871). Literary reconstructions of the prehistoric past became common, and so did speculations regarding the possible evolutionary future of humankind. The most famous examples are *The Time Machine: An Invention* (1895), by H. G. Wells, and *The Hampdenshire Wonder* (1911), by John D. Beresford.

The same period saw a revitalization of speculation about the possibilities of social and political reform by virtue of increasing awareness of the extent that technology might encourage—and perhaps even compel—dramatic changes in the social and political order. Edward Bellamy's *Looking Backward: 2000-1887* (1888) became a runaway best-seller in the United States and provoked numerous replies in kind, including *News from Nowhere* (1890), by William Morris, and *Cuesar's Column* (1890), by Ignatius Donnelly. Whereas Morris's novel was one of many offering an alternative manifesto for the future utopia, Donnelly's was the first in what was later to become a thriving tradition of "dystopian" works developing the hypothesis that the world was getting worse and not better and that technology would help to secure its damnation.

The last important stimulus that proved prolific in this period was the anticipation of war in Europe and the fascination of exploring the potential of new weapons. George Griffith, in *The Angel of the Revolution* (1893), presented a dramatic image of war fought with aircraft and submarines, and this too became a continual preoccupation in the work of H. G. Wells, the most eclectic imaginative writer of the period, reflected in such works as *The War in the Air, and Particularly How Mr. Bert Smallways Fared While It Lasted* (1908) and *The World Set Free: A Story of Mankind* (1914).

The perception by readers and writers that these disparate literary subspecies had something fundamental in common sent critics and publishers in search of a category label. The one most widely used at the time was "scientific romance."

The supposedly realistic quality of these stories was prejudiced in several different ways. For one thing, the writers were primarily interested in the more melodramatic implications of the premises on which they worked, and this led them toward the production of highly colored thrillers rather than sober speculations about the role of science and technology in future human affairs. This was largely a matter of the markets for which the authors worked: The advent of scientific romance coincided with an expansion of literacy and a corollary expansion of the kinds of reading matter that were available. It became possible for the first time for a fairly large number of writers to make a living from their work, provided that they appealed to a wide audience, and most of the successful science-fiction writers belonged to this cadre of new professionals.

Second, and perhaps more important, a realistic approach had to be compromised by the use of literary devices. It was not possible for Jules Verne to describe the operation of a genuinely sophisticated submarine or for George Griffith to describe a workable airship. Both writers had to guess what kind of physical principles such craft would depend on. Both, not surprisingly, guessed incorrectly. A more serious problem was faced by Wells in *The Time Machine* when he wished to expose for contemplation the long-term future of the human race and the planet earth. No matter how well based in evolutionary theory his images of the future might be, in order to embed them in a literary work he needed a means of transporting an observer to report back news of them, and that means could only be a pure invention. Spaceships, too, are used in much science fiction simply as a literary device for opening up the immense imaginative territories provided by an infinite range of alien worlds. Whereas Verne, in *From the Earth to the Moon*, was concerned with the spaceship as a vehicle, an artifact in its own right, Wells, in *The First Men in the Moon* (1901), simply wanted a way to get his characters to the moon so that they could investigate the mysteries of Selenite society and provide an eyepiece for a serious exercise in speculative sociology.

Science fiction has no option but to rely upon such literary devices; there is no other way to avoid the logical trap pointed out by Karl Popper in the introduction to *The Poverty of Historicism* (1957)—that it is by definition impossible to know today what new knowledge will materialize tomorrow. Writers attempt to conceal the arbitrariness of these devices by the use of scientific or pseudoscientific jargon, which creates an illusion of plausibility, but this is merely laying a carpet over a hole in the floor.

The imaginative realms to which the writers of scientific romance built literary highways were soon invaded by writers who were not in the least concerned with fidelity to scientific possibility, but who merely wanted new playgrounds to incorporate into their dreams. There grew up, especially in the United States, a tradition of exotic interplanetary romance founded in the works of Edgar Rice Burroughs, author of *A Princess of Mars* (1917). Burroughs was the first of many to exploit a rich new vocabulary of ideas in the service of a purely romantic fiction. He set his fantasies in an imaginary world inside the earth and in a variety of undiscovered islands on its surface, as well as on other planets. The closest British parallel is to be found in Arthur Conan Doyle's novel *The Lost World* (1912), though the tradition has many affinities with the work of H. Rider Haggard.

When, in the 1920's, Hugo Gernsback began publishing pulp magazines in the United States specializing in science fiction, he issued a prospectus that strongly emphasized fidelity to scientific fact and the careful exploration of technological possibility, but in his own and rival magazines exotic interplanetary romance quickly took over. The audience that supported the pulp magazines demanded thrillers, the more highly colored the better. Gernsback's pretensions could not be maintained if the label "science fiction" was to be viable as a brand name for pulp fiction, and they were soon abandoned, although editorial propaganda continued to maintain a hollow pretense.

In Great Britain the situation was rather different. The literary marketplace was organized differently, and following World War I, cheap books displaced popular magazines to a large extent. The category label "science fiction" was not imported until 1945, and even "scientific romance" was not used freely or consistently. World War I had a tremendous impact on the attitudes of the nation, and postwar works of futuristic speculation were often desperately embittered. Their seriousness was rarely in doubt—many are grim stories of alarmism that try hard to impress the reader with the realistic nature of their forebodings.

There appeared a series of future war stories looking forward to the possible self-destruction of civilization, the best of which are *The People of the Ruins* (1920), by Edward Shanks; *Theodore Savage* (1922), by Cicely Hamilton; and *Tomorrow's Yesterday* (1932), by John Gloag. Anxiety about the fruits of progress also ran high, with many European writers producing bitter parables in which the lot of humankind is made worse by unwise meddling with the secrets of nature or by the appropriation by power groups of sophisticated technological means of maintaining their power. Key examples include *Továrna na absolutno* (1922; *The Absolute at Large*, 1927), by Karel Čapek, and *Brave New World* (1932), by Aldous Huxley.

GROWTH OF THE SCIENCE-FICTION NOVEL MARKET

There is a certain irony in the fact that throughout the 1920's and 1930's, the works produced in the United States labeled "science fiction" actually bear far less resemblance to commonly held notions of the nature of the genre than the unlabeled speculative fiction produced in Europe. This situation began to change, however, in the 1940's. The dominant trend in American pulp science fiction from 1938 on—closely associated with the magazine *Astounding Science Fiction* and its editor John W. Campbell, Jr.—was toward a more sensible and more scrupulous development of hypotheses, while from approximately the same date the British literary community became gradually more aware of American science fiction. By the end of the 1940's, the label was used widely in Britain by both publishers and commentators. One of the effects of World War II was that the United States and Britain were brought much more closely together in cultural as well as political terms. American science fiction began to be imported into Europe on a large scale, bringing with it a diffuse cultural context that affected the attitude of literary critics toward futuristic and speculative works.

Although virtually all the science fiction produced in Britain between the wars was in the novel form—cheap books being the main form of mass-produced fiction in Britain—this was not true of American science fiction of that period. American science fiction rarely achieved book publication before 1950, so longer works were produced mainly as magazine serials. Several pulp magazines boasted that they presented a full-length novel in every issue, but "full-length" in this context could mean anything between twenty thousand and fifty thousand words—almost never anything longer. For some thirty years after Gernsback's founding of the first science-fiction magazine in 1926, science fiction's specialist writers devoted themselves first and foremost to the production of short stories and novellas. The long science-fiction novel was virtually nonexistent in the United States until the 1960's, though British writers regularly turned out works well over 100,000 words in length, including such epics as Olaf Stapledon's *Last and First Men* (1930) and Wells's *The Shape of Things to Come: The Ultimate Resolution* (1933).

This situation changed dramatically in the 1960's, mainly because of the spectacular market success of the paperback book. Paperbacks surpassed magazines as the chief medium of popular fiction in the United States and achieved the same degree of success in Britain. Once this happened, it became inevitable that writers would switch their main effort into the writing of novels. The old pulp writers adapted—the most important among them being Campbell's star protégés, Isaac Asimov and Robert A. Heinlein. The postwar generation of magazine writers adapted too, prominent among them being Arthur C. Clarke, Frederik Pohl, Frank Herbert, John Brunner, Robert Silverberg, and Philip K. Dick. In addition, there emerged in the 1960's many new writers who made

their first impact upon the literary scene as writers of science-fiction novels, including J. G. Ballard, Samuel R. Delany, Ursula K. Le Guin, and Norman Spinrad.

There are some novelists who have always tried to avoid the science-fiction label because they consider it to carry a definite stigma by virtue of its longtime association with pulp fiction. These writers include Kurt Vonnegut, Jr., in the United States and John Wyndham in Britain, both of whom have written abundant work that would be covered by any conceivable definition of science fiction. The willingness of American mainstream writers to borrow from the imagery of science fiction and the increasing interest in the genre taken by American academics have helped to overcome this stigma to some extent. Science fiction is no longer written exclusively by specialist writers or read almost exclusively by specialist readers, and the situation of the genre within American culture is now much more similar to the situation that existed in British culture between the wars. Militating against the possibility that the most serious science-fiction novels will be taken as seriously as they deserve, however, is that fact that the invasion of the publishing category by exotic romances of various kinds has never been repelled. The category therefore continues to shelter a great deal of rather crude blood-and-thunder dream fantasy, which, by dint of sheer weight of numbers, is frequently far more evident to onlookers than that fraction of the labeled science fiction that still endeavors to offer the fruits of responsible and realistic speculation.

DYSTOPIA, CYBERPUNK, AND NEW GENRES

Arguably, the main achievement of the science-fiction novel has been in helping people become more aware of the dangers posed by new technological developments. Science fiction has always been most effective in its more alarmist and pessimistic moods, and its literary quality has been at its highest when its anxieties have run similarly high. Two science-fiction novels—Huxley's *Brave New World* and George Orwell's *Nineteen Eighty-Four* (1949)—may arguably be said to have had a greater impact on the popular imagination than any other literary works of the twentieth century. In its anticipations of social and environmental catastrophe, science fiction has been at its strongest: examples include *A Canticle for Leibowitz* (1960), by Walter M. Miller, Jr.; *The Drowned World* (1962), by J. G. Ballard; *Cat's Cradle* (1963), by Kurt Vonnegut, Jr.; *Stand on Zanzibar* (1968), by John Brunner; *Do Androids Dream of Electric Sheep?* (1968), by Philip K. Dick; and James Morrow's *This Is the Way the World Ends* (1986).

Science fiction has also succeeded in emphasizing and popularizing hopeful possibilities. It is impossible to measure the contribution made by the imaginative stimulus of science fiction to the realized dream of putting men on the moon, but there can be no doubt that the inspiration of many rocket scientists originated from their reading of science fiction.

The use of science-fiction ideas as metaphors representing facets of the human condition has increased in scope. These developments, first seen in such novels as Ursula K. Le Guin's *The Left Hand of Darkness* (1969) and Robert Silverberg's *Dying Inside* (1972), have helped open up new common ground between science fiction and the mainstream novel so that a profitable cross-fertilization of images and methods can take place. This influence can clearly be seen in such works as Margaret Atwood's *The Handmaid's Tale* (1985) and Fay Weldon's *The Cloning of Joanna May* (1989), two of the many novels that use science-fiction methods to explore the politics of feminism.

Science fiction is a uniquely changeable kind of fiction because it continually absorbs, with an alacrity that compensates for its lack of any authentic powers of foresight, the implications of contemporary advancements in technology. The rapid elaboration and microminiaturization of information technology, in parallel with the development for medical purposes of partially mechanized human cyborgs, inspired the "cyberpunk" movement in the 1980's, spearheaded by such writers as William Gibson, Bruce Sterling, and Michael Swanwick. This movement combined dystopian ideas of the disintegration of civilization with images of superhumanly enhanced individuals equipped with exotic weaponry and the ability to enter the hypothetical "cyberspace"

in which computer programs operate. Cyberpunk proved controversial because more traditionally inclined writers of "hard" (or technophilic) science fiction such as Gregory Benford and David Brin were critical of the movement's apparent moral nihilism (more reasonably regarded as moral skepticism). The emerging technologies of genetic engineering and hypothetical nanotechnologies (involving machinery whose microminiaturization has advanced by a further order of magnitude) subsequently began to feed into this kind of high-tech picaresque science fiction and soon began to make dramatic changes to the conceptual horizons of hard science fiction, as imagined in such works as Greg Bear's *Eon* (1985) and Gregory Benford's *Tides of Light* (1989).

In the meantime, however, the increasing popularity of horror and heroic fantasy fiction encouraged many writers to straddle genre boundaries in search of wider audiences. The vocabulary of ideas built up over the years by science-fiction writers became a key resource of horror writers such as Stephen King and Dean R. Koontz, while an increasing number of modern science-fiction stories were set in hypothetical alternative pasts rather than foreseeable futures—examples include James Blaylock's *Homunculus* (1986) and Brian Stableford's *The Empire of Fear* (1988). Hybrid works skillfully mixing science fiction and fantasy motifs, such as Tim Powers's *The Anubis Gates* (1983), also became increasingly common. Given that science fiction is also the label under which earnest religious fantasies such as James Morrow's *Only Begotten Daughter* (1990) are marketed, it has become more difficult than ever before to see where the boundaries of the genre lie or to dictate where they ought to lie. As long as contemporary scientific discoveries continue to transform the spectrum of possible futures at a rapid pace, it will be sensible to argue that the science-fiction novel can serve as an essential tool of psychological adaptation for those who find reasons for hope, as well as reasons for anxiety, in the advancement of science and technology.

After 1980, the "science fiction" label—often shortened to "sci-fi"—was primarily applied to films, television shows, and their spinoff merchandise, including long series of tie-in novels. Within the popular genre, text-based materials were increasingly marginalized, a process completed by the successful colonization of the major publishers' science-fiction and fantasy lists by fantasy novels. Although works of serious hard science fiction continued to appear in the 1990's, it became increasingly common for them to be individually marketed as idiosyncratic items rather than as genre products.

The miniaturization of information technology facilitated by microprocessors has demonstrated that the future of space exploration rests with tiny machines that do not require the elaborate ecological support necessary to sustain humans in space. The image of the future as a gradual conquest of space, which obtained a broad consensus among science-fiction novelists of the 1940's that survived the 1980's, has in consequence been banished to the realms of fantasy, although "planetary romances" set on remote worlds remain an effective crucible for thought experiments in social design.

Intellectually respectable science-fiction novels of the 1990's that dealt with extraterrestrial futures were forced to see humankind's expansion into space in terms that were far more problematic, as in Kim Stanley Robinson's trilogy that began with *Red Mars* (1993) and in Stephen Baxter's *Titan* (1997), or more far-reaching, as in Greg Egan's *Diaspora* (1997). Those novelists who accepted that the foreseeable future would be earthbound became, by necessity, more preoccupied with the seemingly high probability that the twenty-first century would be beset by a complex, interlinked series of ecological and sociopolitical crises; notable attempts to plot hypothetical historical routes through these crises include David Brin's *Earth* (1990), Marge Piercy's *He, She, and It* (1991), and Octavia Butler's *Parable of the Sower* (1993). As the intellectually ambitious elements of science fiction are reabsorbed into the literary mainstream, abandoning the "sci-fi" marketing category to films, television shows, computer games, and toys, this will presumably remain the core activity of literary futurists.

Brian Stableford

BIBLIOGRAPHY

Aldiss, Brian W., and David Wingrove. *The Trillion Year Spree: The History of Science Fiction*. London: Victor Gollancz, 1986. An updated version of a history first published in 1973 as *The Billion Year Spree*.

Barron, Neil. *Anatomy of Wonder 4: A Critical Guide to Science Fiction*. New Providence, N.J.: R. R. Bowker, 1995. The fourth edition of a library guide whose chapters are supplemented by extensively annotated bibliographies of key texts. The section dealing with fiction includes a four-part history and a chapter on "young adult" science fiction, while the section "Secondary Literature and Research Aids" includes chapters on general reference works, history and criticism, and author studies.

Bleiler, Everett F., and Richard J. Bleiler, eds. *Science Fiction Writers: Critical Studies of the Major Writers from the Early Nineteenth Century to the Present Day*. 2d ed. New York: Scribner's, 1998. An updated and expanded version of a collection of critical and biographical essays whose first version (edited by the elder Bleiler alone) appeared in 1982.

Clarke, I. F. *The Pattern of Expectation: 1644-2001*. London: Jonathan Cape, 1979. A comprehensive study of the development of rationally based images of the future and their fictional deployment.

Clute, John, and Peter Nicholls, eds. *The Encyclopedia of Science Fiction*. 2d ed. London: Orbit, 1993. The most comprehensive reference book dealing with the field, including articles on all the principal themes of the genre as well as every author to have made a detectable book-length contribution to it.

Lefanu, Sarah. *Feminism and Science Fiction*. London: The Women's Press, 1988. A comprehensive history of the roles of women in science fiction and the use of utopian and dystopian images of the future as instruments of feminist social critique.

Stableford, Brian. *Scientific Romance in Britain: 1890-1950*. London: Fourth Estate, 1985. The definitive history of the distinctive British tradition of speculative fiction.

SELF-REFLEXIVE LONG FICTION

After a few minutes of reading stories that are not self-reflexive, readers sometimes forget what they are doing and feel transported into the world of the book. Considering this experience naïve, authors of self-reflexive fictions thwart it by such devices as commenting on their own composition and focusing on storytellers as characters. To some extent, literary self-awareness has existed at least since *Gilgamesh* (c. 3000 B.C.E.), which mentions its being recorded on stone, but that single reference is not enough to make it very self-reflexive. Truly self-reflexive fictions fall roughly into four levels of introspection: misguided self-consciousness, in which narrators examine their own words, seeking an elusive self-understanding; the *Künstlerroman* (artist's novel), a novel about the education of a writer or some other analogous artist; "self-begetting" fiction, about its own creation; and extended Midrash, which focuses on its position within literature by combining narrative with literary criticism. Self-reflexive authors tend to use language that is surprisingly contrived or casual, or to deviate from convention in countless other ways; this deviation highlights the text itself, thus making its portrayal of the world seem less real. This effect, called metafiction, is common to all self-reflexive works, though it is usually more extreme in each successive level.

MISGUIDED SELF-CONSCIOUSNESS

The malice-devoured narrator of Fyodor Dostoevski's *Zapiski iz podpolya* (1864; *Letters from the Underworld*, 1913; also known as *Notes from the Underground*) set a pattern for misguided self-consciousness in twentieth century fiction: A narrator analyzes his or her own text, indeed is often a would-be artist, but lacks sufficient insight. Irony thus divides author and narrator. For example, Humbert Humbert, the protagonist of Vladimir Nabokov's *Lolita* (1955), wishes to immortalize statutory rape as serious literature; however, his account is classified in the preface as a psychological case, and the novel is ultimately darkly comic, ridiculing Humbert Humbert. Comparably, Clyde Brion Davis's *The Great American Novel*

(1938) purports to be the diaries of a journalist who spends his whole obtuse life planning a never-written novel. The first-person voice of John Gardner's *Grendel* (1971) becomes fascinated with a narrative poet but ultimately rejects art, morality, and any other order. In fictions primarily about misguided self-consciousness, the monstrous or moronic narrator is an artist manqué.

KÜNSTLERROMAN

Near the start of *Metamorphoses* (second century; *The Golden Ass*, 1566), the author, Apuleius, predicts that its protagonist will have adventures worthy of being in a book. Although Apuleius writes the book, he declares his belief that the adventures themselves take precedence over the authorship of the story. Only with the nineteenth century did writers reach such a status that a genre arose to extol them—the *Künstlerroman*. Some of these include Johann Wolfgang von Goethe's *Wilhelm Meisters Lehrjahre* (1795-1796; *Wilhelm Meister's Apprenticeship*, 1825) and Novalis's *Heinrich von Ofterdingen* (1802; *Henry of Ofterdingen*, 1842). Like many twentieth century imitations of this type, Thomas Wolfe's *Look Homeward, Angel* (1929), *Of Time and the River* (1935), *The Web and the Rock* (1939), and *You Can't Go Home Again* (1940) are disguised autobiography, depicting an artist's disaffection from contemporary society. More original are books that try to refresh the formula, such as Hermann Hesse's *Der Steppenwolf* (1927; *Steppenwolf*, 1929). At first it seems to be a novel of misguided self-consciousness, the ravings of a mad diarist, but Hesse portrays outpourings of the unconscious as an artist's proper education. Another variant of the formula is to counterpoise the perspectives of many writer characters, as in Aldous Huxley's *Point Counter Point* (1928), André Gide's *Les Faux-monnayeurs* (1925; *The Counterfeiters*, 1927), or Laurence Durrell's *The Alexandria Quartet* (1962). In America, authors frequently labor to keep self-reflection from turning into preciosity. Consequently, a popular variant of the formula is to disguise it as masculine adventure, as in Orson Scott Card's Ender novels. The first, *Ender's*

Game (1985), seems to be about a prepubescent military leader, although his siblings become famous writers. Then, in the second volume, *Speaker for the Dead* (1986), his education is shown to have prepared him to write the scriptures for a new religion. By the end of the series, his powers as author have reached a magical dimension such that he can make characters literally live merely by imagining them. In the *Künstlerroman*, being a writer is deemed the ultimate expression of a person's potential, whereas the following level, the self-begetting novel, celebrates the author's godlike creation of a whole world.

SELF-BEGETTING NOVEL

In an attempt to define all self-reflexive long fiction, Steven G. Kellman devised the label "self-begetting novel," by which he meant a work that appears to have been written by a character within it. Although he admits that this is actually not the focus of all self-reflexive works, his phrase does suit those fictions that suggest self-enclosure by, for example, ending with references to their beginning.

Kellman sees self-begetting fiction as predominantly French, stemming from Marcel Proust's *À la recherche du temps perdu* (1913-1927; *Remembrance of Things Past*, 1922-1931, 1981). Henry Miller, in *Tropic of Cancer* (1934) and *Tropic of Capricorn* (1939), models his writer-protagonist's resistance to devouring time on Proust's work. Comparably, Jean-Paul Sartre's *La Nausée* (1938; *Nausea*, 1949) concludes with its main character, Antoine Roquentin, wishing to write a novel so that people might one day revere him the way he does a singer on a repeatedly heard record. As Kellman observes, the waitress who plays the record is named Madeleine, an allusion to Proust's madeleine cake, whose taste triggered the protagonist's paranormally vivid recollection of his past. Significantly, Michel Butor, famous for his *La Modification* (1957; *Second Thoughts*, 1958; better known as *A Change of Heart*), and Samuel Beckett, author of *Molloy* (1951; English translation, 1955), *Malone meurt* (1951; *Malone Dies*, 1956), and *L'Innommable* (1953; *The Unnamable*, 1958), have written not only self-begetting fictions but also major essays on Proust.

The aforementioned Proust-like narratives are increasingly constricted and dissatisfied with life. Miller's world is designedly more tawdry and sordid than Proust's. Sartre ventures further still into squalor, inspiring the "nausea" of Roquentin. Two decades later, rather than being by class a writer-intellectual like Roquentin, the protagonist of *A Change of Heart* works for a typewriter company, and Beckett's fictions concern barely human authors in nightmarish worlds. Kellman argues that Beckett's parodies of the tradition bring it to a close.

Anne Rice's best-selling *The Tale of the Body Thief* (1992), however, combines elements of this French tradition (such as slow movement, world-weariness, and prestigious allusion) with American self-begetting narrative (adventure, youthful perspective, and uncouth diction, as in J. D. Salinger's 1951 novel *The Catcher in the Rye*). Her French-American protagonist Lestat alternates between poetic monologues about his centuries-long self-disgust and slang-filled expressions of his immortal youth. As epigraph, Rice quotes William Butler Yeats's poem "Sailing to Byzantium," about the need to leave the transience of life for the eternity of art or of the supernatural. Lestat achieves both: He writes the book and chooses a vampiric identity, which seems the next step beyond Beckett's almost dead narrators.

More purely American is the deliberate vulgarity of Kurt Vonnegut's *Slaughterhouse-Five* (1969), a fictionalized autobiography prefaced and repeatedly interrupted by the author's discussion of its composition. To emphasize circularity, he begins the story by accurately predicting that the final word will be a bird's song endlessly reheard by Billy Pilgrim, the time-shifting protagonist.

A frequent metaphor in American self-begetting novels (including Rice's) compares the self-begetting to physically sterile but psychologically productive sexual adventures. Two groundbreaking works of this sort are Philip Roth's *Portnoy's Complaint* (1969) and Erica Jong's *Fear of Flying* (1973). These forays are fraught with shame and angst. Roth's persona ends by wondering if he has allowed the irrational to govern his writings, and Jong's protagonist at least once dreads being caught in her own book. Sexual explicitness brought *Fear of Flying* its notoriety; nonetheless, it has much in common with more restrained, feminist, self-begetting novels such as Doris Lessing's masterpiece *The Golden Notebook* (1962). Therein, the protagonist writes a series of notebooks culminating in the novel itself. This shows the closeness of the notebook form and self-begetting fiction. For example, Rainer Maria Rilke's *Die Aufzeichnungen des Malte Laurids Brigge* (1910; *The Notebooks of Malte Laurids Brigge*, 1930; also known as *The Journal of My Other Self*), although not precisely circular, frequently doubles back on itself, as Brigge keeps referring to earlier sections. His final discussion of the Prodigal Son involves the idea of cyclic return. Comparably, the diarylike structure of Kōbō Abe's *Hako otoko* (1973; *The Box Man*, 1974) is possibly solipsistic and pervaded by metaphoric use of the box as an emblem of self-containment. Despite the form's fascination with autonomy, throughout the world variants of self-begetting fiction take on local color, as N. Scott Momaday's *House Made of Dawn* (1968) does from the Native American chant that begins and ends it, making the whole into the eternally repeating song of its protagonist.

EXTENDED MIDRASH

Because of its use by such critics as Harold Bloom, the term *Midrash* has come to denote literary interpretation in narrative form. Before there was a critical term for it, extended Midrash became fashionable through James Joyce's *Ulysses* (1922), based on a massive analogy between itself and Homer's *Odyssey* (c. 800 B.C.E.), though it links itself to a vast number of other works as well. For example, its character Stephen Dedalus (protagonist of Joyce's *Künstlerroman* of 1916, *A Portrait of the Artist as a Young Man*) spends a long chapter discussing William Shakespeare's *Hamlet* in a manner applicable to *Ulysses* itself. In the same year that Joyce published the even more metafictional *Finnegans Wake* (1939), Flann O'Brien issued the almost equally experimental *At Swim-Two-Birds*, a parody of Irish literary tradition. The appearance of these works did not mark the opening of floodgates, since *Ulysses*-like extended Midrash requires readers who are able to comprehend a vertiginous play of allusions. Consequently, works of this sort are hardly plentiful. Even the most erudite readers do not always esteem them. In *Remembrance of Things Past*, for example, Proust's narrator condemned theorizing about art within a novel, likening it to leaving a price tag on a purchase.

Midrash first developed as an ancient form of Jewish biblical criticism. Some modern fictions continue applying Midrash to scriptures. For example, biblical hermeneutics are repeatedly foregrounded in Thomas Mann's multivolume *Die Geschichten Jaakobs* (1933; *Joseph and His Brothers*, 1934; also known as *The Tales of Jacob*, 1934), thereby underlining the fact that his retelling of Genesis is a speculation or even a fantasy. Its protagonist is himself both storyteller and dream interpreter, analogous to Mann himself. Comparably, Salman Rushdie's *The Satanic Verses* (1988) contains a Midrash-like dream about a character named Salman (Rushdie?) who finds that the Koran is imperfect, destroying Salman's belief in everything. This sense of unreality spreads into the dreamer's life, eventually causing him to kill himself. He has been an actor in religious roles, a part of the public's collective dreams, which mingle with their interpretation of scriptures. Caught in their pious fantasies, for much of the book he is transformed into an angel with a halo, a stereotyping that contributes to his suicidal depression.

Although stories about scriptures, myths, and fairy tales are the most common varieties of extended Midrash, authors' involvement with academia has resulted in other uses. For example, to his college class, Vladimir Nabokov presented an analysis of an apartment's structure in Franz Kafka's novela *Die Verwandlung* (1915; *The Metamorphosis*, 1936). This analysis found its way into a poem, on which a crazed exegete then expatiates, in Nabokov's novel *Pale Fire* (1962). From an even more abstract source—a structuralist conference—Italo Calvino gleaned the idea of arranging tarot cards at random. The narrators of his *Il castello dei destini incrociati* (1969, 1973; *The Castle of Crossed Destinies*, 1976) connect these arrangements simultaneously to characters in the novel and to ones from world literature. In Julian Barnes's *Flaubert's Parrot* (1984), the narrator's obsessions with love and with scholarship on Gustave Flaubert converge. Samuel Delany's series of fantasies beginning with *Tales of Nevèrÿon* (1979) wanders among his personal problems as an openly homosexual African American author, the Conan parody he is writing, and the literary theories (particularly deconstruction) that inspire the narrative. In extended Midrash, nonfiction (criticism, autobiography) and fiction converge ambiguously, creating a feeling of uncertainty that life often gives as well.

Because of its ambiguities, ironies, and complexities, extended Midrash cannot be treated as if it were a simple statement of an author's opinions. Milan Kundera, for example, objects vociferously when critics treat the essays within his fictions as if they were his own views. Rather, he insists that their function is to reveal how he invents his characters. For example, as he reveals in *L'Art du roman* (1986; *The Art of the Novel*, 1988), his ruminations on the Romantic tradition led to his devising an imaginary member of it, the character Jaromil of *La Vie est ailleurs* (1973; *Life Is Elsewhere*, 1974). In that novel, Kundera's remarks about Romanticism are meant to create this character from the outside rather than through the devices of psychological fiction. His practice has its roots in eighteenth century characterization through recognizable types. Nonetheless, Kundera's version is significantly different from this conventional stereotyping. He not only breaks the illusion of reality by spending much of his novels explaining how he devises characters, but also, through meditations on language and literature, constructs new types and narratives about them. Certain words and scenes thus repeat as motifs.

Some comparable repetition pervades all self-reflexive fiction. As *Ulysses* and *Finnegans Wake* prove, despite this iteration, self-reflexive fiction can have great length without being necessarily tedious. Nonetheless, as Robert Scholes observes, it more commonly presents its complexity within the limits of the short novel, novella, or even short story, as in the metaphysical fictions of Jorge Luis Borges. Consequently, it tends toward unconventional, multilayered, integrated condensation reminiscent of experimental poetry.

James Whitlark

BIBLIOGRAPHY

Christenson, Inger. *The Meaning of Metafiction*. Bergen: Universitetsforlaget, 1981. In addition to analyzing twentieth century metafictions, this study shows some awareness of their precursors, though not to the extent of Doody's study.

Doody, Margaret Anne. *The True Story of the Novel*. New Brunswick, N.J.: Rutgers University Press, 1996. Doody traces self-consciousness in modern fiction to that in ancient fiction, connected to the mystery religions that fostered it.

Hornby, Richard. *Drama, Metadrama, and Perception*. Cranbury, N.J.: Bucknell University Press, 1986. Although Hornby's examples come primarily from theater, the approach of this study is applicable to narrative.

Hutcheon, Linda. *Narcissistic Narrative: The Metafictional Paradox*. New York: Methuen, 1984. Hutcheon distinguishes the overt narcissism of metafiction from the covert narcissism of mystery novels, fantasy, eroticism, game structures, and puns.

Kellman, Steven G. *The Self-Begetting Novel*. New York: Columbia University Press, 1980. Although it tries to do more, this study does especially well in tracing the self-begetting strand of metafiction.

Scholes, Robert. *Fabulation and Metafiction*. Urbana: University of Illinois Press, 1979. An excellent basic resource.

Waugh, Patricia. *Metafiction: The Theory and Practice of Self-Conscious Fiction*. London: Methuen, 1984. Waugh lists and discusses typical features of metafiction.

CRITICAL
SURVEY OF
LONG FICTION

GLOSSARY OF LITERARY TERMS

Absurdism: A philosophical attitude pervading much of modern drama and fiction, which underlines the isolation and alienation that humans experience, having been thrown into what absurdists see as a godless universe devoid of religious, spiritual, or metaphysical meaning. Conspicuous in its lack of logic, consistency, coherence, intelligibility, and realism, the literature of the absurd depicts the anguish, forlornness, and despair inherent in the human condition. Counter to the rationalist assumptions of traditional humanism, absurdism denies the existence of universal truth or value.

Allegory: A literary mode in which a second level of meaning, wherein characters, events, and settings represent abstractions, is encoded within the surface narrative. The allegorical mode may dominate the entire work, in which case the encoded message is the work's primary excuse for being, or it may be an element in a work otherwise interesting and meaningful for its surface story alone. Elements of allegory may be found in Jonathan Swift's *Gulliver's Travels* (1726) and Thomas Mann's *The Magic Mountain* (1924).

Anatomy: Literally the term means the "cutting up" or "dissection" of a subject into its constituent parts for closer examination. Northrop Frye, in his *Anatomy of Criticism* (1957), uses the term to refer to a narrative that deals with mental attitudes rather than people. As opposed to the novel, the anatomy features stylized figures who are mouthpieces for the ideas they represent.

Antagonist: The character in fiction who stands as a rival or opponent to the *protagonist.*

Antihero: Defined by Seán O'Faoláin as a fictional figure who, deprived of social sanctions and definitions, is always trying to define himself and to establish his own codes. Ahab may be seen as the antihero of Herman Melville's *Moby Dick* (1851).

Archetype: The term "archetype" entered literary criticism from the psychology of Carl G. Jung, who defined archetypes as "primordial images" from the "collective unconscious" of humankind. Jung believed that works of art derived much of their power from the unconscious appeal of these images to an-

cestral memories. In his extremely influential *Anatomy of Criticism* (1957), Northrop Frye gave another sense of the term wide currency, defining the archetype as "a symbol, usually an image, which recurs often enough in literature to be recognizable as an element of one's literary experience as a whole."

Atmosphere: The general mood or tone of a work; it is often associated with setting but can also be established by action or dialogue. A classic example of atmosphere is the primitive, fatalistic tone created in the opening description of Egdon Heath in Thomas Hardy's *The Return of the Native* (1878).

Bildungsroman: Sometimes called the "novel of education," the *Bildungsroman* focuses on the growth of a young *protagonist* who is learning about the world and finding his or her place in life; typical examples are James Joyce's *A Portrait of the Artist as a Young Man* (serial 1914-1915, book 1916) and Thomas Wolfe's *Look Homeward, Angel* (1929).

Biographical criticism: Criticism that attempts to determine how the events and experiences of an author's life influence his work.

Bourgeois novel: A novel in which the values, preoccupations, and accoutrements of middle-class or bourgeois life are given particular prominence. The heyday of the bourgeois novel was the nineteenth century, when novelists as varied as Jane Austen, Honoré de Balzac, and Anthony Trollope both criticized and unreflectingly transmitted the assumptions of the rising middle class.

Canon: An authorized or accepted list of books. In modern parlance, the literary canon comprehends the privileged texts, classics, or great books that are thought to belong permanently on university reading lists. Recent theory—especially feminist, Marxist, and poststructuralist—critically examines the process of canon formation and questions the hegemony of white male writers. Such theory sees canon formation as the ideological act of a dominant institution and seeks to undermine the notion of canonicity itself, thereby preventing the exclusion of works by women, minorities, and oppressed peoples.

Character: Characters in fiction can be presented

as if they were real people or as stylized functions of the plot. Usually characters are a combination of both factors.

Classicism: A literary stance or value system consciously based on the example of classical Greek and Roman literature. While the term is applied to an enormous diversity of artists in many different periods and in many different national literatures, "classicism" generally denotes a cluster of values including formal discipline, restrained expression, reverence for tradition, and an objective rather than a subjective orientation. As a literary tendency, classicism is often opposed to *Romanticism*, although many writers combine classical and romantic elements.

Climax/Crisis: Whereas climax refers to the moment of the reader's highest emotional response, crisis refers to a structural element of plot. Crisis refers to a turning point in fiction, a point when a resolution must take place.

Complication: The point in a novel when the conflict is developed or when the already existing conflict is further intensified.

Conflict: The struggle that develops as a result of the opposition between the *protagonist* and another person, the natural world, society, or some force within the self.

Contextualist criticism: A further extension of formalist criticism, which assumes that the language of art is constitutive. Rather than referring to preexistent values, the artwork creates values only inchoately realized before. The most important advocates of this position are Eliseo Vivas (*The Artistic Transaction*, 1963) and Murray Krieger (*The Play and Place of Criticism*, 1967).

Conventions: All those devices of stylization, compression, and selection that constitute the necessary differences between art and life. According to the Russian Formalists, these conventions constitute the "literariness" of literature and are the only proper concern of the literary critic.

Deconstruction: An extremely influential contemporary school of criticism based on the works of the French philosopher Jacques Derrida. Deconstruction treats literary works as unconscious reflections of the reigning myths of Western culture. The primary myth

is that there is a meaningful world that language signifies or represents. The deconstructionist critic is most often concerned with showing how a literary text tacitly subverts the very assumptions or myths on which it ostensibly rests.

Defamiliarization: Coined by Viktor Shklovsky in 1917, the term denotes a basic principle of Russian Formalism. Poetic language (by which the Formalists meant artful language, in prose as well as in poetry) defamiliarizes or "makes strange" familiar experiences. The technique of art, says Shklovsky, is to "make objects unfamiliar, to make forms difficult, to increase the difficulty and length of perception. . . . Art is a way of experiencing the artfulness of an object; the object is not important."

Detective story: The so-called classic detective story (or mystery) is a highly formalized and logically structured mode of fiction in which the focus is on a crime solved by a detective through interpretation of evidence and ratiocination; the most famous detective in this mode is Arthur Conan Doyle's Sherlock Holmes. Many modern practitioners of the genre, however, such as Dashiell Hammett, Raymond Chandler, and Ross Macdonald, have deemphasized the puzzlelike qualities of the detective story, stressing instead characterization, theme, and other elements of mainstream fiction.

Determinism: The belief that an individual's actions are essentially determined by biological and environmental factors, with free will playing a negligible role. (See *Naturalism*.)

Dialogue: The similitude of conversation in fiction, dialogue serves to characterize, to further the plot, to establish conflict, and to express thematic ideas.

Displacement: Popularized in criticism by Northrop Frye, the term refers to the author's attempt to make his story psychologically motivated and realistic, even as the latent structure of the mythical motivation moves relentlessly forward.

Dominant: A term coined by Roman Jakobson to refer to that which "rules, determines, and transforms the remaining components in the work of a single artist, in a poetic canon, or in the work of an epoch." The shifting of the dominant in a *genre* accounts for the creation of new generic forms and new poetic epochs. For example, the rise of realism in the mid-nineteenth century indicates realistic conventions becoming dominant and romance or fantasy conventions becoming secondary.

Doppelgänger: A double or counterpart of a person, sometimes endowed with ghostly qualities. A fictional character's *Doppelgänger* often reflects a suppressed side of his or her personality. One of the classic examples of the *Doppelgänger* motif is found in Fyodor Dostoevski's novella *The Double* (1846); Isaac Bashevis Singer and Jorge Luis Borges, among others, offer striking modern treatments of the *Doppelgänger.*

Epic: Although this term usually refers to a long narrative poem that presents the exploits of a central figure of high position, the term is also used to designate a long novel that has the style or structure usually associated with an epic. In this sense, for example, Herman Melville's *Moby Dick* (1851) and James Joyce's *Ulysses* (1922) may be called epic.

Episodic narrative: A work that is held together primarily by a loose connection of self-sufficient episodes. *Picaresque novels* often have an episodic structure.

Epistolary novel: A novel made up of letters by one or more fictional characters. Samuel Richardson's *Pamela* (1740-1741) is a well-known eighteenth century example. In the nineteenth century, Bram Stoker's *Dracula* (1897) is largely epistolary. The technique allows for several different points of view to be presented.

Euphuism: A style of writing characterized by ornate language that is highly contrived, alliterative, and repetitious. Euphuism was developed by John Lyly in his *Euphues, an Anatomy of Wit* (1578) and was emulated frequently by writers of the Elizabethan Age.

Existentialism: A philosophical, religious, and literary term, emerging from World War II, for a group of attitudes surrounding the pivotal notion that existence precedes essence. According to Jean-Paul Sartre, "man is nothing else but what he makes himself." Forlornness arises from the death of God and the concomitant death of universal values, of any source of ultimate or a priori standards. Despair arises from the fact that an individual can reckon only with what depends on his or her will, and the sphere of that will is severely limited; the number of things on which he or she can have an impact is pathetically small. Existentialist literature is antideterministic in the extreme and rejects the idea that heredity and environment shape and determine human motivation and behavior.

Exposition: The part or parts of a fiction that provide necessary background information. Exposition not only provides the time and place of the action but also introduces readers to the fictive world of the story, acquainting them with the ground rules of the work.

Fantastic: In his study *The Fantastic* (1970), Tzvetan Todorov defines the fantastic as a *genre* that lies between the "uncanny" and the "marvelous." All three *genres* embody the familiar world but present an event that cannot be explained by the laws of the familiar world. Todorov says that the fantastic occupies a twilight zone between the uncanny—when the reader knows that the peculiar event is merely the result of an illusion—and the marvelous—when the reader understands that the event is supposed to take place in a realm controlled by laws unknown to humankind. Thus, the fantastic is essentially unsettling, provocative, even subversive.

Feminist criticism: A criticism advocating equal rights for women in a political, economic, social, psychological, personal, and aesthetic sense. On the thematic level, the feminist reader should identify with female characters and their concerns. The object is to provide a critique of phallocentric assumptions and an analysis of patriarchal ideologies inscribed in a literature that is male-centered and male-dominated. On the ideological level, feminist critics see gender, as well as the stereotypes that go along with it, as a cultural construct. They strive to define a particularly feminine content and to extend the *canon* so that it might include works by lesbians, feminists, and women writers in general.

Flashback: A scene in a fiction that depicts an earlier event; it can be presented as a reminiscence by a character in the story or it can simply be inserted into the narrative.

Foreshadowing: A device to create suspense or dramatic irony by indicating through suggestion what will take place in the future.

Formalist criticism: There were two particularly influential formalist schools of criticism in the twentieth century: the Russian Formalists and the American New Critics. The Russian Formalists were concerned with the conventional devices used in literature to defamiliarize that which habit has made familiar. The New Critics believed that literary criticism is a description and evaluation of its object and that the primary concern of the critic is with the work's unity. Both schools of criticism, at their most extreme, treated literary works as artifacts or constructs divorced from their biographical and social contexts.

Genre: In its most general sense, the term "genre" refers to a group of literary works defined by a common form, style, or purpose. In practice, the term is used in a wide variety of overlapping and, to a degree, contradictory senses. Thus, tragedy and comedy are described as distinct genres; the novel (a form that includes both tragic and comic works) is a genre; and various subspecies of the novel, such as the *gothic* and the *picaresque*, are themselves frequently treated as distinct genres. Finally, the term *genre fiction* refers to forms of popular fiction in which the writer is bound by more or less rigid conventions. Indeed, all these diverse usages have in common an emphasis on the manner in which individual literary works are shaped by the expectations and conventions of a particular genre: This is the subject of genre criticism.

Genre fiction: Categories of popular fiction such as the mystery, the romance, and the Western. Although the term can be used in a neutral sense, "genre fiction" is often pejorative, used dismissively to refer to fiction in which the writer is bound by more or less rigid conventions.

Gothic novel: A form of fiction developed in the eighteenth century that focuses on horror and the supernatural. In his preface to *The Castle of Otranto* (1764), the first gothic novel in English, Horace Walpole claimed that he was trying to combine two kinds of fiction, with events and story typical of the medieval romance and character delineation typical of the realistic novel. Other examples of the form are Matthew Lewis's *The Monk* (1796) and Mary Shelley's *Frankenstein* (1818).

Grotesque: According to Wolfgang Kayser (*The Grotesque in Art and Literature*, 1963), the grotesque is an embodiment in literature of the estranged world. Characterized by a breakup of the everyday world by mysterious forces, the form differs from fantasy in that the reader is not sure whether to react with humor or with horror and in that the exaggeration manifested exists in the familiar world rather than in a purely imaginative world.

Hebraic/Homeric styles: Terms coined by Erich Auerbach in *Mimesis: The Representation of Reality in Western Literature* (1953) to designate two basic fictional styles: the Hebraic, which focuses only on the decisive points of narrative and leaves all else obscure, mysterious, and "fraught with background," and the Homeric, which places the narrative in a definite time and place and externalizes everything in a perpetual foreground.

Historical criticism: In contrast to *formalist criticism*, which treats literary works to a great extent as self-contained artifacts, historical criticism emphasizes the historical context of literature; these approaches, however, need not be mutually exclusive. Ernst Robert Curtius's *European Literature and the Latin Middle Ages* (1940) is a prominent example of historical criticism.

Historical novel: A novel that depicts past historical events, usually public in nature, and features real as well as fictional people. Sir Walter Scott's Waverley novels established the basic type, but the relationship between fiction and history in the form varies greatly depending on the practitioner.

Implied author: According to Wayne Booth (*The Rhetoric of Fiction*, 1961), the novel often creates a kind of second self who tells the story—a self who is wiser, more sensitive, and more perceptive than any real person could be.

Interior monologue: Defined by Édouard Dujardin as the speech of a character designed to introduce the reader directly to the character's internal life, the form differs from other monologues in that it attempts to reproduce thought before any logical organization is imposed upon it. See, for example, Molly Bloom's long interior monologue at the conclusion of James Joyce's *Ulysses* (1922).

Irrealism: A term often used to refer to modern or postmodern fiction that is presented self-consciously as a fiction or a fabulation rather than a mimesis of external reality. The best-known practitioners of irrealism are John Barth, Robert Coover, and Donald Barthelme.

Local colorists: A loose movement of late nineteenth century American writers whose fiction emphasized the distinctive folkways, landscapes, and dialects of various regions. Important local colorists included Bret Harte, Mark Twain, George Washington Cable, Kate Chopin, and Sarah Orne Jewett. (See *Regional novel*.)

Marxist criticism: Based on the nineteenth century writings of Karl Marx and Friedrich Engels, Marxist criticism views literature as a product of ideological forces determined by the dominant class. However, many Marxists believe that literature operates according to its own autonomous standards of production and reception: It is both a product of ideology and able to determine ideology. As such, literature may overcome the dominant paradigms of its age and play a revolutionary role in society.

Metafiction: The term refers to fiction that manifests a reflexive tendency, such as Vladimir Nabokov's *Pale Fire* (1962) and John Fowles's *The French Lieutenant's Woman* (1969). The emphasis is on the loosening of the work's illusion of reality to expose the reality of its illusion. Such terms as *irrealism*, *postmodernist fiction*, "antifiction," and "surfiction" are also used to refer to this type of fiction.

Modernism: An international movement in the arts that began in the early years of the twentieth century. Although the term is used to describe artists of widely varying persuasions, modernism in general was characterized by its international idiom, by its interest in cultures distant in space or time, by its emphasis on formal experimentation, and by its sense of dislocation and radical change.

Motif: A conventional incident or situation in a fiction that may serve as the basis for the structure of the narrative itself. The Russian Formalist critic Boris Tomashevsky uses the term to refer to the smallest particle of thematic material in a work.

Motivation: Although this term is usually used in reference to the convention of justifying the action of a character from his or her psychological makeup, the Russian Formalists use the term to refer to the network of devices that justify the introduction of individual *motifs* or groups of *motifs* in a work. For example, compositional motivation refers to the principle that every single property in a work contributes to its overall effect; realistic motivation refers to the realistic devices used to make the work plausible and lifelike.

Multiculturalism: The tendency to recognize the perspectives of those traditionally excluded from the canon of Western art and literature. In order to promote multiculturalism, publishers and educators have revised textbooks and school curricula to incorporate material by and about women, minorities, non-Western cultures, and homosexuals.

Myth: Anonymous traditional stories dealing with basic human concepts and antinomies. Claude Lévi-Strauss says that myth is that part of language where the "formula *tradutore, traditore* reaches its lowest truth value. . . . Its substance does not lie in its style, its original music, or its syntax, but in the story which it tells."

Myth criticism: Northrop Frye says that in myth, "we see the structural principles of literature isolated." Myth criticism is concerned with these basic principles of literature; it is not to be confused with mythological criticism, which is primarily concerned with finding mythological parallels in the surface action of the *narrative*.

Narrative: Robert Scholes and Robert Kellogg, in *The Nature of Narrative* (1966), say that by narrative they mean literary works that include both a story and a storyteller. Narrative usually implies a contrast to "enacted" fiction such as drama.

Narratology: The study of the form and functioning of narratives; it attempts to examine what all *narratives* have in common and what makes individual *narratives* different from one another.

Narrator: The character who recounts the *narrative*, or story. Wayne Booth describes various dramatized narrators in *The Rhetoric of Fiction* (1961): unacknowledged centers of consciousness, observers, narrator-agents, and self-conscious narrators. Booth suggests that the important elements to consider in narration are the relationships among the narrator, the author, the characters, and the reader.

Naturalism: As developed by Émile Zola in the late nineteenth century, naturalism is the application of the principles of scientific *determinism* to fiction. Although it usually refers more to the choice of subject matter than to technical conventions, those conventions associated with the movement center on the author's attempt to be precise and scientifically objective in description and detail, regardless of whether the events described are sordid or shocking.

New Criticism. See *Formalist criticism.*

Novel: Perhaps the most difficult of all fictional forms to define because of its multiplicity of modes. Edouard, in André Gide's *The Counterfeiters* (1926), says the novel is the freest and most lawless of all *genres:* he wonders if fear of that liberty is not the reason the novel has so timidly clung to reality. Most critics seem to agree that the novel's primary area of concern is the social world. Ian Watt (*The Rise of the Novel*, 1957) says that the novel can be distinguished from other fictional forms by the attention it pays to individual characterization and detailed presentation of the environment. Moreover, says Watt, the novel, more than any other fictional form, is interested in the "development of its characters in the course of time."

Novel of manners: The classic example of the form might be the novels of Jane Austen, wherein the customs and conventions of a social group of a particular time and place are realistically, and often satirically, portrayed.

Novella, novelle, nouvelle, novelette, novela: Although these terms often refer to the short European tale, especially the Renaissance form employed by Giovanni Boccaccio, the terms often refer to that form of fiction that is said to be longer than a short story and shorter than a novel. "Novelette" is the term usually preferred by the British, whereas "novella" is the term usually used to refer to American works in this *genre*. Henry James claimed that the

main merit of the form was the "effort to do the complicated thing with a strong brevity and lucidity."

Phenomenological criticism: Although best known as a European school of criticism practiced by Georges Poulet and others, this so-called criticism of consciousness is also propounded in America by such critics as J. Hillis Miller. The focus is less on individual works and *genres* than it is on literature as an act; the work is not seen as an object, but rather as part of a strand of latent impulses in the work of a single author or an epoch.

Picaresque novel: A form of fiction that centers on a central rogue figure or picaro who usually tells his or her own story. The plot structure is normally *episodic*, and the episodes usually focus on how the picaro lives by his or her wits. Classic examples of the mode are Henry Fielding's *Tom Jones* (1749) and Mark Twain's *Adventures of Huckleberry Finn* (1884).

Plot/Story: Story is a term referring to the full narrative of character and action, whereas plot generally refers to action with little reference to character. A more precise and helpful distinction is made by the Russian Formalists, who suggest that plot refers to the events of a *narrative* as they have been artfully arranged in the literary work, subject to chronological displacement, ellipses, and other devices, while story refers to the sum of the same events arranged in simple, causal-chronological order. Thus, story is the raw material for plot. By comparing the two in a given work, the reader is encouraged to see the *narrative* as an artifact.

Point of view: The means by which the story is presented to the reader, or, as Percy Lubbock says in *The Craft of Fiction* (1921), "the relation in which the narrator stands to the story"—a relation that Lubbock claims governs the craft of fiction. Some of the questions the critical reader should ask concerning point of view are: Who talks to the reader? From what position does the narrator tell the story? At what distance does he or she place the reader from the story? What kind of person is he or she? How fully is he or she characterized? How reliable is he or she? For further discussion, see Wayne Booth, *The Rhetoric of Fiction* (1961).

Postcolonialism: Postcolonial literature emerged in the mid-twentieth century when colonies in Asia, Africa, and the Caribbean began gaining their independence from the European nations that had long controlled them. Postcolonial authors, such as Salman Rushdie and V. S. Naipaul, tend to focus on both the freedom and the conflict inherent in living in a postcolonial state.

Postmodernism: A ubiquitous but elusive term in contempory criticism, "postmodernism" is loosely applied to the various artistic movements that followed the era of so-called high modernism, represented by such giants as James Joyce and Pablo Picasso. In critical discussions of contemporary fiction, the term "postmodernism" is frequently applied to the works of writers such as Thomas Pynchon, John Barth, and Donald Barthelme, who exhibit a self-conscious awareness of their modernist predecessors as well as a reflexive treatment of fictional form.

Protagonist: The central character in a fiction, the character whose fortunes most concern the reader.

Psychological criticism: While much modern literary criticism reflects to some degree the impact of Sigmund Freud, Carl Jung, Jacques Lacan, and other psychological theorists, the term "psychological criticism" suggests a strong emphasis on a causal relation between the writer's psychological state, variously interpreted, and his or her works. A notable example of psychological criticism is Norman Fruman's *Coleridge, the Damaged Archangel* (1971).

Psychological novel: A form of fiction in which character, especially the inner life of characters, is the primary focus. The form has been of primary importance, at least since Henry James, and it characterizes much of the work of James Joyce, Virginia Woolf, and William Faulkner. For a detailed discussion, see *The Modern Psychological Novel* (1955) by Leon Edel.

Realism: A literary technique in which the primary convention is to render an illusion of fidelity to external reality. Realism is often identified as the primary method of the novel form: It focuses on surface details, maintains a fidelity to the everyday experiences of middle-class society, and strives for a one-to-one relationship between the fiction and the action

imitated. The realist movement in the late nineteenth century coincides with the full development of the novel form.

Reception aesthetics: The best-known American practitioner of reception aesthetics is Stanley Fish. For the reception critic, meaning is an event or process; rather than being embedded in the work, it is created through particular acts of reading. The best-known European practitioner of this criticism, Wolfgang Iser, says indeterminacy is the basic characteristic of literary texts; the reader must "normalize" the text either by projecting his or her standards into it or by revising his or her standards to "fit" the text.

Regional novel: Any novel in which the character of a given geographical region plays a decisive role. Although regional differences persist in America, there has been a considerable leveling in speech and customs, so that the sharp regional distinctions evident in nineteenth century American fiction have all but disappeared. Only in the South has a strong regional tradition persisted to the present. (See *Local colorists.*)

Rhetorical criticism: The rhetorical critic is concerned with the literary work as a means of communicating ideas and the means by which the work affects or controls the reader. Such criticism seems best suited to didactic works such as satire.

Roman à clef: A fiction wherein actual people, often celebrities of some sort, are thinly disguised.

Romance: The romance usually differs from the novel form in that the focus is on symbolic events and representational characters rather than on "as-if-real" characters and events. Richard Chase says that in the romance, character is depicted as highly stylized, a function of the plot rather than as someone complexly related to society. The romancer is more likely to be concerned with dreamworlds than with the familiar world, believing that reality cannot be grasped by the traditional novel.

Romanticism: A widespread cultural movement in the late eighteenth and early nineteenth centuries, the influence of which is still felt. As a general literary tendency, Romanticism is frequently contrasted with *classicism.* Although there were many varieties of

Romanticism indigenous to various national literatures, the term generally suggests an assertion of the preeminence of the imagination. Other values associated with various schools of Romanticism include primitivism, an interest in folklore, a reverence for nature, and a fascination with the demoniac and the macabre.

Scene: The central element of narration; specific actions are narrated or depicted that make the reader feel he or she is participating directly in the action.

Science fiction: Fiction in which certain givens (physical laws, psychological principles, social conditions: any one or all of these) form the basis of an imaginative projection into the future or, less commonly, an extrapolation in the present or even into the past.

Semiotics: The science of signs and sign systems in communication. Roman Jakobson says that semiotics deals with the principles that underlie the structure of signs, their use in language of all kinds, and the specific nature of various sign systems.

Sentimental novel: A form of fiction popular in the eighteenth century in which emotionalism and optimism are the primary characteristics. The best-known examples are Samuel Richardson's *Pamela* (1740-1741) and Oliver Goldsmith's *The Vicar of Wakefield* (1766).

Setting: Setting refers to the circumstances and environment, both temporal and spatial, of a *narrative.*

Spatial form: An author's attempt to make the reader apprehend the work spatially in a moment of time rather than sequentially. To achieve this effect, the author breaks up the *narrative* into interspersed fragments. Beginning with James Joyce, Marcel Proust, and Djuna Barnes, the movement toward spatial form is concomitant with the modernist effort to supplant historical time in fiction with mythic time. For the seminal discussion of this technique, see Joseph Frank, *The Widening Gyre* (1963).

Stream of consciousness: The depiction of the thought processes of a character, insofar as this is possible, without any mediating structures. The metaphor of consciousness as a "stream" suggests a rush of thoughts and images governed by free association rather than by strictly rational development. The term "stream of consciousness" is often used loosely as a synonym for *interior monologue.* The most celebrated example of stream of consciousness in fiction is the monologue of Molly Bloom in James Joyce's *Ulysses* (1922); other notable practitioners of the stream-of-consciousness technique include Dorothy Richardson, Virginia Woolf, and William Faulkner.

Structuralism: As a movement of thought, structuralism is based on the idea of intrinsic, self-sufficient structures that do not require reference to external elements. A structure is a system of transformations that involves the interplay of laws inherent in the system itself. The study of language is the primary model for contemporary structuralism. The structuralist literary critic attempts to define structural principles that operate intertextually throughout the whole of literature as well as principles that operate in *genres* and in individual works. The most accessible survey of structuralism and literature is Jonathan Culler's *Structuralist Poetics* (1975).

Summary: Those parts of a fiction that do not need to be detailed. In *Tom Jones* (1749), Henry Fielding says "If whole years should pass without producing anything worthy of . . . notice . . . we shall hasten on to matters of consequence."

Thematics: Northrup Frye says that when a work of fiction is written or interpreted thematically, it becomes an illustrative fable. Murray Krieger defines thematics as "the study of the experiential tensions which, dramatically entangled in the literary work, become an existential reflection of that work's aesthetic complexity."

Tone: Tone usually refers to the dominant mood of the work. (See *Atmosphere.*)

Unreliable narrator: A narrator whose account of the events of the story cannot be trusted, obliging readers to reconstruct—if possible—the true state of affairs themselves. Once an innovative technique, the use of the unreliable narrator has become commonplace among contemporary writers who wish to suggest the impossibility of a truly "reliable" account of any event. Notable examples of the unreliable narrator can be found in Ford Madox Ford's *The Good Soldier* (1915) and Vladimir Nabokov's *Lolita* (1958).

Victorian novel: Although the Victorian period extended from 1837 to 1901, the term "Victorian novel" does not include the later decades of Queen Victoria's reign. The term loosely refers to the sprawling works of novelists such as Charles Dickens and William Makepeace Thackeray—works that frequently appeared first in serial form and are characterized by a broad social canvas.

Vraisemblance/Verisimilitude: Tzvetan Todorov defines vraisemblance as "the mask which conceals the text's own laws, but which we are supposed to take for a relation to reality." When one speaks of vraisemblance, one refers to the work's attempts to make the reader believe that it conforms to reality rather than to its own laws.

Western novel: Like all varieties of *genre fiction*, the Western novel—generally known simply as the "Western"—is defined by a relatively predictable combination of conventions, *motifs*, and recurring themes. These predictable elements, familiar from the many Western series on television and in film, differentiate the Western from *historical novels* and idiosyncratic works such as Thomas Berger's *Little Big Man* (1964) that are also set in the Old West. Conversely, some novels set in the contemporary West are regarded as Westerns because they deal with modern cowboys and with the land itself in the manner characteristic of the *genre*.

Charles E. May

CHRONOLOGICAL LIST OF AUTHORS

This chronology of the authors covered in these volumes serves as a time line for students interested in the development of long fiction from ancient to modern times. The arrangement is chronological on the basis of birth years, and the proximity of writers provides students with some insights into potential influences and contemporaneous developments.

BORN UP TO 1700

Malory, Sir Thomas (early fifteenth century)
Rabelais, François (c. 1494)
Cervantes, Miguel de (September 29, 1547)
Bunyan, John (November, 1628)
Behn, Aphra (July [?], 1640)
Defoe, Daniel (1660)
Swift, Jonathan (November 30, 1667)
Richardson, Samuel (July 31 [?], 1689)
Voltaire (November 21, 1694)

BORN 1701-1800

Fielding, Henry (April 22, 1707)
Johnson, Samuel (September 18, 1709)
Diderot, Denis (October 5, 1713)
Sterne, Laurence (November 24, 1713)
Smollett, Tobias (March 19, 1721)
Goldsmith, Oliver (November 10, 1728 or 1730)
Goethe, Johann Wolfgang von (August 28, 1749)
Burney, Fanny (June 13, 1752)
Rowson, Susanna (1762)
Radcliffe, Ann (July 9, 1764)
Edgeworth, Maria (January 1, 1767)
Chateaubriand, François René de (September 4, 1768)
Brown, Charles Brockden (January 17, 1771)
Scott, Sir Walter (August 15, 1771)
Lewis, Matthew Gregory (July 9, 1775)
Austen, Jane (December 16, 1775)
Maturin, Charles Robert (September 25, 1780)
Stendhal (January 23, 1783)
Manzoni, Alessandro (March 7, 1785)
Peacock, Thomas Love (October 18, 1785)
Cooper, James Fenimore (September 15, 1789)
Shelley, Mary Wollstonecraft (August 30, 1797)
Balzac, Honoré de (May 20, 1799)
Pushkin, Alexander (June 6, 1799)

BORN 1801-1820

Hugo, Victor (February 26, 1802)
Dumas, Alexandre, *père* (July 24, 1802)
Sand, George (July 1, 1804)
Hawthorne, Nathaniel (July 4, 1804)
Simms, William Gilmore (April 17, 1806)
Gogol, Nikolai (March 31, 1809)
Gaskell, Elizabeth (September 29, 1810)
Stowe, Harriet Beecher (June 14, 1811)
Thackeray, William Makepeace (July 18, 1811)
Dickens, Charles (February 7, 1812)
Le Fanu, Joseph Sheridan (August 28, 1814)
Trollope, Anthony (April 24, 1815)
Brontë, Charlotte (April 21, 1816)
Brontë, Emily (July 30, 1818)
Turgenev, Ivan (November 9, 1818)
Melville, Herman (August 1, 1819)
Eliot, George (November 22, 1819)
Fontane, Theodor (December 30, 1819)

BORN 1821-1840

Dostoevski, Fyodor (November 11, 1821)
Flaubert, Gustave (December 12, 1821)
Collins, Wilkie (January 8, 1824)
De Forest, John William (March 31, 1826)
Verne, Jules (February 8, 1828)
Meredith, George (February 12, 1828)
Tolstoy, Leo (September 9, 1828)
Carroll, Lewis (January 27, 1832)
Alcott, Louisa May (November 29, 1832)
Twain, Mark (November 30, 1835)
Butler, Samuel (December 4, 1835)
Howells, William Dean (March 1, 1837)
Machado de Assis, Joaquim Maria (June 21, 1839)
Pater, Walter (August 4, 1839)
Zola, Émile (April 2, 1840)
Hardy, Thomas (June 2, 1840)
Verga, Giovanni (September 2, 1840)

BORN 1841-1860

Hudson, W. H. (August 4, 1841)
James, Henry (April 15, 1843)
Pérez Galdós, Benito (May 10, 1843)
France, Anatole (April 16, 1844)
Cable, George Washington (October 12, 1844)
Sienkiewicz, Henryk (May 5, 1846)
Strindberg, August (January 22, 1849)
Jewett, Sarah Orne (September 3, 1849)
Stevenson, Robert Louis (November 13, 1850)
Chopin, Kate (February 8, 1851)
Moore, George (February 24, 1852)
Wilde, Oscar (October 16, 1854)
Frederic, Harold (August 19, 1856)
Gissing, George (November 22, 1857)
Conrad, Joseph (December 3, 1857)
Chesnutt, Charles Waddell (June 20, 1858)
Lagerlöf, Selma (November 20, 1858)
Doyle, Arthur Conan (May 22, 1859)
Hamsun, Knut (August 4, 1859)
Garland, Hamlin (September 14, 1860)

BORN 1861-1880

Wharton, Edith (January 24, 1862)
Kipling, Rudyard (December 30, 1865)
Rolland, Romain (January 29, 1866)
Wells, H. G. (September 21, 1866)
Bennett, Arnold (May 27, 1867)
Pirandello, Luigi (June 28, 1867)
Galsworthy, John (August 14, 1867)
Gorky, Maxim (March 28, 1868)
Tarkington, Booth (July 29, 1869)
Gide, André (November 22, 1869)
Norris, Frank (March 5, 1870)
Proust, Marcel (July 10, 1871)
Dreiser, Theodore (August 27, 1871)
Crane, Stephen (November 1, 1871)
Azuela, Mariano (January 1, 1873)
Jensen, Johannes V. (January 20, 1873)
Colette (January 28, 1873)
Glasgow, Ellen (April 22, 1873)
Richardson, Dorothy (May 17, 1873)
Cather, Willa (December 7, 1873)
Ford, Ford Madox (December 17, 1873)
Maugham, W. Somerset (January 25, 1874)

Stein, Gertrude (February 3, 1874)
Chesterton, G. K. (May 29, 1874)
Mann, Thomas (June 6, 1875)
Buchan, John (August 26, 1875)
London, Jack (January 12, 1876)
Anderson, Sherwood (September 13, 1876)
Hesse, Hermann (July 2, 1877)
Döblin, Alfred (August 10, 1878)
Sinclair, Upton (September 20, 1878)
Forster, E. M. (January 1, 1879)
Cabell, James Branch (April 14, 1879)
Asch, Sholem (November 1, 1880)

BORN 1881-1900

Martin du Gard, Roger (March 23, 1881)
Macaulay, Rose (August 1, 1881)
Wodehouse, P. G. (October 15, 1881)
Woolf, Virginia (January 25, 1882)
Joyce, James (February 2, 1882)
Fauset, Jessie Redmon (April 27, 1882)
Undset, Sigrid (May 20, 1882)
Lewis, Wyndham (November 18, 1882)
Kazantzakis, Nikos (February 18, 1883)
Kafka, Franz (July 3, 1883)
Compton-Burnett, Ivy (June 5, 1884)
Lewis, Sinclair (February 7, 1885)
Ferber, Edna (August 15, 1885)
Lawrence, D. H. (September 11, 1885)
Tanizaki, Jun'ichirō (July 24, 1886)
Roberts, Elizabeth Madox (October 30, 1886)
Wilson, Ethel (January 20, 1888)
Chandler, Raymond (July 23, 1888)
Cary, Joyce (December 7, 1888)
Cocteau, Jean (July 5, 1889)
Aiken, Conrad (August 5, 1889)
Čapek, Karel (January 9, 1890)
Pasternak, Boris (February 10, 1890)
Porter, Katherine Anne (May 15, 1890)
Werfel, Franz (September 10, 1890)
Christie, Agatha (September 15, 1890)
Richter, Conrad (October 13, 1890)
Hurston, Zora Neale (January 7, 1891)
Lagerkvist, Pär (May 23, 1891)
Miller, Henry (December 26, 1891)
Tolkien, J. R. R. (January 3, 1892)

Buck, Pearl S. (June 26, 1892)
Cain, James M. (July 1, 1892)
Andrič, Ivo (October 10, 1892)
West, Rebecca (December 21, 1892)
Sayers, Dorothy L. (June 13, 1893)
Céline, Louis-Ferdinand (May 27, 1894)
Hammett, Dashiell (May 27, 1894)
Huxley, Aldous (July 26, 1894)
Rhys, Jean (August 24, 1894)
Priestley, J. B. (September 13, 1894)
Giono, Jean (March 30, 1895)
Graves, Robert (July 24, 1895)
Gordon, Caroline (October 6, 1895)
Hartley, L. P. (December 30, 1895)
Dos Passos, John (January 14, 1896)
Cronin, A. J. (July 19, 1896)
Rawlings, Marjorie Kinnan (August 8, 1896)
Fitzgerald, F. Scott (September 24, 1896)
Wilder, Thornton (April 17, 1897)
Faulkner, William (September 25, 1897)
Powell, Dawn (November 28, 1897)
O'Brien, Kate (December 3, 1897)
Remarque, Erich Maria (June 22, 1898)
Lewis, C. S. (November 29, 1898)
Nabokov, Vladimir (April 23, 1899)
Bowen, Elizabeth (June 7, 1899)
Kawabata, Yasunari (June 11, 1899)
Hemingway, Ernest (July 21, 1899)
Asturias, Miguel Ángel (October 19, 1899)
Silone, Ignazio (May 1, 1900)
Saint-Exupéry, Antoine de (June 29, 1900)
Wolfe, Thomas (October 3, 1900)
Pritchett, V. S. (December 16, 1900)

BORN 1901-1910

Lehmann, Rosamond (February 3, 1901)
Wescott, Glenway (April 11, 1901)
Malraux, André (November 3, 1901)
Boyle, Kay (February 19, 1902)
Steinbeck, John (February 27, 1902)
Stead, Christina (July 17, 1902)
Waters, Frank (July 25, 1902)
Bontemps, Arna (October 13, 1902)
Paton, Alan (January 11, 1903)
Simenon, Georges (February 13, 1903)

Nin, Anaïs (February 21, 1903)
Callaghan, Morley (February 22, 1903)
Yourcenar, Marguerite (June 8, 1903)
Orwell, George (June 25, 1903)
Horgan, Paul (August 1, 1903)
Mallea, Eduardo (August 14, 1903)
Cozzens, James Gould (August 19, 1903)
West, Nathanael (October 17, 1903)
Waugh, Evelyn (October 28, 1903)
Caldwell, Erskine (December 17, 1903)
Farrell, James T. (February 27, 1904)
Singer, Isaac Bashevis (July 14 or November 21, 1904)
Gombrowicz, Witold (August 4, 1904)
Greene, Graham (October 2, 1904)
Carpentier, Alejo (December 26, 1904)
O'Hara, John (January 31, 1905)
Rand, Ayn (February 2, 1905)
Warren, Robert Penn (April 24, 1905)
Sholokhov, Mikhail (May 24, 1905)
Sartre, Jean-Paul (June 21, 1905)
Canetti, Elias (July 25, 1905)
Renault, Mary (September 4, 1905)
Koestler, Arthur (September 5, 1905)
Snow, C. P. (October 15, 1905)
Green, Henry (October 29, 1905)
Powell, Anthony (December 21, 1905)
Beckett, Samuel (April 13, 1906)
White, T. H. (May 29, 1906)
Narayan, R. K. (October 10, 1906)
Michener, James A. (February 3, 1907[?])
MacLennan, Hugh (March 20, 1907)
Du Maurier, Daphne (May 13, 1907)
Stuart, Jesse (August 8, 1907)
Moravia, Alberto (November 28, 1907)
Beauvoir, Simone de (January 9, 1908)
L'Amour, Louis (March 22, 1908)
Prokosch, Frederic (May 17, 1908)
Saroyan, William (August 31, 1908)
Wright, Richard (September 4, 1908)
Pavese, Cesare (September 9, 1908)
Stegner, Wallace (February 18, 1909)
Algren, Nelson (March 28, 1909)
Welty, Eudora (April 13, 1909)
Lowry, Malcolm (July 28, 1909)

Himes, Chester (July 29, 1909)
Clark, Walter Van Tilburg (August 3, 1909)
Agee, James (November 27, 1909)
Morris, Wright (January 6, 1910)
De Vries, Peter (February 27, 1910)
Doerr, Harriet (April 8, 1910)
Genet, Jean (December 19, 1910)
Bowles, Paul (December 30, 1910)

BORN 1911-1920

Goodman, Paul (September 9, 1911)
Golding, William (September 19, 1911)
O'Brien, Flann (October 5, 1911)
Mahfouz, Naguib (December 11, 1911)
Durrell, Lawrence (February 27, 1912)
Sarton, May (May 3, 1912)
Cheever, John (May 27, 1912)
White, Patrick (May 28, 1912)
McCarthy, Mary (June 21, 1912)
Amado, Jorge (August 10, 1912)
Pym, Barbara (June 2, 1913)
Wilson, Angus (August 11, 1913)
Cyrano de Bergerac (August 28, 1913)
Simon, Claude (October 10, 1913)
Camus, Albert (November 7, 1913)
Burroughs, William S. (February 5, 1914)
Ellison, Ralph (March 1, 1914)
Duras, Marguerite (April 4, 1914)
Malamud, Bernard (April 26, 1914)
Hersey, John (June 17, 1914)
Cortázar, Julio (August 26, 1914)
Wouk, Herman (May 27, 1915)
Bellow, Saul (June 10, 1915)
Gonzalez, N. V. M. (September 8, 1915)
Macdonald, Ross (December 13, 1915)
Fielding, Gabriel (March 25, 1916)
Cela, Camilo José (May 11, 1916)
Percy, Walker (May 28, 1916)
Yerby, Frank (September 5, 1916)
McCullers, Carson (February 19, 1917)
Burgess, Anthony (February 25, 1917)
Powers, J. F. (July 8, 1917)
Auchincloss, Louis (September 27, 1917)
Clarke, Arthur C. (December 16, 1917)
Böll, Heinrich (December 21, 1917)

Spark, Muriel (February 1, 1918)
Sturgeon, Theodore (February 26, 1918)
Settle, Mary Lee (July 29, 1918)
Solzhenitsyn, Aleksandr (December 11, 1918)
Salinger, J. D. (January 1, 1919)
Murdoch, Iris (July 15, 1919)
Levi, Primo (July 31, 1919)
Lessing, Doris (October 22, 1919)
Tutuola, Amos (1920)
Asimov, Isaac (January 2, 1920)
Adams, Richard (May 9, 1920)
James, P. D. (August 3, 1920)
Bradbury, Ray (August 22, 1920)

BORN 1921-1930

Highsmith, Patricia (January 19, 1921)
Harris, Wilson (March 24, 1921)
Moore, Brian (August 25, 1921)
Lem, Stanisław (September 12, 1921)
Jones, James (November 6, 1921)
Kerouac, Jack (March 12, 1922)
Amis, Kingsley (April 16, 1922)
Robbe-Grillet, Alain (August 18, 1922)
Vonnegut, Kurt, Jr. (November 11, 1922)
Gaddis, William (December 29, 1922)
Kemal, Yashar (1923)
Mailer, Norman (January 31, 1923)
Dickey, James (February 2, 1923)
Heller, Joseph (May 1, 1923)
Jolley, Elizabeth (June 4, 1923)
Purdy, James (July 14, 1923)
Calvino, Italo (October 15, 1923)
Gordimer, Nadine (November 20, 1923)
Berger, Thomas (July 20, 1924)
Gass, William H. (July 30, 1924)
Baldwin, James (August 2, 1924)
Connell, Evan S., Jr. (August 17, 1924)
Škvorecký, Josef (September 27, 1924)
Capote, Truman (September 30, 1924)
Donoso, José (October 5, 1924)
Mishima, Yukio (January 14, 1925)
Wain, John (March 14, 1925)
O'Connor, Flannery (March 25, 1925)
Styron, William (June 11, 1925)
Vidal, Gore (October 3, 1925)

Leonard, Elmore (October 11, 1925)
Williams, John A. (December 5, 1925)
Lispector, Clarice (December 10, 1925)
Fowles, John (March 31, 1926)
Donleavy, J. P. (April 23, 1926)
Lee, Harper (April 28, 1926)
Laurence, Margaret (July 18, 1926)
Lurie, Alison (September 3, 1926)
Knowles, John (September 16, 1926)
Wallant, Edward Lewis (October 19, 1926)
Jhabvala, Ruth Prawer (May 7, 1927)
Matthiessen, Peter (May 22, 1927)
Grass, Günter (October 16, 1927)
Kennedy, William (January 16, 1928)
García Márquez, Gabriel (March 6, 1928)
Ozick, Cynthia (April 17, 1928)
Trevor, William (May 24, 1928)
Brookner, Anita (July 16, 1928)
Wiesel, Elie (September 30, 1928)
Fuentes, Carlos (November 11, 1928)
Dick, Philip K. (December 16, 1928)
Hinojosa, Rolando (January 21, 1929)
Potok, Chaim (February 17, 1929)
Wolf, Christa (March 18, 1929)
Kundera, Milan (April 1, 1929)
Marshall, Paule (April 9, 1929)
Grau, Shirley Ann (July 8, 1929)
Le Guin, Ursula K. (October 21, 1929)
Highwater, Jamake (probably early 1930's)
West, Paul (February 23, 1930)
Elkin, Stanley (May 11, 1930)
Barth, John (May 27, 1930)
Bradley, Marion Zimmer (June 3, 1930)
McElroy, Joseph (August 21, 1930)
Ballard, J. G. (November 15, 1930)
Achebe, Chinua (November 16, 1930)
O'Brien, Edna (December 15, 1930)

BORN 1931-1940

Doctorow, E. L. (January 6, 1931)
Richler, Mordecai (January 27, 1931)
Morrison, Toni (February 18, 1931)
Wolfe, Tom (March 2, 1931)
Barthelme, Donald (April 7, 1931)
Weldon, Fay (September 22, 1931)

Le Carré, John (October 19, 1931)
Coover, Robert (February 4, 1932)
Updike, John (March 18, 1932)
Dunne, John Gregory (May 25, 1932)
Naipaul, V. S. (August 17, 1932)
Hoagland, Edward (December 21, 1932)
Puig, Manuel (December 28, 1932)
Gaines, Ernest J. (January 15, 1933)
Price, Reynolds (February 1, 1933)
Lively, Penelope (March 17, 1933)
Roth, Henry (March 19, 1933)
Kosinski, Jerzy (June 14, 1933)
McCarthy, Cormac (July 20, 1933)
Gardner, John (July 21, 1933)
Madden, David (July 25, 1933)
Malouf, David (March 20, 1934)
Soyinka, Wole (July 13, 1934)
Berry, Wendell (August 5, 1934)
Didion, Joan (December 5, 1934)
Lodge, David (January 28, 1935)
Brautigan, Richard (January 30, 1935)
Ōe, Kenzaburō (January 31, 1935)
Kesey, Ken (September 17, 1935)
Keneally, Thomas (October 7, 1935)
Vargas Llosa, Mario (March 28, 1936)
McMurtry, Larry (June 3, 1936)
DeLillo, Don (November 20, 1936)
Wambaugh, Joseph (January 22, 1937)
McGinley, Patrick (February 8, 1937)
Pynchon, Thomas (May 8, 1937)
Godwin, Gail (June 18, 1937)
Desai, Anita (June 24, 1937)
Stone, Robert (August 21, 1937)
Anaya, Rudolfo A. (October 30, 1937)
Kelley, William Melvin (November 1, 1937)
Harrison, Jim (December 11, 1937)
Ngugi wa Thiong'o (January 5, 1938)
Reed, Ishmael (February 22, 1938)
Oates, Joyce Carol (June 16, 1938)
Armah, Ayi Kwei (1939)
Bambara, Toni Cade (March 25, 1939)
Young, Al (May 31, 1939)
Drabble, Margaret (June 5, 1939)
Chase-Riboud, Barbara (June 26, 1939)
Atwood, Margaret (November 18, 1939)

McGuane, Thomas (December 11, 1939)
Coetzee, J. M. (February 9, 1940)
Plante, David (March 4, 1940)
Carter, Angela (May 7, 1940)
Chatwin, Bruce (May 13, 1940)

BORN SINCE 1941

Theroux, Paul (April 10, 1941)
Wideman, John Edgar (June 14, 1941)
Rice, Anne (October 4, 1941)
Tyler, Anne (October 25, 1941)
Woiwode, Larry (October 30, 1941)
Irving, John (March 2, 1942)
De la Mare, Walter (April 1, 1942)
Hannah, Barry (April 23, 1942)
Allende, Isabel (August 2, 1942)
Handke, Peter (December 6, 1942)
Ondaatje, Michael (September 12, 1943)
Walker, Alice (February 9, 1944)
Ford, Richard (February 16, 1944)
Brown, Rita Mae (November 28, 1944)
Butler, Robert Olen (January 20, 1945)
Banville, John (December 8, 1945)
Barnes, Julian (January 19, 1946)

O'Brien, Tim (October 1, 1946)
Auster, Paul (February 3, 1947)
Rushdie, Salman (June 19, 1947)
Butler, Octavia E. (June 22, 1947)
Helprin, Mark (June 28, 1947)
Beattie, Ann (September 8, 1947)
King, Stephen (September 21, 1947)
Boyle, T. Coraghessan (1948)
Silko, Leslie Marmon (March 5, 1948)
Johnson, Charles (April 23, 1948)
Turow, Scott F. (April 12, 1949)
Kincaid, Jamaica (May 25, 1949)
Amis, Martin (August 25, 1949)
Smiley, Jane (September 26, 1949)
Gordon, Mary (December 8, 1949)
Campbell, Bebe Moore (1950)
Naylor, Gloria (January 25, 1950)
Wilson, A. N. (October 27, 1950)
Hijuelos, Oscar (August 24, 1951)
Tan, Amy (February 19, 1952)
Erdrich, Louise (June 7, 1954)
Grisham, John (February 8, 1955)
Kingsolver, Barbara (April 8, 1955)
Wallace, David Foster (February 21, 1962)

GEOGRAPHICAL LIST OF AUTHORS AND ESSAYS

AFRICA. *See also* **GHANA, KENYA, NIGERIA, SOUTH AFRICA**
African Long Fiction

ANTIGUA
Kincaid, Jamaica

ARGENTINA
Cortázar, Julio
Hudson, W. H.
Mallea, Eduardo
Puig, Manuel

AUSTRALIA
Jolley, Elizabeth
Keneally, Thomas
Malouf, David
Stead, Christina
White, Patrick
The Australian Novel

AUSTRIA
Canetti, Elias
Handke, Peter

BELGIUM
Simenon, Georges
Yourcenar, Marguerite

BRAZIL
Amado, Jorge
Lispector, Clarice
Machado de Assis, Joaquim
    Maria

BULGARIA
Canetti, Elias

CANADA
Atwood, Margaret
Bellow, Saul
Callaghan, Morley

Davies, Robertson
Laurence, Margaret
MacLennan, Hugh
Richler, Mordecai
Wilson, Ethel
Canadian Long Fiction

CARIBBEAN. *See also* **ANTIGUA, CUBA, GUYANA, TRINIDAD**
The Caribbean Novel

CHILE
Allende, Isabel
Donoso, José

CHINA. *See also* **SOUTH ASIA**
Chinese Long Fiction

COLOMBIA
García Márquez, Gabriel

CUBA
Carpentier, Alejo

CZECHOSLOVAKIA
Čapek, Karel
Kafka, Franz
Kundera, Milan
Škvorecký, Josef
Werfel, Franz

DENMARK
Jensen, Johannes V.

EGYPT
Mahfouz, Naguib

ENGLAND
Adams, Richard
Amis, Kingsley
Amis, Martin
Austen, Jane

Ballard, J. G.
Barnes, Julian
Behn, Aphra
Bennett, Arnold
Bowen, Elizabeth
Brontë, Charlotte
Brontë, Emily
Brookner, Anita
Bunyan, John
Burgess, Anthony
Burney, Fanny
Butler, Samuel
Carroll, Lewis
Carter, Angela
Cary, Joyce
Chatwin, Bruce
Chesterton, G. K.
Christie, Agatha
Clarke, Arthur C.
Collins, Wilkie
Compton-Burnett, Ivy
Conrad, Joseph
Defoe, Daniel
De la Mare, Walter
Dickens, Charles
Doyle, Arthur Conan
Drabble, Margaret
Du Maurier, Daphne
Durrell, Lawrence
Edgeworth, Maria
Eliot, George
Fielding, Gabriel
Fielding, Henry
Ford, Ford Madox
Forster, E. M.
Fowles, John
Galsworthy, John
Gaskell, Elizabeth
Gissing, George
Golding, William
Goldsmith, Oliver
Graves, Robert
Green, Henry

GUATEMALA
Asturias, Miguel Ángel

GUYANA
Harris, Wilson

INDIA. *See also* SOUTH ASIA
Desai, Anita
Jhabvala, Ruth Prawer
Narayan, R. K.
Rushdie, Salman

IRELAND
Banville, John
Beckett, Samuel
Goldsmith, Oliver
Joyce, James
Le Fanu, Joseph Sheridan
McGinley, Patrick
Maturin, Charles Robert
Moore, Brian
Moore, George
O'Brien, Edna
O'Brien, Flann
O'Brien, Kate
Swift, Jonathan
Trevor, William
Irish Long Fiction

ITALY
Calvino, Italo
Levi, Primo
Manzoni, Alessandro
Moravia, Alberto
Pavese, Cesare
Pirandello, Luigi
Silone, Ignazio
Italian Long Fiction

JAPAN
Kawabata, Yasunari
Mishima, Yukio
Ōe, Kenzaburō
Tanizaki, Jun'ichirō
Japanese Long Fiction

KENYA
Ngugi wa Thiong'o

LATIN AMERICA. *See also* ARGENTINA, BRAZIL, CHILE, COLOMBIA, CUBA, GUATEMALA, GUYANA, MEXICO, PANAMA, PERU
Latin American Long Fiction

MEXICO
Azuela, Mariano

MIDDLE EAST. *See also* EGYPT, TURKEY
The Middle Eastern Novel

NIGERIA
Achebe, Chinua
Soyinka, Wole
Tutuola, Amos

NORWAY
Hamsun, Knut
Undset, Sigrid

PANAMA
Fuentes, Carlos

PERU
Vargas Llosa, Mario

PHILIPPINES
Gonzalez, N. V. M.

POLAND
Asch, Sholem
Gombrowicz, Witold
Lem, Stanisław
Sienkiewicz, Henryk
Singer, Isaac Bashevis

ROMANIA
Wiesel, Elie

ROME. *See also* ITALY
Long Fiction in the Ancient Greco-Roman World

RUSSIA
Dostoevski, Fyodor
Gogol, Nikolai
Gorky, Maxim
Nabokov, Vladimir
Pasternak, Boris
Pushkin, Alexander
Sholokhov, Mikhail
Solzhenitsyn, Aleksandr
Tolstoy, Leo
Turgenev, Ivan
Russian Long Fiction

SCANDINAVIA. *See also* DENMARK, NORWAY, SWEDEN
Scandinavian Long Fiction

SCOTLAND
Buchan, John
Cronin, A. J.
Scott, Sir Walter
Smollett, Tobias
Spark, Muriel
Stevenson, Robert Louis

SICILY. *See also* ITALY
Verga, Giovanni

SOUTH AFRICA
Coetzee, J. M.
Gordimer, Nadine
Paton, Alan

SOUTH ASIA. *See also* CHINA, INDIA, SRI LANKA
South Asian Long Fiction

SPAIN
Cela, Camilo José
Cervantes, Miguel de

Pérez Galdós, Benito
Spanish Long Fiction

SRI LANKA
Ondaatje, Michael

SWEDEN
Lagerkvist, Pär
Lagerlöf, Selma
Strindberg, August

TRINIDAD
Naipaul, V. S.

TURKEY
Kemal, Yashar

UNITED STATES
Agee, James
Aiken, Conrad
Alcott, Louisa May
Algren, Nelson
Anaya, Rudolfo A.
Anderson, Sherwood
Asimov, Isaac
Auchincloss, Louis
Auster, Paul
Baldwin, James
Bambara, Toni Cade
Barth, John
Barthelme, Donald
Beattie, Ann
Berger, Thomas
Berry, Wendell
Bontemps, Arna
Bowles, Paul
Boyle, Kay
Boyle, T. Coraghessan
Bradbury, Ray
Bradley, Marion Zimmer
Brautigan, Richard
Brown, Charles Brockden
Brown, Rita Mae
Buck, Pearl S.
Burroughs, William S.

Butler, Octavia E.
Butler, Robert Olen
Cabell, James Branch
Cable, George Washington
Cain, James M.
Caldwell, Erskine
Campbell, Bebe Moore
Capote, Truman
Cather, Willa
Chandler, Raymond
Chase-Riboud, Barbara
Cheever, John
Chesnutt, Charles Waddell
Chopin, Kate
Clark, Walter Van Tilburg
Connell, Evan S., Jr.
Cooper, James Fenimore
Coover, Robert
Cozzens, James Gould
Crane, Stephen
De Forest, John William
Delany, Samuel R.
DeLillo, Don
De Vries, Peter
Dick, Philip K.
Dickey, James
Didion, Joan
Doctorow, E. L.
Doerr, Harriet
Donleavy, J. P.
Dos Passos, John
Dreiser, Theodore
Dunne, John Gregory
Elkin, Stanley
Ellison, Ralph
Erdrich, Louise
Farrell, James T.
Faulkner, William
Fauset, Jessie Redmon
Ferber, Edna
Fitzgerald, F. Scott
Ford, Richard
Frederic, Harold
Gaddis, William
Gaines, Ernest J.

Gardner, John
Garland, Hamlin
Gass, William H.
Glasgow, Ellen
Godwin, Gail
Goodman, Paul
Gordon, Caroline
Gordon, Mary
Grau, Shirley Ann
Grisham, John
Hammett, Dashiell
Hannah, Barry
Harrison, Jim
Hawthorne, Nathaniel
Heller, Joseph
Helprin, Mark
Hemingway, Ernest
Hersey, John
Highsmith, Patricia
Highwater, Jamake
Hijuelos, Oscar
Himes, Chester
Hinojosa, Rolando
Hoagland, Edward
Horgan, Paul
Howells, William Dean
Hurston, Zora Neale
Irving, John
James, Henry
Jewett, Sarah Orne
Johnson, Charles
Jones, James
Kelley, William Melvin
Kennedy, William
Kerouac, Jack
Kesey, Ken
King, Stephen
Kingsolver, Barbara
Knowles, John
Kosinski, Jerzy
L'Amour, Louis
Lee, Harper
Le Guin, Ursula K.
Leonard, Elmore
Lewis, Sinclair

London, Jack
Lurie, Alison
McCarthy, Cormac
McCarthy, Mary
McCullers, Carson
Macdonald, Ross
McElroy, Joseph
McGuane, Thomas
McMurtry, Larry
Madden, David
Mailer, Norman
Malamud, Bernard
Marshall, Paule
Matthiessen, Peter
Melville, Herman
Michener, James A.
Miller, Henry
Morris, Wright
Morrison, Toni
Nabokov, Vladimir
Naylor, Gloria
Nin, Anaïs
Norris, Frank
Oates, Joyce Carol
O'Brien, Tim
O'Connor, Flannery
O'Hara, John
Ozick, Cynthia
Percy, Walker
Plante, David
Porter, Katherine Anne
Potok, Chaim
Powell, Dawn
Powers, J. F.
Price, Reynolds

Prokosch, Frederic
Purdy, James
Pynchon, Thomas
Rand, Ayn
Rawlings, Marjorie Kinnan
Reed, Ishmael
Rice, Anne
Richter, Conrad
Roberts, Elizabeth Madox
Roth, Henry
Roth, Philip
Salinger, J. D.
Saroyan, William
Sarton, May
Settle, Mary Lee
Silko, Leslie Marmon
Simms, William Gilmore
Sinclair, Upton
Smiley, Jane
Stegner, Wallace
Stein, Gertrude
Steinbeck, John
Stone, Robert
Stowe, Harriet Beecher
Stuart, Jesse
Sturgeon, Theodore
Styron, William
Tan, Amy
Tarkington, Booth
Theroux, Paul
Turow, Scott F.
Twain, Mark
Tyler, Anne
Updike, John
Vidal, Gore

Vonnegut, Kurt, Jr.
Walker, Alice
Wallace, David Foster
Wallant, Edward Lewis
Wambaugh, Joseph
Warren, Robert Penn
Waters, Frank
Welty, Eudora
Wescott, Glenway
West, Nathanael
Wharton, Edith
Wideman, John Edgar
Wiesel, Elie
Wilder, Thornton
Williams, John A.
Woiwode, Larry
Wolfe, Thomas
Wolfe, Tom
Wouk, Herman
Wright, Richard
Yerby, Frank
Young, Al
African American Long Fiction
The American Novel
Asian American Long Fiction
The Euro-American Immigrant
    Experience in Long Fiction
Jewish American Long Fiction
Latino Long Fiction
Native American Long Fiction
The Southern Novel
The Western Novel

YUGOSLAVIA
Andrič, Ivo

CATEGORIZED LIST OF AUTHORS

ADVENTURE NOVEL
Brown, Charles Brockden
Buchan, John
Conrad, Joseph
Cooper, James Fenimore
Dickey, James
Kemal, Yashar
Melville, Herman
Stevenson, Robert Louis
Verne, Jules

AFRICAN AMERICAN CULTURE
Baldwin, James
Bontemps, Arna
Butler, Octavia
Cable, George Washington
Campbell, Bebe Moore
Chase-Riboud, Barbara
Chesnutt, Charles Waddell
Crane, Stephen
Ellison, Ralph
Faulkner, William
Fauset, Jessie Redmon
Gaines, Ernest J.
Grau, Shirley Ann
Himes, Chester
Hurston, Zora Neale
Johnson, Charles
Kelley, William Melvin
Lee, Harper
Naylor, Gloria
Reed, Ishmael
Stowe, Harriet Beecher
Styron, William
Walker, Alice
Wideman, John Edgar
Williams, John A.
Wright, Richard
Yerby, Frank
Young, Al

ASIAN CULTURE
Buck, Pearl S.
Döblin, Alfred
Malraux, André
Tan, Amy

BEAT NOVEL
Burroughs, William S.
Kerouac, Jack

BILDUNGSROMAN
Atwood, Margaret
Cronin, A. J.
Dickey, James
Giono, Jean
Goethe, Johann Wolfgang von
Golding, William
Handke, Peter
Hartley, L. P.
Hesse, Hermann
Horgan, Paul
Joyce, James
Kingsolver, Barbara
Kosinski, Jerzy
Lagerlöf, Selma
London, Jack
Madden, David
Mann, Thomas
Maugham, W. Somerset
Ngugi wa Thiong'o
Roberts, Elizabeth Madox
Roth, Henry
Roth, Philip
Salinger, J. D.
Sand, George
Snow, C. P.
Stendhal
Strindberg, August
Swift, Jonathan
Thackeray, William Makepeace
Vargas Llosa, Mario
Woolf, Virginia

CHRISTIANITY. *See also* RELIGIOUS NOVEL
Cary, Joyce
Cervantes, Miguel de
Diderot, Denis
Gordon, Mary
Greene, Graham
Lagerkvist, Pär
Lewis, C. S.
Moore, George
O'Brien, Kate
O'Connor, Flannery
Pater, Walter
Powers, J. F.
Werfel, Franz

CIVIL WAR
Crane, Stephen
De Forest, John William
Gordon, Caroline
Madden, David

COLONIALISM
Achebe, Chinua
Armah, Ayi Kwei
Behn, Aphra
Conrad, Joseph
Ngugi wa Thiong'o

COMMUNISM
Buck, Pearl S.
Farrell, James T.
Koestler, Arthur

DETECTIVE AND MYSTERY NOVEL
Asimov, Isaac
Auster, Paul
Barnes, Julian
Brown, Rita Mae
Cain, James M.
Chandler, Raymond
Chesterton, G. K.

Christie, Agatha
Collins, Wilkie
Desai, Anita
Doyle, Arthur Conan
Dunne, John Gregory
Hammett, Dashiell
Highsmith, Patricia
James, P. D.
Le Carré, John
Lewis, Wyndham
Macdonald, Ross
McGinley, Thomas
Sayers, Dorothy L.
Simenon, Georges
Wambaugh, Joseph

DIDACTIC NOVEL
Alcott, Louisa May
Bunyan, John
Chateaubriand, René de
Fielding, Henry
Gissing, George
Richardson, Samuel

DOMESTIC REALISM. *See also* REALISM
Agee, James
Austen, Jane
Burney, Fanny
Compton-Burnett, Ivy
Eliot, George
Moore, Brian
Morris, Wright

DYSTOPIAN NOVEL
Burroughs, William S.
Huxley, Aldous
Vonnegut, Kurt, Jr.

EPISTOLARY NOVEL
Barth, John
Goethe, Johann Wolfgang de
Richardson, Samuel
Walker, Alice

EROTIC NOVEL
Cabell, James Branch
Chopin, Kate
Delany, Samuel R.
Durrell, Lawrence
Lawrence, D. H.
Lehmann, Rosamond
Miller, Henry
Moravia, Alberto
O'Hara, John
Sand, George
Tanizaki, Jun'ichirō

EXISTENTIALISM
Beauvoir, Simone de
Bowles, Paul
Camus, Albert
Céline, Louis-Ferdinand
Döblin, Alfred
Donoso, José
Fielding, Gabriel
Gardner, John
Genet, Jean
Gombrowicz, Witold
Kazantzakis, Nikos
Kosinski, Jerzy
Mallea, Eduardo
Pavese, Cesare
Percy, Walker
Wright, Richard

EXPRESSIONISM
Dos Passos, John
Werfel, Franz

FANTASY. *See also* SCIENCE FICTION
Adams, Richard
Bradbury, Ray
Bradley, Marion Zimmer
Brontë, Charlotte
Carroll, Lewis
Carter, Angela
Defoe, Daniel
De la Mare, Walter

Donoso, José
Fuentes, Carlos
Hartley, L. P.
Le Guin, Ursula K.
Lem, Stanisław
Lewis, C. S.
O'Connor, Flannery
Tolkien, J. R. R.
Wilde, Oscar

FASCISM
Boyle, Kay
Calvino, Italo
Cary, Joyce
Moravia, Alberto
Pavese, Cesare
Sartre, Jean-Paul
Silone, Ignazio
Wilson, Angus
Yourcenar, Marguerite

FEMINIST NOVEL
Atwood, Margaret
Bradley, Marion Zimmer
Brontë, Charlotte
Brookner, Anita
Brown, Rita Mae
Burney, Fanny
Chopin, Kate
Compton-Burnett, Ivy
Drabble, Margaret
Fauset, Jessie Redmon
Ferber, Edna
Gaskell, Elizabeth
Gissing, George
Glasgow, Ellen
Godwin, Gail
Gordon, Mary
Graves, Robert
James, Henry
Kincaid, Jamaica
Kingsolver, Barbara
Laurence, Margaret
Lessing, Doris

Lurie, Alison
Macaulay, Rose
McCarthy, Mary
Naylor, Gloria
Nin, Anaïs
Oates, Joyce Carol
O'Brien, Edna
Richardson, Dorothy
Stead, Christina
Stein, Gertrude
Weldon, Fay
West, Rebecca
Woolf, Virginia

GAY AND LESBIAN NOVEL
Baldwin, James
Boyle, Kay
Brown, Rita Mae
Burgess, Anthony
Burroughs, William S.
Cheever, John
Compton-Burnett, Ivy
Durrell, Lawrence
Forster, E. M.
Genet, Jean
Gide, André
Goodman, Paul
Hammett, Dashiell
Jolley, Elizabeth
Lawrence, D. H.
Le Fanu, Joseph Sheridan
Lehmann, Rosamond
Lurie, Alison
McCullers, Carson
Mann, Thomas
Naylor, Gloria
Nin, Anaïs
O'Hara, John
Plante, David
Price, Reynolds
Proust, Marcel
Puig, Manuel
Purdy, James
Rice, Anne
Sarton, May

Sartre, Jean-Paul
Stead, Christina
Stein, Gertrude
Vidal, Gore
White, Patrick
Yourcenar, Marguerite

GOTHIC NOVEL
Atwood, Margaret
Brontë, Charlotte
Brontë, Emily
Brown, Charles Brockden
Collins, Wilkie
De la Mare, Walter
Desai, Anita
Du Maurier, Daphne
Gogol, Nikolai
Hartley, L. P.
Hawthorne, Nathaniel
Hugo, Victor
Lewis, Matthew Gregory
Maturin, Charles Robert
Oates, Joyce Carol
Rice, Anne
Shelley, Mary Wollstonecraft

HISTORICAL NOVEL
Armah, Ayi Kwei
Azuela, Mariano
Banville, John
Chase-Riboud, Barbara
Doctorow, E. L.
Doyle, Arthur Conan
Dumas, Alexandre, *père*
Fowles, John
Gordon, Caroline
Graves, Robert
Jewett, Sarah Orne
Keneally, Thomas
Koestler, Arthur
Le Fanu, Joseph Sheridan
Macaulay, Rose
Manzoni, Alessandro
Maturin, Charles Robert
Michener, James

O'Brien, Kate
Pater, Walter
Prokosch, Frederic
Scott, Sir Walter
Settle, Mary Lee
Škvorecký, Josef
Vidal, Gore
Werfel, Franz
Yerby, Frank
Yourcenar, Marguerite

HORROR NOVEL
Bradbury, Ray
King, Stephen
Le Fanu, Joseph Sheridan

IMPRESSIONISM
Conrad, Joseph
Crane, Stephen
Ford, Ford Madox
Hartley, L. P.
Joyce, James
Matthiessen, Peter
Rhys, Jean
Wolfe, Thomas

ISLAM. *See also* **RELIGIOUS NOVEL**
Cary, Joyce
Rushdie, Salman

JUDAISM. *See also* **RELIGIOUS NOVEL**
Asch, Sholem
Bellow, Saul
Levi, Primo
Malamud, Bernard
Ozick, Cynthia
Potok, Chaim
Richler, Mordecai
Roth, Philip
Singer, Isaac Bashevis
White, Patrick
Wiesel, Elie
Wouk, Herman

LATINO CULTURE

Anaya, Rudolfo
Carpentier, Alejo
Cortázar, Julio
Donoso, José
Hijuelos, Oscar
Hinojosa, Rolando

LOCAL COLOR

Berry, Wendell
Buchan, John
Cable, George Washington
Cather, Willa
Chesnutt, Charles Waddell
Chopin, Kate
Garland, Hamlin
Giono, Jean
Grau, Shirley Ann
Hudson, W. H.
Jewett, Sarah Orne
Kipling, Rudyard
Pavese, Cesare
Rawlings, Marjorie Kinnan
Richter, Conrad
Twain, Mark

MAGICAL REALISM. *See also* REALISM

Allende, Isabel
Amado, Jorge
Asturias, Miguel Ángel
Carpentier, Alejo
Erdrich, Louise
García Márquez, Gabriel

MANNERS, FICTION OF

Auchincloss, Louis
Austen, Jane
Bowen, Elizabeth
Burney, Fanny
Edgeworth, Maria
Fontane, Theodor
Glasgow, Ellen
Howells, William Dean
O'Hara, John

METAFICTION

Calvino, Italo
Coover, Robert
Gardner, John
O'Brien, Flann

MINIMALISM

Beattie, Ann
Ford, Richard

MODERNISM

Cary, Joyce
Donleavy, J. P.
Durrell, Lawrence
Ellison, Ralph
Faulkner, William
Joyce, James
Kafka, Franz
Lagerkvist, Pär
Lewis, Wyndham
Lowry, Malcolm
Nin, Anaïs
O'Brien, Flann
Pérez Galdós, Benito
Pirandello, Luigi
Prokosch, Frederic
Stein, Gertrude
Woolf, Virginia

NATIVE AMERICAN CULTURE

Berger, Thomas
Cooper, James Fenimore
Erdrich, Louise
Garland, Hamlin
Highwater, Jamake
Horgan, Paul
Kingsolver, Barbara
Roberts, Elizabeth Madox
Silko, Leslie Marmon
Simms, William Gilmore
Warren, Robert Penn
Waters, Frank
Woiwode, Larry

NATURALISM

Algren, Nelson
Armah, Ayi Kwei
Caldwell, Erskine
Callaghan, Morley
Calvino, Italo
Cela, Camilo José
Crane, Stephen
Dreiser, Theodore
Farrell, James T.
Flaubert, Gustave
Fontane, Theodor
Garland, Hamlin
Gissing, George
Jensen, Johannes V.
Jones, James
Kafka, Franz
Kennedy, William
London, Jack
Maugham, W. Somerset
Norris, Frank
Pérez Galdós, Benito
Pirandello, Luigi
Simenon, Georges
Sinclair, Upton
Steinbeck, John
Strindberg, August
Turgenev, Ivan
Verga, Giovanni
Yourcenar, Marguerite
Zola, Émile

NEOREALISM

Calvino, Italo
Green, Henry
Moravia, Alberto
Pavese, Cesare
Silone, Ignazio

NEW JOURNALISM

Callaghan, Morley
Capote, Truman
Chatwin, Bruce
Dreiser, Theodore
Hemingway, Ernest

Hersey, John
Wambaugh, Joseph
Wolfe, Tom

NEW NOVEL

Duras, Marguerite
Giono, Jean
Robbe-Grillet, Alain
Simon, Claude
Spark, Muriel

NOBEL PRIZE WINNERS

Andrić, Ivo
Asturias, Miguel Ángel
Beckett, Samuel
Bellow, Saul
Böll, Heinrich
Buck, Pearl S.
Camus, Albert
Canetti, Elias
Cela, Camilo José
Faulkner, William
France, Anatole
Galsworthy, John
García Márquez, Gabriel
Gide, André
Golding, William
Gordimer, Nadine
Hamsun, Knut
Hemingway, Ernest
Hesse, Hermann
Jensen, Johannes V.
Kawabata, Yasunari
Kipling, Rudyard
Lagerkvist, Pär
Lagerlöf, Selma
Lewis, Sinclair
Mahfouz, Naguib
Mann, Thomas
Martin du Gard, Roger
Morrison, Toni
Ōe, Kenzaburō
Pasternak, Boris
Rolland, Romain
Sartre, Jean-Paul

Sholokhov, Mikhail
Sienkewicz, Henryk
Simon, Claude
Singer, Isaac Bashevis
Solzhenitsyn, Aleksandr
Soyinka, Wole
Steinbeck, John
Undset, Sigrid
White, Patrick

PICARESQUE NOVEL

Auster, Paul
Barth, John
Berger, Thomas
Boyle, T. Coraghessan
Diderot, Denis
Elkin, Stanley
Fielding, Gabriel
Gogol, Nikolai
Hesse, Hermann
Kafka, Franz
Levi, Primo
Madden, David
Prokosch, Frederic
Rushdie, Salman
Saroyan, William
Voltaire

POLITICAL NOVEL

Asturias, Miguel Ángel
Beauvoir, Simone de
Calvino, Italo
Carpentier, Alejo
Conrad, Joseph
Cooper, James Fenimore
Cortázar, Julio
Dick, Philip K.
Diderot, Denis
Donoso, José
Dostoevski, Fyodor
Fontane, Theodor
Gaskell, Elizabeth
Gissing, George
Gogol, Nikolai
Gorky, Maxim

Kundera, Milan
London, Jack
Moravia, Alberto
Ngugi wa Thiong'o
Orwell, George
Pasternak, Boris
Pavese, Cesare
Rushdie, Salman
Silone, Ignazio

POSTMODERNISM

Auster, Paul
Banville, John
Barth, John
Barthelme, Donald
Beckett, Samuel
Burgess, Anthony
Coover, Robert
Gass, William
Lively, Penelope
McCarthy, Cormac
McElroy, Joseph
O'Connor, Flannery
Ondaatje, Michael
Purdy, James
Pynchon, Thomas
Reed, Ishmael
Vonnegut, Kurt, Jr.
Wallace, David Foster

PROBLEM NOVEL

Chopin, Kate
Cooper, James Fenimore

PSYCHOLOGICAL NOVEL

Aiken, Conrad
Chopin, Kate
Cocteau, Jean
Conrad, Joseph
Diderot, Denis
Sterne, Laurence
Tutuola, Amos

PSYCHOLOGICAL REALISM.

See also **REALISM**
Anderson, Sherwood
Davies, Robertson
Dostoevski, Fyodor
Durrell, Lawrence
Eliot, George
Faulkner, William
Flaubert, Gustave
Gide, André
Hawthorne, Nathaniel
James, Henry
Laurence, Margaret
Melville, Herman
Mishima, Yukio
Murdoch, Iris
Proust, Marcel
Saint-Exupéry, Antoine de
Simenon, Georges
Trevor, William
Wescott, Glenway
West, Paul
West, Rebecca
Wilder, Thornton
Wilson, Ethel
Wolf, Christa

RACISM

Buck, Pearl S.
Cable, George Washington
Campbell, Bebe Moore
Crane, Stephen
Garland, Hamlin
Gordimer, Nadine
Grau, Shirley Ann
Hannah, Barry
Hurston, Zora Neale
Michener, James
Paton, Alan
Price, Reynolds
Waters, Frank
White, Patrick
Williams, John A.

REALISM

Balzac, Honoré de
Bennett, Arnold
Camus, Albert
Capote, Truman
Cary, Joyce
Cheever, John
Chopin, Kate
Clark, Walter Van Tilburg
Connell, Evan S., Jr.
Cozzens, James Gould
Cronin, A. J.
De Forest, John William
Dick, Philip K.
Dickens, Charles
Dickey, James
Donoso, José
Dos Passos, John
Fielding, Gabriel
Gardner, John
Garland, Hamlin
Gordon, Caroline
Harris, Wilson
Hartley, L. P.
Howells, William Dean
Hudson, W. H.
Jensen, Johannes V.
Jewett, Sarah Orne
Joyce, James
Lagerlöf, Selma
Lehmann, Rosamond
Lewis, Sinclair
Naipaul, V. S.
Paton, Alan
Pérez Galdós, Benito
Prokosch, Frederic
Pym, Barbara
Rabelais, François
Renault, Mary
Silone, Ignazio
Simms, William Gilmore
Smollett, Tobias
Snow, C. P.
Stendhal
Sterne, Laurence

Stowe, Harriet Beecher
Thackeray, William Makepeace
Tolstoy, Leo
Trollope, Anthony
Twain, Mark
Undset, Sigrid
Wain, John
Wallant, Edward Lewis
Waugh, Evelyn
Werfel, Franz
Wharton, Edith

RELIGIOUS NOVEL

Bunyan, John
Cary, Joyce
Chateaubriand, Rene de
Cronin, A. J.
Defoe, Daniel
De Forest, John William
De Vries, Peter
Diderot, Denis
Dostoevski, Fyodor
Greene, Graham
Hardy, Thomas
Hartley, L. P.
Kazantzakis, Nikos
Lagerkvist, Pär
Lewis, Sinclair
Macaulay, Rose
Mann, Thomas
Martin du Gard, Roger
Meredith, George
Moore, George
O'Brien, Kate
O'Connor, Flannery
Pater, Walter
Powers, J. F.
Rushdie, Salman
Vidal, Gore
Werfel, Franz
Yerby, Frank

ROMANCE

Buchan, John
Capote, Truman

Colette
Cooper, James Fenimore
Jhabvala, Ruth Prawer
Lodge, David
Malory, Sir Thomas
White, T. H.
Wodehouse, P. G.

ROMANTIC NOVEL
Chateaubriand, Rene de
Ellison, Ralph
Flaubert, Gustave
Hesse, Hermann
Machado de Assis, Joaquim
    Maria
Priestley, J. B.
Pushkin, Alexander
Sand, George
Sarton, May
Stendhal
Sterne, Laurence
Stevenson, Robert Louis
Stowe, Harriet Beecher
Strindberg, August
Twain, Mark
White, Patrick

SATIRE
Amado, Jorge
Amis, Kingsley
Amis, Martin
Atwood, Margaret
Auchincloss, Louis
Austen, Jane
Burroughs, William S.
Butler, Samuel
Carter, Angela
Cortázar, Julio
Cyrano de Bergerac
Dickens, Charles
Diderot, Denis
Donleavy, J. P.
Gaddis, William
Gide, André
Gogol, Nikolai

Goldsmith, Oliver
Jolley, Elizabeth
Kelley, William Melvin
McCarthy, Mary
Nabokov, Vladimir
Orwell, George
Peacock, Thomas Love
Powell, Dawn
Pritchett, V. S.
Rabelais, François
Roth, Philip
Smiley, Jane
Smollett, Tobias
Sterne, Laurence
Stuart, Jesse
Swift, Jonathan
Thackeray, William
    Makepeace
Trollope, Anthony
Voltaire
Waugh, Evelyn
Wilson, A. N.
Wolfe, Tom

SCIENCE FICTION. *See also*
    FANTASY
Asimov, Isaac
Auster, Paul
Ballard, J. G
Bradbury, Ray
Bradley, Marion Zimmer
Butler, Octavia
Calvino, Italo
Čapek, Karel
Carter, Angela
Clarke, Arthur C.
Delany, Samuel R.
Dick, Philip K.
Doyle, Arthur Conan
Durrell, Lawrence
Le Guin, Ursula K.
Lem, Stanisław
Lewis, C. S.
Orwell, George
Sturgeon, Theodore

Tolkien, J. R. R.
Verne, Jules
Wells, H. G.

SOCIAL ACTIVISM
Dick, Philip K.
Dickens, Charles
Gaskell, Elizabeth
Gissing, George
Gogol, Nikolai
Gorky, Maxim
Hersey, John
Hugo, Victor

SOCIAL REALISM. *See also*
    REALISM
Fitzgerald, F. Scott
Forster, E. M.
Frederic, Harold
Gorky, Maxim
Howells, William Dean
Huxley, Aldous
O'Hara, John
Sholokhov, Mikhail
Tarkington, Booth
Updike, John

SOUTHERN UNITED STATES
Cable, George Washington
Chesnutt, Charles Waddell
Caldwell, Erskine
De Forest, John William
Ellison, Ralph
Gaines, Ernest J.
Glasgow, Ellen
Godwin, Gail
Gordon, Caroline
Grau, Shirley Ann
Hannah, Barry
Lee, Harper
Settle, Mary Lee
Simms, William Gilmore
Stowe, Harriet Beecher
Tyler, Anne
Warren, Robert Penn

Welty, Eudora
Yerby, Frank

SURREALISM
Cocteau, Jean
Grass, Günter
Hesse, Hermann
Kennedy, William
Prokosch, Frederic
Sartre, Jean-Paul

SUSPENSE
Grisham, John
Le Carré, John
Turow, Scott F.

SYMBOLISM
Conrad, Joseph
Cronin, A. J.
Gide, André
Goethe, Johann Wolfgang von

TRAGICOMEDY
De Vries, Peter
McCullers, Carson
Meredith, George

UTOPIAN NOVEL
Brautigan, Richard
Cyrano de Bergerac
Sturgeon, Theodore

VERISM
Pirandello, Luigi
Verga, Giovanni

VICTORIAN NOVEL
Dickens, Charles
Galsworthy, John
Gaskell, Elizabeth

Gissing, George
Hardy, Thomas

VIETNAM WAR
Butler, Robert Olen
Coetzee, J. M.
Laurence, Margaret
O'Brien, Tim
Stone, Robert

WESTERN
Berger, Thomas
Clark, Walter Van Tilburg
Cooper, James Fenimore
Doctorow, E. L.
Horgan, Paul
L'Amour, Louis
Leonard, Elmore
McGuane, Thomas
McMurtry, Larry
Ondaatje, Michael
Stegner, Wallace

WIT AND HUMOR
De Vries, Peter
Didion, Joan
Irving, John
Jolley, Elizabeth
Narayan, R. K.
Wilson, A. N.

WORLD WAR I
Andrič, Ivo
Auchincloss, Louis
Cary, Joyce
Céline, Louis-Ferdinand
Döblin, Alfred
Dos Passos, John
Ford, Ford Madox
Hesse, Hermann

Lewis, Sinclair
MacLennan, Hugh
Malouf, David
Mann, Thomas
Martin du Gard, Roger
Porter, Katharine Anne
Remarque, Erich Maria

WORLD WAR II
Beauvoir, Simone de
Berry, Wendell
Böll, Heinrich
Bowen, Elizabeth
Boyle, Kay
Buck, Pearl S.
Cary, Joyce
Durrell, Lawrence
Fielding, Gabriel
Gombrowicz, Witold
Gonzalez, N. V. M.
Grass, Günter
Heller, Joseph
Jones, James
Knowles, John
Koestler, Arthur
Kosinski, Jerzy
Levi, Primo
Macaulay, Rose
Mailer, Norman
Michener, James
Ondaatje, Michael
Prokosch, Frederic
Saroyan, William
Styron, William
Vonnegut, Kurt, Jr.
Wilson, Angus
Wouk, Herman
Yourcenar, Marguerite

CRITICAL SURVEY

OF

LONG FICTION

INDEX